W9-CEV-949

DATABASE PROCESSING

DATABASE PROCESSING

Fundamentals, Design & Implementation

Eighth Edition

David M. Kroenke

PRENTICE HALL
Upper Saddle River, NJ 07458

Library of Congress Cataloging-in Publication Data

Kroenke, David.
Database processing : fundamentals, design & implementation / David M. Kroenke.—8th ed.
p. cm.
Includes bibliographical references and index.
ISBN 0-13-064839-6
1. Database management. I. Title.

QA76.9.D3K76 2001
005.74—dc21

2001041423

Publisher: Natalie E. Anderson
Executive Editor, MIS: Bob Horan
Associate Editor: Kyle Hannon
Media Project Manager: Joan Waxman
Marketing Manager: Sharon K. Turkovich
Marketing Assistant: Jason Smith
Managing Editor (Production): Gail Steier de Acevedo
Production Editor: Vanessa Nuttry
Associate Director, Manufacturing: Vincent Scelta
Manufacturing Buyer: Natacha St. Hill Moore
Manager, Print Production: Christy Mahon
Design Manager: Pat Smythe
Designer: Steve Frim
Interior Design: Jill Little
Cover Design: John Romer
Composition and Project Management: Progressive Publishing Alternatives
Printer/Binder: Quebecor World
Cover Printer: Phoenix Color

10 9 8 7 6 5 4 3 2 1
ISBN 0-13-064839-6

BRIEF CONTENTS

CONTENTS

PREFACE

According to Alan Greenspan, Chairman of the U.S. Federal Reserve, information technology has enabled unprecedented increases in business productivity. While the Internet takes most of the credit, behind the scenes database technology plays a vital role. After all, the Internet is only a communication system; much of its value lies in the data and information transmitted to and from databases.

News of the dot-com bust may cause students to wonder if the value of these technologies will decline accordingly. Nothing could be further from the truth. Lou Gestner, Chairman of IBM, stated several years ago that the true benefits of the Internet and related technologies will occur only after those technologies have been embraced by mainstream, corporate America—-by the so-called "old economy" companies. Major opportunities for database technology (and for future database practitioners) lie in applying this technology now, to every kind of business and business activity.

All of which means there has never been a better time to study database processing. From personal databases on desktops to large interorganizational databases distributed on computers worldwide, databases are increasingly important business assets. Marketing, sales, production, operations, finance, accounting, management, and indeed all business disciplines, are using database technology to gain increased productivity in their respective activities.

Moreover, after the frenzy of new technologies and products in recent years, the key elements of modern database management have now become clear. Conceptual knowledge of data modeling and database design continue to be essential; equally, the relational model and SQL are as important as in the past. Database administration, especially the technology supporting multi-user database management, has increased in importance because all databases that use the new technologies are multi-user.

Additionally, technology for publishing databases on the web, especially three-tier and multi-tier architectures, XML, Active Server Pages (ASP), and Java Server Pages (JSP) have emerged as winners among many contenders for database publishing. In concert with these technologies, both ODBC with OLE DB and JDBC continue their importance.

In short, database technology is more important than ever, and the basic technologies that need to be taught have become clearer than any time in the past five years.

FEATURES OF THIS EDITION

In accordance with these remarks, the second half of this text has been completely rewritten. Almost all of Chapters 11 through 16 is new. The major tasks of database administration are surveyed in Chapter 11 and then illustrated for Oracle in Chapter 12, and again for SQL Server in Chapter 13. Then, Chapter 14 surveys the basic technologies for database publishing on the Web and these technologies are then illustrated for ODBC, OLE DB, IIS, and ASP in Chapter 15 and again for JDBC, JSP, and MySQL in Chapter 16. Chapter 17 includes information on OLAP, while Chapter 18 introduces Oracle's new object-relational constructs.

Addressing all of these topics in a single term is a challenge, and I believe we need seriously to consider devoting a full year to the database class. Meanwhile, if you have just one term and time is short, this edition has been written to enable you to choose among three sets of alternative technologies.

Specifically, regarding data modeling, the text addresses the entity-relationship model and the semantic object model. If time is short, you might want to cover only the E-R model because it is far more popular. Similarly, regarding multi-user databases, pick either Oracle in Chapter 12 or SQL Server in Chapter 13 depending on the needs of graduates in your community[1]. Finally, regarding Web publishing, if time constrains your course, choose either IIS, ASP, and ODBC in Chapter 15; or Java, JDBC, and JSP in Chapter 16. No loss of continuity will occur if you select only one of any of these three pairs. Of course, if you're not constrained by time, all of these topics are important.

Concept	**Alternative 1**	**Alternative 2**
Data Modeling	Entity-relationship model Chapters 3 and 6	Semantic Object Model Chapters 4 and 7
Multi-user DBMS	Oracle Chapter 13	SQL Server Chapter 14
Web Publishing	IIS, ASP, ODBC Chapter 15	Java, JDBC, JSP Chapter 16

This edition also includes a new series of end-of-chapter exercises. These concern a small company that markets, sells, produces, and supports a line of camping stoves. The goal of these exercises is to enable the students to apply the knowledge gained from each chapter to a small, realistic, but constrained application.

Chapter-by-Chapter Overview

This text consists of seven parts. Part I introduces database processing. Chapter 1 illustrates sample applications, defines basic terms, and sketches the history of database processing. Chapter 2 then illustrates the development of a simple database and application using Microsoft Access XP.

The second part concerns data modeling. Chapter 3 discusses the entity-relationship model and shows how this model has been integrated with UML, or the Uniform Modeling Language. Chapter 4 presents the semantic object model, a data modeling alternative to the E-R model. Database design is the subject of Part III. Chapter 5 discusses the relational model and normalization. Chapter 6 then applies the ideas from Chapters 3 and 5 to transform entity-relationship models into relational database designs. Chapter 7 applies the ideas from Chapters 4 and 5 to transform semantic object models into relational database designs.

The next part addresses the fundamentals of relational database implementation. Chapter 8 presents an overview, Chapter 9 addresses procedural SQL, and Chapter 10 describes the design of relational database applications. Part V considers multi-user database management. Chapter 11 describes database administration and discusses important issues of multi-user database processing including concurrency control, security, and backup and recovery. The ideas presented in

[1]You can order a version of this text that includes either Oracle 8i or SQL Server 2000. Oracle 8i is unconstrained; SQL Server 2000 has a 120-day license. For the Oracle version order ISBN 0-13-065628-3 and for the SQL Server version order ISBN 0-13-066083-3.

Chapter 11 are then illustrated for Oracle in Chapter 12. Chapter 12 also illustrates SQL for data definition. Chapter 13 also mirrors the discussion of Chapter 11 to illustrate multi-user database management using SQL Server.

Database publishing on the Web is next addressed in Part VI. Chapter 14 lays the foundations of network processing, multi-tier architectures and XML. Chapter 15 then applies these concepts using Microsoft technology including ODBC, OLE DB, IIS, and ASP. Chapter 16 applies the concepts of Chapter 14 using Java; it includes JDBC, JSP, and MySQL. Concepts are illustrated with example using Linux and Apache Tomcat. Chapter 17 then addresses issues of data administration and discusses OLAP.

Part VII contains only one chapter which addresses object-oriented database processing. New to this chapter is a discussion of Oracles object-relational features and functions. Appendix A contains a brief survey of data structures and Appendix B illustrates the use of Tabledesigner, a product that can be used to develop semantic object models and covert them into database designs and ASP pages.

Acknowledgements

The dramatic change in the second half of this edition is due to constructive and helpful conversations with my editor, Bob Horan, and to exceptionally useful and insightful reviews from the following individuals:

Jack Becker, University of North Texas
William D. Burg, University of Alabama at Birmingham
Bhushan Kapoor, California State University — Fullerton
Donald R. Moscato, Iona College
Nancy L. Russo, Northern Illinois University
Behrooz Saghafi, Chicago State University
Joseph L. Sessum, Kennesaw State University
Ashraf Shirani, San Jose State University
Ludwig Slusky, California State University — Los Angeles

In addition, Marty Murray of Portland Community College encouraged and helped me to develop the material on Oracle in Chapter 12. I am indebted to Warner Schyerer of SoundDev Corporation in Seattle, for the idea of including JSP and MySQL in Chapter 16. Thanks also to Jude Stoller, also of SoundDev, who reviewed that material. I thank especially Chris Wilkens of SafariDog.com, who led me through the process of setting up Linux, Apache, and Tomcat.

Thanks to Oracle and to Microsoft for making the student versions of their products available. Thanks also to Thorsten Ganz, President of Coolstrategy.com, who made Tabledesigner available to students using this text and to Kenji Kawai, who continues to play a crucial role in the development of products based on the semantic object model. Special thanks to Kyle Hannon of Prentice-Hall who manages the text and its supporting components and ensures that they all successfully come together and also to Vanessa Nuttry of Prentice-Hall who skillfully managed the production process. Finally, I thank Lynda for her love, support, and encouragement.

Database processing is a fascinating topic that has developed and evolved for more than thirty years. I believe it will continue to do so for at least as many years to come, and I wish you great success in exploring the many opportunities on the road ahead!

David Kroenke
Seattle, Washington

INTRODUCTION

The two chapters in Part I introduce the topic of database processing. Chapter 1 describes four typical database applications and discusses the advantages of databases over earlier file-processing systems. It also defines the term *database* and surveys the history of database processing. Chapter 2 then describes the elements of a database and surveys the functions of a database management system (DBMS). Chapter 2 concludes this introduction by summarizing the tasks necessary to develop a database and its related applications.

Part I provides an overview of the need for databases and the nature of the components of databases and their applications. Its purpose is to set the stage for your study of the details of database concepts and technology in subsequent chapters.

Introduction to Database Processing

Database processing has always been an important topic in the study of information systems. In recent years, however, the explosion of the Internet and the dramatic development of new technology for the Internet has made knowledge of database technology one of the hottest career paths. Database technology enables Internet applications to step beyond the simple brochure publishing that characterized early applications. At the same time, Internet technology provides a standardized and readily accessible means of publishing database content to users. None of these new developments takes away from the need for classical database applications that were vital to business interests prior to the rise of the Internet. They simply amplify the importance of database knowledge.

Many students find this subject enjoyable and interesting, even though it can be challenging. Database design and development involve both art and engineering. Understanding user requirements and translating them into effective database designs is an artistic process. Transforming those designs into physical databases with functionally complete, high performance applications is an engineering process. Both aspects are full of challenging and enjoyable intellectual puzzles.

Because of the immense need for database technology, the skills you develop and the knowledge you gain in this course will be in great demand. The goal of this text is to provide a solid foundation in the fundamentals of database technology so that you can begin a successful career in this field if you choose to do so.

➤ FOUR DATABASE EXAMPLES

The purpose of a database is to help people keep track of things. The classical database applications concern the tracking of items like orders, customers, jobs, employees, phone calls, or other things of interest to a business person. Recently, database technology has been applied on the Internet not only for these classical applications, but also for new applications like displaying advertisements targeted to customer characteristics and tracking customer viewing and purchasing habits on Web pages. These databases include picture, audio, and video data as well as traditional scalar data like names, dates, and phone numbers. The following four examples illustrate the use of database technology across this wide range of applications.

Mary Richards Housepainting

Mary Richards is a professional housepainter who owns and operates a small company consisting of herself, another professional painter, and, when needed, part-time painters. Mary has been in business for ten years and has earned a reputation as a high-quality painter who works for a reasonable rate. Mary gets most of her work through repeat business from customers who hire her to paint their houses and also from their word-of-mouth referrals. In addition, Mary gets some work from building contractors and professional interior designers.

Customers remember Mary far better than she remembers them. Indeed, sometimes she is embarrassed when a customer calls and says something like, "Hi Mary, this is John Maples. You painted my house three years ago." Mary knows she is supposed to remember the caller and the work she did for him, but since she paints more than 50 houses a year, it is difficult for her to do so. This situation becomes worse when the customer says something like, "My neighbor liked the job you did on our house and would like something similar done to her house."

In order to help her memory and to keep better track of her business records, Mary had a consultant develop a database and database application that she uses on her personal computer. The database stores records regarding customers, jobs, and referral sources in the form of tables, as shown in the example in Figure 1-1.

It is the job of a program called a database management system (DBMS) to store and retrieve the data in these tables. Unfortunately, when such data are in the form of tables, they are not very useful to Mary. Rather, she would like to

Tables of Data for Mary Richards Housepainting

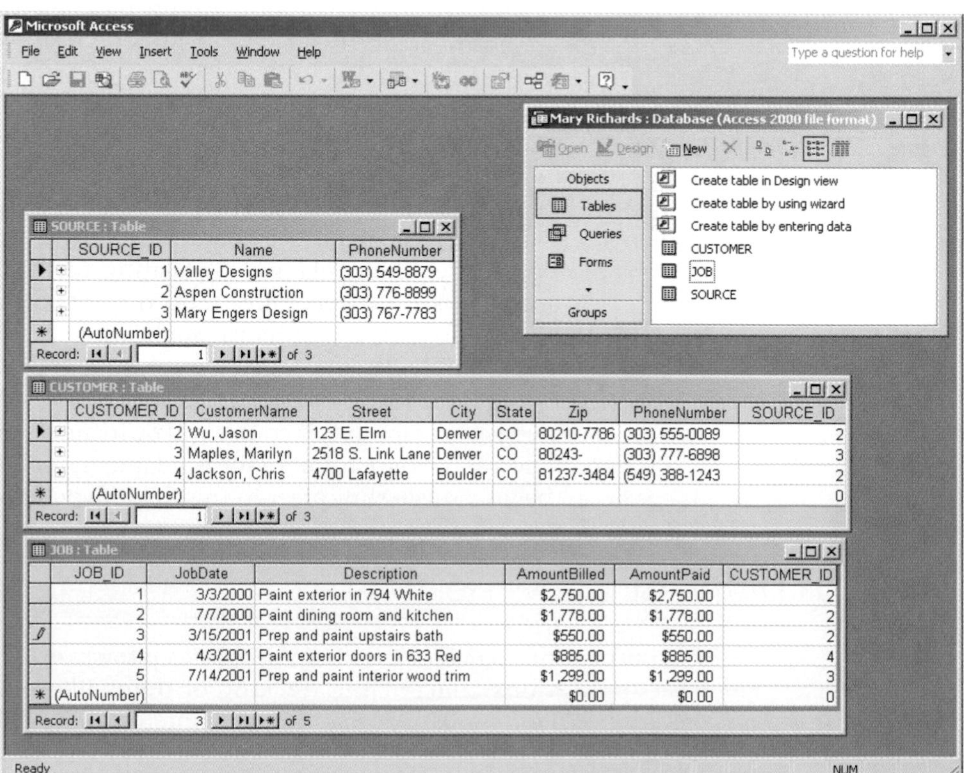

➤ FIGURE 1-2

Example Data Entry Form for Mary Richards Housepainting

CUSTOMER

Customer: Wu, Jason

Phone: (303) 555-0089

Street: 123 E. Elm

City: Denver

State: CO Zip: 80210-7786

Referral Source: Aspen Construction — Phone: (303) 776-8899

JOB

JobDate	Description	AmountBilled	AmountPaid
3/3/2000	Paint exterior in 794 White	$2,750	$2,750
7/7/2000	Paint dining room and kitchen	$1,778	$1,778
3/15/2001	Prep and paint upstairs bath	$550	$550
		$0	$0

Record: 1 of 3

Record: 1 of 3

know how customers and jobs and referrals relate to one another—for example, what jobs she has done for a particular customer or what customers have been referred by a particular person.

To provide this capability, Mary's consultant created a database application that processes data entry forms and produces reports. Consider the example form in Figure 1-2. Here, Mary keys in data about customers such as name, phone, and address. She also links the customer to a particular referral source and keys in data about jobs performed for the customer. This data can then be displayed in reports like the one shown in Figure 1-3. Other uses of the database include recording bid estimates, tracking referral sources, and producing mailing labels for the direct sales literature that Mary sends out from time to time.

➤ FIGURE 1-3

Example Report for Mary Richards Housepainting

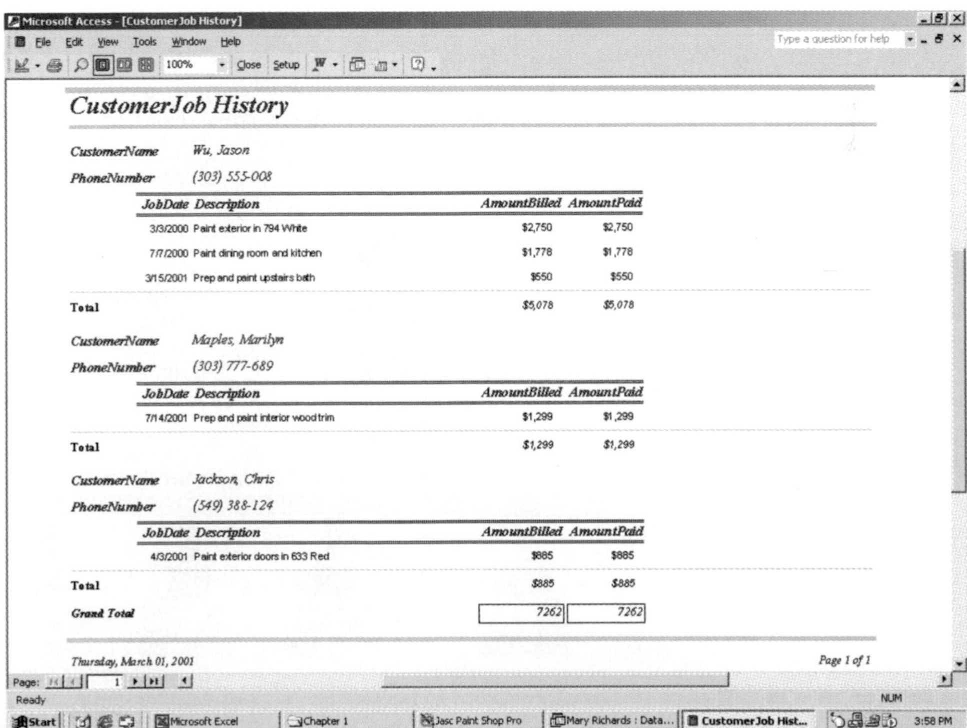

Microsoft Access - [CustomerJob History]

CustomerJob History

CustomerName: Wu, Jason
PhoneNumber: (303) 555-008

JobDate	Description	AmountBilled	AmountPaid
3/3/2000	Paint exterior in 794 White	$2,750	$2,750
7/7/2000	Paint dining room and kitchen	$1,778	$1,778
3/15/2001	Prep and paint upstairs bath	$550	$550
Total		$5,078	$5,078

CustomerName: Maples, Marilyn
PhoneNumber: (303) 777-689

JobDate	Description	AmountBilled	AmountPaid
7/14/2001	Prep and paint interior wood trim	$1,299	$1,299
Total		$1,299	$1,299

CustomerName: Jackson, Chris
PhoneNumber: (549) 388-124

JobDate	Description	AmountBilled	AmountPaid
4/3/2001	Paint exterior doors in 633 Red	$885	$885
Total		$885	$885
Grand Total		7262	7262

Thursday, March 01, 2001 — Page 1 of 1

The database application and the DBMS process the form and store the data that are entered into tables like those in Figure 1-1. Similarly, the application and DBMS extract data from tables like those in Figure 1-1 to create a report like the one in Figure 1-3.

Consider again the data in Figure 1-1, and notice that the rows in the tables cross-reference and thus are linked to one another. Each JOB contains the CUSTOMER_ID of the CUSTOMER who purchased that JOB, and each CUSTOMER contains the SOURCE_ID of the person who referred that customer. These references are used to combine the data to produce forms and reports like those shown in Figures 1-2 and 1-3.

As you can imagine, Mary is unlikely to know how to design the tables in Figure 1-1, how to use a DBMS to create those tables, and how to develop the application to create the forms and reports. But by the time you have finished this course, you should know how to use database technology to create this database and its application. You should also know how to design and manipulate tables to create forms and reports of greater complexity.

TREBLE CLEF MUSIC

Mary Richards's database is called a *single-user* database because only one user accesses the database at a given time. In some cases, this limitation is too restrictive; multiple people need to access the database simultaneously from multiple computers. Such *multi-user* databases are more complicated because the DBMS and the application must keep one user's work from interfering with another's.

Treble Clef Music uses a database application to keep track of musical instruments that it rents. It needs a multi-user database application because, during busy periods, several salespeople may rent musical instruments at the same time. Also, the store manager needs to access the rental database to determine when to order more instruments of a given type. She does not want to interrupt the rental process when she does this.

The Treble Clef store has a local area network that connects several personal computers to a server computer that holds the rental database as shown in Figure 1-4. Each clerk has access to a database application that has the three forms illustrated in Figure 1-5. The Customer form is used to maintain customer data, the

➤ FIGURE 1-4

Local Area Network with Database Server Used by Treble Clef Music

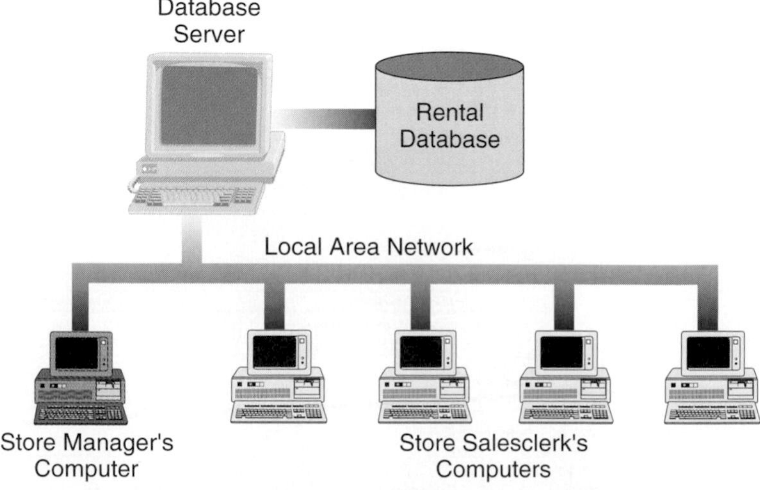

FIGURE 1-5

Three Forms Used by Treble Clef Music: (a) Customer Form, (b) Rental Agreement Form, and (c) Instrument Form

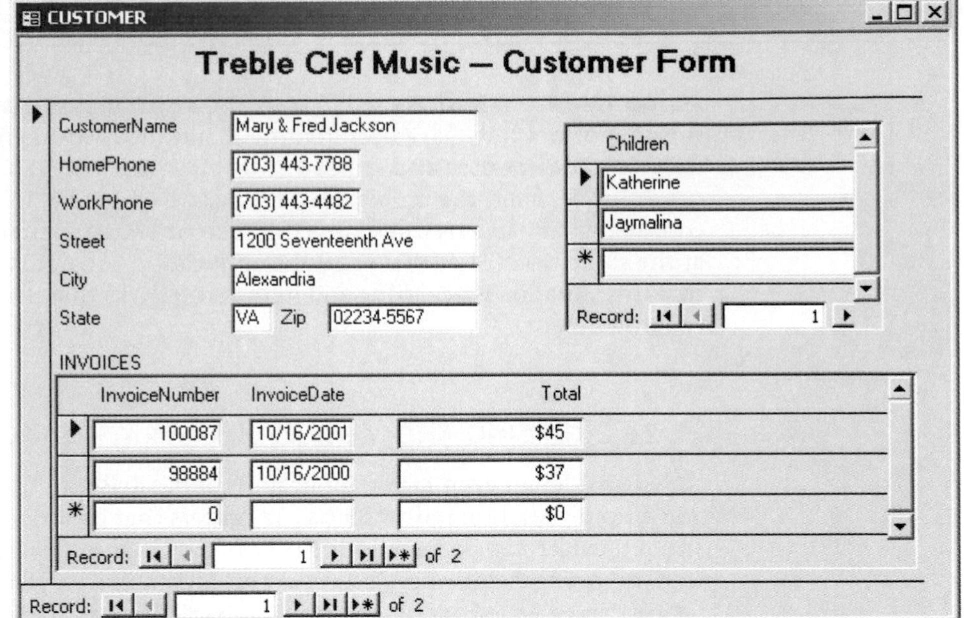
CUSTOMER
Treble Clef Music — Customer Form
CustomerName Mary & Fred Jackson
HomePhone (703) 443-7788
WorkPhone (703) 443-4482
Street 1200 Seventeenth Ave
City Alexandria
State VA Zip 02234-5567
Children
Katherine
Jaymalina
Record: 1
INVOICES
InvoiceNumber InvoiceDate Total
100087 10/16/2001 $45
98884 10/16/2000 $37
0 $0
Record: 1 of 2
Record: 1 of 2

(a)

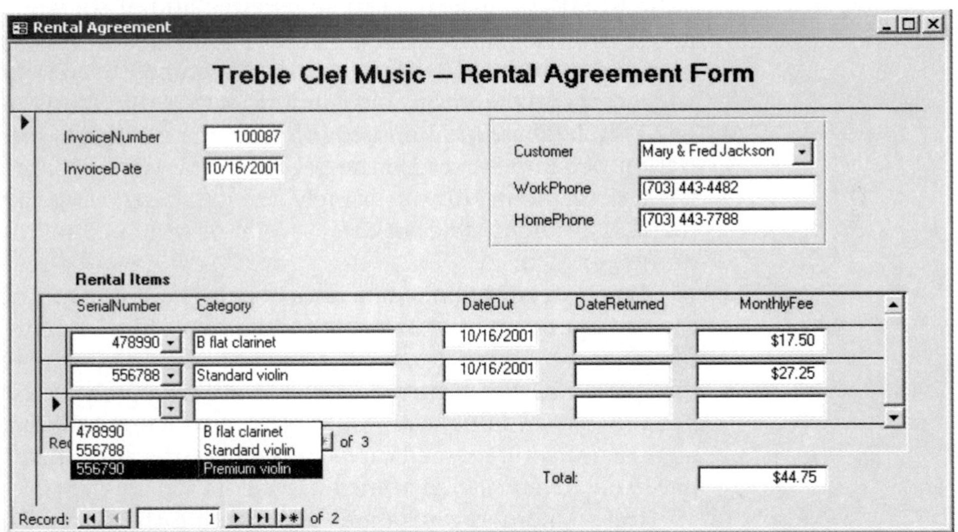
Rental Agreement
Treble Clef Music — Rental Agreement Form
InvoiceNumber 100087
InvoiceDate 10/16/2001
Customer Mary & Fred Jackson
WorkPhone (703) 443-4482
HomePhone (703) 443-7788
Rental Items
SerialNumber Category DateOut DateReturned MonthlyFee
478990 B flat clarinet 10/16/2001 $17.50
556788 Standard violin 10/16/2001 $27.25
478990 B flat clarinet
556788 Standard violin
556790 Premium violin
of 3
Total: $44.75
Record: 1 of 2

(b)

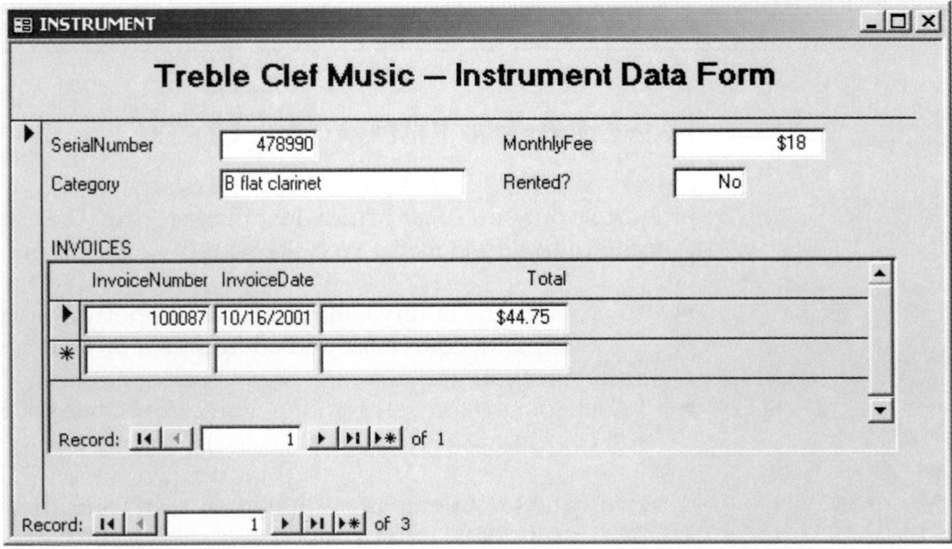
INSTRUMENT
Treble Clef Music — Instrument Data Form
SerialNumber 478990
MonthlyFee $18
Category B flat clarinet
Rented? No
INVOICES
InvoiceNumber InvoiceDate Total
100087 10/16/2001 $44.75
Record: 1 of 1
Record: 1 of 3

(c)

Rental Agreement form is used to track the instruments that have been rented and whether or not they have been returned, and the Instrument Data form is used to show instrument data and rental history.

To understand the problems that must be overcome in a multi-user database, consider what happens when two customers attempt to rent the same B-flat clarinet at the same time. The DBMS and the application programs must somehow detect that this situation is occurring and inform the clerks that they must choose a different instrument.

State Licensing and Vehicle Registration Bureau

Now consider an even larger application of database technology, a state licensing and auto registration bureau. It has 52 centers that conduct drivers' tests and issue and renew drivers' licenses and also 37 offices that sell vehicle registrations.

The personnel in these offices access a database to perform their jobs. Before people can be issued or can renew their driver's licenses, their records in the database are checked for traffic violations, accidents, or arrests. These data are used to determine whether the license can be renewed and, if so, whether it should carry any limitations. Similarly, personnel in the auto registration department access the database to determine whether an auto has been registered before and, if so, to whom, and whether there are any outstanding matters that should prohibit the registration.

This database has hundreds of users, including not only the license and registration personnel but also the people in the state department of revenue and in law enforcement. Not surprisingly, the database is large and complex, with more than 40 different tables of data, several of which contain hundreds of thousands of rows of data.

Large organizational databases like the licensing and registration bureau were the first applications of database technology. These systems have been in existence for 20 or 30 years and have been modified to meet changing requirements over that period. Other examples of organizational databases concern account processing at banks and financial institutions, production and material supply systems at large manufacturers, medical records processing at hospitals and insurance companies, and governmental agencies.

Today, many organizations are adapting their organizational database applications to enable customers to access and even to change their own data over the Internet. If you work for a large organization, you could likely be assigned to such a project.

Calvert Island Reservations Centre

Calvert Island is a little known, beautiful island on the west coast of Canada. To promote tourism to a worldwide market, the Calvert Island Chamber of Commerce has developed a Web site with three purposes:

- To promote the beauty and recreational opportunities on Calvert Island
- To obtain and store name and address data of Web site visitors for follow-up postal promotions
- To obtain and store reservation requests for hotels, lodges, and tourist services and communicate those requests to the appropriate vendors

Two databases are used to support this web site. The first, the promotional database, stores data, photos, video clips, and sound bites of places, events, and facilities on Calvert Island. This database has two types of user. Normal users access this database in read-only mode. Using standard browsers, these users can point and click around the Web site to view activities and facilities in which they have an interest. Behind the scenes, a database application is extracting data and multimedia elements from the promotional database (See Figure 1-6).

The second type of user of the promotional database is an employee of the Chamber of Commerce who maintains the site. Employees add, change, and delete data and multimedia files in the database as promotions change, vendors enter and leave the program, and in response to user requests.

In addition to the promotional database, applications at the Web site process a customer and reservation database. This database stores data entered when Web site visitors complete a customer survey form and when they request a reservation. Customer name, postal and e-mail addresses, interests, preferences, and reservation requests are maintained in this database. When a reservation request is entered, the database application forwards it to the appropriate vendor via

Calvert Island Reservation Centre Web Page

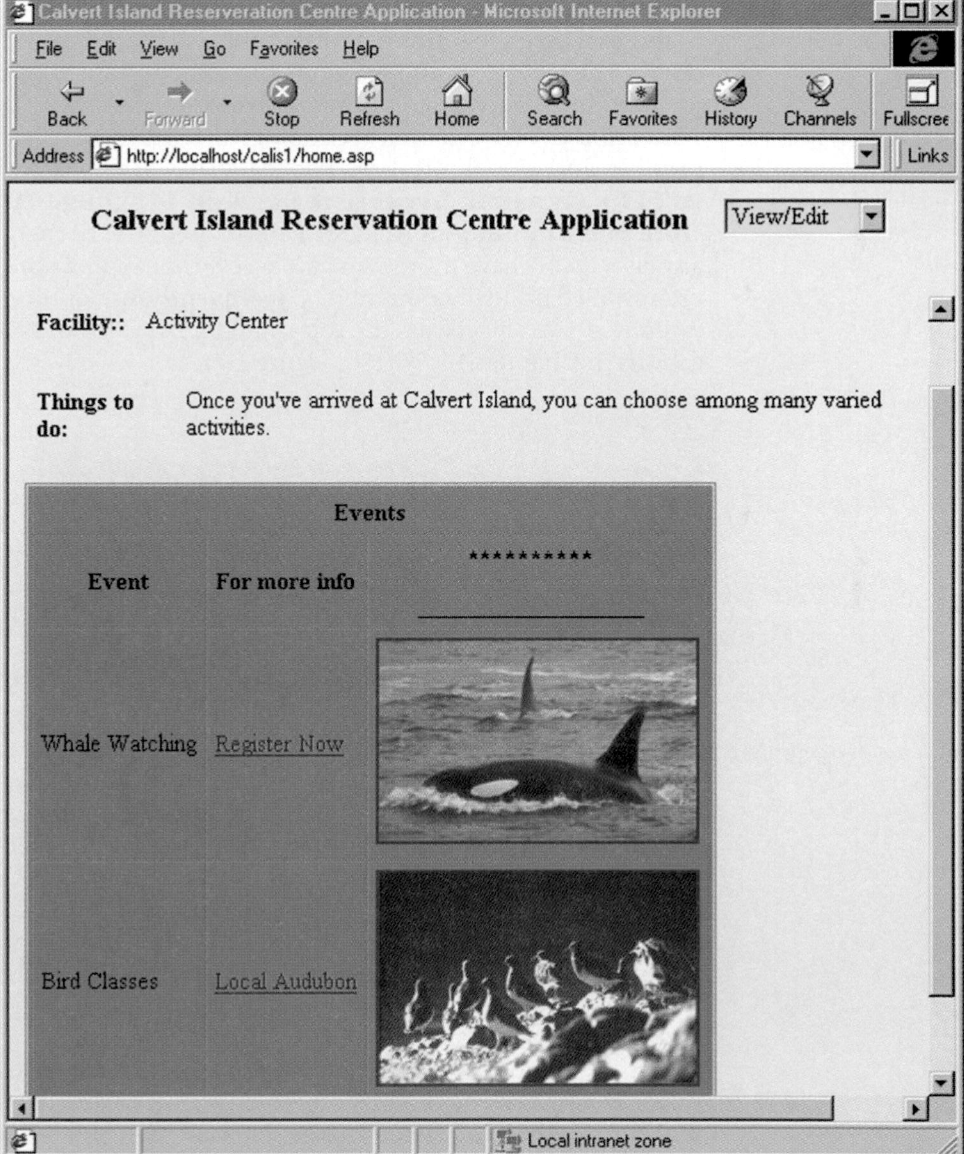

FIGURE 1-7

Characteristics of Internet Technology Applications

- Include both structured data and multi-media data
- Forms and reports displayed via a standard browser
- Data transfer via internet standards such as HTTP, DHTML, and XML.

e-mail. Periodically, summary reservation reports are prepared and e-mailed to vendors for follow-up and other management purposes.

Three primary characteristics of the Calvert Island database differentiate it from the other applications we have discussed. First, a large portion of the first database contains not only structured data like vendor names and addresses, but also nonstructured bit streams of multimedia files. Second, application content is delivered to the user via a standardized browser. The forms used for Mary Richards, Treble Clef, and the driver's license bureau are fixed in format by the designer and change only when the application is modified. In contrast, Calvert Island users see the form in a format that is determined not only by the application but also by the brand, version, and local options used in their browsers.

The third differentiating characteristic of the Calvert Island application is that standardized Web-oriented technology is used to transfer the data between the browser and the application and database. **Hypertext transfer protocol (HTTP), dynamic hypertext markup language (DHTML),** and **extensible markup language (XML)** are all used. Use of these standards means that any users who have a browser can access this application. No software must be pre-installed on their computers. Consequently, use of this application is virtually unlimited. We will discuss the role of HTTP, DHTML, and XML for database applications in Chapters 14–16. (See Figure 1-7).

Comparison of Database Applications

These examples represent a sampling of the uses of database technology. Hundreds of thousands of databases are like the one used by Mary Richards House Painting, single-user databases with a relatively small amount of data—say, fewer than 10 megabytes. The forms and reports for these are generally simple and straightforward.

Other databases are like the one used by Treble Clef Music; they have more than one user but usually fewer than 20 or 30 users altogether. They contain a moderate amount of data, say, 50 or 100 megabytes. The forms and reports need to be complex enough to support several different business functions.

The largest databases are like those in the auto registration case, which have hundreds of users and trillions of bytes of data. Many different applications are in use, each application having its own forms and reports. Finally, some databases involve use of Internet technology and process both character and multimedia data such as pictures, sounds, animations, movies, and the like. The characteristics of these types of databases are summarized in Figure 1-8.

When you finish this book, you should be able to design and create databases and database applications like those used by Mary Richards and Treble Clef. You will probably not be able to create one as large and complicated as the vehicle registration database, but you will be able to serve as an effective member of a team that does design and create such a database. You should also be able to create a small to medium database using Internet technology.

➤ FIGURE 1-8

Characteristics of Different Types of Databases

Type	Example	Typical Number of Concurrent Users	Typical Size of Database
Personal	Mary Richards House Painting	1	<10 Megabytes
Workgroup	Treble Clef Music	<25	<100 Megabytes
Organizational	Licensing and Registration	Hundreds to Thousands	>1 Trillion Bytes
Internet	Calvert Island Reservations	Hundreds to Thousands	<Any

➤ THE RELATIONSHIP OF APPLICATION PROGRAMS AND THE DBMS

All of the preceding examples and, indeed, all database applications have the general structure shown in Figure 1-9: The user interacts with a database application, which in turn interfaces with the DBMS, which accesses the database data.

At one time, the boundary between the application program and the DBMS was clearly defined. Applications were written in third-generation languages like COBOL, and those applications called on the DBMS for data management services. In fact, this still is done, most frequently on large mainframe databases.

Today, however, the features and functions of many DBMS products have grown to the point where the DBMS itself can process sizable portions of the application. For example, most DBMS products contain report writers and form generators that can be integrated into an application. This fact is important to us for two reasons. First, although the bulk of this text considers the design and

Relationships of Users, Database Applications, DBMS, and Database

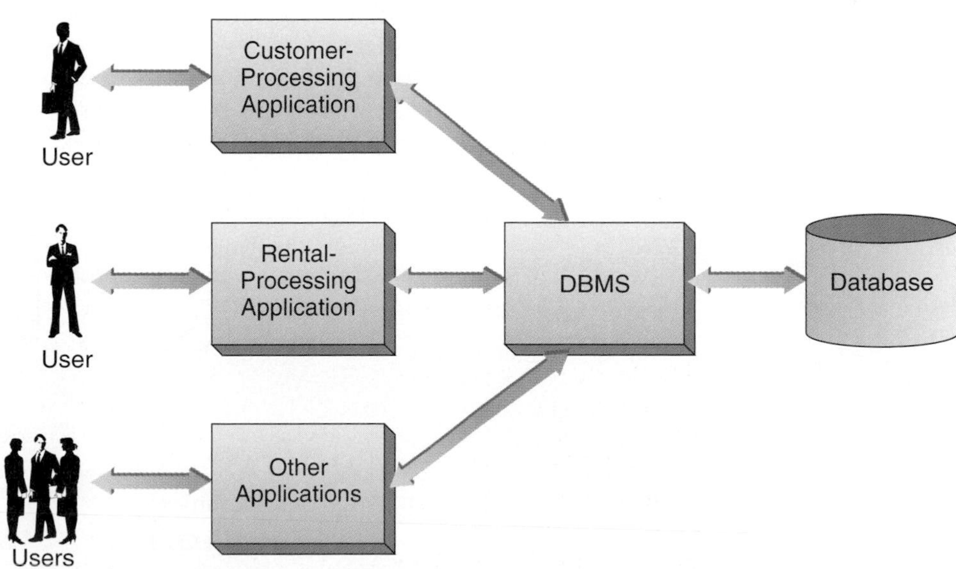

development of databases, we will often refer to the design and development of database applications. After all, no user wants just a database. Instead, users want forms, reports, and queries that are based on their data.

Second, from time to time you will note an overlap between the material discussed in this class and that discussed in your systems development class because developing effective database applications requires many of the skills that you have learned or will learn in your systems development class. Likewise, most systems development classes today include the design of databases. The difference between the two courses is one of emphasis. Here, our emphasis is on the design, construction and processing of the database. In a systems class, the emphasis is on the development of information systems, most of which use database technology.

➤ FILE-PROCESSING SYSTEMS

The best way to understand the general nature and characteristics of databases today is to look at the characteristics of systems that predated the use of database technology. These systems reveal the problems that database technology has solved.

The first business information systems stored groups of records in separate files and were called file-processing systems. Figure 1-10, for example, depicts two file-processing systems that Treble Clef could use. One system processes CUSTOMER data, and the other one processes RENTAL data.

Although file-processing systems are a great improvement over manual record-keeping systems, they have important limitations:

- Data are separated and isolated.
- Much data is duplicated.
- Application programs are dependent on file formats.
- Files are often incompatible with one another.
- It is difficult to represent data in the users' perspectives.

SEPARATED AND ISOLATED DATA

The salespeople at Treble Clef need to relate their customers to the instruments that they rent. For the system in Figure 1-10, the data need to be extracted somehow from CUSTOMER and RENTAL files and combined into a third file. With file-processing, this is difficult. First, systems analysts and computer programmers must determine which parts of each of the files are needed; then they must decide how the files are related to one another; last, they must coordinate the processing of the files so that the correct data are extracted. Coordinating two

Two File-Processing Systems

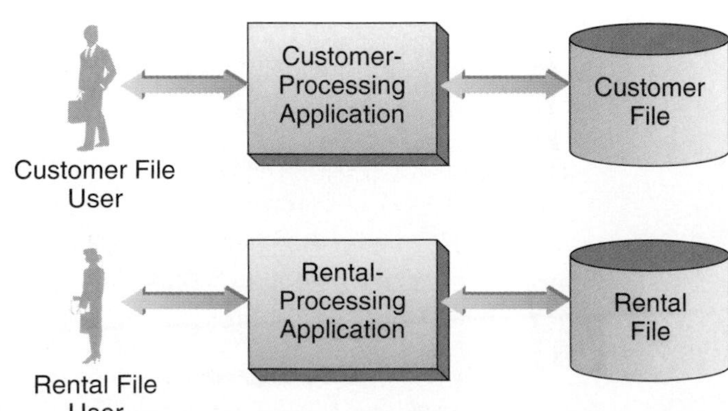

files is difficult enough, but imagine the task of coordinating 10 or more of them!

Data Duplication

In the Treble Clef example, a customer's name, address, and other data may be stored many times. That is, the data are stored once for CUSTOMER and again for each RENTAL agreement the customer has. Although these duplicate data waste file space, that is not the most serious problem; rather, the most serious problem with duplicated data concerns **data integrity.**

A collection of data has integrity if the data are logically consistent. Poor data integrity often results when data are duplicated. For example, if a customer changes his or her name or address, then all the files containing that data must be updated, but the danger is that all of the files might *not* be updated, causing discrepancies among them. In the Treble Clef example, the customer might have one address for one RENTAL record and a different address for a second RENTAL record.

Data integrity problems are serious. If data items differ, they will produce inconsistent results and uncertainty. If a report from one application disagrees with a report from another application, who will be able to tell which one is correct? When results are inconsistent, the credibility of the stored data, and even the MIS function itself, comes into question.

Application Program Dependency

With file processing, application programs depend on the file formats. Usually in file-processing systems the physical formats of files and records are part of the application code. In COBOL, for example, file formats are written in the DATA DIVISION. The problem with this arrangement is that when changes are made in the file formats, the application programs also must be changed.

For example, if the customer record is modified to expand the ZIP code field from five to nine digits, all programs using that customer record must be modified, even if they do not use the ZIP code field. Because there might be 20 programs that process the customer file, such a change means that a programmer has to identify all the affected programs, modify them, and then retest them—all time-consuming and error-prone tasks. Also, requiring programmers to modify programs that do not use the field whose format has changed is a waste of money.

Incompatible Files

One of the consequences of program data dependency is that file formats depend on the language or product used to generate them. Thus, the format of a file processed by a COBOL program is different from the format of a file processed by a Visual Basic program, which is different still from the format of a file processed by a C++ program.

As a result, files cannot be readily combined or compared. Suppose, for example, FILE-A contains CUSTOMER data that includes CustomerNumber, and FILE-B contains RENTAL data that also includes CustomerNumber. Suppose an application requires that we combine records that have matching CustomerNumbers. If FILE-A were processed by a Visual Basic program and FILE-B were processed by a C++ program, we would need to convert both files to a common structure before we could combine the records. This would be time consuming and sometimes difficult. Such problems grow worse as the number of files to be combined increases.

THE DIFFICULTY OF REPRESENTING DATA IN THE USERS' PERSPECTIVES

It is difficult to represent file-processing data in a form that seems natural to users. Users want to see RENTAL data in a format like that in Figure 1-5(b). But in order to show the data in this way, several different files need to be extracted, combined, and presented together. This difficulty arises because with file processing, relationships among records are not readily represented or processed. Since a file-processing system cannot quickly determine which CUSTOMERs have rented which instruments, producing a form showing CUSTOMER preferences is quite difficult.

➤ DATABASE PROCESSING SYSTEMS

Database technology was developed to overcome the limitations of file-processing systems. To understand how, compare the file-processing system in Figure 1-10 with the database system in Figure 1-9. File-processing programs directly access files of stored data. In contrast, database-processing programs call the DBMS to access the stored data. This difference is significant because it makes application programming easier; that is, application programmers do not have to be concerned with the ways in which data are physically stored. Rather, they are free to concentrate on matters important to the user instead of matters important to the computer system.

INTEGRATED DATA

In a database system, all the application data are stored in a single facility called the **database.** An application program can ask the DBMS to access customer data or sales data or both. If both are needed, the application programmer specifies only how the data are to be combined, and the DBMS performs the necessary operations to do it. Thus, the programmer is not responsible for writing programs to consolidate the files, as must be done for the system in Figure 1-10.

REDUCED DATA DUPLICATION

With database processing, the duplication of data is minimal. For example, in Treble Clef's database, the customer's number, name, and address are stored only once. Whenever these data are needed, the DBMS can retrieve them, and when they are modified, only one update is necessary. Because data are stored in only one place, data integrity problems are less common—there is less opportunity for discrepancies among multiple copies of the same data item.

PROGRAM/DATA INDEPENDENCE

Database processing reduces the dependency of programs on file formats. All record formats are stored in the database itself (along with the data), and they are accessed by the DBMS, not by application programs. Unlike file-processing programs, database application programs need not include the format of all the files and records they process. Instead, application programs must contain only a definition (the length and data type) of each of the data items they need from the database. The DBMS maps the data items into records and handles other similar transformations.

Program/data independence minimizes the impact of data format changes on application programs. Format changes are input into the DBMS, which in turn updates the data it maintains concerning the structure of the database. For the most part, application programs are unaware that the format has changed. This also means that whenever data items are added, changed, or deleted from the database, only those programs that use these particular data items have to be modified. For applications consisting of dozens of programs, this can be a considerable savings of time.

EASIER REPRESENTATION OF THE USERS' PERSPECTIVES

As you will discover throughout this text, database technology makes it possible to represent, in a straightforward fashion, the objects found in the user's world. The forms in Figure 1-5 can readily be produced from a database because the relationships among the records of data are stored as part of the database.

➤ DEFINITION OF A DATABASE

The term *database* suffers from many different interpretations. It has been used to refer to everything from a collection of index cards to the volumes and volumes of data that a government collects about its citizens. In this text, we use this term with a specific meaning: *A database is a self-describing collection of integrated records.* It is important to understand each part of this definition.

A DATABASE IS SELF-DESCRIBING

A database is self-describing: It contains, in addition to the users' source data, a description of its own structure. This description is called a **data dictionary** (also called a **data directory** or **metadata**).

In this sense, a database is similar to a library, which can be thought of as a self-describing collection of books. In addition to the books, the library contains a card catalog describing them. In the same way, the data dictionary (which is part of the database, just as the card catalog is part of the library) describes the data contained in the database.

Why is this self-describing characteristic of a database so important? First, it promotes program–data independence. That is, it makes it possible to determine the structure and content of the database by examining the database itself. We do not need to guess what the database contains, nor do we need to maintain external documentation of the file and record formats (as is done in file-processing systems).

Second, if we change the structure of the data in the database (such as adding new data items to an existing record), we enter only that change in the data dictionary. Few, if any, programs will need to be changed. In most cases, only those programs that process the altered data items must be changed.

A DATABASE IS A COLLECTION OF INTEGRATED RECORDS

The standard hierarchy of data is as follows: Bits are aggregated into bytes or characters; characters are aggregated into fields; fields are aggregated into records; and records are aggregated into files (see Figure 1-11(a)). It is tempting to follow the pattern of that statement and say that files are aggregated into databases. Although this statement is true, it does not go far enough.

A database does include files of user data, but it also contains more. As we mentioned earlier, a database contains a description of itself in metadata. In addition, a database includes **indexes** that are used to represent relationships among the data and also to improve the performance of database applications. Finally, the database often contains data about the applications that use the database. The

FIGURE 1-11

Hierarchy of Data Elements in (a) File-Processing Systems and (b) Database Systems

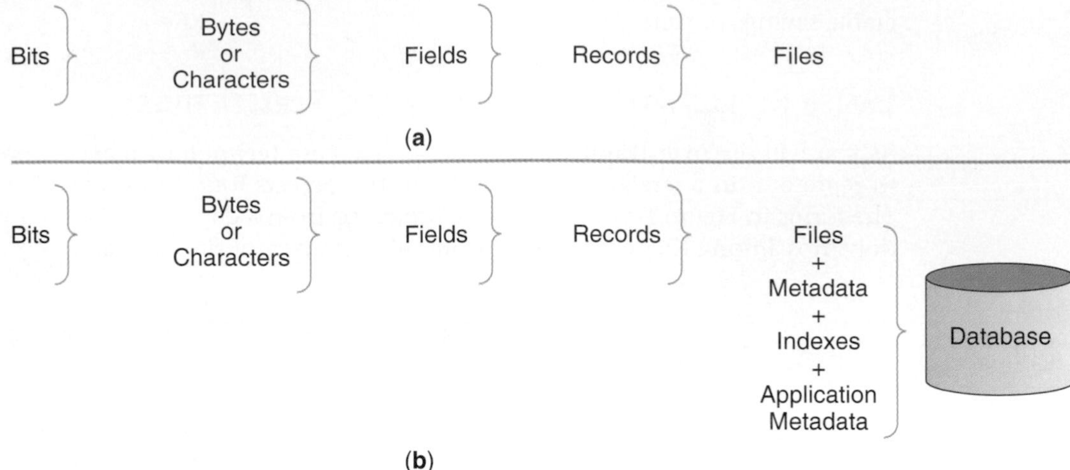

structure of a data entry form, or a report, is sometimes part of the database. This last category of data we call **application metadata.** Thus a database contains the four types of data shown in Figure 1-11(b): files of user data, metadata, indexes, and application metadata.

A Database Is a Model of a Model

A database is a model. It is tempting to say that a database is a model of reality or of some portion of reality as it relates to a business. This, however, is not true. A database does not model reality or some portion thereof. Instead, a database is a model of the *users' model.* For example, Mary Richards's database is a model of the way in which Mary Richards views her business. As she sees it, her business has customers, jobs, and referrals. Her database, therefore, contains representations of facts concerning those entities. The names and addresses of customers, the dates and descriptions of her jobs, and the names of her referral sources all are measurements that are important to her view of her business.

Databases vary in their level of detail. Some are simple and crude. A list of customers and the amounts they owe is an approximate representation of Mary's mental model. A more detailed representation includes jobs, referrals, and the trips made for each job. And a very detailed representation contains the amount and type of paint used on each job, the number of paintbrushes required, and the hours of labor on specific job tasks such as taping, painting woodwork, painting walls, cleanup, and the like.

The degree of detail that should be incorporated into a database depends on the information desired. Clearly, the more information that is wanted, the more detail the database must have. Deciding on the appropriate amount of detail is an important part of the job of designing a database. As you will discover, the principal criterion is the level of detail that exists in the minds of the users.

The database is a dynamic model because businesses change. People come and go. Products are introduced and phased out. Money is earned and spent. As these changes occur, the data that represent the business also must be altered. If not, the data will become outdated and inaccurately represent the business.

Transactions are representations of events. When events take place, the transactions for the events must be processed against the database. To do this, someone (a data entry clerk, a salesperson, or a teller, for example) activates a transaction-processing program and enters the transaction data. The program then calls on the DBMS to alter the database. Transaction-processing programs usually produce displays or print responses such as order confirmations or receipts.

➤ THE HISTORY OF DATABASE PROCESSING

Database processing was originally used in major corporations and large organizations as the basis of large transaction-processing systems. An example is the licensing and vehicle registration example considered earlier. Later, as microcomputers gained popularity, database technology migrated to micros and was used for single-user, personal database applications like that described for Mary Richards. Next, as micros were connected together in work groups, database technology moved to the workgroup setting such as in the Treble Clef example. Finally, databases are being used today for Internet and intranet applications.

THE ORGANIZATIONAL CONTEXT

The initial application of database technology was to resolve problems with the file-processing systems discussed earlier in this chapter. In the mid-1960s, large corporations were producing data at phenomenal rates in file-processing systems, but the data were becoming difficult to manage, and new systems were becoming increasingly difficult to develop. Furthermore, management wanted to be able to relate the data in one file system to those in another.

The limitations of file processing prevented the easy integration of data. Database technology, however, held out the promise of a solution to these problems, and so large companies began to develop organizational databases. Companies centralized their operational data, such as orders, inventory, and accounting data, in these databases. The applications were primarily organization-wide, transaction-processing systems.

At first, when the technology was new, database applications were difficult to develop, and there were many failures. Even those applications that were successful were slow and unreliable: The computer hardware could not handle the volume of transactions quickly; the developers had not yet discovered more efficient ways to store and retrieve data; and the programmers were still new at accessing databases, and sometimes their programs did not work correctly.

Companies found another disadvantage of database processing: vulnerability. If a file-processing system fails, only that particular application will be out of commission. But if the database fails, all of its dependent applications will be out of commission.

Gradually, the situation improved. Hardware and software engineers learned how to build systems powerful enough to support many concurrent users and fast enough to keep up with the daily workload of transactions. New ways of controlling, protecting, and backing up the database were devised. Standard procedures for database processing evolved, and programmers learned how to write more efficient and more maintainable code. By the mid-1970s, databases could efficiently and reliably process organizational applications. Many of those applications are still running today, more than 25 years after their creation!

THE RELATIONAL MODEL

In 1970, E. F. Codd published a landmark paper[1] in which he applied concepts from a branch of mathematics called relational algebra to the problem of storing large amounts of data. Codd's paper started a movement in the database community that in a few years led to the definition of the **relational database model.** This model is a particular way of structuring and processing a database, and we discuss it at length in Chapters 5 and 9 through 14.

The advantage of the relational model is that data are stored in a way that minimizes duplicated data and eliminates certain types of processing errors that can occur when data are stored in other ways. Data are stored as tables, with rows and columns, like the data in Figure 1-1.

According to the relational model, not all tables are equally desirable. Using a process called *normalization,* a table that is not desirable can be changed into two or more that are. You will learn about the normalization process in detail in Chapter 5.

Another key advantage of the relational model is that columns contain data that relate one row to another. For example, in Figure 1-1, CUSTOMER_ID in the JOB table relates to CUSTOMER_ID in the CUSTOMER table. This makes the relationships among rows visible to the user.

At first, it was thought that the relational model would enable users to obtain information from databases without the assistance of MIS professionals. Part of the rationale of this idea was that tables are simple constructs that are intuitively understandable. Additionally, since the relationships are stored in the data, the users would be able to combine rows when necessary. For example, to access a RENTAL record, a user at Treble Clef would be able to combine a row of the CUSTOMER table with rows of a RENTAL table.

It turned out that this process was too difficult for most users. Hence, the promise of the relational model as a means for nonspecialists to access a database was never realized. In retrospect, the key benefit of the relational model has turned out to be that it provides a standard way for specialists (like you!) to structure and process a database.

MICROCOMPUTER DBMS PRODUCTS

In 1979, a small company called Ashton-Tate introduced a microcomputer product, dBase II (pronounced "d base two"), and called it a relational DBMS. In an exceedingly successful promotional tactic, Ashton-Tate distributed—nearly free of charge—more than 100,000 copies of its product to purchasers of the then-new Osborne microcomputer. Many of the people who bought these computers were pioneers in the microcomputer industry. They began to invent microcomputer applications using dBase, and the number of dBase applications grew quickly. As a result, Ashton-Tate became one of the first major corporations in the microcomputer industry. Later, Ashton-Tate was purchased by Borland, which now sells the dBase line of products.

The success of this product, however, confused and confounded the subject of database processing. The problem was this: According to the definition prevalent in the late 1970s, dBase II was neither a DBMS nor relational. In fact, it was a programming language with generalized file-processing capabilities. The systems that were developed with dBase II appeared much more like those in Figure 1-10 than the ones in Figure 1-9. The million or so users of dBase II thought they were using a relational DBMS when, in fact, they were not.

---

[1]E. F. Codd, "A Relational Model of Data for Large Shared Databanks," *Communications of the ACM,* June 1970, pp. 377–387.

Thus, the terms *database management system* and *relational database* were used loosely at the start of the microcomputer boom. Most of the people who were processing a microcomputer database were really managing files and were not receiving the benefits of database processing, although they did not realize it. Today, the situation has changed as the microcomputer marketplace has become more mature and sophisticated. dBase IV and the dBase products that followed it such as Foxpro are truly *relational* DBMS products.

Although dBase did pioneer the application of database technology on microcomputers, at the same time other vendors began to move their products from the mainframe to the microcomputer. Oracle, Focus, and Ingress are three examples of DBMS products that were ported down to microcomputers. They are truly DBMS programs, and most would agree that they are truly relational as well.

One impact of the move of database technology to the micro was the dramatic improvement in DBMS user interfaces. Users of microcomputer systems will not put up with the clumsy and awkward user interfaces common on mainframe DBMS products. Thus, as DBMS products were devised for micros, user interfaces were made easier to use. This was possible because micro DBMS products operate on dedicated computers and because more computer power is available to process the user interface. Today, DBMS products are rich and robust with graphical user interfaces such as Microsoft Windows.

The combination of microcomputers, the relational model, and vastly improved user interfaces enabled database technology to move from an organizational context to a personal-computing context. When this occurred, the number of sites that used database technology exploded. In 1980 there were about 10,000 sites using DBMS products in the United States. Today there are well over 40 million such sites!

Client–Server Database Applications

In the middle to late 1980s, end users began to connect their separated microcomputers using local area networks (LANs). These networks enabled computers to send data to one another at previously unimaginable rates. The first applications of this technology shared peripherals, such as large-capacity fast disks, expensive printers, and plotters, and facilitated intercomputer communication via electronic mail. In time, however, end users wanted to share their databases as well, which led to the development of multi-user database applications on LANs.

The LAN-based multi-user architecture is considerably different from the multi-user architecture used on mainframe databases. With a mainframe, only one CPU is involved in database application processing, but with LAN systems, many CPUs can be simultaneously involved. Because this situation was both advantageous (greater performance) and more problematic (coordinating the actions of independent CPUs), it led to a new style of multi-user database processing called the **client–server database architecture.**

Not all database processing on a LAN is client–server processing. A simple, but less robust, mode of processing is called **file-sharing architecture.** A company like Treble Clef could most likely use either type since it is a small organization with modest processing requirements. Larger workgroups, however, would require client–server processing. We will describe these approaches and discuss them in detail in Chapter 17.

Databases Using Internet Technology

As shown in the Calvert Island Reservations Centre example, database technology is being used in conjunction with Internet technology to publish database data on the Web. This same technology is used to publish applications over corporate and organizational intranets. Some experts believe that, in time, all database applications will be delivered using browsers and related Internet technologies—even personal databases that are "published" to a single person.

Thus there are two categories of database applications that use Internet technology. One category consists of pure Web database applications such as the Calvert Island applications. Another category consists of traditional personal, workgroup, and organizational databases that are not published on the Internet, but do use technology like browsers, DHTML, and XML. Because it is incorrect to refer to this second category as Internet databases, this text will refer to both categories as *databases using Internet technology.*

This category stands on the leading edge of database technology today. As will be described in Chapter 14, XML in particular serves the needs of database applications exceptionally well, and is the basis of many new database products and services.

Distributed Database Processing

Before concluding this survey of the history of database processing, we need to discuss two aspects of database technology that are important in theory but have not been, at least so far, widely adopted. The first is distributed database processing, and the second is object-oriented databases. We discuss these topics in more detail in Chapters 17 and 18, respectively.

Organizational database applications solve the problems of file processing and allow more integrated processing of organizational data. Personal and workgroup database systems bring database technology even closer to users by allowing them access to locally managed databases. **Distributed databases** combine these types of database processing by allowing personal, workgroup, and organizational databases to be combined into integrated but distributed databases. As such, in theory, they offer even more flexible data access and processing, but they also unfortunately pose many unsolved problems.

The essence of distributed databases is that all of the organization's data are spread over many computers—micros, LAN servers, and mainframes—that communicate with one another as they process the database. The goals of distributed database systems are to make it appear to each user that he or she is the only user of the organization's data and to provide the same consistency, accuracy, and timeliness that he or she would have if no one else were using the distributed database.

Among the more pressing problems with distributed databases are those of security and control. Enabling so many users to access the database (there can be hundreds of concurrent users) and controlling what they do to that distributed database are complicated tasks.

Coordinating and synchronizing processing can be difficult. If one user group downloads and updates part of the database and then transmits the changed data back to the mainframe, how does the system prevent, in the meantime, another user from attempting to use the version of the data it finds on the mainframe? Imagine this problem involving dozens of files and hundreds of users using scores of pieces of computer equipment.

Whereas the transitions from organizational to personal to workgroup database processing were relatively easy, the difficulties facing the database designers and engineers of the distributed DBMS are monumental. In truth, even though work on distributed database systems has been underway for more than 25 years, significant problems remain. Microsoft has defined and is building a distributed processing architecture and set of supporting products called the **Microsoft**

Transaction Server (MTS). While MTS has promise and, of all companies, Microsoft has the resources to develop and market such a system, it is still unknown whether truly distributed databases can meet the needs of day-to-day organizational processing. See the discussion of OLE DB in Chapter 15 for more on this topic.

OBJECT-ORIENTED DBMS (ODBMS)

In the late 1980s a new style of programming called *object-oriented programming* (OOP) began to be used, which has a substantially different orientation from that of traditional programming, as is explained in Chapter 18. In brief, the data structures processed with OOP are considerably more complex than those processed with traditional languages. These data structures also are difficult to store in existing relational DBMS products. As a consequence, a new category of DBMS products called *object-oriented database systems* is evolving to store and process OOP data structures.

For a variety of reasons, OOP has not yet been widely used for business information systems. First, it is difficult to use, and it is very expensive to develop OOP applications. Second, most organizations have millions or billions of bytes of data already organized in relational databases, and they are unwilling to bear the cost and risk required to convert those databases to an ODBMS format. Finally, most ODBMS have been developed to support engineering applications, and they do not have features and functions that are appropriate or readily adaptable to business information applications.

Consequently, for the foreseeable future, ODBMSs are likely to occupy a niche in commercial information systems applications. We will discuss OOP, object-oriented databases and a hybrid from Oracle Corporation called object-relational databases in Chapter 18, but the bulk of the discussion in this text will concern the relational model, since it concerns technologies that you are likely to use in the first five years of your career.

➤ SUMMARY

Database processing is one of the most important courses in the information systems curriculum. Database skill and knowledge are in high demand not only for traditional applications but also for applications that use Internet technology for public and private networks.

Database technology is used in a variety of applications. Some serve only a single user on a single computer; others are used by work groups of 20 or 30 people on a LAN; still others are used by hundreds of users and involve trillions of bytes of data. Recently, database technology has been combined with Internet technology to support multimedia applications over public and private networks.

The components of a database application are the database, the database management systems (DBMSs), and application programs. Sometimes the application programs are entirely separate from the DBMS; other times substantial portions of the application are provided by features and functions of the DBMS.

File-processing systems store data in separate files, each of which contains a different type of data. File-processing systems have several limitations. With separated files, it is difficult to combine data stored in separate files, as the data are often duplicated among files, leading to data integrity problems. Application programs are dependent on file formats, causing maintenance problems when the formats change and the files become incompatible, requiring file conversions. And it is difficult to represent data from the users' perspectives.

Database processing systems were developed to overcome these limitations. In the database environment, the DBMS is the interface between application programs and the database. The data are integrated, and their duplication is reduced. Only the DBMS is affected by changes in the physical formats of stored data. And if data items are changed, added, or deleted, few application programs will require maintenance. With database technology, it is easier to represent objects in the users' environments.

A database is a self-describing collection of integrated records. It is self-describing because it contains a description of itself in a data dictionary. A data dictionary is also known as a data directory or metadata. A database is a collection of integrated records because the relationships among the records are stored in the database. This arrangement enables the DBMS to construct even complicated objects by combining data on the basis of the stored relationships. Relationships are often stored in overhead data. Thus, the three parts of a database are the application data, the data dictionary, and the overhead data.

Database technology developed in several stages. Early databases focused on the transaction processing of organizational data. Then, the relational model, together with the microcomputer, led to the use of personal database applications. With the advent of LANs, departments began to implement workgroup client–server databases. Today, Internet and traditional database applications are being delivered using Internet technology. Distributed processing and object-oriented databases are important topics in database processing. To date, however, neither has been commercially successful or seen widespread use in business applications.

➤ GROUP I QUESTIONS

1.1 Why is database processing an important subject?

1.2 Describe the nature and characteristics of a single-user database application used by an individual like Mary Richards.

1.3 Describe the nature and characteristics of a database application used by a workgroup like Treble Clef Music.

1.4 Describe the nature and characteristics of a database application used by an organization like the state's driver's licensing and vehicle registration bureau.

1.5 Describe the nature and characteristics of a database application used by an organization like the Calvert Island Reservation Centre.

1.6 Explain the nature and function of each of the components of Figure 1-9.

1.7 How is the relationship between application programs and the DBMS changing over time?

1.8 List the limitations of file-processing systems as described in this chapter.

1.9 Explain how database technology overcomes the limitations you listed in your answer to Question 1.8.

1.10 Define the term *database.*

1.11 What are metadata? What are indexes? What are application metadata?

1.12 Explain why a database is a model. Describe the difference between a model of reality and a model of a user's model of reality. Why is this difference important?

1.13 Give an example, other than one in this chapter, of a personal database application.

1.14 Give an example, other than one in this chapter, of a workgroup database application.

1.15 Give an example, other than one in this chapter, of a large-enterprise database application.

1.16 What were some of the weaknesses of early organizational database applications?

1.17 What are the two primary advantages of the relational model?

1.18 Summarize the events in the development of microcomputer DBMS products.

1.19 What was the major factor that gave rise to workgroup database applications?

1.20 How does the client–server architecture differ from mainframe multi-user architectures?

1.21 What is the difference between an Internet database application and a database application that uses Internet technology?

1.22 Explain the general nature of distributed processing. What are some of the difficult problems to be faced?

1.23 Describe the purpose of an object-oriented database. Why have such databases not been more accepted for information systems applications?

➤ PROJECTS

A. Access the Web site of a computer manufacturer such as Dell (www.dell.com). Use the Web site to determine which model of laptop computer you would recommend for under $2500. Do you think one or more databases are used to support this site? If so, which features and functions of the Web site do you think would be most helped by database technology, keeping in mind both the definition of a database and the advantages of database processing?

B. Access the Web site of a retail bookseller such as Amazon (www.amazon.com). Use the Web site to locate the most recently published biography of William Wordsworth. Do you think one or more databases are used to support this site? If so, which features and functions of the Web site do you think would be most helped by database technology, keeping in mind both the definition of a database and the advantages of database processing?

➤ FIREDUP PROJECT QUESTIONS

FiredUp, Inc., is a small business owned by Curt and Julie Robards. Based in Brisbane, Australia, FiredUp manufacturers and sells a lightweight camping stove, called the FireNow. Curt, who previously worked as an aerospace engineer, invented and patented a burning nozzle that enables the stove to stay lit in very high wind—up to 90 miles per hour. Julie, an industrial designer by training, developed an elegant folding design that is small, lightweight, easy to set up, and very stable. The Robards manufacture the stove in their garage and they sell it directly to their customers over the Internet, by fax, and through postal mail service.

The Owners of FiredUp need to keep track of the stoves they have sold in case they should ever need to contact their users regarding product failures or other product liability matters. They also think that someday they may use their customer list for marketing additional products if and when they develop any.

A. Do you think a database might be appropriate for FiredUp to use to keep track of their stove and customer data? Explain the circumstances for which you think a database would be appropriate and those for which it would not be appropriate. Describe the circumstances under which you think a personal database would be appropriate. Under what circumstances would a workgroup database be appropriate? What are the circumstances for which an Internet database would be appropriate for FiredUp?

B. Address the same problem for the registration of a product sold by Starbucks coffee. Say, for example, that Starbucks wants to develop the ability to track the purchasers of espresso machines from their stores. How do your answers to the questions in part A change?

Introduction to Database Development

This chapter presents an overview of the development of a database and a database application. We begin with a description of the elements of a database and a discussion of the features and functions of a DBMS. Next, we illustrate the creation of a database and a database application. Finally, we discuss common strategies of database development. The goal of this chapter is to create a perspective for the detailed descriptions of the technology in following chapters.

➤ THE DATABASE

Figure 2-1 shows the main components of a database system. The **database** is processed by the **DBMS,** which is used by both developers and users, who can access the DBMS either directly or indirectly via **application programs.** We discuss the database in this section and the DBMS and applications in subsequent sections.

As described in Chapter 1, a database contains four main elements: user data, metadata, indexes, and application metadata.

USER DATA

Today, most databases represent user data as relations. We formally define the term *relation* in Chapter 5. For now, consider a relation to be a table of data. The columns of the table contain fields or attributes, and the rows of the table contain records for particular entities in the business environment.

Not all relations are equally desirable; some relations are better structured than others. Chapter 5 describes a process called normalization that is used to create well-structured relations. To get an idea of the difference between poorly

➤ FIGURE 2-1

Components of Database Systems

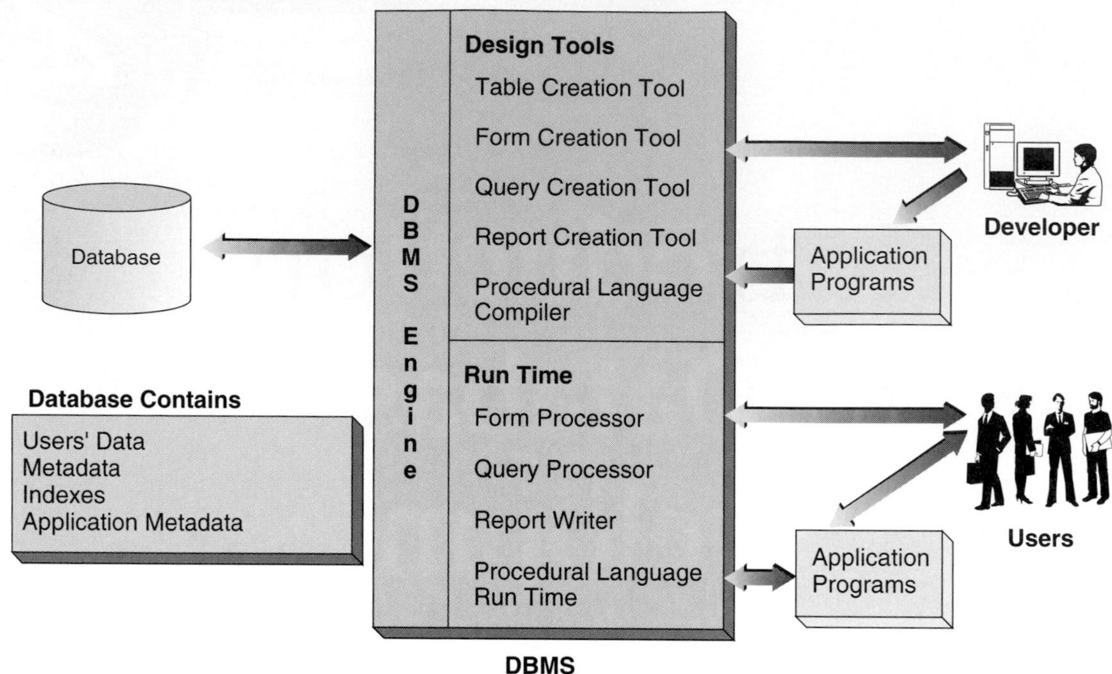

structured and well-structured relations, consider the relation R1 (StudentName, StudentPhone, AdviserName, AdviserPhone) with the following data:

StudentName	StudentPhone	AdviserName	AdviserPhone
Baker, Rex	232-8897	Parks	236-0098
Charles, Mary	232-0099	Parks	236-0098
Johnson, Beth	232-4487	Jones	236-0110
Scott, Glenn	232-4444	Parks	236-0098
Zylog, Frita	232-5588	Jones	236-0110

The problem with this relation is that it has data concerning two different topics—students and advisers. A relation structured in this way presents several problems when it is updated. For example, if adviser Parks changes his or her telephone number, three rows of data must be changed. For this reason, the data would be better represented by the two relations R2 (StudentName, Student-Phone, AdviserName) with data:

StudentName	StudentPhone	AdviserName
Baker, Rex	232-8897	Parks
Charles, Mary	232-0099	Parks
Johnson, Beth	232-4487	Jones
Scott, Glenn	232-4444	Parks
Zylog, Frita	232-5588	Jones

and R3 (AdviserName, AdviserPhone) with data:

AdviserName	AdviserPhone
Parks	236-0098
Jones	236-0110

Now if an adviser changes his or her phone, only one row of R3 has to be changed. Of course, to produce a report that shows the names of students along with their advisers' phone numbers, the rows of these two tables will need to be combined. It turns out, however, that it is far better to store the relations separately and combine them when producing a report than to store them as one combined table.

METADATA

As defined in Chapter 1, a database is self-describing, which means that it contains a description of its structure as part of itself. This description of the structure is called **metadata.** Since DBMS products are designed to store and manipulate tables, most products store the metadata in the form of tables, sometimes called **system tables.**

Figure 2-2 shows an example of metadata stored in two system tables. The first stores a list of tables that are in the database, indicating how many columns are in each table and what column(s) is the primary key. Such a column is the unique identifier of a row. The second table stores a list of columns in each table and the data type and length of each column. These two tables are typical of

➤ FIGURE 2-2

Examples of Metadata

SysTables Table

Table Name	Number of Columns	Primary Key
Student	4	StudentNumber
Adviser	3	AdviserName
Course	3	ReferenceNumber
Enrollment	3	{StudentNumber, ReferenceNumber}

SysColumns Table

Column Name	Table Name	Data Type	Length*
StudentNumber	Student	Integer	4
FirstName	Student	Text	20
LastName	Student	Text	30
Major	Student	Text	10
AdviserName	Adviser	Text	25
Phone	Adviser	Text	12
Department	Adviser	Text	15
ReferenceNumber	Course	Integer	4
Title	Course	Text	10
NumberHours	Course	Decimal	4
StudentNumber	Enrollment	Integer	4
ReferenceNumber	Enrollment	Integer	4
Grade	Enrollment	Text	2

* Lengths are stated in bytes, which are the same as characters of text data.

system tables; other such tables store lists of indexes, keys, stored procedures and the like.

Storing metadata in tables is not only efficient for the DBMS; it is also convenient for developers because they can use the same query tools for metadata as they do for user data. In Chapter 9 we discuss a language called SQL (pronounced "sequel") that is used to query and update tables for both metadata and user data.

As an example of how you might use SQL for this purpose, suppose that you have developed a database with 15 tables and 200 columns. You remember that several of the columns have the data type *currency,* but you cannot remember which ones. By using SQL, you can access the SysColumns Table to find out which columns have that data type.

INDEXES

A third type of database data improves the performance and accessibility of the database. These data, which are sometimes called **overhead data,** consist principally of indexes, although other types of data structures, such as linked lists, are sometimes used (see Appendix A for a discussion of indexes and linked lists).

Figure 2-3 shows a table of student data and two indexes. To demonstrate the utility of having these indexes, suppose that the data are stored on disk in ascending order of StudentNumber and that the user wants to print a report of student data sorted by LastName. To do this, all of the data could be extracted from the source table and sorted, but unless the table is small, this is a time-consuming process. Alternatively, an index like the LastName index in Figure 2-3 could be

➤ FIGURE 2-3

Examples of Database Indexes

Example STUDENT Table

Student Number	FirstName	LastName	Major
100	James	Baker	Accounting
200	Mary	Abernathy	Info Systems
300	Beth	Jackson	Accounting
400	Eldridge	Johnson	Marketing
500	Chris	Tufte	Accounting
600	John	Smathers	Info Systems
700	Michael	Johnson	Accounting

LastName Index

LastName	StudentNumber
Abernathy	200
Baker	100
Jackson	300
Johnson	400, 700
Smathers	600
Tufte	500

Major Index

Major	StudentNumber
Accounting	100, 300, 500, 700
Info Systems	200, 600
Marketing	400

created. The entries in this index are sorted by value of LastName, so the entries of the index can be read and used to access the student data in sorted order.

Now suppose that student data must also be printed in order of student major. Again, the data could be extracted from the source table and sorted, or an index like the Major index could be constructed and used as just described.

Indexes are used not only for sorting but also for quick access to data. For example, a user wants to access only those students who have the value "Info Systems" for Major. Without an index, the entire source table must be searched. But with the index, the index entry can be found and used to find all of the qualifying rows. Although indexes are not needed for a table with as few rows as the STUDENT table in Figure 2-3, consider a table that has 10,000 or 20,000 rows of data. In that case, sorting or searching the entire table would be slow.

Indexes are helpful for sorting and searching operations, but at a cost. Every time a row in the STUDENT table is updated, the indexes must also be updated. This is not necessarily bad; it just means that indexes are not free and so should be reserved for cases in which they are needed.

APPLICATION METADATA

The fourth and final type of data in the database is **application metadata,** which are used to store the structure and format of user forms, reports, queries, and other application components. Not all DBMS products support application components and, of those products that do, not all store the structure of those components as application metadata in the database. However, most of the modern DBMS products do store such data as part of the database. In general, neither the database developers nor the users access the application metadata directly. Instead, they use tools in the DBMS to process it.

➤ THE DBMS

DBMS products vary considerably in the features and functions that they provide. The first such products were developed for use on mainframes in the late 1960s, and they had very primitive features. Since then, DBMS products have been continually enhanced and improved not only to process database data better but also to incorporate features that facilitate the creation of database applications.

In this chapter we use Microsoft Access 2002 to illustrate the capabilities of DBMS products. This is done because Access 2002 provides features and functions that typify the characteristics of a modern DBMS. Access 2002 is not, however, the only such DBMS, and our selecting it is not meant as an endorsement of it over other, similar products, such as Lotus Approach.

As shown in Figure 2-1, the features and functions of a DBMS can be divided into three subsystems: the design tools subsystem, the run-time subsystem, and the DBMS engine.

THE DESIGN TOOLS SUBSYSTEM

The design tools subsystem has a set of tools to facilitate the design and creation of the database and its applications. It typically includes tools for creating tables, forms, queries, and reports. DBMS products also provide programming languages and interfaces to programming languages. For example, Access has two languages, a macro language that does not require in-depth programming knowledge and a version of BASIC called Visual Basic.

RUN-TIME SUBSYSTEM

The run-time subsystem[1] processes the application components that are developed using the design tools. For example, Access 2002 has a run-time facility that materializes forms and connects form elements with table data. Suppose a form has been defined that includes a text box to display the value of StudentNumber of the STUDENT table. During execution, when the form is opened, the form run-time processor extracts the value of StudentNumber from the current STUDENT row and displays it in the form. All of this is automatic; neither the user nor the developer need do anything once the form is created. Other run-time processors answer queries and print reports. In addition, there is a run-time component that processes application program requests for reading and writing database data.

Although not shown in Figure 2-1, DBMS products must also provide an application program interface for standard languages such as C++ and Java. You will learn more about this in Chapters 15 and 16.

THE DBMS ENGINE

The third component of the DBMS is the DBMS engine, which is the intermediary between the design tools and run-time subsystems and the data. The DBMS engine receives requests from the other two components—stated in terms of tables, rows, and columns—and translates those requests into commands to the operating system to read and write data on physical media.

The DBMS engine is also involved with transaction management, locking, and backup and recovery. As we show in Chapter 11, actions against the database often must be made as a complete unit. When processing an order, for example, changes in the CUSTOMER, ORDER, and INVENTORY tables should be made as a group: Either all of them should be made, or none of them should be made. The DBMS engine helps coordinate the activities to ensure that either all of the group or none of the group is applied.

Microsoft provides two different engines for Access 2002: the Jet Engine and SQL Server. The Jet Engine is used for smaller personal and workgroup databases. SQL Server, which is an independent Microsoft product, is used for larger departmental and small to medium-size organizational databases. When you create a database using the native Access 2002 table generation capabilities (databases stored with the suffix.mdb), you are using the Jet Engine. When you create Access 2002 projects (with suffix.adp), you are creating an application interface to the SQL Server engine.

➤ CREATING THE DATABASE

A *database schema* defines a database's structure, its tables, relationships, domains, and business rules. A database schema is a design, the foundation on which the database and the applications are built.

---

[1]Do not confuse the term *run-time subsystem* with the term *run-time product*. Some vendors use the term *run-time product* to refer to a product that includes the run-time and DBMS engine components but not the design tools subsystem. Such a product can be used to process an application that has already been developed. The purpose of run-time products is to reduce the cost of the application to the end user. Normally, the run-time product is much less expensive (sometimes free) than the full DBMS product. Hence, only the developer buys the full product that includes the design tools subsystem; the end users buy only the run-time product.

An Example of a Schema

To illustrate a schema and why it is important, consider an example. Highline College is a small liberal arts college in the Midwest. Its student activities department sponsors intramural athletic leagues, but it has a problem keeping track of the athletic equipment that has been checked out to various team captains. The following schema components are used for this system:

TABLES The database contains two tables[2]:

CAPTAIN (CaptainName, Phone, Street, City, State, Zip)

and

ITEM (Quantity, Description, DateOut, DateIn)

where the table names are shown outside the parentheses and the column names are shown inside the parentheses.

Neither CaptainName nor Description is necessarily a unique name, as two captains could easily be named 'Mary Smith' and there certainly are many items called "Soccer Balls." In order to make sure that each row can be identified (the importance of this will be made clearer in later chapters), we add two columns of unique numbers to these tables, as follows:

CAPTAIN (CAPTAIN_ID, CaptainName, Phone, Street, City, State, Zip)
ITEM (ITEM_ID, Quantity, Description, DateOut, DateIn)

RELATIONSHIPS The relationship between these two tables is as follows: One row of CAPTAIN relates to many rows of ITEM, but a row of ITEM relates to one, and only one, row of CAPTAIN. The notation for a relationship like this is **1:N** and is pronounced "one to N" or "one to many." The term **1:N** means that one row of the first table is related to many rows of the second.

For the tables shown here, there is no way to tell which row of CAPTAIN relates to which rows of ITEM. Therefore, to show that relationship, we add CAPTAIN_ID to ITEM. The complete structure of the two tables is as follows:

CAPTAIN (CAPTAIN_ID, CaptainName, Phone, Street, City, State, Zip)
ITEM (ITEM_ID, Quantity, Description, DateOut, DateIn, CAPTAIN_ID)

With this structure, it is easy to determine which captain has checked out a given ITEM. For example, to find out who has checked out item 1234, we examine the row for item 1234 and find the value of CAPTAIN_ID stored in that row. We can then use that value to determine the name and phone number of that captain.

DOMAINS A domain[3] is a set of values that a column may have. Consider the domains for the columns of ITEM. Suppose that both ITEM_ID and Quantity are integer numbers, that Description is text of length 25, that both DateOut and DateIn have the domain of date, and that CAPTAIN_ID also has the domain of integer numbers. In addition to the physical format, we also need to decide whether any of the domains are to be unique to the table. For our example, we want ITEM_ID to be unique and so must specify its domain in that way. Since a

---

[2]As we show in Chapters 3 through 7, the most important and difficult task in database development is designing the table structure. By starting this example with the tables already defined, we have skipped a major portion of the project.

[3]This discussion is simplified considerably so as to focus on the components of a database system. A more complete discussion of domains appears in Chapter 4.

captain may have more than one ITEM checked out, CAPTAIN_ID is not unique to the ITEM table.

The domains of the columns of CAPTAIN also must be specified. CAPTAIN_ID is integer, and all the rest of the columns are text of different lengths. CAPTAIN_ID must be unique in the CAPTAIN table.

BUSINESS RULES The last element of a database schema is business rules, which are restrictions on the business's activities that need to be reflected in the database and database applications. The following are examples of business rules for Highline College:

1. In order to check out any equipment, a captain must have a local phone number.
2. No captain may have more than seven soccer balls checked out at any one time.
3. Captains must return all equipment within five days after the end of each semester.
4. No captain may check out more equipment if he or she has any overdue.

Business rules are an important part of the schema because they specify the constraints on allowed data values that must be enforced no matter how the data changes reach the DBMS engine. Regardless of whether the request for a data change comes from the user of a form, a query/update request, or from an application program, the DBMS must ensure that the change violates no rules.

Unfortunately, business rules are enforced in different ways by different DBMS products. With Access 2002, some rules can be defined in the schema and enforced automatically. With products like SQL Server and ORACLE, additional business rules are enforced via a facility called *stored procedures*. In some cases, the DBMS product does not have the capability to enforce the necessary business rules and they must be coded into application programs. We will discuss this topic in greater detail in Chapter 10.

Creating Tables

Once the schema has been designed, the next step is creating the database tables using the DBMS's table creation tools. Figure 2-4 shows the form used with Microsoft Access to create the ITEM table. Each table column name is typed in the Field Name form column, and the data type of the column is specified in the Data Type column. Description is used to record optional documentation and comments about the table column. Additional data—such as text length, field format, caption, and others—are specified in the entry fields in the lower left-hand column of the form.

In Figure 2-4, the focus is on the ITEM_ID column. Observe that the indexed property at the bottom of the form has been set to Yes (No Duplicates), which means that an index of unique values is to be created for the ITEM_ID column. To complete the database definition, the CAPTAIN table is created in a similar way.

Defining Relationships

The relationship between CAPTAIN and ITEM is 1:N, which we represent in the schema by placing the key of CAPTAIN in ITEM. In Figure 2-4, we place CAPTAIN_ID in the ITEM table. A column like CAPTAIN_ID in the ITEM table is sometimes called a **foreign key** because it is the key of a table that is foreign to the table in which it resides. When creating forms, queries, and reports, the DBMS can provide more services and help to the developer if it knows that CAPTAIN_ID in ITEM is a foreign key of CAPTAIN.

DBMS products vary in the way that they declare this status. With Microsoft Access, the declaration is made by drawing the relationship between the key and

FIGURE 2-4

Creating a Table with Microsoft Access 2002

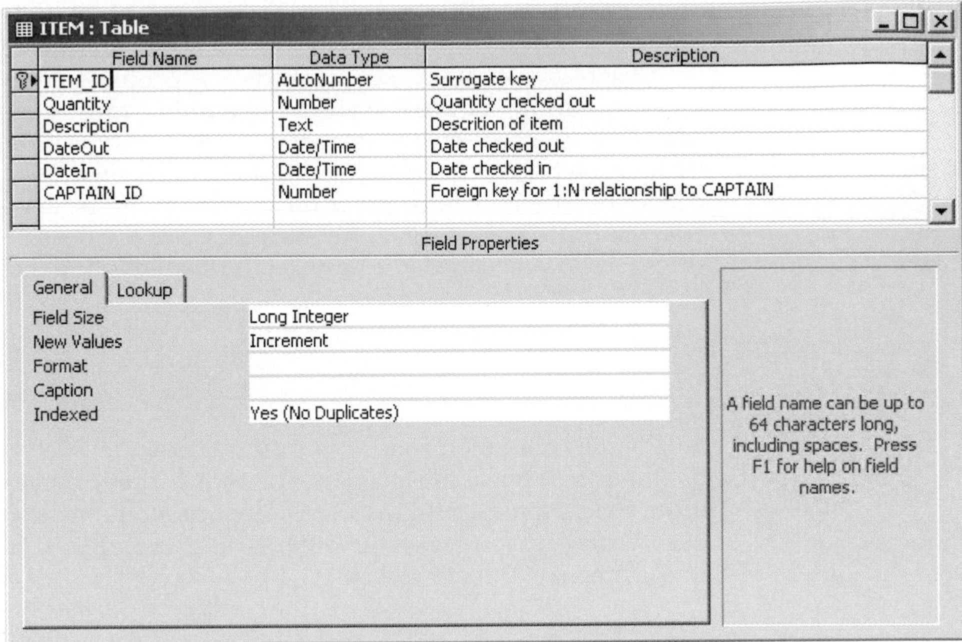

FIGURE 2-5

Declaring a Relationship with Microsoft Access 2002

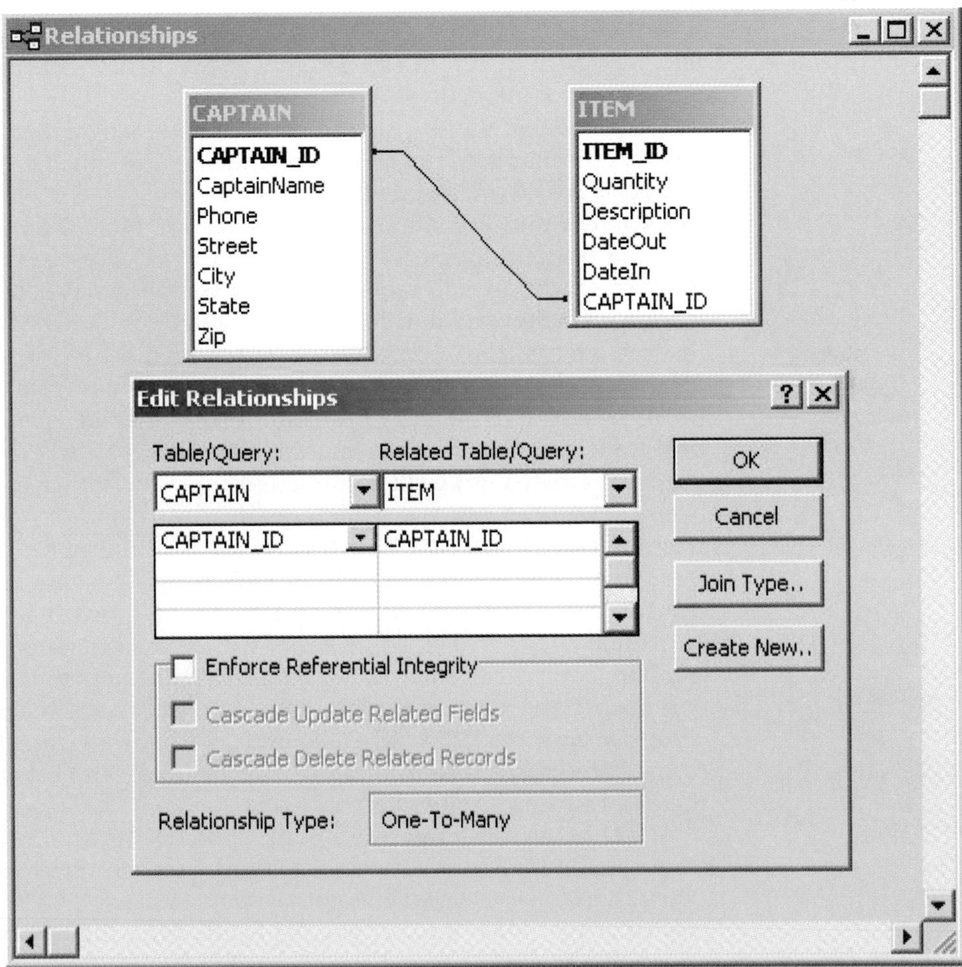

the foreign key, as shown in Figure 2-5. CAPTAIN_ID of the primary table (CAPTAIN) is set to match CAPTAIN_ID of the related table (ITEM).

One of the advantages of declaring a relationship to the DBMS is that whenever columns from the two tables are placed in a form, query, or report, the DBMS will know how to relate the rows of the tables. Although this can be declared each time for each form, query, or report, declaring it once saves time and reduces the chance of errors. For now, ignore other elements in the Edit Relationships window. You will learn about them as we proceed. Once the tables, columns, and relationships have been defined, the next step is to build the application components.

➤ COMPONENTS OF APPLICATIONS

A database application consists of forms, queries, reports, menus, and application programs. As shown in Figure 2-1, the forms, queries, and reports can be defined using tools supplied with the DBMS. Application programs must be written either in a language that is part of the DBMS or in a standardized language and connected to the database through the DBMS.

FORMS

Figure 2-6 shows three different presentations of the data in the CAPTAIN and ITEM tables. In Figure 2-6(a), the data is shown in spreadsheet or tabular format. The user can click on the plus sign at the start of each row to display the ITEM records that are related to a particular CAPTAIN row. This has been done for the data for Abernathy in the second row in this figure. Observe that two ITEM rows are related to Abernathy.

Figure 2-6(b) shows a second presentation using a data entry form. This form displays the data for a single captain at a time. Untrained users will most likely find it easier to use than the tabular format.

The Captain Registration Page shown in Figure 2-6(c) can be used over the Internet or the university's intranet and can be accessed via Microsoft's Internet Explorer. Such use will require it to be stored on a Web server like the Internet Information Server. You will learn more about this in Chapters 14 to 16. For now, just realize that the Access 2002 form tool can be used to create such forms.

Access 2002 automatically generates the tabular form for each table defined in the database. Data entry forms, however, must be created using form generation tools. Figure 2-7 shows one way of creating such a form. Here, a new form has been created using the form design tool. The source of data for the form has been set to the CAPTAIN table (not shown in Figure 2-7). Access then shows a window, called a *field list*, that displays the columns of the CAPTAIN table. In this figure, the user has dragged and dropped CaptainName from the field list onto the form. In response, Access creates a label control with the caption CaptainName and a textbox control that will be used to enter and display values for CaptainName. At this point, the textbox is said to be *bound to* the CaptainName column of the CAPTAIN table. Other columns are bound in the same way; columns from the ITEM table are bound to the form using a facility called a subform. Access also has a form design wizard that can be used to create forms like the one in Figure 2-6(b).

Neither of these forms displays the CAPTAIN_ID or ITEM_ID columns. Such IDs have been hidden from the user. Behind the scenes, however, the DBMS automatically assigns new values whenever the user causes a new CAPTAIN or ITEM row to be created. Thus, when the user opens a blank form, the DBMS automatically creates a new row in CAPTAIN and assigns a value for CAPTAIN_ID. When the user then

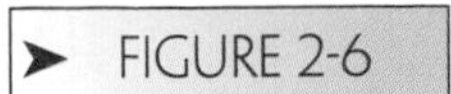
➤ FIGURE 2-6

Presentations of CAPTAIN and ITEM Data

CAPTAIN : Table

CaptainName	Phone	Street	City	State	Zip
+ Miyamoto, Mary	398.232.1770	McGilvra Hall #544	Campus		
− Abernathy, Mary Jayne	223.768.3378	777 East Fiftieth	Chicago	IL	323398
+ Jackson, Stephen	331.442.1454	300 East Centerview Apt 22	Evanston	IL	22343

Quantity	Description	DateOut	DateIn
14	Soccer Shirts	3/22/2001	6/3/2001
5	Soccer Balls	3/22/2001	6/3/2001
0			

Record: 1 of 3

(a) Tabular Form

Captain Checkout Form

CaptainName: Abernathy, Mary Jayne
Street: 777 East Fiftieth
Phone: 223.768.337
City: Chicago
State: IL
Zip: 323398

ITEM

Quantity	Description	DateOut	DateIn
14	Soccer Shirts	3/22/2001	6/3/2001
5	Soccer Balls	3/22/2001	6/3/2001
0			

Record: 1 of 2

Record: 2 of 3

(b) Data Entry Form

Captain Registration Page1

Captain Registration Page

CaptainName: Jackson, Stephen
Phone: 331.442.1
Street: 300 East Centerview Apt 22
City: Evanston
State: IL
Zip: 22343

CAPTAIN 2 of 3

(c) Browser Data Entry form

adds new ITEM rows for that captain, the DBMS creates new values of ITEM_ID for each new ITEM row and places the current value of CAPTAIN_ID in the CAPTAIN_ID column in the ITEM row. Examine Figure 2-4 again. The data type of ITEM_ID has been set to AutoNumber. This instructs Access to assign values to ITEM_ID when new rows are created. When the CAPTAIN table was created (not shown), a similar

FIGURE 2-7

Creating a Form with Microsoft Access 2002

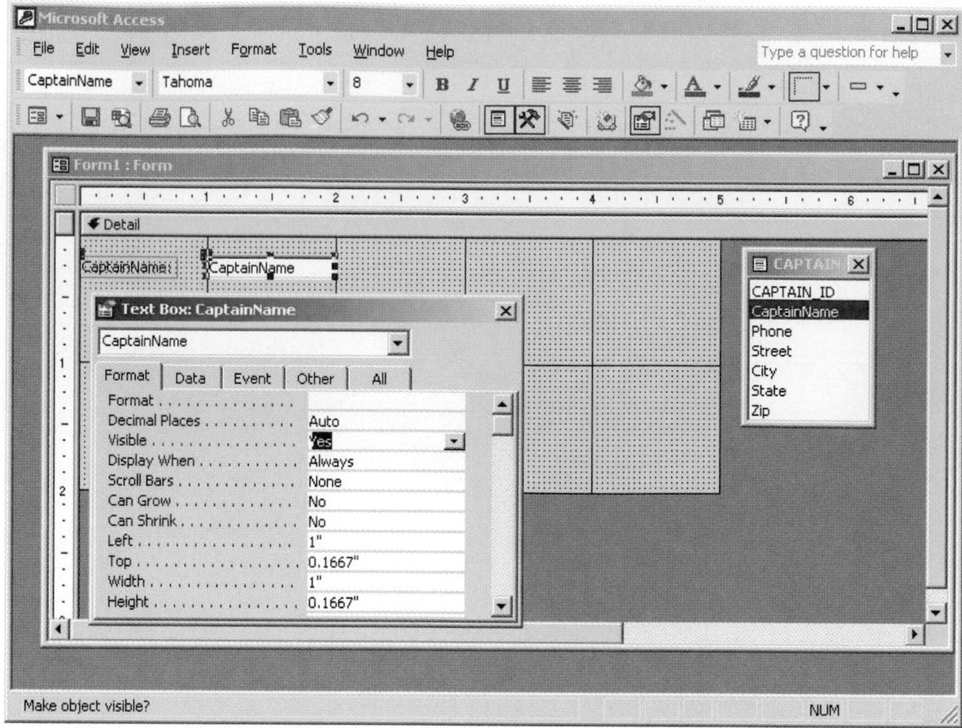

setting was given to CAPTAIN_ID. Note, however, that CAPTAIN_ID in the ITEM table is not set to AutoNumber. This is because the value of CAPTAIN_ID is created when the CAPTAIN row is created; that value is then copied into the CAPTAIN_ID field in the ITEM table when an ITEM row is connected to a particular captain.

Why are these IDs hidden? The reason is that they have no meaning to the users. Highline does not assign IDs to captains or to particular items that are checked out. If they did, then these IDs would be used and made visible. Instead, these IDs have been created only so that each row of each table will be uniquely identifiable to Access. Since these IDs have no meaning to the user, they are hidden. Identifiers like this are called **surrogate keys.**

QUERIES

From time to time, users want to query the data to answer questions or to identify problems or particular situations. For example, suppose that at the start of the fall semester 2001, one of the users wants to know whether any equipment that was checked out before September 1, 2001, has not yet been checked back in. If it has not, the user wants to know the name of the captain, his or her phone number, and the quantity and description of the items checked out.

There are a number of ways that such a query can be expressed. One is to use the data access language SQL, which is explained in Chapter 9. Another way is to use **query by example (QBE).** Figure 2-8 shows the creation of this query using QBE in Microsoft Access. To create a query, the user places into the query window the names of the tables that are to be queried. This has already been done in the upper section of the form shown in Figure 2-8. Since the relationship between CAPTAIN and ITEM has already been defined for Access (in Figure 2-5), Access knows that the two tables are linked by CAPTAIN_ID, as shown by the line drawn between CAPTAIN_ID in the two table boxes in Figure 2-8.

Next the query creator indicates which columns of data are to be returned by the query. With Access, this is done by dragging and dropping the names of the

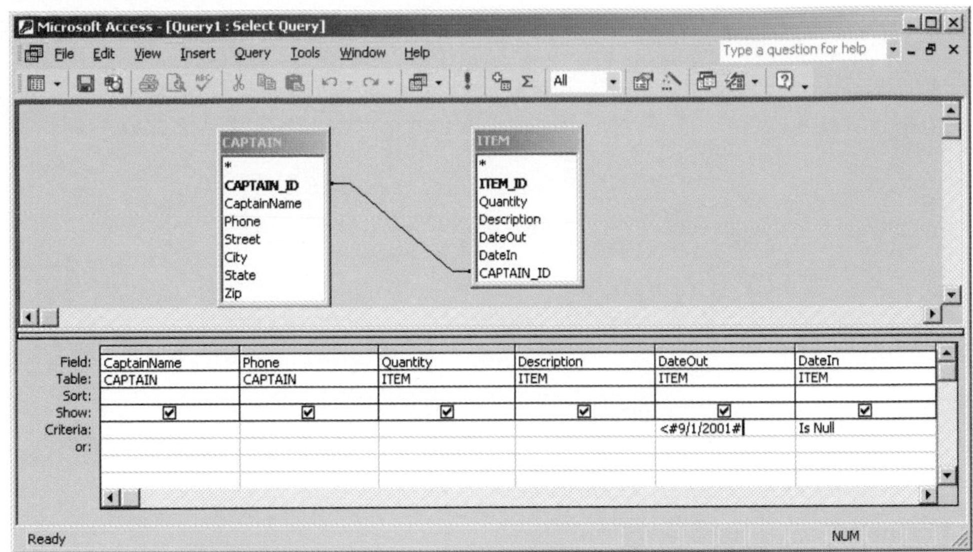

➤ FIGURE 2-8

Creating a Query with Microsoft Access 2002

columns from the table boxes into the grid in the bottom half of the form. In Figure 2-8, the columns CaptainName, Phone, Quantity, Description, DateOut, and DateIn have been placed into the query. Then the query criteria are specified in the row labeled Criteria. These criteria are that data must be before (<) 9/1/2001. (In Access, dates are surrounded by pound signs [#].) Also, the value of DateIn is to be equal to null, which means that no value for DateIn has been specified. The result of this query for sample data is shown in Figure 2-9. Note that all of the equipment shown was checked out before 9/1/2001, as was required in the query definition.

With Access and most other DBMS products, queries can be saved as part of the application so that they can be rerun as necessary. In addition, queries can be parameterized, meaning that they can be constructed so as to accept criteria values at the time they are run. For example, the query in Figure 2-8 can be parameterized so that the user enters the value of DateOut when the query is run. Any items that were checked out before that date but that have not yet been checked back in will be shown.

A third type of query, one that is easier for users, is called **query by form.** With it, the user types query constraints on a data entry form and presses the search button. The DBMS finds all instances that meet the given constraints. For the example query, for the form in Figure 2-6, the user would enter <#9/1/2001# in the DateOut field and Is Null in the DateIn field and press the QueryByForm button. The DBMS would find the records for all captains who meet the query constraints. Query by form is a newer and more modern way to query data than query by example and is likely to replace query by example in many applications.

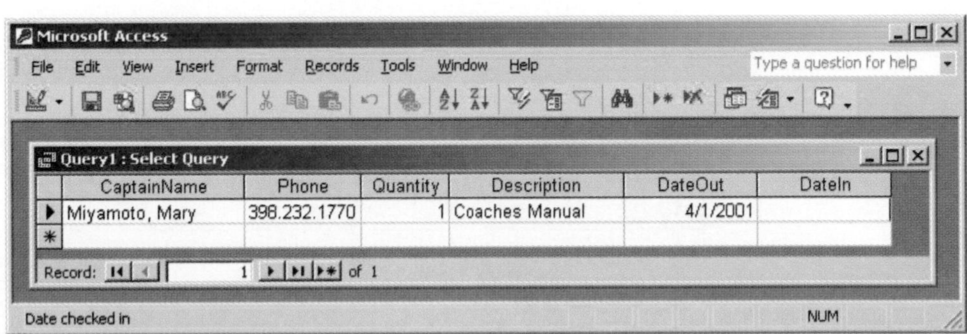

➤ FIGURE 2-9

Result of Example Query in Figure 2-8

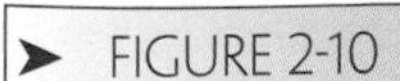
FIGURE 2-10

Example Report for Highline College

Captain Equipment Report

CaptainName *Miyamoto, Mary*

Phone *398.232.1770*

DateOut	Quantity	Description	DateIn
4/1/2001	1	Coaches Manual	
4/1/2001	7	Soccer Balls	6/10/2001
4/10/2001	25	Blue Soccer Shirts	6/10/2001

CaptainName *Abernathy, Mary Jayne*

Phone *223.768.3378*

DateOut	Quantity	Description	DateIn
3/22/2001	5	Soccer Balls	6/3/2001
3/22/2001	14	Soccer Shirts	6/3/2001

Reports

A report is a formatted display of database data. The report in Figure 2-10 contains a section for each team captain and a list of the items checked out by that captain in the section. For example, the items checked out by captain 'Miyamoto Mary' are shown in the first section of the report.

Developing a report is similar to developing a data entry form, although in some ways it is easier because a report is used only for displaying data. In other ways, constructing a report is more difficult because reports often have a more complicated structure than forms do.

Figure 2-11 shows the display of the Access 2002 report definition for the report shown in Figure 2-10. This is an example of a **banded report writer;** it is

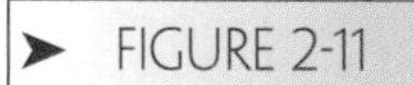
FIGURE 2-11

Developing a Report with Microsoft Access 2002

called that because the report is divided into sections or bands. As shown, there are header bands, a detail band, and footer bands. The report header band displays the name of the report and the report footer band shows the time the report was printed, the page number and the total number of pages. The page header is empty, but the CAPTAIN_ID header has captain data and labels for the detail section. The detail section shows the items checked out by a captain.

There is a problem with this report in that the two date fields are separated from each other. A better report would be to move DateOut between Description and DateIn. This can readily be done by dragging and dropping the labels and text boxes and is typical of the kinds of changes made using such tools.

In general, reports can have many sections. In a more complex example, say, course/student enrollment, a report could be grouped by COLLEGE, by DEPARTMENT, by COURSE, and by STUDENT. In this case the report would have three header sections and a detail line.

Menus

Menus are used to organize the application components so as to make them more accessible to the end user and to provide control over the user's activities. Figure 2-12 shows an example menu for the Highline application. The line across the top of the form presents the highest-level options: File, Forms, Queries, Reports, and Help. The underlined letters represent keyboard shortcut keys. If the user types ⟨Alt⟩ plus the underlined letter, the submenu choices will be displayed.

In Figure 2-12, the user has keyed ⟨Alt⟩ plus the letter *S*. The submenu choices are Select All Records, Select by Name, and Select by Phone. Again, keyboard shortcut keys can be used to select one of these items by typing ⟨Alt⟩ and the underlined letter of the choice. Menus make the application more accessible to the user by showing what options are available and helping the users select those actions they want performed. Menus can also be used to control user access to forms, reports, and programs. Some applications take advantage of this by dynamically changing menu items after the user signs on.

Application Programs

The final component of a database application is application programs. As we mentioned earlier, such programs can be written in a language that is specific to the DBMS or in a standard language that interfaces with the DBMS through a predefined

➤ FIGURE 2-12

Example Menu

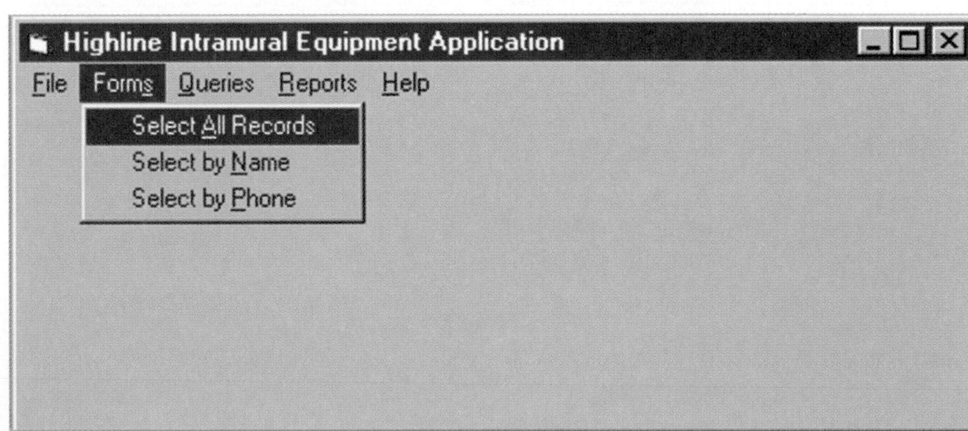

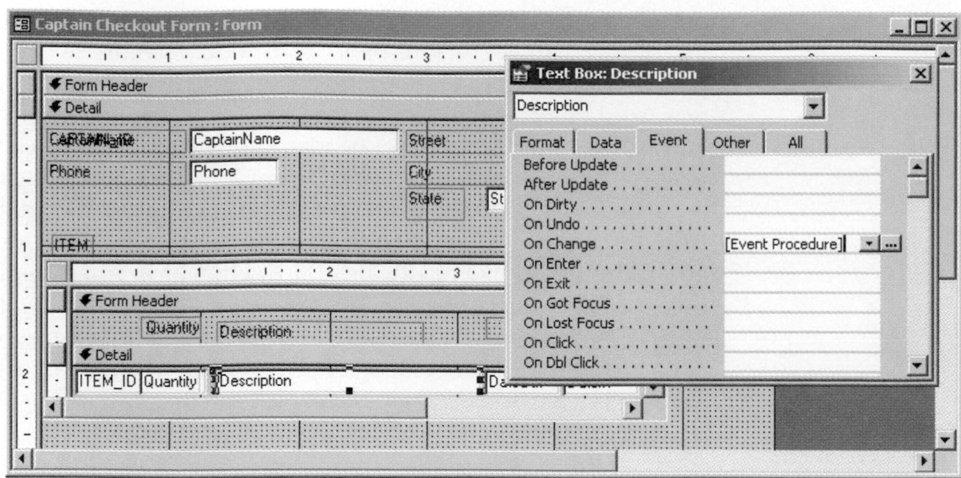

➤ FIGURE 2-13

Trapping an Event on the Caption Checkout Form

program interface. Here we will use Microsoft Visual Basic in conjunction with Access 2002.

Suppose that Highline has a business rule that captains who live off campus cannot check out a coach's manual. We do not know the reason for this rule; perhaps the manual contains secret instructions that give Highline teams a competitive advantage and Highline is attempting to control the distribution of the manuals. Maybe the manuals are expensive and students who live on campus are easier to bill if a manual is lost. For whatever reason, Highline wants the database application to enforce this rule.

There are many ways to do this. One way, shown in Figure 2-13, is to trap the change event on the Description textbox in the Item subform of the Captain Checkout Form and to insert code to enforce the rule whenever the Description changes. In Figure 2-13, the developer has opened the properties for the Description textbox and set the On Change event to Event Procedure. When this was done, Access opened the coding window shown in Figure 2-14.

The developer wrote a section of Visual Basic that will be run when the change event occurs. The code first determines if the value of City is not equal to the string "Campus." If so, then the InStr function is called to determine if the contents of the textbox (Description.Text) contains the string "Coaches Manual."

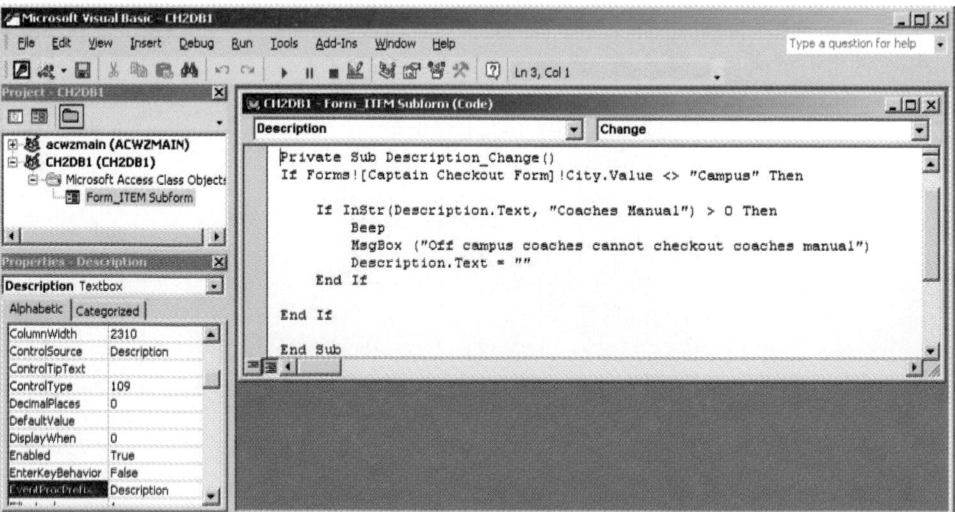

➤ FIGURE 2-14

Visual Basic Code to Enforce Business Rule

If so, a beep is issued, a message box is generated, and the Description textbox is set to blank.

This code is executed whenever the user changes the value of the Description textbox. Other, more efficient means of enforcing this rule exist, but the point here is just to show you how application code can be integrated with database forms.

Of course, it is also possible to write code that runs independently of any form or report. Programs can be written to read and update database data in the same sense that they read and update other types of files. You will see examples of this later in this text, particularly in Chapter 15 where we show the use of Microsoft ADO to read and update data from a Web server, and in Chapter 16 where we use Java for the same purpose.

➤ DATABASE DEVELOPMENT PROCESSES

Volumes and volumes have been written on the development of information systems in general and on the development of database applications in particular. Therefore, we do not need to discuss here systems development processes in any depth, but we will conclude this chapter with an overview of the processes used to develop databases and database applications.

General Strategies

A database is a model of the users' model of their business activities. Therefore, in order to build an effective database and related applications, the development team must thoroughly understand the users' model. To do this, the team builds a data model that identifies the things to be stored in the database and defines their structure and the relationships among them. This understanding must be obtained early in the development process by interviewing the users and building a statement of requirements. Most such statements include the use of **prototypes,** which are sample databases and applications that represent various aspects of the system to be created.

There are two general strategies for developing a database: top-down and bottom-up. **Top-down development** proceeds from the general to the specific. It begins with a study of the strategic goals of the organization, the means by which those goals can be accomplished, the information requirements that must be satisfied to reach those goals, and the systems necessary to provide that information. From such a study, an abstract data model is constructed.

Using this high-level model, the development team progressively works downward toward more and more detailed descriptions and models. Intermediate-level models also are expanded with more detail until the particular databases and related applications can be identified. One or more of these applications is then selected for development. Over time, the entire high-level data model is transformed into lower-level models, and all of the indicated systems, databases, and applications are created.

Bottom-up development operates in the reverse order of abstraction, by beginning with the need to develop a specific system. The means of selecting the first system vary from organization to organization. In some organizations, a steering committee chooses the application; in others, the users may choose it themselves; in still others, the loudest voice in the executive office wins out.

By whatever means, a particular system is selected for development. The development team then obtains statements of requirements by considering the outputs and inputs of any existing computer-based systems, by analyzing the forms and reports for existing manual systems, and by interviewing the users to find out their need for new reports, forms, queries, and other requirements. From all of this, the team develops the information system. If the system involves a database, the team uses the requirement specifications to build a data model, and from the model, it designs and implements the database. When this system is finished, other projects are started in order to build additional information systems.

Proponents of the top-down approach claim that it is superior to the bottom-up approach because the data models (and subsequent systems) are constructed with a global perspective. They believe that such systems have better interfaces to one another, are more consistent, and require far less rework and modification.

Proponents of the bottom-up approach claim that it is superior to top-down because it is faster and less risky. They assert that top-down modeling results in many studies that are difficult to complete and that the planning process often ends in analysis paralysis. Although bottom-up modeling does not necessarily produce the best set of systems, it does produce useful systems quickly. The benefits of these systems begin accruing much faster than with top-down modeling, and they can more than compensate for any rework or modification that will need to be done to adjust the system to a global perspective.

This text explains the tools and techniques that can be used with either style of systems development. For example, although both entity-relationship modeling (Chapter 3) and semantic object modeling (Chapter 4) work with either top-down or bottom-up development, the entity-relationship approach is particularly effective with top-down development, and the semantic object approach is particularly effective with bottom-up development.

Data Modeling

As we stated, the most important goal of the requirements phase is creating a model of the users' data. Whether this is done in top-down or bottom-up fashion, it involves interviewing users, documenting requirements, and, from those requirements, building the data model and prototypes. Such a model identifies what is to be stored in the database and defines their structure and the relationships among them.

For example, consider Figure 2-15(a), a list of orders made by a salesperson during a specific period of time. For this report to be produced by a database application, the database must contain the data shown, so the database developers need to examine the report and work backward to the data that must be stored in the database. In this case, there must be data concerning salespeople (name and region) and data concerning orders (company, order date, and amount).

Database development is complicated by the fact that there is not just one requirement but many and that the requirements usually overlap. The report in Figure 2-15(b) is also about salespeople, but, instead of orders, it lists commission checks. From this report, we can surmise that there are different types of orders and that each type has a different commission rate.

The orders implied by the report in Figure 2-15(b) somehow relate to the orders listed in Figure 2-15(a), but how they do so is not entirely clear. The development team must determine this relationship by inference from reports and forms, from interviews with users, from the team's knowledge of the subject matter, and from other sources.

DATA MODELING AS INFERENCING When the users say they need forms and reports with specific data and structures, their statement implies a model that the users have of the things in their world. The users may not, however, be able to describe exactly what that model is. If a developer were to ask the typical user, "What is the structure of the data model in your brain regarding salespeople?"

FIGURE 2-15

Examples of Two Related Reports: (a) Sample SALES Report and (b) Sample COMMISSION Report

Salesperson Order List
03-Oct-2001

Name	Region	CompanyName	OrderDate	Amount
Kevin Dougherty	**Western**			
		Cabo Controls	9/12/2001	$2,349.88
				$2,349.88
Mary B. Wu	**Western**			
		Ajax Electric	9/17/2001	$23,445.00
		American Maxell	9/24/2001	$17,339.44
				$40,784.44
			Grand Total:	**$43,134.32**

(a)

Salesperson Commission Check Report
03-Oct-2001

Name	LocalNumber	CheckDate	CType	CAmount
Kevin Dougherty	**232-9988**			
		9/30/2001	XZ	$487.38
				$487.38
Mary B. Wu	**232-9987**			
		9/30/2001	C	$237.44
		9/30/2001	A	$1,785.39
				$2,022.83
			Grand Total:	**$2,510.21**

(b)

the user would, at best, look quizzical, because most users do not think in that way.

Instead, the developers must infer, from the users' statements about forms and reports, the structure and relationships of the things to be stored in the database. The developers then record these inferences in a data model that is transformed into a database design, and that design is implemented using a DBMS. Applications that produce the reports and forms for the users are then constructed.

Building a data model is thus a process of inference. Reports and forms are like shadows projected on a wall. The users can describe the shadows, but they cannot describe the shapes that give rise to the shadows. Therefore the developers must infer, work backward, and reverse-engineer the structures and relationships of those shapes from the shadows.

This inferencing process is, unfortunately, more art than science. It is possible to learn the tools and techniques for data modeling; in fact, such tools and techniques are the subject of the next two chapters, but using those tools and techniques is an art that requires experience guided by intuition.

The quality of the model is important. If the documented data model accurately reflects the data model in the users' minds, there is an excellent chance that the resulting applications will be close to the users' needs. But if the documented data model inaccurately reflects this data model, it is unlikely that the application to be produced will be close to what the users really want.

MODELING IN MULTI-USER SYSTEMS The data modeling process becomes even more complicated for multi-user workgroup and organizational databases, because many users may envision many different data models. Occasionally these data models are inconsistent, although most times the inconsistencies can be resolved. For example, the users may be employing the same term for different things or different terms for the same things.

Sometimes, however, the differences cannot be reconciled. In such cases, the database developer must document the differences and help the users resolve them, and this usually means that some people have to change the way they view their world.

An even greater challenge is presented by large systems in which no single user has a model of the complete structure. Each user understands some of the workgroup's or organization's data model, but no single user understands all of it. In such cases, the database becomes the logical union of the pieces of the workgroup's or organization's model, and the developers must document that logical union in the data model. And this can be quite difficult.

CONFUSION ABOUT THE TERM *MODEL* The next two chapters present two alternative tools for building data models: the entity-relationship model and the semantic object model. Both models are structures for describing and documenting users' data requirements. To avoid confusion, note the different uses of the term *model*. The development team analyzes the requirements and builds a *users' data model* or a *requirements data model*. This model is a representation of the structure and relationships of what needs to be in the database to support the users' requirements. To create the users' data model, the development team uses tools called entity-relationship and the semantic object data models, which consist of language and diagramming standards for representing the users' data model. Their role in database development is similar to that of flowcharting and pseudocode in programming.

➤ SUMMARY

The components of a database system are the database, the DBMS, and application programs, which are used by both developers and users. A database contains data, metadata, indexes, and application metadata. Most databases today represent data as relations or tables, although not all relations are equally desirable. Undesirable relations can be improved through a process called normalization. Metadata is often stored in special tables called system tables.

A DBMS's features and functions can be grouped into three subsystems. The design tools subsystem defines the database and the structure of applications or application components. The functions of the run-time subsystem are to materialize the forms, reports, and queries by reading or writing database data. The DBMS engine is the intermediary between the other two subsystems and the operating system. It receives requests stated in terms of tables and rows and columns and translates those requests into read and write requests.

A schema is a description of the structure of a database and includes descriptions of tables, relationships, domains, and business rules. The rows of one table can be related to the rows of other tables. This chapter illustrated a 1:N relationship between table rows; there are other relationship types as well, as we will discuss in the next chapter.

A domain is a set of values that a column may have. We must specify a domain for each column of each table.

Finally, business rules are restrictions on the business's activities that must be reflected in the database and database applications.

The facilities of the DBMS are used to create table structures, to define relationships, and to create forms, queries, reports, and menus. DBMS products also include facilities for interacting with application programs written in either DBMS-specific languages or standard languages like Java.

Since a database is a model of the users' model of the business, database development begins by learning and recording this model. Sometimes it is expressed in prototypes of the application or application components to be constructed.

The two general styles of development are top-down development, which proceeds from the general to the specific, and bottom-up development, which proceeds from the specific to the general. With top-down, applications are developed with a global perspective; with bottom-up, applications are developed more quickly. Sometimes a combination of the two approaches is used.

Data models are constructed by a process that involves inferencing from users' statements. Forms, reports, and queries are gathered, and the developers work backward to infer the structures that the users envision. This is necessary because most users cannot describe their data models directly. Data modeling can be especially difficult and challenging in multi-user applications, in which the users' views may contradict one another's and no single user can visualize the entire view of the business activity.

The term *data model* is used in two ways, to refer to a model of the users' view of their data and to refer to the tools used to define the users' view of their data.

➤ GROUP I QUESTIONS

2.1 Name the major components of a database system, and briefly explain the function of each.

2.2 Give an example, other than the one in this chapter, of a relation that is likely to have problems when it is updated. Use relation R1 as an example.

2.3 Transpose the relation in your answer to Question 2.2 into two or more relations that do not have update problems. Use relations R2 and R3 as examples.

2.4 Explain the roles of metadata and system tables.

2.5 What is the function of indexes? When are they desirable, and what is their cost?

2.6 What is the function of application metadata? How does it differ from metadata?

2.7 Explain the features and functions of the design tools subsystem of a DBMS.

2.8 Describe the features and functions of a DBMS's run-time subsystem.

2.9 Explain the features and functions of the DBMS engine.

2.10 What is a database schema? List its components.

2.11 How are relationships represented in a relational database design? Give an example of two tables with a 1:N relationship, and explain how the relationship is expressed in the data.

2.12 What is a domain, and why is it important?

2.13 What are business rules? Give an example of possible business rules for the relations in your answer to Question 2.11.

2.14 What is a foreign key? Which column(s) in your answer to Question 2.11 is a foreign key?

2.15 Explain the purpose of forms, reports, queries, and menus.

2.16 Explain the difference between query by example and query by form.

2.17 What is the first important task in developing a database and related applications?

2.18 What is the role of a prototype?

2.19 Describe top-down development. What are its advantages and disadvantages?

2.20 Describe bottom-up development. What are its advantages and disadvantages?

2.21 Explain the two different meanings of the term *data model*.

➤ GROUP II QUESTIONS

2.22 Implement a database with the relations CAPTAIN and ITEM in any DBMS to which you can gain access. Use one of the DBMS products facilities to enter data into each of these relations. Create and process a query to use the DBMS's facility to process a query that identifies those items checked out before September 1, 2001, that have not yet been checked back in. Print the name of the captain, his or her phone number, and the quantity and description of any such items.

2.23 Interview a professional database application developer, and find out the process that this person uses to develop databases. Is this top-down development, bottom-up development, or some other strategy? How does this developer build data models and with what tools? What are the biggest problems usually encountered in developing a database?

2.24 Consider the statement "A database is a model of the users' model of reality." How does it differ from "A database is a model of reality"? Suppose two developers disagree about a data model, and one of them asserts, "My model is a better representation of reality." What does this person really mean? What differences are likely to result when a developer believes the first statement more than the second statement?

➤ FIREDUP PROJECT QUESTIONS

Consider the situation of FiredUp, Inc., the company introduced at the end of Chapter 1. Each of the stoves is accompanied by a product registration form that includes the following data:

PurchaserName, StreetAddress, ApartmentNumber, City, State/Province, Zip/PostalCode, Country, EmailAddress, PhoneNumber, DateOfPurchase, and SerialNumber

Assume that FiredUp decides to create a personal database with the following tables:

CUSTOMER (Name, StreetAddress, ApartmentNumber, City, State/Province, Zip/PostalCode, Country, EmailAddress, PhoneNumber)

and

PURCHASE (DateOfPurchase, SerialNumber)

A. Construct a table of sample data that conforms to the CUSTOMER structure. Include at least four rows in your table. For Questions A through G, just list the data using a word processor.

B. Which of the columns of the CUSTOMER table could be used to identify a unique row of the table? Such a column is sometimes called a *primary key,* as you will learn later in this text.

C. Construct a table of data that conforms to the PURCHASE structure. Include at least four rows in your table.

D. Which of the columns of the PURCHASE table could be used as a primary key of PURCHASE?

E. Using the tables defined above, there is no way to relate a particular customer to his or her stove. One way to do that would be to add SerialNumber of PURCHASE to CUSTOMER. The CUSTOMER table would then appear as:

CUSTOMER (Name, StreetAddress, ApartmentNumber, City, State/Province, Zip/PostalCode, Country, EmailAddress, PhoneNumber, SerialNumber)

Copy your sample CUSTOMER data and add the SerialNumber column to it. Call this new table CUSTOMER1

F. An alternative technique for representing the relationship of the two tables would be to place EmailAddress of CUSTOMER in PURCHASE. The PURCHASE table would then appear as:

PURCHASE (DateOfPurchase, SerialNumber, EmailAddress) Copy your sample PURCHASE data and add the EmailAddress column to it. Call this new table PURCHASE1.

G. You now have three possible database structures:

DB1: CUSTOMER1 with PURCHASE

DB2: CUSTOMER with PURCHASE1 and

DB3: CUSTOMER1 with PURCHASE1

Under what circumstances would you recommend the structure in DB1? Under what circumstances would you recommend the structure in DB2?

H. Under what circumstances would you recommend the structure in DB3?

DATA MODELING

Data modeling is the process of creating a logical representation of the structure of a database. To be correct, the data model must support all of the users' views of the data. Data modeling is the most important task in the development of effective database applications. If the data model incorrectly represents the users' view of the data, the users will find the applications difficult to use, incomplete, and very frustrating. Data modeling is the basis for all subsequent work in the development of databases and their applications.

Part II describes two different data modeling tools: Chapter 3 considers the entity-relationship (E-R) model, which has a considerable following among database professionals, and Chapter 4 describes the semantic-object model, which has a smaller following, but some consider it to be richer and easier to use than the E-R model.

These models provide a language to express the structure of data and relationships in the users' environment. Data modeling expresses a logical data design just as flowcharting expresses a logical program design.

The Entity-Relationship Model

This chapter describes and illustrates the use of the **entity-relationship model (E-R model)** which was introduced by Peter Chen in 1976.[1] In this paper, Chen set out the foundation of the model, which has since been extended and modified by Chen and many others.[2,3] In addition, the E-R model has been made part of a number of CASE tools, which also have modified it. Today, there is no single, generally accepted standard E-R model but, instead, a set of common constructs from which most of the E-R variants are derived. This chapter describes these common constructs and shows how they are used. The symbols used to express the E-R model differ considerably. We will discuss not only the traditional symbols, but also those symbols used by the Unified Modeling Language (UML), a design tool that is gaining prominence among object-oriented programmers and that incorporates the E-R model.

➤ ELEMENTS OF THE ENTITY-RELATIONSHIP MODEL

Key elements of the E-R model are entities, attributes, identifiers, and relationships. Consider each of these in turn.

[1]P. P. Chen, "The Entity-Relationship Model—Towards a Unified View of Data," *ACM Transactions on Database Systems,* January 1976, pp. 9–36.
[2]T. J.Teorey, D. Yang, and J. P. Fry, " A Logical Design Methodology for Relational Databases Using the Extended Entity-Relationship Model," *ACM Computing Surveys,* June 1986, pp. 197–222.
[3]Thomas A. Bruce, *Designing Quality Databases with IDEF1X Information Models* (New York: Dorset House Publishing, 1992).

ENTITIES

An **entity** is something that can be identified in the users' work environment, something that the users want to track. Example entities are EMPLOYEE Mary Doe, CUSTOMER 12345, SALES-ORDER 1000, SALESPERSON John Smith, and PRODUCT A4200. Entities of a given type are grouped into **entity classes.** Thus, the EMPLOYEE entity class is the collection of all EMPLOYEE entities. In this text, entity classes are printed in capital letters.

It is important to understand the differences between an entity class and an entity instance. An *entity class* is a collection of entities and is described by the structure or format of the entities in that class. An *instance* of an entity class is the representation of a particular entity, such as CUSTOMER 12345; it is described by the values of attributes of the entity. There are usually many instances of an entity in an entity class. For example, within the class CUSTOMER, there are many instances—one for each customer represented in the database. An entity class and two of its instances are shown in Figure 3-1.

ATTRIBUTES

Entities have **attributes** or, as they are sometimes called, **properties** that describe the entity's characteristics. Examples of attributes are EmployeeName, DateOfHire, and JobSkillCode. In this text, attributes are printed in both uppercase and lowercase letters. The E-R model assumes that all instances of a given entity class have the same attributes.

The original E-R model definition includes both composite and multi-value attributes. An example of a composite attribute is Address which consists of the group of attributes {Street, City, State/Province, Zip/PostalCode}. An example of a multi-value attribute is ContactName in CUSTOMER, where more than one person's name is associated with a given Customer. An attribute can be both multi-value and composite; for example, the composite attribute Phone {AreaCode, Number} could be multi-value to allow for multiple phone numbers. Most implementations of the E-R model ignore single-value composite attributes. They require multi-value attributes (whether composite or not) to be transformed into entities as will be shown below.

➤ FIGURE 3-1

CUSTOMER: An Example of an Entity

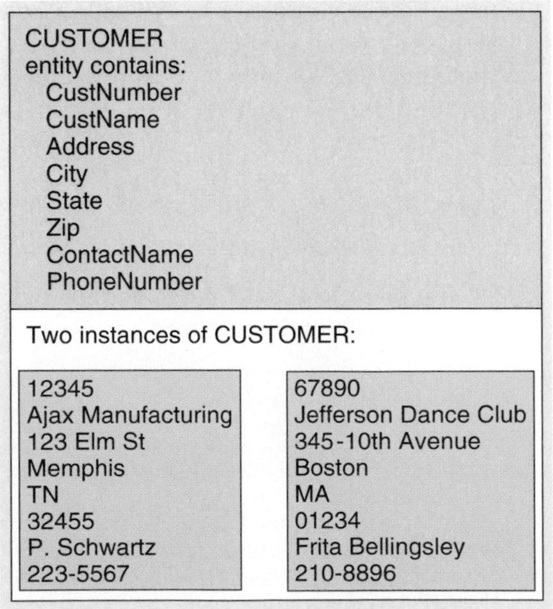

CUSTOMER
entity contains:
CustNumber
CustName
Address
City
State
Zip
ContactName
PhoneNumber

Two instances of CUSTOMER:

12345	67890
Ajax Manufacturing	Jefferson Dance Club
123 Elm St	345-10th Avenue
Memphis	Boston
TN	MA
32455	01234
P. Schwartz	Frita Bellingsley
223-5567	210-8896

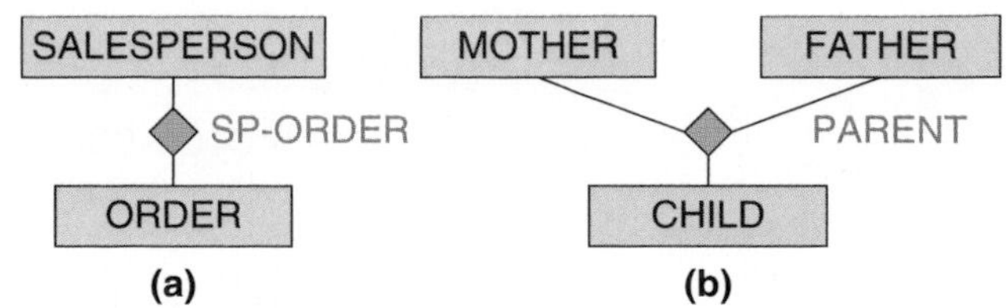

FIGURE 3-2

Relationships of Different Degrees: (a) Example Relationship of Degree 2 and (b) Example Relationship of Degree 3

IDENTIFIERS

Entity instances have **identifiers,** which are attributes that name, or identify, entity instances. For example, EMPLOYEE instances could be identified by SocialSecurityNumber, EmployeeNumber, or EmployeeName. EMPLOYEE instances are not likely to be identified by attributes like Salary or DateOfHire because normally these attributes are not used in a naming role. Similarly, CUSTOMERs could be identified by CustomerNumber or CustomerName, and SALES-ORDERs could be identified by OrderNumber.

The identifier of an entity instance consists of one or more of the entity's attributes. An identifier may be either **unique** or **nonunique.** If it is unique, its value will identify one, and only one, entity instance. If it is nonunique, the value will identify a set of instances. EmployeeNumber is most likely a unique identifier, while EmployeeName is most likely a nonunique identifier (there may be many John Smiths, for example).

Identifiers that consist of two or more attributes are called **composite identifiers.** Examples are {AreaCode, LocalNumber}, {ProjectName, TaskName}, and {FirstName, LastName, PhoneExtension}.

RELATIONSHIPS

Entities can be associated with one another in **relationships.** The E-R model contains both relationship classes and relationship instances.[4] *Relationship classes* are associations among entity classes, and *relationship instances* are associations among entity instances. Relationships can have attributes.

A relationship class can involve many entity classes. The number of entity classes in the relationship is the **degree** of the relationship. In Figure 3-2(a), the SP-ORDER relationship is of degree 2 because it involves two entity classes, SALESPERSON and ORDER. The PARENT relationship in Figure 3-2(b) is of degree 3, because it involves three entity classes: MOTHER, FATHER, and CHILD. Relationships of degree 2 are very common and are often referred to by the term **binary relationships.**

THREE TYPES OF BINARY RELATIONSHIPS Figure 3-3 shows the three types of binary relationships. In a 1:1 (read "one-to-one") relationship, a single-entity instance of one type is related to a single-entity instance of another type. In Figure 3-3(a), the AUTO-ASSIGNMENT relationship associates a single EMPLOYEE with a single AUTO. According to this diagram, no employee has more than one automobile assigned, and no automobile is assigned to more than one employee.

Figure 3-3(b) shows the second type of relationship, 1:N (read "one to N" or "one to many"). In this relationship, called a DORM-OCCUPANT relationship, a single instance of DORMITORY relates to many instances of STUDENT.

---

[4]For brevity, we sometimes drop the word *instance* when the context makes it clear that an instance rather than an entity class is involved.

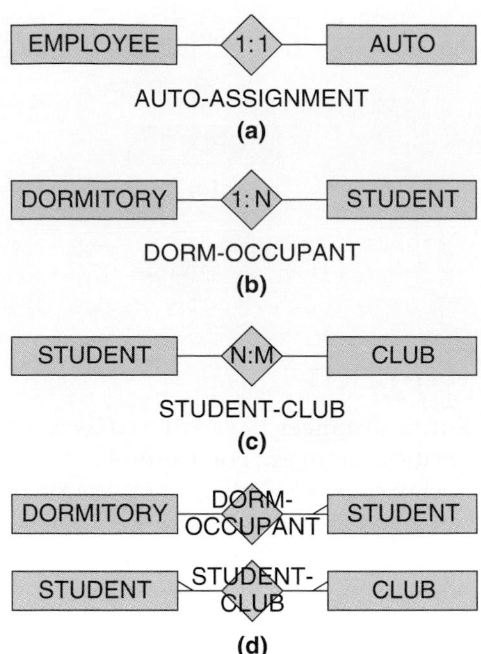

FIGURE 3-3

Three Types of Binary Relationships: (a) 1:1 Binary Relationship, (b) 1:N Binary Relationship, (c) N:M Binary Relationship, and (d) Relationship Representation with Crow's Feet

According to this sketch, a dormitory has many students, but a student has only one dormitory.

The positions of the 1 and the N are significant. The 1 is close to the line connecting DORMITORY, which means that the 1 refers to the DORMITORY side of the relationship, and the N is close to the line connecting STUDENT, which means that the N refers to the STUDENT side of the relationship. If the 1 and the N were reversed and the relationship were written N:1, a DORMITORY would have one STUDENT, and a STUDENT would have many DORMITORIES. This is not, of course, the case.

Figure 3-3(c) shows the third type of binary relationship, N:M (read "N to M" or "many to many"). This relationship is named STUDENT-CLUB, and it relates instances of STUDENT to instances of CLUB. A student can join more than one club, and a club can have many students as members.

The numbers inside the relationship diamond show the maximum number of entities that can occur on one side of the relationship. Such constraints are called the relationship's **maximum cardinality.** The relationship in Figure 3-3(b), for example, is said to have a maximum cardinality of 1:N. But the cardinalities are not restricted to the values shown here. It is possible, for example, for the maximum cardinality to be other than 1 and N. The relationship between BASKETBALL-TEAM and PLAYER, for example, could be 1:5, indicating that a basketball team has at most five players.

Relationships of the types shown in Figure 3-3 are sometimes called **HAS-A relationships.** This term is used because an entity *has a* relationship with another entity. For example, an EMPLOYEE has an AUTO; a STUDENT has a DORMITORY; and a CLUB has STUDENTs.

ENTITY-RELATIONSHIP DIAGRAMS The sketches in Figure 3-3 are called **entity-relationship** or **E-R diagrams**. Such diagrams are standardized, but only loosely. According to this standard, entity classes are shown by rectangles, relationships are shown by diamonds, and the maximum cardinality of the rela-

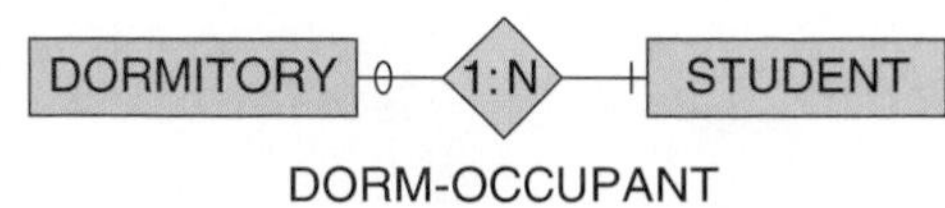

➤ FIGURE 3-4

Relationship with Minimum Cardinality Shown

tionship is shown inside the diamond.[5] The name of the entity is shown inside the rectangle, and the name of the relationship is shown near the diamond.

Although in some E-R diagrams the name of the relationship is shown inside the diamond, this can make the diagram look awkward, since the diamonds may have to be large and out of scale in order to include the relationship name. To avoid this, relationship names are sometimes written over the diamond. When the name is placed inside or on top of the diamond, the relationship cardinality is shown by placing crow's feet on the lines connecting to the entity(ies) on the many side of the relationship. Figure 3-3(d) shows the DORM-OCCUPANT and STUDENT-CLUB relationships with such crow's feet.

As we stated, the maximum cardinality indicates the maximum number of entities that can be involved in a relationship. The diagrams do not indicate the minimum. For example, Figure 3-3(b) shows that a student is related, at maximum, to one dormitory, but it does not show whether a student *must be* related to a dormitory instance.

Several different ways are used to show **minimum cardinality.** One way, illustrated in Figure 3-4, is to place a hash mark across the relationship line to indicate that an entity must exist in the relationship and to place an oval across the relationship line to indicate that there may or may not be an entity in the relationship. Accordingly, Figure 3-4 shows that a DORMITORY must have a relationship with at least one STUDENT but that a STUDENT is not required to have a relationship with a DORMITORY. The complete relationship restrictions are that a DORMITORY has a minimum cardinality of one and a maximum cardinality of many STUDENT entities. A STUDENT has a minimum cardinality of zero and a maximum cardinality of one DORMITORY entity.

A relationship may exist among entities of the same class. For example, the relationship ROOMS-WITH could be defined on the entity STUDENT. Figure 3-5(a) shows such a relationship, and Figure 3-5(b) shows instances of entities that conform to this relationship. Relationships among entities of a single class are sometimes called **recursive relationships.**

SHOWING ATTRIBUTES IN ENTITY-RELATIONSHIP DIAGRAMS In some versions of E-R diagrams, the attributes are shown in ellipses and are connected to the entity or relationship to which they belong. Figure 3-6(a) shows the DORMITORY and STUDENT entities and the DORM-OCCUPANT relationship with the attributes. As shown, DORMITORY has DormName, Location, and NumberOfRooms attributes, and STUDENT has StudentNumber, StudentName, and StudentYear attributes. The relationship DORM-OCCUPANT has the attribute Rent, which shows the amount of rent paid by a particular student in a particular dorm.

If an entity has many attributes, listing them in this way on the E-R diagram may make the diagram cluttered and difficult to interpret. In these cases, entity attributes are listed separately, as shown in Figure 3-6(b). Many CASE tools show such attributes in pop-up windows.

---

[5]The graphical symbols that originated with the model (which are the symbols described here) are not the best ones for displaying a model in a Graphical User Interface (GUI) system such as the Macintosh or Microsoft Windows. In fact, the E-R model was developed long before any GUI system was popular. The UML symbols shown later in this chapter are more easily used in a graphical environment.

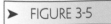

➤ FIGURE 3-5

Recursive Relationship

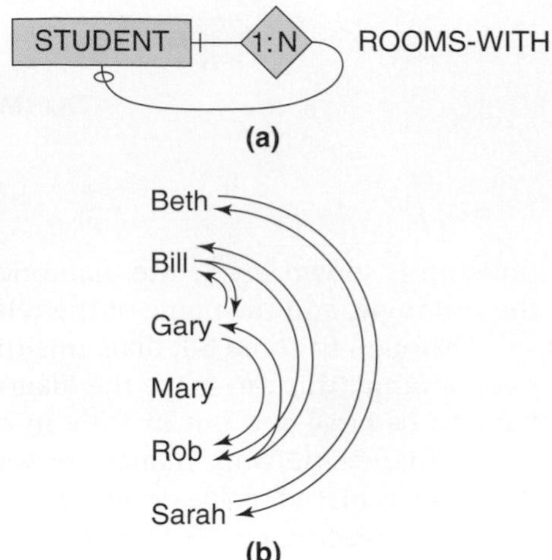

WEAK ENTITIES

The entity-relationship model defines a special type of entity called a **weak entity.** Such entities are those that cannot exist in the database unless another type of entity also exists in the database. An entity that is not weak is called a **strong entity.**

To understand weak entities, consider a human resource database with EMPLOYEE and DEPENDENT entity classes. Suppose the business has a rule that an EMPLOYEE instance *can exist* without having a relationship to any DEPENDENT entity, but a DEPENDENT entity *cannot exist* without having a relationship to a particular EMPLOYEE entity. In such a case, DEPENDENT is a weak entity. This means that DEPENDENT data can be stored in the database only if the DEPENDENT has a relationship with an EMPLOYEE entity.

➤ FIGURE 3-6

Showing Properties in Entity-Relationship Diagrams: (a) Entity-Relationship Diagram with Properties Shown and (b) Entity-Relationship Diagram with Properties Listed Separately

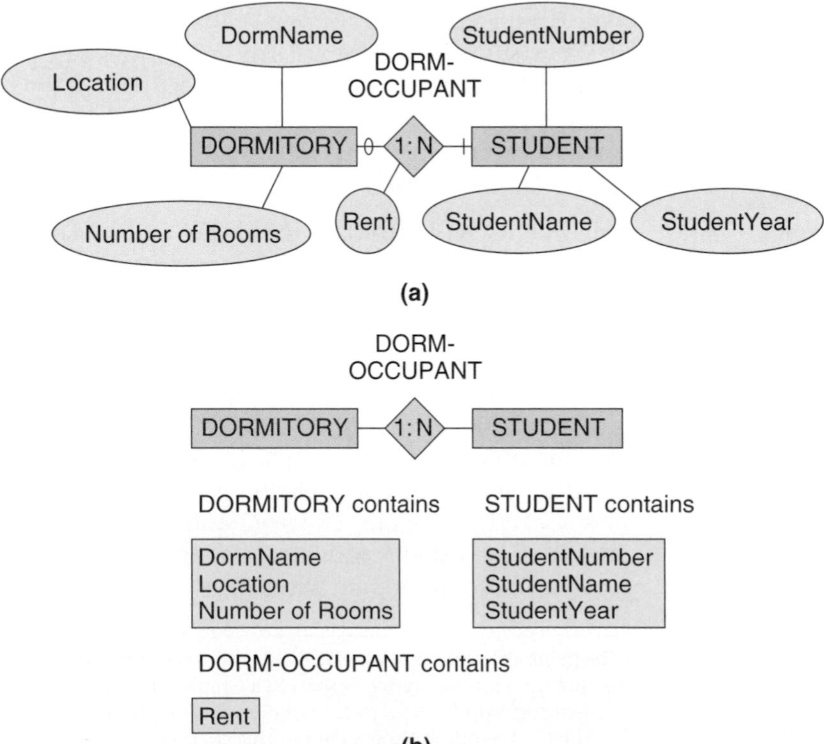

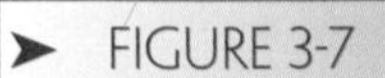

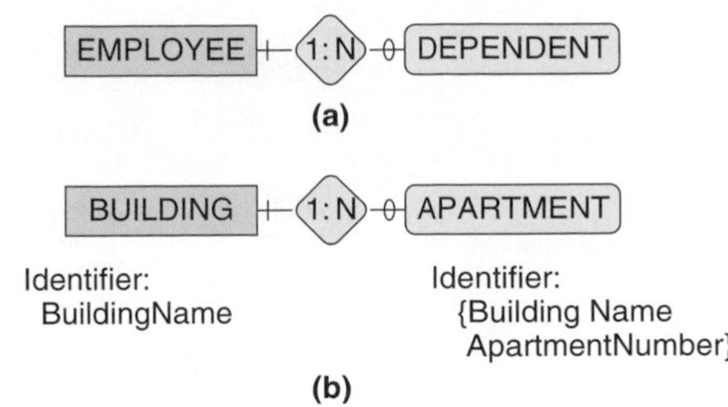

Weak Entities: (a) Example of a Weak Entity and (b) ID-Dependent Entity

As shown in Figure 3-7(a), weak entities are signified by rounding the corners of the entity rectangle. In addition, the relationship on which the entity depends for its existence is shown in a diamond with rounded corners. Alternatively, in some E-R diagrams (not shown here), weak entities are depicted by using a double line for the boundary of the weak entity rectangle and double diamonds for the relationship on which the entity depends.

The E-R model includes a special type of weak entity called an **ID-dependent entity.** Such an entity is one in which the identifier of one entity includes the identifier of another entity. Consider the entities BUILDING and APARTMENT. Suppose the identifier of BUILDING is BuildingName, and the identifier of APARTMENT is the composite identifier {BuildingName, ApartmentNumber}. Since the identifier of APARTMENT contains the identifier of BUILDING (BuildingName), then APARTMENT is ID-dependent on BUILDING. Contrast Figure 3-7(b) with Figure 3-7(a). Another way to think of this is that, both logically and physically, an APARTMENT cannot exist unless a BUILDING exists.

ID-dependent entities are common. Another example is the entity VERSION in the relationship between PRODUCT and VERSION, where PRODUCT is a software product and VERSION is a release of that software product. The identifier of PRODUCT is ProductName, and the identifier of VERSION is {ProductName, ReleaseNumber}. A third example is EDITION in the relationship between TEXTBOOK and EDITION. The identifier of TEXTBOOK is Title, and the identifier of EDITION is {Title, EditionNumber}.

Unfortunately, there is an ambiguity hidden in the definition of weak entity, and this ambiguity is interpreted differently by different database designers (as well as different textbook authors). The ambiguity is this: In a strict sense, if a weak entity is defined as any entity whose presence in the database depends on another entity, then any entity that participates in a relationship having a minimum cardinality of 1 to a second entity is a weak entity. Thus, in an academic database, if a STUDENT must have an ADVISER, then STUDENT is a weak entity, because a STUDENT entity cannot be stored without an ADVISER. This interpretation, however, seems too broad to some people. A STUDENT is not physically dependent on an ADVISER (unlike APARTMENTs and BUILDINGs), and a STUDENT is not logically dependent on an ADVISER (in spite of how it might appear to either the student or the adviser!); therefore, a STUDENT should be considered a strong entity.

To avoid such situations, some people interpret the definition of weak entity more narrowly. To be a weak entity, an entity must *logically* depend on another entity. According to this definition, both DEPENDENT and APARTMENT would be considered weak entities, but STUDENT would not. A DEPENDENT cannot be a dependent unless it has someone to depend on, and an APARTMENT cannot exist without a BUILDING to reside in. A STUDENT, however, can logically exist without an ADVISER, even if a business rule requires it.

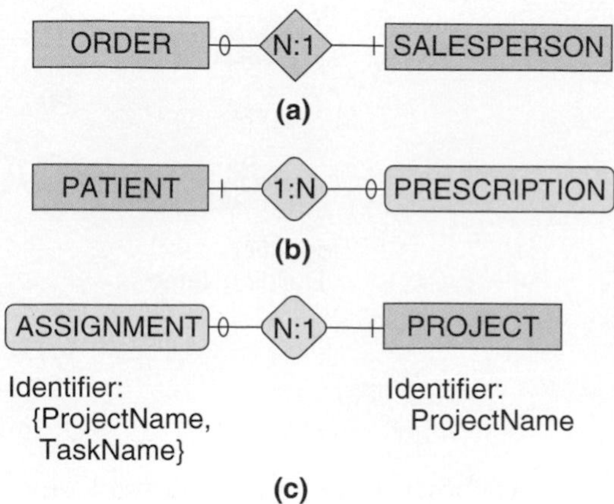

FIGURE 3-8

Examples of Required Entities

To illustrate this interpretation, consider several examples. Suppose a data model includes the relationship between an ORDER and a SALESPERSON [Figure 3-8(a)]. While we might say that an ORDER must have a SALESPERSON, it does not necessarily require one for its existence (the ORDER could be a cash sale in which the salesperson is not recorded). Hence, the minimum cardinality of 1 arises from a business rule, not from logical necessity. Thus, ORDER requires a SALESPERSON but is not existence-dependent on it, and ORDER would be considered a strong entity.

Now, however, consider the relationship of PATIENT and PRESCRIPTION in Figure 3-8(b). Here, a PRESCRIPTION cannot logically exist without a PATIENT. Hence, not only is the minimum cardinality 1, but also the PRESCRIPTION is existence-dependent on PATIENT. PRESCRIPTION is thus a weak entity. Finally, consider ASSIGNMENT in Figure 3-8(c), where the identifier of ASSIGNMENT contains the identifier of PROJECT. Here, not only does ASSIGNMENT have a minimum cardinality of 1, and not only is ASSIGNMENT existence-dependent on PROJECT, but it is also ID-dependent on PROJECT, since its key includes the key of another entity. Thus, ASSIGNMENT is a weak entity.

In this text we define weak entities as those that must logically depend on another entity. Hence, not all entities that have a minimum cardinality of 1 in relationship to another entity are weak. Only those that are logically dependent are termed weak. This definition also implies that all ID-dependent entities are weak. Additionally, every weak entity has a minimum cardinality of 1 on the entity on which it depends, but every entity that has a minimum cardinality of 1 need not necessarily be weak.[6]

REPRESENTING MULTI-VALUE ATTRIBUTES WITH WEAK ENTITIES

Multi-value attributes are represented in the E-R by creating a new weak entity to represent the multi-value attribute and constructing a one-to-many relationship. For example, Figure 3-9(a) shows the representation of the multi-value attribute ContactName in CUSTOMER. A new weak entity called CONTACTNAME is created with a single attribute ContactName. The relationship between CUSTOMER and CONTACTNAME is one-to-many. The constructed entity must be weak because it is logically dependent on the entity that had the multi-value attribute.

Figure 3-9(b) shows the representation of the multi-value composite attribute Address. The new weak entity ADDRESS contains all of the attributes of the composite, namely, Street, City, State/Province, Zip/PostalCode.

---

[6] This discussion omits the cases in which the minimum cardinality is greater than 1. The logic is similar, but the entity depends on a set of entities.

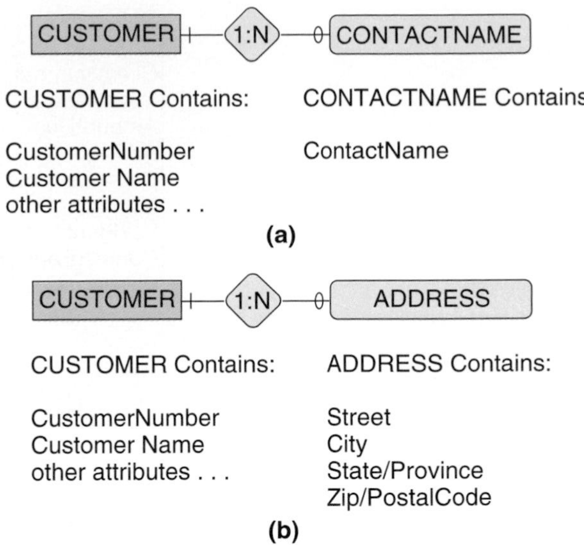

➤ FIGURE 3-9

Representing Multi-Value Attributes with Weak Entities

Subtype Entities

Some entities contain optional sets of attributes; these entities are often represented using subtypes.[7] Consider, for example, CLIENT, with attributes ClientNumber, ClientName, and AmountDue. Suppose that a CLIENT can be an individual, a partnership, or a corporation and that additional data are to be stored depending on the type. Assume that these additional data are as follows:

INDIVIDUAL-CLIENT:
Address, SocialSecurityNumber
PARTNERSHIP-CLIENT:
ManagingPartnerName, Address, TaxIdentificationNumber
CORPORATE-CLIENT:
ContactPerson, Phone, TaxIdentificationNumber

One possibility is to allocate all of these attributes to the entity CLIENT, as shown in Figure 3-10(a). In this case, some of the attributes are not applicable. ManagingPartnerName has no meaning for an individual or corporate client, and so it cannot have a value.

A closer-fitting model would instead define three subtype entities, as shown in Figure 3-10(b). Here the INDIVIDUAL-CLIENT, PARTNERSHIP-CLIENT, and CORPORATE-CLIENT entities are shown as **subtypes** of CLIENT. CLIENT, in turn, is a **supertype** of the INDIVIDUAL-CLIENT, PARTNERSHIP-CLIENT, and CORPORATE-CLIENT entities.

The ∈ next to the relationship lines indicates that INDIVIDUAL-CLIENT, PARTNERSHIP-CLIENT, and CORPORATE-CLIENT are subtypes of CLIENT. Each subtype entity must belong to the supertype CLIENT. The curved line with a 1 next to it indicates that a CLIENT entity must belong to one, and only one, subtype. It means that the subtypes are exclusive and that one of them is required.

---

[7] Subtypes were added to the E-R model after the publication of Chen's initial paper, and they are part of what is called the *extended E-R model*.

FIGURE 3-10

Subtype Entities: (a) CLIENT Without Subtype Entities, (b) CLIENT with Subtype Entities, and (c) Nonexclusive Subtypes with Optional Supertype

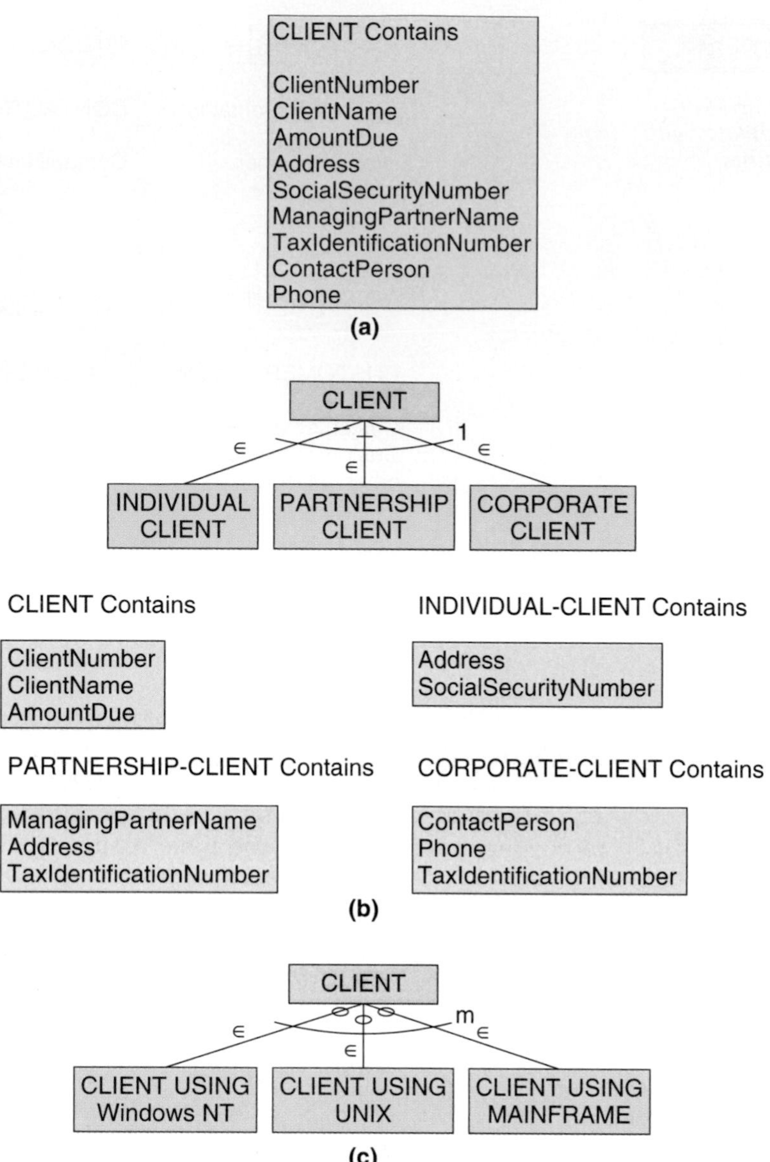

Entities with an *IS-A* relationship should have the same identifier since they represent different aspects of the same thing. In this case, that identifier is Client Number. Contrast this situation with the HAS-A relationships shown in Figure 3-3 where the entities represent aspects of different things.

Generalization hierarchies have a special characteristic called **inheritance,** which means that the entities in subtypes inherit attributes of the supertype entity class. PARTNERSHIP-CLIENT, for example, inherits ClientName and AmountDue from CLIENT.

The reasons for using subtypes in data modeling differ from the reasons for using them in object-oriented programming. In fact, the only reason to use them in a data model is to avoid situations in which some attributes are required to be null. For example, in Figure 3-10(a), if SocialSecurityNumber has a value, then the last four attributes must be null. The situation can be more obvious in medical applications—asking a male patient for the number of his pregnancies, for example. Null values are discussed in greater detail in Chapter 6.

FIGURE 3-11

Example Entity-Relationship Diagram

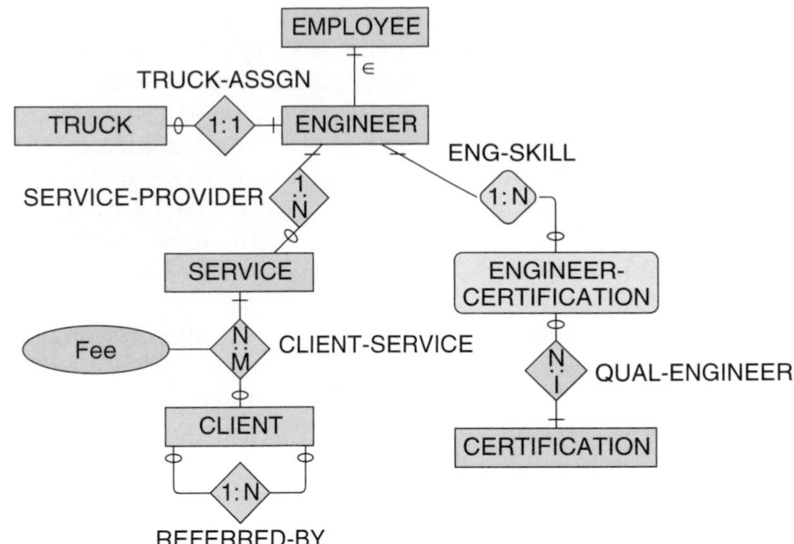

Example E-R Diagram

Figure 3-11 is an example E-R diagram that contains all of the elements of the E-R model that we have been discussing. It shows the entities and relationships for an engineering consulting company that analyzes the construction and condition of houses and other buildings and facilities.

There is an entity class for the company's employees. Because some EMPLOYEEs are ENGINEERs, there is a subtype relationship between EMPLOYEE and ENGINEER. Every ENGINEER must be an EMPLOYEE; ENGINEER has a 1:1 relationship to TRUCK; and each TRUCK must be assigned to an ENGINEER, but not all ENGINEERs have a TRUCK.

ENGINEERs provide SERVICEs to CLIENTs. An ENGINEER can provide from zero to many services, but a given SERVICE must be provided by an ENGINEER and can be provided by only that ENGINEER. CLIENTs have many SERVICEs, and a SERVICE can be requested by many CLIENTs. A CLIENT must have purchased at least one SERVICE, but SERVICE need not have any CLIENTs. The CLIENT-SERVICE relationship has an attribute Fee, which shows the amount that a particular client paid for a particular SERVICE. (Other attributes of entities and relationships are not shown in this diagram.)

Sometimes CLIENTs refer one another, which is indicated by the recursive relationship REFERRED-BY. A given CLIENT can refer one or more other CLIENTs. A CLIENT may or may not have been referred by another client, but a CLIENT may be referred by only one other CLIENT.

The ENGINEER-CERTIFICATION entity shows that a given ENGINEER has completed the education and testing required to earn a particular certificate. An ENGINEER may have earned CERTIFICATIONs. ENGINEER-CERTIFICATION's existence is dependent on ENGINEER through the relationship ENG-SKILL. CERTIFICATION is the entity that describes a particular certification.

Documentation of Business Rules

Chapter 2 defined a database schema as consisting of tables, relationships, domains, and business rules. We can obtain or infer the first three of these from an E-R model, but we cannot obtain business rules from the model. Thus, these rules are sometimes added to the E-R model during the data modeling stage.

The E-R model is developed from an analysis of requirements obtained from users. During this analysis, business rules often are brought up, and, indeed, systems analysts should make it a point to ask about them.

Consider the entities TRUCK and ENGINEER in Figure 3-11. Does the business have rules concerning who is assigned a TRUCK? If there are not enough TRUCKs for one to be assigned to every ENGINEER, what rules determine who gets a TRUCK? It might be that the database application is to assign trucks on the basis of which ENGINEER has the most number of SERVICEs scheduled during some period of time, the most number of SERVICEs out of the office, or some other rule.

Another example concerns the allocation of ENGINEERs to SERVICEs. There probably are rules concerning the type of ENGINEERING-CERTIFICATION that an ENGINEER must have in order to be assigned to particular types of SERVICE. To inspect an apartment building, for example, the ENGINEER may need to be licensed as a professional ENGINEER. Even if there is no law that dictates this rule, it may be the policy of the company to enforce it.

Business rules may or may not be enforced by the DBMS or by the application program. Sometimes business rules are written in manual procedures that the users of the database application are to follow. At this point, the way in which the rules are to be enforced is not important. What is important is to document these rules so that they become part of the system's requirements.

The Entity-Relationship Model and CASE Tools

Developing a data model using the entity-relationship model has become easier in recent years, because the tools for building E-R diagrams are included in many popular CASE products. Products such as IEW, IEF, DEFT, ER-WIN, and Visio have drawing and diagramming facilities to create E-R diagrams. Such products also integrate entities with the database relations that represent them, which can facilitate the administration, management, and maintenance of the database.

We do not assume the use of a CASE tool for the discussions in this text. But if your university has such a tool, by all means use it to create E-R diagrams for exercises you are assigned. The E-R diagrams created using these tools are generally more visually pleasing, and they are far easier to change and adapt.

➤ UML-Style Entity-Relationship Diagrams

The Unified Modeling Language (UML) is a set of structures and techniques for modeling and designing object-oriented programs (OOP) and applications. UML is both a methodology for developing OOP systems and a set of tools to support the development of such systems. UML has received prominence via the Object Management Group, an organization that has been developing OOP models, technology, and standards since the 1980s. It has also begun to receive widespread use among OOP practitioners. UML is the basis of the object-oriented design tools from Rational Systems.

Because it is an application development methodology, UML is a subject for a course on systems development and is of limited concern to us. You may, however, encounter UML-style entity-relationship diagrams, so you should be familiar with their style. Realize that when it comes to database design, they are treated just the same as traditional entity-relationship diagrams.

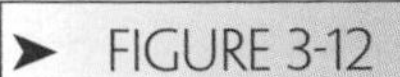
FIGURE 3-12

a. UML Representation of a 1:1 Relationship, b. UML Representation of a 1:N Relationship, and c. UML Representation of an N:M Relationship

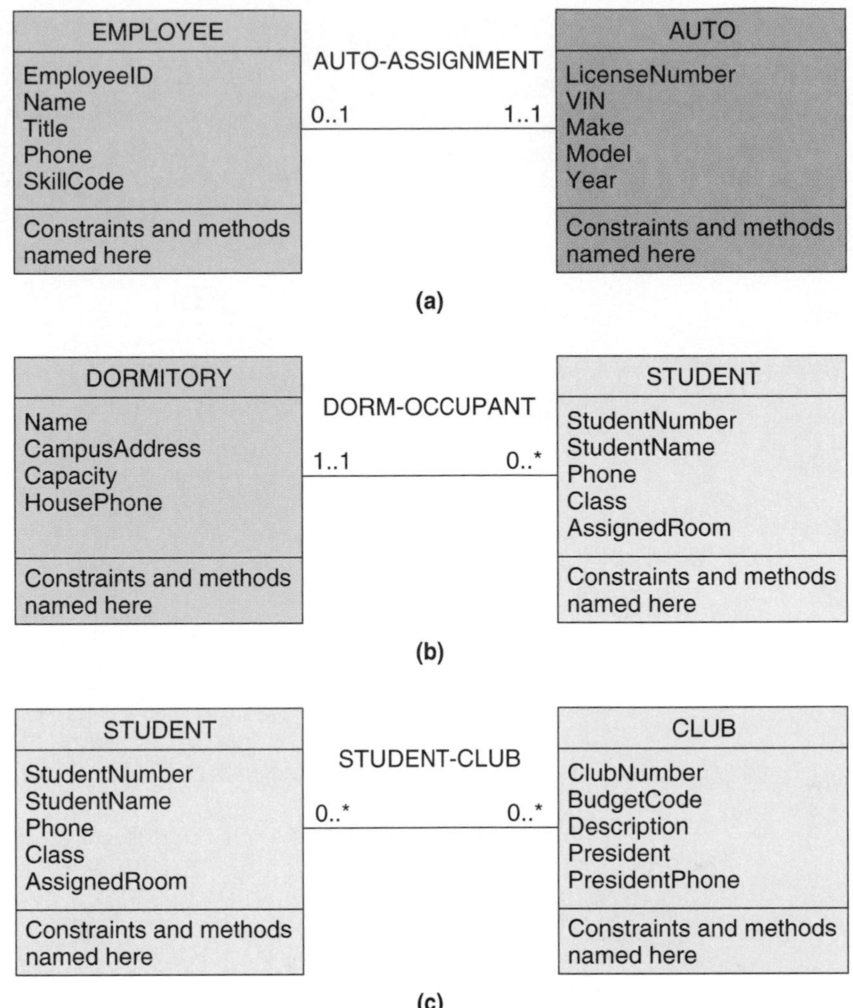

UML Entities and Relationships

Figure 3-12 shows the UML representation of the designs in Figure 3-3. Each entity is represented by an **entity class,** which is shown as a rectangle with three segments. The top segment shows the name of the entity and other data that we will discuss. The second segment lists the names of the attributes in the entity, and the third documents constraints and lists methods (program procedures) that belong to the entity.

Relationships are shown with a line between two entities. Cardinalities are represented in the format *x..y,* where *x* is the minimum required and *y* is the maximum allowed. Thus, 0..1 means that no entity is required and at most one is allowed. An asterisk represents an unlimited number. Thus, 1..* means that one is required and an unlimited number is allowed. Examine Figures 3-12(a)–(c) for examples of 1:1, 1:N, and N:M maximum cardinality relationships.

REPRESENTATION OF WEAK ENTITIES Figure 3-13 shows the UML representation of weak entities. A filled-in diamond is placed on the line to the parent of the weak entity (the entity on which the weak entity depends). In Figure 3-13(a), PRESCRIPTION is the weak entity and PATIENT is the parent entity. All weak entities have a parent, and thus the cardinality on their side of the weak

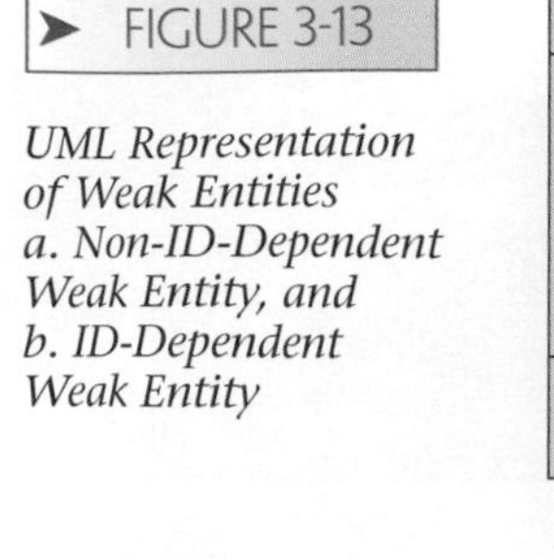

FIGURE 3-13

UML Representation of Weak Entities a. Non-ID-Dependent Weak Entity, and b. ID-Dependent Weak Entity

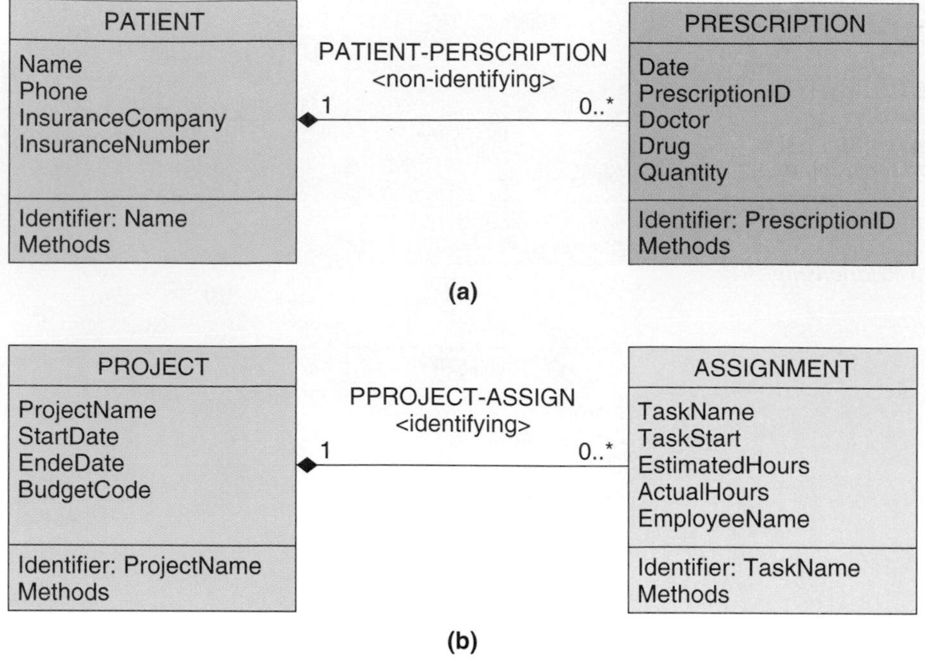

relationship is always 1..1. Because this is so, the cardinality on the parent entity is shown simply as 1.

Figure 3-13(a) shows a weak entity that is not an ID-dependent entity. This is denoted by the expression <non-identifying> on the PATIENT-PRESCRIPTION relationship. Figure 3-13(b) shows a weak entity that is ID-dependent. That is denoted with the label <identifying>.

REPRESENTATION OF SUBTYPES UML represents subtypes as shown in Figure 3-14. In this figure, INDIVIDUAL, PARTNERSHIP, and CORPORATE subtypes of CLIENT are allowed. According to this figure, a given CLIENT could be one, two, or three of these subtypes. For this situation, this does not make sense; a CLIENT should be one and only one of these types. The current version of UML

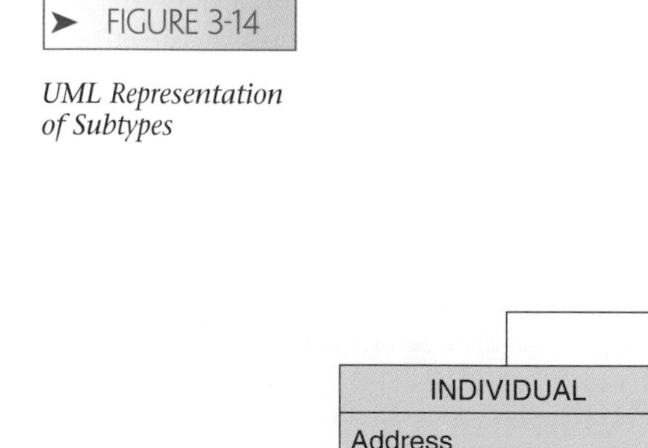

FIGURE 3-14

UML Representation of Subtypes

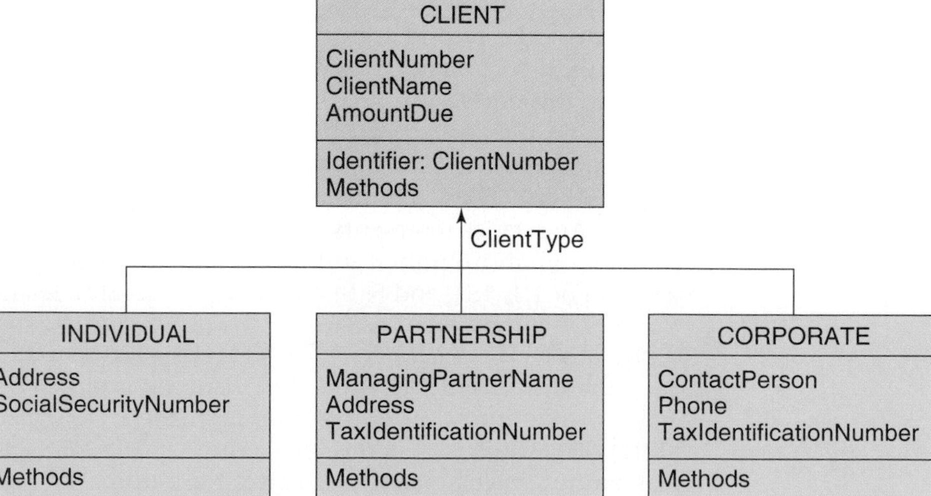

➤ FIGURE 3-15

UML Version of E-R Diagram in Figure 3-11

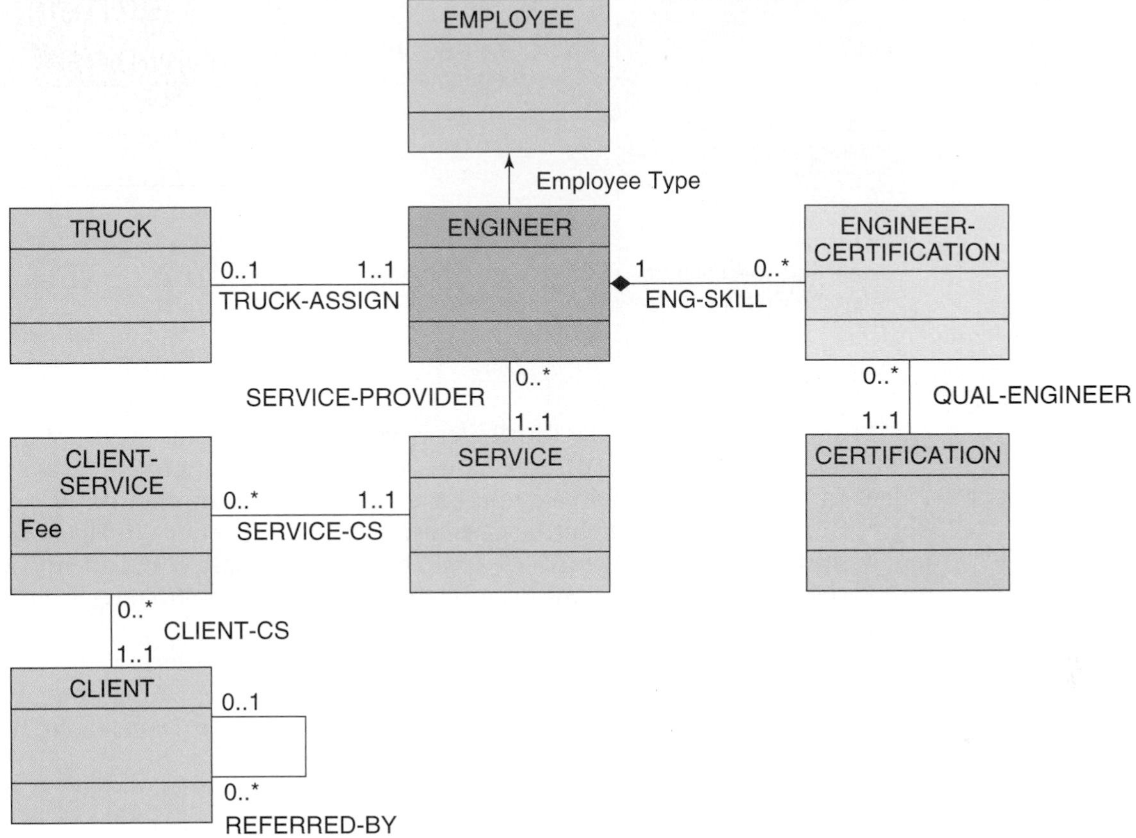

does not provide a means to document exclusivity. Such notation could be added to a UML diagram, however.

Figure 3-15 presents a UML version of the entity-relationship diagram shown previously as Figure 3-11. Because the relationship between SERVICE and CLIENT has an attribute—Fee—a separate entity CLIENT-SERVICE has been defined to carry that attribute. This is standard practice when using UML tools. Also note the representation of the recursive relationship, REFERRED-BY.

OOP Constructs Introduced by UML

Because UML is an object-oriented technology, several OOP constructs have been added to UML entity classes. We will touch on these ideas here and develop them further in Chapter 18. First, the classes of all entities that are to be stored in the database are labeled with the keyword <Persistent>. This simply means that data should continue to exist even if the object that processes it is destroyed. In simpler terms, it means that the entity class is to be stored in the database.

Next, UML entity classes allow for **class attributes.** Such attributes differ from entity attributes because they pertain to the class of all entities of a given type. Thus, in Figure 3-16, PatientCount of PATIENT is an attribute of the collection of all PATIENTs in the database. PatientSource is an attribute that documents the source of all of the PATIENTs in the database.

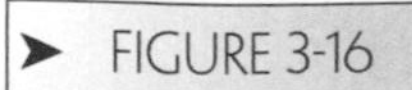

UML Entity Classes with OOP Constructs

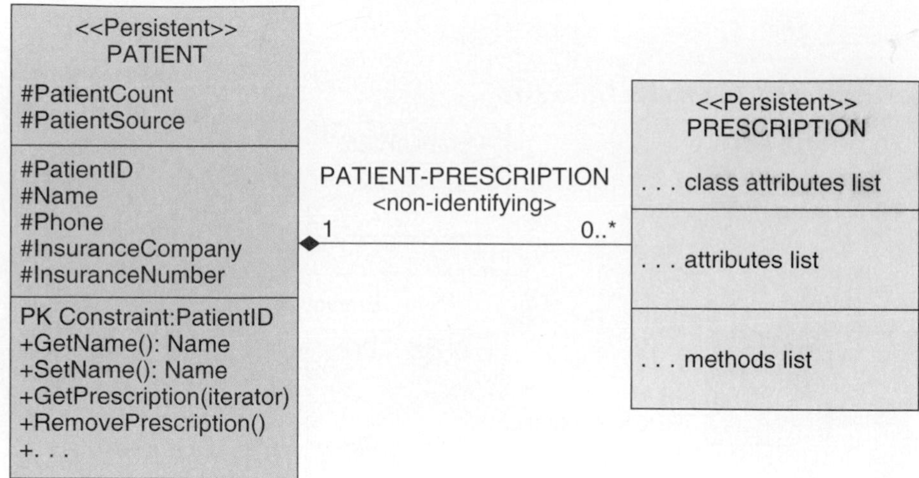

As you will learn, such class attributes have no place to reside when using the relational model. Instead, in some cases, attributes like PatientCount are not stored in the database but are computed at run-time. Or, in other cases, a new entity is introduced to contain the class attributes. For the entity in Figure 3-16, a new entity called PATIENT-SOURCE could be defined to hold both PatientCount and PatientSource attributes. In this case all of the entities in PATIENT would be connected to PATIENT-SOURCE.

A third new feature is that UML uses object-oriented notation for the visibility of attributes and methods. Attributes preceded by a + are public; those with a # are protected, and those with a − are private. In Figure 3-16, Name in PATIENT is a protected attribute.

These terms arise from the discipline of object-oriented programming. A *public* attribute can be accessed and changed by any method of any object. A public method can be invoked by any method of any object. *Protected* means that the attribute or method is accessible only by methods of this class or of its subclasses, and *private* means that the attribute or method is accessible only by methods of this class.

Finally, UML entities specify constraints and methods in the third segment of the entity classes. In Figure 3-16, a primary key constraint is placed on PatientID. This simply means that PatientID is a unique identifier. Additionally, Figure 3-16 documents that GetName() is to be created to provide public access (note the + in front of GetName) to the Name attribute; SetName() is to be used to set its value and the method GetPrescription() can be used to iterate over the set of Prescription entities related to this PATIENT entity.

The Role of UML in Database Processing Today

The ideas illustrated in Figure 3-16 lie in the murky water where database processing and object thinking merge. Such object-oriented notation doesn't fit with the practices and procedures of commercial database processing today. The notion that an entity attribute can be hidden in an object doesn't make sense unless only object-oriented programs are processing the database, and, even then, those programs must process the data in conformance with that policy. Except for special-purpose object-oriented DBMS (OODBMS) products and applications, this is never done.

Instead, most commercial DBMS products have features that allow all types of programs to access the database and process any data for which they have security authority. Moreover, with facilities like the query generator of Microsoft Access

2002 (Figure 2-8), there is no way to limit access to attribute values to a single object.

So, the bottom line is that you should know how to interpret UML-style entity-relationship diagrams. They can be used for database design just as traditional-style E-R diagrams can. At present, however, the object-oriented notation they introduce is of limited practical value. See Chapter 18 for more on this topic.

➤ EXAMPLES

The best way to gain proficiency with any modeling tool is to study examples and to use the tool to make your own models. The remainder of this chapter presents two case applications to help you with the first task. After working through these examples, you should then work the example problems at the end of the chapter.

EXAMPLE 1: THE JEFFERSON DANCE CLUB

The Jefferson Dance Club teaches social dancing and offers both private and group lessons. Jefferson charges $45 per hour per student (or couple) for a private lesson and $6 per hour per student for a group lesson. Private lessons are offered throughout the day, from noon until 10 P.M., six days a week. Group lessons are offered in the evenings.

Jefferson employs two types of instructor: full-time salaried instructors and part-time instructors. The full-time instructors are paid a fixed amount per week, and the part-time instructors are paid either a set amount for an evening or a set amount for teaching a particular class.

In addition to the lessons, Jefferson sponsors two weekly social dances featuring recorded music. The admission charge is $5 per person. The Friday night dance is the more popular and averages around 80 people; the Sunday night dance attracts about 30 attendees. The purpose of the dances is to give the students a place in which to practice their skills. No food or drinks are served.

Jefferson would like to develop an information system to keep track of students and the classes they have taken. Jefferson's managers would also like to know how many and which types of lessons each teacher has taught and to be able to compute the average cost per lesson for each of their instructors.

ENTITIES

The best way to begin an entity-relationship model is to determine potential entities. Entities are usually represented by nouns (places, persons, concepts, events, equipment, and so on) in documents or interviews. A search of the previous example for important nouns that relate to the information system reveals the following list:

- Private lesson
- Group lesson
- Teacher
- Full-time teacher
- Part-time teacher
- Dance
- Customer

Clearly, the nouns *private lesson* and *group lesson* have something in common, as do the nouns *teacher, full-time teacher,* and *part-time teacher.* One solution is to define an entity LESSON, with subtypes PRIVATE-LESSON and GROUP-LESSON, and another entity TEACHER, with subtypes FULL-TIME-TEACHER and PART-TIME-TEACHER. Additional entities are DANCE and CUSTOMER.

As stated in Chapter 2, data modeling is as much art as it is science. The solution just described is one of several feasible solutions. A second solution is to eliminate LESSON and TEACHER from the list in the preceding paragraph and to eliminate all subtypes. A third solution is to eliminate LESSON (since lesson was never mentioned by itself as a noun) but to keep TEACHER and its subtypes. Here we choose the third case because it seems to be the best fit for the information we have. Thus, the list of entities is PRIVATE-LESSON, GROUP-LESSON, TEACHER, FULL-TIME-TEACHER, PART-TIME-TEACHER, DANCE, and CUSTOMER.

Choosing among these alternatives requires analyzing the requirements and considering the design implications of each of them. Sometimes it helps to consider the attributes of the entities. If, for example, the entity LESSON has no attributes other than its identifier, then it is not necessary.

Relationships

To begin, TEACHER has two subtype entities, FULL-TIME-TEACHER and PART-TIME-TEACHER. A given teacher must be one or the other, so the subtypes are mutually exclusive.

Consider next the relationships between TEACHER and PRIVATE-LESSON and GROUP-LESSON. A TEACHER can teach many PRIVATE-LESSONs, and normally a PRIVATE-LESSON is taught by a single TEACHER. However, further discussion with Jefferson's management reveals that for advanced dancers, especially those preparing for competitions, sometimes two teachers are involved in a private lesson. Therefore the relationship between TEACHER and PRIVATE-LESSON must be many to many. Assume, however, that only one teacher is involved in a group lesson. The relationships just described are shown in Figure 3-17.

CUSTOMERs can take either PRIVATE-LESSONs or GROUP-LESSONs. Sometimes a lesson is taken by an individual and sometimes by a couple. There are two ways in which this situation can be modeled. An entity COUPLE can be defined as having a one-to-two relationship with CUSTOMER, or either CUSTOMER or COUPLE can have a relationship with PRIVATE-LESSON. We assume that couples do not take group lessons or that if they do, it is not important to store that fact in the database. This alternative is shown in Figure 3-18(a).

PRIVATE-LESSON's existence is dependent on CUSTOMER or COUPLE. That is, a lesson cannot exist unless it is given to either a CUSTOMER or a COUPLE. The 1 next to the horizontal line underneath CUSTOMER and COUPLE indicates

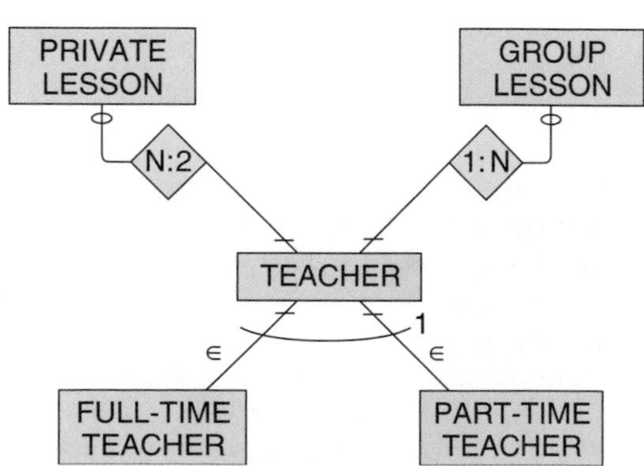

➤ FIGURE 3-17

Initial E-R Diagram for the Jefferson Dance Club

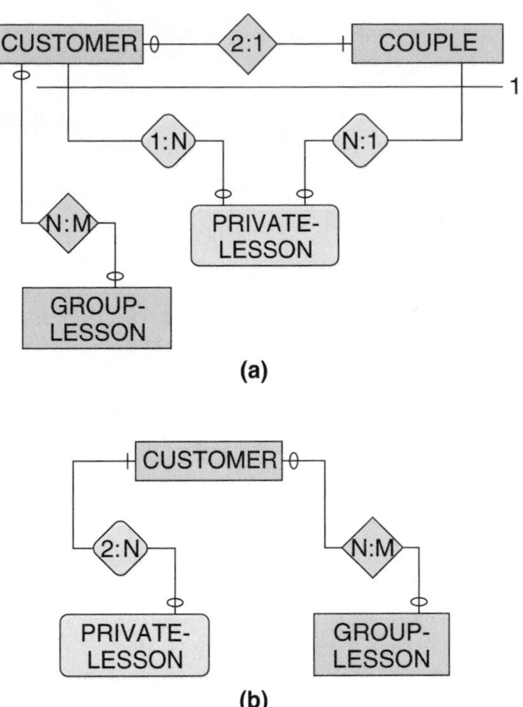

➤ FIGURE 3-18

Alternatives for Representing CUSTOMER: (a) E-R Diagram Showing COUPLE Entity and (b) E-R Diagram Without Couples

that PRIVATE-LESSON must have at least one CUSTOMER or one COUPLE, which makes sense, since PRIVATE-LESSON is dependent on them.

Another alternative is not to represent couples but, instead, to model the relationship between CUSTOMER and PRIVATE-LESSON as many to many. More precisely, this relationship is one or two to many and is shown in Figure 3-18(b). Although the model is not as detailed as that in Figure 3-18(a), it may very well suffice for Jefferson's purposes.

The last relationship possibility is that between DANCE and other entities. Both customers and teachers attend dances, and the developers must decide whether it is important to store these relationships. Does Jefferson really need to know which customers attended which dances? Do Jefferson's managers really want to record attendance in a computer-based information system as customers enter the door? Do the customers want that fact recorded? Most likely, this is not a relationship that needs to be or should be stored in the database.

The situation between DANCE and TEACHER is different. Jefferson likes some of its teachers to be present at each dance. In order to be fair about this requirement, Jefferson's management has drawn up a schedule for the teachers' attendance at dances. Developing and recording this schedule requires that the database contain the DANCE-TEACHER relationship, which is many to many.

Final E-R Diagram for the Jefferson Dance Club

Figure 3-19 shows an E-R diagram for the model described in this section. We have not named the relationships in this diagram. Although doing so would make the diagrams more true to form, for our data, naming relationships would add little.

PRIVATE-LESSON's existence is dependent on CUSTOMER, but GROUP-LESSON's is not, because group lessons are scheduled long before any customer signs up, and they will be held even if no customers show up. This situation is not true, however, for private lessons, as they are scheduled only at the customer's request. Also notice that this model does not represent couples.

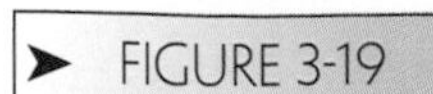
FIGURE 3-19

The Final E-R Diagram for Jefferson Dance Club

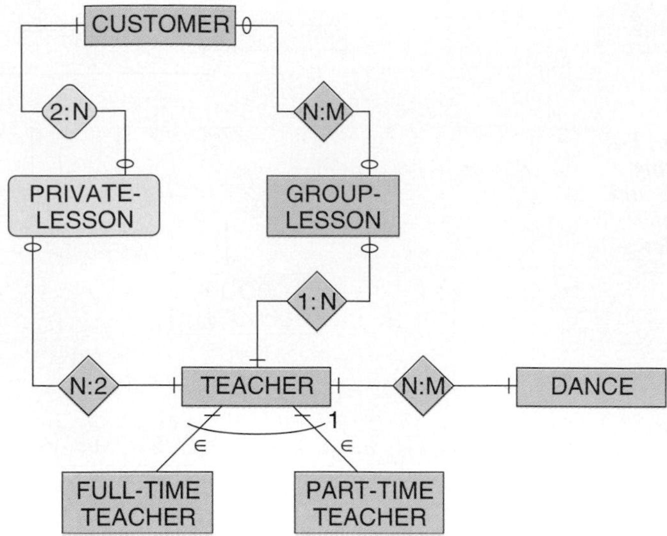

Once a model such as this is developed, its accuracy and completeness in regard to the requirements should be verified. Usually this is done with the users.

Evaluating the E-R Data Model

It is easier and cheaper to correct errors early in the database development process rather than later. For example, changing the maximum cardinality of a relationship from 1:N to N:M in the data modeling stage is simply a matter of recording the change in the E-R diagram. But once the database has been designed and loaded with data and application programs written to process the database, making such a change requires considerable rework, possibly even weeks of labor. It is important, therefore, to evaluate the data model before designing it.

One evaluation technique is to consider the E-R data model in the context of possible queries that might be posed to a database with the structure implied by the model. For example, look at the diagram in Figure 3-19. What questions could be answered from a database that was implemented according to this design?

- Who has taught which private lessons?
- Which customers have taken a private lesson from Jack?
- Who are the full-time teachers?
- Which teachers are scheduled to attend the dance on Friday?

When evaluating an E-R data model, you can construct such questions and show them to the users, who can then be asked to draw up their own list of questions. Their questions can then be posed against the design in order to check its appropriateness. For example, suppose that the users asked which customers attended last week's Friday night dance. The designers of the data model in Figure 3-19 would conclude that their design was not correct, because it is not possible to answer this question using their E-R model. If it must be answered, a relationship between CUSTOMER and DANCE must be constructed.

Clearly, such an informal and loosely structured process cannot be used to *prove* that a design is correct. It is, however, a pragmatic technique that can be used to verify the potential correctness of a design. And it is far better than no evaluation at all!

Example 2: San Juan Sailboat Charters

San Juan Sailboat Charters is an agent that leases sailboats to customers for a fee. San Juan does not own any sailboats but instead leases them on behalf of boat owners who wish to earn income when they are not using their boats. San Juan charges a fee for its service. San Juan specializes in boats that can be used for multi-day or weekly charters—the smallest sailboat in their inventory is 28 feet and the largest is 51 feet.

Each sailboat is fully equipped at the time it is leased. Most of the equipment is provided by the owners, but some is added by San Juan. The owner-provided equipment includes what is fixed on the boat, such as radios, compasses, depth indicators and other instrumentation, stoves, and refrigerators. Other owner-provided equipment is not installed as part of the boat. Such equipment includes sails, lines, anchors, dinghies, life preservers, and, in the cabin, dishes, silverware, cooking utensils, bedding, and the like. San Juan provides consumable equipment, which could also be considered supplies, such as charts, navigation books, tide and current tables, soap, dish towels, toilet paper, and similar items.

An important part of San Juan's responsibilities is keeping track of the equipment on the boat. Much of it is expensive, and some of it, particularly what is not attached to the boat, can easily be lost or stolen. Customers are responsible for all equipment during the period of their charter.

San Juan likes to keep accurate records of its customers and the charters, not only for marketing but also for recording the trips that customers have taken. Some itineraries and weather conditions are more dangerous than others, and so San Juan likes to know which customers have what experience.

Most of San Juan's business is bare-boat chartering, which means that no skipper or other crew is provided. In some cases, however, customers request the services of a skipper or other crew member, and so San Juan hires such personnel on a part-time basis.

Sailboats often need maintenance. San Juan is required by its contracts with the boat owners to keep accurate records of all maintenance activities and costs, including normal activities, such as cleaning or engine-oil changes, and unscheduled repairs. In some cases, repairs are necessary during a charter. A boat engine, for example, might fail while the boat is far away from San Juan's facility. In this case, the customers radio the San Juan dispatcher, who determines the best facility to make the repair and sends the facility's personnel to the disabled boat. To make these decisions, the dispatchers need information about repair facilities as well as past histories of repair quality and costs.

Before you continue reading, try to produce an entity-relationship diagram on your own. Examine the preceding statements and look for nouns that seem important to the design. Then check the possible relationships among the entities. Finally, list the likely attributes for each entity or relationship.

Entities

The data model required for San Juan Charters is more complicated than that for the Jefferson Dance Club. Potential entities are shown in Figure 3-20(a).

Consider first the equipment-related entities. There are several different kinds of equipment, and this fact suggests the possibility of modeling subtypes. However, why does San Juan care about equipment? It does not really want to know the characteristics of each item—the chain length on each anchor, for example. Instead, its goal is to keep track of the items and their type so that it can determine if any has been lost or damaged. This can be done without keeping detailed records of the particular subtypes of equipment. Thus, for this design, we place all types of equipment into the entity EQUIPMENT.

➤ FIGURE 3-20

Entities for San Juan Charters

LEASE
BOAT
CUSTOMER
OWNER
EQUIPMENT
OWNER-PROVIDED-EQUIPMENT
FIXED OWNER-EQUIPMENT
REMOVABLE OWNER-EQUIPMENT
SAN-JUAN-PROVIDED-EQUIPMENT
ITINERARY/WEATHER
CHARTER
PART-TIME-CREW
SCHEDULED-MAINTENANCE
UNSCHEDULED-MAINTENANCE
REPAIRS
REPAIR-FACILITY

(a) Possible entities for San Juan Charters

LEASE or CHARTER(synonyms)
BOAT
CUSTOMER
OWNER
EQUIPMENT
ITINERARY/WEATHER
PART-TIME-CREW
SCHEDULED-MAINTENANCE
REPAIR or UNSCHEDULED-MAINTENANCE(synonyms)
REPAIR-FACILITY

(b) Entities selected for the E-R design

Ownership of equipment is established by defining a relationship between EQUIPMENT and OWNER. If San Juan Charters is allowed to be an instance of OWNER, all of the equipment that it owns can be carried by this relationship. Similarly, from the case description, there is no reason to define the equipment that is attached to the boat differently from that not attached. An accurate list can be produced without this division. Figure 3-20(b) shows the final list of entities. Note that LEASE and CHARTER are synonyms; they refer to the same transaction. We show both names here so that they can be related to the case description.

It is possible that SCHEDULED-MAINTENANCE should be combined with UNSCHEDULED-MAINTENANCE. One way to decide is to examine the attributes of each of these entities. If they are the same, the two entity classes should be merged into one. Also observe that REPAIR and UNSCHEDULED-MAINTENANCE are defined as synonyms.

Relationships

Figure 3-21 is an entity-relationship diagram for San Juan Charters. For the most part, the relationships in this diagram are straightforward, but the relationship between EQUIPMENT and LEASE is arguable. One might say that EQUIPMENT should be related to BOAT and not to LEASE or that some EQUIPMENT should be related to BOAT (the equipment that stays with the boat) and the other equip-

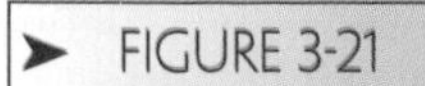

FIGURE 3-21

E-R Diagram for San Juan Charters

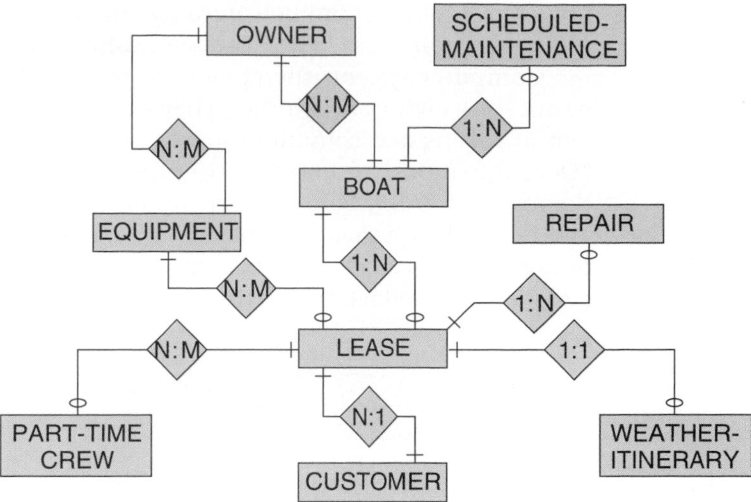

ment should be related to LEASE. These changes would be feasible alternatives to the design shown in Figure 3-21.

Notice, too, that SCHEDULED-MAINTENANCE is related to BOAT but that REPAIR (UNSCHEDULED-MAINTENANCE) is related to LEASE. This implies that no repair action is required when the boat is not being leased. Perhaps this is unrealistic.

Finally, LEASE and ITINERARY-WEATHER have a 1:1 relationship, and they also have the same identifying attributes. Therefore, it would be possible, and might even be preferable, to combine them into one entity class.

DATABASES AS MODELS OF MODELS

As you can see, there are many different ways of modeling a business situation, and the variety becomes even greater as the application grows more complex. Often, dozens of models are feasible, and it can be difficult to choose among them.

Sometimes when evaluating alternatives, project team members discuss and argue about which data model best represents the real world. These discussions are misguided. Databases do not model the real world, although it is a common misconception that they do. Rather, databases are models of the users' models of the world (or, more to the point, of their business world). The question to ask when evaluating alternative data models is not "Does this design accurately represent the real world?" but, rather, "Does this design accurately represent the users' model of his or her environment?" The goal is to develop a design that fits the users' mental conception.

In fact, Immanuel Kant and other philosophers argued that it is impossible for humans to build models of what actually exists, claiming that the essence of things is forever unknowable by humans.[8] Extending this line of argument to computer systems, Winograd and Flores stated that in societies, humans construct systems of tokens that enable them to operate successfully in the world. A series of tokens is

[8] "We cannot, indeed, beyond all possible experience, form a definitive concept of what things in themselves may be. Yet we are not at liberty to abstain entirely from inquiring into them; for experience never satisfies reason fully, but in answering questions, refers us further and further back and leaves us dissatisfied with regard the complete solution." Immanuel Kant, *Prolegomena to Any Future Metaphysics* (Indianapolis: Bobbs-Merrill, 1950), p. 100.

not a model of the infinitude of reality but, rather, only a social system that enables users to coordinate their activities successfully, and nothing more can be said.[9]

Computer systems therefore need to model and represent their users' communications with one another. They do not model anything other than that system of tokens and communications. So learn to ask these questions of yourself: "Does this model accurately reflect the users' perceptions and mental models of their world? Will it help the users respond consistently and successfully with one another and with their customers?" It is pointless for one analyst to claim that his or her model is a better representation of reality. Instead, the point is to develop a model that well represents the user's model of his or her business environment.

➤ SUMMARY

The entity-relationship model was developed by Peter Chen. With this model, entities—which are identifiable things of importance to the users—are defined. All of the entities of a given type form an entity class. A particular entity is called an instance. Entities have attributes that describe their characteristics, and one or more attributes identify an entity.

Relationships are associations among entities. The E-R model explicitly defines relationships; each relationship has a name; and there are relationship classes as well as relationship instances. Relationships may have attributes.

The degree of the relationship is the number of entities participating in the relationship. Most relationships are binary. The three types of binary relationships are 1:1, 1:N, and N:M.

In entity-relationship diagrams, the entities are shown in rectangles, and the relationships are shown in diamonds. The maximum cardinality of the relationship is shown inside the diamond. The minimum cardinality is indicated by a hash mark or an oval. Relationships that connect entity instances of the same class are recursive. Attributes can be shown in an E-R diagram in ellipses or in a separate table.

A weak entity is one whose existence depends on another entity; an entity that is not weak is called a strong entity. Weak entities are shown in rectangles with rounded corners, and the relationship on which the entity depends is indicated by a diamond with rounded corners. In this text, we further define a weak entity to be an entity that logically depends on another entity. An entity can have a minimum cardinality of 1 in a relationship with another entity and not necessarily be a weak entity. Multi-value attributes are represented with weak entities.

Some entities have subtypes that define subsets of similar entities. Subtypes inherit attributes from their parent, the supertype. HAS-A relationships connect entities of different types, and the identifiers of the entities are different. IS-A relationships are subtypes, and the identifiers of the entities are the same.

Once a data model is developed, the designers should consider business rules that may restrict processing against entities. Each entity in the model should be evaluated in light of possible data additions, changes, and deletions. Deletions, in particular, often are the source of important processing restrictions. When business rules are discovered, they should be documented in the data model.

The E-R model is an important part of many CASE products. These products provide tools for constructing and storing E-R diagrams. Some CASE tools integrate the E-R constructs with data constructs in the CASE repository. The Unified Modeling Language (UML) has defined a new style of entity-relationship

[9]Terry Winograd and F. Flores, *Understanding Computers and Cognition* (Reading, MA: Addison-Wesley, 1986).

diagrams. You should be familiar with diagrams of that style; but also realize that when creating a database design, there is no fundamental difference between the traditional style and the UML style.

Once they are completed, E-R models should be evaluated. One technique is to list queries that could be answered using the data model. This list is then shown to the users, who are asked to think of additional questions. The design is then evaluated against these questions to ensure that the model can answer them.

Databases do not model the real world but instead model the users' model of their business world. The appropriate criterion for judging a data model is whether the model fits the users' model. Arguing about which model best fits the real world is pointless.

➤ GROUP I QUESTIONS

3.1 Define *entity* and give an example.

3.2 Explain the difference between an entity class and an entity instance.

3.3 Define *attribute* and give examples for the entity you described in Question 3.1.

3.4 Explain what a composite attribute is and give an example.

3.5 Which attribute defined in your answer to Question 3.3 identifies the entity?

3.6 Define *relationship* and give an example.

3.7 Explain the difference between a relationship class and a relationship instance.

3.8 Define *degree of relationship*. Give an example, other than the one in this text, of a relationship greater than degree 2.

3.9 List and give an example of the three types of binary relationships. Draw an E-R diagram for each.

3.10 Define the terms *maximum cardinality* and *minimum cardinality*.

3.11 Name and sketch the symbols used in entity-relationship diagrams for (a) entity, (b) relationship, (c) weak entity and its relationship, (d) recursive relationship, and (e) subtype entity.

3.12 Give an example E-R diagram for the entities DEPARTMENT and EMPLOYEE, which have a 1:N relationship. Assume that a DEPARTMENT does not need to have any EMPLOYEE but that every EMPLOYEE does have a DEPARTMENT.

3.13 Give an example of a recursive relationship and show it in an E-R diagram.

3.14 Show example attributes for DEPARTMENT and EMPLOYEE (from Question 3.12). Use UML-style symbols.

3.15 Define the term *weak entity* and give an example other than the one in this text.

3.16 Explain the ambiguity in the definition of the term *weak entity*. Explain how this text interprets this term. Give examples, other than those in this text, of each type of weak entity.

3.17 Define the term *ID-dependent entity* and give an example other than one in this text.

3.18 Show how to use a weak entity to represent the multi-value attribute Skill in an EMPLOYEE entity. Indicate both the maximum and minimum cardinalities on both sides of the relationship. Use traditional symbols.

3.19 Show how to use a weak entity to represent the multi-value composite attribute Phone that contains the single-value attributes AreaCode, PhoneNumber. Assume Phone appears in an entity called SALESPERSON.

Indicate both the maximum and minimum cardinalities on both sides of the relationship. Use UML-style symbols.

3.20 Describe subtype entities and give an example other than those in this text.

3.21 Explain the term *inheritance* and show how it applies to your answer to Question 3.20.

3.22 Explain the difference between a HAS-A relationship and an IS-A relationship, and give an example of each.

3.23 How are business rules treated in an E-R model?

3.24 Describe why it is important to evaluate a data model once it has been created. Summarize one technique for evaluating a data model, and explain how that technique could be used to evaluate the data model in Figure 3-21.

➤ GROUP II QUESTIONS

3.25 Change the E-R diagram in Figure 3-19 to include an entity LESSON. Let PRIVATE-LESSON and GROUP-LESSON be subtypes of LESSON. Modify the relationships as necessary. Use traditional symbols.

3.26 Change the E-R diagram in Figure 3-19 to exclude TEACHER. Modify the relationships as necessary. Use UML-style symbols.

3.27 Which of the models in Figure 3-19 and in your answers to Questions 3.25 and 3.26 do you prefer? Explain the reason for your preference.

3.28 Change the E-R diagram in Figure 3-21 to include subtypes of equipment. Assume that the equipment owned by San Juan Charters pertains to LEASE and that other equipment pertains to BOAT. Model the differences between the BOAT-related EQUIPMENT that is fixed on the boats and the BOAT-related EQUIPMENT that is not fixed. What benefits does the added complexity of this model bring?

➤ PROJECTS

A. Develop an E-R diagram for a database to support the tracking needs of the following organization: The Metropolitan Housing Agency (MHA) is a nonprofit organization that advocates the development and improvement of low-income housing. The MHA operates in a metropolitan area of approximately 2.2 million people in a midwestern city.

The MHA maintains data about the location, availability, and condition of low-income housing in 11 different census tracts in the metropolitan area. Within the boundaries of these tracts are approximately 250 different buildings that provide low-income housing. On average, each building contains 25 apartments or other units.

The MHA keeps data about each census tract, including geographic boundaries, median income of the population, elected officials, principal businesses, principal investors involved in attributes in that tract, and other demographic and economic data. It also maintains a limited amount of data about crime. For each building, the MHA stores the name, address, size, owner(s)'s name and address, mortgagor(s)'s name and address, renovations and repairs, and availability of facilities for handicapped people. In addition, the MHA keeps a list of each of the units within each building, including the type of unit, size, number of bedrooms, number of baths, kitchen and dining facilities, location in the building, and any special remarks. The MHA would like to maintain data regarding the average occupancy rates for each unit, but, to date, it has been unable to collect or store such data. The MHA does, however, keep data about whether a given unit is occupied.

The MHA serves as an information clearinghouse and offers three basic services. First, it works with politicians, lobbyists, and advocacy groups to support legislation that encourages the development of low-income housing through tax incentives, developmental zoning preferences, and other legislative inducements. To accomplish this, the MHA provides information about low-income housing to state, county, and city governments. Second, through speeches, seminars, displays at conventions, and other public relations activities, the MHA officials strive to raise the community's consciousness about the need for low-income housing. Finally, the MHA provides information about the availability of low-income housing to other agencies that work with the low-income and homeless populations.

B. Access the Web site for a computer manufacturer such as Dell (www.dell.com). Use the Web site to determine which laptop computer you would buy for a power user who has a budget of $10,000. As you use the Web site, think about the structure of a possible database of computer systems and subsystems to support this site.

Develop an E-R diagram of computer system and subsystem database for this Web site. Show all entities and relationships and at least two or three attributes per entity. Indicate minimum and maximum cardinalities for both sides of each relationship. Possible entities are BASE-SYSTEM, MEMORY-OPTION, VIDEO-CARD, and PRINTER. Of course there are many more possible entities. Model any multi-value attributes as shown in the text. Use subtypes where appropriate. To keep this project from exploding in size, constrain your design to the needs of someone who is making a purchase decision.

C. Access the Web site for a bookseller such as Amazon (www.amazon.com). Use the Web site to determine the three best books on XML (Extended Markup Language) for someone who is just learning that subject. As you use the Web site, think about the structure of a possible database of books, authors, subjects, and related topics.

Develop an E-R diagram of a book database for this for this Web site. Show all entities and relationships and at least two or three attributes per entity. Indicate minimum and maximum cardinalities for both sides of each relationship. Possible entities are TITLE, AUTHOR, PUBLISHER, COPY, and SUBJECT. Of course there are many more possible entities. Model any multi-value attributes as shown in the text. Use subtypes where appropriate. To keep this project from exploding in size, assume that only books are to be tracked. Further, constrain your design to the needs of someone who is looking for books to purchase. Do not consider customer ordering, order fulfillment, purchase ordering, and other such business processes.

➤ FIREDUP PROJECT QUESTIONS

Consider the situation of FiredUp discussed at the end of Chapters 1 and 2. Assume that FiredUp has now developed a line of three different stoves: FiredNow, FiredAlways, and FiredAtCamp. Further, assume that the owners are selling spare parts for each of their stoves and that they also are making stove repairs. Some repairs are at no charge because they are within the stove warranty period; other repairs are made at a charge for parts only; and still others are made for parts and labor. FiredUp wants to keep track of all of these data. When asked for further details, the owners made the following list:

CUSTOMER: Name, StreetAddress, ApartmentNumber, City, State/Province, Zip/PostalCode, Country, EmailAddress, PhoneNumber

STOVE: SerialNumber, Type, ManufactureDate, InspectorInitials

INVOICE: InvoiceNumber, Date, Customer, with a list of items and prices that were sold, TotalPrice

REPAIR: RepairNumber, Customer, Stove, Description, with a list of items that were used in the repair and the charge for them, if any, and TotalAmount of the repair

PART: Number, Description, Cost, SalesPrice

A. Create an entity-relationship diagram of a database for FiredUp. Set the minimum and maximum cardinality of the relationships among entities as you think is appropriate. Explain your rationale for each cardinality value. Use week entities as you see appropriate. Do not use subtypes. Name any ID-dependent entities, if any.

B. Modify your entity-relationship diagram in your answer to Question A by representing INVOICE and REPAIR with appropriate subtypes. Under what circumstances is this design better than the one in your answer to question A?

C. Suppose that FiredUp wants to keep track of home, fax, and cell phone numbers as well as multiple e-mail addresses for each of their customers. Modify your E-R diagram to allow for multiple values of PhoneNumber and EmailAddress.

D. Suppose that FiredUp develops different versions of the same stove product. Thus, they develop a FiredNow Version 1 and a FiredNow Version 2, and so on. Modify your entity-relationship diagram from Question A, above, as necessary to account for this situation.

E. When asking users for the data they want to track, they will not necessarily remember everything they need. Using your knowledge of small business operations, make a list of entities that they may have forgotten. Show potential relationships among these entities in an E-R diagram. How would you go about determining if any of these additional data are needed at FiredUp?

The Semantic Object Model

This chapter discusses the semantic object model, which, like the E-R model discussed in Chapter 3, is used to create data models. As shown in Figure 4-1, the development team interviews users; analyzes the users' reports, forms, and queries; and from these constructs a model of the users' data. This data model is later transformed into a database design.

The particular form of the data model depends on the constructs used to build it. If an E-R model is used, the model will have entities, relationships, and the like. If a semantic model is used, the model will have semantic objects and related constructs, which are discussed in this chapter.

The E-R model and the semantic object model are like lenses through which the database developers look when studying and documenting the users' data. Both lenses work, and they both ultimately result in a database design. They use different lenses to form that design, however, and because the lenses create different images, the designs they produce may not be exactly the same. When developing a database, you must decide which approach to use, just as a photographer needs to decide which lens to use. Each approach has strengths and weaknesses, which we discuss at the end of this chapter.

The semantic object model was first presented in the third edition of this text, in 1988. It is based on concepts that were developed and published by Codd and by Hammer and McLeod.[1] The semantic object model is a data model. It is different from **object-oriented database processing,** which we will discuss in Chapter 18. There you will learn how the purposes, features, and constructs of semantic object modeling differ from object-oriented database processing.

---

[1]E. F. Codd, "Extending the Relational Model to Capture More Meaning," *ACM Transactions on Database Systems,* December 1976, pp. 397–424; and Michael Hammer and Dennis McLeod, "Database Description with SDM: A Semantic Database Model," *ACM Transactions on Database Systems,* September 1981, pp. 351–386.

FIGURE 4-1

Using Different Data Models for Database Designs

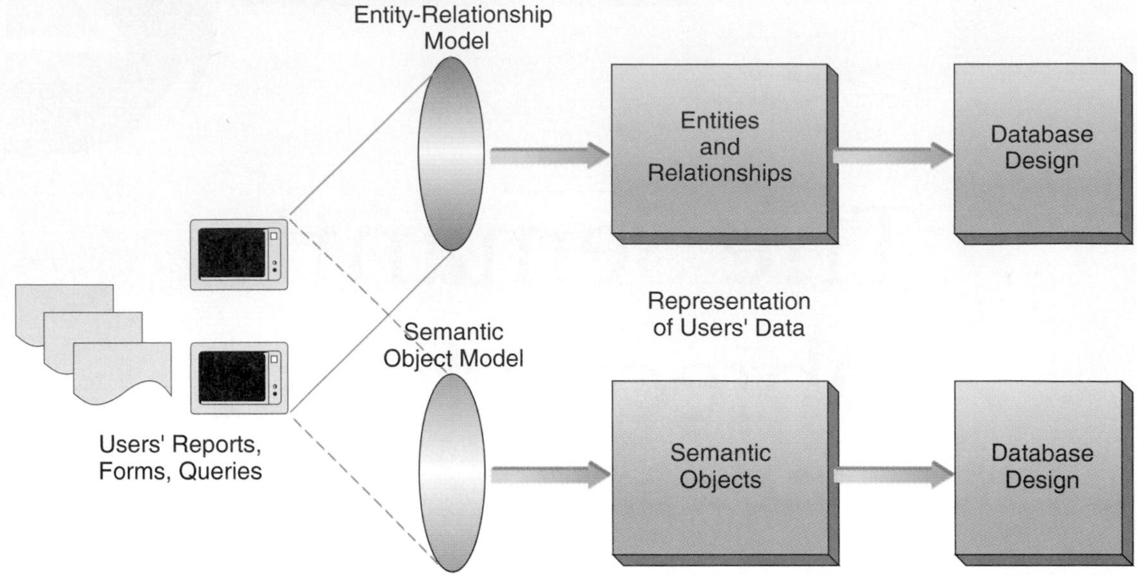

SEMANTIC OBJECTS

The purpose of a database application is to provide forms, reports, and queries so that the users can track entities or objects important to their work. The goals of the early stages of database development are to determine the things to be represented in the database, to specify the characteristics of those things, and to establish the relationships among them.

In Chapter 3, we referred to these things as entities. In this chapter, we refer to them as **semantic objects,** or sometimes as just objects. The word *semantic* means meaning, and a semantic object is one that models, in part, the meaning of the users' data. Semantic objects model the users' perceptions more closely than does the E-R model. We use the adjective *semantic* with the word *object* to distinguish the objects discussed in this chapter from the objects defined in object-oriented programming (OOP) languages.

DEFINING SEMANTIC OBJECTS

Entities and objects are similar in some ways, and they are different in other ways. We begin with the similarities. A semantic object is a representation of some identifiable thing in the users' work environment. More formally, a semantic object is a *named collection of attributes that sufficiently describes a distinct identity.*

Like entities, semantic objects are grouped into classes. An object class has a *name* that distinguishes it from other classes and that corresponds to the names of the things it represents. Thus, a database that supports users who work with student records has an object class called STUDENT. Note that object class names, like entity class names, are spelled with capital letters. A particular semantic object is an instance of the class. Thus, 'William Jones' is an instance of the STUDENT class, and 'Accounting' is an instance of the DEPARTMENT class.

Like entities, an object has a *collection of attributes.* Each attribute represents a characteristic of the identity being represented. For instance, the STUDENT object could have attributes like Name, HomeAddress, CampusAddress, DateOfBirth, DateOfGraduation, and Major. This collection of attributes also is a *sufficient description,* which means that the attributes represent all of the characteristics that the users need in order to do their work. As we stated at the end of Chapter 3, things in the world have an infinite set of characteristics; we cannot represent all of them. Instead, we represent those necessary for the users to satisfy their information needs so that they can successfully perform their jobs. Sufficient description also means that the objects are complete in themselves. All of the data required about a CUSTOMER, for example, is located in the CUSTOMER object, so we need not look anywhere else to find data about CUSTOMERs.

Objects represent *distinct identities;* that is, they are something that users recognize as independent and separate and that users want to track and report. These identities are the nouns about which the information is to be produced. To understand better the term *distinct identity,* recall that there is a difference between objects and object instances. CUSTOMER is the name of an object, and 'CUSTOMER 12345' is the name of an instance of an object. When we say that an object represents a distinct identity, we mean that users consider each *instance* of an object to be unique and identifiable in its own right.

Finally, note that the identities that the objects represent may or may not have a physical existence. For example, EMPLOYEEs physically exist, but ORDERs do not. Orders are, themselves, models of a contractual agreement to provide certain goods or services under certain terms and conditions. They are not physical things but, rather, representations of agreements. Thus, something need not be physical in order to be considered an object; it need only be identifiable in its own right in the minds of the users.

ATTRIBUTES

Semantic objects have attributes that define their characteristics. There are three types of attributes. **Simple attributes** have a single element. Examples are DateOfHire, InvoiceNumber, and SalesTotal. **Group attributes** are composites of other attributes. One example is Address, which contains the attributes {Street, City, State, Zip}; another example is FullName, which contains the attributes {FirstName, MiddleInitial, LastName}. **Semantic object attributes** are attributes that establish a relationship between one semantic object and another.

To understand these statements better, look at Figure 4-2(a), which is an example of a **semantic object diagram,** or **object diagram.** Such diagrams are used by development teams to summarize the structures of objects and to present them visually. Objects are shown in portrait-oriented rectangles. The name of the object appears at the top, and attributes are written in order after the object name.

The DEPARTMENT object contains an example of each of the three types of attributes. DepartmentName, PhoneNumber, and FaxPhoneNumber are simple attributes, each of which represents a single data element. CampusAddress is a group attribute containing the simple attributes Building and OfficeNumber. Finally, COLLEGE, PROFESSOR, and STUDENT each are semantic object attributes, which means that those objects are connected to and logically contained in DEPARTMENT.

The object attributes, or **object links** as they are sometimes called, mean that when a user thinks about a DEPARTMENT, he or she thinks not only about DepartmentName, CampusAddress, PhoneNumber, and FaxPhoneNumber but also about the COLLEGE, PROFESSORs, and STUDENTs who are related to that department. Since COLLEGE, PROFESSOR, and STUDENT also are objects, the complete data model contains object diagrams for them, too. The COLLEGE

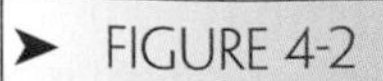
FIGURE 4-2

DEPARTMENT Object Diagram: (a) DEPARTMENT Object and (b) DEPARTMENT Object with Cardinalities

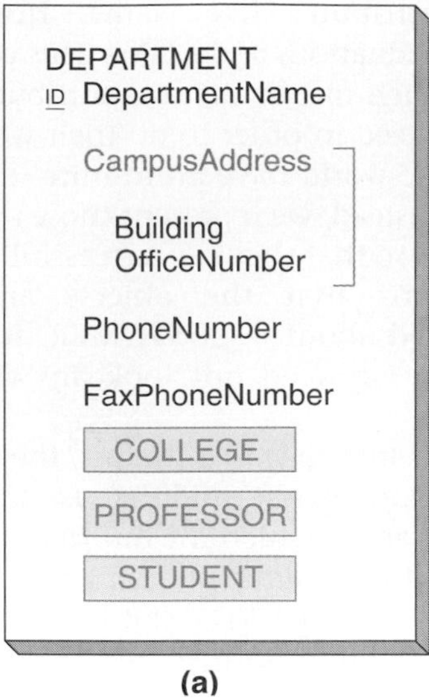

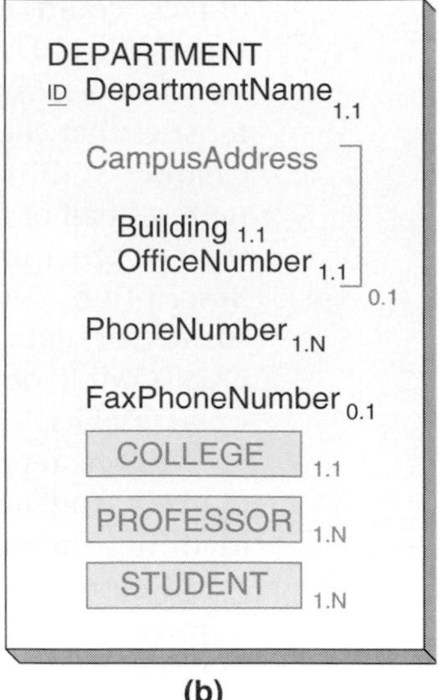

object contains attributes of the college; the PROFESSOR object contains attributes of the faculty; and the STUDENT object contains attributes of the students.

ATTRIBUTE CARDINALITY Each attribute in a semantic object has both a minimum cardinality and a maximum cardinality. The minimum cardinality indicates the number of instances of the attribute that must exist in order for the object to be valid. Usually this number is either 0 or 1. If it is 0, the attribute is not required to have a value. If it is 1, the attribute must have a value. Although it is unusual, the minimum cardinality can sometimes be larger than 1. For example, the attribute PLAYER in an object called BASKETBALL-TEAM might have a minimum cardinality of 5, since this is the smallest number of players required to make up a basketball team.

The maximum cardinality indicates the maximum number of instances of the attribute that the object may have. It is usually either 1 or N. If it is 1, the attribute can have no more than one instance; if it is N, the attribute can have many values, and the absolute number is not specified. Sometimes the maximum cardinality is a specific number such as 5, meaning the object can contain no more than exactly five instances of the attribute. For example, the attribute PLAYER in BASKETBALL-TEAM might have a maximum cardinality of 15, which would indicate that no more than 15 players could be assigned to a team's roster.

Cardinalities are shown as subscripts of attributes in the format **N.M,** where N is the minimum cardinality and M is the maximum. In Figure 4-2(b), the minimum cardinality of DepartmentName is 1 and the maximum is also 1, which means that exactly one value of DepartmentName is required. The cardinality of PhoneNumber is 1.N, meaning that a DEPARTMENT is required to have at least one PhoneNumber but may have many. The cardinality of 0.1 in FaxPhoneNumber means that a DEPARTMENT may have either zero or one FaxPhoneNumber.

The cardinalities of groups and the attributes in groups can be subtle. Consider the attribute CampusAddress. Its cardinalities are 0.1, meaning a DEPARTMENT need not have an address and has at most one. Now examine the attributes inside CampusAddress. Both Building and OfficeNumber have the cardinalities 1.1. You might be wondering how a group can be optional if the attributes in that group are required. The answer is that the cardinalities operate only between the attribute and the container of that attribute. The minimum cardinality of CampusAddress indicates that there need not be a value for address in DEPARTMENT. But the minimum cardinalities of Building and OfficeNumber indicate that both Building and

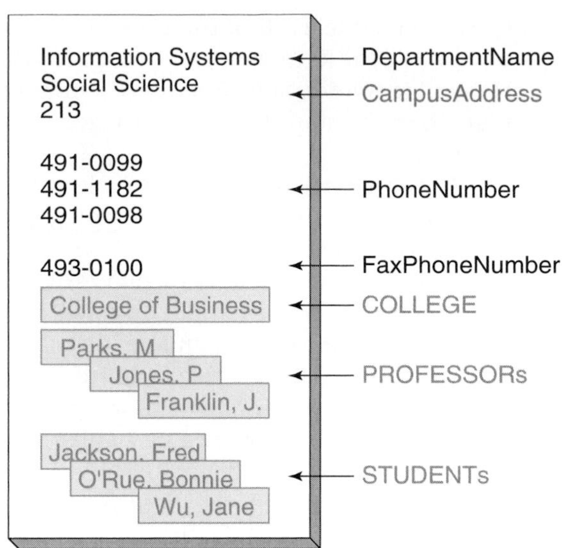

➤ FIGURE 4-3

An Instance of the DEPARTMENT Object in Figure 4-2

OfficeNumber must exist in CampusAddress. Thus a CampusAddress group need not appear, but if one does, it must have a value for both Building and OfficeNumber.

OBJECT INSTANCES The object diagrams for DEPARTMENT shown in Figure 4-2 are a format, or general structure, that can be used for any department. An instance of the DEPARTMENT object is shown in Figure 4-3, with each attribute's value for a particular department. The DepartmentName is Information Systems, and it is located in Room 213 of the Social Science Building. Observe that there are three values for PhoneNumber—the Information Systems Department has three phone lines in its office. Other departments may have fewer or more, but every department has at least one.

Furthermore, there is one instance of COLLEGE, the College of Business, and there are multiple values for the PROFESSOR and STUDENT object attributes. Each of these object attributes is a complete object; each has all the attributes defined for an object of that type. To keep this diagram simple, only the identifying names are shown for each of the instances of object attribute.

An object diagram is a picture of the user's perception of an object in the work environment. Thus, in the user's mind, the DEPARTMENT object includes all of this data. A DEPARTMENT logically contains data about the COLLEGE in which it resides, as well as the PROFESSORs and STUDENTs who are related to that department.

PAIRED ATTRIBUTES The semantic object model has no one-way object relationships. If an object contains another object, the second object will contain the first. For example, if DEPARTMENT contains the object attribute COLLEGE, then COLLEGE will contain the matching object attribute DEPARTMENT. These object attributes are called **paired attributes,** since they always occur as a pair.

Why must object attributes be paired? The answer lies in the way in which human beings think about relationships. If Object A has a relationship with Object B, then Object B will have a relationship with Object A. At the least, B is related to A in the relationship of "things that are related to B." If this argument seems obscure, try to envision a one-way relationship between two objects. It cannot be done.

Object Identifiers

An **object identifier** is one or more object attributes that the users employ to identify object instances. Such identifiers are potential names for a semantic object. In CUSTOMER, for example, possible identifiers are CustomerID and

CustomerName. Each of these are attributes that users consider to be valid names of CUSTOMER instances. Compare these identifiers with attributes like DateOfFirstOrder, StockPrice, and NumberOfEmployees. Such attributes are not identifiers because the users do not think of them as names of CUSTOMER instances.

A **group identifier** is an identifier that has more than one attribute. Examples are {FirstName, LastName}, {FirstName, PhoneNumber} and {State, License Number}.

Object identifiers may or may not be unique, depending on how the users view their data. For example, InvoiceNumber is a unique identifier for ORDER, but StudentName is not a unique identifier for STUDENT. There may, for example, be two students named "Mary Smith." If so, the users will employ StudentName to identify a group of one or more students and then, if necessary, use values of other attributes to identify a particular member of that set.

In semantic object diagrams, object identifiers are denoted by the letters *ID* in front of the attribute. If the identifier is unique, these letters will be underlined. In Figure 4-2(b), for example, the attribute DepartmentName is a unique identifier of DEPARTMENT.

Normally, if an attribute is to be used as an identifier, its value is required. Also, generally there is no more than one value of an identifier attribute for a given object. In most cases, therefore, the cardinality of an ID attribute is 1.1, and so we use this value as a default.

There are (relatively few) cases, however, in which the cardinality of an identifier is other than 1.1. Consider, for example, the attribute Alias in the semantic object PERSON. A person need not have an alias, or he or she may have several aliases. Hence, the cardinality of Alias would be 0.N.

Showing the subscripts of all attributes clutters the semantic object diagram. To simplify, we will assume the cardinalities of simple-value identifier attributes are 1.1 and the cardinalities of other simple-value attributes are 0.1. If the cardinality of the simple-value attribute is other than these assumptions, we will show it on the diagram. Otherwise subscripts on simple-value attributes will be omitted.

Attribute Domains

The **domain** of an attribute is a description of an attribute's possible values. The characteristics of a domain depend on the type of the attribute. The domain of a simple attribute consists of both a physical and a semantic description. The physical description indicates the type of data (for example, numeric versus string), the length of the data, and other restrictions or constraints (such as the first character must be alphabetic, or the value must not exceed 9999.99). The semantic description indicates the function or purpose of the attribute—it distinguishes this attribute from other attributes that might have the same physical description.

For example, the domain of DepartmentName could be defined as "the set of strings of up to seven characters that represent names of departments at Highline University." The phrase *strings of up to seven characteristics* is the physical description of the domain, and the phrase *that represent names of departments at Highline University* is the semantic description. The semantic description differentiates strings of seven characters that represent names of departments from similar strings that represent, say, names of courses or buildings or some other attribute.

In some cases, the physical description of a simple attribute domain is an **enumerated list,** the set of an attribute's specific values. The domain of the attribute PartColor, for example, might be the enumerated list {'Blue', 'Yellow', 'Red'}.

The domain of a group attribute also has a physical and a semantic description. The physical description is a list of all of the attributes in the group and the order of those attributes. The semantic description is the function or purpose of the group.

Thus the physical domain description of CampusAddress (in Figure 4-2) is the list {Building, OfficeNumber}; the semantic description is *the location of an office at Highline University.*

The domain of an object attribute is the set of object instances of that type. In Figure 4-2, for example, the domain of the PROFESSOR object attribute is the set of all PROFESSOR object instances in the database. The domain of the COLLEGE object is the set of all COLLEGEs in the database. In a sense, the domain of an object attribute is a dynamically enumerated list; the list contains all of the object instances of a particular type.

SEMANTIC OBJECT VIEWS

Users access the values of object attributes through database applications that provide data entry forms, reports, and queries. In most cases, such forms, reports, and queries do not require access to all of an object's attributes. For example, Figure 4-4 shows two application views of DEPARTMENT. Some attributes of DEPARTMENT (its DepartmentName, for example) are visible in both application views. Other attributes are visible in only one. For example, STUDENT is seen only in the StudentListing View, but PROFESSOR is visible in only the Staff View.

The portion of an object that is visible to a particular application is called the **semantic object view** or simply the **view.** A view consists of the name of the object plus a list of all of the attributes visible from that view.

Views are used in two ways. When you are developing a database, you can use them to develop the data model. Look at Figure 4-1 again. As shown, when developing the data model, the database and application developers work backward. That is, they begin with the forms, reports, and queries that the users say they need and then work backward to the database design. To do this, the team selects a required form, report, or query and determines the view that must exist in order for the form, report, or query to be created. Then the team selects the next form, report, or query and does the same. These two views are then integrated. This process is repeated until the structure of the entire database has been created.

The second way in which views are used occurs after the database structure has been created. At this point, views are constructed to support new forms, reports, and queries based on the existing database structure. Examples of this second use are shown in Part IV when we discuss SQL Server and Oracle.

FIGURE 4-4

StudentListing and Staff Views of the DEPARTMENT Semantic Object

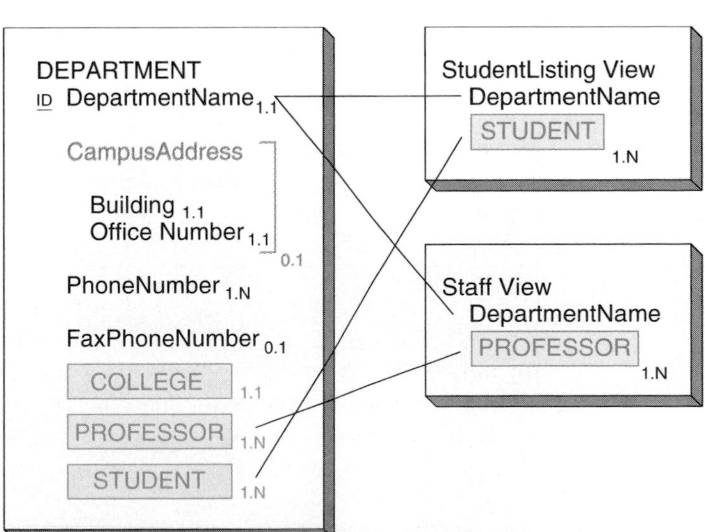

➤ CREATING DATA MODELS WITH SEMANTIC OBJECTS

This section illustrates a process for developing semantic objects in which the developers examine the application interface—forms, reports, and queries—and work backward (or reverse-engineer) to derive the object structure. For example, to model the structure of a DEPARTMENT object, we first gather all of the reports, forms, and queries based on DEPARTMENT. From them, we define a DEPARTMENT object that enables those reports, forms, and queries to be constructed.

For a totally new application, however, there will be no computer-based reports, forms, or queries to examine. In this case, the developers begin by determining what objects the users need to track. Then through interviews with the users, the team finds out what object attributes are important. From this, prototypes of forms and reports can be constructed that are then used to refine the data model.

AN EXAMPLE: THE HIGHLINE UNIVERSITY ADMINISTRATION DATABASE

Suppose that the administration at Highline University wants to keep track of department, faculty, and student major data. Suppose further that the application needs to produce four reports (Figures 4-5, 4-7, 4-9, and 4-11). Our goal is to examine these reports and, using reverse engineering, determine the objects and attributes that must be stored in the database.

THE COLLEGE OBJECT The example report in Figure 4-5 is about a college—specifically, the College of Business. This example is only one instance of the report; Highline University has similar reports about other colleges, such as the College of Arts and Sciences and the College of Social Sciences. When creating a data model, it is important to gather enough examples to form a representative sample of all of the college reports. Here we assume that the report in Figure 4-5 is representative.

In examining the report, we find data specific to the college—such as the name, dean, telephone number, and campus address—and also facts about each of the departments within the college. This *suggests* that the database might contain COLLEGE and DEPARTMENT objects, with a relationship between the two.

These preliminary findings are documented in the object diagrams in Figure 4-6. Notice that we have omitted cardinalities from simple attributes having a cardinality of 0.1.

➤ FIGURE 4-5

Example COLLEGE Report

College of Business
Mary B. Jefferson, Dean

Phone: 232-1187 | Campus Address: Business Building, Room 100

Department	Chairperson	Phone	Total Majors
Accounting	Jackson, Seymour P.	232-1841	318
Finance	HeuTeng, Susan	232-1414	211
Info Systems	Brammer, Nathaniel D.	236-0011	247
Management	Tuttle, Christine A.	236-9988	184
Production	Barnes, Jack T.	236-1184	212

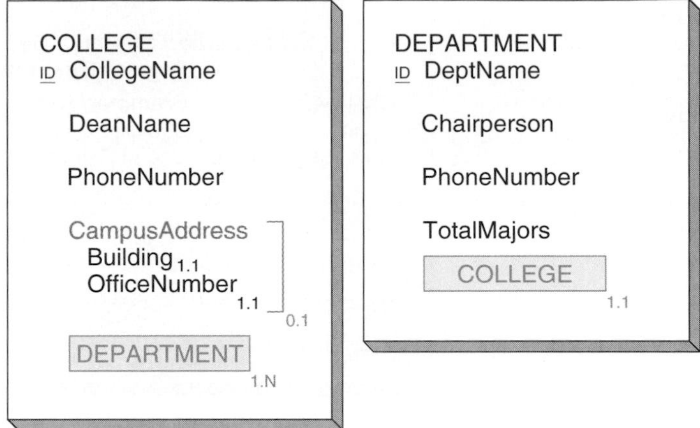

➤ FIGURE 4-6

First Version of COLLEGE and DEPARTMENT Objects

The cardinality of DEPARTMENT within COLLEGE is 1.N, indicating that a COLLEGE must have at least one DEPARTMENT and that it may have many. This minimum cardinality cannot be deduced from the report in Figure 4-5; rather, it was obtained by asking the users whether a college could exist with no departments. Their answer was no.

Also note that the structure of DEPARTMENT is inferred from the data shown in Figure 4-5. Since object attributes are always paired, COLLEGE is shown in DEPARTMENT, even though, strictly speaking, this fact cannot be determined from Figure 4-5. As with the DEPARTMENT attribute in COLLEGE, the users were asked to determine the cardinalities of the COLLEGE attribute. They are 1.1, meaning that a DEPARTMENT must be related to one, and only one, COLLEGE.

As an aside, we have interpreted the report in Figure 4-5 to mean that the groups of repeating data refer to DEPARTMENT as an independent object. In fact, such repeating groups are often a signal that another object exists. *This is not always the case, however.* The repeating group can also be a group attribute that happens to have several values.

You may be wondering how to tell the difference between repeating-object data and repeating-group data. There is no hard and fast rule, because the answer depends on the ways that the users view their world. Consequently, the best approach is to consult the users about the semantics of the data. Ask whether these repeating-group data are only a part of the college or whether they refer to something else that stands on its own. If the former, they constitute a group attribute; if the latter, a semantic object. Also, look for other reports (or forms or queries). Do the users have one for departments? If so, then the assumption that DEPARTMENT is a semantic object would be confirmed. In fact, the personnel at Highline use two reports regarding DEPARTMENTs. This fact further substantiates the notion that a DEPARTMENT object must be defined.

Also, groups of attributes that represent an independent object generally have obvious identifying attribute(s). Automobiles have a VINNumber or LicenseNumber; products have a ProductNumber or SKU. Orders have an OrderNumber. However, the group of attributes {DateOfMeasure, TirePressure} does not have an obvious identifier. When you ask a user about that group's identifier, he or she will say something like "Tire pressure of what?" It will be tire pressure of a car or a truck or a trailer or some vehicle. Hence, such a group would be a group attribute within another object—the object that is the answer to the "of what" question.

THE DEPARTMENT OBJECT The DEPARTMENT report shown in Figure 4-7 contains departmental data, along with a list of the professors who are assigned to

➤ FIGURE 4-7

Example DEPARTMENT Report

Information Systems Department
College of Business

Chairperson: Brammer, Nathaniel D
Phone: 236-0011
Campus Address: Social Science Building, Room 213

Professor	Office	Phone
Jones, Paul D.	Social Science, 219	232-7713
Parks, Mary B	Social Science, 308	232-5791
Wu, Elizabeth	Social Science, 207	232-9112

those departments. Note that this report contains data concerning the department's campus address. Since these data do not appear in the object in Figure 4-6, we need to add them to the DEPARTMENT object, as has been done in Figure 4-8. This adjustment is typical of the data modeling process. That is, the semantic objects are continually adjusted as new reports, forms, and queries are identified and analyzed.

THE PROFESSOR OBJECT The report in Figure 4-7 not only indicates that a DEPARTMENT object needs to be modeled, but also it suggests that another object may be needed to represent professor data. Accordingly, a PROFESSOR object was added to the model, as shown in Figure 4-8. The ID of PROFESSOR, which is ProfessorName, is not unique; this is denoted by not underlining the ID in Figure 4-8.

According to the object diagrams in Figure 4-8, a DEPARTMENT must have at least one PROFESSOR and may have several, but a PROFESSOR must have one, and only one, DEPARTMENT. Thus, according to this model, joint appointments are prohibited. This restriction is part of the business rules that must be obtained from interviews with the users.

Figure 4-9 shows a second report about a department. This one concerns a department and the students who major in that area. Having two reports about an object is typical; they are simply documenting different views of the same thing. Moreover, the existence of this second report strengthens the notion that department is an object in the minds of the users.

THE STUDENT OBJECT The report in Figure 4-9 gives data about students who major in a department's area, implying that students are also an object.

➤ FIGURE 4-8

Adjusted DEPARTMENT and New PROFESSOR Objects

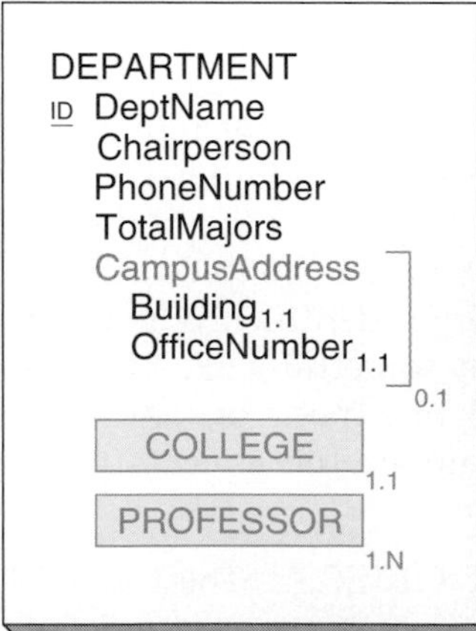

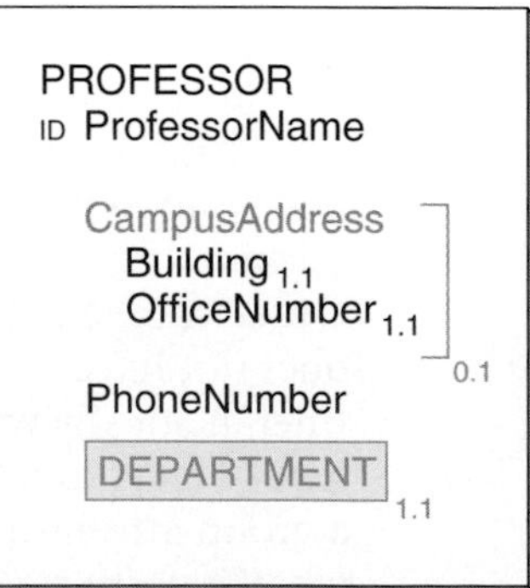

➤ FIGURE 4-9

Second Example DEPARTMENT Report

Student Major List
Information Systems Department

Chairperson: Brammer, Nathaniel D Phone: 236-0011

Major's Name	Student Number	Phone
Jackson, Robin R.	12345	237-8713
Lincoln, Fred J.	48127	237-8713
Madison, Janice A.	37512	237-8713

Therefore the DEPARTMENT object must contain a STUDENT object as well as a PROFESSOR object, as in Figure 4-10.

The STUDENT object in Figure 4-10 contains the attributes StudentName, StudentNumber, and PhoneNumber, the attributes listed on the report in Figure 4-9. Note that both StudentName and StudentNumber are identifiers. StudentNames are not unique, but StudentNumbers are.

Figure 4-11 is an example of another report about a student—the acceptance letter that Highline sends to its incoming students. Even though this is a letter, it is also a report; the letter was probably produced using mail merge with a word-processing program.

Those data items in the letter that should be stored in the database are shown in boldface type. In addition to data regarding the student, the letter also contains data regarding the student's major DEPARTMENT and the student's adviser. Since an adviser is a PROFESSOR, this letter substantiates the need for a separate PROFESSOR object. Object diagrams from the revised PROFESSOR and STUDENT objects are shown in Figure 4-12. According to the STUDENT object, both DEPARTMENT and PROFESSOR are single value (they have a maximum cardinality of 1). Hence, a student at this university has, at most, one major department and one adviser and is required to have both.

The STUDENT object in Figure 4-12 corresponds to the data shown in the letter in Figure 4-11. It may turn out, however, that the student actually has more than one major, in which case both DEPARTMENT and PROFESSOR would be multi-value. This fact cannot be determined from this single form letter, so additional letters and interviews are needed to find out whether multiple majors are permitted. Here we assume that only one major is allowed.

➤ FIGURE 4-10

Adjusted DEPARTMENT and New STUDENT Objects

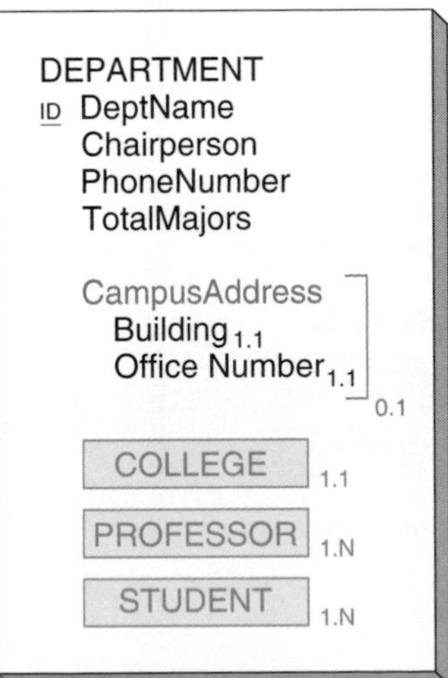

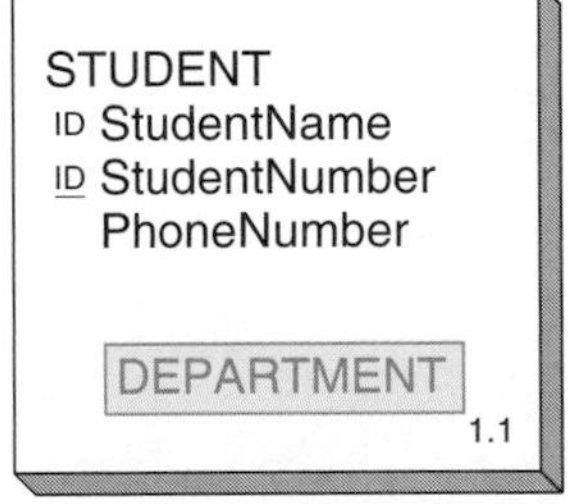

➤ FIGURE 4-11

Acceptance Letter

Mr. Fred Parks
123 Elm Street
Los Angeles, CA 98002

Dear **Mr. Parks**:

You have been admitted as a major in the **Accounting** Department at Highline University, starting in the **Fall Semester**, **2000**. The office of the Accounting Department is located in the **Business** Building, Room **210**.

Your adviser is professor **Elizabeth Johnson**, whose telephone number is **232-8740** and whose office is located in the **Business** building, Room **227**. Please schedule an appointment with your adviser as soon as you arrive on campus.

Congratulations and welcome to Highline University!

Sincerely,

Jan P. Smathers
President

JPS/rkp

The format of the student's name is given first in the format *first name last name* at the top of the letter and then in the format *last name* in the salutation. If presenting names in this format is a requirement, then the single attribute StudentName (in Figure 4-10) will not suffice, and instead the group FirstName, LastName must be defined. This has been done in Figure 4-12. Note also that the adviser's name is in the format {FirstName, LastName}, which means that the name of PROFESSOR should be changed as well.

In addition, this letter indicates that names in addresses and salutations must be preceded by the title "Mr." or "Ms." If this is to be done, an additional attribute must be placed in STUDENT. One alternative is to record the gender of the student

➤ FIGURE 4-12

Adjusted PROFESSOR and STUDENT Objects

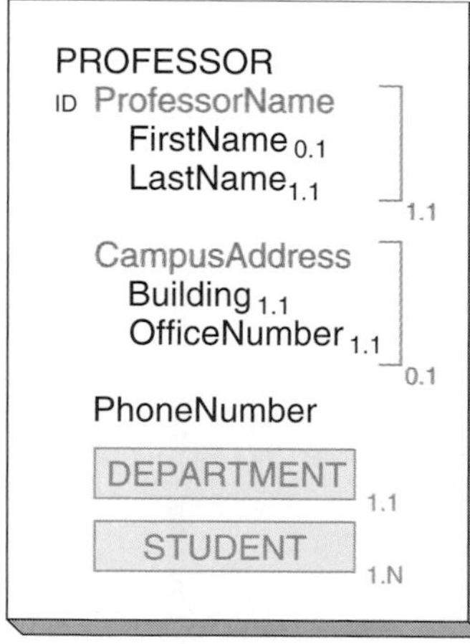

STUDENT
ID StudentName
FirstName 0.1
LastName 1.1
1.1
ID StudentNumber
PhoneNumber
HomeAddress
Street 0.1
City 1.1
State 1.1
Zip 1.1
1.1
Title
EnrollmentDate
DEPARTMENT
1.1
PROFESSOR
1.1

and to select the title based on this attribute. Another alternative is to store the title itself. The advantage of this second alternative is that titles other than "Mr." and "Ms.," such as "Dr.," can be stored.

As currently documented, the model does not require a title other than Mr. or Ms. It seems plausible, however, that additional titles might be needed; hence, the second alternative seems more robust, and therefore the attribute Title has been added to STUDENT in Figure 4-12.

Again, these changes illustrate the iterative nature of data modeling. Design decisions often need to be rethought and revised again and again. Such iteration does not mean that the design process is faulty; in fact, it is typical and expected.

SPECIFYING OBJECTS

Figure 4-13 shows the completed object diagrams for the Highline University database. A few changes have been made: Both DeanName and Chairperson have been modeled in the format {FirstName, LastName} so that all names are in a similar format. And to improve the precision of the model, the PROFESSOR

➤ FIGURE 4-13

A Complete Set of Semantic Object Diagrams

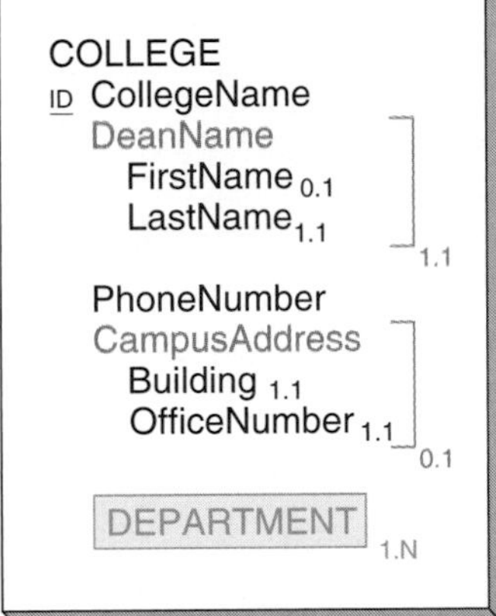

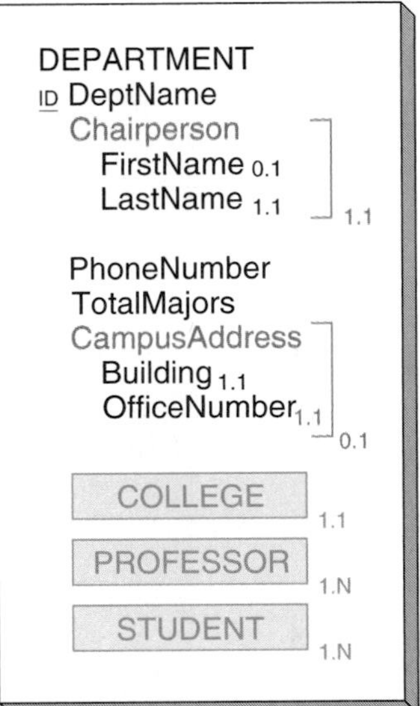

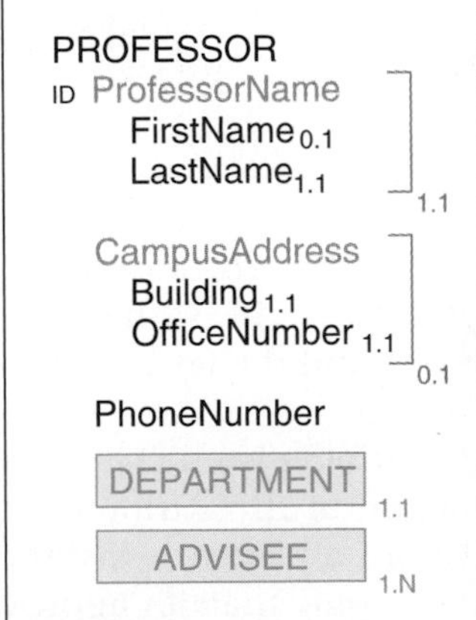

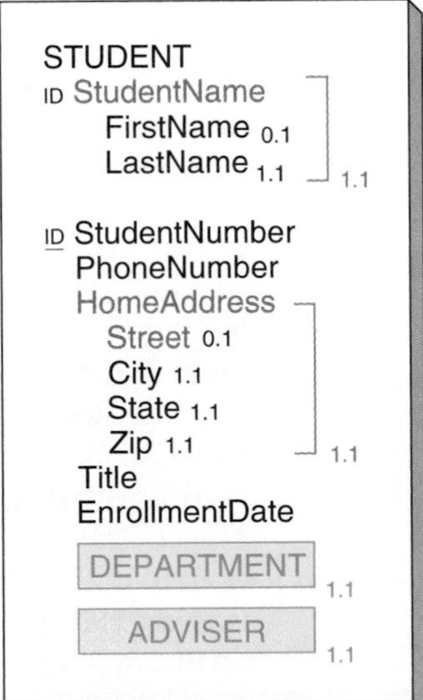

➤ FIGURE 4-14

Object Specifications for the Highline University Database: (a) Semantic Object Specifications and (b) Domain Specifications

Object Name	Property Name	Min Card	Max Card	ID Status	Domain Name
COLLEGE	CollegeName	1	1	ID	CollegeName
	DeanName	1	1		PersonName
	FirstName	0	1		FirstName
	LastName	1	1		LastName
	PhoneNumber	0	1		Phone
	CampusAddress	0	1		CampusAddress
	Building	1	1		Building
	OfficeNumber	1	1		OfficeNumber
	DEPARTMENT	1	N		DEPARTMENT
DEPARTMENT	DeptName	1	1	ID	DeptName
	Chairperson	1	1		PersonName
	FirstName	0	1		FirstName
	LastName	1	1		LastName
	PhoneNumber	0	1		Phone
	TotalMajors	0	1		MajorCount
	CampusAddress	0	1		CampusAddress
	Building	1	1		Building
	OfficeNumber	1	1		OfficeNumber
	COLLEGE	1	1		COLLEGE
	PROFESSOR	1	N		PROFESSOR
	STUDENT	1	N		STUDENT
PROFESSOR	ProfessorName	1	1	ID	PersonName
	FirstName	0	1		FirstName
	LastName	1	1		LastName
	CampusAddress	0	1		CampusAddress
	Building	1	1		Building
	OfficeNumber	1	1		OfficeNumber
	PhoneNumber	0	1		Phone
	DEPARTMENT	1	1		DEPARTMENT
	ADVISER	1	N		STUDENT
STUDENT	StudentName	1	1	ID	PersonName
	FirstName	0	1		FirstName
	LastName	1	1		LastName
	StudentNumber	1	1	ID	StudentNumber
	PhoneNumber	0	1		Phone
	HomeAddress	1	1		Address
	Title	0	1		Title
	EnrollmentDate	0	1		QuarterDate
	DEPARTMENT	1	1		DEPARTMENT
	ADVISER	1	1		PROFESSOR

(a)

attribute in STUDENT has been renamed ADVISER. The PROFESSOR instance that is connected to a STUDENT instance through this attribute is not just any of the STUDENT's professors; it is the particular PROFESSOR who serves as that STUDENT's adviser, and the term *ADVISER* is more precise than the term *PROFESSOR*.

The domain of this attribute is unchanged. The domain of ADVISER is PROFESSOR, just as the domain of the attribute PROFESSOR was PROFESSOR. This attribute still points to or connects to instances of the PROFESSOR semantic object. The name change is only that: an improvement in specifying the role that the PROFESSOR domain plays in the STUDENT semantic objects. A similar change was made in PROFESSOR. The STUDENT attribute was renamed ADVISEE, but this attribute is still connected to objects from the STUDENT domain.

➤ FIGURE 4-14

(Continued)

Domain Name	Type[a]	Semantic Description	Physical Description
Address	G	A U.S. address	Street City State Zip
Building	S	A name of a building on campus	Text 20
CampusAddress	G	An address on campus	Building OfficeNumber
City	S	A city name	Text 25
COLLEGE	SO	One of Highline's ten colleges	See semantic object specification table
CollegeName	S	The official name of a college at Highline	Text 25
DEPARTMENT	SO	An academic department on campus	See semantic object specification table
DeptName	S	The official name of an academic department	Text 25
FirstName	S	The first-name portion of PersonName	Text 20
LastName	S	The last-name portion of PersonName	Text 30
MajorCount	F	Count of the students assigned to a given department	Integer; values {0 to 999}; format 999.
OfficeNumber	S	The number of an office on campus	Text 4
PersonName	G	First and last names of an administrator, professor, or student	FirstName LastName
Phone	S	Phone number within local area code	Text 4
PROFESSOR	SO	The name of a full-time member of Highline's faculty	See semantic object specification table
QuarterDate	S	An academic quarter and year	Text 3; values {*q01*, where *q* = one of {'F', 'W', 'S', 'M'} and *01* is decimal number from 00 to 99.}
State	S	A two-digit state abbreviation	Text 2
Street	S	A street address	Text 30
STUDENT	SO	A person who has been admitted for study at Highline	See semantic object specification table
StudentNumber	S	The ID assigned to a student admitted to Highline	Integer; values {10000 to 99999}; format 99999
Title	S	The title of individuals to be used in addresses	Text 3; values {Mr., Ms.}
Zip	S	A nine-digit zip code	Text 10; format 99999-9999

[a]F = formula
G = Group
S = Simple
SO = semantic object

(b)

Figure 4-14 presents a tabular specification of the data model. The semantic objects and attributes are defined in the semantic object specification, and the domains are defined in the domain specification. The first table is an alternative presentation of the information in the semantic object diagrams, and its interpretation is straightforward.

The second table, the domain table, supplies information about domains that is not available from the semantic object diagrams. As we stated earlier, a domain has both a semantic and a physical description. The semantic description of each domain is shown in the Description column, and the physical description is shown in the Specification column. The Description column is self-explanatory.

The specification for domains includes a physical description and, in some cases, a set of values and a format. StudentNumber, for example, is specified as an integer with values between 10,000 and 99,999 and with a format of five decimal digits. (In this table, a 9 in a format specification means a decimal digit.) Other domains are documented in a similar way. Title is an example of an enumerated domain whose values for Title are Mr., Ms. The physical description of a group domain consists of a list of the domains included in the group. The physical description of a semantic object domain is just a reference to the semantic object description.

The domain of TotalMajors is an example of a fourth type of domain, the **formula domain.** Formulas represent attributes computed from other values. The MajorCount domain is the count of the STUDENT objects that are connected to a given DEPARTMENT object. We shall not try to document the means by which this computation is to be carried out in the domain definition. At this point, all that is important is documenting the need for and the specification of the formula.

➤ TYPES OF OBJECTS

This section describes and illustrates seven types of objects. For each type, we examine a report or form and show how to model that report or form with an object. Later, in Chapter 7, we transform each of these types of objects into database designs.

Three new terms are used in this section. A **single-value attribute** is an attribute whose maximum cardinality is 1. A **multi-value attribute** is one whose maximum cardinality is greater than 1. And a **nonobject attribute** is a simple or group attribute.

SIMPLE OBJECTS

A **simple object** is a semantic object that contains only single-value, simple or group attributes. An example is shown in Figure 4-15. Part a of this figure shows two instances of a report called an *Equipment Tag*. Such tags are applied to items of office equipment in order to help keep track of inventory. These tags can be considered a report.

Figure 4-15(b) shows a simple object, EQUIPMENT, that models Equipment Tag. The attributes of the object include the items shown on the tag: EquipmentNumber, Description, AcquisitionDate, and PurchaseCost. Note that none of these attributes is multi-value, and none is an object attribute. Hence, EQUIPMENT is a simple object.

FIGURE 4-15

Example of a Simple Object: (a) Reports Based on a Simple Object and (b) EQUIPMENT Simple Object

Composite Objects

A **composite object** is a semantic object that contains one or more multi-value, simple or group attributes but no object attributes. The Hotel Bill shown in Figure 4-16(a) gives rise to the need for a composite object. The bill includes data that concerns the bill as a whole: InvoiceNumber, ArrivalDate, CustomerName, and TotalDue. It also contains a group of attributes that is repeated for services provided to the guest. Each group includes ServiceDate, ServiceDescription, and Price.

Figure 4-16(b) shows an object diagram for the HOTEL-BILL object. The attribute LineItem is a group attribute having a maximum cardinality of N, which means that the group ServiceDate, ServiceDescription, Price can occur many times in an instance of the HOTEL-BILL semantic object.

FIGURE 4-16

Example of a Composite Object: (a) Report Based on a Composite Object and (b) HOTEL-BILL Composite Object

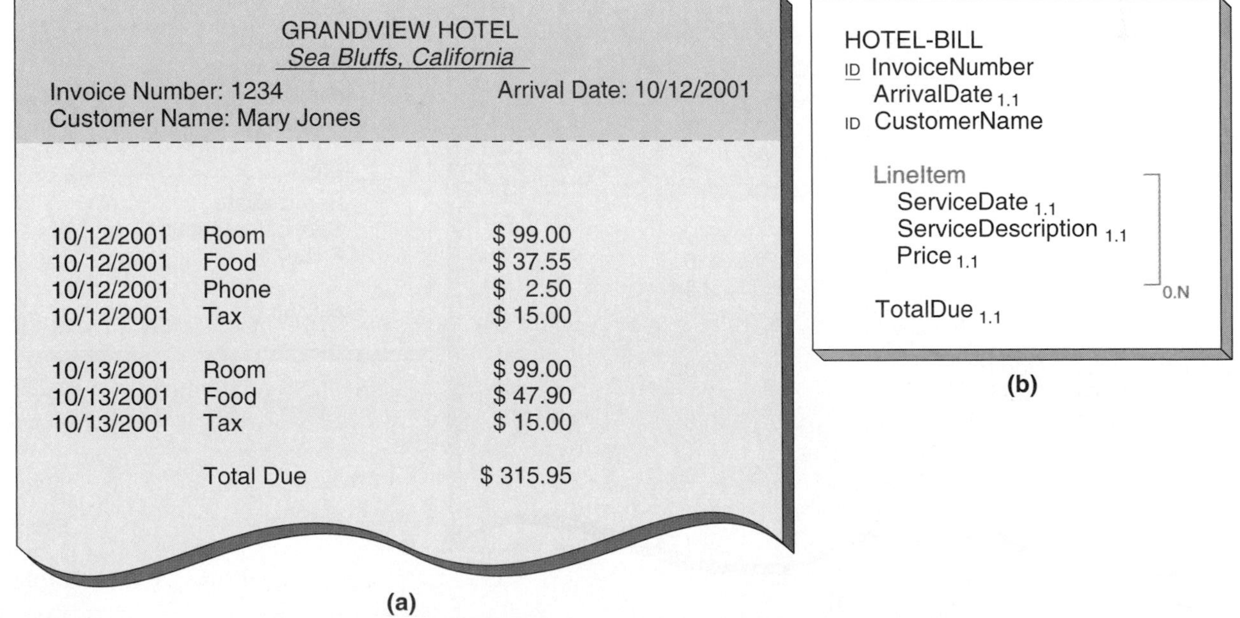

LineItem is not modeled as an independent semantic object; instead, it is considered to be an attribute within a HOTEL-BILL. This design is appropriate because the hotel does not view one line of a guest's charges as a separate thing, so line items on the guest's bill do not have identifiers of their own. No employee attempts to enter a LineItem except in the context of a bill. The employee enters the data for bill number 1234 and then, in the context of that bill, enters the charges. Or the employee retrieves an existing bill and enters additional charges in the context of that bill.

The minimum cardinality of LineItem is 0, which means that a HOTEL-BILL object can exist without any LineItem data. This allows a bill to be started when the customer checks in and before there are any charges. If the minimum cardinality were 1, then no HOTEL-BILL could be started until there was at least one charge. This design decision must be made in light of the business rules. It may be that the hotel's policy is not to start the bill until there has been a charge. If so, then the minimum cardinality of LineItem should be 1.

A composite object can have more than one multi-value attribute. Figure 4-17(a) shows a hotel bill that has a multi-value attribute for CustomerName, as well as a multi-value group for service charges. Each of these groups is independent of the other. The second instance of CustomerName, for example, is not logically associated with the second LineItem.

Figure 4-17(b) is an object diagram for the hotel bill in Figure 4-17(a). CustomerName is shown as a multi-value attribute. It is not included in the bracket of service charges because the repetitions of CustomerName have nothing to do with the repetitions of services. The two are independent, as we just noted.

Both simple and group attributes can be multi-value. In Figure 4-17(a), for example, CustomerName is a multi-value, simple attribute. By itself, it is sufficient for the object to be considered a composite object.

Multi-value attributes can also be nested within one another. For example, suppose it is important to keep track of individual expenses within a LineItem. In

➤ FIGURE 4-17

A Composite Objecct with Two Groups: (a) HOTEL-BILL with Multivalued Customer Names and (b) HOTEL-BILL with Two Multivalued Groups

GRANDVIEW HOTEL
Sea Bluffs, California

Invoice Number: 1234 Arrival Date: 10/12/2001
Customer Name: Mary Jones
Fred Jones
Sally Jones

10/12/2001	Room	$ 99.00
10/12/2001	Food	$ 37.55
10/12/2001	Phone	$ 2.50
10/12/2001	Tax	$ 15.00
10/13/2001	Room	$ 99.00
10/13/2001	Food	$ 47.90
10/13/2001	Tax	$ 15.00
	Total Due	$ 315.95

(a)

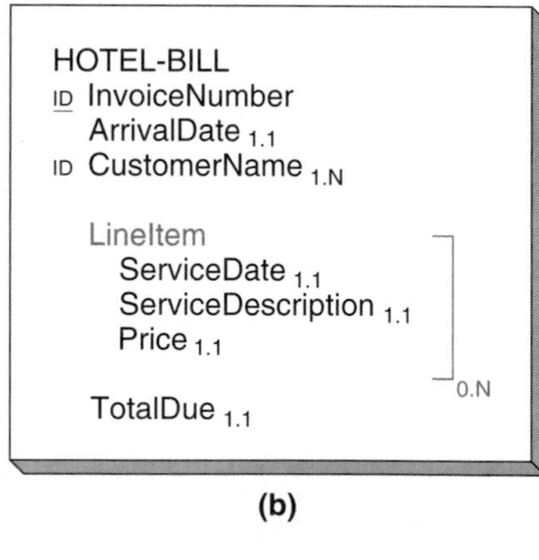

(b)

➤ FIGURE 4-18

A Composite Object with Nested Groups: (a) HOTEL-BILL with Service Subdescriptions and (b) HOTEL-BILL with Nested Multivalued Groups

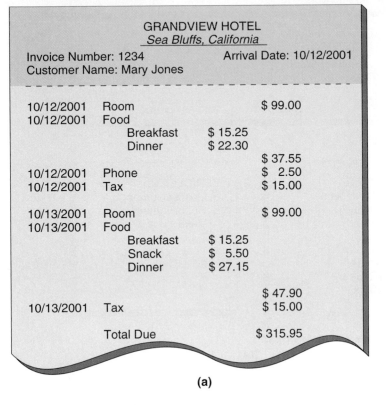

GRANDVIEW HOTEL
Sea Bluffs, California

Invoice Number: 1234 Arrival Date: 10/12/2001
Customer Name: Mary Jones

10/12/2001	Room			$ 99.00
10/12/2001	Food			
		Breakfast	$ 15.25	
		Dinner	$ 22.30	
				$ 37.55
10/12/2001	Phone			$ 2.50
10/12/2001	Tax			$ 15.00
10/13/2001	Room			$ 99.00
10/13/2001	Food			
		Breakfast	$ 15.25	
		Snack	$ 5.50	
		Dinner	$ 27.15	
				$ 47.90
10/13/2001	Tax			$ 15.00
	Total Due			$ 315.95

(a)

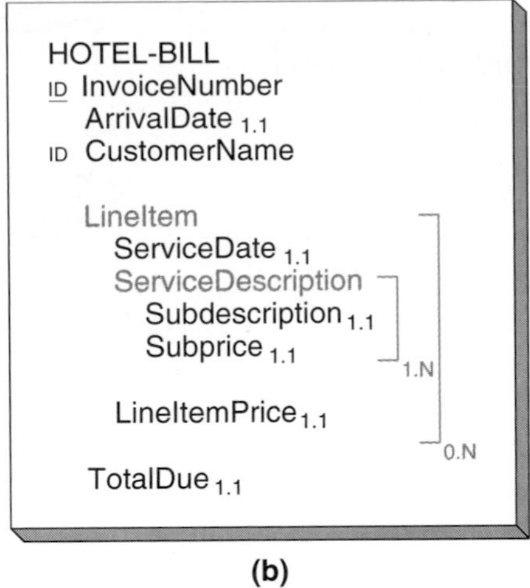

(b)

the form in Figure 4-18(a), the charges are subdivided. Food, for example, is broken down by meal. An object diagram for such nested attributes is presented in Figure 4-18(b) and shows that any service charge can have subitems.

To repeat, a composite object is an object that contains one or more multi-value simple or group attributes. It has no object attributes.

Compound Objects

A **compound object** contains at least one object attribute. Figure 4-19(a) shows two different data entry forms. One form, used by the company's motor pool, is used to keep track of the vehicles. The second form is used to maintain data about the employees. According to these forms, a vehicle is assigned to at most one employee, and an employee has at most one auto assigned.

We cannot tell from these forms whether an auto must be assigned to an employee or whether every employee must have an auto. To obtain that information, we would have to ask the users in the motor pool or human resources departments. Assume that we find out that an EMPLOYEE need not have a VEHICLE but that a VEHICLE must be assigned to an employee.

Figure 4-19(b) shows object diagrams for EMPLOYEE and VEHICLE. An EMPLOYEE contains VEHICLE as one of its attributes, and VEHICLE, in turn, contains EMPLOYEE as one of its attributes. Since both EMPLOYEE and VEHICLE contain object attributes, they both are compound objects. Furthermore, since neither attribute is multi-value, the relationship from EMPLOYEE to VEHICLE is one to one, or 1:1.

➤ FIGURE 4-19

Compound Objects with 1:1 Paired Properties: (a) Example Vehicle and Employee Data Entry Forms and (b) EMPLOYEE and VEHICLE Compound Objects

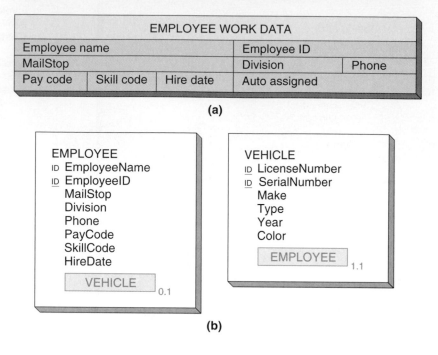

VEHICLE DATA			
License number	Serial number		
Make	Type	Year	Color
Employee assignment			

EMPLOYEE WORK DATA			
Employee name		Employee ID	
MailStop		Division	Phone
Pay code	Skill code	Hire date	Auto assigned

(a)

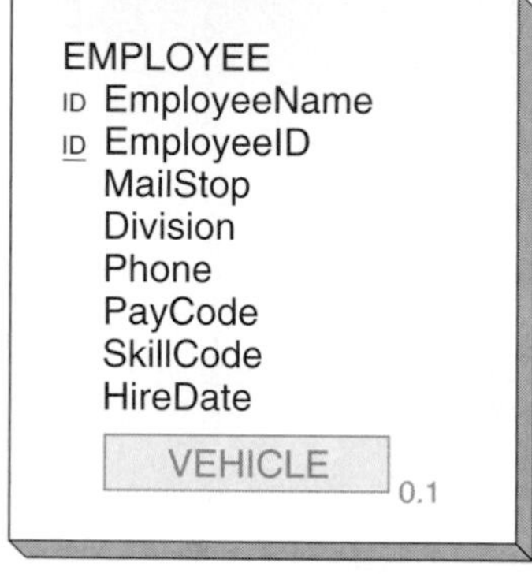

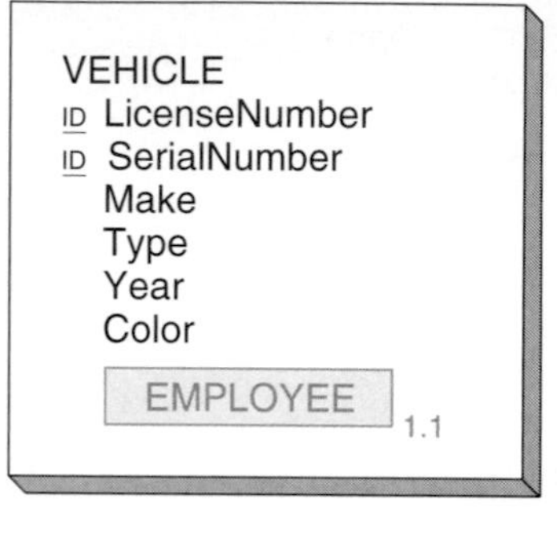

(b)

In Figure 4-19(a) the Employee and Vehicle forms contain each other. That is, VEHICLE DATA has a field Employee assignment, and EMPLOYEE WORK DATA has a field Auto assigned. But this is not always the case; sometimes the relationship can appear in only one direction. Consider the report and form in Figure 4-20(b), which concern two objects: DORMITORY and STUDENT. From the Dormitory Occupancy Report, we can see that users think of a dorm as having attributes regarding the dorm (Dormitory, ResidentAssistant, Phone) and also attributes regarding the students (StudentName, StudentNumber, Class) who live in the dorm.

On the other hand, the Student Data Form shows only student data; it does not include any dormitory data. (The campus address might contain a dorm address, but this, if true, is apparently not important enough to document on the form. In a database development project, this possibility should be checked out with the users in an interview. Here we will assume that the Student Data Form does not include dormitory data.)

As we stated earlier, object attributes always occur in pairs. Even if the forms, reports, and queries indicate that only one side of the relationship can be seen, both sides of the relationship always exist. By analogy, a bridge that connects two islands touches both islands and can be used in both directions, even if the bridge is, by custom or law, a one-way bridge.

When no form or report can be found to document one side of a relationship, the development team must ask the users about the cardinality of that relationship. In this case, the team would need to find out how many DORMITORYs a STUDENT could have and whether a STUDENT must be related to a DORMITORY. Here let us suppose the answers to these questions are that a STUDENT is related to just one DORMITORY and may be related to no DORMITORY. Thus in Figure 4-20(b), DORMITORY contains multiple values of STUDENT, and STUDENT

➤ FIGURE 4-20

Compound Objects with 1:N Paired Properties: (a) Example Dormitory Report and Student Data Form and (b) DORMITORY and STUDENT Compound Objects

DORMITORY OCCUPANCY REPORT

Dormitory	Resident Assistant	Phone
Ingersoll	Sarah and Allen French	3-5567

Student name	Student Number	Class
Adams, Elizabeth	710	SO
Baker, Rex	104	FR
Baker, Brydie	744	JN
Charles, Stewart	319	SO
Scott, Sally	447	SO
Taylor, Lynne	810	FR

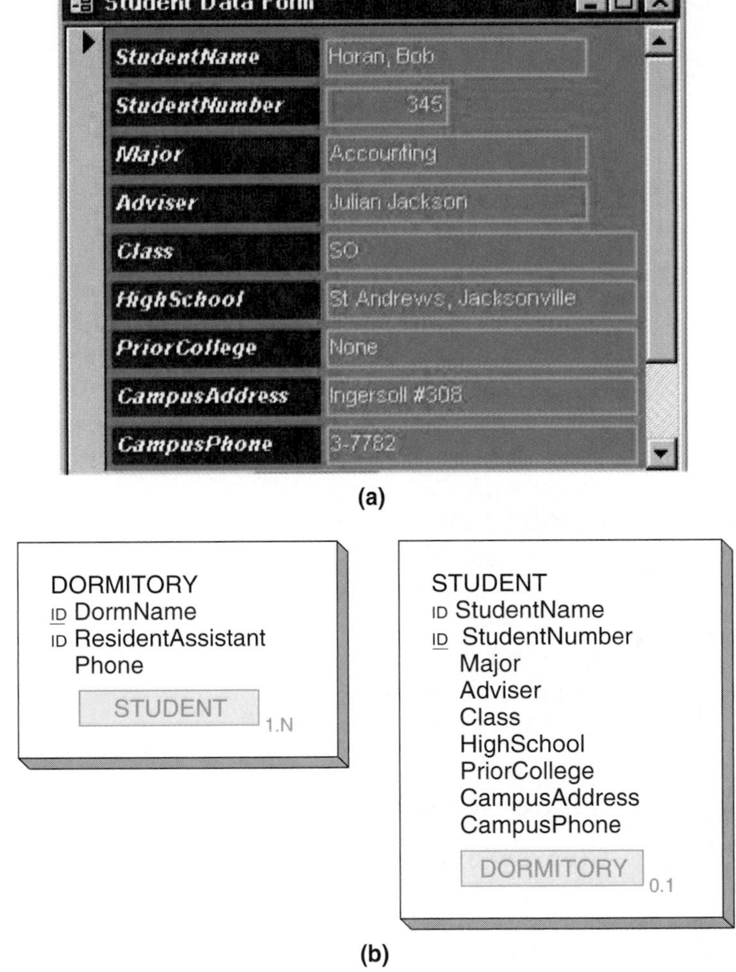

contains one value of DORMITORY, so the relationship from DORMITORY to STUDENT is one to many, or 1:N.

A third illustration of compound objects appears in Figure 4-21(a). From these two forms, we can deduce that one book can be written by many authors (from the Book Stock Data form) and that one author can write many books (from the Books in Stock, by Author form). Thus, in Figure 4-21(b), the BOOK object contains many values of AUTHOR, and AUTHOR contains many values of BOOK. Hence the relationship from BOOK to AUTHOR is many to many, or N:M. Furthermore, a BOOK must have an AUTHOR, and an AUTHOR (to be an author)

➤ FIGURE 4-21

Compound Objects with N:M Paired Properties: (a) Bookstore Data Entry Forms and (b) BOOK and AUTHOR Objects

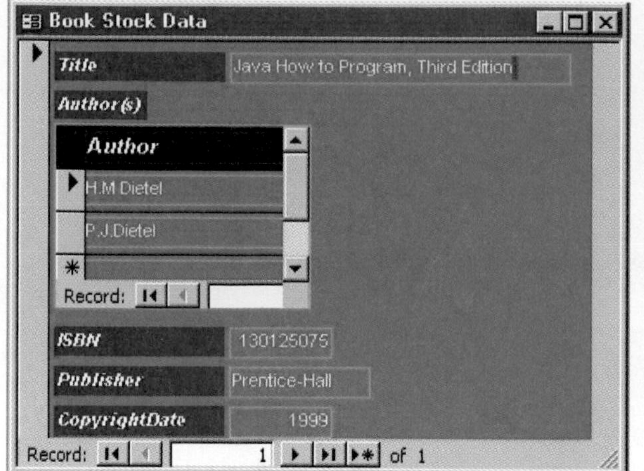

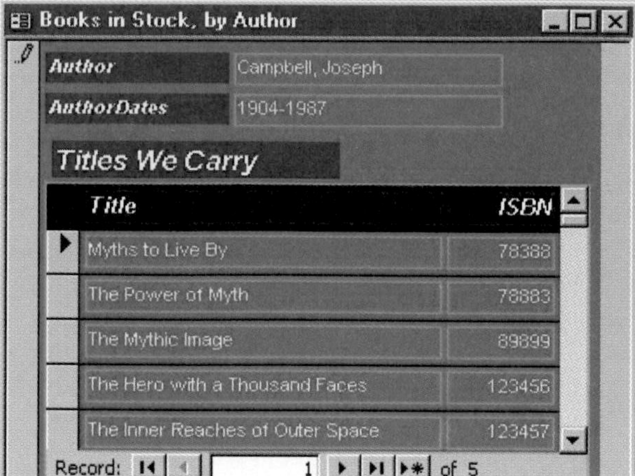

(a)

BOOK
ID Title
AUTHOR 1.N
ID ISBN
Publisher
Copyright Date

AUTHOR
ID AuthorName
AuthorDates
BOOK 1.N

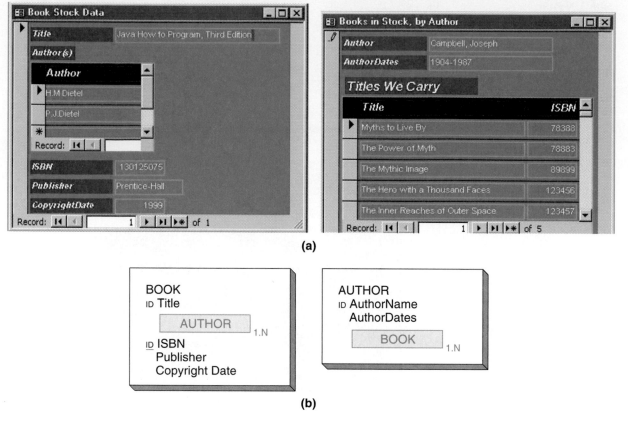

(b)

must have written at least one BOOK. Therefore, both of these objects have a minimum cardinality of one.

Figure 4-22 summarizes the four types of compound objects. In general, OBJECT-1 can contain a maximum of one or many OBJECT-2s. Similarly, OBJECT-2 can contain one or many OBJECT-1s. We use this table when we discuss database design in Chapter 7.

Hybrid Objects

Hybrid objects are combinations of composite and compound objects. In particular, a hybrid object is a semantic object with at least one multi-value group attribute that includes a semantic object attribute.

Figure 4-23(a) is a second version of the report about dormitory occupancy shown in Figure 4-20(a). The difference is that the third column of the student data contains Rent instead of Class. This is an important difference because rent is not an attribute of STUDENT but pertains to the combination of STUDENT and DORMITORY and is an attribute of DORMITORY.

➤ FIGURE 4-22

Four Types of Compound Objects

		Object1 Can Contain	
Object2		One	Many
Can	One	**1:1**	**1:N**
Contain	Many	**M:1**	**M:N**

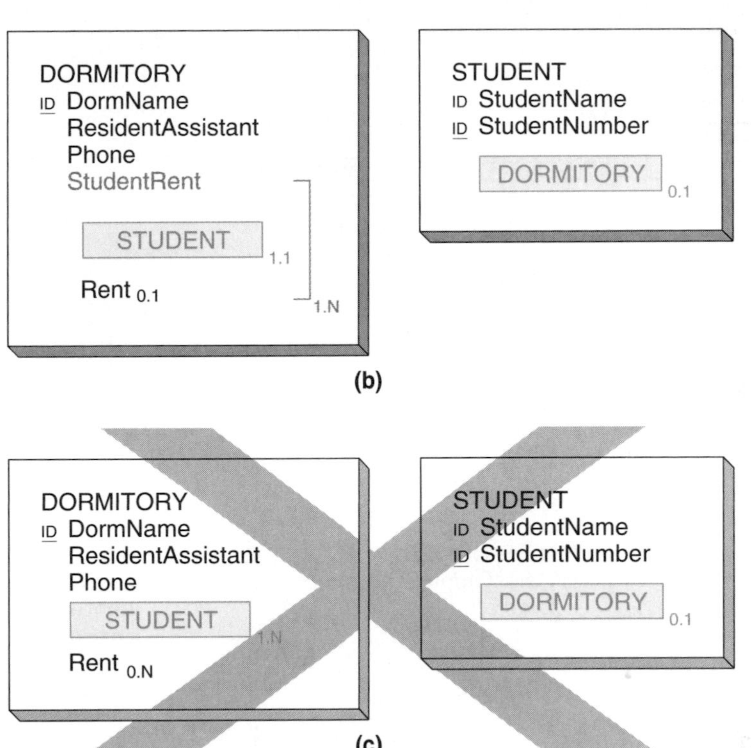

➤ FIGURE 4-23

DORMITORY Hybrid Object: (a) Dormitory Report with Rent Property, (b) Correct DORMITORY and STUDENT Objects, and (c) Incorrect DORMITORY and STUDENT Objects

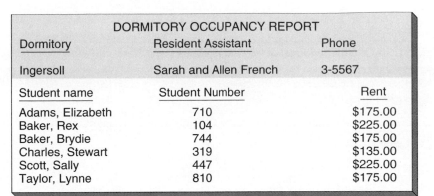

Figure 4-23(b) is an object diagram that models this form. DORMITORY contains a multi-value group having the object attribute STUDENT and the nonobject attribute Rent. This means that Rent is paired with STUDENT in the context of DORMITORY.

Now examine the alternative DORMITORY object in Figure 4-23(c). This is an *incorrect* model of the report in Figure 4-23(a), as it shows that Rent and STUDENT are independently multi-value, which is incorrect because Rent and STUDENT are multi-value as a pair.

Figure 4-24(a) shows a form based on another hybrid object. This Sales Order Form contains data about an order (Sales Order Number, Date, Subtotal, Tax, and Total), data about a CUSTOMER and a SALESPERSON, and a multi-value group that itself contains data about items on the order. Furthermore, ITEM data (Item Number, Description, and Unit Price) appear within the multi-value group.

Figure 4-24(b) shows the SALES-ORDER semantic object. It contains the nonobject attributes SalesOrderNumber, Date, Subtotal, Tax, and Total. It also contains the CUSTOMER and SALESPERSON object attributes and a multi-value

➤ FIGURE 4-24

Hybrid SALES-ORDER and Related Objects: (a) Sales Order Form and (b) Objects to Model Sales Order Form

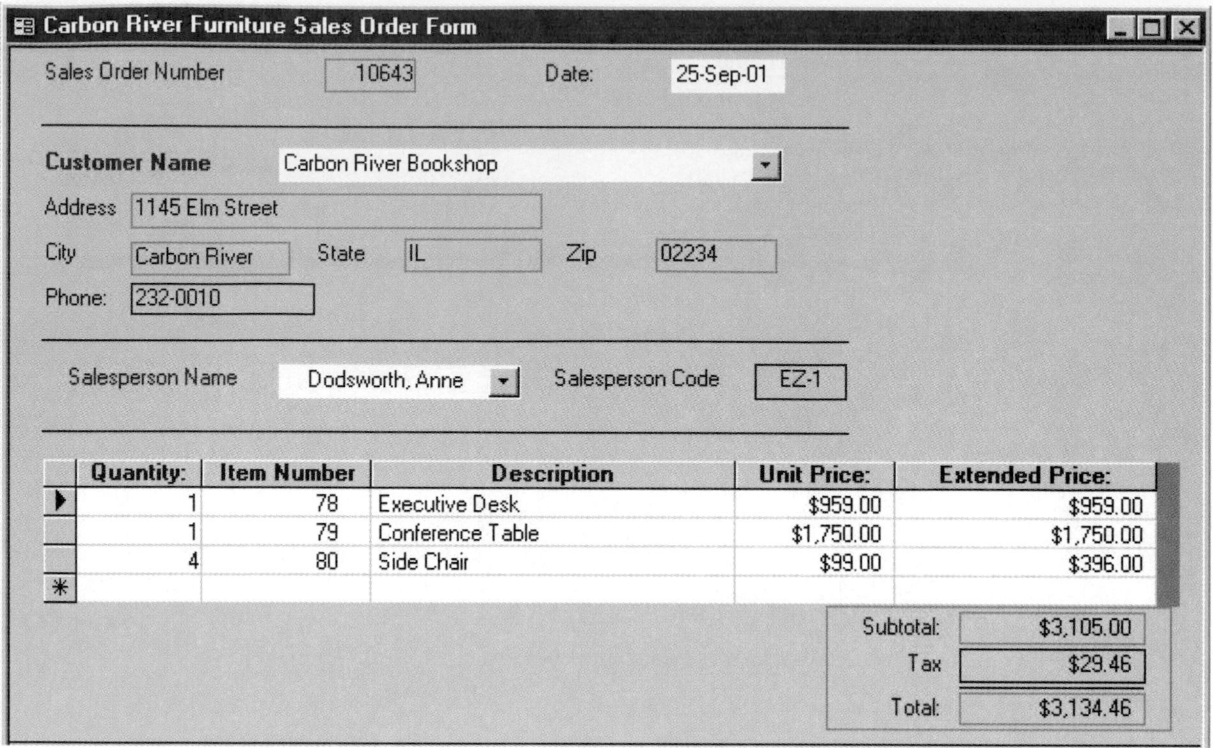

Carbon River Furniture Sales Order Form

Sales Order Number 10643 Date: 25-Sep-01

Customer Name Carbon River Bookshop

Address 1145 Elm Street

City Carbon River State IL Zip 02234

Phone: 232-0010

Salesperson Name Dodsworth, Anne Salesperson Code EZ-1

Quantity:	Item Number	Description	Unit Price:	Extended Price:
1	78	Executive Desk	$959.00	$959.00
1	79	Conference Table	$1,750.00	$1,750.00
4	80	Side Chair	$99.00	$396.00

Subtotal: $3,105.00

Tax $29.46

Total: $3,134.46

(a)

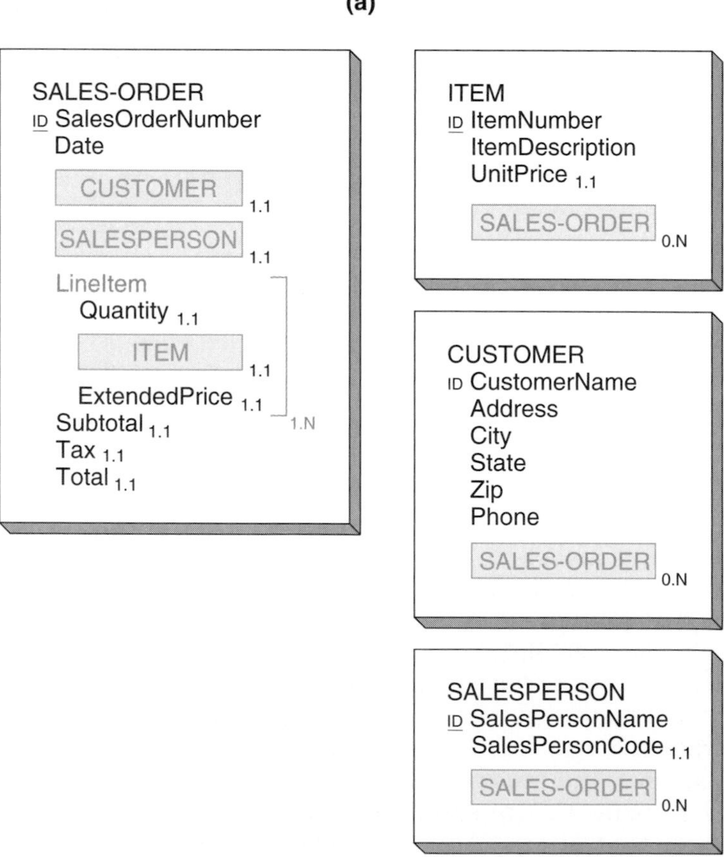

(b)

group that represents each line item on the sales order. The group contains nonobject attributes Quantity and ExtendedPrice and the object attribute ITEM.

The object diagrams in Figure 4-24(b) are ambiguous in one aspect that may or may not be important, depending on the application. According to the ITEM object diagram, an ITEM can be connected to more than one SALES-ORDER. But since the multi-value group LineItem is encapsulated (hidden within) SALES-ORDER, it is not clear from this diagram whether an ITEM can occur *once or many times* on the same SALES-ORDER.

In general, there are four interpretations of maximum cardinality for the paired attributes in the SALES-ORDER hybrid object:

1. An ITEM can appear on only one SALES-ORDER and in only one of the LineItems within that SALES-ORDER.
2. An ITEM can appear on only one SALES-ORDER but in many different LineItems within that SALES-ORDER.
3. An ITEM can appear on many different SALES-ORDERs but in only one LineItem within each of those SALES-ORDERs.
4. An ITEM can appear on many different SALES-ORDERs and in many different LineItems within those SALES-ORDERs.

When it is important to distinguish among these cases, the following notation should be used: If either Case 1 or 2 is in force, the maximum cardinality of the hybrid object attribute should be set to 1. Thus, for this example, the maximum cardinality of SALES-ORDER in ITEM is set to 1. If an ITEM is to appear in only one LineItem of the SALES-ORDER (Case 1), it should be marked as having a unique ID in that group. Otherwise (Case 2), it need not be marked. These two cases are shown in Figure 4-25(a) and (b).

If either Case 3 or 4 is in force, the maximum cardinality of the hybrid object attribute is set to N. Thus, for this example, the maximum cardinality of SALES-ORDER in ITEM is set to N. Furthermore, if an ITEM is to appear in only one LineItem of a SALES-ORDER (Case 3), it should be marked as having a unique ID in that group. Otherwise (Case 4), it need not be marked. These two cases are shown in Figure 4-25(c) and (d).

ASSOCIATION OBJECTS

An **association object** is an object that relates two (or more) objects and stores data that are peculiar to that relationship. Figure 4-26(a) on page 105 shows a report and two data entry screens that give rise to the need for an association object. The report contains data about an airline flight and data about the particular airplane and pilot assigned to that flight. The two data entry forms contain data about a pilot and an airplane.

In Figure 4-26(b), the object FLIGHT is an association object that associates the two objects AIRPLANE and PILOT and stores data about their association. FLIGHT contains one each of AIRPLANE and PILOT, but both AIRPLANE and PILOT contain multiple values of FLIGHT. This particular pattern of associating two (or more) objects with data about the association occurs frequently, especially in applications that involve the assignment of two or more things. Other examples are a JOB that assigns an ARCHITECT to a CLIENT, a TASK that assigns an EMPLOYEE to a PROJECT, and a PURCHASE-ORDER that assigns a VENDOR to a SERVICE.

For the example in Figure 4-26, the association object FLIGHT has an identifier of its own, the group {FlightNumber, Date}. Often association objects do not have identifiers of their own, in which case the identifier is the combination of the identifiers of the objects that are associated.

Examples of the Four Cases of Maximum Cardinality in a Hybrid Object: (a) ITEM in One ORDER, (b) ITEM in (Possibly) Many LineItems of One ORDER, (c) ITEM in One LineItem of (Possibly) Many ORDERs, and (d) ITEM in (Possibly) Many LineItems of (Possibly) Many ORDERs

(a)

```
SALES-ORDER
ID SalesOrderNumber
   Date
   [CUSTOMER] 1.1
   [SALESPERSON] 1.1
   LineItem
      Quantity 1.1
   ID [ITEM] 1.1
      ExtendedPrice 1.1   1.N
   Subtotal 1.1
   Tax 1.1
   Total 1.1

ITEM
ID ItemNumber
   ItemDescription
   UnitPrice 1.1
   [SALES-ORDER] 0.1
```

(b)

```
SALES-ORDER
ID SalesOrderNumber
   Date
   [CUSTOMER] 1.1
   [SALESPERSON] 1.1
   LineItem
      Quantity 1.1
      [ITEM] 1.1
      ExtendedPrice 1.1   1.N
   Subtotal 1.1
   Tax 1.1
   Total 1.1

ITEM
ID ItemNumber
   ItemDescription
   UnitPrice 1.1
   [SALES-ORDER] 0.1
```

(c)

```
SALES-ORDER
ID SalesOrderNumber
   Date
   [CUSTOMER] 1.1
   [SALESPERSON] 1.1
   LineItem
      Quantity 1.1
   ID [ITEM] 1.1
      ExtendedPrice 1.1   1.N
   Subtotal 1.1
   Tax 1.1
   Total 1.1

ITEM
ID ItemNumber
   ItemDescription
   UnitPrice 1.1
   [SALES-ORDER] 0.N
```

(d)

```
SALES-ORDER
ID SalesOrderNumber
   Date
   [CUSTOMER] 1.1
   [SALESPERSON] 1.1
   LineItem
      Quantity 1.1
      [ITEM] 1.1
      ExtendedPrice 1.1   1.N
   Subtotal 1.1
   Tax 1.1
   Total 1.1

ITEM
ID ItemNumber
   ItemDescription
   UnitPrice 1.1
   [SALES-ORDER] 0.N
```

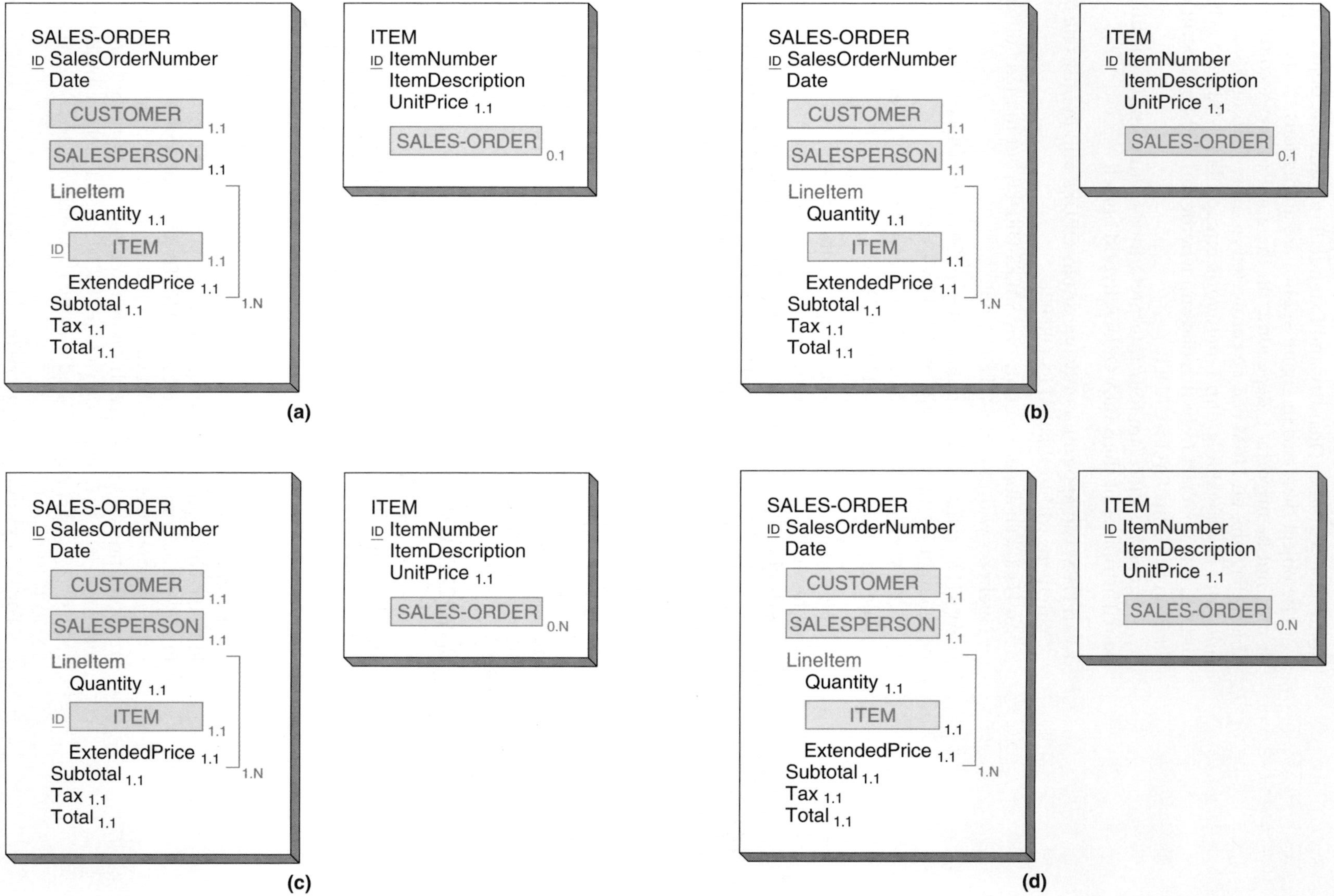

➤ FIGURE 4-26

Examples of an Association Object: (a) Example Flight Report and Forms, and (b) FLIGHT, PILOT, AIRPLANE Objects

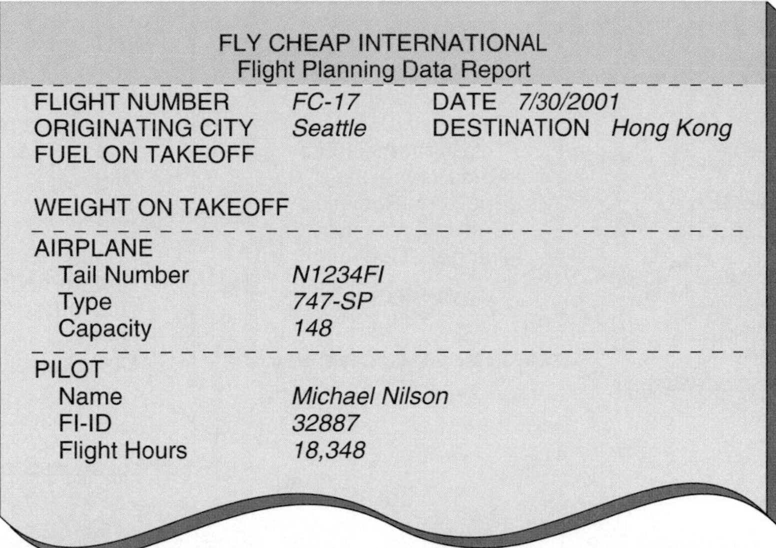

FLY CHEAP INTERNATIONAL
Flight Planning Data Report

FLIGHT NUMBER *FC-17* DATE *7/30/2001*
ORIGINATING CITY *Seattle* DESTINATION *Hong Kong*
FUEL ON TAKEOFF

WEIGHT ON TAKEOFF

AIRPLANE
Tail Number *N1234FI*
Type *747-SP*
Capacity *148*

PILOT
Name *Michael Nilson*
FI-ID *32887*
Flight Hours *18,348*

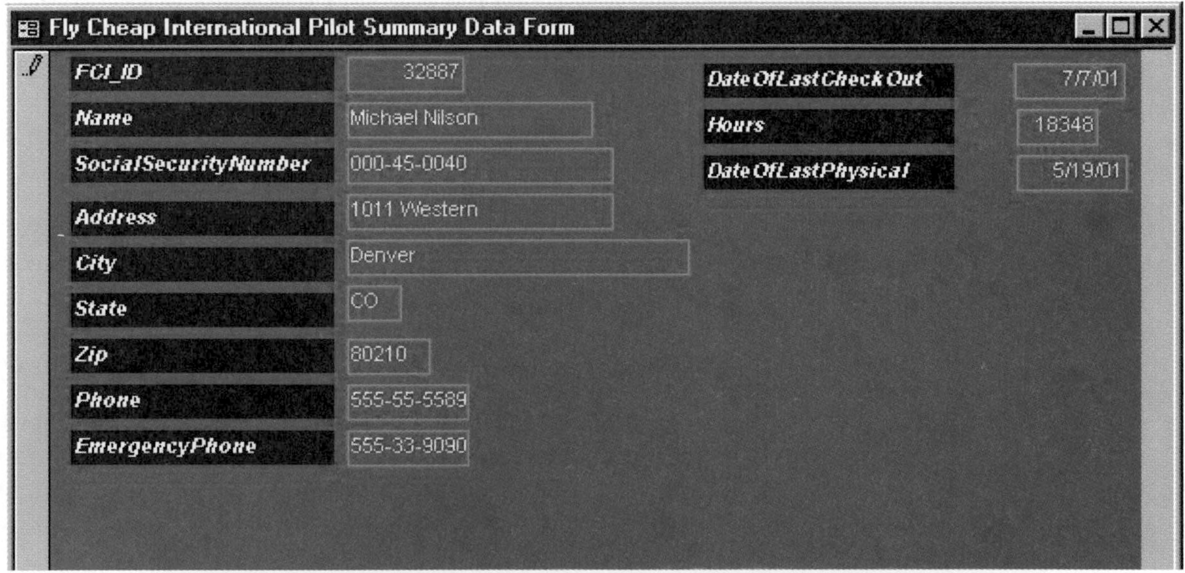

Fly Cheap International Pilot Summary Data Form

FCI_ID	32887
Name	Michael Nilson
SocialSecurityNumber	000-45-0040
Address	1011 Western
City	Denver
State	CO
Zip	80210
Phone	555-55-5589
EmergencyPhone	555-33-9090
DateOfLastCheckOut	7/7/01
Hours	18348
DateOfLastPhysical	5/19/01

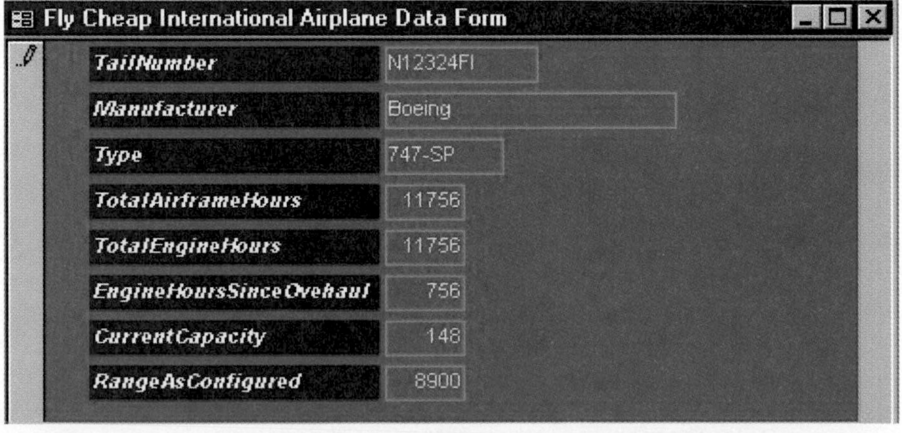

Fly Cheap International Airplane Data Form

TailNumber	N12324FI
Manufacturer	Boeing
Type	747-SP
TotalAirframeHours	11756
TotalEngineHours	11756
EngineHoursSinceOvehaul	756
CurrentCapacity	148
RangeAsConfigured	8900

(a)

(continued)

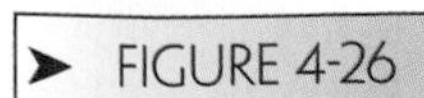
FIGURE 4-26

(Continued)

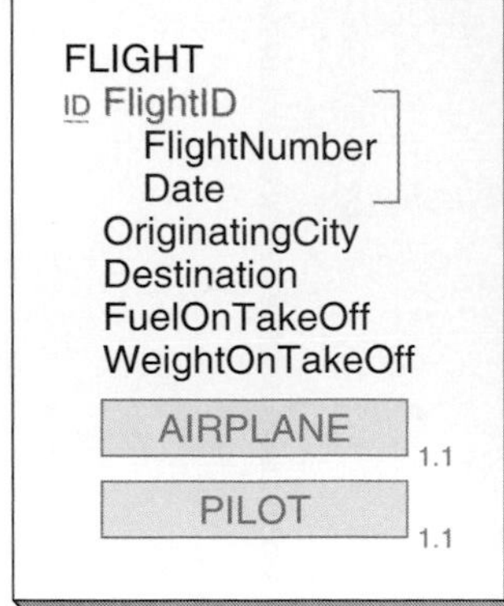

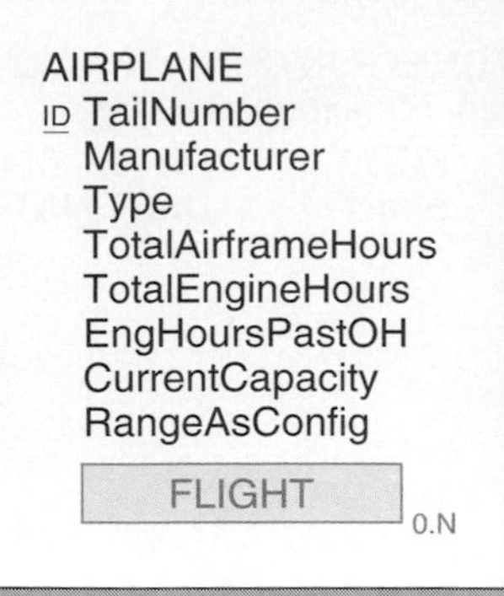

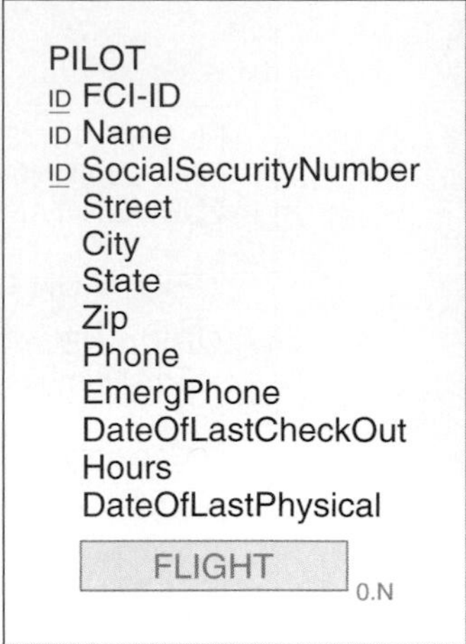

(b)

To understand this better, consider Figure 4-27(a), which shows a report about the assignment of architects to projects. Although the assignment has no obvious identifier, in fact the identifier is the combination {ProjectName, ArchitectName}. These attributes, however, belong to PROJECT and ARCHITECT and not to ASSIGNMENT. The identifier of ASSIGNMENT is thus the combination of those identifiers of the things that are assigned.

Figure 4-27(b) shows the object diagrams for this situation. Both PROJECT and ARCHITECT are object attributes of ASSIGNMENT, and the group {PROJECT, ARCHITECT} is the identifier of ASSIGNMENT. This means that the combination of an instance of PROJECT and an instance of ARCHITECT identifies a particular ASSIGNMENT.

Note that the AssignmentID identifier in Figure 4-27(b) is not unique, thereby indicating that an architect may be assigned to a project more than once. If this is not correct, the identifier should be declared to be unique. Also, if an employee may be assigned to a project more than once and if for some reason it is important to have a unique identifier for an ASSIGNMENT, the attribute Date or some other time-indicating attribute (Week, Quarter, and so forth) should be added to the group.

Parent/Subtype Objects

To understand parent and subtype objects, consider the object EMPLOYEE in Figure 4-28(a). Some of the attributes in EMPLOYEE pertain to all employees, and others pertain only to employees who are managers. The object in Figure 4-28(a) is not very precise because the manager-oriented attributes are not suitable for nonmanager employees.

A better model is shown in Figure 4-28(b), in which the EMPLOYEE object contains a subtype object, MANAGER. All of the manager-oriented attributes have been moved to the MANAGER object. Employees who are not managers have one EMPLOYEE object instance and no MANAGER object instances. Employees who are managers have both an EMPLOYEE instance and a MANAGER instance. In this example, the EMPLOYEE object is called a **parent object** or **supertype object,** and the MANAGER object is called a **subtype object.**

➤ FIGURE 4-27

ASSIGNMENT Association Object: (a) Example Assignment Report and (b) ASSIGNMENT Object with Semantic Object ID

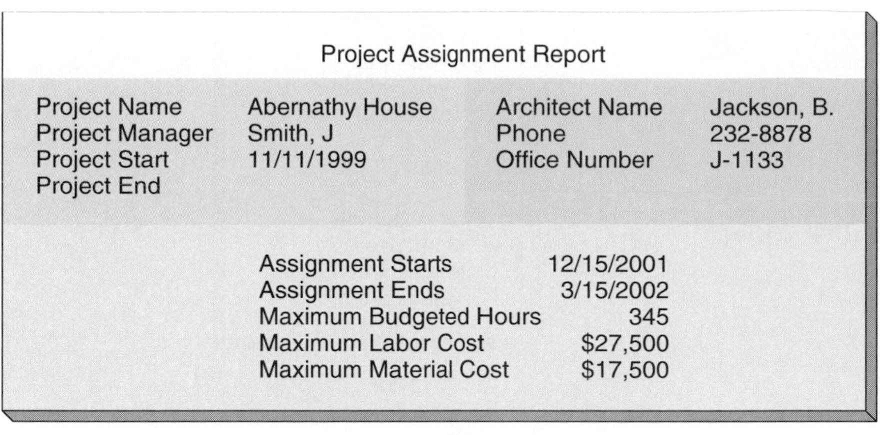

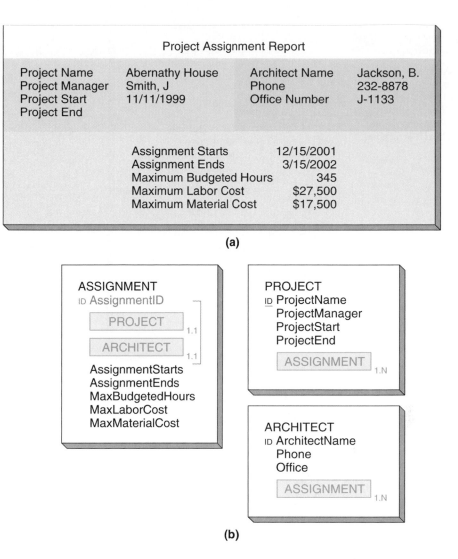

Project Assignment Report

Project Name	Abernathy House	Architect Name	Jackson, B.
Project Manager	Smith, J	Phone	232-8878
Project Start	11/11/1999	Office Number	J-1133
Project End			

Assignment Starts	12/15/2001
Assignment Ends	3/15/2002
Maximum Budgeted Hours	345
Maximum Labor Cost	$27,500
Maximum Material Cost	$17,500

(a)

ASSIGNMENT
ID AssignmentID
PROJECT 1.1
ARCHITECT 1.1
AssignmentStarts
AssignmentEnds
MaxBudgetedHours
MaxLaborCost
MaxMaterialCost

PROJECT
ID ProjectName
ProjectManager
ProjectStart
ProjectEnd
ASSIGNMENT 1.N

ARCHITECT
ID ArchitectName
Phone
Office
ASSIGNMENT 1.N

(b)

The first attribute of a subtype is the parent attribute and is denoted by the subscript P. Parent attributes are always required. The identifiers of the subtype are the same as the identifiers of the parent. In Figure 4-28, EmployeeNumber and EmployeeName are identifiers of both EMPLOYEE and MANAGER.

Subtype attributes are shown with the subscript 0.ST or 1.ST. The first digit (0 or 1) is the minimum cardinality of the subtype. If 0, the subtype is optional, and if 1, the subtype is required. (A required subtype does not make sense for this example but will for the more complicated examples to follow.) The *ST* indicates that the attribute is a subtype, or IS-A attribute.

Parent/subtype objects have an important characteristic called inheritance. A subtype acquires, or *inherits,* all of the attributes of its parent, and therefore a MANAGER inherits all of the attributes of an EMPLOYEE. In addition, the parent acquires all of the attributes of its subtypes, and an EMPLOYEE who is a MANAGER acquires all of the attributes of MANAGER.

A semantic object may contain more than one subtype attribute. Figure 4-29 shows a second EMPLOYEE object that has two subtype attributes, MANAGER and PROGRAMMER. Since all of these attributes are optional, an EMPLOYEE can have neither, one, or both of these subtypes. This means that some employees are neither managers nor programmers, some are managers but not programmers, some are programmers but not managers, and some are both programmers and managers.

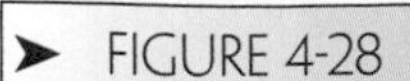

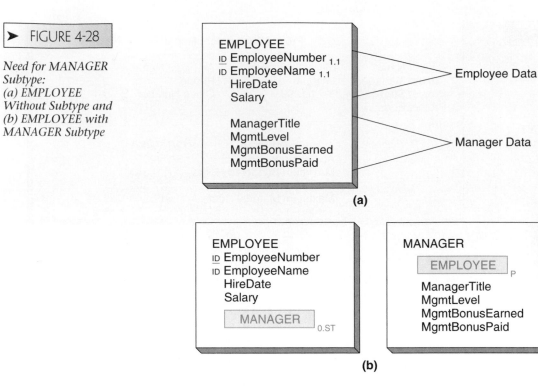

Need for MANAGER Subtype: (a) EMPLOYEE Without Subtype and (b) EMPLOYEE with MANAGER Subtype

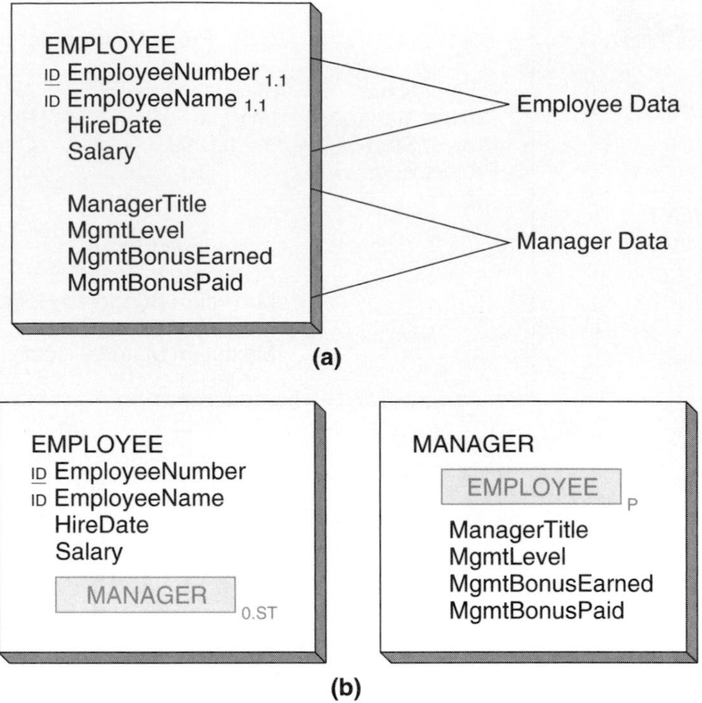

Sometimes subtypes exclude one another. That is, a VEHICLE can be an AUTO or a TRUCK, but not both. A CLIENT can be an INDIVIDUAL, a PARTNERSHIP, or a CORPORATION, but only one of these three types. When subtypes exclude one another, they are placed into a subtype group, and the group is assigned a subscript of the format *X.Y.Z*. X is the minimum cardinality and is 0 or 1, depending on whether or not the subtype group is required. Y and Z are counts of the number of attributes in the group that are allowed to have a value. Y is the minimum number required, and Z is the maximum number allowed.

Figure 4-30(a) shows three types of CLIENT as a subtype group. The subscript of the group, 0.1.1, means that the subtype is not required, but if it exists, a minimum of one and a maximum of one (or exactly one) of the subtypes in the group must exist. Note that each of the subtypes has the subscript 0.ST, meaning that

EMPLOYEE with Two Subtype Properties

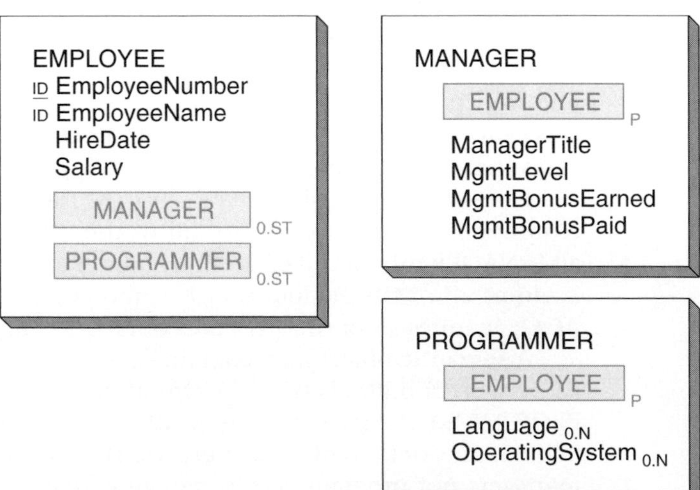

FIGURE 4-30

Exclusive (a) and Nested (b) Subtypes

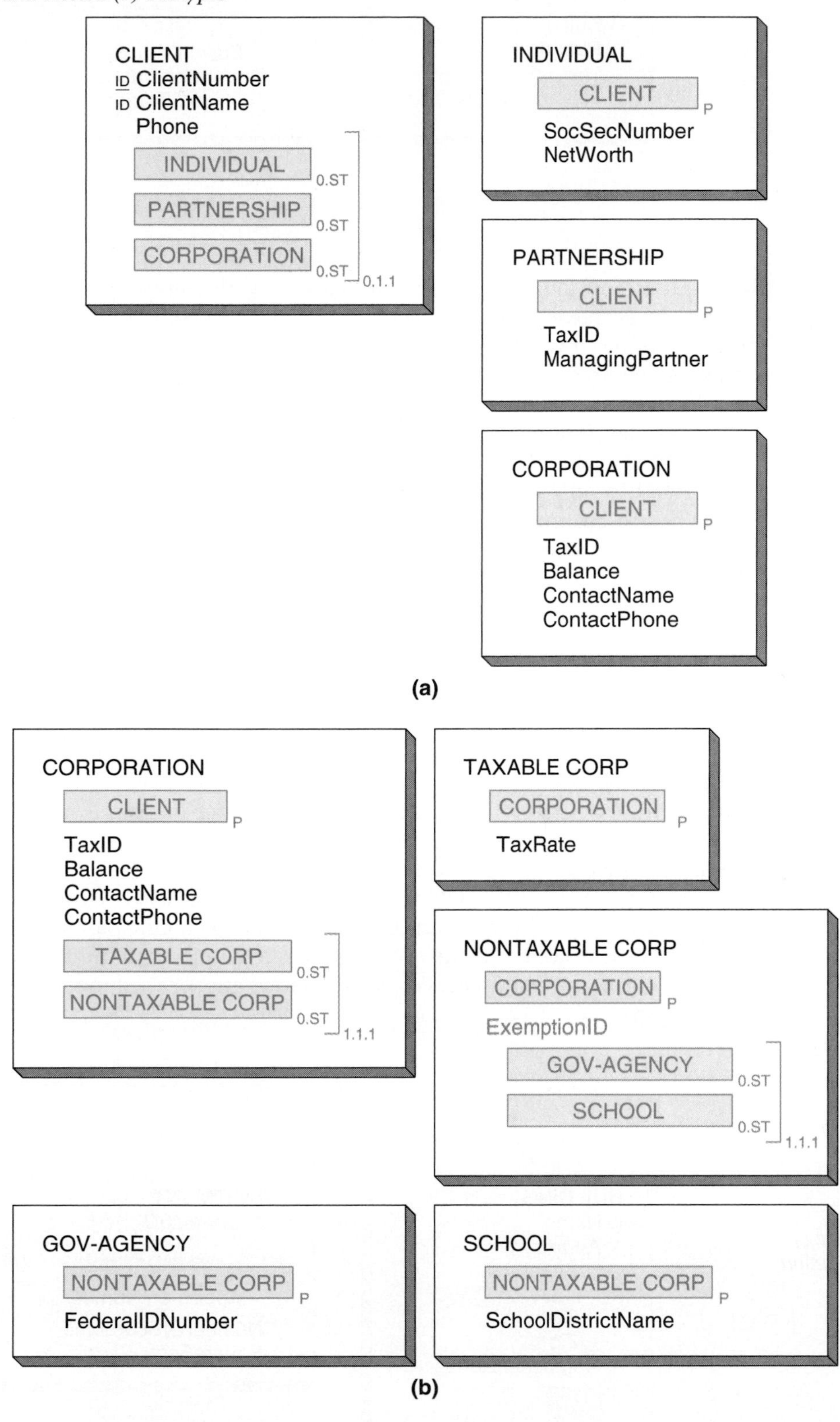

FIGURE 4-31

Example of an Archetype/Version Object

they all are optional, as they must be. If they all were required, the maximum count would have to be three, not one. This notation is robust enough to allow for situations in which three out of five or seven out of 10 of a list of subtypes must be required.

Even more complex restrictions can be modeled when subtypes are nested. The subtype group in Figure 4-30(b) models a situation in which the subtype CORPORATION must be either a TAXABLE-CORP or a NONTAXABLE-CORP. If it is a NONTAXABLE-CORP, it must be either GOV-AGENCY or a SCHOOL. Only a few nonobject attributes are shown in this example. In reality, if such a complex structure were required, there would likely be more attributes.

ARCHETYPE/VERSION OBJECTS

The final type of object is the **archetype/version object.** An archetype object is a semantic object that produces other semantic objects that represent versions, releases, or editions of the archetype. For example, in Figure 4-31, the archetype object TEXTBOOK produces the version objects EDITIONs. According to this model, the attributes Title, Author, and Publisher belong to the object TEXTBOOK, and the attributes EditionNumber, PublicationDate, and NumberOfPages belong to the EDITION of the TEXTBOOK.

The ID group in EDITION has two portions, TEXTBOOK and EditionNumber; this is the typical pattern for an ID of a version object. One part of the ID contains the archetype object, and the second part is a simple attribute that identifies the version within the archetype. Figure 4-32 shows another instance of archetype/version objects.

FIGURE 4-32

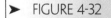

Another Example of an Archetype/Version Object

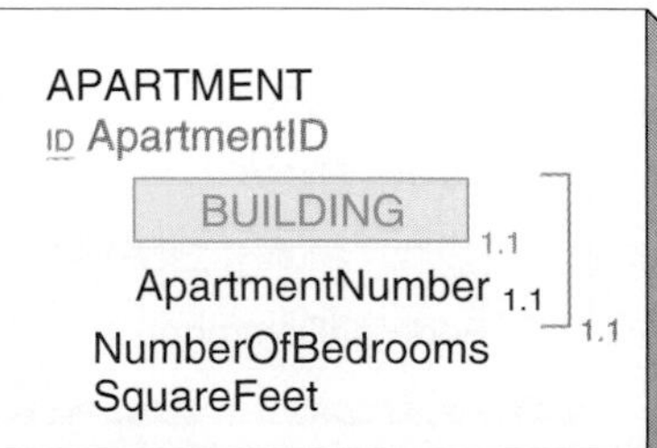

➤ COMPARING THE SEMANTIC OBJECT AND THE E-R MODEL

The E-R model and the semantic object model have both similarities and differences. They are similar in that they both are tools for understanding and documenting the structure of the users' data. They both strive to model the structure of the things in the users' world and the relationships among them.

The principal difference between the two models is one of orientation. The E-R model sees the concept of *entity* as basic. Entities and their relationships are considered the atoms, if you will, of a data model. These atoms can be combined to form what the E-R model calls *user views,* which are combinations of entities whose structure is similar to that of semantic objects.

The semantic object model takes the concept of *semantic object* as basic. The set of semantic objects in a data model is a map of the essential structure of the things that the user considers important. These objects are the atoms of the users' world and are the smallest distinguishable units that the users want to process. They may be decomposed into smaller parts inside the DBMS (or application), but those smaller parts are of no interest or utility to the users.

According to the semantic object perspective, entities, as defined in the E-R model, do not exist. They are only pieces or chunks of the real entities. The only entities that have meaning to users are, in fact, semantic objects. Another way to state this is to say that semantic objects are *semantically self-contained* or *semantically complete.* Consider an example. Figure 4-33 shows four semantic objects, SALES-ORDER, CUSTOMER, SALESPERSON, and ITEM. When a user says, "Show me sales order number 2000," he or she means show SALES-ORDER as modeled in Figure 4-33. That includes, among other attributes, CUSTOMER data. Because CUSTOMER is part of SALES-ORDER, the SALES-ORDER object includes CUSTOMER.

Figure 4-34 is an E-R model of this same data and contains the SALES-ORDER, CUSTOMER, SALESPERSON, LINE-ITEM, and INVENTORY entities.

➤ FIGURE 4-33

SALES-ORDER and Related Semantic Objects

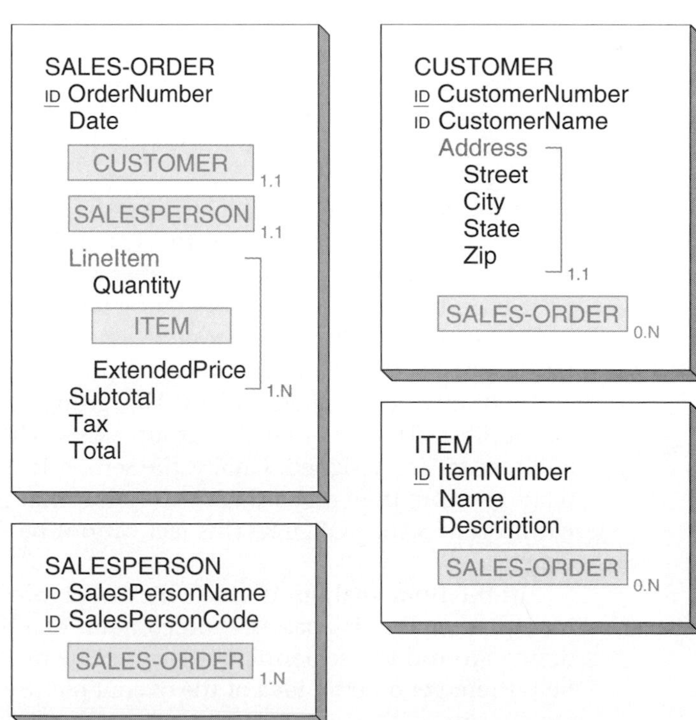

➤ FIGURE 4-34

Entity-Relationship Model of SALES-ORDER and CUSTOMER

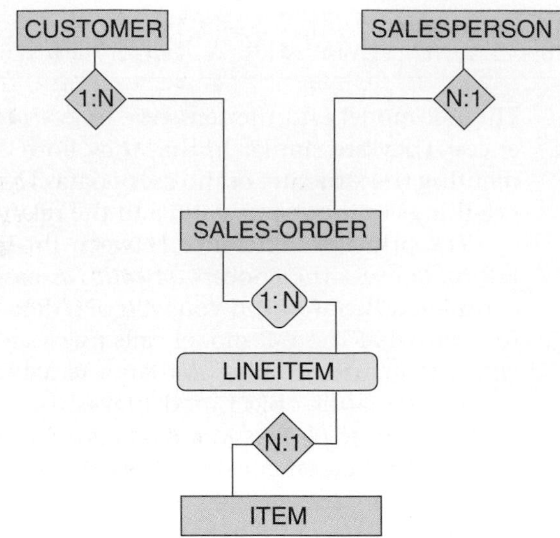

The SALES-ORDER entity includes the attributes OrderNumber, Date, Subtotal, Tax, and Total. Now if a user were to say, "Show me sales order number 2000" and be given only the attributes Date, Subtotal, Tax, and Total, he or she would be disappointed. Most likely the user's response would be, "Where's the rest of the data?" That is, the entity SALES-ORDER does not represent the user's meaning of the distinct identity SALES-ORDER. The entity is only a part of SALES-ORDER.

At the same time, when a user (perhaps even the same user) says, "Show me customer 12345," he or she means show all of the data modeled for CUSTOMER in Figure 4-33, including CustomerName, all of the attributes of the group Address, and all of the SALES-ORDERs for that CUSTOMER. The entity CUSTOMER in Figure 4-34 has only the attributes CustomerName, Street, City, State, Zip. If the user were to say, "Show me customer ABC" and be given only this data, he or she again would be disappointed: "No, that's only part of what I want."

According to the semantic object view, E-R entities are unnecessary. Semantic objects can be readily transformed into database designs without ever considering E-R model entities. They are halfway houses, so to speak, constructed in the process of moving away from the paradigm of computer data structures to the paradigm of the user.

Another difference is that the semantic objects contain more metadata than do the entities. In Figure 4-33, the semantic object model records the fact that CustomerNumber is a unique identifier in the users' minds. It may or may not be used as an identifier for the underlying table, but that fact is not important to the data model. In addition, CustomerName is a nonunique identifier to the users. Furthermore, the semantic objects represent the fact that there is a semantic group of attributes called *Address*. This group contains other attributes that form the address. The fact that this group exists will become important when forms and reports are designed. Finally, the semantic objects indicate that an ITEM may relate to more than one SALES-ORDER but that it can relate to only one LineItem within that SALES-ORDER. This fact cannot be shown on the entity-relationship diagram.

In the final analysis, decide which of Figures 4-33 and 4-34 gives you a better idea of what the database should contain. Many people find that the boundaries drawn around the semantic objects and the brackets around the group attributes help them get a better idea of the overall picture of the data model.

➤ SUMMARY

Both the E-R and the semantic object models are used to interpret requirements and to build models of the users' data. These models are like lenses through which developers look when studying and documenting the users' data. Both ultimately lead to a database design.

A semantic object is a named collection of attributes that sufficiently describes a distinct identity. Semantic objects are grouped into classes, and both classes and instances of semantic objects have names. For example, the name of a class is EMPLOYEE, and the name of an instance is Employee 2000.

Attributes represent characteristics of the identities being represented. The set of attributes is sufficient in that it represents all of the characteristics that the users need to do their work. Objects represent distinct identities, instances that the users view as independent and separate. The distinct identities represented may or may not be physical; indeed, they may themselves be representative, such as a contract.

Object attributes can be simple data items, groups, or other semantic objects. Object diagrams summarize the structure of objects. Object names are spelled in capital letters at the top of the diagram. Nonobject attributes are written with initial capitals, and attribute groups are indicated by brackets.

All attributes have a minimum cardinality that indicates how many instances of the attribute must exist in order for the object to be valid. They also have a maximum cardinality that indicates the maximum number of instances of the attribute allowed. Cardinality is written in the format N.M, where N is the minimum cardinality and M is the maximum. To reduce the clutter in an object diagram, if the cardinality of a simple value attribute is 0.1, it is not shown. But cardinality is always shown for group and object attributes.

Object attributes are always paired. If one object has a relationship with a second, the second must have a relationship with the first. Object identifiers are attributes that serve, in the users' minds, to identify objects. Identifiers can be unique or not unique. Any type of attribute can be an identifier. Identifiers are shown with the letters ID in front of the attribute. If the attribute is unique, then the letters ID are underlined. The cardinalities of an identifier are normally 1.1.

The domain of an attribute is the set of all possible values that the attribute can have. Domains have both a physical and a semantic definition. There are three types of domains: simple, group, and semantic object.

Applications process objects through users' views. A view of an object consists of the name of the object and all of the attributes visible from that view. View and object definition is often an iterative process.

The process of developing a set of object diagrams is iterative. Reports or forms are examined; an initial set of objects is documented; and the new reports and forms are then checked to reveal new objects and changes in existing objects. This process continues until all the forms and reports have been examined.

There are seven types of objects. Simple objects have no multi-value attributes and no object attributes. Composite objects have multi-value attributes but no object attributes. Compound objects have object attributes, and hybrid objects combine composite and compound objects. Association objects relate two or more other objects. Subtype objects are used to represent the specializations of objects. Finally, archetype/version objects are used to model objects that contain base data along with multiple variations, or versions.

The E-R model considers entities as basic, whereas the semantic object model considers semantic objects as basic. The semantic object model also contains more information about the meaning of the data than does the E-R model.

➤ GROUP I QUESTIONS

4.1 Explain why the E-R model and the semantic object model are like lenses.

4.2 Define *semantic object.*

4.3 Explain the difference between an object class name and an object instance name. Give an example of each.

4.4 What is required for a set of attributes to be a sufficient description?

4.5 Explain the words *distinct identity* as they pertain to the definition of a semantic object.

4.6 Explain why a line item of an order is not a semantic object.

4.7 List the three types of attributes.

4.8 Give an example of each of the following:

a. a simple, single-value attribute
b. a group, single-value attribute
c. a simple, multi-value attribute
d. a group, multi-value attribute
e. a simple object attribute
f. a multi-value object attribute

4.9 What is minimum cardinality? How is it used? Which types of attributes have minimum cardinality?

4.10 What is maximum cardinality? How is it used? Which types of attributes have maximum cardinality?

4.11 What are paired attributes? Why are they needed?

4.12 What is an object identifier? Give an example of a simple attribute object identifier and an example of a group attribute object identifier.

4.13 Define *attribute domain.* What are the types of attribute domain? Why is a semantic description necessary?

4.14 What is a semantic object view? Give an example of an object and two views other than those in this text.

4.15 Give an example of a simple object other than the one discussed in this chapter.

4.16 Give three examples of composite objects other than those in this chapter. One of your examples should have just one multi-value simple attribute; one should have two independent multi-value groups; and the third should have nested multi-value groups.

4.17 Give an example of four sets of compound objects other than those in this chapter. One set should have a 1:1 relationship; one set should have a 1:N relationship; one set should have an M:1 relationship; and one set should have an M:N relationship.

4.18 Give an example of a hybrid object other than the one in this chapter.

4.19 Give an example of one association and two compound objects other than those in this chapter.

4.20 Give an example of a supertype object with three subtype objects other than those in this chapter.

4.21 Give an example of archetype/version objects other than those in this chapter.

4.22 Explain the similarities between the E-R model and the semantic object model.

4.23 Explain the major differences between the E-R model and the semantic object model.

4.24 Explain the reasoning that entities, as defined in the E-R model, do not truly exist.

4.25 Show how both the E-R model and the semantic object model would represent the data underlying the SALES-ORDER form in Figure 4-24(a), and explain the main differences.

➤ GROUP II QUESTIONS

4.26 Modify the semantic object diagram in Figure 4-13 to include CLASS, CLASS-OFFERING, and ENROLLMENT objects. Assume ENROLLMENT is an association object that relates a STUDENT to a CLASS.

4.27 Modify the semantic object diagram in Figure 4-13 to include a COMMITTEE object. Assume that many PROFESSORs are assigned to a committee and that a COMMITTEE includes many PROFESSORs. Create a MEETING object as an archetype/version object that represents the meetings of a COMMITTEE.

4.28 Modify your answer to Question 4.27 to create MEETING as a multi-value group within COMMITTEE. Is this model a better model than the one in Question 4.27? Justify your answer.

➤ PROJECTS

A. Develop a semantic object model for the MHA case in Project A at the end of Chapter 3.

B. Access the Web site for a computer manufacturer such as Dell (www.dell.com). Use the Web site to determine which laptop computer you would buy for a power user who has a budget of $10,000. As you use the Web site, think about the structure of a possible database of computer systems and subsystems to support this site.

Develop a semantic object model of computer system and subsystem database for this Web site. Possible objects are BASE-SYSTEM, MEMORY-OPTION, VIDEO-CARD, and PRINTER. Show object relationships and at least two or three attributes per object. Indicate the type of each semantic object. To keep this project from exploding in size, constrain your design to the needs of someone who is making a purchase decision.

C. Access the Web site for a bookseller such as Amazon (www.amazon.com). Use the Web site to determine the three best books on XML (Extended Markup Language) for someone who is just learning that subject. As you use the Web site, think about the structure of a possible database of books, authors, subjects, and related topics.

Develop a semantic object model of a book database for this Web site. Possible objects are TITLE, AUTHOR, PUBLISHER, and SUBJECT. Show object relationships and at least two or three attributes per object. Indicate the type of each semantic object. To keep this project from exploding in size, assume that only books are to be tracked. Further, constrain your design to the needs of someone who is looking for books to purchase. Do not consider customer ordering, order fulfillment, purchase ordering, and other such business processes.

➤ FIREDUP PROJECT QUESTIONS

Consider the situation of FiredUp discussed at the end of Chapters 1 and 2. Assume that FiredUp has now developed a line of three different stoves: FiredNow, FiredAlways, and FiredAtCamp. Further, assume that the owners are selling spare parts for each of their stoves and they are also making stove repairs. Some repairs are at no charge because they are within the stove warranty period; other repairs are made at a charge for parts only; and still others are made for parts and labor. FiredUp wants to keep track of all of these data. When asked for further details, the owners made the following list:

CUSTOMER: Name, StreetAddress, ApartmentNumber, City, State/Province, Zip/PostalCode, Country, EmailAddress, PhoneNumber

STOVE: SerialNumber, Type, ManufactureDate, InspectorInitials

INVOICE: InvoiceNumber, Date, Customer, with a list of items and prices that were sold, TotalPrice

REPAIR: RepairNumber, Customer, Stove, Description, with a list of items that were used in the repair and the charge for them, if any, and TotalAmount of the repair

PART: Number, Description, Cost, SalesPrice

A. Create a set of semantic objects for a database at FiredUp. Set the minimum and maximum cardinality of all attributes as you think is appropriate. Explain your rationale for each cardinality value. Use as many types of semantic object as you think appropriate, but do not use subtypes. (This task is easier if you download Tabledesigner, the semantic object diagramming tool described in Appendix B. Use it to define your semantic objects and print object reports to submit to your instructor. See Appendix B and ask your instructor before you do this, however.)

B. Modify your object diagrams in your answer to Question A by representing INVOICE and REPAIR as subtypes. Under what circumstances is this design better than the one in your answer to Question A?

C. Suppose that FiredUp wants to keep track of home, fax, and cell phone numbers as well as multiple e-mail addresses for each of their customers. Modify your objects to allow for muliple values of PhoneNumber and EmailAddress.

D. Suppose that FiredUp develops different versions of the same stove product. Thus, they develop a FiredNow Version 1 and FiredNow Version 2, and so on. Modify your objects in Question A, above, as necessary to account for this situation.

E. When asking users for the data they want to track, they will not necessarily remember everything they need. Using your knowledge of small business operations, make a list of semantic objects they may have forgotten. Be sure to show relationships among the objects. How would you go about determining if any of this additional data is needed at FiredUp?

F. If you answered the FiredUp questions at the end of Chapter 3, compare the entity-relationship model developed for that chapter with the semantic object model developed here. Which do you prefer? Which do you think the owners of FiredUp would be able to understand better?

DATABASE DESIGN

The chapters in Part III discuss database design. Chapter 5 presents the relational model and normalization. The relational model is important because it is the standard in which most database designs are expressed; it is also the foundation of most of today's DBMS products.

Normalization is important because it is a technique for checking the quality of a relational design. Given the groundwork in Chapter 5, we then consider, in Chapter 6, the process of transforming entity-relationship data models into DBMS-independent, relational designs. Next, Chapter 7 describes the process for transforming semantic object data models into such designs.

The Relational Model and Normalization

The relational model is important for two reasons. First, because the constructs of the relational model are broad and general, it can be used to express DBMS-independent database designs. Second, the relational model is the basis for almost all DBMS products. Understanding the concepts of this model is therefore essential.

This chapter presents the basics of the relational model and explains the fundamental concepts of *normalization.* We begin with the fact that not all relations are equal, that some are better than others. Normalization is a process for converting a relation that has certain problems to two or more relations that do not have these problems. Even more important, normalization can be used as a guideline for checking the desirability and correctness of relations. Much theoretical work has been done on the question of what a well-structured relation is. This work is termed *normalization* because one of the pioneers in database technology, E. F. Codd, defined various *normal forms* of relations. In this chapter we survey normalization, including the results of theorems that are useful and significant to database practitioners. The proofs of these theorems and a formal, more rigorous treatment of this subject can be found in the work of C. J. Date and of J. D. Ullman.[1]

---

[1]C. J. Date, *An Introduction to Database Systems,* Sixth Edition (Reading, MA: Addison-Wesley, 1994); and J. D. Ullman and Jennifer Widom, *A First Course in Database Systems* (Upper Saddle River, NJ: Prentice Hall, 1997).

THE RELATIONAL MODEL

A **relation** is a two-dimensional table. Each row in the table holds data that pertain to some thing or a portion of some thing. Each column of the table contains data regarding an attribute. Sometimes rows are called **tuples** (rhymes with "couples"), and columns are called **attributes.**

The terms *relation, tuple,* and *attribute* arose from relational mathematics, which is the theoretical source of this model. MIS professionals find more comfortable the analogous terms *file, record,* and *field,* and most users find the terms *table, row,* and *column* most sensible. Figure 5-1 summarizes this terminology.

For a table to be a relation, it must meet certain restrictions.[2] First, the cells of the table must be of single value; neither repeating groups nor arrays are allowed as values.[3] All of the entries in any column must be of the same kind. For example, if the third column in the first row of a table contains EmployeeNumbers, then the third column must contain EmployeeNumbers in all other rows of the table as well. Each column has a unique name, and the order of the columns in the table is insignificant. Finally, no two rows in a table may be identical, and the order of the rows is insignificant.

Figure 5-2 is a sample table. Notice that it has seven rows made up of four columns. If we were to rearrange the order of the columns (say, by placing EmployeeNumber at the far left) or to reorder the rows (perhaps in ascending sequence on Age), we would have an equivalent table.

Figure 5-2 shows one occurrence, or instance, of a table. The generalized format, EMPLOYEE (Name, Age, Sex, EmployeeNumber), is called the relation structure, and it is what most people mean when they use the term *relation.*

To understand normalization, we need to define two important terms, **functional dependency** and **key.**

FUNCTIONAL DEPENDENCIES

A *functional dependency* is a relationship between or among attributes. Suppose that if we are given the value of one attribute, we can obtain (or look up) the value of another attribute. For example, if we know the value of CustomerAccountNumber, we can find the value of CustomerBalance. If this is true, we can say that CustomerBalance is *functionally dependent* on CustomerAccountNumber.

In more general terms, attribute Y is functionally dependent on attribute X if the value of X determines the value of Y. Stated differently, if we know the value of X, we can obtain the value of Y.

Equations represent functional dependencies. For example, if we know the price of an item and the quantity of items purchased, we can calculate the total price of those items, as follows:

TotalPrice = ItemPrice × Quantity

FIGURE 5-1

Equivalent Relational Terminology

Relational Model	Programmer	User
Relation	File	Table
Tuple (Row)	Record	Row
Attribute	Field	Column

[2]E. F. Codd, "A Relational Model of Data for Large Shared Databanks, "*Communications of the ACM,* June 1970, pp. 377–387.

[3]This does not mean that the values must be a fixed length. A variable-length memo field, for example, is a perfectly legitimate value. Only *one* such value is allowed, however.

➤ FIGURE 5-2

EMPLOYEE Relation

	Attribute1 Name	Attribute2 Age	Attribute3 Sex	Attribute4 EmployeeNumber
Tuple 1	Anderson	21	F	010110
Tuple 2	Decker	22	M	010100
.	Glover	22	M	101000
.	Jackson	21	F	201100
.	Moore	19	M	111100
.	Nakata	20	F	111101
Tuple 7	Smith	19	M	111111

In this case, we would say that TotalPrice is functionally dependent on ItemPrice and Quantity.

The functional dependencies between attributes in a relation usually do not involve equations. For example, suppose that students have a unique identification number, SID, and that every student has one, and only one, major. Given the value of an SID, we can find out that student's major, so Major is functionally dependent on SID. Or consider microcomputers in a computer lab. Each has one, and only one, size of main memory, so MemorySize is functionally dependent on ComputerSerialNumber.

Unlike an equation, such functional dependencies cannot be solved using arithmetic; instead, they are listed in the database. In fact, one can argue that the storage and retrieval of functional dependencies is the only reason for having a database.

Functional dependencies are written using the following notation:

SID → Major

ComputerSerialNumber → MemorySize

The first expression is read as "SID functionally determines Major," "SID determines Major," or "Major is dependent on SID." The attributes on the left side of the arrow are called **determinants.**

As stated, if SID determines Major, a particular value of SID will be paired with only *one* value of Major. Conversely, however, a value of Major may be paired with *one or more* different values of SID. Suppose a student has a SID value of 123 majors in accounting. Whenever SID and Major are found together in a relation, the SID value of 123 will always be paired with the Major value of Accounting. The opposite is not true, however, as the Major Accounting may be paired with many values of SID (many students may major in accounting). Consequently, we can say that the relationship of SID with Major is many to one (N:1). In general, we can say that if A determines B, the relationship of the values of A to B is N:1.

Functional dependencies can involve groups of attributes. Consider the relation GRADES (SID, ClassName, Grade). The combination of a SID and a ClassName determines a grade, a functional dependency that is written

(SID, ClassName) → Grade

Note that both SID and ClassName are needed to determine a Grade. We cannot subdivide the functional dependency because neither SID nor ClassName determines Grade by itself.

Notice the difference in the following two patterns: If X → (Y, Z), then X → Y and X → Z. For example, if SID → (StudentName, Major), then SID → StudentName and SID → Major. But if (X, Y) → Z, then in general, it is not true

FIGURE 5-3

ACTIVITY Relation

ACTIVITY (SID, Activity, Fee)
Key: SID
Sample Data

SID	Activity	Fee
100	Skiing	200
150	Swimming	50
175	Squash	50
200	Swimming	50

that X → Y or Y → Z. Hence, if (SID, ClassName) → Grade, then neither SID nor ClassName by itself determines Grade.

KEYS

A *key* is a group of one or more attributes that uniquely identifies a row. Consider the relation ACTIVITY in Figure 5-3, whose attributes are SID, Activity, and Fee. The meaning of a row is that a student engages in the named activity for the specified fee. Assume that a student is allowed to participate in only one activity at a time. In this case, a value of SID determines a unique row, and so it is a key.

Keys can also be composed of a group of attributes taken together. For example, if students were allowed to enroll in many activities at the same time, it would be possible for one value of SID to appear in two or more rows of the table, so SID could not uniquely identify the row. Some combination of attributes, perhaps (SID, Activity), would be required.

As an aside, there is a subtle but important point in the preceding paragraph. Whether or not attributes are keys and whether or not they are functional dependencies are determined not by an abstract set of rules but, rather, by the users' mental models and by the business rules of the organization using the database. In this example, whether SID is the key or whether (SID, Activity) is the key or whether some other combination is the key is determined entirely by the underlying semantics of the people in the organization using the database. We must ask the users to resolve these questions. As we continue, keep in mind that all the assumptions we make about functional dependencies, keys, constraints, and the like are determined by the users' mental models.

After interviewing the users, suppose we discover that students are, in fact, allowed to participate in several activities at one time. This situation is represented by the relation ACTIVITIES, shown in Figure 5-4. As we stated, SID is *not* a key of this relation. Student 100, for example, has enrolled in both skiing and golf, and the SID value of 100 occurs in two different rows. In fact, for this relation,

FIGURE 5-4

ACTIVITIES Relation

SID	Activity	Fee
100	Skiing	200
100	Golf	65
150	Swimming	50
175	Squash	50
175	Swimming	50
200	Swimming	50
200	Golf	65

no single attribute is a key, so the key must be a combination of two or more attributes.

Consider the combinations of two attributes from this table. There are three possibilities: (SID, Activity), (SID, Fee), and (Activity, Fee). Is any one of these combinations a key? To be a key, it must uniquely identify a row. Again, to decide questions like this, we must ask the users. We cannot simply depend on sample data like those in Figure 5-4 or rely on our own assumptions to make the decision.

After talking with the users, suppose we find out that several activities might charge the same fee. Since this is the case, the combination (SID, Fee) cannot determine a unique row. Student 100, for example, could engage in two different activities, both of which cost $200. This would mean that the combination (100, $200) occurs twice in the table, so this combination cannot be a key.

Can the combination (Activity, Fee) be a key? Does the combination (Skiing, $200) determine a unique row? No, it does not, because many students can participate in skiing. What about (SID, Activity)? Given what we know from the users, can a combination of values for SID and Activity determine a unique row? Yes, it can, so long as we are not required to keep records of the different occasions on which a student is enrolled in a given activity. In other words, is this table to be used to record only a student's current activities, or is it supposed to keep records of past activities as well?

Again, we must consult the users to answer this question. Suppose we learn that only records of current activities are to be kept. Then the combination (SID, Activity) can determine a unique row and, consequently (SID, Activity) is the key for this relation. If the users specified that records of current and past activities were to be kept, the relation in Figure 5-3 would have duplicate rows. Because this is prohibited by the definition of relation, we would need to add other attributes such as Date.

This brings up an important point. Every relation has at least one key. This must be true because no relation can have duplicate rows and hence, at the extreme, the key consists of all of the attributes of the relation.

Functional Dependencies, Keys, and Uniqueness

Many students confuse the concepts of functional dependencies, keys, and uniqueness. To avoid that confusion, consider the following: A determinant of a functional dependency may or may not be unique in a relation. If we know that A determines B and that A and B are in the same relation, we still do not know whether A is unique in that relation. We only know that A determines B.

For example, in the ACTIVITIES relation, Activity functionally determines Fee, and yet there can be many instances of a particular Activity in the relation. The functional dependency states only that wherever Activity occurs with Fee, it always occurs with the same value of Fee. That is, skiing always costs $200, regardless of how many times the value Skiing occurs in the table.

Unlike determinants, keys are always unique. A key functionally determines the entire row. If the value of the key were duplicated, the entire tuple would be duplicated. But this is not allowed because, by definition, rows in a relation must be unique. Thus, when we say that an attribute (or combination) is a key, we know that it will be unique. If (SID, Activity) is a key, then, for example, the combination (100, Skiing) will occur only once in a relation.

To test your understanding of these concepts, try to explain why, in the ACTIVITY relation in Figure 5-3, SID is both a determinant and a key but Activity is a determinant and not a key. (Keep in mind that the relation in Figure 5-3 reflects the policy that a student may participate in, at most, one activity at a time.)

➤ NORMALIZATION

Unfortunately, not all relations are equally desirable. A table that meets the minimum definition of a relation may not have an effective or appropriate structure. For some relations, changing the data can have undesirable consequences, called **modification anomalies.** Anomalies can be eliminated by redefining the relation into two or more relations. In most circumstances, the redefined, or **normalized,** relations are preferred.

MODIFICATION ANOMALIES

Again consider Activity in Figure 5-3. If we delete the tuple for Student 100, we will lose not only the fact that Student 100 is a skier but also the fact that skiing costs $200. This is called a **deletion anomaly;** that is, by deleting the facts about one entity (that Student 100 is a skier), we inadvertently delete facts about another entity (that skiing costs $200). With one deletion, we lose facts about two entities.

The same relation can be used to illustrate an **insertion anomaly.** Suppose we want to store the fact that scuba diving costs $175, but we cannot enter this data into the ACTIVITY relation until a student takes up scuba diving. This restriction seems silly. Why should we have to wait until someone takes the activity before we can record its price? This restriction is called an insertion anomaly. We cannot insert a fact about one entity until we have an additional fact about another entity.

The relation in Figure 5-3 can be used for some applications, but it obviously has problems. We can eliminate both the deletion and the insertion anomalies by dividing the ACTIVITY relation into two relations, each one dealing with a different theme. For example, we can put the SID and Activity attributes into one relation (we will call the new relation STU-ACT for student activity), and we can put the Activity and Fee attributes into a relation called ACT-COST (for activity cost). Figure 5-5 shows the same sample data stored in these two new relations.

Now if we delete Student 100 from STU-ACT, we do not lose the fact that skiing costs $200. Furthermore, we can add scuba diving and its fee to the ACT-COST relation even before anyone enrolls. Thus, the deletion and the insertion anomalies have been eliminated.

Separating one relation into two relations has a disadvantage, however. Suppose a student tries to sign up for a nonexistent activity. For instance, Student 250 wants to enroll in racquetball. We can insert this new tuple in STU-ACT (the row would contain 250, Racquetball), but should we? Should a student be allowed to enroll in an activity that is not in the relation ACT-COST? Put another way, should the system somehow prevent student rows from being added if the value of the ACTIVITY is not in the ACT-COST table? The answer to this question lies with the users' requirements. If the action should be prohibited, this constraint (a type of business rule) must be documented as part of the schema design. Later, in

➤ FIGURE 5-5

The Division of ACTIVITY into Two Relations

STU-ACT (SID, Activity)
Key: SID

SID	Activity
100	Skiing
150	Swimming
175	Squash
200	Swimming

ACT-COST (Activity, Fee)
Key: Activity

Activity	Fee
Skiing	200
Swimming	50
Squash	50

implementation, the constraint will be defined to the DBMS if the product in use provides such constraint checking. If not, the constraint must be enforced by application programs.

Suppose the user specifies that activities can exist before any student enrolls in them but that no student may enroll in an activity that does not have a fee assigned to it (that is, no activities that are not in the ACT-COST table). We can document this constraint in any of several ways in the database design: Activity in STU-ACT is a subset of Activity in ACT-COST, or STU-ACT [Activity] is a subset of ACT-COST [Activity], or STU-ACT [Activity] ⊆ ACT-COST [Activity].

According to this notation, the brackets [ ] denote a column of data that is extracted from a relation. These expressions simply mean that the values in the Activity attribute of STU-ACT must exist in the Activity attribute of ACT-COST. It also means that before we allow an Activity to be entered into STU-ACT, we must check to make sure that it is already present in ACT-COST. Constraints like this are called **referential integrity constraints or inter-relation constraints.**

Essence of Normalization

The anomalies in the ACTIVITY relation in Figure 5-3 can be stated in the following intuitive way: Problems occur because ACTIVITY contains facts about two different themes:

- the students who participate in each activity
- how much each activity costs

When we add a new row, we must add data about two themes at once, and when we delete a row, we are forced to delete data about two themes at once.

Remember your eighth-grade English teacher? He or she claimed that a paragraph should have a single theme. If a paragraph had more than one theme, you were taught to break up the paragraph into two or more paragraphs so that each paragraph would have only one theme. Similar statements apply to relations. Every normalized relation has a single theme. Any relation having two or more themes should be broken up into two or more relations, each of which has a single theme. This process is the essence of normalization. When we find a relation with modification anomalies, we eliminate them by splitting the relation into two or more separate ones, each containing a single theme.

Every time we break up a relation, however, we may create referential integrity constraints. Hence, remember to check for such constraints every time you break a relation into two or more.

In the remainder of this chapter, you will learn several rules about normalization. All of these rules are special cases of the process just described.

Classes of Relations

Relations can be classified by the types of modification anomalies to which they are vulnerable. In the 1970s, relational theorists chipped away at these types. Someone would find an anomaly, classify it, and think of a way to prevent it. Each time this happened, the criteria for designing relations improved. These classes of relations and the techniques for preventing anomalies are called **normal forms.** Depending on its structure, a relation may be in first normal form, second normal form, or some other normal form.

In the work that followed his landmark 1970 paper, Codd and others defined first, second, and third normal forms (1NF, 2NF, 3NF). Later, Boyce–Codd normal form (BCNF) was specified, and then fourth and fifth normal forms were defined. As shown in Figure 5-6, these normal forms are nested. That is, a relation in second

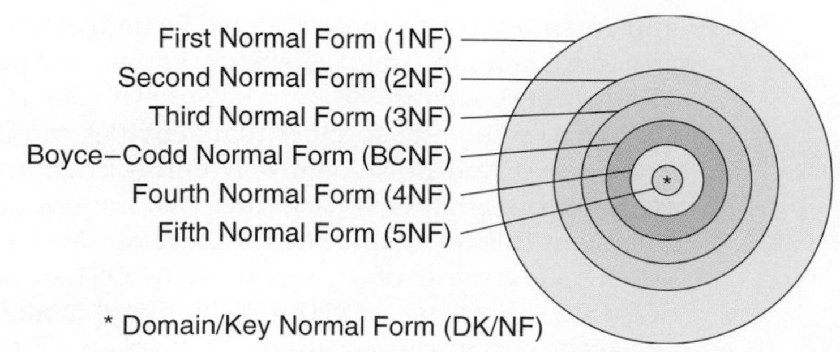

FIGURE 5-6

Relationship of Normal Forms

normal form is also in first normal form, and a relation in 5NF (fifth normal form) is also in 4NF, BCNF, 3NF, 2NF, and 1NF.

These normal forms were helpful, but they had a serious limitation. No theory guaranteed that any of them would eliminate all anomalies; each form could eliminate just certain ones. This changed, however, in 1981 when R. Fagin defined a new normal form called **domain/key normal form (DK/NF).** In an important paper, Fagin showed that a relation in DK/NF is free of all modification anomalies, regardless of their type.[4] He also showed that any relation that is free of modification anomalies must be in DK/NF.

Until DK/NF was defined, it was necessary for relational database theorists to continue looking for more and more anomalies and more and more normal forms. Fagin's proof, however, simplified the situation. If we can put a relation in DK/NF, then we can be sure that it will have no anomalies. The trick is knowing how to put relations in DK/NF.

FIRST THROUGH FIFTH NORMAL FORMS

Any table of data that meets the definition of a relation is said to be in **first normal form.** Remember that for a table to be a relation, the following must hold: The cells of the table must be of single value, and neither repeating groups nor arrays are allowed as values. All entries in any column (attribute) must be of the same kind. Each column must have a unique name, but the order of the columns in the table is insignificant. Finally, no two rows in a table may be identical, and the order of the rows is insignificant.

The relation in Figure 5-3 is in first normal form. As we have seen, however, relations in first normal form may have modification anomalies. To eliminate those anomalies, we split the relation into two or more relations. When we do this, the new relations are in some other normal form—just which one depends on the anomalies we have eliminated, as well as the ones to which the new relations are vulnerable.

SECOND NORMAL FORM

To understand second normal form, consider the ACTIVITIES relation in Figure 5-4. This relation has modification anomalies similar to the ones we examined earlier. If we delete the tuple for Student 175, we will lose the fact that squash costs $50. Also, we cannot enter an activity until a student signs up for it. Thus, the relation suffers from both deletion and insertion anomalies.

[4]R. Fagin, "A Normal Form for Relational Databases That Is Based on Domains and Keys," *ACM Transactions on Database Systems,* September 1981, pp. 387–415.

The problem with this relation is that it has a dependency involving only part of the key. The key is the combination (SID, Activity), but the relation contains a dependency, Activity → Fee. The determinant of this dependency (Activity) is only part of the key (SID, Activity). In this case, we say that Fee is *partially dependent* on the key of the table. There would be no modification anomalies if Fee were dependent on all of the key. To eliminate the anomalies, we must separate the relation into two relations.

This example leads to the definition of second normal form: *A relation is in second normal form if all its nonkey attributes are dependent on all of the key.* According to this definition, if a relation has a single attribute as its key, then it is automatically in second normal form. Because the key is only one attribute, by default, every nonkey attribute is dependent on *all* of the key; there can be no partial dependencies. Thus, second normal is of concern only in relations that have composite keys.

ACTIVITIES can be decomposed to form two relations in second normal form. The relations are the same as those in Figure 5-5, namely, STU-ACT and ACT-COST. We know the new relations are in second normal form because they both have single-attribute keys.

Third Normal Form

Relations in second normal form can also have anomalies. Consider the HOUSING relation in Figure 5-7(a). The key is SID, and the functional dependencies are SID → Building and Building → Fee. These dependencies arise because each student lives in only one building and each building charges only one fee. Everyone living in Randolph Hall, for example, pays $3,200 per quarter.

➤ FIGURE 5-7

Elimination of Transitive Dependency: (a) Relation with Transitive Dependency and (b) Relations Eliminating the Transitive Dependency

HOUSING (SID, Building, Fee)
Key: SID
Functional dependencies: Building → Fee
SID → Building → Fee

SID	Building	Fee
100	Randolph	3200
150	Ingersoll	3100
200	Randolph	3200
250	Pitkin	3100
300	Randolph	3200

(a)

STU-HOUSING (SID, Building)
Key: SID

SID	Building
100	Randolph
150	Ingersoll
200	Randolph
250	Pitkin
300	Randolph

BLDG-FEE (Building, Fee)
Key: Building

Building	Fee
Randolph	3200
Ingersoll	3100
Pitkin	3100

(b)

Since SID determines Building and Building determines Fee, then indirectly SID → Fee. An arrangement of functional dependencies like this is called a **transitive dependency,** since SID determines Fee through the attribute Building.

The key of HOUSING is SID, which is a single attribute, and hence the relation is in second normal form (both Building and Fee are determined by SID). Despite this, however, HOUSING has anomalies because of the transitive dependency.

What happens if we delete the second tuple shown in Figure 5-7(a)? We lose not only the fact that Student 150 lives in Ingersoll Hall but also the fact that it costs \$3,100 to live there. This is a deletion anomaly. And how can we record the fact that the Fee for Carrigg Hall is \$3,500? We cannot until a student decides to move in. This is an insertion anomaly.

To eliminate the anomalies from a relation in second normal form, the transitive dependency must be removed, which leads to a definition of third normal form: *A relation is in third normal form if it is in second normal form and has no transitive dependencies.*

The HOUSING relation can be divided into two relations in third normal form. This has been done for the relations STU-HOUSING (SID, Building) and BLDG-FEE (Building, Fee) in Figure 5-7(b).

The ACTIVITY relation in Figure 5-3 also has a transitive dependency. In ACTIVITY, SID determines Activity and Activity determines Fee. Therefore, ACTIVITY is not in third normal form. Decomposing ACTIVITY into the relations STU-ACT (SID, Activity) and ACT-COST (Activity, Fee) eliminates the anomalies.

Boyce–Codd Normal Form

Unfortunately, even relations in third normal form can have anomalies. Consider the ADVISER relation in Figure 5-8(a). Suppose the requirements underlying this relation are that a student (SID) can have one or more majors (Major), a major can have several faculty members (Fname) as advisers, and a faculty member (Fname) advises in only one major area. Also assume no two faculty members have the same name.

Since students can have several majors, SID does not determine Major. Moreover, since students can have several advisers, SID also does not determine Fname. Thus, SID, by itself, cannot be a key.

The combination (SID, Major) determines Fname, and the combination (SID, Fname) determines Major. Hence, either of the combinations can be a key. Two or more attributes or attribute collections that can be a key are called **candidate keys.** Whichever of the candidates is selected to be *the* key is called the **primary key.**

In addition to the candidate keys, there is another functional dependency to consider: Fname determines Major (any faculty member advises in only one major. Therefore, given the Fname, we can determine the Major). Thus, Fname is a determinant.

By definition, ADVISER is in first normal form. It is also in second normal form, since it has no nonkey attribute (all attributes are part of at least one key). And it also is in third normal form because it has no transitive dependencies. Despite all this, however, it has modification anomalies.

Suppose Student 300 drops out of school. If we delete Student 300's tuple, we will lose the fact that Perls advises in psychology. This is a deletion anomaly. Similarly, how can we store the fact that Keynes advises in economics? We cannot until a student majors in economics. This is an insertion anomaly.

Situations like this lead to the definition of Boyce–Codd normal form (BCNF): *A relation is in BCNF if every determinant is a candidate key.* ADVISER is not in BCNF, because the determinant, Fname, is not a candidate key.

➤ FIGURE 5-8

Boyce–Codd Normal Form: (a) Relation in Third Normal Form But Not in Boyce–Codd Normal Form and (b) Relations in Boyce–Codd Normal Form

ADVISER (SID, Major, Fname)

Key (primary): (SID, Major)
Key (candidate): (SID, Fname)

Functional
dependencies: Fname→Major

SID	Major	Fname
100	Math	Cauchy
150	Psychology	Jung
200	Math	Riemann
250	Math	Cauchy
300	Psychology	Perls
300	Math	Riemann

(a)

STU-ADV (SID, Fname)
Key: SID, Fname

SID	Fname
100	Cauchy
150	Jung
200	Riemann
250	Cauchy
300	Perls
300	Riemann

ADV-SUBJ (Fname, Subject)
Key: Fname

Fname	Subject
Cauchy	Math
Jung	Psychology
Riemann	Math
Perls	Psychology

(b)

As with the other examples, ADVISER can be decomposed into two relations having no anomalies. For example, the relations STU-ADV (SID, Fname) and ADV-SUBJ (Fname, Subject) have no anomalies.

Relations in BCNF have no anomalies in regard to functional dependencies, and this seemed to put the issue of modification anomalies to rest. It was soon discovered, however, that anomalies can arise from situations other than functional dependencies.

Fourth Normal Form

Consider the STUDENT relation in Figure 5-9, showing the relationship among students, majors, and activities. Suppose that students can enroll in several different majors and participate in several different activities. Because this is so, the only key is the combination of attributes (SID, Major, Activity). Student 100 majors in music and accounting, and she also participates in swimming and tennis. Student 150 majors only in math and participates in jogging.

What is the relationship between SID and Major? It is not a functional dependency because students can have several majors. A single value of SID can have many values of Major. Also, a single value of SID can have many values of Activity.

This attribute dependency is called a **multi-value dependency.** Multi-value dependencies lead to modification anomalies. To begin, note the data redundancy in Figure 5-9. Student 100 has four records, each of which shows one of her majors paired with one of her activities. If the data were stored with fewer rows—say, there were only two tuples, one for music and swimming and one for accounting

➤ FIGURE 5-9

Relation with Multi-Value Dependencies

STUDENT (SID, Major, Activity)
Key: (SID, Major, Activity)

Multivalued dependencies: SID →→ Major
SID →→ Activity

SID	Major	Activity
100	Music	Swimming
100	Accounting	Swimming
100	Music	Tennis
100	Accounting	Tennis
150	Math	Jogging

and tennis—the implications would be misleading. It would *appear* that Student 100 swam only when she was a music major and played tennis only when she was an accounting major. But this interpretation is not logical. Her majors and her activities are completely independent of each other. So to prevent such a misleading conclusion, we store all the combinations of majors and activities.

Suppose that because Student 100 decides to sign up for skiing, we add the tuple [100, MUSIC, SKIING], as in Figure 5-10(a). The relation at this point implies that Student 100 skis as a music major but not as an accounting major. In order to keep the data consistent, we must add one row for each of her majors paired with skiing. Thus, we must also add the row [100, ACCOUNTING, SKIING], as in Figure 5-10(b). This is an update anomaly—too much updating needs to be done to make a simple change in the data.

In general, a multi-value dependency exists when a relation has at least three attributes, two of them are multi-value, and their values depend on only the third attribute. In other words, in a relation R (A, B, C), a multi-value dependency exists

➤ FIGURE 5-10

STUDENT Relations with Insertion Anomalies: (a) Insertion of a Single Tuple and (b) Insertion of Two Tuples

STUDENT (SID, Major, Activity)
Key: (SID, Major, Activity)

SID	Major	Activity
100	Music	Skiing
100	Music	Swimming
100	Accounting	Swimming
100	Music	Tennis
100	Accounting	Tennis
150	Math	Jogging

(a)

SID	Major	Activity
100	Music	Skiing
100	Accounting	Skiing
100	Music	Swimming
100	Accounting	Swimming
100	Music	Tennis
100	Accounting	Tennis
150	Math	Jogging

(b)

➤ FIGURE 5-11

Elimination of Multi-Value Dependency

STU-MAJOR (SID, Major)
Key: (SID, Major)

SID	Major
100	Music
100	Accounting
150	Math

STU-ACT (SID, Activity)
Key: (SID, Activity)

SID	Activity
100	Skiing
100	Swimming
100	Tennis
150	Jogging

if A determines multiple values of B, A determines multiple values of C, and B and C are independent of each other. As we saw in the previous example, SID determines multiple values of Major and SID determines multiple values of Activity, but Major and Activity are independent of each other.

Refer again to Figure 5-9. Notice how multi-value dependencies are written: SID →→ Major, and SID →→ Activity. This is read "SID multi-determines Major, and SID multi-determines Activity." This relation is in BCNF (2-NF because it is all key; 3NF because it has no transitive dependencies; and BCNF because it has no nonkey determinants). However, as we have seen, it has anomalies: If a student adds a major, we must enter a tuple for the new major, paired with each of the student's activities. The same holds true if a student enrolls in a new activity. If a student drops a major, we must delete each of his records containing that major. If he participates in four activities, there will be four tuples containing the major he has dropped, and each of them must be deleted.

To eliminate these anomalies, we must eliminate the multi-value dependency. We do this by creating two relations, each one storing data for only one of the multi-value attributes. The resulting relations do not have anomalies. They are STU-MAJOR (SID, Major) and STU-ACT (SID, Activity), as seen in Figure 5-11.

From these observations, we define fourth normal form in the following way: *A relation is in fourth normal form if it is in BCNF and has no multi-value dependencies*. After we have discussed domain/key normal form later in this chapter, we will return to describe multi-value dependencies in another, more intuitive way.

Fifth Normal Form

Fifth normal form concerns dependencies that are rather obscure. It has to do with relations that can be divided into subrelations, as we have been doing, but then cannot be reconstructed. The condition under which this situation arises has no clear, intuitive meaning. We do not know what the consequences of such dependencies are or even if they have any practical consequences. For more information about fifth normal form, refer to the work by Date that was cited earlier in this chapter.

➤ DOMAIN/KEY NORMAL FORM

Each of the normal forms we have discussed was identified by researchers who found anomalies with some relations that were in a lower normal form: Noticing modification anomalies with relations in second normal form led to the definition of third normal form, and so on. Although each normal form solved some of the problems that had been identified with the previous one, no one could know what problems had not yet been identified. With each step, progress was made toward a well-structured database design, but no one could guarantee that no more anomalies would be found. In this section we study a normal form that guarantees that there will be no anomalies of any type. When we put relations into that form, we know that even the obscure anomalies associated with fifth normal form cannot occur.

In 1981, Fagin published an important paper in which he defined domain/key normal form (DK/NF).[5] He showed that a relation in DK/NF has no modification anomalies and, furthermore, that a relation having no modification anomalies must be in DK/NF. This finding establishes a bound on the definition of normal forms, and so no higher normal form is needed, at least in order to eliminate modification anomalies.

Equally important, DK/NF involves only the concepts of key and domain, concepts that are fundamental and close to the heart of database practitioners. They are readily supported by DBMS products (or could be, at least). In a sense, Fagin's work formalized and justified what many practitioners believed intuitively but were unable to express precisely.

Definition

In concept, DK/NF is quite simple: A relation is in DK/NF if every constraint on the relation is a logical consequence of the definition of keys and domains. Consider the important terms in this definition: constraint, key, and domain.

Constraint in this definition is intended to be very broad. Fagin defines a constraint as any rule governing static values of attributes that is precise enough so that we can ascertain whether or not it is true. Edit rules, intrarelation and interrelation constraints, functional dependencies, and multi-value dependencies are examples of such constraints. Fagin expressly excludes constraints pertaining to changes in data values, or time-dependent constraints. For example, the rule "Salesperson salary in the current period can never be less than salary in the prior period" is excluded from Fagin's definition of constraint. Except for time-dependent constraints, Fagin's definition is both broad and inclusive.

A **key** is a unique identifier of a tuple, as we have already defined. The third significant term in the definition of DK/NF is **domain.** In Chapter 4, we stated that a domain is a description of an attribute's allowed values. It has two parts: a physical description and a semantic, or logical, description. The physical description is the set of values the attribute can have, and the logical description is the meaning of the attribute. Fagin's proof refers to both parts.

Informally, a relation is in DK/NF if enforcing key and domain restrictions causes all of the constraints to be met. Moreover, because relations in DK/NF cannot have modification anomalies, the DBMS can prohibit them by enforcing key and domain restrictions.

Unfortunately, there is no known algorithm for converting a relation to DK/NF, nor is it even known which relations can be converted to DK/NF. Finding, or designing, DK/NF relations is more of an art than a science.

In spite of this, in the practical world of database design, DK/NF is an exceedingly useful design objective. If we can define relations in a way that constraints on them are logical consequences of domains and keys, then there will be no modification anomalies. For many designs, this objective can be accomplished. When it cannot, the constraints must be built into the logic of application programs that process the database. We will see more of this later in this chapter and in Chapter 10.

The following three examples illustrate DK/NF.

---

[5] *Ibid.*

➤ FIGURE 5-12

Example 1 of DK/NF

STUDENT (SID, GradeLevel, Building, Fee)

Key: SID

Constraints: Building → Fee
SID must not begin with digit 1

Example 1 of Domain/Key Normal Form

Consider the STUDENT relation in Figure 5-12, which contains attributes SID, GradeLevel, Building, and Fee. Building is the building in which the student lives, and Fee is the amount the student pays to live in that building.

SID functionally determines the other three attributes, so SID is a key. Assume we also know, from the requirements definition, that Building → Fee and that SIDs must not begin with 1. If we can express these constraints as logical consequences of domain and key definitions, we can be certain, according to Fagin's theorem, that there will be no modification anomalies. For this example, it will be easy.

To enforce the constraint that student numbers not begin with 1, we simply define the domain for student numbers to incorporate this constraint (Figure 5-13). Enforcing the domain restriction guarantees that this constraint will be met.

Next we need to make the functional dependency Building → Fee a logical consequence of keys. If Building were a key attribute, Building → Fee would be a logical consequence of a key. Therefore, the question becomes how to make Building a key. It cannot be a key in STUDENT because more than one student lives in the same building, but it can be a key of its own relation. Thus, we define the relation BLDG-FEE with Building and Fee as its attributes. Building is the key of this relation. Having defined this new relation, we can remove Fee from STUDENT. The final domain and relation definitions for this example appear in Figure 5-13.

This is the same result we obtained when converting a relation from 2NF to 3NF to remove transitive dependencies. In this case, however, the process was simpler and the result more robust. It was simpler because we did not need to know that we were eliminating a transitive dependency. We simply needed to find creative ways to make all the constraints logical consequences of domain and key

➤ FIGURE 5-13

Domain/Key Definition of Example 1

Domain Definitions

SID	in	CDDD, where C is decimal digit not = 1; D = decimal digit
GradeLevel	in	{'FR', 'SO', 'JR', 'SN', 'GR'}
Building	in	CHAR(4)
Fee	in	DEC(4)

Relation and Key Definitions

STUDENT (SID, GradeLevel, Building)
Key: SID

BLDG-FEE
(Building, Fee)
Key: Building

➤ FIGURE 5-14

Example 2 of DK/NF

```
PROFESSOR (FID, Fname, Class, SID, Sname)
Key: (FID, Class, SID)
Constraints:     FID → Fname
                 Fname → FID
                 FID →→ Class | SID
                 Fname →→ Class | SID
                 SID → FID
                 SID → Fname
                 SID → Sname
                 FID must start with 1; SID must not start with 1
```

definitions. The result was more robust because when converting the relation to 3NF, we knew only that it had fewer anomalies than when it was in 2NF. By converting the relation to DK/NF, we know that the relations have no modification anomalies whatsoever.

EXAMPLE 2 OF DOMAIN/KEY NORMAL FORM

The next, more complicated, example involves the relation in Figure 5-14. The PROFESSOR relation contains data about professors, the classes they teach, and the students they advise. FID (for Faculty ID) and Fname uniquely identify a professor. SID uniquely identifies a student, but Sname does not necessarily identify a SID. Professors can teach several classes and advise several students, but a student is advised by only one professor. FIDs start with a 1, but SIDs must not start with a 1.

These statements can be expressed more precisely by the functional and multivalue dependencies shown in Figure 5-14. FID and Fname functionally determine each other (in essence, they are equivalent). FID and Fname multidetermine Class and SID. SID functionally determines FID and Fname. SID determines Sname.

In more complex examples such as this one, it is helpful to consider DK/NF from a more intuitive light. Remember that the essence of normalization is that every relation should have a single theme. Considered from this perspective, there are three themes in PROFESSOR. One is the correspondence between FIDs and Fnames. Another concerns the classes that a professor teaches, and the third concerns the identification number, name, and adviser of a given student.

Figure 5-15 shows three relations that reflect these themes. The FACULTY relation represents the equivalence of FID and Fname. FID is the key and Fname is an alternative key, which means that both attributes are unique to the relation. Because both are keys, the functional dependencies FID → Fname and Fname → FID are logical consequences of keys.

The PREPARATION relation contains the correspondence of faculty and classes; it shows the classes that a professor is prepared to teach. The key is the combination (Fname, Class). Both attributes are required in the key because a professor may teach several classes and a class may be taught by several professors. Finally, STUDENT represents the student and adviser names for a particular SID. Observe that each of these relations has a single theme. These relations express all of the constraints of Figure 5-14 as a logical consequence of domains and key definitions. These relations are, therefore, in DK/NF.

Note that separating the PREPARATION theme from the STUDENT theme has eliminated the multi-value dependencies. When we examined fourth normal form, we found that in order to eliminate multi-value dependencies, we had to

➤ FIGURE 5-15

Domain/Key Definition of Example 2

Domain Definitions

FID	in	CDDD, C = 1; D = decimal digit
Fname	in	CHAR(30)
Class	in	CHAR(10)
SID	in	CDDD, C is decimal digit, not = 1; D = decimal digit
Sname	in	CHAR(30)

Relation and Key Definitions

FACULTY (FID, Fname)
Key (primary): FID
Key (candidate): Fname

PREPARATION (Fname, Class)
Key: Fname, Class

STUDENT (SID, Sname, Fname)
Key: SID

separate the multi-value attributes into different relations. Our approach here is to break a relation with several themes into several relations, each with one theme. In doing that, we eliminated a multi-value dependency. In fact, we arrived at the same solution using both approaches.

Example 3 of Domain/Key Normal Form

The next example concerns a situation that was not addressed by any of the other normal forms but that occurs frequently in practice. This relation has a constraint among data values within a tuple that is neither a functional dependency nor a multi-value dependency.

Consider the constraints in the relation STU-ADVISER in Figure 5-16. This relation contains information about a student and his or her adviser. SID determines Sname, FID, Fname, and GradFacultyStatus and is therefore the key. FID and Fname identify a unique faculty member and are equivalent to each other, as in Example 2. Both FID and Fname determine GradFacultyStatus. Finally, the new

➤ FIGURE 5-16

Example 3 of DK/NF

STU-ADVISER (SID, Sname, FID, Fname, GradFacultyStatus)

Key: SID

Constraints:
FID → Fname
Fname → FID
FID and Fname → GradFacultyStatus
Only graduate faculty can advise graduate students
FID begins with 1
SID must not begin with 1
SID of graduate student begins with 9
GradFacultyStatus = { 0 for undergraduate faculty
1 for graduate faculty

type of constraint is that only members of the graduate faculty are allowed to advise graduate students.

The domain restrictions are that SID must not begin with a 1, SID must begin with a 9 for graduate students, FID must begin with a 1, and GradFacultyStatus is 0 for undergraduate faculty and 1 for graduate faculty. With these domain definitions, the constraint that graduate students must be advised by graduate faculty can be expressed as a constraint on row values. Specifically, if the SID starts with 9, the value of GradFacultyStatus must be 1.

To put this relation in DK/NF, we proceed as in Example 2. What are the basic themes of this relation? There is one regarding faculty personnel that relates FID, Fname, and GradFacultyStatus. Since FID and Fname determine GradFacultyStatus, either of these attributes can be the key, and this relation is in DK/NF (see Figure 5-17).

Now consider the data regarding students and advisers. Although it may first appear that there is only one theme, that of advising, the constraint that only graduate faculty can advise graduate students implies otherwise. Actually, there are two themes: graduate advising and undergraduate advising. Thus, Figure 5-17 contains a G-ADV relation for graduate students and a UG-ADV relation for undergraduates. Look at the domain definitions: GSID starts with a 9; Gfname is the Fname of a FACULTY tuple with GradFacultyStatus equal to 1; and UGSID must not begin with 1 or 9. All the constraints described in Figure 5-16 are implied by the key and domain definitions in Figure 5-17. These relations are therefore in DK/NF and have no modification anomalies.

To summarize, Figure 5-18 lists the normal forms and presents the defining characteristic of each.

➤ FIGURE 5-17

Domain/Key Definition of Example 3

Domain Definitions

FID	in CDDD, where C = 1; D = decimal digit
Fname	in CHAR (30)
Grad-faculty-status	in [0, 1]
GSID	in CDDD, where C = 9; D = decimal digit; graduate student
UGSID	in CDDD, WHERE C ≠ 1 and C ≠ 9; D = decimal digit; undergraduate student
Sname	in CHAR (30)

Additional Domain Definitions

Gfname	in {Fname of FACULTY, where GradFacultyStatus = 1}

Relations and Key Definitions

FACULTY (FID, Fname, GradFacultyStatus)
Key: FID or Fname

G-ADV (GSID, Sname, Gfname)
Key: GSID

UG-ADV (UGSID, Sname, Fname)
Key: UGSID

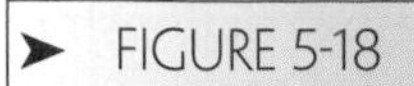
FIGURE 5-18

Summary of Normal Forms

Form	Defining Characteristic
1NF	Any relation
2NF	All nonkey attributes are dependent on all of each key.
3NF	There are no transitive dependencies.
BCNF	Every determinant is a candidate key.
4NF	There are no multivalued dependencies.
5NF	Not described in this discussion.
DK/NF	All constraints on relations are logical consequences of domains and keys.

➤ THE SYNTHESIS OF RELATIONS

In the previous section, we approached relational design from an analytical perspective. The question we asked was, Given a relation, is it in good form? Does it have modification anomalies? In this section, we look at relational design from a different perspective—a synthetic one. From this perspective, we ask, "Given a set of attributes with certain functional dependencies, what relations should we form?"

First, observe that two attributes, say, A and B, can be related in three ways:

1. They determine each other:
A → B and B → A
Hence, A and B have a one-to-one attribute relationship.

2. One determines the other.
A → B, but B not → A
Hence, A and B have a many-to-one relationship.

3. They are functionally unrelated.
A not → B and B not → A
Hence, A and B have a many-to-many attribute relationship.

ONE-TO-ONE ATTRIBUTE RELATIONSHIPS

If A determines B and B determines A, the values of the attributes have a one-to-one relationship. This must be because if A determines B, the relationship between A and B is many to one. It is also true, however, that if B determines A, the relationship between B and A must be many to one. For both statements to be true at the same time, the relationship between A and B must actually be one to one (which is a special case of many to one), and the relationship between B and A is also actually one to one. Therefore, the relationship is one to one.

This case is illustrated by FID and Fname in Examples 2 and 3 in the previous section on domain/key normal form. Each of these attributes uniquely identifies a faculty person. Consequently, one value of FID corresponds to exactly one value of Fname, and vice versa.

Three equivalent statements can be drawn from the example of FID and Fname:

- ➤ If two attributes functionally determine each other, the relationship of their data values is one to one.
- ➤ If two attributes uniquely identify the same thing (entity or object), the relationship of their data values is one to one.
- ➤ If two attributes have a one-to-one relationship, they functionally determine each other.

When creating a database with attributes that have a one-to-one relationship, the two attributes must occur together in at least one relation. Other attributes that are functionally determined by these (an attribute that is functionally determined by one of them is functionally determined by the other as well) may also reside in this same relation.

Consider FACULTY (FID, Fname, GradFacultyStatus) in Example 3 in the previous section. FID and Fname determine each other. GradFacultyStatus can also occur in this relation because it is determined by FID and Fname. Attributes that are not functionally determined by these attributes may not occur in a relation with them. Consider the relations FACULTY and PREPARATION in Example 2, in which both FID and Fname occur in FACULTY, but Class (from PREPARATION) may not. Class can have multiple values for a faculty member, so Class is not dependent on FID or Fname. If we added Class to the FACULTY relation, the key of FACULTY would need to be either (FID, Class) or (Fname, Class). In this case, however, FACULTY would not be in DK/NF because the dependencies between FID and Fname would not be logically implied by either of the possible keys.

These statements are summarized in the first column of Figure 5-19, and the record definition rules are listed in Figure 5-20. If A and B have a 1:1 relationship, they can reside in the same relation, say R. A determines B, and B determines A. The key of the relation can be either A or B. A new attribute, C, can be added to R if either A or B functionally determines C.

Attributes having a one-to-one relationship must exist together in at least one relation in order to establish their equivalence (FID of 198, for example, refers to Professor Heart). It is generally undesirable to have them occur together in more than one relation, however, because this causes needless data duplication. Often, one or both of the two attributes occur in other relations. In Example 2, Fname occurs in both PREPARATION and STUDENT. Although it would be possible to place Fname in PREPARATION and FID in STUDENT, this generally is bad practice, because when attributes are paired in this way, one of them should be selected to represent the pair in all other relations. Fname was selected in Example 2.

Many-to-One Attribute Relationships

If attribute A determines B but B does not determine A, the relationship among their data values is many to one. In the adviser relationship in Example 2, SID determines FID. Many students (SID) are advised by a faculty member (FID), but each student is advised by only one faculty member. This, then, is a many-to-one relationship.

For a relation to be in DK/NF, all constraints must be implied by keys, and thus every determinant must be a key. If A, B, and C are in the same relation and if A determines B, then A must be the key (meaning it also determines C). If,

➤ FIGURE 5-19

Summary of Three Types of Attribute Relationships

	Type of Attribute Relationship		
	One to One	Many to One	Many to Many
Relation Definition*	R(A,B)	S(C,D)	T(E,F)
Dependencies	A → B B → A	C → D D ↛ C	E ↛ F F ↛ E
Key	Either A or B	C	(E,F)
Rule for Adding Another Attribute	Either A or B → C	C → E	(E,F) → G

* The letters used in these relation definitions match those used in Figure 5-20

➤ FIGURE 5-20

Summary of Rules for Constructing Relations

Concerning One-to-One Attribute Relationships

- Attributes that have a one-to-one relationship must occur together in at least one relation. Call the relation *R* and the attributes *A* and *B*.
- Either *A* or *B* must be the key of *R*.
- An attribute can be added to *R* if it is functionally determined by *A* or *B*.
- An attribute that is not functionally determined by *A* or *B* cannot be added to *R*.
- *A* and *B* must occur together in *R*, but should not occur togehter in other relations.
- Either *A* or *B* should be consistently used to represent the pair in relations other than *R*.

Concerning Many-to-One Attribute Relationships

- Attributes that have a many-to-one relationship can exist in a relation together. Assume *C* determines *D* in relation *S*.
- *C* must be the key of *S*.
- An attribute can be added to *S* if it is determined by *C*.
- An attribute that is not determined by *C* cannot be added to *S*.

Concerning Many-to-Many Attribute Relationships

- Attributes that have a many-to-many relationship can exist in a relation together. Assume two such attributes, *E* and *F*, reside together in relation *T*.
- The key of *T* must be (*E*, *F*).
- An attribute can be added to *T* if it is determined by the combination (*E*, *F*).
- An attribute may not be added to *T* if it is not determined by the combination (*E*, *F*).
- If adding a new attribute, *G*, expands the key to (*E*, *F*, *G*), then the theme of the relation has been changed. Either *G* does not belong in *T* or the name of *T* must be changed to reflect the new theme.

instead, (A, B) determines C, then (A, B) must be the key. In this latter case, no other functional dependency, such as A determines B, is allowed.

You can apply these statements to database design in the following way: When constructing a relation, if A determines B, the only other attributes you can add to the relation must also be determined by A. For example, suppose you have put SID and Building together in a relation called STUDENT. You may add any other attribute determined by SID, such as Sname, to this relation. But if the attribute Fee is determined by Building, you may not add it to this relation. Fee can be added only if SID → Fee.

These statements are summarized in the center column of Figure 5-19. If C and D have an N:1 relationship, they may reside together in a relation, say, S. C will determine D, but D will not determine C. The key of S will be C. Another attribute, E, can be added to S only if C determines E.

Many-to-Many Attribute Relationships

If A does not determine B and B does not determine A, the relationship among their data values is many to many. In Example 2, Fname and Class have a many-to-many relationship. A professor teaches many classes, and a class is taught by many professors. In a many-to-many relationship, both attributes must be a key of the relation. For instance, the key of PREPARATION in Example 2 is the combination (Fname, Class).

When constructing relations that have multiple attributes as keys, you can add new attributes that are functionally dependent on all of the key.

NumberOfTimesTaught is functionally dependent on both (Fname, Class) and can be added to the relation. FacultyOffice, however, cannot be added because it would be dependent only on Fname, not on Class. If FacultyOffice needs to be stored in the database, it must be added to the relation regarding faculty, not to the relation regarding preparations.

These statements are summarized in the right column of Figure 5-19. If E and F have an M:N relationship, E does not determine F, and F does not determine E. Both E and F can be put into a relation T, and if this is done, the key of T will be the composite (E, F). A new attribute, G, can be added to T if it is determined by all of (E, F). It cannot be added to T if it is determined by only one of E or F.

Consider a similar example. Suppose we add Classroom Number to PREPARATION. Is ClassroomNumber functionally determined by the key of PREPARATION, (Fname, Class)? Most likely it is not, because a professor could teach a particular class in many different rooms.

The composite (Fname, Class) and ClassroomNumber have an M:N relationship. Since this is so, the rules in Figure 5-19 can be applied, but with E representing (Fname, Class) and F representing ClassroomNumber. Now we can compose a new relation, T, with attributes Fname, Class, and ClassroomNumber. The key becomes (Fname, Class, ClassroomNumber). In this situation, we have created a new relation with a new theme. Consider relation T, which contains faculty names, classes, and classroom numbers. The theme of this relation is therefore no longer PREPARATION but, rather, WHO-WHAT-WHERE-TAUGHT.

Changing the theme may or may not be appropriate. If ClassroomNumber is important, the theme does need to be changed. In that case, PREPARATION is the wrong relation, and WHO-WHAT-WHERE-TAUGHT is a more suitable theme.

On the other hand, depending on user requirements, PREPARATION may be completely suitable as it is. If so, then if ClassroomNumber belongs in the database at all, it should be located in a different relation—perhaps SECTION-NUMBER, CLASS-SECTION, or some similar relation.

➤ MULTI-VALUE DEPENDENCIES, ITERATION 2

The discussion about many-to-many attribute value relationships may make the concept of multi-value dependencies easier to understand. The problem with the relation STUDENT (SID, Major, Activity) in Figure 5-9 is that it has *two* different many-to-many relationships—one between SID and Major and the other between SID and Activity. Clearly, a student's various majors have nothing to do with his or her various activities. Putting both of these many-to-many relationships in the same relation, however, makes it appear as if there is some association.

Major and Activity are independent, and there would be no problem if a student had only one of each. SID would functionally determine Major and Activity, and the relation would be in DK/NF. In this case, both the relationships between Major and SID and Activity and SID would be many to one.

Another way of perceiving the difficulty is to examine the key (SID, Major, Activity). Since STUDENT has many-to-many relationships, all of the attributes have to be in the key. Now what theme does this key represent? We might say the combination of a student's studies and activities. But this is not one thing; it is plural. One row of this relation describes only part of the combination, and in order to get the whole picture, we need all of the rows about a particular student. *In general, a row should have all of the data about one instance of the relation's theme.* A row of Customer, for example, should have all the data we want about a particular customer.

Consider PREPARATION in Example 2 in the section on domain/key normal form. The key is (Fname, Class). The theme this represents is that a particular professor is prepared to teach a particular class. We need only one row of the relation to get all of the information (the relation might include NumberOfTimesTaught, AverageCourseEvaluationScore, and so on) we have about the combination of that professor and that class. Looking at more rows will not generate any more information about it.

As you know, the solution to the multi-value dependency constraint problem is to split the relation into two relations, each with a single theme. STU-MAJOR shows the combination of a student and a major. Everything we know about the combination is in a single row, and we will not gain more information about that combination by examining more rows.

➤ OPTIMIZATION

In this chapter we examined the concepts of normalization and demonstrated how to create tables that are in DK/NF. The process we used is usually suitable, but sometimes the result of normalization is not worth the cost. In this last section we look at two ways in which that can happen.

DE-NORMALIZATION

As stated, normalized relations avoid modification anomalies, and on that ground they are preferred to unnormalized relations. Judged on other grounds, however, normalization is sometimes not worth it.

Consider this relation:

CUSTOMER (CustNumber, CustName, City, State, Zip),

where CustNumber is the key.

This relation is not in DK/NF because it contains the functional dependency Zip → (City, State), which is not implied by the key, CustNumber. Hence, there is a constraint not implied by the definition of keys.

This relation can be transformed into the following two DK/NF relations:

CUSTOMER (CustNumber, CustName, Zip)

where the key is CustNumber

CODES (Zip, City, State)

where the key is Zip

These two tables are in domain/key normal form, but they most likely do not represent a better design. The unnormalized table is probably better because it will be easier to process and the disadvantages of duplicating the City and State data are not very important.

For another example of de-normalization, consider the relation

COLLEGE (CollegeName, Dean, AssistantDean)

and suppose that a college has one dean and from one to three assistant deans. In this case, the key of the table is (CollegeName, AssistantDean). This table is not in domain/key normal form because the constraint, CollegeName → Dean, is not a logical consequence of the table's key.

COLLEGE can be normalized into the relations

DEAN (CollegeName, Dean)

and

ASSISTANT-DEAN(CollegeName, AssistantDean)

But now whenever a database application needs to obtain data about the college, it must read at least two rows and possibly as many as four rows of data. An alternative to this design is to place all three AssistantDeans into the COLLEGE table, each in a separate attribute. The table would then be

COLLEGE1 (CollegeName, Dean, AssistantDean1, AssistantDean2, AssistantDean3)

COLLEGE1 is in DK/NF because all of its attributes are functionally dependent on the key CollegeName. But something has been lost. To see what, suppose that you wanted to determine the names of the COLLEGEs that had an assistant dean named 'Mary Abernathy.' To do this, you would have to look for this value in each of the three AssistantDean columns. Your query would appear something like this:[6]

```
SELECT   CollegeName
FROM     COLLEGE1
WHERE    AssistantDean1 = 'Mary Abernathy' OR
         AssistantDean2 = 'Mary Abernathy' OR
         AssistantDean3 = 'Mary Abernathy'
```

Using the normalized design with ASSISTANT-DEAN, you would need only to state

```
SELECT   CollegeName
FROM     ASSISTANT-DEAN
WHERE    AssistantDean = 'Mary Abernathy'
```

In this example there are three possible solutions, each with advantages and disadvantages. The choice among them is an artistic one; there is no hard-and-fast rule stating how to select among them. The best choice depends on the processing characteristics of the applications that use this database.

In summary, relations are sometimes purposely left unnormalized or are normalized and then de-normalized. Often this is done to improve performance. Whenever data must be combined from two separate tables, the DBMS must perform additional work. In most cases, at least two reads are required instead of one.

Controlled Redundancy

One of the advantages of normalized relations is that data duplication is minimized (only key values appear in more than one relation). For performance reasons, however, it is sometimes appropriate to duplicate data intentionally. Consider, for example, an order-processing application that accesses the ITEM table having the following columns:

PartNumber
PartName
PartColor
PartDescription
PartPicture
QuantityOnHand
QuantityOnOrder

---

[6]These statements are examples of SQL, a relational language that we will discuss in detail in Chapter 9. For now, just think of them intuitively; you will learn the format of them in that chapter.

StandardPrice
StandardCost
BuyerName

Assume that PartNumber is the key and that the table is in DK/NF. Also assume the attribute PartDescription is a potentially long memo field, and PartPicture is a binary column at least 256K bytes in length.

The order-processing application will need to access this table to obtain PartName, PartColor, StandardPrice, and QuantityOnHand. Assume it does not need PartDescription or PartPicture. Depending on the characteristics of the DBMS in use, it is possible that the presence of these two large columns will slow processing considerably. If this is the case, the database designers might decide to duplicate some of the data in a second table that contains only data required for the ordering process. They might define a table like ORDERITEM (PartNumber, PartName, PartColor, StandardPrice, QuantityOnHand) that is used only for the order-processing application.

In this case, the designers are creating a potential for serious data integrity problems. They will need to develop both programmatic and manual controls to ensure that such problems do not occur. They would only create such a design if they judged the increased performance was worth the cost of the controls and the risk of the integrity problems.

Another reason for controlled redundancy is to create tables that are used for reporting and decision support purposes only. We will address this topic further in Chapter 17.

➤ SUMMARY

The relational model is important for two reasons: It can be used to express DBMS-independent database designs, and it is the basis for an important category of DBMS-products. Normalization can be used as a guideline for checking the desirability and correctness of relations.

A relation is a two-dimensional table that has single-value entries. All entries in a given column are of the same kind; columns have a unique name; and the order of the columns is not important. Columns are also called attributes. No two rows of a table are identical, and the order of the rows in the table is not important. Rows are also called tuples. The terms *table, file,* and *relation* are synonymous; the terms *column, field,* and *attribute* are synonymous; and the terms *row, record,* and *tuple* are synonymous.

A functional dependency is a relationship between attributes. Y is functionally dependent on X if the value of X determines the value of Y. A determinant is a group of one or more attributes on the left-hand side of a functional dependency. For example, if X determines Y, then X is the determinant. A key is a group of one or more attributes that uniquely identifies a tuple. Every relation has at least one key; because every row is unique, in the most extreme case the key is the collection of all of the attributes in the relation. Although a key is always unique, the determinant in a functional dependency need not be. Whether or not attributes are keys and whether or not they are attributes are determined not by an abstract set of rules but by the users' semantics.

When updated, some relations suffer from undesirable consequences called modification anomalies. A deletion anomaly occurs when the deletion of a row loses information about two or more entities. An insertion anomaly occurs when the relational structure forces the addition of facts about two entities at the same time. Anomalies can be removed by splitting the relation into two or more relations.

There are many types of modification anomalies. Relations can be classified by the types of anomaly that they eliminate. Such classifications are called normal forms.

By definition, every relation is in first normal form. A relation is in second normal form if all nonkey attributes are dependent on all of the key. A relation is in third normal form if it is in second normal form and has no transitive dependencies. A relation is in Boyce–Codd normal form if every determinant is a candidate key. A relation is in fourth normal form if it is in Boyce–Codd normal form and has no multi-value dependencies. The definition of fifth normal form is intuitively obscure, and so we did not define it.

A relation is in domain/key normal form if every constraint on the relation is a logical consequence of the definition of domains and keys. A constraint is any constraint on the static values of attributes whose truth can be evaluated. As we defined them, domains have both a physical and a semantic part. In the context of DK/NF, however, domain refers only to the physical description.

An informal way of expressing DK/NF is to say that every relation must have only a single theme. For example, it might concern PROFESSORs or STUDENTs but not both PROFESSORs and STUDENTs at the same time.

Normalization is a process of analyzing relations. It is also possible to construct relations by a process of synthesis by considering the relationships among attributes. If two attributes functionally determine each other, they have a one-to-one relationship. If one attribute functionally determines the other, but not the reverse, the attributes have a one-to-many relationship. If neither attribute determines the other, they have a many-to-many relationship. These facts can be used when constructing relations as summarized in Figure 5-20.

In some cases, normalization is not desirable. Whenever a table is split into two or more tables, referential integrity constraints are created. If the cost of the extra processing of the two tables and their integrity constraint is greater than the benefit of avoiding modification anomalies, then normalization is not recommended. In addition, in some cases, creating repeating columns is preferred to the standard normalization techniques, and in other cases controlled redundancy is used to improve performance.

➤ GROUP I QUESTIONS

5.1 What restrictions must be placed on a table for it to be considered a relation?

5.2 Define the following terms: *relation, tuple, attribute, file, record, field, table, row, column.*

5.3 Define *functional dependency.* Give an example of two attributes that have a functional dependency, and give an example of two attributes that do not have a functional dependency.

5.4 If SID functionally determines Activity, does this mean that only one value of SID can exist in the relation? Why or why not?

5.5 Define *determinant.*

5.6 Give an example of a relation having a functional dependency in which the determinant has two or more attributes.

5.7 Define *key.*

5.8 If SID is a key of a relation, is it a determinant? Can a given value of SID occur more than once in the relation?

5.9 What is a deletion anomaly? Give an example other than one in this text.

5.10 What is an insertion anomaly? Give an example other than one in this text.

5.11 Explain the relationship of first, second, third, Boyce–Codd, fourth, fifth, and domain/key normal forms.

5.12 Define *second normal form.* Give an example of a relation in 1NF but not in 2NF. Transform the relation into relations in 2NF.

5.13 Define *third normal form.* Give an example of a relation in 2NF but not in 3NF. Transform the relation into relations in 3NF.

5.14 Define *BCNF.* Give an example of a relation in 3NF but not in BCNF. Transform the relation into relations in BCNF.

5.15 Define *multi-value dependency.* Give an example.

5.16 Why are multi-value dependencies not a problem in relations with only two attributes?

5.17 Define *fourth normal form.* Give an example of a relation in BCNF but not in 4NF. Transform the relation into relations in 4NF.

5.18 Define *domain/key normal form.* Why is it important?

5.19 Transform the following relation into DK/NF. Make and state the appropriate assumptions about functional dependencies and domains.

EQUIPMENT (Manufacturer, Model, AcquisitionDate, BuyerName, BuyerPhone, PlantLocation, City, State, ZIP)

5.20 Transform the following relation into DK/NF. Make and state the appropriate assumptions about functional dependencies and domains.

INVOICE (Number, CustomerName, CustomerNumber, CustomerAddress, ItemNumber, ItemPrice, ItemQuantity, SalespersonNumber, SalespersonName, Subtotal, Tax, TotalDue)

5.21 Answer Question 5.20 again, but this time add attribute CustomerTaxStatus (0 if nonexempt, 1 if exempt). Also add the constraint that there will be no tax if CustomerTaxStatus = 1.

5.22 Give an example, other than one in this text, in which you would judge normalization to be not worthwhile. Show the relations and justify your design.

5.23 Explain two situations in which database designers might intentionally choose to create data duplication. What is the risk of such designs?

➤ GROUP II QUESTIONS

5.24 Consider the following relation definition and sample data:

PROJECT Relation

ProjectID	EmployeeName	EmployeeSalary
100A	Jones	64K
100A	Smith	51K
100B	Smith	51K
200A	Jones	64K
200B	Jones	64K
200C	Parks	28K
200C	Smith	51K
200D	Parks	28K

PROJECT (ProjectID, EmployeeName, EmployeeSalary)
Where ProjectID is the name of a work project

EmployeeName is the name of an employee who works on that project
EmployeeSalary is the salary of the employee whose name is EmployeeName

Assuming that all of the functional dependencies and constraints are apparent in this data, which of the following statements is true?

a. ProjectID → EmployeeName
b. ProjectID → EmployeeSalary
c. (ProjectID, EmployeeName) → EmployeeSalary
d. EmployeeName → EmployeeSalary
e. EmployeeSalary → ProjectID
f. EmployeeSalary → (ProjectID, EmployeeName)

Answer these questions:

g. What is the key of PROJECT?
h. Are all nonkey attributes (if any) dependent on all of the key?
i. In what normal form is PROJECT?
j. Describe two modification anomalies from which PROJECT suffers.
k. Is ProjectID a determinant?
l. Is EmployeeName a determinant?
m. Is (ProjectID, EmployeeName) a determinant?
n. Is EmployeeSalary a determinant?
o. Does this relation contain a transitive dependency? If so, what is it?
p. Redesign this relation to eliminate the modification anomalies.

5.25 Consider the following relation definition and sample data:

PROJECT-HOURS Relation

EmployeeName	ProjectID	TaskID	Phone	TotalHours
Don	100A	B-1	12345	12
Don	100A	P-1	12345	12
Don	200B	B-1	12345	12
Don	200B	P-1	12345	12
Pam	100A	C-1	67890	26
Pam	200A	C-1	67890	26
Pam	200D	C-1	67890	26

PROJECT-HOURS (EmployeeName, ProjectID, TaskID, Phone, TotalHours)
Where EmployeeName is the name of an employee
ProjectID is the name of a project
TaskID is the name standard work task
Phone is the employee's telephone number
TotalHours is the hours worked by the employee on this project

Assuming that all of the functional dependencies and constraints are apparent in this data, which of the following statements is true?

a. EmployeeName → ProjectID
b. EmployeeName → ProjectID
c. EmployeeName → TaskID

d. EmployeeName →→ TaskID
e. EmployeeName → Phone
f. EmployeeName → TotalHours
g. (EmployeeName, ProjectID) → TotalHours
h. (EmployeeName, Phone) → TaskID
i. ProjectID → TaskID
j. TaskID → ProjectID

Answer these questions:

k. List all of the determinants.
l. Does this relation contain a transitive dependency? If so, what is it?
m. Does this relation contain a multi-value dependency? If so, what are the unrelated attributes?
n. Describe the deletion anomaly that this relation contains.
o. How many themes does this relation have?
p. Redesign this relation to eliminate the modification anomalies. How many relations did you use? How many themes does each of your new relations contain?

5.26 Consider the following domain, relation, and key definitions:

Domain Definitions

EmployeeName	in	CHAR(20)
PhoneNumber	in	DEC(5)
EquipmentName	in	CHAR(10)
Location	in	CHAR(7)
Cost	in	CURRENCY
Date	in	YYMMDD
Time	in	HHMM where HH between 00 and 23 and MM between 00 and 59

Definitions of Relation, Key, and Constraint

EMPLOYEE (EmployeeName, PhoneNumber)
Key: EmployeeName
Constraints: EmployeeName → PhoneNumber

EQUIPMENT (EquipmentName, Location, Cost)
Key: EquipmentName
Constraints: EquipmentName → Location
EquipmentName → Cost

APPOINTMENT (Date, Time, EquipmentName, EmployeeName)
Key: (Date, Time, EquipmentName)
Constraints: (Date, Time, EquipmentName) → EmployeeName

a. Modify the definitions to add this constraint: An employee may not sign up for more than one equipment appointment.
b. Define nighttime to refer to the hours between 2100 and 0500. Add an attribute Employee Type whose value is 1 if the employee works during nighttime. Change this design to enforce the constraint that only employees who work at night can schedule nighttime appointments.

➤ FIREDUP PROJECT QUESTIONS

FiredUp hired a team of database designers (who should have been fired!) who created the following relations for a database to keep track of their stove, repair, and customer data. See the projects at the ends of Chapters 1 through 3 to review their needs. For each of the following relations, specify candidate keys, functional dependencies, and multi-valued dependencies (if any). Justify these specifications unless they are obvious. Given your specifications about keys and so on, what normal form does each relation have? Transform each relation into two or more relations that are in domain/key normal form. Indicate the primary key of each table, candidate keys, foreign keys, and specify any referential integrity constraints.

In answering these questions, assume the following:

- Stove type and version determine tank capacity.
- A stove can be repaired many times, but never more than once on a given day.
- Each stove repair has its own repair invoice.
- A stove can be registered to different users, but never at the same time.
- A stove has many component parts and each component part can be used on many stoves. Thus, FiredUp maintains records about part types, such as *burner valve,* and not about particular parts such as burner valve number 41734 manufactured on 12 December 2001.

A. PRODUCT1 (SerialNumber, Type, VersionNumber, TankCapacity, DateOfManufacture, InspectorInitials)

B. PRODUCT2 (SerialNumber, Type, TankCapacity, RepairDate, RepairInvoiceNumber, RepairCost)

C. REPAIR1 (RepairInvoiceNumber, RepairDate, RepairCost, RepairEmployeeName, RepairEmployeePhone)

D. REPAIR2 (RepairInvoiceNumber, RepairDate, RepairCost, RepairEmployeeName, RepairEmployeePhone, SerialNumber, Type, TankCapacity)

E. REPAIR3 (RepairDate, RepairCost, SerialNumber, DateOfManufacture)

F. STOVE1 (SerialNumber, RepairInvoiceNumber, ComponentPartNumber)

G. STOVE2 (SerialNumber, RepairInvoiceNumber, RegisteredOwnerID)
Assume there is a need to record the owner of a stove, even if it has never been repaired.

H. Given the assumptions of this case, the relations and attributes in items A–G, and your knowledge of small business, construct a set of domain/key relations for FiredUp. Indicate primary keys, foreign keys, and inter-relation constraints.

Database Design Using Entity-Relationship Models

In Chapter 3 we discussed the specification of data models using the entity-relationship model, and in Chapter 5 we studied the relational model and normalization. In this chapter, we bring these subjects together to illustrate the transformation of users' requirements expressed in entity-relationship models into relational database designs. These designs are independent of any particular DBMS.

This chapter has three sections. In the first, we show techniques for transforming entity-relationship data models into relational designs. Normalization has an important role, as you will see. The second section applies these techniques to transform four data structures that occur frequently in database applications. Finally, a discussion of surrogate keys and null values concludes this chapter.

➤ TRANSFORMATION OF ENTITY-RELATIONSHIP MODELS INTO RELATIONAL DATABASE DESIGNS

According to the entity-relationship model, things that users want to track are represented by **entities,** and relationships among those entities are represented by explicitly defined **relationships.** This section describes how to transform those entities and relationships into the terms of the relational model.

REPRESENTING ENTITIES WITH THE RELATIONAL MODEL

The representation of entities by means of a relational model is straightforward. We begin by defining a relation for each entity. The name of the relation is the name of the entity, and the attributes of the relation are the attributes of

FIGURE 6-1

Representation of an Entity with a Relation: (a) CUSTOMER Entity and (b) Relation Representing CUSTOMER Entity

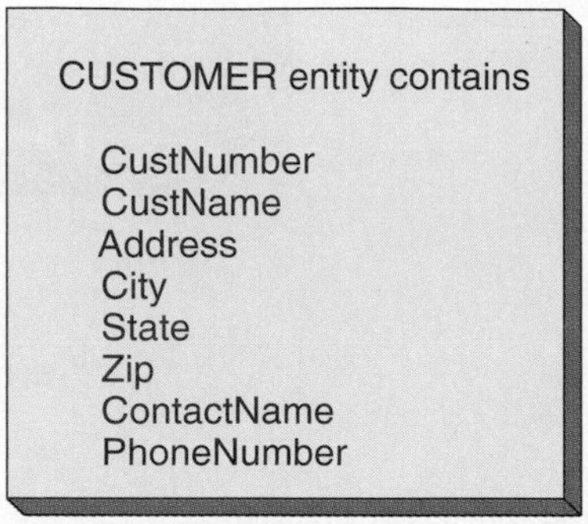

CUSTOMER entity contains

CustNumber
CustName
Address
City
State
Zip
ContactName
PhoneNumber

(a)

CUSTOMER (<u>CustNumber</u>, CustName, Address, City, State, Zip, ContactName, PhoneNumber)

(b)

the entity. Then we examine each relation according to the normalization criteria discussed in Chapter 5. It may or may not be necessary to change this initial design.

The example in Figure 6-1(a) is the entity shown in Figure 3-1. The CUSTOMER entity contains the following attributes: CustNumber, CustName, Address, City, State, Zip, ContactName, and PhoneNumber. To represent this entity with a relation, we define a relation for the entity and place the attributes in it as columns in the relation. If we know from the data model which attribute identifies this entity, that attribute will become the key of the relation. Otherwise, we must ask the users or otherwise investigate the requirements to determine what attribute or attributes can identify an entity. In this case, we assume that CustNumber is the key. In this figure, as in others to follow, the keys of the relations are underlined.

THE ROLE OF NORMALIZATION During the requirements phase, the only stipulation placed on an entity is that it be important to the user. No attempt is made to determine whether the entity fits any of the criteria for normalization discussed in Chapter 5. Therefore, once a relation has been defined for an entity, it should be examined according to the normalization criteria.

Consider, for example, the CUSTOMER relation in Figure 6-1(b). Is it in domain key/normal form (DK/NF)? To find out, we need to know the constraints on this relation. Without a full description of the underlying requirements, we do not know all of the constraints, such as all of the domain constraints. But we can discover some of the requirements just from the names of the attributes and knowledge about the nature of the business.

First, CustNumber determines all of the other attributes, because the unique values of CustName, Address, City, State, Zip, ContactName, and PhoneNumber can be determined from a given value of CustNumber. There are other constraints, however, that arise from other functional dependencies. Zip determines City and State, and ContactName determines PhoneNumber. To create a set of relations in DK/NF, we need to make these additional functional dependencies a logical consequence of domains and keys, and we can do that by defining the three relations shown in Figure 6-2. Observe that the key of CUSTOMER is CustNumber, the key of ZIP-TABLE is Zip, and the key of CONTACT is ContactName. Also note the referential integrity constraints.

The design in Figure 6-2 is in DK/NF, and there will be no modification anomalies. That is, we can add new zip codes and new contacts without having to add

➤ FIGURE 6-2

Representing the Customer Entity with Relations in Domain/Key Normal Form

CUSTOMER (<u>CustomerNumber</u>, Address, Zip, ContactName)

ZIP-TABLE (<u>Zip</u>, City, State)

CONTACT (<u>ContactName</u>, PhoneNumber)

Referential integrity constraints:

Zip in CUSTOMER must exist in Zip in ZIP-TABLE
ContactName in CUSTOMER must exist in ContactName in CONTACT

a customer with the new zip code or contact. Furthermore, when we delete the last customer in a given zip code, we do not lose the city and state for that zip code. But as we pointed out at the end of Chapter 5, most practitioners would consider this design too pure; breaking out Zip, City, and State will make the design hard to use. Hence, a better design would probably result by leaving Zip, City, and State in the CUSTOMER relation.

What about CONTACT? If the relationship between a contact and a company is 1:1 then little is gained by placing contact data in a table of its own. The relation in Figure 6-1(b) is acceptable. If the relationship is not 1:1, then CONTACT should be made into an entity, with the appropriate relationship to CUSTOMER (which could be N:1 or 1:N), and the E-R model revised accordingly.

In other examples the DK/NF design is preferable. Consider the SALES-COMMISSION entity in Figure 6-3(a). If we attempt to represent this entity with one relation, as shown in Figure 6-3(b), the result is a confused mess of attributes with many potential modification anomalies.

This relation obviously contains more than one theme. On examination, it contains a theme about salespeople, a theme about sales during some period, and a theme about sales commission checks. The relations in DK/NF that represent this entity are shown in Figure 6-3(c). Intuitively, this design seems superior to that in Figure 6-3(b); it is more straightforward and better fitting.

To summarize the discussion so far, when representing an entity with the relational model, the first step is to construct a relation that has all of the entity's attributes as columns. Then the relation is examined against the normalization criteria. In many cases, the design can be improved by developing sets of relations in DK/NF.

DK/NF relations are not always preferred, however. If the relations are contrived and difficult to work with, a non-DK/NF design may be better. Performance can also be a factor. Having to access two or three relations to obtain the data needed about a customer may be prohibitively time-consuming.

Regardless of our decision about whether to normalize, we should examine every entity's relation(s) against the normalization criteria. That is, if we are going to sin, we should make an informed and conscious decision to do so. In the process, we also learn the types of modification anomalies to which the relations are vulnerable.

REPRESENTATION OF WEAK ENTITIES Weak entities require special treatment when creating the relational design. Recall that a weak entity depends for its existence on another entity. If the weak entity is existence dependent but not ID dependent, it can be represented using the techniques described in the last section. The existence dependency needs to be recorded in the relational design so that no application will create a weak entity without its proper parent (the entity on which the weak entity depends). Moreover, a business rule needs to be

➤ FIGURE 6-3

Entity with Appropriate Normalization: (a) SALES-COMMISSION Entity, (b) Representing SALES-COMMISSION with a Single Relation, and (c) Representing SALES-COMMISSION with Domain/Key Normal Form Relations

SALES-COMMISSION entity contains

SalespersonNumber
SalespersonName
Phone
CheckNumber
CheckDate
CommissionPeriod
TotalCommissionSales
CommissionAmount
BudgetCategory

(a)

SALES-COMMISSION (SalespersonNumber, SalespersonName, Phone, <u>CheckNumber</u>, CheckDate, CommissionPeriod, TotalCommissionSales, CommissionAmount, BudgetCategory)

Functional dependencies:
CheckNumber is key
SalespersonNumber determines SalespersonName, Phone, BudgetCategory
(SalespersonNumber, CommissionPeriod) determines TotalCommissionSales, CommissionAmount

(b)

SALESPERSON(<u>SalespersonNumber</u>, SalespersonName, Phone, BudgetCategory)
SALES (<u>SalespersonNumber</u>, <u>CommissionPeriod</u>, TotalCommissionSales, CommissionAmount)
COMMISSION-CHECK (<u>CheckNumber</u>, CheckDate, SalespersonNumber, CommissionPeriod)

Referential integrity constraints:
SalespersonNumber in SALES must exist in SalespersonNumber in SALESPERSON
(SalespersonNumber, CommissonPeriod) in COMMISSION-CHECK must exist in (SalespersonNumber, CommissionPeriod) in SALES

(c)

implemented so that when the parent is deleted, the weak entity is also deleted. These rules should be described in the relational design.

This situation is slightly different if the weak entity also is ID dependent. In Figure 6-4(a), LINE-ITEM is an ID-dependent weak entity. It is weak because its logical existence depends on INVOICE, and it is ID dependent because its identifier contains the identifier of INVOICE.

When creating a relation for an ID-dependent entity, we must ensure that both the key of the parent and the key of the entity itself appear in the relation. For example, consider what would happen if we merely established a relation for LINE-ITEM and did not include the key of INVOICE. Such a relation is shown in Figure 6-4(b). What is the key of this relation? Because LINE-ITEM is ID dependent, it does not have a complete key, and, in fact, this relation could very well have duplicate rows. (This would happen if two invoices had the same quantity of the same item on the same line.)

Thus, for an ID-dependent weak entity, it is necessary to add the key of the parent entity to the weak entity's relation, and this added attribute becomes part of the weak entity's key. In Figure 6-4(c), we have added InvoiceNumber, the key

➤ FIGURE 6-4

Relational Representation of a Weak Entity: (a) Example Weak Entity, (b) Relation Representing LINE-ITEM with Improper Key, and (c) LINE-ITEM Relation with Proper Key

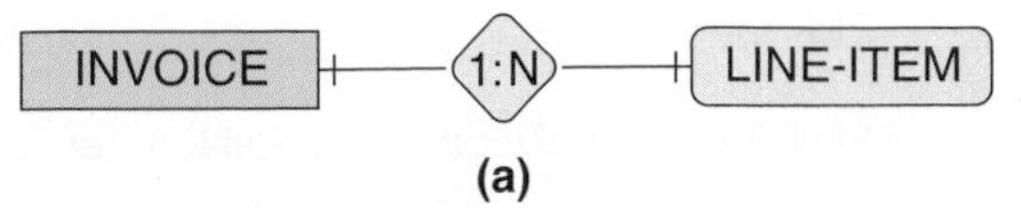

(a)

LINE-ITEM (LineNumber, Qty, ItemNumber, Description, Price, ExtPrice)

(b)

LINE-ITEM (InvoiceNumber, LineNumber, Qty, ItemNumber, Description, Price, ExtPrice)

(c)

of INVOICE, to the attributes in LINE-ITEM. The key of LINE-ITEM is the composite {InvoiceNumber, LineNumber}.

Representing HAS-A Relationships

There are two types of relationships in the E-R model: HAS-A relationships among entities of different logical types and IS-A relationships among entities that are subtypes of a common logical type. In this section we consider HAS-A relationships; later we discuss IS-A relationships. There are three types of HAS-A relationships: one-to-one, one-to-many, and many-to-many.

REPRESENTING ONE-TO-ONE RELATIONSHIPS The simplest form of binary relationship is a one-to-one (1:1) relationship, in which an entity of one type is related to no more than one entity of another type. In the example of EMPLOYEE and AUTO, suppose that an employee is assigned exactly one automobile and an auto is assigned to exactly one employee. An E-R diagram for this relationship is shown in Figure 6-5.

Representing a 1:1 relationship with the relational model is straightforward. First each entity is represented with a relation, and then the key of one of the relations is placed in the other. In Figure 6-6(a), the key of EMPLOYEE is stored in AUTO, and in Figure 6-6(b), the key of AUTO is stored in EMPLOYEE.

When the key of one relation is stored in a second relation, it is called a **foreign key.** In Figure 6-6(a), EmployeeNumber is a foreign key in AUTO, and in Figure 6-6(b), LicenseNumber is a foreign key in EMPLOYEE. In this figure, foreign keys are shown in italics, but sometimes you may see foreign keys depicted by a dashed underline. In still other cases, foreign keys are not denoted in any special way. In this text, when there is a danger of confusion, we show foreign keys in italics, but most of the time, they do not receive any special notation.

For a 1:1 relationship, the key of either table can be placed as a foreign key in the other table. In Figure 6-6(a) the foreign key LicenseNumber is placed in EMPLOYEE. With this design, we can navigate from EMPLOYEE to AUTO or from AUTO to EMPLOYEE. In the first case, we have an employee and want the auto assigned to that employee. To get the employee data, we use EmployeeNumber to obtain the employee's row in EMPLOYEE. From this row, we obtain the LicenseNumber of the auto assigned to that employee. We then use this number to look up the auto data in AUTO.

➤ FIGURE 6-5

Example of a 1:1 Relationship

EMPLOYEE — 1:1 — AUTO

Alternatives for Representing 1:1 Relationships: (a) Placing the Key of AUTO in EMPLOYEE and (b) Placing the Key of EMPLOYEE in AUTO

EMPLOYEE (EmployeeNumber, EmployeeName, Phone, . . . *LicenseNumber*)

AUTO (LicenseNumber, SerialNumber, Color, Make, Model, . . .)

Referential integrity constraint:
LicenseNumber in EMPLOYEE must exist in LicenseNumber in AUTO

(a)

EMPLOYEE (EmployeeNumber, EmployeeName, Phone, . . .)

AUTO (LicenseNumber, SerialNumber, Color, Make, Model, . . . *EmployeeNumber*)

Referential integrity constraint:
EmployeeNumber in AUTO must exist in EmployeeNumber in EMPLOYEE

(b)

Now consider the other direction. Assume that we have an auto and want the employee assigned to that auto. Using the design in Figure 6-6(a), we access the EMPLOYEE table and look up the row that has the given license number. The data about the employee who has been assigned that auto appear in that row.

We take similar actions to travel in either direction for the alternative design, in which the foreign key of EmployeeNumber is placed in AUTO. Using this design, to go from EMPLOYEE to AUTO, we go directly to the AUTO relation and look up the row in AUTO that has the given employee's number as its value of EmployeeNumber. To travel from AUTO to EMPLOYEE, we look up the row in AUTO having a given LicenseNumber. From this row, we extract the EmployeeNumber and use it to access the employee data in EMPLOYEE. Here we are using the term *look up* to mean "find a row given a value of one of its columns." Later, when we discuss particular DBMS models, we demonstrate how this is done.

Although the two designs in Figure 6-6 are equivalent in concept, they may be different in performance. For instance, if a query in one direction is more common than a query in the other, we may prefer one design to the other. Also, if the DBMS product is much faster in lookups on primary keys versus lookups on foreign keys, we might also prefer one design to another.

QUESTIONABLE 1:1 RELATIONSHIPS Figure 6-7 shows another 1:1 relationship, in which each EMPLOYEE has a JOB-EVALUATION and each JOB-EVALUATION corresponds to a particular employee. Observe from the hash marks that the relationship is mandatory in both directions. When the relationship is 1:1 and is mandatory in both directions, it is likely that the records are describing different aspects of the same entity, especially if, as is the case in Figure 6-7, both entities have the same key. When this occurs, the records should generally be combined into one relation. Learn to regard such 1:1 mandatory relationships with suspicion.

The separation of an entity into two relations can, however, sometimes be justified. One justification concerns performance. For example, suppose that the JOB-EVALUATION data are lengthy and are used far less frequently than are the other employee data. In these circumstances it may be appropriate to store

➤ FIGURE 6-7

EMPLOYEE — 1:1 — JOB-EVALUATION

Suspect 1:1 Relationship

JOB-EVALUATIONs in a separate table so that the more common requests for nonevaluation employee data can be processed faster.

Better security is the second justification for separating a single logical entity into two. If the DBMS does not support security at the data-item level, the JOB-EVALUATION data may need to be separated in order to prevent unauthorized users from accessing them. Or it may be desirable to place JOB-EVALUATION in a separate table so that the table can be placed on disk media that are accessible by certain users.

Do not conclude from this discussion that all 1:1 relationships are questionable; only those that appear to describe different aspects of the same entity are suspect. For example, the 1:1 mandatory relationship between EMPLOYEE and AUTO is quite suitable because each relation describes a logically different thing.

REPRESENTING ONE-TO-MANY RELATIONSHIPS The second type of binary relationship is one to many (1:N), in which an entity of one type can be related to many entities of another type. Figure 6-8 is an E-R diagram of a one-to-many relationship between professors and students. In this relationship, PROFESSOR is related to the many STUDENTs that he or she advises. As stated in Chapter 3, the oval means that the relationship between PROFESSOR and STUDENT is optional; that is, a professor need not have any advisees. The bar across the line at the other end means that a STUDENT row must correspond to a PROFESSOR row.

The terms **parent** and **child** are sometimes applied to relations in 1:N relationships. The parent relation is on the *one* side of the relationship, and the child relation is on the *many* side. In Figure 6-8(a), PROFESSOR is the parent entity, and STUDENT is the child entity.

Figure 6-8 shows two other one-to-many relationships. In Figure 6-8(b), a DORMITORY entity corresponds to many STUDENT entities, but a STUDENT entity corresponds to one DORMITORY. Furthermore, a dormitory does not have to have any students assigned to it, nor is a student required to live in a dormitory.

In Figure 6-8(c), a CUSTOMER is related to many APPOINTMENT entities, and a particular APPOINTMENT corresponds to only one CUSTOMER. Moreover, a CUSTOMER may or may not have an APPOINTMENT, but every APPOINTMENT must correspond to a CUSTOMER.

Representing 1:N relationships is simple and straightforward. First each entity is represented by a relation, and then the key of the relation representing the parent entity is placed in the relation representing the child entity. Thus, to represent the ADVISES relationship of Figure 6-8(a), we place the key of PROFESSOR, ProfessorName, in the STUDENT relation as shown in Figure 6-9.

Figure 6-9 is an example of what is sometimes called a **data structure diagram,** in which relations are shown in rectangles with lines representing

➤ FIGURE 6-8

Examples of One-to-Many Relationships: (a) Optional-to-Mandatory 1:N Relationship, (b) Optional-to-Optional 1:N Relationship, and (c) 1:N Relationship with Weak Entity

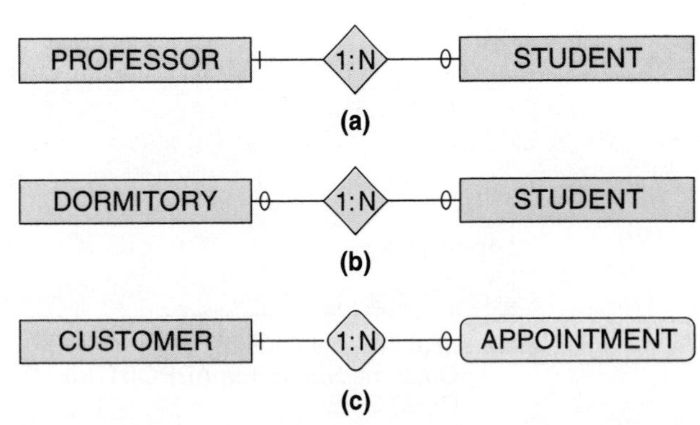

➤ FIGURE 6-9

Relational Representation of PROFESSOR and STUDENT Entities in Figure 6-8(a)

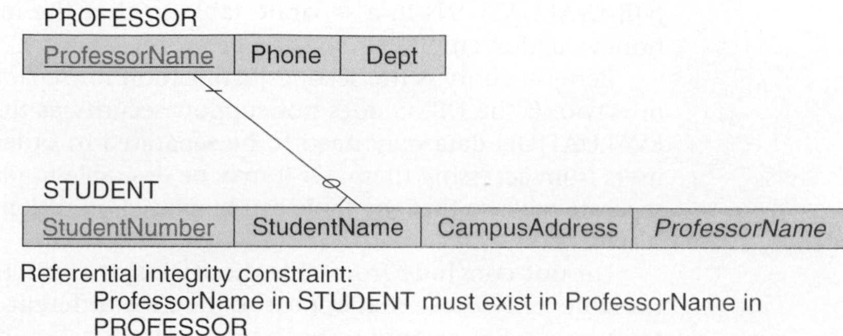

relationships and the key attributes are underlined. A fork, or crow's foot, on a relationship line indicates a many relationship.

In Figure 6-9, the fork at the STUDENT end of the relationship line means that there can be many STUDENT rows for each PROFESSOR. No fork at the other end means that each STUDENT can be advised by, at most, one PROFESSOR. As with E-R diagrams, hash lines are used to denote mandatory relationships, and ovals denote optional ones.

Notice that with ProfessorName stored as a foreign key in STUDENT, we can process the relationship in both directions. Given a StudentNumber, we can look up the appropriate row in STUDENT and get the name of his or her adviser from the row data. To obtain the rest of the PROFESSOR data, we use the professor name obtained from STUDENT to look up the appropriate row in PROFESSOR. To determine all of the students advised by a particular faculty member, we look up all rows in STUDENT having the professor's name as a value for ProfessorName. Student data is then taken from those rows.

Contrast this situation with one representing 1:1 relationships. In both cases, we store the key of one relation as a foreign key in the second relation. In a 1:1 relationship, however, it does not matter which key is moved to the second relation. But in a 1:N relationship, it does matter. *The key of the parent relation must be placed in the child relation.*

To understand this better, notice what would happen if we tried to put the key of the child into the parent relation (placing StudentNumber in PROFESSOR). Because attributes in a relation can have only a single value, each PROFESSOR record has room for only one student. Consequently, such a structure cannot be used to represent the "many" side of the 1:N relationship. Hence, to represent a 1:N relationship, we must place the key of the parent relation in the child relation.

Figure 6-10 shows the representation of the CUSTOMER and APPOINTMENT entities. We represent each entity with a relation. APPOINTMENT is an

➤ FIGURE 6-10

Relational Representation of the Weak Entity in Figure 6-8(c)

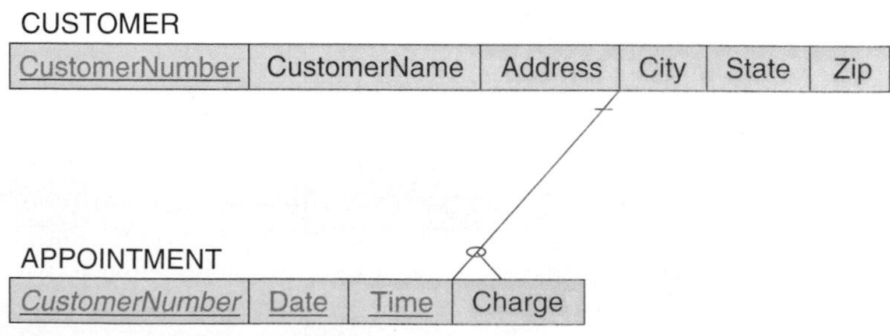

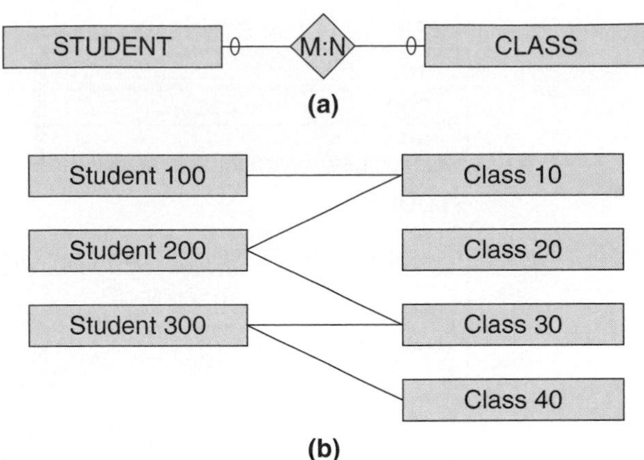

➤ FIGURE 6-11

Example of an M:N Relationship: (a) E-R Diagram of STUDENT to CLASS Relationship and (b) Sample Data for STUDENT to CLASS Relationship

ID-dependent weak entity, so it has a composite key consisting of the key of the entity on which it depends plus at least one attribute from itself. Here the key is (CustomerNumber, Date, Time). To represent the 1:N relationship, we would normally add the key of the parent to the child. In this case, however, the key of the parent (CustomerNumber) is already part of the child, so we do not need to add it.

REPRESENTING MANY-TO-MANY RELATIONSHIPS The third and final type of binary relationship is many to many (M:N), in which an entity of one type corresponds to many entities of the second type, and an entity of the second type corresponds to many entities of the first type.

Figure 6-11(a) presents an E-R diagram of the many-to-many relationship between students and classes. A STUDENT entity can correspond to many CLASS entities, and a CLASS entity can correspond to many STUDENT entities. Notice that both participants in the relationship are optional: A student does not need to be enrolled in a class, and a class does not need to have any students. Figure 6-11(b) gives sample data.

Many-to-many relationships cannot be directly represented by relations in the same way that one-to-one and one-to-many relationships are. To understand why this is so, try using the same strategy we did for 1:1 and 1:N relationships—placing the key of one relation as a foreign key in the other relation. First, define a relation for each of the entities; call them STUDENT and CLASS. Now try to put the key of STUDENT (say StudentNumber) in CLASS. Because multiple values are not allowed in the cells of a relation, we have room for only one StudentNumber, so we have no place to record the StudentNumber of the second and subsequent students.

The same problem will occur if we try to put the key of CLASS (say ClassNumber) in STUDENT. We can readily store the identifier of the first class in which a student is enrolled, but we have no place to store the identifier of additional classes.

Figure 6-12 shows another (*but incorrect*) strategy. In this case, we have stored a row in the CLASS relation for each STUDENT enrolled in one class, so there are two records for Class 10 and two for Class 30. The problem with this scheme is that we duplicate the class data and thus create modification anomalies. Many rows will need to be changed if, say, Class 10's schedule is modified. Also consider the insertion and deletion anomalies: How can we schedule a new class until a student has enrolled? And what will happen if Student 300 drops out of Class 40? Obviously, this strategy is unworkable.

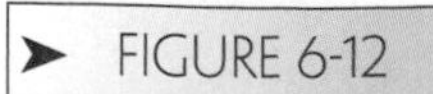

Incorrect Representation of an M:N Relationship

STUDENT

SID	Other STUDENT Data
100	. . .
200	. . .
300	. . .

CLASS

ClassNumber	ClassTime	Other CLASS Data	SID
10	10:00 MWF	. . .	100
10	10:00 MWF	. . .	200
30	3:00 TH	. . .	200
30	3:00 TH	. . .	300
40	8:00 MWF	. . .	300

The solution to this problem is to create a third relation that represents the relationship itself. Relation STU-CLASS has been defined in Figure 6-13(a). An instance of this relation is shown in Figure 6-13(b). Such relations are called **intersection relations** because each row documents the intersection of a particular student with a particular class. Notice in Figure 6-13(b) that there is one row in the intersection relation for each line between STUDENT and CLASS in Figure 6-11(b).

The data structure diagrams for the STUDENT-CLASS relationship appear in Figure 6-14. The relationship from CLASS to STU-CLASS is 1:N, and the relationship from STUDENT to STU-CLASS is also 1:N. In essence, we have decomposed the M:N relationship into two 1:N relationships. The key of STU-CLASS is the combination of the keys of both of its parents, (SID, ClassNumber). The key for an intersection relation is always the combination of parent keys. Also, note the parent relations are both required. A parent now must exist for each key value in the intersection relation.

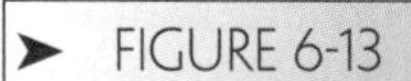

Representing an M:N Relationship: (a) Relations Needed to Represent STUDENT to CLASS Relationship and (b) Example Data for STUDENT to CLASS Relationship

STUDENT (StudentNumber, StudentName)

CLASS (ClassNumber, ClassName)

STU-CLASS (*StudentNumber*, *ClassNumber*)

Referential integrity constraints:
ClassNumber in STU-CLASS must exist in ClassNumber in CLASS
StudentNumber in STU-CLASS must exist in StudentNumber in STUDENT

(a)

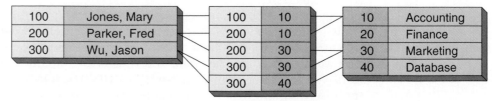

100	Jones, Mary
200	Parker, Fred
300	Wu, Jason

100	10
200	10
200	30
300	30
300	40

10	Accounting
20	Finance
30	Marketing
40	Database

(b)

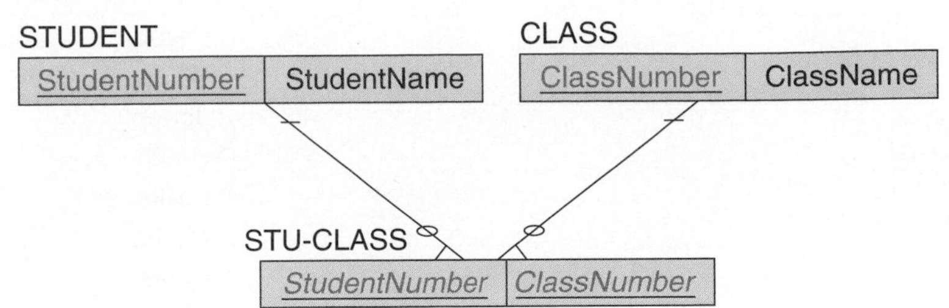

➤ FIGURE 6-14

Data Structure Diagram for STUDENT to CLASS Relationship

REPRESENTING RECURSIVE RELATIONSHIPS

A **recursive relationship** is a relationship among entities of the same class. Recursive relationships are not fundamentally different from other HAS-A relationships and can be represented using the same techniques. As with nonrecursive HAS-A relationships, there are three types of recursive relationships: 1:1, 1:N, and N:M; Figure 6-15 shows an example of each.

Consider first the SPONSOR relationship in Figure 6-15(a). As with a 1:1 relationship, one person can sponsor another person, and each person is sponsored by no more than one person. Figure 6-16(a) shows sample data for this relationship.

To represent 1:1 recursive relationships, we take an approach nearly identical to that for regular 1:1 relationships: We can place the key of the person being sponsored in the row of the sponsor, or we can place the key of the sponsor in the row of the person being sponsored. Figure 6-16(b) shows the first alternative, and Figure 6-16(c) shows the second. Both work, and so the choice depends on performance issues.

This technique is identical to that for nonrecursive 1:1 relationships, except that both the child and parent rows reside in the same relation. You can think of the process as follows: Pretend that the relationship is between two different relations. Determine where the key goes, and then combine the two relations into a single one.

To illustrate, consider the REFERRED-BY relationship in Figure 6-15(b). This is a 1:N relationship, as shown in the sample data in Figure 6-17(a). When this data is placed in a relation, one row represents the referrer, and the other rows represent those who have been referred. The referrer row takes the role of the parent, and the referred rows take the role of the child. As with all 1:N relationships, we place the key of the parent in the child. In Figure 6-17(b), we place the number of the referrer in all the rows that have been referred.

Now consider M:N recursive relationships. The TREATED-BY relationship in Figure 6-15(c) represents the situation in which doctors give treatments to each

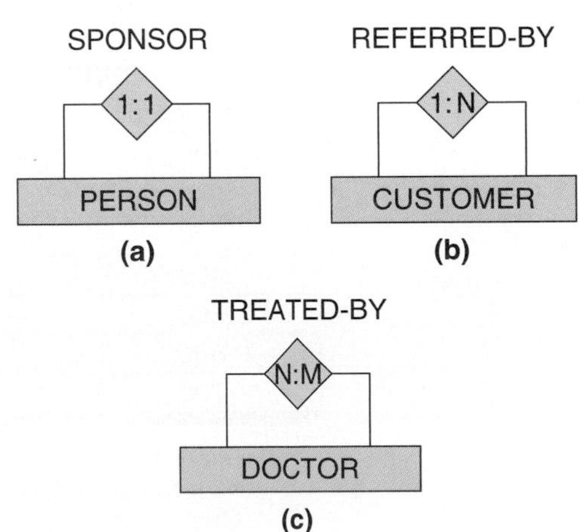

➤ FIGURE 6-15

Examples of Recursive Relationships: (a) 1:1 Recursive Relationship, (b) 1:N Recursive Relationship, and (c) N:M Recursive Relationship

➤ FIGURE 6-16

Example of a 1:1 Recursive Relationship: (a) Sample Data for 1:1 Recursive Relationship, (b) First Alternative for Representing a 1:1 Recursive Relationship, and (c) Second Alternative for Representing a 1:1 Recursive Relationship

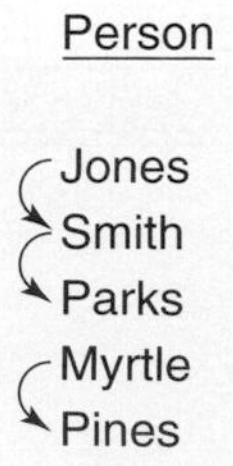

(a)

PERSON1 Relation

Person	PersonSponsored
Jones	Smith
Smith	Parks
Parks	null
Myrtle	Pines
Pines	null

Referential integrity constraint:
PersonSponsored in PERSON1 must exist in Person in PERSON1

(b)

PERSON2 Relation

Person	PersonSponsoredBy
Jones	null
Smith	Jones
Parks	Smith
Myrtle	null
Pines	Myrtle

Referential integrity constraint:
PersonSponsoredBy PERSON2 must exist in Person in PERSON2

(c)

➤ FIGURE 6-17

Example of a 1:N Recursive Relationship: (a) Sample Data for the REFERRED-BY Relationship and (b) Representing a 1:N Recursive Relationship by Means of a Relation

Customer Number	Referred These Customers
100	200, 400
300	500
400	600, 700

(a)

CUSTOMER Relation

CustomerNumber	CustomerData	ReferredBy
100	...	null
200	...	100
300	...	null
400	...	100
500	...	300
600	...	400
700	...	400

Referential integrity constraint:
ReferredBy in CUSTOMER must exist in CustomerNumber in CUSTOMER

(b)

Provider	Receiver
Jones	Smith
Parks	
Smith	Abernathy
Abernathy	Jones
Franklin	Franklin

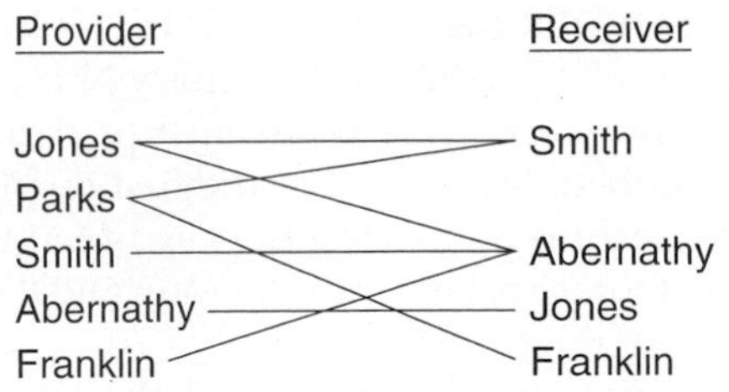

(a)

DOCTOR relation

Name	Other Attributes
Jones	...
Parks	...
Smith	...
Abernathy	...
O'Leary	...
Franklin	...

TREATMENT-INTERSECTION relation

Physician	Patient
Jones	Smith
Parks	Smith
Smith	Abernathy
Abernathy	Jones
Parks	Franklin
Franklin	Abernathy
Jones	Abernathy

Referential integrity constraints:

Physician in TREATMENT-INTERSECTION must exist in Name in DOCTOR

Patient in TREATMENT-INTERSECTION must exist in Name in DOCTOR

(b)

➤ FIGURE 6-18

Example of an M:N Recursive Relationship: (a) Sample Data for the TREATED-BY Relationship and (b) Representing an M:N Recursive Relationship by Means of Relations

other. Sample data is shown in Figure 6-18(a). As with other M:N relationships, we must create an intersection table that shows pairs of related rows. The name of the doctor in the first column is the one who provided the treatment, and the name of the doctor in the second column is the one who received the treatment. This structure is shown in Figure 6-18(b).

Recursive relationships are thus represented in the same way as are other relationships. The rows of the tables can take two different roles, however. Some are parent rows, and others are child rows. If a key is supposed to be a parent key and if the row has no parent, its value will be null. If a key is supposed to be a child key and the row has no child, its value will be null.

Representing Ternary and Higher-Order Relationships

Ternary relationships are represented using the techniques just described, but there is often a special consideration that needs to be documented as a business rule. Consider, for example, the entities ORDER, CUSTOMER, and SALESPERSON. In most cases, we can treat this ternary relationship as two separate binary relationships.

For example, assume an ORDER has a single CUSTOMER, but a CUSTOMER can have many ORDERs. Hence, that relationship is binary N:1. Similarly, suppose the ORDER has just one SALESPERSON, and a SALESPERSON has many ORDERs. That relationship is also binary N:1.

Both of these relationships can be represented using the techniques just described. We represent the first by placing the key of CUSTOMER in ORDER and the second by placing the key of SALESPERSON in ORDER. Thus, we have treated the ternary relationship among ORDER:CUSTOMER:SALESPERSON as two separate binary relationships.

Suppose, however, that the business has a rule that states that each CUSTOMER can place orders only with a particular SALESPERSON. In this case, the ternary relationship ORDER:CUSTOMER:SALESPERSON is constrained by an additional binary N:1 relationship between CUSTOMER and SALESPERSON. To represent the constraint, we need to add the key of SALESPERSON to CUSTOMER. The three relations will be as follows:

ORDER (OrderNumber, nonkey data attributes, *CustomerNumber, SalespersonNumber*)
CUSTOMER (CustomerNumber, nonkey data attributes, *SalespersonNumber*)
SALESPERSON (SalespersonNumber, nonkey data attributes)

The constraint that a particular CUSTOMER is called only by a particular SALESPERSON means that only certain values of CustomerNumber and SalespersonNumber can exist together in ORDER. Unfortunately, there is no way to express this constraint using the relational model. It must be documented in the design, however, and enforced either by stored procedures or by application programs. See Figure 6-19(a).

Other types of such binary constraints are MUST NOT and MUST COVER constraints. In a MUST NOT constraint, the binary relationship indicates combinations that are not allowed to occur in the ternary relationship. For example, the ternary relationship PRESCRIPTION:DRUG:CUSTOMER can be constrained by a

➤ FIGURE 6-19

Examples of Binary Constraints on Ternary Relationships (a) Example of MUST Binary Constraint on a Ternary Relationship

SALESPERSON Table

SalespersonNumber	Other nonkey data
10	
20	
30	

CUSTOMER Table

CustomerNumber	Other nonkey data	*SalespersonNumber*
1000		10
2000		20
3000		30

Binary MUST Constraint

ORDER Table

OrderNumber	Other nonkey data	*SalespersonNumber*	*CustomerNumber*
100		10	1000
200		20	2000
300		10	1000
400		30	3000
500			2000

Only 20 is allowed here

(a)

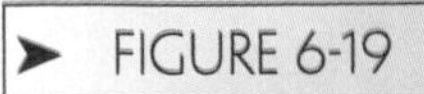
FIGURE 6-19

(Continued)

(b) Example of Binary MUST NOT Constraint on a Ternary Relationship

DRUG Table

DrugNumber	Other nonkey data
10	
20	
30	
45	
70	
90	

ALLERGY Table

CustomerNumber	DrugNumber	Other nonkey data
1000	10	
1000	20	
2000	20	
2000	45	
3000	30	
3000	45	
3000	70	

Binary MUST NOT Constraint

PRESCRIPTION Table

PrescriptionNumber	Other nonkey data	*DrugNumber*	*CustomerNumber*
100		45	1000
200		10	2000
300		70	1000
400		20	3000
500			2000

Neither 20 nor 45 can appear here

(b)

binary relationship in the ALLERGY table that indicates drugs that a customer is not allowed to take. See Figure 6-19(b).

In a MUST COVER constraint, the binary relationship indicates all combinations that must appear in the ternary relationship. For example, consider the relationship AUTO:REPAIR:TASK. Suppose that a given repair consists of a number of TASKs, all of which must be performed for the REPAIR to be successful. In this case, in the relation AUTO-REPAIR, when a given auto has a given REPAIR, then all of the TASKs for that repair must appear as rows in that relation. See Figure 6-19(c).

None of the three types of binary constraints discussed here can be represented in the relational design. Instead, all of the relationships must be treated as a combination of binary relationships. The constraints, however, must be documented as part of the design.

Representing IS-A Relationships (Subtypes)

The strategy for representing subtypes, or IS-A relationships, is somewhat different from the strategy used for HAS-A relationships. Consider the example of CLIENT with attributes ClientNumber, ClientName, and AmountDue. Suppose that there are three subtypes of CLIENT, namely, INDIVIDUAL-CLIENT, PARTNERSHIP-CLIENT, and CORPORATE-CLIENT, with the following attributes:

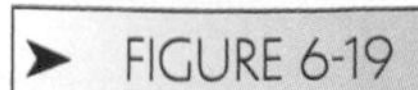

(Continued)

(c) Example of Binary MUST COVER Constraint on a Ternary Relationship

REPAIR Table

RepairNumber	Other nonkey data
10	
20	
30	
40	

TASK Table

TaskNumber	Other nonkey data	*RepairNumber*
1001		10
1002		10
1003		10
2001		20
2002		20
3001		30
4001		40

Binary MUST COVER Constraint

AUTO-REPAIR Table

InvoiceNumber	RepairNumber	TaskNumber	Other nonkey data
100	10	1001	
200	10	1002	
300	10	1003	
400	20	2001	
500	20		

2002 must appear here

(c)

INDIVIDUAL-CLIENT: Address, SocialSecurityNumber
PARTNERSHIP-CLIENT: ManagingPartnerName, Address, TaxIdentificationNumber
CORPORATE-CLIENT: ContactPerson, Phone, TaxIdentificationNumber

To represent this structure by means of relations, we define one relation for the supertype (CLIENT) and one relation for each subtype. Then we place each of the attributes of the supertype into the relation that represents it and each of the attributes of the subtypes into the relations that represent them. At this point, the subtype relations do not have a key. To create a key, we add the key of the supertype, or ClientNumber, to each of the subtypes. The final list of relations is

CLIENT (ClientNumber, ClientName, AmountDue)
INDIVIDUAL-CLIENT (ClientNumber, Address, SocialSecurityNumber)
PARTNERSHIP-CLIENT (ClientNumber, ManagingPartnerName, Address, TaxIdentificationNumber)
CORPORATE-CLIENT (ClientNumber, ContactPerson, Phone, TaxIdentificationNumber)

Note that with this structure, the relationship between a row in CLIENT and a row in one of the subtypes is 1:1. No client has more than one row in a subtype relation, and each subtype corresponds uniquely to one row of the supertype. Depending on the restrictions of the application, it might be possible for a row in CLIENT to correspond to multiple rows, each in a different subtype. But no row of CLIENT can correspond to more than one row in the *same* subtype relation.

It is possible for one or more of the subtypes to have a key of its own. For example, the application may call for a CorporateClientNumber that is distinct from ClientNumber. In that case, the key of CORPORATE-CLIENT is CorporateClientNumber. Since the relationship between CLIENT and CORPORATE-CLIENT is 1:1, it can be established by placing the key of one in the other. Most often, it is considered better design to place the key of the supertype relation in the key of the subtype relation. For this case, the structure of CORPORATE-CLIENT is

CORPORATE-CLIENT (<u>CorporateClientNumber</u>, ClientNumber, ContactPerson, Phone, TaxIdentificationNumber)

➤ EXAMPLE DESIGN

Figure 6-20(a) is a copy of the E-R diagram introduced in Chapter 3 as Figure 3-9. It contains all of the basic elements used in E-R diagrams. To represent this diagram by means of relations, we begin by establishing one relation for each entity. We assume the keys as follows:

RELATION	**KEY**
EMPLOYEE	EmployeeNumber
ENGINEER	EmployeeNumber
TRUCK	LicenseNumber
SERVICE	InvoiceNumber
CLIENT	ClientNumber
CLIENT-SERVICE	(InvoiceNumber, ClientNumber)
ENGINEER-CERTIFICATION	(EmployeeNumber, CertificationName)
CERTIFICATION	CertificationName

The next step is to examine each of these relations against the normalization criteria. The example does not tell us what attributes must be represented, so we cannot determine the constraints. We will assume that these relations are in DK/NF, although in practice we would need to check out that assumption against the attribute lists and constraints. For now, we will focus on the representation of relationships. The relations and their key attributes (including foreign keys) are listed in Figure 6-20(b).

The relationship between EMPLOYEE and ENGINEER is already represented because the relations have the same key, EmployeeNumber. ENGINEER and TRUCK have a 1:1 relationship and so can be related by placing the key of one in the other. Because a truck must be assigned to an employee, there will be no null values if we place EmployeeNumber in TRUCK, and so we will do that.

For the 1:N relationship between ENGINEER and SERVICE, we place the key of ENGINEER (the parent) in SERVICE (the child). The relationship between SERVICE and CLIENT is M:N, so we must create an intersection relation. Because this relationship has an attribute, Fee, we add that attribute to the intersection relation, CLIENT-SERVICE. For the 1:N recursive relationship, REFERRED-BY, we add the attribute ReferredBy to CLIENT. The name *ReferredBy* implies, correctly, that the key of the parent—the one client doing the referring—is being placed in the relation.

Because ENGINEER-CERTIFICATION is ID dependent on ENGINEER, we know that EmployeeNumber must be part of its key; thus, the key is a composite (EmployeeNumber, CertificationName). The dependency relationship is 1:N and so will be carried by EmployeeNumber. Finally, the relationship between CERTIFICATION and ENGINEER-CERTIFICATION is 1:N, so we would normally add the

➤ FIGURE 6-20

Relational Representation of an Example E-R Diagram: (a) E-R Diagram from Chapter 3 and (b) Relations Needed to Represent This E-R Diagram

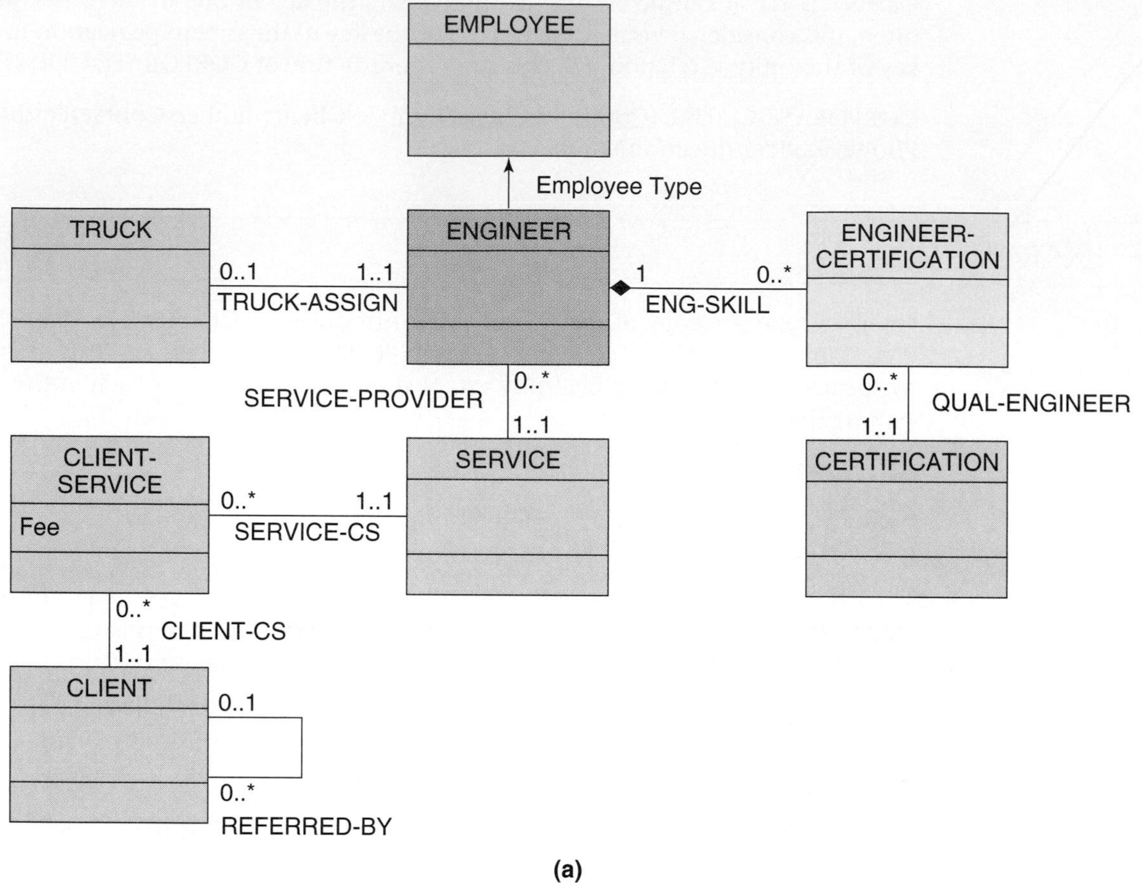

(a)

EMPLOYEE (<u>EmployeeNumber</u>, other nonkey EMPLOYEE attributes . . .)

ENGINEER (<u>EmployeeNumber</u>, other nonkey ENGINEER attributes . . .)

TRUCK (<u>LicenseNumber</u>, other nonkey TRUCK attributes, *EmployeeNumber*)

SERVICE (<u>InvoiceNumber</u>, other nonkey SERVICE attributes, *EmployeeNumber*)

CLIENT (<u>ClientNumber</u>, other nonkey CLIENT attributes, *ReferredBy*)

CLIENT-SERVICE (<u>InvoiceNumber</u>, <u>ClientNumber</u>, Fee)

ENGINEER-CERTIFICATION (<u>EmployeeNumber</u>, <u>CertificationName</u>, other nonkey ENGINEER-CERTIFICATION attributes)

CERTIFICATION (<u>CertificationName</u>, other nonkey CERTIFICATION attributes)

(b)

key of CERTIFICATION (the parent) to ENGINEER-CERTIFICATION. But that key is already part of the relation, so we need not do this.

Study this example to make sure that you understand the various types of relationships and how they are expressed in terms of the relations. All of the elements of the E-R model are present in Figure 6-20. See Question 6.40 regarding referential integrity constraints.

➤ TREES, NETWORKS, AND BILLS OF MATERIALS

Although neither the E-R model nor the semantic object model makes any assumptions about patterns of relationships among entities, some patterns do occur often enough that they have been given special names. These patterns are trees, simple networks, complex networks, and bills of materials. We introduce the concept of these patterns here, in the context of the E-R model.

TREES

A **tree,** or **hierarchy,** as it is sometimes called, is a data structure in which the elements of the structure have only one-to-many relationships with one another. Each element has at most one parent. Figure 6-21 is an example of a tree. According to standard terminology, each element is called a **node,** and the relationships among the elements are called **branches.** The node at the top of the tree is called the **root** (what a metaphor—the roots of real trees are normally at the bottom!). In Figure 6-21, Node 1 is the root of the tree.

Every node of a tree, except the root, has a **parent,** which is the node immediately above it. Thus, Node 2 is the parent of Node 5; Node 4 is the parent of Node 8; and so on. As we stated earlier, trees are distinguished from other data structures in that every node has at most one parent. We say at most one parent because the root node has no parent.

The descendants of a node are called **children.** In general, there is no limitation on the number of children that a node may have. Node 2 has two children, Nodes 5 and 6; Node 3 has no children; and Node 4 has three children, Nodes 7, 8, and 9. Nodes having the same parent are called **twins,** or **siblings.** For example, Nodes 5 and 6 are twins or siblings.

Figure 6-22(a) illustrates a tree of entities in which you can see several one-to-many relationships among entities in a university system. Colleges consist of many departments, which in turn have many professors and many administrative employees. Finally, professors advise many students who have received many grades. There are six different entity types in this structure, but all of the relationships are 1:N.

To represent a tree of entities using the relational model, we simply apply the concepts described in earlier sections of this chapter. First we transform each entity into a relation. Then we examine the relations generated against the normalization criteria and subdivide the relations if necessary. We represent the 1:N

➤ FIGURE 6-21

Example of a Tree

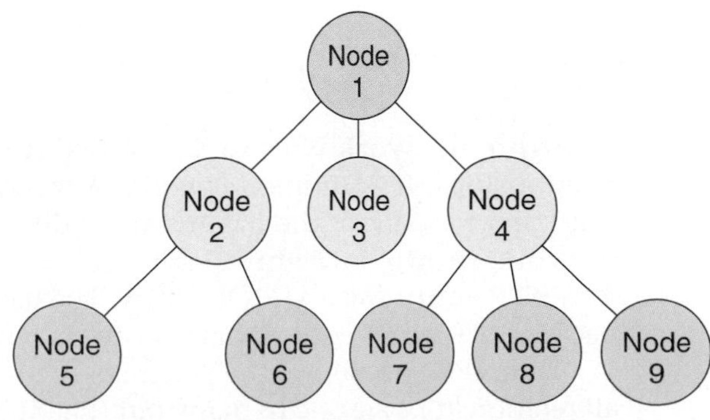

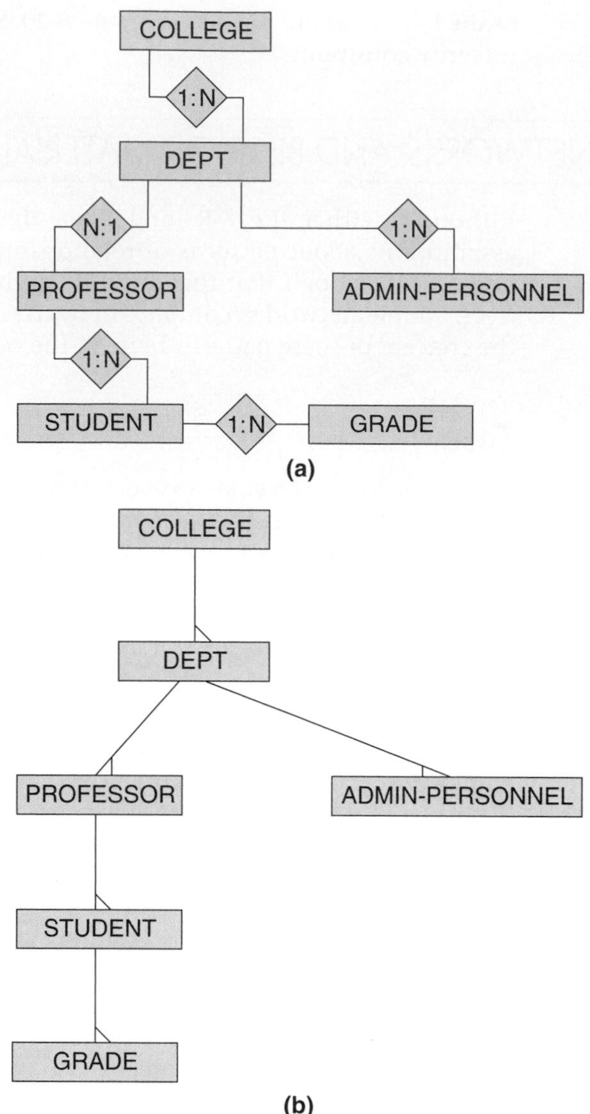

➤ FIGURE 6-22

Representation of a Tree by Means of Relations: (a) Tree Composed of Entities and (b) Representation of This Tree by Means of Relations

relationships by storing the key of the parent in the child. Figure 6-22(b) is a data structure diagram corresponding to the tree in Figure 6-22(a).

In summary, a hierarchy, or tree, is a collection of records organized in such a way that all relationships are 1:N. All records have exactly one parent, except the root, which has no parent. A hierarchy can be represented by a set of relations using the methods defined earlier. Hierarchies are common in businesses, especially in manufacturing applications.

Simple Networks

A **simple network** is also a data structure of elements having only one-to-many relationships. In a simple network, however, the elements may have more than one parent as long as the parents are of different types. For example, in the simple network shown in Figure 6-23, each STUDENT entity has two parents, an ADVISER entity and a MAJOR entity. The data structure in Figure 6-23 is not a tree because STUDENT entities have more than one parent.

Figure 6-24(a) shows the general structure of this simple network. Notice that all relationships are one to many but that STUDENT has two parents. In this figure,

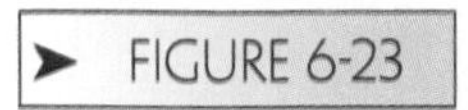

Example of a Simple Network

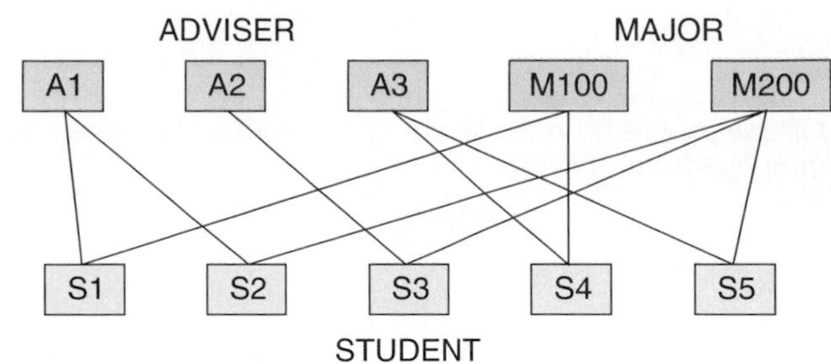

the parent records are on top, and the children records are beneath them. This arrangement is convenient but not essential. You may see simple networks depicted with parents beside or below the children. You can identify simple networks in such arrangements by the fact that a single record type participates as a child in two (or more) one-to-many relationships.

To represent a simple network of entities with the relational model, we follow the procedures described earlier. First we transform each entity into a relation and normalize the relations if necessary. Then we represent each 1:N relationship by storing the key of the parent relation in the child relation. The result of this process for the network in Figure 6-24(a) is shown in Figure 6-24(b).

Complex Networks

A **complex network** is a data structure of elements in which at least one of the relationships is many-to-many. The complex network in Figure 6-25(a) illustrates the relationships among invoices, line items, parts, and suppliers. Two of the three relationships are 1:N, and the third is M:N. Because there is at least one many-to-many relationship, this structure is called a complex network.

As discussed, M:N relationships have no direct representation in the relational model. Consequently, before this structure can be stored in relational form, we must define an intersection relation. In Figure 6-25(b), the intersection relation is Part-Supplier.

Bills of Materials

A **bill of materials** is a special data structure that occurs frequently in manufacturing applications. In fact, such structures provided a major impetus for the development of database technology in the 1960s.

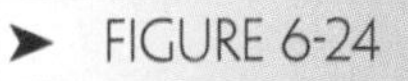

Representation of a Simple Network by Means of Relations: (a) Simple Network Composed of Entities and (b) Its Representation by Means of Relations

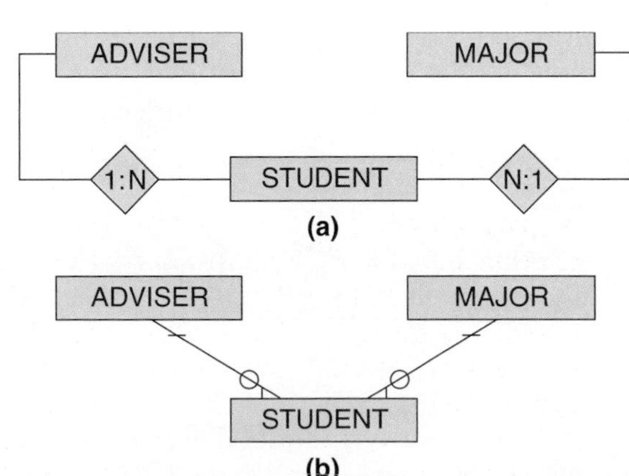

➤ FIGURE 6-25

Representation of a Complex Network by Means of Relations: (a) Complex Network Composed of Entities and (b) Its Representation by Means of Relations

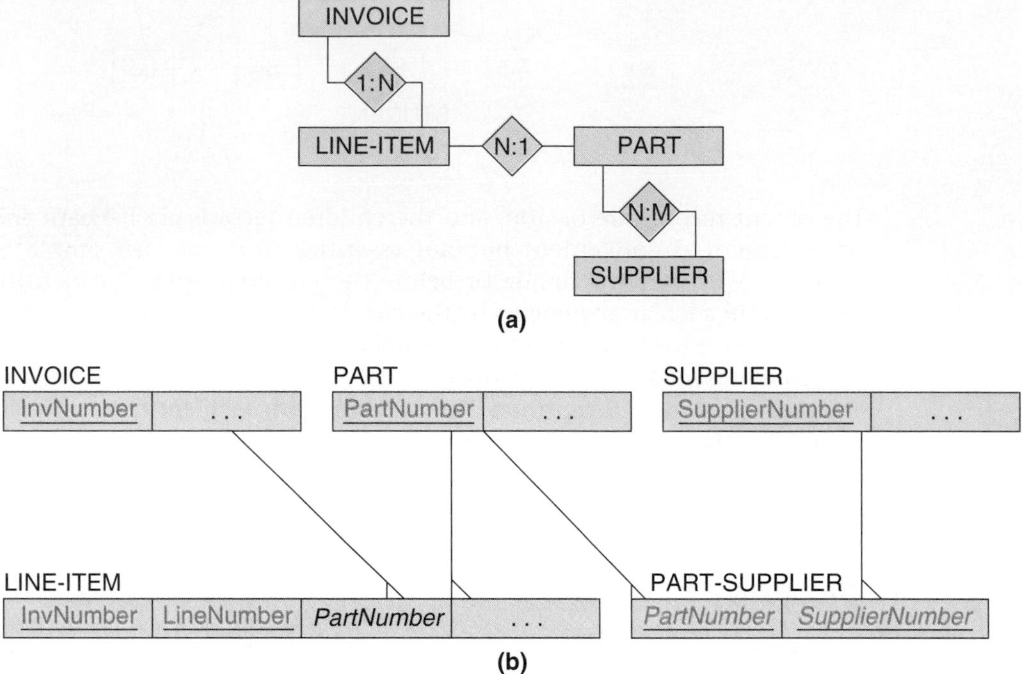

Figure 6-26 is an example of a bill of materials, which shows the parts that constitute products. When viewed from the standpoint of a given product, say, Product A, this data structure is a hierarchy. But because a part can be used in more than one product, this structure is actually a network. For example, the part ABC100 has two parents, Product A and Product B.

A bill of materials can be represented by means of relations in several ways. The most common is to consider it as an M:N recursive relationship. A part (or product or assembly or subassembly or whatever) contains many elements. At the same time, there may be many elements that contain it. Figure 6-27(a) shows the

➤ FIGURE 6-26

Example of a Bill of Materials

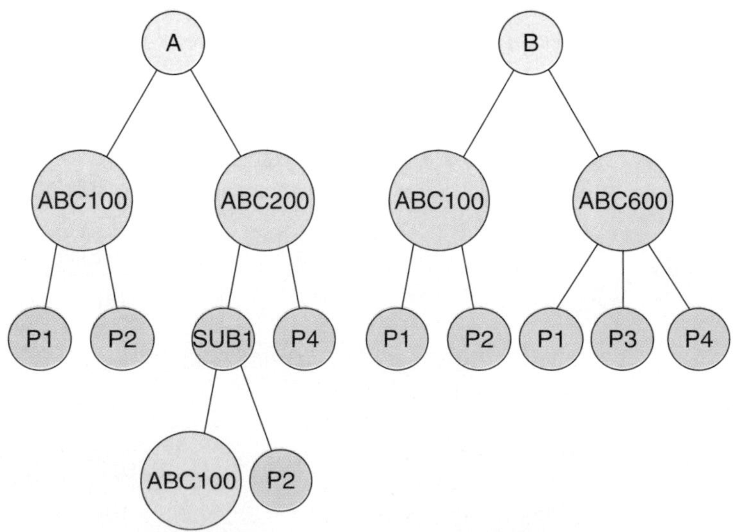

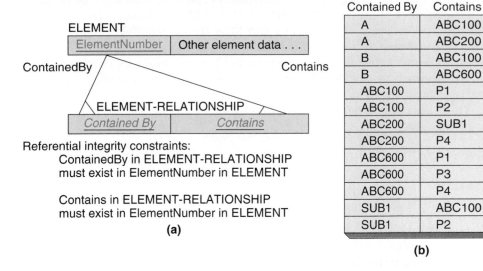

➤ FIGURE 6-27

Representation of a Bill of Materials with Relations: (a) Relations Representing a Bill of Materials and (b) Data for the ELEMENT-RELATIONSHIP Intersection Relation

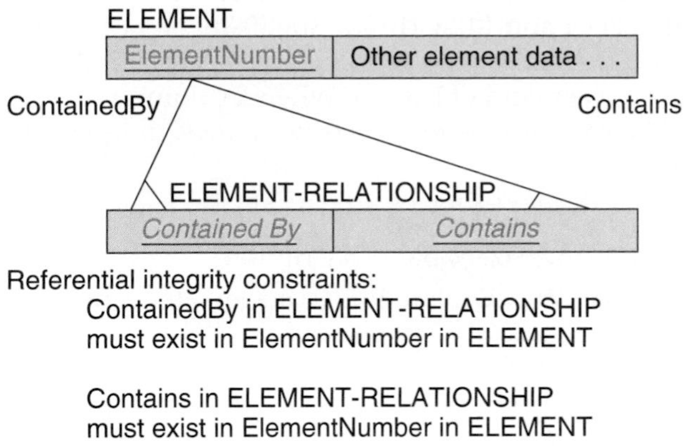

Contained By	Contains
A	ABC100
A	ABC200
B	ABC100
B	ABC600
ABC100	P1
ABC100	P2
ABC200	SUB1
ABC200	P4
ABC600	P1
ABC600	P3
ABC600	P4
SUB1	ABC100
SUB1	P2

Observe element A contains an ABC100 and element ABC100 is contained by an A

(b)

general data structure of the M:N recursive relationship, and Figure 6-27(b) shows an instance of the intersection relation created to represent this bill of materials.

Before concluding this chapter, we need to address two more important topics: surrogate keys and null values.

SURROGATE KEYS

A **surrogate key** is a unique, system-supplied identifier used as the primary key of a relation. The values of a surrogate key have no meaning to the users and are usually hidden on forms and reports. The DBMS will not allow the value of a surrogate key to be changed.

There are two reasons for using surrogate keys, one pragmatic and one philosophical. Consider the pragmatic reason first.

THE PRAGMATIC REASON Suppose there is an M:N relationship between the following two tables:

SHELLFISH (<u>ShellfishName</u>, Size, Color, Description)

and

BEACH (<u>BeachName</u>, Type, WaveOrientation, AverageWaterTemp)

The relationship between these two tables is M:N because a shellfish can be found on many beaches and a beach may support many types of shellfish. Suppose that shellfish names are text data like *Cyrtopleura costata* and so are modeled with a physical domain of Text 50. Further suppose that beach names are also text, like *Whidbey Island, Crescent Beach, East End,* and so are modeled with a physical domain of Text 75. Clearly, the indexes that will need to be created to enforce uniqueness on these columns will be large. (See Appendix A for more information on this use of indexes.)

The greater problem, however, concerns the intersection table that would represent the M:N relationship. The two columns of this table are (ShellfishName, BeachName), which are represented as Text 50 and Text 75, respectively. The data and indexes of this intersection table will be enormousl For example, if the shellfish database contains 1,000 shellfish, which appear on average on 100 beaches, the intersection table will have 100,000 rows of 125 characters of text. To add agony to insult, all of these data duplicate ShellfishName in SHELLFISH and BeachName in BEACH.

The storage and processing of these indexes can be greatly reduced by defining a surrogate key on both the SHELLFISH and BEACH tables. This is done by defining new columns in SHELLFISH and BEACH, say, ShellfishID and BeachID, respectively. These columns are defined to the DBMS as type AutoNumber (or something similar, depending on the brand of DBMS). When a column is defined this way, every time the DBMS creates a new row, it creates a new, unique value for that column of the new row.

Thus, a revised design for these tables using a surrogate key is

SHELLFISH (<u>ShellfishID</u>, ShellfishName, Size, Color, Description)
BEACH (<u>BeachID</u>, BeachName, Type, WaveOrientation, AverageWaterTemp)

and

SHELL_BEACH_INT (<u>ShellfishID</u>, <u>BeachID</u>)

The surrogate key values that are generated are typically 32 bit integers or something similar. Such values are compact and easy to index and will result in not only dramatically reduced file space, but also better performance.

Thus, for pragmatic reasons, any time a table has a primary key that is lengthy text, or has a composite key having lengthy text elements, consider using a surrogate key.

THE PHILOSOPHICAL REASON The philosophical reason for employing surrogate keys is that they serve to maintain entity identity. When the user stores a row in a table it represents something. The something must exist until a user deletes it. The existence of that something shouldn't depend on the presence or absence of certain data values. Since surrogate keys cannot be changed by the user, and since they are guaranteed to be unique, they represent the identity of a row (or entity).

To clarify this, consider the two tables in Figure 6-28(a), which use data keys rather than surrogate keys. There is a 1:N relationship from ADVISER to STUDENT. The relationship is carried by the AdviserName foreign key in STUDENT. Now, assume that Professor Sessions wants to change his or her name to Johnson. Suppose that change is allowed, and suppose our application is smart enough to propagate that change through the foreign key so that all Sessions values are changed to Johnson in AdviserName in STUDENT. The data will appear as shown in Figure 6-28(b).

We have a mess. We've overloaded the name Johnson so that it is impossible to determine which students are advised by the Johnson in Accounting and which students are advised by the Johnson in Law. Even worse, this confusion is an artifact of our design and not due to any problem among the users.

(As an aside, you may be thinking that the problem is that AdviserName should be defined as unique. Such a definition would indeed prohibit this problem, but it begs the question. Who are we, as database developers, to say that advisers cannot have duplicate names? If the semantics of the underlying business allow advisers to have the same name, then we ought not to construct a database that prohibits duplicate names. Contorting the users' behavior for the benefit of the database is bad design.)

Consider this same scenario with surrogate keys. Figure 6-29(a) shows the data prior to the name change, and Figure 6-29(b) shows the data after the name change. There is no confounding of keys because surrogate keys are used to represent the relationship.

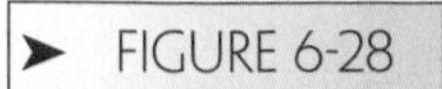

Example of Key Confounding

ADVISER Relation

Name	Department
Johnson	Acounting
Eldridge	Law
Sessions	Law

STUDENT Relation

Name	Major	AdviserName
Franklin	Law	Eldridge
Jefferson	Accounting	Johnson
Washington	Law	Sessions
Lincoln	Law	Sessions

(a) ADVISER and STUDENT Relations Without Surrogate Keys, Before Change

ADVISER Relation

Name	Department
Johnson	Acounting
Eldridge	Law
Johnson	Law

STUDENT Relation

Name	Major	AdviserName
Franklin	Law	Eldridge
Jefferson	Accounting	Johnson
Washington	Law	Johnson
Lincoln	Law	Johnson

(b) ADVISER and STUDENT Relations Without Surrogate Keys, After Change

There are numerous other ways of expressing the notion that surrogate keys protect identity. The object-oriented programming world also makes this same argument in different ways for object programming objects. The arguments all come down to the fact that as long as a row has an unchanging identifier that lasts as long as the row lasts, then the identity of that row will never be lost.

This benefit is gained at a cost, however. For the design in Figure 6-28(a), you can look at a STUDENT row and know immediately who the adviser is. With data keys like these, you don't have to do a lookup in the ADVISER table to determine the Adviser's name like you do for the data in Figure 6-29(b). Also, if a database exchanges data with other databases that do use data keys, then the use of surrogate keys may create problems.

SURROGATE KEYS OR NOT? So what's the bottom line? Experts differ. While no one argues with the pragmatic reasons for using them, some say the use of surrogate keys should be limited to cases where they must be used, like the shellfish example. Others say surrogate keys should be used all of the time, and that data keys should never be used.

My own practice is to use surrogate keys almost all of the time. I hesitate to use surrogate keys for tables that have a natural, easy-to-index data key, such as a PRODUCT table that has a ProductNumber column holding unique, integer values. Also, I sometimes do not define surrogate keys on tables that are regularly used to exchange data with other databases.

This policy means that some databases I've designed have a mixture of data and surrogate keys. I don't like this and it can be confusing. To some extent, this

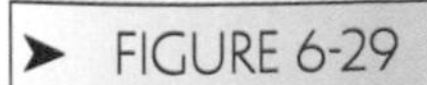

Example of No Key Confounding with Surrogate Keys

ADVISER Relation

AdviserID	Name	Department
1	Johnson	Acounting
2	Eldridge	Law
3	Sessions	Law

STUDENT Relation

StudentID	Name	Major	AdviserFK
20	Franklin	Law	2
21	Jefferson	Acounting	1
22	Washington	Law	3
23	Lincoln	Law	3

(a) ADVISER and STUDENT Relations with Surrogate Keys, Before Change

ADVISER Relation

AdviserID	Name	Department
1	Johnson	Acounting
2	Eldridge	Law
3	Johnson	Law

STUDENT Relation

StudentID	Name	Major	AdviserFK
20	Franklin	Law	2
21	Jefferson	Acounting	1
22	Washington	Law	3
23	Lincoln	Law	3

(b) ADVISER and STUDENT Relations with Surrogate Keys, After Change

confusion can be reduced by consistently naming surrogate key columns. I usually use a naming scheme of *TableName*ID or *TableName*_SK for surrogate key columns.

Discuss this issue with your professor; he or she will undoubtedly have other ideas and opinions. It's an artistic decision that in my opinion needs to be made one table at a time.

NULL VALUES

A **null value** is an attribute value that has never been supplied. The problem of null values is that they are ambiguous. A null value can mean (a) the value is unknown, (b) the value is not appropriate, or (c) the value is known to be blank. For example, consider the attribute DeceasedDate in a CUSTOMER relation. What does a null value for DeceasedDate mean? It could mean the users don't know if the customer is alive or not; it could mean the customer is a corporation and DeceasedDate is inappropriate; or it could mean that it is known both that the customer is a person and that she is alive.

There are several ways of eliminating these ambiguities. The first is not to allow them. Define the attribute as required. This is fine as long as, in the minds of the users, the attribute truly is required. The users, however, will be aggravated to be forced to provide a value of CustomerColorPreference, if such a value is inessential to their business function.

In Chapter 3, we saw a means for eliminating value-inappropriate nulls, and that is to define subtypes. Defining MALE-PATIENT and FEMALE-PATIENT as subtypes of PATIENT will eliminate male patients from having to provide number of pregnancies, and females from being asked the condition of their prostate, for example. This solution, however, is expensive in that it forces the definition of two new tables and requires them to be joined together to have all of the PATIENT data.

Yet a third solution is to define each attribute as having an initial value that is recognized as blank. A text attribute, for example, could be given the initial value (*unknown*). Users could subsequently give it the value (*not appropriate*), for not appropriate, when the value is inappropriate. This will be more effective if such choices appear in drop-down text boxes (see Chapter 10). While this solution works for text attributes, it leaves the problem for numeric, date, boolean and other, nontext attributes. Of course, a solution for them is to model them as text data so that the value of (*unknown*) and (*not appropriate*) can be entered. In that case, however, you will have to write your own editing code to ensure that valid numbers or dates are entered. You'll also have to cast the values in program code before performing numeric or date operations on them.

Sometimes, the best solution is to do nothing about null values. If the users can deal with the ambiguity, or if the solution is more costly than it is worth, just document the fact that the problem exists and move on. Also, see Chapter 9 for more information about the consequences of null values in join operations.

➤ SUMMARY

To transform entity-relationship data models, each entity is represented by a relation. The attributes of the entity become the attributes of the relation. Once the relation has been created, it must be examined against normalization criteria and divided into two or more relations if necessary.

There are three types of binary HAS-A relationships in the E-R model: 1:1, 1:N, and N:M. To represent a 1:1 relationship, we place the key of one relation into the other relation. One-to-one relationships sometimes indicate that two relations have been defined on the same entity and so should be combined into one relation.

To represent a 1:N relationship, we place the key of the parent in the child. Finally, to represent an M:N relationship, we create an intersection relation that contains the keys of the other two relations.

Recursive relationships are relationships in which the participants in the relationship arise from the same entity class. There are three types: 1:1, 1:N, and N:M. The types are represented in the same way as are nonrecursive relationships. For 1:1 and 1:N relationships, we add a foreign key to the relation that represents the entity. For an N:M recursion, we create an intersection table that represents the M:N relationship.

Ternary and higher-order relationships can be treated as combinations of binary relationships. If this is done, however, any binary constraints on the ternary relationship must also be represented in the design. Because it is not possible to enforce the constraint by the relational design, it must be documented as a business rule. Three types of such constraints occur: MUST, MUST NOT, and MUST COVER.

Supertype and subtype entities (IS-A relationships) are also represented by relations. One relation is defined for the supertype entity, and other relations are defined for each subtype. Usually the keys of the relations are the same, and the relationship among the rows is defined through those keys. If they are not the same, the key of the subtype relation can be placed in the supertype relation or the key of the supertype relation can be placed in the subtype. Most often, the key of the supertype relation is placed in the subtype relation.

Binary relationships can be combined to form three types of more complicated structures. A tree is a collection of record types in which each record has exactly one parent, except the root, which has no parent. In a simple network, records may have multiple parents, but the parents must be of different types. In a complex network, records have multiple parents of the same type. Another way of saying this is that in a complex network, at least one of the binary relationships is M:N.

A bill of materials is a data structure frequently seen in manufacturing applications. Such structures can be represented by M:N recursive relationships.

Surrogate keys are unique, system-supplier identifiers used as the primary key of a relation. They are used for pragmatic reasons to reduce the size of keys and foreign keys and to improve performance. They are also used for more philosophical reasons that serve to maintain entity identity. Such keys are generally recommended.

A null value is a value that has not been supplied for an attribute. Such values are ambiguous. They can mean the value is unknown, inappropriate, or known to be blank. They can be avoided by requiring attribute values, by using subtypes, and by supplying initial values. They can also be ignored if the attendant ambiguity is not a problem to the users.

➤ GROUP I QUESTIONS

6.1 Explain how E-R entities are transformed into relations.

6.2 Why is it necessary to examine relations transformed from entities against normalization criteria? Under what conditions should the relations be altered if they are not in DK/NF? Under what conditions should they not be altered?

6.3 Explain how the representation of weak entities differs from the representation of strong entities.

6.4 List the three types of binary relationships and give an example of each. Do not use the examples in this text.

6.5 Define *foreign key* and give an example.

6.6 Show two different ways to represent the 1:1 relationship in your answer to Question 6.4. Use data structure diagrams.

6.7 For your answers to Question 6.6, describe a method for obtaining data about one of the entities, given the key of the other. Describe a method for obtaining data about the second entity, given the key of the first. Describe answers for both of your alternatives in Question 6.6.

6.8 Why are some 1:1 relationships considered suspicious? Under what conditions should relations in a 1:1 relationship be combined into one relation?

6.9 Define the terms *parent* and *child* and give an example of each.

6.10 Show how to represent the 1:N relationship in your answer to Question 6.4. Use a data structure diagram.

6.11 For your answer to Question 6.10, describe a method for obtaining data for all of the children, given the key of the parent. Describe a method for obtaining data for the parent, given a key of the child.

6.12 For a 1:N relationship, explain why you must place the key of the parent in the child, rather than placing the key of the child in the parent.

6.13 Give examples of binary 1:N relationships, other than those in this text, for

a. An optional-to-optional relationship.
b. An optional-to-mandatory relationship.
c. A mandatory-to-optional relationship.
d. A mandatory-to-mandatory relationship.

Illustrate your answer using data structure diagrams.

6.14 Show how to represent the N:M relationship in your answer to Question 6.4. Use a data structure diagram.

6.15 For your answer to Question 6.14, describe a method for obtaining the children for one entity, given the key of the other. Also describe a method for obtaining the children for the second entity, given the key of the first.

6.16 Why is it not possible to represent N:M relationships with the same strategy used to represent 1:N relationships?

6.17 Explain the meaning of the term *intersection relation.*

6.18 Define three types of recursive binary relationships and give an example of each.

6.19 Show how to represent the 1:1 recursive relationship in your answer to Question 6.18. How does this differ from the representation of 1:1 non-recursive relationships?

6.20 Show how to represent the 1:N recursive relationship in your answer to Question 6.18. How does this differ from the representation of 1:N non-recursive relationships?

6.21 Show how to represent the M:N recursive relationship in your answer to Question 6.18. How does this differ from the representation of M:N non-recursive relationships?

6.22 Explain how to use binary relationships to represent a ternary relationship. Give an example other than the ones in this text.

6.23 In your answer to question 6.22, define a binary constraint on the ternary relationship. Explain how to represent the constraint. Since the constraint cannot be enforced in the relational model, what should be done?

6.24 Give examples of MUST NOT and MUST COVER binary constraints other than the ones in this text.

6.25 Give an example of a supertype and two or more subtypes, and show how to represent it using relations.

6.26 Define *tree, simple network,* and *complex network.*

6.27 Give an example of a tree structure other than one in this text, and show how to represent it by means of relations.

6.28 Give an example of a simple network other than one in this text, and show how to represent it by means of relations.

6.29 Give an example of a complex network other than one in this text, and show how to represent it by means of relations.

6.30 What is a bill of materials? Give an example other than the one in this text, and show how to represent your example by means of relations.

6.31 Define *surrogate key* and describe two reasons for using one.

6.32 Describe a situation other than one in this text for which there are good pragmatic reasons for using surrogate keys.

6.33 Explain the statement "Surrogate keys serve to maintain entity identiy." Explain why this is important.

6.34 What are the three possible interpretations of null values?

6.35 Describe three different ways to avoid null values.

6.36 When are null values not a problem?

➤ GROUP II QUESTIONS

6.37 Transform the entity-relationship diagram for the Jefferson Dance Club (Figure 3-19) into relations. Express your answer with a data structure diagram, and show the referential integrity constraints.

6.38 Transform the entity-relationship diagram for San Juan Charters (Figure 3-21) into relations. Express your answer with a data structure diagram, and show the referential integrity constraints.

6.39 Some of the relations in Figure 6-19 are not in DK/NF. Identify them and explain why not. What normal form do they have? How can this design be justified? How else could the database application enforce the binary constraints?

6.40 State all referential integrity constraints for the relations in Figure 6-20(b).

➤ PROJECTS

A. Complete Project A at the end of Chapter 3 if you have not already done so. Transform your E-R diagram into a set of relations. If any of your relations are not in DK/NF, justify your decision to create un-normalized relations.

B. Complete Project B at the end of Chapter 3 if you have not already done so. Transform your E-R diagram into a set of relations. If any of your relations are not in DK/NF, justify your decision to create un-normalized relations.

C. Complete Project C at the end of Chapter 3 if you have not already done so. Transform your E-R diagram into a set of relations. If any of your relations are not in DK/NF, justify your decision to create un-normalized relations.

➤ FIREDUP PROJECT QUESTIONS

If you have not already done so, create entity-relationship diagrams for Questions A and C in the FiredUp Project at the end of Chapter 3.

A. Transform the entity-relationship diagram from Question A at the end of Chapter 3 into a set of relations in domain/key normal form. For each relation, specify the primary key, candidate keys, if any, and foreign keys. Specify all referential integrity constraints. If necessary, make and justify assumptions regarding the underlying semantics of the application.

B. Adjust your answer to Question A to allow un-normalized relations if you think such relations are appropriate. Justify any non-normalized relations you have. If necessary, make and justify assumptions regarding the underlying semantics of the application.

C. Transform the entity-relationship diagram from Question C at the end of Chapter 3 into a set of relations, preferably in domain/key normal form. If any of your relations is not in domain/key normal form, explain why not. For each relation, specify the primary key, candidate keys, if any, and foreign keys. Specify all interrelation constraints.

D. Adjust your answer to Question C, above, to assume that home, fax, and cell phone are to be represented by separate, single-value attributes. Is this a better design than in your answer to Question C? Explain why or why not.

Database Design with Semantic Object Models

This chapter discusses the transformation of semantic object models into relational database designs. First we describe the transformation of each of seven common types of semantic objects. Then we illustrate these concepts by showing the semantic object modeling and relational representation of several real-world objects. Since the best way to learn this subject is to work examples yourself, you are strongly encouraged to do the projects at the end of this chapter.

➤ TRANSFORMATION OF SEMANTIC OBJECTS INTO RELATIONAL DATABASE DESIGNS

Chapter 4 introduced the semantic object data model and defined seven types of semantic objects. In this section, we present methods for transforming each of those seven types into relations. When working with semantic objects, normalization problems are less likely than they are when working with the E-R models because the definition of semantic objects usually separates semantic themes into group attributes or objects. Thus, when transforming an object into relations, the relations are generally either already in DK/NF or are in very close to domain/key normal form.

SIMPLE OBJECTS

Figure 7-1 illustrates the transformation of a simple object into a relation. Recall that a simple object has no multi-value attributes and no object attributes.

➤ FIGURE 7-1

Relational Representation of Example Simple Object: (a) EQUIPMENT Object Diagram and (b) Relation Representing EQUIPMENT

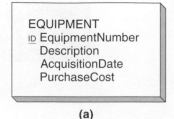

EQUIPMENT
ID EquipmentNumber
Description
AcquisitionDate
PurchaseCost

(a)

EQUIPMENT (EquipmentNumber, Description, AcquisitionDate, PurchaseCost)

(b)

Consequently, simple objects can be represented by a single relation in the database.

Figure 7-1(a) is an example of a simple object, EQUIPMENT, which can be represented by a single relation, as shown in Figure 7-1(b). Each attribute of the object is defined as an attribute of the relation, and the identifying attribute, EquipmentNumber, becomes the key attribute of the relation, denoted by underlining EquipmentNumber in Figure 7-1(b).

The general transformation of simple objects is illustrated in Figure 7-2. Object OBJECT1 is transformed into relation R1. The attribute that identifies OBJECT1 instances is O1; it becomes the key of relation R1. Nonkey data is represented in this and subsequent figures with ellipses (. . .).

Because a key is an attribute that uniquely identifies a row of a table, only unique identifiers—those with the ID underlined—can be transformed into keys. If there is no unique identifier in the object, then one must be created, by combining the existing attributes to form a unique identifier, or by defining a surrogate key.

Composite Objects

A composite object is an object that has one or more multi-value simple or group attributes but no object attributes. Figure 7-3(a) shows an example composite object, HOTEL-BILL. To represent this object, one relation is created for the base object, HOTEL-BILL, and an additional relation is created for the repeating group attribute, DailyCharge. This relational design is shown in Figure 7-3(b).

In the key of DAILY-CHARGE, InvoiceNumber is underlined because it is part of the key of DAILY-CHARGE, and it is italicized because it is also a foreign key. (It is a key of HOTEL-BILL.) ChargeDate is underlined because it is part of the key of DAILY-CHARGE, but it is not italicized because it is not a foreign key.

In general, composite objects are transformed by defining one relation for the object itself and another relation for each multi-value attribute. In Figure 7-4(a), object OBJECT1 contains two groups of multi-value attributes, each of which is represented by a relation in the database design. The key of each of these tables is the composite of the identifier of the object plus the identifier of the group. Thus,

➤ FIGURE 7-2

General Transformation of Simple Object into a Relation

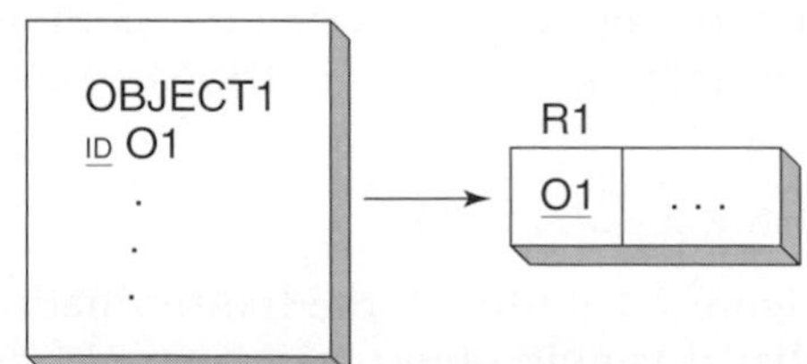

➤ FIGURE 7-3

Relational Representation of Example Composite Object: (a) HOTEL-BILL Object Diagram and (b) Relations Representing HOTEL-BILL

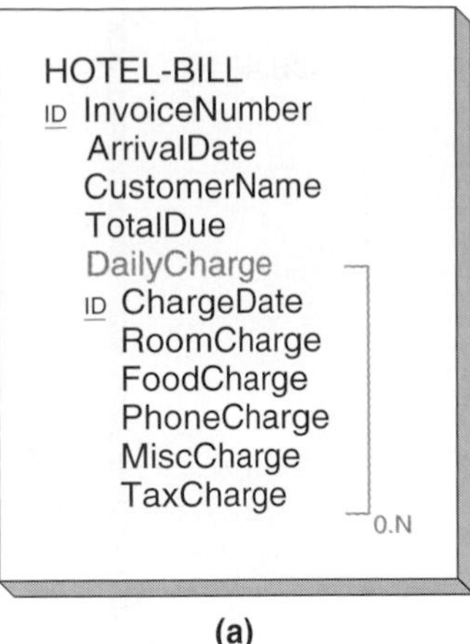

(a)

HOTEL-BILL (InvoiceNumber, ArrivalDate, CustomerName, TotalDue)

DAILY-CHARGE (*InvoiceNumber*, ChargeDate, RoomCharge, FoodCharge, PhoneCharge, MiscCharge, TaxCharge)

Referential integrity constraint:

InvoiceNumber in DAILY-CHARGE must exist in InvoiceNumber in HOTEL-BILL

(b)

the representation of OBJECT1 is a relation R1 with key O1, a relation R2 with key (O1, G1), and a relation R3 with key (O1, G2).

The minimum cardinality from the object to the group is specified by the minimum cardinality of group attribute. In Figure 7-4(a), the minimum cardinality of Group1 is 1 and that of Group2 is 0. These cardinalities are shown as a hash mark (on R2) and an oval (on R3) in the data structure diagram. The minimum cardinality from the group to the object is, by default, always 1, because a group cannot exist if the object that contains that group does not exist. These minimum cardinalities are shown by hash marks on the relationship lines into R1.

As noted in Chapter 4, groups can be nested. Figure 7-4(b) shows an object in which Group2 is nested within Group1. When this occurs, the relation representing the nested group is made subordinate to the relation that represents its containing group. In Figure 7-4(b), relation R3 is subordinate to relation R2. The key of R3 is the key of R2, which is (O1, G1) plus the identifier of Group2, which is G2; thus the key of R3 is (O1, G1, G2).

Make sure that you understand why the keys in Figure 7-4(b) are constructed as they are. Also note that some attributes are underlined and italicized and some are simply underlined, because some attributes are both local and foreign keys and some are just local keys.

Compound Objects

The relational representation of compound objects is similar to the representation of entities. In fact, compound objects and entities are in many ways quite similar.

As we stated in Chapter 4, an object, OBJECT1, can contain one or many instances of a second object, OBJECT2, and OBJECT2 can contain one or many

FIGURE 7-4

General Transformation of Composite Objects: (a) Composite Object with Seperate Groups and (b) Composite Object with Nested Groups

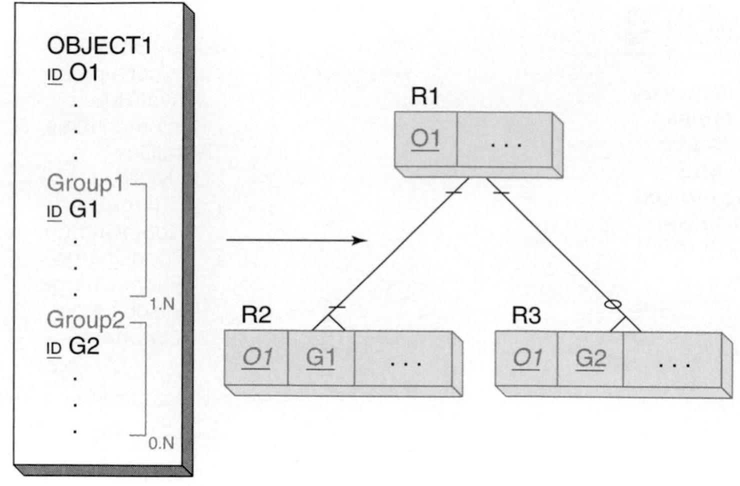

Referential integrity constraints:

O1 in R2 must exist in O1 in R1
O1 in R3 must exist in O1 in R1

(a)

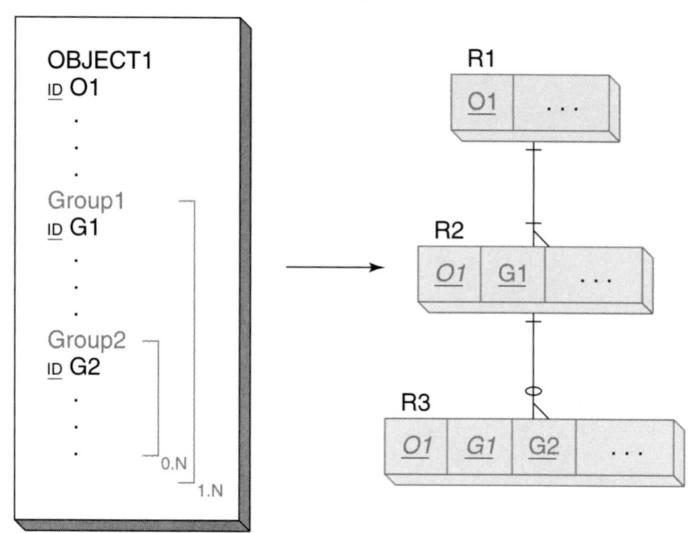

Referential integrity constraints:

O1 in R2 must exist in O1 in R1
(O1, G1) in R3 must exist in (O1, G1) in R2

(b)

instances of the first object, OBJECT1. This leads to the object types shown in Figure 7-5.

All of these relationships involve some variation of one-to-one, one-to-many, or many-to-many relationships. Specifically, the relationship from OBJECT1 to

FIGURE 7-5

Four Types of Compound Objects

		Object1 Can Contain	
Object2		One	Many
Can	One	**1:1**	**1:N**
Contain	Many	**M:1**	**M:N**

➤ FIGURE 7-6

Example Relational Representation of 1:1 Compound Objects: (a) Example 1:1 Compound Objects and (b) Their Representaion

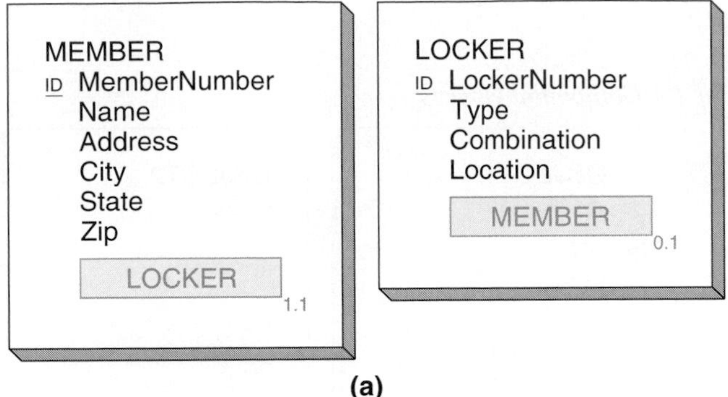

MEMBER (MemberNumber, Name, Address, City, State, Zip, *LockerNumber*)

LOCKER (LockerNumber, Type, Combination, Location)

Referential integrity constraint:

LockerNumber in MEMBER must exist in
LockerNumber in LOCKER

(b)

OBJECT2 can be 1:1, 1:N, or N:M, whereas the relationship from OBJECT2 to OBJECT1 can be 1:1, 1:M, or M:N. To represent any of these, we need only address these three types of relationships.

Representing One-to-One Compound Objects

Consider the assignment of a LOCKER to a health club MEMBER. A LOCKER is assigned to one MEMBER, and each MEMBER has one, and only one, LOCKER. Figure 7-6(a) shows the object diagrams. To represent these objects with relations, we define a relation for each object, and, as with 1:1 entity relationships, we place the key of either relation in the other relation. That is, we can place the key of MEMBER in LOCKER or the key of LOCKER in MEMBER. Figure 7-6(b) shows the placement of the key of LOCKER in MEMBER. Note that LockerNumber is underlined in LOCKER because it is the key of LOCKER and is italicized in MEMBER because it is a foreign key in MEMBER.

In general, for a 1:1 relationship between OBJECT1 and OBJECT2, we define one relation for each object, R1 and R2. Then we place the key of either relation (O1 or O2) as a foreign key in the other relation, as in Figure 7-7.

Representing One-to-Many and Many-to-One Relationships

Now consider 1:N relationships and N:1 relationships. Figure 7-8(a) shows an example of a 1:N object relationship between EQUIPMENT and REPAIR. An item of EQUIPMENT can have many REPAIRs, but a REPAIR can be related to only one item of EQUIPMENT.

The objects in Figure 7-8(a) are represented by the relations in Figure 7-8(b). Observe that the key of the parent (the object on the one side of the relationship) is placed in the child (the object on the many side of the relationship).

FIGURE 7-7

General Transformation of 1:1 Compound Objects

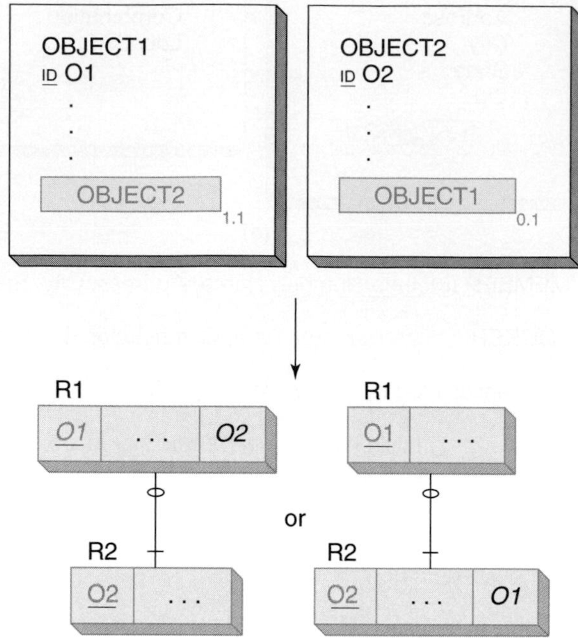

Referential integrity constraint:

O2 in R1 must exist in O2 in R2

Referential integrity constraint:

O1 in R2 must exist in O1 in R1

FIGURE 7-8

Example Relational Representation of 1:N Compound Objects: (a) Example 1:N Compound Objects and (b) Their Reperesentation

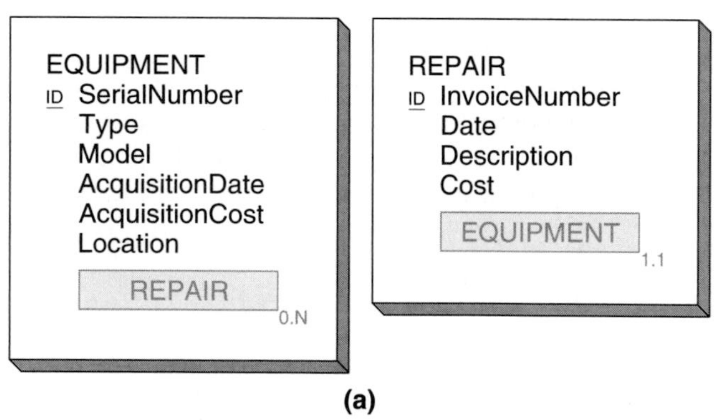

(a)

EQUIPMENT (<u>SerialNumber</u>, Type, Model, AcquisitionDate, AcquisitionCost, Location)

REPAIR (<u>InvoiceNumber</u>, Date, Description, Cost, *SerialNumber*)

Referential integrity constraint:

SerialNumber in REPAIR must exist in SerialNumber in EQUIPMENT

(b)

FIGURE 7-9

General Transformation of 1:N Compound Objects

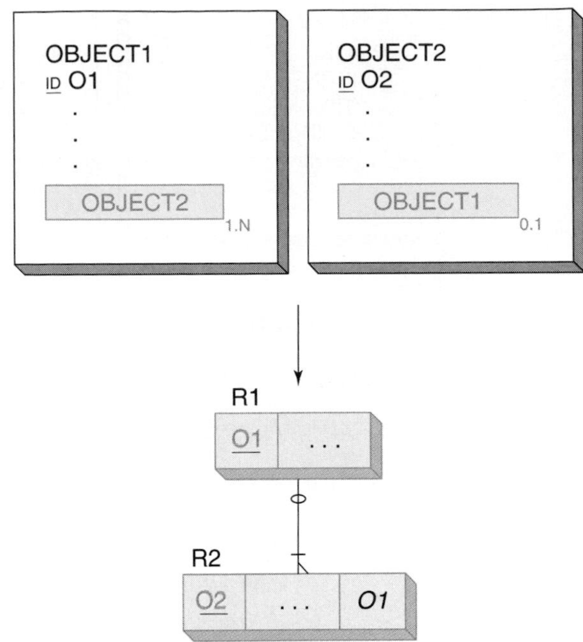

Figure 7-9 shows the general transformation of 1:N compound objects. Object OBJECT1 contains many objects OBJECT2, and object OBJECT2 contains just one OBJECT1. To represent this structure by means of relations, we represent each object with a relation and place the key of the parent in the child. Thus, in Figure 7-9 the attribute O1 is placed in R2.

If OBJECT2 were to contain many OBJECT1s and OBJECT1 were to contain just one OBJECT2, we would use the same strategy but reverse the role of R1 and R2. That is, we would place O2 in R1.

The minimum cardinalities in either case are determined by the minimum cardinalities of the object attributes. In Figure 7-9, OBJECT1 requires at least one OBJECT2, but OBJECT2 does not necessarily require an OBJECT1. These cardinalities are shown in the data structure diagram as an oval on the R1 side of the relationship and as a hash mark on the R2 side of the relationship. These minimum cardinality values are simply examples; either or both objects could have a cardinality of 0, 1, or some other number.

Representing Many-to-Many Relationships

Finally, consider M:N relationships. As with M:N entity relationships, we define three relations, one for each of the objects and a third intersection relation. The intersection relation represents the relationship of the two objects and consists of the keys of both of its parents. Figure 7-10(a) shows the M:N relationship between BOOK and AUTHOR. Figure 7-10(b) depicts the three relations that represent these objects: BOOK, AUTHOR, and BOOK-AUTHOR-INT, the intersection relation. Notice that BOOK-AUTHOR-INT has no nonkey data. Both the attributes ISBN and SocialSecurityNumber are underlined and in italics because they both are local and foreign keys.

➤ FIGURE 7-10

Relational Representation of Example N:M Compound Objects: (a) BOOK and AUTHOR Objects and (b) Their Relational Representation

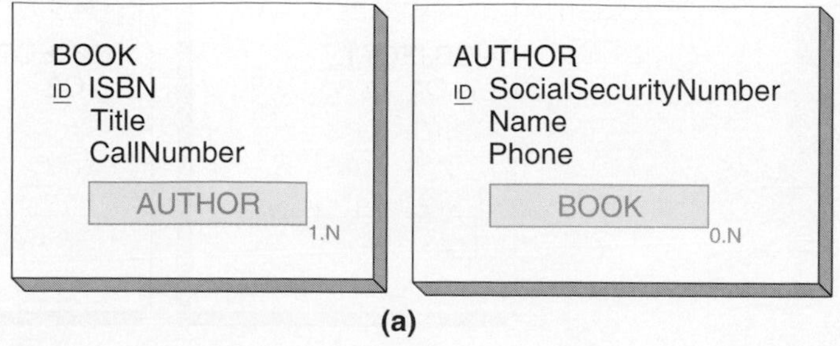

(a)

BOOK (<u>ISBN</u>, Title, CallNumber)

AUTHOR (<u>SocialSecurityNumber</u>, Name, Phone)

BOOK-AUTHOR-INT (<u>*ISBN*</u>, <u>*SocialSecurityNumber*</u>)

Referential integrity constraints:

ISBN in BOOK-AUTHOR-INT must exist in
ISBN in BOOK

SocialSecurityNumber in BOOK-AUTHOR-INT must exist in
SocialSecurityNumber in AUTHOR

(b)

In general, for two objects that have an M:N relationship, we define a relation R1 for object OBJECT1, a relation R2 for object OBJECT2, and a relation R3 for the intersection relation. The general scheme is shown in Figure 7-11. Note that the attributes of R3 are only O1 and O2. For M:N compound objects, R3 never contains nonkey data. The importance of this statement will become clear when we contrast M:N compound relationships with association relationships.

➤ FIGURE 7-11

General Transformation of M:N Compound Objects into Relations

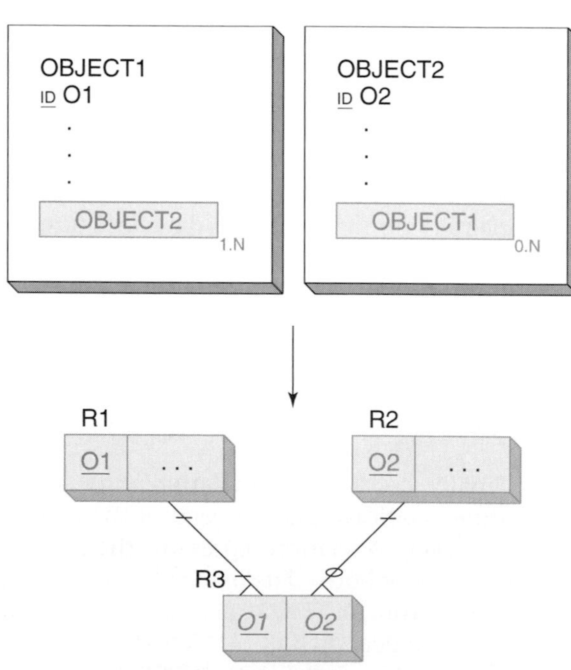

Referential integrity constraints:

O1 in R3 must exist in O1 in R1
O2 in R3 must exist in O2 in R2

Considering minimum cardinality, the parents of the intersection relation are always required. The minimum cardinalities of the relationships into the intersection relation are determined by the minimum cardinalities of the object links. In Figure 7-11, for example, a row in R1 requires a row in R3 because the minimum cardinality of OBJECT2 in OBJECT1 is 1. Similarly, a row in R2 does not require a row in R3 because the minimum cardinality of OBJECT1 in OBJECT2 is 0.

Hybrid Objects

Hybrid objects can be transformed into relational designs using a combination of the techniques for composite and compound objects. Figure 7-12(a) shows SALES-ORDER, a hybrid object, and related objects. To represent this object by means of relations, we establish one relation for the object itself and another relation for each of the contained objects CUSTOMER and SALESPERSON. Then, as with a composite object, we establish a relation for the multi-value group, which is LineItem. Since this group contains another object, ITEM, we also establish a relation for ITEM. All of the one-to-many relationships are represented by placing the key of the parent relation in the child relation, as shown in Figure 7-12(b).

The example in Figure 7-12 is deceptively simple. As we mentioned in Chapter 4, there are actually four cases of hybrid objects, which are summarized in Figure 7-13.

Cases 3 and 4 are more common than Cases 1 and 2, so we consider them first. OBJECT1 in Figure 7-14 shows two groups; Group1 illustrates Case 3 and Group2 illustrates Case 4.

Group1 has a maximum cardinality of N, which means that there can be many instances of Group1 within an OBJECT1. Furthermore, since OBJECT2 is marked as ID unique, this means that a particular OBJECT2 can appear in only one of the Group1 instances within an OBJECT1. Thus OBJECT2 acts as an identifier for Group1 within OBJECT1.

(The SALES-ORDER in Figure 7-12 illustrates this case. ITEM is an identifier of LineItem, so a given ITEM can appear on only one LineItem in a particular ORDER. But an ITEM can appear on many ORDERs.)

Consider the relational representation of Group1 in Figure 7-14. A relation, R1, is created for OBJECT1, and a relation, R2, is created for OBJECT2. In addition, a third relation, R-G1, is created for Group1. The relationship between R1 and R-G1 is 1:N, so we place the key of R1 (which is O1) into R-G1; the relationship between R2 and R-G1 is also 1:N, so we place the key of R2 (which is O2) in R-G1. Because an OBJECT2 can appear with a particular value of OBJECT1 only once, the composite (O1, O2) is unique to R-G1 and can be made the key of that relation.

Now consider Group2. OBJECT3 does not identify Group2, so OBJECT3 can appear in many Group2 instances in the same OBJECT1. (The SALES-ORDER in Figure 7-12 would be like this if ITEM were not ID unique in LineItem. This means that an ITEM could appear many times on the same ORDER.) Since OBJECT3 is not the identifier of Group2, we assume that some other attribute, G2, is the identifier.

In Figure 7-14, we create a relation R3 for OBJECT3 and another relation R-G2 for Group2. The relationship between R1 and R-G2 is 1:N, so place the key of R1 (which is O1) into R-G2. The relationship between R3 and R-G2 is also 1:N, so place the key of R3 (which is O3) into R-G2.

Now, however, unlike Group1, (O1, O3) cannot be the key of R-G2 because an O3 can be paired with a given O1 many times. That is, the composite (O1, O3) is not unique to R-G2, so the key of R-G2 must be (O1, G2).

Case 1 is similar to Case 3 except for the restriction that an OBJECT2 can be related to only one OBJECT1. The relations in Figure 7-14 will still work, but we

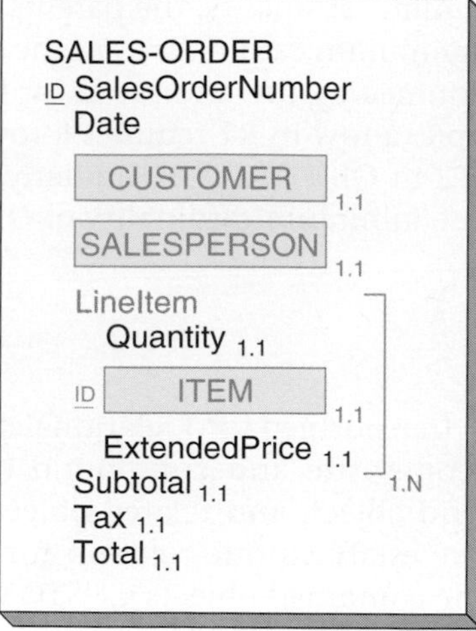
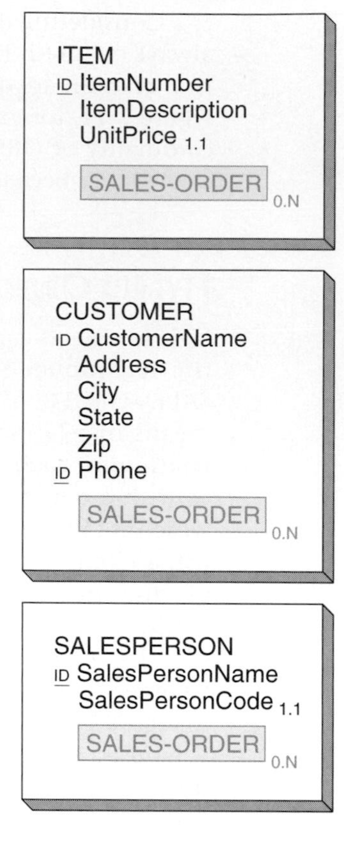

(a)

SALES-ORDER (SalesOrderNumber, Date, Subtotal, Tax, Total, *Phone*, *SalesPersonName*)

CUSTOMER (CustomerName, Address, City, State, Zip, Phone)

SALESPERSON (SalesPersonName, SalesPersonCode)

LINE-ITEM (*SalesOrderNumber*, *ItemNumber*, Quantity, ExtendedPrice)

ITEM (ItemNumber, ItemDescription, UnitPrice)

Referential integrity constraints:

SalesPersonName in SALES-ORDER must exist in SalesPersonName in SALESPERSON

Phone in SALES-ORDER must exist in Phone in CUSTOMER

SalesOrderNumber in LINE-ITEM must exist in SalesOrderNumber in SALES-ORDER

ItemNumber in LINE-ITEM must exist in ItemNumber in ITEM

(b)

➤ FIGURE 7-12

Relational Representation of Example Hybrid Object: (a) Example Hybrid Object and (b) Relational Representation of SALES-ORDER and Related Objects

must add the key of R1 (which is O1) to R2 and establish the restriction that (O1, O2) of R-G1 must equal (O1, O2) of R2.

Case 2 is similar to Case 4 except for the restriction that an OBJECT3 can be related to only one OBJECT1. Again, the relations in Figure 7-14 will work,

➤ FIGURE 7-13

Four Cases of Hybrid Object Cardinality

Case	Description	Example
1	OBJECT2 relates to one instance of OBJECT1 and appears in only one group instance within that object.	ITEM relates to one ORDER and can appear on only one LineItem of that ORDER.
2	OBJECT2 relates to one instance of OBJECT1 and appears in possibly many group instances within that object.	ITEM relates to one ORDER and can appear on many LineItems of that ORDER.
3	OBJECT2 relates to possibly many instances of OBJECT1 and appears in only one group instance within each object.	ITEM relates to many ORDERs and can appear on only one LineItem of that ORDER.
4	OBJECT2 relates to possibly many instances of OBJECT1 and appears in possibly many group instances within those objects.	ITEM relates to many ORDERs and can appear on many LineItems of that ORDER.

➤ FIGURE 7-14

General Transformation of Hybrid Object into Relations

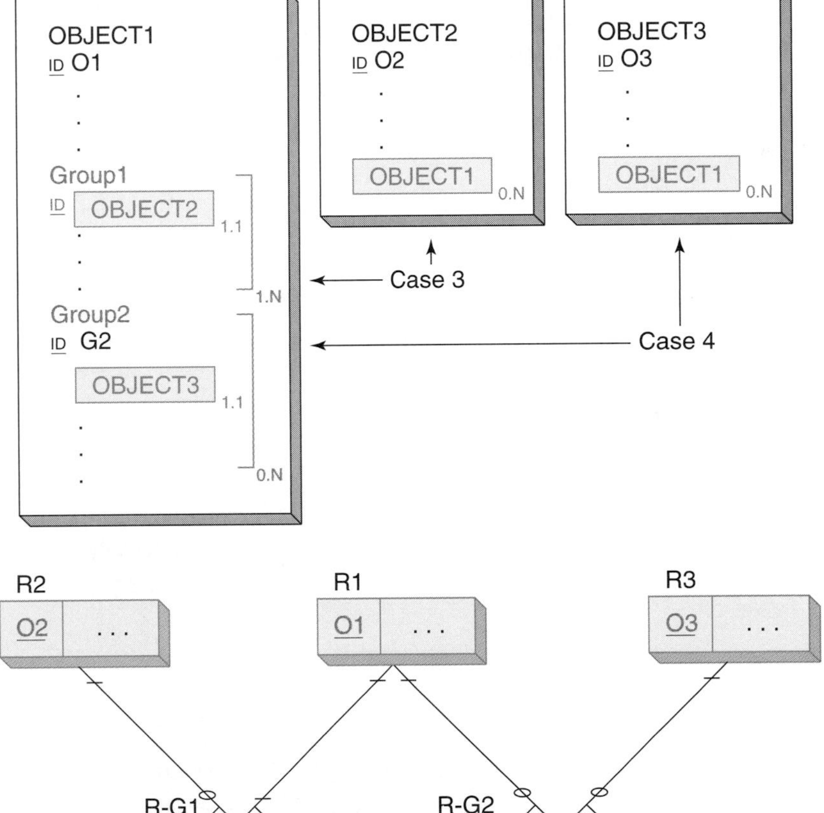

Referential integrity constraints:

O1 in R-G1 must exist in O1 in R1
O2 in R-G1 must exist in O2 in R2
O1 in R-G2 must exist in O1 in R1
O3 in R-G2 must exist in O3 of R3

but we must add the key of R1 (which is O1) to R3 and establish the restriction that (O1, O3) of R-G2 is a subset of (O1, O3) in R3 (see Questions 7.7 and 7.8).

Association Objects

An association object is an object that associates two other objects. It is a special case of compound objects that most often occurs in assignment situations. Figure 7-15(a) shows a FLIGHT object that associates an AIRPLANE with a PILOT.

To represent association objects, we define a relationship for each of the three objects, and then we represent the relationships among the objects using one of the strategies used with compound objects. In Figure 7-15(b), for example, one relation is defined for AIRPLANE, one for PILOT, and one for FLIGHT. The relationships between FLIGHT and AIRPLANE and between FLIGHT and PILOT are 1:N, so we place the keys of the parent in the children. In this case, we place the key of AIRPLANE and the key of PILOT in FLIGHT.

FLIGHT contains a key of its own. Although it contains foreign keys, these keys are only attributes and are not part of FLIGHT's key. But this is not always the case. If FLIGHT had no key of its own, its key would be the combination of the foreign keys of the objects that it associates. Here that combination would be {TailNumber, PilotNumber, Date}.

In general, when transforming association object structures into relations, we define one relation for each of the objects participating in the relationship.

➤ FIGURE 7-15

Relational Representation of Example Association Object: (a) FLIGHT Association Object and Related Objects and (b) Relational Representation of AIRPLANE, PILOT, and FLIGHT Objects

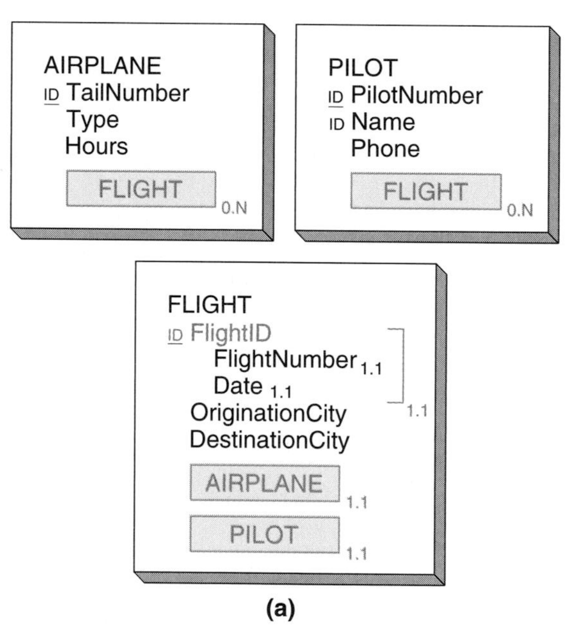

(a)

AIRPLANE (<u>TailNumber</u>, Type, Hours)

PILOT (<u>PilotNumber</u>, Name, Phone)

FLIGHT (<u>FlightNumber</u>, <u>Date</u>, OriginationCity, DestinationCity, *TailNumber*, *PilotNumber*)

Referential integrity constraints:

TailNumber in FLIGHT must exist in TailNumber in AIRPLANE
PilotNumber in FLIGHT must exist in PilotNumber in PILOT

(b)

➤ FIGURE 7-16

General Transformation of Association Objects into Relations

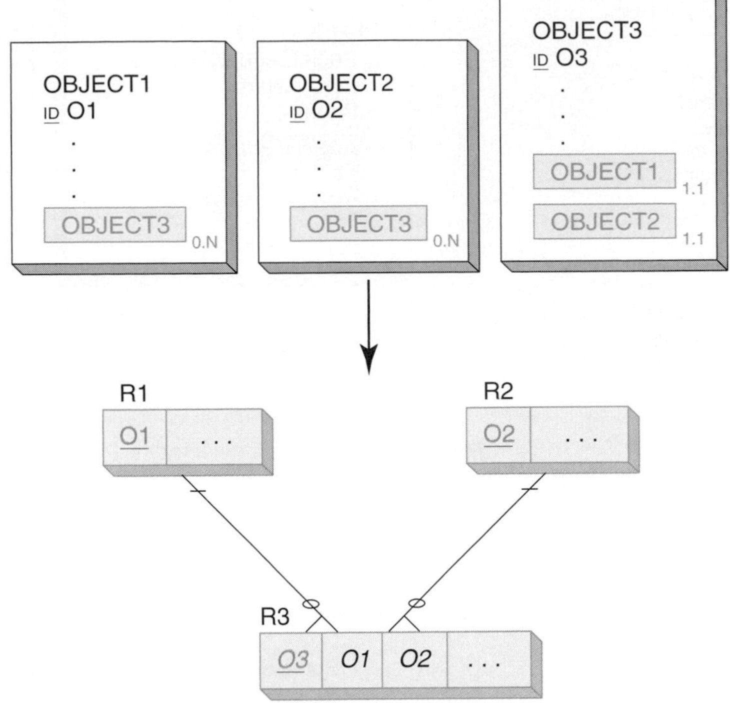

In Figure 7-16, OBJECT3 associates OBJECT1 and OBJECT2. In this case, we define R1, R2, and R3, as shown. The key of each of the parent relations, O1 and O2, appears as foreign key attributes in R3, the relation representing the association object. If the association object has no unique identifying attribute, the combination of the attributes of R1 and R2 will be used to create a unique identifier.

Note the difference between the association relation in Figure 7-16 and the intersection relation in Figure 7-11. The principal distinction is that the association table carries data that represent some aspect of the combination of the objects. The intersection relation carries no data; its only reason for existence is to specify which objects have a relationship with one another.

PARENT/SUBTYPE OBJECTS

Parent (also called *supertype*) and subtype objects are represented in a way similar to that for parent and subtype entities. We define a relation for the parent object and one for each of the subtype objects. The key of each of these relations is the key of the parent.

Figure 7-17(a) shows a parent object, PERSON, that includes two mutually exclusive subtypes, STUDENT and PROFESSOR. Figure 7-17(b) shows a relational representation of these three objects. Each object is represented by a table, and the key of all of the tables is the same.

The relations in Figure 7-17(b) pose a problem, however. The application program still needs to look in both the STUDENT and PROFESSOR tables to determine the type of PERSON. If an entry is found in STUDENT, the person is a student; if an entry is found in PROFESSOR, the person is a professor. This is an

➤ FIGURE 7-17

Representation of Example Parent and Subtypes: (a) PERSON Parent and STUDENT and PROFESSOR Subtypes, (b) Relational Representation of Parent and Subtypes, and (c) Alternative Representations of the Parent Relation

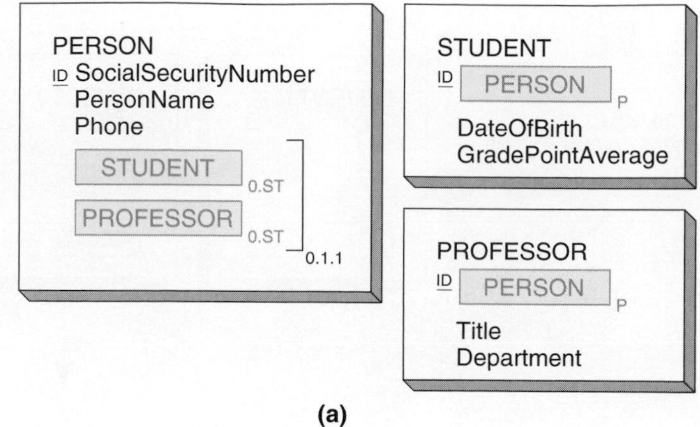

(a)

PERSON (<u>SocialSecurityNumber</u>, PersonName, Phone)

STUDENT (<u>SocialSecurityNumber</u>, DateOfBirth, GradePointAverage)

PROFESSOR (<u>SocialSecurityNumber</u>, Title, Department)

Referential integrity constraints:

> SocialSecurityNumber in STUDENT must exist in SocialSecurityNumber in PERSON
>
> SocialSecurityNumber in PROFESSOR must exist in SocialSecurityNumber in PERSON

(b)

PERSON1 (<u>SocialSecurityNumber</u>, PersonName, Phone, PersonType)

PERSON2 (<u>SocialSecurityNumber</u>, PersonName, Phone, StudentType, ProfessorType)

(c)

indirect and possibly slow way to determine the type of a person, and if, as may happen, the PERSON is of neither type, both tables will have been searched for no reason. Because of this problem, a type indicator attribute is sometimes placed in the parent table.

Figure 7-17(c) shows two variations of a type indicator. In the first variation, relation PERSON1, the type of object is stored in the attribute PersonType. Possible values of this attribute are 'Neither', 'STUDENT', or 'PROFESSOR'. The application would obtain the value of this attribute and thereby determine whether a subtype exists and, if so, which type it is.

A second possibility is shown in the relation PERSON2, to which two attributes have been added, one for StudentType and another for ProfessorType. Each of the attributes is a Boolean variable; the allowed values are true or false. Note that if, as is the case here, a person can be of only one type, then if one of these values is true, the other one must be false.

In general, designs of type PERSON1 are better when the subtypes are mutually exclusive. Designs of type PERSON2 are better when the subtypes are not exclusive.

A general scheme for representing subtypes is shown in Figure 7-18. One relation is created for the parent and one each for the subtypes. The key of all of the relations is the identifier of the parent. All relationships between the parent

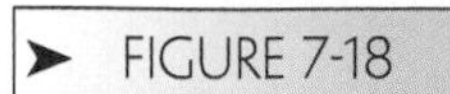
FIGURE 7-18

General Transformation of Parent/Subtype Objects into Relations

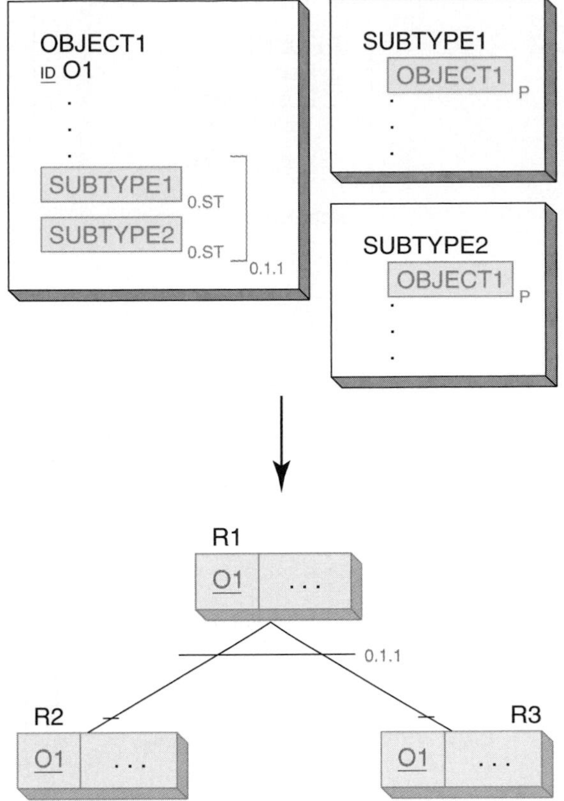

and the subtype are 1:1. Note the bar across the relationship lines and the presence of the subtype group's cardinality. The value shown, 0.1.1, means that no subtype is required but, if present, at most one of the subtypes is allowed.

(Recall that in general, the format of group cardinality is **r.m.n.**, where ***r*** is a Boolean true or false depending on whether or not the subtype group is required, ***m*** is the minimum number of subtypes that must have a value within the group, and ***n*** is the maximum number of subtypes that may have a value within the group. In a group of five subtypes, therefore, the cardinality of 1.2.4 indicates that the subtype group is required, that at least two subtypes must have a value, and that a maximum of four subtypes may have a value.)

Archetype/Version Objects

Archetype/version objects are compound objects that model various iterations, releases, or instances of a basic object. The objects in Figure 7-19(a) model software products for which there are various releases. Examples of such products are Microsoft Internet Explorer or Netscape Navigator. Examples of releases are Access 2000 and Access 2002.

The relational representation of PRODUCT and RELEASE is shown in Figure 7-19(b). One relation is created for PRODUCT, and another is created for

➤ FIGURE 7-19

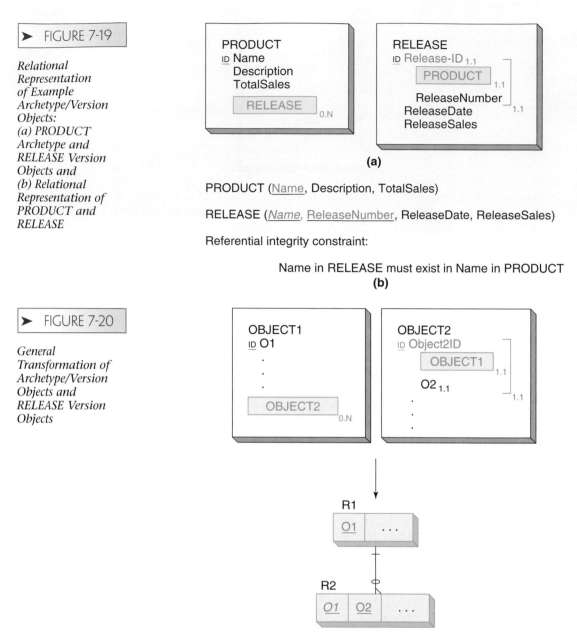

Relational Representation of Example Archetype/Version Objects: (a) PRODUCT Archetype and RELEASE Version Objects and (b) Relational Representation of PRODUCT and RELEASE

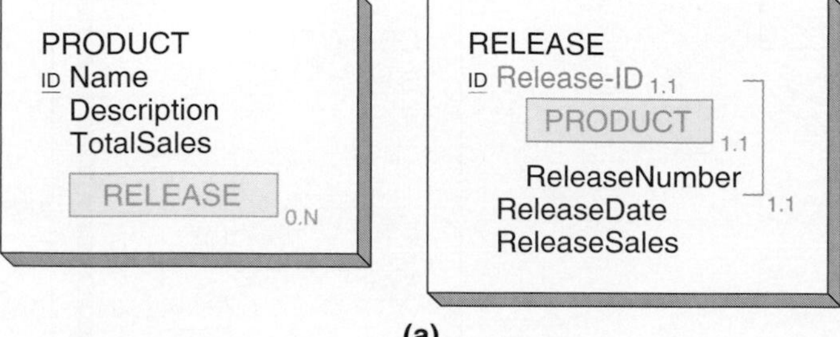

(a)

PRODUCT (<u>Name</u>, Description, TotalSales)

RELEASE (<u>*Name*</u>, <u>ReleaseNumber</u>, ReleaseDate, ReleaseSales)

Referential integrity constraint:

Name in RELEASE must exist in Name in PRODUCT

(b)

➤ FIGURE 7-20

General Transformation of Archetype/Version Objects and RELEASE Version Objects

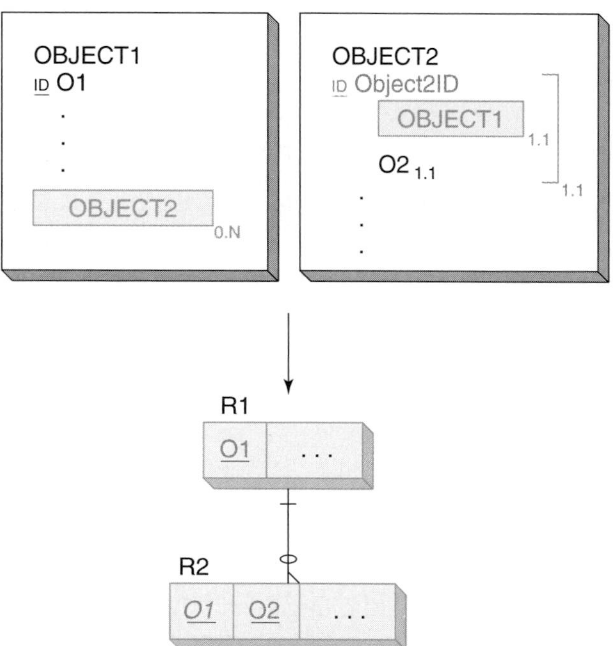

Referential integrity constraint:

O1 in R2 must exist in O1 in R1

RELEASE. The key of RELEASE is the combination of the key of PRODUCT and the local key (ReleaseNumber) of RELEASE.

Figure 7-20 shows the general transformation of archetype/version objects. Attribute O1 of R2 is both a local and a foreign key, but O2 is only a local key.

➤ SAMPLE OBJECTS

To reinforce the concepts presented so far, we now consider several example objects taken from actual businesses, presented in increasing order of complexity. We model the underlying object and represent it in relations using the methods described in this chapter. The specification of referential integrity constraints is left for Questions 7.20, 7.21, and, 7.22.

Subscription Form

Figure 7-21(a) shows a magazine subscription form. At least two object structures could represent this form. If the publishers of *Fine Woodworking* consider a subscriber to be an attribute of a subscription, a subscription could be a simple object represented as a single relation, as in Figure 7-21(b).

If this company has only a single publication and no plans to produce additional publications, the design in Figure 7-21(b) will work. If, however, this company has several publications and if a customer may subscribe to more than one of them, this design will duplicate the customer data for each publication. This will not only waste file space for the publisher but will also exasperate the customer because, for example, he or she will be required to submit address changes for each publication of the same publisher.

If the publisher has several publications or plans to have several publications, a better design would be to model subscriber as a separate object, as shown in Figure 7-21(c). CUSTOMER is a 1:N compound object and is represented by the relations in this figure.

Product Description

Figure 7-22(a) shows the description of a popular packaged-goods product. Whereas Figure 7-21(a) shows a generic form with no data, Figure 7-22(a) shows an instance of a specific report with data about a cereal product. The reports for all of Kellogg's cereal products use this format.

Figure 7-22(b) shows a composite object that could underlie this report. We say *could* because there are many different ways that this object might be represented. Also, further investigation may reveal other objects that are not apparent in this one report. For example, USDA Recommendation may be a semantic object in its own right.

For illustration purposes, we make different assumptions about the Nutrient and USDARecDailyAllow groups. The CEREAL-PRODUCT object assumes that every element of the Nutrient group—namely, calories, protein, carbohydrate, fat, cholesterol, sodium, and potassium—is required in every instance of this object. We do not assume this for the USDARecDailyAllow group, because only one instance of this group must exist.

The report in Figure 7-22(a) has many interpretations and could be modeled in several different ways. In an actual development project, it would be important to obtain as many other reports about other cereal products and about the ingredients and nutritional information in this report. These other documents would most likely give additional structure to this semantic object.

Figure 7-22(c) shows the relational representation for the CEREAL-PRODUCT object. The minimum cardinality of 7 is shown by placing the numeral *7* next to the required hash mark on the relationship line. Foreign keys have been placed as described previously for composite objects.

Traffic-Warning Citation

Figure 7-23(a) shows an instance of the traffic-warning citation form used in the state of Washington. The designer of this form has given us important clues to the underlying objects of this form. Notice that portions of the form are distinguished by rounded corners, indicating that different sections pertain to different objects. Also, some groups of attributes have names, indicating the need for group attributes.

Figure 7-23(b) is one way to illustrate the underlying objects of the traffic-warning citation. Although we cannot be certain from just this one form, there are certain clues that lead us to believe that the driver, vehicle, and officer are

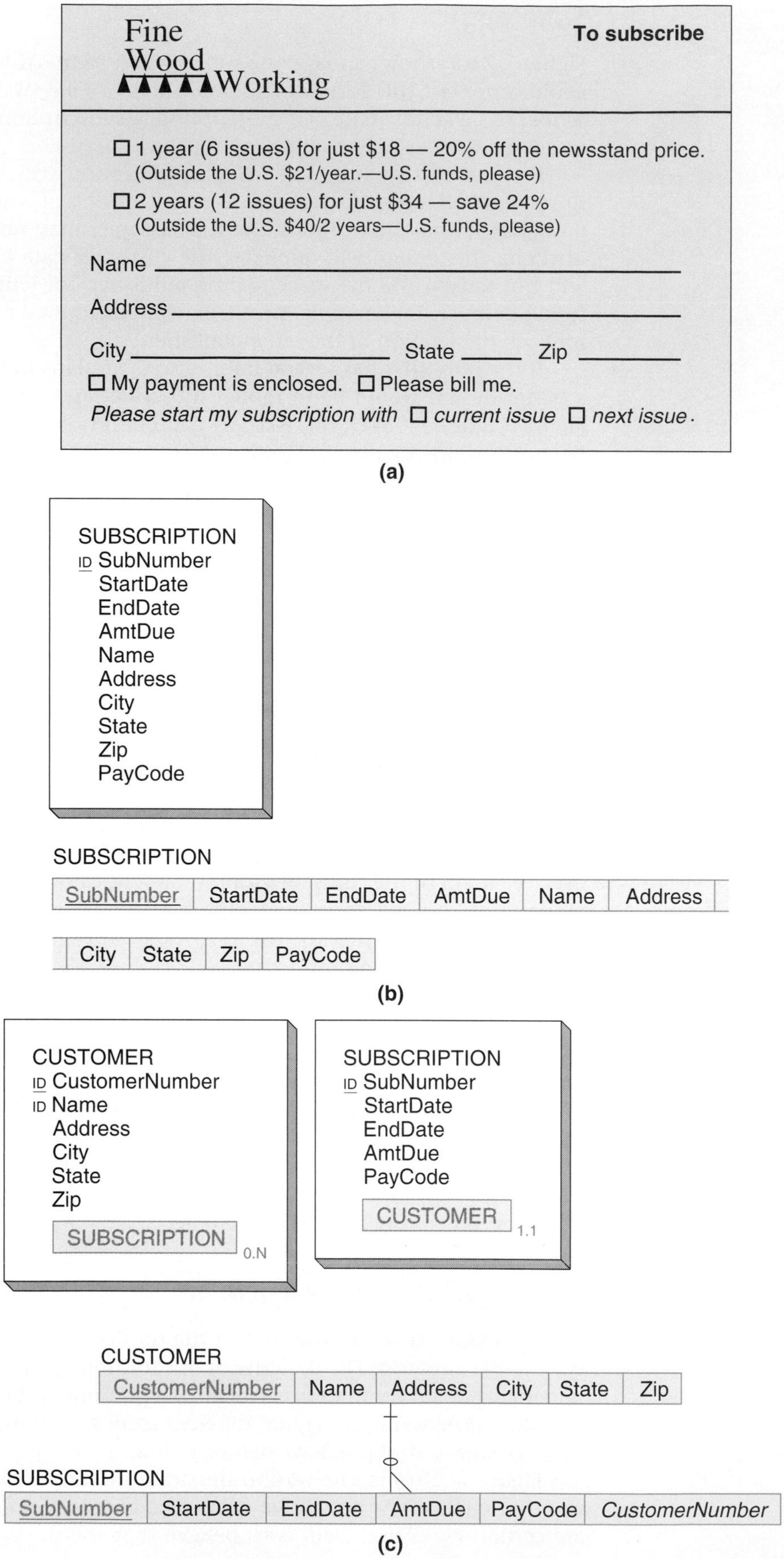

➤ FIGURE 7-21

Alternative Representations of Subscription: (a) Subscription Order Form, (b) Subscription Modeled As One Object, and (c) Subscription Modeled As Two Objects

Fine Wood Working

To subscribe

☐ 1 year (6 issues) for just $18 — 20% off the newsstand price.
(Outside the U.S. $21/year.—U.S. funds, please)

☐ 2 years (12 issues) for just $34 — save 24%
(Outside the U.S. $40/2 years—U.S. funds, please)

Name ______

Address ______

City ______ State ______ Zip ______

☐ My payment is enclosed. ☐ Please bill me.

Please start my subscription with ☐ *current issue* ☐ *next issue.*

(a)

SUBSCRIPTION
ID SubNumber
StartDate
EndDate
AmtDue
Name
Address
City
State
Zip
PayCode

SUBSCRIPTION

SubNumber	StartDate	EndDate	AmtDue	Name	Address	City	State	Zip	PayCode

(b)

CUSTOMER
ID CustomerNumber
ID Name
Address
City
State
Zip
SUBSCRIPTION 0.N

SUBSCRIPTION
ID SubNumber
StartDate
EndDate
AmtDue
PayCode
CUSTOMER 1.1

CUSTOMER

CustomerNumber	Name	Address	City	State	Zip

SUBSCRIPTION

SubNumber	StartDate	EndDate	AmtDue	PayCode	*CustomerNumber*

(c)

➤ FIGURE 7-22

Cereal Product Representation: (a) Cereal Product Report, (b) CEREAL-PRODUCT Object Diagram, and (c) Relational Representation of CEREAL-PRODUCT

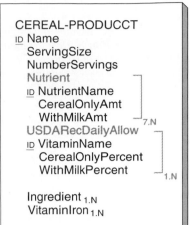

NUTRITION INFORMATION

SERVING SIZE: 1 OZ. (28.4 g, ABOUT 1 CUP)

SERVINGS PER PACKAGE: 13

	CEREAL	WITH ½ CUP VITAMINS A & D SKIM MILK
CALORIES	110	150*
PROTEIN	2 g	6g
CARBOHYDRATE	25 g	31g
FAT	0 g	0g*
CHOLESTEROL	0 mg	0mg*
SODIUM	290 mg	350mg
POTASSIUM	35 mg	240mg

PERCENTAGE OF U.S. RECOMMENDED DAILY ALLOWANCES (U.S. RDA)

PROTEIN	2	10
VITAMIN A	25	30
VITAMIN C	25	25
THIAMIN	35	40
RIBOFLAVIN	35	45
NIACIN	35	35
CALCIUM	**	15
IRON	10	10
VITAMIN D	10	25
VITAMIN B_6	35	35
FOLIC ACID	35	35
PHOSPHORUS	4	15
MAGNESIUM	2	6
ZINC	2	6
COPPER	2	4

*WHOLE MILK SUPPLIES AN ADDITIONAL 30 CALORIES, 4 g FAT, AND 15 mg CHOLESTEROL.

**CONTAINS LESS THAN 2% OF THE U.S. RDA OF THIS NUTRIENT.

INGREDIENTS: RICE, SUGAR, SALT, CORN SYRUP, MALT FLAVORING,

VITAMINS AND IRON: VITAMIN C (SODIUM ASCORBATE AND ASCORBIC ACID), NIACINAMIDE, IRON, VITAMIN B_6 (PYRIDOXINE HYDROCHLORIDE), VITAMIN A (PALMITATE), VITAMIN B_2 (RIBOFLAVIN), VITAMIN B_1 (THIAMIN HYDROCHLORIDE), FOLIC ACID, AND VITAMIN D.
TO KEEP THIS CEREAL FRESH, BHT HAS BEEN ADDED TO THE PACKAGING.

(a)

CEREAL-PRODUCCT
ID Name
ServingSize
NumberServings
Nutrient
ID NutrientName
CerealOnlyAmt
WithMilkAmt
7.N
USDARecDailyAllow
ID VitaminName
CerealOnlyPercent
WithMilkPercent
1.N
Ingredient 1.N
VitaminIron 1.N

(b)

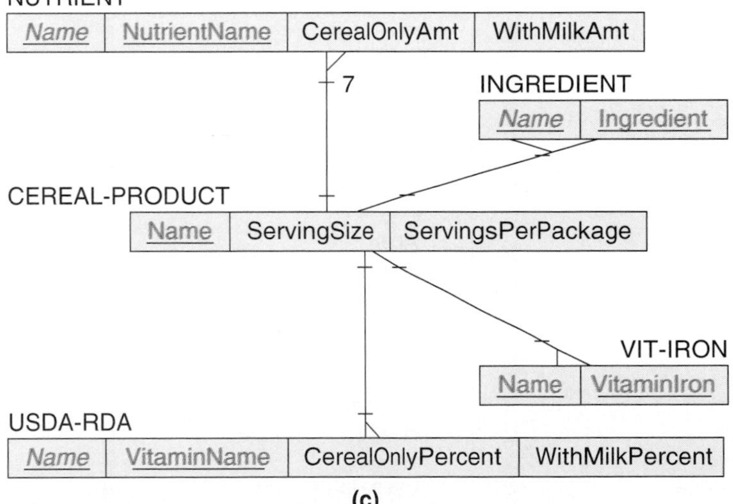

(c)

independent objects. First, the data concerning each of these subjects are in a separate section on the form. But more important, each section has fields that are undoubtedly identifying attributes of something apart from CORRECTION-NOTICE. For example, {DriversLicense, State} uniquely identifies a driver; VehicleLicense, State and VIN (Vehicle Identification Number) identify registered

➤ FIGURE 7-23

Representation of a Correction Notice: (a) Example Form, (b) CORRECTION-NOTICE Object Diagram, and (c) Relational Representation of CORRECTION-NOTICE

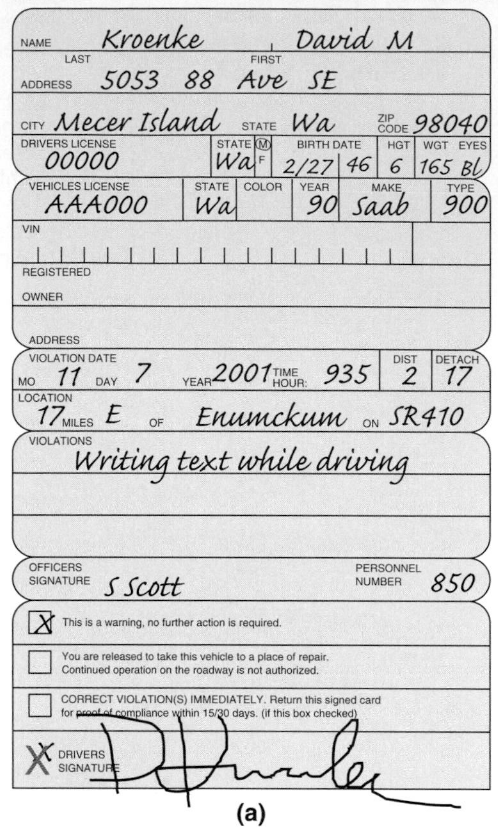
WASHINGTON STATE PATROL CORRECTION NOTICE

NAME Kroenke , David M
LAST FIRST

ADDRESS 5053 88 Ave SE

CITY Mecer Island STATE Wa ZIP CODE 98040

DRIVERS LICENSE	STATE	M F	BIRTH DATE	HGT	WGT	EYES
00000	Wa	M	2/27/46	6	165	Bl

VEHICLES LICENSE	STATE	COLOR	YEAR	MAKE	TYPE
AAA000	Wa		90	Saab	900

VIN

REGISTERED

OWNER

ADDRESS

VIOLATION DATE MO 11 DAY 7 YEAR 2001 TIME HOUR: 935 DIST 2 DETACH 17

LOCATION 17 MILES E OF Enumckum ON SR410

VIOLATIONS Writing text while driving

OFFICERS SIGNATURE S Scott PERSONNEL NUMBER 850

[X] This is a warning, no further action is required.

[ ] You are released to take this vehicle to a place of repair. Continued operation on the roadway is not authorized.

[ ] CORRECT VIOLATION(S) IMMEDIATELY. Return this signed card for proof of compliance within 15/30 days. (if this box checked)

X DRIVERS SIGNATURE

(a)

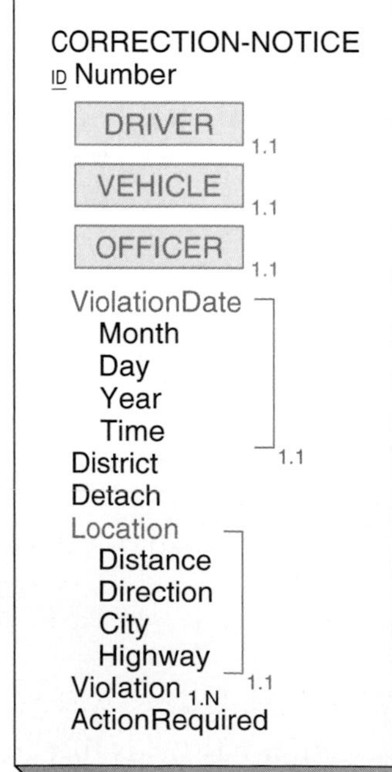

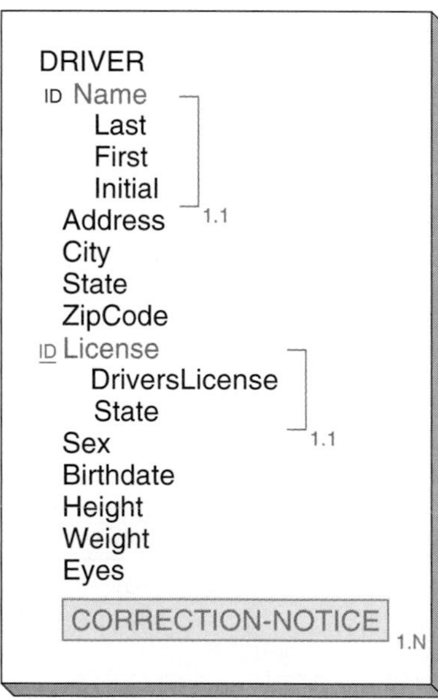

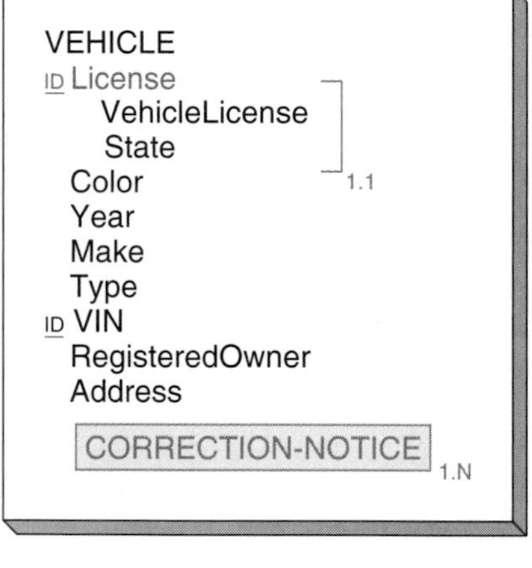

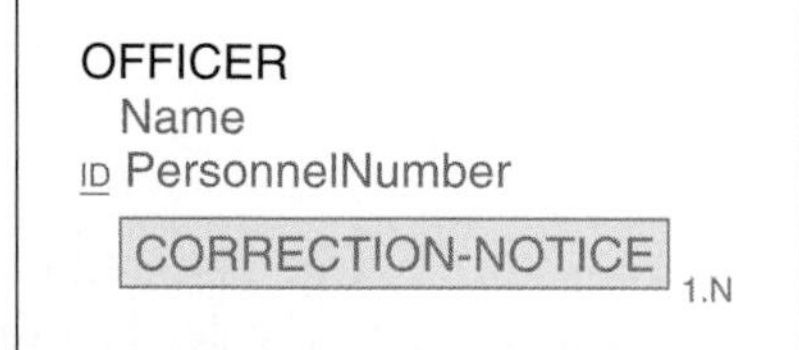

(b)

FIGURE 7-23

(Continued)

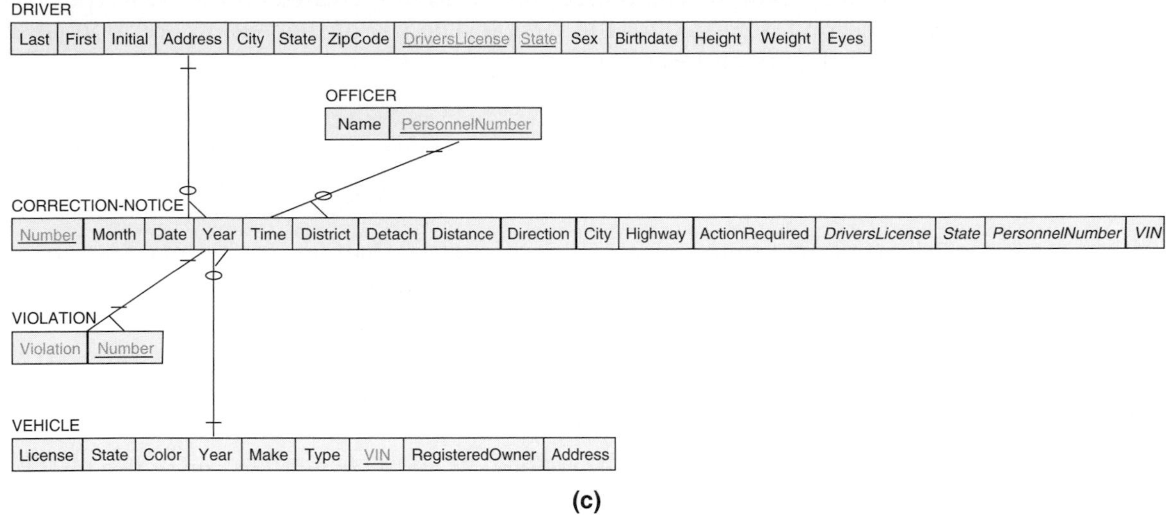

(c)

vehicles; and PersonnelNumber identifies an officer. These key fields obviously are determinants, so objects were defined for each. The relation representation of these diagrams appears in Figure 7-23(c).

SUMMARY

The transformation of semantic objects into relations depends on the type of object. Simple objects are represented by a single relation. The nonobject attributes are carried as attributes of the relation.

Composite objects require two or more relations for their representation. One relation contains the single-value attributes of the object. Another relation is constructed for each multi-value simple or group attribute. The key of the relations representing the multi-value attributes is always a composite key that contains the key of the object plus an identifier of the composite group within that object.

At least two relations are required to represent a compound object. Each relation has its own distinct key. There are four different types of compound objects—one to one, one to many, many to one, and many to many—which are represented by inserting foreign keys. For one-to-one relationships, the key of either table is placed in the other table, and for one-to-many and many-to-one relationships, the key of the parent is placed in the child relation. Finally, for many-to-many relationships, an intersection table is created that carries the keys of both relations.

Hybrid objects are represented by creating a table for the multi-value group attribute of the composite object and placing the key of the relation representing the noncomposite object into that table. The four cases of hybrid are listed in Figure 7-13.

Association objects require at least three relations for their representation, one for each of the objects involved. Each relation has its own key, and the relation representing the association object contains, as foreign keys, the keys of the other two objects.

Parent and subtype objects are represented by creating a relation for the parent and one for each subtype. The key of all relations is normally the same. An identifier attribute is sometimes placed in the parent to indicate the object's type.

For archetype/version objects, one relation is created for the archetype object and a second is created for the version. The key of the version's relation always contains the key of the archetype.

➤ GROUP I QUESTIONS

7.1 Give an example of a simple object other than one in this text. Show how to represent this object by means of a relation.

7.2 Give an example of a composite object other than one in this text. Show how to represent this object by means of relations.

7.3 Give an example of a 1:1 compound object other than one in this text. Show two ways to represent it by means of relations.

7.4 Give an example of a 1:N compound object other than one in this text. Show how to represent it by means of relations.

7.5 Give an example of an M:1 compound object other than one in this text. Show how to represent it by means of relations.

7.6 Give an example of an M:N compound object other than one in this text. Show how to represent it by means of relations.

7.7 Give an example of a Case 1 (see Figure 7-13) hybrid object. Show how to represent it by means of relations.

7.8 Give an example of a Case 2 (see Figure 7-13) hybrid object. Show how to represent it by means of relations.

7.9 Give an example of an association and related objects other than one in this text. Show how to represent these objects by means of relations. Assume that the association object has an identifier of its own.

7.10 Do the same as for Question 7.9, but assume that the association object does not have an identifier of its own.

7.11 Give an example of a parent object with at least two exclusive subtypes. Show how to represent these objects by means of relations. Use a type indicator attribute.

7.12 Give an example of a parent object with at least two nonexclusive subtypes. Show how to represent these objects by means of relations. Use a type indicator attribute.

7.13 Find an example of a form on your campus that would be appropriately modeled with a simple object. Show how to represent this object by means of a relation.

7.14 Find an example of a form on your campus that would be appropriately modeled with a composite object. Show how to represent this object by means of relations.

7.15 Find an example of a form on your campus that would be appropriately modeled with one of the types of a compound object. Show how to represent these objects by means of relations.

7.16 Find an example of a form on your campus that would be appropriately modeled with a hybrid object. Classify the object according to Figure 7-13, and show how to represent these objects by means of relations.

7.17 Find an example of a form on your campus that would be appropriately modeled with an association and related objects. Show how to represent these objects by means of relations.

7.18 Find an example of a form on your campus that would be appropriately modeled with parent/subtypes objects. Show how to represent these objects by means of relations.

7.19 Find an example of a form on your campus that would be appropriately modeled with archetype/version objects. Show how to represent these objects by means of relations.

7.20 What referential integrity constraints, if any, should be specified for the designs in Figure 7-21(b) and (c)?

7.21 What referential integrity constraints, if any, should be specified for the design in Figure 7-22(c)?

7.22 What referential integrity constraints, if any, should be specified for the design in Figure 7-23(c)?

7.23 Suppose object O1 has a 1:N relationship to object O2 and that O1 has a second 1:N relationship to object O3. Further suppose that O2 is required in O1, but O3 is optional in O1. Is there a difference between the referential integrity constraint for the relationship of O1 and O2 and the referential integrity constraint for the relationship of O1 and O3? If so, what is it?

➤ GROUP II QUESTIONS

7.24 In Figure 7-13, give a different example for each of the four cases in the right-hand column. Show how each of your examples would be represented with relations.

7.25 Modify Figure 7-22(b) and (c) to add the reports shown in Figure 7-24.

➤ FIGURE 7-24

Reports for Question 7.25

FDA REPORT #6272
Date: 06/30/2001
Issuer: Kellogg's Corporation
Report Title: Product Summary by Ingredient

Corn	Corn Flakes
	Krispix
	Nutrigrain (Corn)
Corn syrup	Rice Krispies
	Frosted Flakes
	Sugar Pops
Malt	Rice Krispies
	Sugar Smacks
Wheat	Sugar Smacks
	Nutrigrain (Wheat)

(a)

SUPPLIERS LIST
Date: 06/30/2001

Ingredient	Supplier	Price
Corn	Wilson	2.80
	J. Perkins	2.72
	Pollack	2.83
	McKay	2.80
Wheat	Adams	1.19
	Kroner	1.19
	Schmidt	1.22
Barley	Wilson	0.85
	Pollack	0.84

(b)

➤ FIGURE 7-25

Report for Question 7.26

West Side Story
Based on a conception of Jerome Robbins

Book by ARTHUR LAURENTS
Music by LEONARD BERNSTEIN
Lyrics by STEPHEN SONDHEIM

Entire Original Production Directed and Choreographed by JEROME ROBBINS

Originally produced on Broadway by Robert E. Griffith and Harold S. Prince by arrangement with Roger L. Stevens
Orchestration by Leonard Bernstein with Sid Ramin and Irwin Kostal

HIGHLIGHTS FROM THE COMPLETE RECORDING

Maria . . . . KIRI TE KANAWA
Tony . . . . JOSE CARRERAS
Anita . . . . TATIANA TROYANOS
Riff . . . . KURT OLLMAN
and MARILYN HORNE singing "Somewhere"

Rosalia . . . . Louise Edeiken
Consuela . . . . Stella Zambalis
Fancisca . . . . Angelina Reaux
Action . . . . David Livingston
Diesel . . . . Marty Nelson
Baby John . . . . . . Stephen Bogardus
A-rab . . . . Peter Thom
Snowboy . . . . Todd Lester
Bernardo. . . . Richard Harrell

1	**Jet Song** (Riff, Action, Baby John, A-rab, Chorus)	[3'13]
2	**Something's Coming** (Tony)	[2'33]
3	**Maria** (Tony)	[2'56]
4	**Tonight** (Maria, Tony)	[5'27]
5	**America** (Anita, Rosalia, Chorus)	[4'47]
6	**Cool** (Riff, Chorus)	[4'37]
7	**One Hand, One Heart** (Tony, Maria)	[5'38]
8	**Tonight** (Ensemble) (Entire Cast)	[3'40]
9	**I Feel Pretty** (Maria, Chorus)	[3'22]
10	**Somewhere** (A Girl)	[2'34]
11	**Gee OFicer Krupke** (Action, Snowboy, Diesel, A-rab, Baby John, Chorus)	[4'18]
12	**A Boy Like That** (Anita, Maria)	[2'05]
13	**I Have a Love** (Maria, Anita)	[3'30]
14	**Taunting Scene** (Orchestra)	[1'21]
15	**Finale** (Maria, Tony)	[2'40]

7.26 Using the CD cover shown in Figure 7-25 as a guide, perform the following tasks:

a. Draw the object diagrams for the underlying objects ARTIST, ROLE, and SONG.

b. Identify the relationships among those objects. What types of objects are they (simple, composite, and so on)?

c. Indicate for each participant in a relationship whether it is optional or mandatory.

d. Transform the object diagrams into relation diagrams.

What is the key of each relation? What foreign keys appear in each relation?

➤ PROJECTS

A. Complete project A at the end of Chapter 4 if you have not already done so. Transform your semantic object model into a set of relations. If any of your relations are not in DK/NF, justify your decision to create un-normalized relations.

B. Complete project B at the end of Chapter 4 if you have not already done so. Transform your semantic object model into a set of relations. If any of your relations are not in DK/NF, justify your decision to create un-normalized relations.

C. Complete project C at the end of Chapter 4 if you have not already done so. Transform your semantic object model into a set of relations. If any of your relations are not in DK/NF, justify your decision to create un-normalized relations.

➤ FIREDUP PROJECT QUESTIONS

If you have not already done so, create semantic objects for Questions A and C in the FiredUp Project at the end of Chapter 4.

A. Transform the semantic object design from Question A at the end of Chapter 4 into a set of relations in domain/key normal form. For each relation, specify the primary key, candidate keys, if any, and foreign keys. Specify all referential integrity constraints. If necessary, make and justify assumptions regarding the underlying semantics of the application.

B. Adjust your answer to question A to allow un-normalized relations if you think just relations are appropriate. Justify any non-normalized relations you have. If necessary, make and justify assumptions regarding the underlying semantics of the application.

C. Transform the semantic objects design from Question C at the end of Chapter 4 into a set of relations, preferably in domain/key normal form. If any of your relations are not in domain/key normal form, explain why not. For each relation, specify the primary key, candidate keys, if any, and foreign keys. Specify all referential integrity constraints.

D. Adjust your answer to Question C, above, to assume that home, fax and cell phone are to be represented by separate, single-value attributes. Is this a better design than in your answer to Question C? Explain why or why not.

PART IV

DATABASE IMPLEMENTATION WITH THE RELATIONAL MODEL

Part IV considers database implementation using the relational model. Chapter 8 begins with a discussion of relational data manipulation. First we look at the types of relational data manipulation languages, and then we explain the basic operators of relational algebra and illustrate their use.

Chapter 9 describes Structured Query Language, or SQL. This language has been endorsed by the American National Standards Institute as a standard for manipulating relational databases, and it also is the primary data manipulation language for commercial relational DBMS products. Chapter 10 concludes this part with a discussion of the design of database applications.

Foundations of Relational Implementation

This chapter introduces the implementation of relational databases. We begin by describing relational data definition, reviewing relational terminology, and explaining how a design is defined to the DBMS. Next we turn to space allocation and database data creation. The remainder of the chapter addresses relational data manipulation: first, a survey of four types of relational data manipulation language (DML), then the three common modes of DML interfaces to the DBMS, and finally, the basic operators of relational algebra and example queries expressed in terms of relational algebra.

➤ DEFINING RELATIONAL DATA

Several tasks must be performed when implementing a relational database. First, the structure of the database must be defined to the DBMS. To do this, the developer uses a data definition language (DDL) or some equivalent means (such as a graphical display) to describe the structure. Then the database is allocated to physical storage media and filled with data. In this section we discuss each of these tasks, but first we review the relational terminology.

REVIEW OF TERMINOLOGY

As stated in Chapter 5, a **relation** is a table that has several properties:

1. The entries in the relation are single value; multiple values are not allowed. Hence, the intersection of a row and a column contains only one value.
2. All the entries in any column are of the same kind. For example, one column may contain customer names and another, birthdates. Each column has a unique name, and the order of the columns is not important to the relation.

FIGURE 8-1

Occurrence of PATIENT Relation Structure

	Col 1 (or Attribute 1)	Col 2	Col 3	Col 4	Col 5
	Name	Date Of Birth	Gender	Account Number	Physician
Row 1 (or Tuple 1)	Riley	01/19/1946	F	147	Lee
Row 2	Murphy	12/28/1981	M	289	Singh
Row 3	Krajewski	10/21/1973	F	533	Levy
Row 4	Ting	05/23/1938	F	681	Spock
Row 5	Dixon	04/15/1987	M	704	Levy
Row 6	Abel	06/19/1957	M	193	Singh

The columns of a relation are called **attributes.** Each attribute has a **domain,** which is a physical and logical description of allowed values.

3. No two rows in the relation are identical, and the order of the rows is not important (see Figure 8-1). Each row of the relation is known as a tuple.

Figure 8-1 is an example, or occurrence. The generalized format, PATIENT (Name, DateOfBirth, Gender, <u>AccountNumber</u>, Physician), is the relation structure and is what most people mean when they use the term *relation.* (Recall from Chapter 5 that an underlined attribute is a key.) If we add constraints on allowable data values to the relation structure, we then have a **relational schema.** These terms are summarized in Figure 8-2.

CONFUSION REGARDING THE TERM *KEY* The term **key** is a common source of confusion because it has different meanings in the design and the implementation stages. During the design, the term *key* refers to one or more columns that uniquely identify a row in a relation. As we explained in Chapter 5, we know every relation has a key because every row is unique; at the limit, the composite of every column in the relation is the key. Usually the key is composed of one or two columns, however.

During implementation, the term *key* is used differently. For most relational products, a key is a column on which the DBMS builds an index or other data structure. This is done to access rows quickly by means of that column's value. Such keys need not be unique, and often, in fact, they are not. They are constructed only to improve performance. (See the Appendix A for information about such data structures.)

For example, consider the relation ORDER (<u>OrderNumber</u>, OrderDate, CustNumber, Amount). From the standpoint of relational *design,* the key of this relation is OrderNumber, since the underline means OrderNumber uniquely identifies rows of the relation. From the standpoint of relational *implementation,* however, any of the four columns could be a key. OrderDate, for example, could be defined as a key. If it is, the DBMS will create a data structure so that ORDER rows can be quickly accessed by the value of OrderDate. Most likely, there will be many rows for a given value of OrderDate. Defining it as this type of key says nothing about its uniqueness.

Sometimes the terms **logical key** and **physical key** are used to distinguish between these two meanings of key. A logical key is a unique identifier, whereas a physical key is a column that has an index or other data structure defined for it in order to improve performance.

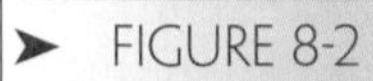

FIGURE 8-2

Summary of Relational Terminology

Term	Meaning
Relation (or Table) (or File)	Two-dimensional table
Attribute (or Column) (or Field) (or Data Item)	Column of a relation
Tuple (or Row) (or Record)	Row in a relation
Domain	Physical and logical description of allowed values
Relation structure	Format of relation
Occurrence	Relation structure with data
Relational schema	Relation structure plus constraints
Key	Group of one or more attributes that uniquely identifies a tuple in a relation
Logical key	Same as key
Physical key (or Index)	A group of one or more attributes that is supported by a data structure that facilitates fast retrieval or rapid sequential access

INDEXES Since a physical key is usually an index, some people reserve the term *key* for a logical key and use the term *index* for a physical key. In this text, we will do exactly that—use the term *key* to mean a logical key, and use the term *index* to mean a physical key.

There are three reasons for defining indexes. One is to allow rows to be quickly accessed by means of the indexed attribute's value. The second is to facilitate sorting rows by that attribute. For instance, in ORDER, OrderDate might be defined as a key so that a report showing orders by dates can be more quickly generated.

A third reason for building an index is to enforce uniqueness. Although indexes do not have to be unique, when the developer wants a column to be unique, an index is created by the DBMS. With most relational DBMS products, a column or group of columns can be forced to be unique by using the keyword UNIQUE when defining the appearance of a column in a table.

Implementing a Relational Database

In this text, we use the relational model to express database designs. Since we have done so, we can proceed directly from designing the database to implementing it. There is no need to transform the design during the implementation stage; we simply define the existing relational design to the DBMS.

The situation is different when we implement databases using DBMS products based on data models other than the relational model. For example, when implementing a database for DL/I, we must convert the relational design to hierarchical design and then define the converted design to the DBMS product.

DEFINING THE DATABASE STRUCTURE TO THE DBMS There are several different means by which the structure of the database is described to the DBMS, depending on the DBMS product being used. With some products, a text file is constructed that describes the database structure. The language used to describe such a structure is sometimes called the **data definition language,** or DDL. The DDL text file names the tables in the database, names and describes the columns of those tables, defines indexes, and describes other structures such as constraints and security restrictions. Figure 8-3 shows the typical data definition language used for defining a simple relational database for a hypothetical DBMS. More realistic examples using a standard called SQL are shown in Chapters 12 and 13.

Some DBMS products do not require that the database be defined by DDL in text file format. One common alternative is to provide a graphical means for defining the structure of the database. With Access 2002, for example, the developer is shown a graphical list structure and asked to fill in the table and column names in the appropriate places. We saw an example of this in Chapter 2 (Figure 2-4).

In general, graphical definition facilities are common for DBMS products on personal computers. Both graphical and textual DDL are common for DBMS products on servers and mainframes. ORACLE and SQL Server, for example, employ both. Figure 8-4 summarizes the database definition process.

Regardless of the means by which the database structure is defined, the developer must name each table, define the columns in that table, and describe the physical format (for example, TEXT 10) of each column. Also, depending on the facilities of the DBMS, the developer may specify constraints that the DBMS is to enforce. Column values can be defined to be NOT NULL or UNIQUE, for example. Some products also allow the definition of range and value constraints (Part less than 10000 or Color equal to one of ['Red', 'Green', 'Blue'], for example). Finally, interrelation constraints can be defined. An example is that DeptNumber in EMPLOYEE must match a value of DeptNumber in DEPARTMENT.

➤ FIGURE 8-3

Example DDL Text File for Database Definition

```
CREATE SCHEMA PHYSICIAN

CREATE TABLE PATIENT

  ( Name                 CHARACTER VARYING (35) NOT NULL,
    Date Of Birth        DATE/TIME,
    Gender               CHARACTER VARYING (10),
    AccountNumber        INTEGER NOT NULL,
    PhysicianName_FK1    CHARACTER VARYING (35) NOT NULL,

    PRIMARY KEY ( AccountNumber ),
    FOREIGN KEY ( PhysicianName_FK1 )
        REFERENCES PHYSICIAN
  )

CREATE TABLE PHYSICIAN

  ( PhysicianName        CHARACTER VARYING (35) NOT NULL,
    AreaCode             CHARACTER VARYING (3),
    LocalNumber          CHARACTER VARYING (8) NOT NULL,

    PRIMARY KEY (PhysicianName)
  )
```

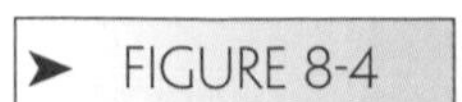
FIGURE 8-4

Database Definition Process

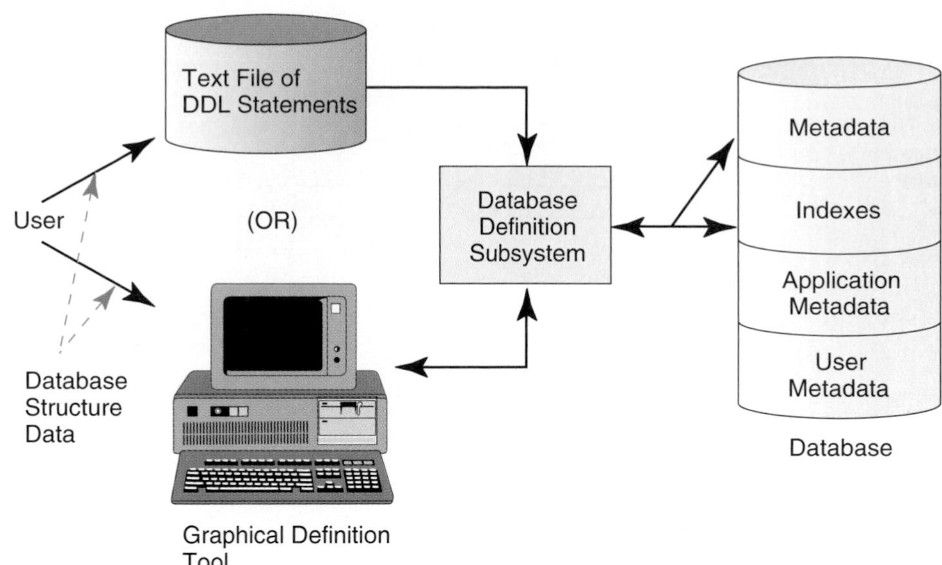

With many products, the developer can also define passwords and other control and security facilities. As shown in Chapter 11, a number of different strategies can be used. Some strategies place controls on data constructs (passwords on tables, for example), and others place controls on people (the user of password X can read and update tables T1 and T2).

ALLOCATING MEDIA SPACE In addition to defining the structure of the database, the developer must allocate database structures to physical media. Again, the specific tasks depend on the particular DBMS product used. For a personal database, all that needs to be done is to assign the database to a directory and give the database a name. The DBMS then allocates storage space automatically.

Other DBMS products, especially those used for servers and mainframes, require more work. To improve performance and control, the distribution of the database data across disks and channels must be carefully planned. For example, depending on the nature of application processing, it may be advantageous to locate certain tables on the same disk, or it may be important to ensure that certain tables are not located on the same disk.

Consider, for example, an order object that is composed of data from ORDER, LINE-ITEM, and ITEM tables. Suppose that when processing an order, the application retrieves one row from ORDER, several rows from LINE-ITEM, and one row from ITEM for each LINE-ITEM row. Furthermore, the LINE-ITEM rows for a given order tend to be clustered together, but the ITEM rows are not at all clustered. Figure 8-5 illustrates this situation.

Now suppose that an organization concurrently processes many orders and has one large, fast disk and one smaller, slower disk. The developer must determine the best place to locate the data. One possibility is that the performance will be better if the ITEM table is stored on the larger, faster disk and the ORDER and LINE-ITEM data on the smaller, slower disk. Or perhaps the performance will be better if the ORDER and LINE-ITEM data for prior months' orders are placed on the slower disk and all the data for this month's orders are placed on the faster disk.

We cannot answer this question here, as the answer depends on the amount of data, the processing characteristics of the DBMS and the operating system, the size and speed of the disks and channels, and the application-processing requirements of all applications that use the database. The point is that factors such as these must be considered when allocating media space to the database.

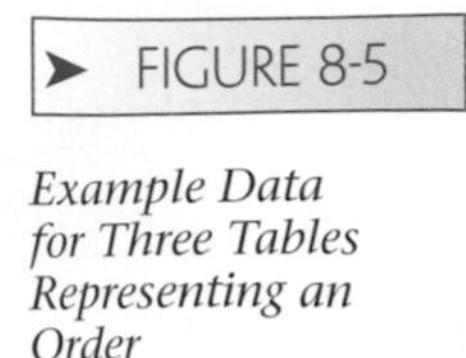

➤ FIGURE 8-5

Example Data for Three Tables Representing an Order

ORDER table

Order Number
100
200
300

LINE-ITEM table

Order-Number	LINE-Number	ITEM-Number
100	1	10
100	2	70
100	3	50
200	1	50
200	2	10
300	1	60
300	2	10
300	3	50
300	4	20
300	5	30

ITEM table

ITEM-Number	ITEM-DESCRIPTION
10	A
20	B
30	C
40	D
50	E
60	F
70	G

Note: For a given order, LINE-ITEM rows are clustered, but ITEM rows are not.

In addition to specifying the location and amount of space for user's data, the developer may also need to declare whether or not the file space should be increased as needed, and if so, by how much. Typically, the amount of space to increase is expressed as either a specific amount or as a percentage of the initial space.

At database creation, the developer will also need to allocate file space for the database logs. You will learn about logging in Chapters 11 through 13; for now, just realize that the DBMS will log changes to data that it can later use to recover the database if necessary. Space for those logs is defined when the database is created.

CREATING A DATABASE MAINTENANCE PLAN A maintenance plan is a schedule of activities to be performed on a recurring basis. Such tasks include backing up the database, dumping the contents of the database log to backup files, checking for violations of referential integrity, optimizing disk space for user data and indices, and the like. Again, we will address this issue in Chapter 11, but be aware that a maintenance plan should be developed when the database is created, or shortly thereafter.

CREATING THE DATABASE DATA Once the database has been defined and allocated to physical storage, it can be filled with data. The means by which this is done depends on the application requirements and the features of the DBMS product. In the best case, all of the data are already in a computer-sensible format, and the DBMS has features and tools to facilitate importing the data from magnetic media. In the worst case, all of the data must be entered via manual key entry using application programs created from scratch by the developers. Most data conversions lie between these two extremes.

Once the data are input, they must be verified for accuracy. Verification is a labor-intensive and tedious but important task. Often, especially for large databases, it is well worth the time and expense for the development team to write verification programs. Such programs count the number of records of various categories, compute control totals, perform reasonableness checks on data item values, and provide other kinds of verification.

➤ RELATIONAL DATA MANIPULATION

So far, we have discussed the design of relational databases and the means by which such designs are defined to the DBMS. Whenever we have referred to processing relations, we have done so in a general and intuitive manner. Although this is fine for discussing designs, to implement applications we need clear, unambiguous languages for expressing processing logic. Such languages are called **data manipulation languages (DML).**

Categories of Relational Data Manipulation Languages

To date, four different strategies for relational data manipulation have been proposed. **Relational algebra,** the first of the strategies, defines operators that work on relations (akin to the operators +, −, and so forth of high school algebra). Relations can be manipulated using these operators to achieve a desired result. But relational algebra is hard to use, partly because it is procedural. That is, when using relational algebra we must know not only *what* we want but also *how* to get it.

Relational algebra is not used in commercial database processing. Although no commercially successful DBMS product provides relational algebra facilities, we will discuss relational algebra here, as it helps clarify relational manipulation and establishes a foundation on which to learn SQL.

Relational calculus is a second type of relational data manipulation. Relational calculus is nonprocedural; it is a language for expressing what we want without expressing how to get it. Recall the variable of integration in calculus, which ranges over an interval to be integrated. Relational calculus has a similar variable. For tuple relational calculus, the variable ranges over the tuples of a relation, and for domain relational calculus, the variable ranges over the values of a domain. Relational calculus is derived from a branch of mathematics called predicate calculus.

Unless you are going to become a theoretician of relational technology, you will probably not need to learn relational calculus. It is never used in commercial database processing, and learning it is not instructive for our purposes. Thus,we do not discuss it in this text.

Although relational calculus is hard to understand and use, its nonprocedural property is highly desirable. Therefore, DBMS designers looked for other nonprocedural techniques, which led to the third and fourth categories of relational DML.

Transform-oriented languages are a class of nonprocedural languages that transform input data expressed as relations into results expressed as a single relation. These languages provide easy-to-use structures for expressing what is desired regarding the data supplied. SQUARE, SEQUEL, and SQL are all transform-oriented languages. We study SQL in depth in Chapters 9, 12, and 13.

The fourth category of relational DML is graphical. **Query-by-Example** and **Query-by-Form** fall into this category. Products that support this category include Approach (from Lotus) and Access. With a graphical interface, the user is presented a materialization of one or more relations. The materialization might be a data entry form, it might be a spreadsheet, or it might be some other structure. The DBMS maps the materialization to the underlying relation and constructs queries (most likely in SQL) on behalf of the user. The users are then causing the execution of DML statements, but they are unaware of that fact. The four categories of relational DML are listed in Figure 8-6.

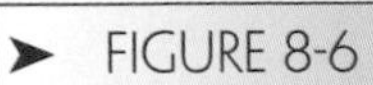

Four Categories of Relational DML

- Relational algebra
- Relational calculus
- Transform-oriented languages (such as SQL)
- Query-by-example/Query-by-form

➤ FIGURE 8-7

Example of a Tabular Default Screen Form

Name	DateOfBirth	Gender	AccountNumber	Physician
Riley	1/19/46	F	147	Lee
Abel	6/19/57	M	193	Singh
Murphy	12/28/81	M	289	Singh
Krajewski	10/21/73	F	533	Levy
Ting	5/23/38	F	661	Spock
Dixon	4/15/87	M	704	Levy

DML Interfaces to the DBMS

In this section, we consider four different interfaces for manipulating database data.

DATA MANIPULATION BY MEANS OF FORMS Most relational DBMS products include tools for building forms. Some of these are created automatically when a table is defined, but others must be created by the developer, perhaps with intelligent assistance like that provided by Access's Wizards. A form may be tabular, like a spreadsheet, in which case it shows multiple rows at a time, or the form may show each row as an independent entity. Figures 8-7 and 8-8 show an example of each for the PATIENT table in Figure 8-1. With most products, some flexibility is provided in the processing of the forms and reports. For example, rows can be selected for processing based on column values, and they can also be sorted. The table in Figure 8-7 is sorted by AccountNumber.

Many of the default forms present data from only a single relation at a time. If data are required from two or more relations, then usually customized forms must be created using DBMS tools. It is possible for both multi-table and multi-row forms to be created using such tools. The use of such tools is very specific to the product, however, and so we do not discuss them further here.

QUERY/UPDATE LANGUAGE INTERFACE The second type of interface to a database is via a **query/update language,** or simply a **query language.** (Although most such languages perform both query and update, they are generally referred to as query languages.) With this type, the user enters query commands that specify actions on the database. The DBMS decodes the commands and carries out the appropriate actions. Figure 8-9 shows the programs involved in query processing.

The single most important query language is SQL. To give you an idea of query languages, consider the following SQL statement that processes the relation PATIENT shown in Figure 8-1:

```
SELECT   Name, DateOfBirth
FROM     PATIENT
WHERE    Physician = 'Levy'
```

➤ FIGURE 8-8

Example of a Single-Row Default Screen Form

PATIENT

Name	Krajewski
DateOfBirth	10/21/73
Gender	F
AccountNumber	533
Physician	Levy

Record: 4

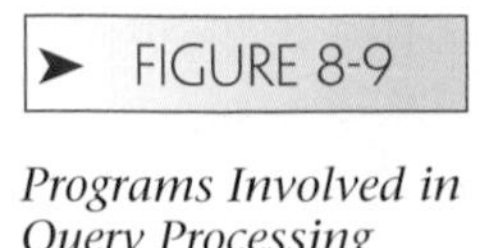

Programs Involved in Query Processing

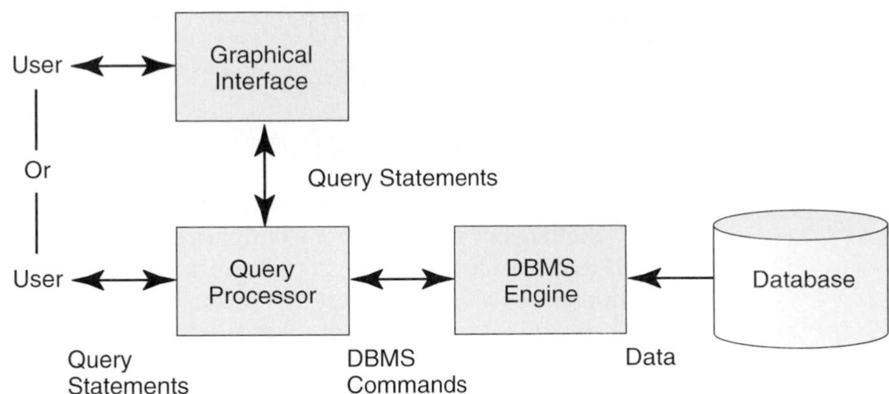

This SQL query statement extracts all the rows from the relation PATIENT for which the physician is 'Levy.' It then displays the Name and DateOfBirth for the qualifying rows in a second table.

STORED PROCEDURES Over time, users and database developers found that certain sequences of SQL commands needed to be performed on a regular basis. The only change from period to period was the use of different values in WHERE clauses. For example, end-of-month billing involves processing the same SQL statements, but with a different closing date. To accommodate this need, DBMS vendors developed **stored procedures,** which are collections of SQL statements stored as a file that can be invoked by a single command. Parameters can be passed to these procedures to be filled into WHERE clauses and so on, when the procedure is invoked. An example use is

```
DO BILLING STORED_ PROCEDURE FOR BILLDATE = "9/1/2000"
```

As developers gained experience, a problem became clear. SQL was created as a data sublanguage and no attempt was ever made to give it a full set of programming features. Some of these missing features were needed for stored procedures, however, and so DBMS vendors extended SQL to add them. One such language, PL/SQL, was developed for Oracle; another, called TRANSACT-SQL was developed for SQL Server. You will learn about these languages in Chapters 12 and 13.

A special type of stored procedure, called a **trigger,** is invoked by the DBMS when a specified condition occurs. For example, in an order entry application, a developer might create a trigger that is to be run whenever the QuantityOnHand of an item in inventory falls below its associated ReOrderQuantity. You will learn more about stored procedures and triggers in Chapters 12 and 13.

APPLICATION PROGRAM INTERFACE The fourth type of data access interface is through application programs written in programming languages such as COBOL, BASIC, Perl, Pascal, and C++. In addition, some application programs are written in languages provided by the DBMS vendors, of which the dBASE programming language is the best known.

There are two styles of application program interface to the DBMS. In one, the application program makes function calls to routines in a function library provided with the DBMS. For example, to read a particular row of a table, the application program calls the DBMS read function and passes parameters that indicate the table to be accessed, the data to be retrieved, the criteria for row selection, and the like.

In some cases, object-oriented syntax is used rather than function calls. In the following Access code, the object reference *db* is set to the currently opened database and a second object reference *rs* is set to point to the rows in the PATIENT table.

```
set db = currentdb( )
set rs = db.OpenRecordset("PATIENT")
```

Properties of the open record set can then be accessed and methods executed using the reference variable. For example, the property *rs.AllowDeletions* can be referenced to determine whether records in the PATIENT record set can be deleted. The method *rs.MoveFirst* can be used to position a cursor to the first row.

A second, older style of interface is sometimes used with mainframe and server DBMS products. Here, a set of high-level data access commands is defined by the DBMS vendor. These commands—which are peculiar to database processing and not part of any standard language—are embedded in the application program code.

The application program, with embedded commands, is then submitted to a precompiler provided by the DBMS vendor. This precompiler translates the data access statements into valid function calls and data structure definitions. In this process, the precompiler sets up parameter sequences for the calls and defines data areas that will be shared between the application program and the DBMS. The precompiler also inserts program logic to maintain the data areas. Then the precompiled routine is submitted to the language compiler. Figure 8-10 shows the relationships of the programs involved in this process.

In addition to its role in query processing, SQL is also used as a data access language in application programs. In this mode, SQL statements are embedded in the programs and translated into function calls by a precompiler. Training costs and learning time are reduced, because the same language can be used for access to both query and application programs. There is one problem to be overcome, however. SQL is a transform-oriented language that accepts relations, manipulates them, and outputs a result relation. Thus, it deals with relations one at a time. Almost all application programs are row (record) oriented; that is, they read one row, process it, read the next row, and so forth. Such programs deal with a row at a time.

Thus, there is a mismatch in the basic orientation of SQL and application program languages. To correct for this mismatch, the results of SQL statements are

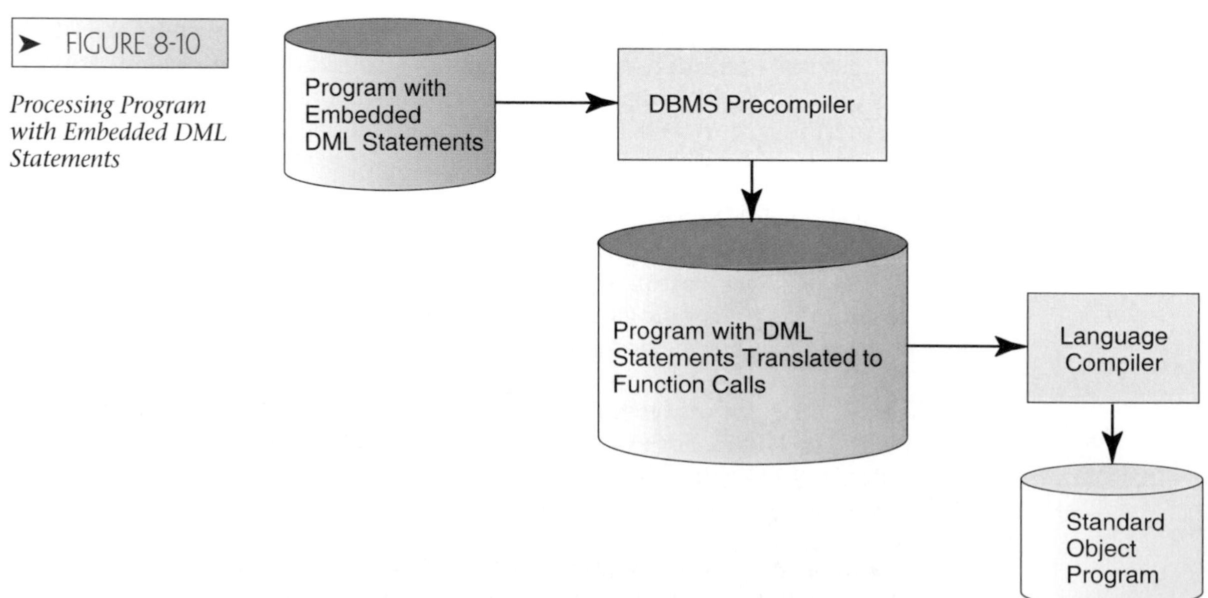

➤ FIGURE 8-10

Processing Program with Embedded DML Statements

assumed, in the application program, to be files. To illustrate, assume that the following SQL statement (the same as that earlier) is embedded in an application program:

```
SELECT   Name, DateOfBirth
FROM     PATIENT
WHERE    Physician = 'Levy'
```

The result of these statements is a table with two columns and *N* rows. In order to accept the results of this query, the application program is written to assume that these statements have produced a file with *N* records. The application opens the query, processes the first row, processes the next row, and so forth, until the last row has been processed. This logic is the same as that for processing a sequential file. You will see examples of such application programs in Chapters 12,13,15 and 16. For now, just be aware that there is a mismatch in the basic orientation of SQL (relation oriented) and programming languages (row, or record, oriented) and that this mismatch must be corrected when programs access a relational database via SQL.

➤ RELATIONAL ALGEBRA

Relational algebra is similar to the algebra you learned in high school, but with an important difference. In high school algebra, variables represented numbers, and operators like +, −, ×, and / operated on numeric quantities. In relational algebra, however, the variables are relations, and the operators manipulate relations to form new relations. For example, the union operation combines the tuples of one relation with the tuples of another relation, thereby producing a third relation. In fact, relational algebra is *closed,* which means that the results of one or more relational operations are *always* a relation.

Relations are sets. The tuples of a relation can be considered elements of a set, and so operations that can be performed on sets can also be performed on relations. We first show four such set operators and then discuss other operators that are peculiar to relational algebra. Before proceeding, however, consider the following sample relations that we will use in this and the next chapter.

RELATIONAL OPERATORS

Figure 8-11 shows six relations and their attribute and domain definitions. Note that the attribute Name is used in several relations. When we refer to a specific attribute, we qualify it with its relation name. Accordingly, Name in CLASS is sometimes denoted as CLASS.Name.

In the following discussion, character values are shown in single quotes, and those characters not in quotes represent names. Thus "ROOM" differs from Room because "ROOM" is a value, whereas Room is, say, a domain name. In regard to numeric data, those numbers not in quotes refer to numeric quantities, and those numbers in quotes refer to character strings. Thus, 123 is a number, and "123" is a string of the characters "1," "2," and "3."

UNION The **union** of two relations is formed by adding the tuples from one relation to those of a second relation to produce a third relation. The order in which the tuples appear in the third relation is not important, but duplicate tuples must be eliminated. The union of relations A and B is denoted A + B.

For this operation to make sense, the relations must be **union compatible;** that is, each relation must have the same number of attributes, and the attributes in corresponding columns must come from the same domain. If, for example, the

FIGURE 8-11

Examples of Relations and Domains: (a) Relation Definitions, (b) Attribute Domains, and (c) Domain Definitions

1. JUNIOR (<u>Snum</u>, Name, Major)
2. HONOR-STUDENT (<u>Number</u>, Name, Interest)
3. STUDENT (<u>SID</u>, Name, Major, GradeLevel)
4. CLASS (<u>Name</u>, Time, Room)
5. ENROLLMENT (<u>StudentNumber</u>, <u>ClassName</u>, PositionNumber)
6. FACULTY (<u>FID</u>, Name, Department)

(a)

	Attribute	*Domain*
1.	Snum	PeopleIdentifiers
	JUNIOR.Name	PeopleNames
	Major	SubjectNames
2.	Number	PeopleIdentifiers
	HONOR-STUDENT.Name	PeopleNames
	Interest	SubjectNames
3.	SID	PeopleIdentifiers
	STUDENT.Name	PeopleNames
	Major	SubjectNames
	GradeLevel	Classes
4.	CLASS.Name	ClassNames
	Time	ClassTimes
	Room	Rooms
5.	StudentNumber	PeopleIdentifiers
	ClassName	ClassNames
	PositionNumber	ClassSizes
6.	FID	PeopleIdentifiers
	FACULTY.Name	PeopleNames
	Department	SubjectNames

(b)

Domain Name	*Format*
PeopleIdentifiers	Decimal (3)
PeopleNames	Char (8) (unrealistic, but handy for these examples)
SubjectNames	Char (10)
Classes	One of [FR, SO, JR, SN, GR]
ClassNames	Char (10)
ClassTimes	Char (5) format: DDDHH, where D is one of [M, T, W, R, F, or blank], and HH is decimal between 1 and 12
Rooms	Char (5) format: BBRRR, where BB is a building code, and RRR, is a room number
ClassSizes	Decimal from 0 to 100

(c)

➤ FIGURE 8-12

JUNIOR and HONOR-STUDENT Relations and Their Union: (a) Example JUNIOR Relation, (b) Example HONOR-STUDENT Relation, and (c) Union of JUNIOR and HONOR-STUDENT Relations

Snum	Name	Major
123	JONES	HISTORY
158	PARKS	MATH
271	SMITH	HISTORY

(a)

Number	Name	Interest
105	ANDERSON	MANAGEMENT
123	JONES	HISTORY

(b)

Snum or Number	Name	Major or Interest
123	JONES	HISTORY
158	PARKS	MATH
271	SMITH	HISTORY
105	ANDERSON	MANAGEMENT

(c)

third attribute of one relation comes from the Rooms domain, the third attribute of the second relation must also come from the Rooms domain.

In Figure 8-11, the JUNIOR and the HONOR-STUDENT relations are union compatible because they both have three attributes, and the corresponding attributes come from the same domain. JUNIOR.Snum and HONOR-STUDENT.Number come from the domain PeopleIdentifiers; JUNIOR.Name and HONOR-STUDENT.Name have the domain PeopleNames; and JUNIOR.Major and HONOR-STUDENT.Interest have the domain SubjectNames. The relations JUNIOR and CLASS both have three attributes, but they are **union incompatible** because the three attributes do not have the same domain.

Figure 8-12 shows the union of the JUNIOR and HONOR-STUDENT relations. Note that the tuple [123, JONES, HISTORY], which occurs in both relations, is not duplicated in the union.

DIFFERENCE The **difference** of two relations is a third relation containing tuples that occur in the first relation but not in the second. The relations must be union compatible. The difference of JUNIOR and HONOR-STUDENT is shown in Figure 8-13. As in arithmetic, the order of the subtraction matters, and so A − B *is not* the same as B − A.

INTERSECTION The **intersection** of two relations is a third relation containing the tuples that appear in both the first and second relations. Again, the relations must be union compatible. In Figure 8-14 the intersection of JUNIOR and

➤ FIGURE 8-13

JUNIOR Minus HONOR-STUDENT Relation

Snum	Name	Major
158	PARKS	MATH
271	SMITH	HISTORY

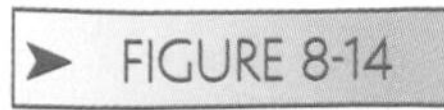

FIGURE 8-14

Intersection of JUNIOR and HONOR-STUDENT Relations

Snum or Number	Name	Major or Interest
123	JONES	HISTORY

HONOR-STUDENT is the single tuple [123, JONES, HISTORY], which is the only tuple that occurs in both JUNIOR and HONOR-STUDENT.

PRODUCT The **product** of two relations (sometimes called the **Cartesian product**) is the concatenation of every tuple of one relation with every tuple of a second relation. The product of relation A (having *m* tuples) and relation B (having *n* tuples) has *m* times *n* tuples. The product is denoted A × B or A TIMES B. In Figure 8-15, the relation STUDENT has four tuples, and the relation ENROLLMENT has three. STUDENT TIMES ENROLLMENT therefore has twelve tuples, which are shown in Figure 8-16. (The resulting relation in Figure 8-16 contains some meaningless tuples. Other operations, shown later, would need to be performed in order to extract any meaningful information from this relation. This is simply an illustration of the product operator.)

PROJECTION **Projection** is an operation that selects specified attributes from a relation. The result of the projection is a new relation with the selected attributes; in other words, a projection chooses columns from a relation. For example, consider the STUDENT relation data in Figure 8-15(a), from which the projection of STUDENT on Name and Major attributes, denoted with brackets as STUDENT [Name, Major], is shown in Figure 8-17(a). The projection of STUDENT on Major and GradeLevel, denoted as STUDENT [Major, GradeLevel], appears in Figure 8-17(b).

Note that although STUDENT has four tuples to begin with, the projection STUDENT [Major, GradeLevel] has only three. A tuple was eliminated because after the projection was completed, the tuple [HISTORY, JR] occurred twice. Because the result of projection is a relation and because relations cannot contain duplicate tuples, the redundant tuple is eliminated.

Projection can also be used to change the order of attributes in a relation. For example, the projection STUDENT [GradeLevel, Major, Name, SID] reverses the order of STUDENT attributes (see Figure 8-11 for the original order). This feature can sometimes be used to make two relations union compatible.

FIGURE 8-15

Examples of (a) STUDENT and (b) ENROLLMENT Relations

SID	Name	Major	GradeLevel
123	JONES	HISTORY	JR
158	PARKS	MATH	GR
105	ANDERSON	MANAGEMENT	SN
271	SMITH	HISTORY	JR

(a)

StudentNumber	ClassName	PositionNumber
123	H350	1
105	BA490	3
123	BA490	7

(b)

➤ FIGURE 8-16

Product of the STUDENT and ENROLLMENT Relations in Figure 8-15

SID	Name	Major	GradeLevel	Student-Number	Class-Name	Position-Number
123	JONES	HISTORY	JR	123	H350	1
123	JONES	HISTORY	JR	105	BA490	3
123	JONES	HISTORY	JR	123	BA490	7
158	PARKS	MATH	GR	123	H350	1
158	PARKS	MATH	GR	105	BA490	3
158	PARKS	MATH	GR	123	BA490	7
105	ANDERSON	MANAGEMENT	SN	123	H350	1
105	ANDERSON	MANAGEMENT	SN	105	BA490	3
105	ANDERSON	MANAGEMENT	SN	123	BA490	7
271	SMITH	HISTORY	JR	123	H350	1
271	SMITH	HISTORY	JR	105	BA490	3
271	SMITH	HISTORY	JR	123	BA490	7

SELECTION Whereas the projection operator takes a vertical subset (columns) of a relation, the **selection** operator takes a horizontal subset (rows). Projection identifies those *attributes* to be included in the new relation, and selection identifies those *tuples* to be included in the new relation. Selection is denoted by specifying the relation name, followed by the keyword WHERE, followed by a condition involving attributes. Figure 8-18(a) shows the selection of the relation STUDENT WHERE Major = 'MATH,' and Figure 8-18(b) shows the selection of STUDENT WHERE GradeLevel = 'JR'.

JOIN The **join** operation is a combination of the product, selection, and (possibly) projection operations. The join of two relations, say, A and B, operates as follows: First, form the product of A times B. Then do a selection to eliminate some tuples (the criteria for the selection are specified as part of the join). Then (optionally) remove some attributes by means of projection.

Consider the STUDENT and ENROLLMENT relations shown in Figure 8-15. Suppose we want to know the Name and Position Number of each student. To find this out, we need to join STUDENT tuples by matching ENROLLMENT tuples based on the SID. We denote such a join as STUDENT JOIN (SID = StudentNumber) ENROLLMENT. The meaning of this expression is "Join a STUDENT tuple to an ENROLLMENT tuple if SID of STUDENT equals StudentNumber of ENROLLMENT."

To form this join, we first find the product of STUDENT and ENROLLMENT, an operation that was shown in Figure 8-16. Next we SELECT those tuples from the product where SID of STUDENT equals StudentNumber of ENROLLMENT (there are only three). This operation leads to the relation in Figure 8-19(a). Note that two attributes are identical: SID and StudentNumber. One of these is redundant, so we eliminate it (in this case, we choose StudentNumber) with projection.

➤ FIGURE 8-17

Projections of STUDENT Relations: (a) STUDENT [Name, Major] and (b) STUDENT [Major, GradeLevel]

Name	Major
JONES	HISTORY
PARKS	MATH
ANDERSON	MANAGEMENT
SMITH	HISTORY

(a)

Major	GradeLevel
HISTORY	JR
MATH	GR
MANAGEMENT	SN

(b)

Examples of Relational Selection: (a) STUDENT WHERE Major = `Math' and (b) STUDENT WHERE GradeLevel = `JR'

SID	Name	Major	GradeLevel
158	PARKS	MATH	GR

(a)

SID	Name	Major	GradeLevel
123	JONES	HISTORY	JR
271	SMITH	HISTORY	JR

(b)

The result is the join in Figure 8-19(b). The join in Figure 8-19(a) is called the **equijoin,** and the one in Figure 8-19(b) is called the **natural join.** Unless otherwise specified, when people say join, they mean the natural join.

Because forming the product of two large relations is time-consuming, the algorithm used by a DBMS to join two relations will be different from that described here. The result will be identical, however.

Joining on conditions other than equality also is possible. For example, STUDENT JOIN (SID not = StudentNumber) ENROLLMENT, or STUDENT JOIN (SID < FID) FACULTY. The latter join would result in tuples in which the student numbers are lower than the faculty numbers. Such a join may have meaning if, say, PeopleIdentifiers were assigned in chronological order. Such a join would portray pairs of students and teachers in such a way that the student would appear to have been at the institution longer than the teacher had.

There is one important limit on the conditions of a join: The attributes in the condition must arise from a common domain, so STUDENT JOIN (Major =

➤ FIGURE 8-19

Examples of Joining STUDENT and ENROLLMENT Relations: (a) Equijoin and (b) Natural Join (c) Left Outer Join

SID	Name	Major	Grade-Level	Student-Number	Class-Name	Position-Number
123	JONES	HISTORY	JR	123	H350	1
123	JONES	HISTORY	JR	123	BA490	7
105	ANDERSON	MANAGEMENT	SN	105	BA490	3

(a)

SID	Name	Major	GradeLevel	ClassName	PositionNumber
123	JONES	HISTORY	JR	H350	1
123	JONES	HISTORY	JR	BA490	7
105	ANDERSON	MANAGEMENT	SN	BA490	3

(b)

SID	Name	Major	Grade-Level	Student-Number	Class-Name	Position-Number
123	JONES	HISTORY	JR	123	H350	1
123	JONES	HISTORY	JR	123	BA490	7
158	PARKS	MATH	GR	null	null	null
105	ANDERSON	MANAGEMENT	SN	105	BA490	3
271	SMITH	HISTORY	JR	null	null	null

(c)

CLASS.Name) CLASS is *illogical.* Even though the values of Major and CLASS.Name are both Char (10), they do not arise from the same domain. Semantically, this type of a join makes no sense. (Unfortunately, many relational DBMS products permit such a join.)

OUTER JOIN The join operation will produce a relation of students and the classes that they are taking. Students who are not taking any class will, however, be omitted from the result. If we want to include all students, an **outer join** can be used. Thus, STUDENT LEFT OUTER JOIN (SID = StudentNumber) ENROLLMENT will include every student row. The result is shown in Figure 8-19(c). Student Smith is included even though he or she enrolled in no class. The keyword LEFT specifies that all rows in the table on the left-hand side of the expression (STUDENT) will appear in the result. The STUDENT RIGHT OUTER JOIN (SID = StudentNumber) ENROLLMENT specifies that all rows in ENROLLMENT are to be included in the result. Outer joins are useful when working with relationships in which the minimum cardinality is zero on one or both sides. When ambiguity can arise between the two types of join, the term INNER JOIN is sometimes used instead of JOIN.

Expressing Queries in Relational Algebra

Figure 8-20 summarizes the basic relational operations just discussed. Standard set operations include +, −, intersection, and product. Selection chooses specific tuples (rows) from a relation in accordance with the conditions for attribute values. Projection chooses specific attributes (columns) from a relation by means of the attribute name. Finally, join concatenates the tuples of two relations in accordance with a condition on the values of attributes.

We now turn to how relational operators can be used to express queries, using the relations STUDENT, CLASS, and ENROLLMENT from Figure 8-11; sample data are shown in Figure 8-21. Our purpose is to demonstrate the use of relations. Although you will probably never use relational algebra in a commercial environment, these examples will help you understand how relations can be manipulated.

➤ FIGURE 8-20

Summary of Relational Algebra Operations

Type	*Format*	*Example*
Set operations	+, −, intersection, product	STUDENT [Name] – JUNIOR [Name]
Selection	Relation WHERE condition	CLASS WHERE Name = 'A'
Projection	relation [list of attributes]	STUDENT [Name, Major]
Join	relation 1 JOIN (condition) relation 2	STUDENT JOIN (SID = StudentNumber) ENROLLMENT
Inner Join	Synonymous with join	
Outer Join	relation 1 LEFT OUTER JOIN (condition) relation 2 or relation 1 RIGHT OUTER JOIN (condition) relation 2	STUDENT LEFT OUTER JOIN (SID = StudentNumber) ENROLLMENT STUDENT RIGHT OUTER JOIN (SID = StudentNumber) ENROLLMENT

FIGURE 8-21

Example Data for Relations Defined in Figure 8-11: (a) STUDENT Relation, (b) ENROLLMENT Relation, and (c) CLASS Relation

SID	Name	Major	GradeLevel
100	JONES	HISTORY	GR
150	PARKS	ACCOUNTING	SO
200	BAKER	MATH	GR
250	GLASS	HISTORY	SN
300	BAKER	ACCOUNTING	SN
350	RUSSELL	MATH	JR
400	RYE	ACCOUNTING	FR
450	JONES	HISTORY	SN

(a)

StudentNumber	ClassName	PositionNumber
100	BD445	1
150	BA200	1
200	BD445	2
200	CS250	1
300	CS150	1
400	BA200	2
400	BF410	1
400	CS250	2
450	BA200	3

(b)

Name	Time	Room
BA200	M-F9	SC110
BD445	MWF3	SC213
BF410	MWF8	SC213
CS150	MWF3	EA304
CS250	MWF12	EB210

(c)

1. What are the names of all students?

   STUDENT [Name]

   This is simply the projection of the Name attribute of the STUDENT relation, and the result is

JONES
PARKS
BAKER
GLASS
RUSSELL
RYE

Duplicate names have been omitted. Although the names JONES and BAKER actually occur twice in the relation STUDENT, repetitions have been omitted because the result of a projection is a relation, and relations may not have duplicate tuples.

2. What are the student numbers of all students enrolled in a class?

   ENROLLMENT [StudentNumber]

   This is similar to the first query, but the projection occurs on the relation ENROLLMENT. The result is

100
150
200
300
400
450

   Again, duplicate tuples have been omitted.

3. What are the student numbers of all students not enrolled in a class?

   STUDENT [SID] – ENROLLMENT [StudentNumber]

   This expression finds the difference of the projection of two relations: STUDENT [SID] has the student numbers of all students, and ENROLLMENT [StudentNumber] has the student numbers of all students enrolled in a class. The difference is the number of students not enrolled in a class. The result is

250
350

4. What are the numbers of students enrolled in the class 'BD445'?

   ENROLLMENT WHERE ClassName = 'BD445' [StudentNumber]

   This expression selects the appropriate tuples and then projects them onto the attribute StudentNumber. The result is

250
350

5. What are the names of the students enrolled in class 'BD445'?

   STUDENT JOIN (SID = StudentNumber) ENROLLMENT WHERE ClassName = 'BD445' [STUDENT.Name]

   To answer this query, data from both STUDENT and ENROLLMENT are needed. Specifically, student names must come from STUDENT, whereas the condition "enrolled in BD445" must be checked in ENROLLMENT. Since both relations are needed, they must be joined. After STUDENT and ENROLLMENT have been joined, the selection is applied, followed by a projection on student names. The result is

   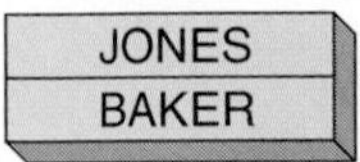

JONES
BAKER

   As we stated earlier, when two or more relations are considered, attribute names can be duplicated. Therefore, for clarity, the relation name may be prefixed to the attribute name. Thus, in our example, the projection is on [STUDENT.Name]. In this example, this prefix was added only for clarity, since the attribute names are different. But when attribute names are identical (a join involving STUDENT and CLASS yields two attributes, both called Name), the prefix is required. Consider the following query:

6. What are the names and meeting times of 'PARKS' classes?

To answer this, we must bring together data in all three relations. We need STUDENT data to find PARKS's student number; we need ENROLLMENT data to learn which classes PARKS is in; and we need CLASS data to determine the class meeting times.

STUDENT WHERE Name = 'PARKS' JOIN (SID = StudentNumber) ENROLLMENT JOIN (ClassName = Name) CLASS [CLASS.Name, Time]

This expression first selects PARKS's tuple and joins it to matching ENROLLMENT tuples. Then the result is joined to matching CLASS tuples. Finally, the projection is taken to print classes and times. The result is

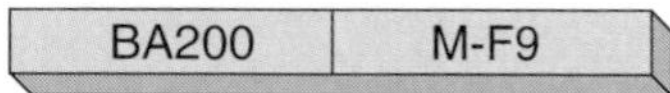

BA200	M-F9

We must specify CLASS.Name; simply specifying Name is ambiguous because both STUDENT and CLASS have an attribute called Name.

There are other, equivalent ways of responding to this query. One is

STUDENT JOIN (SID = StudentNumber) ENROLLMENT JOIN (ClassName = Name) CLASS WHERE STUDENT.Name = 'PARKS' [CLASS.Name, Time]

This expression differs from the first one because the selection on PARKS is not done until after all of the joins have been performed. Assuming that the computer performs the operations as stated, this expression will be slower than the earlier one because many more tuples will be joined.

Such differences are a major disadvantage of relational algebra. To the user, two equivalent queries should take the same amount of time (and hence cost the same). Imagine the frustration if one form of a query costs $1.17 and another costs $4,356. To the unwary and unsophisticated user, the cost difference appears capricious.

7. What are the grade levels and meeting rooms of all students, including students not enrolled in a class?

Since all students are to be included, this query requires the use of an outer join. The syntax is straightforward:

STUDENT LEFT OUTER JOIN (SID = StudentNumber) ENROLLMENT JOIN (ClassName = Name) CLASS [GradeLevel, Room].

The result includes the GradeLevels of Glass and Russell, who are not enrolled in any class.

GR	SC213
SO	SC110
GR	EB210
SN	Null
SN	EA304
JR	Null
FR	SC110
FR	SC213
FR	EB210
SN	SC110

➤ SUMMARY

Several tasks must be carried out when implementing a relational database. First, the structure of the database must be defined to the DBMS. Then file space needs to be allocated, and finally the database is filled with data.

The relational model represents and processes data in the form of tables called relations. The columns of the tables are called attributes, and the rows are called tuples. The values of the attributes arise from domains. The terms *table, column,* and *row* and *file, field,* and *record* are used synonymously with the terms *relation, attribute,* and *tuple,* respectively.

The use of the term *key* can be confusing because it is used differently in the design and implementation stages. During design, the term means a logical key, which is one or more attributes that uniquely define a row. During implementation, the term means a physical key, which is a data structure used to improve performance. A logical key may or may not be a physical key, and a physical key may or may not be a logical key. In this text we use key to mean logical key and index to mean physical key.

Because we are using the relational model to express database designs, there is no need to transform the design during the implementation stage. We simply define the relational design to the DBMS. Two ways of defining the design are to express it in a DDL text file and to use a graphical data definition tool. In either case, the tables, columns, indexes, constraints, passwords, and other controls are defined to the DBMS.

In addition to defining the database structure, the developers must allocate media space for the database. With multiuser systems, such allocation can be important to the DBMS's effective performance. Finally, the database is filled with data using tools provided by the DBMS vendor, programs developed by the vendor, or both.

The four categories of relational data manipulation language are relational algebra, relational calculus, transform-oriented languages, and query-by-example. Relational algebra consists of a group of relational operators that can be used to manipulate relations to obtain a desired result. Relational algebra is procedural. The transform-oriented languages offer a nonprocedural means to transform a set of relations into a desired result. SQL is the most common example.

There are three means of accessing a relational database. One is to use the form and report facilities provided by the DBMS. A second is to use a query/update language, of which SQL is the most common. A third is through application programs.

Application program interfaces can be either by function call, object methods, or special-purpose database commands that are translated by a precompiler. The processing orientation of the relational model is relation at a time, but the orientation of most programming languages is row at a time. Some means must be devised to correct for this mismatch.

Relational algebra is used to manipulate relations to obtain a desired result. The operators are union, difference, intersection, product, projection, selection, (inner) join, and outer join.

➤ GROUP I QUESTIONS

8.1 Name and describe the three tasks necessary to implement a relational database.

8.2 Define *relation, attribute, tuple,* and *domain.*

8.3 Explain the use of the terms *table, column, row, file, field,* and *record.*

8.4 Explain the difference between a relational schema and a relation.

8.5 Define *key, index, logical key,* and *physical key.*

8.6 Describe three reasons for using indexes.

8.7 Under what conditions is it necessary to transform the database design during the implementation stage?

8.8 Explain the term *data definition language.* What purpose does it serve?

8.9 How can a database structure be defined other than through a text file?

8.10 What aspects of a database design need to be defined to the DBMS?

8.11 Give an example, other than the one in this text, in which the allocation of the database to physical media is important.

8.12 Describe the best and worst extremes for loading the database with data.

8.13 Name and briefly explain four categories of relational DML.

8.14 Describe how relational data can be manipulated by means of forms.

8.15 Explain the role of query languages in relational data manipulation. How do stored queries differ from application programs? Why are they used?

8.16 Describe the two styles of application program interface to the database. In your answer, explain the role of a precompiler.

8.17 Describe the mismatch between the orientation of the SQL and the orientation of most programming languages. How is this mismatch corrected?

8.18 How does relational algebra differ from high school algebra?

8.19 Why is relational algebra *closed?*

8.20 Define *union compatible.* Give an example of two relations that are union compatible and two that are union incompatible.

Questions 8.21 through 8.23 refer to the following two relations:

COMPANY (<u>Name</u>, NumberEmployees, Sales)
MANUFACTURERS (<u>Name</u>, PeopleCount, Revenue)

8.21 Give an example of a union of these two relations.

8.22 Give an example of a difference of these two relations.

8.23 Give an example of an intersection of these two relations.

Questions 8.24 through 8.28 refer to the following three relations:

SALESPERSON (<u>Name</u>, Salary)
ORDER (<u>Number</u>, CustName, SalespersonName, Amount)
CUSTOMER (<u>Name</u>, City, IndustryType)

An instance of these relations is shown in Figure 8-22. Use the data in those tables for the following problems:

8.24 Give an example of the product of SALESPERSON and ORDER.

8.25 Show an example of

SALESPERSON [Name, Salary]
SALESPERSON [Salary]

Under what conditions will SALESPERSON [Salary] have fewer rows than SALESPERSON does?

8.26 Show an example of a select on SALESPERSON Name, on SALESPERSON Salary, and on both SALESPERSON Name and Salary.

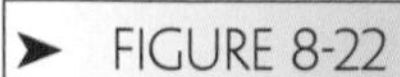
FIGURE 8-22

Sample Data for Questions 8.24 Through 8.28

Name	Salary
Abel	120,000
Baker	42,000
Jones	36,000
Murphy	50,000
Zenith	118,000
Kobad	34,000

SALESPERSON

Number	CustName	SalespersonName	Amount
100	Abernathy Construction	Zenith	560
200	Abernathy Construction	Jones	1800
300	Manchester Lumber	Abel	480
400	Amalgamated Housing	Abel	2500
500	Abernathy Construction	Murphy	6000
600	Tri-City Builders	Abel	700
700	Manchester Lumber	Jones	150

ORDER

Name	City	IndustryType
Abernathy Construction	Willow	B
Manchester Lumber	Manchester	F
Tri-City Builders	Memphis	B
Amalgamated Housing	Memphis	B

CUSTOMER

8.27 Show an example of an equijoin and a natural join of SALESPERSON and ORDER in which the Name of SALESPERSON equals the SalespersonName of ORDER.

8.28 Show relational algebra expressions for

a. The names of all salespeople

b. The names of all salespeople having an ORDER row

c. The names of salespeople not having an ORDER row

d. The names of salespeople having an order with Abernathy Construction

e. The salaries of salespeople having an order with Abernathy Construction

f. The city of all CUSTOMERS having an order with salesperson Jones

g. The names of all salespeople with the names of customers who have ordered from them. Include salespeople who have no orders.

Structured Query Language

Structured Query Language, or SQL, is the most important relational data manipulation language in use today. It has been endorsed by the American National Standards Institute (ANSI) as the language of choice for manipulating relational databases, and it is the data access language used by many commercial DBMS products, including DB2, SQL/DS, Oracle, INGRES, SYBASE, SQL Server, dBASE for Windows, Paradox, Microsoft Access, and many others. Because of its popularity, SQL has become the standard language for information interchange among computers. Since there is a version of SQL that can run on almost any computer and operating system, computer systems are able to exchange data by passing SQL requests and responses to one another.

The development of SQL began at IBM's San Jose research facilities in the mid-1970s under the name SEQUEL. Several versions of SEQUEL were released, and in 1980 the product was renamed SQL. Since then, IBM has been joined by many other vendors in developing products for SQL. The American National Standards Institute has taken over the role of maintaining SQL and periodically publishes updated versions of the SQL standard. This chapter discusses the core of SQL as described in the 1992 ANSI standard, which is often referred to as SQL92.[1] The most recent version, SQL3, concerns extensions to the language for object-oriented programming. That version is discussed in Chapter 18.

The constructs and expressions in a particular implementation of SQL (for example, in Oracle or SQL Server) may differ in minor ways from the ANSI standard, in part because many of the DBMS products were developed before there was agreement on the standard and also because vendors added capabilities to their products to gain a competitive advantage. From a marketing perspective, simply supporting the ANSI standard was at times judged as not having enough sizzle.

SQL commands can be used interactively as a query language, or they can be embedded in application programs. Thus SQL is not a programming language (like COBOL); rather, it is a *data sublanguage,* or *data access language,* that is embedded in other languages.

---

[1]International Standards Organization Publication ISO/IEC 9075: 1992, *Database Language SQL.*

In this chapter, we present interactive SQL statements, which need to be adjusted and modified when they are embedded in programs, as illustrated in Chapters 12 and 13. This chapter is concerned only with data manipulation statements; data definition statements are discussed in Chapters 12 and 13.

SQL is a transform-oriented language that accepts one or more relations as input and produces a single relation as output. The result of every SQL query is a relation; even if the result is a single number, that number is considered to be a relation with a single row and a single column. Thus SQL, like relational algebra, is *closed*.

➤ QUERYING A SINGLE TABLE

In this section, we consider SQL facilities for querying a single table. We will discuss multiple tables and update statements later in this chapter. By custom, SQL reserved words such as SELECT and FROM are written in capital letters. Also, SQL statements are normally written in multiple lines as illustrated in this chapter. SQL language compilers do not require either capitals or multiple lines, however. These conventions are used only to provide better clarity to humans who read the SQL statements.

We use the same set of six relations with which we illustrated relational algebra in Chapter 8. The structure of those relations is shown in Figure 9-1, and sample data for three of them appears in Figure 9-2.

➤ FIGURE 9-1

Relations Used for SQL Examples

1. JUNIOR (Snum, Name, Major)
2. HONOR-STUDENT (Number, Name, Interest)
3. STUDENT (SID, Name, Major, GradeLevel)
4. CLASS (Name, Time, Room)
5. ENROLLMENT (StudentNumber, ClassName, PositionNumber)
6. FACULTY (FID, Name, Department)

	Attribute	*Domain*
1.	Snum	PeopleIdentifiers
	JUNIOR.Name	PeopleNames
	Major	SubjectNames
2.	Number	PeopleIdentifiers
	HONOR-STUDENT.Name	PeopleNames
	Interest	SubjectNames
3.	SID	PeopleIdentifiers
	STUDENT.Name	PeopleNames
	Major	SubjectNames
	GradeLevel	Classes
4.	CLASS.Name	ClassNames
	Time	ClassTimes
	Room	Rooms
5.	StudentNumber	PeopleIdentifiers
	ClassName	ClassNames
	PositionNumber	ClassSizes
6.	FID	PeopleIdentifiers
	FACULTY.Name	PeopleNames
	Department	SubjectNames

➤ FIGURE 9-2

Sample Data Used for SQL Examples: (a) STUDENT Relation, (b) ENROLLMENT Relation, and (c) CLASS Relation

SID	Name	Major	GradeLevel
100	JONES	HISTORY	GR
150	PARKS	ACCOUNTING	SO
200	BAKER	MATH	GR
250	GLASS	HISTORY	SN
300	BAKER	ACCOUNTING	SN
350	RUSSELL	MATH	JR
400	RYE	ACCOUNTING	FR
450	JONES	HISTORY	SN

(a)

StudentNumber	ClassName	PositionNumber
100	BD445	1
150	BA200	1
200	BD445	2
200	CS250	1
300	CS150	1
400	BA200	2
400	BF410	1
400	CS250	2
450	BA200	3

(b)

Name	Time	Room
BA200	M-F9	SC110
BD445	MWF3	SC213
BF410	MWF8	SC213
CS150	MWF3	EA304
CS250	MWF12	EB210

(c)

Projections Using SQL

To form a projection with SQL, we name the relation to be projected and list the columns to be shown. Using standard SQL syntax, the projection STUDENT [SID, Name, Major] is specified as

```
SELECT    SID, Name, Major
FROM      STUDENT
```

The keywords SELECT and FROM are always required; the columns to be obtained are listed after the keyword SELECT; and the table to be used is listed after the keyword FROM. The result of this projection for the data in Figure 9-2 is

100	JONES	HISTORY
150	PARKS	ACCOUNTING
200	BAKER	MATH
250	GLASS	HISTORY
300	BAKER	ACCOUNTING
350	RUSSELL	MATH
400	RYE	ACCOUNTING
450	JONES	HISTORY

Do not confuse the keyword SELECT with the relational algebra operator selection. SELECT is an SQL verb that can be used to perform a relational algebra projection, selection, and to specify other actions. Selection, on the other hand, differs from SELECT because it is the relational algebra operation of obtaining a subset of rows from a table.

Consider another example:

```
SELECT    Major
FROM      STUDENT
```

The result of this operation is the following:

HISTORY
ACCOUNTING
MATH
HISTORY
ACCOUNTING
MATH
ACCOUNTING
HISTORY

As you can see, this table contains duplicate rows, and consequently, in a strict sense, this table is not a relation. In fact, SQL does not automatically eliminate duplicates because such removal can be very time-consuming and, in many cases, is not desirable or necessary.

If duplicate rows must be removed, the qualifier DISTINCT must be specified, as follows:

```
SELECT    DISTINCT Major
FROM      STUDENT
```

The result of this operation is the relation

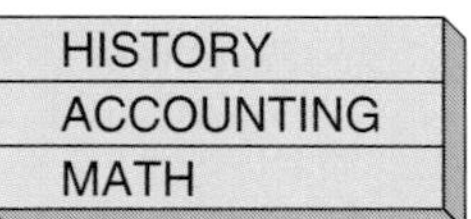

HISTORY
ACCOUNTING
MATH

Selections Using SQL

The relational algebra selection operator is also performed with the SQL SELECT command. An example is the following:

```
SELECT    SID, Name, Major, GradeLevel
FROM      STUDENT
WHERE     Major = 'MATH'
```

This SELECT expression specifies the names of all the table's columns. FROM specifies the table to be used, and the new phrase, WHERE, provides the condition(s) for the selection. The format SELECT—FROM—WHERE is the fundamental structure of SQL statements. The following is an equivalent form of the preceding query:

```
SELECT    *
FROM      STUDENT
WHERE     Major = 'MATH'
```

The asterisk (*) means that all columns of the table are to be obtained. The result of both of these queries is

200	BAKER	MATH	GR
350	RUSSELL	MATH	JR

We can combine the selection and projection as follows:

```
SELECT    Name, GradeLevel
FROM      STUDENT
WHERE     Major = 'MATH'
```

The result is

BAKER	GR
RUSSELL	JR

Several conditions can be expressed in the WHERE clause. For example, the expression

```
SELECT    Name, GradeLevel
FROM      STUDENT
WHERE     Major = 'MATH' AND GradeLevel = 'GR'
```

obtains the following:

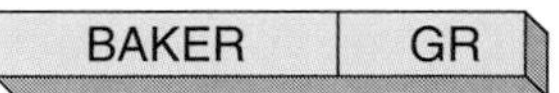

BAKER	GR

The conditions in WHERE clauses can refer to a set of values. To do this, the keywords IN or NOT IN may be used. Consider

```
SELECT    Name
FROM      STUDENT
WHERE     Major IN ['MATH', 'ACCOUNTING']
```

Notice that multiple values can be placed inside the brackets. This expression means "Display the names of students who have either a math or an accounting major." The result is

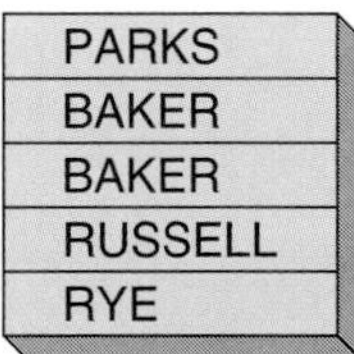

PARKS
BAKER
BAKER
RUSSELL
RYE

The expression

```
SELECT    Name
FROM      STUDENT
WHERE     Major NOT IN ['MATH', 'ACCOUNTING']
```

causes the names of students other than math or accounting majors to be presented. The result is

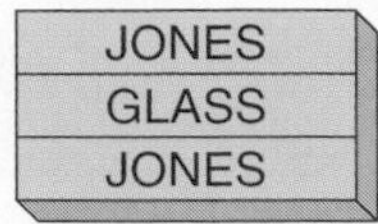

JONES
GLASS
JONES

The expression MAJOR IN means the value of the Major column can equal *any* of the listed majors. This is equivalent to the logical OR operator. The expression MAJOR NOT IN means the value must be different from *all* the listed majors.

WHERE clauses can also refer to ranges and to partial values. The keyword BETWEEN is used for ranges. For example, the statement

```
SELECT    Name, Major
FROM      STUDENT
WHERE     SID BETWEEN 200 AND 300
```

will obtain the following result

BAKER	MATH
GLASS	HISTORY
BAKER	ACCOUNTING

This expression is equivalent to

```
SELECT    Name, Major
FROM      STUDENT
WHERE     SID >= 200 AND SID <= 300
```

Thus, the end values of BETWEEN (here 200 and 300) are included in the selected range.

The LIKE keyword is used in SQL expressions to select on partial values. The symbol _ (underscore) represents a single unspecified character. The symbol % represents a series of one or more unspecified characters. Thus the result of the expression

```
SELECT    Name, GradeLevel
FROM      STUDENT
WHERE     GradeLevel LIKE '_R'
```

is a relation having Name and GradeLevel columns and where GradeLevel consists of two characters, the second of which is the character R:

JONES	GR
BAKER	GR
RUSSELL	JR
RYE	FR

Similarly, the following expression will find students whose last names end with S:

```
SELECT    Name
FROM      STUDENT
WHERE     Name LIKE '%S'
```

the result is

JONES
PARKS
GLASS
JONES

(Microsoft Access uses a different set of wildcard symbols than the ANSI standard. A "?" is used in place of the underscore, and an "*" is used in place of "%.")

Finally, the keywords IS NULL are used to search for null (or missing) values. The expression

```
SELECT    Name
FROM      STUDENT
WHERE     GradeLevel IS NULL
```

will obtain the names of students who do not have a recorded value of GradeLevel. For the data in Figure 9-2, all students have a GradeLevel and this expression will return a relation with no rows.

SORTING

The rows of the result relation can be sorted by the values in one or more columns. Consider the following example:

```
SELECT    Name, Major, GradeLevel
FROM      STUDENT
WHERE     Major = 'ACCOUNTING'
ORDER BY  Name
```

This query will list the accounting majors in ascending sequence by value of name. The result is

BAKER	ACCOUNTING	SN
PARKS	ACCOUNTING	SO
RYE	ACCOUNTING	FR

More than one column can be chosen for sorting. If so, the first column listed will be the major sort field, the next column the next major sort field, and so on. Columns can also be declared to be ascending (ASC) or descending (DESC), as shown in the next statement:

```
SELECT    Name, Major, GradeLevel
FROM      STUDENT
WHERE     GradeLevel IN ['FR', 'SO', 'SN']
ORDER BY  Major ASC, GradeLevel DESC
```

The result is

PARKS	ACCOUNTING	SO
BAKER	ACCOUNTING	SN
RYE	ACCOUNTING	FR
GLASS	HISTORY	SN
JONES	HISTORY	SN

ORDER BY can be combined with any of the SELECT statements.

SQL Built-in Functions

SQL provides five built-in functions: COUNT, SUM, AVG, MAX, and MIN.[2] Although COUNT and SUM sound similar, they actually are different. COUNT computes the number of rows in a table, whereas SUM totals numeric columns. AVG, MAX, and MIN also operate on numeric columns: AVG computes the average value, and MAX and MIN obtain the maximum and minimum values of a column in a table.

The query expression

```
SELECT    COUNT(*)
FROM      STUDENT
```

counts the number of STUDENT rows and displays this total in a table with a single row and single column:

8

Consider the expressions

```
SELECT    COUNT (Major)
FROM      STUDENT
```

and

```
SELECT    COUNT (DISTINCT Major)
FROM      STUDENT
```

The first expression counts all majors, including duplicates, and the second counts only unique majors. The results are

8

and

3

respectively.

With the exception of GROUP BY (considered below), built-in functions cannot be mixed with column names in the SELECT statement. Thus,

```
SELECT    Name, COUNT (*)
```

is not allowed.

The built-in functions can be used to request a result, as in the preceding examples. In most implementations of SQL, and in the ANSI standard SQL, the built-in functions *cannot* be used as part of a WHERE clause.

Built-In Functions and Grouping

To increase their utility, built-in functions can be applied to groups of rows within a table. Such groups are formed by collecting those rows (logically, not physically) that have the same value of a specified column. For example, students can be grouped by major, which means that one group will be formed for each value of

---

[2]Sometimes built-in functions are referred to as *aggregate functions* to distinguish them from program languages' built-in functions such as SUBSTRING.

MAJOR. For the data in Figure 9-2, there is a group of HISTORY majors, a group of ACCOUNTING majors, and a group of MATH majors.

The SQL keyword GROUP BY instructs the DBMS to group together those rows that have the same value of a column. Consider

```
SELECT      Major, COUNT (*)
FROM        STUDENT
GROUP BY    Major
```

The result of this expression is

HISTORY	3
ACCOUNTING	3
MATH	2

The rows of the STUDENT table have been logically grouped by the value of MAJOR, and the COUNT function sums the number of rows in each group. The result is a table with two columns, the major name and the sum. For subgroups, both columns and built-in functions can be specified in the SELECT statement.

In some cases, we do not want to consider all of the groups. For example, we might form groups of students having the same major and then wish to consider only those groups that have more than two students. In this case, we use the SQL HAVING clause to identify the subset of groups we want to consider.

The following SQL statements can list the majors that have more than two students and also the count of students in each of those majors.

```
SELECT      Major, COUNT (*)
FROM        STUDENT
GROUP BY    Major
HAVING      COUNT (*) > 2
```

Here, groups of students having the same major are formed, and then groups having more than two students are selected. (Other groups are ignored.) The major and the count of students in these selected groups are produced. The result is

HISTORY	3
ACCOUNTING	3

For even greater generality, WHERE clauses can be added as well. Doing so, however, can create ambiguity. For example,

```
SELECT      Major, MAX (SID)
FROM        STUDENT
WHERE       GradeLevel = 'SN'
GROUP BY    Major
HAVING      COUNT (*) > 1
```

The result of this expression will differ depending on whether the WHERE condition is applied before or after the HAVING condition. To eliminate this uncertainty, the SQL standard specifies that WHERE clauses are to be applied first. Accordingly, in the preceding statement, the operations are: select the senior students; form the groups; select the groups that meet the HAVING condition; display the results. In this case, the result is

HISTORY	450

(This query is not valid for all implementations of SQL. For some implementations, the only attributes that can appear in the SELECT phrase of a query with GROUP BY are attributes that appear in the GROUP BY phrase and built-in functions of those attributes. Thus in this query, only MAJOR and built-in functions of MAJOR would be allowed.)

➤ QUERYING MULTIPLE TABLES

In this section we extend our discussion of SQL to include operations on two or more tables. The STUDENT, CLASS, and ENROLLMENT data in Figure 9-2 are used to illustrate these SQL commands.

RETRIEVAL USING SUBQUERY

Suppose we need to know the names of those students enrolled in the class BD445. If we know that students with SIDs of 100 and 200 are enrolled in this class, the following will produce the correct names:

```
SELECT    Name
FROM      STUDENT
WHERE     SID IN [100, 200]
```

Usually we do not know the SIDs of students in a class, but we do have a facility for finding those out. Examine the expression

```
SELECT    StudentNumber
FROM      ENROLLMENT
WHERE     ClassName = 'BD445'
```

The result of this operation is

100
200

These are the student numbers we need. Combining the last two queries, we obtain the following:

```
SELECT    Name
FROM      STUDENT
WHERE     SID IN
              (SELECT   StudentNumber
               FROM     ENROLLMENT
               WHERE    ClassName = 'BD445' )
```

The second SELECT, which is called a **subquery**, is enclosed in parentheses.

It may be easier to understand these statements if you work from the bottom and read up. The last three statements obtain the student numbers for people enrolled in BD445, and the first three statements produce the names for the two students selected. The result of this query is

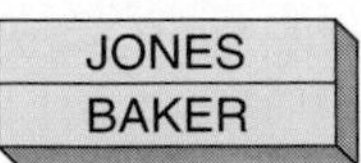

JONES
BAKER

For this operation to be semantically correct, SID and StudentNumber must come from the same domain.

Subqueries can consist of three or even more tables. For example, suppose we want to know the names of the students enrolled in classes on Monday, Wednesday, and Friday at 3 o'clock (denoted as MWF3 in our data). First, we need the names of those classes that meet at that time:

```
SELECT    CLASS.Name
FROM      CLASS
WHERE     Time = 'MWF3'
```

(Since we are dealing with three different tables, we qualify the column names with table names to avoid confusion and ambiguity. Thus, CLASS.Name refers to the column Name in the relation CLASS.)

Now we get the identifying numbers of students in these classes with the following expression:

```
SELECT    ENROLLMENT.StudentNumber
FROM      ENROLLMENT
WHERE     ENROLLMENT.ClassName IN
              (SELECT    CLASS.Name
              FROM       CLASS
              WHERE      Time = 'MWF3')
```

This yields

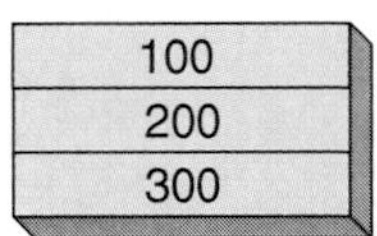

100
200
300

which are the numbers of the students in the class MWF3. To get the names of those students, we specify

```
SELECT    STUDENT.Name
FROM      STUDENT
WHERE     STUDENT.SID IN
              (SELECT ENROLLMENT.StudentNumber
              FROM ENROLLMENT
              WHERE ENROLLMENT.ClassName IN
                  (SELECT    CLASS.Name
                  FROM       CLASS
                  WHERE      CLASS.Time = 'MWF3'))
```

The result is

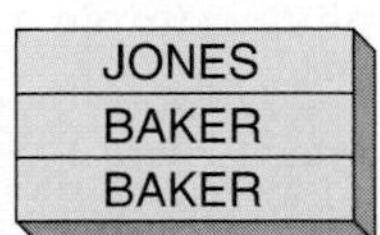

JONES
BAKER
BAKER

This strategy works well as long as the attributes in the answer come from a single table. If, however, the result comes from two or more tables, we have a problem. For example, suppose we want to know the names of students and the names of their classes. Say we need SID, StudentName, and ClassName. In this case, the results come from two different tables (STUDENT and ENROLLMENT), and so the subquery strategy will not work.

Joining with SQL

To produce the SID, Name, and ClassName for every student, we must join the STUDENT table with the ENROLLMENT table. The following statements will do this:

```
SELECT    STUDENT.SID, STUDENT.Name, ENROLLMENT.ClassName
FROM      STUDENT, ENROLLMENT
WHERE     STUDENT.SID = ENROLLMENT.StudentNumber
```

Recall that a join is the combination of a product operation, followed by a selection, followed (usually) by a projection. In this expression, the FROM statement expresses the product of STUDENT and ENROLLMENT, and then the WHERE statement expresses the selection. The meaning is "Select from the product of STUDENT and ENROLLMENT those rows in which SID of STUDENT equals StudentNumber of ENROLLMENT." Finally, after the selection, the projection of the student number, name, and class name is taken. The result is

100	JONES	BD445
150	PARKS	BA200
200	BAKER	BD445
200	BAKER	CS250
300	BAKER	CS125
400	RYE	BA200
400	RYE	BF410
400	RYE	CS250
450	JONES	BA200

The WHERE clause can contain qualifiers in addition to those needed for the join. For example,

```
SELECT    STUDENT.SID, ENROLLMENT.ClassName
FROM      STUDENT, ENROLLMENT
WHERE     STUDENT.SID = ENROLLMENT.StudentNumber
AND       STUDENT.Name = 'RYE'
AND       ENROLLMENT.PositionNumber = 1
```

The additional qualifiers here are STUDENT.Name = 'RYE' and ENROLLMENT.PositionNumber = 1. This operation will list the student number and class name of all students named RYE who were first to enroll in a class. The result is

400	BF410

When data are needed from more than two tables, we can use a similar strategy. In the next example, three tables are joined:

```
SELECT    STUDENT.SID, CLASS.Name, CLASS.Time,
          ENROLLMENT.PositionNumber
FROM      STUDENT, ENROLLMENT, CLASS
WHERE     STUDENT.SID = ENROLLMENT.StudentNumber
AND       ENROLLMENT.ClassName = CLASS.Name
AND       STUDENT.Name = 'BAKER'
```

The result of this operation is

200	BD445	MWF3	2
200	CS250	MWF12	1
300	CS150	MWF3	1

Comparison of SQL Subquery and Join

A join can be used as an alternative way of expressing many subqueries. For example, we used a subquery to find the students enrolled in the class BD445. We can also use a join to express this query:

```
SELECT    STUDENT.Name
FROM      STUDENT, ENROLLMENT
WHERE     STUDENT.SID = ENROLLMENT.StudentNumber
AND       ENROLLMENT.ClassName = 'BD445'
```

Similarly, the query "What are the names of the students in class MWF at 3?" can be expressed as

```
SELECT    STUDENT.NAME
FROM      STUDENT, ENROLLMENT, CLASS
WHERE     STUDENT.SID = ENROLLMENT.StudentNumber
AND       ENROLLMENT.ClassName = CLASS.Name
AND       CLASS.Time = 'MWF3'
```

Although join expressions can substitute for many subquery expressions, they cannot substitute for all of them. For instance, subqueries that involve EXISTS and NOT EXISTS (discussed in the next section) cannot be represented by joins.

Similarly, subqueries cannot be substituted for all joins. When using a join, the displayed columns may come from any of the joined tables, but when using a subquery, the displayed columns may come from only the table named in the FROM expression in the first SELECT. For example, suppose we want to know the names of classes taken by undergraduates. We can express this as a subquery:

```
SELECT    DISTINCT ClassName
FROM      ENROLLMENT
WHERE     StudentNumber IN
              (SELECT SID
              FROM STUDENT
              WHERE GradeLevel NOT = 'GR')
```

or as a join:

```
SELECT    DISTINCT ENROLLMENT.ClassName
FROM      ENROLLMENT, STUDENT
WHERE     ENROLLMENT.StudentNumber = STUDENT.SID
AND       STUDENT.GradeLevel NOT = 'GR'
```

But if we want to know both the names of the classes and the grade levels of the undergraduate students, we must use a join. A subquery will not suffice because the desired results come from two different tables. That is, the names of the classes are stored in ENROLLMENT, and the names of the students are stored in STUDENT. The following obtains the correct answer:

```
SELECT   DISTINCT ENROLLMENT.ClassName, STUDENT.GradeLevel
FROM     ENROLLMENT, STUDENT
WHERE    ENROLLMENT.StudentNumber = STUDENT.SID
AND      STUDENT.GradeLevel NOT = 'GR'
```

The result is

BA200	SO
CS150	SN
BA200	FR
BF410	FR
CS250	FR
BA200	SN

Outer Join

ANSI standard SQL does not support outer joins. They are, however, supported by many DBMS products. Here we will illustrate the use of one of them.

Suppose we want a list of all students and the names of the classes that they are taking. Further, suppose that we want to include all students, even those who are taking no class. The following SQL expression will obtain this result using Microsoft Access

```
SELECT   Name, ClassName
FROM     STUDENT LEFT JOIN ENROLLMENT
         ON SID = StudentNumber;
```

The result is

JONES	BD445
PARKS	BA200
BAKER	BD445
BAKER	CS250
GLASS	Null
BAKER	CS150
RUSSELL	Null
RYE	BA200
RYE	BF410
RYE	CS250
JONES	BA200

Observe the differences in Access SQL and ANSI standard notation. The join conditions are specified using the keyword ON. Also, all SQL expressions are terminated with a semicolon.

➤ EXISTS AND NOT EXISTS

EXISTS and NOT EXISTS are logical operators whose value is either true or false depending on the presence or absence of rows that fit the qualifying conditions. For example, suppose we want to know the student numbers of students enrolled in more than one class.

```
SELECT     DISTINCT StudentNumber
FROM       ENROLLMENT A
WHERE      EXISTS
              (SELECT     *
              FROM        ENROLLMENT B
              WHERE       A.StudentNumber = B.StudentNumber
                 AND      A.ClassName NOT = B.ClassName)
```

In this example, both the query and the subquery refer to the ENROLLMENT table. To prevent ambiguity, these two uses of ENROLLMENT have been assigned a different name. In the first FROM statement, ENROLLMENT is assigned the temporary and arbitrary name A, and in the second FROM statement, it is assigned another temporary and arbitrary name, B.

The meaning of the subquery expression is this: Find two rows in ENROLLMENT having the same student number but different class names. (This means that the student is taking more than one class.) If two such rows exist, then the logical value of EXISTS is true. In this case, we present the student number in the answer. Otherwise, the logical value of the EXISTS is false, so we do not present that SID in the answer.

Another way of viewing this query is to imagine two separate and identical copies of the ENROLLMENT table. Call one copy Table A and the other copy Table B. We compare each row in A with each row in B. First we look at the first row in A and the first row in B. In this case, since the two rows are identical, both the StudentNumbers and the ClassNames are the same, so we do not display the SID.

Now look at the first row in A and the second row in B. If the StudentNumbers are the same and the ClassNames are different, we display the StudentNumber. Essentially, we are comparing the first row of ENROLLMENT with the second row of ENROLLMENT. For the data in Figure 9-2, neither the StudentNumbers nor the ClassNames are the same.

We continue comparing the first row of A with each row of B. If the conditions are ever met, we print the StudentNumber. When all of the rows in B have been examined, we move to the second row of A and compare it with all the rows in B (actually, if we are considering the *n*th rows in A, only those rows greater than *n* need to be considered in B).

The result of this query is

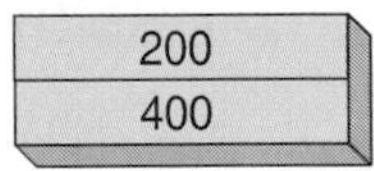

To illustrate the application of NOT EXISTS, suppose we want to know the names of students taking all classes. Another way of stating this is that we want the names of students such that there are no classes that the student did not take. The following expresses this:

```
SELECT     STUDENT.Name
FROM       STUDENT
WHERE      NOT EXISTS
              (SELECT *
              FROM    ENROLLMENT
              WHERE   NOT EXISTS
                 (SELECT     *
                 FROM        CLASS
                 WHERE       CLASS.Name = ENROLLMENT.ClassName
                 AND         ENROLLMENT.StudentNumber = STUDENT.SID))
```

This query has three parts. In the bottom part, it finds classes the student did take. The middle part determines whether any classes were found that the student did not take. If not, then the student is taking all classes, and his or her name is displayed.

This query may be difficult to understand. If you have trouble with it, use the data in Figure 9-2 and follow the instructions. For that data, the answer is that no student is taking all classes. You might try to change the data so that a student does take all classes. Another way to look at this query is to try to solve it in a way other than with NOT EXISTS. The problems you encounter will help you understand why NOT EXISTS is necessary.

➤ CHANGING DATA

SQL has provisions for changing data in tables by inserting new rows, deleting rows, and modifying values in existing rows. SQL also can change the data structure, although we will not explore this until Chapters 12 and 13.

INSERTING DATA

Rows can be inserted into a table one at a time or in groups. To insert a single row, we state

```
INSERT      INTO ENROLLMENT
            VALUES (400, 'BD445', 44)
```

If we do not know all of this data—for instance, if we do not know PositionNumber—we could say

```
INSERT      INTO ENROLLMENT
            (StudentNumber, ClassName)
            VALUES (400, 'BD445')
```

PositionNumber could then be added later. Note that this causes the value of PositionNumber to have a null value in the new row.

We can also copy rows in mass from one table to another. For example, suppose we want to fill the JUNIOR table defined in Figure 9.1.

```
INSERT      INTO JUNIOR
                VALUES
                (SELECT SID, Name, Major
                FROM        STUDENT
                WHERE       GradeLevel = 'JR')
```

The contained SELECT, and all of the SQL SELECT expressions developed in the previous two sections, can be used to identify the rows to be copied. This feature offers quite powerful capabilities.

DELETING DATA

As with insertion, rows can be deleted one at a time or in groups. The following example deletes the row for Student 100:

```
DELETE   FROM STUDENT
WHERE    STUDENT.SID = 100
```

Note that if Student 100 is enrolled in classes, this delete will cause an integrity problem, as the ENROLLMENT rows having StudentNumber = 100 will have no corresponding STUDENT row.

Groups of rows can be deleted as shown in the next two examples, which delete all enrollments for accounting majors as well as all accounting majors.

```
DELETE   FROM ENROLLMENT
WHERE    ENROLLMENT.StudentNumber IN
            (SELECT   STUDENT.SID
             FROM     STUDENT
             WHERE    STUDENT.Major = 'Accounting')
DELETE   FROM STUDENT
WHERE    STUDENT.Major = 'Accounting'
```

The order of these two operations is important, for if it were reversed, none of the ENROLLMENT rows would be deleted because the matching STUDENT rows would already have been deleted.

Modifying Data

Rows can also be modified one at a time or in groups. The keyword SET is used to change a column value. After SET, the name of the column to be changed and then the new value or way of computing the new value is specified. Consider two examples:

```
UPDATE   ENROLLMENT
SET      PositionNumber = 44
WHERE    SID = 400
```

and

```
UPDATE   ENROLLMENT
SET      PositionNumber = MAX(PositionNumber) + 1
WHERE    SID = 400
```

In the second UPDATE statement, the value of the column is calculated using the MAX built-in function. Some implementations of SQL, however, may not allow the built-in function to be used as an argument in the SET command.

To illustrate mass updates, suppose the name of a course has been changed from BD445 to BD564. In this case, to prevent integrity problems, both the ENROLLMENT and the CLASS tables must be changed.

```
UPDATE   ENROLLMENT
SET      ClassName = 'BD564'
WHERE    ClassName = 'BD445'
UPDATE   CLASS
SET      ClassName = 'BD564'
WHERE    ClassName = 'BD445'
```

Remember that mass updates can be quite dangerous. The user is given great power—power that when used correctly can rapidly perform the task at hand but when used incorrectly can cause serious problems.

➤ SUMMARY

SQL is today's most important relational data manipulation language. It has become the standard for information exchange among computers, and its popularity continues to grow. SQL statements that operate on a single table include SELECT, SELECT with WHERE, SELECT with GROUP BY, and SELECT with GROUP BY and HAVING. SQL also contains the built-in functions of COUNT, SUM, AVG, MAX, and MIN.

Operations on two or more tables can be done using subquery, joins, EXISTS, and NOT EXISTS. Subqueries and joins perform many of the same operations, but they do not completely substitute for each other. Subqueries require that the attributes retrieved arise from a single relation, but joins do not. On the other hand, some queries are possible with subqueries and EXISTS and NOT EXISTS that are impossible with joins.

The SQL statements for data modification include INSERT, DELETE, and UPDATE commands, which are used to add, remove, and change data values.

In this chapter we presented the basic SQL commands in generic form, and in Chapters 13, 14, and 16 we use these commands to process a database using commercial DBMS products.

➤ GROUP I QUESTIONS

The questions in this group refer to the following three relations:

SALESPERSON (<u>Name</u>, PercentOfQuota, Salary)
ORDER (<u>Number</u>, CustName, SalespersonName, Amount)
CUSTOMER (<u>Name</u>, City, IndustryType)

An instance of these relations is shown in Figure 9-3. Use the data in those tables and show the SQL statements to display or modify data as indicated in the following questions:

9.1 Show the salaries of all salespeople.

9.2 Show the salaries of all salespeople but omit duplicates.

9.3 Show the names of all salespeople under 30 percent of quota.

9.4 Show the names of all salespeople who have an order with Abernathy Construction.

9.5 Show the names of all salespeople who earn more than $49,999 and less than $100,000.

9.6 Show the names of all salespeople with PercentOfQuota greater than 49 and less than 60. Use the BETWEEN keyword.

9.7 Show the names of all salespeople with PercentofQuota greater than 49 and less than 60. Use the LIKE keyword.

9.8 Show the names of customers who are located in a City ending with S.

9.9 Show the names and salary of all salespeople who do not have an order with Abernathy Construction, in ascending order of salary.

9.10 Compute the number of orders.

9.11 Compute the number of different customers who have an order.

9.12 Compute the average percent of quota for salespeople.

9.13 Show the name of the salesperson with highest percent of quota.

9.14 Compute the number of orders for each salesperson.

9.15 Compute the number of orders for each salesperson, considering only orders for an amount exceeding 500.

9.16 Show the names and quota percentages of salespeople who have an order with ABERNATHY CONSTRUCTION, in descending order of quota percentage (use a subquery).

9.17 Show the names and quota percentages of salespeople who have an order with ABERNATHY CONSTRUCTION, in descending order of quota percentage (use a join).

9.18 Show the quota percentages of salespeople who have an order with a customer in MEMPHIS (use a subquery).

9.19 Show the quota percentages of salespeople who have an order with a customer in MEMPHIS (use a join).

9.20 Show the industry type and names of the salespeople of all orders for companies in MEMPHIS.

9.21 Show the names of salespeople along with the names of the customers which have ordered from them. Include salespeople who have had no orders. Use Microsoft Access notation.

9.22 Show the names of salespeople who have two or more orders.

➤ FIGURE 9-3

Sample Data for Group I Questions

Name	PercentOfQuota	Salary
Abel	63	120,000
Baker	38	42,000
Jones	26	36,000
Murphy	42	50,000
Zenith	59	118,000
Kobad	27	36,000

SALESPERSON

Number	CustName	SalespersonName	Amount
100	Abernathy Construction	Zenith	560
200	Abernathy Construction	Jones	1800
300	Manchester Lumber	Abel	480
400	Amalgamated Housing	Abel	2500
500	Abernathy Construction	Murphy	6000
600	Tri-City Builders	Abel	700
700	Manchester Lumber	Jones	150

ORDER

Name	City	IndustryType
Abernathy Construction	Willow	B
Manchester Lumber	Manchester	F
Tri-City Builders	Memphis	B
Amalgamated Housing	Memphis	B

CUSTOMER

9.23 Show the names and quota percentages of salespeople who have two or more orders.

9.24 Show the names and ages of salespeople who have an order with all customers.

9.25 Show a SQL statement to insert a new row into CUSTOMER.

9.26 Show a SQL statement to insert a new name and age into SALESPERSON; assume that salary is not determined.

9.27 Show a SQL statement to insert rows into a new table, HIGH-ACHIEVER (Name, Salary), in which, to be included, a salesperson must have a salary of at least 100,000.

9.28 Show a SQL statement to delete customer ABERNATHY CONSTRUCTION.

9.29 Show a SQL statement to delete all orders for ABERNATHY CONSTRUCTION.

9.30 Show a SQL statement to change the salary of salesperson JONES to 45,000.

9.31 Show a SQL statement to give all salespeople a 10 percent pay increase.

9.32 Assume that salesperson JONES changes his name to PARKS. Show the SQL statements that make the appropriate changes.

➤ GROUP II QUESTIONS

9.33 Install Access 2002 and open the Northwind database. Using the Query Design/SQL View tool, write SQL statements for the following queries and print them.

a. List all columns of suppliers.

b. List CompanyName from suppliers with CompanyName starting with "New."

c. List all columns from products supplied by suppliers with CompanyName starting with "New." Show answers using both a join and a subquery.

d. List the ReorderLevel and count for all products.

e. List the ReorderLevel and count for all ReorderLevels having more than one element.

f. List the ReorderLevel and count for all ReorderLevels having more than one element for products from suppliers whose names start with "New."

➤ FIREDUP PROJECT QUESTIONS

Assume FiredUp has created a database with the following tables:

CUSTOMER (<u>CustomerSK</u>, Name, Phone, EmailAddress)
STOVE (<u>SerialNumber</u>, Type, Version, DateOfManufacture)
REGISTRATION (<u>*CustomerSK*</u>, <u>*SerialNumber*</u>, <u>Date</u>)
STOVE_REPAIR (<u>RepairInvoiceNumber</u>, *SerialNumber*, Date, Description, Cost, *CustomerSK*)

Code SQL for the following, assume all dates are in the format *mmddyyyy*.

A. Show all of the data in each of the four FiredUp tables.

B. List the versions of all stoves.

C. List the versions of all stoves of type 'FiredNow.'

D. List the SerialNumber and Date of all registrations in the year 2000.

E. List the SerialNumber and Date of all registrations in February. Use the underscore (_) wildcard.

F. List the SerialNumber and Date of all registrations in February. Use the percent (%) wildcard.

G. List the names and EmailAddresses of all customers who have an e-mail address.

H. List the names of all customers who do not have an EmailAddress; present the results in descending sorted order of Name.

I. Determine the maximum cost of a stove repair.

J. Determine the average cost of a stove repair.

K. Count all stoves.

L. Count all stoves of each type and display the Type and count.

M. List the names and e-mail addresses of all customers who have had a stove repair that cost more than $50. Use subquery.

N. List the names and e-mail addresses of all customers who have registered a stove of type 'FiredNow.' Use subquery.

O. List the names and e-mail addresses of all customers who have had a stove repair that cost more than $50. Use join.

P. List the names and e-mail addresses of all customers who have registered a stove of type 'FiredNow.' Use join.

Q. List the names, e-mail addresses, and registration date of all customer registrations.

R. Show the names and e-mail addresses of all customers who have registered a stove but who have not had any stove repaired.

S. Show the names and e-mail addresses of all customers who have registered a stove but who have not had that stove repaired.

Database Application Design

This chapter introduces the fundamental concepts in database application design. We begin by listing and describing the functions of a database application. Then each of these functions is described in further detail using an example application of an art gallery. The ideas presented in this chapter pertain best to database applications that are developed for use in traditional environments such as Windows. Chapters 14 through 16 will extend these concepts for the design of applications that use Internet technology.

Before we begin, a note on terminology is necessary. In the early days of database processing, it was easy to find a line between the DBMS and the application—applications were separate programs that invoked the DBMS. Today, especially with desktop DBMS products like Microsoft Access, the line has become blurred. To avoid confusion in this chapter, we will assume that all forms, reports, menus, and any program code that is contained in any of those are part of the database application. Additionally, stand-alone programs that call the DBMS are also part of the application. Any structures, rules, or constraints that are part of the table and relationship definitions are managed by the DBMS and are part of the database. Thus, a rule placed on a column of a table in table definition is considered a rule that is enforced by the DBMS. The same rule, placed on a form control, is considered a rule that is enforced by the database application. You will see the importance of this distinction as we proceed.

➤ FUNCTIONS OF A DATABASE APPLICATION

Figure 10-1 lists the functions of a database application. The first is to process views of data. There are four basic processing functions: create, read, update, and delete. These functions are sometimes referred to by the (unfortunate) acronym **CRUD.** Thus, the first function of a database application is to CRUD views.

FIGURE 10-1

Functions of a Database Application

- Create, Read, Update and Delete Views
- Format (or Materialize) Views
  - Forms
  - Reports
  - Inter-process
  - OLAP cubes
  - Other
- Enforce Constraints
  - Domains
  - Uniqueness
  - Relationships
  - Business rules
- Provide Control and Security
- Execute Application Logic

An application view is more than a row of a table and more than the result of a SQL statement. Often the construction of an application view requires two or more SQL statements, as you will see in the next section.

A second application function is to **format** or **materialize** the views that are being processed. Note that there is a difference between the data content (the view) and the appearance of that content (the format or materialization). A given view usually has many different formats. The distinction between content and form is especially important for database applications that use Internet technology.

There are several types of view materialization. Forms and reports are the two most common types. Other types are also important, however. An interprocess materialization is used to send a view from one server to another or from one application to another. The format of such materializations is determined by a standard interface like Microsoft COM or a protocol like XML, which will be introduced in Chapter 14. Electronic data interchange is a good example of the use of this type. Other types of materialization are more specialized. You will see the role of OLAP cubes in Chapter 17. Natural language is an example of yet another type.

Enforcing constraints is a third application function. Such constraints can be structural, such as requiring data values to fit domain specifications, ensuring uniqueness, and enforcing relationship constraints. Other constraints involve business rules, such as "No salesperson can sell to a customer whose billing address is outside of his or her region."

The fourth function of a database application is to provide mechanisms for security and control. The application will work in conjunction with the operating system and the DBMS to augment security provided by user names and passwords. Menus and similar constructs limit what and when users can take particular actions.

The last function of a database application is to execute business logic. For example, in an order entry application, when a customer orders five copies of a book, the application needs to reduce the quantity of that book on hand by five. If insufficient copies are in inventory, or if the quantity on hand is less than the reorder quantity, other action needs to be taken as well.

The last two functions are addressed in detail in systems development classes, and, consequently, we will have the least to say about them in this text. The first three functions, however, are particular to database applications, and we will focus the bulk of our attention on them.

Before learning about these functions in more detail, consider the needs for a database and application at View Ridge Gallery.

➤ CASE APPLICATION: VIEW RIDGE GALLERY

View Ridge Gallery is a small art gallery that sells contemporary fine art, including lithographs, original paintings, and photographs. All of the lithographs and photos are signed and numbered, and most of the art is priced between \$1,000 and \$25,000. View Ridge has been in business for 27 years, has one full-time owner, three salespeople, and two workers who make frames, hang art in the gallery, and prepare art works for shipment.

View Ridge holds openings and other gallery events to attract customers to the gallery. Art is also placed on display in local companies and restaurants and in other public places. View Ridge owns all of the art that it sells; it holds no items on a consignment basis.

APPLICATION REQUIREMENTS

The requirements for the View Ridge application are summarized in Figure 10-2. First, both the owner and the salespeople want to keep track of their customers and their art-purchasing interests. The salespeople need to know whom to contact when new art arrives, and they also need this information so that they can create personal written and verbal communications with their customers.

In addition, the database should record the customers' art purchases so that the salespeople can devote more time to the most active buyers. They also sometimes use the purchase records to identify the location of the art, because the gallery occasionally repurchases hard-to-find art for resale. The database application also should have a form for adding new works that the gallery purchases.

View Ridge wants its database application to provide a list of artists and works that have appeared in the gallery. The owner would also like to be able to determine how fast an artist's work sells and at what sales margins, and the database application should display current inventory on a Web page that customers can access via the Internet. Finally, View Ridge would like the database to produce reports that would reduce the work of the gallery's part-time bookkeeper/accountant.

DATABASE DESIGN

Figure 10-3(a) shows the structure of the objects required to support the gallery's database. CUSTOMER and ARTIST are compound objects, and WORK is a hybrid object whose unique identifier is the group {ARTIST, Title, and Copy}. The multi-value group Transaction represents the gallery's purchase and sale of the work. Because a given work can pass through the gallery several times (because of repurchases and trade-ins), Transaction is multi-value. WORK is a hybrid object

➤ FIGURE 10-2

Summary of Requirements for the View Ridge Gallery Database Applications

Track customers and their purchasing interests.

Record customers' art purchases.

Record gallery's purchases.

List the artists and works that have appeared in the gallery.

Report how fast an artist's works have sold and at what margin.

Show current inventory in a Web page.

List product reports to be used by the gallery's bookkeeper/accountant.

➤ FIGURE 10-3

Database Design for View Ridge Gallery: (a) Semantic Objects, (b) E-R Diagram, (c) Relational Design, (d) Relational Design with Surrogate Keys, (e) Relationship Diagram from Access

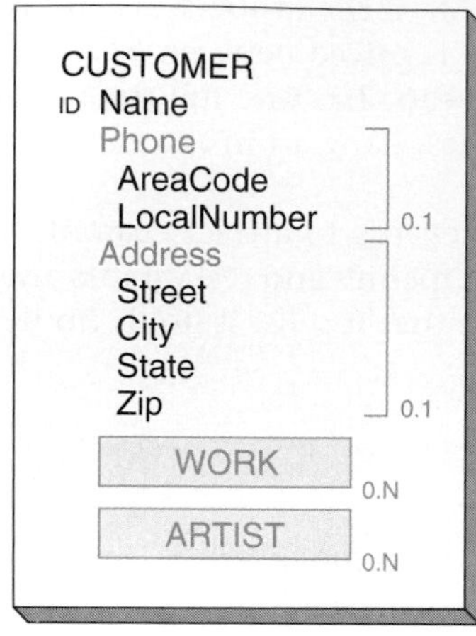

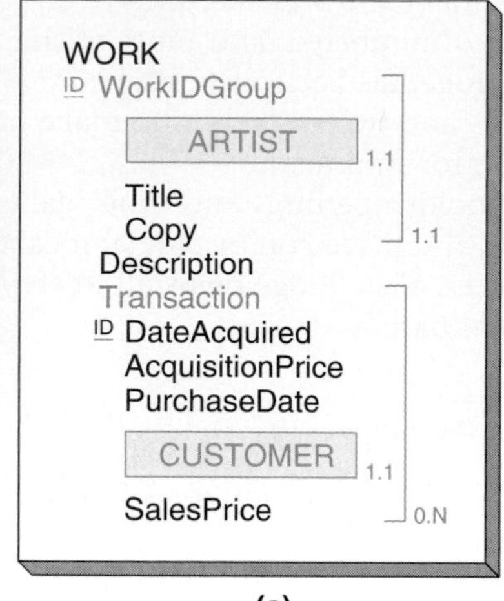

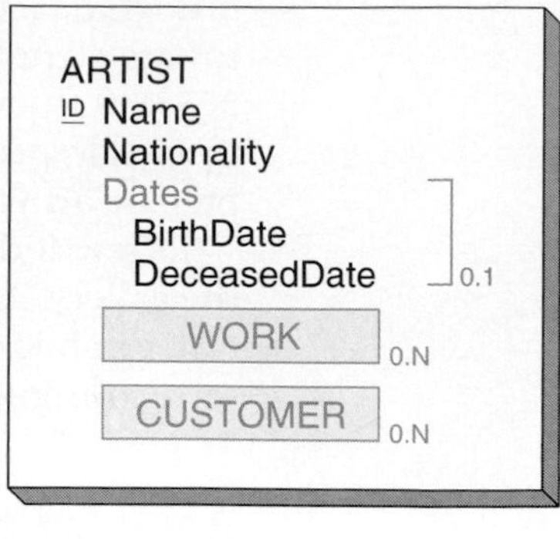

(a)

CUSTOMER
WORK
1 N
1 N
TRANSACTION
N 1
1 N
1 N
CUSTOMER_ARTIST_INT
ARTIST

(b)

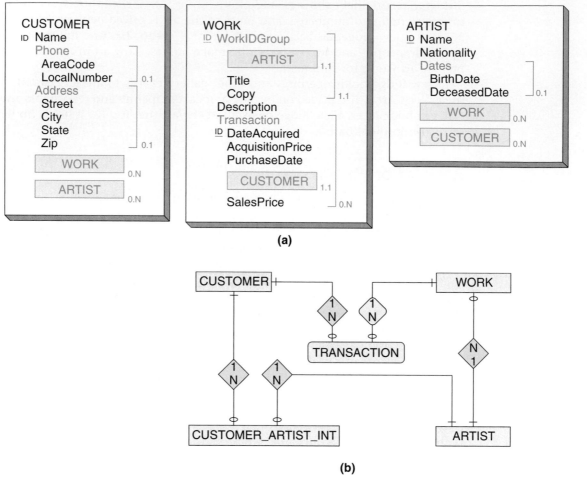

CUSTOMER (CustNumber, Name, AreaCode, LocalNumber, Street, City, State, Zip)

WORK (ArtistName, Title, Copy, Description)

TRANSACTION (*ArtistName*, *Title*, *Copy*, DateAcquired, AcquisitionPrice, PurchaseDate, *CustNumber*, SalesPrice)

ARTIST (ArtistName, Nationality, Birthdate, DeceasedDate)

CUSTOMER_ARTIST_INT (CustNumber, ArtistName)

(c)

because it contains the object attribute CUSTOMER in the multi-value Transaction group.

View Ridge wants to be able to track its customers' interests. In particular, it wants to know the artists in which a particular customer is interested and the customers who have an interest in a particular artist. These requirements are supported by placing the multi-value attribute ARTIST in CUSTOMER and the multi-value attribute CUSTOMER in ARTIST. An E-R diagram appears in Figure 10-3(b).

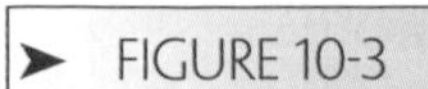
FIGURE 10-3

(Continued)

CUSTOMER (CustomerID, Name, AreaCode, LocalNumber, Street, City, State, Zip)

WORK (WorkID, *ArtistID*, Title, Copy, Description)

TRANSACTION (TransactionID, *WorkID*, DateAcquired, AcquisitionPrice, PurchaseDate, *CustomerID*, SalesPrice)

ARTIST (ArtistID, ArtistName, Nationality, Birthdate, DeceasedDate)

CUSTOMER_ARTIST_INT (*CustomerID*, *ArtistID*)

Referential integrity constraints:

ArtistID in WORK must exist in ArtistID in ARTIST

WorkID in TRANSACTION must exist in WorkID in WORK

CustomerID in TRANSACTION must exist in CustomerID in CUSTOMER

CustomerID in CUSTOMER_ARTIST_INT must exist in CustomerID in CUSTOMER

ArtistID in CUSTOMER_ARTIST_INT must exist in ArtistID in ARTIST

(d)

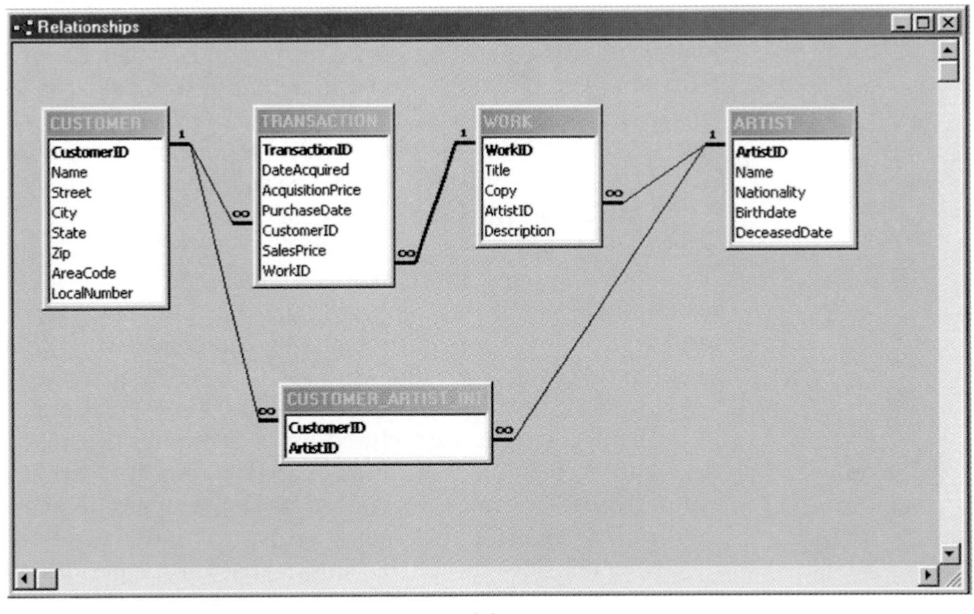

(e)

The relational representation of the View Ridge objects is shown in Figure 10-3(c). Since the CUSTOMER object does not have a unique identifier, one must be created to use as a key. Here we have added an identifying number, CustNumber. The maximum cardinality of the Phone and Address groups is 1, so the attributes in those groups can be placed in the CUSTOMER table. These groups, in fact, do not appear in the table as groups; instead, the group information is used later to construct forms.

The key of WORK consists of the key of ARTIST plus Title and Copy. The only nonkey attribute of WORK is Description. Since the Transaction attribute is multivalue, a table must be created for it. Its key is the key of the object in which it is contained (ArtistName, Title, Copy) plus the key of the group, which is DateAcquired. Note also that CustNumber is carried as a foreign key in TRANSACTION.

The ARTIST object is represented by a single table, and ArtistName can be used as the table key, because artists' names are modeled as being unique. The intersection table CUSTOMER_ARTIST_INT must be created to carry the M:N relationship between CUSTOMER and ARTIST.

Because of the number of text keys, and in particular because of the large composite key of TRANSACTION, this design can be substantially improved by replacing data keys with surrogate keys. This has been done in the design shown in Figure 10-3(d). The names of the surrogate keys are constructed by appending the letters ID to the name of the table.

The design in Figure 10-3(d) is better because less data are duplicated. The columns ArtistName, Title, and Copy need not be copied into the Transaction table. Because there may be many transactions for a given work, this savings may be appreciable. Figure 10-3(e) shows a relationship diagram for the surrogate key design.

➤ CREATING, READING, UPDATING, AND DELETING VIEW INSTANCES

A **view** is a structured list of data items from the entities or semantic objects defined in the data model. A view instance is a view that is populated with data for one entity or semantic object. Figure 10-4(a) shows a sample view for the gallery database in Figure 10-3. This view shows data about a customer, about that customer's transactions, and about that customer's artist interests. In this view, there are potentially many TRANSACTIONs for each CUSTOMER, and each TRANSACTION has one WORK. Also, there can be many ARTIST Names for each CUSTOMER (the artists in which the customer is interested).

Notice that ARTIST.Name occurs twice in this view. The first time it is the name of an artist of a work that the CUSTOMER has purchased. The second time it is the name of an artist in which the CUSTOMER is interested. For the example in Figure 10-4(b), a customer has purchased works by Tobey and Miro, and is interested in work not just by these two artists, but by Dennis Frings as well. In this case, Tobey and Miro each appear twice in the view, once as a value of WORK.ARTIST.Name and once as a value of ARTIST.Name.

Again, a view is a structured list of attributes. Because it is structured, attributes can occur more than once in a view. Also notice that a view is a list of data values only. It can be formatted or materialized in many different ways—as a form, as a report, or in some other type of materialization.

Now consider the CRUD actions that can be performed on a view. We begin with Read.

READING VIEWS INSTANCES

To read an existing view, the application must execute one or more SQL statements to obtain data values and then place the resulting values into the view structure. The Customer View in Figure 10-4 contains data on two paths: one through the TRANSACTION table and another through the CUSTOMER_ARTIST_INT table. The structure of SQL statements is such that only one path through the schema can be followed with a single SQL statement. Thus, this view will require a separate SQL statement for each path. For the first path, the following SQL will obtain the necessary data for the customer named "Jackson, Mary":

```
SELECT    CUSTOMER.CustomerID, CUSTOMER.Name,
          CUSTOMER.AreaCode, CUSTOMER.LocalNumber,
```

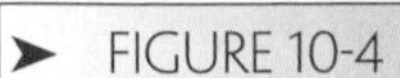

Customer View: (a) Structured List of Attributes, (b) Sample Data

```
CUSTOMER.Name
CUSTOMER.AreaCode
CUSTOMER.LocalNumber
    TRANSACTION.PurchaseDate
    TRANSACTION.SalesPrice . . .
        WORK.ARTIST.Name
        WORK.Title
        WORK.Copy
    ARTIST.Name . . .
```

a. Structured List of Attributes

Jackson, Elizabeth		
206		
284-6783		
	7/15/94	
	4,300	
		Mark Tobey
		Lithograph One
		10/75
	2/5/99	
	2,500	
		Juan Miro
		Poster 14
		5/250
	11/22/97	
	17,850	
		Juan Miro
		Awakening Child
		1/1
	Juan Miro	
	Mark Tobey	
	Dennis Frings	

b. Sample Data

```
         ARTIST.Name, WORK.Title, WORK.Copy,
         TRANSACTION.PurchaseDate, TRANSACTION.SalesPrice
FROM     CUSTOMER, TRANSACTION, WORK, ARTIST
WHERE    CUSTOMER.CustomerID = TRANSACTION.CustomerID
  AND    WORK.WorkID = TRANSACTION.WorkID
  AND    ARTIST.ArtistID = WORK.ArtistID
  AND    CUSTOMER.Name = 'Jackson, Mary'
```

Review this SQL statement while looking at the relationship diagram in Figure 10-3(e). The three joins are necessary to obtain data across the three relationships at the top of the diagram.

In the context of application development, the result of a SQL statement is sometimes termed a **recordset.** To Microsoft, this term means a relation with an object programming wrapper. A recordset has both methods and properties. *Open* is an example recordset method, *CursorType* is an example recordset property. You will learn more about this in Chapter 14.

To obtain the customer's artist interests, a second SQL statement is required to follow the path through CUSTOMER_ARTIST_INT. The SQL statement for this path is

```
SELECT   CUSTOMER.CustomerID, ARTIST.Name
FROM     CUSTOMER, CUSTOMER_ARTIST_INT, ARTIST
WHERE    CUSTOMER.CustomerID = CUSTOMER_ARTIST_INT.CustomerID
  AND    CUSTOMER_ARTIST_INT.ArtistID = ARTIST.ArtistID
  AND    CUSTOMER.Name = 'Jackson, Mary'
```

Because CUSTOMER.Name is not unique, it is possible that the two recordsets from these statements will retrieve data about more than one customer. Hence the application will need to have logic to examine the CustomerID values in the recordsets and to associate the correct rows together.

After executing these two statements, the application has all of the data necessary to construct one or more instances of the view in Figure 10-3. How that is done depends on the language in use. In COBOL, data would be placed in structures defined in the Data Division. In Visual Basic, the data could be placed in a data structure or a series of arrays. In C++ and Java the data would be placed into objects. We are not concerned with those issues here. Rather, you should gain a sense of how the application must execute one or more SQL statements to fill the view data structure. See Chapter 16 for a Java example.

Creating View Instances

To create a new view instance, the application must first obtain the new data values and relationships. This is most likely done via a data entry form, but applications also receive data from other programs and in other ways. In any case, once the application has data values, it then executes SQL statements to store the data in the database.

Consider the New Customer view in Figure 10-5. This view is used when a new customer purchases a painting. It contains data about the customer, about the purchase transaction, and about multiple customer interests. This view differs from that in Figure 10-4 because it has more customer data and it also only allows

➤ FIGURE 10-5

New Customer View

```
CUSTOMER.Name
CUSTOMER.AreaCode
CUSTOMER.LocalNumber
CUSTOMER.Address
CUSTOMER.City
CUSTOMER.State
CUSTOMER.Zip
    TRANSACTION.DateAcquired
    TRANSACTION.AcquisitionPrice
    TRANSACTION.PurchaseDate
    TRANSACTION.SalesPrice
        WORK.ARTIST.Name
        WORK.Title
        WORK.Copy
    ARTIST.Name . . .
```

a single transaction. There can, however, be multiple ARTIST.Name values that record the new customer's interests.

Assume that data values for this view are located in a program structure called NewCust; further suppose that we can access the values in the structure by appending the characters NewCust to the names in the structure. Thus NewCust.CUSTOMER.Name accesses the Name of the CUSTOMER in the NewCust structure.

To create this view in the database, we must store the new customer data in CUSTOMER, store the new transaction data in TRANSACTION, and create a row in the intersection table CUSTOMER_ARTIST_INT for each of the artists in whom the customer is interested.

The following SQL statement will store the new customer data:

```
INSERT   INTO CUSTOMER
         (CUSTOMER.Name,
         CUSTOMER.AreaCode,
         CUSTOMER.LocalNumber,
         CUSTOMER.Address,
         CUSTOMER.City,
         CUSTOMER.State,
         CUSTOMER.Zip)
VALUES   (NewCust.CUSTOMER.Name,
         NewCust.CUSTOMER.AreaCode,
         NewCust.CUSTOMER.LocalNumber,
         NewCust.CUSTOMER.Address,
         NewCust.CUSTOMER.City,
         NewCust.CUSTOMER.State,
         NewCust.CUSTOMER.Zip)
```

Assume that when the new row is created, the DBMS assigns the value of the surrogate key CUSTOMER.CustomerID. We will need the value of this key to finish the creation of the new view instance, so the application will need to obtain it. One way to do so is to execute the following SQL SELECT:

```
SELECT   CUSTOMER.CustomerID, CUSTOMER.AreaCode,
         CUSTOMER.LocalNumber
FROM     CUSTOMER
WHERE    CUSTOMER.Name = NewCust.CUSTOMER.Name
```

Because CUSTOMER.Name is not unique, more than one row can appear in the recordset. In this case, the correct one would be identified by examining the phone data. Assume that this has been done if necessary and the correct value is placed in the program structure as NewCust.CUSTOMER.CustomerID.

An INSERT statement will also be used to store the new TRANSACTION record. However, in this case values for the foreign keys TRANSACTION.WorkID and TRANSACTION.CustomerID will have to be supplied. We already have shown how to obtain the value of CustomerID, so all that remains is to obtain the value of WorkID. The following SQL will do that:

```
SELECT   WORK.WorkID
FROM     WORK, ARTIST
WHERE    WORK.ArtistID = ARTIST.ArtistID
  AND    ARTIST.Name = NewCust.WORK.ARTIST.Name
  AND    WORK.Title = NewCust.WORK.Title
  AND    WORK.Copy = NewCust.WORK.Copy
```

Assume that the returned surrogate key value is stored as NewCust.WORK.WorkID.

The following SQL can be executed to add the new TRANSACTION row:

```
INSERT    INTO TRANSACTION
              (TRANSACTION.WorkID,
              TRANSACTION.DateAcquired,
              TRANSACTION.AcquisitionPrice,
              TRANSACTION.PurchaseDate,
              TRANSACTION.CustomerID,
              TRANSACTION.SalesPrice)
          VALUES
              (NewCust.WORK.WorkID,
              NewCust.TRANSACTION.DateAcquired,
              NewCust.TRANSACTION.AcquisitionPrice,
              NewCust.TRANSACTION.PurchaseDate,
              NewCust.CUSTOMER.CustomerID,
              NewCust.TRANSACTION.SalesPrice)
```

Now all that remains is to create rows for the intersection table CUSTOMER_ARTIST_INT. To do that, we need to obtain the ArtistID for each artist in whom the customer is interested, and then create a new row in the intersection table. The following pseudocode illustrates the logic:

```
For each NewCust.ARTIST.Name
        SELECT    ARTIST.ArtistID
        FROM      ARTIST
        WHERE     ARTIST.Name = NewCust.ARTIST.Name
        INSERT    INTO CUSTOMER_ARTIST_INT
                  (CustomerID, ArtistID)
                  VALUES (NewCust.CUSTOMER.CustomerID,
                  ARTIST.ArtistID)
Next NewCust.ARTIST.Name
```

At this point, the New Customer view has been stored in the database. Of course, a complete application includes logic to catch errors returned from the DBMS and process them. For example, the application must handle the cases of the WORK not existing in the database, and of an ARTIST not existing in the database.

Updating View Instances

The third fundamental action to be performed on a view is update. When updating a view, three types of change are possible. One is a simple value change such as a customer changing his or her phone number. Another is a change to a relationship. An example is when a customer no longer maintains an interest in a particular artist. A third type of update requires the addition of one or more new rows; that would occur in our example when a customer makes a new purchase.

The first type of update can be accomplished with SQL UPDATE statements. For example, assume that a program has a structure named UpdateCust and that this structure has the CustomerID, AreaCode, and LocalNumber. The following SQL will update the new values:

```
UPDATE  CUSTOMER
SET     CUSTOMER.AreaCode = UpdateCust.AreaCode
        CUSTOMER.LocalNumber = UpdateCust.LocalNumber
WHERE   CUSTOMER.CustomerID = UpdateCust.CustomerID
```

Changes to relationships are also straightforward. If the relationship is one-to-many, then the foreign key value just needs to be updated to the new value. For example, assume the relationship from DEPT to EMPLOYEE is 1:N. Then Dept# (or other key) will be stored as a foreign key in EMPLOYEE. To move an EMPLOYEE to a new DEPT, the application need only change the value of Dept# to the new value.

If the relationship is many to many, then the foreign key in the intersection table needs to be modified. For example, at the gallery, if a customer changes his or her interest from Mark Tobey to an interest in Dennis Frings, then the intersection row that represents the connection to Mark Tobey needs to be changed to point to Dennis Frings.

Assume UpdateCust.CustomerID has the ID of the customer, UpdateCust. OldArtistID has the ID of the Mark Tobey row in ARTIST, and UpdateCust. NewArtistID has the ID of the Dennis Frings row in ARTIST. The following SQL will make the necessary change:

```
UPDATE  CUSTOMER_ARTIST_INT
SET     CUSTOMER_ARTIST_INT.ArtistID = UpdateCust.NewArtistID
WHERE   CUSTOMER_ARTIST_INT.CustomerID = UpdateCust.CustomerID
  AND   CUSTOMER_ARTIST_INT.ArtistID = UpdateCust.OldArtistID
```

In a many-to-many relationship, it is also possible to delete a connection without replacing it and to create a new connection without deleting an old one. To delete a connection, we would just delete the appropriate row in the intersection table. To create one, we would add a new row in the intersection table.

The third type of update requires the addition of a new row in one or more tables. If, for example, an existing customer makes a new purchase, then a new row in the TRANSACTION table will need to be created. This can be done in the same way that a new TRANSACTION row was added when creating a new view instance.

Deleting View Instances

Deleting view instances involves removing rows from the tables that make up the view. The trick is to know how much to delete. For example, suppose that the gallery wants to delete data for a Customer whose name is "Jones, Mary." Clearly, the "Jones, Mary" row in CUSTOMER needs to be deleted. Also, all of the intersection rows in CUSTOMER_ARTIST_INT that pertain to her need to be deleted as well. But what about rows in the TRANSACTION table? This table contains CustomerID and if her row is deleted, all rows in TRANSACTION that have her value of CustomerID will have invalid data.

The answers to questions like this are determined from the data model. In the case of the E-R model, all weak entities are deleted if the entity upon which they depend is also deleted. Otherwise, no additional table rows are deleted. In the case of the semantic object model, all data within an object are deleted (there may be many tables in an object if it has multi-value attributes), but no data in a different object is deleted. In addition to these rules, no deletion can be allowed if it will cause a violation of relationship cardinalities. We will touch on that topic here and consider it in more depth later in this chapter.

Consider the model in Figure 10-3. When a customer is deleted, the row in CUSTOMER will be deleted along with all rows in CUSTOMER_ARTIST_INT that pertain to that customer. TRANSACTION data will not be deleted because it resides in a different object—namely, WORK. Note, however, that the minimum cardinality of CUSTOMER in TRANSACTION is 1. Hence, if a given CUSTOMER is bound to a TRANSACTION, then that CUSTOMER is required and its deletion cannot be allowed.

We can also conclude from Figure 10-3, that if a WORK view is deleted, then the WORK row and all TRANSACTION rows relating to that row will be deleted.

Finally, if an ARTIST view is deleted, then only ARTIST and CUSTOMER_ARTIST_INT rows will be deleted. Further, if there are any WORK objects that are bound to that ARTIST, then the deletion cannot be allowed.

Some DBMS products support deletion of dependent rows, usually under the term **cascading deletions.** Figure 10-6 shows the relationship dialog box for Access. Notice that the box Cascade Delete Related Records has been checked. This means that when a WORK row is deleted, Access will automatically delete any connected TRANSACTION rows as well.

As stated, relationship cardinality plays an important role in determining whether or not rows in views can be deleted. We will turn to this subject later in this chapter under the topic of enforcing constraints.

This section surveyed the actions that need to be taken when creating, reading, updating, and deleting view instances. Some of the actions described here can be done automatically by DBMS products. For example, Access has wizards that will generate a form containing Customer and a single path—either to Transactions or to Artist interests. Users of this form can create, read, update, and delete instances of a Customer and data on one of the paths. The Access wizards will not generate a form that will support both paths in the Customer view in Figure 10-3, however. To do that, a developer will need to write program code.

Specifying Cascading Deletions

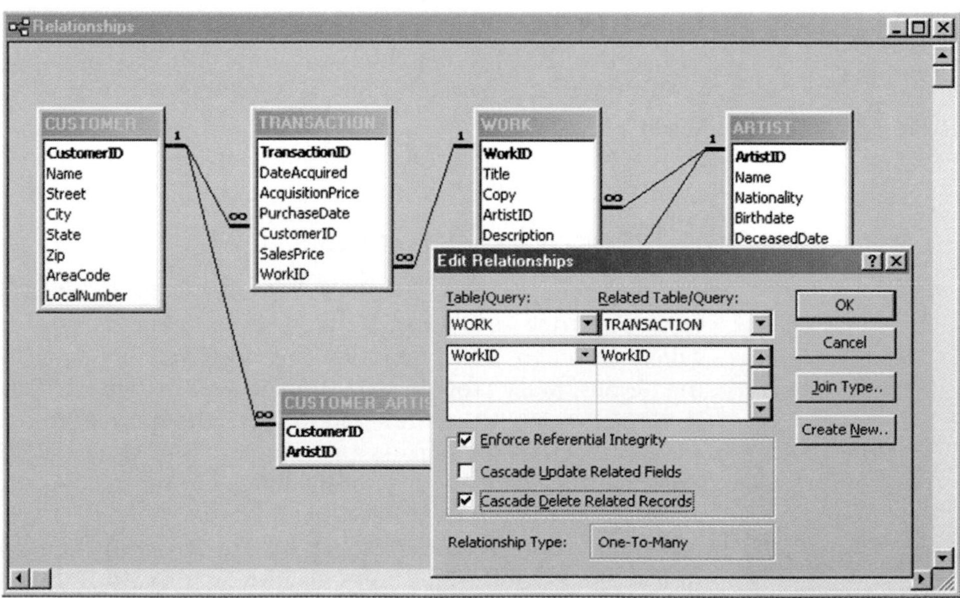

➤ FORM DESIGN

As shown in Figure 10-1, the second major function of a database application is to generate materializations of views. In this chapter we will consider form and report materializations. In Chapter 14 we will consider interprocess materializations using XML, and in Chapter 17 we will consider OLAP cube materializations.

A **form** is a screen display used for data entry and edit. Read-only forms can also be used to report data, but in most cases, when developers speak of forms, they mean those used for data entry and edit.

Some forms are easy to use and result in few data entry errors. Others seem awkward and contrived and are difficult to use without creating errors. In this section, we discuss and illustrate several principles of good form design.

THE FORM STRUCTURE SHOULD REFLECT THE VIEW STRUCTURE

First, to seem natural and be easy to use, *the structure of a form must reflect the structure of the view that it materializes.* Look at the form in Figure 10-7, which is a materialization of the Customer view in Figure 10-4(a).

The structure of this form reflects the structure of the Customer view. One section of the form has the basic customer data such as Name, Phone, and Address. The second section shows the customer's Artist interests. Finally, the third section lists the customer's purchase transactions. Users find this form easy to use because the attributes are grouped in a way that reflects their understanding of the structure of the customer data.

In general, when designing a form, all of the data from a single relation should be placed in one contiguous section of the form. Assuming that the database is in DK/NF, each relation should pertain to a specific theme, and the user should expect to have in one location all of the data for that theme. Thus, there are customer, artist interest, and transaction sections on the form.

➤ FIGURE 10-7

Form Materialization of Customer View in Figure 10-4(a)

There is one exception to this rule: Attributes in the base relation of the view (here, the relation CUSTOMER) are sometimes not placed contiguously. Suppose, for example, that CUSTOMER had a simple attribute named TotalPurchases. If we followed this rule, we would place TotalPurchases in the first section of the form. But it would be more sensible to the users to place that attribute at the end of the form, after all of the purchases have been listed.

The form in Figure 10-7 is not the only acceptable form of this view. Transactions could be placed before Artist Interests, for example. The base CUSTOMER data could be rearranged to be more horizontal in appearance. CustomerName, AreaCode, and LocalNumber could be placed in one column, and Street, City, State, and Zip could be placed in another. All of these alternatives enable the structure of the form to reflect the structure of the underlying objects.

The Semantics of the Data Should Be Graphically Evident

Another characteristic of a well-designed form is that the semantics of the data are graphically evident. Consider the base customer data section of the CUSTOMER form in Figure 10-7. Observe there are rectangles around AreaCode and LocalNumber and around Street, City, State, and Zip.

To understand why this is done, refer again to Figure 10-3(a). The CUSTOMER semantic object has a group attribute named Phone and another group attribute named Address. Since both of these attributes have a maximum cardinality of 1, they are—from the standpoint of the relational design—not really required. In fact, they do not appear in the relations in Figure 10-3(c) or (d). The only purpose of these group attributes is to semantically associate AreaCode with LocalNumber and Street and City, State, and Zip with one another.

The purpose of the rectangles in the Customer Purchase Form is to make these associations graphically clear. Most users are comforted by this arrangement. Knowing that phone number consists of AreaCode and LocalNumber, they find the graphically close association of those two to be very sensible.

The Form Structure Should Encourage Appropriate Action

The structure of forms should make it easy to perform appropriate actions and difficult to perform inappropriate or erroneous actions. For example, the field for entering State in the form in Figure 10-7 is small. Clearly, the user is supposed to enter only a two-digit state abbreviation. But a better design would allow only two digits to be entered, and the best design would present the states in a drop-down list and allow the user to choose from only that list.

In Figure 10-7, some fields are white and some are gray. The forms in this application have been designed so that users can enter data only in the white spaces; the gray data items cannot be changed in the form. Thus, the user cannot type into the Title or Copy fields in the Transaction section. Instead, to select or change a work, the user clicks on the combo box under Artist. When the user clicks on the arrow, a drop-down list of works is displayed, as shown in Figure 10-8. If the user wants to update work or artist data, or add or delete work or artist data, he or she must use a different form.

The reason for this design is that when users are entering new transactions for customers, they should be adding only transaction data, namely, the PurchaseDate and SalesPrice. Allowing them to change ARTIST or WORK data would open the door for accidental and erroneous changes, and such changes need not be made in order to sell a work.

FIGURE 10-8

Use of Drop-Down List Box

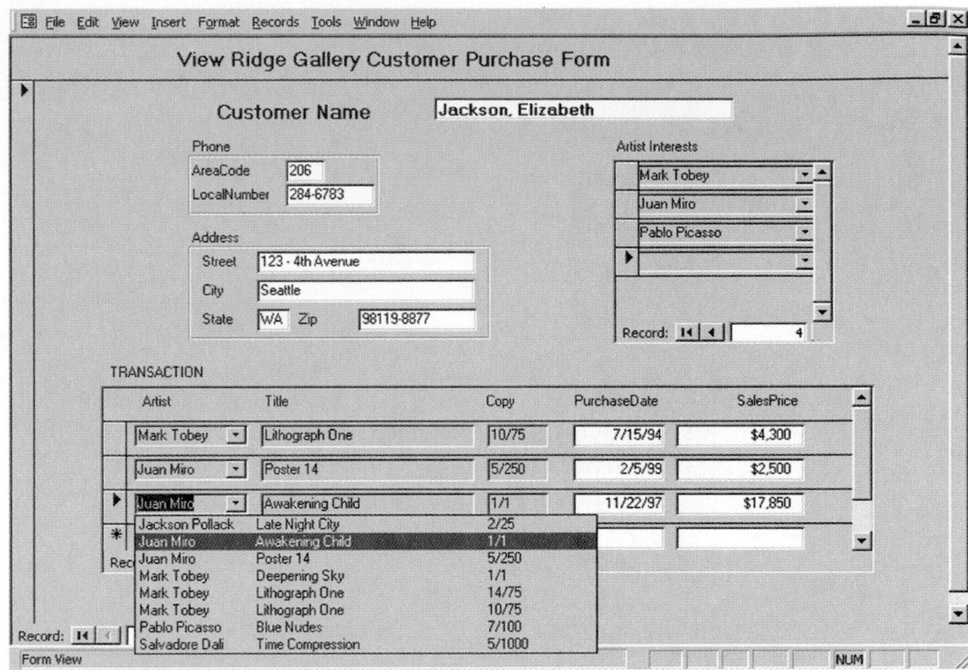

A similar design is used for Artist Interests. Users can only pick from a list. Here, the case is not as strong, however. Salespeople might want to be able to record that a customer has an interest in an artist even if that artist is not in the gallery's database. If so, the form would be changed to allow users to add to the list. In justification of the design in Figure 10-7, the gallery owner may only want to record interests in artists that the gallery has or will represent. He or she may want control over what names can appear.

FORMS IN A GUI ENVIRONMENT

A number of form features peculiar to GUI systems can dramatically facilitate the use of database applications.

DROP-DOWN LIST BOXES A **drop-down list box** is a GUI control that presents a list of items from which the user can choose. A property of the control determines whether the list is fixed or whether users can add to it. Figure 10-9 shows a different version of the Customer Purchase Form in which users can add Artist Names that are not present in the list. Behind the scenes, the application is storing a new ARTIST row in the database. For this to work, of course, only ArtistName can be a required attribute. If there were other required fields, the DBMS would reject the insert of the new row.

List boxes have a number of advantages over data entry boxes. First, people find it easier to *recognize* than to *recollect*. For example, in the Form in Figure 10-8, it is easier to choose an artist's name from the list than it is to remember all of the artists in the database. It is also easier to recognize a name than it is to spell it correctly. Finally, if the list box is set up to display only those values present in the database, the user cannot enter keystroke mistakes. Unfortunately, Juan Miro (one space between the *n* and the *M*) and Juan Miro (two spaces between the *n* and the *M*) will be considered different artists by the DBMS. Fixed-list drop-down list boxes prevent these mistakes.

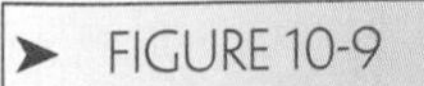
FIGURE 10-9

List Box That Allows New Values

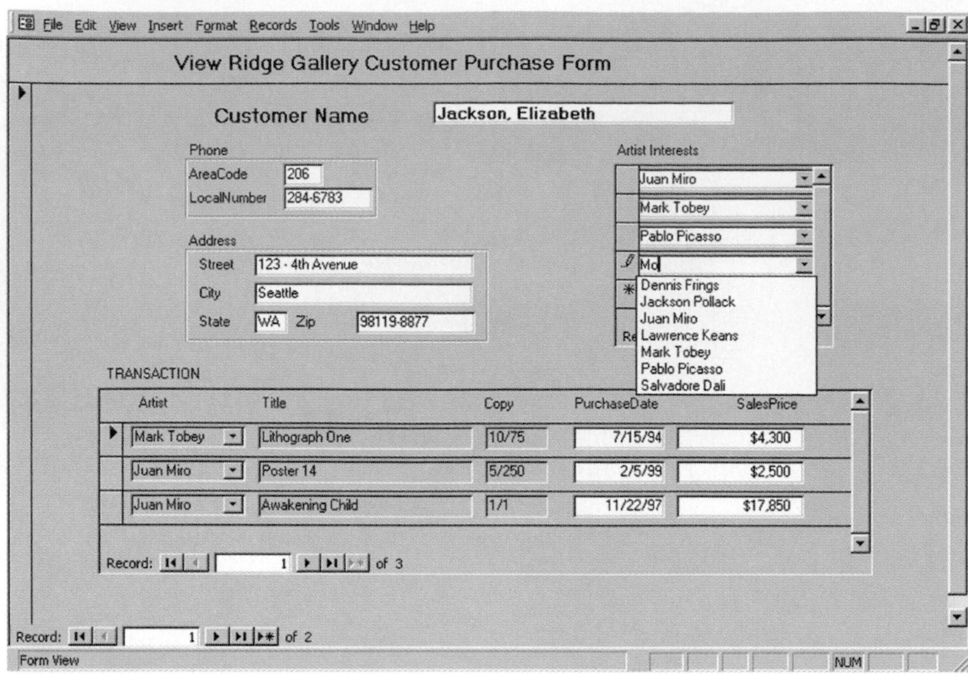

OPTION BUTTONS AND GROUPS An **option button**, or **radio button**, is a display device that enables users to select one alternative condition or state from a list of possibilities. For example, suppose the gallery decides that it needs to track the tax status of its customers. Assume that tax status has two possibilities, Taxable and Nontaxable, and that these possibilities are mutually exclusive. An option group like the one shown in Figure 10-10 could be used to gather this data. Because of the way that the option group works, if the user selects Taxable, then

FIGURE 10-10

Use of Group and Option Buttons

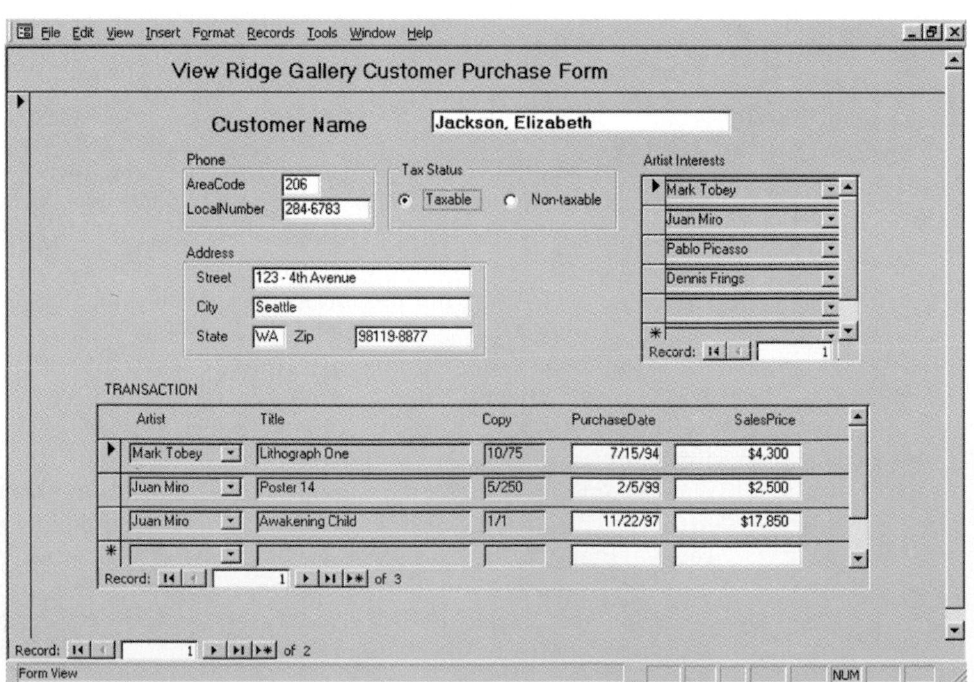

Nontaxable is automatically de-selected. If the user selects Nontaxable, then Taxable is automatically de-selected.

Behind the form, the application program must store data in a table column that represents the radio button selected. For this example, the column is named TaxStatus. One of two possible ways for storing the option button data is used. One is to store an integer number from 1 to the number of buttons. In this example, one of the values 1 or 2 would be stored. The second option is to store a text value that describes the option chosen. The possibilities are Yes or No.

CHECK BOXES **Check boxes** are similar to option buttons except that the alternatives in a group of check boxes are not mutually exclusive—more than one alternative may be chosen. Suppose, for example, that the gallery wants to record the type or types of art in which its customers are interested. The possible types are Lithographs, Oils, Pastels, and Photographs, shown in a series of check boxes in the version of the CUSTOMER form in Figure 10-11. The user selects or checks the appropriate boxes.

There are several ways of representing check boxes in relations. One common and simple way is to define a Boolean-valued column for each item in the check box group. The value of each of such columns is binary; that is, it can be 1 or 0, representing yes or no. There are other possibilities, such as encoding bits in a byte, although they are not important to our discussion.

In Figure 10-11, note the grayed boxes for Pastels and Ceramics. This gray signifies that the values for these choices are null. The users can interpret this form instance to mean that this customer is interested in Lithographs and Photography and is not interested in Oils. Her interest in Pastels and Ceramics is ambiguous. (See the discussion of nulls in Chapter 6.) If it is important to track null status, then the database design must allow for three values for each checkbox: checked, unchecked, and null. Thus discussion also pertains to groups with option buttons.

WEB FORMS Forms used in the browser are GUI forms and all of the above comments pertain to them as well. Web forms have one feature, however, that Windows forms do not have—hyperlinks. Such links are especially useful for

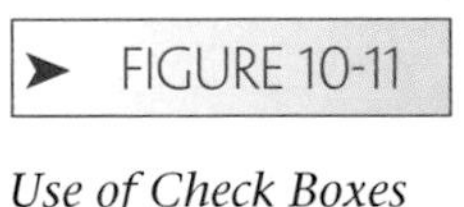

Use of Check Boxes

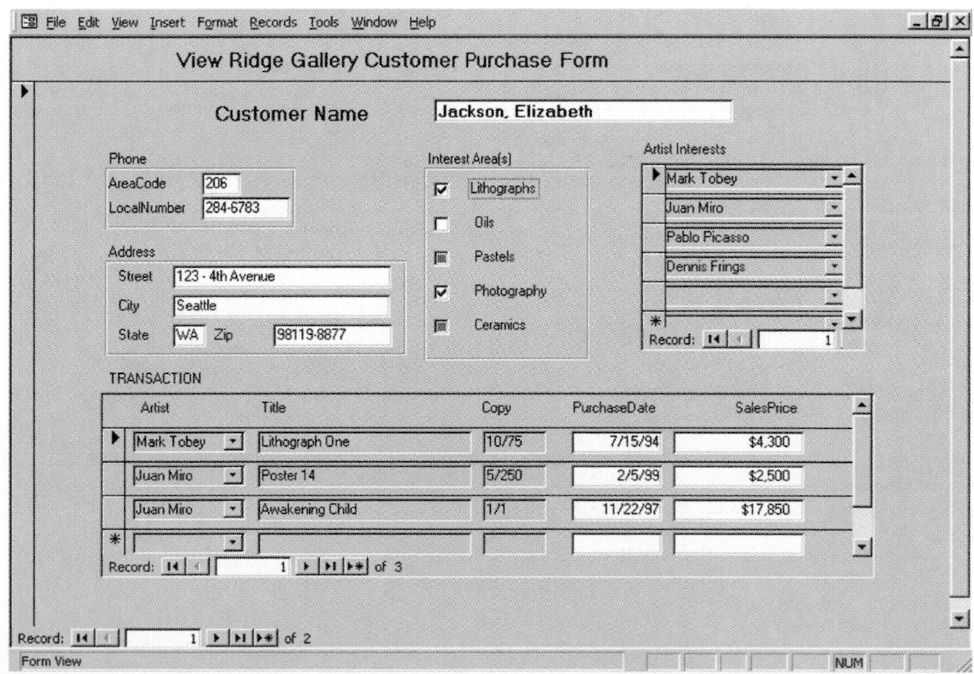

materializing links to other semantic objects or strong entities. For example, in the form in Figure 10-7, the links to artist interests can be replaced by hyperlinks so that when the user clicks on them, they will be taken to an ARTIST form with the appropriate data. The same can be done for links to WORKs.

Cursor Movement and Pervasive Keys

Another consideration in forms design is the action of the cursor. The cursor should move through the form easily and naturally. This usually means that the cursor follows the end user's processing pattern as he or she reads the source data entry documents. If forms are used to enter data over the telephone, the cursor should control the flow of the conversation. In this case, its movement should progress in a manner that the customer finds natural and appropriate.

Cursor movement is especially important during and after an exception condition. Suppose that in using the form in Figure 10-7, an error is made—perhaps an invalid state code is entered. The form should be processed so that the cursor moves to a logical location. For example, the application might display a list box of available state values and place the cursor on a logical position in the list—perhaps on the first state that starts with the first letter the user entered. When the state is selected, the cursor should move back to Zip, the next appropriate space on the form.

The actions of special-purpose keys such as ESC and function keys should be *consistent* and *pervasive*. If ESC is used to exit forms, use it consistently for this purpose and none other (except for actions that are logically equivalent to exiting from forms). The actions of the keys should be consistent throughout the application. That is, if ESC is used to exit from one form, it should be used to exit from all forms. If Cntrl-D is used to delete data in one form, it should be used to delete data in all forms. Otherwise, habits formed in one portion of the application must be disregarded or relearned in other portions of the application. This is wasteful, frustrating, and aggravating, and it causes errors. Although these comments may seem obvious, attention to such details is what makes a form easy and convenient to use.

➤ REPORT DESIGN

The subject of report design, even more so than form design, has been discussed extensively in texts on application development. We will not duplicate or even attempt to summarize those discussions here but, rather, look at several concepts directly related to the notion of a report as a materialization of a database view.

Report Structure

The principles of effective report design are similar to those for form design. Just as with forms, *the structure of a report should reflect the structure of the underlying view.* This means that data from one table should generally be located in one contiguous group on the report. As with forms, one exception to this rule is that the base relation of the view (for example, the CUSTOMER relation for the Customer view) may be separated on the report. Attribute groups, like Phone, should also be located together and distinguished in some way.

Figure 10-12 shows a sample report for the View Ridge Gallery that lists the data for each work of art and the transactions for each work of art, computes the gross margin by work and artist, as well as a grand total.

➤ FIGURE 10-12

Sales Listing Report

Sales Listing
15-Nov-01

ArtistName	Title		Copy		
Dennis Frings	**South Toward Emerald Sea**		**106/195**		
DateAcquired	**AcquisitionPrice**	**DateSold**	**Sold To**	**SalesPrice**	**GrossMargin**
4/17/1986	$750.00	5/3/1986	Heller, Max	$1,000.00	$250.00
3/15/2000	$1,200.00	5/11/2000	Jackson, Elizabeth	$1,800.00	$600.00
	Total margin for South Toward Emerald Seas, Copy 106/195				**$850.00**
			Total margin for Dennis Frings		**$850.00**
Mark Tobey	**Patterns III**		**27/95**		
DateAcquired	**AcquisitionPrice**	**DateSold**	**Sold To**	**SalesPrice**	**GrossMargin**
7/3/1971	$7,500.00	9/11/1971	Cooper, Tom	$10,000.00	$2,500.00
1/4/1986	$11,500.00	3/18/1986	Jackson, Elizabeth	$15,000.00	$3,500.00
9/11/1999	$17,000.00	10/17/1999	Cooper, Tom	$21,000.00	$4,000.00
		Total margin for Patterns III, Copy 27/95			**$10,000.00**
Mark Tobey	**Rhythm**		**2/75**		
DateAcquired	**AcquisitionPrice**	**DateSold**	**Sold To**	**SalesPrice**	**GrossMargin**
4/8/2001	$17,000.00	7/14/2001	Heller, Max	$27,000.00	$10,000.00
			Total margin for Rhythm, Copy 2/75		**$10,000.00**
			Total margin for Mark Tobey		**$20,000.00**
			Grand Total:		**$20,850.00**

The structure of the report in Figure 10-12 reflects the structure of the WORK object. The section for each work begins with the name of the work, which includes artist, title, and copy. Next is a section of repeating lines that shows the transactions for the work. Within each section, the name of the customer has been found from the CUSTOMER table.

Be aware that with most report writers, it is difficult to construct a report that follows more than one multi-value path through the database schema. The report in Figure 10-12 is a materialization of an ARTIST view that follows the path from ARTIST to WORK to TRANSACTION. The relationship diagram in Figure 10-4(e) shows another path—one through the CUSTOMER_ARTIST_INT table to the CUSTOMERs who are interested in a given artist. With most report writers, it will be difficult to construct a report that shows both of these paths.

Reports often have calculated data attributes that are not part of the underlying view and are not stored in the database. The report in Figure 10-12 has calculations for GrossMargin, Total Margin by Work, Total Margin by Artist, and a Grand Total. All of these values are computed on the fly as the report is produced.

While these computed values could be stored in the database, doing so is seldom a good idea because the values used to compute them can change. If for example, a user altered the SalesPrice for a particular transaction and did not recompute GrossMargin and the totals based on it, the stored values would be in error. However, making all of the necessary computations while processing update transactions will probably result in unacceptably slow processing. Hence, totals like this are usually best computed on the fly. Formulae for computing such totals are thus considered part of the materialization of the report and not part of the underlying view.

Implied Objects

Consider the request "Print all ARTISTs Sorted by Total Margin." At first glance, this appears to be a request to print a report about the object ARTIST. The words *sorted by,* however, indicate that more than one ARTIST is to be considered. In fact, this request is not based on the object ARTIST but, rather, is based on the object SET OF ALL ARTISTs. The report in Figure 10-12 shows data for multiple ARTISTs and is, in fact, based on the object SET OF ALL ARTISTs, not on the object ARTIST.

The human mind is so quick to shift from the object *OBJECT-A* to the object *SET OF ALL OBJECTS-A* that we normally do not even know there has been a change. When developing database applications, however, it is important to notice this shift because the application needs to behave differently when it occurs. Consider three ways in which sorting can change the nature of the base object: (1) sorting by object identifier; (2) sorting by non-identifier, nonobject columns; and (3) sorting by attributes contained in object attributes.

SORTED BY OBJECT IDENTIFIER If the report is to be sorted by an attribute that is an identifier of object, the true object is the collection of those objects. Thus, an ARTIST report sorted by ArtistName is a report about the object SET OF ALL ARTISTS. For most DBMS report-writing products, a report about the object SET OF ALL X is no more difficult to produce than a report about object X. It is important to know, however, that there has been a shift in object type.

SORTED BY NON-IDENTIFIER, NONOBJECT COLUMNS When a user needs a report sorted by an attribute that is a non-identifier of the object, the true object in the user's mind is most likely a totally different type of object. For example, the user wants to produce a report about ARTIST sorted by Nationality. Such a report is actually a materialization of a NATIONALITY object, not a materialization of the ARTIST object. Similarly, if the user asks for a report about CUSTOMER sorted by AreaCode, the report is actually based on an object called PHONE-REGION, or some similar object. Figure 10-13 shows an example PHONE-REGION object.

Objects such as NATIONALITY and PHONE-REGION are **implied objects;** that is, their existence can be inferred by the fact that the user asked for such a report. If it makes sense to the user to ask for something as a sort value, then that something must be an object in the user's mind, regardless of whether it is modeled in the database or not.

➤ FIGURE 10-13

PHONE-REGION Object

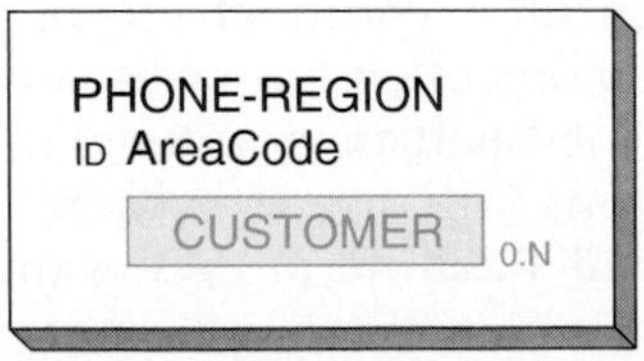

PHONE-REGION
ID AreaCode
CUSTOMER 0.N

SORTED BY ATTRIBUTES CONTAINED IN OBJECT ATTRIBUTES The third way in which reports can be sorted is by attributes contained in object attributes. For example, the user might ask for a report about WORKs sorted by Birthdate of ARTIST. ARTIST is an object attribute of WORK, and Birthdate is an attribute contained in ARTIST. In this case, the user is actually asking for a report about an implied object (say, TIME or ARTISTIC PERIOD) that contains many ARTISTs, each of which includes many WORKs in the gallery.

Understanding this switch in objects may ease the task of developing the report. Proceeding as if WORK were the base object of the report will make the report logic contrived. If WORK is considered the base, the materializations of WORK objects that include ARTIST and Birthdate must be created for all WORK objects, stored on disk, and then sorted by Birthdate. On the other hand, if this report is about an implied object that contains ARTIST, which in turn contains WORK, then ARTIST objects can be created and sorted by Birthdate and WORK objects treated as multi-value rows in each ARTIST object.

➤ ENFORCING CONSTRAINTS

As listed in Figure 10-1, the third major function of a database application is to enforce constraints. In many cases, the DBMS is better able to enforce constraints than the application, and so this is not strictly an application program function. Our concern, here, however, is to describe types of constraints and how they can be enforced, regardless of whether application code or the DBMS enforces them.

First, the reason that the DBMS is often the better place to enforce constraints is that it is a central point through which all data changes must pass. Regardless of the source of a data change (form, another program, bulk data import) the DBMS will have a chance to examine and reject the change, if necessary. Further, certain rules (uniqueness is one) may require the examination of all the rows in a table; the DBMS is better able to perform such a function than an application. Additionally, if the DBMS enforces a rule, then that rule need be coded just once. If the applications enforce a rule, then it will need to be coded for each new application. This is wasteful and generates the possibility that application programs will enforce rules inconsistently.

Having said that, not all DBMS products have the features and functions necessary to enforce constraints. Sometimes, too, it is far more difficult to write and install constraint enforcement code in DBMS facilities than in application code. Further, in some architectures (Microsoft Transaction Server is one) processing is more efficient if constraint checking is removed from the data server. Also, there are some constraints that are application dependent. A user of a particular form, for example, may not be allowed to take certain actions or enter certain data. In that case, the application is better able to enforce the constraint.

Your goal should be to understand the types of constraints and the means by which they are enforced. When possible, enforce them at the DBMS; if not, enforce them in application. We will now consider four types of constraint: domain, uniqueness, referential integrity and business rules.

Domain Constraints

Recall from Chapter 4 that a domain is the set of values that an attribute may have. Domain definitions have a semantic component (the Name of an Artist) and a physical component (Text 25, alphabetic). In general, it is not possible to enforce the semantic component by an automated process. We are not yet at the stage of development in the computer industry that automated processes can determine

FIGURE 10-14

Creating a Domain Constraint with Access

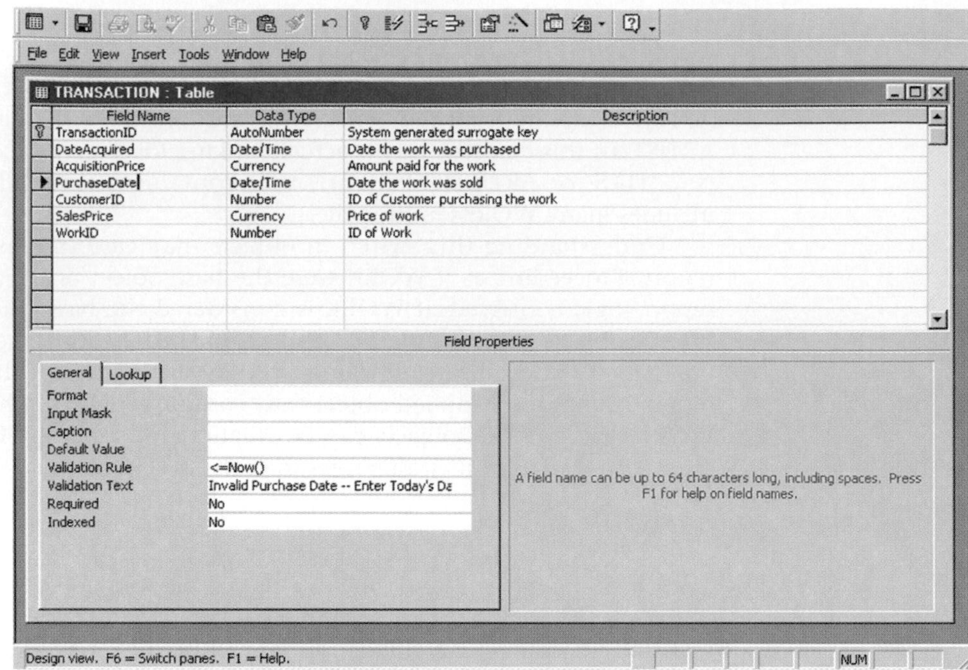

that 3M is the name of a company and not the name of an artist. Therefore, today we are primarily concerned with enforcing the physical part of a domain definition.

Domain constraints arise from the data model as described in Chapter 4. The specificity of domain constraints varies widely. In the View Ridge Gallery database, ARTIST.Name can be any set of 25 or fewer text characters. A domain such as that for Copy, however, is more specific. The format used by the gallery is nn/mm, where nn is a particular copy number and mm is the total number of copies made. Thus, 5/100 means the fifth copy out of a run of 100. Clearly, a value like 105/100 makes no sense. Therefore, validation code should be developed to ensure that this format is followed.

Figure 10-14 shows an example domain constraint in Access. The constraint is that PurchaseDate must be less than or equal to the computer's clock date at the time the purchase is entered. Notice the line labeled Validation Rule. The expression <= Now( ) defines the rule. If the user attempts to enter data that violates this rule, a message box is generated using the text that is entered in the next line (Validation Text). Figure 10-15 shows what happens when the user attempts to enter a date of 10/15/99 when the computer's date was less than 10/15/99. The submitted data is then rejected by Access.

Another type of constraint is whether or not values are required. Strictly speaking, the requirement that a value be provided is a table constraint rather than a domain constraint. A domain is a set of values; whether or not a value is required is a question that arises when the domain appears in a table.

The data model should indicate if attribute values are required. In the semantic object model, if the minimum cardinality of an attribute is 1, then that attribute is required. To enforce this constraint with Access, all that is needed is to set the Required property of a column to Yes. This was done for Name in the ARTIST table definition in Figure 10-16. Other means are used with other DBMS products as you will see.

Required value constraints are important because they eliminate the possibility of null values. Another way to do this is to define an initial value that the DBMS assigns to the column when the row is created. With Access, this is done by placing a value or expression in the Default Value property. See Figure 10-16 and the discussion of null values in Chapter 6.

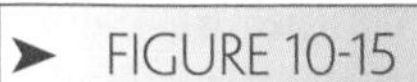

Result of Violating Validation Rule

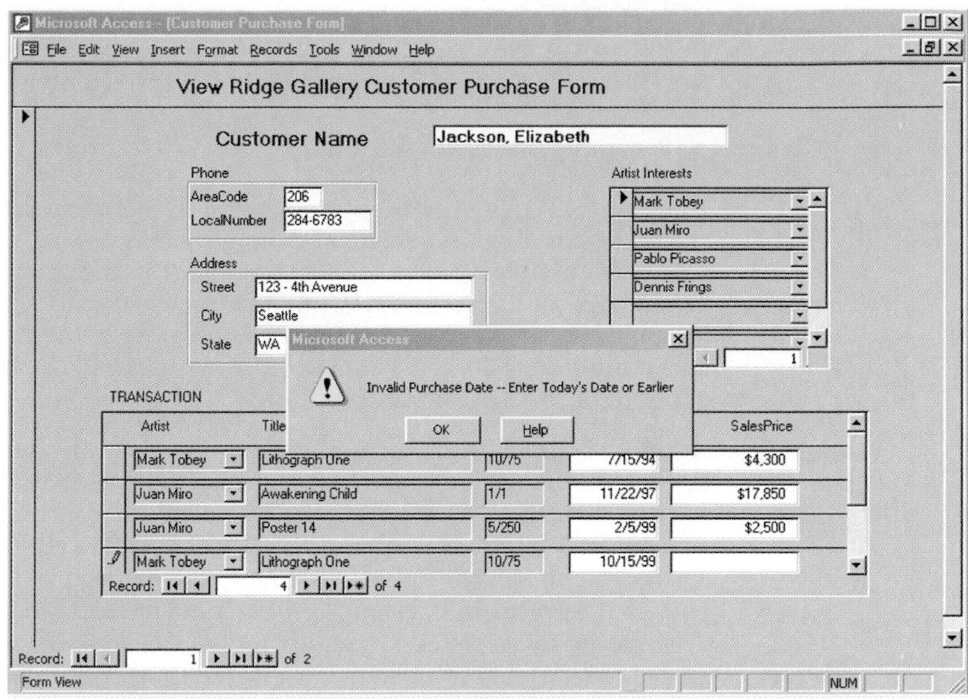

UNIQUENESS CONSTRAINTS

Uniqueness is a second type of constraint. As stated, constraints of this type are best enforced by the DBMS because it can create data structures to make uniqueness checking very fast. See Appendix A for a description of the way that indexes can be used for this purpose.

Defining Uniqueness for Name in ARTIST

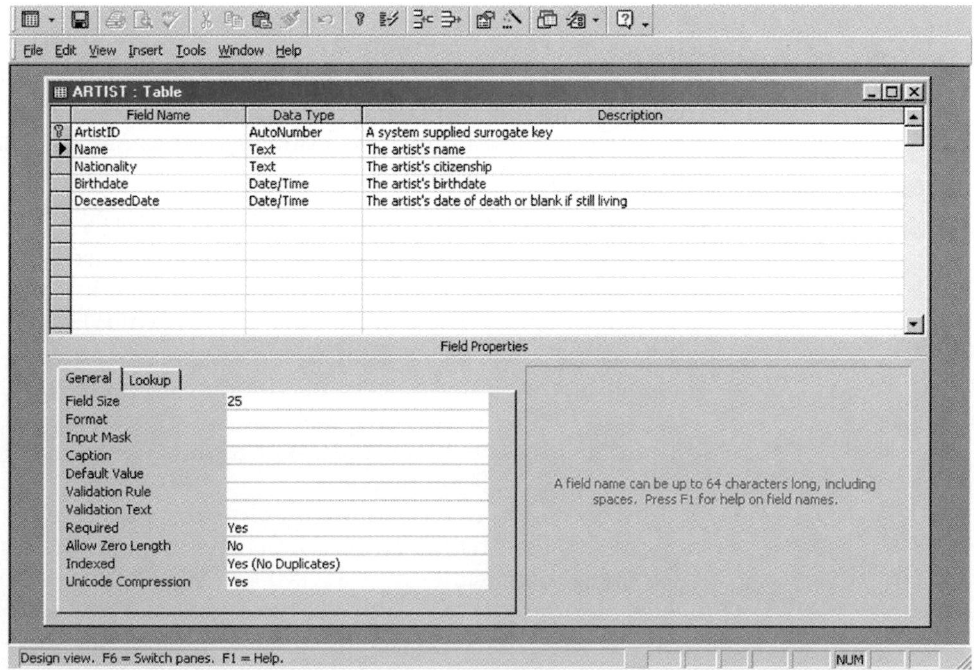

Figure 10-16 shows how Name in ARTIST can be defined as unique in Access. Observe that Indexed has been set to Yes (No Duplicates). With this setting Access will ensure that no duplicate artist names are entered from any source.

Relationship Constraints

There are two types of relationship constraints: **referential integrity** and **relationship cardinality.** Referential integrity refers to constraints on foreign key values. These are the constraints, for example, that arise from normalization when a single relation is split into two, and that occur between strong and weak entities. Relationship cardinality constraints occur because of the values of minimum and maximum cardinality on relationships. We consider both types in this section.

REFERENTIAL INTEGRITY CONSTRAINTS All referential integrity constraints are limitations on foreign key values. Consider the first referential integrity constraint in Figure 10-3(d): ArtistID in WORK must exist in ArtistID in ARTIST. ArtistID in WORK is a foregin key and the constraint just means that its value must be match a value in ArtistID in the ARTIST table, as explained before.

As long as all applications are coded correctly, as long as all transactions are processed correctly, and as long as no user inadvertently deletes an artist without deleting the related WORK (and because of the second constraint, deleting any related TRANSACTION [and because of the third constraint, deleting any related CUSTOMER], as long as all of this happens correctly, then there will never be a foreign key constraint violation. After all, the database starts with no integrity problems—to occur, problems have to be introduced.

This, of course, is hoping for too much. Errors occur. Therefore, DBMS products provide a facility by which such foreign key constraints can be defined to and enforced by the DBMS. This means the DBMS will disallow any insertion, deletion, or modification to foreign key value that causes a foreign key constraint violation. For an example, look ahead to Figure 10-20, where the check in front of Enforce Referential Integrity choice means Access is being asked to enforce the constraint that EmployeeName in

EMPLOYEE_PhoneNumber exist in Name in EMPLOYEE

Similar facilities exist for all DBMS products. In addition, server DBMS products such as ORACLE and SQL Server provide utilities that can be periodically run to ensure that no foreign key constraints have been allowed into the database because of partially completed transactions, imported data, or other mysteries of the universe. These utilities are normally run as part of a database maintenance plan. (See Chapter 11.)

RELATIONSHIP CARDINALITY CONSTRAINTS Relationship cardinality constraints arise from the cardinality settings on object link attributes. For example, in Figure 10-3(a), the CUSTOMER link in WORK.Transaction has cardinality of 1.1; hence a Transaction must have a CUSTOMER link.

In general, such constraints arise from two sources: non-zero settings of minimum cardinality, or settings of maximum cardinality that are neither 1 nor N. Thus, cardinalities of 1.1, 1.N, 2.N will cause cardinality constraints to arise, as will cardinalities of 0.3, 1.4, and 2.4. With one exception, these constraints must be enforced by application code.

The exception is 1.1 cardinalities on the child side of 1:N relationships. In that case, the constraint can be enforced by making the foreign key mandatory. Thus, the 1.1 constraint on CUSTOMER in WORK.Transaction can be enforced by making CustomerID mandatory in the TRANSACTION table.

Other than this exception, the database developer must write code to enforce cardinality constraints. That code can be placed in stored procedures to be

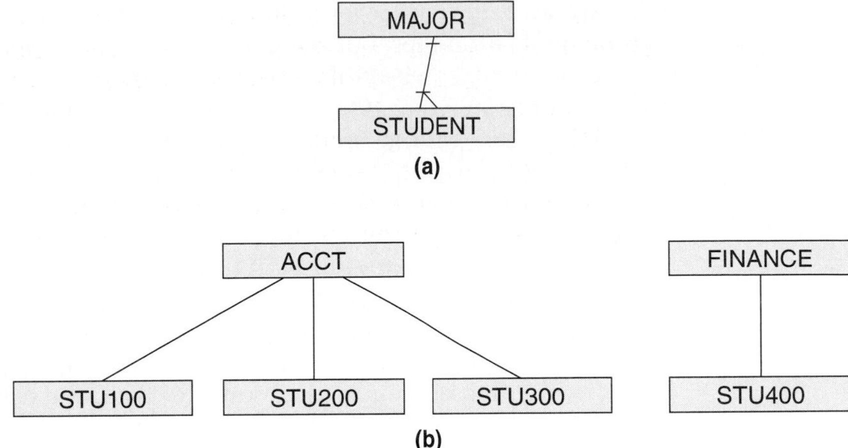

➤ FIGURE 10-17

Example of a Mandatory-to-Mandatory Constraint: (a) Sample Mandatory-to-Mandatory Relationship and (b) Sample Data for It

invoked by the DBMS when relationship changes are made, or it can be placed in application programs, or it can be called during certain form events such as BeforeUpdate (discussed next).

To simplify the discussion, we will only consider 1.1 and 1.N constraints. The logic for the other constraints is a straightforward extension of that presented here.

Figure 10-17 depicts the relationship between MAJOR and STUDENT relations. As shown in Figure 10-17(a), a MAJOR must have at least one STUDENT, and a STUDENT must have exactly one MAJOR. When users update either of these relations, constraint enforcement code must be invoked. In Figure 10-17(b), for example, if a user attempted to delete the row for Student 400, the code should deny this request. If the request were allowed, the row for FINANCE would not have a child row, and the mandatory constraint would be violated. Similarly, a new MAJOR, say BIOLOGY, cannot be added until there is a student who is majoring in that subject.

A row that exists inappropriately without a required parent or child is sometimes called a **fragment,** and child rows that exist without a mandatory parent are sometimes called **orphans.** One of the functions of an application program is to prevent the creation of fragments and orphans.

The means of preventing fragments depends on the type of constraint. Figure 10-18 shows examples of the four possible constraints in 1:N relationships: mandatory to mandatory (M–M), mandatory to optional (M–O), optional to mandatory

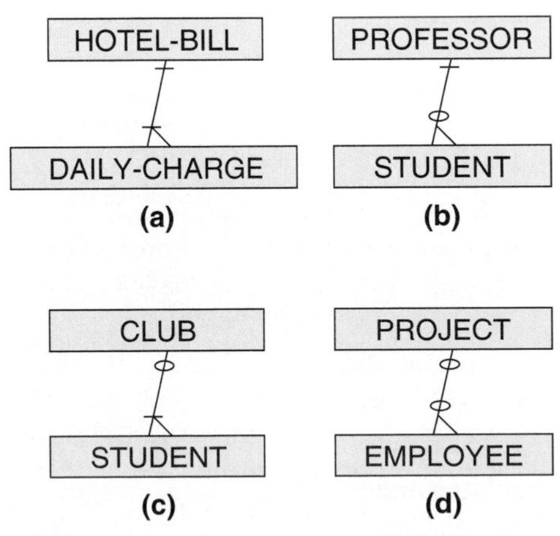

➤ FIGURE 10-18

Example of the Four Types of Relationship Constraints: (a) Mandatory-to-Mandatory (M–M) Constraint, (b) Mandatory-to-Optional (M–O) Constraint, (c) Optional-to-Mandatory (O–M) Constraint, and (d) Optinal-to-Optional (O–O) Constraint

(O–M), and optional to optional (O–O). These constraints are shown on one-to-many relationships, but the same four types also apply to other relationships.

Constraints can be violated whenever there are changes in the key attributes. For example, in Figure 10-17(b), changing the major of Student 300 from ACCT to FINANCE reassigns that student to the finance department. Although this results in a change of parent, it does not cause a constraint violation.

Such a violation will be committed, however, if the major of Student 400 is changed to ACCT. When this is done, FINANCE no longer has any majors, and so the M–M constraint between MAJOR and STUDENT is violated.

Figure 10-19 presents rules for preventing fragments for each of these types of constraints. Figure 10-19(a) concerns actions on the parent row, and Figure 10-19(b) concerns actions on the child rows. As these figures indicate, the possible actions are to insert new rows, modify key data, and delete rows. Figure 10-19 lists

➤ FIGURE 10-19

Rules for Preventing Fragments: (a) Conditions for Allowing Changes in Parent Records and (b) Conditions for Allowing Changes in Child Records

Proposed Action on Parent

Type of Relationship	*Insert*	*Modify (key)*	*Delete*
M-M	Create at least one child	Change matching keys of all children	Delete all children OR Reassign all children
M-O	OK	Change matching keys of all children	Delete all children OR Reassign all children
O-M	Insert new child OR Appropriate child exists	Change key of at least one child OR Appropriate child exists	OK
O-O	OK	OK	OK

(a)

Proposed Action on Child

Type of Relationship	*Insert*	*Modify (key)*	*Delete*
M-M	Parent exists OR Create parent	Parent with new value exists (or create one) AND Sibling exists	Sibling exists
M-O	Parent exists OR Create parent	Parent with new value exists OR Create parent	OK
O-M	OK	Sibling exists	Sibling exists
O-O	OK	OK	OK

(b)

the rules for one-to-many relationships; the rules for one-to-one relationships are similar.

RESTRICTIONS ON UPDATES TO PARENT ROWS The first row of Figure 10-19(a) concerns M–M constraints. A new parent row can be inserted only if at least one child row is being created at the same time, which can be done by inserting a new child row or by reassigning a child from a different parent (however, this latter action may itself cause a constraint violation).

A change in the key of a parent is permitted in an M–M relationship only if the values in the corresponding foreign key in the child rows also are changed in the new value. (It is possible to reassign all of the children to another parent and then create at least one new child for the parent, but this seldom is done.) Thus, changing the Invoice in HOTEL-BILL is allowed as long as the Invoice is changed in all the appropriate DAY-CHARGE rows as well. Note that if surrogate keys are used, this action will never occur.

Finally, a parent of an M–M relationship can be deleted as long as all of the children also are deleted or are reassigned.

In regard to M–O constraints, a new parent can be added without restriction, since parents need not have children. For the relationship in Figure 10-18(b), a new PROFESSOR row can be added without restriction. A change in the parent's key value, however, is permitted only if the corresponding values in the child rows are changed as well. If a PROFESSOR in the relationship in Figure 10-18(b) changes his or her key, the value of Adviser in all of that professor's advisees' rows also must be changed.

Finally, in a relationship with an M–O constraint, the parent row can be deleted only if all the children are deleted or reassigned. For the PROFESSOR-STUDENT relationship, all of the student rows would probably be reassigned.

For O–M constraints, a parent can be inserted only if at least one child is added at the same time or if an appropriate child already exists. For the O–M relationship between CLUB and STUDENT in Figure 10-18(c), for example, a new club can be added only if an appropriate STUDENT row can be created (by either adding a new student or changing the value of CLUB in an existing STUDENT). Alternatively, an appropriate student row may already exist.

Similarly, the key of the parent of an O–M relationship may be changed only if a child is created or if a suitable child row already exists. That is, the Ski Club can change its name to Scuba only if at least one skier is willing to join Scuba or if a student has already enrolled in Scuba. There are no restrictions on the deletion of a parent row in an O–M relationship.

The last type of relationship constraint, O–O, is shown in Figure 10-18(d). There are no restrictions on any type of update on rows in an O–O relationship. Both PROJECT and EMPLOYEE rows can be updated as necessary.

RESTRICTIONS ON UPDATING CHILD ROWS The rules for preventing fragments when updating child rows are shown in Figure 10-19(b) and are similar to those in Figure 10-19(a). The one notable difference is that in several cases, child rows can be modified or deleted as long as sibling rows exist. For example, in an M–M constraint, a child row can be deleted as long as there are siblings in existence. (The last child never leaves home!) For the M–M constraint in Figure 10-18(a), a particular DAILY-CHARGE row can be deleted as long as at least one remains.

With the exception of the considerations regarding siblings, the rules for avoiding fragments when processing child rows are similar to those for parents. Make certain you understand each statement in Figure 10-19(b).

USING THE DBMS TO ENFORCE CARDINALITY CONSTRAINTS Given the preceding discussion, it is useful to consider the constraints in Figure 10-19 in the context of the relationship definition facilities in Access. Suppose a database

Relationship Properties in Access

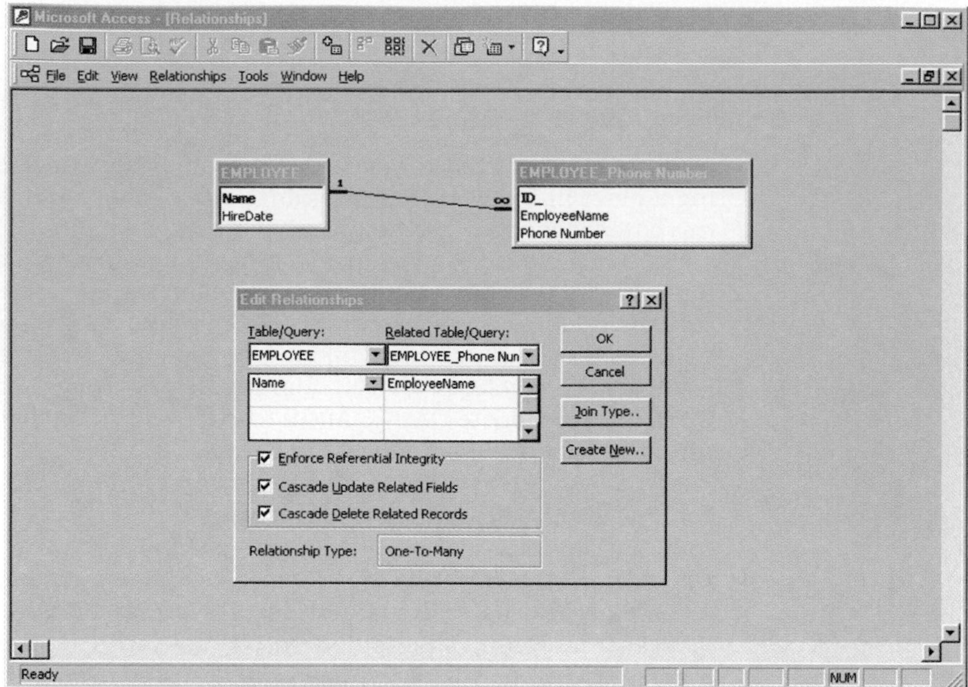

has an EMPLOYEE object with multiple phone numbers. To show the relevance of the middle columns of Figure 10-19, suppose that the key of EMPLOYEE is not a surrogate but is EMPLOYEE.Name instead.

Figure 10-20 shows the relationship definition window for this example. The check in the Enforce Referential Integrity box indicates that Access will not allow a new row of EMPLOYEE_PhoneNumber to be created unless the value of EmployeeName is already present in a row in EMPLOYEE. This is the meaning of referential integrity as discussed previously. The second check, in Cascade Update Related Fields, means that if the name of an employee is changed in the EMPLOYEE table, then that change will be propagated to all related rows in EMPLOYEE_PhoneNumber. This enforces the rules in the middle columns of Figure 10-19. (Again, this would be unnecessary if surrogate keys were used instead.)

The last check, in Cascade Delete Related Records means that when an EMPLOYEE row is deleted, all of the connected EMPLOYEE_PhoneNumber rows will be deleted as well. This is similar to that discussed earlier in the section on deleting view instances.

This feature of Access addresses the rules in the second and third columns of Figure 10-19(a), and those in the first and second columns of Figure 10-19(b). It does not address the rules in the first column of Figure 10-19(a), nor those in the third column of Figure 10-19(b). Those rules will need to be coded in stored procedures or in the application.

Business Rule Constraints

Business rule constraints are particular to the logic and requirements of a given application. They arise from procedures and policies that exist in the organization that will use the database application. Examples of business rules in a sales application are

FIGURE 10-21

Events for Access Forms

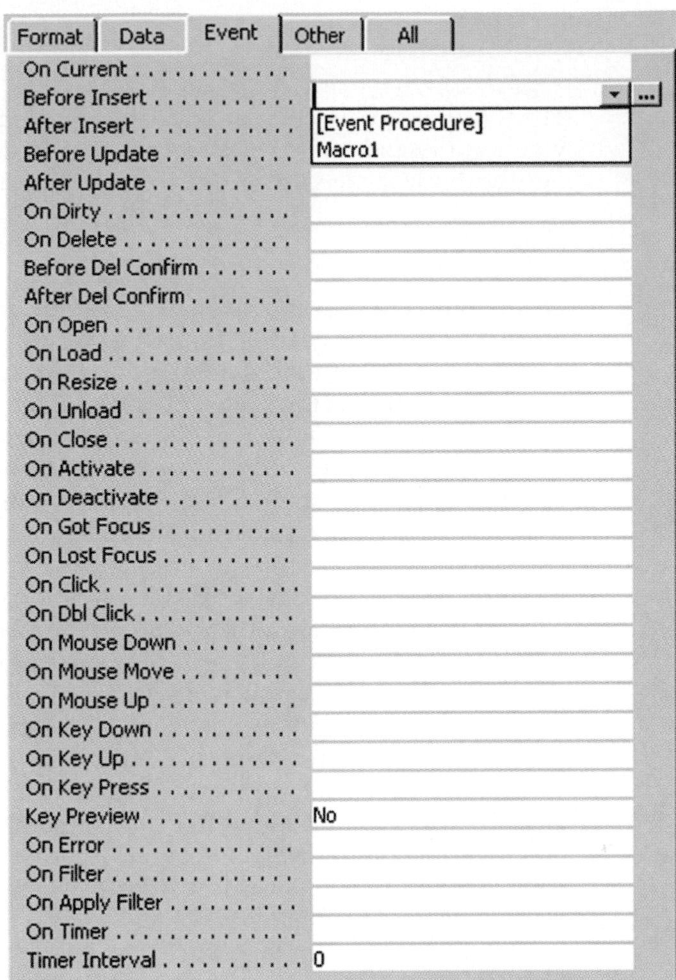

- No commission check can exceed 50 percent of the total commission pool.
- No backorder will be generated if the total value of the ordered items is less than $200.
- Shipping costs are waived for preferred customers.
- Salespeople cannot create orders for themselves.
- To be a sales manager, an employee must first be a salesperson.

Because business rules are application dependent, there are no generic features of DBMS products for enforcing them. Rather, DBMS products provide means for inserting code before or after most important events. Figure 10-21 shows a list of the events that can be trapped on Access forms. In this figure, the developer is in the process of adding logic to the Before Insert event. The logic can take one of several forms: an event procedure in Access's expression language or in a Visual Basic (or other language program), or an Access macro. All of the data in the form and in the database is accessible by the event procedure or macro. Thus, any of the rules listed in the bulleted list could be enforced by trapping events.

With server DBMS products such as Oracle or SQL Server, a similar means is used. Logic can be encoded in triggers, which are stored procedures that are invoked when events occur in the database. The events that can be trapped are similar to those shown in Figure 10-21.

➤ SECURITY AND CONTROL

The fourth major function of a database application listed in Figure 10-1 is to provide security and control mechanisms. The goal is to create applications in which only authorized users can perform appropriate activities at the proper time.

SECURITY

Most DBMS products provide user name and password level of security. Once a user signs in, access can be limited to certain forms, reports, tables, and even columns of tables. This is appropriate and useful as far as it goes. It does not help, however, in limiting the instances of data that users can view.

For example, in a human resources database application, every employee should be able to see only his or her own employee records. Certain human resource employees should be able to see some data about all employees, and senior human resource managers should be able to see all data about all employees.

Limiting access to certain forms and reports does not help. Every employee needs to see the Employee Form; the restriction needs to be that the employee can see only data in that form that pertain to him or her (with the exceptions noted). Sometimes you will hear the terms **horizontal security** and **vertical security.** To understand them, think about a table. Vertical security would limit access to certain columns, but all rows could be seen. Horizontal security would limit access to certain rows, but all columns could be seen.

Applications that limit users to certain forms, reports, tables, or columns provide vertical security. Those that limit users to certain data in forms, reports, tables, or columns provide horizontal security. User name and passwords can be readily used to provide vertical security. Horizontal security generally requires developers to write application code.

To provide horizontal security in the employee application, for example, application code would obtain the user's name from the DBMS security system and limit access to rows that contain that name or are linked to rows that contain that name via joins. One way to do this is to append the user's name as a WHERE clause in SQL statements.

Because every situation is different, we cannot say more. Just be aware that when DBMS products say they support security, most often that only means vertical security via user name and passwords.

CONTROL

Most database applications provide control via menus. Figure 10-22(a) shows a system of menus for a pre-GUI application and Figure 10-22(b) shows the same menus for a GUI application.

The menus in Figure 10-22 are static. More effective control can be provided by dynamically changing menu content as the user changes context. You see menus of that type in Access when the toolbar changes depending on whether you are in the table definition, form definition, or report definition tools. Database application developers can use a similar strategy to change menu choices depending on the form or report that a user is viewing, and even depending on the action that the user is taking in the form. Using Access, a developer could change menu choices by trapping events like those shown in Figure 10-21 and dynamically restructuring the menu choices.

A different type of control concerns transactions. In Chapter 11, you will learn means of controlling multi-user processing so that one user's actions do not have inappropriate side consequences on a second user's actions. A key part of

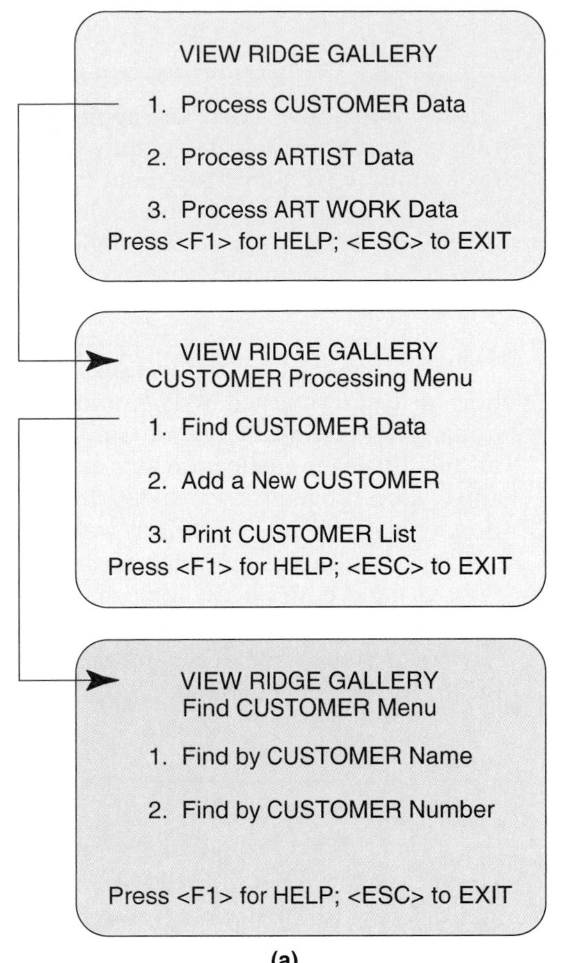

(a)

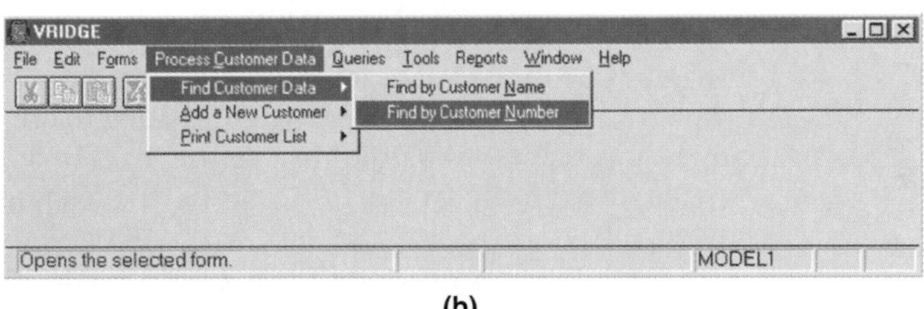

(b)

➤ FIGURE 10-22

Hierarchy of Menus for View Ridge Gallery: (a) Not Using a Graphical User Interface (b) Using a Graphical User Interface

multi-user control is to identify boundaries of work that must be completed as a unit, sometimes called **transaction boundaries.** For example, the series of SQL statements for creating a view shown at the start of this chapter need to be completed as a unit, as a single transaction.

We will not anticipate the discussion in that chapter except to say that it is the job of the application to specify transaction boundaries. It typically does so by executing a statement like BEGIN TRANSACTION at the start of a unit of work and END TRANSACTION when the work is completed.

Setting boundaries is easy if the user views are well designed. The application issues the BEGIN TRANSACTION at the start of the view and the END TRANSACTION at the end of the view. We will hold the rest of this discussion for Chapter 12.

➤ APPLICATION LOGIC

The last function of a database application listed in Figure 10-1 is to execute application logic. This topic is generally discussed in systems development classes and texts; thus, we will say little about it here.

The needs for application logic arise from the systems requirements. In an order-entry system, application logic concerns how to take inventory from stock, how to deal with insufficient stock in inventory, how to schedule a back order, and the like. In a form-based database application like the one for the gallery, code to support this logic is attached to events like those in Figure 10-21.

For other database applications, where forms are materialized by the application instead of by the DBMS (common in mainframe applications), the application processes the data in a way similar to that for file processing. Logic is encoded in-line inside the application as it gets data from and puts data to the DBMS. Some application programs receive data from other programs; in that case, the application logic is contained in-line as well.

Thus, the means by which application logic is embedded in database applications depend both on the logic and the environment. Different means are used for desktop, client-server, mainframe, and Internet technology applications. You have seen how to trap events for desktop applications. We will consider the other means in subsequent chapters.

➤ SUMMARY

The five major functions of a database application are (1) to create, read, update, and delete (CRUD) views, (2) to materialize or format views, (3) to enforce constraints, (4) to provide security and control mechanisms, and (5) to execute business logic.

A view is a structured list of data items from the entities or semantic objects in the data model. A view instance is a view populated with data. Because views are structured, a given data item may appear more than once in a view. To read a view, one or more SQL statements are issued to obtain data values. More than one SQL statement will be required if the view includes two or more relationship paths through the schema. A recordset is a relation with an object programming wrapper.

Creating a view requires storing one or more new rows in tables and possibly creating or changing foreign key values so as to establish relationships. Three types of update are possible: changing existing data, changing relationships, and creating new rows for multi-value attributes. Deleting a view involves removing one or more rows and adjusting foreign keys. The issue when deleting is knowing how much to delete. Weak entities should be deleted if the entity upon which they depend is deleted. Multi-value attributes inside a semantic object should also be deleted. With some DBMS products, relationships can be marked for cascading deletions so that the DBMS will remove appropriate dependent rows.

A form is a screen display used for data entry and edit. Principles of form design are that the form structure should reflect the view structure, the semantics of the data should be graphically evident, and the form structure should encourage appropriate action. Drop-down list boxes, option buttons, and check boxes can be used to increase the usability of forms.

Reports should also be designed so that their structure reflects the structure of the view they materialize. Report sorting often implies the existence of other objects. With most report writers it is difficult to construct reports that follow more than one multi-value path through the schema. Reports often have calculated data attributes; usually it is best not to store those attributes in the database.

Constraints can be enforced by either the DBMS or by application program. In most cases, it is better for the DBMS to enforce them when possible, primarily because the DBMS is a central point through which all data changes must pass. In some cases, the DBMS does not have the features to enforce constraints, however, and they must be enforced by the application. Domain constraints enforce the physical part of domain definitions. Required values are another type of constraint. Making a value required avoids the ambiguity of null values. Uniqueness constraints are best enforced by the DBMS; this is usually done by building indexes.

There are two types of relationship constraints: referential integrity and relationship cardinality. Referential integrity constraints are best enforced by the DBMS. Relationship cardinality constraints arise from cardinality settings on object links; either non-zero settings of minimum cardinality or maximum cardinality values that are neither 1 nor N. Except for 1.1 cardinality on the child side of 1:N relationships, such constraints must be enforced by application code. Rules for constraint enforcement on 1:N relationships are summarized in Figure 10-19. Business rule constraints by application code that is invoked by trapping events, by triggers, or in-line in application programs.

Most DBMS products provide user name and password security. This can be used to provide vertical security; horizontal security must be provided by application code. Most applications provide control via menus. The best control occurs when menus change as the user's context changes. Application programs have the important role of defining transaction boundaries. Application logic is encoded in code and invoked by trapping events and by other means that will be explained in later chapters.

➤ GROUP I QUESTIONS

10.1 List the five major functions of a database application.

10.2 Explain the meaning of the acronym CRUD.

10.3 Define the term *view* as used in this chapter.

10.4 What is a view instance?

10.5 Explain how a view is different from a materialization.

10.6 Can an attribute appear more than once in a view? Why?

10.7 Under what conditions can a view be read with one SQL statement?

10.8 Under what conditions does reading a view require more than one SQL statement?

10.9 Explain the two paths that exist in the Customer view in Figure 10-4.

10.10 Define the term *recordset.*

10.11 Describe in general terms the work that is required when creating a view instance.

10.12 How are new relationships created when creating a view instance?

10.13 What technique can be used to obtain the value of a surrogate key when inserting new rows into a table?

10.14 List the three types of change that can occur when updating a view instance.

10.15 Explain how to change 1:N relationships. Explain how to change N:M relationships.

10.16 What is the major difficulty when writing code to delete a view instance?

10.17 How can an E-R model help determine how much to delete?

10.18 How can a semantic object model help determine how much to delete?

10.19 What are cascading deletions, and why are they important?

10.20 Explain the statement "Form structure should reflect view structure."

10.21 How can forms be designed to make the semantics of the data graphically evident?

10.22 How can forms be designed to encourage appropriate action?

10.23 Explain the role of drop-down list boxes, option groups, and check boxes in form design.

10.24 What limitation exists for report materialization of views?

10.25 Explain why the calculated values on reports should normally not be stored in the database.

10.26 Explain how the request to report objects sorted by a value changes the underlying object of the report.

10.27 Why should constraints normally be enforced by the DBMS and not by a particular form, report, or application program?

10.28 Why are constraints sometimes enforced in application programs?

10.29 Give an example of a domain constraint and explain how it might be enforced by Access.

10.30 Describe the ambiguity that arises when values are null. Describe two ways such values can be eliminated.

10.31 Why should the DBMS normally enforce uniqueness constraints?

10.32 Describe the two sources of cardinality constraints.

10.33 Name two types of relationship constraint.

10.34 What is the best way to enforce constraints on foreign key values?

10.35 How can a 1.1 cardinality constraint on the child side of a 1:N relationship be enforced?

10.36 Define *fragment* and *orphan*.

10.37 Explain the entries in the first column of Figure 10-19(a).

10.38 Explain why the center column of Figure 10-19(a) is unnecessary when surrogate keys are used.

10.39 Explain the entries in the third column of Figure 10-19(a).

10.40 Explain the entries in the first column of Figure 10-19(b).

10.41 Explain the entries in the third column of Figure 10-19(b).

10.42 Explain why the first column of Figure 10-19(a) and the third column of Figure 10-19(b) are not enforced by the Access relationship properties shown in Figure 10-20.

10.43 Give an example of a business rule constraint that could apply to the data model in Figure 10-3. Explain how this constraint could be enforced by trapping an event.

10.44 Define *horizontal* and *vertical* security.

10.45 Which type of security is supported by user name and password?

10.46 Which type of security must be supported by application code?

10.47 Explain why dynamic menus are better than static ones.

10.48 How is business logic connected to a database when using Access?

➤ GROUP II QUESTIONS

Questions 10.49 through 10.52 pertain to the following Artist View, which is based on the data model in Figure 10-3.

ARTIST.Name
ARTIST.Nationality
    TRANSACTION.PurchaseDate
    TRANSACTION.SalesPrice. . .
        CUSTOMER.Name
        CUSTOMER.Phone.AreaCode
        CUSTOMER.Phone.LocalNumber
    CUSTOMER.Name. . .

The ellipses (. . .) refer to structures that can repeat.

10.49 Code SQL statements for reading the "Mark Tobey" instance of this view.

10.50 Code SQL statements to create a new instance of this view. Assume that you have data for ARTIST, one TRANSACTION, and many CUSTOMER.Name(s) for the second instance of CUSTOMER.Name. Assume this data is located in a structure named NewArtist. Use syntax similar to that in the text.

10.51 Code SQL statements to update this view as follows:

a. Change the spelling of Mark Tobey to Mark Toby.
b. Create a new Transaction for Mark Toby. Assume you have the necessary transaction, work, and customer data in a structure named NewTrans.
c. Add new interested customers for Mark Toby. Assume they are stored in a collection that you can access with the command "For Each NewCust.Name."

10.52 Code SQL statements to delete the row for Mark Toby and all related WORK and TRANSACTION rows.

➤ PROJECTS

A. Using Access, create the database shown in Figure 10-3. Create a form for the Artist View shown in Question 10.49. Justify the design of your form using the principles in this chapter. Hint: You can use a wizard to create one of the subforms, but you will need to add the second one manually. Also, add the combo boxes manually, after you have created the forms for the subform.

B. Complete either Project A at the end of Chapters 3 and 4 if you have not already done so.

1. List and describe the purpose of three views, three forms, and three reports that you think would be necessary for this application.
2. Show the structure of a GUI drop-down menu for this application. Using your model, design one of the forms for entering new housing properties. Explain which type of control (text box, drop-down list) is used for each field. Justify the structure of your form using the concepts presented in this chapter.

➤ FIREDUP PROJECT QUESTIONS

Read the FiredUp Project at the end of Chapter 9. In answering the following questions, use the four tables described there.

A. Construct the following views. Use Figure 10-4 as an example.

1. Construct a view starting at STOVE and containing all tables and data. Call that view STOVE_VIEW.
2. Construct a view starting at CUSTOMER and containing all tables and data. Call that view CUSTOMER_VIEW
3. Construct a view starting at REGISTRATION and containing all tables but STOVE_REPAIR. Call that view REGISTRATION_VIEW.
4. Construct a view starting at STOVE_REPAIR and containing all tables and data. Call that view STOVE_REPAIR_VIEW.

B. Construct SQL statements to process views as follows. Use the SQL starting on page 262 as an example.

1. Show SQL statements necessary to read a STOVE_VIEW. Assume you start with a particular SerialNumber.
2. Show SQL statements necessary to construct a new instance of REGISTRATION_VIEW. Assume the necessary stove data is already in the database, but the necessary customer data is not.
3. Show SQL statements to construct a new instance of STOVE_REPAIR. Assume the STOVE data is in the database, but the CUSTOMER data is not. Register the STOVE while recording the repair.
4. Show SQL statements to remove all records concerning a particular stove. Use the STOVE view.

MULTI-USER DATABASE PROCESSING

The three chapters in Part V describe important issues and problems of multi-user databases and illustrate responses and solutions to those issues and problems with two popular DBMS products. We begin in Chapter 11 with a description of database administration and the major tasks and techniques for multi-user database management. The next two chapters illustrate the implementation of these concepts using Oracle 8i in Chapter 12 and SQL Server 2000 in Chapter 13.

Managing Multi-User Databases

While multi-user databases offer great value to the organizations that create and use them, they also pose difficult problems for those same organizations. For one, multi-user databases are complicated to design and develop because they support many overlapping user views. Additionally, requirements change over time, and those changes necessitate other changes to the database structure. Such structure changes must be carefully planned and controlled so that a change made for one group does not cause problems for another. In addition, when users process a database concurrently, special controls are needed to ensure that the actions of one user do not inappropriately influence the results for another. This topic is both important and complicated, as you will see.

In large organizations, processing rights and responsibilities need to be defined and enforced. What happens, for example, when an employee leaves the firm? When can his records be deleted? For the purposes of payroll processing, after the last pay period. For the purposes of quarterly reporting, at the end of the quarter. For the purposes of end-of-year tax record processing, at the end of the year. And so forth. Clearly, no department can decide unilaterally when to delete that data. Similar comments pertain to the insertion and changing of data values. For this and other reasons, security systems need to be developed that enable only authorized users to take only authorized actions at authorized times.

Databases have become key components of organizational operations and even key components of an organization's value. Unfortunately, database failures and disasters do occur. Accordingly, effective backup and recovery plans, techniques, and procedures are essential.

Finally, over time, the DBMS itself will need to be changed to improve performance, to incorporate new features and releases, and to conform to changes made in the underlying operating system. All of this requires attentive management.

In order to ensure that these problems are addressed and solved, most organizations have developed an office of database administration. We begin with a description of the tasks of that office, and then in the rest of this chapter describe the combination of software and manual practices and procedures that is used to perform those tasks. In the next two chapters, we will discuss and illustrate features and functions of Oracle 8i and of SQL Server 2000, respectively, for dealing with these issues as well.

➤ DATABASE ADMINISTRATION

Both the terms **data administration** and **database administration** are used in industry. In some cases the terms are considered synonymous; in other cases, they have different meanings. In this text, we use the term *data administration* to refer to a function that applies to the entire organization. The term *database administration* refers to a function that is specific to a particular database, including the applications that process that database. This chapter addresses database administration. Data administration is discussed in Chapter 17.

Databases vary considerably in size and scope, from a single-user personal database to a large interorganizational database like an airline reservation system. All of these databases have a need for database administration, although the tasks to be accomplished vary in complexity. For example, for a personal database individuals follow simple procedures for backing up their data, and they keep minimal records for documentation. In this case, the person who uses the database also performs the DBA functions, even though he or she is probably unaware of it.

For multi-user database applications, database administration becomes both more important and more difficult. Consequently, it generally has formal recognition. For some applications, one or two people are given this function on a part-time basis. For large Internet or intranet databases, database administration responsibilities are often too time-consuming and too varied to be handled even by a single full-time person. Supporting a database with dozens or hundreds of users requires considerable time as well as both technical knowledge and diplomatic skills and usually is handled by an office of database administration. The manager of the office is often known as the **database administrator;** in this case, the acronym **DBA** refers to either the office or the manager.

The overall responsibility of the DBA is to facilitate the development and use of the database. Usually, this means balancing the conflicting goals of protecting the database and maximizing its availability and benefit to users. The DBA is responsible for the development, operation, and maintenance of the database and its applications. Specific tasks are shown in Figure 11-1. We consider each of these in the following sections.

Summary of Database Administration Tasks

> Managing database structure

> Controlling concurrent processing

> Managing processing rights and responsibilities

> Developing database security

> Providing for database recovery

> Managing the DBMS

> Maintaining the data repository

MANAGING THE DATABASE STRUCTURE

Managing the database structure includes participating in the initial database design and implementation as well as controlling and managing changes to it. Ideally, the DBA is involved early in the development of the database and its applications, participates in the requirements study, helps evaluate alternatives, including the DBMS to be used, and helps design the database structure. For large, organizational applications, the DBA usually is a manager who supervises the work of technically oriented database design personnel.

As described in Chapter 8, creating the database involves several different tasks. First the database is created and space allocated for it and its logs. Then tables are generated, indices are created, and stored procedures and triggers are written. We will discuss examples of all of this in the next two chapters. Once the database structures are created, the database is filled with data. Most DBMS vendors provide utilities for inserting data in bulk.

CONFIGURATION CONTROL After a database and its applications have been implemented, changes in requirements are inevitable. Such changes can arise from new needs, from changes in the business environment, from changes in policy, and so forth. When changes to requirements necessitate changes to the database structure, great care must be used because database structure changes seldom involve just one application.

Hence, effective database administration must include procedures and policies by which users can register their needs for changes, the entire database community can discuss the impacts of the changes, and a global decision can be made whether or not to implement proposed changes.

Because of the size and complexity of a database and its applications, changes sometimes have unexpected results. The DBA thus must be prepared to repair the database and to gather sufficient information to diagnose and correct the problem that caused the damage. The database is most vulnerable to failure after a change in its structure.

DOCUMENTATION The DBA's final responsibility in managing the database structure is documentation. It is extremely important to know what changes have been made, how they were made, and when they were made. A change in the database structure may cause an error that is not revealed for six months; without proper documentation of the change, diagnosing the problem is next to impossible. Dozens of job reruns may be required to identify the point at which certain symptoms first appeared, and for this reason, it also is important to maintain a record of the test procedures and test runs made to verify a change. If standardized test procedures, test forms, and record-keeping methods are used, recording the test results does not have to be time-consuming.

Although maintaining documentation is tedious and unfulfilling, the effort pays off when disaster strikes and the documentation is the difference between solving and not solving a major (and costly) problem. Today, several products are emerging that ease the burden of documentation. Many CASE tools, for example, can be used to document logical database designs. Version control software can be used to track changes. Data dictionaries provide reports and other products to read and interpret the database data structures.

Another reason for carefully documenting changes in the database structure is to use historical data properly. If, for example, marketing wants to analyze three-year-old sales data that have been in the archives for two years, it will be necessary to know what structure was current at the time the data were last active. Records that show the changes in the structure can be used to answer that question. A similar situation arises when a six-month-old backup copy of data must be used to repair a damaged database (although this should not happen, sometimes it does).

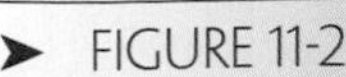

FIGURE 11-2

Summary of the DBA's Responsibilities for Managing the Database Structure

Participate in Database and Application Development
- Assist in requirements stage and evaluation of alternatives.
- Play an active role in database design and creation.

Facilitate Changes to Database Structure
- Seek communitywide solutions.
- Assess impact on all users.
- Provide configuration control forum.
- Be prepared for problems after changes are made.
- Maintain documentation.

The backup copy can be used to reconstruct the database to the state it was in at the time of the backup. Then transactions and structural changes can be made in chronological order to restore the database to its current state. Figure 11-2 summarizes the DBA's responsibilities for managing the database structure.

➤ CONCURRENCY CONTROL

Concurrency control measures are taken to ensure that one user's work does not inappropriately influence another user's work. In some cases, these measures ensure that a user gets the same result when processing with other users as he or she would have received if processing alone. In other cases, it means that the user's work is influenced by other users, but in an anticipated way.

For example, in an order-entry system, a user should be able to enter an order and get the same result regardless of whether there are no other users or hundreds of other users. On the other hand, a user who is printing a report of the most current inventory status may want to obtain in-process data changes from other users, even if there is a danger that those changes may later be aborted.

Unfortunately, no concurrency control technique or mechanism is ideal for all circumstances. They all involve trade-offs. For example, a user can obtain very strict concurrency control by locking the entire database, but while he or she is processing, no other user will be able to do anything. This is strict protection, but at a high cost. As you will see, other measures are available that are more difficult to program or enforce but that allow more throughput. Still other measures are available that maximize throughput, but for a low level of concurrency control. When designing multi-user database applications, you will need to choose among these trade-offs.

THE NEED FOR ATOMIC TRANSACTIONS

In most database applications, users submit work in the form of **transactions,** which are also known as **logical units of work** (LUWs). A transaction (or LUW) is a series of actions to be taken on the database such that either all of them are performed successfully or none of them are performed at all, in which case the database remains unchanged. Such a transaction is sometimes called **atomic,** since it is performed as a unit.

Comparison of the Results of Applying Serial Actions Versus a Multiple-Step Transaction: (a) Two Out of Three Activities Successfully Completed, Resulting in Database Anomalies, and (b) No Change Made Because Entire Transaction Not Successful

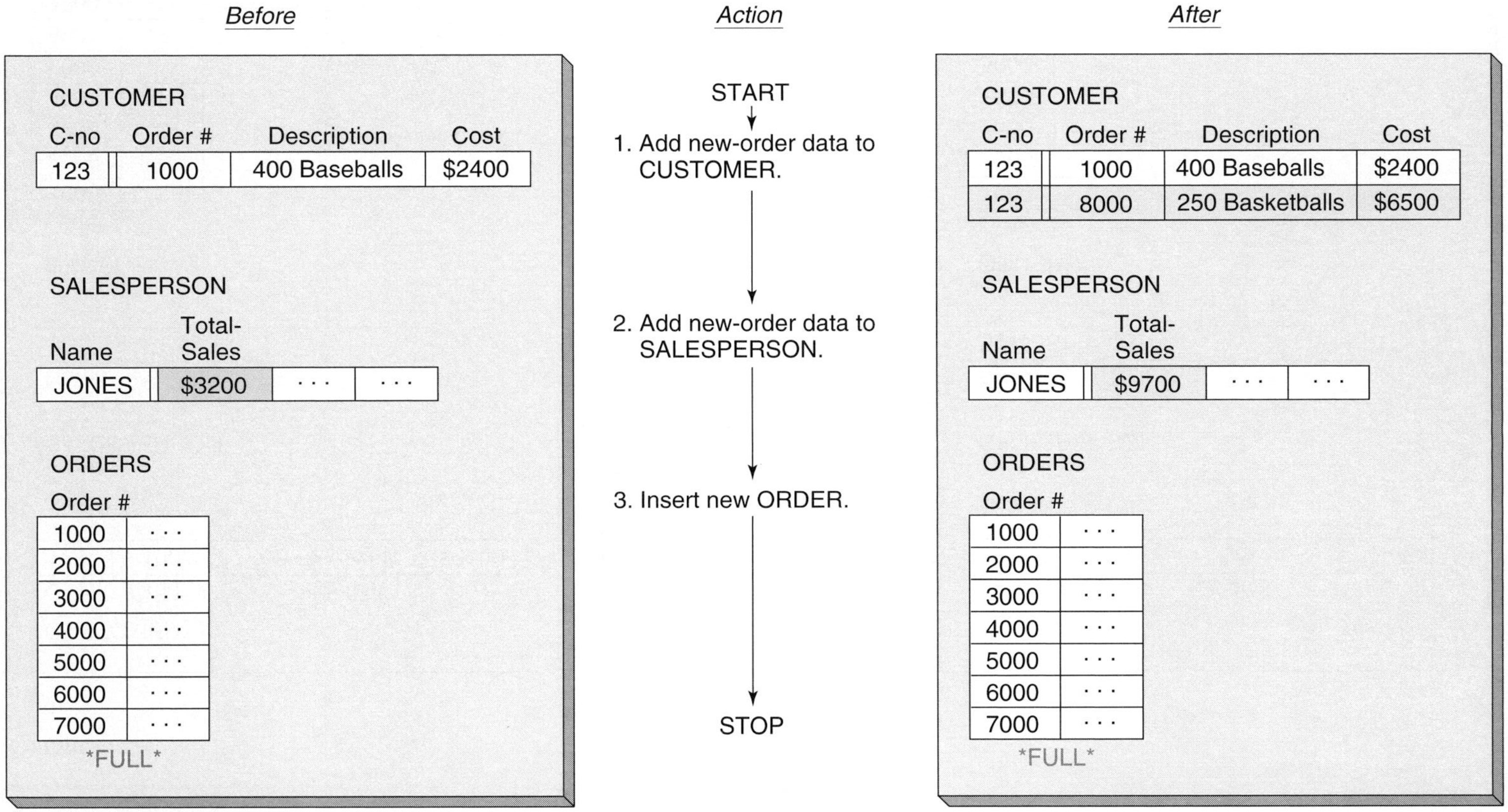

Before

CUSTOMER

C-no	Order #	Description	Cost
123	1000	400 Baseballs	$2400

SALESPERSON

Name	Total-Sales		
JONES	$3200	. . .	. . .

ORDERS

Order #	
1000	. . .
2000	. . .
3000	. . .
4000	. . .
5000	. . .
6000	. . .
7000	. . .

FULL

Action

START

1. Add new-order data to CUSTOMER.
2. Add new-order data to SALESPERSON.
3. Insert new ORDER.

STOP

After

CUSTOMER

C-no	Order #	Description	Cost
123	1000	400 Baseballs	$2400
123	8000	250 Basketballs	$6500

SALESPERSON

Name	Total-Sales		
JONES	$9700	. . .	. . .

ORDERS

Order #	
1000	. . .
2000	. . .
3000	. . .
4000	. . .
5000	. . .
6000	. . .
7000	. . .

FULL

(a)

FIGURE 11-3

(Continued)

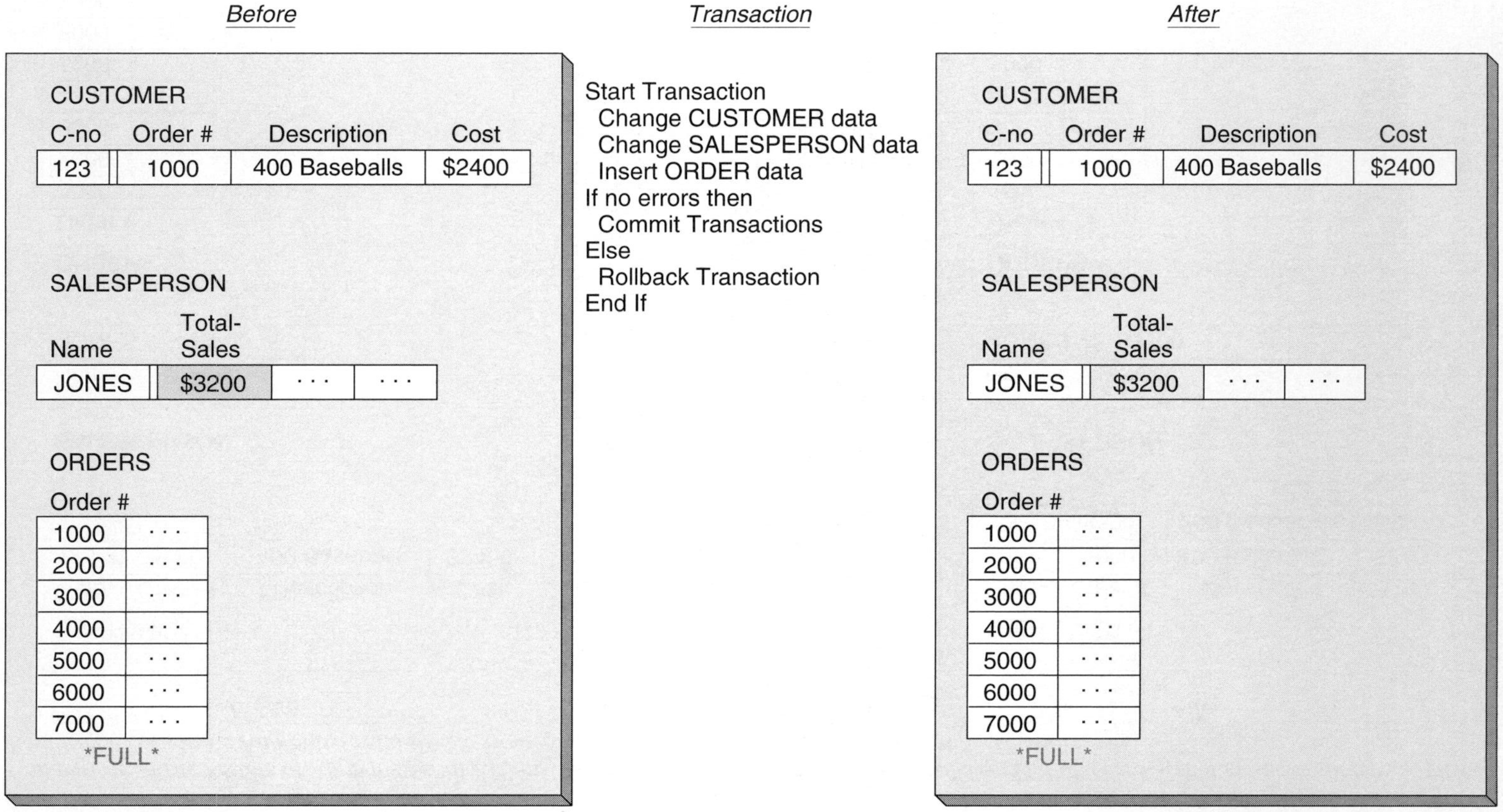

Before

CUSTOMER

C-no	Order #	Description	Cost
123	1000	400 Baseballs	$2400

SALESPERSON

Name	Total-Sales		
JONES	$3200	. . .	. . .

ORDERS

Order #	
1000	. . .
2000	. . .
3000	. . .
4000	. . .
5000	. . .
6000	. . .
7000	. . .

FULL

Transaction

```
Start Transaction
  Change CUSTOMER data
  Change SALESPERSON data
  Insert ORDER data
If no errors then
  Commit Transactions
Else
  Rollback Transaction
End If
```

After

CUSTOMER

C-no	Order #	Description	Cost
123	1000	400 Baseballs	$2400

SALESPERSON

Name	Total-Sales		
JONES	$3200	. . .	. . .

ORDERS

Order #	
1000	. . .
2000	. . .
3000	. . .
4000	. . .
5000	. . .
6000	. . .
7000	. . .

FULL

(b)

Consider the following sequence of database actions that could occur when recording a new order:

1. Change the customer record, increasing Amount Owed.
2. Change the salesperson record, increasing Commission Due.
3. Insert the new order record into the database.

Suppose the last step failed, perhaps because of insufficient file space. Imagine the confusion that would ensue if the first two changes were made but not the third one. The customer would be billed for an order never received, and a salesperson would receive a commission on an order that was never sent to the customer. Clearly, these three actions need to be taken as a unit—either all of them should be done or none of them should be done.

Figure 11-3 compares the results of performing these activities as a series of independent steps [Figure 11-3(a)] and as an atomic transaction [Figure 11-3(b)]. Notice that when the steps are carried out atomically and one fails, no changes are made in the database. Also note that the commands Start Transaction, Commit Transaction, or Rollback Transaction must be issued by the application program to mark the boundaries of the transaction logic. The particular form of these commands varies from one DBMS product to another.

CONCURRENT TRANSACTION PROCESSING When two transactions are being processed against a database at the same time, they are termed *concurrent transactions*. While it may appear to the users that concurrent transactions are being processed simultaneously, this cannot be true, since the CPU of the machine processing the database can execute only one instruction at a time. Usually transactions are interleaved, which means that the operating system switches CPU services among tasks so that some portion of each of them is carried out in a given interval. This switching among tasks is done so quickly that two people seated at browsers side by side, processing the same database, may believe that their two transactions are completed simultaneously, but, in reality, the two transactions are interleaved.

Figure 11-4 shows two concurrent transactions. User A's transaction reads Item 100, changes it, and rewrites it in the database. User B's transaction takes the same actions, but on Item 200. The CPU processes User A until it encounters an I/O interrupt or some other delay for User A. The operating system shifts control to User B. The CPU now processes User B until an interrupt, at which point the operating system passes control back to User A. To the users, the processing appears to be simultaneous, but actually it is interleaved, or concurrent.

➤ FIGURE 11-4

Example of Concurrent Processing of Two Users' Tasks

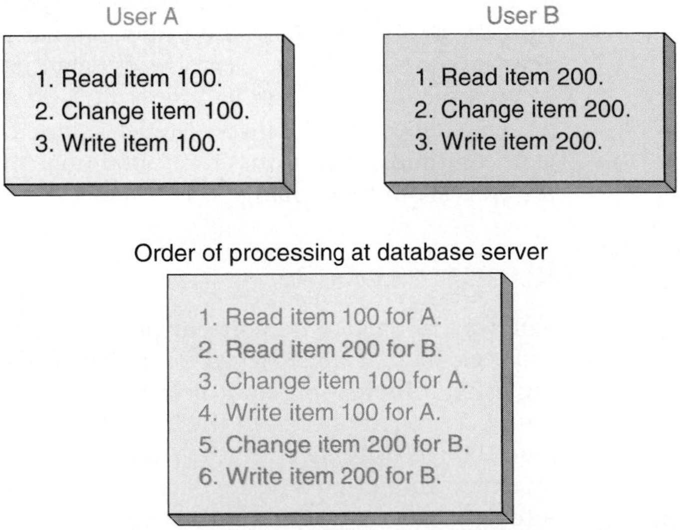

User A

1. Read item 100.
2. Change item 100.
3. Write item 100.

User B

1. Read item 200.
2. Change item 200.
3. Write item 200.

Order of processing at database server

1. Read item 100 for A.
2. Read item 200 for B.
3. Change item 100 for A.
4. Write item 100 for A.
5. Change item 200 for B.
6. Write item 200 for B.

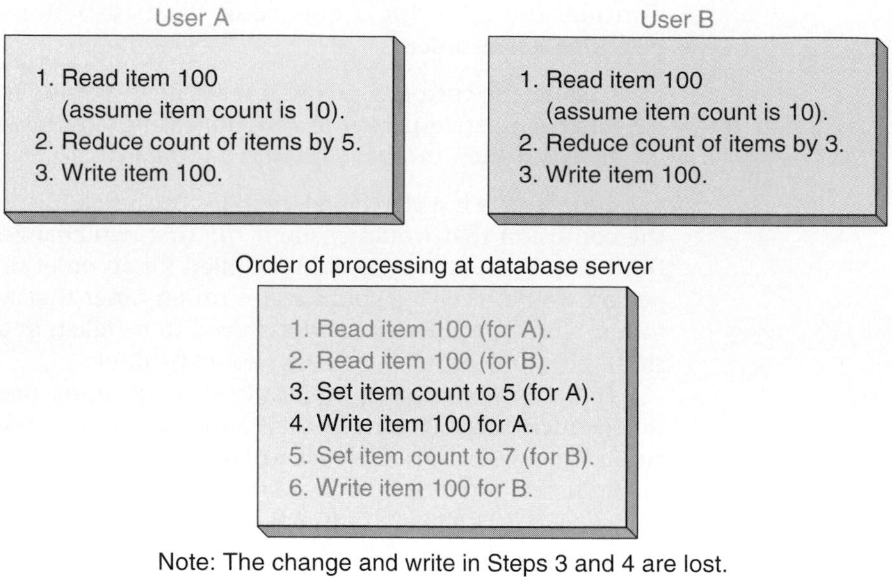

➤ FIGURE 11-5

Lost Update Problem

User A

1. Read item 100
   (assume item count is 10).
2. Reduce count of items by 5.
3. Write item 100.

User B

1. Read item 100
   (assume item count is 10).
2. Reduce count of items by 3.
3. Write item 100.

Order of processing at database server

1. Read item 100 (for A).
2. Read item 100 (for B).
3. Set item count to 5 (for A).
4. Write item 100 for A.
5. Set item count to 7 (for B).
6. Write item 100 for B.

Note: The change and write in Steps 3 and 4 are lost.

LOST UPDATE PROBLEM The concurrent processing illustrated in Figure 11-4 poses no problems because the users are processing different data. But suppose that both users want to process Item 100. For example, User A wants to order five units of Item 100, and User B wants to order three units of the same item.

Figure 11-5 illustrates the problem. User A reads Item 100's record into a user work area. According to the record, there are 10 items in inventory. Then User B reads Item 100's record into another user work area. Again, according to the record there are 10 in inventory. Now User A takes five, decrements the count of items in its user work area to five, and rewrites the record for Item 100. Then User B takes three, decrements the count in its user work area to seven, and rewrites the record for Item 100. The database now shows, incorrectly, that there are seven Item 100s in inventory. To review: We started with 10 in inventory, User A took five, User B took three, and the database shows that seven are in inventory. Clearly, this is a problem.

Both users obtained data that were correct at the time they obtained them. But when User B read the record, User A already had a copy that it was about to update. This situation is called the **lost update problem** or the **concurrent update problem.** There is another, similar problem, called the **inconsistent read problem.** With it, User A reads data that have been processed by a portion of a transaction from User B. As a result, User A reads incorrect data.

One remedy for the inconsistencies caused by concurrent processing is to prevent multiple applications from obtaining copies of the same record when the record is about to be changed. This remedy is called **resource locking.**

Resource Locking

One way to prevent concurrent processing problems is to disallow sharing by locking data that are retrieved for update. Figure 11-6 shows the order of processing using a **lock** command. Because of the lock User B's transaction must wait until User A is finished with the Item 100 data. Using this strategy, User B can read Item 100's record only after User A has completed the modification. In this case, the final item count stored in the database is two, as it should be. (We started with 10, A took five, and B took three, leaving two.)

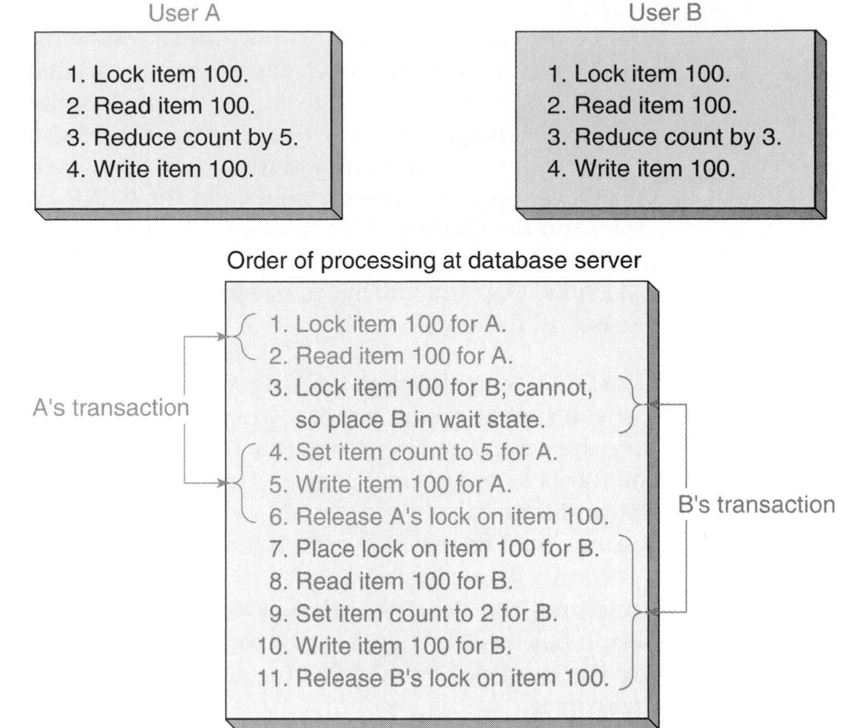

FIGURE 11-6

Concurrent Processing with Explicit Locks

LOCK TERMINOLOGY Locks can be placed either automatically by the DBMS or by a command issued to the DBMS from the application program or query user. Locks placed by the DBMS are called **implicit locks;** those placed by command are called **explicit locks.**

In the preceding example, the locks were applied to rows of data. Not all locks are applied at this level, however. Some DBMS products lock at the page level, some at the table level, and some at the database level. The size of a lock is referred to as the **lock granularity.** Locks with large granularity are easy for the DBMS to administer but frequently cause conflicts. Locks with small granularity are difficult to administer (there are many more details for the DBMS to keep track of and check), but conflicts are less common.

Locks also vary by type. An **exclusive lock** locks the item from access of any type. No other transaction can read or change the data. A **shared lock** locks the item from change but not from read. That is, other transactions can read the item as long as they do not attempt to alter it.

SERIALIZABLE TRANSACTIONS When two or more transactions are processed concurrently, the results in the database should be logically consistent with the results that would have been achieved had the transactions been processed in an arbitrary serial fashion. A scheme for processing concurrent transactions in this way is said to be **serializable.**

Serializability can be achieved by a number of different means. One way is to process the transaction using **two-phased locking.** With this strategy, transactions are allowed to obtain locks as necessary, but once the first lock is released, no other lock can be obtained. Transactions thus have a **growing phase,** in which the locks are obtained, and a **shrinking phase,** in which the locks are released.

A special case of two-phased locking is used with a number of DBMS products. With it, locks are obtained throughout the transaction, but no lock is released until the COMMIT or ROLLBACK command is issued. This strategy is more restrictive than two-phase locking requires, but it is easier to implement.

In general, the boundaries of a transaction should correspond to the definition of the database view it is processing. Following the two-phase strategy, the rows of each relation in the view are locked as needed. Changes are made, but the data are not committed to the database until all of the view has been processed. At this point, changes are made in the actual database, and all locks are released.

Consider an order-entry transaction that involves an object CUSTOMER-ORDER that is constructed from data in the CUSTOMER table, the SALESPERSON table, and the ORDER table. To make sure that the database will suffer no anomalies due to concurrency, the order-entry transaction issues locks on CUSTOMER, SALESPERSON, and ORDER as needed, makes all the database changes, and then releases all its locks.

DEADLOCK Although locking solves one problem, it introduces another. Consider what might happen when two users want to order two items from inventory. Suppose User A wants to order some paper, and if she can get the paper, she wants to order some pencils. Then suppose User B wants to order some pencils, and if he can get the pencils, he wants to order some paper. The order of processing could be that shown in Figure 11-7.

In this figure, users A and B are locked in a condition known as **deadlock,** or sometimes the **deadly embrace.** Each is waiting for a resource that the other person has locked. There are two common ways of solving this problem: preventing the deadlock from occurring or allowing the deadlock to occur and then breaking it.

Deadlock can be prevented in several ways. One way is to allow users to issue only one lock request at a time. In essence, users must lock all the resources they want at once. If User A in the illustration had locked both the paper and the pencil records at the beginning, the embrace would never have taken place. A second way to prevent deadlock is to require all application programs to lock resources in the same order. Even if not all applications lock in that order, deadlock will be reduced for those that do. This philosophy could extend to an organizational programming standard such as "Whenever processing rows from tables in a parent-child relationship, lock the parent before the child rows." This will at least reduce the likelihood of deadlock and it might eliminate it altogether.

Almost every DBMS has algorithms for detecting deadlock. When deadlock occurs, the normal solution is to roll back one of the transactions to remove its

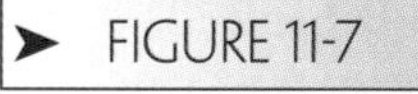

Deadlock

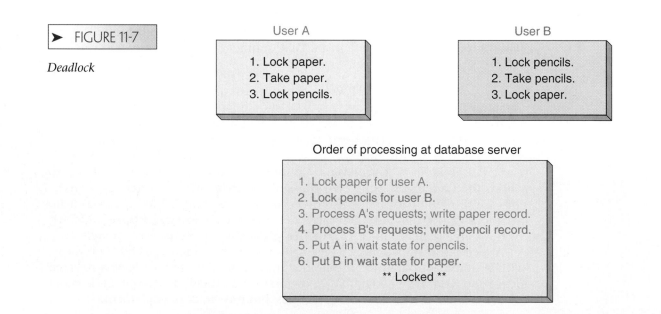

User A

1. Lock paper.
2. Take paper.
3. Lock pencils.

User B

1. Lock pencils.
2. Take pencils.
3. Lock paper.

Order of processing at database server

1. Lock paper for user A.
2. Lock pencils for user B.
3. Process A's requests; write paper record.
4. Process B's requests; write pencil record.
5. Put A in wait state for pencils.
6. Put B in wait state for paper.

** Locked **

changes from the database. You will see variants of this with Oracle and SQL Server in the next two chapters.

Optimistic Versus Pessimistic Locking

Locks can be invoked in two basic styles. With **optimistic locking,** the assumption is made that no conflict will occur. Data is read, the transaction is processed, updates are issued, and then a check is made to see if conflict occurred. If not, the transaction is finished. If so, the transaction is repeated until it processes with no conflict. With **pessimistic locking,** the assumption is made that conflict will occur. First, locks are issued, then the transaction is processed, and then locks are freed.

Figure 11-8 shows an example of each style for a transaction that is reducing the quantity of the pencil row in PRODUCT by five. Figure 11-8(a) shows optimistic locking. First the data are read and the current value of Quantity of pencils is saved in the variable OldQuantity. The transaction is then processed, and, assuming that all is OK, a lock is obtained on PRODUCT. The lock might be only for the pencil row, or it might be at a larger level of granularity. In any case, a SQL statement is then issued to update the pencil row with a WHERE condition that the current value of Quantity equal OldQuantity. If no other transaction has changed the Quantity of the pencil row, then this UPDATE will be successful. If another transaction has changed the Quantity of the pencil row, the UPDATE will fail and the transaction will need to be repeated.

Figure 11-8(b) shows the logic for the same transaction using pessimistic locking. Here, a lock is obtained on PRODUCT (at some level of granularity) before any work is begun. Then values are read, the transaction is processed, the UPDATE occurs, and PRODUCT is unlocked.

The advantage of optimistic locking is that the lock is obtained only after the transaction has processed. Thus, the lock is held for less time than with pessimistic locking. If the transaction is complicated or if the client is slow (due to transmission delays, or the client doing other work, or the user getting a cup of coffee or shutting down without exiting the browser), the lock will be held considerably less time. This advantage will be even more important if the lock granularity lock is large—say, the entire PRODUCT table.

The disadvantage of optimistic locking is that if there is a lot of activity on the pencil row, the transaction may have to be repeated many times. Thus, transactions that involve a lot of activity on a given row (purchasing a popular stock, for example) are poorly suited for optimistic locking.

In general, the Internet is a wild and wooly place, and users are likely to take unexpected actions like abandoning transactions in the middle. So unless Internet users have been prequalified (by enrolling in an online brokerage stock purchase plan, for example), optimistic locking is the better choice. On intranets, however, the decision is more difficult. Probably optimistic locking is still preferred unless there is some characteristic of the application that causes substantial activity on particular rows, or if application requirements make reprocessing transactions particularly undesirable.

Declaring Lock Characteristics

As you can see, concurrency control is a complicated subject; some of the decisions about lock types and strategy have to be made on the basis of trial and error. For this and other reasons, database application programs do not generally explicitly issue locks. Instead, they mark transaction boundaries, and then declare the

Optimistic vs. Pessimistic Locking: (a) Optimistic Locking; (b) Pessimistic Locking

```
SELECT    PRODUCT.Name, PRODUCT.Quantity
FROM      PRODUCT
WHERE     PRODUCT.Name = 'Pencil'

OldQuantity = PRODUCT.Quantity

Set NewQuantity = PRODUCT.Quantity – 5

{process transaction – take exception action if NewQuantity < 0, etc.

Assuming all is OK: }

LOCK PRODUCT {at some level of granularity}

UPDATE    PRODUCT
SET       PRODUCT.Quantity = NewQuantity
WHERE     PRODUCT.Name = 'Pencil'
     AND  PRODUCT.Quantity = OldQuantity

UNLOCK    PRODUCT

{check to see if update was successful;
if not, repeat transaction}
```

(a)

```
LOCK      PRODUCT {at some level of granularity}

SELECT    PRODUCT.Name, PRODUCT.Quantity
FROM      PRODUCT
WHERE     PRODUCT.Name = 'Pencil'

Set NewQuantity = PRODUCT.Quantity – 5

{process transaction – take exception action if NewQuantity < 0, etc.

Assuming all is OK: }

UPDATE    PRODUCT
SET       PRODUCT.Quantity = NewQuantity
WHERE     PRODUCT.Name = 'Pencil'

UNLOCK    PRODUCT

{no need to check if update was successful}
```

(b)

type of locking behavior they want the DBMS to use. In this way, if the locking behavior needs to be changed, the application need not be rewritten to place locks in different locations in the transaction. Instead, the lock declaration is changed.

Figure 11-9 shows the pencil transaction with transaction boundaries marked with, BEGIN TRANSACTION, COMMIT TRANSACTION, and ROLLBACK TRANSACTION statements. These boundaries are the essential information that the DBMS needs in order to enforce different locking strategies. If the developer now declares (via a system parameter or similar means) that he or she wants optimistic locking, the DBMS will implicitly set the locks in the correct place for that locking

Marking Transaction Boundaries

```
BEGIN TRANSACTION:

SELECT     PRODUCT.Name, PRODUCT.Quantity
FROM       PRODUCT
WHERE      PRODUCT.Name = 'Pencil'

Old Quantity = PRODUCT.Quantity

Set NewQuantity = PRODUCT.Quantity – 5

{process part of transaction – take exception action if NewQuantity < 0, etc.}

UPDATE     PRODUCT
SET        PRODUCT.Quantity = NewQuantity
WHERE      PRODUCT.Name = 'Pencil'

{continue processing transaction} . . .


IF transaction has completed normally     THEN

     COMMIT TRANSACTION

ELSE

     ROLLBACK TRANSACTION

END IF

Continue processing other actions not part of this transaction . . .
```

style. If he or she later changes tactics and requests pessimistic locking, the DBMS will implicitly set the locks in a different place.

Consistent Transactions

Sometimes you will see the acronym ACID applied to transactions. An **ACID transaction** is one that is *a*tomic, *c*onsistent, *i*solated, and *d*urable. Atomic and durable are easy to define. As you just learned, an atomic transaction is one in which either all of the database actions occur or none of them do. A durable transaction is one for which all committed changes are permanent. The DBMS will not remove such changes, even in the case of failure. If the transaction is durable, the DBMS will provide facilities to recover the changes of all committed actions when necessary.

The terms *consistent* and *isolated* are not, however, as definitive as the terms *atomic* and *durable*. Consider the following SQL update command:

```
UPDATE   CUSTOMER
SET      AreaCode = '425'
WHERE    ZipCode = '98050'
```

Suppose there are 500,000 rows in the CUSTOMER table and that 500 of them have ZipCode equal to '98050.' It will take some time for the DBMS to find all 500 rows. During that time, will other transactions be allowed to update the AreaCode or ZipCode fields of CUSTOMER? If the SQL statement is consistent, such updates will be disallowed. The update will apply to the set of rows as they existed at the time the SQL statement started. Such consistency is called **statement level consistency.**

Now consider a transaction that contains two SQL update statements:

```
BEGIN TRANSACTION
UPDATE  CUSTOMER
SET     AreaCode = '425'
WHERE   ZipCode = '98050'
{other transaction work}
UPDATE  CUSTOMER
SET     Discount = 0.05
WHERE   AreaCode = '425'
{other transaction work}
COMMIT  TRANSACTION
```

Now, in this context, what does consistent mean? Statement level consistency means that each statement independently processes consistent rows, but that changes from other users to these rows might be allowed during the interval between the two SQL statements. **Transaction level consistency** means that all rows impacted by either of the SQL statements are protected from changes during the entire transaction. Observe, however, that for some implementations of transaction level consistency, a transaction will not see its own changes. In this example, the second SQL statement may not see rows changed by the first SQL statement.

Thus, when you hear the term *consistent,* look further to determine which type of consistency is meant. Be aware as well of the potential trap of transaction level consistency.

The situation is more complicated for the term *isolated.* We consider it next.

Transaction Isolation Level

Locks prevent concurrent processes from causing lost updates, but there are other types of problems that they do not prevent. Specifically, a **dirty read** occurs when one transaction reads a changed record that has not been committed to the database. This can occur, for example, if one transaction reads a row changed by a second uncommitted transaction, and this second transaction later aborts.

Nonrepeatable reads occur when a transaction rereads data it has previously read and finds modification or deletions caused by a committed transaction. Finally, **phantom reads** occur when a transaction rereads data and finds new rows that were inserted by a committed transaction since the prior read.

The 1992 ANSI SQL standard defines four **isolation levels,** which specify which of these problems are allowed to occur. The goal is for the application programmer to be able to declare the type of isolation level he or she wants and then to have the DBMS manage locks so as to achieve that level of isolation.

As shown in Figure 11-10, Read Uncommitted isolation level allows dirty reads, nonrepeatable reads, and phantom reads to occur. With Read Committed isolation, dirty reads are disallowed. The Repeatable Reads isolation level disallows both dirty reads and nonrepeatable reads. Serializable isolation level will not allow any of these three.

Generally, the more restrictive the level, the less the throughput, though much depends on the workload and how the application programs are written. Moreover, not all DBMS products support all of these levels. Products also vary in the manner in which they are supported and the burden they place on the application

FIGURE 11-10

Summary of Isolation Levels

		Isolation Level			
		Read Uncommitted	**Read Committed**	**Repeatable Read**	**Serializable**
Problem Type	**Dirty Read**	Possible	Not Possible	Not Possible	Not Possible
	Nonrepeatable Read	Possible	Possible	Not Possible	Not Possible
	Phantom Read	Possible	Possible	Possible	Not Possible

programmer. You will learn how Oracle and SQL Server support isolation levels in the next two chapters.

Cursor Type

A cursor is a pointer into a set of rows. Cursors are usually defined using SELECT statements. For example, the statement

```
DECLARE CURSOR TransCursor AS
SELECT    *
FROM      TRANSACTION
WHERE     PurchasePrice > '10000'
```

defines a cursor named TransCursor that operates over the set of rows indicated by this SELECT statement. When an application program opens a cursor and reads the first row, the cursor is said to be "pointing at the first row."

A transaction may open several cursors—either in sequence or at the same time. Additionally, two or more cursors may be open on the same table; either directly on the table or through a SQL view on that table. Because cursors require considerable memory, having many cursors open at the same time for, say, a thousand concurrent transactions, can consume considerable memory and CPU time. One way to reduce cursor overhead is to define reduced-capability cursors and use them when a full capability cursor is not needed.

Figure 11-11 lists four cursor types used in the Windows 2000 environment. (Cursor types for other systems are similar.) The simplest cursor is forward only. With it, the application can only move forward through the recordset. Changes made by other cursors in this transaction and by other transactions will be visible only if they occur in rows ahead of the cursor.

The next three types of cursor are called **scrollable cursors** since the application can scroll forward and backward through the recordset. A static cursor processes a snapshot of the relation that was taken when the cursor was opened. Changes made using this cursor are visible to it; changes from any other source are not visible.

Keyset cursors combine some features of static cursors with some features of dynamic cursors. When the cursor is opened, a primary key value is saved for each row in the recordset. When the application positions the cursor on a row, the DBMS uses the key value to read the current value of the row. If the application issues an update on a row that has been deleted either by a different cursor in this transaction or by a different transaction, the DBMS creates a new row with the old key value and places the updated values in the new row (assuming that all required fields are present). Inserts of new rows by other cursors in this transaction or by

➤ FIGURE 11-11

Summary of Cursor Types

CursorType	Description	Comments
Forward only	Application can only move forward through the recordset.	Changes made by other cursors in this transaction or in other transactions will be visible only if they occur on rows ahead of the cursor.
Static	Application sees the data as it was at the time the cursor was opened.	Changes made by this cursor are visible. Changes from other sources are not visible. Backward and forward scrolling allowed.
Keyset	When the cursor is opened, a primary key value is saved for each row in the recordset. When the application accesses a row, the key is used to fetch the current values for the row.	Updates form any source are visible. Inserts from sources outside this cursor are not visible (there is no key for them in the keyset). Inserts from this cursor appear at the bottom of the recordset. Deletions from any source are visible. Changes in row order are not visible. If the isolation level is dirty read, then committed updates and deletions are visible; otherwise only committed updates and deletions are visible.
Dynamic	Changes of any type and from any source are visible.	All inserts, updates, deletions, and changes in recordset order are visible. If the isolation level is dirty read, then uncomitted changes are visible. Otherwise, only committed changes are visible.

other transactions are not visible to a keyset cursor. Unless the isolation level of the transaction is a dirty read, only committed updates and deletions are visible to the cursor.

A dynamic cursor is a fully featured cursor. All inserts, updates, deletions, changes in row order are visible to a dynamic cursor. As with keyset cursors, unless the isolation level of the transaction is a dirty read, only committed changes are visible.

The amount of overhead and processing required to support a cursor is different for each type. In general, the cost goes up as we move down the cursor types in Figure 11-11. In order to improve DBMS performance, therefore, the application developer should create cursors that are just powerful enough to do the job. It is also very important to understand how a particular DBMS implements cursors and whether cursors are located on the server or on the client. In some cases, it might be better to place a dynamic cursor on the client than to have a static cursor on the server. No general rule can be stated because performance depends on the implementation used by DBMS product and the application requirements.

A word of caution: If you do not specify the isolation level of a transaction or do not specify the type of cursors you open, the DBMS will use a default level and types. These defaults may be perfect for your application, but they also may be terrible. Thus, even though these issues can be ignored, the consequences of them cannot be avoided. Learn the capabilities of your DBMS product and use them wisely.

➤ DATABASE SECURITY

The goal of database security is to ensure that only authorized users can perform authorized activities at authorized times. This goal is difficult to achieve, and to make any progress at all, the database development team must, during the project's requirements specification phase, determine the processing rights and responsibilities of all users. These security requirements can then be enforced using the security features of the DBMS and additions to those features written into the application programs.

PROCESSING RIGHTS AND RESPONSIBILITIES

Consider, for example, the needs of View Ridge Gallery, discussed in Chapter 10. There are three types of users: sales personnel, management personnel, and systems administrators. The sales personnel are allowed to enter new customer and transaction data, to change customer data, and to query any of the data. They are not allowed to enter new artist or work data. They are not allowed to delete any data at all.

Management personnel are allowed all of the permissions of sales personnel, plus they are allowed to enter new artist and work data, and to modify transaction data. Even though management personnel have the authority to delete data, they are not given that permission in this application. This restriction is made to prevent the possibility of accidental data loss.

The system administrator is allowed unrestricted access to the data. He or she can create, update, read, and delete any of the database data. The administrator can also grant processing rights to other users and he or she can change the structure of the database elements such as tables, indices, stored procedures, and the like. Figure 11-12 summarizes these requirements.

➤ FIGURE 11-12

Processing Rights at View Ridge Gallery

	Customer	**Transaction**	**Work**	**Artist**
Sales Personnel	Insert, Change, Query	Insert, Query	Query	Query
Management Personnel	Insert, Change, Query	Insert, Change, Query	Insert, Change, Query	Insert, Change, Query
System Administrator	Insert, Change, Query, Delete, Grant rights, Modify Structure	Insert, Change, Query, Delete, Grant rights, Modify Structure	Insert, Change, Query, Delete, Grant rights, Modify Structure	Insert, Change, Query, Delete, Grant rights, Modify Structure

The permissions in this table are given to types of users or **user groups** and not to individuals. This is typical, but not required. It would be possible to say, for example, that the user identified as "Benjamin Franklin" has certain processing rights. Note, too, that when groups are used, it is necessary to have a means for allocating users to groups. When "Mary Smith" signs on to the computer, some means needs to be available to determine which group or groups she belongs to. We will discuss this further in the next section.

In this discussion, we have used the phrase *processing rights and responsibilities.* As this phrase implies, responsibilities go with processing rights. If, for example, the system administrator deletes transaction data, he or she has the responsibility to ensure that these deletions do not adversely impact the gallery's operation, accounting, and so forth.

Processing responsibilities cannot be enforced by the DBMS or the database applications. They are, instead, encoded in manual procedures and explained to users during systems training. These are topics of a systems development text and we will not consider them further here, except to reiterate that *responsibilities* go with *rights.* Such responsibilities must be documented and enforced.

According to Figure 11-1, the DBA has the task of managing processing rights and responsibilities. As this implies, these rights and responsibilities will change over time. As the database is used, as changes are made to the applications and to DBMS structure, the need for new or different rights and responsibilities will arise. The DBA is a focal point for the discussion of such changes and for their implementation.

Once processing rights have been defined, they can be implemented at many levels: operating system, network, Web server, DBMS, and application. In the next two sections we will consider DBMS and application. The others are beyond the scope of this text.

DBMS Security

The terminology, features, and functions of DBMS security depend on the DBMS product in use. Basically, all such products provide facilities that limit certain actions on certain objects to certain users. A general model of DBMS security is shown in Figure 11-13. A user can be assigned to one or more roles and a role can have one or more users. Both users and roles have many permissions. Objects (used in a generic sense) have many permissions assigned to them. Each permission pertains to one user or role and one object.

When a user signs on to the database, the DBMS limits his or her actions to the defined permissions for that user and to the permissions for roles to which that user has been assigned. Determining whether someone actually is who they claim to be is, in general, a difficult task. All commercial DBMS products use some ver-

A Model of DBMS Security

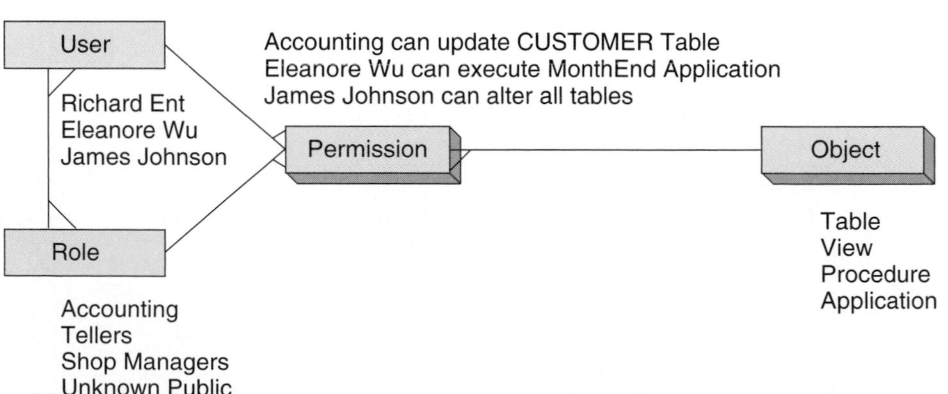

sion of user name and password, even though such security is readily circumvented if users are careless with their identities.

Users can enter their name and password, or, in some applications, the name and password is entered on behalf of the user. For example, the Windows 2000 user name and password can be directly passed to SQL Server. In other cases, an application program provides the name and password.

Internet applications usually define a group like "Unknown Public," and assign anonymous users to that group when they sign on. In this way, companies like Dell Computer need not enter every customer into their security system by name and password.

Models of the security systems used by Oracle and SQL Server are illustrated in Figures 11-14 and 11-15. As you can see, both of these are variants of the general

➤ FIGURE 11-14

Oracle Security (a) Model of Oracle Security (b) Defining an Oracle Profile (c) Oracle User, Roles, and Profiles

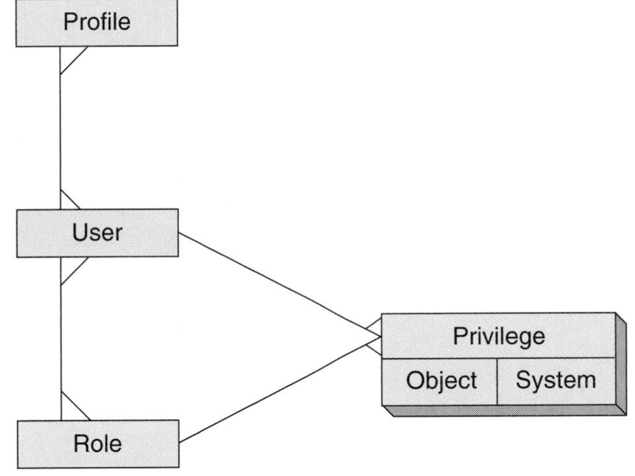

(a) Model of Oracle Security

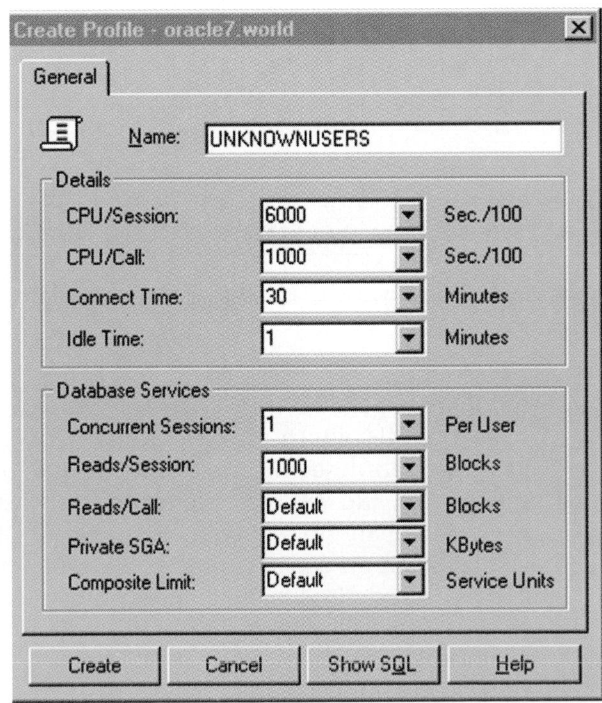

(b)

FIGURE 11-14

(Continued)

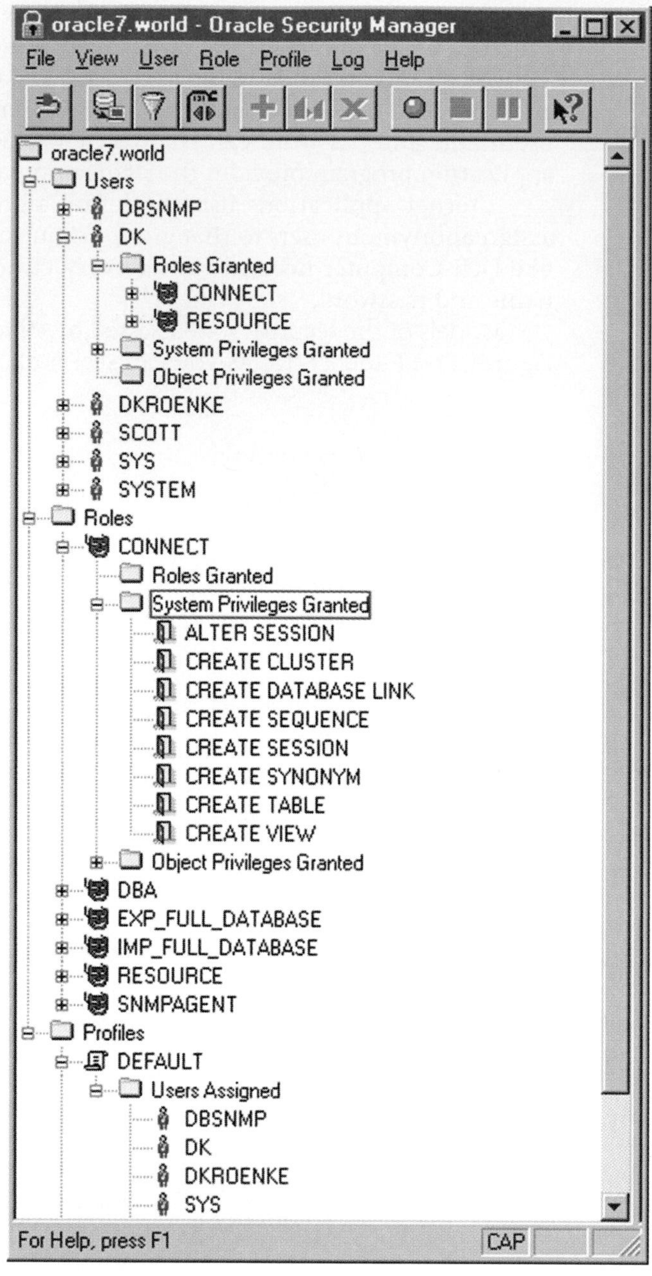

(c)

model in Figure 11-13. Considering the Oracle model in Figure 11-14(a), users have a profile, which is a specification of systems resources that they can use. An example profile definition is shown in Figure 11-14(b). Users can be assigned many roles, and a role is assigned to many users. Each user or role has many privileges. There are two subtypes of privilege: Object privileges concern actions that can be taken on database objects like tables, views, and indexes; system privileges concern the actions using Oracle commands.

An example of this security system is shown in Figure 11-14(c). Observe that the user DK has been granted roles for CONNECT and RESOURCE. Looking further down the list, the CONNECT role has been granted system privileges like ALTER SESSION, CREATE CLUSTER, and others, including CREATE TABLE.

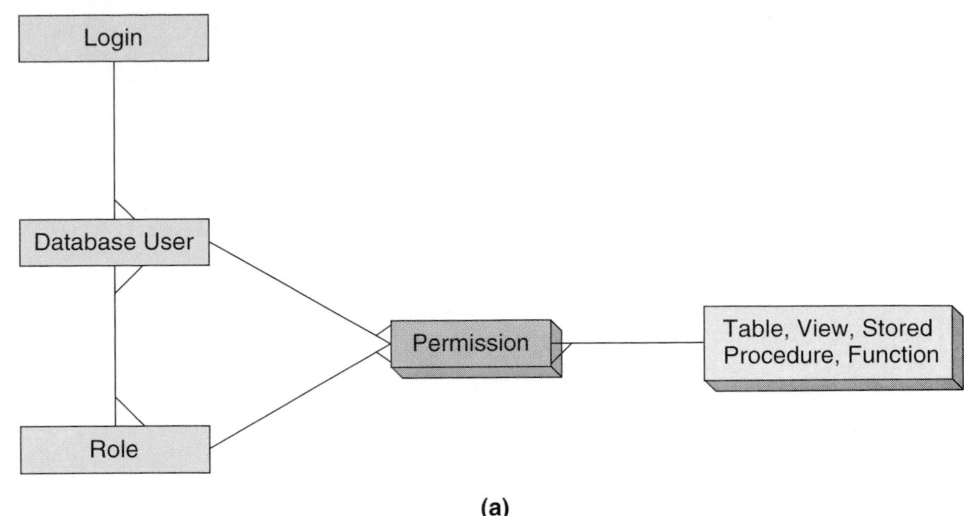

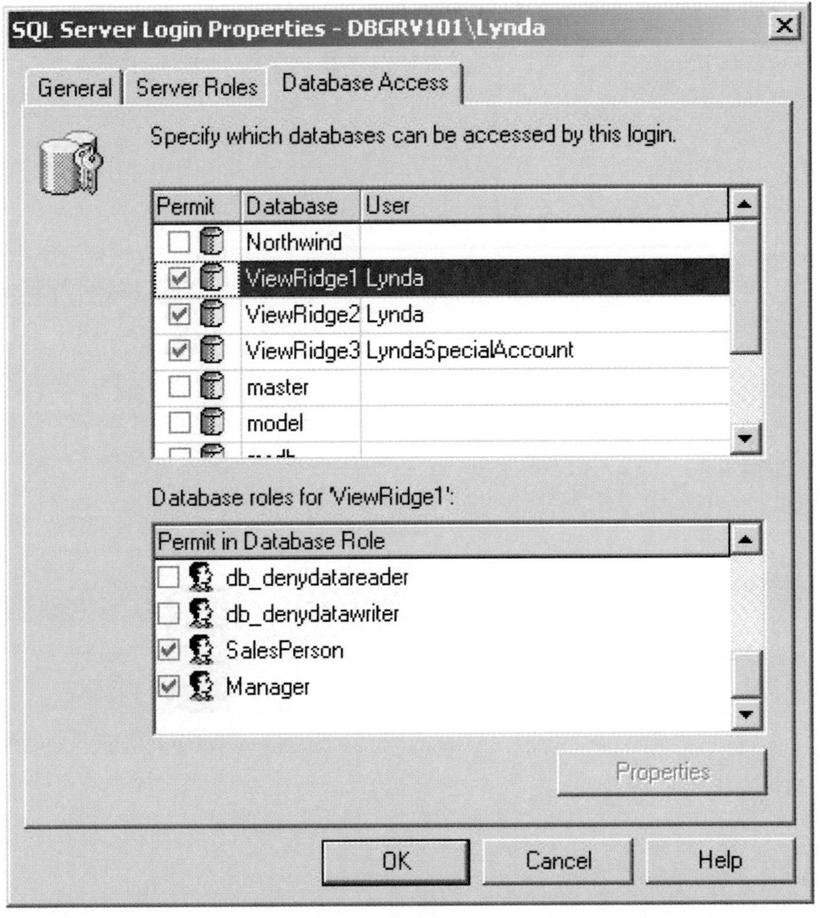

➤ FIGURE 11-15

SQL Server Security: (a) A Model of SQL Server Security, (b) SQL Server Login Example, (c) SQL Server Role Example, and (d) SQL Server User Example

Looking even further down the list, the user DK has been assigned to the DEFAULT profile.

The security scheme for SQL Server is illustrated in Figure 11-15(a). A login account (the name and password used when signing on to SQL Server or onto Windows) may be associated with one or more database/user combinations. In

➤ FIGURE 11-15

(Continued)

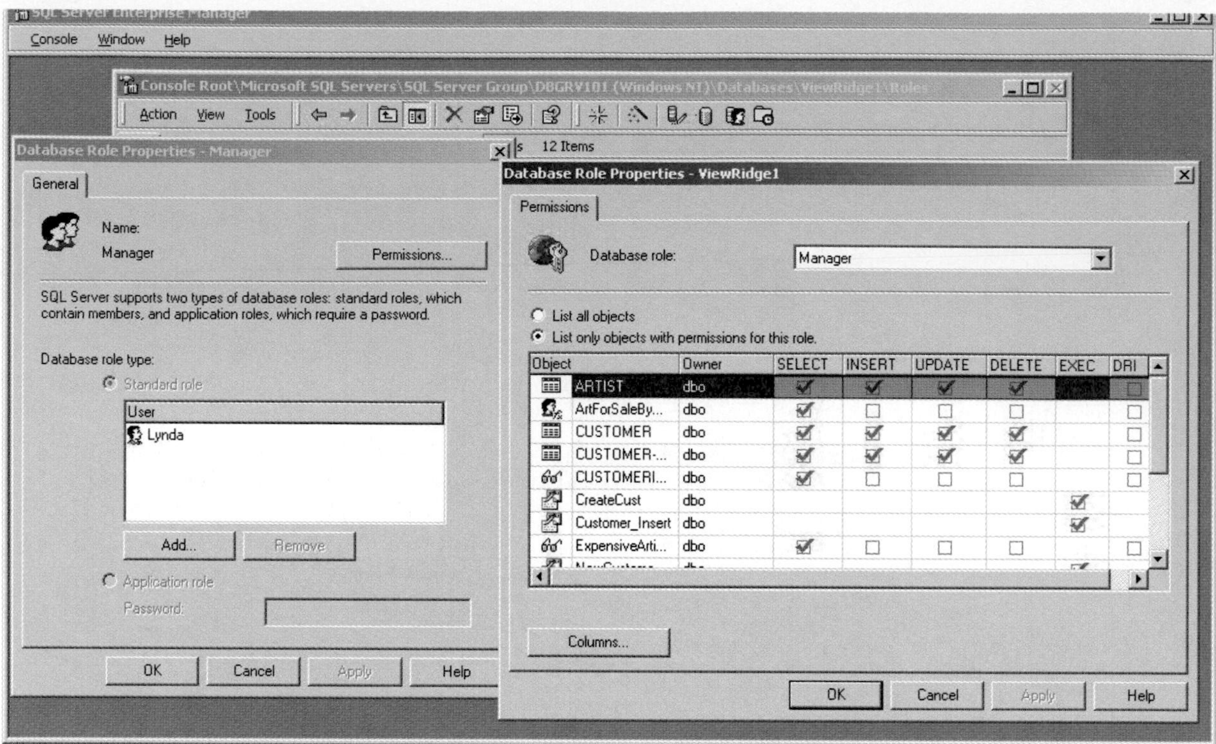

(c)

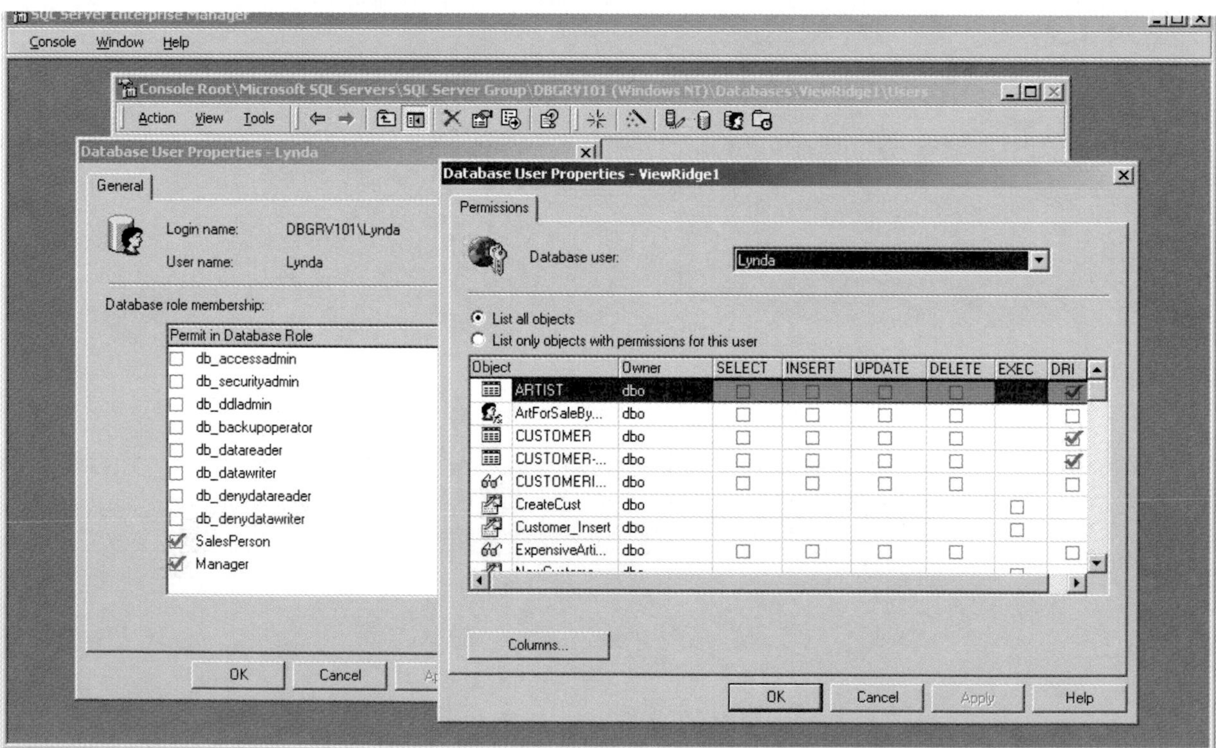

(d)

Figure 11-15(b), for example, the login named Lynda on domain DBGRV101 has been permitted access to the database ViewRidge1 with the user name Lynda, to ViewRidge2 with the user name Lynda, and to ViewRidge3 with the user name LyndaSpecialAccount. As shown in Figure 11-15(a), more than one login can be associated with a given database/user combination.

Figure 11-15(c) shows the permissions of a role named Manager in the database ViewRidge1. A role may have one or more users and in this case it has only one user, Lynda. The permissions of the Manager role are shown with green check marks in the permissions dialog box. EXEC refers to the permission to execute a stored procedure and DRI refers to the permission to create, change, or delete declarative referential integrity constraints such as CustomerID in CUSTOMER-ARTIST-INT must be a subset of CustomerID in CUSTOMER. EXEC is only applicable to stored procedure objects and DRI is only applicable to tables and views.

A given database/user has all of the permissions of the roles to which he or she is assigned as well as any permissions that are particular to that user. Figure 11-15(d) shows that user ViewRidge1/Lynda has been assigned to the SalesPerson and Manager roles and she will have all of the permissions of those roles. In addition, she has been given permission to create, modify, and delete DRI constraints on ARTIST, CUSTOMER, and CUSTOMER-ARTIST-INT tables (a portion of the name of this last table is cut off in this figure).

Application Security

While DBMS products like Oracle and SQL Server do provide substantial database security capabilities, by their very nature, they are generic. If the application requires specific security measures such as "No user can view a row of a table or of a join of a table that has an employee name other than his or her own," the DBMS facilities will not be adequate. In these cases, the security system must be augmented by features in the database application.

For example, as you will learn in Chapter 14, application security in Internet applications is often provided on the Web server computer. Executing application security on this server means that sensitive security data need not be transmitted over the network.

To understand this better, suppose an application is written such that when users click a particular button on a browser page, the following query is sent to the Web server and then to the DBMS:

```
SELECT   *
FROM     EMPLOYEE
```

This statement will, of course, return all EMPLOYEE rows. If the application security limits employees to access only their own data, then a Web server could add the where clause shown below to this query:

```
SELECT   *
FROM     EMPLOYEE
WHERE EMPLOYEE.Name = '<%=SESSION("EmployeeName")%>'
```

As you will learn in Chapters 15 and 16, an expression like this will cause the Web server to fill the employee's name into the WHERE clause. For a user signed in under the name 'Benjamin Franklin,' the statement that results from this expression is

```
SELECT   *
FROM     EMPLOYEE
WHERE EMPLOYEE.Name = "Benjamin Franklin"
```

Because the name is inserted by a program on the Web server, the browser user does not know that it is occurring and cannot interfere with it even if he or she did.

Such security processing can be done as shown here on a Web server, but it can also be done within the application programs themselves, or written as stored procedures or triggers to be executed by the DBMS at the appropriate times.

This idea can be extended by storing additional data in a security database that is accessed by the Web server, or by stored procedures and triggers. That security database could contain, for example, the identities of users paired with additional values of WHERE clauses. For example, suppose that the users in the personnel department can access more than just their own data. The predicates for appropriate WHERE clauses could be stored in the security database, read by the application program, and appended to SQL SELECT statements as necessary.

Many other possibilities exist for extending DBMS security with application processing. In general, however, you should use the DBMS security features first. Only if they are inadequate for the requirements, should you add to them with application code. The closer the security enforcement is to the data, the less chance there is for infiltration. Also, using the DBMS security features is faster, cheaper, and probably results in higher quality results than developing your own.

➤ DATABASE RECOVERY

Computer systems can fail. Hardware breaks. Programs have bugs. Human procedures contain errors, and people make mistakes. All of these failures can and do occur in database applications. Since a database is shared by many people and since it often is a key element of an organization's operations, it is important to recover it as soon as possible.

Several problems must be addressed. First, from a business standpoint, business functions must continue. For example, customer orders, financial transactions, and packing lists must be completed manually. Later, when the database application is operational again, the new data can be entered. Second, computer operations personnel must restore the system to a usable state as quickly as possible and as close as possible to what it was when the system crashed. Third, users must know what to do when the system becomes available again. Some work may need to be reentered, and users must know how far back they need to go.

When failures occur, it is impossible simply to fix the problem and resume processing. Even if no data are lost during a failure (which assumes that all types of memory are nonvolatile—an unrealistic assumption), the timing and scheduling of computer processing are too complex to be accurately recreated. Enormous amounts of overhead data and processing would be required for the operating system to be able to restart processing precisely where it was interrupted. It is simply not possible to roll back the clock and put all the electrons in the same configuration they were in at the time of the failure. Two other approaches are possible: recovery via reprocessing, and recovery via rollback/rollforward.

RECOVERY VIA REPROCESSING Since processing cannot be resumed at a precise point, the next best alternative is to go back to a known point and reprocess the workload from there. The simplest form of this type of recovery is to make a copy periodically of the database (called a **database save**) and to keep a record of all transactions that have been processed since the save. Then, when there is a failure, the operations staff can restore the database from the save and reprocess all the transactions.

Unfortunately, this simple strategy is normally unfeasible. First, reprocessing transactions takes the same amount of time as did processing them in the first place. If the computer is heavily scheduled, the system may never catch up.

Second, when transactions are processed concurrently, events are asynchronous. Slight variations in human activity, such as a user inserting a floppy disk more slowly or a user reading an electronic mail message before responding to an application prompt, may change the order of the execution of concurrent transactions. Therefore, whereas Customer A got the last seat on a flight during the original processing, Customer B may get the last seat during reprocessing. For these reasons, reprocessing is normally not a viable form of recovery from failure in concurrent processing systems.

RECOVERY VIA ROLLBACK/ROLLFORWARD A second approach is periodically to make a copy of the database (the database save) and to keep a log of the changes made by transactions against the database since the save. Then, when there is a failure, one of two methods can be used. Using the first method, called **rollforward,** the database is restored using the saved data, and all valid transactions since the save are reapplied. (We are not reprocessing the transactions, as the application programs are not involved in the rollforward. Instead, the processed changes, as recorded in the log, are reapplied.)

The second method is **rollback,** in which we undo changes made by erroneous or partially processed transactions by undoing the changes they have made in the database. Then the valid transactions that were in process at the time of the failure are restarted.

Both of these methods require that a **log** of the transaction results be kept. This log contains records of the data changes in chronological order. Transactions must be written to the log before they are applied to the database. That way, if the system crashes between the time a transaction is logged and the time it is applied, then at worst there is a record of an unapplied transaction. If, on the other hand, the transactions were to be applied before they were logged, it would be possible (as well as undesirable) to change the database but have no record of the change. If this happened, an unwary user might reenter an already completed transaction.

In the event of a failure, the log is used both to undo and to redo transactions, as shown in Figure 11-16. To undo a transaction, the log must contain a copy of every database record (or page) before it was changed. Such records are called **before-images.** A transaction is undone by applying before-images of all its changes to the database.

To redo a transaction, the log must contain a copy of every database record (or page) after it was changed. These records are called **after-images.** A transaction is redone by applying after-images of all its changes to the database. Possible data items of a transaction log are shown in Figure 11-17(a).

For this example log, each transaction has a unique name for identification purposes. Furthermore, all images for a given transaction are linked together with pointers. One pointer points to the previous change made by this transaction (the reverse pointer), and the other points to the next change made by this transaction (the forward pointer). A zero in the pointer field means that this is the end of the list. The DBMS recovery subsystem uses these pointers to locate all records for a particular transaction. Figure 11-17(b) shows an example of the linking of log records.

Other data items in the log are: the time of the action; the type of operation (START marks the beginning of a transaction, and COMMIT terminates a transaction, releasing all locks that were in place); the object acted on, such as record type and identifier; and finally, the before-images and after-images.

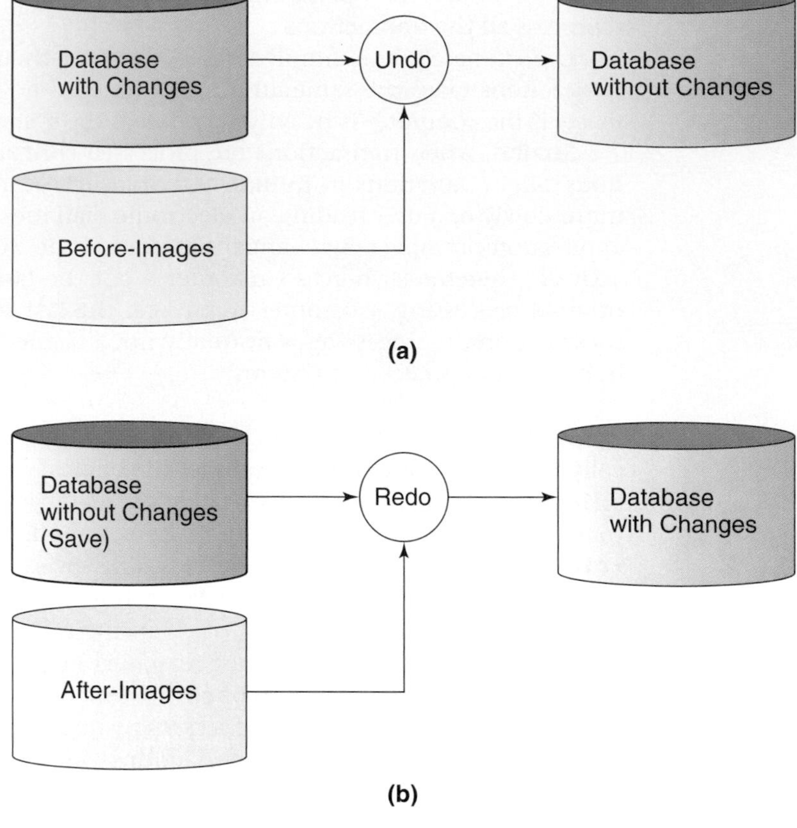

➤ FIGURE 11-16

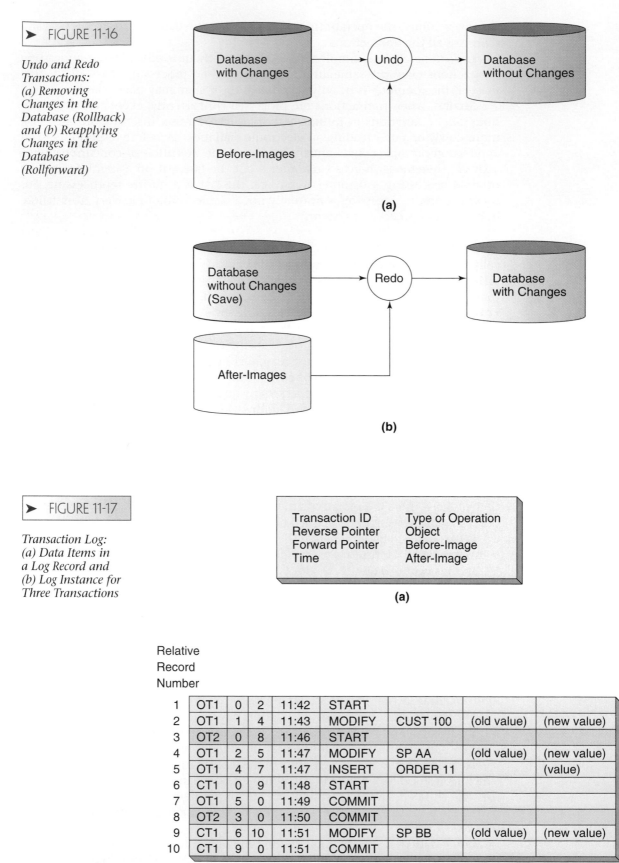

Undo and Redo Transactions: (a) Removing Changes in the Database (Rollback) and (b) Reapplying Changes in the Database (Rollforward)

➤ FIGURE 11-17

Transaction Log: (a) Data Items in a Log Record and (b) Log Instance for Three Transactions

Transaction ID	Type of Operation
Reverse Pointer	Object
Forward Pointer	Before-Image
Time	After-Image

(a)

Relative Record Number								
1	OT1	0	2	11:42	START			
2	OT1	1	4	11:43	MODIFY	CUST 100	(old value)	(new value)
3	OT2	0	8	11:46	START			
4	OT1	2	5	11:47	MODIFY	SP AA	(old value)	(new value)
5	OT1	4	7	11:47	INSERT	ORDER 11		(value)
6	CT1	0	9	11:48	START			
7	OT1	5	0	11:49	COMMIT			
8	OT2	3	0	11:50	COMMIT			
9	CT1	6	10	11:51	MODIFY	SP BB	(old value)	(new value)
10	CT1	9	0	11:51	COMMIT			

(b)

Given a log with both before-images and after-images, the undo and redo actions are straightforward (to describe, anyway). To undo the transaction in Figure 11-18, the recovery processor simply replaces each changed record with its before-image. When all before-images have been restored, the transaction is undone. To redo a transaction, the recovery processor starts with the version of the database at the time the transaction started and applies all after-images. As stated, this action assumes that an earlier version of the database is available from a database save.

Restoring a database to its most recent save and reapplying all transactions may require considerable processing. To reduce the delay, DBMS products sometimes use checkpoints. A **checkpoint** is a point of synchronization between the database and the transaction log. To perform a checkpoint, the DBMS refuses new requests, finishes processing outstanding requests, and writes its buffers to disk. The DBMS then waits until the operating system notifies it that all outstanding write requests to the database and to the log have been successfully completed. At this point, the log and the database are synchronized. A checkpoint record is then written to the log. Later, the database can be recovered from the checkpoint and only after-images for transactions that started after the checkpoint need to be applied.

➤ FIGURE 11-18

Example of a Recovery Strategy: (a) ORDER Transaction and (b) Recovery Processing to Undo an ORDER Record

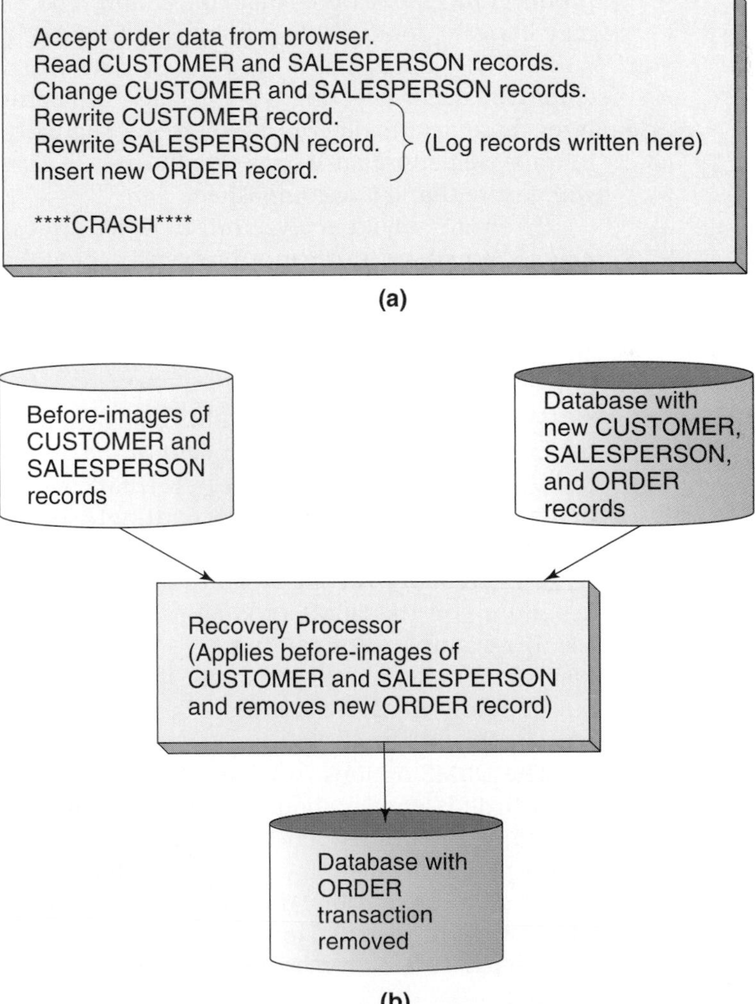

Checkpoints are inexpensive operations, and it is feasible to take three or four (or more) per hour. In this way, no more than 15 or 20 minutes of processing need to be recovered. Most DBMS products automatically checkpoint themselves, making human intervention unnecessary.

You will see specific examples of backup and recovery techniques for Oracle and SQL Server in the next two chapters. For now, you just need to understand the basic ideas and to realize that it is the responsibility of the DBA to ensure that adequate backup and recovery plans have been developed and that database saves and logs are generated as required.

Managing the DBMS

In addition to managing data activity and the database structure, the DBA must manage the DBMS itself. He or she should compile and analyze statistics concerning the system's performance and identify potential problem areas. Keep in mind that the database is serving many user groups. The DBA needs to investigate all complaints about the system's response time, accuracy of data, ease of use, and so forth. If changes are needed, the DBA must plan and implement them.

The DBA must periodically monitor the users' activity on the database. DBMS products include features that collect and report statistics. Some of these reports may indicate, for example, which users have been active, which files and perhaps which data items have been used, and which access methods have been employed. Error rates and types can also be captured and reported. The DBA analyzes these data to determine whether a change to the database design is needed to improve performance or to ease the users' tasks. If change is necessary, the DBA will ensure that it is accomplished.

The DBA should analyze run-time statistics on database activity and performance. When a performance problem is identified (by either a report or a user's complaint), the DBA must determine whether a modification of the database structure or system is appropriate. Examples of possible structure modifications are establishing new keys, purging data, deleting keys, and establishing new relationships among objects.

When the vendor of the DBMS being used announces new product features, the DBA must consider them in light of the overall needs of the user community. If she decides to incorporate the new DBMS features, the developers must be notified and trained in their use. Accordingly, the DBA must manage and control changes in the DBMS, as well as in the database structure.

Other changes in the system for which the DBA is responsible vary widely, depending on the DBMS product as well as on other software and hardware in use. For example, changes in other software (such as the operating system or the Web server) may mean that some DBMS features, functions, or parameters must be changed. The DBA must therefore also tune the DBMS product to other software in use.

The DBMS options (such as transaction isolation levels) are initially chosen when little is known about how the system will perform in the particular user environment. Consequently, operational experience and performance analysis over a period of time may reveal that changes are necessary. Even if the performance seems acceptable, the DBA may want to alter the options and observe the effect on performance. This process is referred to as *tuning*, or *optimizing*, the system. Figure 11-19 summarizes the DBA's responsibilities for managing the DBMS product.

Summary of the DBA's Responsibilities for Managing the DBMS

- Generate database application performance reports.
- Investigate user performance complaints.
- Assess need for changes in database structure or application design.
- Modify database structure.
- Evaluate and implement new DBMS features.
- Tune the DBMS.

Maintaining the Data Repository

Consider a large and active Internet database application like those used by e-commerce companies, for instance, an application that is used by a company that sells music over the Internet. Such a system may involve data from several different databases, dozens of different Web pages, and hundreds, or even thousands, of users.

Suppose the company using this application decides to expand its product line to include the sale of sporting goods. Senior management of this company might ask the DBA to develop an estimate of the time and other resources required to modify the database application to support this new product line.

For the DBA to respond to this request, he or she needs accurate metadata about the database, about the database applications and application components, about the users and their rights and privileges, and about other system elements. The database does carry some of this metadata in system tables, but this metadata is inadequate to answer the questions senior management poses. The DBA needs additional metadata about COM and ActiveX objects, script procedures and functions, ASP pages, stylesheets, document type definitions, and the like. Furthermore, while DBMS security mechanisms do document users, groups, and privileges, they do so in a highly structured and often inconvenient form.

For all of these reasons, many organizations develop and maintain **data repositories,** which are collections of metadata about databases, database applications, Web pages, users, and other application components. The repository may be virtual in that it is composed of metadata from many different sources: the DBMS, version control software, code libraries, Web page generation and editing tools, and so forth. Or, the data repository may be an integrated product from a CASE tool vendor or from other companies such as Microsoft or Oracle.

Either way, the time for the DBA to think about constructing such a facility is long before senior management asks questions. In fact, the repository should be constructed as the system is developed and should be considered an important part of the system deliverables. If not, the DBA will always be playing catchup, trying to maintain the existing applications, adapt them to new needs, and somehow gather together the metadata to form a repository.

The best repositories are **active;** they are part of the system development process in such a way that metadata is created automatically as the system components are created. Less desirable, but still effective, are **passive repositories** that are filled only when someone takes the time to generate the needed metadata and place it in the repository.

The Internet has created enormous opportunities for businesses to expand their customer base and increase their sales and profitability. The databases and database applications that support these companies are an essential element of that success. Unfortunately, there will be organizations whose growth is stymied for lack of ability to grow their applications or adapt them to changing needs. Often, building a new system is easier than adapting an existing one; certainly building a new system that integrates with an old one while it replaces that old one can be very difficult.

➤ SUMMARY

Multi-user databases pose difficult problems for the organizations that create and use them and most organizations have created an office of database administration to ensure that such problems are solved. In this text, the term *database administrator* refers to the person or office that is concerned with a single database. The term *data administrator* is used to describe a similar function that is concerned with all of an organization's data assets. Data administration will be discussed in Chapter 17. Major functions of the database administrator are listed in Figure 11-1.

The DBA is concerned with the development of the initial database structures and with providing configuration control over them as requests for changes arise. Keeping accurate documentation of the structure and changes to it is an important DBA function.

The goal of concurrency control is to ensure that one user's work does not inappropriately influence another user's work. No single concurrency control technique is ideal for all circumstances. Trade-offs need to be made between level of protection and throughput. A transaction or logical unit of work is a series of actions taken against the database that occur as an atomic unit; either all of them occur or none of them do. The activity of concurrent transactions is interleaved on the database server. In some cases, updates can be lost if concurrent transactions are not controlled. Another concurrency problem concerns inconsistent reads.

To avoid concurrency problems, database elements are locked. Implicit locks are placed by the DBMS; explicit locks are issued by the application program. The size of the locked resource is called lock granularity. An exclusive lock prohibits other users from reading the locked resource; a shared lock allows other users to read the locked resource, but they cannot update it.

Two transactions that run concurrently and generate results that are consistent with the results that would have occurred if they had run separately are referred to as serializable transactions. Two-phased locking, in which locks are acquired in a growing phase and released in a shrinking phase, is one scheme for serializability. A special case of two-phase locking is to acquire locks throughout the transaction, but not to free any lock until the transaction is finished.

Deadlock, or the deadly embrace, occurs when two transactions are each waiting on a resource that the other transaction holds. Deadlock can be prevented by requiring transactions to acquire all locks at the same time; once it occurs, the only way to cure it is to abort one of the transactions (and back out partially completed work). Optimistic locking assumes no transaction conflict will occur and deals with the consequences if it does. Pessimistic locking assumes that conflict will occur and so prevents it ahead of time with locks. In general, optimistic locking is preferred for the Internet and for many intranet applications.

Most application programs do not explicitly declare locks. Instead, they mark transaction boundaries with BEGIN, COMMIT, and ROLLBACK transaction statements and declare the concurrent behavior they want. The DBMS then places locks for the application that will result in the desired behavior.

An ACID transaction is one that is atomic, consistent, isolated, and durable. Durable means that database changes are permanent. Consistency can mean either statement level or transaction level consistency. With transaction level consistency, a transaction may not see its own changes. The 1992 SQL standard defines four transaction isolation levels: read uncommitted, read committed, repeatable read, and serializable. The characteristics of each are summarized in Figure 11-10.

A cursor is a pointer into a set of records. Four cursor types are prevalent: forward only, static, keyset, and dynamic. Developers should select isolation levels and cursor types that are appropriate for their application workload and for the DBMS product in use.

The goal of database security is to ensure that only authorized users can perform authorized activities at authorized times. To develop effective database security, the processing rights and responsibilities of all users must be determined.

DBMS products provide security facilities. Most involve the declaration of users, groups, objects to be protected, and permissions or privileges on those objects. Almost all DBMS products use some form of user name and password security. DBMS security can be augmented by application security.

In the event of system failure, that database must be restored to a usable state as soon as possible. Transactions in process at the time of the failure must be reapplied or restarted. While in some cases recovery can be done by reprocessing, the use of logs and rollback and rollforward is almost always preferred. Checkpoints can be taken to reduce the amount of work that needs to be done after a failure.

In addition to these tasks, the DBA manages the DBMS product itself, measuring database application performance, and assessing needs for changes in database structure or DBMS performance tuning. The DBA also ensures that new DBMS features are evaluated and used as appropriate. Finally, the DBA is responsible for maintaining the data repository.

➤ GROUP I QUESTIONS

11.1 Briefly describe five difficult problems for organizations that create and use multi-user databases.

11.2 Explain the difference between a database administrator and a data administrator.

11.3 List seven important tasks for a DBA.

11.4 Summarize the DBA's responsibilities for managing database structure.

11.5 What is configuration control? Why is it necessary?

11.6 Explain the meaning of the word *inappropriately* in the phrase "one user's work does not inappropriately influence another user's work."

11.7 Explain the trade-off that exists in concurrency control.

11.8 Define an atomic transaction and explain why atomicity is important.

11.9 Explain the difference between concurrent transactions and simultaneous transactions. How many CPUs are required for simultaneous transactions?

11.10 Give an example, other than the one in this text, of the lost update problem.

11.11 Explain the difference between an explicit and an implicit lock.

11.12 What is lock granularity?

11.13 Explain the difference between an exclusive lock and a shared lock.

11.14 Explain two-phased locking.

11.15 How does releasing all locks at the end of the transaction relate to two-phase locking?

11.16 In general, how should the boundaries of a transaction be defined?

11.17 What is deadlock? How can it be avoided? How can it be resolved once it occurs?

11.18 Explain the difference between optimistic and pessimistic locking.

11.19 Explain the benefits of marking transaction boundaries, declaring lock characteristics, and letting the DBMS place locks.

11.20 Explain the use of BEGIN, COMMIT, and ROLLBACK TRANSACTION statements.

11.21 Explain the meaning of the expression ACID transaction.

11.22 Describe statement level consistency.

11.23 Describe transaction level consistency. What disadvantage can exist with it?

11.24 What is the purpose of transaction isolation levels?

11.25 Explain read uncommitted isolation level. Give an example of its use.

11.26 Explain read committed isolation level. Give an example of its use.

11.27 Explain repeatable read isolation level. Give an example of its use.

11.28 Explain serializable isolation level. Give an example of its use.

11.29 Explain the term *cursor*.

11.30 Explain why a transaction may have many cursors. Also, how is it possible that a transaction may have more than one cursor on a given table?

11.31 What is the advantage of using different types of cursors?

11.32 Explain forward only cursors. Give an example of their use.

11.33 Explain static cursors. Give an example of their use.

11.34 Explain keyset cursors. Give an example of their use.

11.35 Explain dynamic cursors. Give an example of their use.

11.36 What happens if you do not declare transaction isolation level and cursor type to the DBMS? Is this good or bad?

11.37 Explain the necessity of defining processing rights and responsibilities. How are such responsibilities enforced?

11.38 Explain the relationships of USERS, GROUPS, PERMISSION, and OBJECTS for a generic database security system.

11.39 Describe the advantages and disadvantages of DBMS-provided security.

11.40 Describe the advantages and disadvantages of application-provided security.

11.41 Explain how a database could be recovered via reprocessing. Why is this generally not feasible?

11.42 Define *rollback* and *rollforward*.

11.43 Why is it important to write to the log before changing the database values?

11.44 Describe the rollback process. Under what conditions should it be used?

11.45 Describe the rollforward process. Under what conditions should it be used?

11.46 What is the advantage of taking frequent checkpoints of a database?

11.47 Summarize the DBA's responsibilities for managing the DBMS.

11.48 What is a data repository? A passive data repository? An active data repository?

11.49 Explain why a data repository is important. What is likely to happen if one is not available?

➤ GROUP II QUESTIONS

11.50 Visit www.microsoft.com and search for information about transaction isolation levels and cursor types. For now, ignore information about RDS, ADO, ODBC, and OLE/DB and focus instead on the features and functions of SQL Server. Compare and contrast its capabilities with those described in this text.

11.51 Visit www.oracle.com and search for information about transactions isolation levels and cursor types. Ignore information about ODBC, and focus instead of the features and functions of Oracle. Compare and contrast its capabilities with those described in this text.

11.52 Describe the advantages and disadvantages of user name and password security. In what ways might users be careless with their identities? How can such carelessness compromise the security of the database? What steps could be taken to reduce the risk of such problems?

11.53 Search the Web for CASE tools that provide repositories and for repository products. Find what you think is the best one and list its major functions and features. Explain how those functions and features could be used to help the DBA of an e-commerce company that is adding new product lines to its business.

➤ PROJECT

A. Consider the Customer view in Figure 10-4.

1. Suppose that you are developing an application to create new instances of this view. What transaction isolation level would you use? Name the cursors involved and recommend a cursor type for each.
2. Suppose that you are developing an application to modify the values (only values, not relationships) in this view. What transaction isolation level would you use? Name the cursors involved and recommend a cursor type for each.
3. Suppose that you are developing an application to modify both data values and relationships in this view. How does your answer to Question A.2 change?
4. Suppose that you are developing an application to delete instances of inactive customers (defined as customers who have never purchased art). What transaction isolation level would you use? Name the cursors involved and recommend a cursor type for each.

➤ FIREDUP PROJECT QUESTIONS

A. Assume that FiredUp, Inc., has hired you as a database consultant to develop their operational database having the four tables described at the end of Chapter 9. Assume that FiredUp personnel are the two owners, an office administrator, a repair technician, and two employees in production. The office administrator processes all registration forms. The repair technician inputs repair data, and the production employees enter stove data on stoves they have produced. Prepare a 3 to 5 page memo to FiredUp management that addresses the following issues:

1. The need for database administration at FiredUp.
2. Your recommendation for who should serve as database administrator. Assume FiredUp is not sufficiently large to need or afford a full-time database administrator.
3. Using Figure 11-1 as a guide, describe the nature of database administration activities at FiredUp. As an aggressive consultant, keep in mind that you can recommend yourself for performing some of the DBA functions.

B. For the employees described in Question A, define users, groups, and permissions on data in the four tables described at the end of Chapter 9. Use the security scheme shown in Figure 11-13 as an example. Again, don't forget to include yourself.

C. Consider the REGISTRATION_VIEW and STOVE_REPAIR_VIEW defined at the end of Chapter 10.

1. Give an example of a dirty read, a non-repeatable read, and a phantom read when processing the REGISTRATION_VIEW.
2. What concurrency control measures do you think would be appropriate for a transaction that updates the REGISTRATION_VIEW? What concurrency control measures do you think would be appropriate for a transaction that deletes REGISTRATION_VIEW data? State your assumptions.
3. Answer question 2 for the CUSTOMER_VIEW. Justify any differences from your answer to question 2.
4. What isolation level would you use for a transaction that prints a report listing all stove repairs in a given period. What cursor type would you use?

Managing Databases with Oracle

Oracle is a powerful and robust DBMS that runs on many different operating systems including Windows 98, Windows 2000, several variations of UNIX, several different mainframe operating systems, and Linux. It is the world's most popular DBMS and has a long history of development and use. Oracle exposes much of its technology to the developer, and consequently can be tuned and tailored in many ways.

All of this means, however, that Oracle can be difficult to install and that there is a lot to learn. A gauge of Oracle's breadth is that one of the most popular references, *Oracle 8i, The Complete Reference* by Loney and Koch, is over 1,300 pages long, and it does not contain everything. Moreover, techniques that work with a version of Oracle on one operating system may need to be altered when working with a version on a different operating system. You will need to be patient with Oracle and with yourself and not expect to master this subject overnight.

There are many configurations of the Oracle program suite. To start, there are two different versions of the Oracle DBMS engine: Personal Oracle and Enterprise Oracle. It addition, there are Forms and Reports and also Oracle Designer, and a host of tools for publishing Oracle databases on the Web. Add to this the need for these to operate on many different operating systems, over networks using several different communication protocols, and you can see why there is considerable complexity to learn.

Oracle SQL Plus is a utility for processing SQL and creating components like stored procedures and triggers. It is also one component that is constant through all of these product configurations. Consequently, we will focus the bulk of our attention on it. SQL Plus can be used to submit both SQL and PL/SQL statements to Oracle. The latter, PL/SQL, is a programming language that adds programming constructs to the SQL language. We will use PL/SQL to create tables, constraints, relationships, views, stored procedures, and triggers.

This chapter uses the View Ridge example from Chapter 10, and the discussion will roughly parallel the discussion of database administration in Chapter 11.

➤ INSTALLING ORACLE

If you purchased the version of this book that includes Oracle, you should install it now. As we go along, mirror the actions described in this chapter. You should have two versions of Personal Edition: one for Windows 98 and the other for Windows 2000. Install the version for the operating system you have. Do not attempt to install Oracle Designer or Forms and Reports. You will not need them for the purposes of this chapter, and they can be difficult to install and configure. You will have your hands full with basic Oracle.

➤ CREATING AN ORACLE DATABASE

There are three ways to create an Oracle database: via the Oracle Database Configuration Assistant, via the Oracle-supplied database creation procedures, or via the SQL CREATE DATABASE command. The Oracle Database Configuration Assistant is by far the easiest, and you should use it.

You can find the Database Configuration Assistant in one of the directories created when Oracle was installed. Depending on your operating system, you will find it by clicking Start/Programs/Oracle—OraHome81/Database Administration, or something similar. Your directories may not be named exactly as these; search through the directories under Start/Programs to find Database Configuration Assistant.

When you start the Configuration Assistant, you will see Figure 12-1. Click *Create a database,* and select typical; choose to copy existing database files from the cd; and then select a name for your database. This chapter uses the database name VR1. Click Finish and your database will be created.

➤ FIGURE 12-1

Creating an Oracle Database

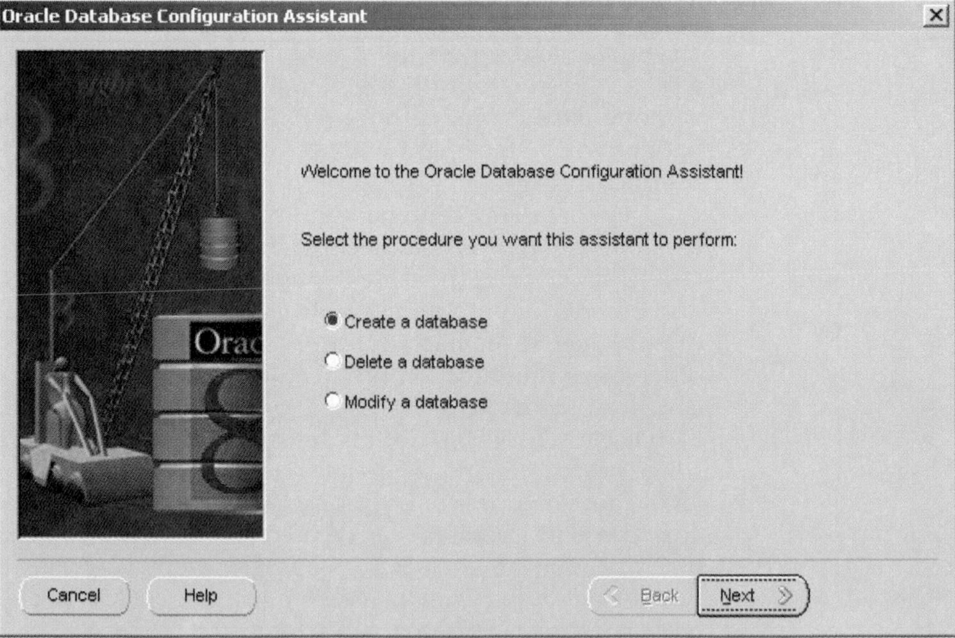

FIGURE 12-2

Oracle Login

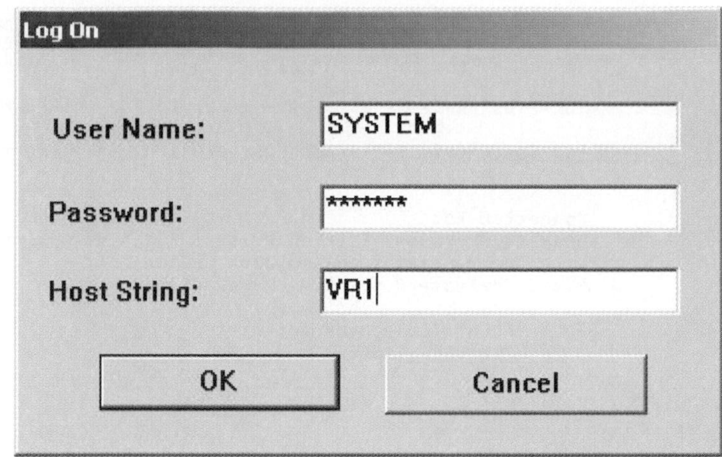

By default, Oracle creates three accounts in your new database: *INTERNAL* with password *ORACLE, SYS* with password *CHANGE_ON_INSTALL,* and *SYSTEM* with password *MANAGER*. (The account names and passwords are case insensitive.)

Oracle will create default files for your data and for logs of data activity. The developer has great control over how and where these files are created, but we will omit discussion of that topic here. You can investigate these topics once you have learned Oracle basics.

Using SQL Plus

To use SQL Plus, find its icon under the Start/Programs menus and click it. Sign on to your database using the SYSTEM account and enter the name of your database under Host String as shown in Figure 12-2. (This procedure might be different if you are using a version of Oracle set up by someone else. If this is the case, check with your database administrator.) Click OK and you should see a window similar to the one in Figure 12-3.

Among its many functions, SQL Plus is a text editor. Working with Oracle will be easier if you learn a bit about this editor. First, when you type into SQL Plus, your keystrokes are placed into a buffer. When you press enter, SQL Plus will save

SQL Plus Prompt

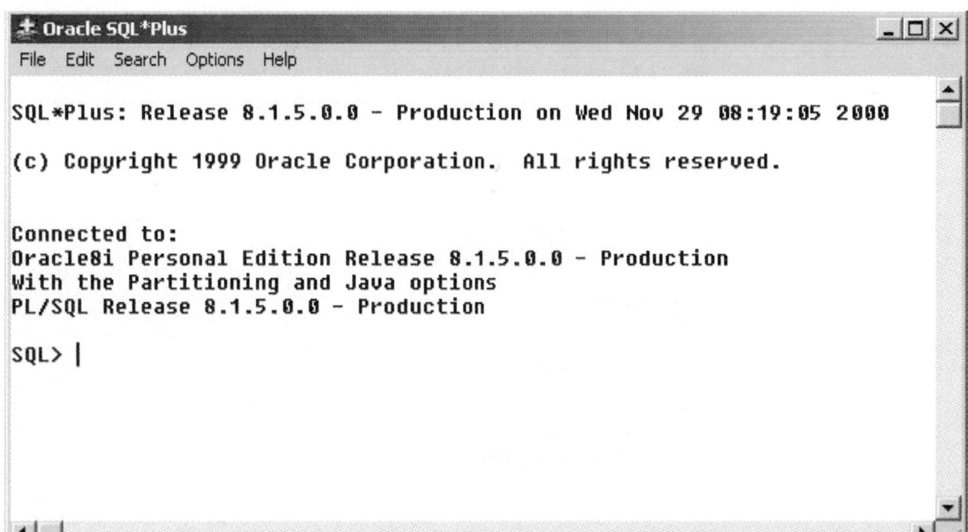

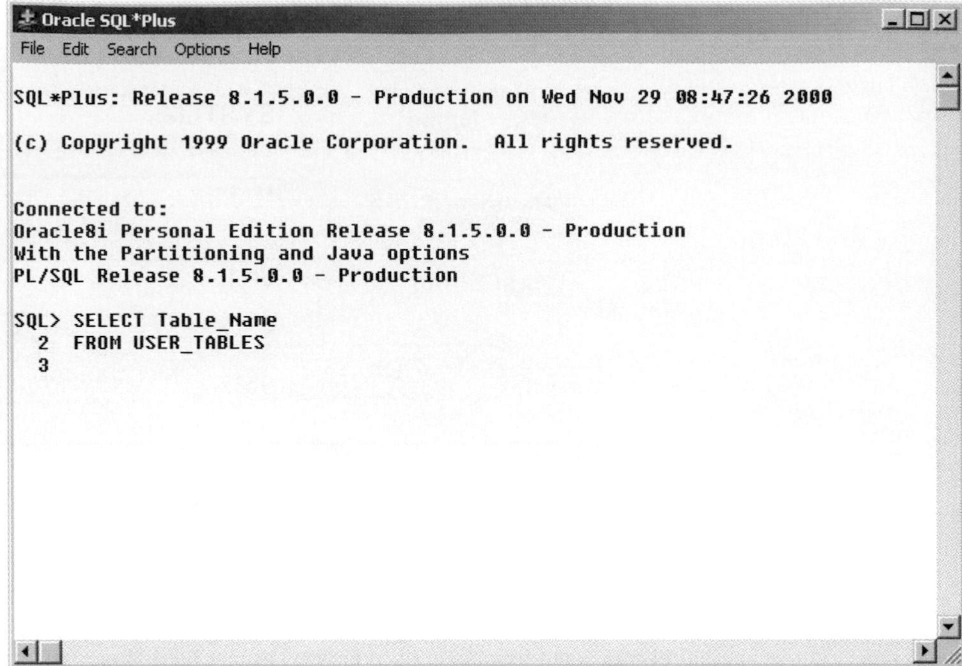

SQL Plus Multi-line Buffer

what you just typed into a line in the buffer, and go to a new line, but it will neither finish nor execute the statement.

THE SQL PLUS BUFFER For example, in Figure 12-4, the user has entered two lines of a SQL statement. The user can enter more lines if necessary. When the user types a semicolon and presses {Enter}, SQL Plus will finish the statement

➤ FIGURE 12-5

Using LIST

```
Oracle SQL*Plus
File Edit Search Options Help
REPCAT$_RESOLUTION_METHOD

TABLE_NAME
------------------------------
REPCAT$_RESOLUTION_STATISTICS
REPCAT$_RESOL_STATS_CONTROL
REPCAT$_RUNTIME_PARMS
REPCAT$_SNAPGROUP
REPCAT$_TEMPLATE_OBJECTS
REPCAT$_TEMPLATE_PARMS
REPCAT$_TEMPLATE_SITES
REPCAT$_USER_AUTHORIZATIONS
REPCAT$_USER_PARM_VALUES
SQLPLUS_PRODUCT_PROFILE
T1
TRANSACTION
WORK

55 rows selected.

SQL> LIST
  1  SELECT Table_Name
  2  FROM USER_TABLES
  3*
SQL> |
```

and then execute it. Try this, but ignore the results—we'll worry about them later.

To see the contents of the buffer, type LIST as shown in Figure 12-5. The line shown with an asterisk, here line 3, is the current line. You can change the current line by entering LIST followed by a line number, such as LIST 1. At that point, line 1 is the current line.

To change the contents of the current line, enter change */astring/bstring/*, where astring is the string you want to change and bstring is what you want to change it to. In Figure 12-6, the user has entered

change/Table_Name/*/

This expression will replace the string 'Table_Name' with the string '*'.

Now when the user types list, the expression in line 1 of the buffer has been changed from SELECT Table_Name to SELECT *. Type LIST to see the complete statement. Enter the right-leaning slash (/), followed by {Enter} and the command in the buffer will be executed.

Before going on you should know that Oracle commands, column names, table names, view names, and all other database elements are case insensitive. *LIST* is the same as *list* as demonstrated in Figure 12-6. The only time that case matters is inside quotations of strings. Thus,

SELECT * from ARTIST;

and

select * FROM artist;

are identical. But

SELECT * FROM ARTIST WHERE Name='Miro';

and

SELECT * FROM ARTIST WHERE Name='MIRO';

are different. Case matters inside quotations when used for data values.

There is also a difference between the semicolon and the right-leaning slash (/). The semicolon terminates a SQL statement; the right-leaning slash tells Oracle to execute whatever statement is in the buffer. If there is only one statement and no ambiguity about what is wanted, Oracle will treat the semicolon and slash as the same. Thus, in

Select * from USER_TABLES;

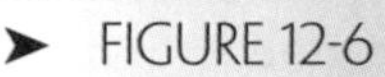
FIGURE 12-6

Changing a Buffer Line

```
SQL> LIST
   1  SELECT Table_Name
   2  FROM USER_TABLES
   3*
SQL> LIST 1
   1* SELECT Table_Name
SQL> change /Table_Name/*/
   1* SELECT *
SQL> list
   1  SELECT *
   2  FROM USER_TABLES
   3*
SQL> l
```

the semicolon both terminates the statement and causes Oracle to execute the statement. Type / at this point, and that statement will be executed again.

USING A TEXT EDITOR This facility is fine for making small changes, but it becomes unworkable for editing longer expressions such as stored procedures. For that purpose, you can set up SQL Plus to connect to your text editor. Before doing this, however, you should create a directory for your code and point SQL Plus to that directory.

First, exit SQL Plus by typing exit at the SQL> prompt. Now, create a directory for your Oracle code, say, c:\MyDirectory\OracleCode. Find the SQL Plus icon on your computer, right click on it to reveal properties, and enter the name of your new directory in the Start In text box. Click OK. Restart SQL Plus.

Click on the Edit item in the SQL Plus window menu, and then select Editor/Define Editor. You can enter the name of your editor here. Notepad is offered as the default and will be fine for our purposes, so click OK.

At this point, you've defined Notepad as your default editor to SQL Plus and set it to point to your directory. Now, whenever you type *Edit,* SQL Plus will invoke Notepad (or your editor, if you selected a different one). You can now create, save, and edit files of code in that directory. For example, reenter the statements:

```
SELECT Table_Name
FROM USER_TABLES;
```

After the results appear, type *Edit*. SQL Plus will bring up Notepad with the contents of the buffer. Use Save As to give this file a new name, say EX1.txt. Close Notepad and you will return to SQL Plus. To edit the file you just created, type *Edit EX1.txt* and you will enter your editor with that file. When you exit your editor and return to SQL Plus, EX1.txt will be stored in the SQL Plus buffer. To cause the buffer contents to execute, enter the right-leaning slash (/) key.

By the way, the default file extension for SQL Plus is *.sql*. If you name a file EX1.sql then you can simply enter *Edit EX1* and SQL Plus will add the extension for you.

Armed with this knowledge of SQL Plus, we can now investigate some of the characteristics of Oracle. In the next section we will use the View Ridge Gallery example introduced in Chapter 10 and create the surrogate key database schema shown in Figure 10-3(d).

Creating Tables

The basic syntax for the CREATE TABLE SQL statement is illustrated in Figure 12-7. It consists of the expression CREATE TABLE, followed by the table name, followed by a list of column names, types, and properties enclosed in parentheses. The statement terminates with a semicolon as all Oracle SQL statements do.

Figure 12-7 shows two different ways of creating a primary key. The structure of table CUSTOMER is created without a primary key and then one is defined using the ALTER TABLE statement that follows. The name of the primary key constraint used here is CustomerPK. A second means of creating a primary key is to set it as a property of a column in the CREATE TABLE statement. This is done for the ARTIST table in Figure 12-7. (In this chapter, text that you key into your text editor will appear as plain text in the format of Figure 12-7. Displays of SQL Plus screen views will be boxed like that shown in Figure 12-6.)

If the table has a composite primary key, then only the ALTER TABLE method of creating the primary key can be used because the CREATE TABLE syntax only allows for one column to have the PRIMARY KEY property. Thus, the primary key for CUSTOMER_ARTIST_INT table (use underscores instead of hyphens with Oracle), which is a composite key, must be defined using an ALTER statement as shown.

To create these tables, open Notepad and key them in. Save them under a file name, say, Create1.sql. Now, start SQL Plus and enter

Creating the CUSTOMER, ARTIST, and CUSTOMER_ARTIST _INT Tables

```
CREATE TABLE CUSTOMER(
        CustomerID          int            NOT NULL,
        Name                varchar(25)    NOT NULL,
        Street              varchar(30)    NULL,
        City                varchar(35)    NULL,
        State               varchar(2)     NULL,
        Zip                 varchar(5)     NULL,
        Area_Code           varchar(3)     NULL,
        Phone_Number        varchar(8)     NULL);

ALTER TABLE CUSTOMER
 ADD CONSTRAINT CustomerPK PRIMARY KEY ( CustomerID );

CREATE INDEX CustomerNameIndex ON CUSTOMER(Name);

CREATE TABLE ARTIST(
        ArtistID            int            PRIMARY KEY,
        Name                varchar(25)    NOT NULL,
        Nationality         varchar(30)    NULL,
        Birthdate           date           NULL,
        DeceasedDate        date           NULL);

CREATE UNIQUE INDEX ArtistNameIndex ON ARTIST(Name);


CREATE TABLE CUSTOMER_ARTIST_INT(
        ArtistID        int            NOT NULL,
        CustomerID      int            NOT NULL);

ALTER TABLE CUSTOMER)_ARTIST_INT
 ADD CONSTRAINT CustomerArtistPK PRIMARY KEY  (  ArtistID, CustomerID );
```

```
Start Create1
```

at the SQL prompt. (If you used a file extension other than .sql, you'll have to add it, e.g., Start Create1.txt.).

SQL Plus will open the file Create1.sql and read the SQL into the buffer. It will not, however, execute these statements until you press the right-leaning slash (/). Do that now and your tables will be created.

If there is a problem, type

```
Edit Create1
```

and your editor will be opened with your file. Make necessary changes, save them, and exit your editor. SQL Plus will have your changed statements in its buffer. To execute them, enter slash.

If you want your statements to be automatically executed at the end of the file, place the slash after the semicolon of your last statement. When you type Start *filename,* the statement in your file will be executed automatically.

You can obtain the structure of a table using the DESCRIBE or DESC command. Enter *DESC CUSTOMER* and the structure of the table will be displayed. Your tables should appear as shown in Figure 12-8. Observe that SQL standard data type varchar was changed to varchar2; Oracle prefers that name. Also, the surrogate keys, which were defined as by the standard type int were changed to number of length 38. A partial list of Oracle data types is shown in Figure 12-9.

SURROGATE KEYS USING SEQUENCES A sequence is an object that generates a sequential series of unique numbers. Sequences are most often used to provide values for surrogate keys. The following statement defines a sequence called CustID that starts at 1000 and is incremented by 1 each time it is used.

➤ FIGURE 12-8

Using the Describe (desc) Command

```
SQL> desc customer;
 Name                                   Null?      Type
 -------------------------------------- ---------- ----------------
 CUSTOMERID                             NOT NULL   NUMBER(38)
 NAME                                   NOT NULL   VARCHAR2(25)
 STREET                                            VARCHAR2(30)
 CITY                                              VARCHAR2(35)
 STATE                                             VARCHAR2(2)
 ZIP                                               VARCHAR2(5)
 AREA_CODE                                         VARCHAR2(3)
 PHONE_NUMBER                                      VARCHAR2(8)

SQL> desc artist
 Name                                   Null?      Type
 -------------------------------------- ---------- ----------------
 ARTISTID                               NOT NULL   NUMBER(38)
 NAME                                   NOT NULL   VARCHAR2(25)
 NATIONALITY                                       VARCHAR2(30)
 BIRTHDATE                                         DATE
 DECEASEDDATE                                      DATE

SQL> desc customer_artist_int;
 Name                                   Null?      Type
 -------------------------------------- ---------- ----------------
 ARTISTID                               NOT NULL   NUMBER(38)
 CUSTOMERID                             NOT NULL   NUMBER(38)
```

Create Sequence CustID Increment by 1 start with 1000;

Two methods of sequences are important to us. The method NextVal provides the next value in a sequence and the method CurrVal provides the current value in a sequence. Thus, CustID.NextVal provides the next value of the CustID sequence. You can insert a row into CUSTOMER using a sequence as follows:

```
INSERT INTO CUSTOMER
    (CustomerID, Name, Area_Code, Phone_Number)
    VALUES
    (CustID.NextVal, 'Mary Jones', '350', '555-1234');
```

➤ FIGURE 12-9

Commonly Used Oracle Data Types

Data Type	Description
BLOB	Binary large object. Up to 4 gigabytes in length.
CHAR (n)	Fixed length character field of length n. Maximum 2,000 characters.
DATE	7-byte field containing both date and time.
INT	Whole number of length 38.
NUMBER(n,d)	Numeric field of length n, d places to the right of the decimal
VARCHAR(n) or VARCHAR2(n)	Variable length character field up to n characters long. Maximum value of n = 4,000

A CUSTOMER row will be created with the next value in the sequence as the value for CustomerID. Once this statement has been executed, you can retrieve the row just created with the CurrVal method as follows:

```
SELECT   *
FROM     CUSTOMER
WHERE    CustomerID = CustID.CurrVal
```

Here, CustID.CurrVal returns the current value of the sequence, which is the value just used.

Unfortunately, using sequences does not guarantee valid surrogate key values. For one, any developer can use a defined sequence for any purpose. If a sequence is used for purposes other than the surrogate key, some values will be missing. A second, more serious, problem is that there is nothing in the schema that prevents someone from issuing an insert statement that does not use the sequence. Thus, Oracle will accept

```
INSERT INTO CUSTOMER
   (CustomerID, Name, Area_Code, Phone_Number)
   VALUES
   (350, 'Mary Jones', '350', '555–1234);
```

When this is done, it is possible that duplicate values of a surrogate could occur. In this case, Oracle will disallow the duplicate insertion because CustomerID is defined as a primary key. Still, however, this means code may need to be written to deal with this exception. Finally, it is possible that someone could accidentally use the wrong sequence when inserting into the table. In spite of these possible problems, sequences are the best way to work with surrogate keys in Oracle.

We will use the following sequences in the View Ridge database. Create them now using SQL Plus.

```
Create Sequence CustID Increment by 1 start with 1000;
Create Sequence ArtistID Increment by 1 start with 1;
Create Sequence WorkID Increment by 1 start with 500;
Create Sequence TransID Increment by 1 start with 100;
```

ENTERING DATA We can now use these sequences to add data. Figure 12-10 shows a file of insert statements created in Notepad. Type these in your editor,

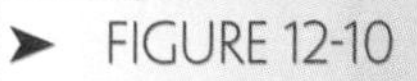
FIGURE 12-10

Inserting Data into the ARTIST and CUSTOMER Tables

```
INSERT INTO ARTIST (ArtistID, Name, Nationality) Values
 (ArtistID.NextVal, 'Tobey', 'US');
INSERT INTO ARTIST (ArtistID, Name, Nationality) Values
 (ArtistID.NextVal, 'Miro', 'Spanish');
INSERT INTO ARTIST (ArtistID, Name, Nationality) Values
 (ArtistID.NextVal, 'Frings', 'US');
INSERT INTO ARTIST (ArtistID, Name, Nationality) Values
 (ArtistID.NextVal, 'Foster', 'English');
INSERT INTO ARTIST (ArtistID, Name, Nationality) Values
 (ArtistID.NextVal, 'van Vronkin', 'US');

INSERT INTO CUSTOMER (CustomerID, Name, Area_Code, Phone_Number) Values
 (CustID.NextVal, 'Jeffrey Janes', '206', '555-1234');
INSERT INTO CUSTOMER (CustomerID, Name, Area_Code, Phone_Number) Values
 (CustID.NextVal, 'David Smith', '206', '555-4434');
INSERT INTO CUSTOMER (CustomerID, Name, Area_Code, Phone_Number) Values
 (CustID.NextVal, 'Tiffany Twilight', '360', '555-1040');
```

place a slash at the end of the file, and save the file using the name *ACIns.sql*. Enter

```
Start ACIns;
```

and the statements in ACIns will be executed. Your data should appear as shown in Figure 12-11.

DROP AND ALTER STATEMENTS You can use the drop statement to remove structures from the database. For example, the statements

```
DROP TABLE MYTABLE;
DROP SEQUENCE MySequence;
```

will drop the table MYTABLE and the sequence MySequence, respectively. Any data in the MYTABLE table will be lost.

You can drop a column with the ALTER statement as follows:

```
ALTER TABLE MYTABLE DROP COLUMN MyColumn;
```

We will show other uses for DROP and ALTER as the discussion proceeds.

Creating Relationships

With Oracle, you create relationships among tables by defining foreign key constraints. For example, the following SQL statements will define the relationships between CUSTOMER and CUSTOMER_ARTIST_INT and between ARTIST and CUSTOMER_ARTIST_INT:

```
ALTER TABLE CUSTOMER_ARTIST_INT ADD CONSTRAINT ArtistIntFK
FOREIGN KEY(ArtistID) REFERENCES ARTIST ON DELETE CASCADE;

ALTER TABLE CUSTOMER_ARTIST_INT ADD CONSTRAINT CustomerIntFK
FOREIGN KEY(CustomerID) REFERENCES CUSTOMER ON DELETE CASCADE;
```

The names of the constraints are ArtistIntFK and CustomerIntFK. These names have no particular significance to Oracle; they can be chosen by the developer. Note only the foreign key column of the child table is specified. Oracle assumes the foreign key will relate to the primary key of the parent table and so the primary key column need not be named. Also, the phrase ON DELETE CASCADE specifies that child rows should be deleted when a parent row is

➤ FIGURE 12-11

ARTIST and CUSTOMER after Insert

```
SQL> SELECT ArtistID, Name, Nationality FROM ARTIST;

  ARTISTID  NAME                          NATIONALITY
----------  ----------------------------  ------------------------------
         2  Miro                          Spanish
         3  Frings                        US
         4  Foster                        English
         5  van Vronkin                   US
         1  Tobey                         US

SQL> SELECT CustomerID, Name, Area_Code, Phone_Number FROM CUSTOMER;

CUSTOMERID  NAME                          ARE  PHONE_NU
----------  ----------------------------  ------------------------------
      1001  David Smith                   206  555-4434
      1002  Tiffany Twilight              360  555-1040
      1000  Jeffrey Janes                 206  555-1234
```

deleted. The term *cascade* is used because the deletion cascades from the parent table to the child table.

Enter these statements into SQL Plus and then enter several intersection table rows. If you then delete a customer or an artist, any intersection table rows for that customer or artist will be deleted as well.

Figure 12-12 shows create statements necessary to create the WORK and TRANSACTION tables. Observe there is no ON DELETE CASCADE clause in the foreign key constraint specifications. Thus, the constraint ArtistFK will prohibit the deletion of ARTIST rows that have child WORK rows. WorkFK and CustomerFK function similarly.

You can also use the ALTER statement to remove a constraint. The statement:

```
ALTER TABLE MYTABLE DROP CONTRAINT MyConstraint;
```

will remove the constraint MyConstraint from the table MYTABLE.

In Figure 12-12, the notation numeric (7, 2) means a number with seven digits, two of which are to the right of the decimal point. Numeric(7), on the other hand, means that an integer number of seven digits is being defined.

Creating Indexes

Indexes are created to enforce uniqueness on columns, to facilitate sorting, and to enable fast retrieval by column values. Columns that are frequently used with equal conditions in WHERE clauses are good candidates for indexes. The equal clause could be either a simple condition in a WHERE clause or it could occur in a join. Both are shown in the following two statements:

```
SELECT *
FROM MYTABLE
WHERE Column1=100;
```

and

```
SELECT *
FROM MYTABLE1, MYTABLE2
WHERE MYTABLE1.Column1=MYTABLE2.Column2;
```

➤ FIGURE 12-12

Creating WORK and TRANSACTION Tables

```
CREATE TABLE        WORK (
        WorkID              int                 PRIMARY KEY,
        Description         varchar(1000)       NULL,
        Title               varchar(25)         NOT NULL,
        Copy                varchar(8)          NOT NULL,
        ArtistID            int                 NOT NULL);

ALTER TABLE WORK ADD CONSTRAINT ArtistFK
FOREIGN KEY (ArtistID) REFERENCES ARTIST;

CREATE TABLE        TRANSACTION (
        TransactionID       int                 PRIMARY KEY,
        DateAcquired        date                NOT NULL,
        AcquisitionPrice    number(7, 2)        NULL,
        PurchaseDate        date                NULL,
        SalesPrice          number(7, 2)        NULL,
        CustomerID          int                 NULL,
        WorkID              int                 NOT NULL);

ALTER TABLE TRANSACTION ADD CONSTRAINT WorkFK
FOREIGN KEY (WorkID) REFERENCES WORK;

ALTER TABLE TRANSACTION ADD CONSTRAINT CustomerFK
FOREIGN KEY (CustomerID) REFERENCES CUSTOMER;
```

If statements like these are frequently executed, then Column1 and Column2 are good candidates for indexes.

The following statement creates an index on the Name column of the CUSTOMER table:

```
CREATE INDEX CustNameIdx ON CUSTOMER(Name);
```

The index will be called CustNameIdx. Again, the name has no particular significance to Oracle. To create a unique index, add the keyword UNIQUE before the keyword INDEX. For example, to ensure that no work is added twice to the WORK table, we can create a unique index on (Title, Copy, ArtistID) as follows:

```
CREATE UNIQUE INDEX WorkUniqueIndex ON WORK(Title, Copy, ArtistID);
```

Changing Table Structure

After a table has been created, its structure can be modified using the ALTER TABLE command. Be careful when you do this, however, because it is possible to lose data.

Adding or dropping a column is straightforward, as shown below:

```
ALTER TABLE MYTABLE ADD C1 NUMBER(4);
ALTER TABLE MYTABLE DROP COLUMN C1;
```

The first statement will add a new column named C1 and give it a numeric data type with a length of four characters. The second statement will drop the column just added. Note that the key word *column* is omitted when adding a new column.

When you issue these commands, you will receive the brief message "Table altered" in response. To ensure the desired changes were made, use the DESCRIBE command to see the table's structure.

RESTRICTIONS ON TABLE COLUMN MODIFICATIONS You can drop a column at any time. All data will be lost when doing so, however. You can add a column at any time as long as it is a NULL column.

To add a NOT NULL column, first add it to the table as NULL, then fill the new column in every row with data, and then change its structure to NOT NULL using the modify clause. For example, suppose you have just added column C1 to table T1. After you have filled C1 in every row of T1, you can issue the following:

```
ALTER TABLE T1 MODIFY C1 NOT NULL;
```

Values will now be required for column C1.

When modifying a column, you can increase the number of characters in character columns or the number of digits in numeric columns. You can also increase or decrease the number of decimal places at any time. If the values of all rows of a given column are NULL, you can decrease the width of character and numeric data and you can change the column's data type.

Check Constraints

Check constraints are used to constrain the values that columns may have. Check constraints must be written so that they evaluate to either true or false and so that they can be evaluated using only constants and values from the current row of the table in which they are defined. Check constraints cannot contain subqueries nor sequences, nor can they refer to the function SysDate.

Check constraints can be created when the table is created or they can be added later. An example of the former is

```
CREATE TABLE MYTABLE(
    Name VARCHAR(50)    NOT NULL,
    State CHAR(2)       NULL CHECK (State IN ('CA', 'CO', 'NY')));
```

With this definition, the only values allowed for State are 'CA,' 'CO,' and 'NY.'

An example of a CHECK constraint that is added with ALTER is

```
ALTER TABLE TRANSACTION ADD CONSTRAINT DateCheck CHECK
(DateAcquired <= PurchaseDate);
```

For this to work, both DateAcquired and PurchaseDate must reside in the TRANSACTION table.

Constraints can be dropped with the ALTER TABLE statement as well:

```
ALTER TABLE TRANSACTION DROP CONSTRAINT DateCheck;
```

Using Alter Table and Check Constraints

We can use what we just discussed to modify the definition of the ARTIST table. In Figure 12-7 we set the data type of the columns BirthDate and DeceasedDate to Date. Suppose the users of this database do not care about storing a particular date for these columns. Instead, they just want to record the year of the artist's birth and death. Suppose also that none of the gallery's artists was born or died before 1400 or after 2100.

Since we have not yet stored any data in these columns, they are both NULL, and we can change their data types without dropping them. To do that, submit the following commands via SQL Plus:

```
ALTER TABLE ARTIST MODIFY Birthdate Number(4);
ALTER TABLE ARTIST MODIFY DeceasedDate Number(4);
```

Now, the following two statements will set the limits on Birthdate and DeceasedDate values:

```
ALTER TABLE ARTIST ADD CONSTRAINT BDLimit CHECK (Birthdate
    BETWEEN 1400 AND 2100);
ALTER TABLE ARTIST ADD CONSTRAINT DDLimit CHECK (DeceasedDate
    BETWEEN 1400 AND 2100);
```

Consider the following two update commands:

```
UPDATE ARTIST SET BirthDate = 1870 WHERE Name = 'Miro';
UPDATE ARTIST SET BirthDate = 1270 WHERE Name = 'Tobey';
```

The first update will process normally, but the second one will cause the check violation and will not be processed. Try them to see the results.

Views

As mentioned in Chapter 10, views in SQL are different from what we have called database views. A view in SQL is the result of a SQL expression that uses selection, projection, and join. For example, a view can join ARTIST, WORK, and TRANS rows, select certain columns from those rows, and apply WHERE conditions to the resulting relation.

FIGURE 12-13

Creating a View

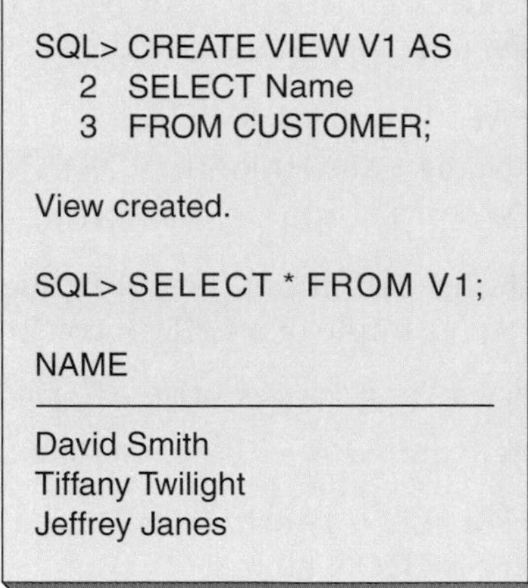

```
SQL> CREATE VIEW V1 AS
  2  SELECT Name
  3  FROM CUSTOMER;

View created.

SQL> SELECT * FROM V1;

NAME
--------------------------------
David Smith
Tiffany Twilight
Jeffrey Janes
```

The important limitation of SQL views is that they can contain no more than one multi-value path. It is not possible, for example, to represent a view that has CUSTOMER, TRANS, and CUSTOMER_ARTIST_INT data with a SQL view (as is done in Figure 10-4). We will return to this topic when we describe XML in Chapter 14.

In spite of this limitation, SQL views are useful. One use is to provide more comprehensive security. To do this, define a view that has all of the columns of a table, but give the users of the new view different security permissions than the users of the table or users of other views on the table. Another purpose is to define a view of a table that omits certain columns or certain rows. For example, you can define a view on an EMPLOYEE table that omits the Salary column and that omits all of the data for executives. Yet a third purpose of a view is to join tables so that users of the view need not perform the join; they can simply query the view instead. This use of a view also hides table structure from users, which is sometimes desired.

CREATING VIEWS Figure 12-13 shows the creation and use of a simple view. View V1 is defined as having only the Name column from the CUSTOMER table. When the user selects all columns from the view (with *), only the Name column is presented. None of the other columns in CUSTOMER is shown because they are not present in the view.

A more complicated view is shown in Figure 12-14(a). This view joins three tables together and then applies a condition on AcqusitionPrice and CustomerID. Views like this are sometimes called **join views** because they are based on joins. Note the Select statement in Figure 12-14(b) contains neither the join nor the where clause. They were applied behind the scenes when the view was constructed.

In general it is possible to update data from a view that is based on a single table. If this is not desired, you can create a read-only view by adding the expression *with read only* to the end of the view definition. Thus,

FIGURE 12-14

Example of a Join View: (a) Creating the View

```
CREATE VIEW ExpensiveArt AS

        SELECT  Name, Copy, Title
        FROM    ARTIST, WORK, TRANSACTION
        WHERE   ARTIST.ArtistID     =   WORK.ArtistID AND
                WORK.WorkID         =   TRANSACTION.WorkID AND
                AcquisitionPrice    >   10000 AND
                CustomerID IS NULL;
```

(continued)

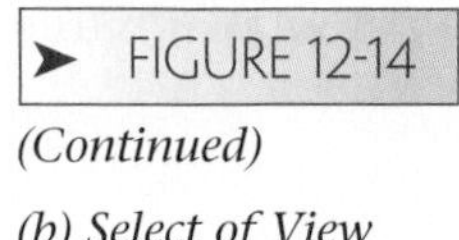
(Continued)

(b) Select of View

```
SQL> select * from expensiveart;

NAME                        COPY     TITLE
--------------------------- -------- -------------------------
Tobey                       4/40     Mystic Fabric
Tobey                       4/40     Mystic Fabric
Miro                        79/122   Mi Vida
```

```
CREATE VIEW V1 AS
    SELECT *
    FROM ARTIST
    WITH READ ONLY;
```

will create a read-only view.

The SQL UPDATE statement can sometimes be used for updating values via a view, but only under special circumstances and then only if the change involves just one table.

In general, to make updates via a view, you cannot use the UPDATE command. Instead, you must write a special type of trigger called an INSTEAD OF trigger. We will consider such triggers in the next section.

APPLICATION LOGIC

There are many ways of processing an Oracle database from an application. One is to create application code in C++, C#, Java, Visual Basic, or some other programming language and make calls to Oracle programs. As mentioned in Chapter 8, this can be done using either native Oracle libraries or via the ODBC or JDBC industry standards. We will illustrate examples of the latter in Chapters 15 and 16.

Another way of processing an Oracle database is to write procedures in PL/SQL. These procedures can be saved as files and executed via the START command in SQL Plus; they can be stored in the database as stored procedures; and they can be stored as triggers to be fired when specified database events occur. Consider each in turn.

PROCESSING FILES OF PL/SQL

If the database user has access to SQL Plus, he or she can save PL/SQL statement in files and process them directly using START. A file containing the statement

```
SELECT    *
FROM      ExpensiveArt;
/
```

could be stored under the name ToSell.sql. The user would then open SQL Plus, and type the command

```
Start ToSell;
```

Data from the ExpensiveArt view would then be displayed.

Realistically, however, most business users do not have access to SQL Plus and they would probably not like it if they did. This style of processing is used, however, by database administrators and database developers to automate routine database administration tasks.

Stored Procedures

A stored procedure is a PL/SQL or Java program that is stored within the database. Stored procedures are programs; they can have parameters, they can invoke other procedures and functions, they can return values, and they can raise exceptions. Stored procedures can be invoked remotely. You will see examples of invoking stored procedures using Internet technology in Chapters 15 and 16. Here we will consider two stored procedure examples.

Customer_Insert STORED PROCEDURE Suppose the View Ridge Gallery wants to be able to add a new customer to its database and record the customer's artist interests. In particular, the gallery wants to record the customer's name and phone data, and then to connect the customer to all artists of a specified nationality.

Figure 12-15 shows a stored procedure that will accomplish this task. The procedure, named Customer_Insert, receives four parameters: newname, newareacode, newphone, and artistnationality. The key word *IN* signifies that these are input parameters. *OUT* would signify an output parameter and *IN OUT* signifies a parameter used for both input and output. Notice the data type is given for the parameter, but not its length. Oracle will determine the length from the context.

Variables are declared after the keyword *AS*. A **cursor variable** named *artistcursor* is defined on the SELECT statement shown. This cursor will be used to process all of the rows for an artist of the input nationality.

The first section of the procedure checks to determine if the customer data already exists. If so, nothing is done and an output message is printed using the Oracle package DBMS_OUTPUT.

Before continuing with this procedure, note that this message can be seen only if the procedure is invoked from SQL Plus. If the procedure were invoked differently, say, over the Internet using a browser, then this message would not be seen. The developer would need to use an output parameter or raise an error exception. These topics are beyond the scope of the present discussion, however. Although not shown, the syntax for printing a string and a variable value is: DBMS_OUTPUT.PUT_LINE ('string' // variable).

Additionally, to see such messages, execute the following:

```
Set serveroutput on;
```

If you are not receiving output from your procedures when using SQL Plus, it is likely you have not executed this statement.

The remainder of the procedure in Figure 12-15 inserts the new customer data and then loops through all artists of the given nationality. Observe the use of the special PL/SQL construct *FOR artist IN artistcursor.* This construct does several tasks. It opens the cursor and fetches the first row. Then it iterates through all rows in the cursor and when there are no more, transfers control to the next statement after the FOR. Also notice that the ArtistID value of the current cursor row can be accessed with the syntax artist.ArtistID, where artist is the name of the variable in the FOR statement and *not* the name of the cursor.

Once you have written this procedure, you must first compile and store it in the database. Code the procedure using your editor and save it under a name, say, SP_CI.sql. If you include a slash as your last line, then the procedure will be compiled and stored when you enter the command:

```
Start SP_CI
```

FIGURE 12-15

The Procedure Customer_Insert

```
CREATE OR REPLACE PROCEDURE Customer_Insert
        (
        newname             IN      char,
        newareacode         IN      char,
        newphone            IN      char,
        artistnationality   IN      char
        )

AS

        rowcount integer(4);

        CURSOR          artistcursor IS
                        SELECT ArtistID
                        FROM ARTIST
                        WHERE Nationality=artistnationality;

BEGIN

        SELECT          Count (*) INTO rowcount
        FROM            CUSTOMER
        WHERE           Name=newname AND Area_Code=newareacode AND
                        Phone_Number = newphone;

        IF rowcount > 0 THEN
            BEGIN
                  DBMS_OUTPUT.PUT_LINE ('Customer Already Exists -- No Action Taken');
                  RETURN;
            END;
        END IF;

        INSERT INTO CUSTOMER
               (CustomerID, Name, Area_Code, Phone_Number)
               VALUES
               (CustID.NextVal, newname, newareacode, newphone);

        FOR artist IN artistcursor
               LOOP
                        INSERT INTO CUSTOMER_ARTIST_INT
                        (CustomerID, ArtistID)
                        VALUES
                        (CustID.CurrVal, artist.ArtistID);
               END LOOP;

        DBMS_OUTPUT.PUT_LINE ('New Customer Successfully Added') ;
END;
/
```

If you have made a mistake, you may have compile errors. Unfortunately, SQL Plus will not automatically show them to you. Instead, it will give you the message "Warning: Procedure created with compilation errors." To see the errors, enter

```
Show errors;
```

If there are no syntax errors, you will receive the message "Procedure created." Now you can invoke the procedure with the Execute or Exec command as follows:

```
Exec Customer_Insert ('Selma Warning', '206', '555-0099', 'US');
```

If you have execution time errors, the line numbers reported differ from the line numbers you see in your text editor. You can adjust these line numbers to conform to yours, but the process is too complicated to describe here. For the simple procedures we will do, just work around the issue. Do not assume the line numbers match, however.

NewCustomerWithTransaction STORED PROCEDURE Chapter 10 described SQL statements necessary for creating, reading, modifying, and deleting the database view shown in Figure 10-4. An Oracle stored procedure for implementing the create view logic described in Chapter 10 is shown in Figure 12-16.

The logic of this procedure, named NewCustomerWithTransaction, is as follows. First create new customer data and then search for TRANSACTION rows for the purchased work that have null values for CustomerID. That search involves the join of the ARTIST, WORK, and TRANSACTION tables because the Name of the artist is stored in ARTIST, and Title and Copy of the work are stored in WORK. If one, and only one, such row is found, update CustomerID, SalesPrice, and PurchaseDate in that row. Then, insert a row in the intersection table to record the customer's interest in this artist. Otherwise, make no changes to the database.

NewCustomerWithTransaction accepts parameters having customer and purchase data as shown. Next, several variables and a cursor are declared. The cursor defines the join of ARTIST, WORK, and TRANSACTION tables. It selects TransactionID and ARTIST.ArtistID of rows that match the input artist and work data and that have a null value for CustomerID.

The procedure first checks if the input customer data already exists in the database. If not, it inserts the new customer data. In PL/SQL, there is no BEGIN TRANSACTION[1] statement; the first database action automatically starts a transaction. Here, the customer data insert will start a new transaction.

Note, also, that comments are enclosed between /* and */. Such comments can extend over multiple lines, and if you begin a comment with /* and fail to terminate it with */, then your entire program will be treated as a comment.

After the customer data is inserted, the TransCursor is processed. The variable rowcount is used to count the rows, the value of TransactionID is stored in *tid,* and the value of ArtistID is stored in *aid*. Observe that the assignment operator in Oracle is :=. Thus, tid := trans. TransactionID means to assign the value of trans.TransactionID to the variable tid.

According to this logic, if only one qualifying row is found, then *tid* and *aid* will have the values we need to continue. If zero or more than one qualifying rows are found, then the transaction will be aborted, but neither *tid* nor *aid* will be used.

We could use Count(*) to count the qualifying rows, and then, if Count(*) = 1, execute another SQL statement to obtain the values of *tid* and *aid* we need. The logic in Figure 12-16 saves this second SQL statement.

If RowCount is greater than 1 or equal to zero, then an error message is generated and the transaction is rolled back to remove the prior insert to CUSTOMER. If RowCount equals 1, then the appropriate TRANSACTION row is updated. Note the use of the function SysDate to store the current date. Finally, an intersection row is inserted for this customer and the artist of the purchased work (*aid*).

This stored procedure can be invoked with a command like

Exec NewCustomerWithTransaction ('Susan Wu', '206', '555-1000', 'Miro', 'Mi Vida', '79/122', '65000');

---

[1]Watch out here! We are using the word *TRANSACTION* in two ways in the section: as the name of one of the View Ridge tables and as the name of a group of statements to be executed atomically. The context will make the usage clear, but be aware of the possible confusion.

➤ FIGURE 12-16

The Procedure NewCustomerWith Transaction

```
CREATE OR REPLACE PROCEDURE NewCustomerWithTransaction
        (
        newname IN char,
        newareacode IN char,
        newphone IN char,
        artistname IN char,
        worktitle IN char,
        workcopy IN char,
        price IN number
        )
AS

        rowcount integer (2) ;
        tid      int;
        aid      int;

              CURSOR    transcursor IS
                SELECT  TransactionID, ARTIST.ArtistID
                FROM    ARTIST, WORK, TRANSACTION
                WHERE   Name=artistname AND Title=worktitle AND Copy=workcopy AND
                        TRANSACTION.CustomerID IS NULL AND
                        ARTIST.ArtistID = WORK.ArtistID AND
                        WORK.WorkID = TRANSACTION.WorkID;

BEGIN

        /* Does Customer Already exist? */

        SELECT  Count (*) INTO rowcount
        FROM    CUSTOMER
        WHERE   Name=newname AND Area_Code=newareacode AND Phone_Number = newphone;

        IF rowcount > 0 THEN
             BEGIN
                   DBMS_OUTPUT.PUT_LINE ('Customer Already Exists -- No Action Taken');
                   RETURN;
             END;
        END IF;

        /* Customer not exist, add new customer data */
        INSERT INTO CUSTOMER
                (CustomerID, Name, Area_Code, Phone_Number)
                VALUES
                (CustID.NextVal, newname, newareacode, newphone);

        /* Look for one and only one available TRANSACTION row. */
        rowcount := 0;
        FOR trans In transcursor
                LOOP
                        tid := trans.TransactionID;
                        aid := trans.ArtistID;
                        rowcount := rowcount + 1;
                END LOOP;

        IF rowcount > 1 Then
            BEGIN
                /* Too many available rows -- undo with message and return */
                ROLLBACK;
                DBMS_OUTPUT.PUT_LINE ('Invalid Artist/Work/Transaction data -- No Action Taken');
                RETURN;
            END;
        END IF;
```

(continued)

➤ FIGURE 12-16

(Continued)

```
        IF rowcount = 0 Then
            BEGIN
                /* No available row exists -- undo with message and return */
                ROLLBACK;
                DBMS_OUTPUT.PUT_LINE ('No available transaction row -- No Action Taken');
                RETURN;
            END;
        END IF;

        /* Exactly one exists -- use it with tid obtained from transcursor above */
        DBMS_OUTPUT.PUT_LINE (tid);
        UPDATE TRANSACTION
                SET       CustomerID = CustID.Currval, Salesprice = price, PurchaseDate = SysDate
                WHERE  TransactionID = tid;
        DBMS_OUTPUT.PUT_LINE ('Customer created and transaction data updated') ;

        /* Now create interest in this artist for this customer */
        /* Use aid from transcursor above and CurrVal of sequence*/

        INSERT INTO CUSTOMER_ARTIST_INT (ArtistID, CustomerID)
                        VALUES (aid, CustID.CurrVal);
END;
/
```

The following two SQL statements display the data after the update:

```
SELECT   CUSTOMER.Name, Copy, Title, ARTIST.Name
FROM     CUSTOMER, TRANSACTION, WORK, ARTIST
WHERE    CUSTOMER.CustomerID = TRANSACTION.CustomerID AND
         TRANSACTION.WorkID = WORK.WorkID AND
         WORK.ArtistID = ARTIST.ArtistID;
```

and

```
SELECT   CUSTOMER.Name, ARTIST.Name
FROM     CUSTOMER, CUSTOMER_ARTIST_INT, ARTIST
WHERE    CUSTOMER.CustomerID = CUSTOMER_ARTIST_INT.CustomerID
         AND
         ARTIST.ArtistID = CUSTOMER_ARTIST_INT.ArtistID;
```

Observe that two SQL statements are required because this view is a database view having two multi-valued paths. It cannot be represented with a single SQL statement (or SQL view).

The results of these queries are shown in Figure 12-17. Susan Wu's data is included correctly in both the TRANSACTION and CUSTOMER_ARTIST_INT data.

Triggers

Oracle triggers are PL/SQL or Java procedures that are invoked when specified database activity occurs. Oracle supports several trigger types; some are fired on SQL commands that create new database structures like tables, some are fired once at the table level when a change is made to rows in a table, and others are fired once for each row that is changed in a table. The latter are called **row triggers** and we will consider them here. Oracle supports BEFORE, AFTER, and INSTEAD OF row triggers. Consider an example of each.

Data after Customer Insert

```
SQL> SELECT CUSTOMER.Name, Copy, Title, ARTIST.Name
  2  FROM CUSTOMER, TRANSACTION, WORK, ARTIST
  3  WHERE CUSTOMER.CustomerID = TRANSACTION.CustomerID AND
  4      TRANSACTION.WorkID = WORK.WorkID AND
  5      WORK.ArtistID = ARTIST.ArtistID;

NAME                 COPY      TITLE           NAME
-------------------- --------- --------------- ----------
Tiffany Twilight     4/40      Mystic Fabric   Tobey
David Smith          4/40      Mystic Fabric   Tobey
Jeffrey Janes        5/40      Mystic Fabric   Tobey
Tiffany Twilight     79/122    Mi Vida         Miro
Susan Wu             79/122    Mi Vida         Miro

SQL> SELECT CUSTOMER.Name, ARTIST.Name
  2  FROM CUSTOMER, CUSTOMER_ARTIST_INT, ARTIST
  3  WHERE CUSTOMER.CustomerID = CUSTOMER_ARTIST_INT.CustomerID
  4      AND
  5      ARTIST.ArtistID = CUSTOMER_ARTIST_INT.ArtistID;

NAME                 NAME
-------------------- ------------------------------
Susan Wu             Miro
Fred Smathers        Frings
Selma Warning        Frings
Fred Smathers        van Vronkin
Selma Warning        van Vronkin
Fred Smathers        Tobey
Selma Warning        Tobey

7 rows selected.
```

BEFORE TRIGGER EXAMPLE Figure 12-18 shows a BEFORE TRIGGER that is used to set a value in a row prior to update. To use this trigger, first create a new column in TRANSACTION called AskingPrice. You can do that with the command

ALTER TABLE TRANSACTION ADD AskingPrice Number(7, 2);

In Figure 12-18, the New_Price trigger is defined with the phrase "Before Insert or Update of AcquisitionPrice ON TRANSACTION." That phrase, which is correct, contains an ambiguity. It means "Before (any) Insert ON TRANSACTION or BEFORE an update of AcquisitionPrice IN TRANSACTION," fire the trigger.

➤ FIGURE 12-18

BEFORE TRIGGER New_Price

```
CREATE OR REPLACE TRIGGER New_Price

        BEFORE INSERT OR UPDATE of AcquisitionPrice ON TRANSACTION

        FOR EACH ROW

                /* set AskingPrice before insert or update */

        BEGIN

                :new.AskingPrice := :new.AcquisitionPrice * 2;

        END;
```

Thus, any insert will fire the trigger and an update of AcquisitionPrice will fire the trigger. Updates of other columns will not fire the trigger.

The phrase "FOR EACH ROW" identifies this as a row trigger. The logic is simple: Compute the new value of AskingPrice as two times the new value of AcquisitionPrice.

The prefix *:new* is available only to triggers. It references the new value for a column of the insert or update command. Thus, :new.AcquisitionPrice refers to the new value of AcquisitionPrice (as supplied by the user). For updates and deletes, there is also a prefix *:old* that references the value of columns prior to the update or delete command.

To create this trigger, type it using your editor and save it in a file, say, Trig1.sql. Then, in SQL Plus, type *start Trig1* and the trigger will be compiled. If there are no compilation errors, the trigger will be stored in the database and will be active. Update the AcquisitionPrice column and then select the rows you've updated. AskingPrice will have been set by the trigger.

If you have compilation errors, you can see them by entering *Show Errors* as was done previously with stored procedures.

AFTER TRIGGER EXAMPLE Figure 12-19 shows an AFTER TRIGGER example. The logic of this trigger is the following: View Ridge defines a work for sale as any work having a TRANSACTION row with a null value of CustomerID. The purpose of this trigger is to ensure that such a TRANSACTION row exists whenever a work is added to the database. This trigger, which is fired whenever a WORK row is

➤ FIGURE 12-19

AFTER TRIGGER On_Work_Insert

```
CREATE OR REPLACE TRIGGER On_WORK_Insert
      AFTER INSERT ON WORK

FOR EACH ROW

DECLARE
          rowcount        integer(2) ;

BEGIN

          /* Count Available Rows */

          SELECT     Count (*) INTO rowcount
          FROM       TRANSACTION
          WHERE      CustomerID IS NULL AND WorkID=:new.WorkID;

          IF rowcount > 0 Then /* Row exists do nothing */

                DBMS_OUTPUT.PUT_LINE ('Suitable transaction row exists; nothing done.');
                RETURN;

          ELSE /* Need to add new row */

                INSERT INTO TRANSACTION (TransactionID, DateAcquired, WorkID)
                VALUES (TransID.NextVal, SysDate, :new.WorkID);

          END IF;

END;
/
```

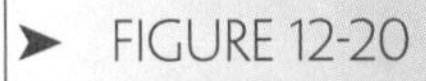

FIGURE 12-20

CustomerPurchases View: (a) View Definition and (b) View Data

```
CREATE VIEW CustomerPurchases AS

    SELECT    CUSTOMER.Name CustName, Copy, Title, ARTIST.Name ArtistName
    FROM      CUSTOMER, TRANSACTION, WORK, ARTIST
    WHERE     CUSTOMER.CustomerID = TRANSACTION.CustomerID AND
              TRANSACTION.WorkID = WORK.WorkID AND
              WORK.ArtistID = ARTIST.ArtistID;
```

(a)

```
SQL> SELECT * FROM CustomerPurchases;

CUSTNAME              COPY        TITLE              ARTISTNAME
____________________  __________  _________________  __________

Tiffany Twilight      4/40        Mystic Fabric      Tobey
David Smith           4/40        Mystic Fabric      Tobey
Jeffrey Janes         5/40        Mystic Fabric      Tobey
Tiffany Twilight      79/122      Mi Vida            Miro
Susan Wu              79/122      Mi Vida            Miro
```

(b)

created, checks the TRANSACTION table and does nothing if it finds a suitable TRANSACTION row. Otherwise, it creates a new row in the TRANSACTION table.

The logic is straightforward. A count is made of suitable rows and if the count is greater than zero, nothing is done. If the count is zero, a new TRANSACTION row is created with appropriate data. Notice how the *:new* prefix is used in the VALUES portion of the INSERT statement.

INSTEAD OF TRIGGER EXAMPLE INSTEAD OF TRIGGERS are used to update views. Consider the view defined in Figure 12-20(a). This view joins four tables together and, as a join view, is not updatable unless an INSTEAD OF TRIGGER is defined for it.

Notice the SELECT phrase in this view definition. It specifies synonyms for CUSTOMER.Name (synonym CustName) and ARTIST.Name (synonym ArtistName). If this were not done, this view would have two columns named Name. This is not allowed. Figure 12-20(b) shows how the synonyms are used when this view is processed. Note the CUSTNAME and ARTISTNAME column headings.

Examine the data in Figure 12-20(b); consider what should happen when the user tries to update the Title column. The title "Mystic Fabric" appears in three rows, yet the underlying WORK table only has two rows with this value. When the user updates a Title, what is Oracle to do? Should it update the WORK rows that underlie this view? Should it create new rows in WORK and connect them to the rows in this view? Or something else? It is not possible to write generalized code in the DBMS to handle correctly every possibility.

INSTEAD OF TRIGGERS allow the developer to specify the application-unique actions to take when an attempt is made to update a view. Figure 12-21 shows one such trigger that processes updates on the Title column of the CustomerPurchases view. Because INSTEAD OF TRIGGERS cannot have the UPDATE OF phrase like we used in the BEFORE TRIGGER example, we have to write code to determine if the Title column has been changed.

If the user is updating Title, then an appropriate update is made to the WORK table. Notice that the trigger fires on an update of the view CustomerPurchases,

➤ FIGURE 12-21

INSTEAD OF TRIGGER Title_Update

```
CREATE OR REPLACE TRIGGER Title_Update
        INSTEAD OF UPDATE ON CustomerPurchases

        FOR EACH ROW

        BEGIN
                /* Do nothing unless update is on title column */


                IF :new.Title = :old.Title THEN
                     RETURN;
                END IF;


                UPDATE      WORK
                SET         Title = :new.Title
                WHERE       Title = :old.Title;

        END;
```

but the update is made on WORK, one of this view's underlying tables. This action is exactly what such triggers are designed to do.

This trigger might generate surprising results. If the user enters

UPDATE CustomerPurchases SET Title='aa', Copy='1/3' WHERE Title='bb';

an update will be made to the Title column but nothing will be done to the Copy column. It would be better practice to send a warning message to this effect back to the user.

EXCEPTION HANDLING This discussion has omitted a discussion of PL/SQL exception handling. This is unfortunate because exception handling is both important and useful. There's just too much to do. If you program in PL/SQL in the future, however, be sure to learn about this important topic. It can be used in all types of PL/SQL programming, but it is especially useful in BEFORE and INSTEAD OF TRIGGERS for canceling pending updates. Exceptions are necessary because, in Oracle, transactions cannot be rolled back in triggers. Exceptions can be used instead to generate error and warning messages. They also keep Oracle better informed about what the trigger has done.

For example, the trigger in Figure 12-21 has an odd characteristic. If you enter

UPDATE CustomerPurchases SET Copy='5/5' WHERE Title='Mystic Fabric;

the trigger will update no rows. Oracle will report, however, that all of the rows in the view having a Title equal to "Mystic Fabric" were updated. That is because all of those rows were passed to the trigger and Oracle doesn't know which caused an update and which did not. If you write code in this trigger to fire an exception event, however, Oracle would know that the row was not updated and would report a correct count of updated rows.

➤ DATA DICTIONARY

Oracle maintains an extensive data dictionary of metadata. This dictionary describes the structures of tables, sequences, views, indexes, constraints, columns, stored procedures and much more. It also contains the source code of procedures, functions, and triggers. And it contains much more.

The dictionary contains metadata about itself in the table DICT. You can query this table to learn more about the contents of the data dictionary, but be

➤ FIGURE 12-22

Some Useful Tables in the Oracle Data Dictionary

Table Name	Contents
DICT	Data dictionary metadata
USER_CATALOG	List of tables, views, sequences, and other structures owned by the user
USER_TABLES	User table structures
USER_TAB_COLUMNS	A child of USER_TABLES. Has data about table columns. Synonym is COLS.
USER_VIEWS	User views
USER_CONTRAINTS	User constraints
USER_CONS_COLUMNS	A child of USER_CONTRAINTS. Has columns in constraints
USER_TRIGGERS	Has trigger metadata. Query Trigger_Name, Trigger_Type, and Trigger_Event. Warning: Trigger_Body does not provide a useful listing.
USER_SOURCE	To obtain the text of procedure MY TRIGGER, SELECT Text FROM USER_SOURCE WHERE Name='MYTRIGGER' AND Type='PROCEDURE'

warned that it is a big table. For example, over 800 rows will be returned if you query for the names of all tables in the data dictionary.

Suppose you want to know what tables the data dictionary contains about user or system tables. The following query obtains that result:

```
SELECT    Table_Name, Comments
FROM      DICT
WHERE     Table_Name LIKE ('%TABLES%');
```

Twenty-five or so rows will be returned. One of those tables is named USER_TABLES. To display the columns of that table, enter

```
DESC      USER_TABLES;
```

You can use this strategy of query and describe to obtain the dictionary's metadata for objects and structures you want. Figure 12-22 lists many of the views and their purposes. The tables USER_SOURCE and USER_TRIGGERS are useful when you want to know what source code is currently stored in the database for procedures and triggers.

By now you should know enough SQL to navigate your way around the dictionary. Be aware that Oracle stores all names in uppercase. If you're looking for a trigger named On_Customer_Insert, search for ON_CUSTOMER_INSERT.

➤ CONCURRENCY CONTROL

Oracle supports three different transaction isolation levels and, in addition, allows applications to place locks explicitly. Explicit locking is not recommended, however, because such locking can interfere with Oracle's default locking behavior and also because it increases the likelihood of transaction deadlock.

Before discussing transaction isolation levels, we need to summarize how Oracle processes database changes. Oracle maintains a **System Change Number (SCN),** which is a database-wide value that is incremented by Oracle whenever database changes are made. When a row is changed, the current value of SCN is stored along with the row. At the same time, the before image of the row is placed in a **rollback segment,** which is a buffer maintained by Oracle for the purpose of rolling back and logging transactions. The before image includes the SCN that was in the row prior to the change. After completing the update, Oracle increments the SCN.

When an application issues a SQL statement, say,

```
UPDATE   MYTABLE
SET      MyColumn1='NewValue'
WHERE    MyColumn2='Something';
```

The value of SCN that was current at the time the statement started is recorded. Call this value the Statement SCN. While processing the query, in this case while looking for rows with MyColumn2 = 'Something,' Oracle will select only rows that have committed changes with an SCN value less than or equal to the Statement SCN. When it finds a row with a committed change and SCN value greater than the Statement SCN, it looks in the rollback segment to find an earlier version of the row. It will search the rollback segments until it finds a version of the row with a committed change having an SCN less than the Statement SCN.

In this way, SQL statements always read a consistent set of values—those that were committed at or before the time the statement was started. As you will see, this strategy is sometimes extended to apply to transactions. In that case, all of the statements in a transaction read rows having an SCN value less than the SCN that was current when the transaction started.

Observe that Oracle only reads committed changes. Hence, dirty reads are not possible.

Oracle supports Read Committed, Serializable, and Read Only transaction isolation levels. The first two are defined in the 1992 ANSI standard; Read Only is unique to Oracle. Figure 12-23 summarizes these isolation levels.

➤ FIGURE 12-23

Summary of Oracle Concurrency Control Facilities

Read Committed Transaction Isolation	The default Oracle isolation level. Dirty reads are not possible, but repeated reads may yield different data. Phantoms are possible. Each statement reads consistent data. When blocked for updates, statements are rolled back and restarted when necessary. Deadlock is detected and one of the blocking statements is rolled back.
Serializable Transaction Isolation	Dirty reads are not possible, repeated reads yield the same results, and phantoms are not possible. All statements in the transaction read consistent data. "Cannot serialize" error occurs when a transaction attempts to update or delete a row with a committed data change that occurred after the transaction started. Also occurs when blocking transactions or statements commit their changes or when the transaction is rolled back due to deadlock. Application programs need to be written to handle the "Cannot serialize" exception.
Read Only Transaction Isolation	All statements read consistent data. No inserts, updates, or deletions are possible.
Explicit Locks	Not recommended.

Read Committed Transaction Isolation Level

Recall from Chapter 11 that with Read Committed isolation, dirty reads are not allowed, but reads may not be repeatable, and phantoms are possible. Read Committed is Oracle's default transaction isolation level because Oracle never reads uncommitted data changes.

With Read Committed isolation, each statement is consistent, but two different statements in the same transaction may read inconsistent data. This is the same as statement level consistency as defined in the last chapter. If transaction level consistency is required, then Serializable isolation must be used. Do not confuse statement consistency with the lost update problem, however. Oracle prohibits lost updates because it never reads dirty data.

Because of the way that it uses the SCN, Oracle never needs to place read locks. When a row is to be changed or deleted, however, Oracle will place an exclusive lock on the row before making the change or deletion. If another transaction has an exclusive lock on the row, the statement will wait. If the blocking transaction rolls back, the change or deletion proceeds.

If the blocking transaction commits, then the new SCN value is given to the statement and the statement (not the transaction) rolls back and starts over. When a statement is rolled back, changes already made by the statement are removed using the rollback segments.

Because exclusive locks are used, deadlock can occur. When that happens, Oracle detects the deadlock using a wait-for graph and rolls back one of the conflicting statements.

Serializable Transaction Isolation Level

As you learned in Chapter 11, with serializable transaction isolation, dirty reads are not possible, reads are always repeatable, and phantoms cannot occur. Oracle supports serializable transaction isolation, but for it to work, the application program must play a role.

Use the Set command to change the transaction isolation level within a transaction. The following statement will establish serializable isolation for the duration of the transaction:

```
SET TRANSACTION ISOLATION LEVEL SERIALIZABLE;
```

To change the isolation level for all transactions in a session, use the ALTER command:

```
ALTER SESSIONS SET ISOLATION_LEVEL SERIALIZABLE;
```

When the isolation level is serializable, Oracle saves the SCN at the time the transaction started. Call this value the Transaction SCN. As the transaction proceeds, Oracle only reads committed changes that have an SCN value less than or equal to the Transaction SCN. Hence, reads are always repeatable and phantoms are not possible.

As long as the transaction does not attempt to update or delete any row having a committed change with an SCN greater than the Transaction SCN, the transaction will proceed normally. If, however, the transaction does attempt to update or delete such a row, then Oracle will issue a "Cannot serialize" error when the update or delete occurs. At that point, the application program must play a role. It can commit changes made to that point, or roll back the entire transaction, or take some other action. Any program that executes under serializable isolation must include such exception handling code.

Also, when a transaction running under serializable isolation attempts to update or delete a row that has been locked exclusively by a different transaction or statement, the transaction waits. If the blocking transaction or statement later rolls back, then the transaction can continue. If, however, the blocking transaction commits, then Oracle will generate the "Cannot serialize" error and the application will need to process that exception.

Similarly, if a serializable transaction is rolled back due to deadlock, the "Cannot serialize" error will also be generated.

READ ONLY TRANSACTION ISOLATION

With this isolation level, the transaction reads only rows having committed changes with an SCN value less than or equal to the Transaction SCN. If the transaction encounters rows with committed changes having an SCN value greater than the Transaction SCN, Oracle will root around in the rollback segments and reconstruct the row as it was prior to the Transaction SCN. With this level of transaction isolation, no inserting, updating, or deleting is allowed.

ADDITIONAL LOCKING COMMENTS

The application can invoke locks explicitly using the SELECT FOR UPDATE form of the select statement. This is not recommended and you should not use it until you have learned much more about Oracle locking than we have described here.

Behind the scenes, Oracle uses quite a wide variety of locks to provide the isolation levels described here. There is a row share lock as well as several different types of table locks. There are other locks used internally within Oracle. You can learn more about these in the Oracle documentation.

To reduce the likelihood of lock conflict, Oracle does not promote locks from one level to another. Row locks remain row locks, even if there are hundreds of them on hundreds of rows of a table. This strategy is different from SQL Server, as you will learn in the next chapter. Oracle Corporation claims not promoting locks is an advantage, and it probably is, especially given the rest of the Oracle lock architecture.

➤ ORACLE SECURITY

As described in Chapter 11, the database administrator defines users by creating a user account with name and password. Each user is assigned a profile, which is a list of system resource limits assigned to that user. Such limits include total CPU time that can be used per session or per Oracle call and other similar limits.

Oracle defines system and object privileges. System privileges are rights to general tasks such as SELECT ANY TABLE, and UPDATE ANY TABLE. Object privileges concern actions on particular database elements constructs like tables, views, and sequences. A GRANT statement may be used to give a privilege to another user.

An Oracle role is a set of privileges and other roles. A role may be assigned to many users and a user may have many roles. An example of a role for View Ridge Gallery is MANAGER. This role would be given all system and object privileges necessary to perform the management function at View Ridge. Certain View Ridge employees would then be given user accounts that have been granted that role.

You can learn more about Oracle security by searching the documentation for User, Roles, or Privileges.

➤ ORACLE BACKUP AND RECOVERY

Oracle provides a sophisticated set of facilities and utilities for backup and recovery processing. These can be used in many different ways to provide appropriate backup and recovery for databases ranging from a small workgroup database that can be backed up when it is unused at night to large interorganizational databases that must be operational 24 hours per day, 7 days a week (24/7) and can never be shut down.

ORACLE RECOVERY FACILITIES

Oracle maintains three types of files that are important for backup and recovery. **Datafiles** contain user and system data. Because of the way that Oracle writes data buffers to disk, at an arbitrary moment in time, the datafiles may contain both committed and uncommitted changes. Of course Oracle processes transactions so that these uncommitted changes are eventually either committed or removed, but a snapshot of the datafiles at any arbitrary moment will include uncommitted changes. Thus, when Oracle shuts down or when certain types of backups are made, the datafiles must be cleaned up so that only committed changes remain in them.

ReDo files contain logs of database changes; they are backups of the rollback segments used for concurrent processing. **Control files** are small files that describe the name, contents, and locations of various files used by Oracle. Control files are frequently updated by Oracle and they must be available for a database to be operational.

There are two types of ReDo files. **OnLine ReDo** files are maintained on disk and contain the rollback segments from recent database changes. **Offline** or **Archive ReDo** files are backups of the OnLine ReDo files. They are stored separately from the OnLine ReDo files, and need not necessarily reside on disk media. Oracle can operate in either ARCHIVELOG or NOARCHIVELOG mode. If it is running in ARCHIVE mode, when the OnLine ReDo files fill up, they are copied to the Archive ReDo files.

Control files and OnLine ReDo files are so important that Oracle recommends that two active copies of them be kept, a process called **multiplexing** in Oracle terminology.

TYPES OF FAILURE

Oracle recovery techniques depend on the type of failure. When an **application failure** occurs, say, because of application logic errors, Oracle simply rolls back uncommitted changes made by that application using the in-memory rollback segments and OnLine ReDo files as necessary.

Other types of failure recovery are more complicated and depend on the failure type. An **instance failure** occurs when Oracle itself fails due to an operating system or computer hardware failure. A **media failure** occurs when Oracle is unable to write to a physical file. This may occur because of a disk head crash or other disk failure, because needed devices are not powered on, or because a file is corrupt.

INSTANCE FAILURE RECOVERY When Oracle is restarted after an instance failure, it looks first to the control file to find out where all the other files are located. Then, it processes the OnLine ReDo logs against the datafiles. It rolls forward all changes in the ReDo log that were not yet written to the datafiles at the time of failure. In the process of rolling forward, rollback segments are filled with records of transactions in the ReDo log.

After rollforward, the datafiles may contain uncommitted changes. These uncommitted changes could have been in the datafiles at the time of the instance failure or they could have been introduced by rollforward. Either way, Oracle eliminates them by rolling back such uncommitted changes using the rollback segments that were created during rollforward. So that transactions do not need to wait for rollback to complete, all uncommitted transactions are marked as DEAD. If a new transaction is blocked by a change made by a DEAD transaction, the locking manager destroys the locks held by the DEAD transaction.

The Archive ReDo logs are not used for instance recovery. Accordingly, instance recovery can be done in either ARCHIVELOG or NOARCHIVELOG mode.

MEDIA FAILURE RECOVERY To recover from a media failure, the database is restored from a backup. If the database was running in NOARCHIVELOG, then nothing else can be done. The OnLine ReDo log will not be useful because it will concern changes made long after the backup was made. The organization must find another way to recover changes to the database. (This would be the wrong time to start thinking about this, by the way.)

If Oracle was operating in ARCHIVELOG mode, then the OnLine ReDo logs will have been copied to the archive. To recover, the database is restored from a backup and then the database is rolled forward by applying Archive ReDo log files. After this rollforward finishes, changes made by uncommitted transactions are removed by rolling them back as described above.

Two kinds of backups are possible. A **consistent backup** is one in which all uncommitted changes have been removed from the datafiles. Database activity must be stopped, all buffers must be flushed to disk, and changes made by any uncommitted transactions removed. Clearly, this type of backup cannot be done if the database supports 24/7 operations.

An **inconsistent backup** may contain uncommitted changes. It is sort of flying backup, made while Oracle is processing the database. For recovery, such backups can be made consistent by applying the archive log records to commit or roll back all transactions that were in process when the backup was made. Inconsistent backups can be made on portions of the database. For example, in a 24/7 application, every night one-seventh of the database can be backed up. Over a week's time, a copy of the entire database will have been made.

The Oracle Recovery Manager (RMAN) is a utility program used to create backups and to perform recovery. RMAN can be instructed to create a special recovery database that contains data about recovery files and operations. The specifics of this program are beyond the scope of this discussion.

➤ TOPICS NOT DISCUSSED IN THIS CHAPTER

There are several important Oracle features that we have not discussed in this chapter. For one, Oracle supports object-oriented structures, and developers can use them to define their own abstract data types. Oracle can also be used to create and process databases that are hybrids of traditional databases and object databases. Such hybrids are called object-relational databases and we will describe them in Chapter 18.

Also, Enterprise Oracle supports distributed database processing, in which the database is stored on more than one computer. This topic will be introduced in Chapter 17. Additionally, there are quite a few Oracle utilities that we have not discussed. The Oracle Loader is a utility program for inputting bulk data into an

Oracle database. Other utilities can be used to measure and tune Oracle performance.

We have, however, discussed the most important Oracle features and topics here. If you have understood these concepts, you are well on your way to becoming a successful Oracle developer.

➤ SUMMARY

Oracle is a powerful and robust DBMS that runs on many different operating systems and has many different products. This chapter addresses the use of the Oracle utility SQL Plus, which can be used to create and process SQL and PL/SQL with all versions of Oracle. PL/SQL is a language that adds programming facilities to the SQL language.

You can create a database using the Database Configuration Assistant, using the Oracle-supplied database creation procedures, and using the SQL CREATE DATABASE command. The Database Configuration Assistant creates default database and log files. SQL Plus has a limited text editor that keeps the current statement in a multiline buffer. SQL Plus can be configured to invoke text editors such as Notepad.

The SQL CREATE TABLE command is used to create Oracle tables. This command names the new table and creates table columns according to a list of column names, data types, and properties that are enclosed in parentheses. In Oracle, surrogate keys can be maintained using sequences. Sequence objects have a NextVal method, which provides the next value of a sequence, and a CurrVal method, which provides the current value of a sequence. Unfortunately, implementing surrogate keys with sequences does not guarantee that the table will have valid surrogate key values.

Tables (and their data) can be removed from the database with the DROP command. Table columns can be removed with the ALTER TABLE command. Relationships are declared by defining foreign key constraints using the ALTER TABLE . . . ADD CONSTRAINT . . . command. The deletion of parent rows can be propagated to tables having dependent foreign keys using the ON DELETE CASCASE phrase.

Indexes are created to enforce uniqueness and to enable fast retrieval by column values. They are created with the CREATE INDEX command. Columns can be added, modified, or removed from a table with the ALTER command. CHECK CONSTRAINTS are used to constrain values that columns may have. The conditions in such constraints must evaluate to true or false using only constants and column values in the current row of the table in which they are defined. Constraints are added and dropped with the ALTER TABLE command.

A SQL view is the result of a SQL SELECT expression that uses selection, projection, and join. Such views can have at most one multi-valued path. Views are constructed with the CREATE VIEW command. Join views are constructed using a join and are generally not updatable with INSERT, UPDATE, and DELETE commands. They can be updated with INSTEAD OF TRIGGERS, however.

PL/SQL statements can be saved in files and processed using SQL Plus. They can also be recorded in the database as stored procedures and invoked from other PL/SQL programs or from application programs. Examples of stored procedures are shown in Figures 12-15 and 12-16. Oracle triggers are PL/SQL or Java programs that are invoked when specified database activity occurs. Examples of BEFORE, AFTER, and INSTEAD OF TRIGGERS are shown in Figures 12-18, 12-19, and 12-20, respectively.

Oracle maintains a data dictionary of metadata. The metadata of the dictionary itself is stored in the table DICT. You can query this table to determine the dictionary's contents.

Oracle supports read committed, serializable, and read-only transaction isolation levels. Because of the way SCN values are processed, Oracle never reads dirty data. Serializable isolation is possible, but the application program must be written to process the "Cannot serialize" exception. Applications can place locks explicitly using SELECT FOR UPDATE commands, but this is not recommended.

With Oracle the DBA defines users and privileges. A role is a group of privileges and other roles. A user may be given many roles and a role has many users.

Three types of files are used in Oracle recovery: Datafiles, OnLine and OffLine ReDo log files, and Control files. If running in ARCHIVELOG mode, Oracle logs all changes to the database. Oracle can recover from application failure and instance failure without using the archived log file. Archive logs are required, however to recover from media failure. Backups can be consistent or inconsistent. An inconsistent backup can be made consistent by processing an archive log file.

➤ GROUP I QUESTIONS

12.1 Describe the general characteristics of Oracle and the Oracle suite of products. Explain why these characteristics mean there is considerable complexity to master.

12.2 What is SQL Plus and what is its purpose?

12.3 Name three ways of creating an Oracle database. Which is the easiest?

12.4 Explain how to change a row in the SQL Plus buffer. Assume there are three statements in the buffer, the focus is on statement 3, and you want to change the second statement from CustID=1000 to CustomerID=1000.

12.5 How do you set the default directory for SQL Plus to use?

12.6 Show the SQL statement necessary to create a table named T1 with columns C1, C2, and C3. Assume C1 is a surrogate key. Assume C2 has character data of maximum length 50 and C3 contains a date.

12.7 Show the statement necessary to create a sequence starting at 50 and incremented by 2. Name your sequence T1Seq.

12.8 Show how to insert a row into table T1 (Question 12.6) using the sequence created in Question 12.7.

12.9 Show a SQL statement for querying the row created in Question 12.8.

12.10 Explain the problems inherent in using sequences for surrogate key columns.

12.11 Show SQL statements for dropping table T1 and for dropping SeqT1.

12.12 Show SQL statements for dropping column C3 of table T1.

12.13 Show SQL statements for creating a relationship between table T2 and table T3. Assume that T3 has a foreign key column named FK1 that relates to T2 and that deletions in T2 should force deletions in T3.

12.14 Answer Question 12.13 but do not force deletions.

12.15 Show how to eliminate a relationship with SQL.

12.16 Show SQL statements to create a unique index on columns C2 and C3 of table T1.

12.17 Under what circumstances should indexes be used?

12.18 Show SQL statements to add a new column C4 to table T1. Assume T1 will have currency values up to $1 million.

12.19 Under what conditions can you drop a column in an existing table?

12.20 Under what conditions can you add a column to an existing table?

12.21 Explain how to add a NOT NULL column to an existing table.

12.22 Under what conditions can you change the width of a character or numeric column?

12.23 Under what conditions can you change a column's data type?

12.24 Show how to add a constraint to specify that column C4 of table T1 cannot be less than 1,000.

12.25 Show how to add a constraint to specify that column C4 of table T1 cannot be less than column C5 of table T1.

12.26 For the View Ridge database discussed in this chapter, construct a view that contains Name, City, and State of a customer. Name your view CustView.

12.27 For the View Ridge database, construct a view that has customer name and artist name for all art that the customer has purchased.

12.28 For the View Ridge database, construct a view that has customer name and artist name for all artists in which the customer is interested. Explain the difference between this view and the view in Question 12.27.

12.29 Can you combine the views in Questions 12.27 and 12.28 into one view? Why or why not?

12.30 How can you update a join view using Oracle?

12.31 Create a file of PL/SQL statements that describes the structure of the CUSTOMER, ARTIST, WORK, TRANSACTION, and CUSTOMER_ARTIST_INT tables. Store the file with the name VRTabs.sql and show how to invoke the PL/SQL procedure using SQL Plus.

12.32 In a PL/SQL procedure, what do the keywords IN, OUT, and IN OUT signify?

12.33 What must be done to be able to see output generated by the Oracle DBMS_OUTPUT package? What limits exist on such output?

12.34 Explain how the PL/SQL statement FOR *variable* IN *cursorname* work.

12.35 What statement is used to obtain errors when compiling stored procedures and triggers?

12.36 What is the syntax of the BEGIN TRANSACTION statement in PL/SQL? How is a transaction started?

12.37 In the stored procedure in Figure 12-16, how are the values of the variables tid and aid used if there are no suitable TRANSACTION rows in the database? How are they used if there is just one suitable TRANSACTION row in the database?

12.38 Explain the purpose of BEFORE, AFTER, and INSTEAD OF triggers.

12.39 When an update is in progress, how can the trigger code obtain the value of a column, say, C1, before the update began? How can the trigger code obtain the value that the column is being set to?

12.40 Explain why INSTEAD OF TRIGGERS are needed for join views.

12.41 Explain what would happen if the IF statement in the trigger in Figure 12-21 was removed.

12.42 Show a SQL statement to obtain the names of tables the data dictionary contains about triggers.

12.43 What three levels of transaction isolation are supported by Oracle?

12.44 Explain how Oracle uses the system change number to read data that are current at a particular point in time.

12.45 Under what circumstances will Oracle read dirty data?

12.46 Explain how conflicting locks are handled by Oracle when a transaction is operating in READ COMMITTED isolation mode.

12.47 Show the SQL statement necessary to set the transaction isolation level to SERIALIZABLE for an entire session.

12.48 What happens when a transaction in serializable mode tries to update data that have been updated by a different transaction? Assume the SCN is less than the transaction's SCN. Assume the SCN is greater than the transaction's SCN.

12.49 Describe three circumstances under which a transaction could receive the "Cannot serialize" exception.

12.50 Explain how Oracle processes the read only transaction isolation level.

12.51 Explain the use of user, privilege, and role in Oracle security.

12.52 What three types of files are important for Oracle backup and recovery processing?

12.53 What is the difference between the OnLine ReDo logs and the OffLine or Archive ReDo logs? How is each type used?

12.54 What does multiplexing mean in the context of Oracle recovery?

12.55 Explain how Oracle recovers from application failure.

12.56 What is instance failure and how does Oracle recover from it?

12.57 What is media failure and how does Oracle recover from it?

➤ PROJECTS

For the following projects, use Oracle to create the View Ridge Gallery database as described in this chapter. Consider the database view named Artist View that is shown for the Group II Questions at the end of Chapter 10.

A. Write a PL/SQL procedure to read the ARTIST table portion of this view. Display the data you read. Accept the name of the artist as an input parameter.

B. Write a PL/SQL procedure to read the ARTIST, TRANSACTION, and CUSTOMER (under TRANSACTION) tables in this view. Display the data you read using DBMS_OUTPUT. Accept the name of the artist as an input parameter.

C. Write a PL/SQL procedure to read all of the view tables. Display the data you read using DBMS_OUTPUT. Accept the name of the artist as an input parameter.

D. Write a PL/SQL procedure to assign a new customer interest to an artist. Assume the name of the artist and the name of the customer are input. If the customer name is not unique, display an error message. Check for duplication in the CUSTOMER_ARTIST_INT table before you insert the new row. Display an error message if there is duplication.

E. Code a BEFORE TRIGGER that checks inserts and modifications on ARTIST Nationality. If the new value is 'British' change it to 'English.'

➤ FIREDUP PROJECT QUESTIONS

Use Oracle to create a database with the following four tables:

CUSTOMER (<u>CustomerID</u>, Name, Phone, EmailAddress)
STOVE (<u>SerialNumber</u>, Type, Version, DateOfManufacture)
REGISTRATION (<u>*CustomerID*, *SerialNumber*, RDate</u>)
STOVE-REPAIR (<u>RepairInvoiceNumber</u>, *SerialNumber*, RepairDate, Description, Cost, *CustomerID*)

Assume the primary keys of CUSTOMER, STOVE, and STOVE-REPAIR are surrogate keys and create sequences for each of them. Create relationships to enforce the following referential integrity constraints:

- CustomerID of REGISTRATION is a subset of CustomerID of CUSTOMER
- SerialNumber of REGISTRATION is a subset of SerialNumber of STOVE
- SerialNumber of STOVE-REPAIR is a subset of SerialNumber of STOVE
- CustomerID of STOVE-REPAIR is a subset of CustomerID of CUSTOMER

Do not cascade deletions.

A. Fill your tables with sample data and display them.

B. Create a stored procedure to register a stove. The procedure receives the customer's name, phone, e-mail address, and stove serial number. If the customer already exists in the database (name, phone, and e-mail match), use that customer's CustomerID for the REGISTRATION. Otherwise, create a new CUSTOMER row for the customer. Assume a stove with the input serial number already exists in the database. If not, print an error and roll back changes to the CUSTOMER table. Code and test your procedure.

C. Create a stored procedure to record a stove repair. The procedure receives customer's name, phone, e-mail address, stove serial number, repair description, and cost. Assume you are given a valid stove serial number; print an error message and make no database changes if not. Use an existing CUSTOMER row if name, phone, and e-mail match; otherwise, create a new CUSTOMER record. Assume that the STOVE_REPAIR row must be created. Register the stove if necessary.

D. Create a view that contains all of the FiredUp data for a given customer. Name this view CustomerRecord. This view must join CUSTOMER, REGISTRATION, STOVE, and STOVE_REPAIR data. Write a stored procedure that accepts a customer's Name and displays all of the data for the given customer.

Managing Databases with SQL Server 2000

This chapter describes the basic features and functions of Microsoft SQL Server 2000. The discussion uses the example of View Ridge Gallery from Chapter 10 and it parallels the discussion of the database administration tasks in Chapter 11. The presentation is similar in scope and orientation to that for Oracle in the prior chapter. In fact, because the SQL language has been standardized by the American National Standards Institute (ANSI), almost everything you learned about SQL processing with Oracle will pertain to SQL Server as well. Since this is so, we will focus more on the graphical design tools that are available with SQL Server than on SQL statements.

SQL Server is a large and complicated product. In this one chapter, we will be able only to scratch the surface. The goal is to prepare you to use SQL Server for projects of your own, and to learn sufficient basics so that you can continue learning on your own or in other classes.

➤ INSTALLING SQL SERVER 2000

If you purchased the version of this book that has SQL Server, you should install it now. The SQL Server CD that comes with this text contains an evaluation copy that has a license valid for 120 days. It requires Windows NT with Service Pack 5 or later, or Windows 2000 Professional, Windows 2000 Server, Windows 2000 Advanced Server, or Windows 2000 Datacenter Server. It also needs at least 64MB of RAM and about 250MB of disk space (less is possible, but not recommended for our purposes).

To install this software, log in to your computer with Administrator privileges and insert the CD-ROM. The install program should start automatically. If not, double click on the autorun executable at the top level of the CD. Click on SQL Server Components and then click on Install Database Server. The rest of the installation process is a typical Windows program installation.

FIGURE 13-1

SQL Server Enterprise Manager

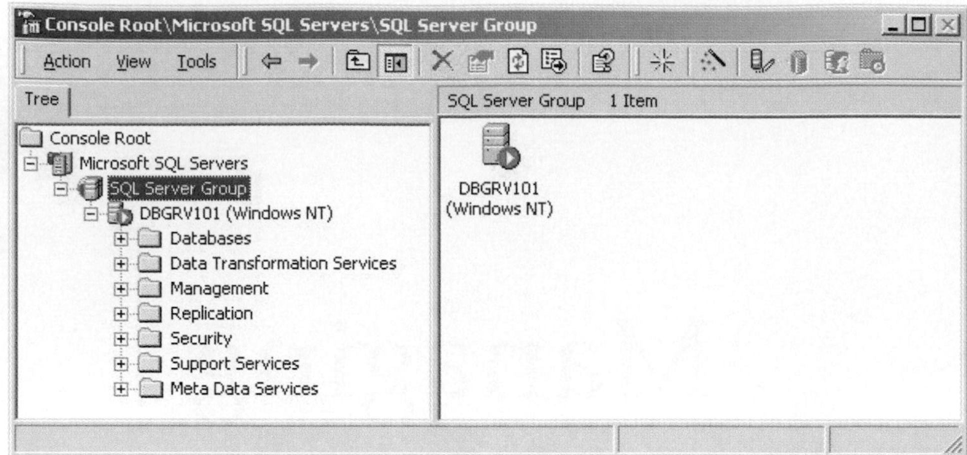

Once you've installed the software, you can start to work with SQL Server by clicking Start/Programs/Microsoft SQL Server/Enterprise Manager. After you have done this, find the icon labeled Microsoft SQL Server in the left-hand pane. Click on the plus sign to open it; then open SQL Server Group in the same way. You'll next see the name of your computer followed by (Windows NT). Open this and you should see the display shown in Figure 13-1. In this figure, you see the name of the computer used to make this figure, which was DBGRV101.

➤ CREATING A SQL SERVER 2000 DATABASE

To create a new database, right-click on Databases and select New Database. Type the name of your database (here, ViewRidge1) into the Name text box as shown in Figure 13-2.

By default, SQL Server will create one data file and one log file for each database. You can create multiple files for both data and logs, and assign particular tables and logs to particular files and file groups. All of this is beyond the scope of this discussion, however. To learn more about it on your own, right-click on Databases and select Help. In the left-hand pane of the Help menu, search on *File Groups* in the Search Text box to get started.

For now, take the default sizes and files that SQL Server offers. You can see what they are by clicking on the Data Files and Transaction Log tabs.

Once you've created your database, open the Databases folder and then open the folder with the name of your database. Then open Tables. Your screen should look like the one in Figure 13-3, but you will not yet have any user tables in it. All the tables listed in your display are system tables used by SQL Server 2000 to manage your database. By the way, *dbo* stands for database owner. That will be you, if you installed SQL Server and created this database.

CREATING TABLES

There are two ways to create and modify tables (and most SQL Server 2000 structures, for that matter). The first is to write SQL code using either the CREATE or ALTER SQL statements as we did in the last chapter for Oracle. The second is to use the graphical facilities of SQL Server. Because the graphical means is different from that discussed previously, we will use it most of the time in this chapter.

➤ FIGURE 13-2

Creating a SQL Server Database

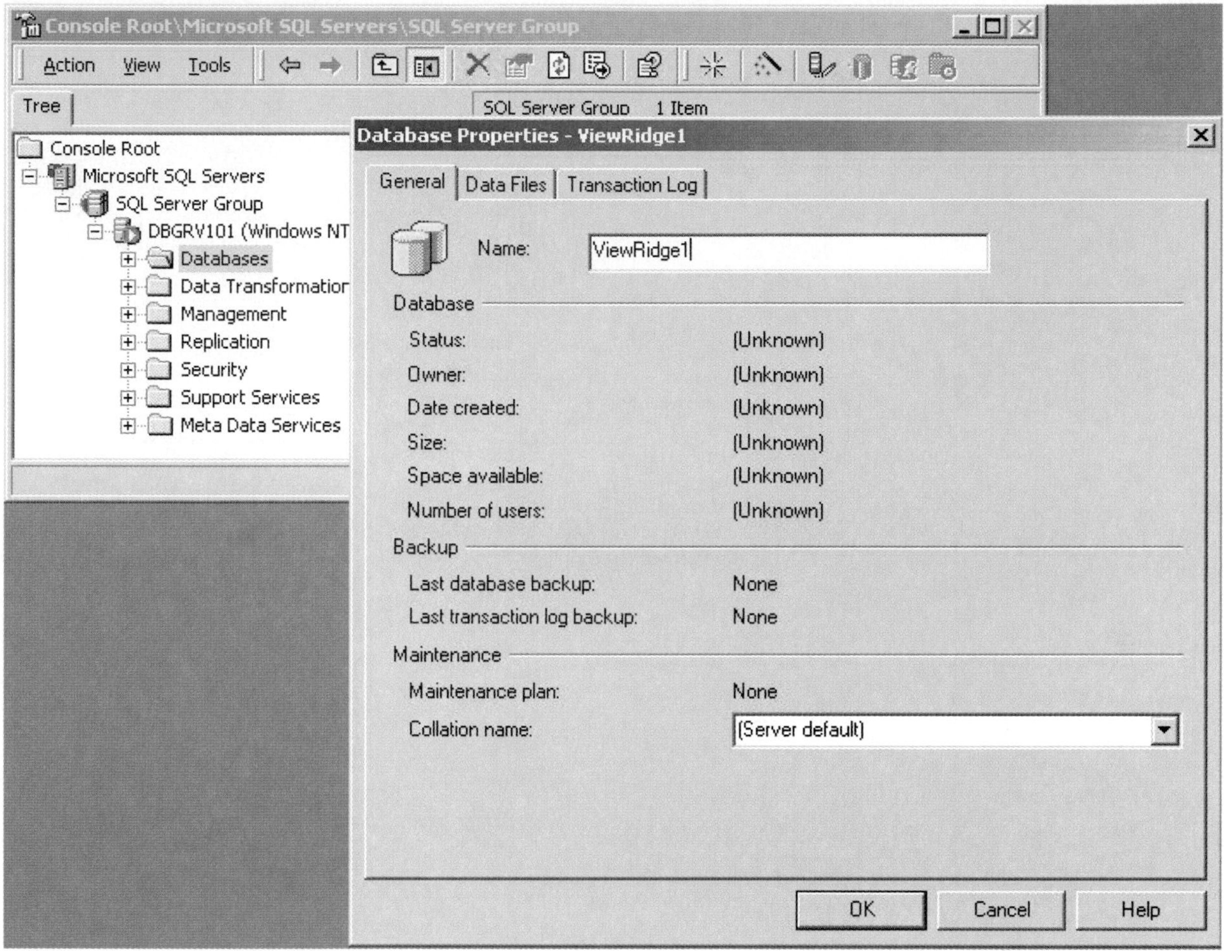

Keep in mind, however, that SQL statements are the only way to create database structures programmatically, so you should know how to use both.

USING THE CREATE SQL STATEMENT Figure 13-4 shows a typical SQL CREATE TABLE statement. As described in the last chapter, such statements always begin with CREATE TABLE followed by the name of the new table. Next, a list of the table columns is presented, enclosed in parentheses. Each column has a name, a data type, and then any special properties. Column descriptions are separated by commas, but there is no comma after the last column.

In Figure 13-4, the name of the table is CUST and it has four columns: CustomerID, Name, AreaCode, and LocalNumber. CustomerID has type *int* and is the primary key of the table. Name is of type character and is 50 bytes in length. Name is NOT NULL, which means null values are not allowed. If neither NULL or NOT NULL appears, the column is assumed to be NULL.

Name is enclosed in brackets as [Name]. This is necessary because *Name* is a SQL Server reserved word. If not placed in brackets, SQL Server will try to interpret *Name* as the name of one of its constructs. Hence, anytime you are using a SQL Server reserved word as a user identifier, place the word in brackets. If you're not sure a word is reserved, place it in brackets. There is no harm in doing so.

➤ FIGURE 13-3

Viewing the Tables in a Database

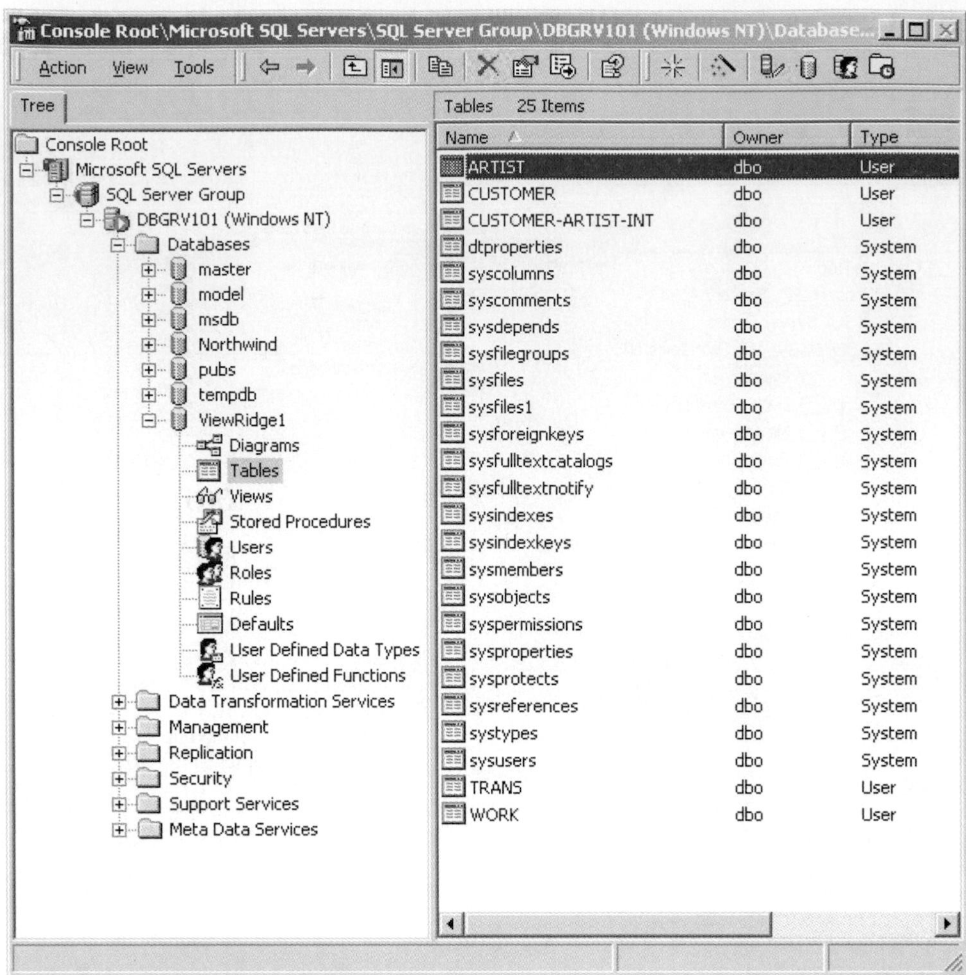

➤ FIGURE 13-4

Creating a Table with SQL in the SQL Query Analyzer

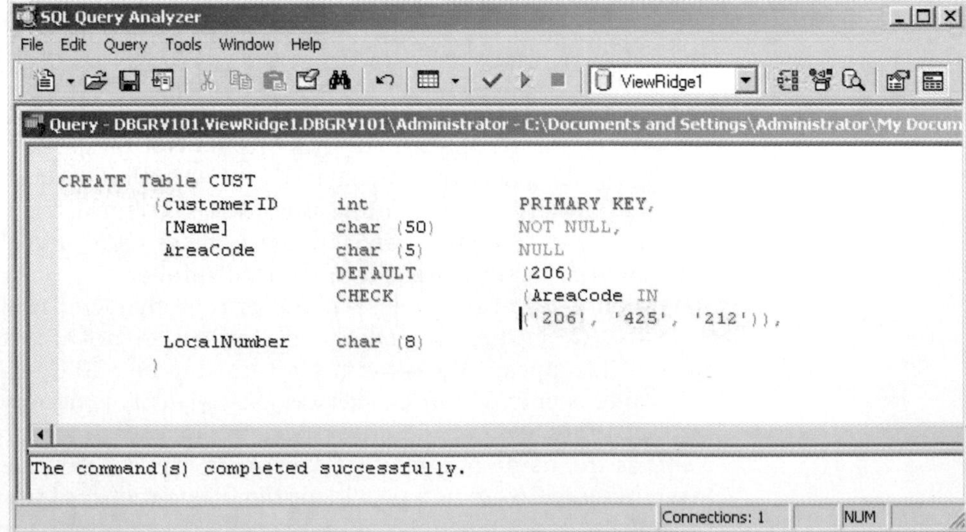

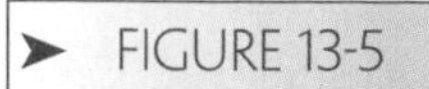
FIGURE 13-5

Invoking the Query Analyzer

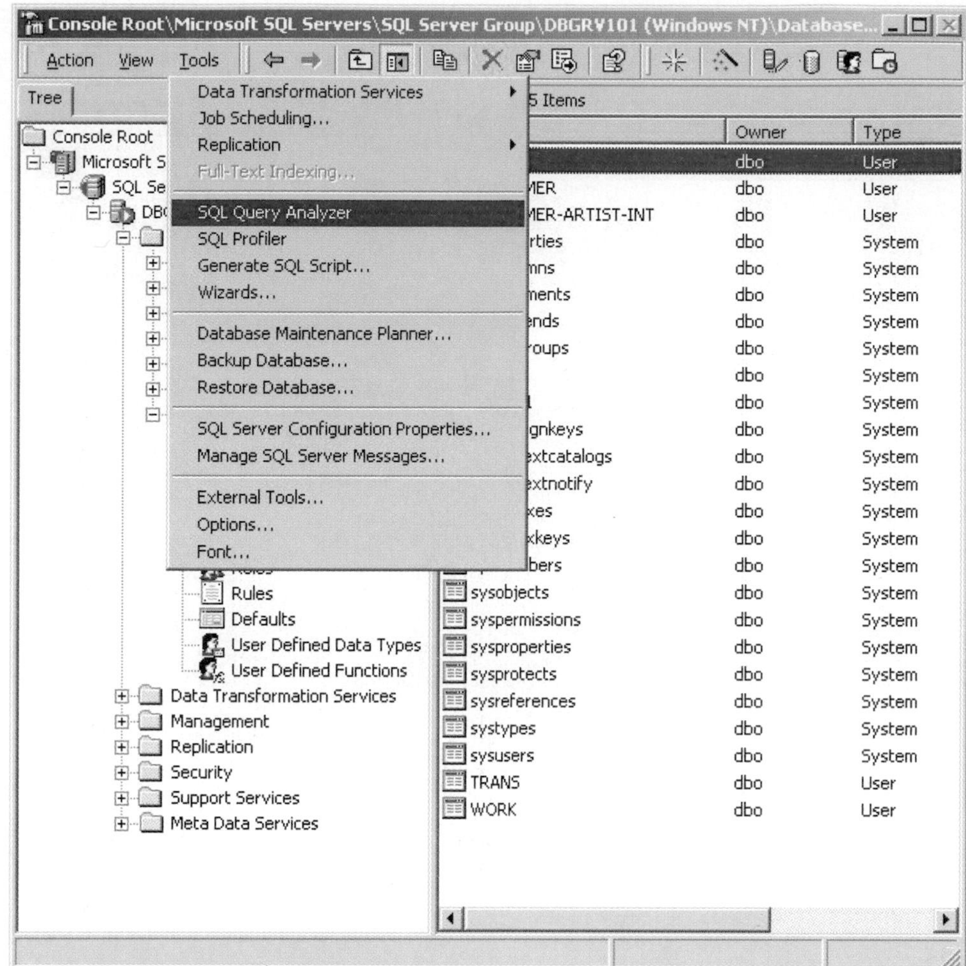

In this example, the default value for AreaCode is defined as (206). Furthermore, the CHECK constraint limits the values of AreaCode to those listed. AreaCode values can be NULL. LocalNumber is defined as char(8) and because no indication is given about NULL or NOT NULL, the default of NULL will be used.

There are several ways to pass this CREATE statement to SQL Server. The simplest is to use the Query Analyzer. To do that, click on Tools and then select SQL Query Analyzer as shown in Figure 13-5. Type the CREATE Table statement into the window and then click on the blue check mark. If your statement has syntax errors, they will be reported in the pane underneath the statement. Once you have removed syntax errors, click the green right-facing diamond and the table will be created.

To see that the table has, in fact, been created, go back to the Enterprise Manager window, right-click on Tables, and select Refresh. The new table should appear in the list in the right-hand pane. Right-click on the new table and select Design Table. You will see a display like that in Figure 13-6. Notice that the default of AreaCode is indeed (206) and that both AreaCode and LocalNumber are allowed to be null. Further, the primary key (denoted by the key symbol) of the table is CustomerID.

USING THE GRAPHICAL TABLE CREATION WINDOW The second way to create a table is similar to that used in Microsoft Access. Right-click on Tables in the Enterprise Manager and select New Table. A blank form will appear into which you can type Column Names and Data Types. For some Data Types you can set

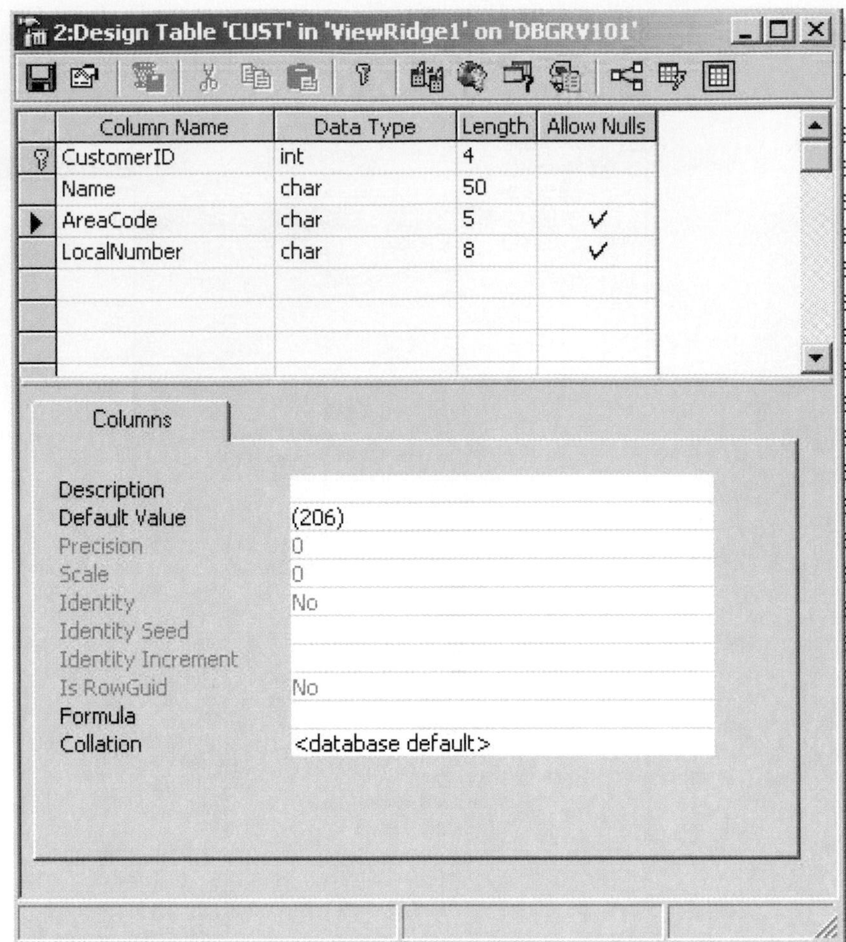

➤ FIGURE 13-6

SQL Server Table Created by SQL in Figure 13-4

the length (char, for example), but for others the length is determined by the Data Type (int, for example).

In Figure 13-7, ArtistID is a surrogate key. To cause SQL Server to supply values for ArtistID, its Identity Property has been set to Yes. The starting value is specified by the Identity Seed; the amount to add to the surrogate key when adding a new row is specified by the Identity Increment. Here, ArtistID will start with 1 and will be incremented by 1. Only one column in a table can be an identity column. SQL Server does not have sequence objects like those in Oracle.

To make this column the table key, click anywhere in the ArtistID row to highlight it and then click the key symbol in the design window menu bar. To make a composite key, highlight all of the columns that comprise the key and then click on the key symbol.

The system-supplied data types for SQL Server 2000 are listed in Figure 13-8 You can select any of these types when defining a column.

USER-DEFINED DATA TYPES SQL Server 2000 implements User-Defined Data Types, an important facility that can be used to represent domains. For example, in the View Ridge application, suppose that the domain of both Birthdate and Deceaseddate are not true dates, but are four digit years instead.

To implement this with SQL Server 2000, a User-Defined Data Type can be defined. To do this in the Enterprise Manager, right-click on User-Defined Data Types and select New User-Defined Data Type. A dialog box like that in Figure 13-9

Creating a Table with the Graphical Design Tool

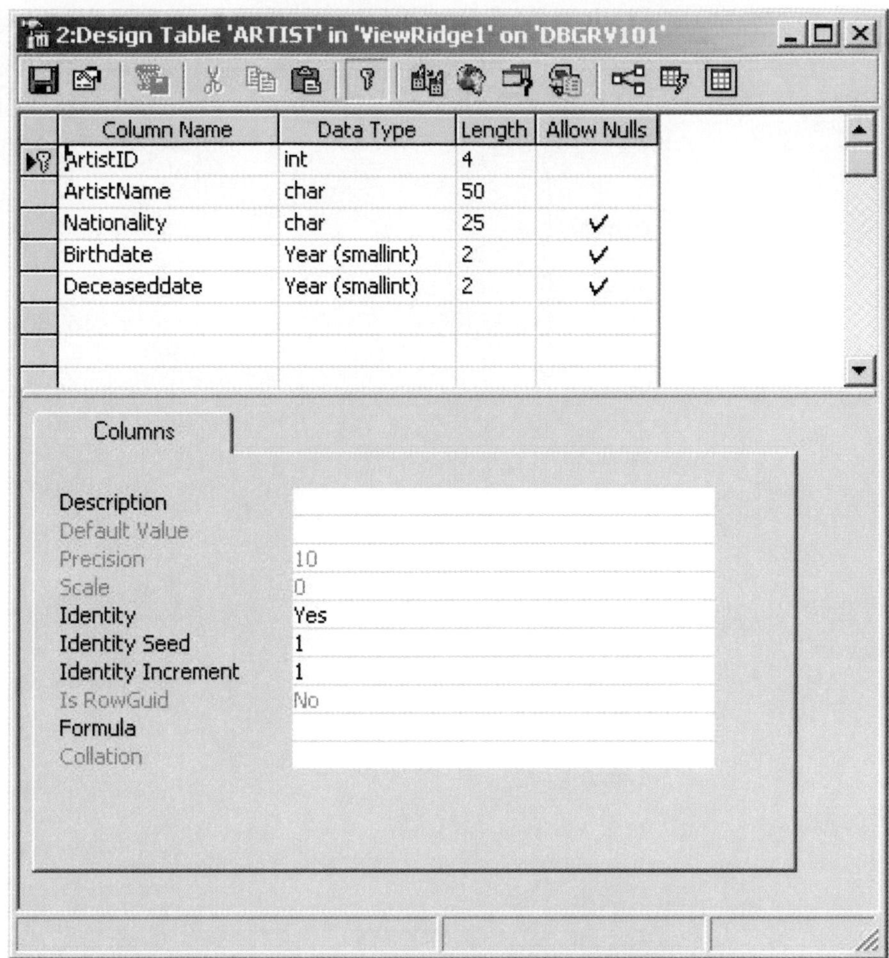

will appear. Enter the name of the new data type in the Name: text box and set its data type. Here, *Year* is defined and given the type *smallint*.

Once you have defined a data type, it will appear in the drop-down list that appears when you click in the Data Types column—just as if it were one of the system-supplied data types. In Figure 13-7, the Year data type was selected for both Birthdate and Deceaseddate columns.

User-Defined Types are even more useful when combined with Rules.

RULES Rules are declarative expressions that limit data values. The general format of them is @variablename <rule expression>. Figure 13-10 shows the definition of the rule @year BETWEEN 1400 AND 2100. You can use any SQL predicate expression (limiting expressions found in WHERE clauses) as the rule expression. The name of the variable is unimportant. You can define a rule by right-clicking on Rules under your database Name and selecting New Rule.

One particularly useful expression is @List IN (list of values). For example, @State IN ('CA', 'OR', 'WA', 'AZ') limits a column or User-Defined Data Type to those values.

The rule in Figure 13-10 is bound to the Year User-Defined Data Type. Once that has been done, all of the columns that use the Year data type will have values restricted by this rule.

Rules serve the same purpose as CHECK clauses of CREATE and ALTER statements; you can use either with SQL Server. CHECK clauses are part of the 1992

Common SQL Server Data Types

Binary	Binary, length 0 to 8000 bytes.
Char	Character, length 0 to 8000 bytes.
Datetime	8-byte datetime. Range from January 1, 1753, through December 31, 9999, with an accuracy of three-hundredths of a second.
Decimal	Decimal—can set precision and scale. Range −10^38 +1 through 10^38 −1.
Float	8-byte floating point number. Value range −1.79E + 308 through 1.79E + 308.
Image	Variable length binary data. Maximum length 2,147,483,647 bytes.
Int	4-byte integer. Value range from −2,147,483,648 through 2,147,483,647.
Money	8-byte money. Range from −922,337,203,685,477.5808 through +922,337,203,685,477.5807, with accuracy to a ten-thousandth of a monetary unit.
Numeric	Same as decimal.
Real	4-byte floating pointnumber. Value range: −3.40E + 38 through 3.40E + 38.
Smalldatetime	4-byte datetime. Range from January 1, 1900, through June 6, 2079, with an accuracy of one minute.
Smallint	2-byte integer. Range from −32,768 through 32,767.
Smallmoney	4-byte money. Range from 214,748.3648 through +214,748.3647, with accuracy to a ten-thousandth of a monetary unit.
Text	Variable length text, maximum length 2,147,483,647 characters.
Tinyint	1-byte integer. Range from 0 through 255.
Varchar	Variable-length character, length 0 to 8000 bytes.

ANSI standard SQL specification and so they are preferred by some organizations. On the other hand, rules can be graphically defined.

CHANGING TABLE STRUCTURE Table structure can also be changed in two ways. One is to use the ALTER SQL statement as we did in the last chapter. The other is to make changes using the table design form (like Figures 13-6 and 13-7). Figure 13-11 shows several ALTER statements for changing the structure of the CUST table. The first extends the length of the Name column from 50 to 100.

The second ALTER defines a new column, CustomerSince, using the new user-defined data type *year*. The next two statements show a second way for extending the length of a column. Here, the column is first dropped and then it is added back with the new length. Unlike the first ALTER statement, however, data will be lost because the column is physically dropped before it is re-created.

FIGURE 13-9

Defining a User-Defined Data Type

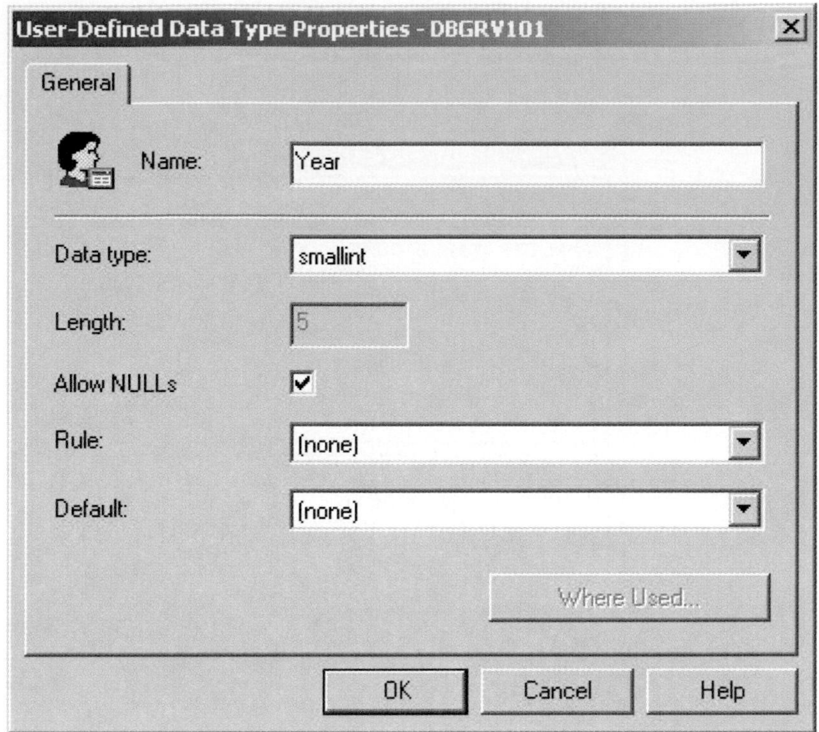

➤ FIGURE 13-10

Creating a Rule and Binding It to a User-Defined Data Type

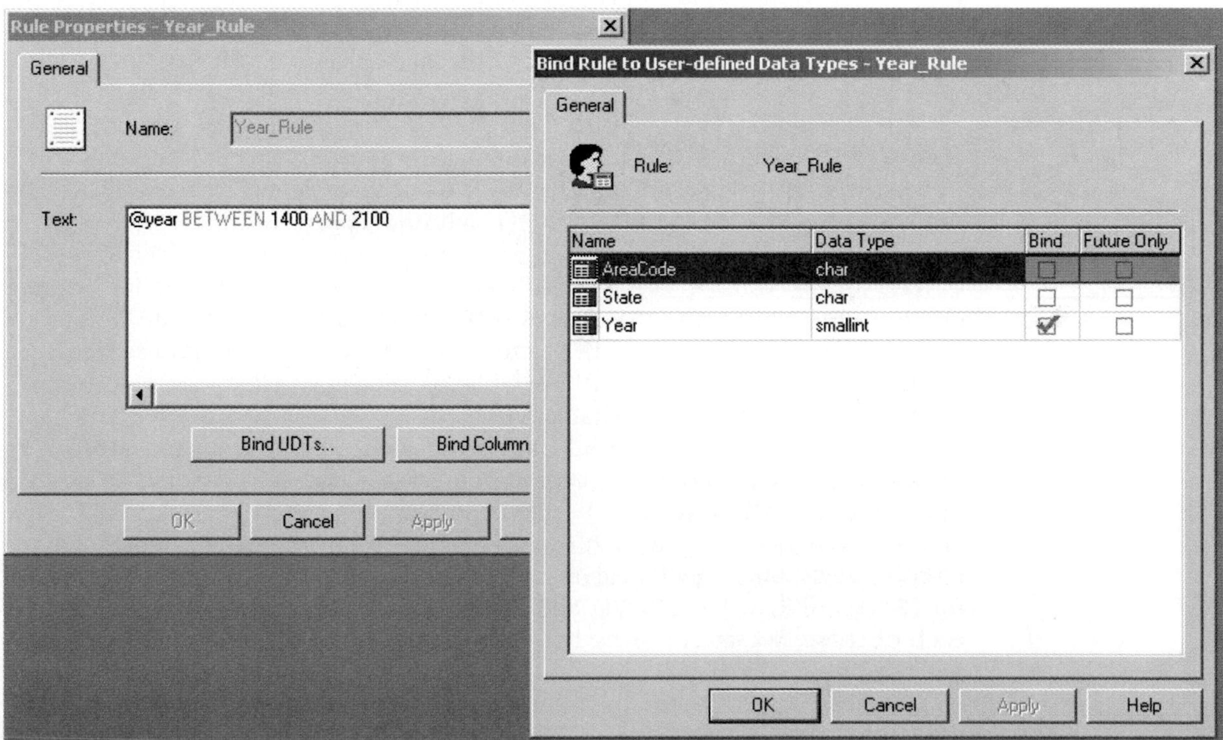

Changing Table Structure with ALTER Statements

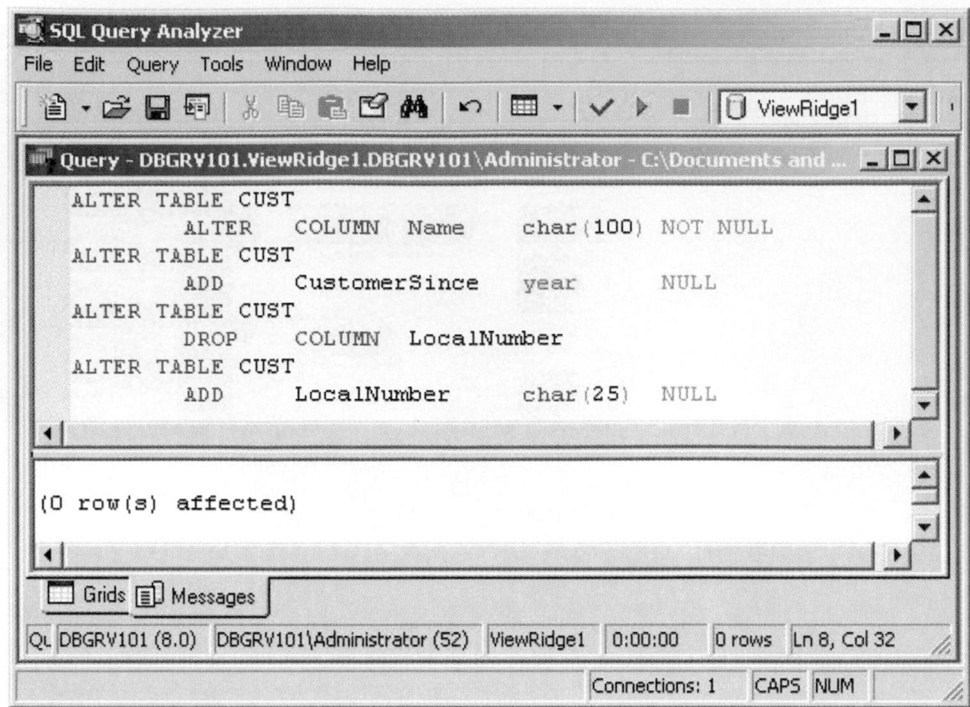

A second way to make these changes is to use the graphical table design window as shown in Figure 13-12. Just open the window and make whatever changes you want to the columns, data types, and lengths. SQL Server will let you know if you try to make unsupported changes.

With SQL Server, you can reduce the length of char, varchar, and similar types, even if the column has data. Doing this, however, will cause data to be truncated. In the process duplicate values may be created that violate uniqueness constraints. This will cause the change to fail, and may result in a mess. Thus, make such size reductions carefully.

Similar comments pertain to changing a column's data type; you can do it even if the column has data, but be careful, as you may lose data. Changing an all-numeric text field like AreaCode to integer is not a problem. Changing a text field such as Name to integer, however, will result in data loss.

CREATING THE EXAMPLE TABLES If you are mirroring the actions in this chapter with your copy of SQL Server, you should now create the five tables shown in Figure 10-3(d). You can delete the CUST table, we will not use it further. (Right-click on the table name in the table list and click Delete.)

Name the TRANSACTION table TRANS instead of TRANSACTION. The name *TRANSACTION* is so special to SQL Server that no stored procedures will work on a table named TRANSACTION, even if you enclose it in brackets. Life is easier if you name it TRANS, instead.

Use surrogate keys for each of these tables. As in the prior chapter, set the identity seeds differently for each table. Use an Identity Seed of 1 for ARTIST, 1000 for CUSTOMER, 500 for WORK, and 100 for TRANS. Leave the Increment at 1 for each of these. Set table keys by highlighting the column(s) and clicking the key symbol.

As with Oracle, if you are creating the tables using SQL statements, then, when creating CUSTOMER_ARTIST_INT, do not give any column the property

FIGURE 13-12

Result of ALTER Statements in Figure 13-11

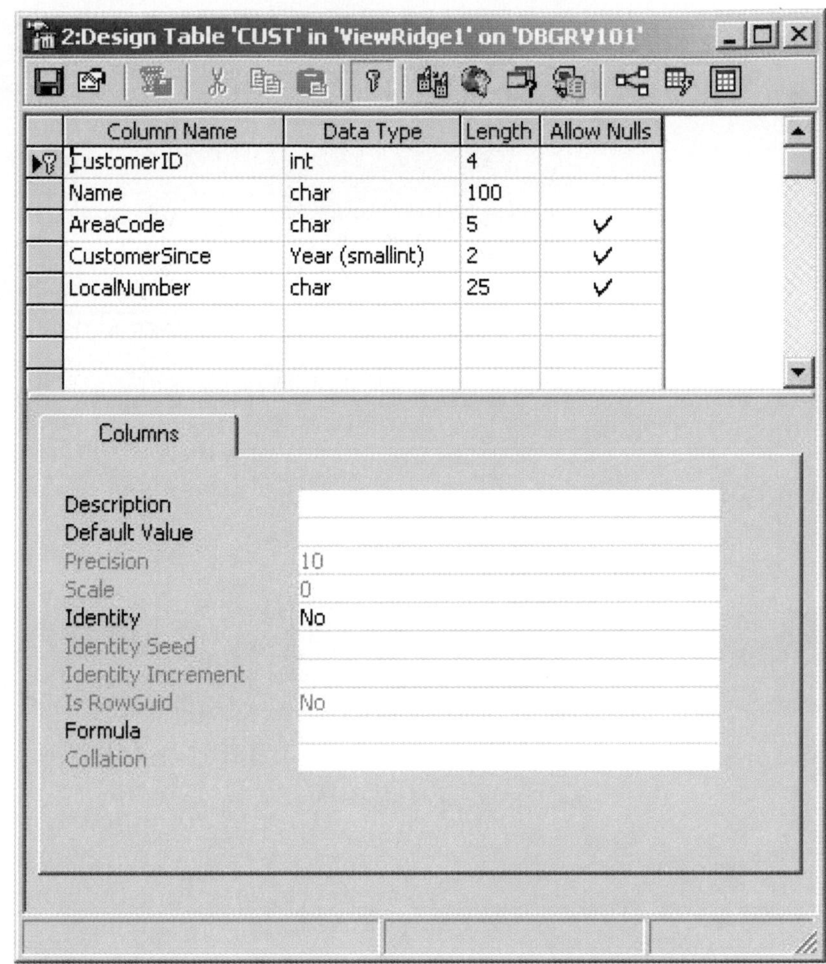

PRIMARY KEY. Instead, after the CREATE TABLE statement, create a primary key constraint with

```
CONSTRAINT pk_constraint PRIMARY KEY (CustomerID, ArtistID)
```

This statement will establish a composite key of (CustomerID, ArtistID) with the name pk_constraint. You can, of course, use any constraint name you want.

Defining Relationships

As with other structures, we can define relationships by defining foreign keys in ALTER TABLE statements or by creating relationships in a database diagram. We did the former in the last chapter, so here we will use a database diagram.

Right-click on Diagrams and choose New Database Diagram. A wizard will start that leads you through the process of adding tables to your diagram. Add all five of the tables from Figure 10-3(d) to the diagram.

Now, to create a relationship, drag a primary key from one table onto a foreign key in the table you want to relate. For example, to create the relationship between ARTIST and CUSTOMER_ARTIST_INT, drag ArtistID in ARTIST and drop it on top of ArtistID in CUSTOMER_ARTIST_INT. This will create the relationship and the dialog box in Figure 13-13 will be displayed. Notice SQL Server provides a default name for the relationship and shows the primary and foreign key

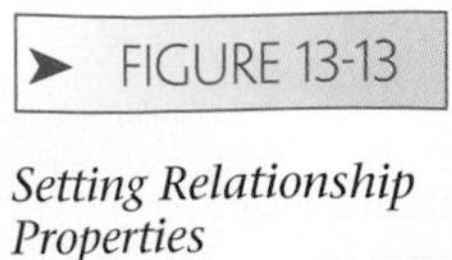

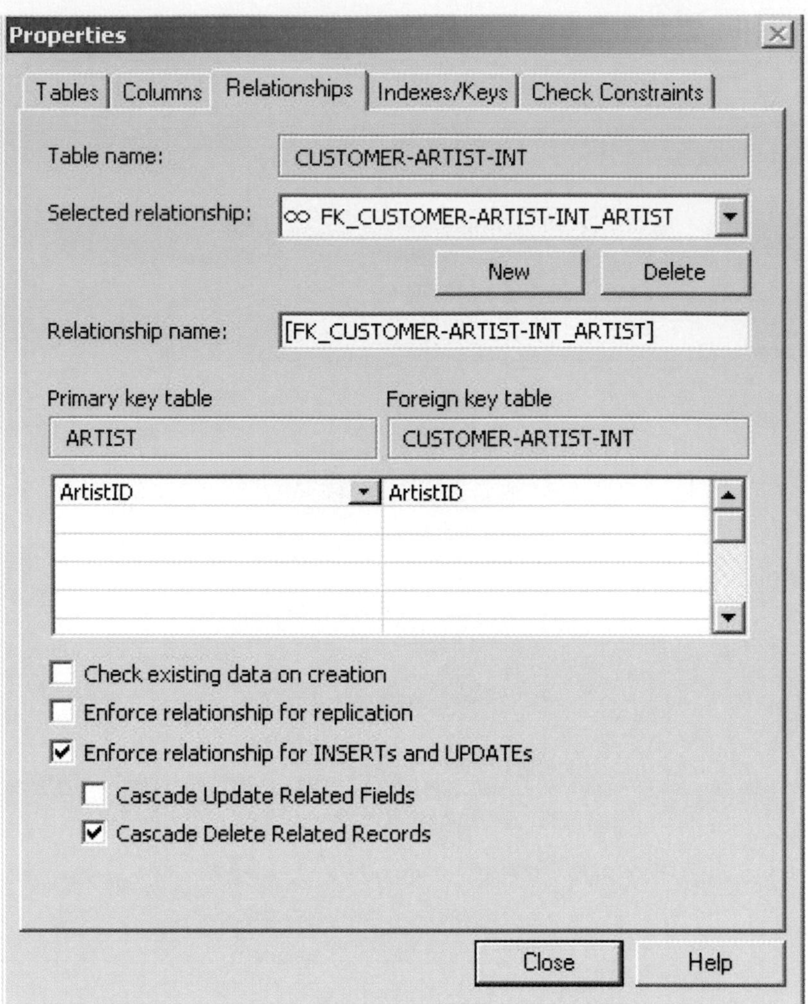

FIGURE 13-13

Setting Relationship Properties

columns. You need do nothing to these, but you do need to think carefully about the referential integrity check boxes that follow.

ENFORCING REFERENTIAL INTEGRITY Recall that referential integrity constraints concern the presence of key values in parent table and child tables. In particular, such constraints ensure that a key value in a child table exists in a related parent table. An example is that ArtistID in CUSTOMER_ARTIST_INT must exist in ArtistID in ARTIST.

The first check box in Figure 13-13 concerns referential integrity checking on existing data. Since we're creating a new database, this box is unimportant to us. If we were creating a relationship on existing data, however, we would check it if we want SQL Server to look for integrity violations in already existing data. If not, SQL Server would only apply the constraint to new data and to data as thereafter modified.

You might not want SQL Server to check integrity on existing data if the database is large because this can be time-consuming. Additionally, you would not want to check this box if you do not know how to fix violations that you find. You may not know how to make up a relationship for existing data.

The next check box, Enforce relationship for replication, has to do with distributed processing and we'll skip that for now.

➤ FIGURE 13-14

Summary of View Ridge Database Referential Integrity Constraints Enforcement

Relationship	Enforce Relationship	Cascade Delete
CUSTOMER to TRANS	Yes	No
CUSTOMER to CUSTOMER-ARTIST-INT	Yes	Yes
ARTIST to WORK	Yes	No
WORK to TRANS	Yes	No
ARTIST to CUSTOMER-ARTIST-INT	Yes	Yes

The third check box, Enforce relationships for INSERTs and UPDATEs, is important for our current purposes. If this box is unchecked, SQL Server will ignore the relationship during updates and deletions. Thus, if this box is unchecked, we could delete an ARTIST and possibly leave CUSTOMER_ARTIST_INT rows with invalid values of ArtistID. This is not desired, so check this box.

Now, if we check neither of the next two boxes, SQL Server will simply disallow any update or deletion that would violate this integrity constraint. We will use this to our advantage in a moment.

The relationship that we're creating concerns an intersection table. If an artist row is deleted, we want the corresponding rows in this intersection table to be deleted as well. Consequently, we check the Cascade Delete Related Records box. By doing this, we instruct SQL Server to delete all related intersection table rows when we delete a row in ARTIST. This has the same effect as the SQL clause ON DELETE CASCADE shown in Chapter 12.

This design uses surrogate keys, and hence no changes to key values are possible. Therefore, we need not worry about the Cascade Update Related Records. No updates to key values are possible.

Now we can define the relationship between CUSTOMER and CUSTOMER_ARTIST_INT in a similar way. Check both the Enforce relationship and the Cascade Delete check boxes.

Consider next the relationships between ARTIST and WORK, between WORK and TRANS, and between CUSTOMER and TRANS. We do not want to cascade deletions in any of these relationships. Instead, we want to disallow any deletion that would cause a referential integrity violation. If, for example, someone attempts to delete a row in WORK that has a TRANS child, we want to prevent the deletion. Because of this, in the relationship properties dialog box, check the Enforce relationships check box, but do not check the Cascade Delete check box. The relationships in this database are summarized in Figure 13-14.

With relationships set up this way, the only way to delete, say, an ARTIST row is first to delete all of the TRANS rows for any works by that artist, then to delete all of the WORK rows for any works by that artist, and then to delete the ARTIST row.

The finished relationship diagram appears as in Figure 13-15. You can determine the properties of any relationship by right-clicking on the line that represents it.

VIEWS

If you have not already done so, read the discussion of views in Chapter 12, pages 341–342. The general comments made there pertain to views expressed in SQL Server as well.

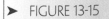

➤ FIGURE 13-15

Database Diagram for the View Ridge Schema

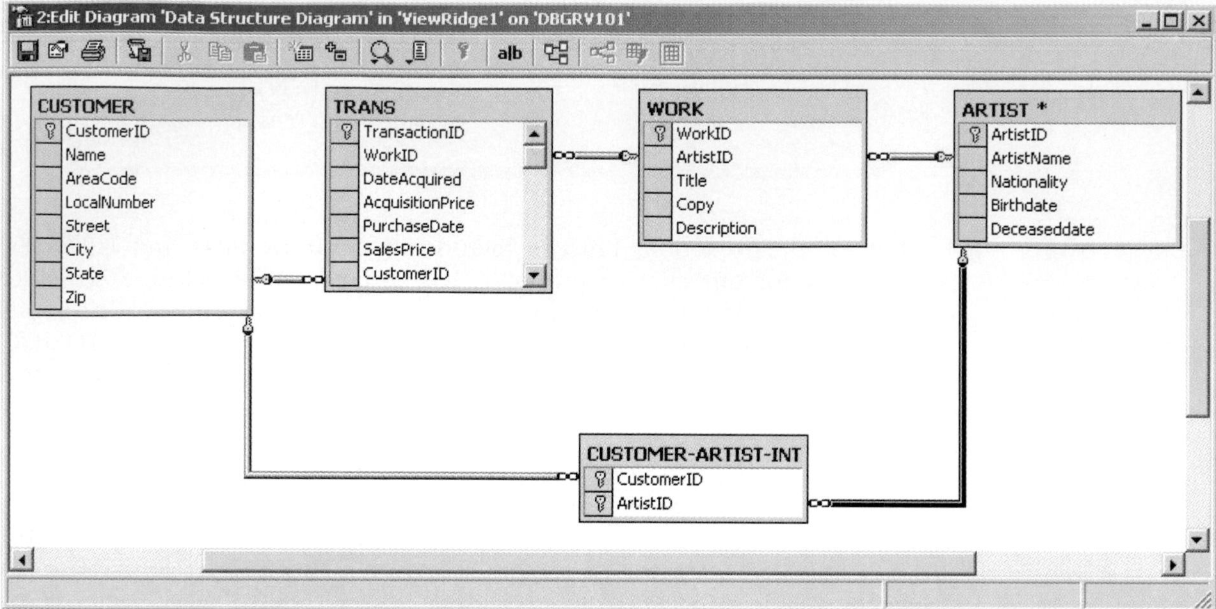

CREATING VIEWS Views can be defined using SQL statements or using the graphical design facilities of SQL Server. Figures 13-16 and 13-17 show both approaches.

The view defined in these figures is called ExpensiveArtistWork. It joins the ARTIST, WORK, and TRANS data for all artists and then selects rows for which the

➤ FIGURE 13-16

Creating a View with SQL Statements

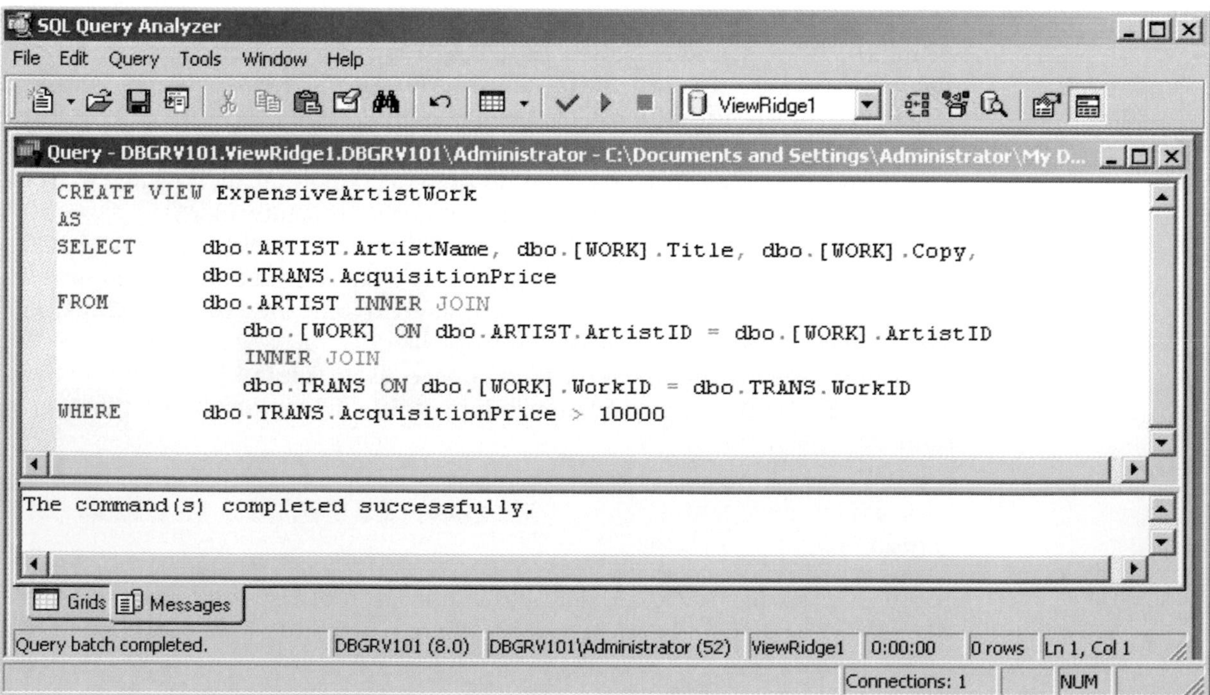

➤ FIGURE 13-17

Creating a View with the Graphical Tool

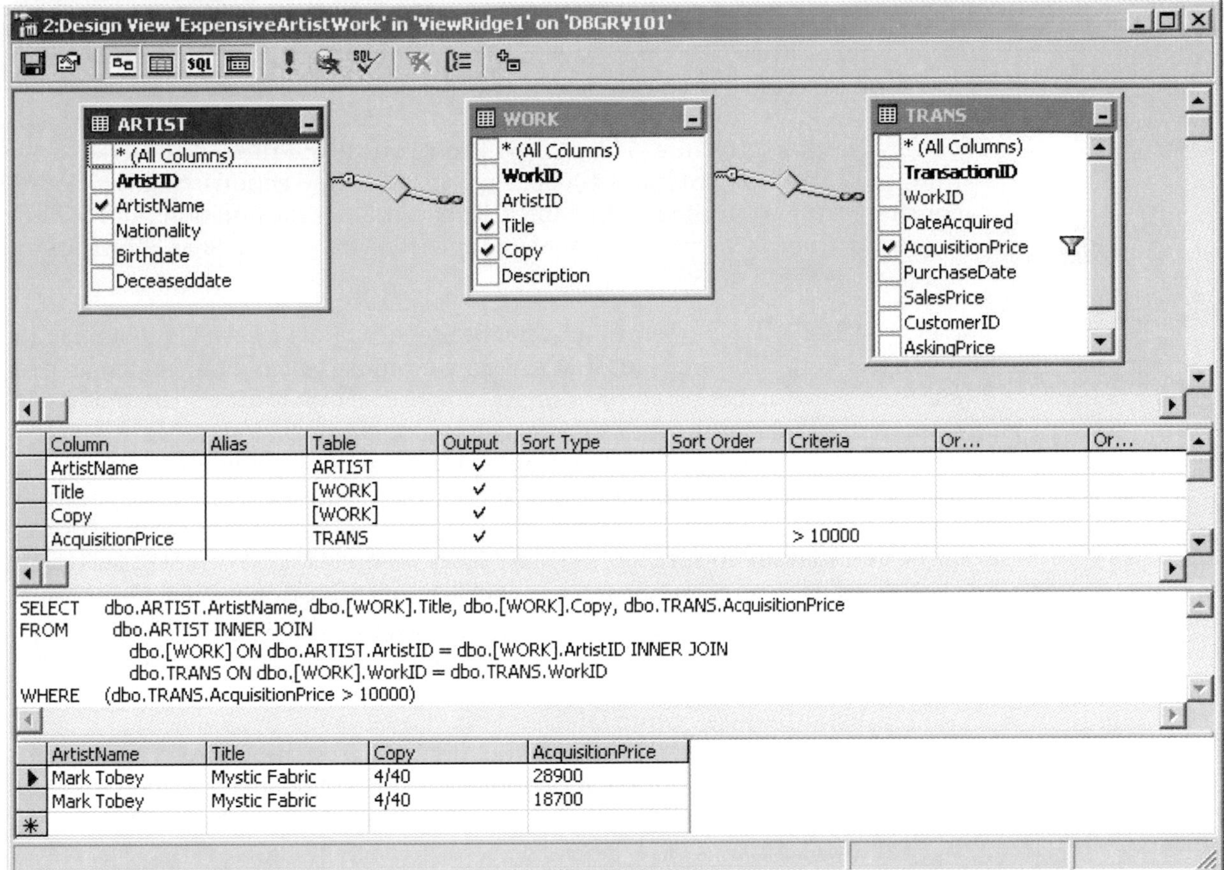

AcquisitionPrice is greater than 10000. Once this view has been created, a user could enter the following SQL to obtain the data:

```
SELECT    *
FROM      ExpensiveArtistView
```

The user would not need to perform the joins on the underlying tables, nor even know that such a join had been performed.

By the way, observe in Figure 13-16 that each table name is qualified with the term *dbo*. This is done for the following reason. By default, every table name has a user name appended to it. If no name appears in a table reference, SQL Server appends the user's name to the reference. Thus, if user John is signed on to SQL Server and makes reference to table CUST, SQL Server will look for the table name John.CUST. However, if user John is signed on to SQL Server and makes reference to table dbo.CUST, SQL Server will look for the table named dbo.CUST, not John.CUST.

The CREATE VIEW statement in Figure 13-16 appends dbo to every table reference so that users other than the dbo can utilize this statement. When the user dbo runs this statement, all of the dbo references are superfluous because they would have been added by SQL Server, anyway. But when user John runs this statement, the presence of the prefix dbo ensures that SQL Server will refer to the tables owned by the dbo and not by those owned by John.

Since no name is appended to ExpensiveArtistWork, when the dbo runs this query, he or she will create a view named dbo.ExpensiveArtistWork. When John runs this query, he will create a view named John.ExpensiveArtistWork. They will be different views. They will have the same data since they are based on the same tables, but there will be two views with two different names.

To create a view using the graphical tool, right click on Views in the Enterprise Manager and then click New View. Right-click in the top, empty pane and select Add Table. To create the view in Figure 13-17, add ARTIST, WORK, and TRANS tables. Check ArtistName, Title, Copy, and AcquisitionPrice. In the grid in the third pane, add the criteria > 10000. As you take these actions, SQL Server will construct the SQL in the fourth pane. Click on the red exclamation point on the menu bar and SQL Server will populate the view with your data as shown in the last pane of Figure 13-17.

UPDATABLE VIEWS Some views can be used for updating data and others cannot. Specifying the conditions that make a view updatable is complicated. In general, any view that is based on a single table can be used for update and delete operations as long as it contains no aggregate functions (like COUNT or MAX) or derived columns in its SELECT clause. Such a view can also be used for inserting data, if the view contains all of the NOT NULL columns. Otherwise, it cannot accept inserts.

Views that are formed on joins are more complicated. With SQL Server, no view that has more than one table in its FROM clause can have deletions. Multi-table views can accept inserts and updates as long as the inserts and updates are made to a single table within the view, and again assuming the view has no aggregate functions or derived columns in its SELECT clause.

Finally, otherwise nonupdatable views can be made updatable if the developer creates an INSTEAD OF trigger for the update operation. Such a trigger is a TRANSACT-SQL procedure that performs the insert, update, or delete operation on behalf of SQL Server. We will discuss this further when we discuss triggers.

Indexes

As stated, indexes are special data structures that are created to improve database performance (see Appendix A). SQL Server automatically creates an index on all primary and foreign keys. The developer can also direct SQL Server to create an index on other columns that are frequently used in WHERE clauses or on columns that are used for sorting data when sequentially processing a table for queries and reports.

To create an index, right-click on the table that has the column you want to index, click on All Tasks, and then click on Manage Indexes. You will see the dialog box shown in the left-hand portion of Figure 13-18. Click New and you will be shown the dialog box in the right-hand portion of this figure. The developer is creating an index on the Zip column of the CUSTOMER table. The index, named CUSTOMER_Zip_Index, is to be padded, filled to 80%, and assigned to the PRIMARY File Group. Padding causes space to be left open for inserts in all levels of the index except the bottom one. Filling refers to the amount of empty space left in the bottom level of the index. See Appendix A and the SQL Server documentation for more information about these choices.

Click Edit SQL in this dialog box and you will see the dialog box in Figure 13-19. This shows the SQL statement that could be entered via the SQL Analyzer to create the index.

SQL Server supports two kinds of indexes: clustered and nonclustered. With a clustered index, the data are stored in the bottom level of the index and in the

➤ FIGURE 13-18

Creating An Index with the Graphical Tool

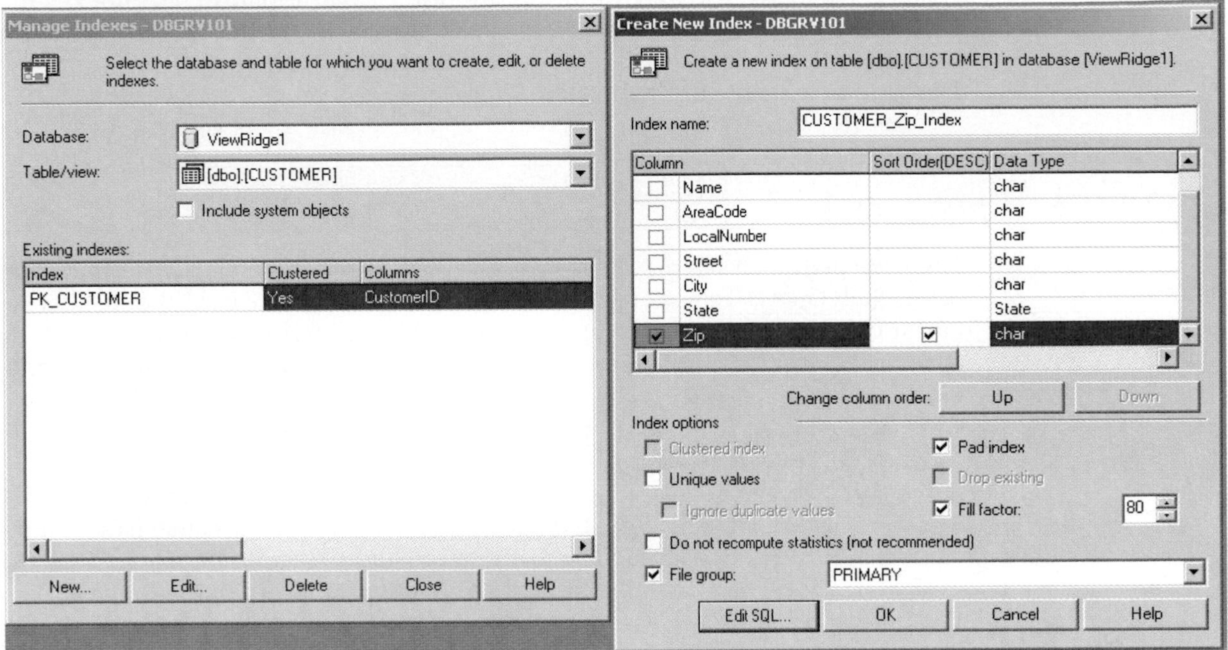

➤ FIGURE 13-19

SQL for Creating an Index

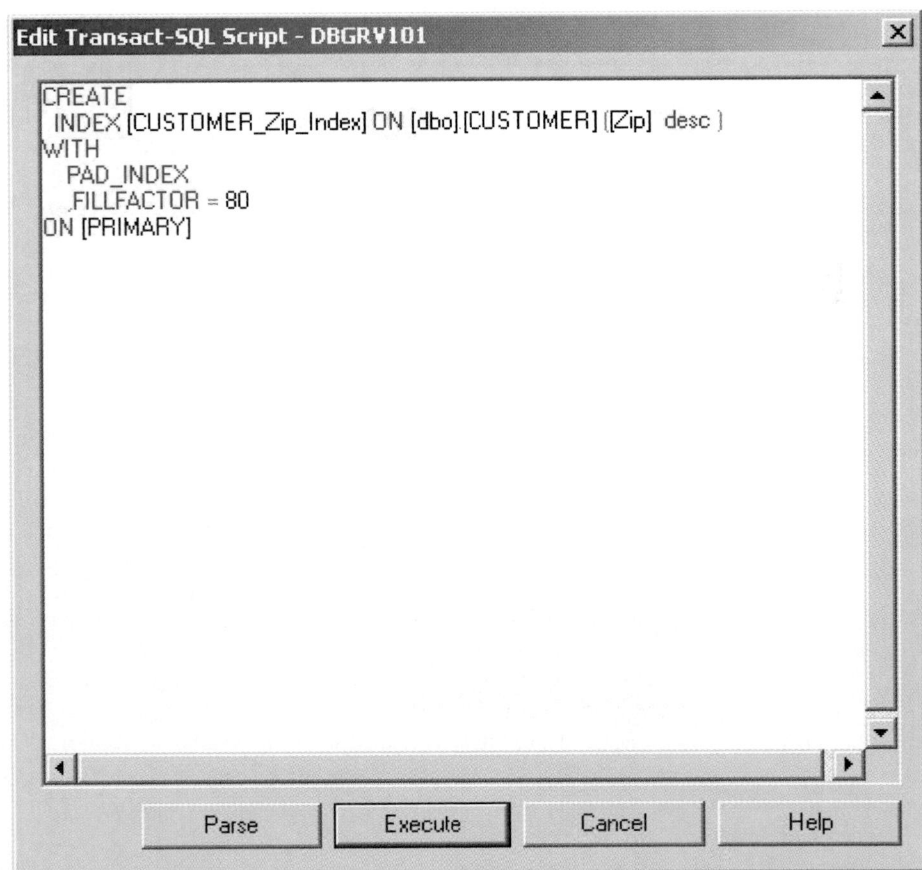

same order as that index. With a nonclustered index, the bottom level of an index does not contain data, but rather it contains pointers to the data. Because rows can be sorted only in one physical order at a time, only one clustered index is allowed per table. Clustered indexes are faster than nonclustered indexes for retrieval. They are normally faster for updating as well, but not if there are many updates in the same spot in the middle of the relation. See the SQL Server documentation for more information.

➤ APPLICATION LOGIC

There are many ways to process a SQL Server database. You've already seen the use of the SQL Query Analyzer to submit SQL statements. We've used that facility so far for creating database structures, but it can be used to process any type of SQL statement. Other means of processing the database are to write application programs in languages like Visual Basic, Java, C#, or C++ and to use Active Data Objects, ODBC, or JDBC to process the database structures and content. We will show examples of that use for Internet processing in Chapter 15.

A third means of accessing the database is to write procedures in TRANSACT-SQL, which is a language that adds programming elements like parameters, variables, IF, WHILE loops, and so forth, to the basic capabilities of SQL. TRANSACT_SQL serves the same role for SQL Server that PL/SQL does for Oracle.

You can write TRANSACT-SQL programs and submit them to the DBMS via the SQL Query Analyzer, via stored procedures, and via triggers. We will consider each of these in this section. You can also invoke TRANSACT/SQL in web script programs as you will see in Chapter 15.

SAVED QUERIES

Suppose every Monday morning the manager of View Ridge wants to obtain a list of all of the works that are currently available for sale. One way to do this is to write the SQL query shown in Figure 13-20. This query lists the ArtistName, Title, and Copy of every work for which the CustomerID in TRANS is null. These rows represent the unsold works.

To avoid having to write this query every week, the manager can write it once and save it to a file. Then, to run it, the user starts the SQL Query Analyzer, opens the query file, and executes the query.

Doing this, however, requires that users have access to the SQL Query Analyzer, which is unlikely, especially if they are processing from a computer other than the one that manages the database. It also exposes the users to considerable complexity. More likely an application program would be written that runs this query and reports the results back to the user in a more user-friendly way.

This style of processing is frequently used, however, by database administrators. They develop procedures in TRANSACT-SQL that perform many database administration tasks. These procedures are saved in files and later used when required.

STORED PROCEDURES

Another approach for processing a SQL Server database is to create procedures of TRANSACT-SQL statements and store them either on the users' computers or in the database. These stored procedures can be invoked via their name and can be passed as parameter values. For example, the statement

```
InsertARTIST @ArtistName='Matisse'
```

➤ FIGURE 13-20

An Example Saved Query

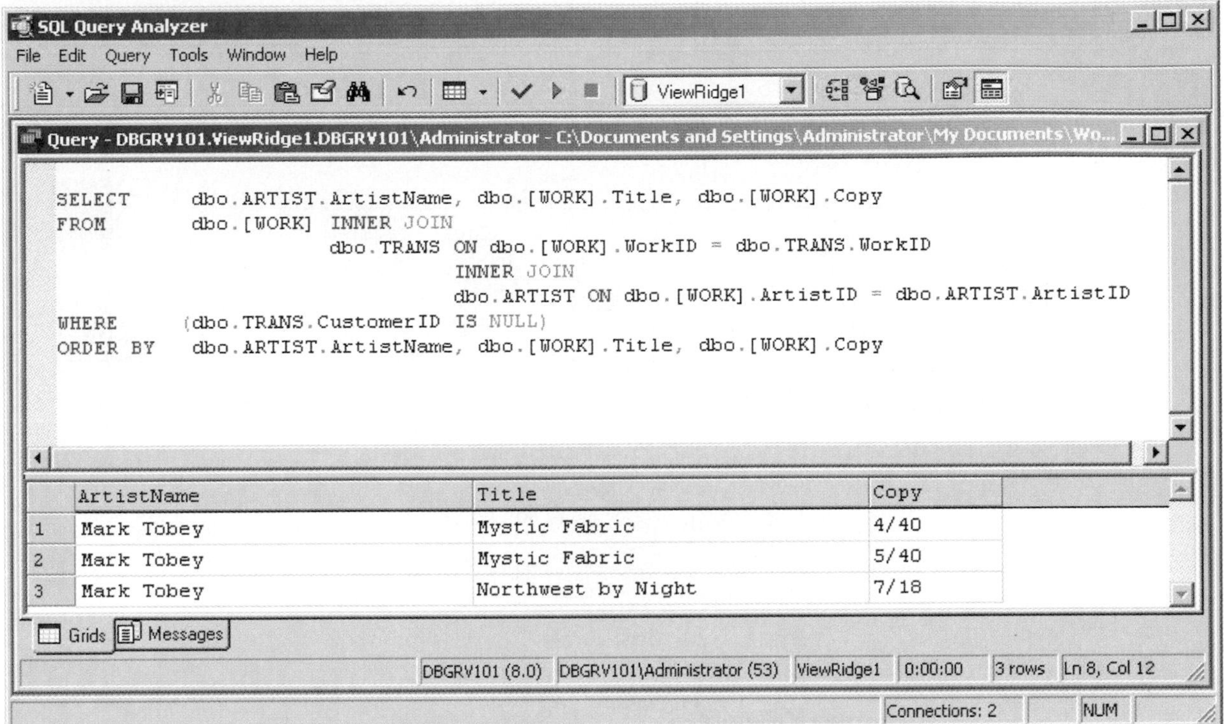

invokes a stored procedure named InsertARTIST and passes it the parameter named @ArtistName with the value "Matisse." Such procedures can have arbitrarily complicated logic; they can process potentially many databases, they can invoke other stored procedures and functions, and so forth.

With the advent of the Internet, it is becoming more common to keep the stored procedures in the database rather than distributing them to the users' computers. Web server and browser code then invoke the procedures and pass parameters via a connection established using Active Data Objects or COM over HTTP. We will illustrate this use further in Chapter 15.

Here, however, we will write stored procedures within SQL Server and then test them using the SQL Query Analyzer. We are doing this for simplicity of illustration. More realistically, the stored procedures would be invoked by an application program over a network or the Internet and not by the SQL Query Analyzer.

THE Customer_Insert STORED PROCEDURE Figure 13-21 illustrates a stored procedure that stores data for a new customer and connects that customer to all artists having a particular nationality. (This is the same logic as shown for Customer_Insert in the last chapter.) Four parameters are input to the procedure: @NewName, @NewAreaCode, @NewPhone, and @Nationality. As you can see, parameters and variables in TRANSACT-SQL are preceded by @ signs. The first three parameters are the new customer data and the fourth one is the nationality of the artists for which the new customer has an interest.

The first task performed by this stored procedure is to determine if the customer already exists. If the count of the first SELECT statement is greater than 0, then a row for that customer already exists. In this case, nothing is done and the stored procedure prints an error message and exits. This error message, by the way,

➤ FIGURE 13-21

Customer_Insert Stored Procedure

```
CREATE PROCEDURE Customer_Insert
        @NewName            char(50),
        @NewAreaCode        char (5),
        @NewPhone           char (8),
        @Nationality        char(25)
AS

DECLARE @Count      as smallint
DECLARE @Aid        as int
DECLARE @Cid        as int

/* Check to see if customer already exists */
SELECT @Count = Count (*)
FROM dbo.CUSTOMER
WHERE [Name]=@NewName AND AreaCode=@NewAreaCode AND LocalNumber=@NewPhone

IF @Count > 0
        BEGIN
                PRINT 'Customer Already Exists -- No Action Taken'
                RETURN
        END

/* Add new Customer data */
INSERT INTO     dbo.CUSTOMER
                ([Name], AreaCode, LocalNumber)
                VALUES
                (@NewName, @NewAreaCode, @NewPhone)

/* Get new surrogate key value */
Select @Cid = CustomerID
FROM dbo.CUSTOMER
WHERE [Name]=@NewName AND AreaCode=@NewAreaCode AND LocalNumber=@NewPhone

/* Now create intersection record for each appropriate artist */
DECLARE Artist_Cursor CURSOR FOR
SELECT ArtistID
FROM dbo.ARTIST
WHERE Nationality=@Nationality

/* process each Artist of specified nationality */
OPEN Artist_Cursor
FETCH NEXT FROM Artist_Cursor INTO @Aid
WHILE @@FETCH_STATUS = 0
BEGIN
        INSERT INTO dbo.[CUSTOMER-ARTIST-INT]
                        (ArtistID,CustomerID)
                VALUES (@Aid, @Cid)
        FETCH NEXT FROM Artist_Cursor INTO @Aid
END

CLOSE Artist_Cursor
DEALLOCATE Artist_Cursor
GO
```

will be visible in the Query Analyzer, but, in general, would not be visible to application programs that invoked this procedure. Instead, a parameter or other facility would need to be used to return the error message back to the user via the application program. We will consider this issue in later chapters.

Next, the procedure inserts the new data into dbo.CUSTOMER and then new value of CustomerID is read into the variable @Cid.

To create the appropriate intersection table rows, a cursor is opened on a SQL Statement that obtains all ARTIST rows where Nationality equals the parameter @Nationality. The cursor is then processed in the WHILE loop and new values are inserted into the intersection table CUSTOMER_ARTIST_INT. The FETCH statement moves the cursor to the next row.

Figure 13-22 shows how to invoke this stored procedure using the SQL Query Analyzer to add a new customer having an interest in US artists. Parameters are passed with the values shown. Figure 13-23 shows database data after the stored procedure has run. Customer Lynda Johnson has been added to the CUSTOMER table and assigned CustomerID 1038. Note that there are three US artists, and that a row for each of them has been inserted into the CUSTOMER_ARTIST_INT table for CustomerID of 1038.

To create a stored procedure, right-click Stored Procedures in a database and select New Stored Procedure. To modify an existing stored procedure, right-click on the procedure in the procedure list and select properties.

THE NewCustomerWithTransaction STORED PROCEDURE A stored procedure that implements the logic for View Ridge view creation pseudocode on page 264 is shown in Figure 13-24. This procedure receives seven parameters having data about the new customer and about the customer's purchase.

The first action is to check if the customer already exists; if so, the procedure exits with an error message. If the customer does not exist, this procedure then starts a transaction. Recall from Chapter 11 that transactions ensure that all of the database activity is committed atomically; either all of the updates will occur or none of them will. The transaction is begun and the new customer row is inserted.

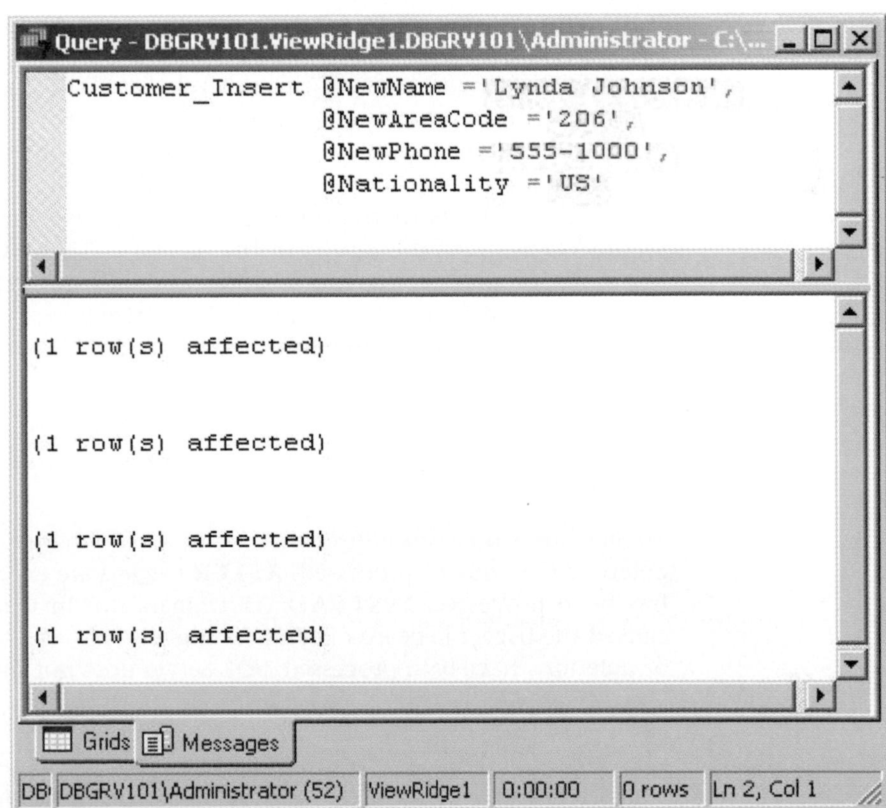
Query - DBGRV101.ViewRidge1.DBGRV101\Administrator - C:\...
Customer_Insert @NewName ='Lynda Johnson',
@NewAreaCode ='206',
@NewPhone ='555-1000',
@Nationality ='US'
(1 row(s) affected)
(1 row(s) affected)
(1 row(s) affected)
(1 row(s) affected)
Grids
Messages
DBGRV101\Administrator (52)
ViewRidge1
0:00:00
0 rows
Ln 2, Col 1

➤ FIGURE 13-22

Invoking the Customer_Insert Stored Procedure from the SQL Query Analyzer

FIGURE 13-23

Results of the Stored Procedure Call in Figure 13-22

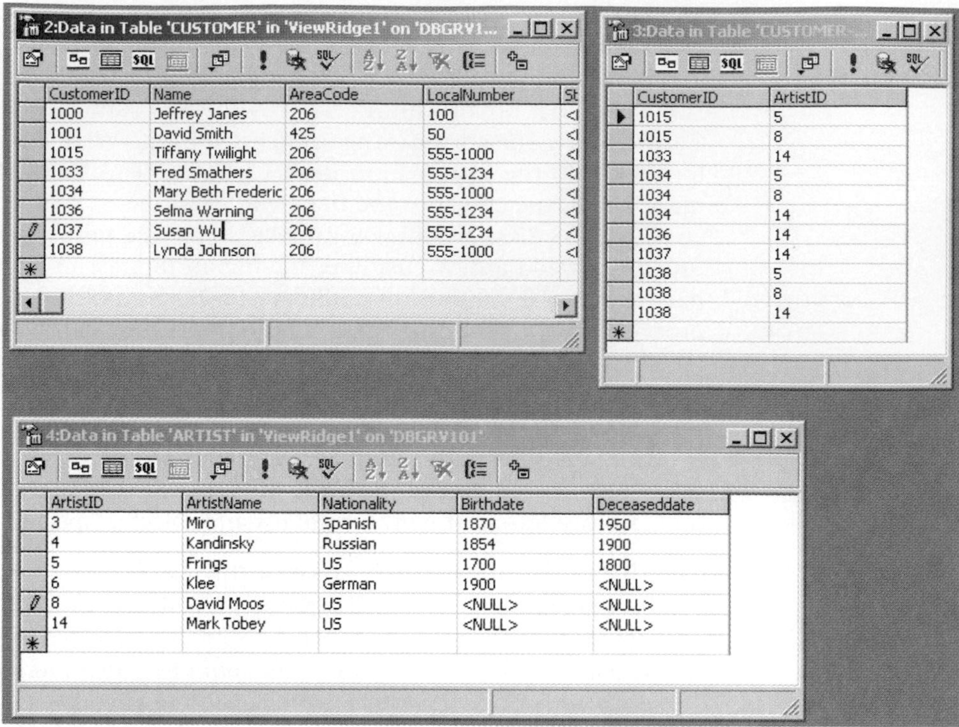

2:Data in Table 'CUSTOMER' in 'ViewRidge1' on 'DBGRV1...

CustomerID	Name	AreaCode	LocalNumber	St
1000	Jeffrey Janes	206	100	<l
1001	David Smith	425	50	<l
1015	Tiffany Twilight	206	555-1000	<l
1033	Fred Smathers	206	555-1234	<l
1034	Mary Beth Frederic	206	555-1000	<l
1036	Selma Warning	206	555-1234	<l
1037	Susan Wu	206	555-1234	<l
1038	Lynda Johnson	206	555-1000	<l

3:Data in Table 'CUSTOMER-...

CustomerID	ArtistID
1015	5
1015	8
1033	14
1034	5
1034	8
1034	14
1036	14
1037	14
1038	5
1038	8
1038	14

4:Data in Table 'ARTIST' in 'ViewRidge1' on 'DBGRV101'

ArtistID	ArtistName	Nationality	Birthdate	Deceaseddate
3	Miro	Spanish	1870	1950
4	Kandinsky	Russian	1854	1900
5	Frings	US	1700	1800
6	Klee	German	1900	<NULL>
8	David Moos	US	<NULL>	<NULL>
14	Mark Tobey	US	<NULL>	<NULL>

The new value of CustomerID is obtained as shown previously. Next, the procedure checks to determine if the ArtistID, WorkID, and TransactionID are valid. If any of them are invalid, the transaction is rolled back.

If all of these are valid, then an UPDATE statement updates PurchaseDate, Price, and CustomerID in the appropriate TRANS row. PurchaseDate is set to system date (via the system-supplied GETDATE() function), SalesPrice is set to the value of @Price, and CustomerID is set to the value of @Cid. Finally, a row is added to CUSTOMER_ARTIST_INT to record the customer's interest in this artist. If everything proceeds normally to this point, then the transaction is committed.

Figure 13-25 shows the invocation of this procedure using sample data and Figure 13-26 shows the results in the database. The new customer was assigned CustomerID 1040 and this id was stored in the CustomerID foreign key column of TRANS as required. PurchaseDate and SalesPrice were also set appropriately. Note the new row in the intersection table that records customer 1040's interest in artist 14 as required.

TRIGGERS

Triggers are stored procedures that are invoked when specified insert, update, or delete commands are processed. **AFTER** triggers are executed after the command has been processed; **INSTEAD OF** triggers run instead of the statement that caused the trigger to be invoked. After triggers are run after any cascading updates or deletions have been processed. SQL Server does not support BEFORE triggers as Oracle does.

New_Price TRIGGER Figure 13-27 shows a trigger that is used to compute the value of the NewPrice column. The CREATE TRIGGER statement indicates that it

➤ FIGURE 13-24

NewCustomerWith Transaction Stored Procedure

```
CREATE PROCEDURE NewCustomerWithTransaction
        @NewName char(50), @NewAreaCode char (3), @NewPhone char (8),
        @ArtistName char(50), @WorkTitle char(50), @WorkCopy char (10),
        @Price smallmoney
AS

DECLARE @Count as smallint
DECLARE @Aid as int
DECLARE @Cid as int
DECLARE @Wid as int
DECLARE @Tid as int

SELECT @Count = Count (*)
FROM dbo.CUSTOMER
WHERE [Name]=@NewName AND AreaCode=@NewAreaCode AND LocalNumber=@NewPhone

IF @Count > 0
        BEGIN  PRINT 'Customer Already Exists -- No Action Taken'
               RETURN
        END

BEGIN TRANSACTION  /* Start transaction rollback everything if cannot complete it. */

INSERT INTO dbo.CUSTOMER
        ([Name], AreaCode, LocalNumber)
        VALUES (@NewName, @NewAreaCode, @NewPhone)

Select @Cid = CustomerID
FROM dbo.CUSTOMER
WHERE [Name]=@NewName AND AreaCode=@NewAreaCode AND LocalNumber=@NewPhone

SELECT @Aid = ArtistID
FROM dbo.ARTIST
WHERE ArtistName=@ArtistName

If @Aid IS NULL   /* Invalid Artist ID */
        BEGIN
               Print 'Artist ID not valid'
               ROLLBACK
               RETURN
        END

SELECT @Wid = WorkID
FROM dbo.[WORK]
WHERE ArtistID = @Aid AND Title = @WorkTitle AND Copy = @WorkCopy
If @Wid IS NULL  /* Invalid Work ID */
        BEGIN
               Print 'Work ID not valid'
               ROLLBACK
               RETURN
        END

SELECT @Tid = TransactionID
FROM dbo.[TRANS]
WHERE WorkID=@Wid AND SalesPrice IS NULL
If @Tid IS NULL /*Invalid Transaction ID */
        BEGIN
               Print 'No valid transaction record'
               ROLLBACK
               RETURN
        END

UPDATE dbo.[TRANS] /* ALL is OK, update TRANS row */
SET PurchaseDate = GETDATE(), SalesPrice = @Price, CustomerID = @Cid
WHERE TransactionID=@Tid

INSERT INTO dbo.[CUSTOMER-ARTIST-INT] /* Create interest for this artist */
        (CustomerID, ArtistID)
        Values (@Cid, @Aid)

COMMIT
GO
```

➤ FIGURE 13-25

Invoking the NewCustomerWithTransaction Stored Procedure from the SQL Query Analyzer

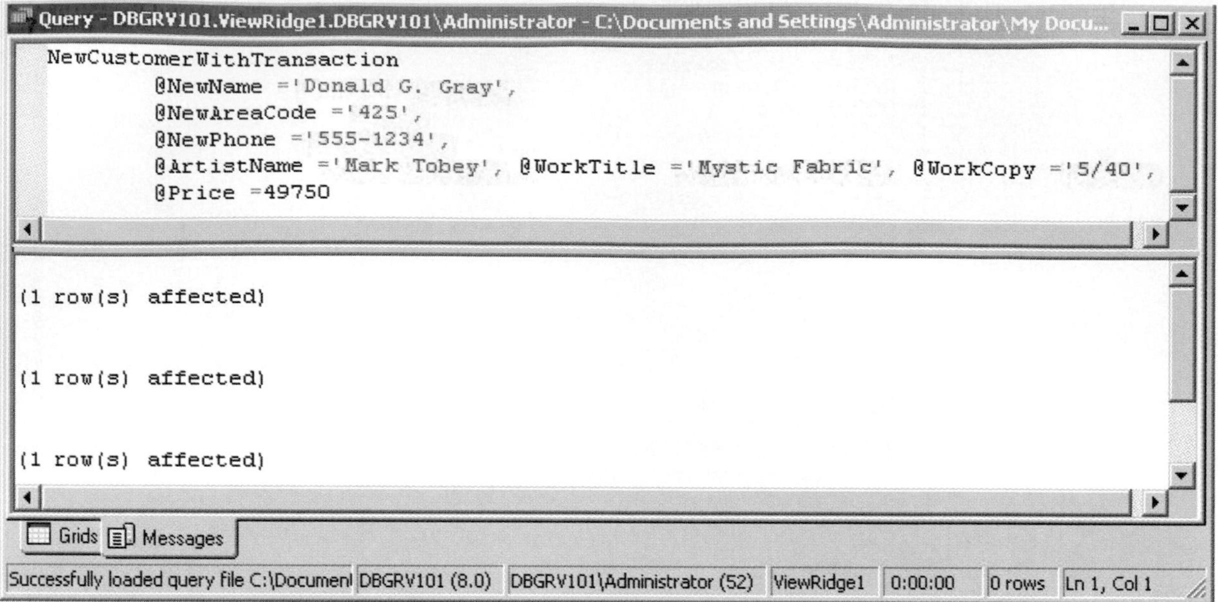
Query - DBGRV101.ViewRidge1.DBGRV101\Administrator - C:\Documents and Settings\Administrator\My Docu...
NewCustomerWithTransaction
@NewName ='Donald G. Gray',
@NewAreaCode ='425',
@NewPhone ='555-1234',
@ArtistName ='Mark Tobey', @WorkTitle ='Mystic Fabric', @WorkCopy ='5/40',
@Price =49750
(1 row(s) affected)
(1 row(s) affected)
(1 row(s) affected)
Grids
Messages
Successfully loaded query file C:\Documen
DBGRV101 (8.0)
DBGRV101\Administrator (52)
ViewRidge1
0:00:00
0 rows
Ln 1, Col 1

➤ FIGURE 13-26

Results of the Stored Procedure Call in Figure 13-25

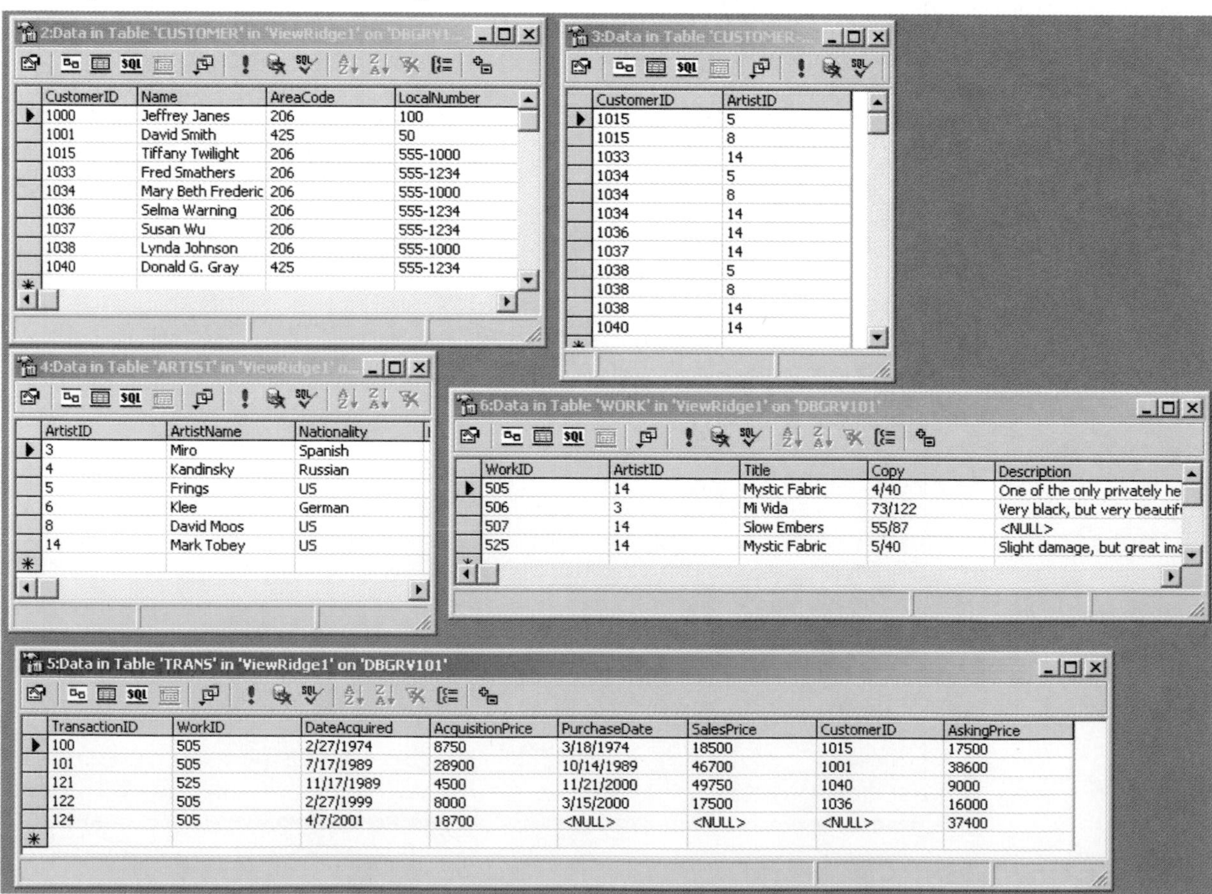

2:Data in Table 'CUSTOMER' in 'ViewRidge1' on 'DBGRV1...

CustomerID	Name	AreaCode	LocalNumber
1000	Jeffrey Janes	206	100
1001	David Smith	425	50
1015	Tiffany Twilight	206	555-1000
1033	Fred Smathers	206	555-1234
1034	Mary Beth Frederic	206	555-1000
1036	Selma Warning	206	555-1234
1037	Susan Wu	206	555-1234
1038	Lynda Johnson	206	555-1000
1040	Donald G. Gray	425	555-1234

3:Data in Table 'CUSTOMER-...

CustomerID	ArtistID
1015	5
1015	8
1033	14
1034	5
1034	8
1034	14
1036	14
1037	14
1038	5
1038	8
1038	14
1040	14

4:Data in Table 'ARTIST' in 'ViewRidge1' o...

ArtistID	ArtistName	Nationality
3	Miro	Spanish
4	Kandinsky	Russian
5	Frings	US
6	Klee	German
8	David Moos	US
14	Mark Tobey	US

6:Data in Table 'WORK' in 'ViewRidge1' on 'DBGRV101'

WorkID	ArtistID	Title	Copy	Description
505	14	Mystic Fabric	4/40	One of the only privately he
506	3	Mi Vida	73/122	Very black, but very beautif
507	14	Slow Embers	55/87	<NULL>
525	14	Mystic Fabric	5/40	Slight damage, but great ima

5:Data in Table 'TRANS' in 'ViewRidge1' on 'DBGRV101'

TransactionID	WorkID	DateAcquired	AcquisitionPrice	PurchaseDate	SalesPrice	CustomerID	AskingPrice
100	505	2/27/1974	8750	3/18/1974	18500	1015	17500
101	505	7/17/1989	28900	10/14/1989	46700	1001	38600
121	525	11/17/1989	4500	11/21/2000	49750	1040	9000
122	505	2/27/1999	8000	3/15/2000	17500	1036	16000
124	505	4/7/2001	18700	<NULL>	<NULL>	<NULL>	37400

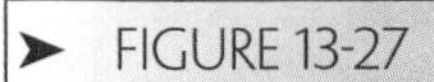
FIGURE 13-27

New_Price Trigger

```
CREATE TRIGGER New_Price ON [dbo].[TRANS]
FOR INSERT, UPDATE
AS

DECLARE @NewPrice as smallmoney
DECLARE @id as int

IF NOT UPDATE (AcquisitionPrice) RETURN /* Only concerned with new values or changes to Acquisition Price */

SELECT @NewPrice = AcquisitionPrice, @id = TransactionID
FROM inserted

Set @NewPrice = @NewPrice * 2 /* Could use a function here for more sophisticated aging of price, etc. */

/* Note: the following will cause a recursive call to this trigger. It will terminate because this update does not
   involve AcqusitionPrice */

UPDATE dbo.TRANS
SET AskingPrice = @NewPrice
WHERE TransactionID = @id
```

is to be invoked for insert and update on the TRANS table. The trigger code first checks to determine if the update (here meaning either insert or update) involves the AcqusitionPrice column. If not, the trigger exits.

If the insert or update does involve the AcquisitionPrice column, then the next statement issues a SELECT that obtains the new value of AcquisitionPrice and the value of TransactionID. This select operates on a pseudo-table that is maintained by SQL Server. This table is called *inserted* and it contains all of the inserted or changed data. There is another similar table (not used here) called *deleted* that contains the data that existed before any delete operation. The inserted and deleted tables are only available in trigger code. They are similar to the *:new* and *:old* prefixes used in Oracle.

Next, the trigger computes the new value of price in the variable @Price. This value is then used to update the AskingPrice column of the row being updated. As the comment states, the UPDATE of TRANS in this trigger will cause the trigger to fire again, recursively. The second time it fires, however, the update will not concern AcquisitionPrice and the second instance of the trigger will exit without making another UPDATE.

This, by the way, is an expensive way to implement such a simple formula. A better solution would be to define this formula as a property of the AskingPrice column in the definition of the TRANS table. However, if the computation of AskingPrice were more complicated, if it involved accessing other tables or even other databases, then this trigger would be necessary.

On_WORK_Insert TRIGGER Figure 13-28 shows a more typical use for trigger code. As stated in Chapter 10, the same work of art may be sold by the gallery several times. Because we are using surrogate keys, however, each time a work is entered into the database, it will be entered as a new row, and will appear to be a different work of art. To prevent this, the On_WORK_Insert trigger is written to check if the new work has been stored in the database before. If so, the WORK row that was just created is removed from the database and the old row is used.

Additionally, the gallery wants each WORK that is available for sale to have a TRANS row with a null value for CustomerID. If the work has never been in the

➤ FIGURE 13-28

On_WORK_Insert Trigger

```
CREATE TRIGGER On_WORK_Insert ON dbo.[WORK] FOR INSERT
AS

DECLARE @NewWorkID as int
DECLARE @Count as smallint
DECLARE @Aid as int
DECLARE @Title as char (50)
DECLARE @Copy as char (10)

SELECT      @NewWorkID = WorkID, @Aid = ArtistID, @Title = Title, @Copy = Copy
FROM        Inserted /* this pseudo-table of inserted data is available to triggers */

SELECT      @Count = Count (*)
FROM        ViewRidge1.dbo.[WORK]
WHERE       ArtistID = @Aid AND Title = @Title AND Copy = @Copy

IF @Count > 2  /* Error -- this work had 2 rows PRIOR to new insert */
        BEGIN
            ROLLBACK
            Print 'Error in work table data; more than one available row for this work.'
            RETURN
        END

IF @Count = 2  /* Means one was available prior to insert -- rollback new insert and use existing row*/
        BEGIN
            ROLLBACK
            SELECT @NewWorkID = WorkID /* Get WorkID of existing row */
            FROM ViewRidge1.dbo.[WORK]
            WHERE ArtistID = @Aid AND Title = @Title AND Copy = @Copy
        END

SELECT @Count = Count(*) /* Check for available TRANS row */
FROM ViewRidge1.dbo.TRANS
WHERE @NewWorkID = WorkID AND CustomerID IS NULL

IF @Count > 0 RETURN /* One is Available */

INSERT INTO ViewRidge1.dbo.TRANS
(WorkID, DateAcquired)
VALUES (@NewWorkID, GETDATE())
```

gallery before, a new TRANS record must be created and connected to the new WORK row. If the work has been in the gallery before, and if there is no TRANS row for that WORK with a null CustomerID, then a new TRANS row must be created. If there is such a TRANS row already, then the work was never sold and the existing TRANS row can to be used.

The first task of the procedure is to obtain the new WORK values from the pseudo-table *inserted*. Then, a SELECT statement is issued to count the number of WORK rows that have the given ArtistID, Title, and Copy. If the count is greater than 2, then an error has occurred previously. There should be at most two rows having these data—the original row and the new row. If there are more than 2, the trigger rolls back the transaction, prints an error message, and exits.

If there are exactly two rows, then the work has been in the gallery before, and the trigger rolls back the transaction to remove the just-inserted WORK row.

Inserts That Will Invoke the Trigger in Figure 13-28

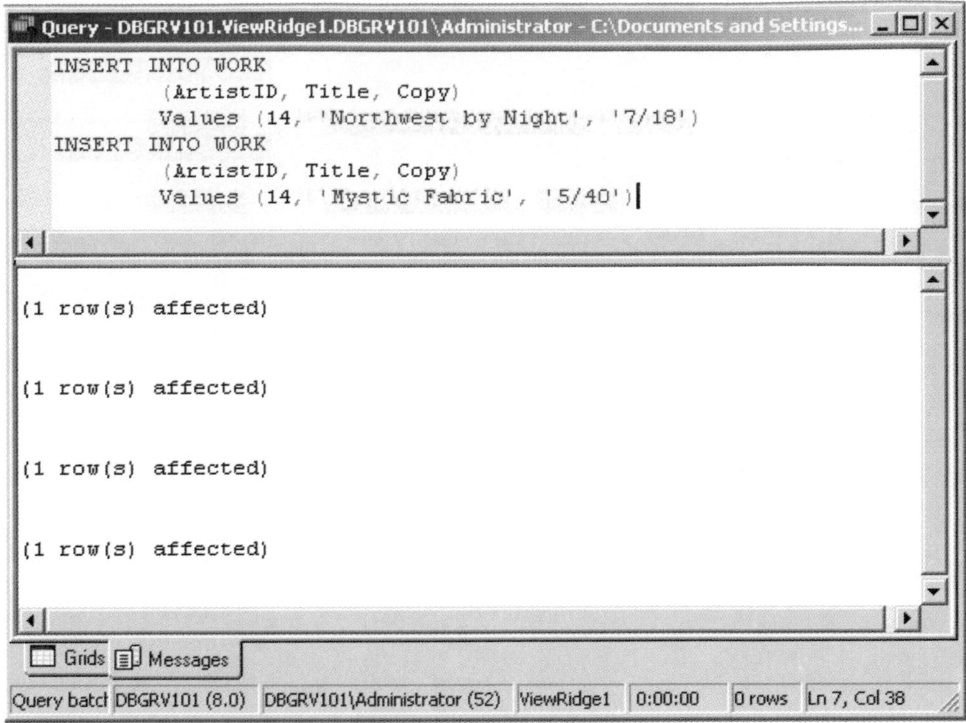

Query - DBGRV101.ViewRidge1.DBGRV101\Administrator - C:\Documents and Settings...
INSERT INTO WORK
(ArtistID, Title, Copy)
Values (14, 'Northwest by Night', '7/18')
INSERT INTO WORK
(ArtistID, Title, Copy)
Values (14, 'Mystic Fabric', '5/40')
(1 row(s) affected)
(1 row(s) affected)
(1 row(s) affected)
(1 row(s) affected)
Grids
Messages
Query batch DBGRV101 (8.0) DBGRV101\Administrator (52) ViewRidge1 0:00:00 0 rows Ln 7, Col 38

By the way, such a rollback eliminates any changes made by the transaction that caused this trigger to be invoked as well. After the rollback, the trigger code obtains the WorkID for the other row that has this work data.

At this point, WorkID either points to the old row for a work that has been in the gallery before, or points to the new row that has been created for a work that is new to the gallery.

The only remaining task is to determine if there is a TRANS row in the database for this work that has a null value of CustomerID. If so, no new TRANS row needs to be created. Otherwise a new TRANS row is inserted into the database.

Figure 13-29 shows the insert of two works into the ViewRidge database. The first work has never been in the gallery before and the second one has. Figure 13-30 shows the WORK and TRANS tables after both of these inserts. A new WORK row was added for the work "Northwest by Night," but no new row was inserted for "Mystic Fabric" Copy "5/40" because this work was already in the database. (You can tell it was in the database previously because the TRANS row with TransactionID of 131 was bound to it.)

Two new rows were added to TRANS; the foreign keys were set to the correct WORK rows. Notice, too, that the function GETDATE supplies both date and time to the DateAcquired column. Apparently, the other values in DateAcquired were set manually because no time appears in their values.

A view that is otherwise not updatable can be made so by defining an INSTEAD OF trigger. In the case, SQL Server will not attempt to execute the insert, update, or delete operation but will instead call the trigger. This is needed because it is not possible for the DBMS vendor to write general-purpose code to, say, insert any arbitrary view instance. With knowledge of the application, however, it can be possible to write code to do so for particular views.

This section has introduced basic stored procedure and trigger functionality. There is much more to learn, but this should give you a sufficient basis to get started. We will see how to invoke stored procedures using Internet technology in Chapter 15.

➤ FIGURE 13-30

Results of the Inserts in Figure 13-29

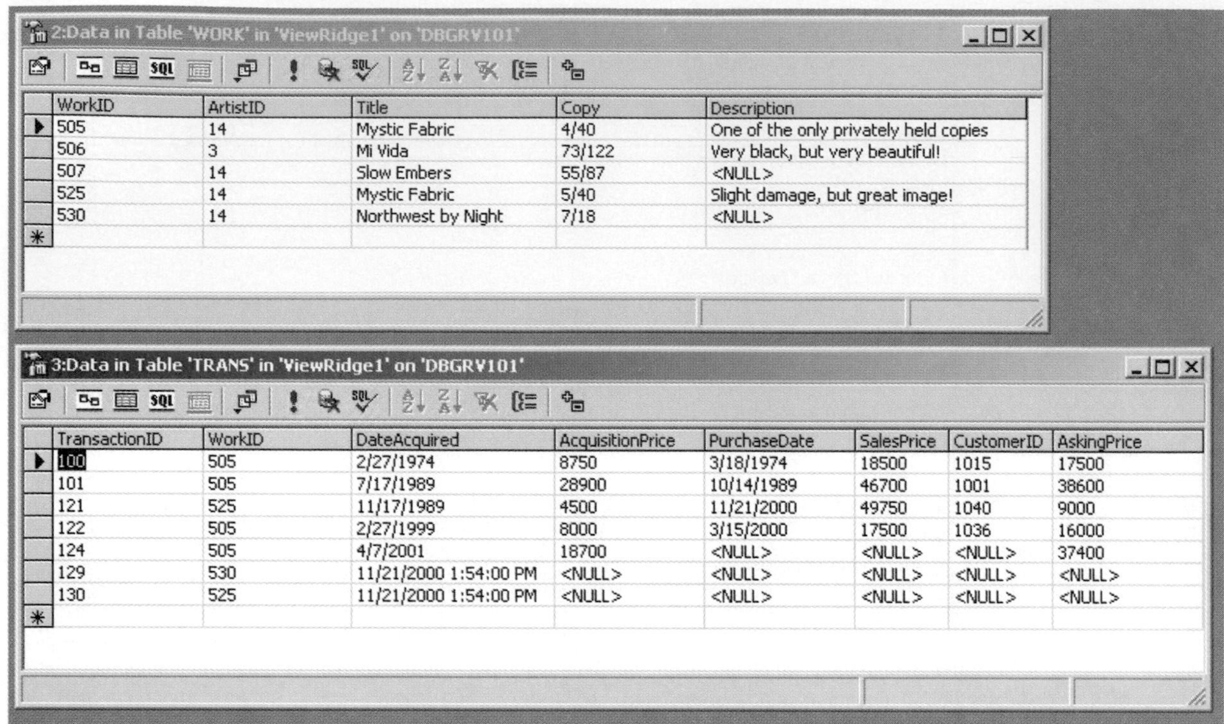

WorkID	ArtistID	Title	Copy	Description
505	14	Mystic Fabric	4/40	One of the only privately held copies
506	3	Mi Vida	73/122	Very black, but very beautiful!
507	14	Slow Embers	55/87	<NULL>
525	14	Mystic Fabric	5/40	Slight damage, but great image!
530	14	Northwest by Night	7/18	<NULL>

TransactionID	WorkID	DateAcquired	AcquisitionPrice	PurchaseDate	SalesPrice	CustomerID	AskingPrice
100	505	2/27/1974	8750	3/18/1974	18500	1015	17500
101	505	7/17/1989	28900	10/14/1989	46700	1001	38600
121	525	11/17/1989	4500	11/21/2000	49750	1040	9000
122	505	2/27/1999	8000	3/15/2000	17500	1036	16000
124	505	4/7/2001	18700	<NULL>	<NULL>	<NULL>	37400
129	530	11/21/2000 1:54:00 PM	<NULL>	<NULL>	<NULL>	<NULL>	<NULL>
130	525	11/21/2000 1:54:00 PM	<NULL>	<NULL>	<NULL>	<NULL>	<NULL>

➤ CONCURRENCY CONTROL

SQL Server 2000 provides a comprehensive set of capabilities to control concurrent processing. There are many choices and options available, and the resulting behavior is determined by the interaction of three factors: transaction isolation level, cursor concurrency setting, and locking hints provided in the SELECT clause. Locking behavior is also dependent on whether the cursor is processed as part of a transaction; whether the SELECT statement is part of a cursor, and whether update commands occur inside of transactions or independently.

In this section, we will just describe the basics. See the SQL Server 2000 documentation for more information.

With SQL Server, developers do not place locks directly. Instead, the developer declares the concurrency control behavior they want, and SQL Server determines where to place the locks. Locks are applied on rows, pages, keys, indexes, tables, and even on the entire database. SQL Server determines what level of lock to use and may promote or demote a lock level while processing. It also determines when to place the lock and when to release it, depending on the declarations made by the developer.

TRANSACTION ISOLATION LEVEL

Figure 13-31 summarizes the concurrency control options. The broadest level of settings is **transaction isolation level.** Options for it are listed in ascending level of restriction in the first row of Figure 13-31. These four options are the four you studied in Chapter 11; they are the SQL-92 standard levels. Note that with

➤ FIGURE 13-31

Concurrrency Options with SQL Server 2000

Type	Scope	Options
Transaction Isolation Level	Connection—all transactions	READ UNCOMMITTED READ COMMITTED (default) REPEATABLE READ SERIALIZABLE
Cursor Concurrency	Cursor	READ_ONLY OPTIMISTIC SCROLL_LOCK
Locking Hints	SELECT	READCOMMITTED READUNCOMMITTED REPEATABLEREAD SERIALIZABLE NOLOCK HOLDLOCK and others ...

SQL Server, it is possible to make dirty reads by setting the isolation level to READ UNCOMMITTED. READ COMMITTED is the default isolation level.

The next most restrictive level is REPEATABLE READ, which means SQL Server places and holds locks on all rows that are read. This means that no other user can change or delete a row that has been read until the transaction commits or aborts. Rereading the cursor may, however, result in phantom reads.

The most strict isolation level is SERIALIZABLE. With it, SQL Server places a range lock on the rows that have been read. This ensures that no read data can be changed or deleted, and that no new rows can be inserted in the range to cause phantom reads. This level is the most expensive to enforce and should only be used when absolutely required.

An example TRANSACT-SQL statement to set the isolation level to, say, REPEATABLE READ is

```
SET TRANSACTION ISOLATION LEVEL REPEATABLE READ
```

This statement could be issued anyplace TRANSACT-SQL is allowed, prior to any other database activity.

Cursor Concurrency

The second way in which the developer can declare locking characteristics is with cursor concurrency. Possibilities are read only, optimistic, and pessimistic, here called SCROLL_LOCK. As described in Chapter 11, with optimistic locking, no lock is obtained until the user updates the data. At that point, if the data have been changed since it was read, the update is refused. Of course, the application program must specify what to do when such a refusal occurs.

SCROLL_LOCK is a version of pessimistic locking. With it, an update lock is placed on a row when the row is read. If the cursor is opened within a transaction, the lock is held until the transaction commits or rolls back. If the cursor is outside of a transaction, the lock is dropped when the next row is read. Recall from Chapter 11 that an update lock will block another update lock, but will not block a shared lock. Thus, other connections can read the row with shared locks.

The default cursor concurrency setting depends on the cursor type (see Chapter 11). It is read only for static and forward only cursors, and is optimistic for dynamic and keyset cursors.

Cursor concurrency is set with the DECLARE CURSOR statement. An example to declare a dynamic, SCROLL_LOCK cursor on all rows of the TRANS table is

```
DECLARE     MY_CURSOR CURSOR DYNAMIC SCROLL_LOCKS
FOR
      SELECT    *
      FROM      TRANS
```

Locking Hints

Locking behavior can be further modified by providing locking hints in the WITH parameter of the FROM clause in SELECT statements. Figure 13-31 lists several of the locking hints available with SQL Server. The first four hints override transaction isolation level; the next two influence the type of lock issued.

Consider the following statements:

```
SET TRANSACTION ISOLATION LEVEL REPEATABLE READ
DECLARE  MY_CURSOR CURSOR DYNAMIC SCROLL_LOCKS
FOR
         SELECT    *
         FROM      TRANS WITH READUNCOMMITTED NOLOCK
```

Without the locking hints, the cursor MY_CURSOR would have REPEATABLE READ isolation and would issue update locks on all rows read. The locks would be held until the transaction committed. With the locking hints, the isolation level for this cursor becomes READ UNCOMMITTED. Furthermore, the specification of NOLOCK changes this cursor from DYNAMIC to READ_ONLY.

Consider another example:

```
SET TRANSACTION ISOLATION LEVEL REPEATABLE READ
DECLARE  MY_CURSOR    CURSOR DYNAMIC SCROLL_LOCKS
FOR
         SELECT    *
         FROM      TRANS WITH HOLDLOCK
```

Here, the locking hint will cause SQL Server to hold update locks on all rows read until the transaction commits. The effect is to change the transaction isolation level for this cursor from REPEATABLE READ to SERIALIZABLE.

In general, the beginner is advised not to provide locking hints. Rather, until you have become an expert, set the isolation level and cursor concurrency to appropriate values for your transactions and cursors and leave it at that.

➤ SECURITY

We discussed SQL Server security in Chapter 11 and will not discuss it again here. To review, a login is an identity used to sign on to SQL Server, or used to sign on to Windows 2000 and then passed to SQL Server. A login is associated with one or more database/user combinations. A role is a group of users like Sales Person or Manager. Users may have zero to many roles, and they have permissions. Roles may have zero to many users and they also have permission.

The permissions associated with a given login are all the permissions held by the user that are associated with the login plus all the permissions of all of the roles to which the user has been assigned. Users may be given permission to give other users permissions with the GRANT option.

➤ BACKUP AND RECOVERY

When you create a SQL Server database, both data and log files are created. As explained in Chapter 11, these files should be backed up periodically. When this is done, it is possible to recover a failed database by restoring it from a prior database save and applying changes in the log.

To recover a database with SQL Server, the database is restored from a prior database backup and log after images are applied to the restored database. When the end of the log is reached, changes from any transaction that failed to commit are then rolled back.

It is also possible to process the log to a particular point in time or to a transaction mark. For example, the statement

```
BEGIN TRANSACTION NewCust WITH MARK
```

will cause a mark labeled NewCust to be placed into the log every time this transaction is run. If this is done, the log can be restored to a point either just before or just after the first NewCust mark or first NewCust mark after a particular point in time. The restored log can then be used to restore the database. Such marks consume log space, however, so they should not be used without good reason.

TYPES OF BACKUP

SQL Server supports several types of backup. To see them, open the Enterprise Manager, open Databases, and right click on a database name. Select All Tasks and then select Backup Database. The dialog shown in Figure 13-32 will appear. At this point you can create a complete or differential backup of the database, you can create a transaction log backup, and you can create a backup of particular files and file groups.

As the name implies, a complete backup makes a copy of the entire database. A **differential backup** makes a copy of the changes that have been made to the database since the last complete backup. This means a complete backup must be made before the first differential backup. Because differential backups are faster, they can be taken more frequently and the chance of data loss is reduced. On the other hand, complete backups take longer but they are slightly simpler to use for recovery, as you will see.

The transaction log also needs to be periodically backed up to ensure that its contents are preserved. Further, the transaction log must be backed up before it can be used to recover a database.

Backups can be made either to disk or tape. When possible, the backups should be made to devices other than those that store the operational database and log. Backing up to removable devices allows the backups to be stored in a location physically removed from the database data center. This is important for recovery in the event of disasters caused by flood, hurricanes, and the like.

SQL SERVER RECOVERY MODELS

SQL Server supports three recovery models: simple, full, and bulk-logged. You can set the recovery model by right-clicking on a database name in the Enterprise Manager and selecting properties. The recovery model is specified under the Options tab. Figure 13-33 shows an example.

With the simple recovery model, no logging is done. The only way to recover a database is to restore the database to the last backup. Changes made since that

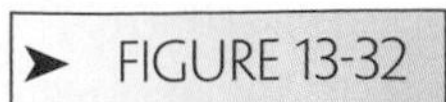
FIGURE 13-32

Dialog for Creating Backups

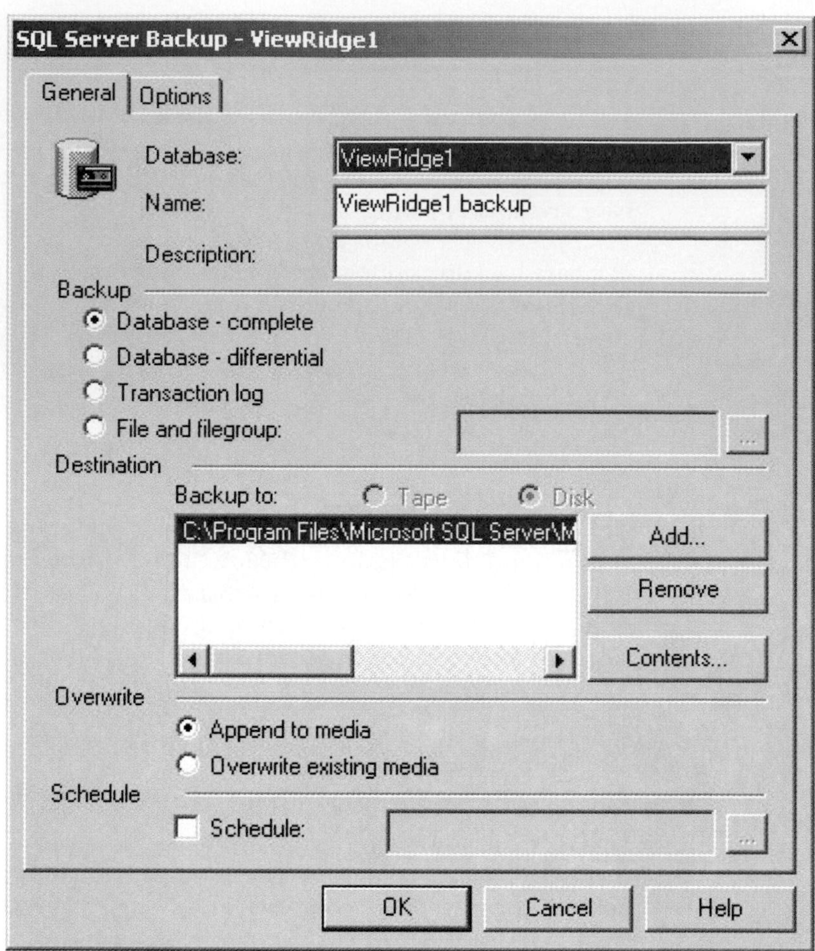

last backup are lost. The simple recovery model could be used for a database that is never changed—say, one having the names and locations of the occupants of a full graveyard. Or, one that is used for read-only analysis of data that is copied from some other transactional database.

With full recovery, all database changes are logged, and with bulk-logged database recovery, all changes are logged except those that cause large log entries. With bulk-logged recovery, changes to large text and graphic data items are not recorded to the log, actions like CREATE INDEX are not logged, and some other bulk-oriented actions are not logged. An organization would use bulk-logged recovery if conserving log space is important and if the data used in the bulk operations is saved in some other way.

Restoring a Database

If the database and log files have been properly backed up, restoring the database is straightforward. First, backup the current log so that changes in the most recent log will be available. Then, right-click on the database name in the Enterprise Manager, select All Tasks and the select Restore Database. The dialog shown in Figure 13-34 will appear.

In this example, database ViewRidge1 is being restored as database ViewRidge3. It is not necessary to change the name of the database. Here, the

FIGURE 13-33

Recovery Model Options

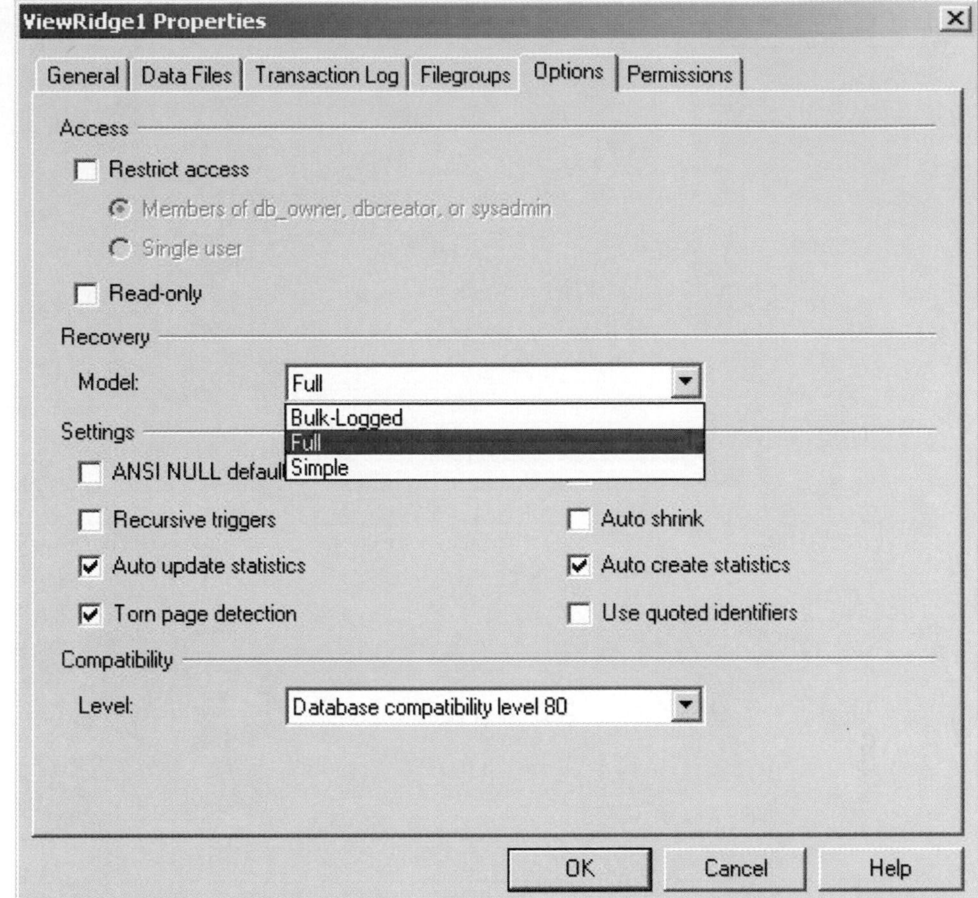

thinking is to restore it under a different name, test the restored database, delete what's left of the old database, and then rename the recovered database ViewRidge1.

This database is being restored to a point in time of 11/24/2000, 2:08:24 P.M. If this entry were left blank, the database would be restored to the end of the log. When OK is clicked, SQL Server starts the restoration and notifies the DBA of progress and completion status.

(As an aside, this restoration was done because in the process of preparing this chapter, I inadvertently submitted the following update:

```
UPDATE    WORK
SET       Copy='99/2000'
```

The query I meant to submit was

```
UPDATE    WORK
SET       Copy='99/2000'
WHERE     WorkID=530
```

I made this mistake just after 2:30 P.M., so I restored to a time that was prior to this, but one in which I knew was after other changes that I wanted to keep.)

FIGURE 13-34

Restoring the Database to a Point In Time

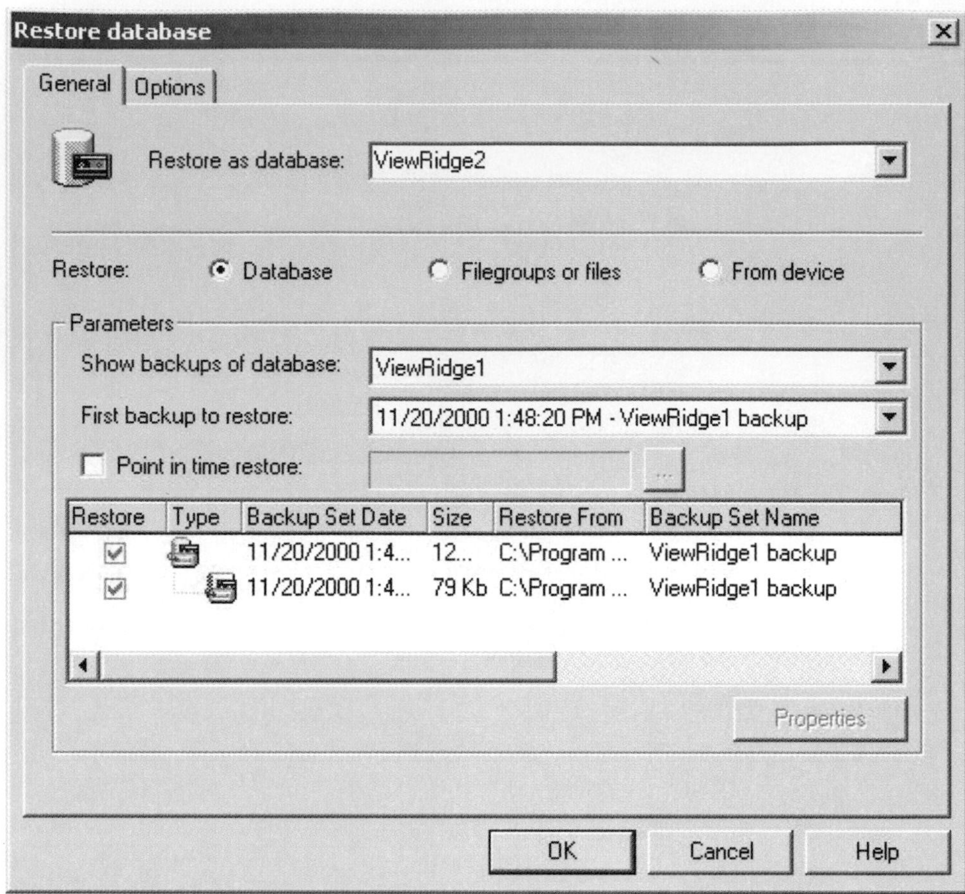

DATABASE MAINTENANCE PLAN

You can create a database maintenance plan to, among other tasks, facilitate the making of database and log backups. SQL Server provides a wizard for this task. To use it, right-click on a database name, select All Tasks, and select Maintenance Plan. The wizard will guide you through the process of scheduling various tasks. Some of these tasks maintain the database by reorganizing indexes and other related activities. Of importance here, however, is that you can schedule the automatic backup of both database data and logs.

➤ TOPICS NOT DISCUSSED IN THIS CHAPTER

There are several important SQL Server topics that are beyond the scope of this discussion. For one, SQL Server provides utilities to measure database activity and performance. The DBA can use these utilities when tuning the database. Another facility not described here is connecting Access to SQL Server. You can check the Access documentation for more information about this topic.

SQL Server 2000 provides facilities to support distributed database processing (called **replication** in SQL Server). These facilities use the publish-subscribe distributed model that we will discuss in Chapter 17. Distributed database processing, while very important in its own right, is beyond the scope of this text. Microsoft provides an OLE DB server called the Distributed Transaction Manager that coordinates distributed transactions. Java supports Enterprise Java Beans for the same purpose. We will touch on these topics in Chapters 15 and 16.

Finally, SQL Server has facilities for processing database views in the form of XML documents. We will discuss XML in detail in the next chapter.

➤ SUMMARY

SQL Server 2000 can be installed on Windows NT and Windows 2000 computers. There are two ways to create tables, views, indexes, and other database structures. One is to use the graphical design tools, which are similar to those in Microsoft Access. The other is to write SQL statements to create the structures and submit them to SQL Server via the SQL Query Analyzer utility. SQL Server data types are listed in Figure 13-8.

SQL Server 2000 implements User-Defined Data Types, which can be used to implement domains. Once defined, such data types can be used for column definition in either the graphical tool or in SQL statements. Rules can be defined and applied to either columns or User-Defined Data Types. If the latter, the rule will be enforced on all columns based on the user data type.

Table structure can be changed using either the graphical tool or the ALTER TABLE SQL statement. Relationships can be defined in Database Diagrams or by defining foreign keys in SQL statements.

Some of the relationship's properties pertain to referential integrity. If Enforce Relationship is checked, SQL Server will not allow foreign key values in child tables that do not match primary key values in parent tables. Both cascade updates and cascade deletes are supported. If the database design uses surrogate keys, cascade updates are never necessary.

SQL Server supports SQL views. Some views can be used for updating data and some cannot. Any view based on a single table is updatable unless the view includes aggregate functions or derived columns. All of the NOT NULL columns must be present in the view for the view to accept inserts. No view that has more than one table can be used for deletion operations. Multi-table views can accept inserts and updates as long as those operations apply to only a single table in the view. Views that are not otherwise updatable can be made so by defining INSTEAD OF triggers.

Indexes are special data structures used to improve performance. SQL Server automatically creates an index on all primary and foreign keys. Additional views can be created using CREATE INDEX or the Manage Index graphical tool. SQL Server supports clustered and nonclustered indexes.

SQL Server supports a language called TRANSACT-SQL, which surrounds basic SQL statements with programming constructs such as parameters, variables, and logic structures such as IF, WHILE, and so forth. Three ways to process application logic with SQL Server are to save queries and TRANSACT-SQL procedures and submit them via the SQL Query Analyzer, to create stored procedures and invoke them via application program or the SQL Query Analyzer, and to write triggers that are invoked by SQL Server when specified database actions occur.

Stored procedures can be stored on the users' computers or they can be kept within the database and invoked by application programs. The latter is more common for Internet applications, as you will learn in Chapter 15. A stored procedure for the logic to store a new customer and transaction is shown in Figure 13-24. Examples of insert and update triggers are shown in Figures 13-25 and 13-26.

Three factors determine the concurrency control behavior of SQL Server: transaction isolation level, cursor concurrency setting, and locking hints provided in the SELECT clause. These factors are summarized in Figure 13-31. Behavior also changes depending on whether actions occur in the context of transactions or cursors or independently. Given these behavior declarations, SQL Server places locks on behalf of the developer. Locks may be placed at many levels of granularity and may be promoted or demoted as work progresses.

SQL Server supports log backups and both complete and differential database backups. Three recovery models are available: simple, full, and, bulk-logged. With simple recovery, no logging is done nor log records applied. Full recovery logs all database operations and applies them for restoration. Bulk-logged recovery omits certain transactions that would otherwise consume large amounts of space in the log.

➤ GROUP I QUESTIONS

13.1 Install SQL Server 2000 and create a database named MEDIA. Use the default settings for file sizes, names, and locations.

13.2 Write a SQL statement to create a table named PICTURE with columns Name, Description, DateTaken, and FileName. Assume Name is char(20), Description is varchar(200), DateTaken is smalldate, and FileName is char(45). Also assume Name and DateTaken are required. Use Name is the primary key. Set the default value of Description to '(None).'

13.3 Use the SQL Query Analyzer to submit the SQL statement in Question 13.2 to create the PICTURE table in the MEDIA database.

13.4 Open the MEDIA database using Enterprise Manager and open the database design window for the PICTURE table. In this window, add a column PictureID and set its identity seed to 300 and identity increment to 25. Change the primary key from Name to PictureID.

13.5 Using the graphical table design tool, set the default value of DateTaken to the system date.

13.6 Create a User-Defined Data Type named Subject with data type char(30). Add a column to PICTURE named Topic that is based on Subject.

13.7 Create a rule called Valid_Subjects that defines the following set of values: {'Home', 'Office', 'Family', 'Recreation', 'Sports', 'Pets'}. Bind this rule to the Subject User-Defined Data Types.

13.8 Write ALTER statements to

  a. Change the length of Name to 50.

  b. Delete the DateTaken column.

  c. Add column TakenBy as char(40).

13.9 Submit your answer to Question 13.8 to SQL Server via the SQL Query Analyzer. Then open the table design window to verify that changes occurred correctly.

13.10 Create table SLIDE-SHOW (ShowID, Name, Description, Purpose). Assume ShowID is a surrogate key. Set the data type of Name and Description however you deem appropriate. Set the data type of Purpose to Subject. Use either a CREATE statement or the graphical table design tool.

13.11 Create table SHOW-PICTURE-INT as an intersection table between PICTURE and SLIDE-SHOW.

13.12 Create appropriate relationships between PICTURE and SHOW-PICTURE-INT and between SLIDE-SHOW and SHOW-PICTURE-INT. Set the referential integrity properties to disallow any deletion of a SLIDE-SHOW row that has any SHOW-PICTURE-INT rows related to it. Set the referential integrity properties to cascade deletions when a PICTURE is deleted.

13.13 Explain how to set the Cascade Update property for the relationships in Question 13.12.

13.14 Write a SQL statement to create a view name PopularShows that has SLIDE-SHOW.Name and PICTURE.Name for all slide shows that have a Purpose of either "Home" or "Pets." Execute this statement using SQL Query Analyzer.

13.15 Open the view design tool and determine that PopularShows was constructed correctly. Modify this view to include Description and FileName.

13.16 Can the SQL DELETE statement be used with the PopularShows view? Why or why not?

13.17 Under what circumstances can PopularShows be used for inserts and modifications?

13.18 Create an index on the Purpose column. Use the Manage Index graphical design tool to do this.

13.19 In Figure 13-21, for what purpose is the @Count variable used?

13.20 Why is the SELECT statement that begins SELECT @Cid necessary?

13.21 Explain how you would change the stored procedure in Figure 13-21 to connect the customer to all artists who either (a) were born before 1900 or (b) had a null value Birthdate.

13.22 Explain the purpose of the transaction in Figure 13-24.

13.23 What happens if an incorrect value of Copy is input to the stored procedure in Figure 13-24?

13.24 Explain why the trigger in Figure 13-27 is recursive. What stops the recursion?

13.25 In Figure 13-28, explain why an @Count value of 2 or greater means that an error was made prior to the invocation of On_WORK_Insert.

13.26 In Figure 13-28, what happens if the ROLLBACK statement is executed.

13.27 What are the three primary factors that influence SQL Server locking behavior?

13.28 Explain the meaning of each of the four transaction isolation levels listed in Figure 13-31.

13.29 Explain the meaning of each of the cursor concurrency settings listed in Figure 13-31.

13.30 What is the purpose of Locking Hints?

13.31 What is the difference between complete and differential backups? Under what conditions are complete backups preferred? Under what conditions are differential backups preferred?

13.32 Explain the differences among simple, full, and bulk-logged recovery models. Under what conditions would you choose each one?

13.33 When is point in time restore necessary?

➤ PROJECTS

For the following projects, use SQL Server to create the View Ridge Gallery database as described in this chapter. Consider the database view named Artist View that is shown for the Group II Questions at the end of Chapter 10.

A. Write a Transact/SQL procedure to read the ARTIST table portion of this view. Display the data you read in Query Analyzer as shown in the chapter. Accept the name of the artist as an input parameter.

B. Write a Transact/SQL procedure to read the ARTIST, TRANSACTION, and CUSTOMER (under TRANSACTION) table portion of this view. Display the data you read via Query Analyzer. Accept the name of the artist as an input parameter.

C. Write a Transact/SQL procedure to read all of the view tables. Display the data you read via Query Analyzer. Accept the name of the artist as an input parameter.

D. Write a Transact/SQL procedure to assign a new customer interest to an artist. Assume the name of the artist and the name of the customer are input. If the customer name is not unique display an error message. Check for duplication in the CUSTOMER_ARTIST_INT table before you insert the new row. Display an error message if there is duplication.

E. Code an AFTER TRIGGER that checks inserts and modifications on ARTIST Nationality. If the new value has been assigned as 'British' change it to 'English'.

➤ FIREDUP PROJECT QUESTIONS

Use SQL Server to create a database with the following four tables:

CUSTOMER (<u>CustomerID</u>, Name, Phone, EmailAddress)
STOVE (<u>SerialNumber</u>, Type, Version, DateOfManufacture)
REGISTRATION (<u>*CustomerID*</u>, <u>*SerialNumber*</u>, <u>RDate</u>)
STOVE_REPAIR (<u>RepairInvoiceNumber</u>, *SerialNumber*, RepairDate, Description, Cost, *CustomerID*)

Assume the primary keys of CUSTOMER, STOVE, and STOVE_REPAIR are surrogate keys. Create relationships to enforce the following referential integrity constraints:

- CustomerID of REGISTRATION is a subset of CustomerID of CUSTOMER
- SerialNumber of REGISTRATION is a subset of SerialNumber of STOVE
- SerialNumber of STOVE_REPAIR is a subset of SerialNumber of STOVE
- CustomerID of STOVE_REPAIR is a subset of CustomerID of CUSTOMER

Do not cascade deletions.

A. Fill your tables with sample data and display it.

B. Create a stored procedure to register a stove. The procedure receives the customer's name, phone, e-mail address, and stove serial number. If the customer already exists in the database (name, phone, and e-mail match), use that customer's CustomerID for the REGISTRATION. Otherwise, create a new CUSTOMER row for the customer. Assume a stove with the input serial number already exists in the database. If not, print an error and rollback changes to the CUSTOMER table. Code and test your procedure.

C. Create a stored procedure to record a stove repair. The procedure receives customer's name, phone, e-mail address, stove serial number, repair description, and cost. Assume you are given a valid stove serial number; print an error message and make no database changes if not. Use an existing CUSTOMER row if name, phone, and e-mail match; otherwise, create a new CUSTOMER record. Assume that the STOVE-REPAIR row must be created. Register the stove, if necessary.

D. Create a view that contains all of the FiredUp data for a given customer. Name this view CustomerRecord. This view must join CUSTOMER, REGISTRATION, STOVE, and STOVE_REPAIR data. Write a stored procedure that accepts a customer's Name and displays all of the data for the given customer.

ENTERPRISE DATABASE PROCESSING

Part VI addresses technologies used to publish and use enterprise databases. Chapters 14 through 16 describe and illustrate database processing using Internet technology. Such applications use technology first developed for the Internet but that today reside both on the Internet and on private intranets. Chapter 14 lays the foundation by describing network environments, three-tier and n-tier architectures, and XML. Chapter 15 then illustrates the use of Microsoft technology for publishing database applications using OLE DB, ADO, and Active Server Pages. Chapter 16 illustrates the use of JDBC, Java, and Java Server Pages for publishing these applications. Finally, Chapter 17 concludes Part VI with a discussion of additional enterprise architectures, OLAP applications, and data administration.

Many of the technologies described in this part are rapidly evolving. You should check www.oracle.com for information regarding new Oracle technologies, www.microsoft.com for the information regarding new Microsoft technologies, www.w3.org for latest information regarding XML and related technologies, and www.sun.com/java for the latest information regarding Java technologies. These sites are merely starting places; search the Web as well, because new sites frequently appear.

Networks, Multi-Tier Architectures, and XML

The Internet has given rise to technologies that are used today to publish database applications on both the Internet and on private intranets. We begin with a short summary of network environments and then describe the multi-tier architectures most often used to support these applications. Next, we consider the role of HTML and DHTML, and then conclude the chapter with a survey and discussion of XML. As you will learn, XML Schema is particularly important for database processing.

➤ NETWORK ENVIRONMENTS

A **network** is a collection of computers that communicate with one another using a standardized protocol. Some networks are **public;** anyone can utilize the network by paying a fee to a vendor who will provide access (or, like students, by joining an organization that has already paid to have access). Other networks are **private.** With these, only users who are preauthorized to connect to the network can gain access. The most widely used public network is the Internet, and we begin with it.

THE INTERNET

The Internet is a public network of computers that communicate using a communications protocol called **Transmission Control Program/Internet Protocol (TCP/IP).** This network was created by the Advanced Research

Projects Agency (ARPA) of the U.S. armed services in the 1960s. Initially, it was called ARPANET, and it connected major computing centers at military, university, and research institutions. Over time, more and more organizations joined the network, and it became desirable for nonresearch, commercially oriented organizations to join as well. Today it is referred to as the Internet.

In 1989, Tim Berners-Lee of the European Particle Physics Laboratory (CERN) began work on a project that would enable researchers to share their work over the Internet. This project led to the development of the **hypertext transfer protocol (HTTP),** which is a TCP/IP–based protocol that enables the sharing of documents with embedded links to other documents over TCP/IP networks.

Two characteristics of the HTTP protocol are noteworthy for database applications. First HTTP is *request-oriented.* HTTP servers wait for requests to arrive; when they do, the HTTP server takes some action and then, possibly, generates a response. Unlike some traditional MIS applications, they do not poll or otherwise solicit application activity.

Second, HTTP applications are *stateless.* The HTTP server receives a request, processes it, and then forgets about the client who made the request. No attempt is made to conduct a continuing session or conversation with a given client. This stateless characteristic poses no problems for Web applications that serve static content to display pages of promotional material and the like.

It *is* a problem for database applications, however, because database applications involve the processing of transactions, which may require several or many exchanges between the client and the server. Thus, HTTP must be augmented in some way to provide a state-oriented environment for database and other applications. A few years ago, Web applications themselves had to perform algorithmic gymnastics to maintain state. Today, IIS with ASP and Java servlets with JSP provide mechanisms to maintain state, as you will learn.

Intranets

The term *intranet* has several different interpretations. Most commonly, the term means a private, local, or wide-area network (LAN or WAN) that uses TCP/IP, HTML, and related browser technology on client computers and Web server technology on servers. Less commonly, the term is used to mean any private LAN or WAN that involves clients and servers.

Two characteristics of intranets differentiate them from the Internet. First, intranets are private. Either they are not connected to a public network at all, or they are connected to a public network via a **firewall,** which is a computer that serves as a security gateway. Firewall computers monitor the source and destination of traffic between the intranet and the Internet and filter it. Some firewalls operate so as to allow only certain traffic through; others operate so as to prohibit certain traffic; still others operate in both modes.

Because intranets are private, security is less of a concern. This does not mean that security is not a concern at all but rather that less elaborate security measures need to be taken. In most cases, computers on an intranet are known and supported by the organization that owns and maintains the intranet. Unauthorized activity and security problems are more easily identified and managed than on a public network.

The second major differentiating characteristic of an intranet is speed. Intranets are fast; many operate in the range of 100,000 kbs (thousands of bits per second). This compares to 56 kbs for users connecting to the Internet via a traditional modem. Even users that have upgraded to DSL or other specialized modem technologies operate at less than 500 kbs. Thus, anyone planning an Internet application needs to size the application's transmission requirements according to the transmission speeds available to the application users.

Because of the speed difference, large bitmaps, sound files, and animations can be included in intranet applications. More important in the database world, large query responses can be transmitted to client computers. In addition, because of the increased speed, it is possible to download large program files to the client computer. This means, as you will see, that more of the application processing can be conducted on the client in an intranet than can be conducted on a client using the Internet.

Wireless Network Access

Users of wireless telephones, wireless personal digital assistants, and other wireless devices want to access the Internet and organizational intranets using wireless technology. Because wireless devices have limited screen size, reduced keyboards, and less memory, standard HTML, XML, and other protocols are inappropriate for wireless use. The **Wireless Application Protocol (WAP)** has been developed to create a worldwide standard for network access from wireless devices. In addition, a variant of XML, called the **Wireless Markup Language (WML),** has been defined to enable Web pages to be displayed on wireless devices.

Figure 14-1 shows the use of all three types of networks for a contact management application. The user wants to be able to access contact name and phone data from her office, from her home, or from a cell phone while in transit. The contact database could be located at her business, in her home, or at a service provider's facility. The user doesn't care where the database is located, she just wants to be able to get to a single source of contact data at all times. We will discuss WML and WAP further in this chapter after we have discussed XML.

Need for Multiple net Access to Data

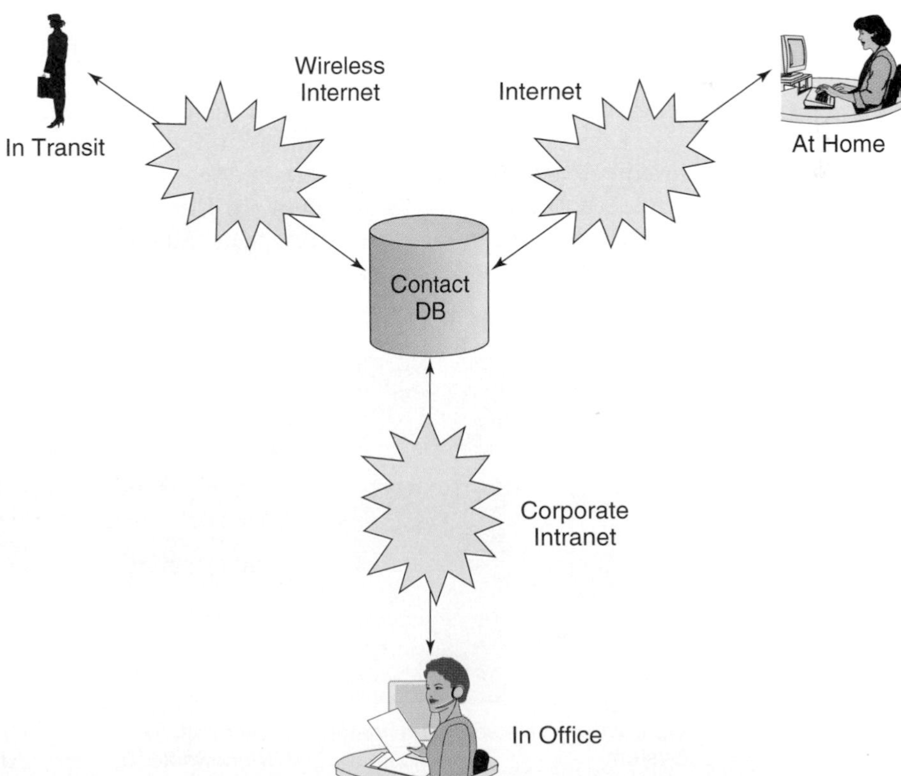

➤ MULTI-TIER ARCHITECTURE

Figure 14-2 shows the three-tier architecture that is used for many Internet technology database applications. We will use many acronyms in this and the three following figures. Do not worry if these terms are strange to you. We will explain the servers (like IIS) and the markup languages (like DHTML) after we describe the general architecture. The database standards (like ODBC) will be explained in Chapters 15 and 16.

Three types of processor, or tiers, are shown in Figure 14-2. From right to left, they are the database server, the Web server, and the browser or client computers. As shown, each of these tiers can run a different operating system. In this example, the database server runs UNIX, the Web server runs Windows 2000, and the browsers are running the Macintosh operating system. These are only examples. More likely, the browsers would be running a mixture of Windows 98, UNIX, Macintosh, and Windows 2000. The Web server and the database server could be either UNIX or Windows 2000.

Example products shown in Figure 14-2 are Oracle on the database server, Microsoft Internet Information Server (IIS) on the Web server, and Netscape Navigator on the clients. Again, these are only examples. The data server could be running any DBMS from Access to DB2. Common Web servers are IIS, Netscape Server, and Apache. Common browsers are Netscape Navigator and Microsoft Internet Explorer.

As shown, the interface between the Web server and the database server transmits SQL statements and relational data. The interface between the Web server and the browser transmits Web pages, client code, and data. We will say much more about each of these interfaces in this and the next three chapters.

The functions of the three tiers are summarized in Figure 14-3. The purpose of the database server is to run the DBMS to process SQL statements and perform database management tasks. Here, the DBMS is operating in its traditional role of serving up data; the application tools capabilities that you have seen with Access are not in use. The DBMS on the data server in Figure 14-3 is not creating forms or reports or menus. Instead, it is a pure data engine; receiving SQL requests and processing rows in tables as described in the previous two chapters.

Figure 14-3 shows the standards and application program interfaces that are used between the data server and the Web server. We will discuss ODBC, OLE DB, and ADO in Chapter 15 and JDBC in Chapter 16. For now, just think of those standards as means of transmitting SQL and relations between the Web server and the database server.

➤ FIGURE 14-2

Three-Tier Architecture

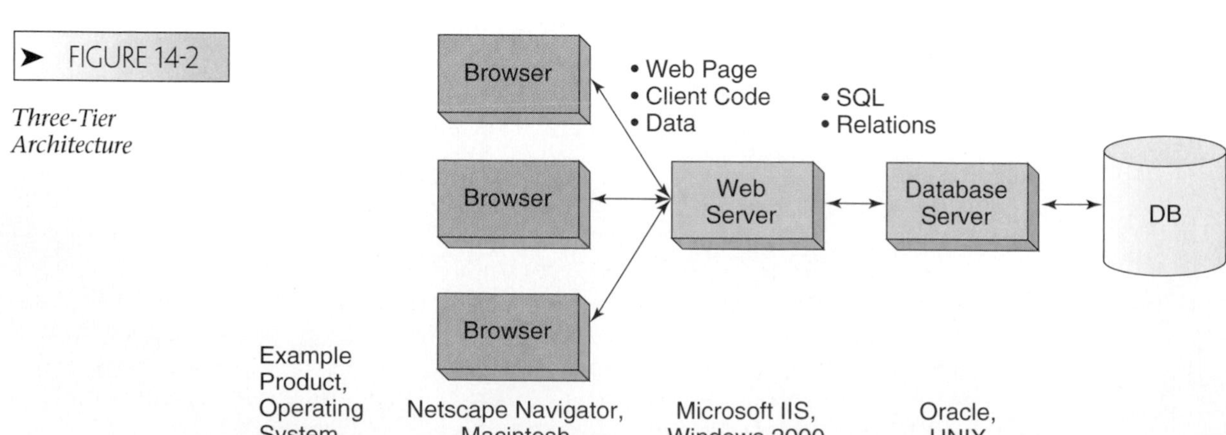

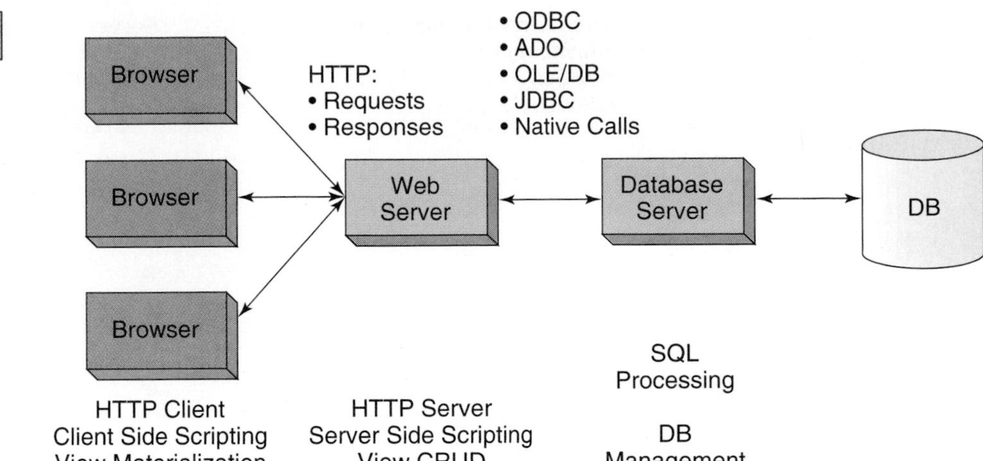

➤ FIGURE 14-3

Functions of Tiers

The Web server performs three major functions. First, it is an HTTP server, meaning that it processes the HTTP protocol, receiving requests and generating responses in HTTP format. The Web server also hosts scripting environments so that developers can write code in languages like VBScript and JavaScript and execute that code on the Web server. Finally, in database applications, the third function of the Web server is to create, read, update, and delete view instances as discussed in Chapter 10. Again, keep in mind the difference between a relation and a view; views are constructions of relations.

In database applications, the browser has three functions that are analogous to those on the Web server. First, the browser is an HTTP client, generating requests for pages and for other activity. It also hosts a scripting environment for executing scripts on the client machine. Finally, the browser materializes views, transforming HTML or other markup language into a display in the client's browser window.

This architecture allows for scripting on both the Web server and client computers. One of the important tasks when developing an Internet technology database application is to decide what work is to be done on which machine. Because there are many browsers and only one server, it is desirable to place as much code on the client as possible. However, if the client needs to keep going back to the Web server to obtain data for its calculations, this advantage can be offset by the time required for the data request and response round trips. Also, the client code needs to be sent down to the browser in the HTTP message. Large chunks of code will require a long time for download. A good rule of thumb is shown in Figure 14-3: Use client code for scripting tasks that support view materialization. Use server code for scripting tasks that support view CRUD. Also, code for immediate calculations (ExtendedPrice = Quantity * Price) is usually processed on the browser.

Windows 2000 Web Server Environment

Figure 14-4 shows the standards and languages that are common when the Web server is running Windows 2000 as its operating system. In this case, the HTTP server will almost always be IIS since it is part of the Windows operating system. IIS provides an interface called Internet Server Application Program Interface (ISAPI) by which other programs can trap and process HTTP messages. The Active Server Processor (ASP) is one such program. It processes all Web pages with the suffix *.asp*. When IIS receives such a page, it sends it to Active Server Processor over the ISAPI interface. ASP then processes the page and sends a response back to the client via the ISAPI interface to IIS.

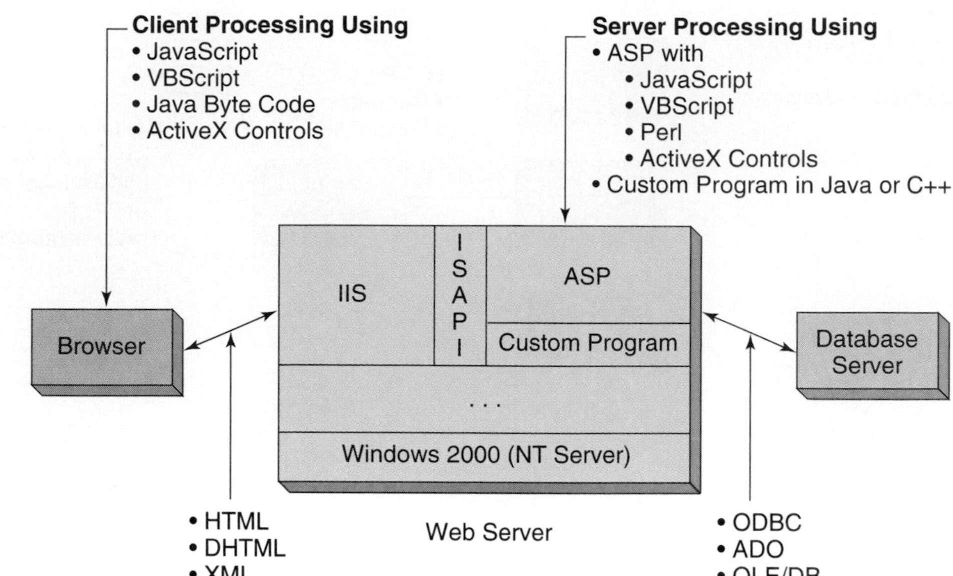

➤ FIGURE 14-4

Standards and Languages Common with Microsoft Web Server

ASP hosts scripting languages; therefore, ASP pages can contain JavaScript, VBScript, Perl, and other scripting language statements. These statements will be executed when ASP processes the page. In addition, ActiveX controls can be embedded in the page and they will be invoked as well.

ASP is not the only program that can use the ISAPI interface. C++ and Java developers can create custom programs for processing HTTP messages instead of using the ASP facility.

When using a Microsoft Web server, the data access standard used will most likely be ODBC, ADO, or OLE DB since these standards are supported and promulgated by Microsoft.

Unix and Linux Web Server Environment

When using a Unix or Linux Web server (Figure 14-5), IIS is not used as the HTTP server. Instead, products like Apache and the Netscape Web servers are used. Apache is the world's most common Web server, in part because it is free. You can find information about Apache at www.apache.org.

In the past, the **common gateway interface (CGI)** was commonly used by applications that process HTTP requests under Apache and similar servers. The problem with CGI is that one copy of the processing program is loaded into memory for each user. If 100 users are accessing the same CGI script, then 100 copies of the script are loaded into memory. This situation becomes untenable for the workload on commercial Web sites. There are other problems with CGI, as you will learn in Chapter 16.

Today, it is more common for database processing applications to use **Java servlets** or **JavaServer Pages (JSP),** or both. These technologies require software that implements the Java servlet or JavaServer Pages specifications. Basic Apache does not do this, but the Apache organization has facilitated the development of Apache Tomcat, a product that does implement these specifications. Tomcat, like Apache, is free (www.jakarta.tomcat.org). You can run Tomcat as a stand-alone Web server for testing your application; you can also install it to run in conjunction with Apache for higher-performance Web applications. The JavaServer Web Development kit is a second free product that can be used

FIGURE 14-5

Standards and Languages Common with Unix Server

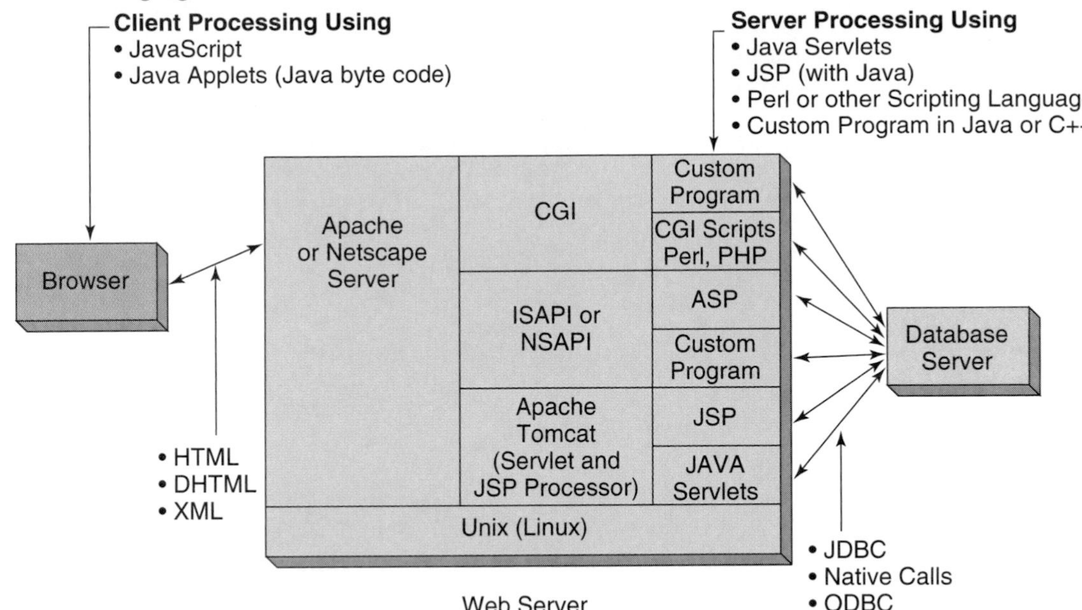

stand-alone for testing servlets and JSP pages. Other products are available as well. Search the Web for Java Servlet 2.2 and JavaServer Pages 1.1. We will discuss the use of these products in detail in Chapter 16.

As an aside, there is an important difference between ASP and JSP technologies. With ASP, you can run any supported scripting language like VBScript and JScript. You cannot, however, directly place C++ or Java into an ASP page. In contrast, with JSP, all coding is done in Java; even if you are only writing snippets of code, those snippets are Java statements.

Apache and other Unix Web servers also support ISAPI and there are versions of ASP that can run with these products as well. Of course, if the ASP pages use ActiveX and other Microsoft components, they will not run correctly (or at all). The Netscape servers provide their own interface, NSAPI, that serves a role similar to that for ISAPI.

JDBC is most commonly used when accessing databases from Java programs. There are also JDBC to ODBC bridges that make it easy for Java programs to utilize ODBC drivers. In addition, DBMS products can be called via native libraries as well. Neither OLE DB nor ADO is implemented on Unix.

Earlier, we mentioned that HTTP is a stateless protocol, meaning that the server processes a request and then forgets about the requestor. Stateless processing is unacceptable for most database applications and the ability to track a session's state has been added to IIS for Windows 2000, and to Tomcat and similar servlet processors in the Unix/Linux world. You will see how this is done in the next two chapters.

N-Tier Processing

For some applications, the three-tier architecture places an unreasonable burden on the Web server. Recall that this server works not only as an HTTP server responding potentially to thousands of requests, but it also creates and manages connections to the database server, generates and transmits SQL requests, accumulates SQL results into views, executes business logic, and enforces business rules. After all of that, it formulates a response back to the user at the browser.

➤ FIGURE 14-6

Examples of n-Tier Architecture: (a) Using Multiple Processors for View and Rule Processing, and (b) Using Multiple Processors for Distributed Processing

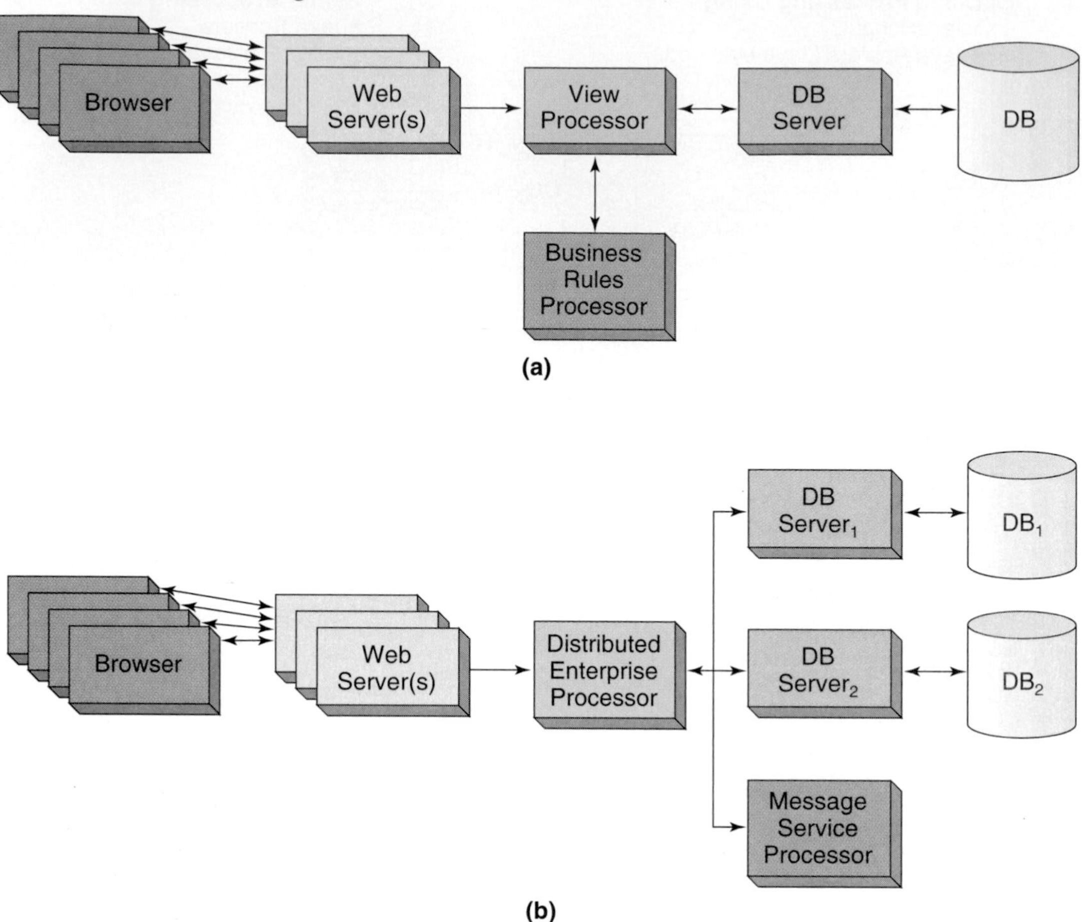

With such a burden, the Web server can become a performance bottleneck. One solution to this problem is to balance the workload across many, perhaps even hundreds of Web servers. This solution can create its own set of problems, however, because it requires that each of the Web servers have all of the programs necessary to perform the functions described above. This can become an administrative headache. Another solution is to utilize the Web server(s) only for HTTP request and response processing, and to off-load the view processing, business rules processing, and the like to other servers. This solution is shown in Figure 14-6(a), where separate computers process views and enforce business rules.

A related problem occurs when the processing of a single transaction is distributed across multiple computers. In Figure 14-6(b), for example, suppose that order data resides in database DB_1 and customer data resides in database DB_2. Furthermore, suppose that for normal order processing, updates need to be made to both of these database and messages need to be sent to production and acknowledgment received before the order can be committed. The solution shown in Figure 14-6(b) is to dedicate one server to managing the distributed transactions, while other servers process the databases and provide message services.

Clearly, many possibilities exist. As organizations gain more experience with Web commerce processing, certain patterns of *n*-tier processing are likely to emerge. For now, just realize that Web database processing is not restricted to three tiers, and there can be more than one server sharing the workload at each tier.

➤ MARKUP LANGUAGES HTML AND DHTML

Markup languages are used to specify the appearance and behavior of a Web page. As noted, the first such language to obtain prominence on the Web was HTML, which is a subset of a more powerful and sophisticated language called SGML. In this section we will consider the markup languages dynamic HTML (DHTML) and XML. In complexity, these languages lie between HTML and SGML. Before delving into them, however, we need to establish an historical context regarding Web standards.

MARKUP LANGUAGE STANDARDS

HTML was tremendous success in that it fostered the development of hundreds of thousands of Web sites and made Web communication a reality for the general computing public. Over time, it became clear, however, that the original version of HTML had significant disadvantages, especially for the development of database applications on the Web. As people worked to overcome these disadvantages, it became apparent that standards were needed. Otherwise, every vendor would make improvements on its own, and soon, only certain browsers would be able to process certain pages, which would take away one of the most important advantages of the Web.

Consequently, starting in 1994, the World Wide Web Consortium (W3C) began to promulgate standards for HTML and other markup languages. These standards have become very important. Visit the consortium's Web site at www.w3.org. There you will find helpful information, tutorials, the endorsed (or recommended) standards, and standards that are in process of development.

The role and importance of standards will be clearer if you understand that vendors of software products have a love/hate relationship with them. On one hand, they love standards because they provide order in the marketplace and establish a base set of capabilities that products need to have. On the other hand, they hate them because they can invalidate features, functions, and technologies in which vendors have made a significant investment.

Also, standards put vendors in a double bind. If they only develop to the standard, then there is no reason for customers to buy their product over their competitors' products. But if they add features and functions to the standard, then they will be criticized for not adhering to the standard. Thus, when Microsoft developed DHTML, it supported the W3C standard called HTML 4.0. It also, however, added features and functions that go beyond that standard. Depending on which hat you wear, those features are wonderful because of their added functionality, or they are terrible because pages that use them may not behave properly in all browsers.

For this reason, when nonstandard features are added to a product, it is done in such a way that products not supporting those additional features will degrade gracefully. For example, an outline will dynamically open and close on browsers that support that feature; it will appear always open on browsers that do not support that feature.

PROBLEMS WITH HTML

The original version of HTML suffered from several problems. For one, the content, layout, and format of pages were confounded; there is no way to separate the definition of content from layout from format. This means that if you want the same content delivered in different ways, you need to create two complete copies of that content, layout, and format. For database applications, it also meant that view data and view materialization were inextricably mixed.

Another disadvantage was the lack of style definitions. It was not possible to say, for example, that all headings would have a particular font, size, and emphasis. Hence, if a Web developer wanted to change the format of all level one headings, he or she would have to find all of the level one headings in the page (or on the Web site) and then change their format one by one. What was needed was a facility to define the style of a given format element.

A third disadvantage of the original HTML was that Web page elements could not be accessed from scripts or other programs. For example, there was no way to refer to the title element of a page in a script to dynamically alter its appearance or layout. Also, code could not be written to respond to Windows events like mouse movements and clicks. Hence, to change the structure or appearance of a page, the browser needed to return to the server to obtain a complete new page. Such round trips were unnecessary, slow, and wasteful.

Finally, and most important to us, there were no constructs to facilitate the caching and data manipulation on the client. Whenever a browser needed to display more data, a round trip had to be made to the server. W3C developed a new standard for HTML called HTML 4.0 to define features and functions to overcome these, and other, disadvantages.

DHTML

DHTML is a Microsoft implementation of HTML 4.0. It includes all of that standard plus additional features and functions. DHTML is supported by Microsoft Internet Explorer 4.0 (and later versions) and by IIS 4.0 (and later versions). Netscape Navigator supports only the HTML 4.0 portion of DHTML; it does not support all of the features that were added to DHTML beyond that standard. Hence, when using DHTML, developers need to be careful to stay within the HTML 4.0 feature set if their users will view the application through non-Microsoft browsers.

There are a number of key features of DHTML that overcome the disadvantages of earlier versions of HTML. First, DHTML provides an object model called the Document Object Model (DOM). This model exposes all page elements as objects. These objects can be manipulated from script to change element attributes and invoke element methods. Thus, an outline can be first shown in compacted form, then fully opened when the user clicks on it.

Because of DOM, page content, layout, and format can be altered through a program without refreshing the page from the server. Not only does this save time, but also the user is not confronted with flashing, changing pages whenever a headline changes. Instead, only the changing text portion is altered.

Another key feature of HTML 4.0 and DHTML is support for Cascading Style Sheets (CSS). This facility enables formats to be defined for the types of elements in a page. Thus, the following DHTML code will set background and color of level one and two headings:

```
<STYLE TYPE="text/class">
<!—
H1 {font-family:Lucida; font-style:normal; color:black}
H2 {font-family:Lucida; font-style:normal; color:green}
—>
</STYLE>
```

In the document, when a level one or two head is encountered, it will appear as defined by the style element. Thus, in the following

```
<H2>
This is an example:
</H2>
```

the level two heading "This is an example:" will appear in green, normal Lucida type. In this case, both styles referred to standard HTML tags (H1 and H2). It is also possible to define styles for developer-defined tags and then insert those tags into the document where needed.

With DHTML, it is possible for an element to have two conflicting styles. For example, a style sheet may specify a particular format for all paragraphs, but within a particular page, a given paragraph may be marked as having a different style. In this case, the style on the paragraph will override the style in the style sheet. As a general rule, the style markings closest to the content will be used. This characteristic is what causes such style sheets to be called *cascading* style sheets.

Style sheets can be contained within the page, or they can be obtained externally, from other documents that contain the style definitions. Thus, with DHTML, content and materialization can be separated.

The combination of style sheets and DOM mean that Web pages can be changed without page refreshes from the server. For example, style can be changed for level two headings as the mouse moves over level one headings; even more dramatic changes are possible.

In conjunction with the development of DHTML, Microsoft developed a set of ObjectX controls called **Remote Data Services (RDS).** With these controls, a developer can cache database data on the client, display it there using a data control, accept updates in the data control, and send the batch back to the server as an update to the database.

In reality, however, RDS is only useful for views that consist of a single table. Updating more complex views can require the execution of two, three, or more SQL statements as you learned in the last chapter. This kind of multi-table updating is not possible with RDS. Instead, developers use ADO.

Even though RDS in itself is not too important for us, the DHTML facility for dynamically changing Web page structure is. For example, with DHTML you can query a view in a database, programmatically determine the number and names of columns in the view, and dynamically configure a Web page to display that data.

DHTML and HTML 4.0 correct many of the deficiencies in the original HTML, but they maintain the same fundamental structure and character. We now turn to a specification having a fundamentally different nature.

➤ XML—EXTENSIBLE MARKUP LANGUAGE

XML is one of the most important developments in information systems in the last ten years. For one, XML provides an extensible standard for materializing documents on Web pages. Beyond that, however, XML has become important for data interchange; it is particularly useful for transmitting database views. XML is also simple, at least the basic XML structures are, and consequently it is used to express many types of standardized text. For example, Tomcat, the Java servlet processor for Apache, uses XML for its configuration files.

XML is even being used as a standard for executing remote procedure calls. DCOM and CORBA vied for years to be the standard for this purpose until the **Simple Object Access Protocol (SOAP)** was defined. SOAP is simply a means of transmitting procedure calls expressed as small XML documents using HTTP. Undoubtedly, many more uses will be found for XML in the future.

XML is a broad subject that deserves a text of its own. Here we will have to confine ourselves to use of XML for Web page materialization and for expressing database views. See the excellent material at www.w3.org and www.xml.org for more information. You can give your career a great boost by learning everything you can about XML.

XML As a Markup Language

As a markup language, XML is significantly better than either HTML or DHTML. There are several reasons for XML's superiority. For one, the designers of XML created a clear separation between document structure, content, and materialization. XML has facilities for dealing with each, and the nature of those facilities is such that they cannot be confounded as they can with HTML.

Additionally, XML is standardized, but as its name implies, the standards allow for extension by developers. With XML, you are not limited to a fixed set of elements like <TITLE>, <H1>, <P>, but can create your own.

One of the problems with HTML and DHTML is that there is too much freedom. Consider the following HTML:

<h2>Hello World </h2>

This <h2> tag can be used to mark a level two heading in an outline. But, it can also be used simply to cause "Hello World" to be displayed with a particular style. Because of this characteristic, we cannot rely on tags to indicate the true structure of an HTML page. Tag use is too arbitrary; <h2> may mean a heading, or it may mean nothing at all.

As you will see, with XML, the structure of the document is formally defined. If we find the tag <street>, we know exactly where that tag belongs and how it relates in the document structure to other tags. Thus, XML documents are said to accurately represent the semantics of their data.

XML Document Type Declarations

Figure 14-7 shows a sample XML document. Notice that the document has two sections. The first section defines the structure of the document; it is referred to as the document type declaration or **DTD.** The second part is the document data.

The DTD begins with the word DOCTYPE and specifies the name of this type of document, which is customer. Then, it calls out the content of the customer document. It consists of two groups: name and address. The name group consists of two elements firstname and lastname. Firstname and lastname are defined as #PCDATA, which means they are strings of character data. Next, the address element is defined to consist of four elements: street, city, state, and zip. Each of these is also defined as character data. The plus sign after street indicates that one value is required and that multiple values are possible.

The data instance of customer shown in Figure 14-7 conforms to the DTD, hence this document is said to be a **type-valid XML document.** If it did not conform to the DTD it would be a **not-type-valid** document. Documents that are not-type-valid can still be perfectly good XML, they are just not valid instances of their type. For example, if the document in Figure 14-7 had two city elements, it would still be valid XML, but it would be not-type-valid.

While DTDs are almost always desirable, they are not required in XML documents. Documents that have no DTD are by definition not-type-valid, since there is no type to validate them against.

FIGURE 14-7

Example XML Document

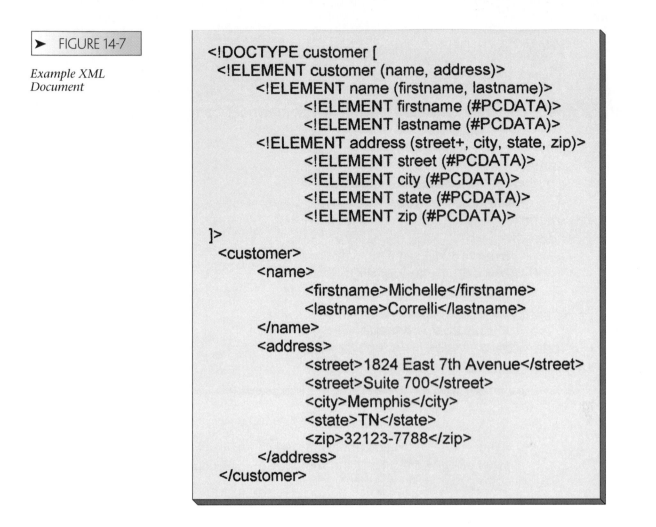

```
<!DOCTYPE customer [
 <!ELEMENT customer (name, address)>
      <!ELEMENT name (firstname, lastname)>
             <!ELEMENT firstname (#PCDATA)>
             <!ELEMENT lastname (#PCDATA)>
      <!ELEMENT address (street+, city, state, zip)>
             <!ELEMENT street (#PCDATA)>
             <!ELEMENT city (#PCDATA)>
             <!ELEMENT state (#PCDATA)>
             <!ELEMENT zip (#PCDATA)>
]>
 <customer>
      <name>
             <firstname>Michelle</firstname>
             <lastname>Correlli</lastname>
      </name>
      <address>
             <street>1824 East 7th Avenue</street>
             <street>Suite 700</street>
             <city>Memphis</city>
             <state>TN</state>
             <zip>32123-7788</zip>
      </address>
 </customer>
```

The DTD does not need to be contained inside the document. Figure 14-8 shows a customer document in which the DTD is obtained from the URL http://www.somewhere.com/dtds/customer.dtd. The advantage of storing the DTD externally is that many documents can be validated against the same DTD.

The creator of a DTD is free to choose any elements he or she wants. Hence, XML documents can be extended, but in a standardized and controlled way. As you will see, DTDs can readily be used to represent database views.

Materializing XML Documents

The XML document in Figure 14-7 shows both the document's structure and content. Nothing in the document, however, indicates how it is to be materialized. The designers of XML created a clean separation among structure, content, and format.

Two facilities are provided for XML document materialization, cascading style sheets, and XSLT. We consider each in turn.

XML MATERIALIZATION WITH CASCADING STYLE SHEETS We discussed CSS (cascading style sheets) in the section on DHTML; its use for XML documents is similar. That is, styles are defined for tags and applied in a cascading manner. Consider the following style definition for the document in Figure 14-7:

```
<STYLE TYPE ="text/class">
<!—
customer  {font-family:Lucida; font-style:normal; color:black}
```

FIGURE 14-8

XML Document with External DTD

```
<!DOCTYPE customer SYSTEM "http://www.somewhere.com/dtds/customer.dtd>

 <customer>
      <name>
           <firstname>Michelle</firstname>
           <lastname>Correlli</lastname>
      </name>
      <address>
           <street>1824 East 7th Avenue</street>
           <street>Suite 700</street>
           <city>Memphis</city>
           <state>TN</state>
           <zip>32123-7788</zip>
      </address>
 </customer>
```

```
name      {font-family:Lucida; font-style:normal; color:green}
lastname  {font-family:Lucida; font-style:normal; color:red}
—>
</STYLE>
```

According to this style specification, the default color for the customer document is black. However, the color for name elements is overridden from black to green, and that for lastname elements is overridden from green to red. Hence the styles cascade over one another.

Currently, there is no standard agreement on where such style definitions are to be placed. They could be placed in the document or in an external file and a reference to them placed in the document. Different products implement them in different ways.

XML MATERIALIZATION WITH EXTENSIBLE STYLE LANGUAGE: TRANSFORMATIONS (XSLT) The second means of materializing XML documents is to use XSLT, or the Extensible Style Language: Transformations. XSLT is a powerful and robust transformation language. It can be used to materialize XML documents into DHTML or HTML and it can be used for many other purposes as well. One common application of XSLT is to transform an XML document in one format into a second XML document in another format. A company could, for example, use XSLT to transform an XML order document in their own format into an equivalent XML order document in their customer's format. There are many features and functions of XSLT that we will be unable to discuss here. See www.w3.org for more information about it.

XSLT is a declarative, transformation language. It is declarative because instead of specifying a procedure for materializing document elements, you create a set of rules that govern how the document is to be materialized. It is transformational because it transforms the input document into another document.

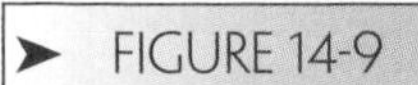

Customer List XML Document

```
<?xml version='1.0'?>
<!DOCTYPE customerlist [
 <!ELEMENT customerlist (customer+)>
       <!ELEMENT customer (name, address) >
       <!ELEMENT name (firstname, lastname)>
       <!ELEMENT firstname (#PCDATA)>
 <!ELEMENT lastname (#PCDATA)>
<!ELEMENT address (street+, city, state, zip)>
<!ELEMENT street (#PCDATA)>
<!ELEMENT city (#PCDATA)>
<!ELEMENT state (#PCDATA)>
<!ELEMENT zip (#PCDATA)>
]>

<?xml:stylesheet type="text/xsl" href="CustomerList.xsl" ?>

<customerlist>
 <customer>
  <name>
   <firstname>Michelle</firstname>
   <lastname>Correlli</lastname>
  </name>
  <address>
   <street>1824 East 7th Avenue</street>
   <street>Suite 700</street>
   <city>Memphis</city>
   <state>TN</state>
   <zip>32123-7788</zip>
  </address>
 </customer>

 <customer>
  <name>
   <firstname>Lynda</firstname>
   <lastname>Jaynes</lastname>
  </name>
  <address>
   <street>2 Elm Street</street>
   <city>New York City</city>
   <state>NY</state>
   <zip>02123-7445</zip>
  </address>
 </customer>
</customerlist>
```

Figure 14-9 shows a customer list XML document with data for two customers. It has a DTD and is a type-valid document. The statement after the DTD invokes the XSL stylesheet named CustomerList.xsl, which is shown in Figure 14-10. The result of the processing of this XML document is shown in Figure 14-11.

➤ FIGURE 14-10

Sample XSL Document

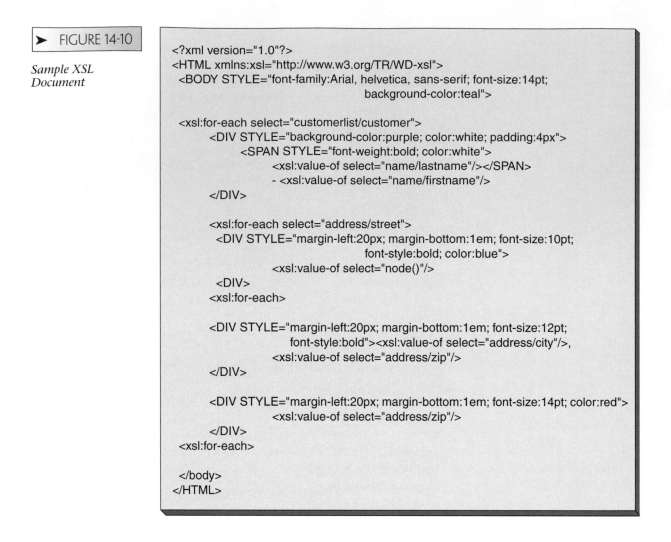

```
<?xml version="1.0"?>
<HTML xmlns:xsl="http://www.w3.org/TR/WD-xsl">
  <BODY STYLE="font-family:Arial, helvetica, sans-serif; font-size:14pt;
                                        background-color:teal">

  <xsl:for-each select="customerlist/customer">
        <DIV STYLE="background-color:purple; color:white; padding:4px">
              <SPAN STYLE="font-weight:bold; color:white">
                    <xsl:value-of select="name/lastname"/></SPAN>
                    - <xsl:value-of select="name/firstname"/>
        </DIV>

        <xsl:for-each select="address/street">
          <DIV STYLE="margin-left:20px; margin-bottom:1em; font-size:10pt;
                                        font-style:bold; color:blue">
                    <xsl:value-of select="node()"/>
          <DIV>
        <xsl:for-each>

        <DIV STYLE="margin-left:20px; margin-bottom:1em; font-size:12pt;
                        font-style:bold"><xsl:value-of select="address/city"/>,
                    <xsl:value-of select="address/zip"/>
        </DIV>

        <DIV STYLE="margin-left:20px; margin-bottom:1em; font-size:14pt; color:red">
                    <xsl:value-of select="address/zip"/>
        </DIV>
  <xsl:for-each>

  </body>
</HTML>
```

This style sheet uses the XSLT facilities in Microsoft's Internet Explorer 5.0, which has an XSLT processor that can be accessed from the stylesheet. In Figure 14-10, for example, any of the elements that begin <xsl: are invoking the Internet Explorer 5.0 XSLT processor.

The structure of an XSL stylesheet is of the form {*match, action*}. The idea is that the XSLT processor will look for a match for an element in the document, and when one is found, take the indicated action. Thus, the first xsl statement

```
<xsl:for-each select="customerlist/customer"/>
```

starts a search in the document for an element labeled customerlist. When one is found, a second search is started for an element labeled customer (it must be within customerlist). If a match is found, the actions indicated in the loop that ends with </xsl:for-each> (third from the bottom in the style sheet) are taken.

Within the loop, styles are set for each element in customer within customerlist. Notice the inner for-each loop that handles the possibility of more than one street element.

XSLT processors are context oriented; each statement is evaluated in the context of the match that has been made. Thus, the statement

```
<xsl:value-of select="name/lastname">
```

operates in the context of the customerlist/customer match that has been made. There is no need to code

<xsl:select="customerlist/customer/name/lastname">/

because the context has already been set to customerlist/customer. In fact, if the select were coded in this second way, nothing would be found. Similarly, <xsl:select "lastname"/> results in no match because lastname occurs only in the context customerlist/customer/name and not in the context customerlist/customer.

This context orientation explains the need for the statement

<xsl:value-of select="node()"/>

➤ FIGURE 14-11

Materialization with XSLT: (a) Result of XSLT Processing of Figure 14-9 with Figure 14-10

```
<HTML xmlns:xsl="http://www.w3.org/TR/WD-xsl">
<BODY STYLE="font-family:Arial, helvetica, sans-serif; font-size:14pt;
      background-color:teal">
<DIV STYLE="background-color:brown; color:white; padding:4px">
<SPAN STYLE="font-weight:bold; color:white">Correlli</SPAN>
      - Michelle
</DIV>
<DIV STYLE="margin-left:20px; margin-bottom:1em; font-size:10pt; font-style:bold;
color:yellow">
1824 East 7th Avenue
</DIV>
<DIV STYLE="margin-left:20px; margin-bottom:1em; font-size:10pt; font-style:bold;
color:yellow">
Suite 700
</DIV>
<DIV STYLE="margin-left:20px; margin-bottom:1em; font-size:12pt; font-style:bold">
Memphis, TN
</DIV>
<DIV STYLE="margin-left:20px; margin-bottom:1em; font-size:14pt; color:blue">
32123-7788
</DIV>
<DIV STYLE="background-color:brown; color:white; padding:4px">
<SPAN STYLE="font-weight:bold; color:white">Jaynes</SPAN>
      - Lynda
</DIV>
<DIV STYLE="margin-left:20px; margin-bottom:1em; font-size:10pt; font-style:bold;
color:yellow">
2 Elm Street
</DIV>
<DIV STYLE="margin-left:20px; margin-bottom:1em; font-size:12pt; font-style:bold">
New York City, NY
</DIV>
<DIV STYLE="margin-left:20px; margin-bottom:1em; font-size:14pt; color:blue">
02123-7445
</DIV>
</BODY>
</HTML>
```

(a)

FIGURE 14-11

Continued

(b) Browser Materialization

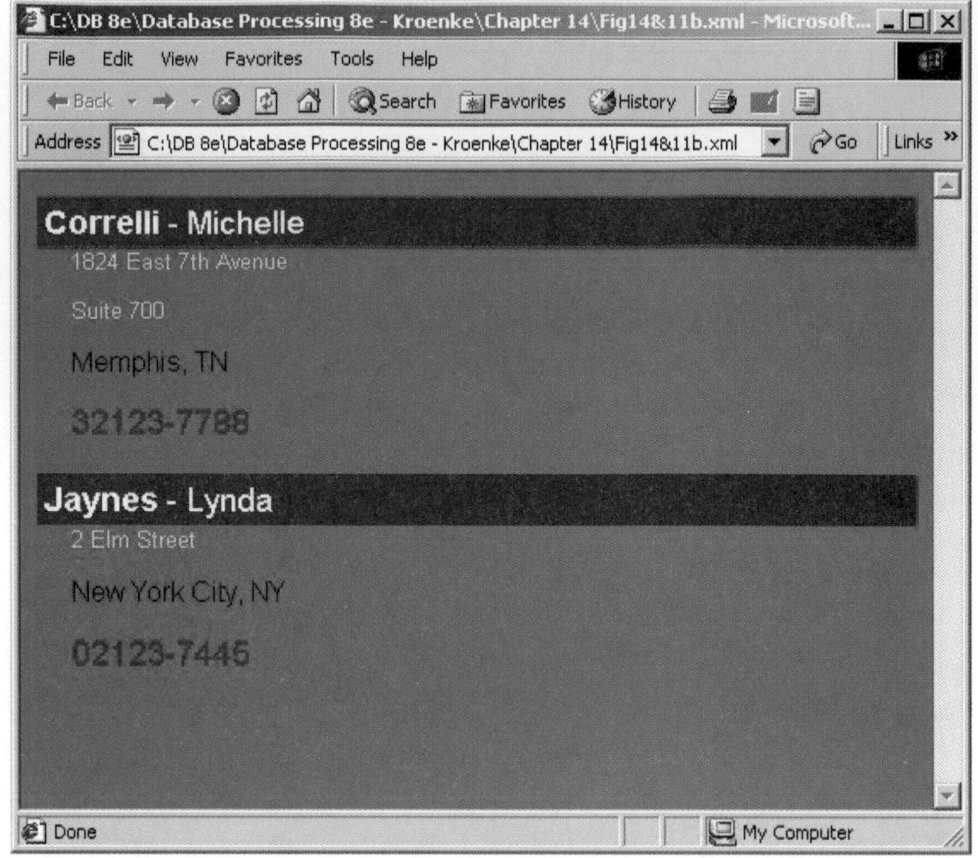

(b)

(in the center of the style sheet). The context at the location of this statement has been set to customerlist/customer/address/street. Hence, the current node is a street element, and this expression indicates that the value of that node is to be produced.

Observe, too, that a small transformation has been made by the stylesheet. The original document has firstname followed by lastname, but the output stream has lastname followed by firstname. The HTML generated by the XSLT parser in Internet Explorer is shown in Figure 14-11(a). You can see how the production rules in the XSL document have been followed for the XML document in Figure 14-9. The materialization of the HTML as it appears in the browser window is shown in Figure 14-11(b).

Microsoft has been updating the XSLT parser in Internet Explorer as the standard evolves. The parser used to generate Figure 14-11 was current as of October 2000. Check the Microsoft Web site for information about XSLT in more recent implementations of Internet Explorer.

XML Terminology and Standards

As you work with XML technology you will encounter a plethora of acronyms and terms. Figure 14-12 lists the major ones. You can find standards, documentation, and some tutorials for these on the www.w3.org and www.xml.org Web sites.

As shown in Figure 14-12, XSL has had two different meanings. Originally it was a facility for transforming XML documents into potentially very complicated formats like those needed by commercial printers. In 1999, the W3 committee decided to split XSL into two parts: the XSLT specification for document transformation and simple formatting and the XSL-FO (formatting objects) specification

➤ FIGURE 14-12

Summary of XML Terminology

Standard	Description
XML	Extensible Markup Language. A document markup language that started the following:
XSL—first meaning	Extensible Style Language. Originally a facility for transforming XML into potentially very complicated styles. Divided into two parts: XSLT for transforming document structure and producing simple formats and XSL-FO for formatting documents in complicated and sophisticated styles.
XSL—current meaning	XSLT Stylesheet. The document that provides the {match, action} pairs and other data for XSLT to use when transforming an XML document.
XSLT	A program (or process) that applies XSLT Stylesheets to an XML document to produce a transformed XML document.
XSL-FO	Extensible Style Language—Formatting Objects. The part of the original XSL left over after XSLT was removed. A very large and complicated standard for sophisticated formatting that is still under development.
XPath	A sublanguage within XSLT that is used to identify parts of an XML document to be transformed. Can also be used for calculations and string manipulation. Comingled with XSLT.
XPointer	A standard for linking one document to another. XPath has many elements from XPointer.
SAX	Simple API (application program interface) for XML. An event based parser that notifies a program when the elements of an XML document have been encountered during document parsing.
DOM	Document Object Model. An API that represents an XML document as a tree. Each node of the tree represents a piece of the XML document. A program can directly access and manipulate a node of the DOM representation.
XQL	A standard for expressing database queries as XML documents. The structure of the query uses XPath facilities and the result of the query is represented in an XML format. Under development and likely to be important in the future.
XML Namespaces	A standard for allocating terminology to defined collections. X:Name is interpreted as the element Name as defined in namespace X. Y:Name is interpreted as the element Name as defined in namespace Y. Useful for disambiguating terms.
XML Schema	An XML-compliant language for constraining the structure of an XML document. Extends and replaces DTDs. Under development and *very* important to database processing.

for sophisticated formatting. Today, the term *XSL* by itself refers to stylesheet documents like that shown in Figure 14-10.

XPath is a standard for addressing elements within documents. In Figure 14-10, expressions like <xsl:value-of-select="name/lastname"> are using the XPath standard for locating a particular element in the document. XPath includes concepts from another standard XPointer, which was developed to provide a sophisticated means for documents to reference elements in other documents.

SAX and DOM refer to different methods of parsing XML documents. The process of parsing consists of reading a document, breaking it into components, and responding to those components in some way—perhaps storing them into a database. XML parsers also validate documents against the DTDs or Schemas (see the next section).

To use the SAX API, an XSLT processor (or other program that is working on an XML document) invokes the SAX-compliant parser and passes it the name of the document to parse. The SAX parser processes the document and calls back objects within the XSLT processor whenever particular structures are encountered. A SAX parser, for example, would call the XSLT parser when it encountered a new element, passing the name of the element, its content, and other relevant items.

The DOM API works from a different paradigm. A DOM-compliant parser processes the entire XML document and creates a tree representation of it. Each element of the document is a node on the tree. The XSLT processor can then call the DOM parser to obtain particular elements using XPath or a similar addressing scheme. DOM requires the entire document to be processed at one time, and may require an unreasonable amount of storage for very large documents. If so, SAX would be a better choice. On the other hand, if all of the document contents need to be available for use at once, then DOM is the only choice.

XQL is an emerging standard for expressing queries in terms of an XML document. It is a way, for example, of representing a SQL statement in XML. This standard may become important in the future.

The last two standards in Figure 14-12 are very important to database practitioners because, among other benefits, they facilitate the representation of domains. The XML Namespaces standard specifies means for declaring and using groups of definitions. Suppose, for example, that one developer defines an Instrument in the context of music. Such an instrument has attributes like Manufacturer, Model, and Material. A second developer also defines Instrument, but in the context of electronics. This type of instrument has attributes Manufacturer, Model, and Voltage.

We can eliminate ambiguities by defining different namespaces for each of these uses. We define a Music namespace with the proper definitions of Manufacturer, Model, and Material for musical applications. We define an Electronics namespace with Manufacturer, Model, and Voltage.

Without namespace support, ambiguity is likely. An element named Model in an XML document could have a value of *Violin* or a value of *Voltage Regulator*. By specifying Music:Model in a DTD or Schema (next section), no ambiguity results.

We used a namespace in Figure 14-10. The expression <HTML xmins:xsl= "http . . ." defined a namespace called xsl. Later in the document, expressions like xsl:value_of select were using that namespace and indicating that the expression *value_of* is defined in the xsl namespace.

To fully understand the importance of name spaces, we need to address the XML Schema standard. We will do that in the next section.

XML Schema

XML Schema[1] is a standard for constraining XML documents. XML Schema serves a role similar to that of DTDs, but it improves and extends the DTD specification. XML Schema is new and changing, and vendors are just now developing parsers that can validate XML documents against XML Schema. At the time of this writing, Microsoft had a beta version of an XML Schema parser for IE 5.0 on its Web site. That version, or one akin to it, may be a supported product by the time you

[1]The use of the word *schema* is unfortunate for us; an XML Schema has no direct relationship to a *database schema*. Think of the term XML Schema in the sense of XML scheme. Now, having said that, it is possible to express the schema of a database in an XML document. Such a document might be based on an XML schema. If that seems too complicated for now, let it go and understand that XML schemas and database schemas are different things used for different purposes.

read this. There are also many other vendors, including Oracle, who have developed XML Schema validating parsers. Search the Web for the latest information. The syntax used in this section was current with the W3 XML Schema Specification as of October 2000.

As mentioned before, a document that conforms to a DTD is called type-valid. Similarly, a document that conforms to an XML Schema is called **schema-valid.** An XML document can be perfectly well-formed and be neither type-valid nor schema-valid.

The most important improvement of XML Schema over DTDs is that XML Schemas are themselves XML documents. Unlike DTDs, which have a syntax of their own, you can use the same syntax for both XML Schema definition and XML documents. This means that you can use an XML Schema validater to check the validity of the XML Schemas you write. (Clearly, there's a chicken-and-the-egg problem here. The ancestor of all XML schemas is located at www.w3.org; it has to be written in DTD format, but no other schema need be.)

XML SCHEMA CONCEPTS Figure 14-13 illustrates important XML Schema expressions and their use in a sample XML document. In XML Schema, there are two types of elements: simple and complex. (These terms are used exactly as we used them in the semantic object model in Chapter 4.) A simple element consists of a single content value. Elements price and purchaseDate in Figure 14-13 are simple elements.

Elements have a type attribute that indicates the domain of the element's content. Here, price arises from the domain dt:decimal. This expression means that values of price are constrained by the *decimal* definition in the dt namespace. Similarly, the type (domain) of purchaseDate is defined by the *date* definition in the dt namespace. We will say more about namespaces shortly. For now, think of it as reference to a location where type definitions are documented.

The third row of Figure 14-13 shows a complexType element. Its name is Address and it contains a sequence of the elements {street, mailStop, city, state, zip.} In XML Schema, the default cardinality of elements is 1.1, meaning values

➤ FIGURE 14-13

Example XML Schema Elements

Schema Definition	Example Document Fragment
<element name="price" type="dt:decimal"/>	<price>27.50</price>
<element name="purchaseDate" type="dt:date"/>	<purchaseDate>2001-12-10</purchaseDate>
<complex Type name="Address"/> <sequence> <element name="street" type="dt:string" maxoccurs="3"/> <element name="mailStop" type="dt:string" minoccurs="0"/> <element name="city" type="dt:string"/> <element name="state" type="dt:string"/> <element name="zip" type="dt:string"/> </sequence> <attribute name="dateLastChanged" type="dt:date"/> </complexType>	<Address dateLastChanged="2001-12-14"> <street>1824 Highland Ave</street> <street>Suite 400</street> <city>Seattle</city> <state>WA</state> <zip>98119</zip> </Address>
<schema targetNamespace xmlns="http://www.kumquat.com/xmldocs/dtd1" xmlns="http://www.kumquat.com/xmldocs/dtd1" xmlns:dt="http://www.w3.org/2000/10/XMLSchema"> <element name="customerView" <element name="part" type="partType"/> <element name="part" type="partType"/> <element name="color" type="dt.string"/> </element> .... </schema>	<?xml version="1.0"?> <customerView xmlns="http://www.kumquat.com/xmldocs/dtd1"> ... <part>12345</part> <color>red</color> ... </customerView>

are required and no more than one value is allowed. These defaults can be overridden with the attributes minoccurs and maxoccurs. In Address, for example, street can occur up to three times (maxoccurs="3") and mailStop is optional (minoccurs="0"). An unlimited number of occurrences is defined by setting maxoccurs equal to "unbounded".

Complex types are allowed to have attributes. Such attributes can be assigned values in the XML document. Attributes differ from element content in that they are intended to carry meta data about the element rather than a content value. Typical attribute examples are a units attribute for a quantity element or a country attribute for an address element. In Figure 14-13 Address has one attribute named dateLast Changed. This attribute is set to "2001-12-10" in the example document fragment.

XML NAMESPACES XML namespaces are one of the most confusing aspects of the XML Schema specification. Part of the reason is that they were intentionally defined to be as general as possible.

Consider the statements in the schema element in the bottom row of Figure 14-13. The first expression defines the **targetNamespace.** This identifies the namespace that the schema is creating. The target namespace is the set of definitions that result from the current schema; this namespace will be used to validate other XML documents. The expression targetNamespace xmlns="http://www.kumquat.com/xml docs/dtd1" tells the parser that this schema is to be used to generate a namespace with the name "http://www.kumquat.com/xmldocs/dtd1". That name can later be invoked by documents that are based on this schema. This is done for the customerView document in the second column of the last row of Figure 14-13.

In addition to the target namespace, every XML document may have zero or one **default namespaces** and zero to many **labeled namespaces.** These namespaces are used by the parser while it is interpreting the schema document in the process of creating the target namespace. The default namespace is indicated with the keyword *xmlns=* followed by the name of the namespace in quotes. A labeled namespace is indicated by the keyword *xmlns* followed by a colon, followed by the label of the namespace, followed by an equal sign and then the name of the namespace in quotes. Thus, xmlns:aviation="http://www.abc.com/dtd" creates a labeled namespace called *aviation* and gives it the name "http://www.abc.com/dtd".

In Figure 14-13, the statement xmlns="http://www.kumquat.com/xml docs/dtd1" defines the default namespace. Unless directed otherwise, the parser will use the default namespace when interpreting the schema contents. Observe that in this case, the targetNamespace and the default namespace are both set equal to "http://www.kumquat.com/xmldocs/dtd1". This arrangement tells the parser to look inside the current schema document for the definitions of any unlabeled elements. As an aside, these two need not always be the same; the target namespace and the default namespace can be different.

In the last row of Figure 14-13, the default namespace is used for defining the element *part*. Its type is "partType", with no label. Since there is no label for partType, the parser will look for the definition of partType somewhere in the current schema document.

The third statement, starting with *xmlns:dt*, sets the name of the labeled namespace *dt* to "http://www.w3.org/2000/10/XMLSchema". This name identifies a namespace that has standard XML element types. (See www.w3.org for a list of them.) This namespace is used later in this schema where color is given the type *dt:string*. This expression tells the parser to go to the namespace indicated by the label dt to find the definition of *string*. You will see a better example of the use of multiple namespaces in the next sections.

Now, here's the tricky part. The namespaces we've used all look like URI addresses. This is not a requirement, however. The only requirement is that the names of namespaces be unique any place the XML Schema will ever be used. If we knew that no one would ever use the identifier BOAT, we could define a namespace, say, *sailing*, with the expression xmlns:sailing="BOAT". This word is unlikely to be a unique, however.

URIs are used for namespace identifiers because they can be chosen so that they will be unique, worldwide. Thus, the identifier "http://www.prenhall.com/databaseprocessing8e/Chapter14/Figure 14-13/dtd" is a valid, worldwide unique identifier. Someone else might use this as a namespace identifier, but Prentice Hall would have the right to object, just as they would if someone made unauthorized use of a Prentice Hall copyright or trademark.

Now, for the continuation of the tricky part,—according to the W3 specification, there is no requirement that a schema document actually be located at the indicated URI. Thus, the URI is only used to give a unique identity to the namespace, and for no other reason. The location of the actual documents required to define the namespace(s) may be indicated to the parser in some other way—perhaps as parameters passed to the parser when it is started, for example. The specification does not indicate how this is to be done.

Keep in mind, however, that particular implementations of XML Schema may use the values of namespace names to locate the necessary documents. If so, that is the choice of the implementer; the standard would allow other mechanisms as well. To recap, the names of namespaces look like URIs, but they need not be. They are only required to be unique.

USING MULTIPLE NAMESPACES TO RESOLVE DOMAIN AMBIGUITY

Earlier, when discussing XML terminology and standards, we introduced the problem that occurs when a single word is used to define two different things. For example, suppose the designer of an XML schema wants to define musicalInstrument with elements {source, model, comment} and to define electricalDevice with elements {source, model, comment}. The elements of the musicalInstrument and those of electricalDevice have the same names, but their domains are different. The source of musicalInstrument is to be only companies that make musical instruments, just as the source of electricalDevice is to be only electronic companies. Comment has an even greater difference. The comment of musicalInstrument is to be the material of the instrument—alloy, silver, brass, and so on, while comment of electricalDevice is to be the voltage of that device.

Figure 14-14 illustrates the use of multiple namespaces to resolve the ambiguity of these names. Two labeled namespaces are defined: music and electronic. The music namespace defines its elements in a way that conforms to the music world; the electronic namespace defines its elements in a way that conforms to the electronics world. The complex type musicalInstrument includes the elements *source, model,* and *comment*, as you would expect. These elements, however, are given the types from the musical namespace, source is music:manufacturer, model is music:model, and comment is music:material.

A similar strategy is used for electrical device. Its elements are defined as type electronic:manufacturer, electronic:model, and electronic:voltage.

The XML Schema standard provides many ways to limit the domain of type definitions. Elements can be constrained to be certain values, to be certain ranges of numbers, to be constant, to have default values, and so forth. Thus, the element manufacturer in the music namespace could be constrained via its type to be {Yamaha, Steinway, Horner} and then only those values would be allowed. Similar techniques can be used for all the other elements. These techniques are beyond the scope of this discussion; see www.w3.org for more information about them.

➤ FIGURE 14-14

Example Use of XML Schema with Multiple Namespaces

Schema Definition

```
<schema targetNamespace xmlns=“http://www.mycompany.com/orders/dtd”
        xmlns=“http://www.mycompany.com/orders/dtd”
        xmlns:dt=“http://www.w3.org/2000/10/XMLSchema”
        xmlns:music=“http://www.musiccompany.com/xml/dtd”
        xmlns:electronic=“http://www.electricalcompany.com/xml/dtd”>

 <complexType name=“equipment”>
  <complexType name=“musicalInstrument” maxoccurs=“unbounded”>
   <sequence>
    <element name=“source” type =“music:manufacturer”/>
    <element name=“model” type =“music:model”/>
    <element name=“comment” type =“music:material” minoccurs=“0”/>
   </sequence>
  </complexType>

 <complexType name=“electronicDevice”/>
   <sequence>
    <element name=“source” type =“electronic:manufacturer”/>
    <element name=“model” type =“electronic:model”/>
    <element name=“comment” type =“electronic:voltage”/>
   </sequence>
  </complexType>
 </complexType>

</schema>
```

Example Document

```
<?xml version=“1.0”?>
<equipment xmlns=“http://www.mycompany.com/orders/dtd>

  <musicalInstrument>
    <source>Yamaha</source>
    <model>Standard Flute</model>
    <comment>Silver</comment>
  </musicalInstrument>

  <musicalInstrument>
    <source>Yamaha</source>
    <model>Piano</model>
   </musicalInstrument>

  <electricalDevice>
    <source>Hewlett-Packard</source>
    <model>HP-2780Z</model>
    <comment>12</comment>
   </electricalDevice>

</equipment>
```

Figure 14-14 illustrates a few other ideas, as well. Given the prior discussion, you should be able to explain why this schema-valid example document can have a musicalInstrument with no material element, and why two such musicalInstruments are allowed. Also, why would a second electricalDevice not be allowed for this to be a schema-valid document?

EDITORIAL COMMENT What we have just described is very, very important to database processing. These XML Schema capabilities provide a standardized, extensible, worldwide solution to a problem that has plagued database processing since its inception: enforcing domains. The only solution heretofore was to write application code, stored procedures, or triggers to enforce domain definitions. This code, however, had a single purpose and had to be rewritten every time a domain changed—say, a new company started producing musical instruments. With XML Schema, the code is written once—in the program that validates XML documents against their schemas, and then the domains are defined in data, using an extensible, standardized means. If a domain changes, the list of allowed domains is updated in the enumerated list. No highly trained, expensive, human (and therefore error-prone) programmer is required.

It will take a few years for products to be developed that implement this standard, and it will take a few more years for companies to learn to use them (here is where you come in!). But, in time, XML Schema, or something very close to it, will see extensive use because it will dramatically simplify application development and maintenance.

AN XML SCHEMA FOR THE VIEWRIDGE GALLERY CustomerView

Figure 14-15 shows an XML schema for the Customer View of View Ridge Gallery (taken from Figure 10-4). The element nameOfArtist is defined at the top of this schema; this was done so that it could be used twice in the body of custView.

This example shows the utility of setting the targetNamespace and the default namespace to be the same. When nameOfArtist is found by the parser, it will

➤ FIGURE 14-15

XML Schema for the ViewRidge Gallery CustomerView

Schema Definition

```
<schema targetNamespace xmlns="http://www.viewridge.com/customer"
        xmlns="http:// www.viewridge.com/customer"
        xmlns:dt="http://www.w3.org/2000/10/XMLSchema"

  <element name="nameOfArtist" type="dt.string"/>
  <complexType name="custView" maxoccurs="unbounded">
   <sequence>
    <complexType name="customer">
     <sequence>
      <element name="name" type ="dt:string"/>
      <element name="areaCode" type ="dt:string" minoccurs="0"/>
      <element name="localNumber" type ="dt:string"/>
      <complexType name="transaction" maxoccurs="unbounded">
       <sequence>
        <element name="purchaseDate" type="dt:date"/>
        <element name="salesPrice" type="dt:decimal"/>
        <complexType name="work">
         <sequence>
          <element name="artistName" type="nameOfArtist"/>
          <element name="workTitle" type="dt:string"/>
          <element name="workCopy" type="dt:string" minoccurs="0">
         </sequence>
        </complexType>
       </sequence>
      </complexType>
      <complexType name="artistInterest" maxoccurs="unbounded"/>
       <element name=artistName type="nameOfArtist"/>
      </complexType>
     </sequence>
    </complexType>
   </sequence>
  </complexType>
```

Example Document

```
<?xml version="1.0"?>
<custView xmins="http://www.viewridge.com/customer">

 <customer>
  <name>Jackson, Elizabeth</name>
  <areaCode>206</areaCode>
  <localNumber>989-4344</localNumber>
  <transaction>
   <purchaseDate>2002-12-10</purchaseDate>
   <salesPrice>4300.00</salesPrice>
   <work>
     <artistName>Juan Miro</artistName>
     <workTitle>Poster</workTitle>
     <workCopy>14/85</workCopy>
   </work>
  </transaction>
  <artistInterest>
   <artistName>Juan Miro</artistName>
   <artistName>Mark Tobey</artistName>
   <artistName>Dennis Frings</artistName>
  </artistInterest>
 </customer>
</customerview>
```

assign it to the targetNamespace. Subsequently, when the two artistName elements are processed, and their type is found to be nameOfArtist, without any label (like dt), the parser will look to the default namespace to find nameOfArtist. It will find it because the targetNamespace and the default namespace are the same.

Defining an element type once like this saves errors because if it is changed, it need only be changed in one place and the change will be propagated to the elements that are defined on it. Also, definitions can be lengthy, and defining multi-use attributes once saves work.

This example doesn't show the full power of XML schema. For example, the domain of workCopy is nnn/mmm, where nnn and mmm are both positive integers and nnn is required to be less than mmm. This complicated domain can be defined in XML Schema syntax and will then be enforced by the parser. Similar comments apply to restrictions on areaCode, localNumber, purchaseDate, and salesPrice.

Wireless Application Protocol

The wireless application protocol has been defined to facilitate the use of Internet technology on wireless devices such as cellular phones and personal digital assistants. We introduced a typical WAP application need earlier in this chapter. In this section we will sketch the essence of WAP; see www.WapForum.org for more information.

Figure 14-16 shows the major components of a WAP system. A WAP Server is an HTTP server that transforms standard Web protocols XML into **wireless markup language** or WML. WML is a subset of XML; hence, WML documents can be validated against DTDs or XML Schemas. In addition, XSLT can be used to

FIGURE 14-16

Use of Wireless Application Protocol (WAP)

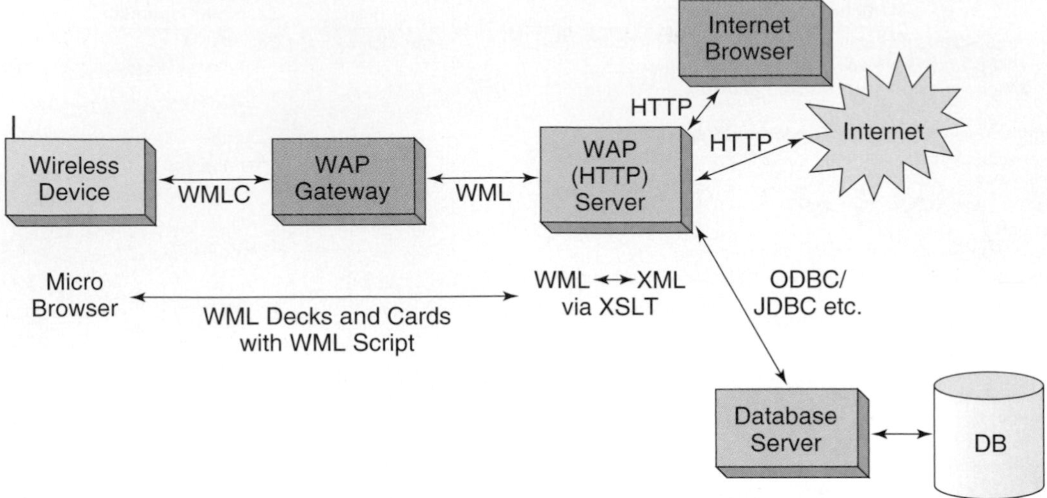

transform XML documents into WML for processing on the wireless device. XSLT can also be used to transform the WML response from the wireless device into standard XML. The WML standard includes a scripting language, **WML Script,** which is a variant of JavaScript.

As shown in Figure 14-16, WML is transformed by a Web Gateway computer into a compressed form called WMLC. This compressed form is akin to a compiled program; it is a much smaller, binary version of the WML document. The purpose of the compression is to reduce the bandwidth required to transmit the document.

At present, wireless devices have insufficient screen space and keyboard capability to support full browsers. **Micro browsers** are ultrathin applications that process WML.

When using WML and XML document is divided into sections that are small enough to be displayed by the microbrowser on the wireless device. Each section is called a **card** and the collection of cards is referred to as a **deck.** Normally, the entire deck is transmitted to the wireless device at one time. Cards are then displayed on the wireless device as they are needed. References to particular cards are written in the format *deck-identifier#card-identifier*. Cards of the current deck can be accessed from the wireless device, while those from other decks require a trip back to the WAP server.

WAP does not require the use of XML; HTML can be used as well. The advantage of using XML, however, is that the WML documents can be validated and that XSLT can be used to convert between WML and XML.

The Importance of XML to Database Applications

XML may be the most important development for database applications since the relational model. Figure 14-17 lists the reasons why. First, XML Schema provides a standardized way of representing domains. Also, XML provides a standard

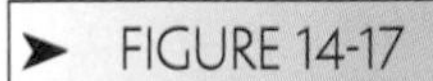

FIGURE 14-17

XML Characteristics Important to Database Processing

> Standard means for representing domains
> Standard means for expressing database views
> Clean separation of structure, content, and materialization
> Facility for document validity checking
> Industry standards for document types

means for expressing the structure of database views. Because of the standard, any application that can process a DTD or XML Schema document can correctly interpret any arbitrary database view.

Consider the XML Schema for the Customer View for View Ridge Galleries in Figure 14-15. Prior to the XML standard, for two programs to exchange this view, they would need to develop a private protocol for specifying its structure. With XML, they need only interpret the XML Schema in Figure 14-15; there need not be any prior agreement on a protocol.

In the past, developers used SQL as a stand-in for a standard way for describing database view data. As you learned in Chapter 10, however, SQL cannot be used for any view that involves more than one multi-valued path through the schema. The view in Figure 14-15 has two multi-valued paths; one through Transaction and one through Artist. Hence, multiple SQL statements are required and there is no standard way to express how they should be connected using SQL. XML overcomes this deficiency.

The third major benefit of XML is the clean break among structure, content, and materialization. The structure of a document can be stored in one place as a DTD or schema and all documents based on that structure can include references to it. Boeing, for example, can place a schema document for airplane part orders on one of its Web sites, and all airplane part purchasers can use that schema when creating order documents.

Companies that order from Boeing can develop their own database applications to construct XML order documents that conform to the schema. The means they use to create such documents is completely hidden from Boeing and everyone else. They might use a database application or they might use a word processor; how the data are created is unknown and unimportant.

Furthermore, Boeing can develop many different XSL stylesheets for materializing this document. They can have one for their Order Entry department, one for their Production Department, one for their Accounting Department, and one for their Marketing Department. They can also provide one for use by their customers. Boeing's customers can also create their own stylesheets for documents based on this schema. Thus, everyone can materialize the content of the standard order document in whatever way is appropriate for them.

Document validity checking is a fourth important characteristic of XML. Using the Boeing example, when a customer creates an order document, they can verify the validity of that document against the DTD or schema. In this way they can ensure that they are transmitting only type-valid or schema-valid orders. Similarly, when Boeing Web sites receive order documents, they can automatically check them against the DTD or schema to ensure that they are accepting only type-valid or schema-valid documents.

Such validity checking can be performed without XML, but it is much more difficult. Boeing would need to develop a specialized program to validate order documents and then send that specialized program to all customers or departments who need it. They would need to create a different specialized program for a second document type, and a third for a third document type, and so forth. With the XML standard, they need only place DTDs or schemas in a public location and all interested parties can validate their own documents of the varying types.

The last important advantage is that with XML, industry groups can develop industry-wide DTDs and schemas. **OASIS (Organization for the Advancement of Structured Information Standards)** serves as a clearinghouse for publication of XML schema standards. It maintains the XML.ORG registry that lists published schemas and a search engine for locating schemas on particular topics. Figure 14-18 lists some of the standards that currently exist.

➤ FIGURE 14-18

Examples of Industry XML Standards

Industry Type	Example Standards
Accounting	• American Institute of Certified Public Accountants (AICPA): Extensible Financial Reporting Markup Language (XFRML)[OASIS Cover page] • Open Applications Group, Inc (OAG)
Architecture and Construction	• Architecture, Engineering, and Construction XML Working Group (aecXML Working Group) • ConSource.com: Construction Manufacturing and Distribution Extensible Markup Language (cmdXML)
Automotive	• Automotive Industry Action Group (AIAG) • Global Automedia: • MSR: Standards for information exchange in the engineering process (MEDOC) • The Society of Automotive Engineers (SAE): XML for the Automotive Industry–SAE J2008[OASIS Cover page] • Open Applications Group, Inc (OAG)
Banking	• Banking Industry Technology Secretariat (BITS): [OASIS Cover page] • Financial Services Technology Consortium (FSTC): Bank Internet Payment System (BIPS)[OASIS Cover page] • Open Applications Group, Inc (OAG)
Electronic Data Interchange	• Data Interchange Standards Association (DISA): [OASIS Cover page] • EEMA EDI/EC Work Group[OASIS Cover page] • European Committee for Standardization/Information Society Standardization System (CEN/ISSS; The European XML/EDI Pilot Project[OASIS Cover page] • XML/EDI Group[OASIS Cover page]
Human Resources	• DataMain: Human Resources Markup Language (hrml) • HR-XML Consortium[OASIS Cover page]: JobPosting, CandidateProfile, Resume • Open Applications Group (OAG): Open Applications Group Interface Specification (OASIS)[OASIS Cover page] • Tapestry.Net: JOB markup language (JOB) • Open Applications Group, Inc (OAG)
Insurance	• ACORD: Property and Casualty[OASIS Cover page], Life (XMLife)[OASIS Cover page] • Lexica: iLingo

EXAMPLE XML FOR BUSINESS-TO-BUSINESS PROCESSING

Figure 14-19 shows the role of XML for the sharing of database documents in a business-to-business application. Company A on the left (say, Boeing) uses one or more database applications to create XML documents. These database applications reference XML schema documents to determine the required view structure. As shown, these documents reside on local sites, in public schema libraries, and in schema libraries kept by Company B (say, one of Boeing's suppliers).

➤ FIGURE 14-18

(Continued)

Industry Type	Example Standards
Real Estate	• OpenMLS: Real Estate Listing Management System (OpenMLS)[OASIS Cover page] • Real Estate Transaction Standard working group (RETS): Real Estate Transaction Standard (RETS)[OASIS Cover page]
Software	• IBM: [OASIS Cover page] • Flashline.com: Software Component Documentation DTD • Flashline.com: • INRIA: Koala Bean Markup Language (KBML)[OASIS Cover page] • Marimba and Microsoft: Open Software Description Format (OSD)[OASIS Cover page] • Object Management Group (OMG): [OASIS Cover page]
Workflow	• Internet Engineering Task Force (IETF): Simple Workflow Access Protocol (SWAP)[OASIS Cover page] • Workflow Management Coalition (MfMC): Wf-XML[OASIS Cover page]

➤ FIGURE 14-19

XML in All Its Glory

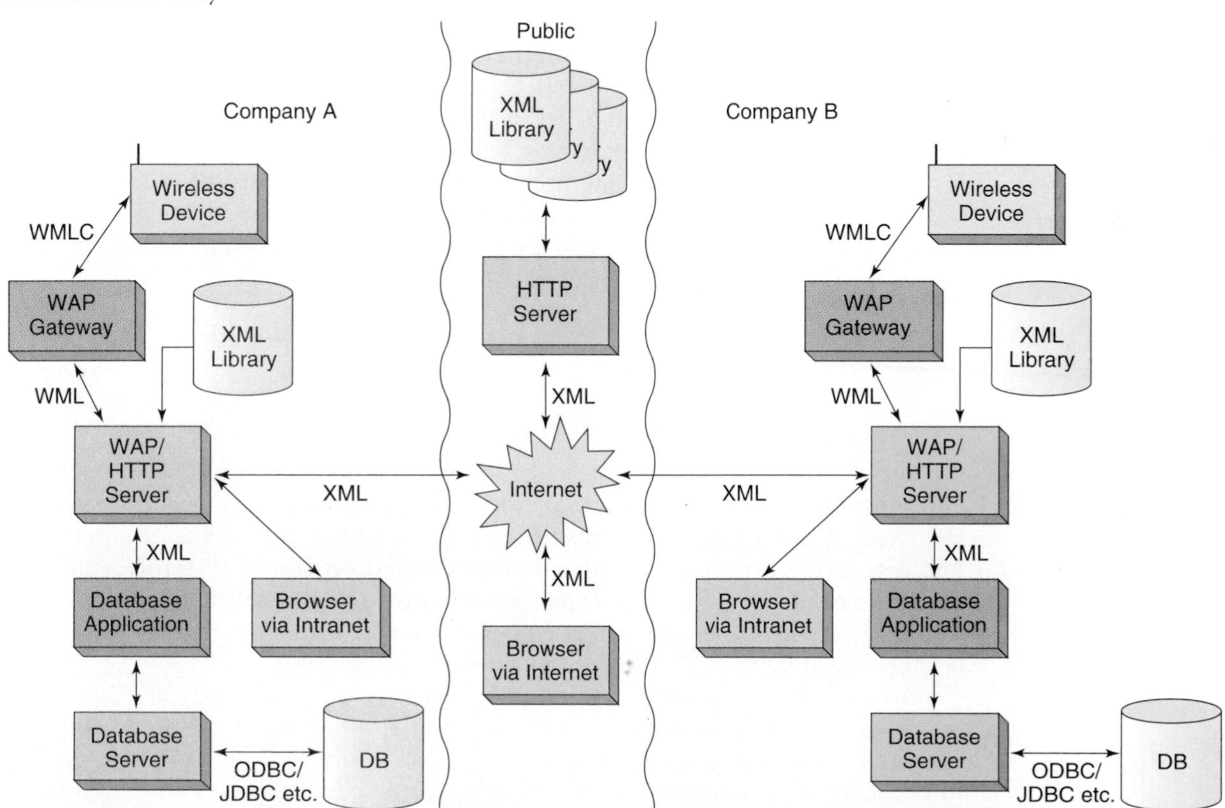

Once the documents have been created, they are passed to a Web server. Here they are passed to either WAP or HTTP servers. There is, of course, no requirement that the documents be accessible by wireless devices; this capability is shown here for illustration. The generated XML documents containing the database view can be directed to internal Company A servers for internal use, they can be published on publicly accessible Web servers maintained by company A or some other company, or they could be transmitted to a server controlled by Company B.

At any stage, the XML document can be validated against the relevant XML Schema to ensure that nothing has been lost. Moreover, at any stage, the XML document can be transformed using XSLT to a different XML format, to WML, to voice, to the format required by manufacturing devices like robots or any other format. If transformed to a form that is itself XML (such as WML), XML Schemas can be utilized to validate the transformed document.

Database applications can be written to use these XML technologies to publish applications in a myriad of ways, using dozens of different formats. And all of this is done using industry standards.

XML Support in Oracle and SQL Server

Both Oracle and SQL Server have begun to incorporate support for XML. Both products include the ability to store XML documents in the database, and they both provide an XML DOM parser for processing XML documents. Using these parsers, developers can write code to extract database fields from XML documents and store those fields as columns of tables.

Further, both products have support for XPath, which enables XML documents to be searched. They also both support means to use SQL queries against database data and have the results materialized as XML documents. Both products enable database-generated XML documents and forms to be processed using Internet technology. Oracle utilizes XSQL pages that can be incorporated with Java Server Pages (discussed in Chapter 16). SQL Server utilizes ADO and ASP pages (discussed in the next chapter).

Support for XML in commercial database products like these is clearly in an early, formative stage. The integration between database constructs and XML is a bit awkward. Clearly, these capabilities will be improved in future versions of both of these products. This topic lies on the leading edge of commercial database processing, and it will be interesting to see how all of this plays out in the future. Stay tuned!

➤ SUMMARY

A computer network is a collection of computers that communicate using a standardized protocol. Public networks can be used by anyone who pays the required fee; users of private networks must be preauthorized to connect to the network. The Internet is a public computer network based on the TCP/IP protocol. The Internet began as a military research project known as ARPANET.

In 1989, the hypertext transfer protocol or HTTP was first developed by Tim Berners-Lee at CERN. HTTP is request oriented and stateless.

An intranet is a private LAN or WAN that uses TCP/IP, HTML, and browsers. Intranets are either not connected to the Internet or are connected via a firewall. Intranets have performance that is orders of magnitude faster than that of the Internet. Wireless network access is possible from cellular phones and other wireless devices using the Wireless Application Protocol.

Database applications using Internet technology most often use either the three tier or *n*-tier architectures. The three-tier architecture consists of a database server, a Web server, and client computers. Each of these tiers can use a different operating system and products from different vendors. The purpose of the database server is to run the DBMS to process SQL and to provide multi-user database services. The Web server is an HTTP server that hosts scripting languages and enables the database application to process database views (CRUD). The client machine operates as an HTTP client that hosts a second scripting environment and materializes database views.

Common Web servers are Microsoft's IIS, Apache, and Netscape Web Server. Active Server Pages are commonly used with IIS on Windows servers and Java servlets and JSP are commonly used with Unix servers.

Standards are important for markup languages so that Web pages can be processed on any browser. The W3C publishes standards and administers the process of developing them. Commercial products extend standards, but when they do, they create problems for users of products that do not support the extensions. HTML 4.0 was developed as a standard to overcome problems in earlier versions of HTML. Microsoft's dynamic HTML (DHTML) implements and extends HTML 4.0. Three features of DHTML are important to database applications: the Document Object Model (DOM), Cascading Style Sheets (CSS), and Remote Data Services (RD), a set of ActiveX controls that allow for caching and materialization of data on the client without round trips to the server.

The Extensible Markup Language (XML) is a markup language that was designed to provide a clear separation among document structure, content, and materialization. It is extendable, but in a standardized way. Document structure is defined by either by document type descriptions (DTDs) or by XML Schema documents. XML documents that conform to their DTDs are type-valid documents. XML documents can be materialized using either CSS or the Extensible Style Language: Transformations (XSLT). XSLT is a declarative, transform facility for manipulating XML documents. XSLT can be used to transform an XML document into HTML or into another XML document having different structure.

Important XML standards are summarized in Figure 14-12. XML Schema is a standard for constraining XML documents; XML documents that conform to their schemas are called schema-valid. XML Schema improves upon DTDs in many ways. For one, XML schema documents are themselves XML documents that can be validated. Additionally, XML schemas provide a generalized extensible means for enforcing domains through the use of XML namespaces.

WML is an XML standard for processing XML documents using micro browsers on wireless devices. With WML, XML pages are divided into sections called cards. A full set of WML cards is called a deck. The scripting language used is WML Script, which is a variant of ECMAScript.

XML is most important to database applications because it provides a standard means for expressing the structure of database views, it cleanly breaks document structure, content, and materialization, it allows for standardized document validly checking, and it enables industry groups to define useful standards for the structure of industry-standard database views. Both Oracle and SQL Server include support for XML.

➤ GROUP I QUESTIONS

14.1 Define the terms *network, public network*, and *private network*.

14.2 Define *Internet.*

14.3 What is TCP/IP and how is it used?

14.4 Explain what it means to say that HTTP is request-oriented and stateless.

14.5 What protocol has been developed to support wireless network processing?

14.6 Name the three tiers of the three-tier architecture and describe the role of each.

14.7 Explain how the three-tier architecture allows for interoperability of operating systems and Web products.

14.8 Explain the functions of each of the components of the Web server in Figure 14-4.

14.9 Explain two uses for the extra tiers in an *n*-tier architecture.

14.10 Why are standards important for markup languages?

14.11 What is W3C, and why is it important?

14.12 Why do vendors have a love/hate relationship with standards?

14.13 Summarize the disadvantages of early versions of HTML.

14.14 What is the difference between DHTML and HTML 4.0?

14.15 Explain the importance of the document object model (DOM).

14.16 Define CSS and explain its importance.

14.17 Define RDS and explain its role.

14.18 Define XML and explain why it is superior to HTML and DHTML.

14.19 Explain why there is too much freedom with HTML.

14.20 What is a DTD, and why is it important?

14.21 Define *type-valid* and *not-type-valid* XML documents.

14.22 Explain how CSS is used with XML documents.

14.23 Define XSLT and explain its importance.

14.24 Why is XSLT declarative? Why is it transformational?

14.25 Explain the importance of context when working with XSLT.

14.26 Describe the difference between DOM and SAX.

14.27 What are two types of elements in XML Schema? Give an example of each.

14.28 Explain the difference between element content and element attributes.

14.29 What is a target namespace and what is its function?

14.30 What is the default namespace and how is it used?

14.31 What is the significance of giving the target namespace and the default namespace the same name?

14.32 Give an example of a labeled namespace.

14.33 Explain how to use namespaces to resolve element name ambiguity.

14.34 Why do namespace names look like Internet addresses? Does the XML Schema standard require that schema documents be located at these addresses?

14.35 Define WAP, WML, WML Script, deck, and card.

14.36 Why is XML important to database applications?

14.37 Why is SQL not an effective way for defining the structure of database views?

➤ GROUP II QUESTIONS

14.38 Visit www.w3.org and determine the current recommended standard for HTML. How does it differ from that described in this chapter? Is there a new standard for HTML underway? If so, what is it and what new features will it have?

14.39 Visit www.w3.org and determine the current recommended standard for XSLT. How does it differ from the implementation of XSLT described in this chapter for Internet Explorer 5.0? What XSLT standards are in process?

14.40 Visit www.w3.org and determine the current recommended standard for XML Schema. How does it differ from that described here?

14.41 Visit either Microsoft's or Oracle's Web site and investigate XML Schema products and technology that they support. How do these products differ from XML Schema described here?

14.42 Visit www.xml.org, go to the registry, and find a standard for an industry type of interest to you. Describe the purpose of the standard. How useful do you believe that standard will become?

14.43 Visit www.wapformum.org and determine the current recommended WAP standard. How does it differ from that described here?

➤ FIREDUP PROJECT QUESTIONS

The Robards decide that they want their customers to register their stoves online. They're not sure how to go about this, so they hire you as a consultant to help them.

Assume they decide to operate their own Web site rather than use a service bureau.

A. Comment on the desirability of their decision to operate their own site. What are the advantages and disadvantages?

B. Consider the three-tier architecture in the light of FiredUp's registration needs. What would be the purpose of each tier?

C. Would you recommend Windows 2000 or Linux for their Web server? Explain the advantages and disadvantages of each.

D. Would you recommend Access, Oracle, or SQL Server for their database server? Explain your rationale.

E. Would it be desirable for FiredUp to combine the Web server and database server on one computer? What are the advantages and disadvantages of this?

F. Create an XML DTD and sample XML registration document. Assume the database tables are:

CUSTOMER (<u>CustomerID</u>, Name, Phone, EmailAddress)
STOVE (<u>SerialNumber</u>, Type, Version, DateOfManufacture)
REGISTRATION (<u>*CustomerID, SerialNumber,* RDate</u>)
STOVE_REPAIR (<u>RepairInvoiceNumber</u>, *SerialNumber*, RepairDate, Description, Cost, *CustomerID*)

G. Create an XML Schema for the registration document.

ODBC, OLE DB, ADO, and ASP

This chapter discusses standard interfaces for accessing database servers. ODBC, or the Open Database Connectivity standard, was developed in the early 1990s to provide a DBMS-independent means for processing relational database data. In the mid-1990s Microsoft announced OLE DB, which is an object-oriented interface that encapsulates data-server functionality. As you will learn, OLE DB was designed not just for relational databases but for many other types of data as well. As a COM interface, OLE DB is readily accessible to C++, C#, and Java programmers, but is not as accessible to Visual Basic and scripting developers. Therefore, Microsoft developed Active Data Objects (ADO), which is a set of objects for utilizing OLE DB that is designed for use by any language, including VB, VBScript, and JScript.

Before considering these standards, we need to gain a perspective on the data environment that surrounds the Web server in Internet technology database applications.

➤ THE WEB SERVER DATA ENVIRONMENT

The environment in which today's Internet technology database applications reside is rich and complicated. As shown in Figure 15-1, a typical Web server needs to publish applications that involve data of dozens of different data types. So far in this text we have considered only relational databases, but as you can see from this figure, there are many other data types as well.

Consider the problems that the developer of Web server applications has when integrating this data. He or she may need to connect to an Oracle database, a DB2 mainframe database, a nonrelational database like IMS, file processing data like VSAM and ISAM, e-mail directories, and so forth. Each one of these products has a different programming interface that the developer must learn. Further,

➤ FIGURE 15-1

Internet Application Data Needs

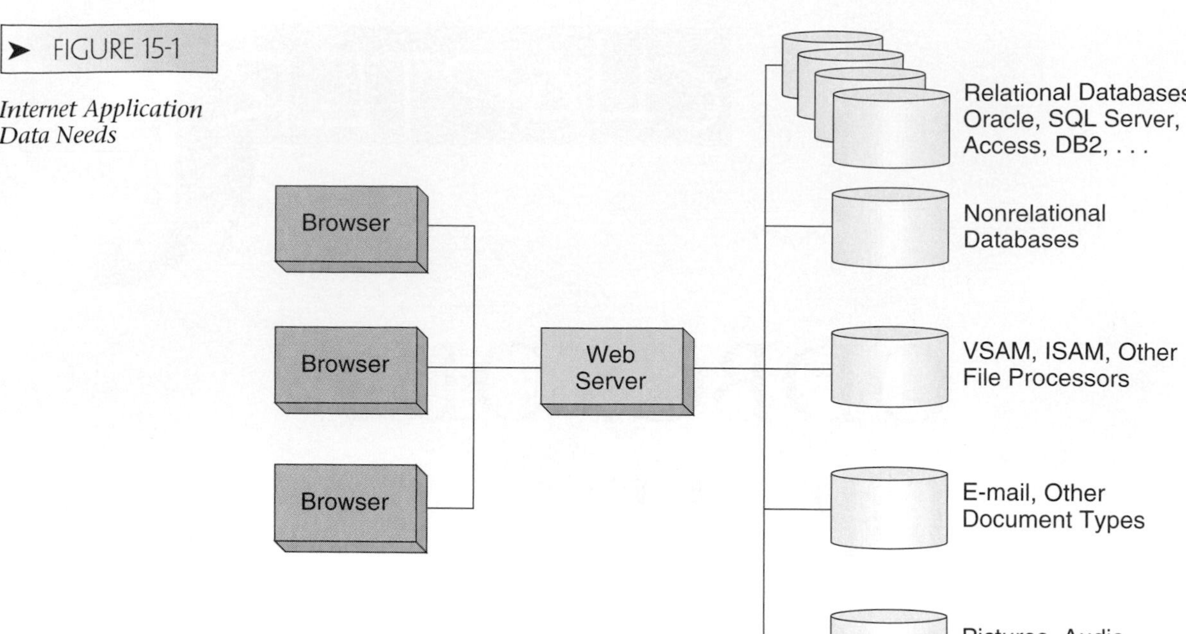

each of these products evolves, so over time new features and functions will be added that will increase the developer's challenge.

ODBC was created to address the part of this problem that concerns relational databases and data sources that are table-like, such as spreadsheets. As shown in Figure 15-2, ODBC is an interface between the Web server (or other database user) and the database server. It consists of a set of standards by which SQL statements also can be issued and results and error messages returned. As shown, developers

➤ FIGURE 15-2

Role of ODBC Standard

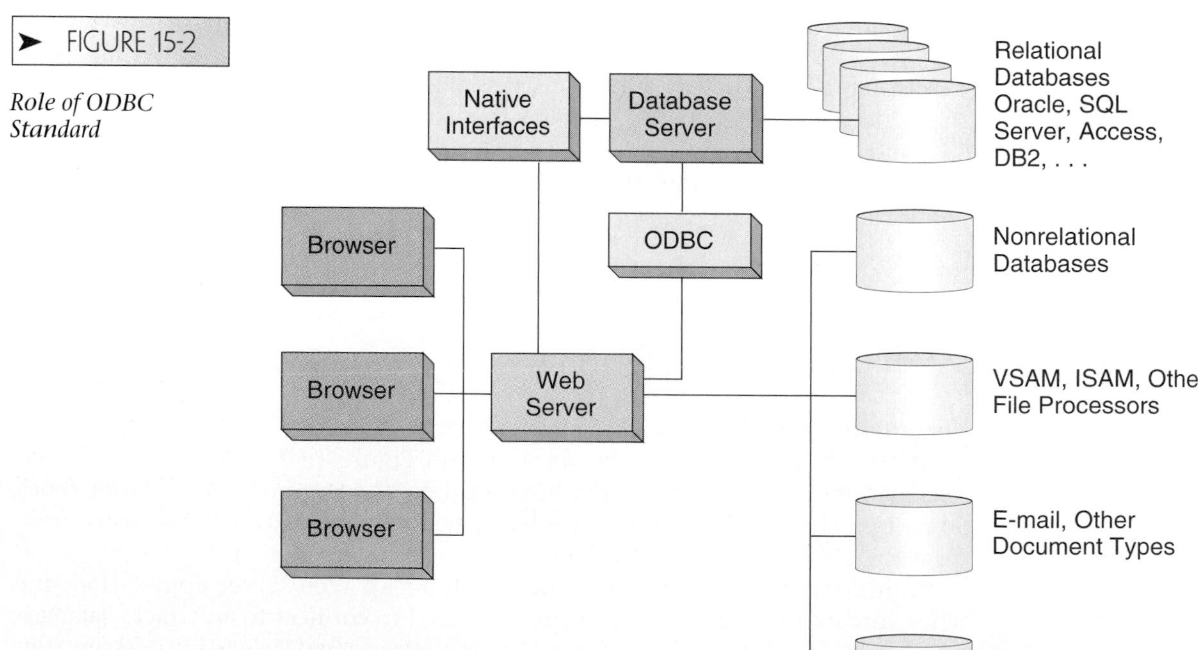

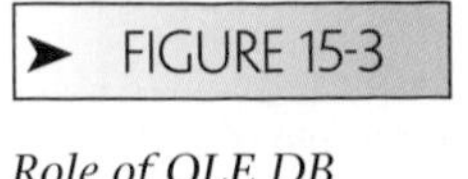
FIGURE 15-3

Role of OLE DB

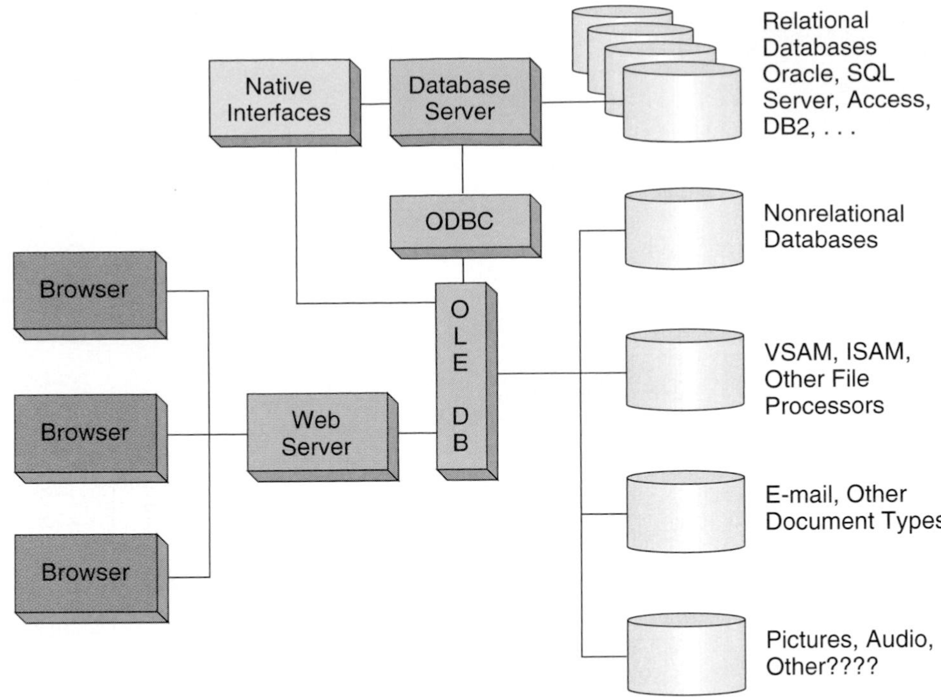

can call data servers using native DBMS interfaces if they want to (sometimes done to increase performance), but the beleaguered developer who does not have the time or desire to learn many different DBMS native libraries can use ODBC instead.

ODBC has been a tremendous success and greatly simplified some database development tasks. As you will learn, it has a substantial disadvantage that was addressed by Microsoft when it developed OLE DB. Figure 15-3 shows the relationship of OLE DB, ODBC, and other data types. OLE DB provides an object-oriented interface to data of almost any type. DBMS vendors can wrap portions of their native libraries in OLE DB objects to expose their product's functionality through this interface. OLE DB can also be used as an interface to ODBC data sources. Finally, OLE DB was developed to support the processing of non-relational data as well.

Because OLE DB is an object-oriented interface, it is particularly suited to object-oriented languages like C++. Many database application developers, however, program in Visual Basic, or scripting languages such as VBScript and JScript. Consequently, Microsoft defined ADO as a cover over OLE DB objects (see Figure 15-4) ADO enables programmers in almost any language to be able to access OLE DB functionality.

You may feel uncomfortable with the strong Microsoft presence in this discussion. Both OLE DB and ADO were developed and promulgated by Microsoft, and even ODBC received prominence in large measure because of support from Microsoft. In fact, other vendors and standards committees did propose alternatives to OLE DB and ADO, but because Microsoft Windows resides on nearly 90 percent of the world's desktops, it is difficult for others to promulgate opposing standards. Furthermore, in defense of Microsoft, both OLE DB and ADO are excellent. They simplify the job of the database developer and they probably would have won out even on a level playing field.

Our aims, here, however, are more pedestrian. You need to learn ADO so that you can build better Internet-technology database applications. To that end, we will now address each of these standards in more detail.

➤ FIGURE 15-4

Role of ADO

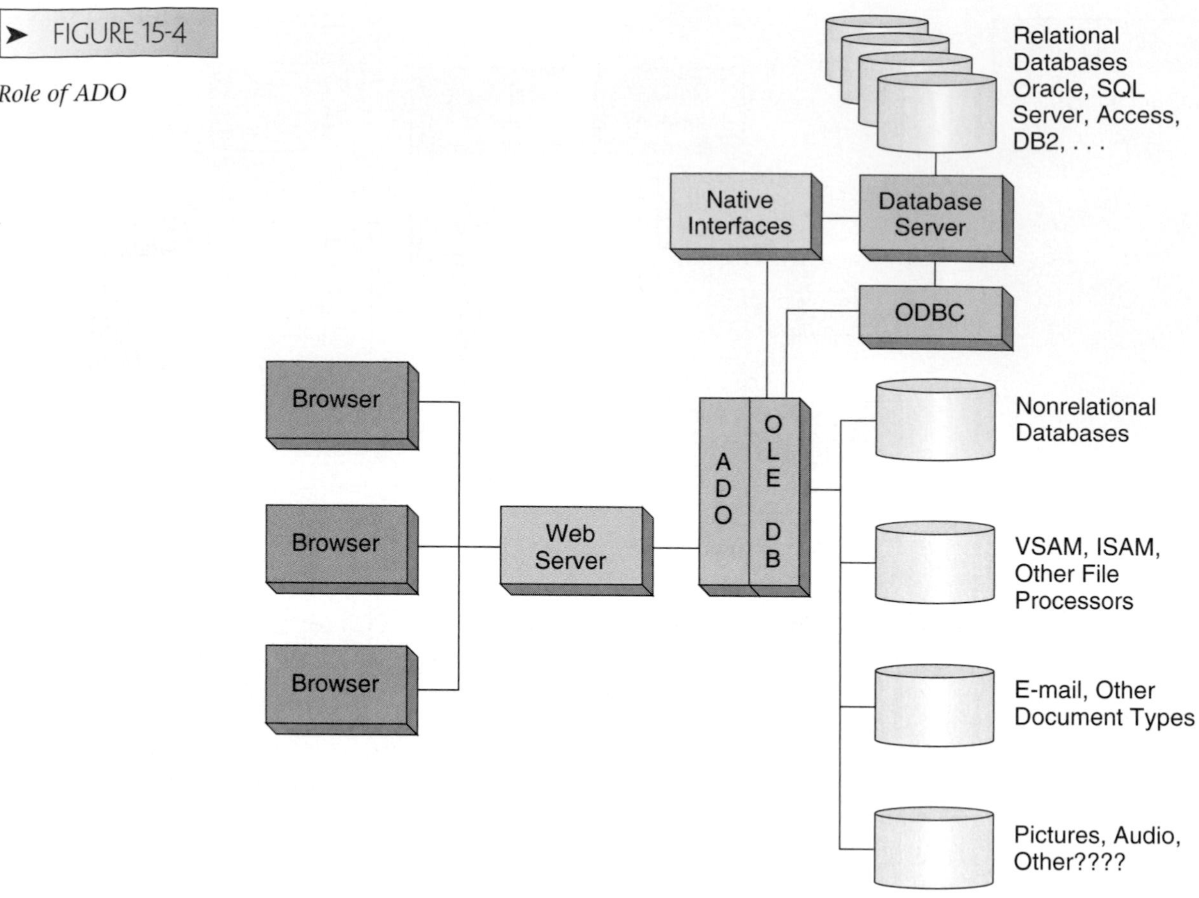

➤ OPEN DATABASE CONNECTIVITY (ODBC) STANDARD

The **open database connectivity (ODBC)** standard is an interface by which application programs can access and process SQL databases in a DBMS-independent manner. This means, for example, that an application that uses the ODBC interface could process an Oracle database, a SYBASE database, an INFORMIX database, and any other database that is ODBC-compliant without any program coding changes. The goal is to allow a developer to create a single application that can access databases supported by different DBMS products without needing to be changed or even recompiled.

ODBC was developed by a committee of industry experts from the X/Open and SQL Access Group committees. Several of such standards were proposed, but ODBC emerged as the winner, primarily because it has been implemented by Microsoft and is an important part of Windows. Microsoft's initial interest in support of such a standard was to allow products like Microsoft Excel to access database data from a variety of DBMS products without having to be recompiled. Of course, Microsoft's interests have changed since the introduction of OLE DB.

ODBC is important to Internet-technology database systems because, in theory, it is possible to develop an application that can process databases that are supported by different DBMS products. We say "in theory" because products vary in the way in which they comply with the standard. Fortunately, variance in conformance levels was anticipated by the ODBC committee, as you will learn.

➤ FIGURE 15-5

ODBC Architecture

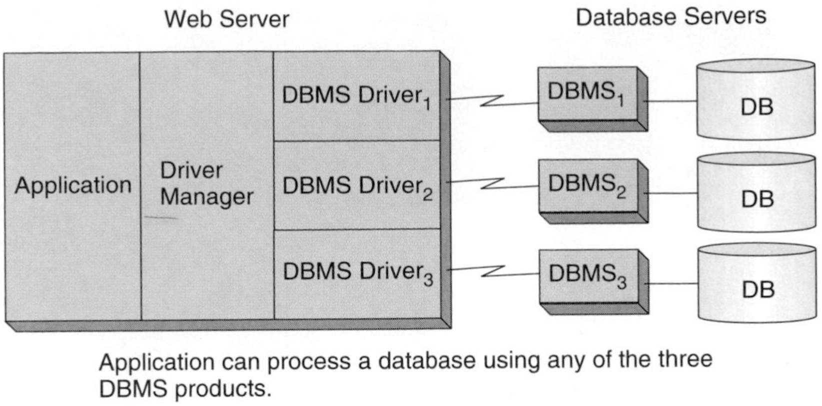

ODBC ARCHITECTURE

Figure 15-5 shows the components of the ODBC standard. The application program, driver manager, and DBMS drivers all reside on the Web server computer. The drivers send requests to data sources, which reside on the database server. According to the standard, a **data source** is the database, its associated DBMS, operating system, and network platform. An ODBC data source can be a relational database; it can also be a file server such as BTrieve, and it can even be a spreadsheet.

The application issues requests to create a connection with a data source, to issue SQL statements and receive results, to process errors, and to start, commit, and rollback transactions. ODBC provides a standard means for each of these requests, and it defines a standard set of error codes and messages.

The **driver manager** serves as an intermediary between the application and the DBMS drivers. When the application requests a connection, the driver determines the type of DBMS that processes a given ODBC data source and loads that driver in memory (if it is not already loaded). The driver manager also processes certain initialization requests and validates the format and order of ODBC requests that it receives from the application. The driver manager is provided by Microsoft and is included with Windows.

A **driver** processes ODBC requests and submits specific SQL statements to a given type of data source. There is a different driver for each data source type. For example, there are drivers for DB2, for Oracle, for Access, and for all of the other products whose vendors have chosen to participate in the ODBC standard. Drivers are supplied by DBMS vendors and by independent software companies.

It is the responsibility of the driver to ensure that standard ODBC commands execute correctly. In some cases, if the data source is itself not SQL-compliant, the driver may need to perform considerable processing to fill in for a lack of capability at the data source. In other cases, where the data source supports full SQL, the driver need only pass the request through for processing by the data source. The driver also converts data source error codes and messages into the ODBC standard codes and messages.

ODBC identifies two types of drivers: single tier and multiple tier. A **single-tier** driver processes both ODBC calls and SQL statements. An example of a single-tier driver is shown in Figure 15-6(a). In this example, the data is stored in Xbase files (the format used by FoxPro, dBase, and others). Since Xbase file managers do not process SQL, it is the job of the driver to translate the SQL request into Xbase file manipulation commands and to transform the results back into SQL form.

A **multiple-tier** driver processes ODBC calls but passes the SQL requests directly to the database server. While it may reformat an SQL request to conform

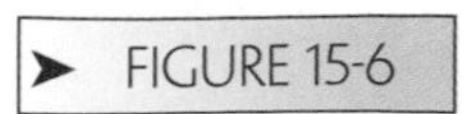

ODBC Driver Types: (a) ODBC Single-Tier Driver (b) ODBC Multiple-Tier Driver

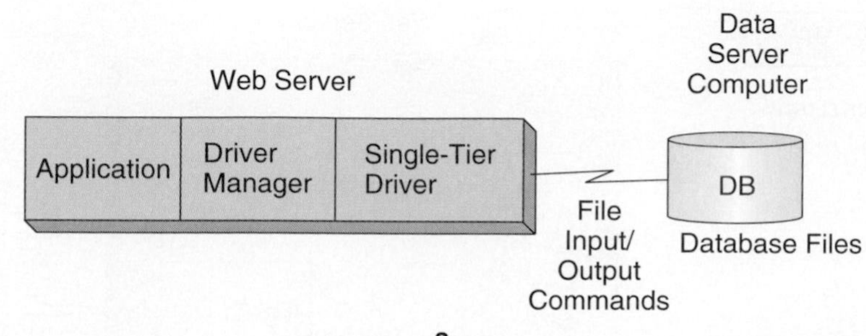

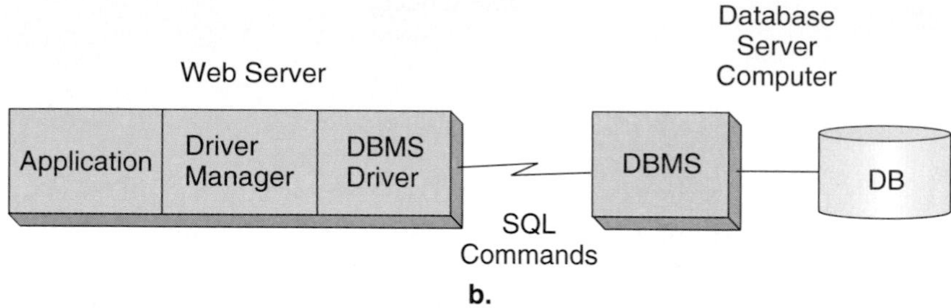

to the dialect of a particular data source, it does not process the SQL. An example of the use of a multiple-tier driver is shown in Figure 15-6(b).

Conformance Levels

The creators of the ODBC standard faced a dilemma. If they chose to describe a standard for a minimal level of capability, many vendors would be able to comply. But if they did so, the standard would represent only a small portion of the complete power and expressiveness of ODBC and SQL. On the other hand, if the standard addressed a very high level of capability, then only a few vendors would be able to comply with the standard, and it would become unimportant. To deal with this dilemma, the committee wisely chose to define levels of conformance to the standard. There are two types: ODBC conformance and SQL conformance.

ODBC CONFORMANCE LEVEL **ODBC conformance levels** concern the features and functions that are made available through the driver's application program interface **(API).** A driver API is a set of functions that the application can call to receive services. Figure 15-7 summarizes the three levels of ODBC conformance that are addressed in the standard. In practice, almost all drivers provide at least Level 1 API conformance, so the core API level is not too important.

An application can call a driver to determine which level of ODBC conformance it provides. If the application requires a level of conformance that is not present, it can terminate the session in an orderly fashion and generate appropriate messages to the user. Or the application can be written to use higher-level conformance features if they are available and to work around the missing functions if a higher level is not available.

For example, drivers at the Level 2 API must provide a scrollable cursor. Using conformance levels, an application could be written to use cursors if they are available, but, if they are not, to work around the missing feature, selecting needed data using very restrictive WHERE clauses. Doing this would ensure that only a few rows were returned at a time to the application, and it would process those rows using a cursor that it maintained itself. Performance would likely be

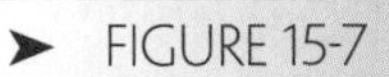

Summary of ODBC Conformance Levels

Core API
- Connect to data sources
- Prepare and execute SQL statements
- Retrieve data from a result set
- Commit or rollback transactions
- Retrieve error information

Level 1 API
- Core API
- Connect to data sources with driver-specific information
- Send and receive partial results
- Retrieve catalog information
- Retrieve information about driver options, capabilities, and functions

Level 2 API
- Core and Level 1 API
- Browse possible connections and data sources
- Retrieve native form of SQL
- Call a translation library
- Process a scrollable cursor

slower in the second case, but at least the application would be able to successfully execute.

SQL CONFORMANCE LEVEL **SQL conformance levels** specify which SQL statements, expressions, and data types a driver can process. Three levels are defined as summarized in Figure 15-8. The capability of the minimum SQL grammar is very limited, and most drivers support at least the core SQL grammar.

As with ODBC conformance levels, an application can call the driver to determine what level of SQL conformance it supports. With that information, the application can then determine which SQL statements can be issued. If necessary, the application can then terminate the session or use alternative, less powerful means of obtaining the data.

Establishing an ODBC Data Source Name

A **data source** is an ODBC data structure that identifies a database and the DBMS that processes it. Data sources identify other types of data such as spreadsheets and other nondatabase data stores, but we are not concerned with that use here.

There are three types of sources: file, system, and user. A **file data source** is a file that can be shared among database users. The only requirement is that the users have the same DBMS driver and privilege to access the database. The data source file can be e-mailed or otherwise distributed to possible users. A **system data source** is one that is local to a single computer. The operating system and any user on that system (with proper privileges) can use a system data source. A **user data source** is only available to the user who created it.

In general, the best choice for Web applications is to create a system data source on the Web server. Browser users then access the Web server, which in turn uses a system data source to set up a connection with the DBMS and the database.

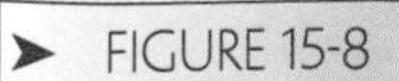

➤ FIGURE 15-8

Summary of SQL Conformance Levels

Minimum SQL Grammar
- CREATE TABLE, DROP TABLE
- simple SELECT (does not include subqueries)
- INSERT, UPDATE, DELETE
- Simple expressions (A > B + C)
- CHAR, VARCHAR, LONGVARCHAR data types

Core SQL Grammar
- Minimum SQL Grammar
- ALTER TABLE, CREATE INDEX, DROP INDEX
- CREATE VIEW, DROP VIEW
- GRANT, REVOKE
- Full SELECT (includes subqueries)
- Aggregate functions such as SUM, COUNT, MAX, MIN, AVG
- DECIMAL, NUMERIC, SMALLINT, INTEGER, REAL, FLOAT, DOUBLE PRECISION data types

Extended SQL Grammar
- Core SQL Grammar
- Outer joins
- UPDATE and DELETE using cursor positions
- Scalar functions such as SUBSTRING, ABS
- Literals for date, time, and timestamp
- Batch SQL statements
- Stored Procedures

➤ FIGURE 15-9

Creating a System Data Source: (a) Selecting the Driver, (b) Selecting the Database

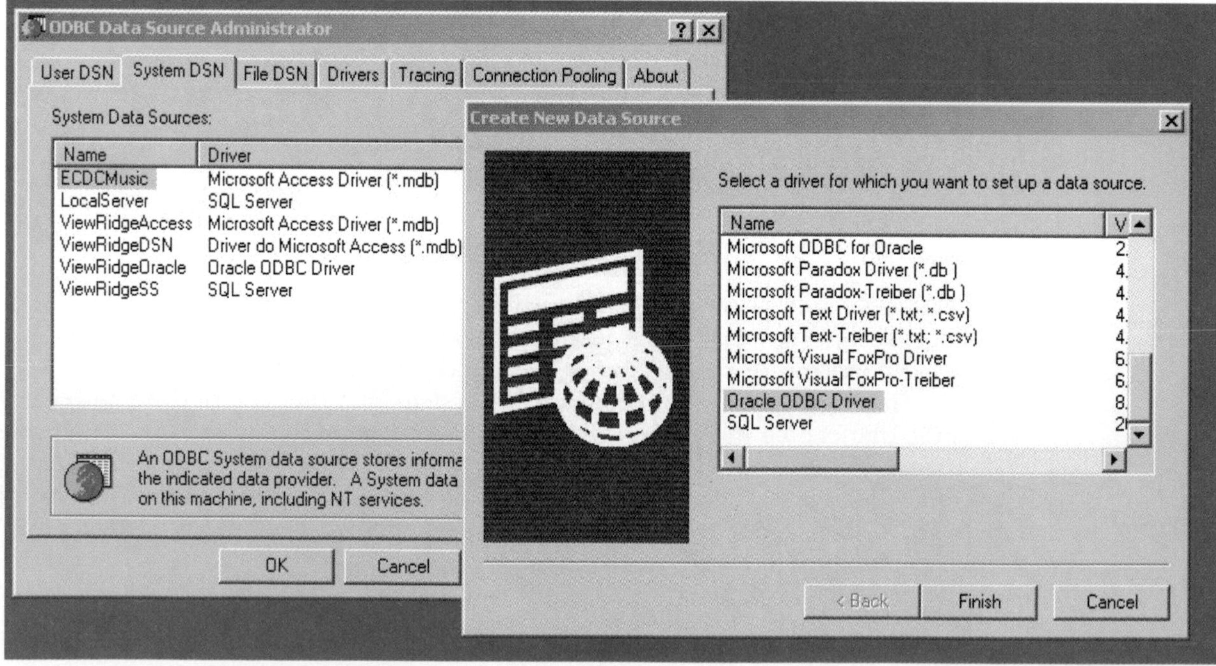

(a)

FIGURE 15-9

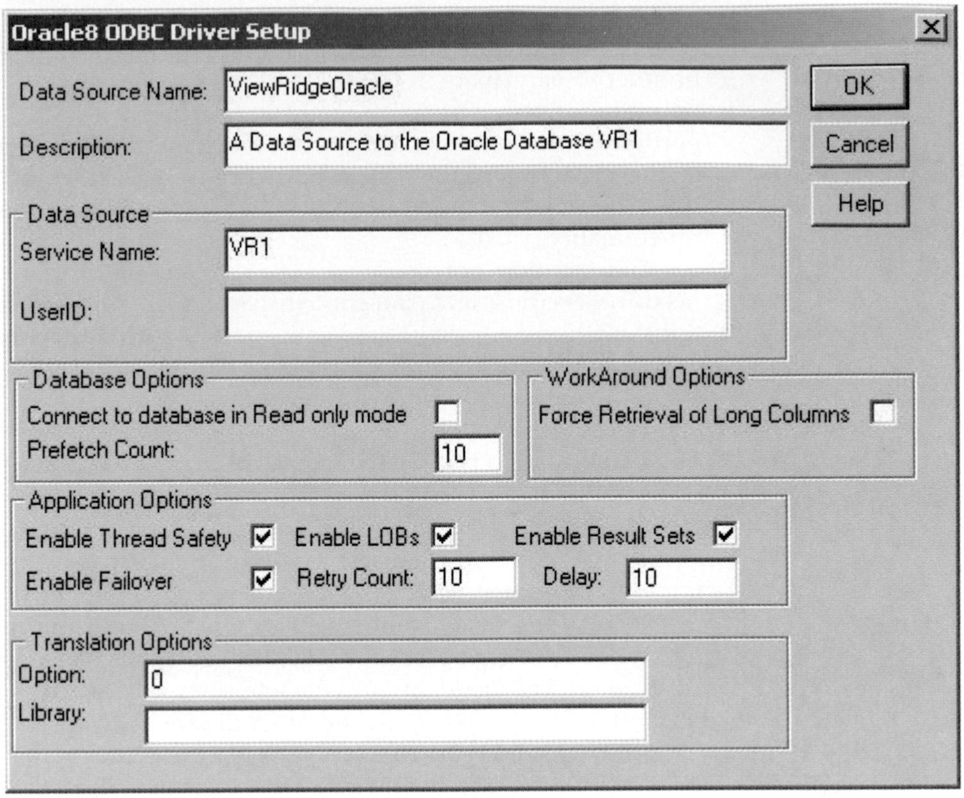

(b)

Figure 15-9 shows the process of creating a system data source using the ODBC Data Source Administrator Service that can be found via the Windows Control Panel. In Figure 15-9(a), the user is selecting a driver for an Oracle database. Notice that there are two such drivers; one is provided by Microsoft and the other is provided by Oracle. The drivers may have different capabilities, and the user should check the documentation for each to determine which is most appropriate for his or her application. Other drivers shown in this figure are for Paradox, text files, and Visual FoxPro.

In Figure 15-9(b), the user is selecting the database. Here, it is VR1, the name given to the database created in Chapter 12. We will use this DSN, named ViewRidgeOracle, later in this chapter to process that database. We will also use a second file DSN named ViewRidgeSS to process the SQL Server database created in Chapter 13.

OLE DB

OLE DB is the foundation of data access in the Microsoft world. As such, it is important to understand the fundamental ideas of OLE DB, even if you will only work with the ADO interfaces that lie on top of it. In this section we present essential OLE DB concepts.

OLE DB is an implementation of the Microsoft OLE object standard. OLE DB objects are COM objects and support all required interfaces for such objects. Fundamentally, OLE DB breaks the features and functions of a DBMS up into COM objects. There can be objects that support query operations, others that perform updates, others that support the creation of database schema constructs such as tables, indexes, and views, and still others that perform transaction management such as optimistic locking.

This characteristic overcomes a major disadvantage of ODBC. With ODBC, a vendor must create an ODBC driver for almost all DBMS features and functions in order to participate in ODBC at all. This is a large task and requires a substantial initial investment. With OLE DB, however, a DBMS vendor can implement portions of their product. One could, for example, implement only the query processor, participate in OLE DB, and hence be accessible to customers using ADO. Later the vendor could add more objects and interfaces to increase their OLE DB functionality.

This text does not assume that you are an object-oriented programmer, so we need to develop a few concepts. In particular, you need to understand abstractions, methods, properties, and collections. An **abstraction** is a generalization of something. ODBC interfaces are abstractions of native DBMS access methods. When we abstract something, we lose detail, but we gain the ability to work with a broader range of types.

For example, a **recordset** is an abstraction of a relation. In this abstraction, a recordset is defined to have certain characteristics that will be common to all recordsets. Every recordset, for instance, has a set of columns, which in this abstraction are called Fields. Now, the goal of abstraction is to capture everything important but omit details that are not needed by users of the abstraction. Thus, Oracle relations may have some characteristic that is not represented in a recordset; the same might be true for relations in SQL Server, AS/400, DB2, and in other DBMS products. These unique characteristics will be lost in the abstraction, but if the abstraction is a good one, no one will care.

Moving up a level, a **rowset** is the OLE DB abstraction of a recordset. Now, why does OLE DB need to define another abstraction? Because OLE DB addresses data sources that are not tables, but have *some of* the characteristics of tables. Consider all e-mail addresses in your personal e-mail file. Are those addresses the same as a relation? No, but they do share some of the characteristics that relations have. Each address is a semantically related group of data items. Like rows of a table, it is sensible to go to the first one, move to the next one, and so forth. But, unlike relations, they are not all of the same type. Some addresses are for individuals and some are for mailing lists. Thus, any action on a recordset that depends on everything in the recordset being the same kind of thing cannot be used on a rowset.

Working from the top down, OLE DB defines a set of data properties and behaviors for rowsets. Every rowset has those properties and behaviors. Furthermore, OLE DB defines a recordset as a subtype of a rowset. Recordsets have all of the properties and behaviors that rowsets have, plus they have some that are uniquely characteristic of recordsets.

Abstraction is both common and useful. You will hear of abstractions of transaction management or abstractions of querying or abstractions of interfaces. This simply means that certain characteristics of a set of things are formally defined as a type.

An object-oriented programming object is an abstraction that is defined by its properties and methods. For example, a recordset object has an AllowEdits property and a RecordsetType property and an EOF property. These **properties** represent characteristics of the recordset abstraction. An object also has actions that it can perform that are called **methods.** A recordset has methods such as Open, MoveFirst, MoveNext, and Close.

Strictly speaking, the definition of an object abstraction is called an **object class,** or just class. An instance of an object class, such as a particular recordset, is called an object. All objects of a class have the same methods and the same properties, but the values of those properties vary from object to object.

The last term we need to address is collection. A **collection** is an object that contains a group of other objects. A recordset has a collection of other objects called Fields. The collection has properties and methods. One of the properties of all collections is Count, which is the number of objects in the collection. Thus, recordset.Fields.Count is the number of fields in the collection. In ADO and OLE DB, collections are named as the plural of the objects they collect. Thus, there is a Fields collection of Field objects, an Errors collection of Error objects, a Parameters collection of Parameters, and so forth. An important method of a collection is an iterator, which is a method that can be used to pass through or otherwise identify the items in the collection.

If you're getting frustrated with all these definitions, don't give up. You will see a practical use of these concepts before the end of this chapter!

Goals of OLE DB

The major goals for OLE DB are listed in Figure 15-10. First, as mentioned, OLE DB breaks DBMS functionality and services into object pieces. This partitioning means great flexibility for both **data consumers** (users of OLE DB functionality) and **data providers** (vendors of products that deliver OLE DB functionality). Data consumers take only the objects and functionality they need; a wireless device for reading a database can have a very slim footprint. Unlike with ODBC, data providers need only implement a portion of DBMS functionality. This partitioning also means that data providers can deliver capabilities in multiple interfaces.

This last point needs expansion. An object interface is a packaging of objects. An **interface** is specified by a set of objects and the properties and methods that they expose. An object need not expose all of its properties and methods in a given interface. Thus, a recordset object would expose only read methods in a query interface, but create, update, and delete methods in a modification interface.

How the object supports the interface, or the **implementation,** is completely hidden from the user. In fact, the developers of an object are free to change the implementation whenever they want. Who will know? But they may not ever change the interface without incurring the justifiable disdain of their users!

OLE DB defines standardized interfaces. Data providers, however, are free to add interfaces on top of the basic standards. Such extensibility is essential for the next goal, which is to provide an object interface to any type of data. Relational

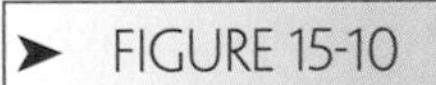

OLE DB Goals

- Create object interfaces for DBMS functionality pieces
  - Query
  - Update
  - Transaction management
  - Etc
- Increase flexibility
  Allow data consumers to use only the objects they need
  Allow data providers to expose pieces of DBMS functionality
  Providers can deliver functionality in multiple interfaces
  Interfaces are standardized and extensible
- Object interface over any type of data
  Relational database
  ODBC or native
  Nonrelational database
  VSAM and other files
  E-mail
  Other
- Do not force data to be converted or moved from where it is

➤ FIGURE 15-11

Two Types of OLE DB Data Providers

- Tabular data provider
  - Exposes data via rowsets
  - Examples: DBMS, spreadsheets, ISAMs, E-mail
- Service provider
  - Does not own data
  - Transforms data through OLE DB interfaces
  - Both a consumer and a provider of data
  - Examples: query processors, XML document creator

databases can be processed through OLE DB objects that use ODBC or that use the native DBMS drivers. OLE DB includes support for the other types as indicated.

The net result of these design goals is that data need not be converted from one form to another, nor need it be moved from one data source to another. The Web server in Figure 15-1 can utilize OLE DB to process data in any of the formats, right where the data resides. This means that transactions may span multiple data sources and may be distributed on different computers. The OLE DB provision for this is the **Microsoft Transaction Manager** (MTS), but discussion of it is beyond the scope of this chapter.

OLE DB Basic Constructs

As shown in Figure 15-11, OLE DB has two types of data providers. **Tabular data providers** present their data via rowsets. Examples are DBMS products, spreadsheets, and ISAM file processors like dbase and FoxPro. Additionally, other types of data like e-mail can also be presented in rowsets. Tabular data providers bring data of some type into the OLE DB world.

A **service provider,** on the other hand, is a transformer of data. Service providers accept OLE DB data from an OLE DB tabular data provider and transform it some way. Service providers are both consumers and providers of transformed data. An example of a service provider is one that obtains data from a relational DBMS and transforms it into XML documents.

The **rowset** object is fundamental to OLE DB; rowsets are equivalent to what we called **cursors** in Chapter 11, and in fact the two terms are used synonymously. Figure 15-12 lists the basic rowset interfaces that are supported. IRowSet

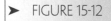

➤ FIGURE 15-12

Rowset Interfaces

- IRowSet
  Methods for sequential iteration through a rowset
- IAccessor
  Methods for setting and determining bindings between rowset and client program variables
- IColumnsInfo
  Methods for determining Information about the columns in the rowset
- Other interfaces
  Scrollable cursors
  Create, update, delete rows
  Directly access particular rows (bookmarks)
  Explicitly set locks
  And so on

provides object methods for forward only sequential movement through a rowset. When you declare a forward only cursor in OLE DB, you are invoking the IRowSet interface. The IAccessor interface is used to bind program variables to rowset fields. When using ADO, this interface is largely hidden because it is used behind the scenes in the scripting engine. If you work with type libraries in VB, however, you may use methods from this interface.

The IColumnsInfo interface has methods for obtaining information about the columns in a rowset. We will use this interface to advantage in two of the ADO examples at the end of this chapter. IRowSet, IAccessor, and IColumnsInfo are the basic rowset interfaces. Other interfaces are defined for more advanced operations like scrollable cursors, update, direct access to particular rows, explicit locks and so forth.

Consider these interfaces in the context of two rowsets—one a traditional relation and another that is a collection of e-mail addresses. The first three interfaces readily pertain to either type of rowset. The last set of interfaces will likely be different in the features and functions between the two rowsets if they pertain at all. One final note—rowsets can contain pointers to objects so quite complicated structures can be created with them.

➤ ADO (ACTIVE DATA OBJECTS)

ADO is a simple object model that can be used by data consumers to process any OLE DB data. It can be called from scripting languages like JScript and VBScript, and from Visual Basic, Java, C#, and C++. Microsoft has stated that it will replace all other data access methods, so that learning it is important not just for Internet-technology database applications, but for any data applications that use Microsoft products.

Because of OLE DB abstractions and object structure, the ADO object model and interfaces are the same regardless of the type of data processed. Thus, a developer who learns ADO for processing a relational database can use that knowledge for processing an e-mail directory as well. Characteristics of ADO are listed in Figure 15-13.

INVOKING ADO FROM ACTIVE SERVER PAGES

In this chapter, we are going to invoke ADO on a Web server using Active Server Pages. Such pages contain a mixture of DHTML (or XML) and program language statements expressed in either VBScript or JavaScript. In this chapter we will use VBScript. ASP pages can be written with any text editor, but they are easier to wirte with FrontPage or some similar Web page authoring product.

Internet Information Server (IIS) is a Web server built into Windows 2000 Professional and Windows NT. As stated in Chapter 14, ASP is an ISAPI extension to IIS. As a practical matter, this simply means that whenever IIS reveives a file with the extension .asp, it sends the file to the ASP program for processing.

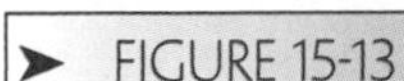
➤ FIGURE 15-13

Characteristics of ADO

- Simple object model for OLE DB data consumers
- Can be used from VBScript, JScript, Visual Basic, Java, C#, C++
- Single Microsoft data access standard
- Data access objects are the same for all types of OLE DB data

Any program language statements enclosed within the characters <% . . . %> will be processed on the Web server computer. Other language statements will be sent to the user's browser for processing. In this chapter, all of our code will be processed on the Web server.

To invoke your ASP pages, place them in some directory, say, C:\MyDirectory. Then, open IIS and set up a virtual directory that points to the directory in which you have placed your ASP pages. You can do this by opening Internet Information Services, and right-clicking on Default Web Site. Choose New/Virtual Directory and a wizard will start that asks you to name your virtual directory and the real directory (here, C:\MyDirectory) in which your ASP pages will reside. Select Read and Run Scripts on the third panel of the wizard. For the examples in this text, we will use the virtual directory name ViewRidgeExample1.

It is not necessary that the DBMS and the Web server be located on the same machine. When you create the ODBC DSN, you can point to a database on a different computer that is accessible from the Web server computer. This will be easier if that other computer runs a Windows operating system, but it can be done with other operating systems as well. Of course, the Web server and the DBMS can be on the same machine.

ADO Object Model

The ADO object model shown in Figure 15-14 is built on top of the OLE DB object model. The Connection object is the first ADO object to be created and the basis for the others. From a connection, a developer can create one or more RecordSet objects and one or more Command objects. In the process of creating or working with any of these objects, ADO will place any errors that are generated in the Errors collection.

Each RecordSet object has a Fields collection; each Field element corresponds to a column in the record set. In addition, each Command object has a Parameters Collection that contains objects for the parameters of the command.

CONNECTION OBJECT The following VBScript code can be embedded in an ASP page to create a connection object. After it runs, the variable objConn will point to an object that is connected to the ODBC data source ViewRidgeSS.

➤ FIGURE 15-14

ADO Object Model

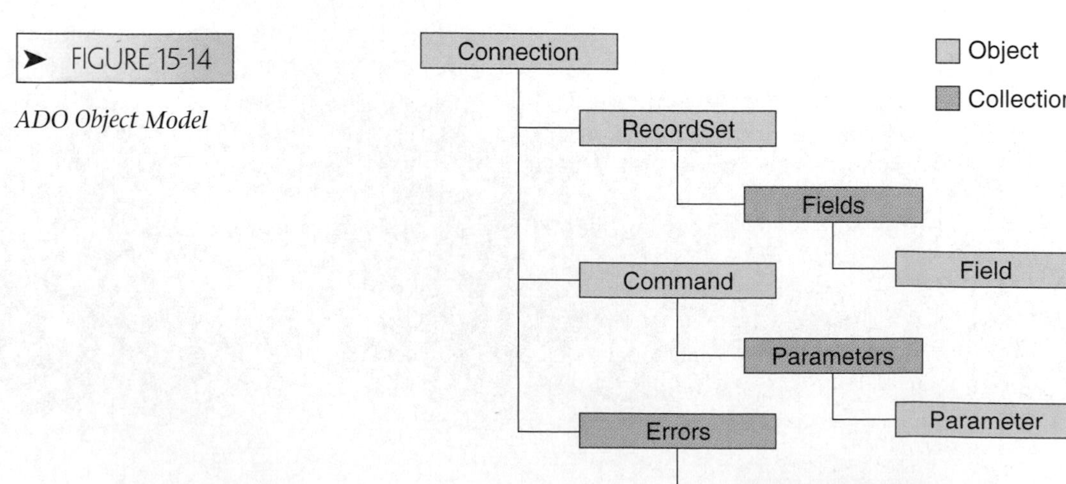

```
<%
Dim objConn
Set objConn = Server.CreateObject ("ADODB.connection")
objConn.IsolationLevel = adXactReadCommitted ' use ADOVBS
objConn.Open "ViewRidgeSS", "sa" 'open the connection
%>
```

In this code, the statement Server.CreateObject is invoking the CreateObject method of the ASP server object. The type of object, here ADODB.connection, is passed as a parameter. After this statement executes, the variable objConn points to the new connection object. Next, the isolation level of this connection is set using a constant from the file ADOVBS. That file can be made available to this script with the following include statement:

```
<!--#include virtual ="ViewRidgeExample1/ADOVBS.inc-->
```

This statement must be part of the ASP file, but **outside** of the <% . . . %>. For this to work, you must copy the file ADOVBS.inc into your directory (find it using Search). Also, substitute the name of your virtual directory if it is other than ViewRidgeExample1.

The names and values of important ADOVBS constants are listed in Figure 15-15. Using the names of the constants rather than their values makes your code more readable. It also makes it easier to adapt your code should Microsoft change the meanings of these values (doubtful, but it could happen).

In the last statement, the open method of the connection is used to open the ODBC data source. The user account "sa" is passed as a parameter. If a password were required, it would be passed as the next parameter. Clearly, this is terrible security, although it's not quite as bad as it looks because this code will be executed on the Web server and never sent over the network. Still, it would be better to obtain the name and password from the user at run-time. That topic is not directly related to database processing and we will not address it.

At this point, a connection has been established to the DBMS via the ODBC data source and the database is open. The objConn pointer can be used to refer to any other methods for a connection (see Figure 15-14), including the creation and use of RecordSet and Command objects. The Errors collection can be processed as well.

RECORDSET OBJECT Given the connection with an open database, the following will create a RecordSet object (we omit the <% and %> from now on, but all of these code examples must be inserted between them or they will not be executed on the Web server):

```
Dim   objRecordSet, varSql
varSQL = "SELECT * FROM ARTIST"
Set objRecordSet = Server.CreateObject ("ADODB.Recordset")
objRecordSet.CursorTye = adOpenStatic
objRecordSet.LockType = adLockReadOnly
objRecordSet.Open varSQL, objConn
```

CursorType and LockType could also be passed as parameters to the recordset open method as follows:

```
Dim   objRecordSet, varSql
varSQL = "SELECT * FROM ARTIST"
Set objRecordSet = Server.CreateObject ("ADODB.Recordset")
objRecordSet.Open varSQL, objConn, adOpenStatic, adLockReadOnly
```

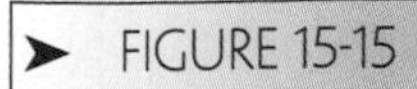

Constant Values for ADO Processing

Isolation Level	Const Name	Value
Dirty reads	adXactReadUncommitted	256
Read committed	adXactReadCommitted	4096
Repeatable read	adXactRepeatableRead	65536
Serializable	adXactSerializable	1048576

(a) Isolation Levels

Cursor Type	Const Name	Value
Forward only	adOpenForwardOnly	0
Keyset	adOpenKeyset	1
Dynamic	adOpenDynamic	2
Static	adOpenStatic	3

(b) Cursor Types

Cursor Type	Const Name	Value
Read only	adLockReadOnly	1
Pessimistic locking	adLockPessimistic	2
Optimistic locking	adLockOptimistic	3
Optimistic with batch updates	adBatchOptimistic	4

(c) Lock Types

Either way, these statements cause the SQL statement in varSQL to be executed using a static, read only cursor. All of the columns of the ARTIST table will be included as fields in the record set. If the SELECT statement named only two columns, say, "SELECT ArtistID, Nationality FROM ARTIST," then only those two columns would be included as fields in the recordset.

By the way, there is a "gotcha" lurking here. With SQL Server, if a table name has spaces or odd characters or is a SQL Server reserved word, you enclose the name in brackets [ ]. To Oracle, however, a table name enclosed in brackets is illegal. For oddly named tables in Oracle, you enclose the name in quotes. Thus, if your database has such tables, you will have to write different code depending on whether you are using an Oracle or SQL Server database.

FIELDS COLLECTION Once the recordset has been created, its fields collection is instantiated. We can process that collection with the following:

```
Dim varI, varNumCols, objField
varNumCols = objRecordSet.Fields.Count
For varI = 0 to varNumCols - 1
  Set objField = objRecordSet.Fields(varI)
  ' objField.Name now has the name of the field
  ' objField.Value now has the value of the field
  ' can do something with them here
Next
```

In the second statement, varNumCols is set to the number of columns in the recordset by accessing the Count property of the Fields collection. Then a loop is executed to iterate over this collection. The property Fields(0) refers to the first column of the record set, so the loop needs to run from 0 to Count − 1.

Nothing is done with the fields objects in this example, but in an actual application, the developer could reference objField.Name to get the name of a column and objField.Value to obtain its value. You will see uses like this in the following examples.

ERRORS COLLECTION Whenever an error occurs, ADO instantiates an errors collection. It must be a collection since more than one error can be generated by a single ADO statement. This collection can be processed in a manner similar to that for the Fields collection:

```
Dim varI, varErrorCount, objError
On Error Resume Next
varErrorCount = objConn.Errors.Count
If varErrorCount > 0 Then
  For varI = 0 to varErrorCount - 1
    Set objError = objConn.Errors(varI)
    ' objError.Description contains
    ' a description of the error
  Next
End If
```

In the loop, objError is set to objConn.Errors(varI). Note that this collection belongs to objConn and not to objRecordSet. Also the Description property of objError can be used to display the error to the user.

Unfortunately, VBScript has quite limited error processing. The code for checking errors (starting with On Error Resume Next) must be placed after every ADO object statement that might cause an error. Because this can bulk up the code undesirably, it would be better to write an error handling function and call it after every ADO object invocation.

COMMAND OBJECT The ADO command object is used to execute queries and stored procedures that are stored with the database. The parameters collection of Command is used to pass parameters. For example, suppose the database opened by objConn has a stored procedure called FindArtist that accepts one parameter which is the nationality of artists to be retrieved. The following code will invoke this stored procedure with the parameter value "Spanish" and create a recordset named objRs that has the results of the stored procedure:

```
Dim objCommand, objParam, objRs

'Create the Command object, connect it to objConn and set its format

Set objCommand = Server.CreateObject("ADODB.command")
Set objCommand.ActiveConnection = objConn
objCommand.CommandText="{call FindArtist (?)}"

'Set up the parameter with the necessary value

Set objParam = objCommand.CreateParameter ("Nationality", adChar,
   ⇒adParamInput, 25)
objCommand.Parameters.Append objParam

objParam.Value = "Spanish"

'Fire the Stored Proc
Set objRs = objCommand.Execute
```

This example first creates an object of type ADODB.command and then sets the connection of that object to objConn. It then declares the format of the call to the stored procedure by setting the CommandText property. This property is used to pass the name of the stored procedure and the number of parameters it has. The question mark denotes a parameter. If there were three parameters, command text would be set to "{call FindArtist (?, ?, ?)}"

Next an object is created for the parameter. The values adChar and adParamInput are from ADOVBS and indicate that the parameter is of type char and is used as input to the stored procedure. The maximum length of the parameter value is 25. Once the parameter has been created, it must be added to the command with the Append method. Finally, the stored procedure is invoked using the Execute method. At this point a recordset named objRs has been created with the results from the stored procedure.

➤ ADO EXAMPLES

The following five examples show how to invoke ADO from VBScript using Active Server Pages. These examples focus on the use of ADO and not on the graphics, presentation, or workflow. If you want a flashy, better-behaving application, you should be able to modify these examples to obtain that result. Here, just learn how ADO is used.

All of these examples process the View Ridge database. In some of them, we connect to ViewRidgeSS, the SQL Server database. In others, we connnect to ViewRidgeOracle, the Oracle database. In fact, in the last example, only one statement need be changed to switch from SQL Server to Oracle! That is amazing, and exactly what the originators of ODBC hoped for when they created the ODBC specification.

As you learned in the last chapter, HTTP is stateless. The ASP processor, however, will maintain transaction state. For each tranction, it keeps a set of session variables. In these examples, we will use session variables to preserve connection objects. The statement

```
Set Session("abc")="Wowzers"
```

creates a session variable named "abc" and gives it the string value "Wowzers." More useful examples follow.

To run any of these pages, open your browser and enter

http://localhost/ViewRidgeExample1/artist.asp

if you are running on the same computer as is IIS. Otherwise, type the name or address of your server instead of "localhost."

Example 1—Reading a Table

Figure 15-16 shows an ASP page that displays the contents of the ARTIST table. In this and the next several figures, statements included within <% %> are shown in red ink. Any code that will be passed to the browser, here primarily HTML, is shown in blue ink. Any other statements are shown in gray.

The top of the page is standard HTML. The first section of the server code creates a connection object and then a recordset object that has the results of the SQL Statement

```
SELECT   ArtistName, Nationality
FROM     ARTIST
```

Because connection objects are expensive—both in terms of time to create them and memory used—this code preserves the connection object in the session variable _conn. The first time a user invokes this page, the connection object will not exist. In this case, the function call IsObject(Session("_conn")) will return false because _conn has not been set. The code after the Else will be executed to create the connection object. Next, the recordset is created for the select statement in variable varSql.

The next section of the ASP page contains HTML for the browser. It is followed by several snippets of server script code intermixed with HTML. The statement On Error Resume Next overrides the ASP script engine's error processing to continue the script. A better page would process the errors instead.

The last part of the page simply produces the HTML and fills in read values. The objRecordSet.MoveFirst. . . . MoveNext loop is the logic for standard sequential processing of a file.

The result of this ASP page is shown in Figure 15-17. There is nothing spectacular about this page nor about this ASP file except the following: If this were on the Internet, any of over 250 million people worldwide would be able to view it! They would need no software other than what is already on their computer.

Example 2—Reading a Table in a Generalized Fashion

The first example made minimal use of the ADO objects in the object model. We can extend this example by using the Fields collection. Suppose we want to take the name of a table as input and display all of the columns in it except the surrogate key.

The ASP page in Figure 15-18 will accomplish this task, except that the name of the table is set in the variable varTableName. The next example will show how to obtain a value for the desired table name using HTML form processing.

The first part of the server script has the same function as that in Figure 15-16. The only difference is that it opens the Oracle data source.

The varSql variable is set using the varTableName variable. The & is an operator that concatenates two strings together. The result of this expression is the string:

```
SELECT * FROM CUSTOMER
```

➤ FIGURE 15-16

Artist.asp

```
<HTML>
<HEAD>
<META HTTP-EQUIV="Content-Type" CONTENT="text/html;charset=windows-1252">
<TITLE>Artist</TITLE>
</HEAD>
<!--#include virtual="ViewRidgeExample1/adovbs.inc"-->
<BODY>
<%
Dim objConn, objRecordSet, varSql

    If IsObject(Session("_conn")) Then ' if already have a connection, use it
        Set objConn = Session("_conn")
    Else
        Set objConn = Server.CreateObject("ADODB.connection") ' get connection
        objConn.open "ViewRidgeSS", "sa"  ' open SQL Server ODBC file as user "sa" with no password
        objConn.IsolationLevel = adXactReadCommitted ' avoid dirty reads
        Set Session("_conn") = objConn
    End If

  Set objRecordSet = Server.CreateObject("ADODB.Recordset") ' create the record set object

  varSql = "SELECT ArtistName, Nationality FROM ARTIST" ' set up SQL command
  objRecordSet.Open varSql, objConn, adOpenStatic, adLockReadOnly ' static with no need to update %>

<TABLE BORDER=1 BGCOLOR=#ffffff CELLSPACING=5><FONT FACE="Arial"
COLOR=#000000><CAPTION><B>ARTIST</B></CAPTION></FONT>
<THEAD>
<TR>
<TH BGCOLOR=#c0c0c0 BORDERCOLOR=#000000 ><FONT SIZE=2 FACE="Arial"
COLOR=#000000>Name</FONT></TH>
<TH BGCOLOR=#c0c0c0 BORDERCOLOR=#000000 ><FONT SIZE=2 FACE="Arial"
COLOR=#000000>Nationality</FONT></TH>

</TR>
</THEAD>
<TBODY>
<%
On Error Resume Next
objRecordSet.MoveFirst
do while Not objRecordSet.eof
 %>
<TR VALIGN=TOP>
<TD BORDERCOLOR=#c0c0c0 ><FONT SIZE=2 FACE="Arial"
COLOR=#000000><%=Server.HTMLEncode(objRecordSet("ArtistName"))%><BR></FONT></TD>
<TD BORDERCOLOR=#c0c0c0 ><FONT SIZE=2 FACE="Arial"
COLOR=#000000><%=Server.HTMLEncode(objRecordSet("Nationality"))%><BR></FONT></TD>

</TR>

<%
End If
Next%>
</TR>
```

FIGURE 15-16

(Continued)

```
<%
objRecordSet.MoveNext
loop%>
</TBODY>
<TFOOT></TFOOT>
</TABLE>
</BODY>
</HTML>
```

Note, too, the table name is included in the HTML table caption with the code ⟨CAPTION⟩⟨B⟩⟨%=varTableName%⟩⟨/B⟩⟨/CAPTION⟩. The code inside the % will cause the value of varTableName to be placed in HTML for the caption.

The next set of server script statements processes the Fields collection. The variable varNumCols is set to the count property of the Fields collection and then the collection is iterated in the loop. Observe how HTML is interspersed in the server code (or server code is interspersed in the HTML, depending on your point of view). Previously varKeyName has been set to the name of the surrogate key, so this loop checks to determine that the name of the current field object is not the name of the surrogate key. If not, HTML is generated to create the table header. A similar loop is used on the next page to populate the table with values from the recordset.

FIGURE 15-17

Result of Artist.asp from Figure 15-16

Artist - Microsoft Internet Explorer

File Edit View Favorites Tools Help

Back Search Favorites History

Address http://localhost/ViewRidgeExample1/artist.asp Go Links

ARTIST

Name	Nationality
Miro	Spanish
Kandinsky	Russian
Frings	US
Klee	German
David Moos	US
Mark Tobey	US
Henri Matisse	French

Done Local intranet

> FIGURE 15-18

CustomerOracle.asp

```
<HTML>
<HEAD>
<META HTTP-EQUIV="Content-Type" CONTENT="text/html;charset=windows-1252">
<TITLE>Table Display Page</TITLE>
</HEAD>
<BODY>
<!--#include virtual="ViewRidgeExample1/adovbs.inc"-->
<%
   Dim objConn, objRecordSet, objField
   Dim varNumCols, varI, varSql
   Dim varTableName, varKeyName

   varTablename = "CUSTOMER"
   varKeyName = "CUSTOMERID"

   If IsObject(Session("_conn")) Then ' if already have a connection, use it
      Set objConn = Session("_conn")
   Else
      Set objConn = Server.CreateObject("ADODB.connection") ' get connection

      ' open Oracle ODBC file using system account with manager password
      objConn.open "ViewRidgeOracle", "system", "manager"
      objConn.IsolationLevel = adXactReadCommitted ' avoid dirty reads
      Set Session("_conn") = objConn
   End If

    Set objRecordSet = Server.CreateObject("ADODB.Recordset")

    varSQL = "SELECT * FROM " & varTableName
    objRecordSet.Open varSql, objConn   ' cursor type and lock type not
                                          supported by Oracle driver
%>

<TABLE BORDER=1 BGCOLOR=#ffffff CELLSPACING=5><FONT FACE="Arial" COLOR=#000000>
<CAPTION><B><%=varTableName%> (in Oracle database)</B></CAPTION></FONT>
<THEAD>
<TR>
<%
varNumCols = objRecordSet.Fields.Count
For varI = 0 to varNumCols - 1
Set objField = objRecordSet.Fields(varI)
If objField.Name <> varKeyName Then  ' omit surrogate key %>
<TH BGCOLOR=#c0c0c0 BORDERCOLOR=#000000 ><FONT SIZE=2 FACE="Arial"
COLOR=#000000><%=objField.Name%></FONT></TH>
<%
End If
Next%>
</TR>
</THEAD>
<TBODY>
<%
On Error Resume Next
objRecordSet.MoveFirst
do while Not objRecordSet.eof
%>
<TR VALIGN=TOP>
<%
varNumCols = objRecordSet.Fields.Count
For varI = 0 to varNumCols - 1
Set objField = objRecordSet.Fields(varI)
If objField.Name <> varKeyName Then  ' omit surrogate key%>
<TD BORDERCOLOR=#c0c0c0 ><FONT SIZE=2 FACE="Arial"
COLOR=#000000><%=Server.HTMLEncode(objField.Value)%><BR></FONT></TD>
```

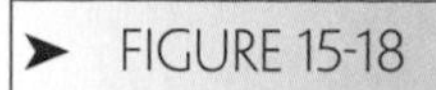

(Continued)

```
<%
End If
Next%>
</TR>
<%
objRecordSet.MoveNext
loop%>
</TBODY>
<TFOOT></TFOOT>
</TABLE>
</BODY>
</HTML>
```

The advantage of this page is that it can process any table, not just a particular one. In fact, using terminology developed earlier, we can say the page in Figure 15-18 is an abstraction of that in Figure 15-16. The results of this page are shown in Figure 15-19. The CUSTOMERID column is not displayed, as we expected.

Example 3—Reading Any Table

Figure 15-20(a) shows a data entry form in which a customer can type the name of the table to be displayed. (A better design would be to use a drop-down list to display valid choices, but that discussion would take us away from the discussion of ADO.) The user of this form has typed *artist.* Assume now that when he or she clicks the Show Table button, the form is to cause script to be executed on the server that will display the ARTIST table in this same browser session. Also, assume the surrogate key is not to be displayed. The desired results are shown in Figure 15-20(b).

Result of CustomerOracle.asp

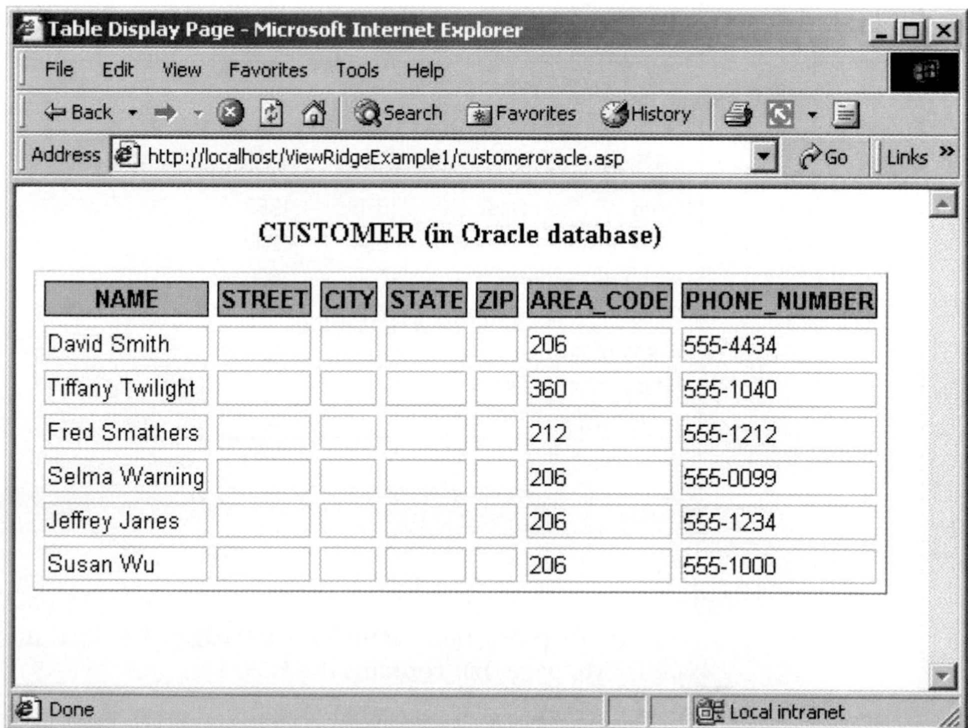

Table Display Page - Microsoft Internet Explorer
File Edit View Favorites Tools Help
Back Search Favorites History
Address http://localhost/ViewRidgeExample1/customeroracle.asp
Go Links
CUSTOMER (in Oracle database)
NAME STREET CITY STATE ZIP AREA_CODE PHONE_NUMBER
David Smith 206 555-4434
Tiffany Twilight 360 555-1040
Fred Smathers 212 555-1212
Selma Warning 206 555-0099
Jeffrey Janes 206 555-1234
Susan Wu 206 555-1000
Done
Local intranet

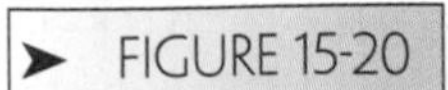

➤ FIGURE 15-20

General Table Display Forms: (a) Table Name Entry Form, (b) Table Display

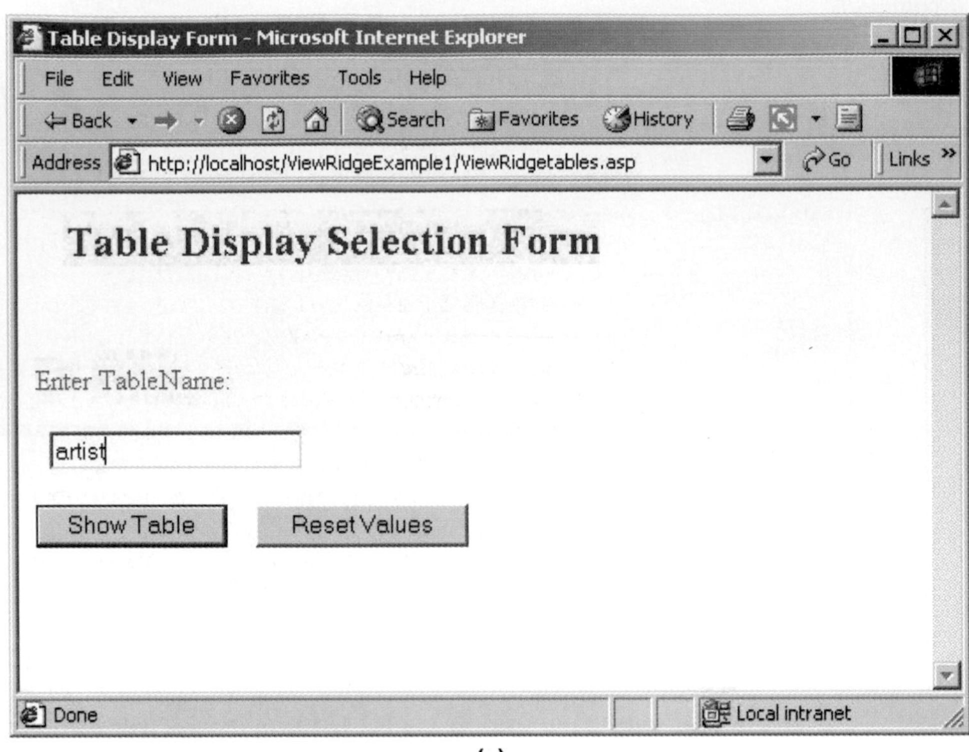

(a)

Table Display Page - Microsoft Internet Explorer

Address http://localhost/ViewRidgeExample1/GeneralTable.asp

View Another Table

ARTIST (in SQL Server Database)

ArtistName	Nationality	Birthdate	Deceaseddate
Miro	Spanish	1870	1950
Kandinsky	Russian	1854	1900
Frings	US	1700	1800
Klee	German	1900	
David Moos	US		
Mark Tobey	US		
Henri Matisse	French		

Done — Local intranet

(b)

This processing necessitates two ASP pages. The first, shown in Figure 15-21(a), is an HTML page that contains the FORM tag

<FORM METHOD="post" ACTION="GeneralTable.asp">

➤ FIGURE 15-21

General Table Display Code: (a) ViewRidgeTables.asp, (b) ViewRidgeTables.asp

```
<HTML>
<HEAD>
<META HTTP-EQUIV="Content-Type" CONTENT="text/html;charset=windows-1252">
<TITLE>Table Display Form</TITLE>
</HEAD>
<BODY>

<FORM METHOD="post" ACTION="GeneralTable.asp">

 <P><STRONG><FONT color=purple face="" size=5>   Table Display
Selection Form</FONT></STRONG>
<P></P>
<P> </P>

<P><FONT style="BACKGROUND-COLOR: #ffffff"><FONT color=forestgreen face=""
style="BACKGROUND-COLOR: #ffffff">Enter
TableName:</FONT>     </FONT></P>

<P></P>

<P><FONT style="BACKGROUND-COLOR: #ffffff"></FONT> 
<INPUT id=text1 name=text1></P>

<P><FONT style="BACKGROUND-COLOR: #ffffff">
<INPUT id=submit1 name=submit1 type=submit value="Show Table"
>   
<INPUT id=reset1 name=reset1 type=reset value="Reset Values"></FONT></P>
</FORM>
</BODY>
</HTML>
```

(a)

This tag defines a form section on the page; the section will contain data entry values. In this form, there is only one: the table name. The post method refers to an HTML process that causes the data in the form (here, the table name *artist*) to be delivered to the ASP server in an object called Form. An alternative method is *get,* which would cause the data values to be delivered via parameters. This distinction is not too important to us here. The second parameter of the FORM tag is ACTION, which is set to GeneralTable.asp. This parameter tells IIS that when it receives the response from this form, it should pass the ASP file GeneralTable.asp to the ASP processor. The values from the form will be passed in an object called Form.

The rest of the page is standard HTML. Note that the name of the text input box is text1.

Figure 15-21(b) shows GeneralTable.asp, the page that will be invoked when the response is received from the form page in Figure 15-21(a). The first executable script statement is

```
varTableName = Request.Form("text1")
```

Request.Form is the name of the object that contains the values sent back from the browser. In this case, text1 will be set to *artist.*

This version of GeneralTable processes the SQL Server View Ridge database. The surrogate key names in SQL Server are in the form ArtistID and not ARTISTID.

➤ FIGURE 15-21 *(Continued)*

```
<HTML>
<HEAD>
<META HTTP-EQUIV="Content-Type" CONTENT="text/html;charset=windows-1252">
<TITLE>Table Display Page</TITLE>
</HEAD>
<BODY>
<!--#include virtual="ViewRidgeExample1/adovbs.inc"-->
<%

Dim objConn, objRecordSet, objField
Dim varNumCols, varI, varSql
Dim varTableName, varRecordSetName, varKeyName
Dim varTableNameFirst, varTableNameRest

varTablename = Request.Form("text1")

' set key name to upper first initial and lower remainder with ID, e.g.,
CustomerID
varTableNameFirst = UCase(Left(varTableName, 1))
varTableNameRest = LCase(Right(varTableName, Len(varTableName)-1))
varKeyName = varTableNameFirst & varTableNameRest &"ID"

varRecordSetName = "_rs_" & varTableName ' use for saving recordset object
pointer

If IsObject(Session("_conn")) Then
    Set objConn = Session("_conn")
Else
   Set objConn = Server.CreateObject("ADODB.connection")
   objConn.IsolationLevel = adXactReadCommitted ' avoid dirty reads
   objConn.open "ViewRidgeSS", "sa"
   Set Session("_conn") = objConn
End If

If IsObject(Session(varRecordSetName)) Then
    Set objRecordSet = Session(varRecordSetName) ' used saved recordset object
if possible
    objRecordSet.Requery
Else
   varSql = "SELECT * FROM " & "[" & varTableName & "]" ' put brackets in case
table name has spaces, etc.
   Set objRecordSet = Server.CreateObject("ADODB.Recordset")
   ' in the next statement, note use of cursor and lock types
   objRecordSet.Open varSql, objConn, adOpenDynamic,   adLockOptimistic ' allow
for updates
   Set Session(varRecordSetName) = objRecordSet

End If
%>

<TABLE BORDER=1 BGCOLOR=#ffffff CELLSPACING=0><FONT FACE="Arial" COLOR=#000000>
<CAPTION><B><%=UCase(varTableName)%> (in SQL Server
Database)</B></CAPTION></FONT>
<THEAD>
<TR>
<%
varNumCols = objRecordSet.Fields.Count
For varI = 0 to varNumCols - 1
Set objField = objRecordSet.Fields(varI)
If objField.Name <> varKeyName Then %>
<TH BGCOLOR=#c0c0c0 BORDERCOLOR=#000000 ><FONT SIZE=2 FACE="Arial"
COLOR=#000000><%=objField.Name%></FONT></TH>
```

(b)

➤ FIGURE 15-21

(Continued)

```
<%
End If
Next%>
</TR>
</THEAD>
<TBODY>
<%
On Error Resume Next
objRecordSet.MoveFirst
do while Not objRecordSet.eof
%>
<TR VALIGN=TOP>
<%
varNumCols = objRecordSet.Fields.Count
For varI = 0 to varNumCols - 1
Set objField = objRecordSet.Fields(varI)
If objField.Name <> varKeyName Then %>
<TD BORDERCOLOR=#c0c0c0 ><FONT SIZE=2 FACE="Arial"
COLOR=#000000><%=Server.HTMLEncode(objField.Value)%><BR></FONT></TD>
<%
End If
Next%>
</TR>

<%
objRecordSet.MoveNext
loop%>
<BR><BR><A HREF="ViewRidgeTables.asp">View Another Table</A>
</TBODY>
<TFOOT></TFOOT>
</TABLE>
</BODY>
</HTML>
```

(b)

Because VBScript comparisons are case sensitive, we need to ensure that varKeyName has the surrogate key name in the required format. The user might enter *ARTIST, artist, Artist, or aRtIsT,* for that matter, so we cannot just append *ID* to the input table name. The three statements starting with varKeyNameFirst employ the UCase and LCase functions to set varKeyName correctly.

The remainder of this page is the same as the Customer.asp page shown in Figure 15-18(b). Note again that varKeyName will be set to ArtistID, which is the name of the surrogate key column that we do not wish to display.

EXAMPLE 4—UPDATING A TABLE

The three previous examples all concern reading data. This next example shows how to update table data by adding a row with ADO. Figure 15-22(a) shows a data entry form that will capture artist name and nationality and create a new row. This form is similar to ViewRidgeTables.asp; it has two data entry fields rather than one. When the user clicks Save New Artist, the artist is added to the database, and if the results are successful, the form in Figure 15-22(b) is produced. The See New List URL will invoke Artist.asp which will display the ARTIST table with the new row as shown in Figure 15-22(c).

➤ FIGURE 15-22

Adding ARTIST Data: (a) ARTIST Data Entry Form, (b) Response Form, (c) ARTIST Table Display

New ARTIST Entry Form - Microsoft Internet Explorer - [Working Offline]
File Edit View Favorites Tools Help
Back Search Favorites History
Address http://localhost/ViewRidgeExample1/NewArtist.asp Go Links

New Artist Data Form

Artist Name: Marc Chagall
Nationality: French

Save New Artist Reset Values

Done Local intranet

(a)

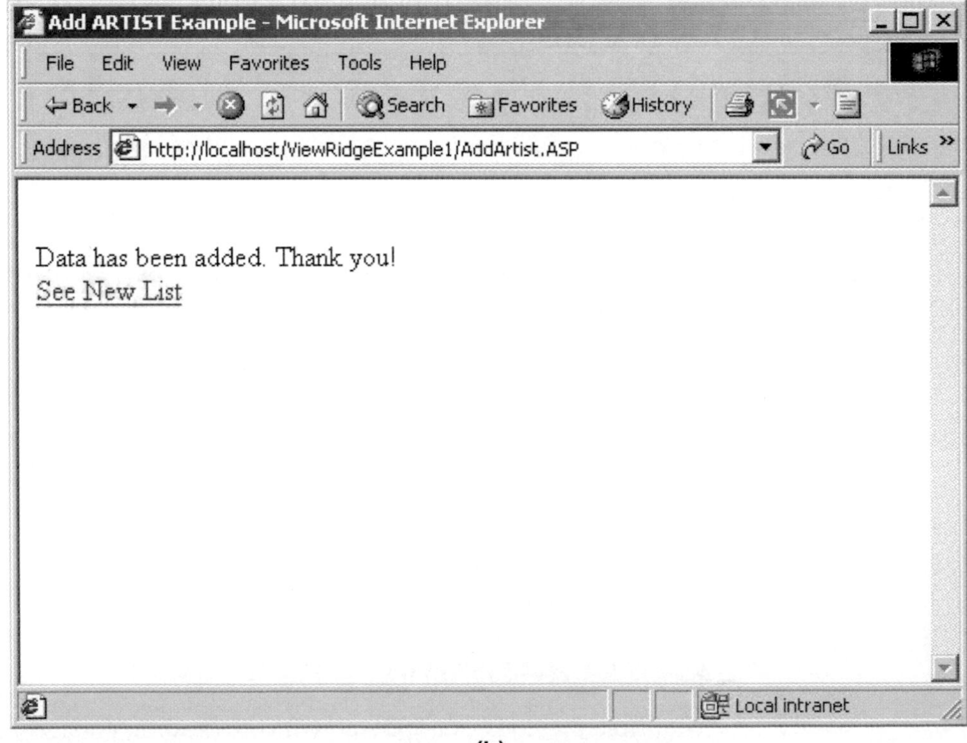

(b)

The ASP pages are shown in Figure 15-23. The first page is a data entry form with two fields, one for artist name (named *Name*) and a second for artist nationality (named *Nation*). When the user clicks the submit button, these data are to be sent back to IIS which in turn is to send it along with the page AddArtist.asp to the ASP processor.

FIGURE 15-22

(Continued)

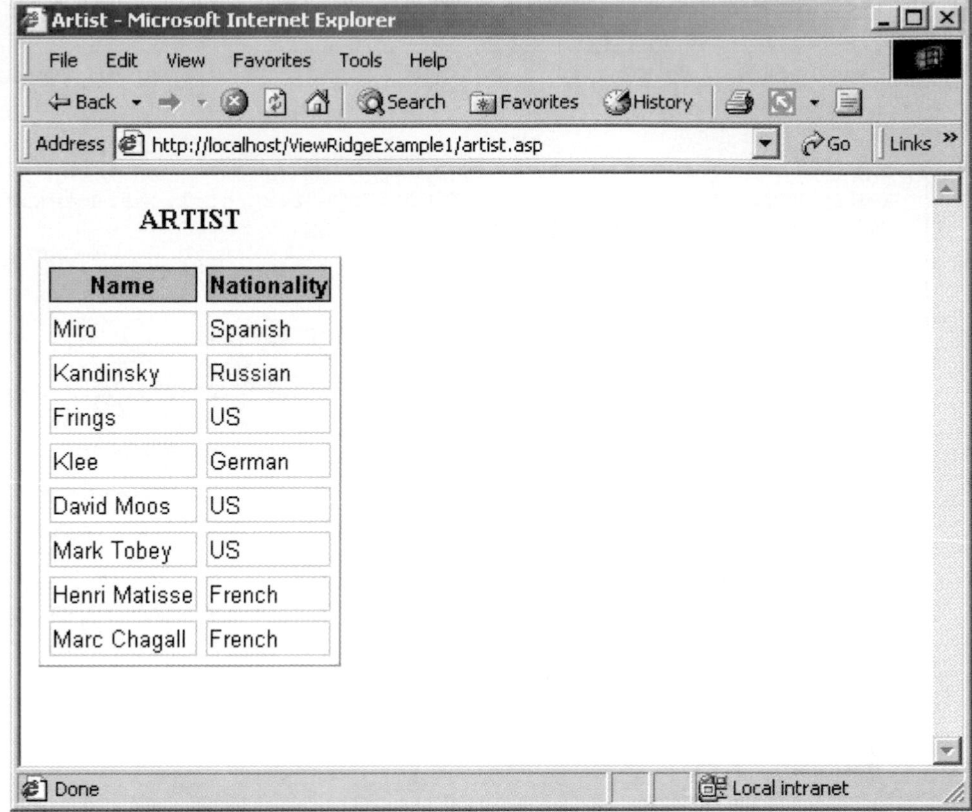

(c)

AddArtist.asp [shown in Figure 15-23(b)] obtains connection and recordset objects. No attempt here is made to save connection and recordset object pointers in session variables. (The assumption is that only one artist will be added per session and saving these would be unnecessary.) If desired, code to save them could certainly be added as shown in the previous examples.

The key difference of this page is shown in the statements

```
objRecordSet.AddNew
objRecordSet("Name")= Request.Form("Name")
objRecordSet("Nationality")= Request.Form("Nation")
objRecordSet.Update
```

The first statement obtains a new row in the objRecordSet object and then values are obtained for the Name and Nationality columns from the Request.Form object. Note there is no need for the column names and Request.Form names to be the same. Here the second column name is Nationality, but the second value from the form is Nation. The objRecordSet.Update call causes the database update. Note the error processing code which will cause error messages to be displayed via the Response.Write statement (this is a method available in the Response object of ASP). The page ends with two calls to send a confirmation message back to the user and to create a URL to Artist.asp if the user wants to see the table with the new values.

➤ FIGURE 15-23

Inserting Data Using ASP: (a) NewArtist.asp, (b) AddArtist.asp

```
<HTML>
<HEAD>
<META HTTP-EQUIV="Content-Type" CONTENT="text/html;charset=windows-1252">
<TITLE>New ARTIST Entry Form</TITLE>
</HEAD>
<BODY>

<FORM METHOD="post" ACTION="AddArtist.ASP">

 <P><STRONG><FONT color=purple face="" size=5>   New Artist Data
Form</FONT></STRONG>
<P></P>
<P> </P>

<P><FONT style="BACKGROUND-COLOR: #ffffff"><FONT color=forestgreen face=""
style="BACKGROUND-COLOR: #ffffff">Artist
Name:</FONT>     
<INPUT id=text1 name=Name style="HEIGHT: 22px; WIDTH: 164px"></FONT></P>

<P><FONT color=forestgreen face=""
style="BACKGROUND-COLOR:
#ffffff">Nationality:       
<INPUT id=text2 name=Nation style="HEIGHT: 22px; WIDTH: 167px"></FONT></P>

<P> </P>

<P><FONT style="BACKGROUND-COLOR: #ffffff">
<INPUT id=submit1 name=submit1 type=submit value="Save New
Artist">   
<INPUT id=reset1 name=reset1 type=reset value="Reset Values"></FONT></P>
</FORM>
</BODY>
</HTML>
```

(a)

EXAMPLE 5—INVOKING A STORED PROCEDURE

We created a stored procedure named Customer_Insert in both the Oracle and SQL Server databases (in Chapters 12 and 13, respectively). In both cases, the stored procedure accepts a new customer name, area code, local number, and the nationality of all artists in whom the customer is interested. It then creates a new row in CUSTOMER and adds appropriate rows to the intersection table.

To invoke the stored procedure using an ASP page, we create a Web page to collect the necessary data, as shown in Figure 15-24(a). Now, when the user clicks Add Customer, we want to invoke an ASP page that calls the stored procedure with the form data. So that the user can verify that the new data has been entered correctly, the ASP page then queries a view that joins customer names with artist names and nationalities. The result is shown in Figure 15-24(b).

Figure 15-25(a) shows the code to generate the form to gather data. The parameter fields are named *text1* through *text4*. The form invokes the asp page CustomerInsertOracle in the FORM METHOD statement, so when the user clicks Add Customer, the data will be sent to CustomerInsertOracle, the page shown in Figure 15-25(b).

➤ FIGURE 15-23

(Continued)

```
<HTML>
<HEAD>
<META HTTP-EQUIV="Content-Type" CONTENT="text/html;charset=windows-1252">
<TITLE>Add ARTIST Example</TITLE>
</HEAD>
<BODY>
<!--#include virtual="ViewRidgeExample1/adovbs.inc"-->
<%

Dim objConn, objRecordSet, objField
Dim varNumCols, varI, varSql

Set objConn = Server.CreateObject("ADODB.connection")
objConn.open "ViewRidgeSS", "sa"  ' open with sa
objConn.IsolationLevel = adXactReadCommitted ' avoid dirty reads

varSql = "SELECT * FROM [ARTIST]"
Set objRecordSet = Server.CreateObject("ADODB.Recordset")
' in the next statement, note use of cursor and lock types
objRecordSet.Open varSql, objConn, adOpenDynamic, adLockOptimistic

objRecordSet.AddNew
objRecordSet("ArtistName")= Request.Form("Name")
objRecordSet("Nationality")= Request.Form("Nation")
objRecordSet.Update

On Error Resume Next
varErrorCount = objConn.Errors.Count
If varErrorCount > 0 Then
   For varI = 0 to varErrorCount - 1
      Response.Write "<BR><I>" & objConn.Errors(varI).Description & "</I><BR>"
   Next
End If

objRecordSet.Close
objConn.Close

Response.Write "<BR>Data has been added.  Thank you!<BR>"
Response.Write "<A HREF="& """" &"artist.asp" & """"& ">See New List</A>"

%>
<BR><BR>
</BODY>
</HTML>
```

(b)

This page looks for a saved connection and, if one is not found, obtains a new one as shown earlier. Then it creates a command object, *objCommand,* and associates it with objConn. It then sets up the call to the Customer_Insert stored procedure with CommandText= "{call Customer_Insert(?, ?, ?, ?)}." This pattern indicates that four parameters will be passed. The next sections of code create the parameters and append them to the command object. Finally, the command is executed which causes the stored procedure to be invoked. No transaction isolation level nor cursor properties are set because the stored procedure will set them for itself.

FIGURE 15-24

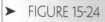

(a) CUSTOMER Data Entry Form, (b) Form Showing Join of Customers and Artist Interest

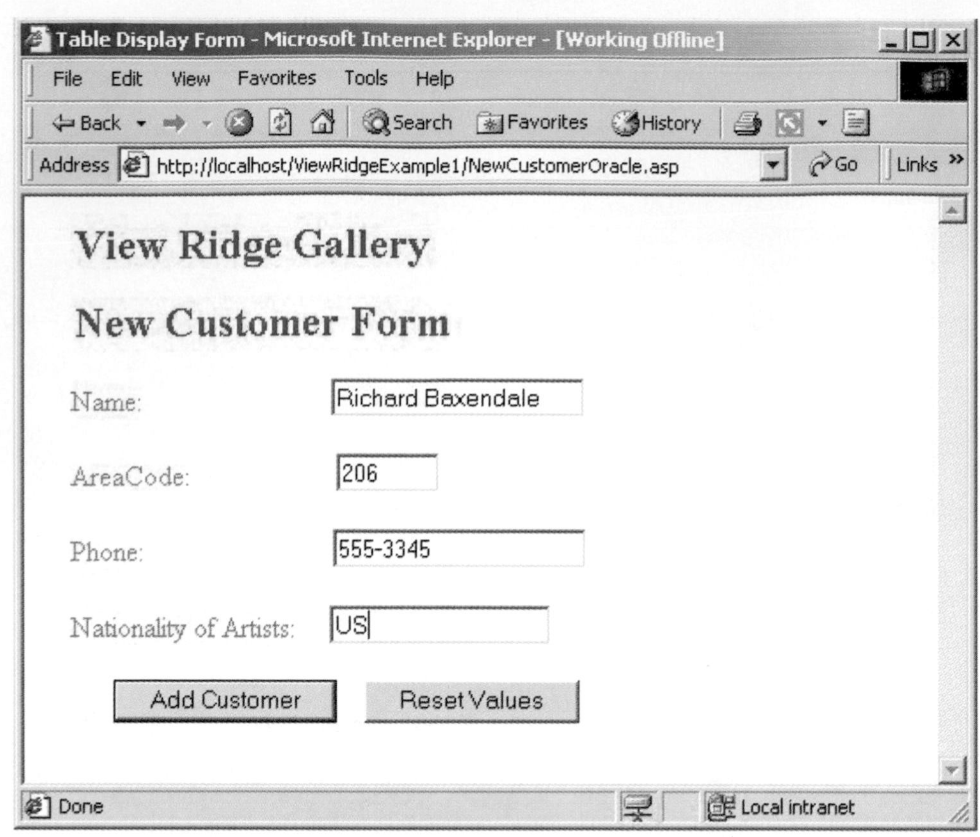

(a)

Customer Update Display Page - Microsoft Internet Explorer

File Edit View Favorites Tools Help

Address http://localhost/ViewRidgeExample1/CustomerInsertOracle.ASP

Customers and Interests After Update

CUSTNAME	ARTISTNAME	NATIONALITY
Fred Smathers	Frings	US
Fred Smathers	van Vronkin	US
Fred Smathers	Tobey	US
Richard Baxendale	Frings	US
Richard Baxendale	van Vronkin	US
Richard Baxendale	Tobey	US
Selma Warning	Frings	US
Selma Warning	van Vronkin	US
Selma Warning	Tobey	US
Susan Wu	Miro	Spanish

Done — Local intranet

(b)

After the command is executed, a recordset is created on a select of all columns of the view CUSTOMERINTERESTS, and finally the columns are displayed in the browser using the techniques shown in earlier examples.

In both the Oracle and SQL Server databases, this view was defined as the join of CUSTOMER and ARTIST over the intersection table. The syntax used for Oracle was

```
CREATE VIEW CUSTOMERINTERESTS AS
   SELECT CUSTOMER.NAME CUSTNAME, ARTIST.NAME
      ARTISTNAME, ARTIST.NATIONALITY
   FROM CUSTOMER, CUSTOMER_ARTIST_INT, ARTIST
   WHERE CUSTOMER.CUSTOMERID = CUSTOMER_ARTIST_
      INT.CUSTOMERID AND
      ARTIST.ARTISTID = CUSTOMER_ARTIST_INT.ARTISTID
   ORDER BY CUSTNAME
```

One very interesting thing about this page is that the only difference between the Oracle version shown here and the SQL Server version is the name of the ODBC data source and the account name and password used. Note the comment line under the objConn.open statement; all of the idiosyncrasies of the DBMS products are contained in the stored procedures and the ASP page developer need know nothing about them.

These examples give you an idea of the use of ADO. The best way to learn more is to write some pages yourself. This chapter has shown all the basic techniques that you will need. You've worked hard to get to this point, and if you are able to understand enough to create some of your own pages, you have come very far indeed since Chapter 1!

➤ FIGURE 15-25

Invoking a Stored Procedure from ASP: (a) NewCustomerOracle.asp, (b) NewCustomerOracle.asp

```
<HTML>
<HEAD>
<META HTTP-EQUIV="Content-Type" CONTENT="text/html;charset=windows-1252">
<TITLE>Table Display Form</TITLE>
</HEAD>
<BODY>

<FORM METHOD="post" ACTION="CustomerInsertOracle.ASP">

 <P><STRONG><FONT color=purple face="" size=5>   View Ridge
Gallery</FONT></STRONG>

 <P>   <strong><font color="purple" face size="5"> New Customer
Form</font></strong><P><font style="background-color: #ffffff"
color="forestgreen" face>   
 Name:   </font><FONT style="BACKGROUND-COLOR:
#ffffff">           &nbs
p;           
 </FONT><INPUT id=text1 name=text1></P>

 <P> <font style="background-color: #ffffff" color="forestgreen"
face>   AreaCode<font style="background-color:
#ffffff">:   </font>       &n
bsp;         
 </font><INPUT id=text2 name=text2 size="6"></P>

 <P><font style="background-color: #ffffff" color="forestgreen"
face>   

Phone:            &
nbsp;            &n
bsp;
 </font><INPUT id=text3 name=text3
size="20">        </P>

 <P>    <font style="background-color: #ffffff"
color="forestgreen" face>Nationality
 of Artists:  </font>   <INPUT id=text4 name=text4
size="17"></P>

 <P> <FONT style="BACKGROUND-COLOR: #ffffff">
   </FONT>     <FONT style="BACKGROUND-
COLOR: #ffffff">
<INPUT id=submit1 name=submit1 type=submit value="Add Customer"
>   
<INPUT id=reset1 name=reset1 type=reset value="Reset Values"></FONT></P>

</FORM>
</BODY>
</HTML>
```

(a)

➤ FIGURE 15-25 *(Continued)*

```
<HTML>
<HEAD>
<META HTTP-EQUIV="Content-Type" CONTENT="text/html;charset=windows-1252">
<TITLE>Customer Update Display Page</TITLE>

</HEAD>
<BODY>

<P><STRONG><FONT color=purple face="" size=5>   Customers and Interests After
Update</FONT></STRONG>
<!--#include virtual="ViewRidgeExample1/adovbs.inc"-->
<%

    Dim objConn, objCommand, objParam, oRs
    Dim objRecordSet, objField
    Dim varI, varSql, varNumCols, varValue

    If IsObject(Session("_conn")) Then
        Set objConn = Session("_conn") ' use current session if available
    Else
        Set objConn = Server.CreateObject("ADODB.connection")
        ' stored procedure will set its own isolation level
        objConn.open "ViewRidgeOracle", "system", "manager" ' use this to update via Oracle
        'objConn.open "ViewRidgeSS", "sa"  ' could use this to update via SQL Server
        Set Session("_conn") = objConn
    End If

    Set objCommand = Server.CreateObject("ADODB.Command") ' create a command object
    Set objCommand.ActiveConnection = objConn ' set the command objects connection

    objCommand.CommandText="{call Customer_Insert (?, ?, ?, ?)}" ' setup call to stored procedure

    ' Set up four parameters with necessary values
    Set objParam = objCommand.CreateParameter("NewName", adChar, adParamInput, 50)
    objCommand.Parameters.Append objParam
    objParam.Value = Request.Form("text1")

    Set objParam = objCommand.CreateParameter("AreaCode", adChar, adParamInput, 5)
    objCommand.Parameters.Append objParam
    objParam.Value = Request.Form("text2")

    Set objParam = objCommand.CreateParameter("PhoneNumber", adChar, adParamInput, 8)
    objCommand.Parameters.Append objParam
    objParam.Value = Request.Form("text3")

    Set objParam = objCommand.CreateParameter("Nationality", adChar, adParamInput, 25)
    objCommand.Parameters.Append objParam
    objParam.Value = Request.Form("text4")

' Fire the Stored Proc

    Set oRs = objCommand.Execute

    ' now read the data from a view having both CUSTOMER and ARTIST
    varSql = "SELECT * FROM CUSTOMERINTERESTS" ' use that joins via the intersection table
    Set objRecordSet = Server.CreateObject("ADODB.Recordset")
    objRecordSet.Open varSql, objConn
```

(b)

➤ FIGURE 15-25

(Continued)

```
%>
<TABLE BORDER=1 BGCOLOR=#ffffff CELLSPACING=5><FONT FACE="Arial"
COLOR=#000000><CAPTION><B><CUSTOMERS AND INTERESTS</B></CAPTION></FONT>
<THEAD>
<TR>
<%
varNumCols = objRecordSet.Fields.Count
For varI = 0 to varNumCols - 1
Set objField = objRecordSet.Fields(varI)
%>
<TH BGCOLOR=#c0c0c0 BORDERCOLOR=#000000 ><FONT SIZE=2 FACE="Arial"
COLOR=#000000><%=objField.Name%></FONT></TH>

<%
Next%>
</TR>
</THEAD>
<TBODY>
<%
On Error Resume Next
objRecordSet.MoveFirst
do while Not objRecordSet.eof
%>
<TR VALIGN=TOP>
<%
varNumCols = objRecordSet.Fields.Count
For varI = 0 to varNumCols - 1
Set objField = objRecordSet.Fields(varI)
If objRecordSet.Fields(varI).Type = adNumeric then
      varValue=CDbl(objField.Value)
      varValue = convert(char, varValue)
else
      varValue=Server.HTMLEncode(objField.Value)
End If
%>
<TD BORDERCOLOR=#c0c0c0 ><FONT SIZE=2 FACE="Arial"
COLOR=#000000><%=(varValue)%><BR></FONT></TD>
<%
varValue=""
Next%>
</TR>

<%
objRecordSet.MoveNext
loop%>
</TBODY>
<TFOOT></TFOOT>
</TABLE>
</BODY>
</HTML>
```

(b)

➤ SUMMARY

Internet technology database applications reside in a rich and complicated environment. In addition to relational databases, there are nonrelational databases, VSAM and other file-processing data, e-mail, and other types of data like pictures, audio, and so forth. To ease the job of the application programmer, various standards have been developed. The ODBC standard is for relational databases; the OLE DB standard is for relational and other databases. ADO was developed to provide easier access to OLE DB data for the non–object-oriented programmer.

ODBC, or the open database connectivity standard, provides an interface by which Web server programs can access and process relational data sources in a DBMS-independent manner. ODBC was developed by an industry committee and has been implemented by Microsoft and many other vendors. ODBC involves applications program, driver manager, DBMS driver, and data source components. Single-tier and multiple-tier drivers are defined. There are three types of data source names: file, system, and user. System data sources are recommended for Web servers. The process of defining a system data source name involves specifying the type of driver and the identity of the database to be processed.

OLE DB is the foundation of the Microsoft data access world. It implements the Microsoft OLE and COM standards and is accessible to object-oriented programs through those interfaces. OLE DB breaks the features and functions of a DBMS into objects, thus making it easier for vendors to implement portions of functionality. Key object terms are abstraction, methods, properties, and collections. A rowset is an abstraction of a recordset, which in turn is an abstraction of a relation. Objects are defined by properties that specify their characteristics and methods that are actions they can perform. A collection is an object that contains a group of other objects. The goals of OLE DB are listed in Figure 15-10. An interface is a set of objects and the properties and methods they expose in that interface. Objects may expose different properties and methods in different interfaces. An implementation is how an object accomplishes its tasks. Implementations are hidden from the outside world and may be changed without impacting the users of the objects. An interface ought not to be changed, ever.

Tabular data providers present data in the form of rowsets. Service providers transform data into another form; such providers are both consumers and providers of data. A rowset is equivalent to a cursor. Basic rowset interfaces are IRowSet, IAccessor, and IColumnsInfo. Other interfaces are defined for more advanced capability.

ADO is a simple object model used by OLE DB data consumers. It can be used from any language supported by Microsoft. The ADO object model has Connection, RecordSet, Command, and Errors collection objects. Recordsets have a Fields collection and Commands have a Parameters collection.

A connection object establishes a connection to a data provider and data source. Connections have an isolation mode. Once a connection is created, it can be used to create RecordSet and Command objects. RecordSet objects represent cursors, they have both CursorType and LockType properties. RecordSets can be created with SQL statements. The Fields collection of a RecordSet can be processed to individually manipulate fields.

The Errors collection contains one or more error messages that result from an ADO operation. The command object is used to execute stored parameterized queries or stored procedures. Input data can be sent to the correct ASP page using the HTML FORM tag. Table updates are made using the RecordSet Update method.

➤ GROUP I QUESTIONS

15.1 Describe why the data environment for Web servers is complicated.

15.2 Explain the relationship of ODBC, OLE DB, and ADO.

15.3 Explain the author's justification for describing Microsoft standards. Do you agree?

15.4 Name the components of the ODBC standard.

15.5 What role does the driver manager serve? Who supplies it?

15.6 What role does the DBMS driver serve? Who supplies it?

15.7 What is a single-tier driver?

15.8 What is a multiple-tier driver?

15.9 Do the uses of the term *tier* in the three-tier architecture and its use in ODBC have anything to do with each other?

15.10 Why are conformance levels important?

15.11 Summarize the three ODBC API conformance levels.

15.12 Summarize the three SQL grammar conformance levels.

15.13 Explain the difference among the three types of data sources.

15.14 Which data source type is recommended for Web servers?

15.15 What are the two tasks to be accomplished when setting up an ODBC data source name?

15.16 Why is OLE DB important?

15.17 What disadvantage of ODBC does OLE DB overcome?

15.18 Define *abstraction* and explain how it relates to OLE DB.

15.19 Give an example of abstraction involving rowset.

15.20 Define object *properties* and *methods*.

15.21 What is the difference between an object class and an object?

15.22 Explain the role of data consumers and data providers.

15.23 What is an interface?

15.24 What is the difference between an interface and an implementation?

15.25 Explain why an implementation can be changed but an interface should not be changed.

15.26 Summarize the goals of OLE DB.

15.27 What is MTS, and what does it do?

15.28 Explain the difference between a tabular data provider and a service provider. Which type is a product that transforms OLE DB data into XML documents?

15.29 In the context of OLE DB, what is the difference between a rowset and a cursor?

15.30 What languages can use ADO?

15.31 List the objects in the ADO object model and explain their relationships.

15.32 What is the function of the Connection object?

15.33 Show a snippet of VBScript for creating a Connection object.

15.34 What is the function of the RecordSet object?

15.35 Show a snippet of VBScript for creating a RecordSet object.

15.36 What does the Fields collection contain? Explain a situation in which you would use it.

15.37 Show a snippet of VBScript for processing the Fields collection.

15.38 What does the Errors collection contain? Explain a situation in which you would use it.

15.39 Show a snippet of VBScript for processing the Errors collection.

15.40 What is the purpose of the Command object?

15.41 Show a snippet of VBScript for executing a stored parameterized query that has two parameters, A and B.

15.42 Explain the purpose of the ⟨% and %⟩ tags in ASP pages.

15.43 Explain the purpose of the _conn variable in Figure 15-16.

15.44 What is the reason for the code that creates varKeyName in Figure 15-21(b).

15.45 Explain the purpose of the ACTION parameter of the FORM tag in Figure 15-21(a).

15.46 Explain what happens when the following statement is executed in the ASP page in Figure 15-21(b).

varTableName = Request.Form("text1")

15.47 Show a VBScript snippet for adding a new record to a recordset name objMyRecordSet. Assume the fields are A and B and their values are to be "Avalue" and "Bvalue" respectively.

15.48 What purpose is served by the Response.Write statement?

➤ GROUP II QUESTIONS

15.49 Microsoft expends much effort to promulgate the OLE DB and ADO standards. It does not directly receive revenue from these standards. IIS is free with Windows NT and Windows 2000. Its Web site has numerous examples of articles to help developers learn more, and all of it is free. Why do you think Microsoft does this? What goal is served?

15.50 In the code in Figure 15-23(b), the cursor type is set to dynamic. What effect will this have on the processing of this and the Customer.asp and Artist.asp pages? Explain how you think the isolation level, cursor type, and lock type parameters should be set for an application that involves all three of these pages.

15.51 Explain how to change the example ASP page in Figure 15-16 to run with the DSN ViewRidgeOracle. Explain how to change the ASP page in Figure 15-18 to run with ViewRidgeSS. While the ease of making these changes is interesting from a technology standpoint, does this capability have any importance in the world of commerce?

15.52 If you have installed Oracle, use your browser to execute the page in Figure 15-18. Now open SQL Plus and delete two rows of CUSTOMER data using the SQL DELETE command. Go back to your browser and execute the page in Figure 15-18 again. Explain the results.

15.53 If you have installed SQL Server, use your browser to execute the page in Figures 15-16. Now open SQL Query Analyzer and delete two rows of CUSTOMER data using the SQL DELETE command. Go back to your browser and execute the page in Figure 15-16 again. Explain the results. If you answered Question 15.52, explain the difference in results you received, if any.

➤ FIREDUP PROJECT QUESTIONS

Create the YourFired database using either Oracle or SQL Server, if you have not already done so. Follow the instructions at the end of Chapters 12 or 13, respectively.

A. Code an ASP page to display the STOVE table

B. Code an ASP page to display any table in the FiredUp database. Use Figure 15.21 as an example.

C. Code an ASP page to enter new STOVE data. Justify your choice of cursor isolation.

D. Code an ASP page to allow customers to register their own stoves. Justify your choice of cursor isolation.

E. Create a stored procedure to enter new stove repair data.

F. Code an ASP page to invoke the stored procedure created in task E, above. Use Figure 15-25 as an example.

JDBC, Java Server Pages, and MySQL

This chapter discusses alternatives to Microsoft's OLE DB, ADO, and IIS technology and products. In particular, we will discuss JDBC, Java Server Pages (JSP) using Apache/Tomcat, and the DBMS product MySQL. The open source movement has played a large role in the development of these technologies, and all of these are open source products. In fact, only open source software was used to develop all of the examples in this chapter.

Open source is not a requirement for use of JDBC, however. You can employ JDBC on Windows 2000 and other operating systems to access SQL Server, Oracle, or other prominent DBMS products. You can run JSP pages and Apache/Tomcat on Windows 2000 as well. In this chapter, however, all of the examples were developed and run on Linux.

As you might guess, the one requirement for using JDBC is that programs be written in Java. Because this text does not assume that you are a Java programmer, we will explain examples at a high level. It will not be important to understand every line of code. Your goal should be to understand the nature and capability of the technologies presented here. If you already program in Java, these examples should stimulate your thinking for more complex and realistic examples. In any case, after reading this chapter, you will be able to compare the capabilities of ODBC, ADO, and ASP to JDBC and JSP.

➤ JDBC

To begin, contrary to many sources, JDBC does *not* stand for Java Database Connectivity. According to Sun, the inventor of Java, and the source of many Java-oriented products, JDBC is not an acronym; it just stands for JDBC. One can only imagine what legal or ego wrangles lie behind that assertion, but JDBC it is.

There are JDBC drivers for almost every conceivable DBMS product. Sun maintains a directory of them at http://java.sun.com/products/jdbc. Some of the drivers are free, and almost all of them have an evaluation edition that can be used free for a limited period of time. The JDBC drivers used for the preparation of this chapter are the MySQL open source drivers developed by Mark Mathews. They can be downloaded from http://worldserver.com/mm.mysql.

So that you do not develop unfortunate habits, we will correct one other possible mistake before we continue. The DBMS product MySQL is pronounced "my ess-queue-lll" and not "my see-quel." This is hardly important, but if you want to be cool, always say "my ess-queue-lll."

Driver Types

Sun defines four driver types. Type 1 drivers are JDBC-ODBC bridge drivers. These drivers provide an interface between Java and regular ODBC drivers. Most ODBC drivers are written in C or C++. For reasons unimportant to us here, there are incompatibilities between Java and C/C++. Bridge drivers resolve these incompatibilities and allow access to ODBC data sources from Java. Because we described the use of ODBC in the last chapter, we will not consider bridge drivers any further here.

Drivers of types 2 to 4 are written entirely in Java; they differ only in how they connect to the DBMS. Type 2 drivers connect to the native-API of the DBMS; they call Oracle, for example, using the standard (non-ODBC) programming interface to Oracle. Drivers of Types 3 and 4 are intended for use over communications networks. A Type 3 driver translates JDBC calls into a DBMS-independent network protocol. This protocol is then translated into the network protocol used by a particular DBMS. Finally, Type 4 drivers translate JDBC calls into DBMS-specific network protocols.

To understand the differences between the driver types 2–4, you must first understand the difference between a **servlet** and an **applet.** As you probably know, Java was designed to be portable. To accomplish portability, Java programs are not compiled into a particular machine language, but instead are compiled into machine-independent bytecode. Sun, Microsoft, and others have written **bytecode interpreters** for each machine environment (Intel 386, Alpha, and so on). These interpreters are referred to as **Java virtual machines.**

To run a compiled Java program, the machine-independent bytecode is interpreted by the virtual machine at run time. The cost of this, of course, is that bytecode interpretation constitutes an extra step and, consequently, such programs can never be as fast as programs that are compiled directly into machine code. This may or may not be a problem depending on application's workload.

An applet is a Java bytecode program that runs on the application user's computer. Applet bytecode is sent to the user via HTTP and is invoked using the HTTP protocol on the user's computer. The bytecode is interpreted by a virtual machine, usually part of the browser. Because of portability, the same bytecode can be sent to a Windows, Unix, or Apple computer.

A servlet is a Java program that is invoked via HTTP on the Web server computer. It responds to requests from browser users. Servlets are interpreted and executed by a Java virtual machine running on the server.

Because they have a connection to a communications protocol, Type 3 and 4 drivers can be used in either applet or servlet code. Type 2 drivers can be used only in situations where the Java program and the DBMS reside on the same machine, or where the Type 2 driver connects to a DBMS program that handles the communications between the computer running the Java program and the computer running the DBMS.

Thus, if you write code that connects to a database from an applet (two-tier), then only a Type 3 or Type 4 driver can be used. In these situations, if your DBMS product has a Type 4 driver, use it because it will be faster than a Type 3 driver.

In three-tier or *n*-tier architecture, if the Web server and the DBMS are running on the same machine, you can use a driver of any of the four types. If the

Summary of JDBC Driver Types

Driver Type	Characteristics
1	JDBC-ODBC bridge. Provides a Java API that interfaces to an ODBC driver. Enables processing of ODBC data sources from Java.
2	A Java API that connects to the native-library of a DBMS product. The Java program and the DBMS must reside on the same machine, or the DBMS must handle the intermachine communication, if not.
3	A JAVA API that connects to a DBMS-independent network protocol. Can be used for servlets and applets.
4	A JAVA API that connects to a DBMS-dependent network protocol. Can be used for servlets and applets.

Web server and the DBMS are running on different machines, then Type 3 and Type 4 drivers can be used without a problem. Type 2 drivers can also be used if the DBMS vendor handles the communications between the Web server and the DBMS. Characteristics of JDBC driver types are summarized in Figure 16-1.

USING JDBC

Unlike ODBC, with JDBC there is no separate utility program for creating a JDBC data source. Instead, all of the work to define a connection is done in Java code via the JDBC driver. The coding pattern for using a JDBC driver is the following:

1. Load the driver.
2. Establish a connection to the database.
3. Create a statement.
4. Do something with the statement.

As you will see, the name of the DBMS product to be used and the name of the database are provided at step 2.

LOADING THE DRIVER To load the driver, you must first obtain the driver library and install it in a directory. You need to ensure that the directory is named in the CLASSPATH for both the Java compiler and for the Java virtual machine. There are several ways to load the driver into program; the most reliable is

```
Class.forName(string).newInstance();
```

The value of the string parameter depends on the driver you use. For the MM MySQL drivers, use

```
Class.forName("org.gjt.mm.mysql.Driver").newInstance();
```

This method will throw an exception, so you should write this code in a try:catch block. (If you're not a Java programmer, don't despair; just understand that these statements are making the JDBC classes available to the program).

ESTABLISHING A CONNECTION TO THE DATABASE Once you have loaded the driver, the next step is to create an object that has a connection to your database. The format is

```
Connection conn = DriverManager.getConnection(string);
```

The DriverManager class is part of the JDBC library you loaded in step 1. It plays the same role as the ODBC driver manager. JDBC drivers register themselves with this class. On a given machine, there may be several drivers registered. When you call DriverManager.getConnection, it looks through its list of JDBC drivers for a suitable driver and uses it. It will pick the first suitable driver it finds, so if more than one driver can process your connection, you may not get the driver you expect.

The string parameter passed to getConnection has three parts, separated by colons. The first part is always "jdbc," the second is a keyword that identifies the DBMS you are using, and the third is a URL to the database you want to process, along with optional parameters such as user and password.

The following statement will connect to a MySQL database named vr1 with user *dk1* and password *sesame*:

```
Connection conn = DriverManager.getConnection
    ("jdbc:mysql://localhost/vr1?user=dk1&password=sesame")
```

The content of the second and third part of this string depends on your JDBC driver. In fact, with some drivers you specify the user name and password as separate parameters. Consult your driver's documentation to find out what to code.

By the way, most of this technology arose in the Unix world. Unix is case sensitive, and almost everything you enter here is also case sensitive. Thus, *jdbc* and *JDBC* are *not* the same. Enter everything in the case that is shown here. There are a few case-insensitive exceptions, but they're not worth mentioning or remembering. Just type the case as shown.

The getConnection method will also throw an exception, so it, too, should appear in a try:catch block.

CREATING A STATEMENT The next step is to create a new Statement object. This is similar to what we did in the last chapter for creating a command object with ADO. The syntax is

```
Statement stmt = conn.createStatement();
```

There are no parameters to pass to this method.

At this point, you can process the statement in various ways as discussed next.

PROCESSING THE STATEMENT The Statement methods are standardized in the JDBC specification. Your driver will process any of the statements shown here (and many more as well). See your driver's API documentation for details. In our examples, we will use the executeQuery and executeUpdate methods as follows:

```
ResultSet rs = stmt.executeQuery(querystring);
```

and

```
int result = stmt.executeUpdate(updatestring);
```

The first statement returns a result set that can be used in the same way we have used cursors in earlier chapters. The second statement returns an integer that indicates the number of rows updated. Specific examples are

```
ResultSet rs = stmt.executeQuery("SELECT * FROM CUSTOMER");
```

and

```
int result = stmt.executeUpdate("UPDATE ARTIST SET Nationality='English'
    WHERE Name='Foster'");
```

Note the use of single quotes to avoid problems with quoting inside quotation marks.

After the executeQuery method has run, the resultset object can be iterated to obtain all rows. The number of columns and the column names in the result set can be obtained from the getMetaData method. Its syntax is

```
ResultSetMetaData rsMeta = rs.getMetaData();
```

At this point, the getColumnCount and getColumnName methods can be invoked on rsMeta as you will see in the examples that follow.

PREPARED STATEMENTS AND CALLABLE STATEMENTS Prepared Statement objects and Callable Statement objects can be used to invoke compiled queries and stored procedures in the database. Their use is similar to the use of the Command object discussed in Chapter 15. Because neither compiled queries nor stored procedures are supported by MySQL we will not use them in the examples in this chapter.

To illustrate a callable statement, however, suppose we are processing the View Ridge database created with Oracle in Chapter 12 and that we want to invoke the CustomerInsert stored procedure. Assume in the following that *conn* has been set to a connection to the Oracle View Ridge database:

```
CallableStatement cs = conn.prepareCall ("{call CustomerInsert(?, ?, ?, ?)}");
cs.setString (1, "Mary Johnson");
cs.setString (2, "212");
cs.setString (3, "555–1234");
cs.setString (4, "US");
cs.execute();
```

This sequence, which would invoke the CustomerInsert stored procedure with the data shown, is very similar to that shown for ODBC in the last chapter. It is possible to receive values back from procedures as well, but that is beyond the scope of our discussion. See http://java.sun.com/products/jdk/1.1/docs/guide/jdbc for more information.

Figure 16-2 summarizes JDBC components. The application creates Connection, Statement, ResultSet, and ResultSetMetaData objects. Calls from these objects are routed via the DriverManager to the proper driver. Drivers then process their databases. Notice that the Oracle database in this figure could be processed via either a JDBC-ODBC bridge or via a pure JDBC driver.

JDBC Examples

Figures 16-3 and 16-4 present two examples using the mm.mysql JDBC drivers and MySQL. Note that both of these programs import java.sql.*. Also, note that the JDBC drivers are not imported; they are loaded instead. If you try to import them, the result is a mess.

The database used in all of these examples is the View Ridge database shown in Figure 10-3(d). Tables in the database are

CUSTOMER(<u>CustomerID</u>, Name, AreaCode, PhoneNumber, Street, City, State, Zip)
ARTIST (<u>ArtistID</u>, Name, Nationality, Birthdate, DeceasedDate)
CUSTOMER_ARTIST_INT (<u>*CustomerID, ArtistID*</u>)
WORK (<u>WorkID</u>, Description, Title, Copy *ArtistID*)
TRANSACTION (<u>TransactionID</u>, DateAcquired, PurchasePrice, SalesPrice, *CustomerID, WorkID*)

Relationships and referential integrity are as described in Chapter 10.

JDBC Components

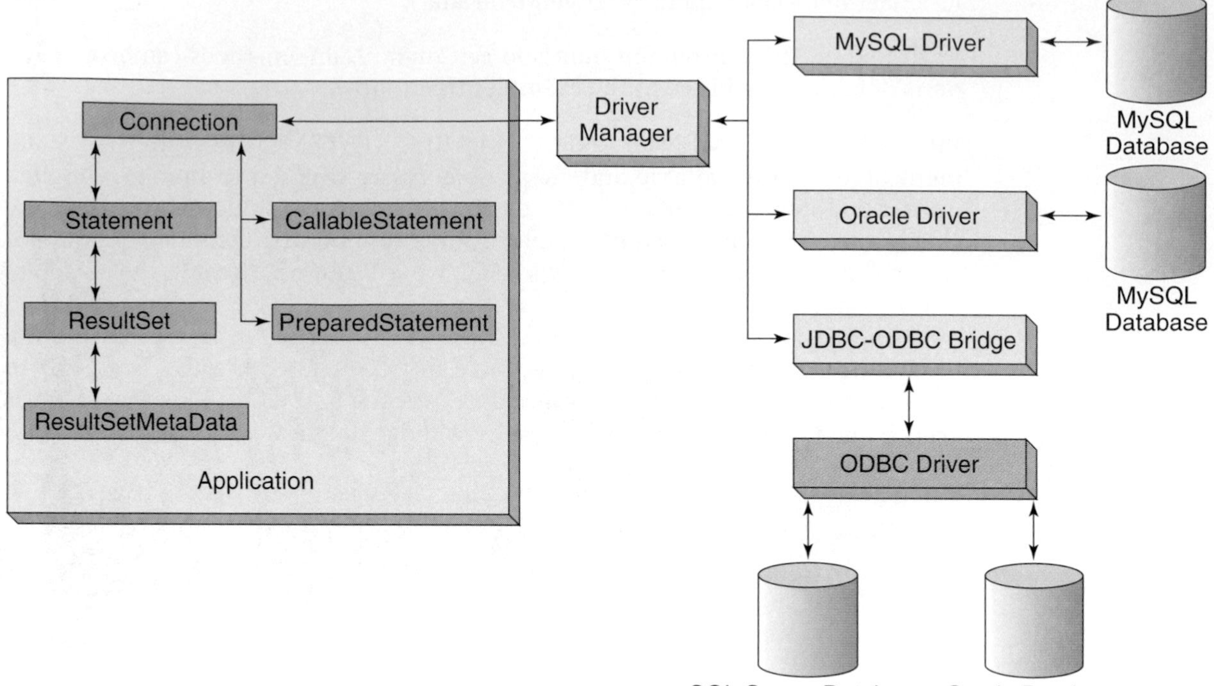

THE GeneralTable CLASS Figure 16-3 shows the Java class GeneralTable. It accepts a single parameter that is the name of a table in the MySQL database vr1. MySQL is case sensitive, and all table names in the database were created in uppercase letters. Thus, the code must convert the input table name to uppercase.

This example is a straightforward application of the concepts we just described. The GeneralTable class has a publicly accessible method that returns no parameters. (That's the meaning of "public static void main.") The program checks for at least one parameter, sets the variable varTableName to the input table name, and converts that name to uppercase. It then processes the database using the JDBC drivers in a try block. A try block is used because many of the methods throw exceptions; these exceptions will be caught in the catch block.

All exception handling is kept generic in these examples. If you program in Java you will see many ways to improve exception handling from that shown here. We're after database concepts, now, however.

If you do not program in Java, just assume that all statements that appear in the try block, denoted by "try { . . . . . }," are what happens under normal circumstances. All statements that appear in the catch block, denoted "catch { . . . }," are what happens when an error occurs. Also, like SQL, in Java a multiline comment is started with "/*" and terminated with "*/." A single line comment is started with "//."

The mm.mysql drivers are loaded as described above and then a Connection object conn and a Statement object stmt are created. The database is vr1 and the user is dk1. There is no password. (For this to work, user dk1 must have been defined in MySQL and granted permission to use database vr1 without a password. We will discuss these actions in the last section.)

A ResultSetMetaData named rsMeta is then created for the result set rs. Once this has been done, the column names are obtained and printed in one long string (varColumnNames). Then rs is iterated and each column in each row is displayed. The output is not pretty, but it works and gets us started.

A typical display is

Showing Table ARTIST

Trying connection with jdbc:mysql://localhost/vr1?user=dk1

Name Nationality Birthdate DeceasedDate ArtistID

Miro Spanish null null 1

➤ FIGURE 16-3

GeneralTable Class

```
import java.io.*;
import java.sql.*;

public class GeneralTable {

      /** A Java program to present the contents of any table
       *  Call with one parameter which is table name --
       *  table name parameter will be converted to uppercase
       */

      public static void main(String[] args) {
            if (args.length <1) {
                  System.out.println ("Insufficient data provided.");
                  return;
            }

            String varTableName = args[0];
            varTableName = varTableName.toUpperCase();
            System.out.println ("Showing Table " + varTableName);
            try {

                  //  Load the MySQL JDBC classes from Mark Mathews
                  //       mm.mysql.jdbc-1.2c

                  Class.forName("org.gjt.mm.mysql.Driver").newInstance();

                  // Set connect string to local MySQL database, user is dk1
                  String connString = "jdbc:mysql://localhost/vr1?user=dk1";

                  System.out.println (" Trying connection with " + connString);
                  Connection conn = DriverManager.getConnection(connString);

                  // Get result set
                  Statement stmt = conn.createStatement();
                  String varSQL = "SELECT * FROM " + varTableName;
                  ResultSet rs = stmt.executeQuery(varSQL);

                  // Get meta data on just opened result set
                  ResultSetMetaData rsMeta = rs.getMetaData();
```

➤ FIGURE 16-3

(Continued)

```
        // Display column names as string
        String varColNames ="";
        int varColCount = rsMeta.getColumnCount();
        for (int col =1; col <= varColCount; col++) {
              varColNames = varColNames + rsMeta.getColumnName(col) +" ";
        }
        System.out.println(varColNames);

        // Display column values
        while (rs.next()) {
              for (int col = 1; col <= varColCount; col++) {
                    System.out.print(rs.getString(col) + "    ");
              }
              System.out.println();
        }

        // Clean up
        rs.close();
        stmt.close();
        conn.close();

  }

  catch (Exception e) {
        e.printStackTrace();
  }
```

Tobey US null null 2
Van Vronken US null null 3
Matisse French null null 4

Like I said, it's not pretty!

THE CustomerInsert CLASS Figure 16-4 shows a second Java program that updates the vr1 database. This program implements the logic for the View Ridge CustomerInsert procedure as described in Chapters 10, 12, 13, and 15. (Are you tired of it yet? At least the logic is familiar!)

As you recall, this procedure accepts four parameters: a new customer's Name, AreaCode, LocalNumber, and the Nationality of all artists in whom the customer maintains an interest. These parameters are received by the main procedure and passed to the method InsertData. The InsertData method is not necessary here; we could have a single method class as in Figure 16-3. The logic is isolated in a separate method here because in the next section we will transform this method into a Java bean. That transformation will be easier if we isolate the code here.

The InsertData method first loads the drivers and then sets up a connection string to vr1 for user dk1. Next it checks for duplicate data by querying vr1 for the input Name, AreaCode, and LocalNumber. If one is found, a message is printed and the resultset, statement, and connection are closed. Otherwise, a new row is inserted in CUSTOMER.

CustomerID, which is the surrogate key column for CUSTOMER, has been defined as an AUTO_INCREMENT column in the database. Thus, no value need be provided for it. MySQL will set it.

If the insert is successful, the variable *result* should not equal zero; if it does, an error occurred during the update. In that case, a message is printed and the objects are cleaned up. Assuming no error occurred, the value of CustomerID is read back from the database, and then rows are inserted in the intersection table CUSTOMER_ARTIST_INT. This is very similar to the logic shown for the CustomerInsert stored procedures in Oracle and SQL Server.

In this code section, the variable *result* is not checked for zero; a better version of this program would do so. And, in fact, if you are a Java programmer, you know

➤ FIGURE 16-4

CustomerInsert Class

```
import java.io.*;
import java.sql.*;

public class CustomerInsert {

      /** A Java implementation of the View Ridge Galleries CustomerInsert procedure.
       *  Receives values Customer Name, AreaCode, LocalNumber and Nationality
       *  Inserts the new customer if not already in the database and then
       *  connects that customer to Artists of the given nationality by
       *  adding appropriate rows to the intersection table.
       */

      public static void main(String[] args) {

            if (args.length < 4) {
                  System.out.println ("Insufficient data provided");
                  return;
            }

            String varName = args[0];
            String varAreaCode = args[1];
            String varLocalNumber = args[2];
            String varNationality = args[3];

            insertData(varName, varAreaCode, varLocalNumber, varNationality);

      }

      public static void insertData(String varName,
                                    String varAreaCode,
                                    String varLocalNumber,
                                    String varNationality) {

            System.out.println ("Adding row for " + varName);
            try {

                  // Load JDBC driver class from Mark Mathews
                  // mm.mysql.jdbc-1.2c

                  Class.forName("org.gjt.mm.mysql.Driver").newInstance();
```

➤ FIGURE 16-4

(Continued)

```
// Set up connection to db vr1 with user dk1, no password
String connString = "jdbc:mysql://localhost/" + "vr1" + "?user=dk1";
System.out.println (" Trying connection with " + connString);
Connection conn = DriverManager.getConnection(connString);

// If we get here, we have a connection.  Now check for duplicated data
Statement stmt = conn.createStatement();
String varSQL = "SELECT Name ";
String varWhere = "FROM CUSTOMER WHERE Name= '";
varWhere = varWhere + varName + "' AND AreaCode = '";
varWhere = varWhere + varAreaCode + "' AND PhoneNumber = '";
varWhere = varWhere + varLocalNumber + "'";
varSQL = varSQL + varWhere;

ResultSet rs = stmt.executeQuery(varSQL);
while (rs.next()) {
      // if get here, there is duplicate data
      System.out.println
      ("Data duplicates an existing customer.  No changes made.");
      rs.close();
      stmt.close();
      conn.close();
      return;
}

// OK to insert new data
varSQL = "INSERT INTO CUSTOMER (Name, AreaCode, PhoneNumber)";
varSQL = varSQL + " VALUES ('" + varName + "', '";
varSQL = varSQL + varAreaCode + "', '";
varSQL = varSQL + varLocalNumber + "')";

int result = stmt.executeUpdate(varSQL);
if (result == 0) {
      System.out.println ("Problem with insert");
      rs.close();
      stmt.close();
      conn.close();
      return;
}
```

that all of these error messages and clean up activities should be done using exceptions. We're stepping around those issues to focus on the database-only matters.

Given this quick introduction to JDBC, we will now discuss its use in Java Server Pages.

➤ FIGURE 16-4

(Continued)

```
        // Update OK, add intersection rows - first get new ID
        varSQL = "SELECT CustomerID " + varWhere;
        rs = stmt.executeQuery(varSQL);
        String varCid ="";
        while (rs.next()) {
              varCid = rs.getString(1);
              if (varCid == "0" ) {
                    System.out.println("Can't find new CustomerID");
                    rs.close();
                    stmt.close();
                    conn.close();
                    return;
              }
        }

        // Now add to intersection table
        varSQL = "SELECT ArtistID FROM ARTIST WHERE Nationality = '" + varNationality +"'";
        String varInsertStart = "INSERT INTO CUSTOMER_ARTIST_INT (CustomerID, ArtistID) VALUES ("
                        →+ varCid +", ";
        String varInsertEnd = ")";
        rs = stmt.executeQuery(varSQL);
        System.out.println("Adding intersection values for customer " + varCid);
        while (rs.next()) {
              result = stmt.executeUpdate(varInsertStart + rs.getString(1) + varInsertEnd);
        }

        // Clean up
        rs.close();
        stmt.close();
        conn.close();

        }

  catch (Exception e){
        e.printStackTrace();
```

➤ JAVA SERVER PAGES

Java Server Pages (JSP) provide a means to create dynamic Web pages using HTML (and XML) and the Java programming language. Java Server Pages look very much like Active Server Pages, but this is deceiving because the underlying technology is quite different. JSP and ASP look similar because they both blend HTML with program code. The difference is that ASP are restricted to using scripting languages like VBScript or JScript. With JSP, however, the coding is done in Java, and only in Java—neither VBScript nor JScript is allowed. With Java, the capabilities of a complete object-oriented language are directly available to the Web page developer.

Because Java is machine independent, JSP pages are also machine independent. With JSP you are not locked into using Windows 2000 and IIS. You can run the same JSP page on a Linux server and on a Windows server and on others as well.

The official specification for JSP can be found at http://java.sun.com/products/jsp.

JSP Pages and Servlets

JSP pages are transformed into standard Java language and then compiled just like a regular program. In particular, they are transformed into Java servlets, which means that, behind the scenes, JSP pages are transformed into subclasses of the HttpServlet class. JSP code thus has access to the HTTP request and response objects, their methods and other HTTP functionality as well.

Because JSP pages are converted into servlet subclasses, you do not need to code complete Java classes or methods in a JSP page. You can insert snippets of Java code wherever you like and they will be placed correctly into a servlet subclass when the page is parsed. Thus, you could plop the following statements into a JSP page without any other Java code and they would execute just fine:

```
<% String partyName ="fiesta";
partyName = partyName.toUpperCase();
out.println ("Come to our " + partyName); %>
```

In this case, the string "Come to our FIESTA" would be displayed in the browser when this section of the JSP page is processed. By the way, note that Java code is isolated between <% and %> just as VBScript and JScript are in ASP pages.

In order to use JSP pages, your Web server must implement the Java servlet 2.1+ and the Java Server Pages 1.0+ specifications. You can check http://java.sun.com/products/servlet/industry.html for a list of servers that support these specifications. There are at least a half a dozen or so possibilities. For the rest of this chapter we will use Apache Tomcat for this purpose.

Apache Tomcat

As of December 2000, the Apache Web server does not support servlets. However, the Apache foundation and Sun cosponsored the Jakarta Project that developed a servlet processor named Apache Tomcat. You can obtain the source and binary of Tomcat from the Jakarta Project Web site at http://jakarta.apache.org.

Tomcat is a servlet processor that can work in conjunction with Apache or can work as a stand-alone Web server. Tomcat has limited Web server facilities, however, so it is normally used in stand-alone mode only for testing servlets and JSP pages. For commercial, production applications, Tomcat should be used in conjunction with Apache.

If you are running Tomcat and Apache separately on the same Web server, they need to use different ports. The default port for a Web server is 80 and normally Apache uses it. When used in stand-alone mode, Tomcat is usually configured to listen to port 8080, though this, of course, can be changed.

In the examples that follow, Tomcat is using port 8080. These examples were run on a private intranet in which the Tomcat server machine was assigned the IP address 10.0.0.3. Thus, to invoke the page *somepage.jsp* we will use the string http://10.0.0.3:8080/somepage.jsp in the browser address field.

Setting Up Tomcat for JSP Processing

When you install Tomcat, it will create a directory structure into which you must place class libraries and Web pages. As of the 3.1 Tomcat release, place class libraries in the *install-dir*/lib directory and place JSP pages in the *install-dir*/webapps/ROOT/WEB-INF/classes directory. On Linux, the RPM utility installs Tomcat in the directory /usr/local/jakarta-tomcat/ by default. Hence, in this case, place the class libraries into /usr/local/jakarta-tomcat/lib and the JSP pages into /usr/local/jakarta-tomcat/webapps/ROOT/WEB-INF/classes. If you are installing with other operating systems, or installing a different servlet processor altogether, you should consult your documentation.

When installing new class files in the lib subdirectory, there is a small "gotcha." Tomcat creates its CLASSPATH when it is started. Therefore, after you have installed a new class file into the lib directory, you must stop and restart Tomcat before it will see your new file. If you just copy the new file into the lib subdirectory without restarting Tomcat, you will receive class not found exceptions. (Trust me, I know. . . .)

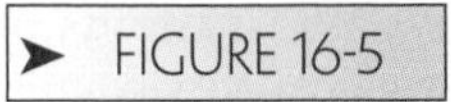
FIGURE 16-5

JSP Compilation Process

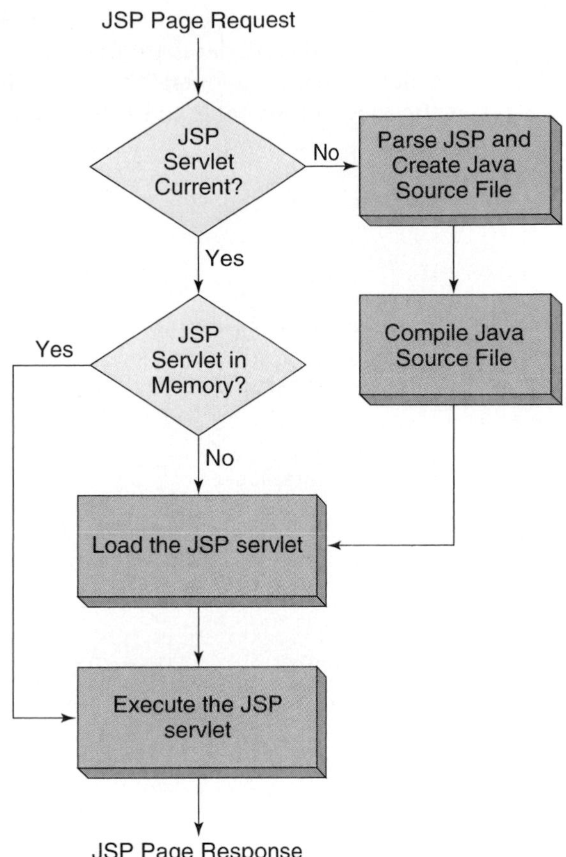

The JSP pages to follow all use the mm.mysql MySQL drivers. To work, the appropriate driver class library must be placed into the lib subdirectory. For these examples, the file "mm_uncomp.jar" was installed in that directory.

Figure 16-5 shows the process by which JSP pages are compiled. When a request for a JSP page is received, a Tomcat (or other) servlet processor finds the compiled version of the page and checks to determine if it is current. It does this by looking for an uncompiled version of the page having a creation date and time later than the compiled page's creation date and time. If the page is not current, the new page is parsed and transformed into a Java source file and that source file is then compiled. The servlet is then loaded and executed. If the compiled JSP page is current, then it is loaded into memory if not already there and then executed. If it is in memory, then it is simply executed.

(By the way, the downside of such automatic compilation is that if you make syntax errors and forget to test your pages, the first user to access your page will receive the compiler errors!)

Unlike CGI files and some other Web server programs, there is a maximum of one copy of a JSP page in memory at a time. Further, pages are executed by one of Tomcat's threads and not by an independent process. This means much less memory and processor time will be required to execute a JSP page than to execute a comparable CGI script.

JSP Examples

This section discusses two simple JSP pages. The first is a JSP version of the GeneralTable class shown in Figure 16-3. The second encapsulates the logic in Figure 16-4 in a Java bean and then invokes that bean from a JSP page.

GeneralTable.JSP Figure 16-6 shows a JSP page that displays the contents of any table in the MySQL database named vr1. The format and logic of this page is very similar to that in GeneralTable.asp in Figure 15-21. Here we assume the user passes the name of the table to be displayed as a parameter to the page.

➤ FIGURE 16-6

GeneralTable.jsp

```
<!DOCTYPE HTML PUBLIC "-//W3C//DTD HTML 4.0 Transitional//EN">
<!-- Example of Database Access from a JSP Page -->
<%@ page import="java.sql.*" %>
<HTML>
<HEAD>
<TITLE>Table Display Using JDBC and MySQL</TITLE>
<META NAME="author" CONTENT="David Kroenke">
<META NAME="keywords"
      CONTENT="JSP,JDBC,Database Access">
<META NAME="description"
      CONTENT="An example of displaying a table using JSP.">
<LINK REL=STYLESHEET HREF="JSP-Styles.css" TYPE="text/css">
</HEAD>
<BODY>
<H2>Database Access Example</H2>
<% String varTableName= request.getParameter("Table");
   varTableName = varTableName.toUpperCase(); %>
<H3>Showing Data from MySQL Database vr1</H3>
<%
try     {
    // Load the Mark Mathew MySQL JDBC Drivers
    Class.forName("org.gjt.mm.mysql.Driver").newInstance();

    // Connect to vr1 with user dk1
    String connString = "jdbc:mysql://localhost/" + "vr1" + "?user=dk1";
         Connection conn = DriverManager.getConnection(connString);

    // Get rs and rsMeta for the SELECT statement
    Statement stmt = conn.createStatement();
    String varSQL = "SELECT * FROM " + varTableName;
    ResultSet rs = stmt.executeQuery(varSQL);
    ResultSetMetaData rsMeta = rs.getMetaData();
%>
<TABLE BORDER=1 BGCOLOR=#ffffff CELLSPACING=5><FONT FACE="Arial" COLOR=#000000
><CAPTION><B><%=varTableName%></B></CAPTION></FONT>
<THEAD>
<TR><%
    String varColNames ="";
    int varColCount = rsMeta.getColumnCount();
    for (int col =1; col <= varColCount; col++) {
         %><TH BGCOLOR=#c0c0c0 BORDERCOLOR=#000000 ><FONT SIZE=2 FACE ="Arial" COLOR=#000000
         ><%=rsMeta.getColumnName(col)%></FONT> </TH>
<%  }%>
</TR>
</THEAD>
<TBODY><%
    while (rs.next()) {
          %><TR VALIGN=TOP><%
                for (int col = 1; col <= varColCount; col++) {
              %><TD BORDERCOLOR=#C0C0C0 ><FONT SIZE=2 FACE="Arial" COLOR=#000000
              ><%=rs.getString(col)%><BR></FONT></TD>
<%       }
    }
         // Clean up
         rs.close();
         stmt.close();
         conn.close();
}
catch (ClassNotFoundException e) {
    out.println("Driver Exception  " + e);
}%>
</TR>
</TBODY>
<TFOOT></TFOOT>
</TABLE>
</BODY>
</HTML>
```

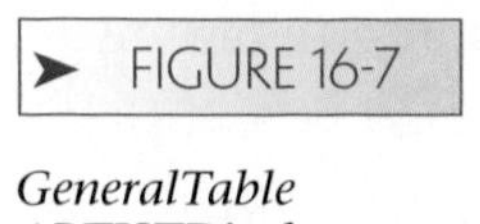

GeneralTable ARTISTDisplay

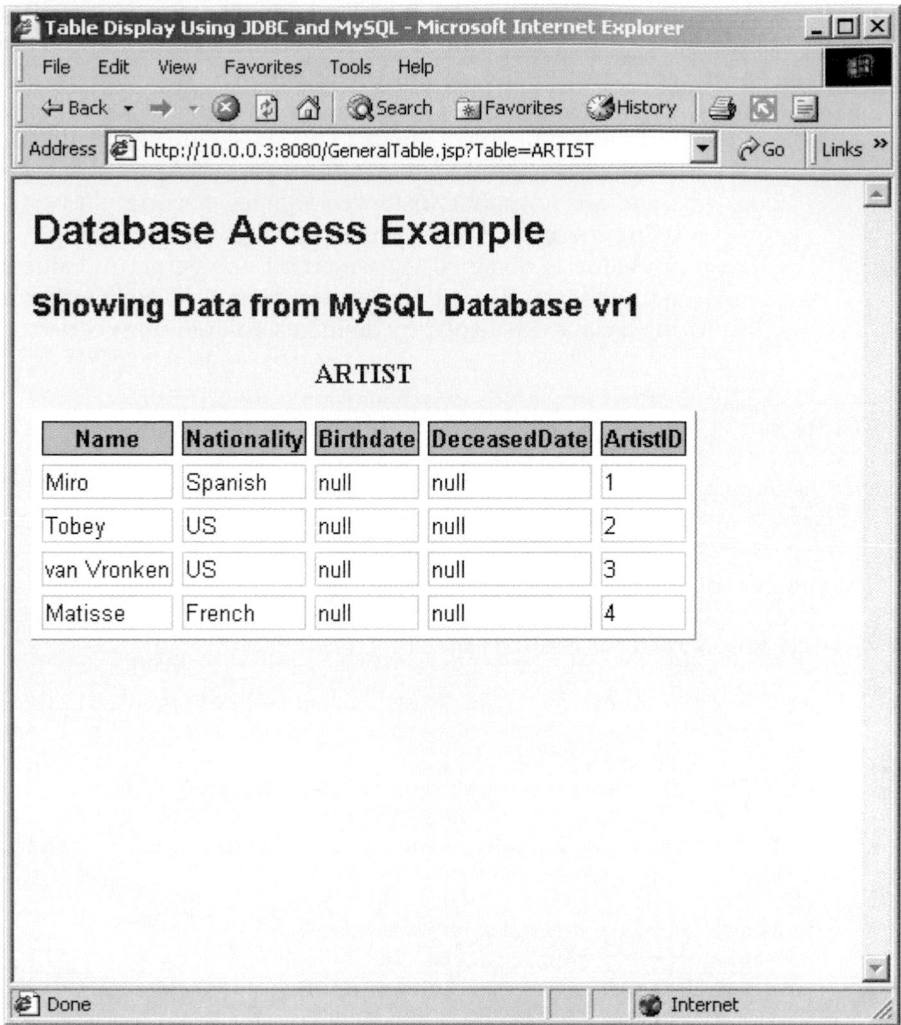

Figure 16-7 shows the results of invoking this page using Internet Explorer on a Windows 2000 computer. The page itself was processed by Tomcat on a Linux computer. Note the call to port 8080; in production, Tomcat would be running with Apache on default port 80 and this port specification would not be needed.

In Figure 16-6, all Java code is shown in red ink. The first line invokes a page directory, which imports the java.sql library. Then, the parameter having the table name is obtained using the HTTP request object method getParameter. The value is set to uppercase. Next, the JDBC classes are loaded as was done in Figure 16-3 and a Connection is created to the vr1 database for user dk1. The rest of the code is the same as that in Figure 16-4—it is just spread among the HTML statements used for displaying results.

Again, this page appears deceptively similar to the ASP version of this page, GeneralTable.asp, shown in Chapter 15. The difference is not just that JDBC is used instead of ADO and ODBC. An even greater difference is that this page will be compiled into a Java program, and hence is portable and will be faster.

CustomerInsertUsingBean.JSP Because Java is used with JSP pages, the full capabilities of an object-oriented program are available. This means that JSP pages can invoke precompiled objects. Doing this is important and useful for a number of reasons. For one, it separates the tasks of writing program logic from generating HTML. Organizations can have different groups and people working on these two, very different, tasks. It also enables logic to be encapsulated into independent modules for reuse and the other benefits of encapsulation. Finally, it reduces the complexity of managing a Web site.

(If you are not a Java programmer, ignore the following paragraph. Think of a bean as a properly mannered Java class. One you could take home to meet Mother.)

In simple terms, a Java bean is a Java class that has three properties: First, there are no public instance variables. Second, all persistent values are accessed using methods named getxxx and setxxx. For example, a persistent value named myValue is obtained via a method named getmyValue() and is set by a method named setmyValue(). Finally, the bean class must either have no constructors or it must have one explicitly defined zero-argument constructor.

➤ FIGURE 16-8

CustomerInsertBean Class

```
import java.io.*;
import java.sql.*;

public class CustomerInsertBean {

      /** A Java bean for the View Ridge Galleries CustomerInsert procedure.
       *  Persistent values obtained by accessors getxxx and setxxx
       *
       *  Inserts the new customer if not already in the database and then
       *  connects that customer to Artists of the given nationality by
       *  adding appropriate rows to the intersection table.
       */

      private String newName = "unknown";
      private String newAreaCode = "";
      private String newLocalNumber = "";
      private String newNationality = "";


      public String getnewName() {
            return(newName);
      }

      public void setnewName(String newName) {
            if (newName != null) {
                  this.newName = newName;
            } else {

                  this.newName = "unknown";
            }
      }

      public String getnewAreaCode() {
            return(newAreaCode);
      }

      public void setnewAreaCode(String newAreaCode) {
            if (newAreaCode != null) {
                  this.newAreaCode = newAreaCode;
            } else {
                  this.newName = "";
```

continued at top of next page

► FIGURE 16-8

(Continued)

```
public String getnewLocalNumber() {
      return(newLocalNumber);
}

public void setnewLocalNumber (String newLocalNumber) {
      if (newLocalNumber != null) {
            this.newLocalNumber = newLocalNumber;
      } else {
            this.newName = "";
      }
}

public String getnewNationality() {
      return(newNationality);
}

public void setnewNationality(String newNationality) {
      if (newNationality != null) {
            this.newNationality = newNationality;
      } else {
            this.newName = "";
      }
}


public String InsertData() {

      try {

            // Load JDBC driver class from Mark Mathews
            // mm.mysql.jdbc-1.2c

            Class.forName("org.gjt.mm.mysql.Driver").newInstance();

            // Set up connection to db vrl with user dkl, no password
            String connString = "jdbc:mysql://localhost/" + "vrl" + "?user=dkl";
            Connection conn = DriverManager.getConnection(connString);

            // If we get here, we have a connection.  Now check for duplicated data
```

continued on following page

Figure 16-8 shows a Java bean named CustomerInsertUsingBean. This class has a method that implements the View Ridge Gallery CustomerInsert procedure (yes, it's BAAAACK!!!, but this is the last time). This class has four persistent values—newName, newAreaCode, newLocalNumber, and newNationality. For each of these persistent values, getXXX and setXXX accessor methods are defined. There are no public persistent values and there is no constructor method. Hence, CustomerInsertUsingBean meets the requirements for a bean.

The actual update procedure is coded in a method named InsertData. This method is identical to the InsertData method in Figure 16-4.

Figure 16-9(a) shows a data entry form to gather the new customer data. The HTML page for this form is shown in Figure 16-9(b). Note that the FORM ACTION value is CustomerInsertUsingBean.jsp. Also observe that the text boxes are named newName, NewAreaCode, NewLocalNumber, and newNationality. These names matter because when the Add Customer button is clicked, CustomerInsertUsingBean.jsp will be passed parameters with those names. JSP

➤ FIGURE 16-8

(Continued)

```
Statement stmt = conn.createStatement();
String varSQL = "SELECT Name ";
String varWhere = "FROM CUSTOMER WHERE Name= '";
varWhere = varWhere + newName + "' AND AreaCode = '";
varWhere = varWhere + newAreaCode + "' AND PhoneNumber = '";
varWhere = varWhere + newLocalNumber + "'";
varSQL = varSQL + varWhere;
ResultSet rs = stmt.executeQuery(varSQL);
while (rs.next()) {
      // if get here, there is duplicate data
      rs.close();
      stmt.close();
      conn.close();
      return ("Duplicate data - no action taken");
}

// OK to insert new data
varSQL = "INSERT INTO CUSTOMER (Name, AreaCode, PhoneNumber)";
varSQL = varSQL + " VALUES ('" + newName + "', '";
varSQL = varSQL + newAreaCode + "', '";
varSQL = varSQL + newLocalNumber + "')";
int result = stmt.executeUpdate(varSQL);
if (result == 0) {
      // if get here, there is a problem with insert
      rs.close();
      stmt.close();
      conn.close();
      return ("Problem with insert");
}

// Update OK, add intersection rows - first get new ID
varSQL = "SELECT CustomerID " + varWhere;
rs = stmt.executeQuery(varSQL);
String varCid ="";
while (rs.next()) {
      varCid = rs.getString(1);
      if (varCid == "0" ) {
            // if get here, can't find new CustomerID
            rs.close();
            stmt.close();
            conn.close();
            return ("Can't find new customer after insert");
```

continued on following page

can match the input parameters with same-named object properties when told to do so, as you will see.

The JSP page CustomerInsertUsingBean.jsp is listed in Figure 16-10. The important statements in this page are the two jsp statements

<jsp:useBean id="insert" class="CustomerInsertBean" />

FIGURE 16-8

(Continued)

```
        }
}

// Now add to intersection table
varSQL = "SELECT ArtistID FROM ARTIST WHERE Nationality = '"
                                    + newNationality +"'";
String varInsertStart = "INSERT INTO CUSTOMER_ARTIST_INT
                        (CustomerID, ArtistID) VALUES
            → (" + varCid +", ";
String varInsertEnd = ")";
rs = stmt.executeQuery(varSQL);
while (rs.next()) {
      result = stmt.executeUpdate
          (varInsertStart + rs.getString(1) + varInsertEnd);
}

// Clean up
rs.close();
stmt.close();
conn.close();
return("Success");
}

catch (Exception e){
      return ("Exception: " + e );
}
```

and

<jsp:setProperty name="insert" property="*" />

The first statement tells the JSP compiler to load the class CustomerInsertBean and to affiliate it with the name *insert*. For this to work with Tomcat 3.1, a compiled version of the bean named CustomerInsertBean.class must reside in the directory *install-dir*/webapps/ROOT/WEB-INF/classes. For the standard RPM install, this would be /usr/local/jakarta-tomcat/webapps/ROOT/WEB-INF/classes.

The second jsp: statement tells the JSP parser to set the class properties using form input parameters. The "*" signals that all properties should be matched with same-named parameters. This statement is a shorthand substitute for the following:

```
<jsp:setProperty name="insert"
      property="newName"
      value='<%= request.getParameter("newName") %>' />
<jsp:setProperty name="insert"
      property="newAreaCode"
      value='<%= request.getParameter("newAreaCode") %>' />
<jsp:setProperty name="insert"
      property="newLocalNumber"
      value='<%= request.getParameter("newLocalNumber") %>' />
<jsp:setProperty name="insert"
      property="newName"
      value='<%= request.getParameter("newNationality") %>' />
```

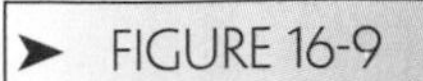

FIGURE 16-9

New Customer Data Entry Form: (a) NewCustomer Form, (b) HTML for NewCustomer Form

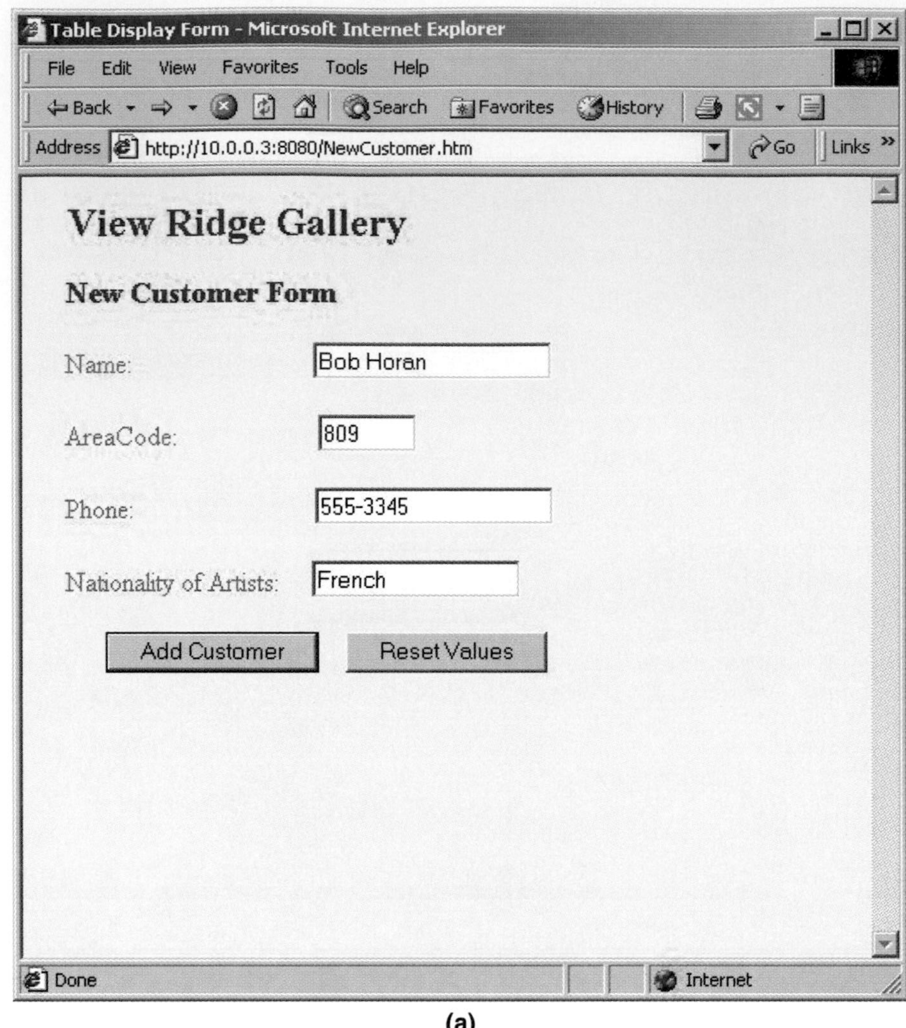

(a)

Of course, either version can be used. In fact, the longer version is required if the names of the form parameters are different from the names of the object properties.

In Figure 16-10, the InsertData method is invoked by the statement

```
String result=insert.InsertData();
```

If the result is not "Success," the result message is printed. Otherwise, the join of the CUSTOMER, CUSTOMER_ARTIST_INT, ARTIST tables is displayed using code very similar to that in Figure 16-3. The result appears as in Figure 16-11.

This is a very short introduction to JSP development. There is much more to use and understand, but a longer discussion is beyond the scope of this text. An excellent reference on this topic is *Core Servlets and Java Server Pages* by Marty Hall.[1]

---

[1]Marty Hall, *Core Servlets and Java Server Pages*. Upper Saddle River, NJ: Prentice Hall, 2000.

➤ FIGURE 16-9

(Continued)

```
<HTML>
<HEAD>
<META HTTP-EQUIV="Content-Type" CONTENT="text/html">
<TITLE>Table Display Form</TITLE>
<LINK REL=STYLESHEET HREF="JSP-Styles.css" TYPE="text/css">
</HEAD>
<BODY>

<FORM METHOD="post" ACTION="CustomerInsertUsingBean.jsp">

 <P><STRONG><FONT color=purple face="" size=5>   View Ridge
Gallery</FONT></STRONG>

 <P>   <strong><font color="purple" face size="4"> New Customer
Form</font></strong><P><font style="background-color: #FDF5EC"
color="forestgreen" face>   
 Name:   </font><FONT style="BACKGROUND-COLOR:
#FDF5EC">           &nbs
p;           
 </FONT><INPUT id=newName name=newName></P>

 <P> <font style="background-color: #FDF5EC" color="forestgreen"
face>   AreaCode<font style="background-color:
#FDF5E6">:   </font>       &n
bsp;         
 </font><INPUT id=newAreaCode name=newAreaCode size="6"></P>

 <P><font style="background-color: #FDF5EC" color="forestgreen"
face>   

Phone:            &
nbsp;            &n
bsp;
 </font><INPUT id=newLocalNumber name=newLocalNumber
size="20">         </P>

 <P>    <font style="background-color: #FDF5EC"
color="forestgreen" face>Nationality
 of Artists:  </font>   <INPUT id=newNationality
name=newNationality size="17"></P>

 <P> <FONT style="BACKGROUND-COLOR: #FDF5EC">
   </FONT>     <FONT style="BACKGROUND-
COLOR: #FDF5EC">
<INPUT id=submit1 name=submit1 type=submit value="Add Customer"
>   
<INPUT id=reset1 name=reset1 type=reset value="Reset Values"></FONT></P>

</FORM>
</BODY>
</HTML>
```

(b)

➤ FIGURE 16-10

Customer Insert Using Bean.jsp

```
<!DOCTYPE HTML PUBLIC "-//W3C//DTD HTML 4.0 Transitional//EN">
<!--
Example of Database Access from a JSP Page
-->
<%@ page import="java.sql.*" %>
<HTML>
<HEAD>
<TITLE>Updating Using a Java Bean</TITLE>
<META NAME="author" CONTENT="David Kroenke">
<META NAME="keywords"
      CONTENT="JSP,JDBC, Database Access">
<META NAME="description"
      CONTENT="An example of invoking a bean and displaying results.">
<LINK REL=STYLESHEET HREF="JSP-Styles.css" TYPE="text/css">
</HEAD>
<BODY>
<H2>Database Update Using JDBC from a Java Bean</H2>
<H3>Processing the View Ridge Customer Insert for MySQL Database vr1</H3>
<jsp:useBean id="insert" class="CustomerInsertBean" />
<jsp:setProperty name="insert" property="*" />
<%
//  Bean properites were set in statement above, now call the
//  bean for insert
String result=insert.InsertData();

if (result != "Success") {
    // print problem and return
    out.println("Problem" + result);
    return;
}
//  Data was inserted successfully; now display the intersection table
try     {
    // Load the Mark Mathew MySQL JDBC drivers
    //

    Class.forName("org.gjt.mm.mysql.Driver").newInstance();
    String connString = "jdbc:mysql://localhost/" + "vr1" + "?user=dk1";

    Connection conn = DriverManager.getConnection(connString);

    // Join Customer to Artist via intersection table
    // Note synonyms for CUSTOMER.Name and ARTIST.Name
    Statement stmt = conn.createStatement();
    String varSQL = "SELECT CUSTOMER.Name Customer, ARTIST.Name  Artist, Nationality ";
    varSQL = varSQL + "FROM CUSTOMER, CUSTOMER_ARTIST_INT, ARTIST ";
    varSQL = varSQL + "WHERE CUSTOMER.CustomerID = CUSTOMER_ARTIST_INT.CustomerID AND ";
    varSQL = varSQL + "ARTIST.ArtistID = CUSTOMER_ARTIST_INT.ArtistID";
    ResultSet rs = stmt.executeQuery(varSQL);
    ResultSetMetaData rsMeta = rs.getMetaData();
%>
<TABLE BORDER=1 BGCOLOR=#ffffff CELLSPACING=5><FONT FACE="Arial" COLOR=#000000>
<CAPTION><B>Customers and Interests</B></CAPTION></FONT>
<THEAD>
<TR><%
    String varColNames ="";
    int varColCount = rsMeta.getColumnCount();
    for (int col =1; col <= varColCount; col++) {
        %><TH BGCOLOR=#c0c0c0 BORDERCOLOR=#000000 ><FONT SIZE=2 FACE ="Arial" COLOR=#000000
        ><%=rsMeta.getColumnName(col)%></FONT> </TH>
<% }%>
</TR>
</THEAD>
<TBODY><%
    while (rs.next()) {
          %><TR VALIGN=TOP><%
        for (int col = 1; col <= varColCount; col++) { %>
                <TD BORDERCOLOR=#C0C0C0 ><FONT SIZE=2 FACE="Arial" COLOR=#000000
                ><%=rs.getString(col)%><BR></FONT></TD><%
```

➤ FIGURE 16-10

(Continued)

```
=rs.getString(col)%><BR></FONT></TD><%
        }
    }
    // Clean up
    rs.close();
    stmt.close();
    conn.close();
}
catch (ClassNotFoundException e) {
    out.println("Driver Exception  " + e);
}%>
</TR>
</TBODY>
<TFOOT></TFOOT>
</TABLE>
</BODY>
</HTML>
```

➤ FIGURE 16-11

Result from CustomerInsertUsingBean.jsp

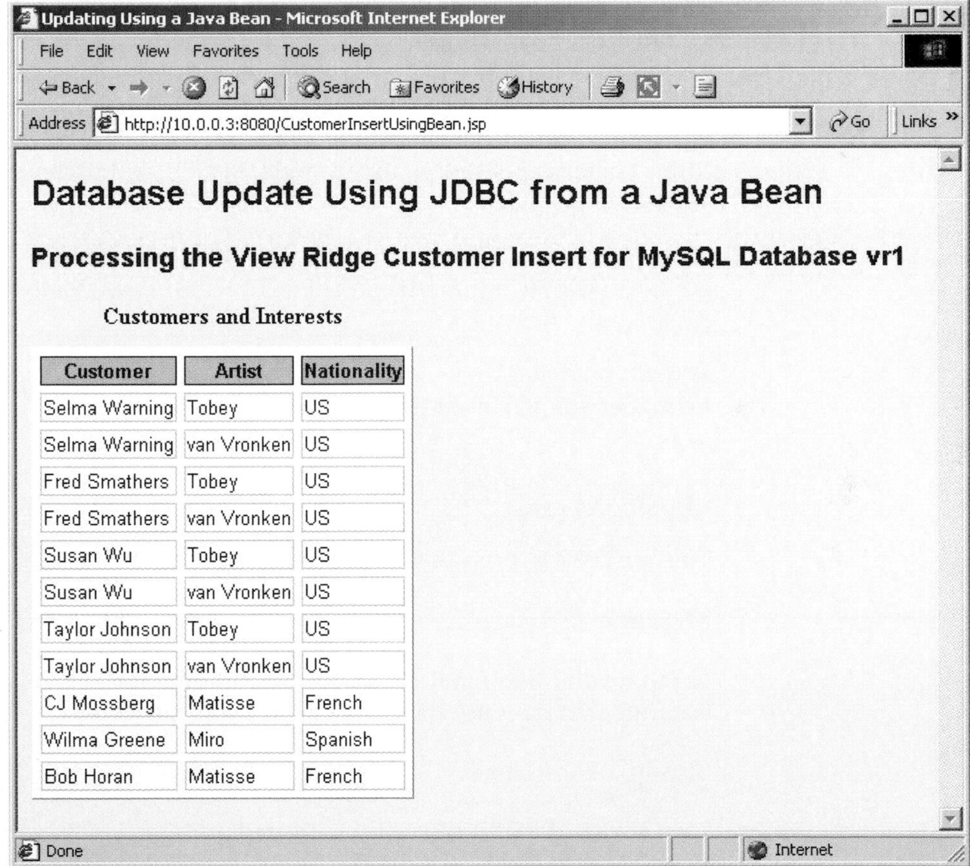

➤ MYSQL

MySQL is an open source DBMS product that runs on Unix, Linux, and Windows. You can download MySQL source and binary code from the MySQL Web site: http://www.mysql.com. The examples in this text were run on MySQL on Linux, but the examples here will work on MySQL on other operating systems as well.

As of December 2000, there was no license fee unless you build MySQL into a commercial application. See the license agreement on the MySQL site for more information.

MySQL is missing many of the capabilities of commercial DBMS products like Oracle and SQL Server, and if you have access to one of those products, you probably should use it. If, however, you're working with a low budget or if you want to participate in the open source movement, then MySQL can be a good choice. In the Linux/Unix environment, MySQL is not only cheaper than Oracle and other commercial products, it is easier to install. A good reference for MySQL is *MySQL* by Paul DuBois.[2]

Ironically, because of its limited transaction management and logging capabilities, MySQL is very fast for pure query applications. There are Web-oriented data publishing companies that maintain their databases using Oracle, but download them to MySQL for query publishing on their Web servers.

MySQL Limitations

As of release 3.x, MySQL does not support views, stored procedures, or triggers. All of these are on the MySQL to-do list, however, so check the latest documentation to determine if some of these features have been added to the product in more recent releases.

In addition, while MySQL will correctly parse foreign key (referential integrity) constraints, it does nothing with them. This means, for example, that it will parse an ON DELETE CASCADE expression in a foreign key constraint, but it will not perform the cascadings deletions that you would expect. In the View Ridge Gallery application, for example, MySQL will parse the following constraint without a problem:

```
ALTER TABLE CUSTOMER_ARTIST_INT ADD CONSTRAINT CustomerIntFK
FOREIGN KEY(CustomerID) REFERENCES CUSTOMER ON DELETE
CASCADE;
```

When you delete a row in CUSTOMER, however, the cascading deletions will not be made. You will need to make them yourself.

Using MySQL

To start MySQL from the command prompt, type

MySQL -u *username* -p

Fill in a valid user name; you will be prompted for a password. If you're using an account that does not have a password, you can enter

MySQL -u username

To see what databases have been created, type

Show databases;

Note that MySQL statements are terminated with a semicolon. Also, MySQL commands are case insensitive, but names of developer-defined constructs such as table names and column names are case sensitive.

[2]Paul DuBois, *MySQL*. Indianapolis, IN: New Riders, 2000.

USING AN EXISTING DATABASE To use one of the existing databases, enter

Use *databasename*;

For example,

Use vr1;

To determine the tables in this database, enter

Show tables;

You can display the table metadata with the describe command

Describe CUSTOMER;

At this point, any standard SQL statement can be used. SELECT, UPDATE, INSERT, and DELETE work as you would expect.

CREATING A NEW DATABASE To create a new database, sign on to MySQL with the account that you want to own the new database. Then enter

Create Database *newdatabasename*;

For example,

Create Database vr2;

The database will be created at that point and you can enter SQL create statements as we have done before. Figure 16-12 shows the statements that you can use to create the View Ridge database. All surrogate keys are given the property AUTO_INCREMENT. This data type is a sequence maintained by MySQL that starts at 1 and increases by increments of 1. Note that MySQL supports a data type of Year. This data type, which is a four-digit integer, is used for the Birthdate and DeceasedDate columns in ARTIST. Also note that no foreign key constraints are defined. As stated earlier, MySQL will parse them correctly, but will do nothing with them.

The schema in Figure 16-12 creates a unique index on (Title, Copy, ArtistID) in WORK. This unique index prevents duplicate work rows from being inserted in the database. This means the logic in the Java programs shown earlier to prevent duplicate rows is unnecessary. It doesn't hurt anything, except perhaps performance just a bit. Still, as stated in Chapter 10, it is always better to enforce integrity rules in the database, if possible.

You can type all of these statements into MySQL. If you have them in a file, however, you can import them into MySQL. Suppose the statements in Figure 16-12 are in a file named VRSQL.txt. To process them, enter the following command at a shell prompt (not in MySQL!):

command prompt$ mysql --user=dk1 --password=sesame < VRSQL.txt

This will start MySQL for user *dk1* and password *sesame* and process the statements in the text file.

Setting Access Permissions for JDBC Use

Once you understand the limitations of MySQL, it is quite easy to use. SQL statements are processed exactly as you would expect. There is one small idiosyncrasy that you should know about, however. Connections from JDBC are treated

➤ FIGURE 16-12

SQL Statements for Creating the View Ridge Database in MySQL

```
CREATE TABLE CUSTOMER(
CustomerID          int           AUTO_INCREMENT PRIMARY KEY,
Name                varchar(25)   NULL,
Street              varchar(30)   NULL,
City                varchar(35)   NULL,
State               varchar(2)    NULL,
Zip                 varchar(9)    NULL,
AreaCode            varchar(3)    NULL,
PhoneNumber         varchar(8)    NULL);

CREATE INDEX CUSTOMER_Name_IDX ON   CUSTOMER(Name);

CREATE TABLE ARTIST(
ArtistID            int           AUTO_INCREMENT PRIMARY KEY,
Name                varchar(25)   NOT NULL,
Nationality         varchar(30)   NULL,
Birthdate           year          NULL,
DeceasedDate        year          NULL);

CREATE UNIQUE INDEX ARTIST_Name_IDX ON ARTIST(Name);

CREATE TABLE WORK(
WorkID              int           AUTO_INCREMENT PRIMARY KEY,
Description         text          NULL,
Title               varchar(25)   NOT NULL,
Copy                varchar(8)    NOT NULL,
ArtistID            int           NOT NULL);

CREATE UNIQUE INDEX WORK_ID_IDX ON WORK (Title, Copy, ArtistID);

CREATE TABLE CUSTOMER_ARTIST_INT(
ArtistID            int           NOT NULL,
CustomerID          int           NOT NULL);

ALTER TABLE CUSTOMER_ARTIST_INT
 ADD
 CONSTRAINT CUST_ARTIST_PK    PRIMARY KEY ( ArtistID, CustomerID );

CREATE TABLE TRANSACTION (
TransactionID       int           AUTO_INCREMENT    PRIMARY KEY,
DateAcquired        date          NOT NULL,
AcquisitionPrice    decimal(7,2)NULL,
PurchaseDate        date          NULL,
SalesPrice          decimal(7,2)NULL,
CustomerID          int           NULL,
WorkID              int           NOT NULL);
```

differently from other user connections. To understand how to deal with this, first consider the MySQL data dictionary.

MySQL maintains metadata in the database *mysql*. Two tables of special interest are *user* and *db*. To see their metadata, open the *mysql* database and use the describe command on *user* and *db*. To see a list of users and their hosts, at the mysql prompt, enter

```
Use mysql;
SELECT Host, User FROM user;
```

To see users, hosts, and their allowed databases, enter

```
SELECT Host, User, Db FROM db;
```

Values of Host are typically "localhost" or names of the MySQL and other computers. They can also be IP addresses. A value of host of "%" means that the user can connect from anywhere.

Now, you would assume that JDBC programs running on the same machine as MySQL would be considered to arise from host localhost. This is not true. The problem is that to MySQL, localhost means connect via a socket and JDBC connections are via TCP/IP. Thus, if you want to connect using JDBC, the simplest (but least secure) method of doing so is to grant access to a database for the account you want from anywhere. The following GRANT will do this:

```
GRANT ALL ON vr1.* TO dk1@"%" IDENTIFIED BY "sesame";
```

This statement will grant all privileges to all tables in the database vr1 to the user account named dk1 with password sesame. The wildcard % indicates that dk1 can connect from any location. For better security, you could replace the wildcard with a specific IP address.

After you have executed this statement, query the db table for User, Host, Db to ensure that there is an entry for your user with host value of %. If so, you should be able to connect via JDBC to that database.

Concurrency Control

MySQL has limited support for concurrency control. As of the 3.0 release, there is no support for transactions, and hence no transaction isolation level support. It is also not possible to roll back transactions. Applications must perform their own rollback, when necessary.

MySQL uses read and write locks at the table level. When executing a SELECT statement, MySQL obtains read locks on all of the tables in the select statement. Such a lock will block other sessions from writing to any of those tables, but it will not block other reads. When executing an INSERT, UPDATE, or DELETE statement, MySQL obtains write looks on all of the tables involved. Such a lock will block other sessions from either reading or writing. The result of this locking strategy is that consistent data is read or updated on a SQL statement-by-statement basis. All of the data read or written is desired.

A programmer can work around the lack of transactions by placing the LOCK TABLES/UNLOCK TABLES commands around transaction boundaries. Thus,

```
LOCK TABLES T1, T2, T3 WRITE;
UPDATE TABLE T1 SET Col1="xzy" WHERE Col1="abc";
```

```
UPDATE TABLE T2 . . .
UPDATE TABLE T3 . . .
. . . do other transaction work on tables T1, T2, T3
UNLOCK TABLES;
```

will keep other users from reading or writing tables T1, T2, T3 while the transaction is processed. All updates between the LOCK and UNLOCK statements are atomic because all of them will be processed before any lock is released.

Unfortunately, when using locks in this manner, throughput will be zero for other users of the locked tables. While the transaction is underway, no one can read or write to T1, T2, T3. For the period of the lock MySQL will be a single user system of these tables. This is likely to be a serious problem if transactions are lengthy and if the application workload involves substantial updating.

A session must lock all tables at once. If it wants to lock more, it must release the lock it has and reacquire a new lock on that includes the additional tables. Thus, no session may have more than one LOCK TABLES statement open at one time. Recall from Chapter 11 that this strategy eliminates the possibility of deadlock.

Dirty reads may or may not be possible, depending on how the applications are written. MySQL does not rollback work, so if no application performs its own rollback, then dirty reads are not possible. If an application does perform its own rollback, and if it and the actions it is rolling back are placed between LOCK TABLES and UNLOCK TABLES statements, then dirty reads are not possible. As mentioned, however, this strategy may result in unacceptable throughput. Finally, if an application performs rollback but does not use LOCK and UNLOCK statements, or does not appear in the same set of LOCK and UNLOCK statements as the statements that it is rolling back, then dirty reads are possible.

Backup and Recovery

MySQL provides limited backup and recovery facilities. It provides a utility for saving the database and for saving individual tables within the database. In some cases, however, it is faster and just as easy to use the operating system copy commands to save the MySQL database files to backup media.

MySQL will maintain a log file of actions that it has processed. This log is one of commands and work, however, and not one of before and after images. To restore a database, an older version of the database is copied back, and the commands in the log reapplied. Bulk changes are logged as commands; only the name of the file used as a source of data changes appears in the log. The individual changes do not appear.

By the way, if you're recovering a database because of a mistake such as an erroneous command like

```
DROP TABLE CUSTOMER;
```

be sure to remove this DROP statement from the log before you reprocess the log. Otherwise, the DROP TABLE will be processed by the log manager and you will have recovered exactly to where you were when you started: without the CUSTOMER table.

MySQL Summary

As you can tell from this section, many features and functions of a modern DBMS product are missing from MySQL. You might be wondering why you should use it at all. As mentioned, it is free and it is also open source; if you want to participate in an open source project in the DBMS domain, this is a good one. Also, MySQL is easy and even fun to use. The features and functions that it does have work well. It would appear the community that is developing MySQL chooses to do only a few things, but to do them well. It is a pleasure to work with such a product.

➤ SUMMARY

JDBC is an alternative to ODBC and ADO that provides database access to programs written in Java. There are JDBC drivers for almost every conceivable DBMS Product. Sun defines four driver types. Type 1 drivers provide a bridge between Java and ODBC. Types 2 through 4 drivers are written entirely in Java. Type 2 drivers rely on the DBMS product for intermachine communication, if any. Type 3 drivers translate JDBC calls into a DBMS-independent network protocol. Type 4 drivers translate JDBC calls into DBMS-dependent network protocol.

An applet is a compiled Java bytecode program that is transmitted to a browser via HTTP and is invoked using the HTTP protocol. A servlet is a Java program that is invoked on the server to respond to HTTP requests. Type 3 and Type 4 drivers can be used for both applets and servlets. Type 2 drivers can be used only in servlets, and only then if the DBMS and Web server are on the same machine or if the DBMS vendor handles the intermachine communication between the Web server and the database server.

There are four steps when using JDBC: (1) Load the driver. (2) Establish a connection to the database. (3) Create a statement. (4) Execute the statement. The driver class libraries need to be in the CLASSPATH for the Java compiler and for the Java virtual machine. They are loaded into a Java program with the forName method of Class. A connection is established using the getConnection method of DriverManager. A connection string includes the literal jdbc: followed by the name of the driver and a URL to the database.

Statement objects are created using the createStatment method of a connection object. Statements can be processed with the executeQuery and executeUpdate methods of a Statement object. ResultSetMetaData objects are created using the getMetaData method of a ResultSet object. Both compiled queries and stored procedures can be processed via JDBC using PreparedStatement and CallableStatement objects.

Java Server Pages (JSP) provide a means to create dynamic Web pages using HTML (and XML) and Java. JSP pages provide the capabilities of a full object oriented language to the page developer. Neither VBScript nor JavaScript can be used in a JSP. JSP pages are compiled into machine independent bytecode.

JSP pages are compiled as subclasses of the HTTPServlet class. Consequently, small snippets of code can be placed in a JSP page, as well as complete Java programs. To use JSP pages, the Web server must implement the Java Servlet 2.1+ and Java Server Pages 1.0+ specifications. Apache Tomcat, an open source product from the Jakarta Project, implements these specifications. Tomcat can work in conjunction with Apache or can operate as a standalone Web server for testing purposes.

When using Tomcat (or any other JSP processor), the JDBC drivers and JSP pages must be located in specified directories. Any Java beans used by the JSP page must also be stored in particular directories. When a JSP page is requested, Tomcat ensures that the most recent page is used. If an uncompiled newer version is available, Tomcat will automatically cause it to be parsed and compiled. There is a maximum of one JSP page in memory at a time, and JSP page requests are executed as a thread of the servlet processor and not as a separate process. The Java code in a JSP can load invoke a compiled Java bean, if desired.

MySQL is an open source DBMS that runs on Unix, Linux, and Windows. There is no license fee. MySQL can provide fast query processing, but it does not support views, stored procedures, or triggers. Referential integrity can be defined, but it is not enforced by MySQL. MySQL maintains a data dictionary in a database named *mysql*. The user and db tables can be queried to determine user permissions. To access MySQL from JDBC, the user account must be granted access to the database either from any location or from a TCP/IP address that represents the local computer.

MySQL provides limited support for concurrent processing. There is no support for transactions and hence no COMMIT or ROLL BACK statements nor transaction isolation. MySQL locks at the table level. Shared read locks are obtained when processing SELECT statements and exclusive locks are obtained when writing. Throughput can be a problem when locking at the table level. Users can surround transaction logic with LOCK TABLES and UNLOCK TABLES commands. Deadlock is prevented by allowing at most one lock statement to be open at a time. Dirty reads are possible if some applications roll back their own work and do not surround their activity with table locks.

MySQL provides limited backup and recovery facilities. There is a backup utility that augments the operating system copy utilities. MySQL maintains a log of commands processed. The log does not include before and after images, nor does it include data values from bulk updates or deletions. Even though it has many limitations, MySQL is easy to use and the features and functions that it does have are well implemented.

➤ GROUP I QUESTIONS

16.1 What is the one major requirement for using JDBC?

16.2 What does JDBC stand for?

16.3 What are the four JDBC driver types?

16.4 Explain the purpose of Type 1 JDBC drivers.

16.5 Explain the purpose of Types 2 through 4 JDBC drivers.

16.6 Define *applet* and *servlet.*

16.7 Explain how Java accomplishes portability.

16.8 List the four steps in using a JDBC driver.

16.9 Show the Java statement for loading the mm.mysql drivers used in this chapter.

16.10 Show the Java statement for connecting to a database using the mm.mysql drivers. Assume the database is named *CustData,* the user is *Lew,* and the password is *Secret.*

16.11 Show the Java statement for creating a Statement object.

16.12 Show the Java statement for creating a ResultSet object that will display the Name and Nationality of the ARTIST table using an already created statement object named s.

16.13 Show Java statements for iterating the resultset created in Question 16.12.

16.14 Show the Java statement for executing an update to change the Nationality of an artist named "Jones" to "French." Use an already created statement object named s.

16.15 In Question 16.14, how can you determine if the update was successful?

16.16 Show a Java statement for creating an object referencing metadata for the resultset created in Question 16.12.

16.17 Show the Java statements necessary to invoke a stored procedure named Customer_Delete. Assume the procedure has three text parameters with values of customer name, area code, and phone number. Pass the values 'Mary Orange,' '206,' and '555-1234' to this procedure.

16.18 What is the purpose of Java Server Pages?

16.19 Describe the differences between ASP and JSP pages.

16.20 Explain how JSP pages are portable.

16.21 How is it possible that small segments of Java can be coded in JSP pages? Why are not complete Java programs required?

16.22 What is the purpose of Tomcat?

16.23 With the standard installation of Tomcat, what actions must be taken before using JSP pages that load JDBC classes?

16.24 When adding new class libraries for Tomcat to use, what must you do to place the library in Tomcat's CLASSPATH?

16.25 Describe the process by which JSP pages are compiled and executed. Can a user ever access an obsolete page? Why or why not?

16.26 Why are JSP programs preferable to CGI programs?

16.27 What conditions are necessary for a Java class to be a bean?

16.28 Show the jsp directive to access a bean named CustomerDeleteBean. Give this bean the identity *custdel*.

16.29 Show the jsp directives to set a bean property named *Prop1* to the value of a form parameter named *Param1*.

16.30 Why is it advantageous to give object properties and form parameters the same names? Show a jsp directive to associate properties and parameters when this is the case.

16.31 What is the difference between invoking a bean from a pure Java program and invoking a bean from Java code in a JSP?

16.32 Under what conditions would you choose to use MySQL?

16.33 For what type of workload does MySQL excel?

16.34 List the major limitations of MySQL.

16.35 How does MySQL 3.0 process referential integrity constraints?

16.36 What statement do you use for creating a new table using MySQL?

16.37 What issue must be addressed when connecting to MySQL using JDBC?

16.38 Show the MySQL command for giving the user *Lew* permission to access any table in the database in the CustData database. Assume the password is *Secret*.

16.39 Describe transaction management facilities in MySQL 3.0.

16.40 How does MySQL use read locks?

16.41 How does MySQL use write locks?

16.42 At what level does MySQL invoke locks? What are the advantages and disadvantages of this?

16.43 Show how an application could provide for transaction atomicity using LOCK TABLES and UNLOCK TABLES.

16.44 What is the disadvantage of the strategy used in your answer to Question 16.43?

16.45 Why is deadlock not possible with MySQL?

16.46 Under what conditions are dirty reads possible with MySQL?

16.47 Describe the MySQL facilities for backup.

16.48 What are the limits on MySQL logging?

16.49 According to the author, why would one choose to use MySQL?

➤ GROUP II QUESTIONS

16.50 Compare and contrast ASP and JSP. Describe the relative strengths and weaknesses of each. Under what circumstances would you recommend one over the other? How important is portability for Web servers? How much of a disadvantage is it to be Microsoft dependent? Some people say preferring one over the other is more a matter of personal preference and values than anything else. Do you agree or disagree?

16.51 Rewrite the Java bean shown in Figure 16-8 to use exceptions rather than the *result* return parameter. Modify the JSP page to correctly process this bean. In what ways is your bean better than the one in Figure 16-8?

➤ PROJECTS

A. Write a Java program to use MySQL and the mm.mysql drivers used in this chapter. Your program should implement the logic of the CustomerInsertWith-Transaction stored procedure described for Oracle in Chapter 12 and SQL Server in Chapter 13. Add logic to your program to display same results as are displayed in the CustomerPurchasesView. Run your program as a stand-alone program.

B. Convert the program you wrote in Project A to a Java bean. Write a JSP page to invoke your bean.

C. Obtain a JDBC Oracle driver and write a Java program to connect to the Oracle version of the View Ridge database and display the contents of any table in the database. Write a Java program to invoke the CustomerInsert stored procedure. Use a JDBC CallableStatement object to invoke that procedure.

D. Convert the program you wrote in Project C to a Java bean. Write a JSP page to invoke your bean.

E. Obtain a JDBC SQL Server driver and write a Java program to connect to the SQL Server version of the View Ridge database and display the contents of any table in the database. Write a Java program to invoke the CustomerInsert stored procedure. Use a JDBC CallableStatement object to invoke that procedure.

F. Convert the program you wrote in Project E to a Java bean. Write a JSP page to invoke your bean.

➤ FIREDUP PROJECT QUESTIONS

Create the FiredUp database using either MySQL or Oracle. If in MySQL, you will not be able to create the referential integrity constraints; otherwise, follow the instructions at the end of Chapters 12 or 13.

A. Code a JSP page to display the STOVE table.

B. Code a JSP page to display any table in the FiredUp database. Use Figure 16-3 as an example.

C. Code a JSP page to enter new STOVE data. Use a Java Bean for the insert; follow Figures 16-8 and 16-9 as an example.

D. Code a JSP page to allow customers to register their own stoves.

E. Create a Java Bean to enter new stove repair data.

F. Code a JSP page to invoke the bean created in Project Question E. Use Figures 16-8 and 16-9 as an example.

Sharing Enterprise Data

So far in this text we have described database processing in the context of personal computing and in the context of Internet technology using the three-tier and *n*-tier architectures. Enterprises also use several other, older, system types. Because you may encounter them, we will survey the characteristics of three such types in the first part of this chapter. A fourth type, distributed database processing, is beginning to be used for commercial database processing. Both Oracle and SQL Server provide support for it, and we will discuss it as well.

Data is an important organizational asset, an asset that can be used not only to facilitate the operations of a company but also for management, planning, forecasting, strategic analysis, and the like. Unfortunately, while many organizations have found that their databases effectively support organizational operations, they know that their databases are ineffectively used for analysis, planning, and other management purposes. In this chapter we address topics that are important in increasing the return of the investment on enterprise data in databases: downloading centralized data, OLAP, data warehousing, and data administration.

➤ ENTERPRISE DATABASE PROCESSING ARCHITECTURES

Several different system architectures are used for enterprise database processing. In the past, teleprocessing systems were the most common. But as microcomputers became common on the desktop and more powerful as data servers, new multi-user database architectures arose. In this section, we introduce teleprocessing, client–server, file-sharing, and distributed, alternatives.

Teleprocessing Systems

The classic method of supporting a multi-user database system is teleprocessing, which uses one computer and one CPU. All processing is done by this single computer.

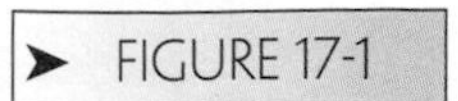
FIGURE 17-1

Relationships of Programs in a Teleprocessing System

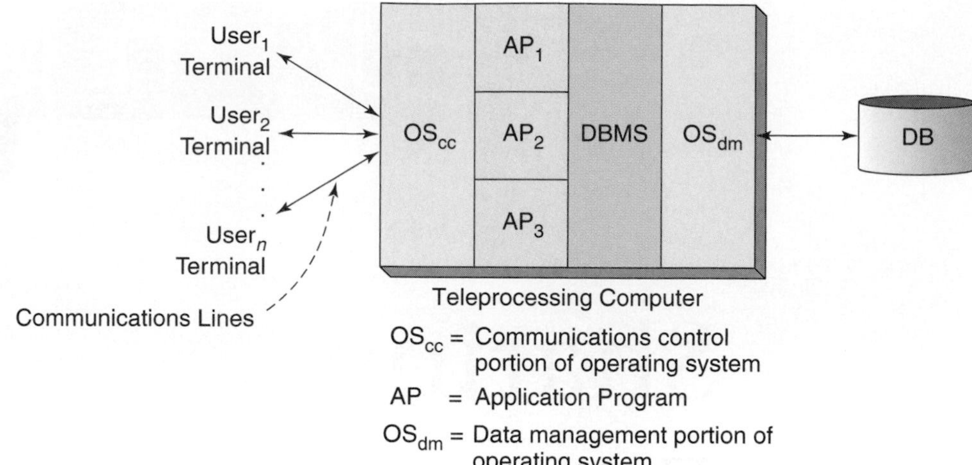

Figure 17-1 shows a typical teleprocessing system. Users operate dumb terminals (or microcomputers that emulate dumb terminals) that transmit transaction messages and data to the centralized computer. The communications control portion of the operating system receives the messages and data and sends them to the appropriate application program. The program then calls on the DBMS for services, and the DBMS uses the data management portion of the operating system to process the database. When a transaction is completed, the results are returned to the users at the dumb terminals via the communications control portion of the operating system.

Figure 17-1 shows *n* users submitting transactions processed by three different application programs. Because there is little intelligence at the users' end (that is, the *terminals* are dumb), all commands for formatting the screen must be generated by the CPU and transmitted over the communication lines. This means that the users' interface is generally character oriented and primitive. Systems like this are called teleprocessing systems, because all inputs and outputs are communicated over a distance (*tele-* means "distance") to the centralized computer for processing.

Historically, teleprocessing systems were the most common alternative for multi-user database systems. But as the price–performance ratio of computers fell and, in particular, with the advent of the personal computer, other alternatives that use multiple computers have supplanted it.

Client–Server Systems

Figure 17-2 is a schematic of one of these alternatives, called a **client–server system.** Unlike teleprocessing, which involves a single computer, client–server computing involves multiple computers connected in a network. Some of the computers process application programs and are designated as *clients*. Another computer processes the database and is designated as the *server.*

Figure 17-2 shows an example in which each of *n* users has his or her own client (application processing) computer: $User_1$ processes AP_1 and AP_2 on Computer 1. $User_2$ processes AP_2 on Computer 2, and $User_n$ processes AP_2 and AP_3 on Computer N. Another computer is the database server.

There are many options regarding computer type. Theoretically, the client computers can be mainframes or microcomputers. Because of cost, however, in almost all cases the client computers are microcomputers. Similarly, any type of computer can be the server, but again, because of cost, the server is most often a microcomputer. The clients and server are connected using either a local area network (LAN) or wide area network (WAN).

FIGURE 17-2

Client–Server Architecture

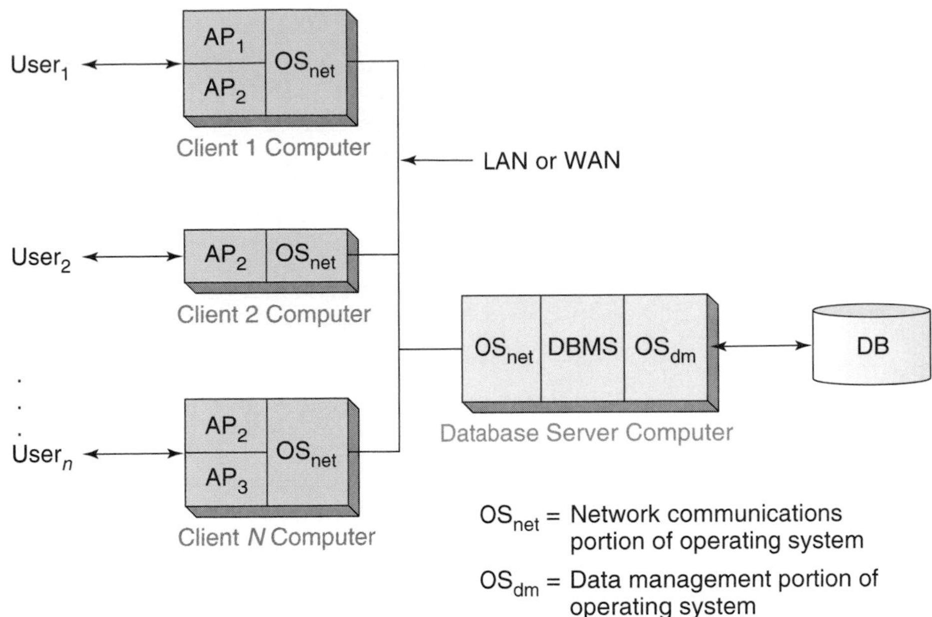

Although it is rare for client computers to be anything other than micros, sometimes the server is a mainframe, especially when considerable power is required from the server or, for reasons of security and control, it is inappropriate to locate the database on a microcomputer.

The system in Figure 17-2 has a single server, although this need not always be the case. Multiple servers may process different databases or provide other services on behalf of the clients. For example, in an engineering consulting firm, one server might process the database while a second server supports computer-assisted design applications.

If there are multiple database processing servers, each one must process a different database in order for the system to be considered a client–server system. When two servers process the same database, the system is no longer called a client–server system; rather, it is termed a distributed database system.

FILE-SHARING SYSTEMS

A second multi-user architecture is shown in Figure 17-3. This architecture, called **file-sharing,** distributes to the users' computers not only the application programs but also the DBMS. In this case, the *server* is a file server and not a database server. Almost all file-sharing systems employ LANs of microcomputers.

The file-sharing architecture was developed before the client–server architecture, and in many ways it is more primitive. With file sharing, the DBMS on each user's computer sends requests to the data management portion of the operating system on the file server for file-level processing. This means that considerably more traffic crosses the LAN than with the client–server architecture.

For example, consider the processing of a query to obtain the Name and Address of all rows in the CUSTOMER table where Zip equals 98033. In a client–server system, the application program would send the following SQL command:

```
SELECT   NAME, ADDRESS
FROM     CUSTOMER
WHERE    ZIP = 98033
```

The server would respond with all qualifying Names and Addresses.

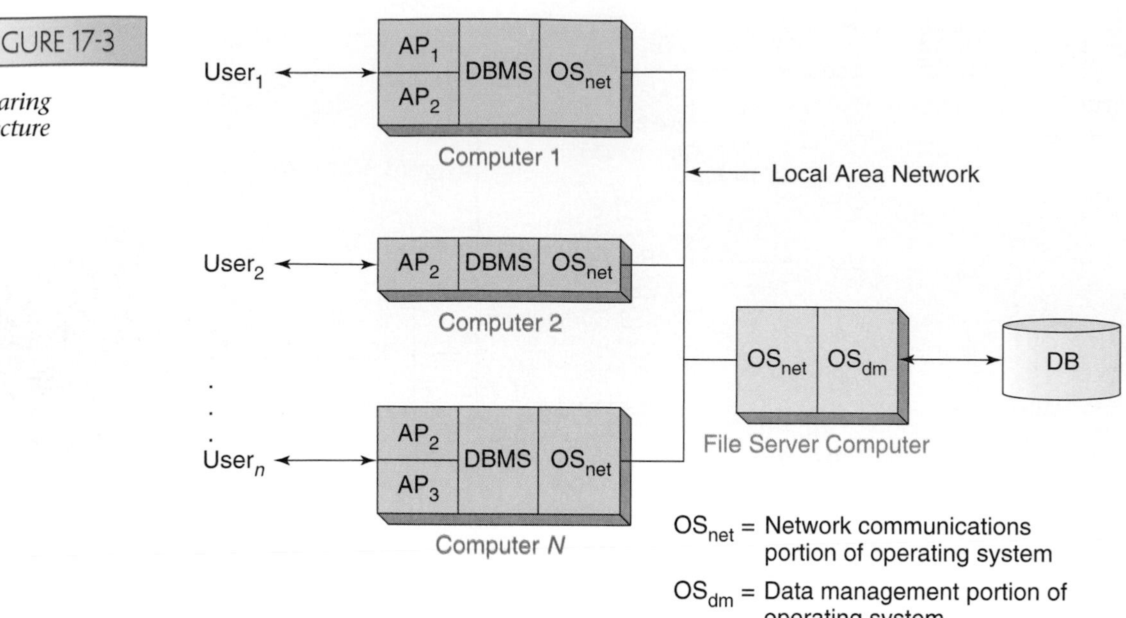

FIGURE 17-3

File-Sharing Architecture

In a file-sharing system, the DBMS is on the local computer, and therefore no program on the file server is capable of processing the SQL statement. All such processing must be done on the user computer, so the DBMS must ask the fil server to transmit the entire CUSTOMER table. If that table has indexes or other overhead associated with it, the overhead structures must be transmitted as well. Clearly, with file sharing, much more data need be transmitted across the LAN.

Because of these problems, file-sharing systems are seldom used for high-volume transaction-oriented processing. Too much data needs to be locked and transmitted for each transaction, and this architecture would result in very slow performance. There is, however, one database application for which this architecture makes sense: the query processing of downloaded, extracted data. If one or more users need access to large portions of the database in order to produce reports or answer queries, it can make sense to have a server that downloads large sections of data. In this case, the downloaded data are not updated and not returned to the database. We show examples of processing extracted data later in this chapter.

File-sharing systems are also used for nondatabase applications, such as those that require large, fast disks to store large files such as large graphics, audio, and animations. They also are used to share expensive printers, plotters, and other peripheral equipment.

Distributed Database Systems

A fourth alternative, shown in Figure 17-4, is a distributed database system, in which the database itself is distributed. In Figure 17-4, the database (or a portion of it) is stored on all *N* computers. As shown, Computers 1, 2, and *N* process both the applications and the database, and Computer 3 processes only the database.

In Figure 17-4, the dashed line around the files indicates that the database is composed of all the segments of the database on all *N* computers. These computers may be physically located in the same facility, on different sides of the world, or somewhere in between.

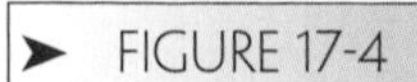

FIGURE 17-4

Distributed Database Architecture

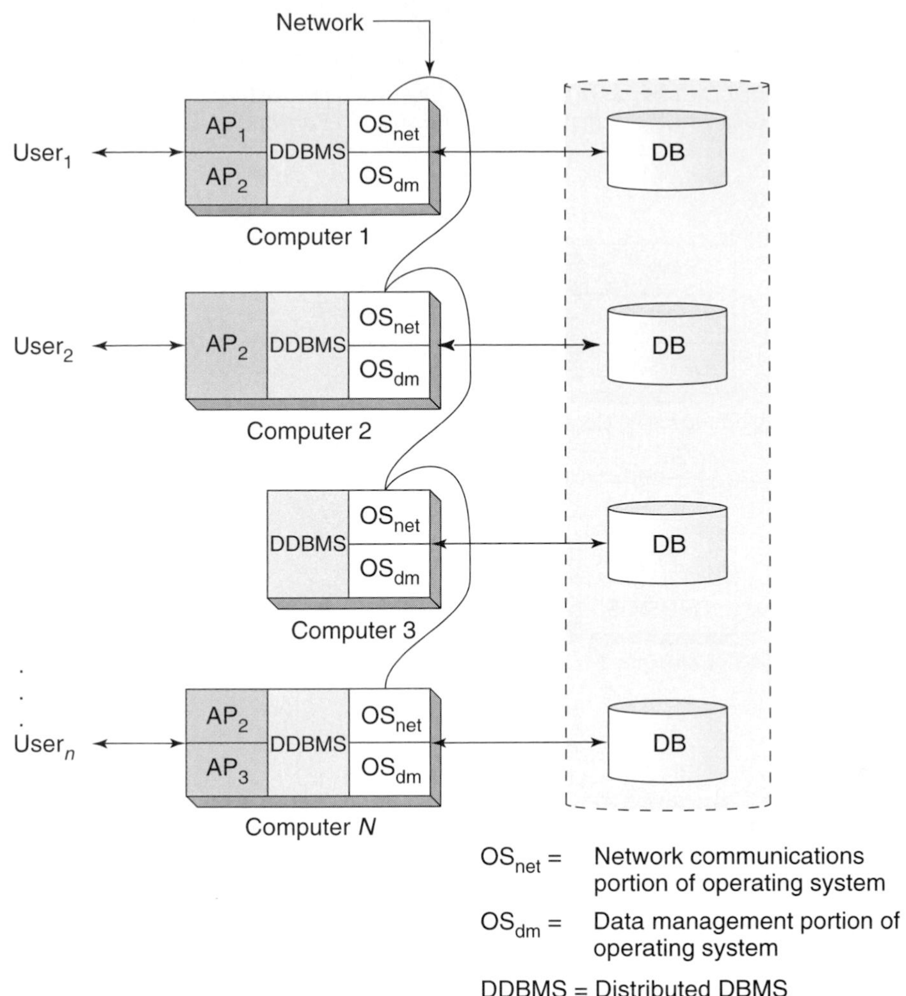

DISTRIBUTED PROCESSING VERSUS DISTRIBUTED DATABASE PROCESSING Consider Figures 17-1, 17-2, 17-3, and 17-4 again. The file-sharing, client–server, and distributed database alternatives all differ from teleprocessing in an important way: They all use multiple computers for applications or DBMS processing. Accordingly, most people would say that all three of these architectures are examples of **distributed systems,** because applications processing has been distributed among several computers.

Observe, however, that the database itself is distributed only in the architecture shown in Figure 17-4. Neither the client–server nor the file-sharing architectures distribute the database to multiple computers. Consequently, most people would *not* refer to the file-sharing or client–server architectures as **distributed database systems.**

TYPES OF DISTRIBUTED DATABASES There are several types of distributed database systems. First look at Figure 17-5(a), which shows a nondistributed database with four pieces, W, X, Y, and Z. All four pieces of these segments are located on a single database, and there is no data duplication.

Now consider the distributed alternatives in Figure 17-5(b) through (d). Figure 17-5(b) shows the first distributed alternative, in which the database has been distributed to two computers; pieces W and X are stored on Computer 1, and

➤ FIGURE 17-5

Types of Distributed Databases: (a) Nonpartitioned, Nonreplicated Alternative; (b) Partitioned, Nonreplicated Alternative; (c) Nonpartitioned, Replicated Alternative; (d) Partitioned, Replicated Alternative

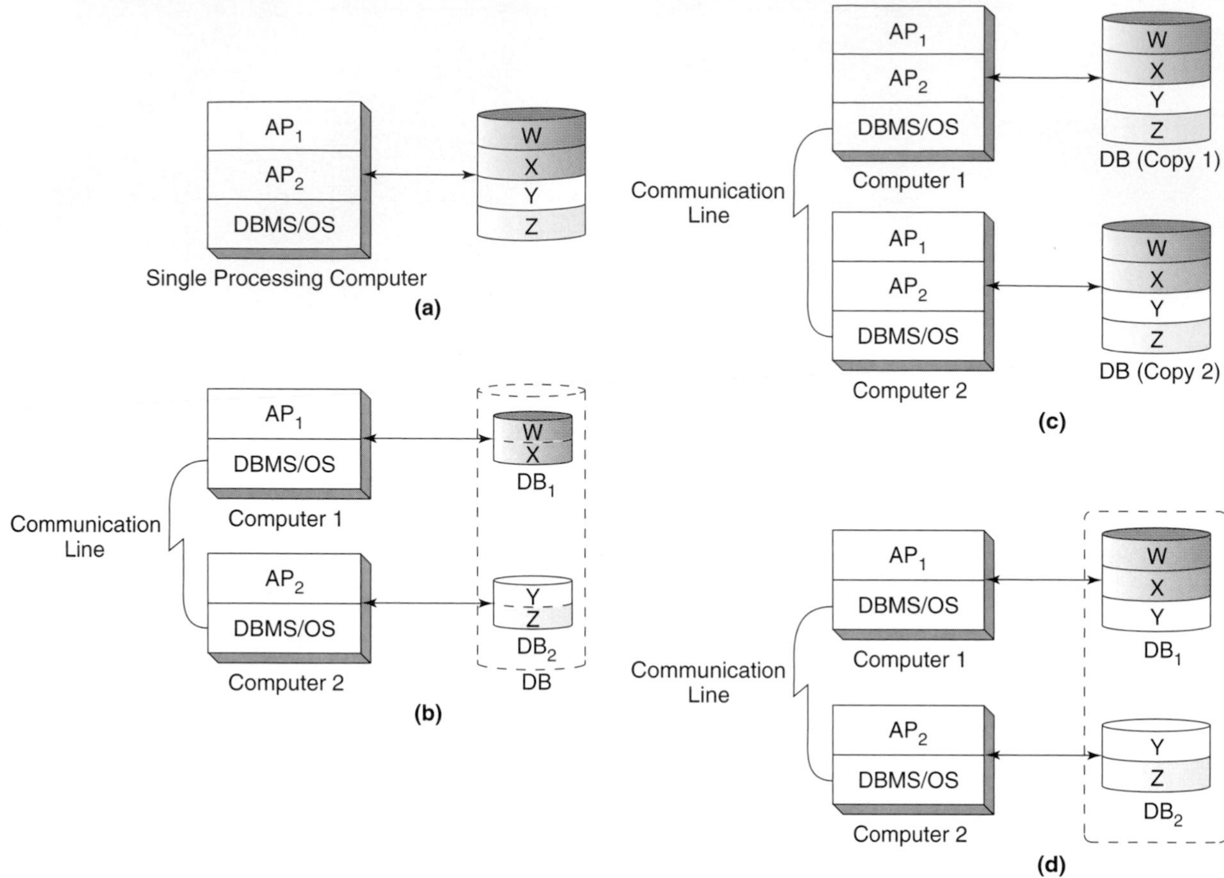

pieces Y and Z are stored on Computer 2. In Figure 17-5(c), the entire database has been replicated on two computers. Finally, in Figure 17-5(d), the database has been partitioned, and a portion (Y) has been replicated.

Two terms are sometimes used with regard to partitioning of databases. A vertical partition or **vertical fragment** refers to a table that is broken into two or more sets of columns. Thus, a table R(C1, C2, C3, C4) could be broken into two vertical partitions of P1(C1, C2) and P2(C3, C4). Depending on the application and the reason for creating the partitions, the key of R would most likely also be placed into P2 to form P2(C1, C3, C4). A horizontal partition or **horizontal fragment** refers to the rows of a table when they are divided into pieces. Thus, in the relation R, if the first 1,000 rows are placed into R1(C1, C2, C3, C4) and the remaining rows are placed into R2(C1, C2, C3, C4), two horizontal partitions will result. Sometimes a database is broken into both horizontal and vertical partitions, and the result is sometimes called a mixed partition.

COMPARISON OF DISTRIBUTED DATABASE ALTERNATIVES These alternatives are summarized on a continuum in Figure 17-6, arranged in increasing degree of distribution, from left to right. The nondistributed database is on the leftmost point of the continuum, and the partitioned, replicated database is on the rightmost point. In between these extremes is a partitioned database.

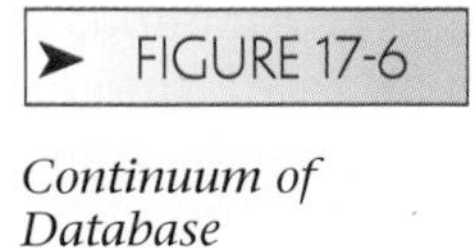

Continuum of Database Distribution Alternatives

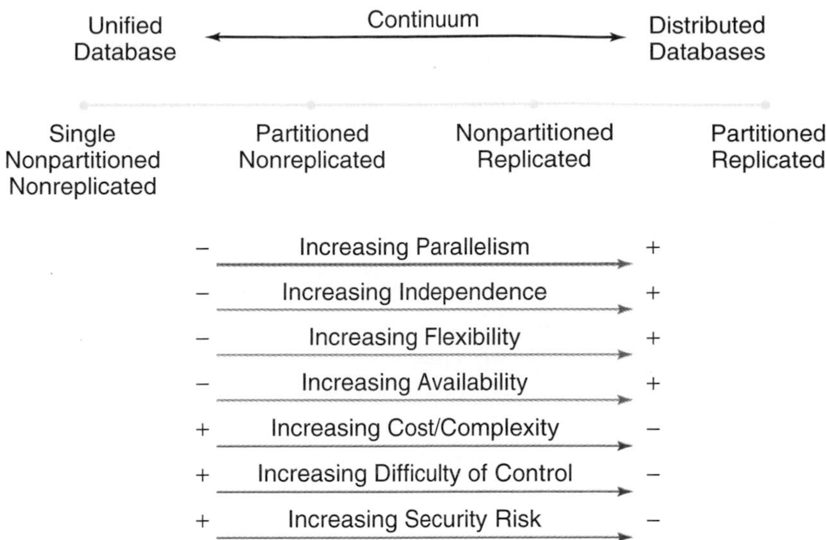

The partitions are allocated to two or more computers and a database that is not partitioned, but each entire database is replicated on two or more computers.

The characteristics of the alternatives on this continuum are listed in Figure 17-6. The alternatives toward the right increase parallelism, independence, flexibility, and availability, but they also mean greater expense, complexity, difficulty of control, and risk to security.

One of these advantages is particularly significant to business organizations. The alternatives on the right of Figure 17-6 provide greater flexibility and hence can be better tailored to the organizational structure and the organizational process. A highly decentralized manufacturing company, for example, in which plant managers have wide latitude in their planning, will never be satisfied with an organizational information system with the structure of Figure 17-5(a) because the structure of the information system architecture and the structure of the company fight with each other. Thus, the alternatives on the right side provide a better and more appropriate fit to that organization than do those on the left.

The greatest disadvantage is the difficulty of control and the resulting potential loss of data integrity. Consider the database architecture in Figure 17-5(d). A user connected to Computer 1 can read and update a data item in Partition Y on Computer 1 at the very same time that a different user connected to Computer 2 can read and update that data item in Partition Y on Computer 2.

DISTRIBUTED PROCESSING TECHNIQUES DBMS vendors provide several techniques for supporting distributed processing. Oracle and SQL Server provide similar types of support, but they use different names for the same things, and the same name for different things. Other DBMS vendors use still other terminology. Here we will focus on the basic ideas.

The simplest type of distributed database processing is the downloading of read-only data. In this case, only one computer updates any of the database data, but multiple computers (maybe even thousands) are sent copies to process in read-only mode. Oracle calls such read-only copies **materialized views.** SQL Server calls such read-only copies **snapshots.** We will address this type of distributed processing in the next section.

A more complex technique for distributed processing is to allow data update requests to originate on multiple computers, but to transmit those update requests to a designated computer for processing. Computer A, for example, could be designated as the only site that can update the EMPLOYEE table (and views based on EMPLOYEE), while Computer B is designated as the only site that can update the CUSTOMER table (and views). From time to time, the updates must be transmitted back to all computers in the distributed net and the databases synchronized.

The most complicated alternative is to allow multiple updates on the same data at multiple sites. In this case, three types of **distributed update conflict** problem can occur. For one, uniqueness can be violated. At View Ridge Galley, two different sites might create a WORK row with the same Copy, Title, and ArtistID. Another possible problem is that akin to the lost update problem. Two sites can each update the same row. A third problem occurs when one site updates a row that has been deleted by a second site.

To deal with conflicting updates, a single site is designated for conflict resolution. All updates are examined by this site, and conflicting updates are resolved using either logic built-in to the DBMS or in application code that is similar to that written for triggers. In the most extreme case, conflicts are written to a log and resolved manually. This latter alternative is not recommended because many rows in operational databases can be left in limbo until the resolutions are resolved. This may unacceptably reduce throughput.

None of these techniques address the problem of providing atomic transactions when database are distributed. This is especially problematical when conflicting updates may occur. At what point is a database action committed? If updates are subject to rollback during distributed update resolution, then the distributed transaction cannot commit for potentially hours of days. This delay is clearly unacceptable.

Setting aside the issue of distributed update conflict, the coordination of distributed transactions is difficult. To be atomic, no update action in a distributed transaction can be committed until all are committed. This means a given site must provisionally commit its updates, pending notification from the distributed transaction manager that all other sites have committed. An algorithm called **two-phased commit** is used for this purpose. Microsoft an OLE service called the **Distributed Transaction Service (DTS)** that implements two-phased commit. In the Java world, **Enterprise Java Beans (EJB)** are used for this purpose. Both of these are beyond the scope of this text, but you should know that they exist. Search on the keyword *replication* in the Oracle and SQL Server documentation.

➤ DOWNLOADING DATA

With the advent of powerful personal computers, it has become feasible to download large quantities of enterprise data to departmental and user computers for local processing. Users can query these data using local DBMS products, and they can also import the data into spreadsheets, financial analysis programs, graphics programs, and other tools with which they are familiar.

In general, downloaded data can be used for query and reporting purposes only. They cannot be updated because once the data are removed from the operational database, they are no longer subject to concurrency control. To understand more about the processing of downloaded data, consider a typical scenario.

UNIVERSAL EQUIPMENT

The Universal Equipment Company manufactures and sells heavy equipment for the construction industry. Its products include bulldozers, graders, loaders, and drilling rigs. Every product is assigned to a product manager in the marketing department who is responsible for product planning, advertising, marketing support, development of sales support material, and so forth. Each product manager is assigned a group of two or three related products.

Advertising is the product managers' largest budget item, so managers want to be able to measure the effectiveness of the ads they run. Universal's ads always contain a mail-in card to request information. The cards have a preprinted number unique to each ad appearance so that this number can be used to identify the ad that generated a particular lead. To facilitate lead tracking, the marketing department has developed a microcomputer database application that the product managers can use.

Figure 17-7(a) shows the semantic objects processed by this application. AD represents an advertisement; AD-APPEARANCE is the occurrence of a particular ad in a particular publication; PRODUCT represents a particular product such as a

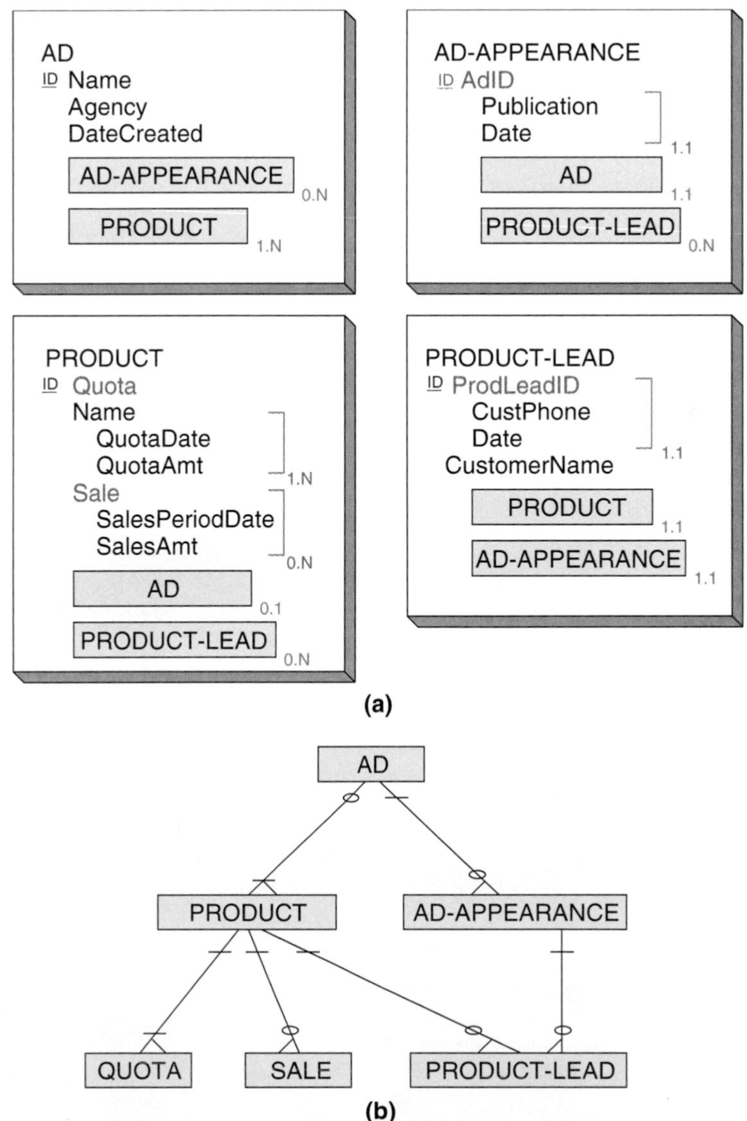

➤ FIGURE 17-7

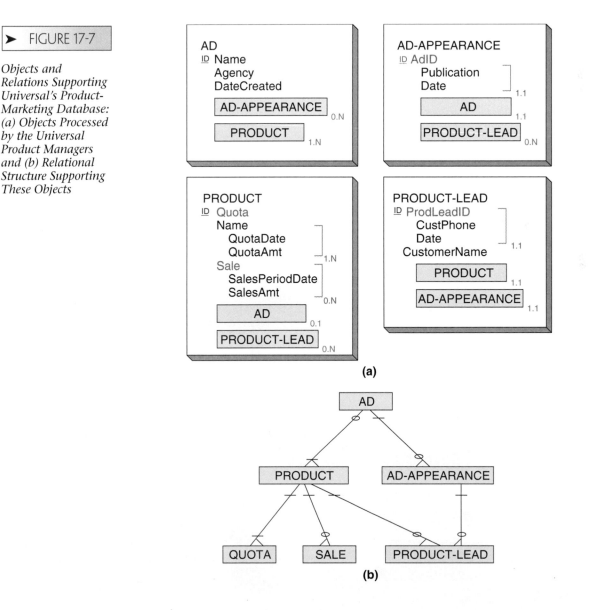

Objects and Relations Supporting Universal's Product-Marketing Database: (a) Objects Processed by the Universal Product Managers and (b) Relational Structure Supporting These Objects

bulldozer; and PRODUCT contains two repeating groups, one on quotas and one on sales. The groups are multi-value because sales quotas are assigned for each quarter and product sales are recorded on a weekly basis.

This view of PRODUCT is quite simple. The complete PRODUCT object actually contains more attributes. But because the other data are not needed for the product managers' application, we have omitted them. The database structure that supports these objects is shown in Figure 17-7(b).

Download Process

The product managers are assigned a personal computer connected to other PCs through a LAN in Universal's marketing department. To obtain sales and product-lead data, the computers call on a file server that serves as a gateway to Universal's mainframe (transaction-processing computer). The architecture is similar to that shown in Figure 17-8.

Every Monday, a key user in the marketing department runs a program developed by Universal's MIS department that updates the SALES, QUOTA, and PRODUCT-LEAD tables on the file server's database with data from the corporation's mainframe database. This program adds to the database the data from the previous week and also makes corrections. Product and sales data are imported for all related products to enable product managers to do comparative studies. Once the data have been downloaded to the file server, each product manager can obtain

➤ FIGURE 17-8

Sharing of Downloaded Data with a Gateway Micro as the File Server

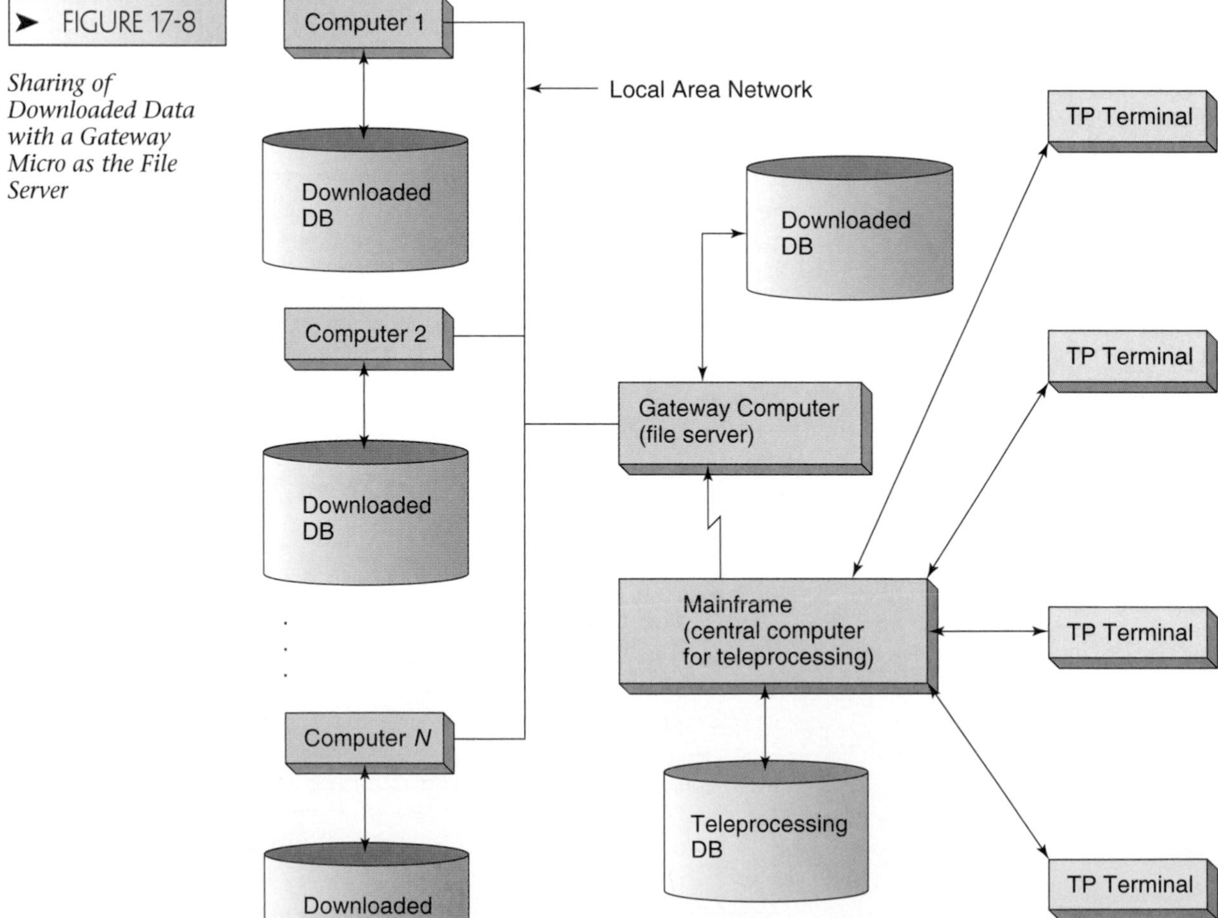

the data of interest to him or her from that server. Controls ensure that the product managers do not obtain data for which access has not been authorized.

Potential Problems in Processing Downloaded Databases

Downloading data moves the data closer to the user and increases the data's utility. Unfortunately, it may cause problems, including coordination, consistency, access control, and computer crime.

COORDINATION First consider coordination, using the PRODUCT-LEAD and AD-APPEARANCE tables for illustration. The PRODUCT-LEAD table is updated from data on the mainframe (leads are handled by sales personnel and are recorded on the mainframe). But the AD-APPEARANCE table is updated "locally" by the key user in the marketing department, who gets the data from reports prepared by the advertising manager and the advertising agency.

This situation could cause problems when an ad is run for the first time in a new issue or publication. For example, the ad could generate leads that are recorded on the mainframe database before the AD-APPEARANCE data is stored on the file server. Then, when those leads are downloaded, the program importing the data will have to reject the lead data, because such data violate the constraint that a PRODUCT-LEAD must have an AD-APPEARANCE parent. Thus, the activities of local updating and downloading must be carefully coordinated: The key user needs to insert AD-APPEARANCE data before importing data from the mainframe. Similar coordination problems can occur when updating SALES and QUOTA data.

CONSISTENCY The second problem with downloaded data concerns **consistency.** Each of the product managers receives downloaded SALES and QUOTA data that they are not supposed to change. But what would happen if a product manager did change the data? In this case, the data in that product manager's database might not match the data in the corporate database, the data in the file server, and possibly the data in other product managers' databases. The reports produced by that product manager could therefore disagree with other reports. And if several product managers update data, many inconsistent data could be generated.

Clearly this situation calls for strict control. The database should be designed so that data cannot be updated. If this is not possible—say, the personal computer database product will not enforce such a restriction, and the costs of writing programs to enforce it are prohibitively high—the solution to this problem is education. Product managers should be aware of the problems that will ensue if they change data, and they should be directed not to do so.

ACCESS CONTROL A third problem is access control. When data are transferred to several computer systems, access control becomes more difficult. At Universal, for example, SALES and QUOTA data may be sensitive. For example, the vice president of sales may not want the sales personnel to learn about upcoming sales quotas until the annual sales meeting. But if 15 product managers have copies of these data in their databases, it can be difficult to ensure that the data will be kept confidential until the appropriate time.

Furthermore, the file server receives all SALES and QUOTA data, which are supposed to be downloaded in such a way that a product manager receives only the SALES and QUOTA data for the products that he or she manages. Product managers can be quite competitive, however, and they may want to find the data for one another's products. Making this data accessible on the file server in the marketing department may thus create management problems.

➤ FIGURE 17-9

Issues and Potential Problems Regarding Downloaded Data Applications

Coordination
- Downloaded data must conform to database constraints.
- Local updates must be coordinated with downloads.

Consistency
- In general, downloaded data should not be updated.
- Applications need features to prevent updating.
- Users should be made aware of possible problems.

Access Control
- Data may be replicated on many computers.
- Procedures to control data access are more complicated.

Potential for Computer Crime
- Illegal copying is difficult to prevent.
- Diskettes and illegal online access are easy to conceal.
- Risk may prevent the development of downloaded data applications.

COMPUTER CRIME The fourth problem, a greater possibility of computer crime, is closely allied to access control. Whereas access control concerns inappropriate but legal activity, crime concerns illegal actions. Data on the corporate mainframe can be very valuable. Universal Equipment's sales and quota data, for example, are of great interest to its competitors.

When data are downloaded in bulk to the file server and then to one or many personal computers, illegal copying becomes difficult to prevent. A diskette or CDROM is easily concealed, and employees sometimes have online connections

➤ FIGURE 17-10

Processing Downloaded Data with a Web Server

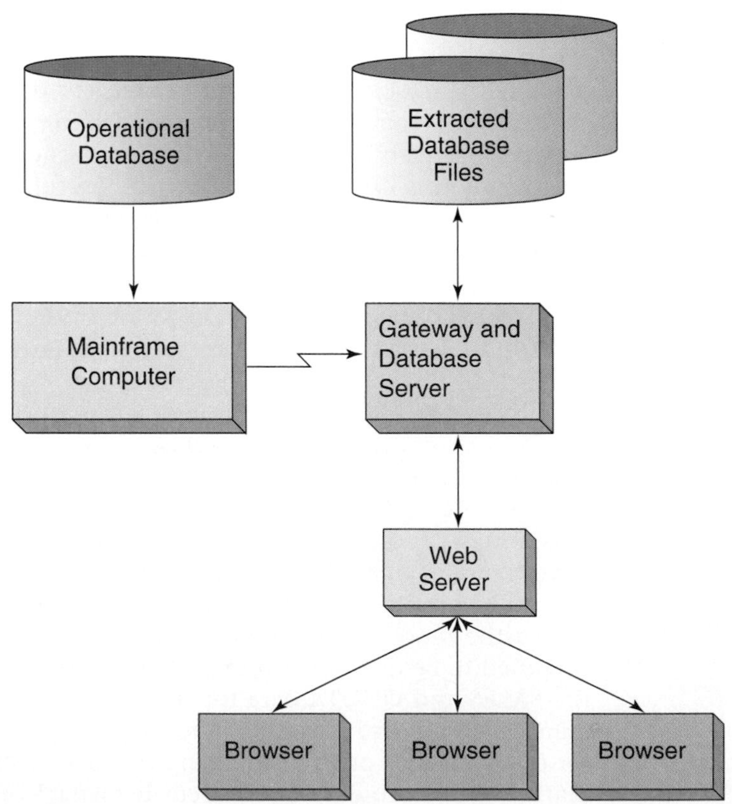

with which they access work computers from off-site locations. In these situations, copying data is nearly impossible to detect or prevent. The risk of computer crime alone might prohibit such a system from being developed, even though it would otherwise be an excellent solution. The potential problems of downloaded databases are summarized in Figure 17-9.

USING A WEB SERVER TO PUBLISH DOWNLOADED DATA

Figure 17-10 shows one way to use a Web server to publish downloaded data. The gateway and database servers are shown here on one computer, but they could reside on two—one computer for the gateway and a second for the server. The Web server communicates with the database server to obtain downloaded data. This data is then published to browser users.

➤ ON LINE ANALYTIC PROCESSING (OLAP)

In recent years a new way of presenting information has emerged that is called **On Line Analytical Processing** or, more frequently, **OLAP.** With OLAP, data is viewed in the frame of a table, or with three axes, in that of a **cube.** OLAP makes no limit on the number of axes, hence, you will sometimes hear the term **OLAP hypercube.** This term means a display with an unlimited number of axes. The term *OLAP cube* is used most frequently.

➤ FIGURE 17-11

Relational Source Data for OLAP Cube

Category	Type	City	State	Date	Sales Price	Asking Price
New	Single Family	San Francisco	California	1/1/2000	679,000	685,000
Existing	Condo	Los Angeles	California	3/5/2001	327,989	350,000
Existing	Single Family	Elko	Nevada	7/17/2001	105,675	125,000
New	Condo	San Diego	California	12/22/2000	375,000	375,000
Existing	Single Family	Paradise	California	11/19/2001	425,000	449,000
Existing	Single Family	Las Vegas	Nevada	1/19/2001	317,000	325,000
New	Single Family	San Francisco	California	1/1/2000	679,000	685,000
Existing	Condo	Los Angeles	California	3/5/2001	327,989	350,000
Existing	Condo	Las Vegas	Nevada	6/19/2001	297,000	305,000
Existing	Single Family	Los Angeles	California	4/1/2000	579,000	625,000
New	Condo	Los Angeles	California	8/5/2001	321,000	320,000
Etc.						

Consider the example relation shown in Figure 17-11. This data concerns the sales of single-family and condo housing properties in California and Nevada. As you can see from the data, the Sales Price and Asking Price for both new construction and existing properties are included.

OLAP TERMINOLOGY An OLAP cube for this data is shown in Figure 17-12. This data has two **axes,** which are columns and rows. The row axis displays the Date **dimension,** and the columns axis displays both the Category and the Location dimensions. When two or more dimensions are shown on an axis, every combination of one is shown with every combination of the other. Thus, Existing Structures is shown for all locations, and New Construction is shown for all locations. The cells of the cube represent the **measures** of the cube, or the data that is to be displayed. In this cube, the measure is average Sales Price. Other measures concern Asking Price or even the difference between Sales Price and Asking Price.

Notice that all of the data in Figure 17-12 concern single-family dwellings. There is no condo data in this cube. In fact, there are two such cubes—one for single family and a second for condos. You could think of the two cubes as one behind the other, as sketched in Figure 17-13. When viewed this way, these

➤ FIGURE 17-12

Example OLAP Cube

Average Sales Price of Single-Family Dwellings ($thousands)										
			Existing Structures				New Construction			
			California			Nevada	California			Nevada
			San Francisco	Los Angeles	San Diego		San Francisco	Los Angeles	San Diego	
2000	Q1	Jan	408	465	375	179	418	468	371	190
		Feb	419	438	382	180	429	437	382	185
		Mar	427	477	380	195	426	471	387	198
	Q2		433	431	382	188	437	437	380	193
	Q3		437	437	380	190	438	439	382	190
	Q4		435	439	377	193	432	434	370	198
2001	Q1	Jan	452	454	368	198	450	457	367	197
		Feb	450	467	381	187	457	464	388	191
		Mar	432	444	373	188	436	446	371	201
	Q2		437	437	368	190	444	432	363	196
	Q3		436	452	388	196	447	455	385	199
	Q4		441	455	355	198	449	455	355	202

➤ FIGURE 17-13

OLAP Cube Slice Dimensions

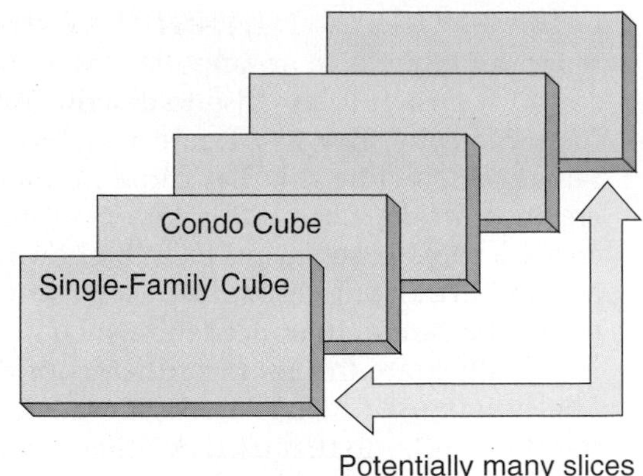

two cubes appear to be slices of data, and, in fact, the dimension(s) that are held constant in a cube are called **slices.** Thus, in this example, the cube is sliced on Type.

The values of a dimension are called **members.** The members of the Type dimension are {Single Family, Condo}, and the members of the Category dimension are {New, Existing}. For this cube, the members of the State dimension are {California, Nevada}, but in general, there could be 50 such members for United States properties. Sometimes there is a very large number of members in a dimension; consider all of the members for the combination {State, City}. Finally, in some cases, members are computed. Date and time are good examples. Given a date, we can compute the month, quarter, year, or century members for that date.

One last important OLAP term is **level.** The level of a dimension is its position in a hierarchy. For example, consider the Date dimension. Its levels are Year, Quarter, Month. The levels in the location dimension are State, City. OLAP terminology is summarized in Figure 17-14.

➤ FIGURE 17-14

OLAP Terminology

Term	Description	Example in Figure 17-12
Axis	A coordinate of the hypercube	Rows, columns
Dimension	A feature of the data to be placed on an axis	Time, Housing Type, Location
Level	A (hierarchical) subset of a dimension	{California, Nevada} {San Francisco, Los Angeles, Other} {Q1, Q2, Q3, Q4}
Member	A data value in a dimension	{New, Existing}, {Jan, Feb, Mar}
Measure	The source data for the hypercube	Sales Price, Asking Price
Slice	A dimension or measure held constant for the display	Housing Type—all shown are for Single Family—another cube exists for Condo

CUBE AND VIEW DEFINITIONS OLAP terminology is evolving and is currently ambiguous in an important way. The term *cube* is used both to describe a semantic structure and also to describe materializations of that underlying structure. The cube shown in Figure 17-12 is one possible view or materialization of a semantic structure that has certain dimensions, levels, and measures. We could create a second cube on this data by exchanging the rows and columns; we could create a third cube on this data by showing Location at the top and then placing a New and Existing column for each Location member. So as you read OLAP documents, be careful to understand which meaning of *cube* is being used.

To illustrate this point further, consider the cube definition in Figure 17-15. The syntax used here is based on Microsoft's OLE DB for OLAP documentation, but it is similar to that used by other vendors as well. This Create Cube statement defines four dimensions and two levels in the logical structure. The Time and Location dimensions have levels, and the HousingCategory and HousingType dimensions do not. Although we do not show it here, it is possible for a dimension to have more than one set of Levels. In that case, two or more hierarchies are defined for that dimension.

The structure shown in Figure 17-15 is a definition of a way to interpret or comprehend housing data. It is not a presentation of data. To define a data presentation or materialization, the OLAP world has extended the syntax of SQL.

➤ FIGURE 17-15

Extended SQL Used for OLAP: (a) Example Create Cube Data Definition Statement

```
CREATE CUBE HousingSalesCube (
    DIMENSION Time TYPE TIME,
        LEVEL Year TYPE YEAR,
        LEVEL Quarter TYPE QUARTER,
        LEVEL Month TYPE MONTH,
    DIMENSION Location,
        LEVEL USA TYPE ALL,
        LEVEL State,
        LEVEL City,
    DIMENSION HousingCategory,
    DIMENSION HousingType,
    MEASURE SalesPrice,
        FUNCTION AVG
    MEASURE AskingPrice,
        FUNCTION AVG
    )
```

(a)

➤ FIGURE 17-15

Extended SQL Used for OLAP: (b) Example Multidimensional SELECT Statement

```
SELECT    CROSSJOIN ({Existing Structure, New Construction}, {California.Children,
          Nevada})
          ON COLUMNS,
          {1998.Q1.Children, 1998.Q2, 1998.Q3, 1998.Q4,
          1999.Q1.Children, 1999.Q2, 1999.Q3, 1999.Q4}
          ON ROWS
FROM      HousingSalesCube
WHERE     (SalesPrice, HousingType = 'SingleFamily')
```

(b)

Figure 17-16(a) shows the OLAP SQL to create the cube materialization shown in Figure 17-11. The only thing confusing about this statement is the CROSSJOIN term. A CROSSJOIN ({A, B}, {1, 2}) results in the following display:

A		B	
1	2	1	2

A CROSSJOIN ({1, 2}, {A, B}) results in this display:

1		2	
A	B	A	B

Extending this idea a bit, the CROSSJOIN ({Existing Structure, New Construction}, {California.Children, Nevada}) results in

Existing Structures				**New Construction**			
California			**Nevada**	**California**			**Nevada**
San Francisco	Los Angeles	San Diego		San Francisco	Los Angeles	San Diego	

The only addition to this last statement was the expression California. Children. This term simply means to breakout all of the children for California for all of the levels defined in the cube.

The SQL in Figure 17-16(b) includes the expression ON COLUMNS and ON ROWS. This declares the axes on which the dimensions are to be placed. Note too that the WHERE clause is used to specify the slicers for the presentation. Only Sales Price and a HousingType of Single Family are to be shown. Note that both a measure and a dimension can serve as a slicer.

One of the key ideas of OLAP is that users be able to dynamically reformat a cube with ease while at their desks (hence the words **on line**). To do this, programs that process cube materializations need to be able dynamically to construct OLAP SQL like that in Figure 17-16(b).

OLAP SCHEMA STRUCTURES All of the data for the OLAP example in Figure 17-11 and 17-12 arise from a single table. This is unusual; normally data for at least some of the dimensions is stored in a table other than the table having the measures. For example, Figure 17-16 shows sample OLAP table structures for View Ridge Gallery. The measure data say, SalesPrice, is stored in the TRANS table but data about the dimensions is stored in parent tables that are connected via foreign keys to TRANS.

A cube based in the data in Figure 17-16(a) could have CUSTOMER, ART_DEALER, SALESPERSON, and WORK dimensions. The member data for those dimensions would be obtained from the related tables. The structure shown in Figure 17-16(a) occurs so frequently in OLAP processing that it has been given the name **star schema,** in reference to the pattern of the dimension tables around the table having the measure data.

Note that this figure does not include ARTIST Name. To include it the OLAP designer has a choice to join Name of ARTIST to the WORK table via the ArtistID key. If that were done, WORK would not be in domain/key normal form and consequently there would be duplicated data.

An alternative to storing such joins is shown in Figure 17-16(b). Here, the ARTIST table is not joined to WORK, but is kept in normalized form. Another table, GENRE, has been added as well. This table structure occurs frequently, too, and has been given the name **snowflake schema.** The difference between the star and the snowflake structures is that with the star, every dimension table is adjacent to the table storing the measure values. These tables may or may not be normalized. With the snowflake structure, there can be multilevels of tables, and each will be normalized.

The choice between these two structures depends on the size and nature of the data and also upon OLAP workload. In general, the star schema requires greater storage but is faster to process. The snowflake is slower, but uses less storage.

OLAP STORAGE ALTERNATIVES (ROLAP, MOLAP, AND HOLAP) No, we are not talking about a high-tech version of the seven dwarves. ROLAP, MOLAP, and HOLAP refer to different means for storing OLAP data. Basically, the question is, in order to gain the best performance, should relational DBMS products be extended to include special facilities for OLAP, or should a special-purpose processing engine be used, or should both be used?

ROLAP storage (relational OLAP) proponents claim that with preprocessing of certain queries and with other extensions, relational DBMS products are more than adequate. Proponents of MOLAP (multidimensional OLAP) storage believe that, while relational DBMS are fine for transaction processing and query and reporting, the processing requirements for OLAP are so specialized that no DBMS can produce acceptable OLAP performance. The third group, HOLAP (hybrid OLAP), believes that both DBMS products and specialized OLAP engines have a role and can be used to advantage.

Microsoft uses these terms more narrowly in the context of SQL Server OLAP. To Microsoft, ROLAP means that the source data and precomputed aggregations of data will be stored in a SQL Server database. With MOLAP, on the other hand, the data, cube structure, and precomputed aggregations of data will be stored in a special-purpose multidimensional data structure. With HOLAP, the data stay in the relational database, but data aggregations are stored in a multidimensional data structure.

➤ FIGURE 17-16

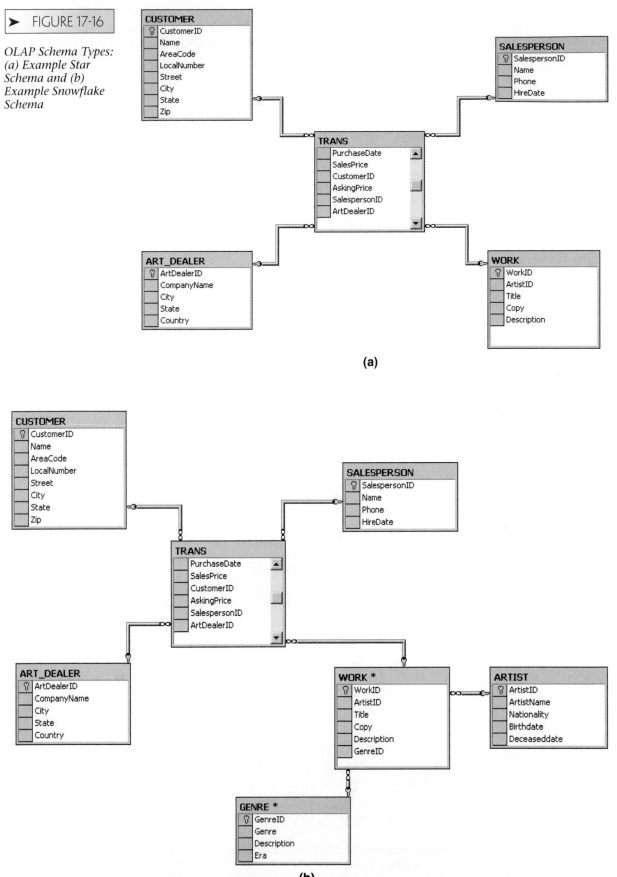

OLAP Schema Types: (a) Example Star Schema and (b) Example Snowflake Schema

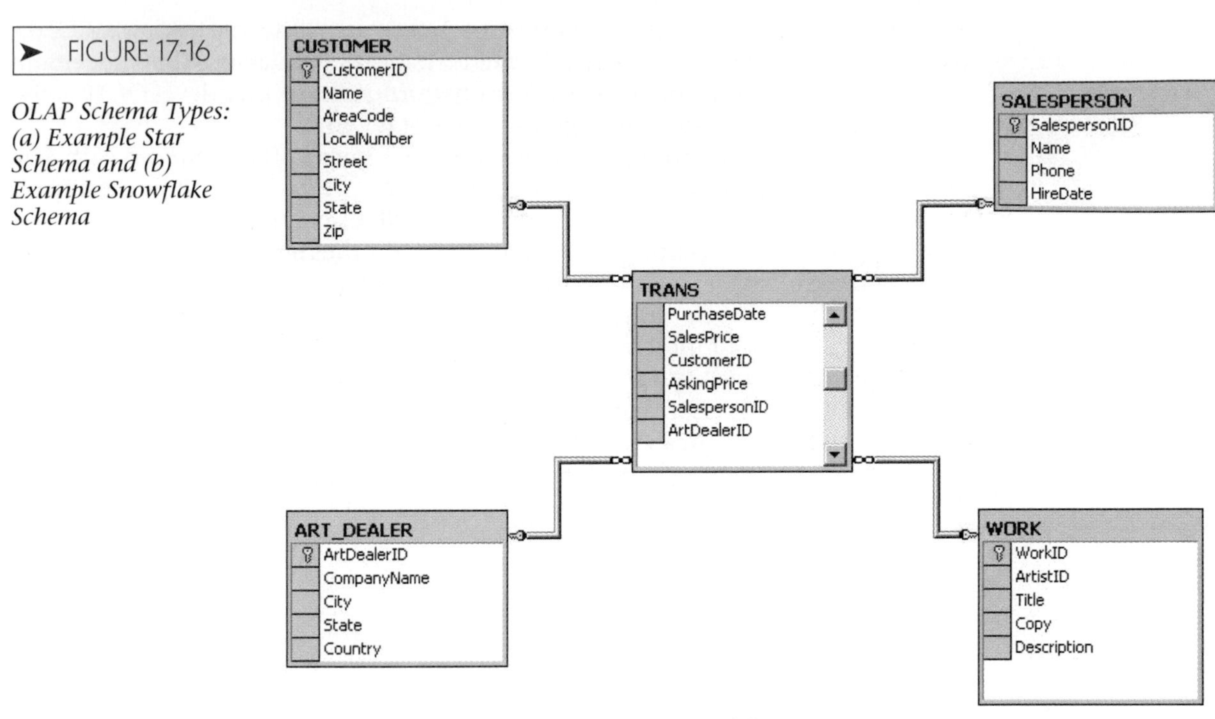

(a)

CUSTOMER
CustomerID
Name
AreaCode
LocalNumber
Street
City
State
Zip

SALESPERSON
SalespersonID
Name
Phone
HireDate

TRANS
PurchaseDate
SalesPrice
CustomerID
AskingPrice
SalespersonID
ArtDealerID

ART_DEALER
ArtDealerID
CompanyName
City
State
Country

WORK *
WorkID
ArtistID
Title
Copy
Description
GenreID

ARTIST
ArtistID
ArtistName
Nationality
Birthdate
Deceaseddate

GENRE *
GenreID
Genre
Description
Era

(b)

MOLAP results in the best performance, but requires the most storage. ROLAP uses less storage, but will be slow. It is intended for large databases that are seldom queried. HOLAP is a compromise with fast performance for high-level OLAP activity, but will be slower for exploring fine levels of detail.

Figure 17-17 shows the OLAP architecture that Microsoft announced with SQL Server 7.0 and Office 2000. This HOLAP architecture involves OLAP processing on central data servers, on the Web server, and on client computers. Enterprise databases are processed by central data servers shown on the right-hand side of this diagram. The results of such processing are then made available to the Pivot Table Service on either a Web server or a client computer. Additionally, either the Web server or the client computer may have local versions of OLAP data.

There are several key elements of this architecture. First, the pivot table service is an OLAP processor that is available as an NT and Windows 2000 service. It is also available on other versions of windows that are running Office 2000. In fact, the pivot table service is invoked whenever creating data access pages in Access. This service is even more frequently used by Excel.

FIGURE 17-17

Microsoft OLAP Architecture

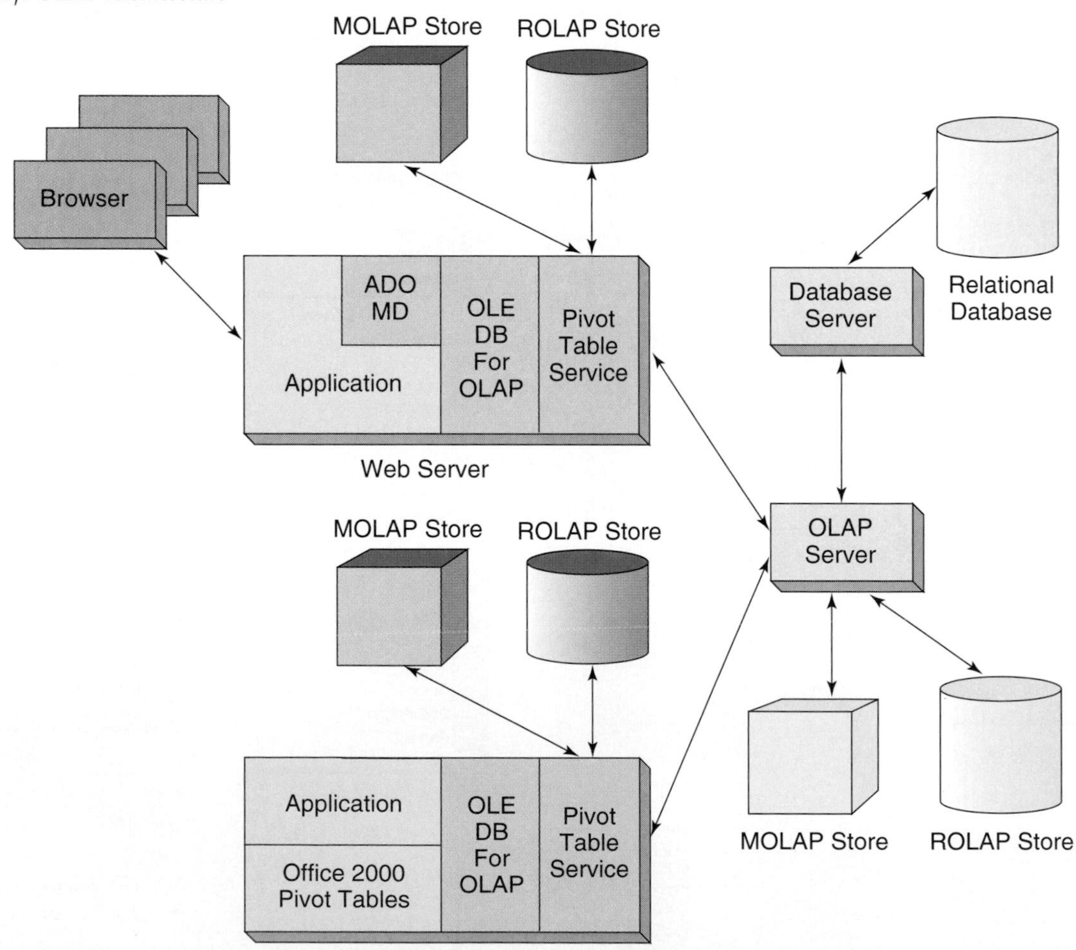

The Pivot Table Service is exposed through an extension to OLE DB called OLE DB for OLAP. This extension builds on the OLE DB that you learned in Chapter 15; basically, it extends the rowset abstraction to include not just recordsets but also to include datasets, which are abstractions of cubes. The ADO extension for processing OLE DB for OLAP is called ADO MD (multidimensional). With ADO MD, Connection and Command objects can open datasets and process them dynamically similarly to the way shown for recordsets in Chapter 15. Data can be both read and written.

This architecture moves as much OLAP processing as possible to the client because the processing requirements of OLAP can be great. There is no disadvantage to this when processing data that is stored locally, but when creating cubes that require data from a central enterprise server, considerable data transmission may occur. This may not be acceptable; certainly, such systems will need to be tuned as experience is gained.

As indicated in Figure 17-17, OLAP processing can be done on centralized, downloaded, or local data. As organizations disburse more of their data to the users, data management problems increase. Data warehousing is a possible solution to this problem, and we consider it next.

➤ DATA WAREHOUSES

Downloading does move the data closer to the user and thereby increase its potential utility. Unfortunately, while one or two download sites can be managed without a problem, if every department wants to have its own source of downloaded data, the management problems become immense. Accordingly, organizations began to look for some means of providing a standardized service for moving data to the user and making them more useful. That service is called data warehousing.

A **data warehouse** is a store of enterprise data that is designed to facilitate management decision making. A data warehouse includes not only data but also tools, procedures, training, personnel, and other resources that make access to the data easier and more relevant to decision makers. The goal of the data warehouse is to increase the value of the organization's data asset.

As shown in Figure 17-18, the role of the data warehouse is to store extracts from operational data and make those extracts available to users in a useful format. The data can be extracts from databases and files, but it can also be document images, recordings, photos, and other nonscalar data. The source data could also be purchased from other organizations. The data warehouse stores the extracted data and also combines it, aggregates it, transforms it, and makes it available to users via tools that are designed for analysis and decision making, such as OLAP.

COMPONENTS OF A DATA WAREHOUSE

The components of a data warehouse are listed in Figure 17-19. As stated, the source of the warehouse is operational data. Hence, the data warehouse needs tools for extracting the data and storing them. These data, however, are not useful without metadata that describe the nature of the data, their origins, their format, limits on their use, and other characteristics of the data that influence the way they can and should be used.

Potentially, the data warehouse contains billions of bytes of data in many different formats. Accordingly, it needs DBMS and OLAP servers of its own to store and process the data. In fact, several DBMS and OLAP products may be used, and the features and functions of these may be augmented by additional in-house

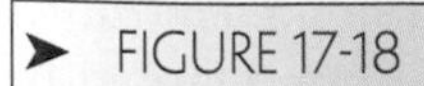
FIGURE 17-18

Data Warehouse

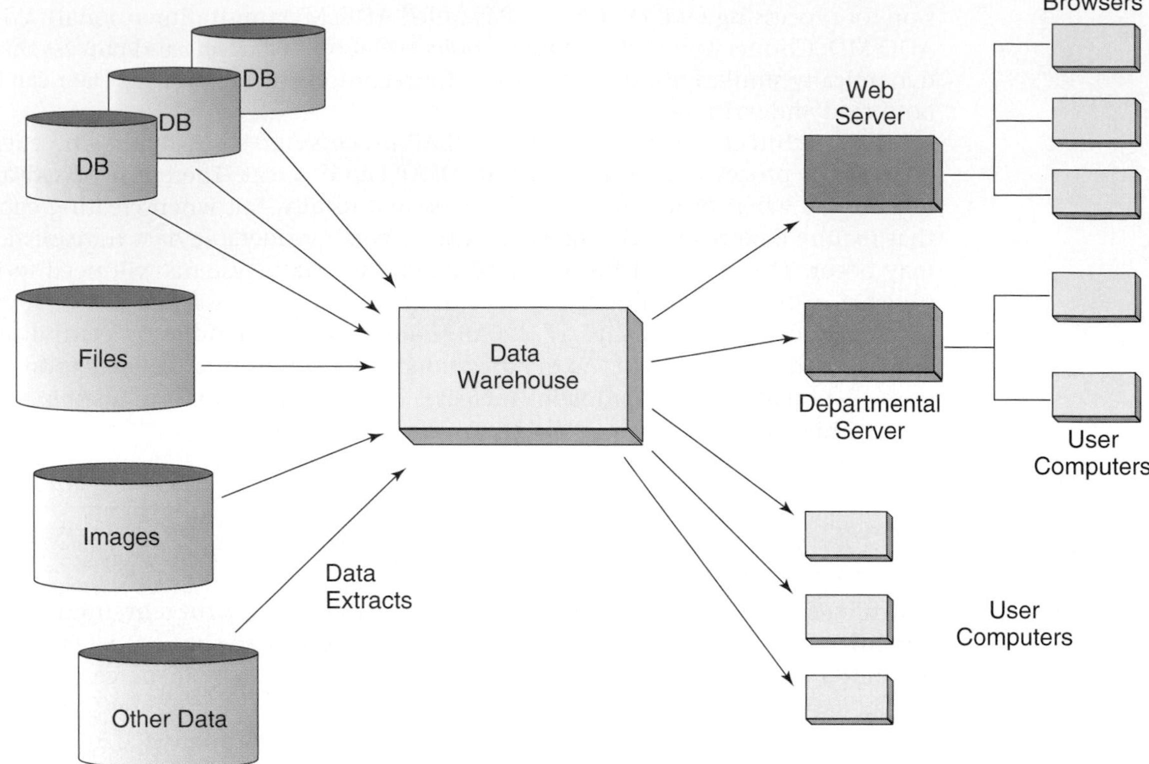

developed software that reformats, aggregates, integrates, and transfers data from one processor to another within the data warehouse. Programs may be needed to store and process nonscalar data like graphics and animations, also.

Because the purpose of the data warehouse is to make organizational data more available, the warehouse must include tools not only to deliver the data to the users but also to transform the data for analysis, query, and reporting, and OLAP for user-specified aggregation and disaggregation.

The data warehouse provides an important, but complicated, set of resources and services. Hence, the warehouse needs to include training courses, training materials, on-line help utilities, and other similar training products to make it

FIGURE 17-19

Components of a Data Warehouse

- Data extraction tools
- Extracted data
- Metadata of warehouse contents
- Warehouse DBMS(s) and OLAP servers
- Warehouse data management tools
- Data delivery programs
- End-user analysis tools
- User training courses and materials
- Warehouse consultants

easy for users to take advantage of the warehouse resources. Finally, the data warehouse includes knowledgeable personnel who can serve as consultants.

Requirements for a Data Warehouse

The requirements for a data warehouse are different from the requirements for a traditional database application. For one, in a typical database application, the structure of reports and queries is standardized. While the data in a report or query vary from month to month, for instance, the structure of the report or query stays the same. Data warehouse users, on the other hand, often need to change the structure of queries and reports.

Consider an example. Suppose a company defines sales territories geographically—for simplicity, say, one salesperson is assigned to each state or province in North America. Now, say, a user of a data warehouse wants to investigate the impact on sales commissions if, instead of allocating salespeople geographically, staff are allocated to specific, named accounts. To compare these alternatives, sales must be grouped by company on the one hand and by state on another. Queries and reports with different structures will need to be created for this purpose.

Another difference is that users want to do their own data aggregation. For example, a user who wants to investigate the impact of different marketing campaigns may want to aggregate product sales according to package color at one time; according to marketing program at another; according to package color within marketing program at a third; and according to marketing program with package color on a fourth. The analyst wants the same data in each report; she simply wants to *slice and dice it differently.*

Not only do data warehouse users want to aggregate data in their own terms; they may also want to disaggregate them in their own terms, or, as it is commonly called, such users want to **drill down** their data. For example, a user may be presented a screen that shows total product sales for a given year. The user may then want to be able to click on the data and have them explode into sales by month; to click again and have the data explode into sales by product by month or sales by region by product by month. While database applications can be written to meet this need for a specific set of drill-down requirements, more often, the requirements vary by user and task. In fact, sometimes the users do not know how they want to drill down until they see the data and start drilling down; hence, drill-down tools need to be flexible.

Graphical output is another common requirement. Users want to see the results of geographic data in geographic form. Sales by state and province should be shown on a map of North America. A reshuffling of employees and offices should be shown on a diagram of office space. Again, these requirements are more difficult because they vary from user to user and from task to task.

Finally, many users of data warehouse facilities want to import warehouse data into domain-specific programs. For example, financial analysts want to import data into their spreadsheet models and into more sophisticated financial analysis programs. Portfolio managers want to import data into portfolio management programs, and oil drilling engineers want to import data into seismic analysis programs. All of this importing usually means that the warehouse data needs to be formatted in specific ways. These requirements are summarized in Figure 17-20.

Challenges for Data Warehouses

So far, we've described data warehouses in an idealized way that makes them appear to be a panacea for management decision making. In point of fact, delivering the capabilities we have described is very difficult. There are a several important challenges that must be met and problems that must be solved.

➤ FIGURE 17-20

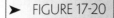

Categories of Requirements for a Data Warehouse

- Queries and reports with variable structure
- User-specified data aggregation
- User-specified drill down
- Graphical outputs
- Integration with domain-specific programs

INCONSISTENT DATA Obviously, the data warehouse is useless, if not downright harmful, if the data that it provides are inaccurate. The issue goes beyond the quality of the data that the warehouse extracts from its sources. The source data can be accurate as extracted, but inaccuracies can be introduced by unwittingly integrating data that are inconsistent in timing or domain.

Consider the example of extracted data in Figure 17-21. One table is an extract of order data, and a second is an extract of checks that were written as bonuses to salespeople. Suppose that a data warehouse user wants to investigate the relationship of sales performance to sales bonuses. At first glance, it would seem that all that need be done is to sum the order amounts for each salesperson and compare the total to the bonus. The following SQL code will accomplish that task:

```
SELECT      SPName, Sum(OrderAmount), BonusAmount
FROM        ORDER, BONUS
WHERE       ORDER.SPNum = BONUS.SP#
GROUP BY    SpNum
```

(As an aside, the typical data warehouse user probably does not know sufficient SQL to write this code, so it would need to be written for him or her or provided indirectly through some type of graphical query interface.)

Now suppose that these data were correct when extracted, and further suppose that they were obtained from two different information systems—order processing and accounts payable. Since they were obtained from two different systems, it is unknown whether the timing of the data is consistent. It might be that the order data were correct as of the last Friday of the month but that the bonus check data were correct as of the last day of the month. There is nothing in the data to indicate that difference, and, in fact, no one may note that such a difference exists. It may have a substantial impact on the results of the analysis, however.

➤ FIGURE 17-21

Example Extracts of Order and Bonus Data

ORDER Table

SPNum	OrderNumber	OrderAmount
100	1000	$12,000
200	1200	$17,000
100	1400	$13,500
300	1600	$11,335

BONUS Table

SP#	SPName	BonusAmount
100	Mary Smith	$3,000
200	Fred Johnson	$2,500
300	Laura Jackson	$3,250

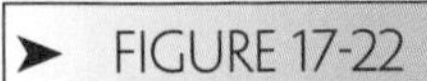
FIGURE 17-22

Salesperson and Region Data for Two Years

SALESPERSON Table

SPName	Region	Year	TotalSales
Johnson	SO	2000	$175,998
Wu	NW	2000	$223,445
O'Connor	NE	2000	$337,665
Abernathy	SE	2000	$276,889
Lopez	SW	2000	$334,557
Johnson	SO	2001	$225,998
Wu	NW	2001	$276,445
O'Connor	NE	2001	$389,737
Abernathy	SO	2001	$362,768
Lopez	SO	2001	$419,334

REGION Table

SalesRegion	Manager
NW	Allen
NE	Brendlmann
SO	Currid

In addition to timing differences, there can also be differences in the underlying domains. Consider the SALESPERSON and REGION tables in Figure 17-22, and suppose that someone wants to produce a report of total sales for each region. To do that, the following SQL needs to be executed:

```
SELECT      SalesRegion, Sum(TotalSales)
FROM        REGION, SALESPERSON
WHERE       REGION.SalesRegion = SALESPERSON.Region
GROUP BY    Region
```

For the data shown, the result of this query will be a table having three rows, one each for the NW, NE, and SO sales regions. Because neither SE nor SW regions had a match in REGION, they were omitted from the join, and the sales from those regions will not appear in the result. This is most likely not what the user intended.

In actuality, between 2000 and 2001, this business changed its sales territories by merging the SE and SW sales regions into the SO region. Hence, all of the sales for salespeople in the SE and SW regions should have been added to the SO row in the query result. Put in database terms, the underlying domain of SalesRegion and Region are different. The domain of SalesRegion is the set of current regions; the domain of Region is the name of the region in which the sale occurred, at the time of the sale.

For the small amounts of data in Figures 17-21 and 17-22, these problems are obvious. If, however, there were thousands of rows of data, such problems could slip past the analyst, and incorrect information would be provided to the decision-making process.

To solve this problem, metadata must be created that describe both the timing and the domains of the source data. These metadata must be made easily accessible to the users of the data warehouse, and those users need to be trained on the importance of considering such issues.

TOOL INTEGRATION Another serious problem for data warehouses concerns the integration of various tools that the users need. The paradigms of different products, in different product categories, are usually different. DBMS products are

➤ FIGURE 17-23

Example of Conceptual Difference Between Spreadsheet and Database Products

EmpNumber	EmpName	DeptNum	Manager	ManagerPhone	DeptCode
1000	Wu	10	Murphy	232-1000	A47
2000	O'Connor	20	Joplin	244-7788	D87
3000	Abernathy	10	Murphy	232-1000	A47
4000	Lopez	20	Joplin	244-7788	D87

(a)

EMPLOYEE(<u>EmpNumber</u>, EmpName, *DeptNum*)
DEPARTMENT(<u>DeptNum</u>, DeptCode, *Manager*)
MANAGER(<u>Manager</u>, ManagerPhone)

(b)

table oriented; OLAP products are cube oriented; spreadsheets are spreadsheet oriented; financial planning packages are plan oriented, and so on. As a result, the user interfaces in the products are dissimilar. Users may need substantial training to learn how to use several products from several categories, and they often have neither the time nor the inclination to learn them.

Even more serious, the process for exporting and importing data across products from different categories may be difficult. Consider the spreadsheet in Figure 17-23(a). This spreadsheet contains data about three themes: Departments, Managers, and Employees. To import this spreadsheet into a normalized database, each of the themes will need to be allocated to separate tables like those in Figure 17-23(b). If the normalization is not done, considerable duplicated data will result as described in Chapter 5. The typical data warehouse user, however, will not understand the need for normalization nor have any idea about how to do it.

Finally, when products are acquired from different vendors, it is often difficult to get to the source of problems when they occur. For example, the vendor of the product that is exporting data may believe that a problem in the export/import process is due to the product that is importing the data, and the vendor of the product that is importing the data may claim the opposite. Since vendors are not experienced in using one another's products, nor are they motivated to encourage the use of other companies' offerings, technical support can be a nightmare.

MISSING WAREHOUSE DATA MANAGEMENT TOOLS While there are many products and tools for extracting data from data sources and many tools for end-user query/reporting and data analysis, there is, at present, a lack of tools for managing the data warehouse itself. If the data warehouse consisted only of extracts from relational databases, and if the problems of timing and domain differences could be solved with training and procedures, then an off-the-shelf DBMS could be used to manage the data warehouse resources. In most instances, however, this is not the case.

Most data warehouses contain extracts from databases, files, spreadsheets, images, and external data sources. Since this is the case, these resources cannot be readily managed by a commercial DBMS, so the organization creating the data warehouse must write its own software. Usually this software has a commercial DBMS at its core, and the in-house data warehouse staff develops the additional features and functions necessary to manage the data warehouse resources.

The management of metadata presents another, similar problem. Few DBMS data dictionaries have sufficient capability to meet the metadata needs of the data warehouse. As stated, users need to know not only what's in the data warehouse but also where it came from, what its timing was, what the underlying domains of the data were, what assumptions were made when the data were extracted, and so forth. Data warehouse personnel will need to write their own metadata management software to augment the capabilities of the DBMS and other data dictionary products that they have.

Writing data management software is difficult and expensive. Once it is written, it must be supported. The vendors of the extraction programs and the data analysis programs will change their products, and any in-house developed software that uses them will need to be altered to conform to new interfaces. Further, the users' requirements will change, and this will necessitate adding new programs that will then need to be integrated with the data warehouse management software.

AD HOC NATURE OF REQUIREMENTS Data warehouses exist to support management decision making. While a good portion of management decisions are regular and recurring, many other decisions are of an ad hoc nature. Questions like, Should we combine sales territories? Sell a product line? Consolidate warehouses? Adopt new Internet-based sales and marketing strategies? are not regular and recurring.

Computer systems, like bureaucracies, are slow and expensive to set up, are relatively inflexible, and work best with needs that follow a pattern. For that reason, such systems excel at tasks like order entry and reservations processing. It is most difficult, however, to design systems that readily respond to changing needs and requirements on an ad hoc basis. Thus, data warehouses have the most success in applications in which the variance in requirements follows a pattern. If a new requirement is similar in structure to an earlier one, that is, "consolidating the northern sales region will be like the process we followed when consolidating the southern region," then the data warehouse will likely be able to respond in a timely fashion. If not, then considerable time, expense, and anguish will probably need to be expended to meet the requirements.

DATA MARTS

Because of the challenges just described, some organizations have decided to limit the scope of the warehouse to more manageable chunks. A **data mart** is a facility akin to a data warehouse but for a much smaller domain. Data marts can be restricted to a particular type of input data, to a particular business function, or to a particular business unit or geographic area.

Restricting a data mart to a particular type of data (e.g., database and spreadsheets) makes the management of the data warehouse simpler and probably means that an off-the-shelf DBMS product can be used to manage the data warehouse. Metadata are also simpler and easier to maintain.

A data mart that is restricted to a particular business function, such as marketing analysis, may have many types of data and metadata to maintain, but all of those data serve the same type of user. Tools for managing the data warehouse and for providing data to the users can be written with an eye toward the requirements that marketing analysts are likely to have.

Finally, a data mart that is restricted to a particular business unit or geographic area may have many types of input and many types of users, but the

➤ FIGURE 17-24

Continuum of Enterprise Data Sharing

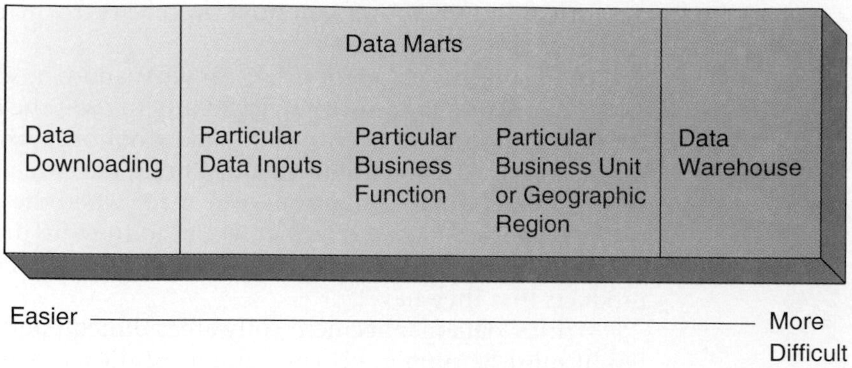

Data Downloading	Data Marts: Particular Data Inputs	Data Marts: Particular Business Function	Data Marts: Particular Business Unit or Geographic Region	Data Warehouse

Easier ——— More Difficult

amount of data to be managed is less than for the entire company. There will also be fewer requests for service, so the data warehouse resources can be allocated to fewer users.

Figure 17-24 summarizes the scope of the alternatives for sharing data that we have addressed in this chapter. Data downloading is the smallest and easiest alternative. Data are extracted from operational systems and delivered to particular users for specific purposes. The downloaded data are provided on a regular and recurring basis, so the structure of the application is fixed, the users are well trained, and problems such as timing and domain inconsistencies are unlikely to occur because users gain experience working with the same data. At the other extreme, a data warehouse provides extensive types of data and services for both recurring and ad hoc requests. Data marts fall in the middle. As we move from left to right in this figure, the alternatives become more powerful but also more expensive and difficult to create.

➤ DATA ADMINISTRATION

An organization's data are as much a resource as are its plant, equipment, and financial assets. Data are time-consuming and expensive to acquire, and they have utility beyond operations. Information derived from data can be used to assess the effectiveness of personnel, products, and marketing programs, and to determine trends in customers' preferences, buying behavior, and so forth. It can be used to simulate the effect of changes in products, sales strategies, and territories. The list of potential applications is so long that, in fact, data often serve to establish and maintain the organization's competitive advantage. Unfortunately, however, as long as the data are locked in operational databases, their utility is limited.

Because of the potential value of the organizational data resource, many organizations have established offices of data administration. The purpose of these offices is not just to guard and protect the data, but also to ensure that they are used effectively.

In some ways, data administration is to data what the controller is to money. The responsibility of a controller is to ensure not only that financial assets are protected and accounted for, but also that they are effectively used. Storing an organization's money in a vault can protect it, but it will not be effectively used. Instead, it must be invested in ways that advance the organization's goals and objectives. Similarly, with data administration, simply protecting the data is not enough. Data administration must also try to increase the utility of the organization's data.

NEED FOR DATA ADMINISTRATION

To understand the need for data administration, consider the analogy of a university library. The typical university library contains hundreds of thousands of books, journals, magazines, government reports, and so forth, but they offer no utility while they are on the bookshelves. To be useful, they must be made available to people who have an interest in and need for them.

Clearly, the library must have some means of describing its collection so that potential users can determine what is available. At first glance, this might seem like a trivial problem. You might say, "Well, build a card catalog." But much work must be done to be able to do that. How should the library's works be identified? How should they be described? Even more basic, what constitutes a work? How can we accommodate different ways of identifying works (ISBN, Dewey decimal system, government report number)? How do we help people find things that they may not know exist?

Other complications arise. Suppose the university is so large that it has several libraries. In this case, how are the collections to be managed as one resource? Furthermore, some departments may maintain their own libraries. Are these to be made part of the university system? Many professors have extensive personal libraries. Should these be part of the system?

CHALLENGES OF DATA ADMINISTRATION

The library analogy does not go far enough, however, as organizational data administration is considerably more difficult than library administration. First, it is not at all clear what constitutes a "work." Libraries contain books, periodicals, and so forth, but organizational data come in myriads of formats. Organizations have traditional data records, but they also have documents, spreadsheets, graphics and illustrations, technical drawings, and audio and video files. How should all of these be described? What are the basic categories of organizational data? These questions are important because their answers determine how the data will be organized, cataloged, managed, protected, and accessed.

Most organizations have many names for the same thing. For instance, a telephone number can be described as a PhoneNumber, Phone, TelephoneNumber, EmployeePhone, or DeptPhone. Which of these names is preferable? When a graphic designer places a telephone number on a new form, what label should he or she use? When a programmer writes a new program, what name should he or she use for the program variable that holds the telephone number? When a user wants to query for a customer area code while developing a buying trend analysis, which name should she use in her query?

There also are many ways of representing the data element. A phone number can be represented as a 10-digit integer, a 10-digit text field, a 13-digit text field in the form *(nnn)nnn-nnnn,* a 12-digit text field in the form *nnn-nnn-nnnn,* or in still other formats. Which of these should be allowed? Which, if any, should be the standard?

Such differences between organizational data and library materials are minuscule, however, when compared with the next difference: People must be able to change organizational data.

Consider what would happen at the library if people checked out books, wrote in them, tore out pages, added pages, and then put the books back on the shelves. Or, even worse, suppose someone checked out three books, made changes in all three, checked them back in, and told the librarian: "Either change all of these or none of them."

Since data are a shared asset, limits must be placed on processing rights and responsibilities. For example, when an employee leaves the company, his or her

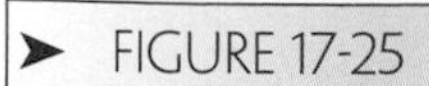

Challenges of Data Administration

- Many types of data exist.
- Basic categories of data are not obvious.
- The same data can have many names.
- The same data can have many descriptions and formats.
- Data are changed — often concurrently.
- Political - organizational issues complicate operational issues.

records cannot be immediately deleted; they need to be maintained for several years for management reporting and tax purposes. Hence, one department cannot delete data from the database just because that department is finished with them. The office of data administration needs to help define users' processing rights and responsibilities. This role is similar to that described for database administration in Chapter 11; there, however, the scope was a particular database. Here, the scope is the entire organization.

In addition to all of these operationally oriented challenges, there are organizational issues. For example, data and processing rights can mean organizational power; hence, changes in data control can mean changes in power. Thus, behind the tasks of data administration lie all sorts of political issues. A discussion of these is beyond the scope of this text, but they are important nonetheless. The challenges for data administration are summarized in Figure 17-25.

Functions of Data Administration

Because of the challenges just described, data administration is complex. To protect the data asset while at the same time increasing its utility to the organization, several different functions or tasks must be performed. As shown in Figure 17-26, these activities can be grouped into several different categories.

MARKETING First and foremost, data administration is responsible for declaring its existence and selling its services to the rest of the organization. Employees need to know that data administration exists and that there are policies, standards, and guidelines that pertain to organizational data and the reasons for them, and they need to be given reasons for respecting and following data administration rules, guidelines, and restrictions.

Data administration must be a service function, and the users must perceive it in that way. Thus, data administration activities must be communicated to the organization in a positive, service-providing light. Employees must believe that they have something to gain from data administration. Otherwise, the function becomes all cost and no benefit to the users, and it will be ignored.

DATA STANDARDS For organizational data to be managed effectively, they must be organized coherently. If each department, function, or employee were to choose a different definition for a data item or for the means by which data items are to be named or described, the result would be chaos. It would be impossible even to compile an inventory of data, let alone manage it. Consequently, many organizations decide that important data items will be described in a standard way. For example, data administration may decide that every data item of importance to the organization will be described by a standard name, definition, description, set of processing restrictions, and the like. Once this structure is determined, the next question is, who will set the values of these standard

Functions of Data Administration

Marketing
- Communicate existence of data administration to organization.
- Explain reason for existence of standards, policies, and guidelines.
- Describe in a positive light the services provided.

Data Standards
- Establish standard means for describing data items. Standards include name, definition, description, processing restrictions, and so forth.
- Establish data proponents.

Data Policies
- Establish organizationwide data policy. Examples are security, data proponency, and distribution.

Forum for Data Conflict Resolution
- Establish procedures for reporting conflicts.
- Provide means for hearing all perspectives and views.
- Have authority to make decision to resolve conflict.

Return on Organization's Data Investment
- Focus attention on value of data investment.
- Investigate new methodologies and technologies.
- Take proactive attitude toward information management.

descriptions? For example, who will decide the standard name or standard-processing restrictions?

In many organizations, the data administration group does not determine the standard descriptions. Instead, each item is assigned a **data proponent,** a department or other organizational unit in charge of managing that data item. The proponent is given the responsibility for establishing and maintaining the official organizational definitions for the data items assigned to it. Even though the data administration group may be the proponent of some data items, most proponents come from other departments.

You may encounter the term *data owner,* which is generally used in the same way that the term *data proponent* is used in this text. We avoid the term here because it implies a degree of propriety that does not exist. Both legally and practically, the organization is the one and only owner of the data. Although some group or groups have a legitimate claim to a greater degree of authority over particular data than others do, these groups do not own those data. Hence, we use the term *data proponent,* instead.

To summarize, the foundation of data administration is a system of data standards. The data administration group is responsible for working with users and management to develop a workable system of standards, which must be documented and communicated to the organization by some effective means. Procedures for assessing the employees' compliance with the standards also must be established.

DATA POLICIES Another group of data administration functions concerns data policies. To illustrate the need for such policies, first consider data security. Every organization has data that are proprietary or sensitive, and data administration is responsible for developing a security system to protect them. Questions like the following need to be addressed: What security schemes should be put in place? Does the organization need a multilevel security system similar to that of the military? Or would a simpler system suffice? The security policy must also decide what is required for people to have access to sensitive data and what agreements they must sign to do so. What about employees of other organizations? Should sensitive data be copied? How should employees be trained with regard to security? What should be done when security procedures are violated?

A second type of data policy concerns data proponents and processing rights. What does being a data proponent mean? What rights does the proponent have that other groups do not? Who decides who will become a data proponent, and how can this be changed?

A third example of the need for data policy concerns the distribution of data, such as whether official data should be distributed on more than one computer and, if so, which, if any, should be the official copy. What processing should be allowed on distributed data? Should data that have been distributed be returned to the official data store? If so, what checks must there be to validate them before accepting them?

FORUM FOR DATA CONFLICT RESOLUTION

To be effective, organizational data must be shared, but humans have difficulty sharing. Consequently, the organization must be prepared to address disputes regarding data proponents, processing restrictions, and other matters.

The first responsibility of data administration in this regard is to establish procedures for reporting conflicts. When one user's or group's needs conflict with another's, the groups need a way to make their conflict known in an orderly manner. Once the conflict has been acknowledged, established procedures should allow all involved parties to present their case. Data administration staff, perhaps in conjunction with the data proponents involved, then must resolve the conflict. This scenario assumes that the organization has granted to data administration the authority to make and enforce the resulting decision.

Data administration provides a forum for resolving conflicts that apply to the entire organization. Database administration also provides a forum for resolving conflicts, but those that pertain to a particular database.

INCREASING THE RETURN ON THE ORGANIZATION'S DATA INVESTMENT

A final function for data administration is the need to increase the organization's return on its data investment. Data administration is the department that asks such questions as, Are we getting what we should be getting from our data resource? If so, can we get more? If not, why not? Is it all worthwhile? This function involves all of the others: It includes marketing, the establishment of standards or policies, conflict resolution, and so forth. Sometimes this function also means investigating new techniques for storing, processing, or presenting data; new methodologies and technology; and the like.

The successful fulfillment of this role requires a *proactive* attitude toward information management. Relevant questions are whether we can use information to increase our market position, our economic competitiveness, and our overall net worth. Data administration must work closely with the organization's planning and development departments to anticipate rather than just react to the need for new information requirements.

Finally, data must be made available to their potential users. Availability means not only making it technically feasible for a highly motivated and skilled person to access data; it means that data must be provided to the users via means that are easy for them to use and in formats that are directly applicable to the work that must be done.

➤ SUMMARY

Teleprocessing is the classic architecture for multi-user database processing. With it, users operate dumb terminals or personal computers that emulate dumb terminals. The communications control program, application programs, DBMS, and operating system all are processed by a single, centralized computer. Because all processing is done by a single computer, the user interface of a teleprocessing system is usually simple and primitive.

A client–server system consists of a network of computers, most often connected via a LAN. In nearly all cases, the user computers, called clients, are personal computers and, in most cases, the server computer is also a personal computer, although mainframes can be used. Application programs are processed on the client computer; the DBMS and the data management portion of the operating system reside on a server.

File-sharing systems also involve networks of computers, and like client–server architectures, they usually consist of micros connected via LANs. The chief difference between file-sharing systems and client–server systems is that the server computer provides fewer services for the user computers. The server, which is called a *file* server and not a *database* server, provides access to files and other resources. Consequently, both the DBMS and the application programs must be distributed to the users' computers.

With a distributed database system, multiple computers process the same database. There are several types of distributed databases: partitioned, nonreplicated; nonpartitioned, replicated; and partitioned, replicated. In general, the greater the degree of partitioning and replication, the greater the flexibility, independence, and reliability will be. At the same time, expense, control difficulty, and security problems increase.

Three types of distributed database processing are the downloading of read-only data, the updating of database data by a designated computer, and the updating of database data by multiple computers. Three types of distributed update conflict can occur: loss of uniqueness, lost updates due to concurrent transactions, and updates of deleted data. If updating is allowed on more than one computer, such problems must be resolved.

Coordination of distributed atomic transactions is difficult and requires a two-phase commit. The OLE Distributed Transaction Server and Java Enterprise Beans are two technologies for dealing with these problems.

With the advent of powerful personal computers, it became possible to download substantial amounts of enterprise data to users for local processing. Users can query and report on downloaded data using DBMS products on their own machines. In most cases, users are not allowed to update and return data because doing so could create data integrity problems. Even when downloaded data are not updated and returned, problems of coordination, consistency, access control, and possible computer crime can occur. A Web server can be used to publish downloaded data.

On Line Analytical Processing (OLAP) is a new way of presenting information. With it, data is viewed in cubes that have axes, dimensions, measures, slices, and levels. Axes refer to the physical structure of the presentation like rows and columns. Dimensions are characteristics of the data that are placed on the axes. Measures are the data values to be displayed. Slices are the attributes of the cube (either dimensions or measures) that are to be held constant in the presentation. Level is an attribute of a dimension that describes its position in a hierarchy.

The term *cube* is used both to refer to the underlying semantic structure that is used to interpret data and to a particular materialization of data in such a semantic structure. Figure 17-15(a) shows one way to define the underlying structure, and Figure 17-15(b) shows one way to define a materialization of a cube structure.

ROLAP, MOLAP, and HOLAP are three of the seven dwarves in OLAP land. Proponents of ROLAP say a relational DBMS with extensions is sufficient to meet OLAP requirements; proponents of MOLAP say a specialized multidimensional processor is necessary; and proponents of HOLAP want to use both.

Microsoft has extended OLE DB and ADO for OLAP. OLE DB for OLAP includes a dataset object; ADO MD has new objects for processing dataset objects in ways similar to recordset objects. The new Pivot Table Service has been added to Office 2000 and Windows 2000. Microsoft's architecture move much OLAP processing to client computers; whether this will be acceptable for the processing of data on enterprise servers is as yet unknown.

A data warehouse is a store of enterprise data that is designed to facilitate management decision making. A data warehouse stores extracts of operational databases, files, images, recordings, photos, external data, and other data and makes these data available to users in a format that is useful to them.

The components of a data warehouse are data extraction tools, data extracts, metadata, one or more DBMS products, in-house developed warehouse data management tools, data delivery programs, user analysis tools, user training, and warehouse consultants. Typical requirements for a data warehouse include variable-structure queries and reports, user-specified data aggregation, drill-down, graphical outputs, and integration with domain-specific programs.

Data warehouses must overcome several important challenges. For one, when data are integrated, inconsistencies can develop due to timing and domain differences. Also, because of the many tools required in a data warehouse, tools will have different user interfaces and inconsistent means of importing and exporting data, and it may be difficult to obtain technical support.

Another challenge is that there is a lack of tools for managing the data warehouse itself. The organization may have to develop its own tools for managing nonrelational data and for maintaining appropriate metadata. Such development is difficult and expensive. Finally, the nature of many requests on the data warehouse is ad hoc; such requests are difficult to satisfy. As a result, some organizations have developed limited-scope warehouses called data marts.

Data are an important organizational asset, one that can support both operations and management decision making. The purpose of the office data administration is not just to guard and protect the data asset but also to ensure that it is effectively used. One of the most important functions of data administration is to document the contents of the organization's data asset. This is a complicated task because data occur in many different formats in many different places in the organization. Data administration needs to help set organizational standards for names and formats of data items and also to define organizational processing rights and responsibilities. Finally, data are an asset, and their use can mean power; because of this, data administration must deal with organizational and political issues.

The specific functions of data administration include marketing its services, facilitating data standards and identifying data proponents, ensuring that appropriate data policies are established, and providing a forum for conflict resolution. All of these functions are aimed at the goal of increasing the return on the organization's data investment.

➤ GROUP I QUESTIONS

17.1 List the architectures that are used to support multi-user databases.

17.2 Sketch the architecture of a teleprocessing system. Name and identify the computer(s) and programs involved, and explain which computer processes which programs.

17.3 Why is the users' interface on teleprocessing applications generally character oriented and primitive?

17.4 Sketch the architecture of a client–server system. Name and identify the computer(s) and programs involved, and explain which computer processes which programs.

17.5 What types of processing hardware are used with client–server systems?

17.6 How many servers can a client–server system have? What restrictions apply to the servers?

17.7 Sketch the architecture of a file-sharing system. Name and identify the computer(s) and programs involved, and explain which computer processes which programs.

17.8 Explain how the processing of the following SQL query would differ in a client–server system and in a file-sharing system:

```
SELECT    StudentName, ClassName
FROM      STUDENT, GRADE
WHERE     STUDENT.StudentNumber = GRADE.StudentNumber
AND       GRADE.Grade = 'A'
```

Assume that the database contains two tables:

STUDENT (StudentNumber, StudentName, StudentPhone)

GRADE (ClassNumber, StudentNumber, Grade)

Also assume that the primary and foreign keys have indexes.

17.9 Explain why file-sharing systems are seldom used for high-volume transaction processing applications.

17.10 Define the terms *partitioned* and *replicated* as they pertain to distributed database applications.

17.11 Explain the difference between a vertical fragment and a horizontal fragment.

17.12 Explain the differences in the four types of distributed databases in Figure 17-5.

17.13 Name and describe three techniques for supporting distributed database processing.

17.14 Describe three types of distributed update conflict.

17.15 What is the purpose of two-phase commit?

17.16 Summarize the coordination problem in processing downloaded databases.

17.17 Summarize the consistency problem in processing downloaded databases.

17.18 Summarize the access control problem in processing downloaded databases.

17.19 Why is computer crime a risk when processing downloaded databases?

17.20 Sketch the components of a system that uses a Web server to publish downloaded data.

17.21 What is an OLAP cube? Give an example other than the one in Figure 17-12.

17.22 Explain the difference between an OLAP axis and an OLAP dimension.

17.23 What is the measure of an OLAP cube?

17.24 What does the term *slice* mean in reference to OLAP cubes?

17.25 What is a member of a dimension? Give examples for Time and Location dimensions.

17.26 Explain the use of levels in Figure 17-12.

17.27 Explain the ambiguity in the term *cube*.

17.28 What is the result of the expression CROSSJOIN ({Mary, Lynda}, {Sailing, Skiing})? Of CROSSJOIN ({Sailing, Skiing}, {Mary, Lynda})?

17.29 Give an SQL SELECT statement to produce a cube similar to that in Figure 17-12 except that the rows and columns are reversed and Location is presented before Category (when reading left to right).

17.30 Explain the difference between the star and the snowflake schemas.

17.31 Define ROLAP, MOLAP, and HOLAP.

17.32 Considering the discussion in this text only, how has OLE been extended for OLAP?

17.33 What does ADO MD stand for and what is its function?

17.34 Define *data warehouse.*

17.35 How does having a data warehouse compare to processing downloaded data?

17.36 List and describe the components of a data warehouse.

17.37 Explain what it means to change the structure of a query or report rather than change the data in a query or report.

17.38 Give an example, other than one in this book, of a user's need to aggregate data.

17.39 Give an example, other than one in this book, of a user's need to drill down data.

17.40 Explain two sources of data inconsistencies, and give an example, other than one in this book, of each.

17.41 Summarize the problems of having tools that use different paradigms and are licensed by different vendors.

17.42 Explain which data warehouse tools must be written in-house.

17.43 Why does the ad hoc nature of data warehouse requests pose a problem?

17.44 What is a data mart, and why would a company develop one?

17.45 List and briefly explain three types of data marts.

17.46 Explain why data are an important organizational asset.

17.47 Describe several example uses of data besides operational systems.

17.48 How is data administration similar to the job of a controller?

17.49 Briefly summarize the necessity for data administration.

17.50 List and briefly explain the challenges of data administration.

17.51 Describe data administration's marketing function.

17.52 What role does data administration take with regard to data standards?

17.53 Define *data proponent.*

17.54 What is the difference between data proponent and data owner?

17.55 Summarize data administration's role in regard to data policy.

17.56 Explain what is involved in establishing a forum for conflict resolution.

17.57 How can data administration help increase the return on an organization's data asset?

➤ GROUP II QUESTIONS

17.58 Consider a company that has a national sales manager and 15 regional salespeople. Each week, the salespeople download sales data from the mainframe and use it to update their sales projections for the next month. When they have done this, they connect via a modem to a server database and store their sales projections into that database. The manager then accumulates the sales data into a companywide forecast. What problems, issues, and difficulties might exist in this situation in terms of coordination, consistency, access control, and computer crime?

17.59 Consider the enterprise data that exist at your college or university. Does it seem to you that your institution makes good use of its data asset? What ways can you identify that the data asset is used for more than operational processing? Describe ways in which you think your college or university could take advantage of its data asset in the areas of

- Student recruitment
- Fund-raising
- Program planning
- Student affairs
- Alumni affairs
- Other areas.

OBJECT-ORIENTED DATABASE PROCESSING

This part consists of one chapter that addresses object-oriented programming and storage with ODBMS. It includes a brief tutorial on object-oriented programming and discussions on Oracle object-relational, on the object extensions to SQL called SQL3, and on an object data management standard called ODMG-93.

This part supplements the discussions of OLE DB, ADO, and JDBC in Chapters 15 and 16. Whereas those chapters presented practical matters on using object interfaces to obtain database services, this chapter presents a more conceptual view on the rationale and purpose of object-oriented database processing.

Object-Oriented Database Processing

This chapter addresses the persistent storage of objects created in programming languages like Java, C#, and C++. As you know, relational databases store data in the form of tables, rows, and columns. As such, relational databases are not well suited to store objects because objects can contain complex structures of data items and also pointers to other objects. Further, objects include executable statements, or methods, and to make objects persistent, some means must be provided to store those methods as well.

Special-purpose DBMS products called **Object-Oriented DBMS** or (**ODBMS** or sometimes **OODBMS**) were developed in the early 1990s to provide persistent object storage. These producs have not been commercially successful, however, because they require that existing data be converted to ODBMS format. Organizations are reluctant to make that conversion because it is very expensive and the gain is not worth the expense.

Object-oriented programming is on the rise, however, and the need for persistent object storage has not disappeared. In response, the traditional DBMS vendors are augmenting the capabilities of their products to allow for object storage as well as traditional relational data storage. Such products are called **object-relational DBMS,** and they are likely to see increased use in the years to come. Oracle, in particular, has developed facilities for object modeling and storage.

Because we do not assume you are an object-oriented programmer, this chapter begins with a sketch of object-oriented terms and concepts. Then we will describe alternatives for providing persistent object storage and illustrate Oracle's support for object persistence. Finally, we will survey two important object standards: SQL3 and ODMG–93.

➤ A SKETCH OF OBJECT-ORIENTED PROGRAMMING

Object-oriented programming (OOP) is a way of designing and coding programs. OOP is substantially different from traditional programming, as it entails a new way of thinking about programming structures. Instead of viewing programs as sequences of instructions to be processed, OOP views programs as sets of data structures that have both data elements and program instructions.

Another way to understand the difference between traditional programming and OOP is that traditional programming is organized around logic first and data second, whereas OOP is organized around data first and logic second. To design a traditional program to create an order, for example, we would first develop a flowchart or pseudocode of the logic of the ordering process. The data to be processed would be documented as a part of the logic.

When developing an object-oriented program to create an order, we would first identify the objects involved, say, ORDER, SALESPERSON, ITEM, and CUSTOMER. We would then design those objects as data elements and programs that are shared or *exposed* to one another. Finally, we would create a flowchart or pseudocode of the behaviors of the objects.

OOP Terminology

An OOP object is an **encapsulated structure** having both **attributes** and **methods.** The term *encapsulated* means that it is complete in itself; programs external to an object know nothing of its structure and need to know nothing of its structure. The external appearance of an object is referred to as its **interface.** The interface consists of the attributes and methods that are visible to the outside world. The encapsulated internals of an object are referred to as its **implementation.** The *attributes*[1] of OOP objects are arranged in a particular structure.

OOP objects contain *methods,* or sequences of instructions that the object executes. For example, an OOP object may have a method to display itself, one to create itself, and one to modify a portion of itself. Consider a method that modifies a CUSTOMER object. This method, which is part of the OOP object, is a program; to modify the OOP object, this program contains instructions to obtain data from the user or other source.

OOP objects interact by calling each other's methods. The CUSTOMER Modify method, for example, invokes other objects' methods to obtain data, perform modifications on itself, and request services. These other objects' methods are called and may invoke yet other methods, and so forth. Because all the objects are encapsulated, none can or need know the structure of any other object. This reduces complexity and promotes effective cohesion.

Many objects have methods in common. To reduce the duplication in programming, objects are subclassed from more general classes. An object, say O_1, that is a subclass of another object, say O_2, **inherits** all the attributes and methods of O_2. For example, an application may have a general class EMPLOYEE with two subtypes, SALESPERSON and ENGINEER. Methods that are common to all three object classes such as GetPhoneNumber are made a part of the EMPLOYEE class. The SALESPERSON and ENGINEER subclasses inherit those methods. Hence, when a program issues a call to GetPhoneNumber on either a SALESPERSON or an ENGINEER, the GetPhoneNumber method in EMPLOYEE is invoked. If the

---

[1]The term *properties* is sometimes used instead of *attribute.* In the ODMG-93 standard, the term *property* is used instead of *attribute,* and *attribute* is used in a more restricted sense, as you will see. When reading the terms *class, type, property,* and *attribute,* pay attention to the context, as different authors use these terms slightly differently. Here we will use the terms in a way that is consistent with the source of the topic.

➤ FIGURE 18-1

Sample of CUSTOMER Object

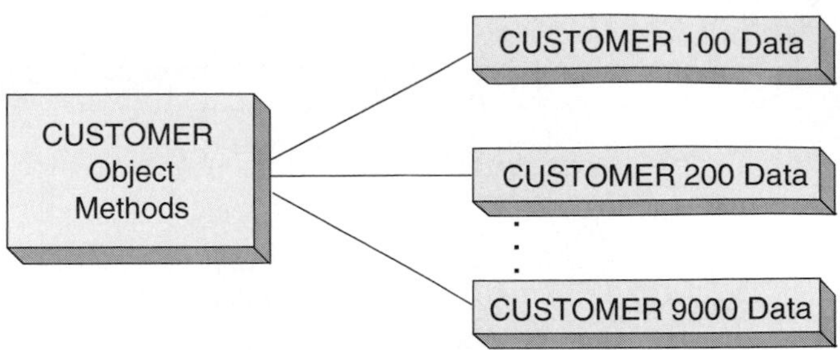

application requirements are such that ENGINEERs have a different way of providing phone numbers than other employees, then ENGINEER can have a special version of GetPhoneNumber as part of its class. That special version will be called when a program invokes GetPhoneNumber on ENGINEER. This characteristic is called **polymorphism.**

Several terms are commonly used in OOP discussions. The logical structure of an object—its name, attributes, and methods—is called an **object class.** A group of object classes is called an **object class library.** And instances of objects are called **object instances,** or simply **objects.**

Objects are created by calling object constructors, programs that obtain main memory and create the structures necessary to instantiate an object. Object destructors are programs that unbind objects and free memory. Objects can be **transient** or **persistent.** A transient object exists only in volatile memory during the execution of a program. When the program terminates, the object is lost. A persistent object is an object that has been saved to permanent storage, such as disk. A persistent object survives the execution of a program and can be read back into memory from storage.

The purpose of an ODBMS is to provide persistent object storage. An object is both data and methods; this means an ODBMS, unlike a traditional DBMS, should store object programs as well as data. Since each object of a given class has the same set of methods, the methods need be stored only once for the class; in contrast, data items must be stored once for each object instance. Figure 18-1 illustrates this point. In point of fact, few ODBMS today provide method persistence, but this is likely to change in the future.

➤ OOP EXAMPLE

Figures 18-2 and 18-3 present a portion of an object-oriented interface and a sample method. To avoid details unimportant to this discussion, the code is written in a generic form that is consistent with object programming but is not in any particular object-oriented language. Consider this code to be something like pseudocode for an object program.

Figure 18-2 shows a portion of the interface of several objects used for order processing. Each object has a set of methods and attributes that it exposes. Every object has a constructor (Create) and a destructor (Destroy) method. Some of the methods take parameters; the Assign method of SALESPERSON, for example, takes a pointer to the ORDER object and a value of ZipCode as its parameters. Attributes

➤ FIGURE 18-2

Sample Objects, Methods, and Attributes

Object	Methods	Attributes
EMPLOYEE	Create Save Destroy ...	Number(R) Name(R) ...
SALESPERSON (subclass of EMPLOYEE)	Create Save Destroy Assign(ORDER, ZipCode) ...	TotalCommission(R) TotalOrders(RW) ...
CUSTOMER	Create Save Destroy Assign(ORDER) Find ...	Name(R) Phone(R) ZipCode(R) CurrentBalance(RW) ...
ITEM	Create Save Destroy Find(Number) Take(ORDER, Quantity) Put(ORDER, Quantity) Find ...	Number(R) Name(R) Description(R) Price ...
ORDER	Create Save Destroy Print ...	Number(R) Date(R) Total(R) CustomerName(R) SalespersonName(R) ...

that are marked with (R) may only be read; attributes marked (RW) may be read or written (changed).

The notation in Figure 18-3 on page 559 needs explanation. First, the braces { } represent remarks. They are used here to describe the function of program code that needs to be written but has been left out of this example for brevity or because it is unimportant to this discussion. The Dim statement is used to declare variables and their types, as it does in Basic. LineItem is declared as a structure having the data elements listed in the brackets [ ]. The exclamation point (!) is used as a separator between an object and one of its methods. Thus, CUSTOMER!Find refers to the Find method of the CUSTOMER object. This character is pronounced "bang." A period is used as a separator between an object and one of its attributes. Thus, CustObj.ZipCode refers to the ZipCode attribute of the object pointed to by CustObj.

Two keywords are also used in Figure 18-3. **Nothing** is a special value of an object pointer that is used to represent a null value. In this figure, the expression

If CustObj = Nothing

means to compare the value of the object variable CustObj to the null object pointer. **Me** is an object pointer that references the object executing the code. When the code in Figure 18-3 is run, it will be run by an instance of the ORDER

➤ FIGURE 18-3

Segment of an Object-Oriented Program

```
ORDER!Create method
Dim CustObj as object, SPObj as object, ItemObj as object
Dim OrderTotal as Currency, OrderDate as Date, OrderNumber as Number
Dim LineItem as Structure
        [
        ItemNumber as Number,
        ItemName as Text(25),
        ItemQuantity as Count,
        QuantityBackOrdered as Count,
        ExtendedPrice as Currency
        ]

        {Get CustomerName from some source}
        Set CustObj = CUSTOMER!Find (CustomerName)
        If CustObj = Nothing then
                Set CustObj = CUSTOMER!Create(CustomerName)
        End If

        CustObj!Assign(Me)
        Set SPObj = SALESPERSON!Assign(Me, CustObj.ZipCode)

        {Get ItemNumber, Quantity of first ITEM from some source}
        Me.OrderTotal = 0
        While Not ItemNumber.EOF

                Me.LineItem!Create
                Me.LineItem.ItemNumber = ItemNumber

                Set ItemObj = ITEM!Find (ItemNumber)
                {process problem if ITEM not exist}

                Me.LineItem.ItemName = ItemObj.Name
                Me.LineItem.Quantity = ITEM!Take (Quantity)
                If Me.LineItem.Quantity <> Quantity Then
                        Me.LineItem.QuantityBackOrdered = Quantity - Me.LineItem.Quantity
                End If

                Me.LineItem.ExtendedPrice = Me.LineItem.Quantity* ITEM.Price
                Me.OrderTotal = Me.OrderTotal + Me.LineItem.ExtendedPrice

                ItemObj!Save
                Me.LineItem!Save
                {Get ItemNumber, Quantity of next ITEM from some source
                assume the source sets EOF to true when there are no more}
        While End

        SPObj.TotalOrders = SPObj.TotalOrders + Me.OrderTotal
        CustObj.CurrentBalance = CustObj.CurrentBalance + Me.OrderTotal

        SPObj!Save
        CustObj!Save
        ME!Save
End ORDER!Create
```

object, since it is an ORDER method. Me refers to the particular ORDER object that is executing the code.

The ORDER!Create method begins by obtaining data about the name of the customer placing the order; it is unimportant to our purposes how this value is obtained—it might be from a text box on a form. The Find method of CUSTOMER is then invoked to find a customer having the given name and to set a pointer to the object that has been found. The particulars of how an instance is found are encapsulated in CUSTOMER!Find, and we do not know how the selection is made, what happens if there is more than one customer that has that name, or other details.

The result of this operation is to set CustObj to either the value of a valid pointer to a CUSTOMER object or to the special value Nothing, which is the null pointer. If CustObj is null, then CustObj is set to a pointer to a new CUSTOMER object created by CUSTOMER!Create. As shown, the code assumes that a pointer to a valid customer object is returned at this point. In fact, CustObj should be checked again to see if it is null, but, for brevity, we will omit all such checking in the rest of this program segment.

CUSTOMER exposes a method Assign that is to be called to assign a CUSTOMER to an ORDER. Because of encapsulation, we do not know what the Assign method does, but we do call it and pass Me, the pointer to the executing object. In fact, in this application, the Assign method is an example of what is called a **callback.** ORDER!Create is giving a pointer to itself to CUSTOMER so that CUSTOMER can keep track of which ORDERs it has. One reason for doing this is that when a CUSTOMER object is to be destroyed, it can call all ORDERs that are linked to it before it departs. In that way, ORDER can destroy its pointer to CUSTOMER when that pointer becomes invalid. There are many other uses for callbacks, as well.

Next, ORDER!Create sets SPObj to a salesperson object. We are passing the value of the customer's ZipCode, so it would seem that ZipCode has something to do with how a salesperson is assigned to us. Again, because of encapsulation, we do not know how this is done, however. By hiding the allocation methodology, the SALESPERSON object is free to change its allocation method without disturbing this or any other program's logic. In fact, no code in Figure 18-3 would need to be changed if SALESPERSON.Assign started using phases of the moon to allocate salespeople!

The next section of code fills in line item values. Observe that the keyword Me is used to refer to local data items. (In fact, in most OO languages, Me would be assumed and would not be necessary; we put it here for explicitness.) At the start of each repetition of the While loop, storage is allocated for another line item in the method LineItem!Create.

The method ITEM!Take is used to withdraw items from inventory. Notice that the logic assumes that if a number of items less than the quantity requested was allocated, then the balance of the items has been backordered. Also, observe that the changed ITEM is saved after each line item has been processed. Also, unlike with CUSTOMER or SALESPERSON, no callback is issued to ITEM. This means that the ITEM objects do not know which ORDERs are connected to them. Apparently, for this application, it is unimportant for the ITEM objects to know which ORDERs are using their data.

The loop continues until there are no more items to be placed on the order. At that point, totals are adjusted in the SALESPERSON and CUSTOMER objects, and both of those objects and Me are saved.

The segment of code in Figure 18-3 is typical of object-oriented code, and it brings to the surface several important issues for object-oriented database systems. In particular, how are the objects to be made persistent?

➤ OBJECT PERSISTENCE

Figure 18-4 summarizes the data structures that exist after an ORDER has been created. In the order object, there are base order data, including ORDER.Number, ORDER.Date, ORDER.Total, as well as a repeating group for line items that have ItemNumber, ItemName, Quantity, a QuantityBackordered, and Extended Price. In addition, the base order data have a pointer to the CUSTOMER object assigned,

➤ FIGURE 18-4

Sample Object Data Structures

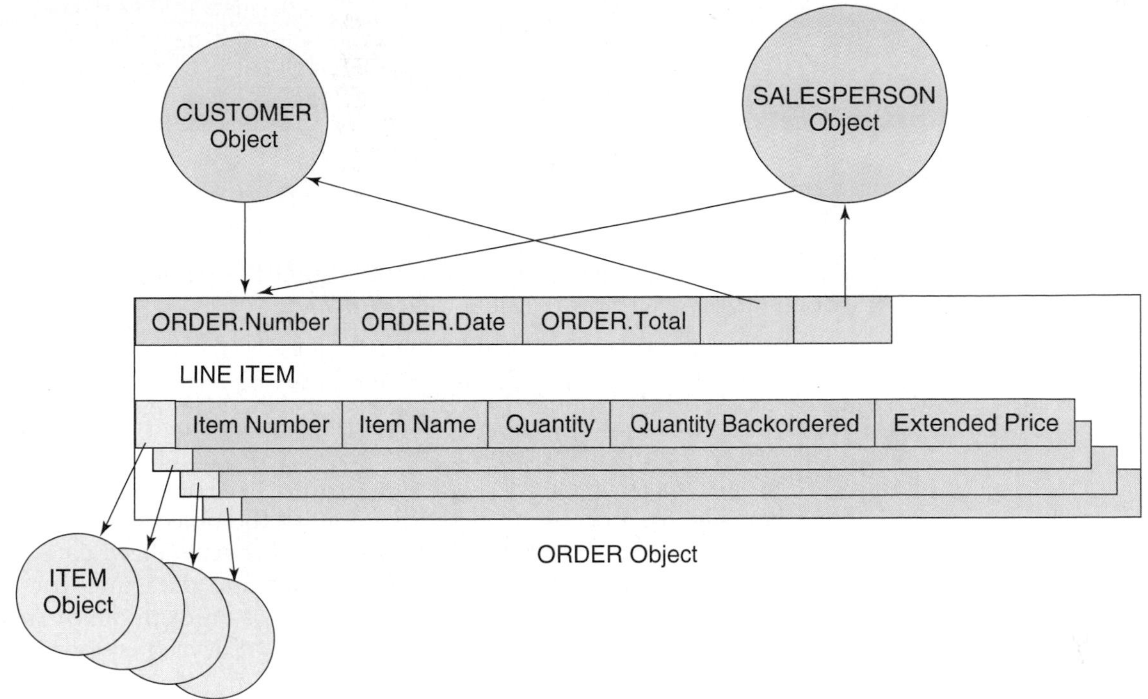

a pointer to the SALESPERSON object assigned, and a pointer to each ITEM for each line item. These pointers are part of the ORDER object's data. To make this object persistent, all of this data must be stored. Further, although we do not know their structure, each CUSTOMER, SALESPERSON, and ITEM object must also be stored. The CUSTOMER and SALESPERSON objects are also storing a pointer back to ORDER as a result of the callbacks (!Assign methods) that were issued.

The pointers pose a particular problem. In most object-oriented languages, pointers are some form of in-memory address. Such addresses are valid only during the execution of the program; if the program terminates and is later restarted, the addresses of the objects will be different. Hence, when storing an object, the in-memory pointers need to be transformed into a permanent unique identifier that will be valid for the lifetime of the object, whether it is in memory or not. The process of transforming permanent identifiers into in-memory addresses is called **swizzling.**

Finally, recall that an object is defined as data values plus methods. Thus, to make an object persistent, we must save both the methods and the object values. Unlike data values, however, every object in a given class has the same methods, so we need to store the methods only once for all object instances in the object class. The requirements for object persistence are listed in Figure 18-5.

➤ FIGURE 18-5

Tasks for Object Persistence

- Save object instance data values
- Convert in-memory object pointers to permanent, unique IDs (swizzling)
- Save object class methods

➤ FIGURE 18-6

Using a Fixed-Length File to Hold Object Data

RecordNumber	RecordCode	Contents	Link
1	ORDER	ORDER 100 data	4
2	SALESPERSON	SALESPERSON Jones data	null
3	CUSTOMER	CUSTOMER 10000 data	null
4	LINEITEM	LineItem of ORDER 100 data	5
5	LINEITEM	LineItem of ORDER 100 DATA	null
...	...	...	...

Objects can be made persistent using traditional file storage, a relational DBMS, or an ODBMS. We now consider each of these.

Object Persistence Using Traditional File Storage

Objects can be saved using traditional file storage, but doing so places a large burden on the programmer. Consider the data in Figure 18-4. The developer might decide to create one file to contain methods for all of the objects and a second file to contain the data for all of the objects. To do this, a generalized data structure will need to be developed to pack the methods and data into the files and to retrieve them when necessary. Figure 18-6 shows an example of such a file for storing just the data items. (Another will need to be developed to store the methods.)

To use such a file, the programmer will write code in the Save methods to pack and unpack object data in these records, to find objects on demand, to manage unused file space, and so forth. Also, the developer will need to devise and implement swizzling and de-swizzling algorithms. Further, there is a bootstrap problem. All methods are stored in files, including the methods that store and read methods. How is the method that reads the first method to be obtained?

All of these problems are surmountable; they have been solved in operating system file-processing subsystems for many years. But, that is just the point. Such programming is slow, tedious, risky, and difficult, and it has already been done for traditional file processing. Why should such programming need to be done one more time?

Because of these problems, traditional file storage is viable for object persistence only when the application has a few simple objects whose structure does not change. Few business applications fall into this category.

Object Persistence Using Relational DBMS

Another approach to object persistence is to use commercial relational DBMS products. This approach places a smaller burden on the developer than traditional file processing, because basic file management issues like record allocation, indexing, space management, and so forth are handled by the DBMS. The data management tasks left to the programmer are to define relational structures to represent the objects and to write the code to interface with the DBMS to get and put objects and to swizzle pointers.

Figure 18-7 shows the tables needed to store ORDER, LINEITEM, CUSTOMER, SALESPERSON, and ITEM objects. We've seen this design before. The only new element is a table to store object methods; this table contains a memo field that stores the method code.

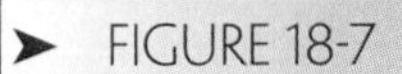

Relations Needed to Store EMPLOYEE, SALESPERSON, CUSTOMER, ITEM, and ORDER Objects

EMPLOYEE (Number, Name,...)
SALESPERSON (*Number*, TotalCommission, TotalOrders,...)
CUSTOMER (Name, Phone, ZipCode, CurrentBalance,...)
ITEM (Number, Name, Description, Price,...)
ORDER (Number, Date, Total, *SALESPERSON.Number*, *CUSTOMER.Name*...)
LINEITEM (*ORDER.Number*, *ITEM.Number*, ItemName, ItemQuantity, QuantityBackOrdered, ExtendedPrice,...)
METHODS (ObjectName, MethodName, MethodCode)

Relational databases represent relationships via foreign keys. This means that the application programmer must devise some means to use foreign keys to make relationships persistent. The most common way of doing this is to code the creation of a unique ID in the object's constructor method. This ID could be stored in the object's base table and exposed as a read-only property. Objects that need to link to the object can save the ID value. This strategy creates the problem that when an object is destroyed, it must notify all objects that are linked to it so that they can remove the pointer to the soon-to-be-destroyed object and take other action as appropriate. This is one reason for having callbacks like those shown in the Assign methods in Figure 18-3.

Object-oriented thinking and design bury relationships in context. Thus, when an ORDER object assigns itself to a SALESPERSON, it is concerned only with its side of that relationship. If the ORDER wants to bind to many SALESPEOPLE, it does so. ORDER has no idea whether a SALESPERSON has a relationship to one or many ORDERs. Such knowledge is encapsulated in the SALESPERSON object and is no part of the ORDER logic.

This characteristic is either an advantage or a disadvantage, depending on how you think about it. Suppose that an ORDER can have several SALESPEOPLE and that a SALESPERSON can have many ORDERs. In database parlance, ORDER and SALESPERSON have an M:N relationship. Consequently, in the relational database world, an intersection table is defined to hold the identifiers of the ORDERs and SALESPEOPLE that are related to one another.

In the object world, SALESPERSON knows it has many ORDERs, and ORDER knows it has many SALESPEOPLE, but they do not know about each other. Hence, the data structures for carrying the relationship will be separated. ORDER will contain storage for many links to SALESPERSON, and SALESPERSON will contain storage for many links to ORDER. The sets of links will be isolated from each other.

Does this matter? No, not as long as there are no errors in the object processing. But there is risk because the object links are separate but not independent. If ORDER 1000 is linked to SALESPERSON A, then, by definition, SALESPERSON A is linked to ORDER 1000. In the relational DBMS world, since the relationship is carried in a row of an intersection table, deleting the row from one side deletes it from the other side automatically. But in the object world, the relationship could be deleted on one side but not on the other. Thus, ORDER 1000 might be linked to SALESPERSON A, but SALESPERSON A might not be linked to ORDER 1000. Clearly, this is an error and should not be allowed to occur, but it is possible if the relationships are defined from a purely object-oriented perspective.

Using a relational DBMS for object persistence is less work for the developer than using traditional file structures. There is still the need, however, for the developer to convert the objects into a relational design, to write SQL (or other code), to get and place the objects using the DBMS, and to swizzle. ODBMS are designed to accomplish these tasks.

➤ FIGURE 18-8

Application Development Work for Object Persistence for Three Alternatives

ODBMS	Relational DBMS	Traditional File Processing
• Invoke ODBMS Save methods	• Convert memory addresses to permanent ID and reverse (swizzling) • Define relational data structures • Create SQL (or other code) • Embed SQL in program	• Convert memory addresses to permanent ID and reverse (swizzling) • Define file data structures • Create object persistence code • Invoke object persistence code • Pack and unpack objects into file structures • Find objects on demand • Manage file space • Other file management tasks

OBJECT PERSISTENCE USING ODBMS

The third alternative for object persistence is to use an ODBMS. Such products are purpose-built for object persistence and hence save the most work for the application programmer.

An ODBMS is designed to be integrated with an object-oriented language. Thus, no special structures, such as SQL, need be embedded in the application code. For the example in Figure 18-4, it is possible that the Save methods are, in fact, methods provided by the ODBMS. Hence, by invoking the Save method, the programmer has invoked the ODBMS.

Further, ODBMS products include a compiler (or are included with the compiler, depending on your point of view) that processes the source code and automatically creates data structures in the object database for storing objects. Hence, unlike with relational database or file processing, the object-oriented programmer need not transform objects into relation or file structures; the ODBMS does that automatically.

Finally, because ODBMSs are designed for object persistence, some form of swizzling is built in. Thus, code like that in Figure 18-3 would be unaware of the problem. An object obtains a link to another object, and that link is a valid one, for all time. If the link takes different forms, the program is unaware of it.

This leads to a characteristic of ODBMS that is called single-level memory. With certain ODBMS, the program (hence, the programmer) need not know whether an object is in memory or not. If ORDER 1000 has a link to SALESPERSON A, then ORDER 1000 can use the exposed properties of SALESPERSON A without ever checking to see if those data are in memory or issuing a read or SQL statement. If SALESPERSON A is in memory, the ODBMS makes the link; if not, the ODBMS reads SALESPERSON A into memory and then makes the link.

Figure 18-8 compares the work required for each of the three alternatives for object persistence. Clearly, an ODBMS provides substantial benefit to the object-oriented programmer, so why are such products not in use everywhere? We consider that question in the next section.

➤ OBJECT PERSISTENCE USING ORACLE

Oracle has extended the facilities of its database products to include support for object modeling and persistent object storage. As mentioned, such databases are sometimes called object-relational databases.

As you read this discussion, reflect about the ways that Oracle has grafted object-oriented thinking onto the relational moel. Even though in some ways the graft is awkward, it does allow organizations to migrate gradually from relational data storage to object data storage. As mentioned earlier, pure object-oriented

ODBMS, which required the abrupt shift from one paradigm to the other, were rejected. In many ways, Oracle has done a masterful job of supporting its current customer base while extending the product to the object world.

This discussion is based on Oracle version 8. These features and functions will certainly be expanded and improved, and you should review the Oracle documentation for newer releases for the latest object storage features.

Object Types and Collections

To develop persistent storage for objects in Oracle, you first create a TYPE that represents the object. That type can then be used in a relation in any of four different ways. The simplest, called a **column object,** is to use the object type to define a table column. The other ways create an object collection of one of three types: **variable length arrays, nested tables,** and **row objects**. We will consider each in turn.

COLUMN OBJECTS The following statement defines an object type named *obj_Apartment:*

```
CREATE TYPE obj_Apartment AS OBJECT (
    BuildingName        VARCHAR2(25),
    ApartmentNumber     CHAR(4),
    NumberBedrooms      NUMBER)
/
```

This type has three columns that use built-in Oracle data types. (Recall that the slash tells SQL Plus to execute the statement just entered. From now on, we will omit showing it at the end of each of these examples.)

The following CREATE statement defines a column object named Location that uses the obj_Apartment object type:

```
CREATE TABLE PERSON (
    Name                VARCHAR (50),
    Location            obj_Apartment)
```

This table can be queried and processed like any relational table. The syntax for insert and update commands is slightly different, however. The following SQL will insert a row into PERSON:

```
INSERT INTO PERSON (Name, Location) VALUES
('Selma Whitbread', obj_Apartment('Eastlake','206', 2));
```

Note the use of the data type name in the values clause. The following SQL will update a row:

```
UPDATE PERSON
SET Location=obj_Apartment('Eastlake', '412', 3)
WHERE Name='Selma Whitebread';
```

Again, note the use of the data type name. Figure 18-9(a) shows the result of a query on this table.

VARIABLE LENGTH ARRAYS Variable length arrays are one of three ways to create collections of object types. To understand the use of such arrays, suppose we want to create a table that contains data for an apartment building. We want

➤ FIGURE 18-9

Example SELECTs for Object Structures (a) Selecting a Column Object; (b) Selecting a Vararray; (c) Selecting a Nested Table; (d) Selecting a Row Object

```
SQL> SELECT * FROM PERSON;

NAME
--------------------------------------------------
LOCATION(BUILDINGNAME, APARTMENTNUMBER, NUMBERBEDROOMS)
-------------------------------------------------------------
Lynda James
OBJ_APARTMENT('Eastlake', '206 ', 2)

Selma Whitbread
OBJ_APARTMENT('Eastlake', '444 ', 3)
```

(a)

```
SQL> SELECT * FROM BUILDING1;

BUILDINGID NAME
---------- --------------------------------------------------
UNITS(APARTMENTNUMBER, NUMBERBEDROOMS)
------------------------------------------------------------------------------
         1 Eastlake
APARTMENT_LIST1(APT_UNIT('100  ', 1), APT_UNIT('200  ', 2), APT_UNIT('300  ', 1))

         2 Westview
APARTMENT_LIST1(APT_UNIT('101  ', 1), APT_UNIT('201  ', 2), APT_UNIT('301  ', 1))
```

(b)

```
SQL> SELECT * FROM BUILDING2;

BUILDINGID NAME
---------- --------------------------------------------------
UNITS(APARTMENTNUMBER, NUMBERBEDROOMS)
------------------------------------------------------------------------------
         1 Eastlake
APARTMENT_LIST2(APT_UNIT('100  ', 1), APT_UNIT('200  ', 2), APT_UNIT('300  ', 1))

         2 Westview
APARTMENT_LIST2(APT_UNIT('101  ', 1), APT_UNIT('201  ', 2), APT_UNIT('301  ', 1))
```

(c)

```
SQL> SELECT * FROM APARTMENTS;

BUILDINGNAME              APAR NUMBERBEDROOMS
------------------------- ---- --------------
Westview                  333               2
Westview                  235               2
```

(d)

to store a surrogate key value, the name of the building, and a list of apartments in the building.

To do this, we first create an object for apartment, and then assign it to a variable length array as follows:

```
CREATE TYPE Apt_Unit AS OBJECT (
    ApartmentNumber      char(5),
    NumberBedrooms       int);
CREATE     TYPE          APARTMENT_LIST1 AS VARRAY(50) OF APT_Unit
```

In this case, the type APARTMENT_LIST1 can have up to 50 elements of the Apt_Unit object type.

The following statement will create a table that uses this varable length array:

```
CREATE     TABLE         BUILDING1 (
    BuildingID           NUMBER,
    Name                 VARCHAR2(50),
    Units                APARTMENT_LIST1);
```

Now, to insert data into the table , we must use the name of both the array and the elements in the array as follows:

```
INSERT INTO BUILDING1 (BuildingID, Name, Units) VALUES
    (1, 'Eastlake',
    APARTMENT_LIST1 (Apt_Unit ('100', 1),
                     Apt_Unit ('200', 2),
                     Apt_Unit ('300', 1)));
```

A normal SELECT statement will work to obtain the values of all columns as long as the WHERE clause does not refer to elements in Apt_Unit. Figure 18-9(b) shows the results of a SELECT * for all rows.

If, however, you want only to obtain values from Apt_Unit or if you want to use elements of Apt_Unit in a WHERE clause, then you must turn the query inside out as follows:

```
SELECT ApartmentNumber
FROM TABLE (
    SELECT UNITS
    FROM BUILDING1
    WHERE Name='Eastlake')
WHERE ApartmentNumber>100;
```

This query selects ApartmentNumber from UNITS, which is the variable length array. The BUILDING table is processed like a subquery. The result will be a table with an ApartmentNumber column and two rows: 200 and 300.

With Oracle Version 8, you cannot update or delete individual rows within a variable array using UPDATE or DELETE statements. You must write a PL/SQL procedure to loop through the array. If you want to use UPDATE and DELETE for this purpose, you must create a nested table instead as shown next.

NESTED TABLES Nested tables are defined in almost the same way as variable length arrays. The difference between them is that whereas variable length array data is stored with the table in which it is defined, nested table data is stored in a separate table. To create the BUILDING table using nested arrays use

```
CREATE TYPE APARTMENT_LIST2 AS TABLE  OF Apt_Unit;
/
CREATE       TABLE          BUILDING2 (
     BuildingID             NUMBER,
     Name                   VARCHAR2(50),
     Units                  APARTMENT_LIST2)
     NESTED TABLE Units STORE AS UNITS_TABLE;
```

The only difference from the vararray syntax is that the nested table must be named. Here it is named UNITS_TABLE.

Figure 18-9(c) shows the result of a SELECT * on all rows of BUILDING2; note it is identical to that from the vararray example. The insert and query statements used with nested tables are also identical to those used for vararrays:

```
INSERT INTO BUILDING2 (BuildingID, Name, Units) VALUES
     (1, 'Eastlake',
     APARTMENT_LIST2 (Apt_Unit ('100', 1),
                      Apt_Unit ('200', 2),
                      Apt_Unit ('300', 1)));
```

and

```
SELECT ApartmentNumber
FROM TABLE (
     SELECT UNITS
     FROM BUILDING2
     WHERE Name='Eastlake')
WHERE ApartmentNumber>100;
```

As promised, however, you can update and delete items in a nested table:

```
UPDATE TABLE (
     SELECT            Units
     FROM              BUILDING2
     WHERE             Name='Eastlake')
SET NumberBedrooms=5
WHERE ApartmentNumber=100;
```

and

```
DELETE FROM TABLE (
     SELECT            Units
     FROM              BUILDING2
     WHERE             Name='Eastlake')
WHERE ApartmentNumber=100;
```

As you can see, variable length arrays and nested tables are very similar, but there are also differences. For one, as stated, UPDATE and DELETE only work with nested tables. Additionally, variable length arrays have a maximum size, but nested tables do not. Also, Oracle stores variable length array data in line with the table but nested table data is stored separately. Finally, the order of rows in a variable length array is maintained; with nested tables, the order of rows may change as new rows are added to the nested table.

ROW OBJECTS Row objects are a fourth way to use object types in tables. A row object table is simply a table that contains only objects. For this example, define obj_Apartment as before:

```
CREATE TYPE obj_Apartment AS OBJECT (
    BuildingName        VARCHAR2(25),
    ApartmentNumber     CHAR(4),
    NumberBedrooms      NUMBER);
```

Then the following will create a table of obj_Apartments:

```
CREATE TABLE APARTMENTS OF obj_Apartment;
```

Selects, inserts, updates, and deletions of rows in this table can be made using regular SQL syntax. Figure 18-9(d) shows a typical SELECT statement. To insert a new row, for example, use

```
INSERT INTO APARTMENTS (BuildingName, ApartmentNumber,
    NumberBedrooms)
VALUES ('Westview', '333',2);
```

The following will update a row in apartments:

```
UPDATE apartments
    Set numberbedrooms=5
    Where ApartmentNumber='100';
```

Finally, to delete a row, use

```
DELETE FROM APARTMENTS
WHERE ApartmentNumber='100';
```

Oracle Objects

So far we have shown how to define object types and use them as elements with tables. These techniques append object structures onto relations; the resulting relations can be processed using variations of SQL. Oracle provides another perspective, however—one that appends relational structures onto objects. SQL cannot be used with these structures. Instead, they are objects that will be stored in a database, but that must be manipulated by object-oriented programs.

OBJECT TYPE DEFINITION Figure 18-10 shows Oracle object definitions for the Order processing example illustrated in Figure 18-4. As shown before, the CREATE TYPE statement is used to define object structures and user-defined types. In this figure, the first two type definitions are used to declare a user-defined address type named obj_ADDRESS and a vararray type named obj_PHONE_LIST of maximum length 5. These two types can now be used in CREATE TYPE AS OBJECT statements in the same way that types were used with table creation statements.

The next definitions in Figure 18-10 are of obj_SALESPERSON and obj_CUSTOMER. Both of these use the obj_ADDRESS and obj_PHONE_LIST user-defined types. This use means that both obj_SALESPERSON and obj_CUSTOMER objects have attributes named Street, City, State, Zip, and Country. They also each have a variable length array of phone numbers.

The next CREATE TYPE statement is an empty one; it is used to inform the Oracle type parser that there will be an obj_ITEM object defined subsequently. This statement allows a type definition like the next one for obj_LINEITEM to use the symbol obj_ITEM, even though obj_ITEM has not yet been defined.

The definition for obj_LINEITEM includes ItemNumber, Quantity, QuantityBackordered, and ExtendedPrice as shown in Figure 18-4. It also includes,

FIGURE 18-10

Oracle Object Definitions

```
CREATE TYPE obj  ADDRESS AS OBJECT (
        Street          VARCHAR2(50),
        City            VARCHAR2(50),
        State           VARCHAR2(2),
        Zip             VARCHAR2(10),
        Country         VARCHAR2(15)
)
/
CREATE TYPE obj_PHONE_LIST AS VARRAY(5) OF VARCHAR2(12)
/
CREATE TYPE obj_SALESPERSON AS OBJECT (
        SalespersonID NUMBER,
        Name            VARCHAR2(50),
        Address         obj_ADDRESS,
        PhoneNums       obj_PHONE_LIST
)
/
CREATE TYPE obj_CUSTOMER AS OBJECT (
        CustomerID      NUMBER,
        Name            VARCHAR2(50),
        Address         obj_ADDRESS,
        PhoneNums       obj_PHONE_LIST
)
/
CREATE TYPE obj_ITEM
/
CREATE TYPE obj_LINEITEM AS OBJECT (
        ItemNumber              NUMBER,
        ItemRef                 REF obj_ITEM,
        Quantity                NUMBER,
        QuantityBackOrdered NUMBER,
        ExtendedPrice           NUMBER

)
/
CREATE TYPE list_LINEITEM AS TABLE OF obj_LINEITEM
/
CREATE TYPE obj_ITEM AS OBJECT (
        ItemNumber              NUMBER,
        ItemName                VARCHAR2(25),
        Price                   NUMBER
)
/
CREATE TYPE obj_ORDER AS OBJECT (
        OrderNumber             NUMBER,
        OrderDate               DATE,
```

➤ FIGURE 18-10

(Continued)

```
        LineItems           list_LINEITEM,
        ShipToAddress       obj_ADDRESS,
        Customer            REF obj_CUSTOMER,
        Salesperson         REF obj_SALESPERSON,

MEMBER FUNCTION totalItems RETURN NUMBER
)
```

however, a definition of a reference pointer attribute. ItemRef is defined as REF obj_ITEM. This means that this attribute willl contain a system-supplied value that references a particular item object. This reference will be valid regardless of whether the referenced item object is in main memory or is on disk storage. If any swizzling is required, Oracle will do it behind the scenes.

Of course, the application program must assign a value to ItemRef. One way to do that is with a SQL statement like the following:

```
INSERT INTO ItemRef
SELECT REF(itemPtr) FROM obj_ITEM itemPtr
WHERE itemPtr.ItemNumber=10000
```

This assumes that only one item has an ItemNumber of 10000.

You may be wondering what is the difference between REF data types and foreign keys. The first difference is that REF values are hidden from the users and have no user meaning. Thus, like surrogate keys, such references have no need for cascading modifications. If, however, the referenced obj_ITEM is deleted, the value here will be invalid. It is up to the program to test it for validity before using it.

Second, such references point to objects, not to rows in tables. The referenced object may itself have a complex data sturcture and will have methods as you will see. Also, Oracle supplied a class library that facilitates the manipulation of such references. A final difference is that such references are one way. The obj_ITEM that is referenced may or may not have a pointer back to the obj_LINEITEM, and in fact, in this example, it does not. This means we can navigate from obj_LINEITEM to obj_ITEM, but not the reverse.

In the next statement, list_LINEITEM is defined as a table of obj_LINEITEMs. This is similar to the definition of APARTMENT_LIST2 earlier. The final type definition describes obj_ORDER. Unlike the definition of BUILDING2, which was a table, obj_ORDER is defined as an object. Because it is an object, the nested table attribute LineItems, which refers to the list_LINEITEM type, need not have a nested table defined for it.

As you examine Figure 18-10, keep in mind that we are defining the data members of an object, and not defining relational tables or anything like relational tables. The data structures in this object will be processed only by object methods.

The last section of the object type definition is to define the interface of this object's methods. In this case, the object has only one method named, totalItems, which returns a single parameter of type NUMBER. In a more realistic example, there would be many methods defined.

OBJECT METHOD DEFINITION Figure 18-11 shows an example Oracle object method. The purpose of this method is to iterate through the LineItems

➤ FIGURE 18-11

Example Oracle Method

```
CREATE OR REPLACE TYPE BODY obj_ORDER AS

  MEMBER FUNCTION totalItems RETURN NUMBER IS
        itemPtr                 obj_ITEM;
        orderTotal              NUMBER :=0;
        i                       INTEGER;

        BEGIN

          FOR i in 1..SELF.LineItems.COUNT LOOP
                UTL_REF.SELECT_OBJECT(LineItems(i).ItemRef, itemPtr);
                orderTotal := orderTotal + SELF.LineItems(i).Quantity * itemPtr.Price;
          END LOOP;
        RETURN orderTotal;

        END;
END;
```

and to total the extended price of each. The function begins by declaring three variables, and then starts a FOR loop over the set of LineItems. The statement

```
FOR i in 1..SELF.LineItems.COUNT LOOP
```

means to set the variable i to 1, to process the instructions through the block terminated by END LOOP, add 1 to i, and to iterate these statements until i is greater than the count of rows in the LineItems attribute.

The statement

```
UTL_REF.SELECT_OBJECT(LineItems(i).ItemRef, itemPtr)
```

invokes a class that is supplied in an Oracle class library. The purpose of this function is to set the value of itemPtr to a valid object pointer to the obj_ITEM object that is referenced by ItemRef in the current row.

After this statement has been executed, itemPtr can be used to refer to any of the properties of obj_ITEM. This is done in the next statement where itemPtr.Price has the value of Price in the obj_ITEM referenced by the current row.

Do not worry if not all of this makes sense. Strive to understand the role and purpose rather than the details of the statements in Figure 18-11. From this discussion, you should understand the general characteristics and nature of Oracle objects and realise how they move traditional relational database management a step or two in the direction of object-oriented programming.

➤ ODBMS STANDARDS

Several groups have been working toward the definition of an object-oriented database standard that could be used as a basis for the construction of ODBMS products. We survey the work of two of those groups here. The first group is a combination of ANSI and ISO (International Standards Organization) committees that has focused on extending the SQL92 standard for object processing. The second group is a consortium of object database vendors and other interested parties that builds on another important standard in the industry, the Object Management Group's Common Object Model and Interface Design Language. As you might expect, the first standard begins with a database perspective and moves toward object thinking. The second standard begins with an object perspective and moves toward data management thinking. Both standards are important.

SQL3

SQL3 is an extension to the SQL92 database standard that includes support for object-oriented database management. Both the ANSI X3H2 and the ISO/IEC JTC1/SC21/WG3 standardization committees have worked to develop the draft of the SQL3 standard that we will discuss here. This standard is very much a work in progress, and changes from this draft are likely. Furthermore, SQL3 is a standard for products and not a product itself. There are, at present, no commercial DBMS products that implement this standard. You should view this section more as a description of the likely evolution of relational DBMS products than as a description of specific product features.

SQL3 arises out of the tradition of database management and not out of the tradition of object thinking. The goal of the committees working on SQL3 has been to describe a standard that is upward compatible with SQL92. This means that all of the features and functions of SQL92 would also work with SQL3. Consequently, SQL3 both looks like and is a relational database facility with object features added to it, as opposed to a new object-oriented database facility.

Three groups of new ideas are incorporated in SQL3: support for abstract data types, enhancements to the definitions of tables, and extensions to the language constructs to make SQL3 computationally complete.

ABSTRACT DATA TYPES In SQL3, an **abstract data type (ADT)** is a user-defined structure that is equivalent to an OOP object. ADTs have methods, data items, and identifiers. ADTs can be subtypes of other ADTs; inheritance is supported. Either SQL (with the new language extensions) or external language, such as Java, C#, and C++ can be used to express the logic of ADT methods.

An ADT can be used in an SQL expression, or it can be stored in a table, or both. If the ADT appears in one or more SQL expressions but is not stored in any table, then the ADT is transient; otherwise, it is made persistent by its storage in a table.

Figure 18-12 shows the definition of a sample ADT for an employee object type. The current syntax of SQL3 is shown in capital letters, and the developer-supplied code is shown in small letters. This specific syntax is unimportant, as it is likely to change. Instead, observe that this ADT, like an OOP object, has data items and functions (methods). The employee data items are name, number, hiredate, currentsalary, and salary, a virtual data item (one that exists only as the result of a computation in a function). The functions are get_salary, change_salary, and remove_employee.

SQL defines two kinds of ADT: OBJECT ADTs and VALUE ADTs. An OBJECT ADT is an identifiable, independent data structure that is assigned an identifier called an **OID.** This identifier is a unique value that persists for the life of the object. If the programmer wants to be able to use the value of the OID to pass to other functions or to store in other tables, the expression WITH OID VISIBLE must be added to the first line of the object definition. This has been done in Figure 18-12.

OID values are pointers to objects; saving an OID value in a table saves a pointer to the object. This can be convenient, but it also creates a problem. When an ADT is destroyed, its OID is invalid, but that particular OID value may

➤ FIGURE 18-12

Sample ADT Definition in SQL3

```
CREATE OBJECT TYPE employee WITH OID VISIBLE
        (name VARCHAR NOT NULL,
        number CHAR(7)
        salary UPDATABLE VIRTUAL GET with get_salary SET WITH change_salary,
        PRIVATE
        hiredate DATE
        currentsalary CURRENCY
        PUBLIC
        ACTOR FUNCTION get_salary (:E employee) RETURNS CURRENCY
        {code to perform security processing
         and return value of currentsalary if appropriate}
        RETURN salary
        END FUNCTION,

        ACTOR FUNCTION change_salary (:E employee) RETURNS employee
        {code to perform security processing
         and compute and set new currentsalary, if appropriate}
        RETURN :E
        END FUNCTION,

        DESTRUCTOR FUNCTION remove_employee (:E employee)
                                                    RETURNS NULL
        {code to get ready to delete employee data}
        DESTROY :E
        RETURN :E
        END FUNCTION,
```

have been stored in rows of tables that are not even in memory when the ADT is destroyed. The SQL3 standard does not indicate what is to happen in this case. Apparently, programs are to be written to test whether an OID is valid before attempting to use it.

The second kind of ADT is a VALUE ADT. VALUE ADTs are not assigned OIDs and cannot exist except in the context in which they are created. If a VALUE ADT is created as a column in a table, it will be saved with that table. It will not be possible to refer to that ADT except through the name of the table. If a VALUE ADT is created in a function, then it will be transient and will be destroyed when memory for the function is released.

The code in Figure 18-12 defines the OBJECT ADT *employee* as a type. As such, the type name can be used in table definitions in the same way that SQL built-in data types can be used. In Figure 18-13, a table Dept is defined; it has a DeptName of type CHAR(10), a Manager of type employee, and an Admin, also of type employee. Thus, the ADT type is used as any other data type is used in a table definition.

When defining a column as having an ADT type, the keyword INSTANCE is used to indicate whether the object or a pointer to the object is to be stored. If INSTANCE is specified, then the object data is stored in the column. If INSTANCE is omitted, then a pointer to the object is stored in the column. If the ADT is a VALUE ADT, then INSTANCE is assumed.

In Figure 18-13, the manager column does not specify INSTANCE, but the admin column does. This means that each row of a dept table will contain

➤ FIGURE 18-13

Table Definition Using the Employee ADT

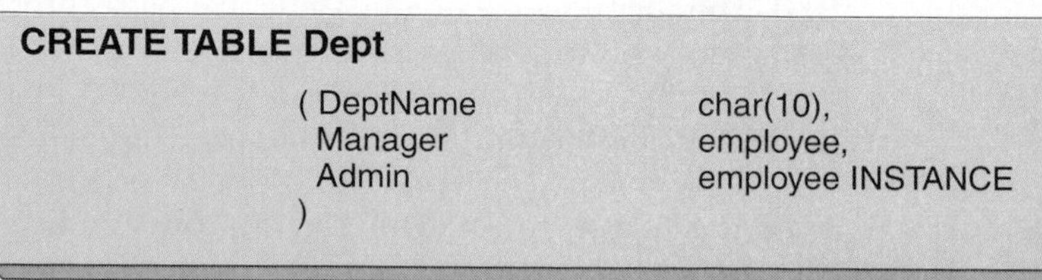

```
CREATE TABLE Dept
            ( DeptName          char(10),
              Manager           employee,
              Admin             employee INSTANCE
            )
```

a pointer to an employee in the Manager column and the actual data and methods for an employee in the Admin column.

The public data items of an object can be used in SQL statements just like regular table columns can be used. For example, consider the table in Figure 18-13 and the following SQL code:

```
SELECT    DeptName, Manager.OID, Manager.Name, Admin.OID, Admin.Name
FROM      Dept
```

When this code is executed, the DeptName, Manager.OID, Admin.OID, and Admin.Name would be extracted from the table. Behind the scenes, the DBMS would use the value of Manager.OID to find the instance of employee that it points to. The DBMS would then extract Manager.Name from that object and return it as part of the response to this SQL statement. The result would be the same as if all of the Manager object were stored in the table. Clearly, if the OID that is stored in the table has become invalid because its object has been deleted, then the DBMS will need to process this error in some fashion.

Consider the SQL statement

```
SELECT    DeptName, Manager.Name, Manager.Salary
FROM      Dept
```

To process this statement, the DBMS will need to access the Dept table, obtain the OID of the manager, obtain the instance of employee that is that manager, and then invoke the get_salary function in employee that materializes the virtual column salary. The get_salary function may perform security checking when it is executed and so the user may be asked to provide a name or password or perform other tasks before the DBMS receives a response from get_salary. Once get_salary has returned a value or an error code indicating that no value will be forthcoming, the DBMS can format the data for that Dept. Similar processing will need to be done for each row of the Dept table.

Private data items are private to the functions in the object. Hence, the following SQL is invalid:

```
SELECT    DeptName, Manager.currentsalary
FROM      Dept
```

The only way currentsalary data can be extracted from an employee object is through the function get_salary.

Values can be assigned to columns just like other SQL statements. Thus, the SQL expression:

```
UPDATE    Dept
SET       Admin.Name = "Fred P. Johnson"
WHERE     DeptName = "Accounting"
```

will set the name of the admin object that is instantiated in the Accounting department.

Since some objects are represented by pointers and not by data values, some surprising results can occur. Consider the following SQL:

```
UPDATE    Dept
SET       Manager.Name = "Fred P. Johnson"
WHERE     DeptName = "Accounting"
```

This statement does not change the employee assignment so that a different employee whose name is "Fred P. Johnson" is assigned to Accounting. Instead, it changes the name of the employee who is currently the manager. The *employee* name is changed; this means that any other table that references this employee object will also have its name changed. If no employee has yet been assigned to Manager in the Accounting row, this statement will generate an error.

In order to replace the manager of the Accounting department with a different employee whose name is "Fred P. Johnson," the Manager object needs to be set to the correct object instance. The following SQL will do this:

```
UPDATE   Dept
SET      Manager =
         SELECT employee.OID
         FROM   employee
         WHERE  name = "Fred P. Johnson"
WHERE    DeptName = "Accounting"
```

Conceptually, this statement is correct. Whether or not it would actually work with a DBMS that implemented SQL3 would, of course, be up to the designers of the DBMS. As stated, since SQL3 is a work in progress and because no product yet implements it, consider the discussion here to indicate the direction of the industry, rather than a fixed, industry-accepted syntax.

The definition of ADTs gives SQL3 the ability to define, store, and manipulate objects. Two other changes to SQL are also proposed in SQL3. We consider them next.

SQL3 TABLE EXTENSIONS SQL3 extends the definition of tables in several ways. First, SQL3 tables have a **row identifier,** which is a unique identifier for each row of a table. This identifier is the same as a *surrogate key,* the term we have used in prior discussions. Applications can use this identifier if it is made explicit by including the expression WITH IDENTITY in the table definition. Any table so defined is given an implicit column named IDENTITY. Values in the column can be used by the application, but it is not included in the results of a SELECT * expression.

Consider the table in Figure 18-14 and the next two SQL expressions:

```
SELECT   ProfessorName, Identity
FROM     PROFESSOR

SELECT   *
FROM     PROFESSOR
```

The result of the first SQL statement is a table with two columns; the first has the name of the professor, and the second has the value of the row identifier. The result of the second SQL expression is a table of three columns, which are ProfessorName, Phone, and Office.

The second extension to the table concept in SQL3 is the definition of three types of table: SET, MULTISET, and LIST. A SET table is a table with no duplicate rows; a MULTISET table may have duplicate rows and is equivalent to the table concept in SQL92. (This definition, of course, ignores the IDENTITY column,

FIGURE 18-14

Table Definition Using WITH IDENTITY

```
CREATE TABLE PROFESSOR WITH IDENTITY
        (ProfessorName        char(10),
         Phone                char(7),
         Office               char(5)
        )
```

➤ FIGURE 18-15

Subtable Definitions

```
CREATE TABLE PROFESSOR WITH IDENTITY
        (ProfessorName          char(10),
         Phone                  char(7),
         Office                 char(5)
        )
CREATE TABLE TENURED-PROFESSOR UNDER PROFESSOR
        (DateTenureGranted      Date)
CREATE TABLE NON-TENURED-PROFESSOR UNDER PROFESSOR
        (NextReviewDate         Date)
```

since with the IDENTITY column, no table has duplicate rows.) Finally, a LIST table is a table that has an order defined by one or more columns.

A third extension to the table concept in SQL3 is the **subtable.** A subtable is a subset of another table, called the **supertable.** A subtable inherits all of the columns of its supertable and may also have columns of its own. A table that has a subtable or a supertable has a row identifier defined implicitly. Figure 18-15 defines two types of professor: TENURED-PROFESSOR and NONTENURED-PROFESSOR. The columns of TENURED-PROFESSOR are ProfessorName, Phone, Office, and DateTenureGranted. The columns of NONTENURED-PROFESSOR are ProfessorName, Phone, Office, and NextReviewDate. Even though WITH IDENTITY is not specified for TENURED-PROFESSOR or NONTENURED-PROFESSOR, both have an IDENTITY column because they are subtypes.

Reflect for a moment on the logical consequences of adding both ADTs and subtypes to the table construct. Both ADTs and tables can have subtypes, and the two are not the same. ADT subtypes define one generalization hierarchy, and table subtypes define another. One hierarchy may be nested in the other or the reverse, or they may be disjoint, or they may partially overlap. SQL3 is open to the criticism of excessive complexity here, and it will be interesting to see how much of this complexity is actually implemented in DBMS products.

SQL LANGUAGE EXTENSIONS According to SQL3, ADT methods can be coded in the SQL language itself. To make this capability more robust, language elements are proposed that will make SQL computationally complete. The proposed additions are summarized in Figure 18-16.

To date, SQL has been a set-oriented language. SELECT statements identify a set of rows and operate upon them. The addition of the language statements in Figure 18-16 will change this characteristic. It will be possible to develop row-at-a-time logic within SQL itself. This change will make SQL more and more like a traditional programming language. This is necessary if SQL is to be used as the language for logic in ADT methods, but it also represents a change in the fundamental character of SQL.

ODMG-93

The Object Data Management Group is a consortium of object database vendors and other interested industry experts that has applied the ideas of another group, the Object Management Group, to the problem of object databases. The first report on ODMG was produced in 1993 and is accordingly referred to as ODMG-93. This heritage of this standard is object programming and not traditional relational

➤ FIGURE 18-16

Proposed SQL3 Language Extensions

Statement	Purpose
DESTROY	Destroy an object ADT; valid only in DESTRUCTOR functions
ASSIGNMENT	Allow the result of an SQL value expression to be assigned to a local variable, column, or ADT attribute
CALL	Invoke an SQL procedure
RETURN	Return a value from a value computation in a procedure or function
CASE	Select execution path on the basis of alternative values
IF THEN ELSE	Allow conditional logic
WHILE LOOP	Allow iterative logic

database management. Hence, it is based on the object as the fundamental construct, rather than on the table as the fundamental construct as we saw for SQL3.

ODMG-93 is a definition of interfaces for object data management products. The implementations of the ideas in ODMG-93 may be quite different. An ODMG-93 product that is designed for C++ object data storage and manipulation might have a completely different implementation from a product that is designed for Smalltalk object storage and manipulation. The two products could be very different and yet still both implement the ODMG-93 interfaces.

Since ODMG-93 arises out of the context of object programming, a detailed description of it requires substantial knowledge of OOP. Such a description is consequently beyond the scope of this text. Instead, we confine this discussion to fundamental ideas behind the ODMG-93 report. Figure 18-17 lists five core concepts as described by Loomis.[2]

OBJECTS ARE FUNDAMENTAL According to the ODMG Object Model, the object is the fundamental entity to be stored and manipulated. Unlike SQL3, in which the fundamental entity is a table and objects are stored in columns of tables, in ODMG-93 the object is the basic entity. The ODMG concept is more like the one we described for the object program in Figure 18-3. That is, the application program defines objects in and of themselves, and it is up to the ODBMS to make those objects persistent. No other structure, such as a table, is required.

According to the ODMG model, objects can be **mutable** or **immutable.** Mutable objects can be changed; immutable objects are fixed, and no application is allowed to alter the state of any immutable object. The ODBMS is required to enforce immutability.

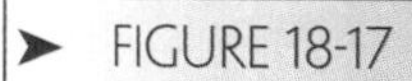

Key Elements of the ODMG Object Model

- Objects are fundamental.
- Every object has a lifelong persistent, unique identifier.
- Objects can be arranged into types and subtypes.
- State is defined by data values and relationships.
- Behavior is defined by object operations.

[2]Mary E. S. Loomis, *Object Databases, The Essentials.* Reading, MA: Addison-Wesley, 1995, pp. 88–110.

EVERY OBJECT HAS A LIFELONG PERSISTENT IDENTIFIER The second fundamental concept in the ODMG object model is that each object is given a unique identifier that is valid for the lifetime of the object. Further, the identifier must be valid whether the object is stored externally or is in memory. The ODBMS is to perform swizzling transparently; the application program can use pointers to objects as if they are always valid.

The standard leaves the particular form of an object identifier open. Thus, different ODBMS vendors can use different means to specify object IDs. This means that object identifiers from different databases from different vendors are not necessarily compatible. For nondistributed databases, this is not likely to be a problem, since all of the objects in a given object database will have been created and stored by the same ODBMS.

In a distributed environment, the object identification problem is more difficult for two reasons: first, because object IDs in different ODBMS may have different formats, and, second, because object IDs are not necessarily unique across different databases. This issue is unaddressed by the ODMG-93 standard.

OBJECTS CAN BE ARRANGED INTO TYPES AND SUBTYPES The ODMG standard object model specifies that objects are arranged into groups by type. Objects are created to be of a given type. All objects of a particular type have the same data characteristics and behavior. Objects can be defined as subtypes of other objects. In this case, they inherit all of the data characteristics and behavior of their parent type. According to the standard, an object is created as an instance of a given type, and that instance cannot change its type.

The terms *type* and *class* are often used synonymously. According to Loomis, this is incorrect. An object class is a logical group of objects as defined in ODMG 93; such classes have subclasses that inherit from them. A type is the implementation of a class in a particular language. Thus, the class Employee is a logical definition of data and methods; it may have subclasses Salesperson and Accountant that inherit from Employee. An implementation of Employee in C++, for example, is called a type; implementations in C++ of Salesperson and Accountant are subtypes.[3] There may be another, different implementation of Employee in, say, Smalltalk. That implementation would be a different Employee type. Distinguishing between *class* and *type* helps to delineate logical definitions from particular implementations of those logical structures.

Object classes (and hence types) can have properties. The ODMG standard specifies that each class has a name and uniqueness constraints as its properties. All of the instances of an object class are called the object's **extent.** Any attribute or combination of attributes can be declared to be unique over the extent. Thus, in Employee, EmployeeNumber can be defined to be unique, as could {FirstName, LastName}, and so on. Since uniqueness requirements apply to the entire extent and not to any given object instance, such requirements are class properties and not class instance properties. Thus, the name Employee and the requirement that EmployeeNumber be unique are class properties. EmployeeNumber itself, however, is a property of an Employee instance.

Since ODMG is a standard for an interface and not for an implementation, no attempt is made to describe how types and subtypes should be stored or manipulated. Rather, the interface simply indicates that objects should be stored and retrieved by class and that inheritance should be provided.

STATE IS DEFINED BY DATA VALUES AND RELATIONSHIPS According to the ODMG standard, the state of any object is represented by its properties. Such properties can be either attributes or relationships. An attribute is a literal value or

[3] *Ibid.*, p. 96.

➤ FIGURE 18-18

ODMG Relationship Operations

Operation	Function
Set	Create a 1:1 relationship
Clear	Destroy a 1:1 relationship
Insert_element	Add an element to the many side of a 1:N or N:M relationship
Remove_element	Remove an element from the many side of a 1:N or N:M relationship
Get	Return a reference to an object in a 1:1 relationship
Traverse	Return a reference to a set of objects on the many side of a 1:N or N:M relationship
Create_iterator	Create a structure to process the elements of a set of objects obtained by a Traverse operation

a set of literal values. DateOfHire and CurrentSalary are literal values. PastSalary is a set of literal values. A relationship is a property that indicates a connection between one object instance and one or more other object instances. Department is an example of a relationship property.

The ODMG specifies a set of operations that can be performed on relationships, which are listed in Figure 18-18. Operations are distinguished by the maximum cardinality of the relationship. This is done because in the case of a 1:1 relationship, the properties are single-value and no set of properties need be considered. In the case of a 1:N or N:M relationship, the number of elements in a property is plural; a set is created, and the program must be able to iterate over the elements of the set.

When objects have a relationship, the relationship must be made persistent when the object is made persistent. The standard does not specify how the relationship is to be represented and what means are to be used to swizzle the pointers among relationships. These issues must be solved when implementing an ODBMS, however.

BEHAVIOR IS DEFINED BY OBJECT OPERATIONS The behavior of an object type is determined by its methods. All objects of a given type have the same methods, and objects of subtypes inherit those methods. If a subtype object redefines a method, then the redefinition will override the inherited method. If, for example, Employee has method Get_Salary, and if Salesperson, a subtype of Employee, also has a method called Get_Salary, the local method will be used for Salesperson!Get_Salary operations.

Objects interact by invoking one another's methods. Sometimes this is expressed by saying that objects pass messages to one another, where a message is a string like Salesperson!Get_Salary that includes the name of the object type and the name of the method of that type. Messages can, of course, include parameters.

The purpose of an ODBMS is to make objects persistent. The ODMG standard indicates that objects include methods, so method storage and management would seem to be included in the functions of an ODMG-compliant ODBMS. In truth, current ODBMSs vary widely in their support for method storage. Some ODBMSs in fact, provide no support whatsoever for method persistence. Others provide some support, but not support for versioning of objects.

Method persistence is important, and likely the capabilities of ODBMS in this area will be improved in the future. No application is static; requirements change, and object behaviors must be adapted. Furthermore, methods can change without changing the underlying data properties of an object. Without method management, two instances of an object could be based on two different versions of methods.

Consider an example: Suppose that an instance of a Salesperson class, say, Salesperson A, is created and stored using a version of the Set_Salary method. Now suppose that the means of computing salesperson salaries changes, and the Set_Salary method is altered accordingly. At this point, Salesperson B is created and stored. Now, Salesperson A and Salesperson B would appear, in their data properties, to be equivalent, but they are not. Without method management on the part of the ODBMS, there is no way to determine that Salespersons A and B represent different versions of the Salesperson object.

This situation is no different from what occurs today with application programs in non-ODBMS environments, so proponents of ODBMS would claim that ODBMS has not made the situation any worse. This, however, seems to be a cop-out. If objects are defined to include data properties and behavior properties, then object persistence cannot be claimed to pertain to one and not to the other. Too much of the promise of object thinking is left on the table if ODBMS do not support method management as well as data management.

➤ SUMMARY

Relational databases are not well suited to store object–oriented programming objects because objects can contain complex structures that do not readily fit into a table. Also, objects include object methods that also need to be stored. Special-purpose Object-Oriented DBMS products were developed to provide persistent object storage, but they have not been commercially successful because existing relational data must be converted into ODBMS format. The gain has not been worth the cost. Instead, DBMS products are beginning to support hybrids of object and relational storage called object-relational databases.

With object-oriented programming (OOP), programs are composed of objects that are encapsulated, logical structures that have data elements and behaviors. An interface is the external appearance of an object; an implementation is the encapsulated interior of an object. Objects can be subclassed; a subclass inherits the attributes and methods of its superclass. Polymorphism allows several versions of the same method to exist; the compiler invokes the proper version at execution time, depending on the class of the object.

An object class is the logical structure of an object; a group of object classes is called an object class library. Instances of an object class are called object instances or simply objects. Object constructors are methods that obtain memory and create object structures; object destructors unbind objects and free memory. Transient objects exist only during the execution of a program; persistent objects are saved to storage and survive the execution of a program.

Objects can be made persistent by using traditional file storage, using relational DBMS, or using ODBMS products. The use of traditional storage places considerable work on the application programmer and is feasible only for applications having a few simple objects whose structure does not frequently change. Relational DBMS can be used for object persistence, but the application developer must convert object structures to relations, write SQL, and develop swizzling algorithms. Using an ODBMS is the most direct and easiest means of object persistence.

Oracle provides support for object persistence with object-relational database facilities. Object types can be defined and then used with table structures as column objects, as variable length arrays, as nested tables, and as row objects. Pure objects can also be defined; such objects can include variable length arrays and nested tables. They also may include object pointers as REF attributes. Finally, such objects include methods, which can use Oracle-supplied class libraries for processing.

SQL3 is an extension to SQL-92 that provides for abstract data types (ADTs), enhancements to tables, and new features in the SQL language. ADTs, which are made persistent by embedding in tables, can be object or value; object ADTs have identifiers called OIDs. In SQL3, tables have a row identifier and can have subtypes. Three types of tables are defined: SET, MULTISET, and LIST. Figure 18-13 shows extensions to the SQL language proposed in SQL3.

The five basic elements of the ODMG-93 standard are that objects are the fundamental data structure, objects are given a lifelong persistent identifier, objects can be arranged in types and subtypes, object state is carried by data values and relationships, and object behavior is defined by object operations. Semantic objects as defined in Chapter 4 implement the ODMG standard for data attributes, but not for object behavior.

➤ GROUP I QUESTIONS

18.1 Explain how object-oriented programming differs from traditional programming.

18.2 Why are relational databases more popular than object databases today?

18.3 Define an OOP object.

18.4 Define the terms *encapsulated, attribute,* and *method.*

18.5 Explain the difference between an interface and an implementation.

18.6 What is inheritance?

18.7 What is polymorphism?

18.8 Define the terms *object class, object class library,* and *object instance.*

18.9 Explain the function of object constructors and object destructors.

18.10 Explain the difference between a transient object and a persistent object.

18.11 Explain the difference in the notation CUSTOMER!Find and CUSTOMER.ZipCode.

18.12 What is the function of the keyword *NOTHING* in Figure 18-3?

18.13 What is the function of the keyword *ME* in Figure 18-3?

18.14 What is a callback, and why is one used?

18.15 What does the term *swizzling* refer to?

18.16 Briefly explain what tasks are required to use traditional file storage for object persistence.

18.17 Briefly explain what tasks are required to use a relational DBMS for object persistence.

18.18 Summarize the advantages and disadvantages of using an ODBMS for object persistence.

18.19 Show the Oracle statements to define an object type named Pname having three attributes: FirstName, MiddleName, and LastName. Use this type as a column object in a table called PERSON.

18.20 Show Oracle statements to create a variable array of up to 100 Pnames. Show statements to create a table named CLUB1 with a surrogate key, a ClubName and the variable array attribute of person names.

18.21 Show Oracle statements to create a CLUB2 table as in Question 18.20, but use a nested table of person names instead of a variable array. Name the storage table Pname_Table.

18.22 Explain the differences between table CLUB1 and table CLUB2.

18.23 Show Oracle statements to create a table having Pname as a row object.

18.24 Explain the purpose of the REF attributes in Figure 18-19. How do these attributes differ from foreign keys?

18.25 Explain the purposes of the following two statements:

a. FOR i in 1..SELF.Lineitems.COUNT LOOP

b. UTI_REF.SELECT_OBJECT(LineItems(i).ItemRef, itemPtr)

18.26 What is SQL3?

18.27 What is an abstract data type (ADT)?

18.28 Explain the difference between an object ADT and a value ADT.

18.29 What is an OID? How can one be used?

18.30 Explain what the DBMS must do when executing the following SQL on the ADT in Figure 18-13:

```
SELECT    DeptName, Manager.Phone, Admin.Phone
FROM      Dept
```

18.31 What happens when the following SQL is executed on the ADT in Figure 18-13:

```
UPDATE    Dept
SET       Manager.Name = "John Jacob Astor"
```

18.32 Code SQL that would need to be executed to change the instance of the manager of a department for the ADT in Figure 18-13.

18.33 What is a row identifier in SQL3?

18.34 Explain the differences among a SET, MULTISET, and LIST in SQL3.

18.35 Explain the differences among a subtable, a supertable, and a table.

18.36 What is ODMG-93?

18.37 List the five core concepts in ODMG-93.

18.38 What is the difference between a type and a class in ODMG-93?

18.39 What is the difference between a property and an attribute in ODMG-93?

18.40 What is an extent?

18.41 What are the properties of a class in ODMG-93?

18.42 In the ODMG standard, what values can properties have?

18.43 In the ODMG standard, what values can attributes have?

18.44 In the ODMG standard, what values can relationship properties have?

18.45 Why is method persistence important? Give an example of a problem that can occur when such persistence is not provided.

18.46 Explain how semantic objects conform to the ODMG standard and how they do not.

➤ GROUP II QUESTIONS

18.47 Review the requirements and relational design for View Ridge Gallery in Chapter 10. Consider the use of Oracle types and column, vararrays, nested tables, and row objects in the context of View Ridge's needs. What changes would you make to the relational design? Would you recommend replacing TRANSACTION or WORK tables with vararrays or nested tables? If so, how? If not, why not? Show how you could use Oracle REF data types to eliminate the need for the intersection table. Would you recommend this course of action?

18.48 Consider Oracle types, vararrays, and nested tables in the context of the semantic object model. Which elements of that model lend themselves to types? To vararrays? To nested tables? Show how you would use Oracle object-relational facilities to model each of the types of semantic objects described in Chapter 7.

Data Structures for Database Processing

All operating systems provide data management services. These services, however, are generally not sufficient for the specialized needs of a DBMS. Therefore, to enhance performance, DBMS products build and maintain specialized data structures, which are topics of this appendix.

We begin by discussing flat files and some of the problems that can occur when such files need to be processed in different orders. Then we turn to three specialized data structures: sequential lists, linked lists, and indexes (or inverted lists). Next, we illustrate how each of three special structures discussed in Chapter 6—trees, simple networks, and complex networks—are represented using various data structures. Finally, we explore how to represent and process multiple keys.

Although a thorough knowledge of data structures is not required to use most DBMS products, this background is essential to database administrators and systems programmers working with a DBMS. Being familiar with the data structures also helps you evaluate and compare database products.

➤ FLAT FILES

A *flat file* is a file that has no repeating groups. Figure A-1 (a) shows a flat file, and (b) shows a file that is not flat because of the repeating field Item. A flat file can be stored in any common file organization such as sequential, indexed sequential, or direct. Flat files have been used for many years in commercial processing. They are usually processed in some predetermined order, say, in an ascending sequence on a key field.

➤ FIGURE A-1

Examples of (a) a Flat and (b) a Nonflat File Enrollment Record

Enrollment Record

StudentNumber	ClassNumber	Semester

Sample Data

200	70	2000S
100	30	2001F
300	20	2001F
200	30	2000S
300	70	2000S
100	20	2000S

(a)

Invoice Record

InvoiceNumber	Item(s)

Sample Data

1000	10	20	30	40
1010	50			
1020	10	20	30	
1030	50	90		

(b)

Processing Flat Files in Multiple Orders

Sometimes users want to process flat files in ways that are not readily supported by the file organization. Consider, for example, the ENROLLMENT records in Figure A-1(a). To produce student schedules, they must be processed in StudentNumber sequence. But to produce class rosters, the records need to be processed in ClassNumber sequence. The records, of course, can be stored in only one physical sequence. For example, they can be in order on StudentNumber or on ClassNumber, but not on both at the same time. The traditional solution to the problem of processing records in different orders is to sort them in student order, process the student schedules, then sort the records in class order, and produce class rosters.

For some applications, such as a batch-mode system, this solution, while cumbersome, is effective. But suppose that both orders need to exist simultaneously because two concurrent users have different views of the ENROLLMENT records. What do we do then?

One solution is to create two copies of the ENROLLMENT file and sort them as shown in Figure A-2. Since the data are listed in sequential order, this data structure is sometimes called a *sequential list*. Sequential lists can be readily stored as sequential files. This, however, is not generally done by DBMS products because sequentially reading a file is a slow process. Further, sequential files cannot be updated in the middle without rewriting the entire file. Also, maintaining several orders by keeping multiple copies of the same sequential list is usually not effective because the duplicated sequential list can create data integrity problems. Fortunately, other data structures allow us to process records in different orders and do not require the duplication of data. These include *linked lists* and *indexes*.

➤ FIGURE A-2

ENROLLMENT Data Stored as Sequential Lists: (a) Stored by StudentNumber and (b) Stored by ClassNumber

Student-Number	Class-Number	Semester
100	30	2001F
100	20	2000S
200	70	2000S
200	30	2000S
300	20	2001F
300	70	2000S

(a)

Student-Number	Class-Number	Semester
300	20	2001F
100	20	2000S
100	30	2001F
200	30	2000S
200	70	2000S
300	70	2000S

(b)

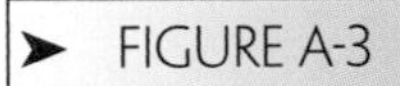

ENROLLMENT Data in StudentNumber Order Using a Linked List

Relative Record Number	Student-Number	Class-Number	Semester	Link
1	200	70	2000S	4
2	100	30	2001F	6
3	300	20	2001F	5
4	200	30	2000S	3
5	300	70	2000S	0
6	100	20	2000S	1

Start of list = 2

A Note on Record Addressing

Usually the DBMS creates large physical records, or blocks, on its direct access files. These are used as containers for logical records. Typically, there are many logical records per physical record. Here we assume that each physical record is addressed by its relative record number (RRN). Thus, a logical record might be assigned to physical record number 7 or 77 or 10,000. The relative record number is thus the logical record's physical address. If there is more than one logical record per physical record, the address must also specify where the logical record is within the physical record. Thus, the complete address for a logical record might be relative record number 77, byte location 100. This means the record begins in byte 100 of physical record 77.

To simplify the illustrations in this text, we assume that there is only one logical record per physical record, so we need not be concerned with byte offsets within physical records. Although this is unrealistic, it simplifies our discussion to the essential points.

Maintaining Order with Linked Lists

Linked lists can be used to keep records in logical order that are not necessarily in physical order. To create a linked list, we add a field to each data record. The *link* field holds the address (in our illustrations, the relative record number) of the *next* record in logical sequence. For example, Figure A-3 shows the ENROLLMENT records expanded to include a linked list; this list maintains the records in StudentNumber order. Notice that the link for the numerically last student in the list is zero.

Figure A-4 shows ENROLLMENT records with two linked lists: One list maintains the StudentNumber order, and the other list maintains the ClassNumber order. Two link fields have been added to the records, one for each list.

➤ FIGURE A-4

ENROLLMENT Data in Two Orders Using Linked Lists

Relative Record Number	Student-Number	Class-Number	Semester	Student Link	Class Link
1	200	70	2000S	4	5
2	100	30	2001F	6	1
3	300	20	2001F	5	4
4	200	30	2000S	3	2
5	300	70	2000S	0	0
6	100	20	2000S	1	3

Start of student list = 2
Start of class list = 6

➤ FIGURE A-5

ENROLLMENT Data After Inserting New Record (in Two Orders Using Linked Lists)

Relative Record Number	Student-Number	Class-Number	Semester	Student Link	Class Link
1	200	70	2000S	4	5
2	100	30	2001F	6	7
3	300	20	2001F	5	4
4	200	30	2000S	7	2
5	300	70	2000S	0	0
6	100	20	2000S	1	3
7	200	45	2000S	3	1

Start of student list = 2
Start of class list = 6

When insertions and deletions are made, linked lists have a great advantage over sequential lists. For example, to insert the ENROLLMENT record for Student 200 and Class 45, both of the lists in Figure A-2 would need to be rewritten. For the linked lists in Figure A-4, however, the new record could be added to the physical end of the list, and only the values of two link fields would need to be changed to place the new record in the correct sequences. These changes are shown in Figure A-5.

When a record is deleted from a sequential list, a gap is created. But in a linked list, a record can be deleted simply by changing the values of the link, or the *pointer* fields. In Figure A-6, the ENROLLMENT record for Student 200, Class 30, has been logically deleted. No other record points to its address, so it has been effectively removed from the chain, even though it still exists physically.

There are many variations of linked lists. We can make the list into a *circular list,* or *ring,* by changing the link of the last record from zero to the address of the first record in the list. Now we can reach every item in the list starting at any item in the list. Figure A-7(a) shows a circular list for the StudentNumber order. A *two-way linked list* has links in both directions. In Figure A-7(b), a two-way linked list has been created for both ascending and descending student orders.

Records ordered using linked lists cannot be stored on a sequential file because some type of direct-access file organization is needed in order to use the link values. Thus, either indexed sequential or direct file organization is required for linked-list processing.

Maintaining Order with Indexes

A logical record order can also be maintained using *indexes* or, as they are sometimes called, *inverted lists.* An index is simply a table that cross-references record

➤ FIGURE A-6

ENROLLMENT Data After Deleting Student 200, Class 30 (in Two Orders Using Linked Lists)

Relative Record Number	Student-Number	Class-Number	Semester	Student Link	Class Link
1	200	70	2000S	7	5
2	100	30	2001F	6	7
3	300	20	2001F	5	2
4	200	30	2000S	7	2
5	300	70	2000S	0	0
6	100	20	2000S	1	3
7	200	45	2000S	3	1

Start of student list = 2
Start of class list = 6

➤ FIGURE A-7

ENROLLMENT Data Sorted by StudentNumber Using (a) a Circular and (b) a Two-Way Linked List

Relative Record Number	Student-Number	Class-Number	Semester	Link
1	200	70	2000S	4
2	100	30	2001F	6
3	300	20	2001F	5
4	200	30	2000S	3
5	300	70	2000S	2
6	100	20	2000S	1

Start of list = 2

(a)

Relative Record Number	Student-Number	Class-Number	Semester	Ascending Link	Descending Link
1	200	70	2000S	4	6
2	100	30	2001F	6	0
3	300	20	2001F	5	4
4	200	30	2000S	3	1
5	300	70	2000S	0	3
6	100	20	2000S	1	2

Start of ascending list = 2
Start of descending list = 5

(b)

addresses with some field value. For example, Figure A-8(a) shows the ENROLLMENT records stored in no particular order, and Figure A-8(b) shows an index on StudentNumber. In this index the StudentNumbers are arranged in sequence, with each entry in the list pointing to a corresponding record in the original data.

➤ FIGURE A-8

ENROLLMENT Data and Corresponding Indexes: (a) ENROLLMENT Data, (b) Index on StudentNumber, and (c) Index on ClassNumber

Relative Record Number	Student-Number	Class-Number	Semester
1	200	70	2000S
2	100	30	2001F
3	300	20	2001F
4	200	30	2000S
5	300	70	2000S
6	100	20	2000S

(a)

Student-Number	Relative Record Number
100	2
100	6
200	1
200	4
300	3
300	5

(b)

Class-Number	Relative Record Number
20	3
20	6
30	2
30	4
70	1
70	5

(c)

As you can see, the index is simply a sorted list of StudentNumbers. To process ENROLLMENT sequentially on StudentNumber, we simply process the index sequentially, obtaining ENROLLMENT data by reading the records indicated by the pointers. Figure A-8(c) shows another index for ENROLLMENT, one that maintains ClassNumber order.

To use an index, the data to be ordered (here, ENROLLMENT) must reside on an indexed sequential or direct file, although the indexes can reside on any type of file. In practice, almost all DBMS products keep both the data and the indexes on direct files.

If you compare the linked list with the index, you will notice the essential difference between them. In a linked list, the pointers are stored along with the data. Each record contains a link field containing a pointer to the address of the next related record. But in an index, the pointers are stored in indexes, separate from the data. Thus, the data records themselves contain no pointers. Both techniques are used by commercial DBMS products.

B-Trees

A special application of the concept of indexes, or inverted lists, is a *B-tree,* a multilevel index that allows both sequential and direct processing of data records. It also ensures a certain level of efficiency in processing, because of the way that the indexes are structured.

A B-tree is an index that is made up of two parts, the sequence set and the index set. (These terms are used by IBM's VSAM file organization documentation. You may encounter other, synonymous, terms.) The *sequence set* is an index containing an entry for every record in the file. This index is in physical sequence, usually by primary key value. This arrangement allows sequential access to the data records as follows: Process the sequence set in order, read the address of each record, and then read the record.

The *index set* is an index pointing to groups of entries in the sequence set index. This arrangement provides rapid direct access to records in the file, and it is the index set that makes B-trees unique.

An example of a B-tree appears in Figure A-9, and an occurrence of this structure can be seen in Figure A-10. Notice that the bottom row in Figure A-9, the sequence set, is simply an index. It contains an entry for every record in the file (although for brevity, both the data records and their addresses have been omitted). Also notice that the sequence set entries are in groups of three. The entries in each group are physically in sequence, and each group is chained to the next one by means of a linked list, as can be seen in Figure A-10.

Examine the index set in Figure A-9. The top entry contains two values, 45 and 77. By following the leftmost link (to RRN2), we can access all the records whose key field values are less than or equal to 45; by following the middle pointer (to RRN3), we can access all the records whose key field values are greater than 45 and less than or equal to 77; and by following the rightmost pointer (to RRN4), we can access all the records whose key field values are greater than 77.

Similarly, at the next level there are two values and three pointers in each index entry. Each time we drop to another level, we narrow our search for a particular record. For example, if we continue to follow the leftmost pointer from the top entry and then follow the rightmost pointer from there, we can access all the records whose key field value is greater than 27 and less than or equal to 45. We have eliminated all that were greater than 45 at the first level.

B-trees are, by definition, balanced. That is, all the data records are exactly the same distance from the top entry in the index set. This aspect of B-trees ensures performance efficiency, although the algorithms for inserting and deleting records are more complex than those for ordinary trees (which can be unbalanced),

➤ FIGURE A-9

General Structure of a Simple B-Tree

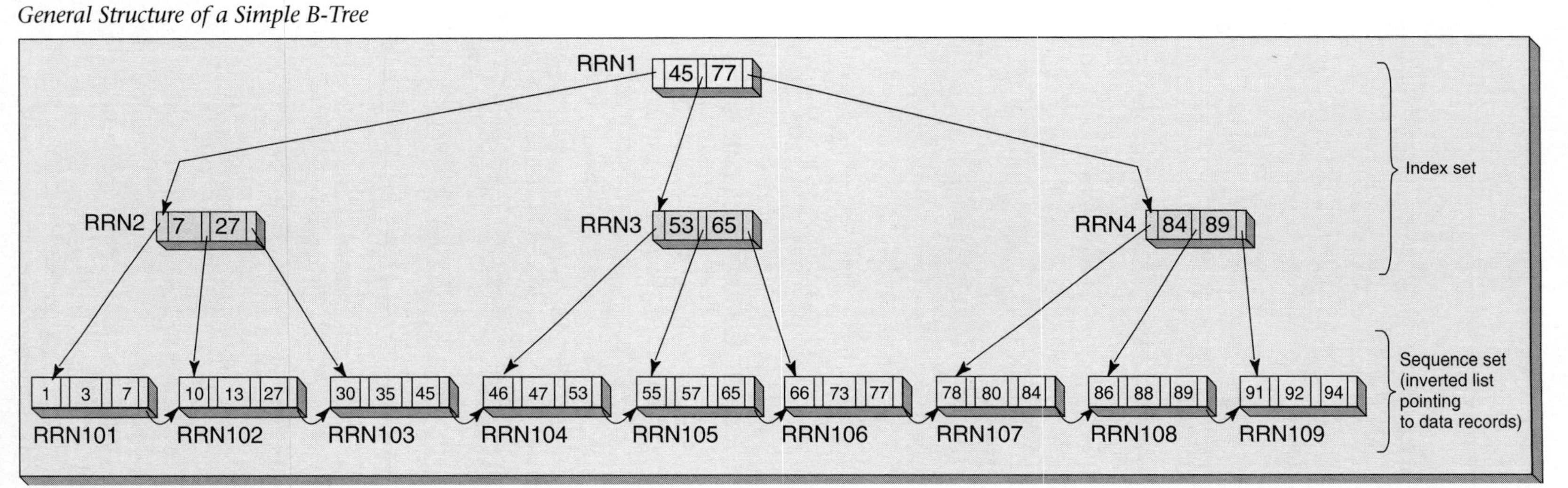

FIGURE A-10

Occurrence of the B-Tree in Figure A-9

RRN	Link1	Value1	Link2	Value2	Link3
1	2	45	3	77	4
2	101	7	102	27	103
3	104	53	105	65	106
4	107	84	108	89	109

Index Set

.
.
.

	R1	Addr1	R2	Addr2	R3	Addr3	Link
101	1	Pointer to 6	3	Pointer to 8	7	Pointer to 12	102
102	10	...	13	...	27	...	103
103	30	...	35	...	45	...	104
104	46	...	47	...	53	...	105
105	55	...	57	...	65	...	106
106	66	...	73	...	77	...	107
107	78	...	80	...	84	...	108
108	86	...	88	...	89	...	109
109	91	...	92	...	94	...	0

Sequence Set (Addresses of data records are omitted)

because several index entries may need to be modified when records are added or deleted to keep all records the same distance from the top index entry.

Summary of Data Structures

Figure A-11 summarizes the techniques for maintaining ordered flat files. Three supporting data structures are possible. Sequential lists can be used, but the data

FIGURE A-11

Summary of Data Structures and Data Organizations Used for Ordered Flat Files

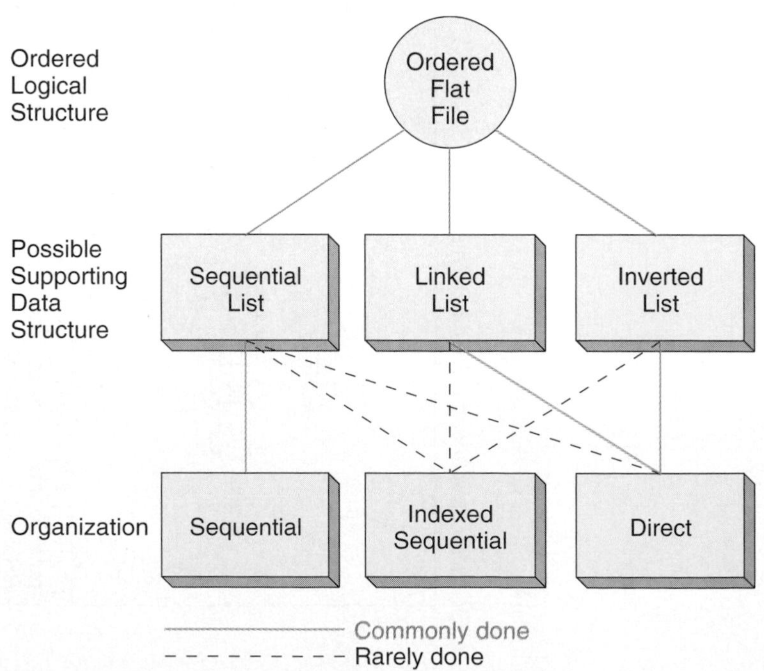

must be duplicated in order to maintain several orders. Because sequential lists are not used in database processing, we will not consider them further. Both linked lists and indexes can be used without data duplication. B-trees are special applications of indexes.

As shown in Figure A-11, sequential lists can be stored using any of three file organizations. In practice, however, they are usually kept on sequential files. In addition, although both linked lists and indexes can be stored using either indexed sequential or direct files, DBMS products almost always store them on direct files.

➤ REPRESENTING BINARY RELATIONSHIPS

In this section we examine how each of the specialized record relationships discussed in Chapter 6—trees, simple networks, and complex networks—can be represented using linked lists and indexes.

REVIEW OF RECORD RELATIONSHIPS

Records can be related in three ways. A *tree* relationship has one or more one-to-many relationships, but each child record has at most one parent. The occurrence of faculty data shown in Figure A-12 illustrates a tree. There are several 1:N relationships, but any child record has only one parent, as shown in Figure A-13.

A *simple network* is a collection of records and the 1:N relationships among them. What distinguishes a simple network from a tree is the fact that in a simple network a child can have more than one parent as long as the parents are different record types. The occurrence of a simple network of students, advisers, and major fields of study in Figure A-14 is represented schematically in Figure A-15.

A *complex network* is also a collection of records and relationships, but the relationships are many to many instead of one to many. The relationship between students and classes is a complex network. An occurrence of this relationship can be seen in Figure A-16, and the general schematic is in Figure A-17.

We saw earlier that we can use linked lists and indexes to process records in orders different from the one in which they are physically stored. We can also use those same data structures to store and process the relationships among records.

➤ FIGURE A-12

Occurrence of a Faculty Member Record

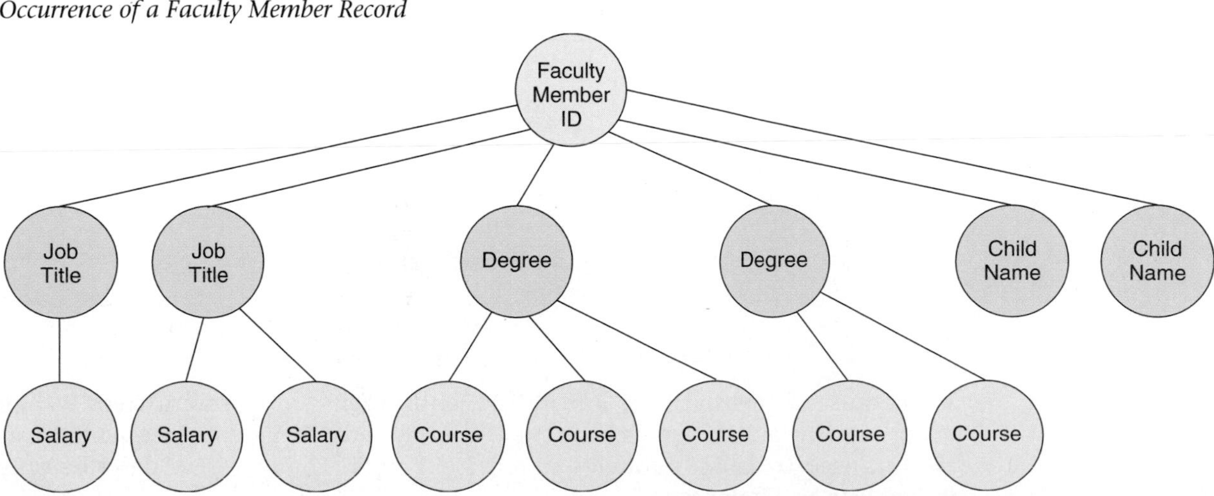

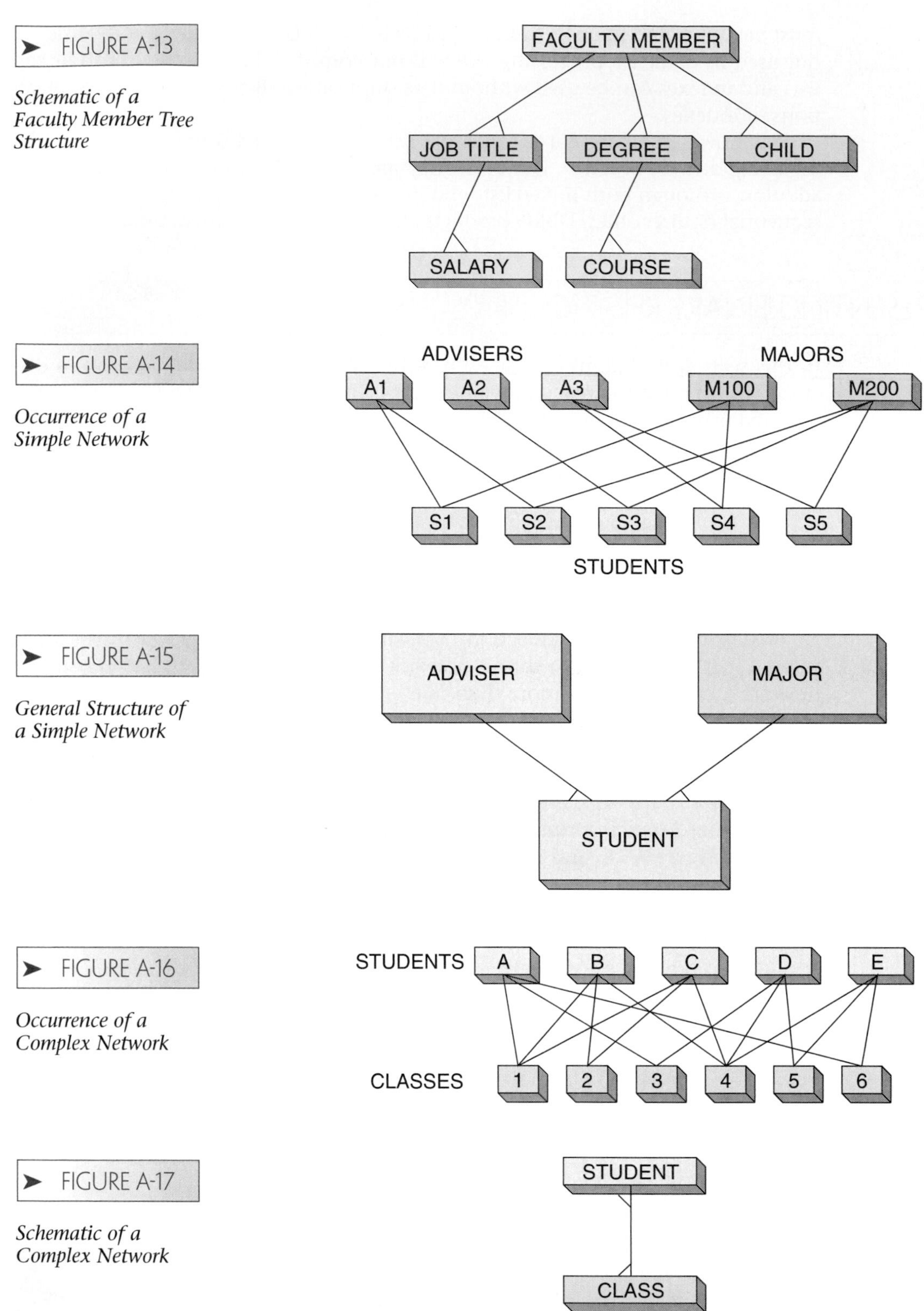

FIGURE A-13

Schematic of a Faculty Member Tree Structure

FIGURE A-14

Occurrence of a Simple Network

FIGURE A-15

General Structure of a Simple Network

FIGURE A-16

Occurrence of a Complex Network

FIGURE A-17

Schematic of a Complex Network

Representing Trees

We can use sequential lists, linked lists, and indexes to represent trees. When using sequential lists, we duplicate many data, and furthermore, sequential lists are not used by DBMS products to represent trees. Therefore, we describe only linked lists and indexes.

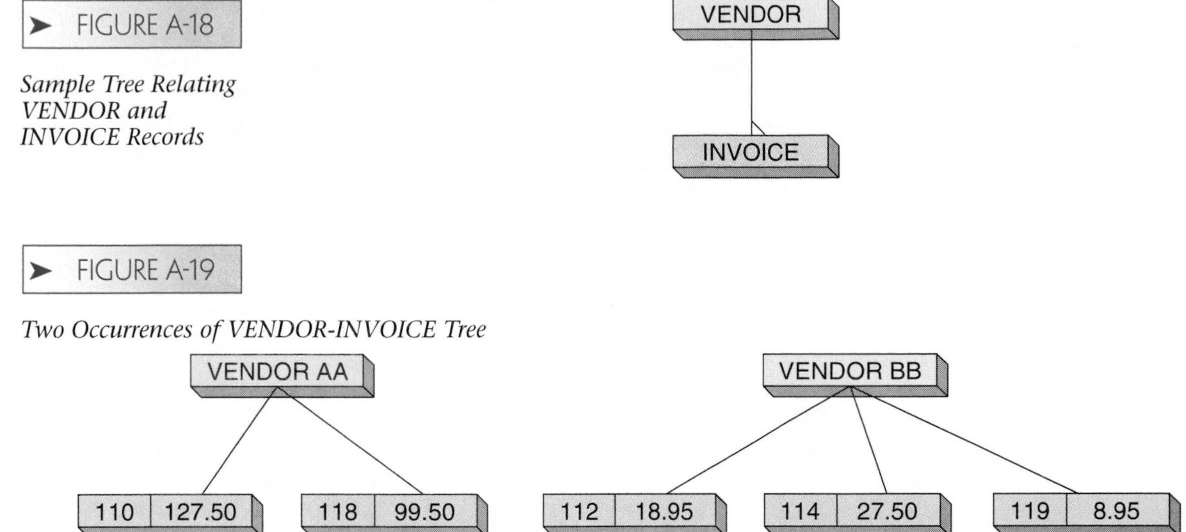

➤ FIGURE A-18

Sample Tree Relating VENDOR and INVOICE Records

➤ FIGURE A-19

Two Occurrences of VENDOR-INVOICE Tree

LINKED-LIST REPRESENTATION OF TREES Figure A-18 shows a tree structure in which the VENDOR records are parents and the INVOICE records are children. Figure A-19 shows two occurrences of this structure, and in Figure A-20, all of the VENDOR and INVOICE records have been written to a direct access file. VENDOR AA is in relative record number 1 (RRN1), and VENDOR BB is in relative record number 2. The INVOICE records have been stored in subsequent records, as illustrated. Note that these records are not stored in any particular order and that they do not need to be.

Our problem is that we cannot tell from this file which invoices belong to which vendors. To solve this problem with a linked list, we add a pointer field to every record. In this field we store the address of some other related record. For example, we place in VENDOR AA's link field the address of the first invoice belonging to it. This is RRN7, which is Invoice 110. Then we make Invoice 110 point to the next invoice belonging to VENDOR AA, in this case RRN3. This slot holds Invoice 118. To indicate that there are no more children in the chain, we insert a 0 in the link field for RRN3.

This technique is shown in Figure A-21. If you examine the figure, you will see that a similar set of links has been used to represent the relationship between VENDOR BB and its invoices.

The structure in Figure A-21 is much easier to modify than is a sequential list of the records. For example, suppose we add a new invoice, say number 111, to VENDOR AA. To do this, we just add the record to the file and insert it into the

➤ FIGURE A-20

File Representation of the Trees in Figure A-19

Record Number	Record Contents	
1	VENDOR AA	
2	VENDOR BB	
3	118	99.50
4	119	8.95
5	112	18.95
6	114	27.50
7	110	127.50

➤ FIGURE A-21

Tree Occurrences Represented by Linked Lists

Relative Record Number	Record Contents		Link Field
1	VENDOR AA		7
2	VENDOR BB		5
3	118	99.50	0
4	119	8.95	0
5	112	18.95	6
6	114	27.50	4
7	110	127.50	3

linked list. Physically, the record can be placed anywhere. But where should it be placed logically? Usually the application will have a requirement like children are to be kept in ascending order on invoice number. If so, we need to make Invoice 110 point to Invoice 111 (at RRN8), and we need to make Invoice 111, the new invoice, point to Invoice 118 (at RRN3). This modification is shown in Figure A-22.

Similarly, deleting an invoice is easy. If Invoice 114 is deleted, we simply modify the pointer in the invoice that is now pointing to Invoice 114. In this case, it is Invoice 112 at RRN5. We give Invoice 112 the pointer that Invoice 114 had before deletion. In this way, Invoice 112 points to Invoice 119 (see Figure A-23). We have effectively cut one link out of the chain and welded together the ones it once connected.

INDEX REPRESENTATION OF TREES A tree structure can readily be represented using indexes. The technique is to store each one-to-many relationship as an index. These lists are then used to match parents and children.

Using the VENDOR and INVOICE records in Figure A-21, we see that VENDOR AA (in RRN1) owns INVOICEs 110 (RRN7) and 118 (RRN3). Thus, RRN1 is the parent of RRN7 and RRN3. We can represent this fact with the index in Figure A-24. The list simply associates a parent's address with the addresses of each of its children.

If the tree has several 1:N relationships, then several indexes will be required, one for each relationship. For the structure in Figure A-13, five indexes are needed.

Representing Simple Networks

As with trees, simple networks can also be represented using linked lists and indexes.

➤ FIGURE A-22

Inserting Invoice 111 into File in Figure A-21

Relative Record Number	Record Contents		Link Field	
1	VENDOR AA		7	
2	VENDOR BB		5	
3	118	99.50	0	
4	119	8.95	0	
5	112	18.95	6	
6	114	27.50	4	
7	110	127.50	8	
8	111	19.95	3	← Inserted Record

➤ FIGURE A-23

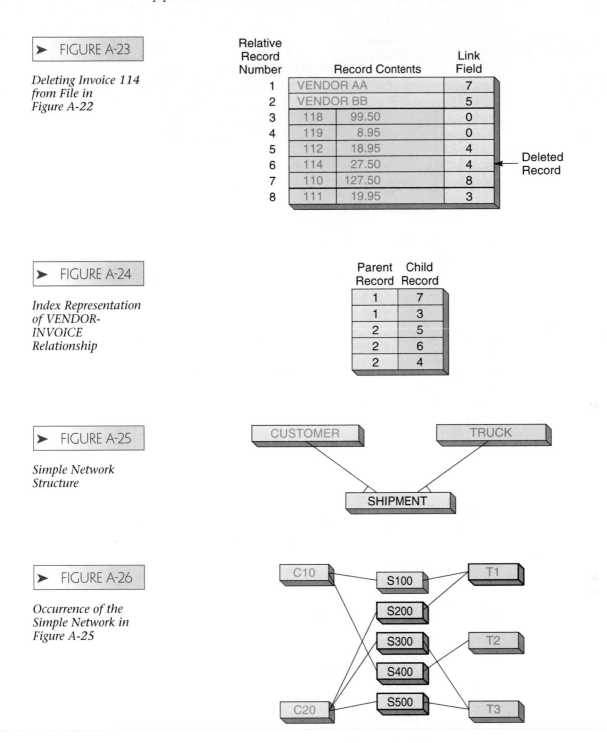

Deleting Invoice 114 from File in Figure A-22

Relative Record Number	Record Contents		Link Field
1	VENDOR AA		7
2	VENDOR BB		5
3	118	99.50	0
4	119	8.95	0
5	112	18.95	4
6	114	27.50	4
7	110	127.50	8
8	111	19.95	3

Deleted Record (← record 6)

➤ FIGURE A-24

Index Representation of VENDOR-INVOICE Relationship

Parent Record	Child Record
1	7
1	3
2	5
2	6
2	4

➤ FIGURE A-25

Simple Network Structure

CUSTOMER
TRUCK
SHIPMENT

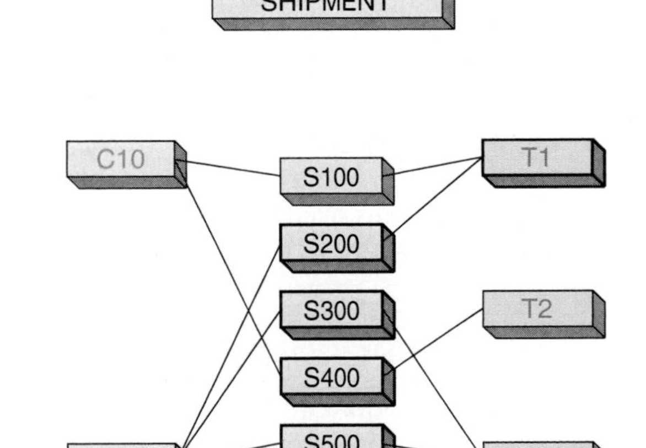

Occurrence of the Simple Network in Figure A-25

LINKED-LIST REPRESENTATION OF SIMPLE NETWORKS Consider the simple network in Figure A-25. It is a simple network because all the relationships are 1:N, and the SHIPMENT records have two parents of different types. Each SHIPMENT has a CUSTOMER parent and a TRUCK parent. The relationship between CUSTOMER and SHIPMENT is 1:N because a customer can have several shipments, and the relationship from TRUCK to SHIPMENT is 1:N because one truck can hold many shipments (assuming that the shipments are small enough to fit in one truck or less). An occurrence of this network is shown in Figure A-26.

➤ FIGURE A-27

Representation of a Simple Network with Linked Lists

Relative Record Number	Record Contents	Link Fields	
1	C10	6	
2	C20	7	
3	T1		6
4	T2		9
5	T3		8
6	S100	9	7
7	S200	8	0
8	S300	10	10
9	S400	0	0
10	S500	0	0
		CUSTOMER Links	TRUCK Links

In order to represent this simple network with linked lists, we need to establish one set of pointers for each 1:N relationship. In this example, that means one set of pointers to connect CUSTOMERs with their SHIPMENTs and another set of pointers to connect TRUCKs with their SHIPMENTs. Thus, a CUSTOMER record will contain one pointer (to the first SHIPMENT it owns); a TRUCK record will contain one pointer (to the first SHIPMENT it owns); and a SHIPMENT record will have two pointers, one for the next SHIPMENT owned by the same CUSTOMER and one for the next SHIPMENT owned by the same TRUCK. This scheme is illustrated in Figure A-27.

A simple network has at least two 1:N relationships, each of which can be represented using an index, as we explained in our discussion of trees. For example, consider the simple network shown in Figure A-25. It has two 1:N relationships, one between TRUCK and SHIPMENT and one between CUSTOMER and SHIPMENT. We can store each of these relationships in an index. Figure A-28 shows the two indexes needed to represent the example in Figure A-26. Assume the records are located in the same positions as in Figure A-27.

Representing Complex Networks

Complex networks can be physically represented in a variety of ways. They can be decomposed into trees or simple networks, and these simpler structures can then be represented using one of the techniques we just described. Alternatively, they

➤ FIGURE A-28

Representation of Simple Network with Index

Customer Record	Shipment Record
1	6
1	9
2	7
2	8
2	10

Truck Record	Shipment Record
3	6
3	7
4	9
5	8
5	10

FIGURE A-29

Decomposition of Complex Network into Simple Network

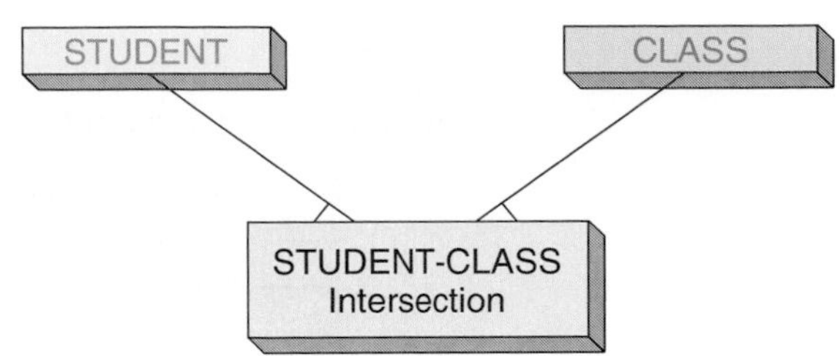

can be represented directly using indexes. Linked lists are not used by any DBMS product to represent complex networks directly. In practice, complex networks are nearly always decomposed into simpler structures, so we consider only those representations using decomposition.

A common approach to representing complex networks is to reduce them to simple networks and then to represent the simple networks with linked lists or indexes. Note, however, that a complex network involves a relationship between two records, whereas a simple network involves relationships among three records. Thus, in order to decompose a complex network into a simple one, we need to create a third record type.

The record that is created when a complex network is decomposed into a simple one is called an *intersection record*. Consider the StudentClass complex network. An intersection record will contain a unique key from a STUDENT record and a unique key from a corresponding CLASS record. It will contain no other application data, although it might contain link fields. The general structure of this relationship is shown in Figure A-29. Assuming that the record names are unique (such as S1, S2, and C1), an instance of the STUDENT-CLASS relationship is illustrated in Figure A-30.

FIGURE A-30

Instance of STUDENT-CLASS Relationship Showing Intersection Records

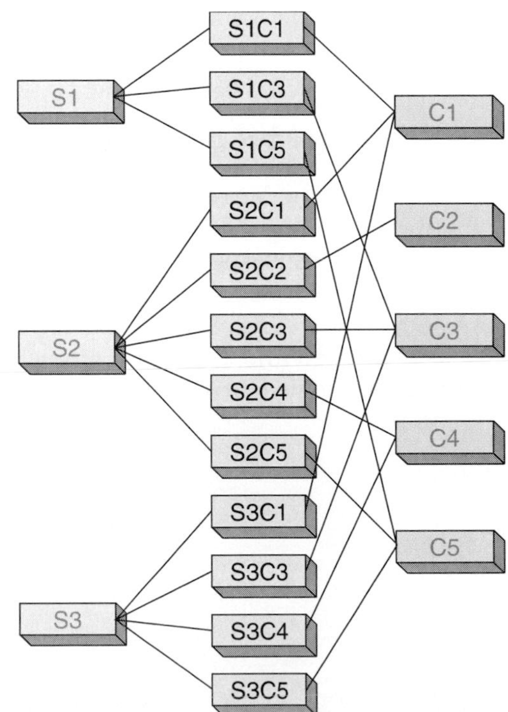

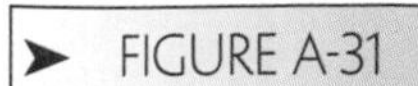

Occurrence of Network in Figure A-30

Relative Record Number	Record Contents	Link Fields (STUDENT Links)	Link Fields (CLASS Links)
1	S1	9	
2	S2	12	
3	S3	17	
4	C1		9
5	C2		13
6	C3		10
7	C4		15
8	C5		11
9	S1C1	10	12
10	S1C3	11	14
11	S1C5	0	16
12	S2C1	13	17
13	S2C2	14	0
14	S2C3	15	18
15	S2C4	16	19
16	S2C5	0	20
17	S3C1	18	0
18	S3C3	19	0
19	S3C4	20	0
20	S3C5	0	0

Notice that the relationship between STUDENT and the intersection record and that between CLASS and the intersection record both are 1:N. Thus, we have created a simple network that can now be represented with the linked-list or index techniques shown earlier. A file of this occurrence using the linked-list technique is shown in Figure A-31.

Summary of Relationship Representations

Figure A-32 summarizes the representations of record relationships. Trees can be represented using sequential lists (although we did not discuss this approach), linked lists, or indexes. Sequential lists are not used in DBMS products. A simple network can be decomposed into trees and then represented, or it can be represented directly using either linked lists or indexes. Finally, a complex network can be decomposed into a tree or a simple network (using intersection records), or it can be represented directly using indexes.

FIGURE A-32

Record Relationships, Data Structures, and File Organizations

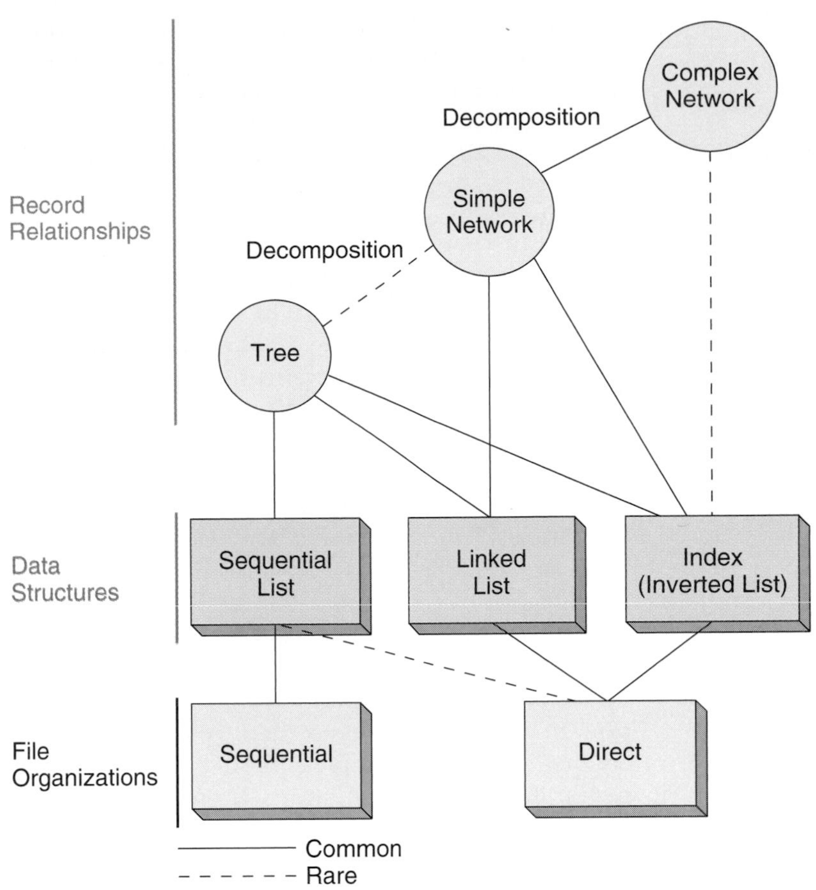

SECONDARY-KEY REPRESENTATIONS

In many cases the word *key* indicates a field (or fields) whose value uniquely identifies a record. This is usually called the *primary key.* Sometimes, however, applications need to access and process records by means of a *secondary key,* one that is different from the primary key. Secondary keys may be unique (such as a professor's name) or nonunique (such as a customer's Zip code). In this section we use the term *set* to refer to all records having the same value of a nonunique secondary key, for example, a set of records having Zip code 98040.

Both linked lists and indexes are used to represent secondary keys, but linked lists are practical only for nonunique keys. Indexes, however, can be used for both unique and nonunique key representations.

LINKED-LIST REPRESENTATION OF SECONDARY KEYS

Consider the example of CUSTOMER records shown in Figure A-33. The primary key is AccountNumber, and there is a secondary key on CreditLimit. Possible CreditLimit values are 500, 700, and 1000. Thus, there will be a set of records for the limit of 500, a set for 700, and a set for 1000.

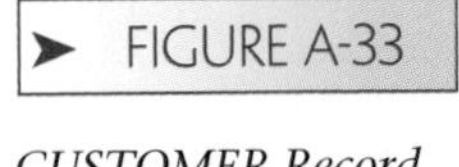

CUSTOMER Record

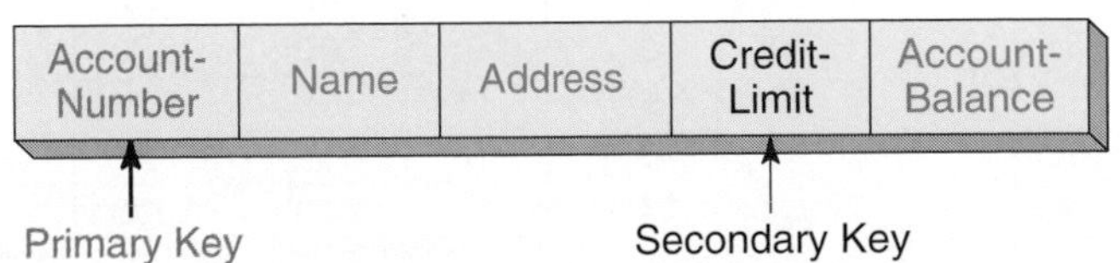

To represent this key using linked lists, we add a link field to the CUSTOMER records. Inside this link field we create a linked list for each set of records. Figure A-34 shows a database of eleven customers, but, for brevity, only AccountNumber and CreditLimit are shown. A link field has been attached to the records. Assume that one database record occupies one physical record on a direct file using relative record addressing.

Three pointers need to be established so that we know where to begin each linked list. These are called *heads* and are stored separate from the data. The head of the $500 linked list is RRN1. Record 1 links to record 2, which in turn links to record 7. Record 7 has a zero in the link position, indicating that it is the end of the list. Consequently, the $500 credit limit set consists of records 1, 2, and 7. Similarly, the $700 set contains records 3, 5, and 10, and the $1000 set contains relative records 4, 6, 8, 9, and 11.

To answer a query such as, How many accounts in the 1000 set have a balance in excess of 900?, the 1000 set linked list can be used. In this way, only those records in the 1000 set need to be read from the file and examined. Although the advantage of this approach is not readily apparent in this small example, suppose there are 100,000 CUSTOMER records, and only 100 of them are in the 1000 set. If there is no linked list, all 100,000 records must be examined, but with the linked list, only 100 records need to be examined, namely, the ones in the 1000 set. Using the linked list, therefore, saves 99,900 reads.

Linked lists are not an effective technique for every secondary-key application. In particular, if the records are processed nonsequentially in a set, linked lists are inefficient. For example, if it often is necessary to find the 10th or 120th or *n*th record in the 500 CreditLimit set, processing will be slow. Linked lists are inefficient for direct access.

In addition, if the application requires that secondary keys be created or destroyed dynamically, the linked-list approach is undesirable. Whenever a new key is created, a link field must be added to every record, which often requires reorganizing the database, a time-consuming and expensive process.

Finally, if the secondary keys are unique, each list will have a length of 1, and a separate linked list will exist for every record in the database. Because this situation is unworkable, linked lists cannot be used for unique keys. For example, suppose that the CUSTOMER records contain another unique field, say, Social Security Number. If we attempt to represent this unique secondary key using a linked list, every Social Security Number will be a separate linked list. Furthermore, each linked list will have just one item in it, the single record having the indicated Social Security Number.

➤ FIGURE A-34

Representing CreditLimit Secondary Key Using Linked List

Relative Record Number	Link	Account-Number	Credit-Limit	Other Data
1	2	101	500	
2	7	301	500	
3	5	203	700	
4	6	004	1000	
5	10	204	700	
6	8	905	1000	
7	0	705	500	
8	9	207	1000	
9	11	309	1000	
10	0	409	700	
11	0	210	1000	

HEAD-500 = 1
HEAD-700 = 3
HEAD-1000 = 4

FIGURE A-35

Representing a Unique Secondary Key with Indexes: (a) Sample CUSTOMER Data (with SSN) and (b) Index for SSN Secondary Key

Relative Record Number	Account-Number	Credit-Limit	Social Security Number (SSN)
1	101	500	000-01-0001
2	301	500	000-01-0005
3	203	700	000-01-0009
4	004	1000	000-01-0003

(a)

SSN	Relative Record Number
000-01-0001	1
000-01-0003	4
000-01-0005	2
000-01-0009	3

(b)

Index Representation of Secondary Keys

A second technique for representing secondary keys uses an index; one is established for each secondary key. The approach varies depending on whether the key values are unique or nonunique.

UNIQUE SECONDARY KEYS Suppose the CUSTOMER records in Figure A-33 contain Social Security Number (SSN) as well as the fields shown. To provide key access to the CUSTOMER records using SSN, we simply build an index on the SSN field. Sample CUSTOMER data are shown in Figure A-35(a), and a corresponding index is illustrated in Figure A-35(b). This index uses relative record numbers as addresses. It would be possible to use AccountNumbers instead, in which case the DBMS would locate the desired SSN in the index, obtain the matching AccountNumber, and then convert the AccountNumber to a relative record address.

NONUNIQUE SECONDARY KEYS Indexes can also be used to represent nonunique secondary keys, but because each set of related records can contain an unknown number of members, the entries in the index are of variable length. For example, Figure A-36 shows the index for the CreditLimit sets for the CUSTOMER data. The $500 set and the $700 set both have three members, so there are three account numbers in each entry. The $1000 set has five members, so there are five account numbers in that entry.

In reality, representing and processing nonunique secondary keys are complex tasks. Several different schemes are used by commercial DBMS products. One common method uses a values table and an occurrence table. Each values table

FIGURE A-36

Index for CreditLimit Key in Figure A-33

CreditLimit	AccountNumber				
500	101	301	705		
700	203	204	409		
1000	004	905	207	309	210

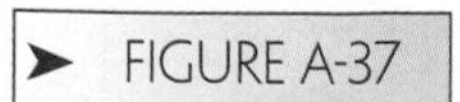

FIGURE A-37

Values and Occurrence Tables for CreditLimit Key in Figure A-33

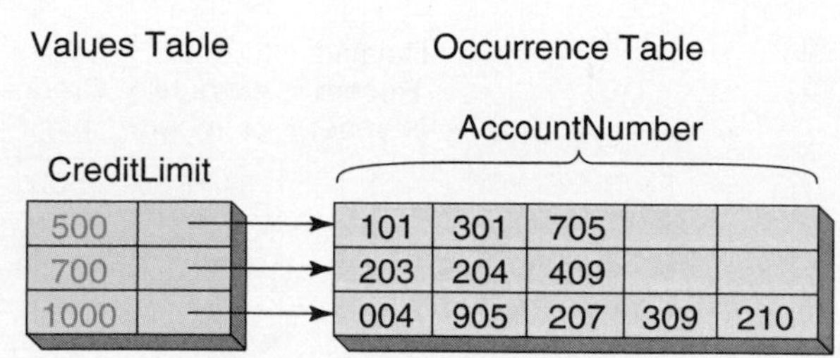

entry consists of two fields, the first of which has a key value. For the CUSTOMER CreditLimit key, the values are 500, 700, and 1000. The second field of the values table entry is a pointer into the occurrence table. The occurrence table contains record addresses, and those having a common value in the secondary-key field appear together in the table. Figure A-37 shows the values and occurrence tables for the CreditLimit key.

To locate records having a given value of the secondary key, the values table is searched for the desired value. Once the given key value is located in the values table, the pointer is followed to the occurrence table to obtain the addresses of those records having that key value. These addresses are then used to obtain the desired records.

When a new record is inserted into the file, the DBMS must modify the indexes for each secondary-key field. For nonunique keys, it must make sure that the new record key value is in the values table; if it is, it will add the new record address to the appropriate entry in the occurrence table. If it is not, it must insert new entries in the values and occurrence tables.

When a record is deleted, its address must be removed from the occurrence table. If no addresses remain in the occurrence table entry, the corresponding values table entry must also be deleted.

When the secondary-key field of a record is modified, the record address must be removed from one occurrence table entry and inserted into another. If the modification is a new value for the key, an entry must be added to the values table.

The index approach to representing secondary keys overcomes the objections to the linked-list approach. Direct processing of sets is possible. For example, the third record in a set can be retrieved without processing the first or second one. Also, it is possible to dynamically create and delete secondary keys. No changes are made in the records themselves; the DBMS merely creates additional values and occurrence tables. Finally, unique keys can be processed efficiently.

The disadvantages of the index approach are that it requires more file space (the tables use more overhead than the pointers do) and that the DBMS programming task is more complex. Note that the *application programming* task is not necessarily any more or less difficult—but it is more complex to write DBMS software that processes indexes than it is to write software that processes linked lists. Finally, modifications are usually processed more slowly because of the reading and writing actions required to access and maintain the values in the occurrence tables.

➤ SUMMARY

In this appendix we surveyed data structures used for database processing. A flat file is a file that contains no repeating groups. Flat files can be ordered using sequential lists (physically placing the records in the sequence in which they will be processed), linked lists (attaching to each data record a pointer to another logically related record), and indexes (building a table, separate from the data records, containing pointers to related records). B-trees are special applications of indexes.

Sequential lists, linked lists, and indexes (or inverted lists) are fundamental data structures. (Sequential lists, however, are seldom used in database processing.) These data structures can be used to represent record relationships as well as secondary keys.

The three basic record structures—trees, simple networks, and complex networks—can be represented using linked lists and indexes. Simple networks can be decomposed into trees and then represented; complex networks can be decomposed into simple networks containing an intersection record and then represented.

Secondary keys are used to access the data on some field besides the primary key. Secondary keys can be unique or nonunique. Nonunique secondary keys can be represented with both linked lists and indexes. Unique secondary keys can be represented only with indexes.

➤ GROUP I QUESTIONS

A.1 Define a flat file. Give an example (other than one in this text) of a flat file and an example of a file that is not flat.

A.2 Show how sequential lists can be used to maintain the file in Question A.1 in two different orders simultaneously.

A.3 Show how linked lists can be used to maintain the file in Question A.1 in two different orders simultaneously.

A.4 Show how inverted lists can be used to maintain the file in Question A.1 in two different orders simultaneously.

A.5 Define a tree, and give an example structure.

A.6 Give an occurrence of the tree in Question A.5.

A.7 Represent the occurrence in Question A.6 using linked lists.

A.8 Represent the occurrence in Question A.6 using indexes.

A.9 Define a simple network and give an example structure.

A.10 Give an occurrence of the simple network in Question A.9.

A.11 Represent the occurrence in Question A.10 using linked lists.

A.12 Represent the occurrence in Question A.10 using indexes.

A.13 Define *complex network,* and give an example structure.

A.14 Give an occurrence of the complex network in Question A.13.

A.15 Decompose the complex network in Question A.14 into a simple network, and represent an occurrence of it using indexes.

A.16 Explain the difference between primary and secondary keys.

A.17 Explain the difference between unique and nonunique keys.

A.18 Define a file containing a unique secondary key. Represent an occurrence of that file using an index on the secondary key.

A.19 Define a nonunique secondary key for the file in Question A.18. Represent an occurrence of that file using a linked list on the secondary key.

A.20 Perform the same task as in Question A.19, but using an index to represent the secondary key.

➤ GROUP II QUESTIONS

A.21 Develop an algorithm to produce a report listing the IDs of students enrolled in each class, using the linked-list structure in Figure A-4.

A.22 Develop an algorithm to insert records into the structure in Figure A-4. The resulting structure should resemble the one in Figure A-5.

A.23 Develop an algorithm to produce a report listing the IDs of students enrolled in each class, using the index structure shown in Figures A-8(a), (b), and (c).

A.24 Develop an algorithm to insert a record into the structure in Figure A-8(a), being sure to modify both of the associated indexes in Figure A-8(b) and (c).

A.25 Develop an algorithm to delete a record from the structure in Figure A-34, which shows a secondary key represented with a linked list. If all records for one of the credit-limit categories (say, $1000) are deleted, should the associated head pointer also be deleted? Why or why not?

A.26 Develop an algorithm to insert a record into the structure shown in Figure A-34. Suppose the new record has a credit-limit value different from those already established. Should the record be inserted and a new linked list established? Or should the record be rejected? Who should make that decision?

Semantic Object Models with Tabledesigner

Tabledesigner is a Windows 95, 98, NT, and Windows 2000 application that you can use to create semantic object models and transform those models into Microsoft Access or other databases. In addition, you can reverse engineer an existing database to create a semantic object model from it. Once you have done this, you can modify the model and Tabledesigner will change the associated database schema (and data) accordingly. Finally, you can use Tabledesigner to generate ASP pages to create, read, update, and delete semantic object views from any browser using pure HTML. For this last function, you will need to place the generated ASP pages on a web server that is running IIS or the Personal Web Server with ASP extensions. A summary of these functions is shown in Figure B-1.

To obtain a copy of Tabledesigner, go to www.prenhall.com/kroenke/ where you will find download instructions. Once you have downloaded the software, install it according to the instructions. There is no charge for using this product in conjunction with your database class. Tabledesigner includes comprehensive documentation. Click help and you will see the display shown in Figure B-2. You may want to supplement the discussion here with that documentation—especially the discussion in the "Learning to Use Tabledesigner Developer" book that is shown open in Figure B-2.

FIGURE B-1

Functions of Tabledesigner

• To Create a SOM model:

Generate an Access database from the model.

Generate a SQL Server database from the model

Generate SQL statements to create or modify a database.

• To Reverse-Engineer an Existing Database:

Create a copy of the database and modify its schema.

Create a copy of the database, with data, and use modeling to modify the schema and data.

Create a copy of the database schema, without data, and use modeling to modify the schema.

Bind to the database and use modeling to modify the schema and data.

• To Generate a Web Application:

Create semantic object views.

Generate ASP pages for create, read, update, and delete actions from those views.

Generated pages can be placed in Microsoft Visual Interdev for customization.

FIGURE B-2

Tabledesigner Help

➤ CREATING A SOM MODEL

To create a new semantic object (SOM) model, pick File/New from the menu or click on the new document button (the first button in the toolbar). Tabledesigner will display the window shown in Figure B-3. Here you can choose a starter kit, which is a list of prebuilt models and domains. In this example, we will choose Generic, but you might want to use the others as well.

The next display will show a list of domains in a list on the left hand side of the screen along with an empty design space on the right. To create a semantic object, hold the left mouse button down in the design space and drag. A rectangle will appear. Release the mouse button and you will see the display shown in Figure B-4. At this point you can name the object whatever you want by typing in the open text box. Name this object STUDENT.

To add attributes to the STUDENT object, click on the Name domain in the left hand list and drag and drop it into STUDENT. Tabledesigner will create an attribute in STUDENT that inherits all of its properties from the Name domain. Click on Name in STUDENT and press the Enter key. Retype Name to be StudentName in the open text box in the semantic object.

All domains and attributes (note that attributes are referred to as *items* in Tabledesigner) have properties. To see them, right click on Name in the domain list. Tabledesigner displays the properties of the Name domain. Now, right click on StudentName in the STUDENT object. Tabledesigner will show the properties

➤ FIGURE B-3

Choosing a Starter Kit

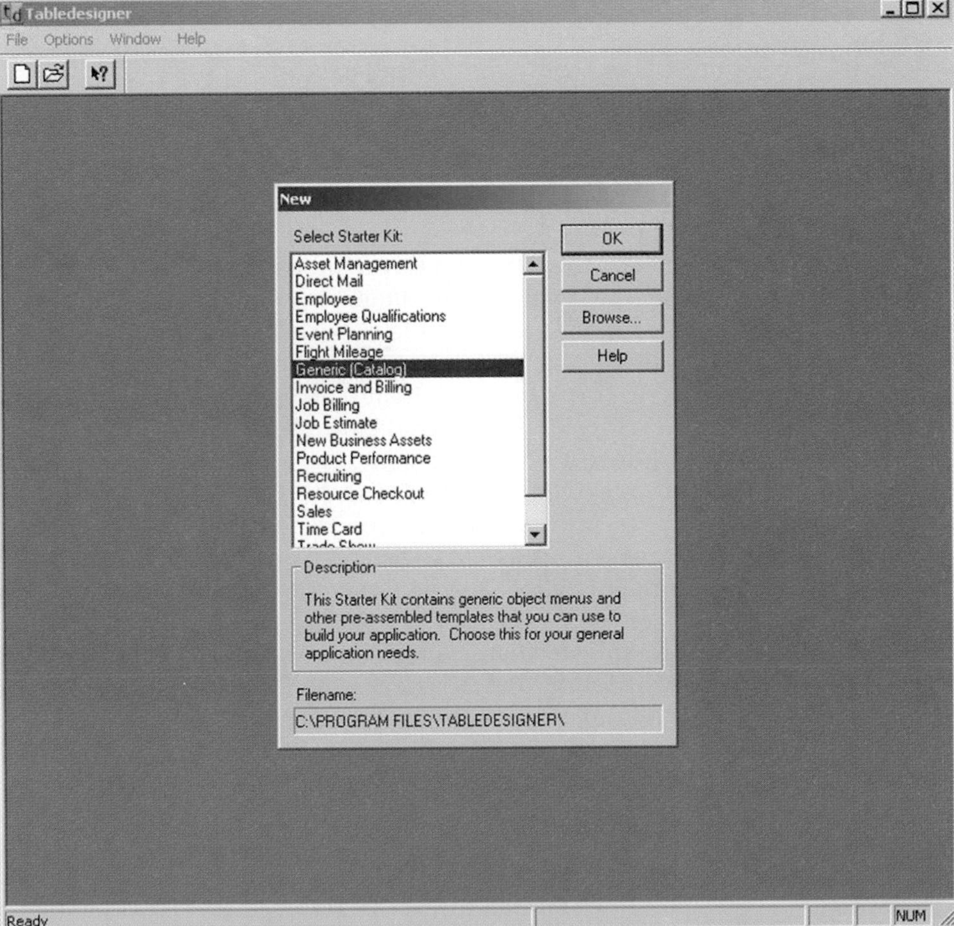

FIGURE B-4

Creating and Naming a Semantic Object

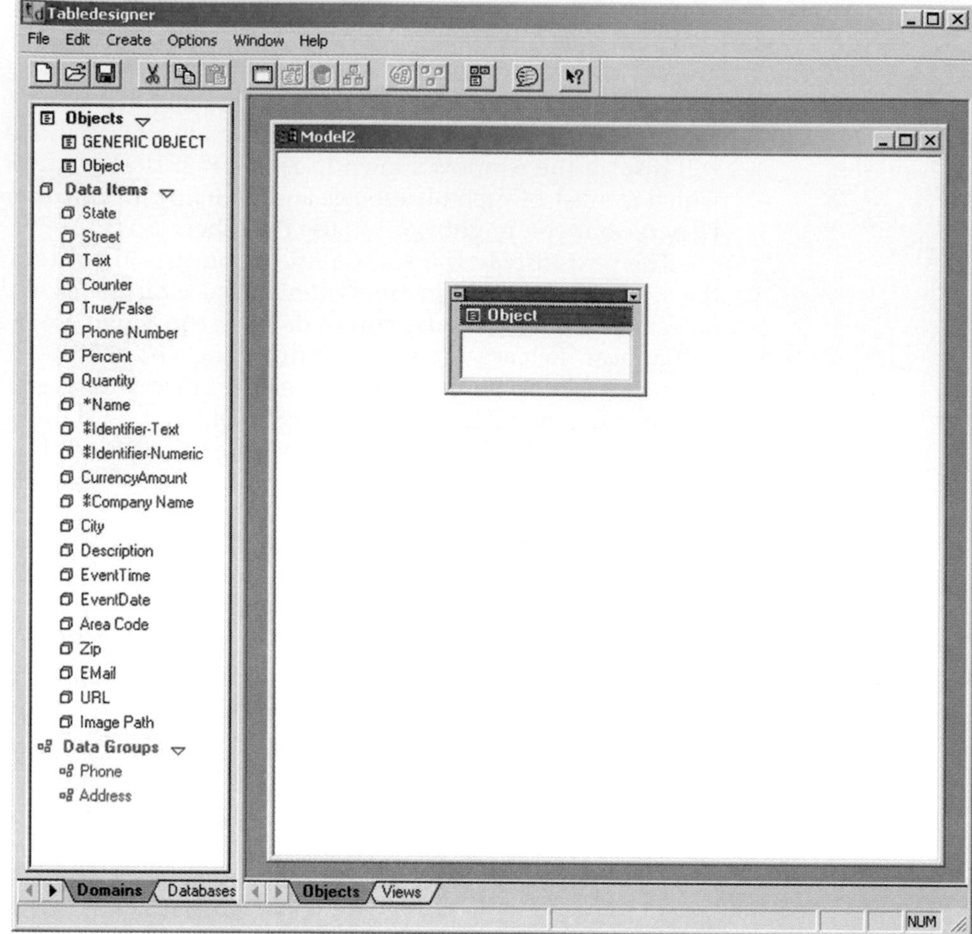

of the StudentName attribute as shown in Figure B-5. These properties will be the same as the Name domain except that the name of the attribute is StudentName. The fact that this property is shown in read means that it has been over-ridden from the property in its underlying domain. Close the property window. Press the <*Ctrl*> and *Z* keys simultaneously to undo the attribute name change. (As an aside, you can undo up to 30 steps of work with Tabledesigner.)

To continue, drag Phone from the Data Group section in the domain list and drop it in STUDENT, just below Name. Click on the arrow next to Phone and it will open to reveal its contents, which are Area Code and Phone Number as shown in Figure B-6. Drag and drop the Address group in the same way.

To continue with the model, create a second object in the design space by dragging another rectangle and name this second object CLASS. Drag Name and drop it in CLASS. Also drag Quantity from the domain list and drop it in CLASS as well. Rename Quantity as CreditHours. If you examine the properties of Quantity, you will see that its Data Type is integer. If your school allows fractions of CreditHours, you can change the Data Type of CreditHours by right clicking to reveal the property sheet and changing the data type to 7 digit Decimal Number.

To create a relationship between two semantic objects, click on the small icon just to the left of the word STUDENT at the top of the STUDENT semantic object. Drag this icon and drop it in CLASS, just below CreditHours. A relationship will be created between STUDENT and CLASS. Your model should now appear as shown in Figure B-7.

The cardinalities of the relationship can be modified by clicking on the 0-1 subscript of either the STUDENT or CLASS object link attributes. When you do

FIGURE B-5

The Properties of Student Name

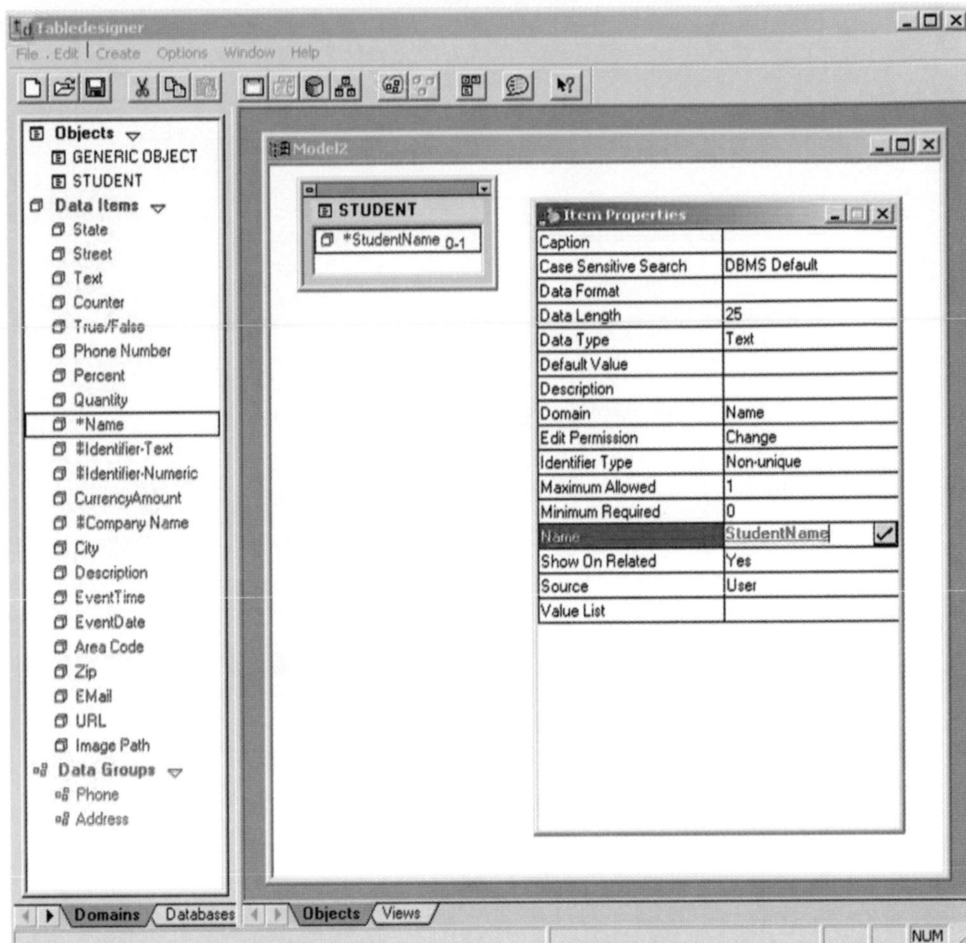

this, the display shown in Figure B-8 will appear. Open the list box labeled "Maximum allowed" to find N. You can enter a specific number like 7, also, if you like. Doing this will have no impact on your schema but it will cause the generated ASP pages to enforce this limit.

Continue with these operations to create a third object, ADVISOR, with the attributes shown in Figure B-9. To observe the consequences of domain inheritance, change the name of Phone in the domain list. Do this by clicking on Phone and then pressing the Enter key. Type Campus Phone as the new name of the domain. Notice that both Phone in STUDENT and Phone in ADVISOR have been changed to Campus Phone. These attributes inherit any change to their domain's properties.

We are now ready to generate a database. Since Tabledesigner can modify your schema once you've created it, you don't need to be finished when you generate your first database. You can generate it incrementally as you go along, if you like.

Click on the small disk in the toolbar (the ninth icon in the toolbar) or select Create/Database from the menu. Save your model under some convenient name; we used Example1 here. After the model has been saved, Tabledesigner will display the window shown in Figure B-10. You can pick the DBMS to be used for the database from this list.

Because we had installed SQL Server prior to this example, it appears in the list. To generate tables in a SQL Server database, click on SQL Server and then log in with SQL Server as discussed in Chapter 13. Use the (local) server, enter *sa* for Login id, and change the default database to be the one in which you want the tables placed. Here we used SQL Server Example Database, which was created

FIGURE B-6

Example of a Group Attribute

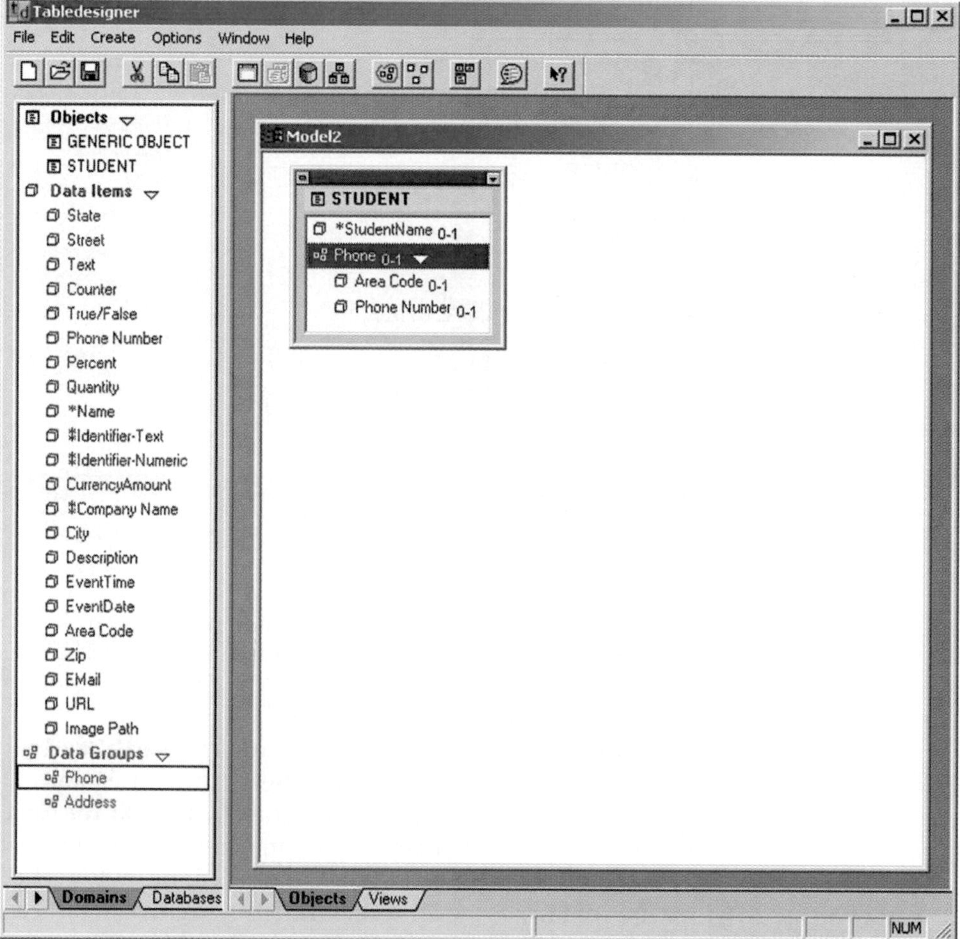

FIGURE B-7

Create a relationship between STUDENT and CLASS

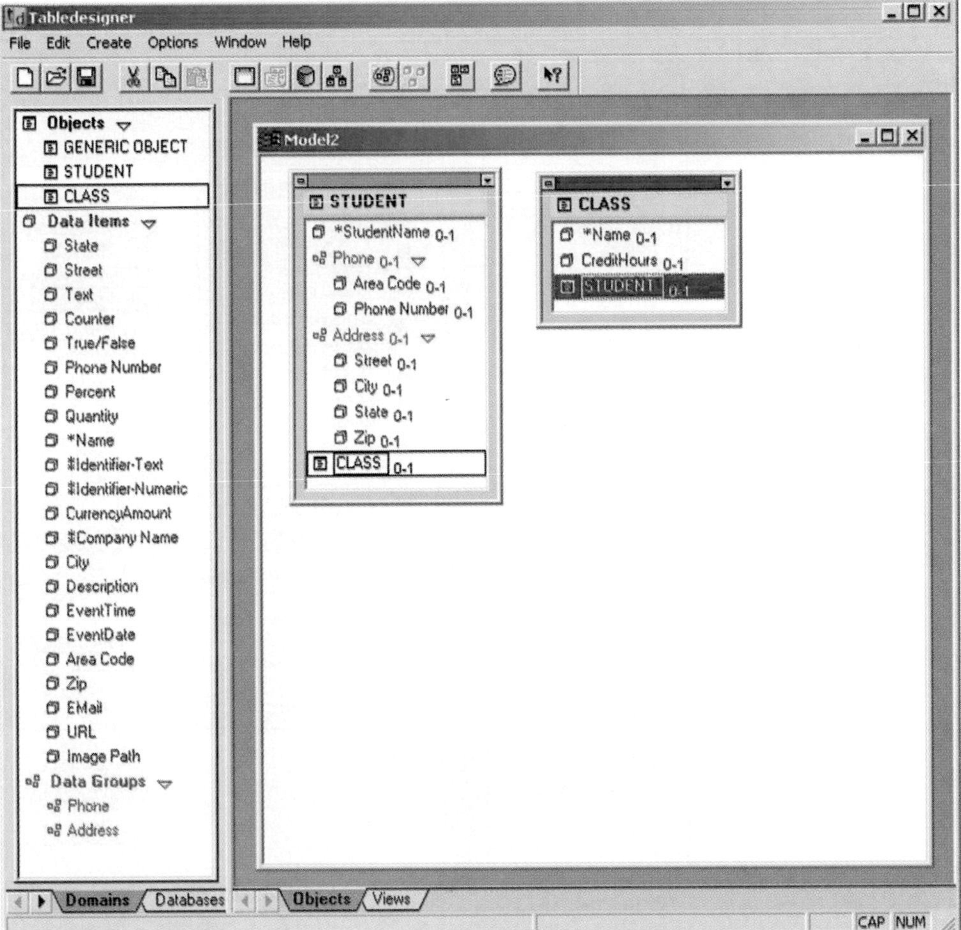

Changing Relationship Cardinalities

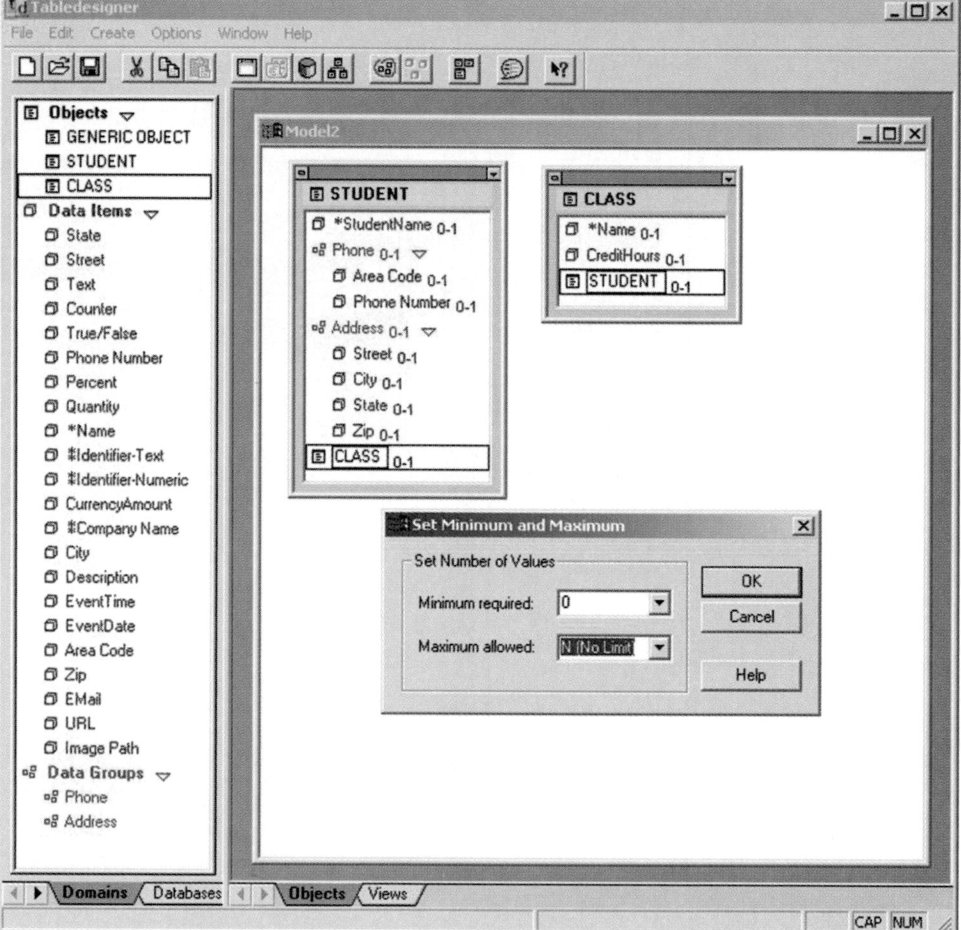

Three Object Model

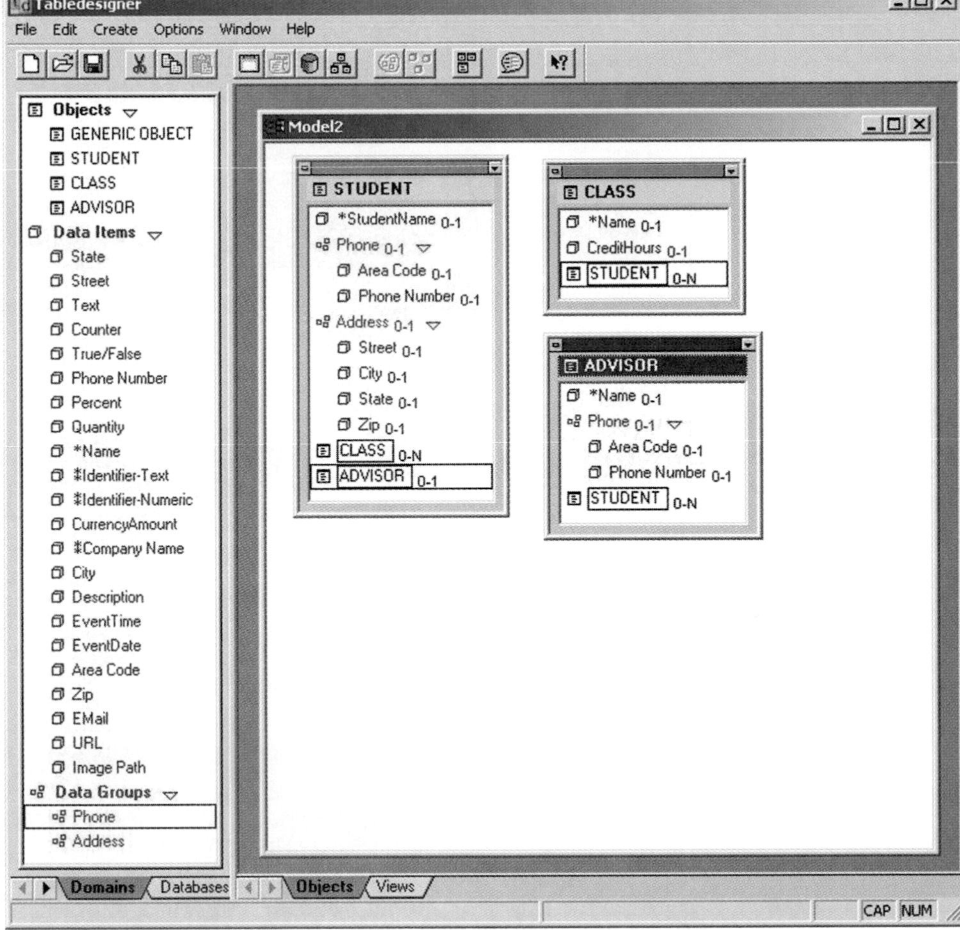

➤ FIGURE B-10

Selecting the DBMS

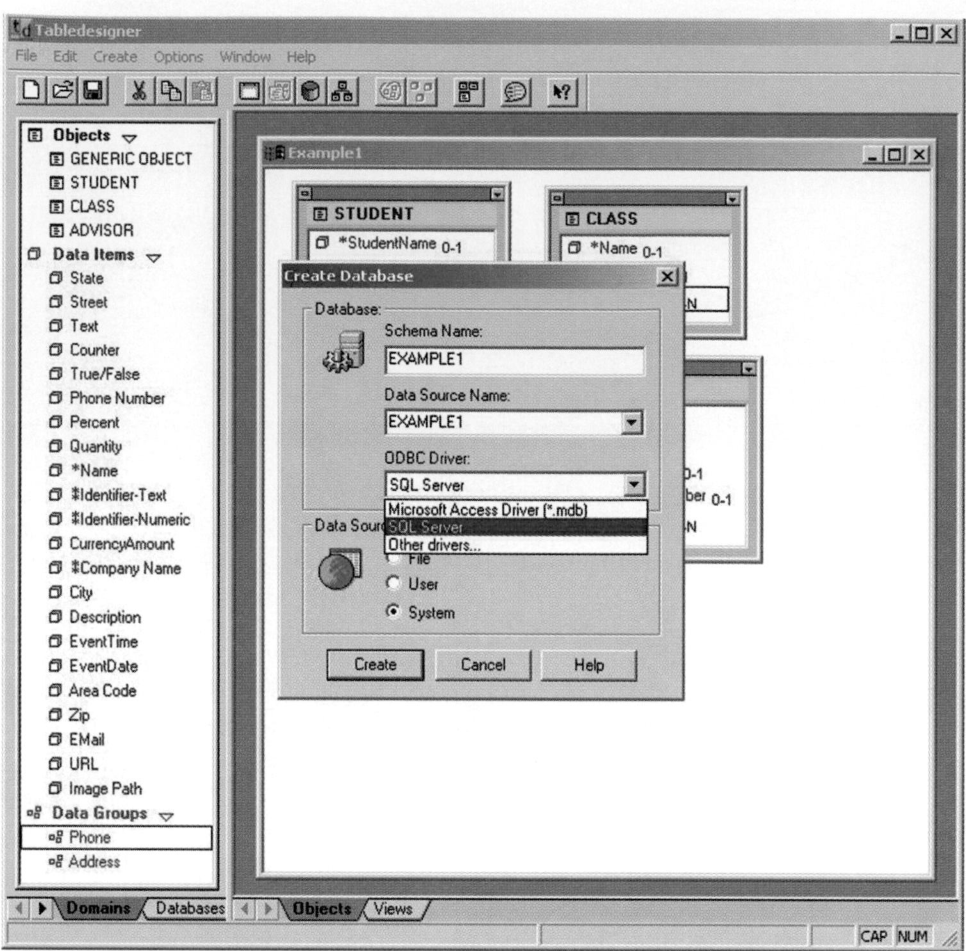

➤ FIGURE B-11

SQL Server Tables for the Model in Figure B-9

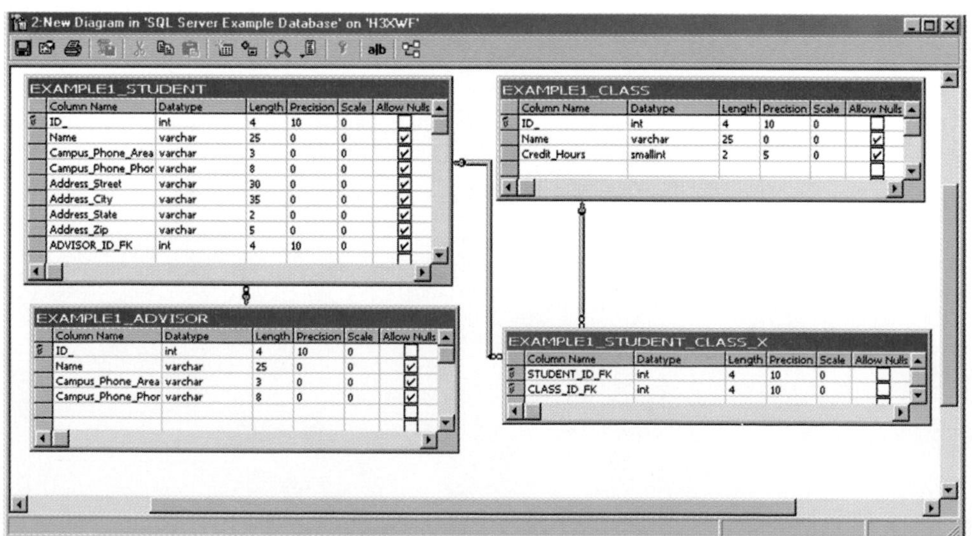

previously. At that point, the tables necessary for the model were created by Tabledesigner and placed into SQL Server Example Database. Figure B-11 shows the tables that were generated for the model in Figure B-9.

If you have not installed SQL Server, but have installed Access, you can select it from the list in Figure B-10 and Tabledesigner will generate an Access database.

You can also cause Tabledesigner to display the SQL statements that it is about to execute before generating a database. To do that, select Create/SQL Text Only and the SQL statements will be placed in a text file in a directory named SQL in the Tabledesigner directory. You must do this before you generate your database; otherwise there is no SQL in the queue awaiting execution.

➤ REVERSE ENGINEERING A SOM MODEL

In addition to creating new models, you can use Tabledesigner to generate a model from all or part of an existing database. To do this, you first need to create an ODBC Data Source Name to the database you wish to reverse engineer. In this example, we will use Northwind.mdb, a database that ships with Microsoft Access.

To set up an ODBC Data Source to Northwind, first open the ODBC Administrator by selecting File/ODBC Administrator from within Tabledesigner. Select the System tab as shown in Figure B-12 and click Add. Select Microsoft Access from the list of drivers, and then click Finish. Enter a name for the data

➤ FIGURE B-12

Using the ODBC Administrator for Creating an ODBC Data Source

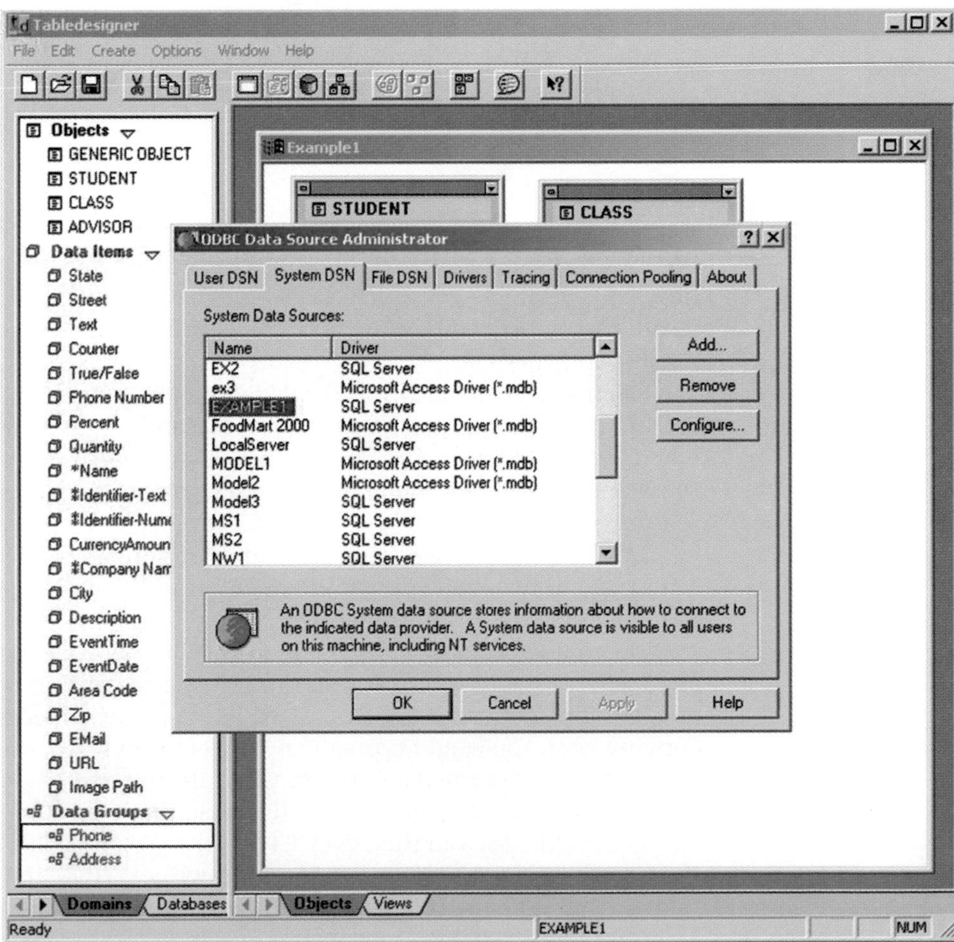

Reverse Engineering Northwind

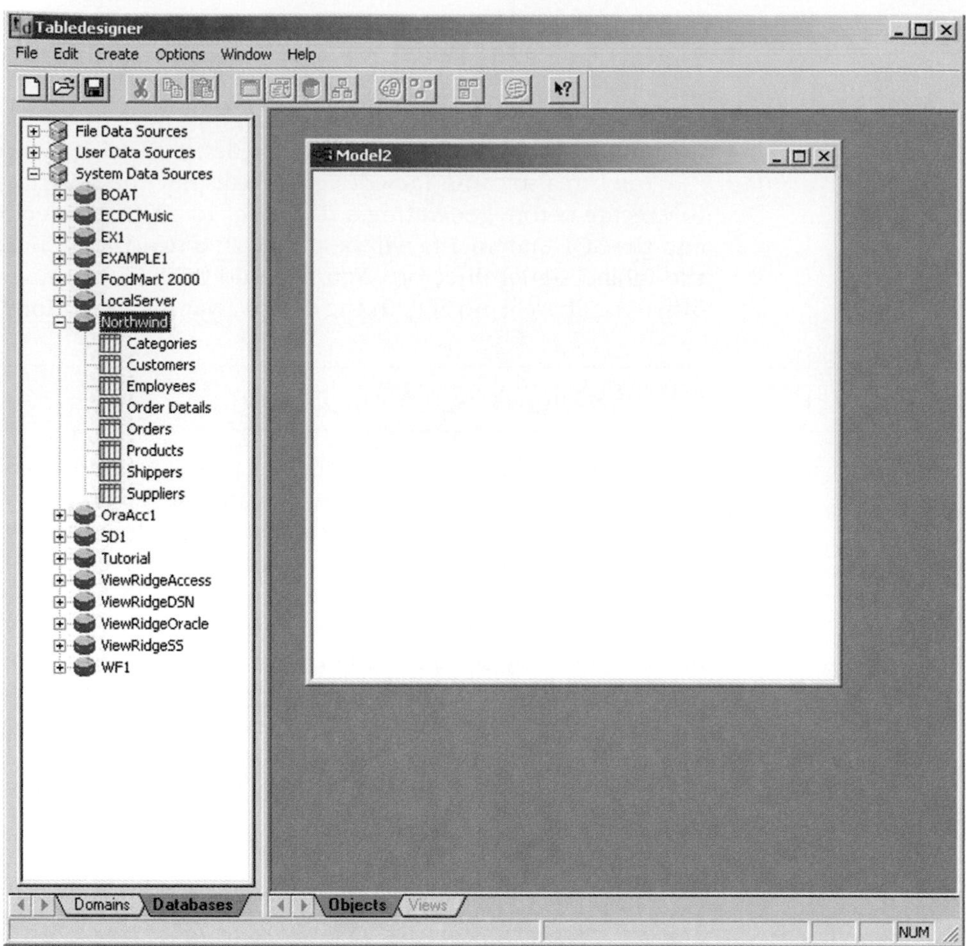

source (we used Northwind in this example) and click the Select button. Browse to the directory where Northwind.mdb is located. This location varies depending on how you installed Access. If you do not know where it is, use Windows Find to locate the file named Northwind.mdb. Go to that directory in the ODBC administrator and click OK.

Open a new model within Tabledesigner. Look to the bottom of the domain list and click on the tab labeled Databases. Tabledesigner will display a list of your File, User, and System data sources. Since we created a System data source, click there and look for the name of your data source. Click on the plus button to the left of it and all of the tables in the database will be shown (as in the left hand window of Figure B-13). Drag the name of your data source (here Northwind) onto the empty design space in the window to the right. Save the model; we used the name RE1 for this example.

The dialog box shown in Figure B-14 will now appear. Click Help to find out about the various options. For now, select the last option which will create a new database but not copy any data; it will set up the Tabledesigner import files for copying later. You would normally use this option if you wanted to apply filters to copy only some of the data, but we will omit this exercise in this Appendix.

Tabledesigner now generates a database that conforms to the model. Select a DBMS from the list and then click Create. The result of this action will be a model like the one shown in Figure B-15 along with a database that has a copy of the tables from Northwind. You can now make changes to this model and use Tabledesigner to change the database structure.

Creating Database Schema without Data

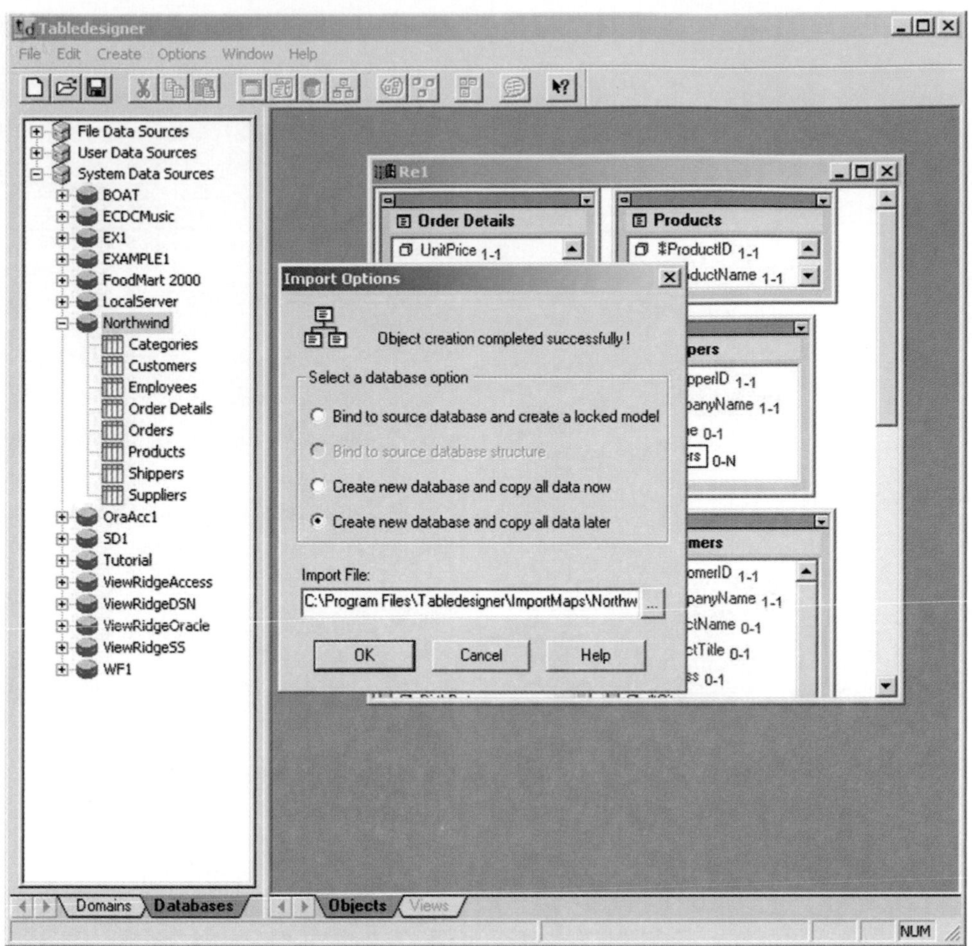

Semantic Object Model of Northwind Using Reverse

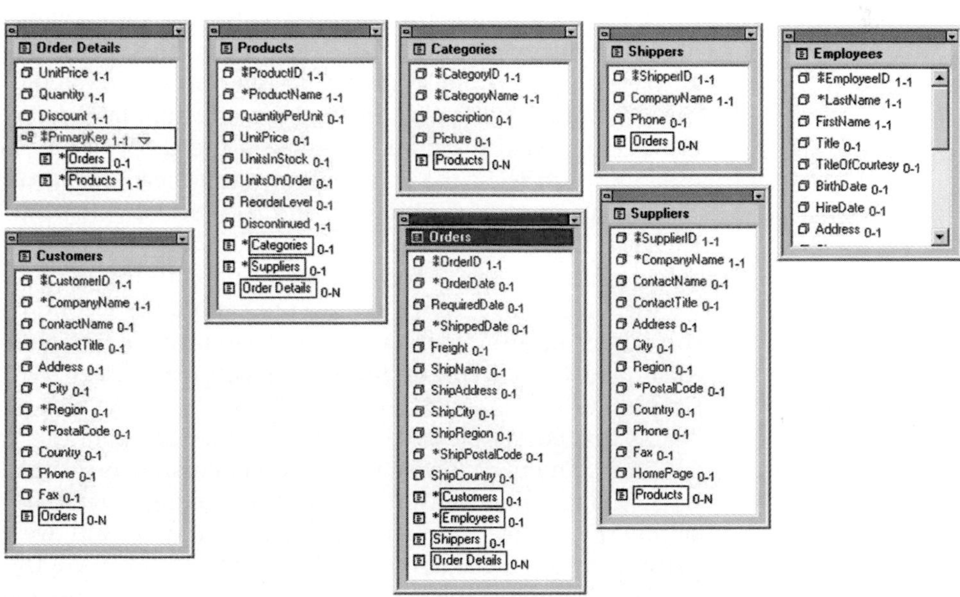

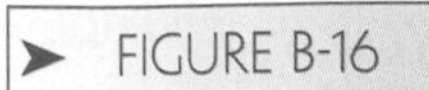

FIGURE B-16

Building a Two-Table Extract from Northwind

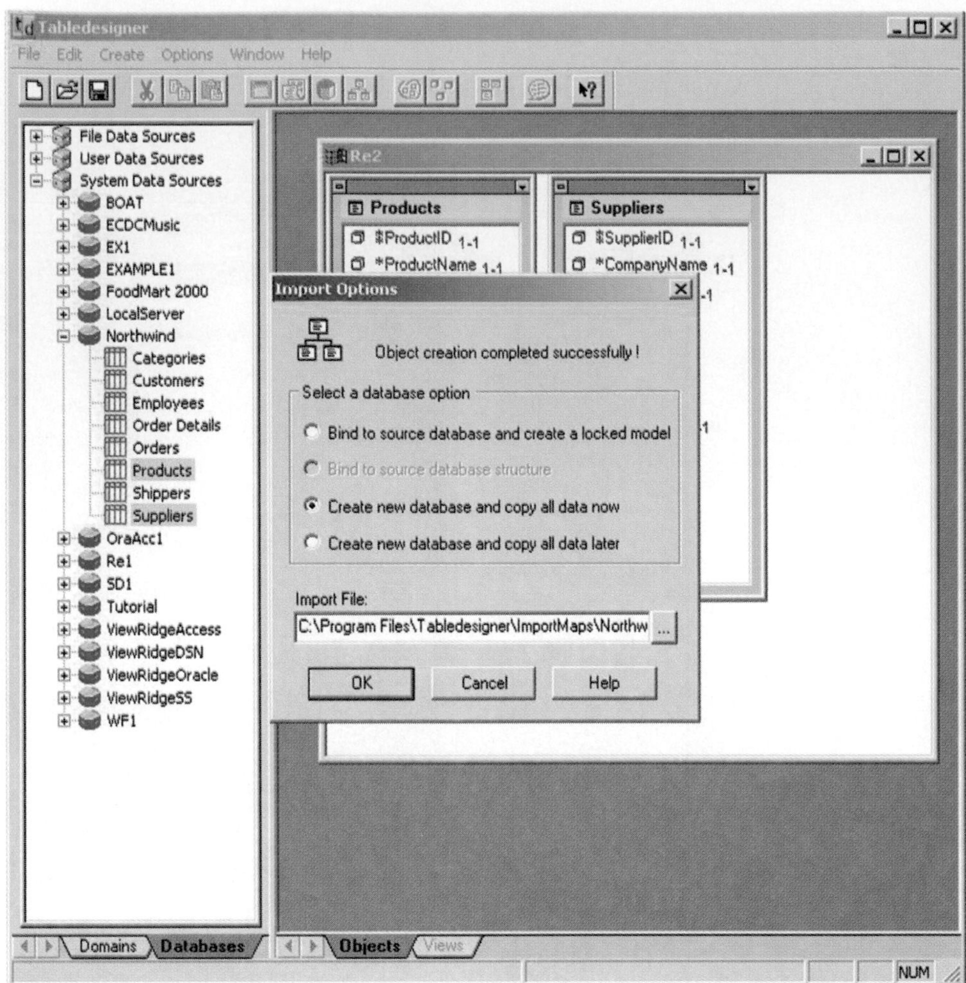

We will use a different example to illustrate the copying of data and the changing of schemas. Close your model and open a new one. Click on the Databases tab and select System Data Sources. Click on Northwind to open the table list. Holding the <Ctrl> key down click on Products and Suppliers. Drag those two tables onto the empty design space and drop them there. Save your model with a name (we used RE2) and select the third option, *Create new database and copy all data now*, as shown in Figure B-16. Click OK and then select your DBMS. We again used SQL Server in this example. You can use Access as well.

If you select SQL Server, you will need to log in three times: the first time via the ODBC driver to set up the connection, the second time just before creating the tables, and the third time when adding data to the tables. Use the Login id *sa* as discussed in Chapter 13. If you use Access the process will be much simpler.

At this point you have a new database with data in two tables: Products and Suppliers. The two tables have a 1:N relationship as shown in the model in Figure B-17. Suppose that we want to make two changes. First, we want to have the possibility of multiple Suppliers for a product and, second, we want to be able to have many Contacts for a given Supplier. We will now make those two changes to the model and observe their consequence in the underlying database.

First, change the maximum cardinality of the Suppliers link in the Products object from 1 to N. Do this by clicking on the 0-1 subscript on Suppliers in

FIGURE B-17

Products and Suppliers Semantic Object Using Reverse Engineering

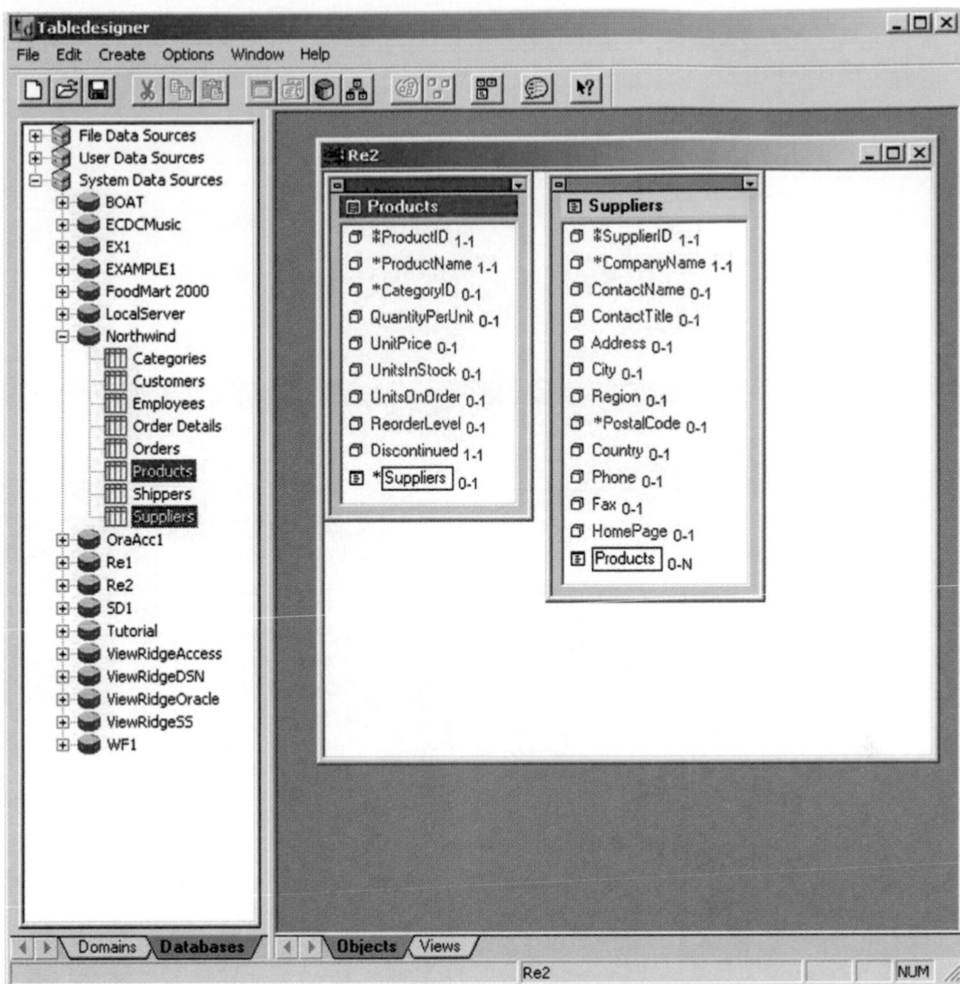

Products and selecting N from the Maximum cardinality list in the dialog box that appears. This is the same process as described before.

Now, to allow for multiple contacts for a supplier, we will first create a group for Contact data and then set the maximum cardinality for that group to N. To create the group, hold the <Shift> key down, click on ContactName and then on ContactTitle. They both should be highlighted as shown in Figure B-18a. Click on the group button, the one that looks like a pizza in the toolbar. The mouse pointer is over that button in Figure B-18a. Enter the name Contact in the dialog box that appears and click OK. You will now have a group containing ContactName and ContactTitle attributes. To allow for multiple contacts, set the maximum cardinality of the Contact group to be greater than one. Again, click on the 0-1 subscript of the Contact group and set the maximum cardinality. In Figure B-18b, the maximum cardinality is being set to N. Click OK.

Before proceeding, consider what Tabledesigner needs to do. Because the relationship between Products and Suppliers has been changed from 1:N to N:M, a new intersection table must be created. The database, however, has data so Tabledesigner will need to move the data into the intersection table to preserve the relationship. Second, a new table will need to be created for the Contact data, and all of the data moved to that new table. All of this will be done when you click on the database icon or select.

Creating a Contact Group

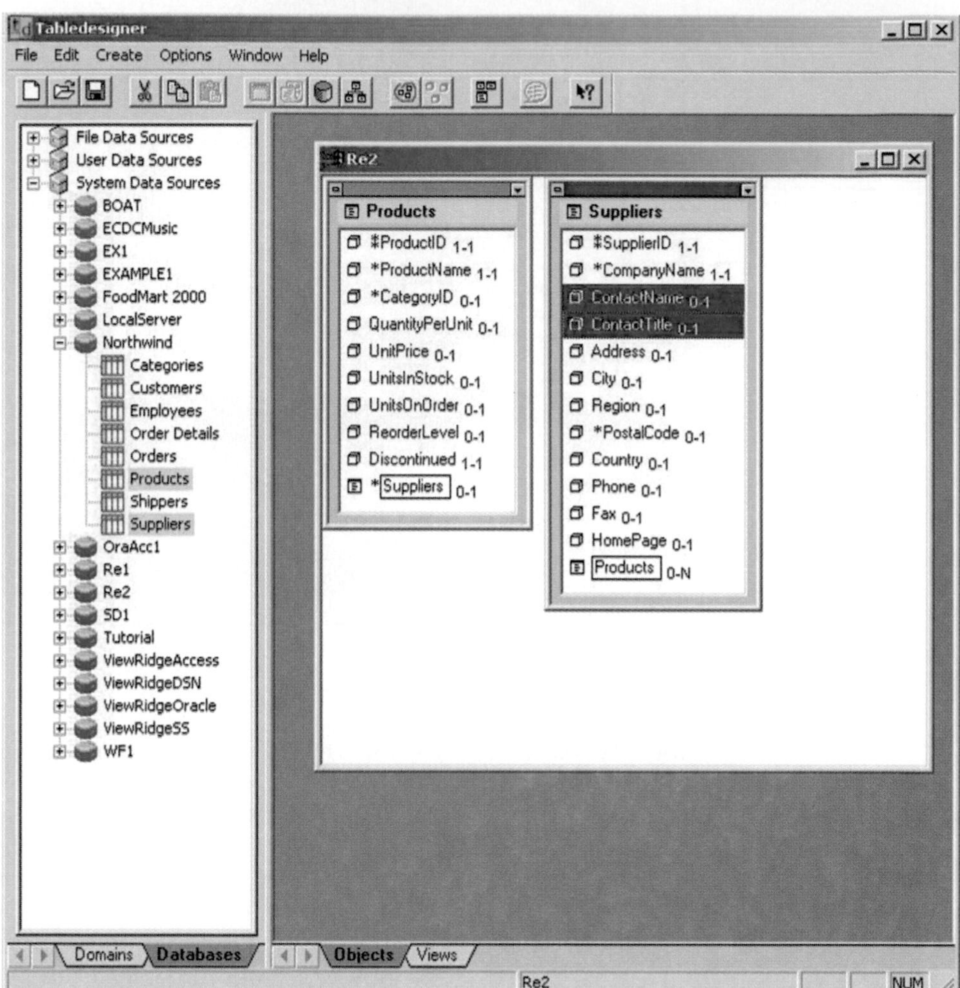

Setting the Maximum Cardinality of the Contact Group

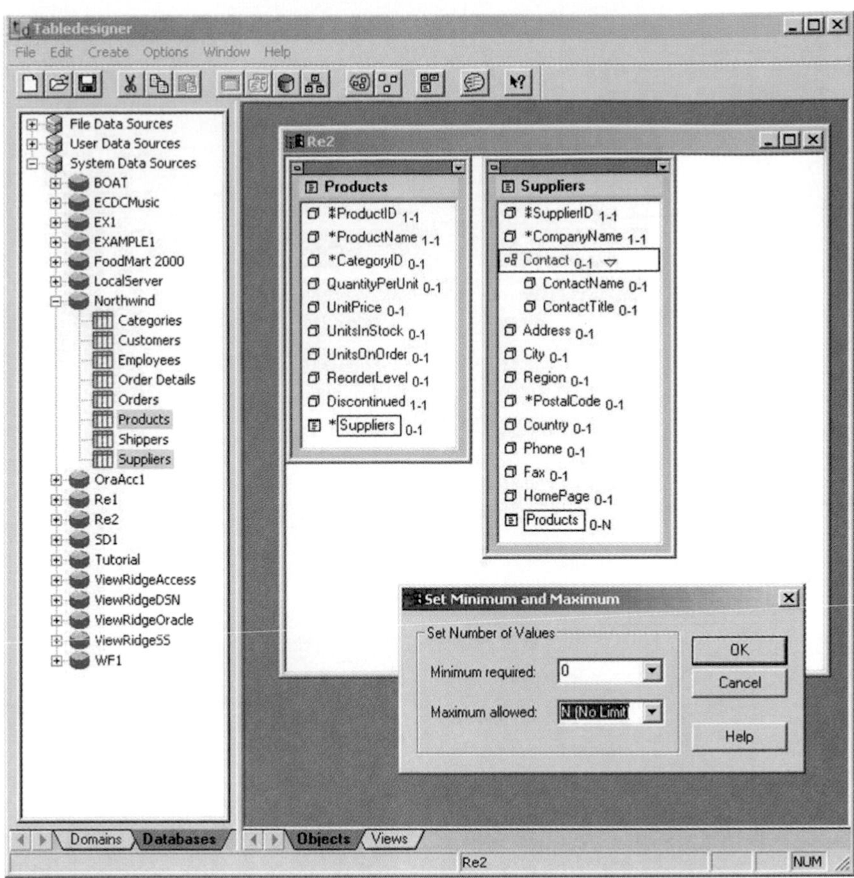

SQL Server Database Structure after Model Changes

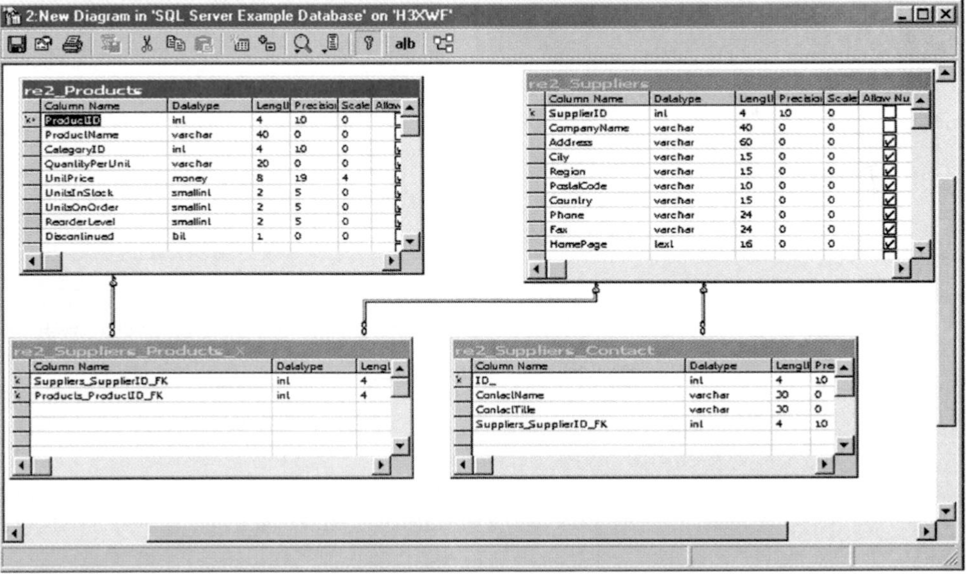

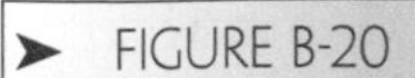

➤ FIGURE B-20

Sample Database Data after Model Changes

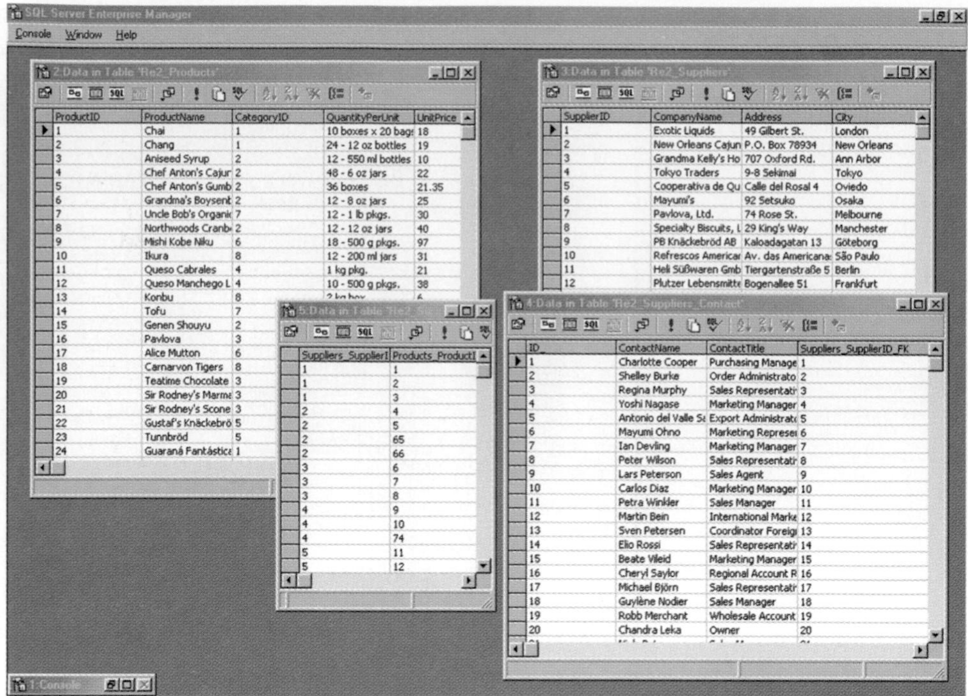

Figure B-19 shows the SQL Server schema that was created by Tabledesigner after these changes. Note that the intersection table has been correctly created and the new table, Contact, has been generated. Figure B-20 shows a portion of the data. Again, observe that the data has been correctly moved to the new tables.

This example shows the benefit of working at the level of a model rather than at the level of a database. Making these changes manually would have required at least several hours of labor.

➤ PUBLISHING DATABASE VIEWS ON THE WEB

In addition to schema creation and modification, Tabledesigner can generate a series of ASP pages that will enable the user to create, read, update, and delete data in database views over the Web. (See Chapter 10 if these terms are unfamiliar to you.) These pages can be processed by IIS running on Windows 2000 and also by the Personal Web Server running on Windows 98 or ME. In the later case, the components necessary for ASP page processing will need to be installed. See the documentation for Personal Web Server for more information.

The process of generating such pages is simple. First, create the views that you want to publish and then run the Tabledesigner Web Publishing wizard to create the pages. Those pages then need to be placed in a directory in which IIS or the Personal Web Server can find them. Since the pages use JScript, the directory will need to be marked for script execution. You can do this by modifying the properties of the application directory. Consult either the Microsoft documentation or the Tabledesigner documentation for more information if necessary.

We will illustrate the page generation process using the RE2 model created in the previous section. Of course, you can use any model you want for this process. To generate a semantic object view, open the model you wish to work with (here

FIGURE B-21

Initial Form and List Views for Products

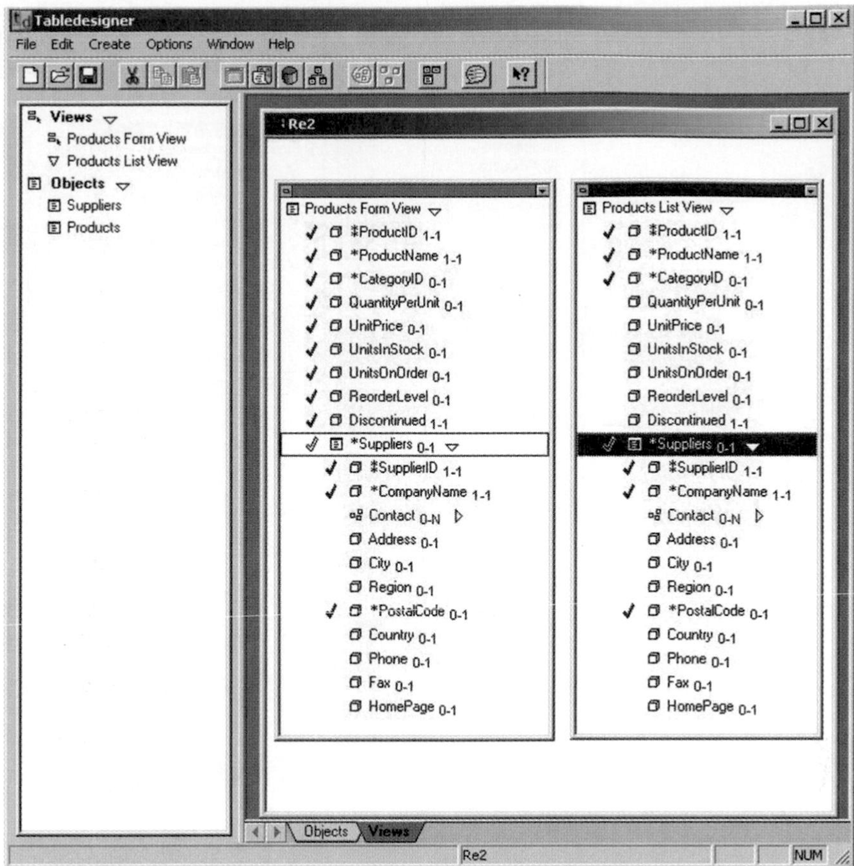

RE2.apm) and click on the View tab at the bottom of your design window. The left hand window now changes to display a list of views and objects.

In the objects section, drag Products and drop it on the empty design space. Two windows will open in the design space as shown in Figure B-21. The Products List View is used to display a set of object instances. It is used most often to display the results of a query. The second view, the Products Form view, is used to enter and change data values. Only one object instance is shown at a time in a Form view.

Consider the List View first. A check mark next to an item indicates that the item will appear in the Web form. In this case, ProductID, ProductName, and CategoryID have been checked by default. Assume we do not want ProductID or CategoryID in our list view. To remove them from the view, double click on their check marks; the check marks will disappear indicating that they have been removed from the view. Now, click on the arrow next to Suppliers to open it. This group represents the Suppliers object link in the semantic object view. Modify the check marks so that CompanyName and Contact will appear in the list view. Expand the Contact group and your screen should look like the one in Figure B-22.

Now consider the Products Form view. Remove check marks so that only ProductID, ProductName, UnitPrice, UnitsinStock, and CompanyName (in Suppliers) are in the view. Your screen should look like the one in Figure B-23.

Follow a similar process for the Suppliers view. Add or remove whatever attributes you deem appropriate. One possible set of Supplier views is shown in Figure B-24. Now we are ready to publish the application on the Web.

To start the Web publishing wizard, select File/Publish Web Application. Save the model when asked to do so and then click Next. The views to be published are

FIGURE B-22

Modifications on the Products' List View

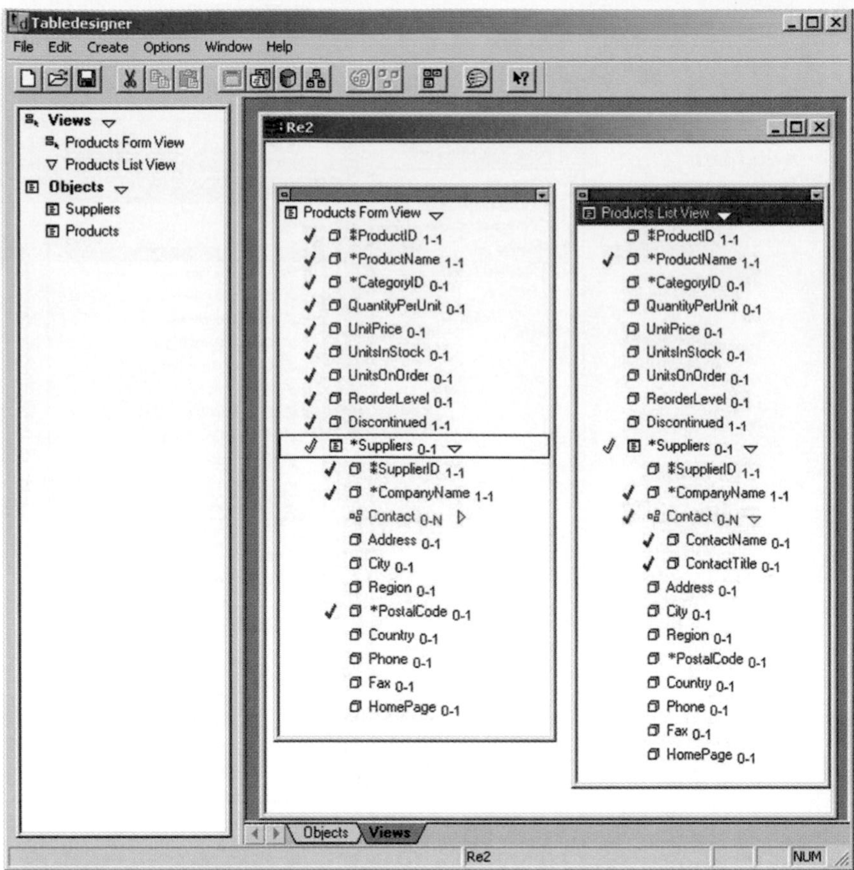

FIGURE B-23

Modification on the Products' Form View

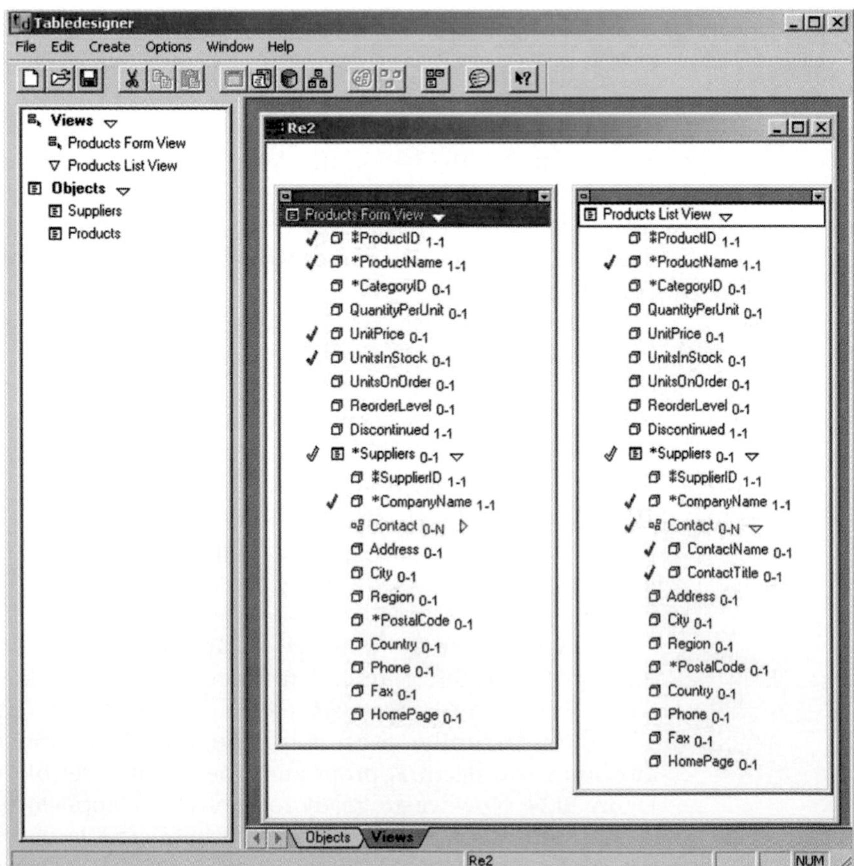

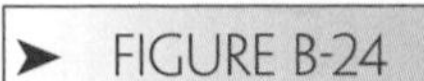

FIGURE B-24

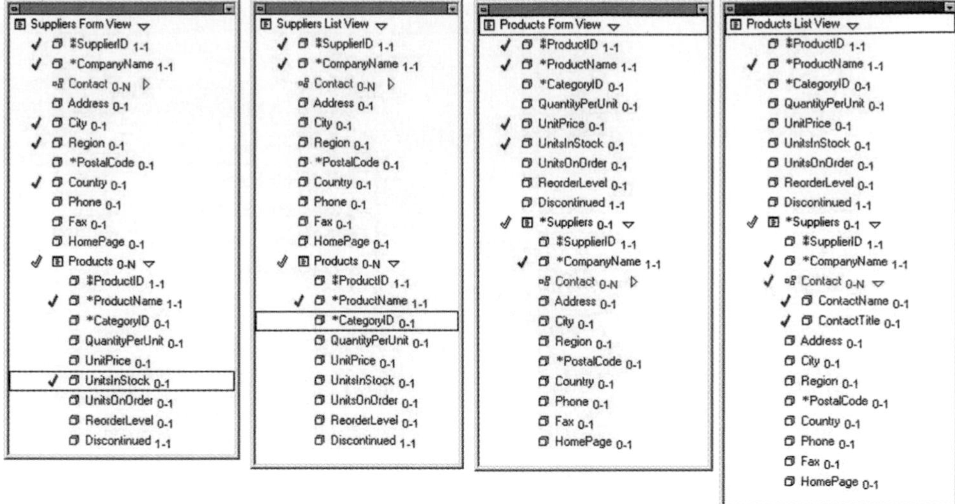

Final Set of Products and Suppliers Views

shown in the next screen. These are the ones we want to publish so click Next again. In the next screen, shown in Figure B-25, Tabledesigner is asking what set of templates you want to use. Select the defaults by clicking Next again.

The wizard next needs to know which directory to store the ASP pages. You should browse to the direction that you have set up with your Web publisher. Alternatively, you can use the directory that Tabledesigner selects and then create web publishing privileges for that directory. Either way, enter a valid directory here and click Next again. In the next screen enter Sample Application or some other title and click Next again.

In the next panel accept the default selection not to register the application now. In the next screen, shown in Figure B-26, you can enter a default Login ID and Password. You would do this if you were creating an application that you wanted strangers to be able to access. Since we are not doing so, enter nothing and click Finish. At this point, Tabledesigner will generate the ASP pages. When it is completed, it will ask if you want to open the Microsoft Web Publishing Wizard. Click No.

To run your generated application, open a browser and enter the directory into which you have placed your ASP pages followed by the keyword *default.asp*. Thus, if you have placed your pages in the directory "mywebs/apps/" then key the characters "/mywebs/apps/default.asp" into the address field of your browser and press <Enter>. You may need to modify this text somewhat depending on how you have set up your Web server.

At this point, your browser should connect with the Web server and present a login page. If you are using SQL Server for your database, enter *sa* with no password or some other valid Login ID and click Login. If you are using Access, enter nothing and click Login.

At this point you can use your pages to process your database. Select the Products page from the list box displayed, and click Query. You will see a display like that in Figure B-27. Since Tabledesigner supports query by form, you can enter search characters into this form. In Figure B-27, the user has entered >0 for UnitsInStock and New* in CompanyName. This user is searching for products for which there are more than zero in stock and in which the name of the supplier begins with the letters *New*.

When the user clicks Search, the list view shown in Figure B-28 will be displayed. Notice that all of the products are supplied by companies whose names start with New. If the user now clicks on one of the products, say the first one, that

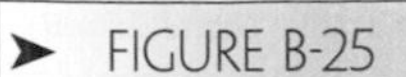

FIGURE B-25

Specifying the Views to Publish

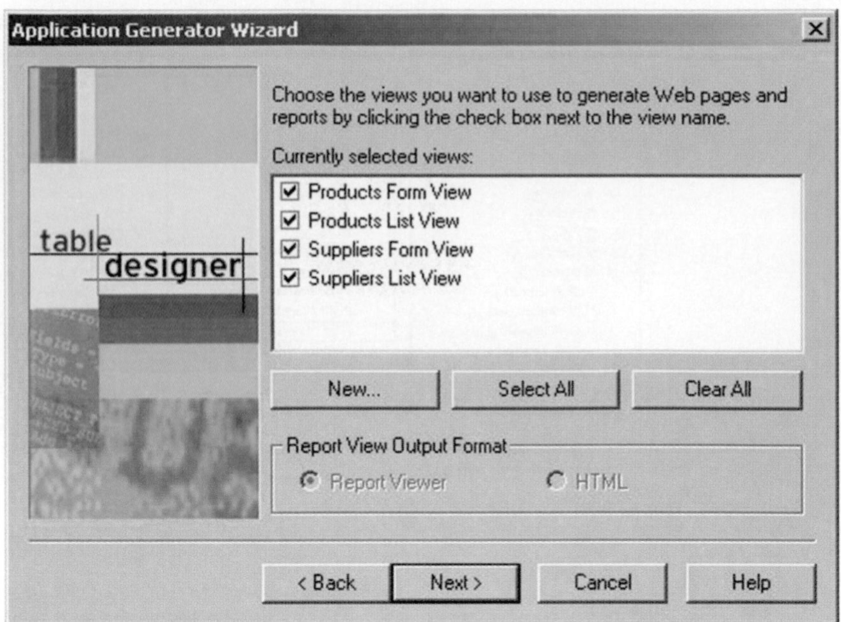

FIGURE B-26

Screen for Setting the Default User Name and Password

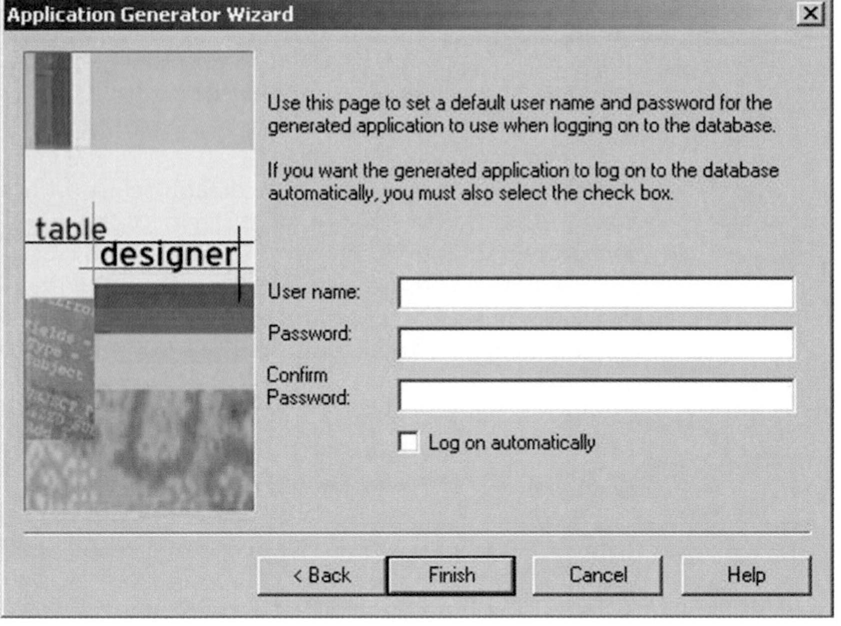

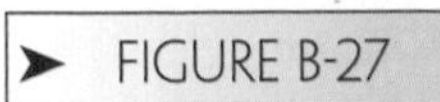

FIGURE B-27

Using Query by Form

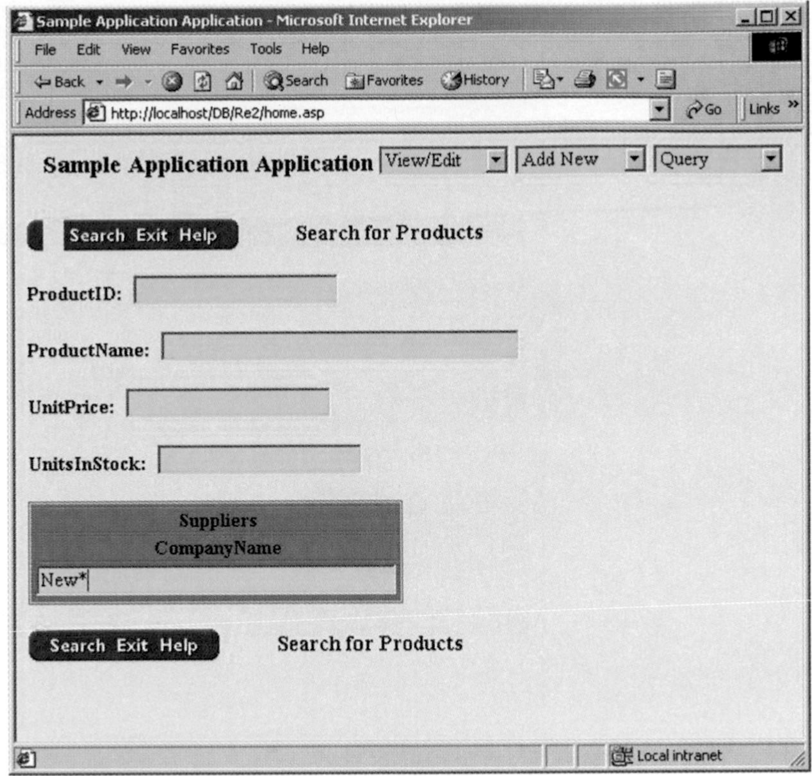

FIGURE B-28

Results for Search in Figure B-27

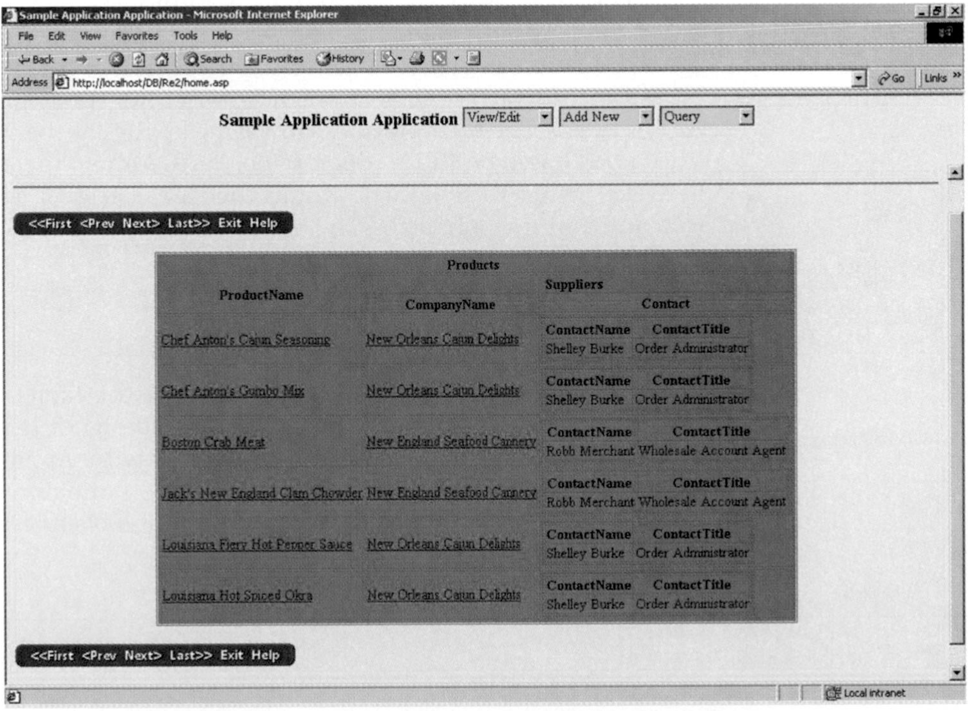

FIGURE B-29

Products Shown in the Products Form View

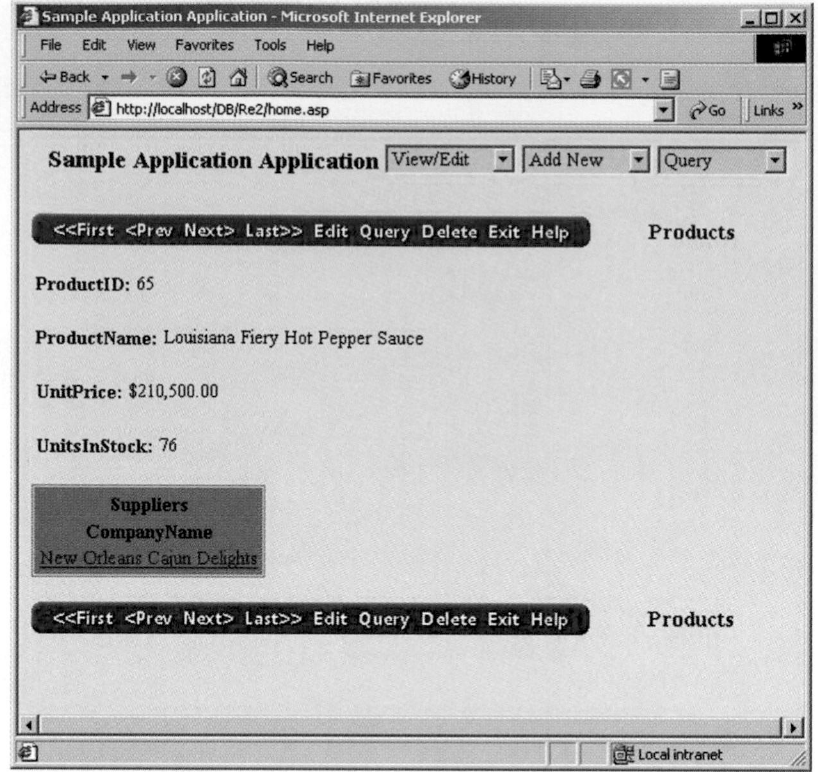

product will be displayed in the Products Form View. This has been done in Figure B-29, The pages generated here are very interactive and you really need to create this application and use it to gain an appreciation of them.

As an aside, reflect for a moment on what Tabledesigner had to do to respond to this query. The filter on CompanyName applies to the Suppliers table, but the list view is based on the Products table. Furthermore, there is a N:M relationship between these two tables. This means that Tabledesigner had to create a left outer join and an inner join across the intersection table to respond to this query.

➤ NEXT STEPS

There are many other features and functions of Tabledesigner besides those described here. You should consult the Tabledesigner help documentation for more information. A good place to start is with Applications/Development Process Overview. You can use Tabledesigner to normalize non-normalized databases and spreadsheet data. See the normalization overview topic for documentation about that process.

➤ EXERCISES

B.1 Use Tabledesigner to create the Highline University model described in Chapter 4. Create the model shown in Figure 14-13. Generate a database in either Access or SQL Server. Examine the resulting schema and explain how each table relates to the model. Change the model so that PROFESSORs can work in more than one DEPARTMENT. Regenerate your database and explain the changes that were made.

B.2 Use Tabledesigner to create a model with an example of each of the following types of semantic object (see Chapter 4):

a. Simple
b. Composite
c. Compound
d. Hybrid
e. Archetype/version
f. Association

Generate a database from your model and examine the resulting tables. Explain how Tabledesigner does or does not use the same design principles as described in Chapter 7.

B.3 Open a new model in Tabledesigner and select the Recruiting starter kit. Examine the model and generate a database. Suggest ways that this model could be improved. Make changes to the model and regenerate a database. Explain changes that were made in the database structure.

B.4 Complete Exercise B.1. Create a Form and List view for each of the objects and use Tabledesigner to generate ASP pages for processing them. Place the generated pages in directory for processing by IIS or the Personal Web Server. Open a browser and use the pages to create sample DEPARTMENT, STUDENT, and PROFESSOR objects. Use the Web pages to link several of the objects. Open the underlying database and examine the foreign key fields. Justify the foreign key values in light of the links that you made among the objects.

B.5 Install SQL Server if you have not already done so. Following the example in this appendix, create an ODBC System data source to the pubs database. You will need to pick SQL Server as the driver and follow the SQL server login process. Enter (local) for server, *sa* for Login id with no password, and change the default database to pubs. Reverse engineer the publishers, authors, titles, and titleauthor tables and create a new Access (use SQL Server if you do not have Access) database and copy data into it. Name your new database pubs2. Change the model (of pubs2) so that a title can have more than one publisher. Regenerate the database and examine the changes. Open the title table in the pubs database and print the rows. Open the title table in pubs2 and print the rows. Also open the new intersection table in pub2 and print the rows. Explain the differences among these tables.

B.6 Create pubs2 as described in Exercise B.5. Generate a view for publisher, author, and title. Be sure that your author view includes all of the titles for that author and that your title view includes the names of all authors for that title. Generate Web pages for these views. Use the Web pages to assign second and third authors to some of the titles. Close your Web application and examine the foreign key values in the database tables. Explain those values in light of the title/author additions you made.

Abstract data type: In SQL3, a user-defined structure having methods, data items, and identifiers; a version of an OOP object. Persistence is provided by binding the ADT to a column of a relation.

Abstraction: A generalization of something that hides some hopefully unimportant details but enables work with a wider class of types. A recordset is an abstraction of a relation. A rowset is an abstraction of a recordset.

ACID transaction: An acronym that stands for atomic, consistent, isolated, and durable. An atomic transaction is one in which all of the database changes are committed as a unit; either all of them are done or none of them are done. A consistent transaction is one in which all actions are taken against rows in the same logical state. An isolated transaction is one that is protected from changes by other users. A durable transaction is one that, once it is committed to the database, is permanent, regardless of subsequent failure. There are different levels of consistency and isolation. See Transaction level consistency and Statement level consistency. Also see Transaction isolation level.

Action/object menu: A system of menus in which the top menu refers to actions and the lowest menus refer to the objects on which those actions are taken.

Active Server Page: See ASP.

ActiveX control: An ActiveX object that supports interfaces that allow the control's properties and methods to be accessed in many different development environments.

ActiveX object: A COM object that supports a slimmed-down version of the OLE object specification.

ADO: Active data objects; an implementation of OLE DB that is accessible via both object and non–object-oriented languages; used primarily as a scripting language (JScript, VBScript) interface to OLE DB.

ADT: See Abstract Data Type.

After-image: A record of a database entity (normally a row or a page) after a change. Used in recovery to perform rollforward.

Anomaly: An undesirable consequence of a data modification used primarily in discussions of normalization. With an insertion anomaly, facts about two or more different themes must be added to a single row of a relation. With a deletion anomaly, facts about two or more themes are lost when a single row is deleted.

API: See Application Program Interface.

Applet: A compiled, machine-independent Java bytecode program that is run by the Java virtual machine embedded in a browser.

Application: A business computer system that processes a portion of a database to meet a user's information needs. It consists of menus, forms, reports, queries, Web pages, and application programs.

Application design: The process of creating the structure of programs and data to meet the application's requirements; also the structure of the users' interface.

Application failure: A failure in the processing of a DBMS statement or in a transaction that is due to application logic errors.

Application metadata: Data dictionary; data concerning the structure and contents of application menus, forms, and reports.

Application program: A custom-developed program for processing a database. It can be written in a standard procedural language such as COBOL, C++, C or Visual Basic, or in a language unique to the DBMS.

Application Program Interface (API): A set of program procedures or functions that can be called to invoke a set of services. The API includes the names of the procedures and functions and a description of the name, purpose, and data type of parameters to be provided. For example, a DBMS product could provide a library of functions to call for database services. The names of procedures and their parameters constitute the API for that library.

Archetype/version object: A structure of two objects that represents multiple versions of a standardized item; for example, a SOFT-PRODUCT (the archetype) and PRODUCT-RELEASE (the version of the archetype). The identifier of the version always includes the archetype object.

ASP: Active Server Page. A file containing markup language, server script, and client script that is processed by the Active Server Processor in Microsoft IIS.

Association object: An object that represents the combination of at least two other objects and that contains data about that combination. It is often used in contracting and assignment applications.

Atomic: A set of actions that is completed as a unit. Either all actions are completed or none is.

Atomic transaction: A group of logically related database operations that is performed as a unit. Either all of the operations are performed, or none of them is.

Attribute: (1) A column of a relation; also called a column, field, or data-item. (2) A property in an entity or semantic object. (3) A data or relationship property in an OOP object. (4) In the ODMG-93 model, an implementation of an object property in an OOP implementation such as C++ or Smalltalk.

Authorization rules: A set of processing permissions that describes which users or user groups can take particular actions against particular portions of the database.

Axis: In OLAP, a coordinate of a cube or hypercube.

Band: The section of a report definition that contains the format of a report section. There normally are bands for the report heading and footing, page heading and footing, and the detail line of the report. There are also bands for group or break points within the report.

Banded report writer: A report writer in which the sections of the reports are defined by bands. Also see Band.

Base table: In relational implementations, the table from which relational views are defined.

Before-image: A record of a database entity (normally a row or a page) before a change. Used in recovery to perform rollback.

Bill of materials: A recursive data structure in which a part (or, in general, any element) can be both an assembly of other parts and a component of other assemblies.

Binary relationship: A relationship between exactly two entities or tables.

Bind: To connect a program variable or a GUI control to a column of a table or query.

Bottom-up database design: The design of a database that works from the detailed and specific to the general. Although this sort of design takes little time, it may result in a database that is too narrow in scope.

Boyce-Codd normal form: A relation in third normal form in which every determinant is a candidate key.

Branch: A subelement of a tree that may consist of one or many nodes.

Buffer: An area of memory used to hold data. For a read, data is read from a storage device into a buffer; for a write, data is written from the buffer to storage.

Built-in function: In SQL, any of the functions COUNT, SUM, AVG, MAX, or MIN.

Callback: An OOP design practice by which an object passes its identity to another object with the expectation that the called object will notify the calling object when some event occurs. Often the event is the destruction of the called object, but used for other purposes as well.

Candidate key: An attribute or group of attributes that identifies a unique row in a relation. One of the candidate keys is chosen to be the primary key.

Card: In the wireless markup language, a portion of an XML document that is small enough to be displayed on a wireless device. See also Deck.

Cardinality: In a binary relationship, the maximum or minimum number of elements allowed on each side of the relationship. The maximum cardinality can be 1:1, 1:N, N:1, or N:M. The minimum cardinality can be optional–optional, optional–mandatory, mandatory–optional, or mandatory–mandatory.

Cartesian product: A relational operation on two relations, A and B, producing a third relation, C, with C containing the concatenation of every row in A with every row in B.

Cascading deletion: A property of a relationship that indicates that when one row is deleted, related rows should be deleted as well.

CGI: See Common Gateway Interface.

Check box: In a GUI environment, an element of the user interface in which a user can select one or more items from a list. Items are selected by clicking on them.

Checkpoint: The point of synchronization between a database and a transaction log. All buffers are force-written to external storage. This is the standard definition of checkpoint, but this term is sometimes used in other ways by DBMS vendors.

Child: A row, record, or node on the many side of a one-to-many relationship.

Class attributes: In the uniform modeling language (UML), attributes that pertain to the class of all entities of a given type.

Client computer: (1) A personal computer on a local area network with client–server architecture. In a database application, the client computer processes database application programs. Requests for actions on the database are sent to the database computer. (2) In the three-tier and multi-tier architecture, a computer that hosts a browser for accessing a Web server.

Client–server database architecture: The structure of a networked computing system in which one computer (usually a personal computer) performs services on behalf of other computers (usually a personal computer). For a database system, the server computer, which is called a database server, processes the DBMS, and client computers process the application programs. All database activities are carried out by the database server.

Client–server system: A system of two or more computers in which at least one computer provides services for one or more other computers. The services can be database services, communication services, printer services, or some other function.

Collection: An object that contains a group of other objects. Examples are the ADO Names, Errors, and Parameters collections.

Column: A logical group of bytes in a row of a relation or a table. The meaning of a column is the same for every row of the relation.

Column object: In Oracle, an object structure that defines and is carried in a table column.

COM: Component Object Model; a Microsoft specification for the development of object-oriented programs that enables such programs to work together readily.

COM object: An object that conforms to the COM standard.

Command: A statement input to a database application by which users specify the activity to be performed. Contrast this with Menu.

Commit: A command issued to the DBMS to make database modifications permanent. Once the command has been processed, the changes are written to the database and to a log in such a way that they will survive system crashes and other failures. A commit is usually used at the end of an atomic transaction. Contrast this with Rollback.

Common Gateway Interface: A standard for defining forms and sending and receiving form data in HTML documents.

Complex network: A collection of entities, objects, or relations and their relationships, of which at least one of the relationships is complex (many to many).

Composite group: A group of attributes in a semantic object that is multi-valued and contains no other object attributes.

Composite key: A key with more than one attribute.

Composite object: An object with at least one multi-value attribute or attribute group. It is called a composite object because the key of the relation that represents the multi-value attribute or group is a composite key.

Compound object: An object that contains at least one other object.

Computed value: A column of a table that is computed from other column values. Values are not stored but are computed when they are to be displayed.

Concurrency: A condition in which two or more transactions are processed against the database at the same time. In a single CPU system, the changes are interleaved; in a multi-CPU system, the transactions may be processed simultaneously, and the changes on the database server are interleaved.

Concurrency transparency: In a distributed database system, the condition in which application programs do not know and do not need to know whether data is being processed concurrently. The DDBMS organizes update activities so that the results produced when concurrent processing is under way are consistent with the results that would occur if there were no concurrent processing.

Concurrent processing: In teleprocessing applications, the sharing of the CPU among several transactions. The CPU is allocated to each transaction in a round robin or in some other fashion for a certain period of time. Operations are performed so quickly that they appear to users to be simultaneous. In local area networks and other distributed applications, concurrent processing is used to refer to the (possibly simultaneous) processing of applications on multiple computers.

Concurrent update problem: An error condition in which one user's data changes are overwritten by another user's data changes. Same as lost update problem.

Conflict: Two operations conflict if they operate on the same data item and at least one of the operations is a write.

Consistency: Two or more concurrent transactions are consistent if the result of their processing is the same as it would have been if they had been processed in some serial order.

Consistent backup: A backup file from which all uncommitted changes have been removed.

Consistent schedule: An ordered list of transaction operations against a database in which the result of the processing is consistent.

Constraint: A rule concerning the allowed values of attributes whose truth can be evaluated. A constraint usually does not include dynamic rules such as "SalesPersonPay can never decrease" or "Salary now must be greater than Salary last quarter."

CPU: Central Processing Unit; the portion of the computer hardware that processes arithmetic and logic instructions. The term CPU usually includes main memory as well.

CRUD: An acronym representing Create, Read, Update, Delete, which are the four actions that can be performed on a database view.

Cube: In OLAP, a presentation structure having axes upon which data dimensions are placed. Measures of the data are shown in the cells of the cube. Also called hypercube.

Cursor: An indicator of the current position or focus. (1) On a computer screen, a blinking box or underscore that indicates the position into which the next entry will be made. (2) In a file or embedded SQL SELECT, the identity of the next record or row to be processed.

Cursor type: A declaration on a cursor that determines how the DBMS places implicit locks. Four types of cursor discussed in this text are forward only, snapshot, keyset, and dynamic.

Data administration: The enterprisewide function that concerns the effective use and control of the organization's data assets. It can be a person but more often is a group. Specific functions include setting data standards and policies and providing a forum for conflict resolution. Also see database administrator.

Data consumer: A user of OLE DB functionality.

Data provider: A provider of OLE DB functionality. Examples are tabular data providers and service data providers.

Database: A self-describing collection of integrated records.

Database administration: The function that concerns the effective use and control of a particular database and its related applications.

Database administrator: The person or group responsible for establishing policies and procedures to control and protect a database. He (she or it) works within guidelines set by data administration to control the database structure, manage data changes, and maintain DBMS programs.

Database data: The portion of a database that contains data of interest and use to the application end users.

Database save: A copy of database files that can be used to restore the database to some previous, consistent state.

Database server: (1) On a local area network with client–server database architecture, the computer that runs the DBMS and processes actions against the database on behalf of its client computers. (2) In the three-tier multi-tier architecture, a computer that hosts a DBMS and responds to database requests from the Web server.

Data Definition Language (DDL): A language used to describe the structure of a database.

Data dictionary: A user-accessible catalog of both database and application metadata. An active data dictionary is a dictionary whose contents are automatically updated by the DBMS whenever changes are made in the database or application structure. A passive data dictionary is one whose contents must be updated manually when changes are made.

Data dictionary and database administration subsystem: A collection of programs in the DBMS used to access the data dictionary and to perform database administration functions such as maintaining passwords and performing backup and recovery.

Data integrity: The state of a database in which all constraints are fulfilled; usually refers to inter-relation constraints in which the value of a foreign key is required to be present in the table having that foreign key as its primary key.

Data-item: (1) A logical group of bytes in a record, usually used with file processing. (2) In the context of the relational model, a synonym for attribute.

Data Manipulation Language (DML): A language used to describe the processing of a database.

Data mart: A facility similar to a data warehouse but for a restricted domain. Often the data are restricted to particular types, business functions, or business units.

Data model: (1) A model of the users' data requirements expressed in terms of either the entity-relationship model or the semantic-object model. It is sometimes called a users' data model. (2) A language for describing the structure and processing of a database.

Data owner: Same as Data proponent.

Data proponent: In data administration, a department or other organizational unit in charge of managing a particular data item.

Data replication: A term that indicates whether any portion or all of a database resides on more than one computer. If so, the data are said to be replicated.

Data source: In the ODBC standard, a database together with its associated DBMS, operating system, and network platform.

Data structure diagram: A graphical display of tables (files) and their relationships. The tables are shown in rectangles, and the relationships are shown by lines. A many relationship is shown with a fork on the end of the line; an optional relationship is depicted by an oval; and a mandatory relationship is shown with hash marks.

Data sublanguage: A language for defining and processing a database intended to be embedded in programs written in another language—in most cases, a procedural language such as COBOL, C++, or Visual Basic. A data sublanguage is an incomplete programming language, as it contains only constructs for data access.

Data warehouse: A store of enterprise data that is designed to facilitate management decision making. A data warehouse includes not only data, but also metadata, tools, procedures, training, personnel, and other resources that make access to the data easier and more relevant to decision makers.

DBA: See Database Administrator.

DBM: Database Manager. In a DDBMS, software that processes some portion of a distributed database in accordance with action requests received from distributed transactions managers (DTMs).

DBMS: Database Management System; a set of programs used to define, administer, and process the database and its applications.

DBMS engine: A DBMS subsystem that processes logical I/O requests from other DBMS subsystems and submits physical I/O requests to the operating system.

DDBMS: Distributed database management system. (1) A commercial DBMS product that supports the processing of a distributed database. Both Oracle and SQL Server provide limited facilities for distributed database processing

DDL: See Data Definition Language.

Deadlock: A condition that can occur during concurrent processing in which each of two (or more) transactions is waiting to access data that the other transaction has locked. It is also called a deadly embrace.

Deadlock detection: The process of determining whether two or more transactions are in a state of deadlock.

Deadlock prevention: A way of managing transactions so that a deadlock cannot occur.

Deadly embrace: See Deadlock.

Deck: In the wireless markup language, the set of all cards that comprise an XML document

Default namespace: In an XML schema document, the namespace that is used for all unlabeled elements.

Definition tools subsystem: The portion of the DBMS program used to define and change the database structure.

Degree: For relationships in the entity-relationship model, the number of entities participating in the relationship. In almost all cases, such relationships are of degree 2.

Deletion anomaly: In a relation, the situation in which the removal of one row of a table deletes facts about two or more themes.

Determinant: One or more attributes that functionally determine another attribute or attributes. In the functional dependency (A, B) → C, the attributes (A, B) are the determinant.

DHTML: A Microsoft implementation of the HTML 4.0 standard. Key features are support for the document object model, cascading style sheets, and remote data services.

Difference: A relational algebra operation performed on two union-compatible relations, A and B, that produces a third relation, C. Each row in C is present in A but not in B.

Differential backup: A backup file that contains only changes made since a prior backup.

Dimension: In OLAP, a feature of data that is placed on an axis.

Dirty read: Reading data that has been changed but not yet committed to the database. Such changes may later be rolled back and removed from the database.

Distributed database: A database stored on two or more computers. Distributed data can be partitioned or not partitioned, replicated or not replicated.

Distributed database application: A business computer system in which the retrieval and updating of data occur across two or more independent and usually geographically distributed computers.

Distributed Database Management System (DDBMS): In a distributed database, the collection of distributed transaction and database managers on all computers.

Distributed database processing: Database processing in which transactions data is retrieved and updated across two or more independent and usually geographically separated computers.

Distributed database system: A distributed system in which a database or portions of a database are distributed across two or more computers.

Distributed system: A system in which the application programs of a database are processed on two or more computers.

Distributed transaction service (DTS): An OLE Service developed by Microsoft that supports distributed processing and, in particular, implements two-phased commit.

Distributed two-phase locking: Two-phase locking in a distributed environment, in which locks are obtained and released across all nodes on the network. See Two-phase locking.

DML: See Data Manipulation Language.

Document Object Model (DOM): An API that represents an XML document as a tree. Each node of the tree represents a piece of the XML document. A program can directly access and manipulate a node of the DOM representation.

Document Type Declaration: A set of markup elements that defines the structure of an XML document.

DOM: See Document Object Model.

Domain: (1) The set of all possible values an attribute can have. (2) A description of the format (data type, length) and the semantics (meaning) of an attribute.

Domain/Key Normal Form (DK/NF): A relation in which all constraints are logical consequences of domains and keys.

Download: Copying database data from one computer to another, usually from a mainframe or mini to a personal computer or LAN.

Drill down: User-directed disaggregation of data used to break higher-level totals into components.

Driver: In ODBC, a program that serves as an interface between the ODBC driver manager and a particular DBMS product. Runs on the client machines in a client–server architecture.

Driver manager: In ODBC, a program that serves as an interface between an application program and an ODBC driver. It determines the driver required, loads it into memory, and coordinates activity between the application and the driver. On Windows systems, it is provided by Microsoft.

DSD: See Data Structure Diagram.

DSS: Decision Support System; an interactive, computer-based facility for assisting decision making, especially for semistructured and unstructured problems. Such a system often includes a database and a query/update facility for processing ad hoc requests.

DTD: See Document Type Declaration.

DTS: See Distributed Transaction Service.

ECMAScript-262: The standard version of an easily learned interpreted language used for both Web server and Web client applications processing. The Microsoft version is called JScript, and the Netscape version is called JavaScript.

Encapsulated data: Properties or attributes contained in a program or object not visible or accessible to other programs or objects.

Encapsulated structure: A portion of an object that is not visible to other objects.

Enterprise Java Beans: A facility for managing distributed objects and distributed processing in the Java development world.

Entity: (1) Something of importance to a user that needs to be represented in a database. (2) In an entity-relationship model, entities are restricted to things that can be represented by a single table. Also see Existence-dependent entity, Strong entity, and Weak entity.

Entity class: A set of entities of the same type, for example, EMPLOYEE and DEPARTMENT.

Entity instance: A particular occurrence of an entity, for example, Employee 100 and the Accounting Department.

Entity-relationship diagram: A graphic used to represent entities and their relationships. Entities are normally shown in squares or rectangles, and relationships are shown in diamonds. The cardinality of the relationship is shown inside the diamond.

Entity-relationship model: The constructs and conventions used to create a model of the users' data (see Data model). The things in the users' world are represented by entities, and the associations among those things are represented by relationships. The results are usually documented in an entity-relationship diagram.

Entry-point relation: Used with regard to the relations representing an object. The entry-point relation is the relation whose key is the same as the key of the object it represents. The entry-point relation is normally the first relation processed. Also, the name of the entry-point relation is normally the same as the name of the object.

Enumerated list: A list of allowed values for a domain, attribute, or column.

Equijoin: The process of joining relation A containing attribute A1 with B containing attribute B1 to form relation C, so that for each row in C, A1 = B1. Both A1 and B1 are represented in C.

E-R diagram: See Entity-relationship diagram.

Exclusive lock: A lock on a data resource that no other transaction can either read or update.

Existence-dependent entity: Same as a weak entity. An entity that cannot appear in the database unless an instance of one or more other entities also appears in the database. A subclass of existence-dependent entities is ID-dependent entities.

Explicit lock: A lock requested by a command from an application program.

Export: A function of the DBMS, to write a file of data in bulk. The file is intended to be read by another DBMS or program.

Extent (of object): In the ODMG model, the union of all object instances. Attributes can be declared to be unique across an object's extent.

Extract: A portion of an operational database downloaded to a local area network or personal computer for local processing. Extracts are created to reduce communications cost and time when querying and creating reports from data created by transaction processing.

Failure transparency: In a distributed database system, the condition in which application programs are isolated from failure.

Field: (1) A logical group of bytes in a record used with file processing. (2) In the context of a relational model, a synonym for attribute.

File data source: An ODBC data source stored in a file that can be E-mailed or otherwise distributed among users.

File-processing system: An information system in which data is stored in separate files. There is no integrated data dictionary. The format of the files is usually stored in application programs.

File server: In a local area network, a personal computer containing a file that it processes on behalf of other personal computers on the network. The term file server is normally used for the resource-sharing architecture. See Client computer, Client-server database architecture, Database server, and Resource-sharing architecture.

Firewall: A computer that serves as a security gateway between an intranet and the Internet. Firewalls monitor the source and destination of network traffic and filter it.

First normal form: Any table that fits the definition of a relation.

Flat file: A file that has only a single value in each field. The meaning of the columns is the same in every row.

Force-write: A write of database data in which the DBMS waits for acknowledgment from the operating system that the after-image of the write has been successfully written to the log.

Foreign key: An attribute that is a key of one or more relations other than the one in which it appears.

Form: (1) A display on a computer screen used to present, enter, and modify data. A form is also called a data entry form or panel. (2) A paper document used in a business system to record data, usually concerning a transaction. Forms are analyzed in the process of building a data model.

Forms generator: A portion of the application development subsystem used to create a data entry form without having to write any application program code.

Formula domain: A domain whose values are computed by an expression containing arguments that are themselves domains.

Fourth normal form: A relation in third Boyce–Codd normal form in which every multi-value dependency is a functional dependency.

Fragment: A row in a table (or record in a file) in which a required parent or child is not present. For example, a row in a LINE-ITEM table for which no ORDER row exists.

FTP: File Transfer Protocol. A standard Internet service for copying files to or from a remote server.

Functional dependency: A relationship between attributes in which one attribute or group of attributes determines the value of another. The expressions $X \rightarrow Y$, "X determines Y," and "Y is functionally dependent on X" mean that given a value of X, we can determine the value of Y.

Generalization hierarchy: A set of objects or entities of the same logical type that are arranged in a hierarchy of logical subtypes. For example, EMPLOYEE has the subtypes ENGINEER and ACCOUNTANT, and ENGINEER has the subtypes ELECTRICAL ENGINEER and MECHANICAL ENGINEER. Subtypes inherit characteristics of their supertypes.

Generalization object: An object that contains subtype objects. The generalization object and its subtypes all have the same key. Subtype objects inherit attributes from the generalization object. A generalization object is also called a supertype object.

Granularity: The size of database resource that can be locked. Locking the entire database is large granularity; locking a column of a particular row is small granularity.

Group identifier: An attribute that identifies a unique instance of a group within a semantic object or another group.

Growing phase: The first stage in two-phase locking in which locks are acquired but not released.

HAS-A relationship: A relationship between two entities or objects that are of different logical types, for example, EMPLOYEE HAS-A(n) AUTO. Contrast this with an IS-A relationship.

Hierarchical data model: A data model that represents all relationships using hierarchies or trees. Network structures must be decomposed into trees before they can be represented by a hierarchical data model. DL/I is the only surviving hierarchical data model.

HOLAP: Hybrid OLAP using a combination of ROLAP and MOLAP for supporting OLAP processing.

Horizontal partition: A subset of a table consisting of complete rows of the table. For example, in a table with 10 rows, the first five rows.

Horizontal security: Limiting access to certain rows of a table or join.

Host variable: A variable in an application program into which a DBMS places a value from the database.

HTML: See Hypertext Markup Language.

HTML 4.0: A World Wide Web consortium standard for an advanced version of HTML. See DHTML.

Hybrid object: An object containing a multi-value group that contains at least one object attribute.

Hypercube: In OLAP, a presentation structure having axes upon which data dimensions are placed. Measures of the data are shown in the cells of the hypercube. Also called cube.

Hypertext Markup Language: A standardized system of tagging text for formatting, locating images and other nontext files, and placing links or references to other documents.

Hypertext Transfer Protocol: HTTP; a standardized means for using TCP/IP for communicating HTML documents over networks.

ID-dependent entity: An entity that cannot logically exist without the existence of another entity. An APPOINTMENT, for example, cannot exist without a CLIENT to make the appointment. The ID-dependent entity always contains the key of the entity on which it depends. Such entities are a subset of a weak entity. See also Strong entity and Weak entity.

IIS: Internet Information Server; a Microsoft product that operates as an HTTP server. IIS requires Windows 2000.

Immutable object: In the ODMG standard, an object whose attributes cannot be changed.

Implementation: In OOP, a set of objects that instantiates a particular OOP interface.

Implicit lock: A lock that is automatically placed by the DBMS.

Implied object: An object that exists in the user's mind when he or she requests a report "sorted by x" or "grouped by x." For example, when the user requests all ORDERs sorted by OrderDate, the implied object is the set of all ORDER objects.

Import: A function of the DBMS, to read a file of data in bulk.

Inconsistent backup: A backup file that contains uncommitted changes.

Inconsistent read problem: An anomaly that occurs in concurrent processing in which transactions execute a series of reads inconsistent with one another. It can be prevented by two-phase locking and other strategies.

Index: Overhead data used to improve access and sorting performance. Indexes can be constructed for a single column or groups of columns. They are especially useful for columns used for control breaks in reports and to specify conditions in joins.

Inheritance: A characteristic of objected-oriented systems in which objects that are subtypes of other objects obtain attributes (data or methods) from their supertypes.

Inner Join: Synonym for join.

Insertion anomaly: In a relation, the condition that exists when, to add a complete row to a table, one must add facts about two or more logically different themes.

Instance failure: A failure in the operating system or hardware that causes the DBMS to fail.

Interface: (1) The means by which two or more programs call each other; the definition of the procedural calls between two or more programs. (2) In OOP, the design of a set of objects that includes the objects' names, methods, and attributes.

Internet: A worldwide, public network of computers that communicate using TCP/IP.

Internet Information Server: See IIS.

Interrelation constraint: A restriction that requires the value of an attribute in a row of one relation to match the value of an attribute found in another relation. For example, CustNumber in ORDER must equal CustNumber in CUSTOMER.

Intersection: A relational algebra operation performed on two union-compatible relations, A and B, forming a third relation, C, so that C contains only rows that appear in both A and B.

Intersection relation: A relation used to represent a many-to-many relationship. It contains the keys of the relations in the relationship. When used to represent many-to-many compound objects, it has no nonkey data. When used to represent entities having a many-to-many relationship, it may have nonkey data if the relationship contains data.

Intranet: (1) A private local or wide area network that uses TCP/IP, HTML, and related browser technology on client computers and Web server technology on serves. (2) Less commonly, any private LAN or WAN that involves clients and servers.

IS-A relationship: A relationship between two entities or objects of the same logical type. In reference to ENGINEER IS-A(n) EMPLOYEE, both of these entities are employees and are of the same logical type. Contrast this with a HAS-A relationship.

Isolation level: See Transaction isolation level.

IUnknown: An ActiveX interface in which one ActiveX program can call another, unknown ActiveX program. Once a connection has been established, the first program can use the Query Interface to determine what objects, methods, and properties the second program supports.

Java: An object programming language that has better memory management and bounds checking than C++; used primarily for Internet applications, but also can be used as a general-purpose programming language. Java compliers generate Java byte code that is interpreted on client computers.

Java bean: A properly mannered Java class, suitable for taking home to Mother. Beans have no public instance variables, all of their persistent values are accessed via accessor methods, and they have either no constructors or only one explicitly defined zero-argument constructors.

JavaScript: A proprietary scripting language owned by Netscape. The Microsoft version is called JScript; the standard version is called ECMAScript-262. These are easily learned interpreted languages used for both Web server and Web-client applications processing. Sometimes written "Java Script."

Java servlet: See Servlet.

Java Server Page (JSP): A combination of HTML and Java that is complied into a Java servlet that is a subclass of the HttpServlet class. Java code embedded into a JSP has access to HTTP objects and methods. JSP pages are used similarly to ASP pages, but are compiled rather than interpreted, as ASP pages are.

Java virtual machine: A Java bytecode interpreter that runs on a particular machine environment, e.g., Intel 386, Alpha. Such interpreters are usually embedded in browsers, included with the operating system, or included as part of a Java development environment.

JDBC: A standard interface by which application programs written in Java can access and process SQL databases (or table structures such as spreadsheets and text tables) in a DBMS-independent manner. It does not stand for Java Database Connectivity.

JScript: A proprietary scripting language owned by Microsoft. The Netscape version is called JavaScript; the standard version is called ECMAScript-262. These are easily learned interpreted languages used for both Web server and Web-client applications processing.

JSP: See Java Server Page.

Join: A relational algebra operation on two relations, A and B, that produces a third relation, C. A row of A is concatenated with a row of B to form a new row in C if the rows in A and B meet restrictions concerning their values. For example, A1 is an attribute in A, and B1 is an attribute in B. The join of A with B in which A1 < B1 will result in a relation, C, having the concatenation of rows in A and B in which the value of A1 is less than the value of B1. See Equijoin and Natural join.

Key: (1) A group of one or more attributes identifying a unique row in a relation. Because relations may not have duplicate rows, every relation must have at least one key, which is the composite of all of the attributes in the relation. A key is sometimes called a logical key. (2) With some relational DBMS products, an index on a column used to improve access and sorting speed. It is sometimes called a physical key.

Labeled namespace: In an XML schema document, a name space that is given a name (label) within the document. All elements preceded by the name of the labeled namespace are assumed to be defined in that labeled namespace.

LAN: Local Area Network; a group of microcomputers connected to one another by means of communications lines in close proximity, usually less than a mile. See Client–server database architecture and Resource-sharing architecture.

Level: In OLAP, a (possibly hierarchical) subset of a dimension.

List box: In a GUI environment, an element of the user interface in which a list of choices is presented in a rectangle. The user moves the cursor to shade the item to be selected from the list.

Location transparency: In a distributed database system, the condition in which application programs do not know and do not need to know where data are located. The DDBMS finds data, wherever they are located, without the involvement of the application program.

Lock: The process of allocating a database resource to a particular transaction in a concurrent-processing system. The size of the resource locked is known as the lock granularity. With an exclusive lock, no other transaction may read or write the resource. With a shared lock, other transactions may read the resource, but no other transaction may write it.

Lock granularity: The size of a locked data element. The lock of a column value of a particular row is a small granularity lock, and the lock of an entire table is a large granularity lock.

Log: A file containing a record of database changes. The log contains before-images and after-images.

Logical key: One or more columns that uniquely determine the row of a table or a record of a file; a synonym for a key. Contrast this with a physical key, which is a synonym for an index.

Look up: The process of obtaining related data by using the value of a foreign key, for example, when processing a row of ORDER (*OrderNumber,* Ord-Date, *CustNumber,* . . .), using the value of CustNumber to obtain the related value of CustName from CUSTOMER (*CustNumber,* CustName, . . .).

Lost update problem: Same as Concurrent update problem.

Materialization: A database view as it appears in a form, report, or Web page.

Maximum cardinality: (1) The maximum number of values that an attribute may have within a semantic object. (2) In a relationship between tables, the maximum number of rows to which a row of one table may relate in the other table.

Me: In OOP, a special pointer to the current object instance. For example, Me.Name refers to the Name attribute of the current object.

Measure: In OLAP, the source data for the cube; data that is displayed in the cells. It may be raw data, or it may be functions of raw data such as SUM, AVG, or other computations.

Media failure: A failure that occurs when the DBMS is unable to write to a disk. Usually caused by a disk head crash or other disk failure.

Members: In OLAP, the values of a dimension.

Menu: A list of options presented to the user of a database (or other) application. The user selects the next action or activity from a list. Actions are restricted to those in the list. Contrast this with Command.

Metadata: Data concerning the structure of data in a database stored in the data dictionary. Metadata are used to describe tables, columns, constraints, indexes, and so forth. Compare this with Application metadata.

Method: (1) A program attached to an object-oriented programming (OOP) object. A method can be inherited by lower-level OOP objects. (2) In OOP, a program attribute of an object.

Minimum cardinality: (1) The minimum number of values that an attribute may have within a semantic object. (2) In a relationship between tables, the number of rows to which a row of one table may relate in the other table.

Mixed partition: A combination of a horizontal and a vertical partition; for example, in a table with five columns and five rows, the first three columns of the first three rows.

Modification anomaly: The situation existing when the storing of one row in a table records two separate facts or when the deletion of one row of a table eliminates two separate facts.

MOLAP: Multidimensional OLAP using a purpose-built processor for supporting OLAP processing.

Multiple-tier driver: In ODBC, a two-part driver, usually for a client–server database system. One part of the driver resides on the client and interfaces with the application; the second part resides on the server and interfaces with the DBMS.

Multi-value attribute: The attribute of a semantic object that has a maximum cardinality greater than one.

Multi-value dependency: A condition in a relation with three or more attributes in which independent attributes appear to have relationships they do not have. Formally, in a relation R (A, B, C), having key (A, B, C) where A is matched with multiple values of B (or of C or both), B does not determine C, and C does not de-termine B. An example is the relation EMPLOYEE (EmpNumber, Emp-skill, Dependent-name), where an employee can have multiple values of Emp-skill and Dependent-name. Emp-skill and Dependent-name do not have any relationship, but they do appear to in the relation.

Mutable object: In the ODMG standard, an object whose attributes may be changed.

Natural join: A join of a relation A having attribute A1 with relation B having attribute B1 where A1 equals B1. The joined relation, C, contains either column A1 or B1 but not both. Contrast this with Equijoin.

Natural language interface: An interface to an application program or DBMS by which users can enter requests in the form of standard English or another human language.

Network: (1) A group of interconnected computers. (2) An intranet. (3) The Internet.

Network database application: A database application in which the clients use an HTML-based browser and the server includes both an Internet-style server and a database. The application could reside on either the Internet or an intranet.

Network data model: A data model supporting at least simple network relationships. The CODASYL DBTG, which supports simple network relationships but not complex relationships, is the most important network data model.

N.M: An abbreviation for a many-to-many relationship between the rows of two tables.

Node: (1) An entity in a tree. (2) A computer in a distributed-processing system.

Nonobject attribute: An attribute of a semantic object that is not an object.

Nonrepeatable reads: The situation that occurs when a transaction reads data it has previously read and finds modifications or deletions caused by a committed transaction.

Normal form: A rule or set of rules governing the allowed structure of relations. The rules apply to attributes, functional dependencies, multi-value dependencies, domains, and constraints. The most important normal forms are 1NF, 2NF, 3NF, BoyceCodd NF, 4NF, 5NF, and domain/key normal form.

Normalization: The process of evaluating a relation to determine whether it is in a specified normal form and, if necessary, of converting it to relations in that specified normal form.

Nothing: In OOP, a null object reference used to set an object pointer to null or test an object pointer to determine if it is null.

Not-type-valid document: An XML document that either does not conform to its DTD or does not have a DTD; contrast with type-valid document.

Null value: An attribute value that has never been supplied. Such values are ambiguous and can mean (a) the value is unknown, (b) the value is not appropriate, or (c) the value is known to be blank.

Object: (1) A semantic object. (2) A structure in an object-oriented program that contains an encapsulated data structure and data methods. Such objects are arranged in a hierarchy so that objects can inherit methods from their parents. (3) In security systems, a unit of data protected by a password or other means.

Object attribute: An attribute of a semantic object that represents a link to an object.

Object class: In object-oriented programming, a set of objects with a common structure.

Object class library: In object-oriented programming, a collection of object classes, usually a collection that serves a particular purpose.

Object constructor: In object-oriented programming, a function that creates an object.

Object destructor: In object-oriented programming, a function that destroys an object.

Object diagram: A portrait-oriented rectangle that represents the structure of a semantic object.

Object identifier: An attribute that is used to specify an object instance. Object identifiers can be unique, meaning that they identify one (and only one) instance, or nonunique, meaning that they identify exactly one object instance.

Object instance: The occurrence of a particular semantic object, for example, the SALESPERSON semantic object having LastName equal to Jones.

Object-oriented Programming: A style of computer programming in which programs are developed as sets of objects that have data members and methods. Objects interface with one another by calling each other's methods.

Object persistence: In object-oriented programming, the characteristic that an object can be saved to nonvolatile memory, such as a disk. Persistent objects exist between executions of a program.

Object-relational DBMS: DBMS products that support both relational and object oriented programming data structures, such as Oracle.

Object view: The portion of a semantic object that is visible to a particular application. A view consists of the name of the semantic object plus a list of the attributes visible in that view.

ODBC: See Open Database Connectivity standard.

ODMG-93: A report issued by the Object Data Management Group, which is a consortium of object database vendors and other interested industry experts. The report applies the ideas of another group, the Object Management Group, to the problem of object databases. The first ODMG report was produced in 1993 and is accordingly referred to as ODMG-93.

OLAP: On-Line Analytical Processing; a form of data presentation in which data is summarized aggregated, de-aggregated, and viewed in the frame of a table or a cube.

OLE DB: The COM-based foundation of data access in the Microsoft world. OLE DB objects support the OLE object standard. ADO is based upon OLE DB.

OLE object: Object Linking and Embedding object. COM objects that support interfaces for embedding into other objects.

1:N: An abbreviation for a one-to-many relationship between the rows of two tables.

On-Line Analytical Processing: See OLAP.

OOP: See Object-oriented Programming.

Open Database Connectivity standard (ODBC): A standard interface by which application programs can access and process SQL databases (or table structures such as spreadsheets and text tables) in a DBMS-independent manner. The driver manager portion of ODBC is incorporated into Windows. ODBC drivers are supplied by DBMS vendors, Microsoft, and by other third-party software developers.

Optimistic locking: A locking strategy that assumes no conflict will occur, processes a transaction, and then checks to determine if conflict did occur. If so, the transaction is aborted. Also see pessimistic locking.

Option button: In a GUI environment, an element of the user interface in which the user can select an item from a list. Clicking on one button deselects the button currently pressed, if any. It operates like the radio buttons on a car radio and is the same as a radio button (see Radio button) but was introduced under a different name to avoid litigation among vendors.

Orphan: Any row (record) that is missing its parent in a mandatory one-to-many relationship.

Outer join: A join in which all the rows of a table appear in the result relation regardless of whether they have a match in the join condition. In a left outer join, all the rows in the left-hand relation appear; in a right outer join, all the rows in the righthand relation appear.

Overhead data: Metadata created by the DBMS to improve performance, for example, indexes and linked lists.

Owner: In data administration, the department or other organizational unit in charge of the management of a particular data item. An owner can also be called a data proponent.

Paired attribute: In a semantic object, object attributes are paired. If object A has an object attribute of object B, then object B will have an object attribute of object A; that is, the object attributes are paired with each other.

Parent: A row, record, or node on the one side of a one-to-many relationship.

Partition: (1) A portion of a distributed database. (2) The portion of a network that is separated from the rest of the network during a network failure.

PERL: The Practical Extraction and Report Language. An interpreted programming language developed by Larry Wall and originally for UNIX. PERL interpreters are now available for Windows and Macintosh. Often used for server programs on the Internet and on intranets.

Persistent object: An OOP object that has been written to persistent storage.

Pessimistic locking: A locking strategy that prevents conflict by placing locks before processing database read and write requests. Also see optimistic locking and deadlock.

Phantom reads: The situation that occurs when a transaction reads data it has previously read and finds new rows that were inserted by a committed transaction.

Physical key: A column that has an index or other data structure created for it; a synonym for an index. Such structures are created to improve searching and sorting on the column values.

PL/SQL: Programming language/SQL. An Oracle-supplied language that augments SQL with programming language structures such as while loops, if-then-else blocks, and other such constructs. PL/SQL is used to create stored procedures and triggers.

Pointer: An address to an instance of a data item in a structure.

Polymorphism: In OOP, the situation in which one name can be used to invoke different functions. Polymorphism in which the functions are distinguished by having different parameter sequences is called parametric polymorphism. For it, names are resolved by the compiler at compile time. Polymorphism in which the functions are distinguished by object inheritance is called inheritance polymorphism. Such names are resolved at run time by determining the type of object being invoked.

Primary key: A candidate key selected to be the key of a relation.

Processing-interface subsystem: The portion of the DBMS routines that executes commands for processing the database. It accepts input from interactive query programs and from application programs written in standard or DBMS-specific languages.

Processing rights and responsibilities: Organiza-tional policies regarding which groups can take which actions on specified data-items or other collections of data.

Product: A relational operation on two relations, A and B, producing a third relation, C, with C containing the concatenation of every row in A with every row in B. It is the same as a Cartesian product.

Program/data independence: The condition existing when the structure of the data is not defined in application programs. Rather, it is defined in the database, and then the application programs obtain it from the DBMS. In this way, changes can be made in the data structures that may not necessarily be made in the application programs.

Projection: A relational algebra operation performed on a relation, A, that results in a relation, B, where B has a (possibly improper) subset of the attributes of A. Projection is used to form a new relation that reorders the attributes in the original relation or that has only some of the attributes from the original relation.

Property: Same as Attribute.

Proponent: See Data proponent.

Prototype: A quickly developed demonstration of an application or portion of an application.

QBE: Query By Example. A style of query interface, first developed by IBM but now used by other vendors, that enables users to express queries by providing examples of the results they seek.

Query Interface: An interface in Microsoft COM that can be used to determine the objects, methods, and properties supported by an ActiveX program.

Query/update language: A language that can be employed by end users to query the database and make changes in the database data.

Radio button: In a GUI environment, an element of the user interface in which the user can select one item from a list. Clicking on one button deselects the button currently pressed if any. It operates like the radio buttons on a car radio.

RDS: See Remote Data Services.

Read committed: A level of transaction isolation that prohibits dirty reads, but allows nonrepeatable reads and phantom reads.

Read uncommitted: A level of transaction isolation that allows dirty reads, nonrepeatable reads, and phantom reads to occur.

Real output: Output transmitted to the client of an information system, such as an order confirmation. When produced in error, such outputs cannot be changed by recovering the database. Instead, compensating transactions must be executed.

Record: (1) A group of fields pertaining to the same entity; used in file-processing systems. (2) In a relational model, a synonym for Row and Tuple.

Recordset: An ADO object that represents a relation; created as the result of the execution of a SQL statement or a stored procedure.

Recursive relationship: A relationship among entities, objects, or rows of the same type. For example, if CUSTOMERs refer other CUSTOMERs, the relationship *refers* is recursive.

ReDo files: In Oracle, backups of rollback segments used for backup and recovery. There are online and offline ReDo files.

Referential integrity constraint: A relationship constraint on foreign key values. A referential integrity constraint specifies that the values of a foreign key must be a proper subset of the values of the primary key to which it refers.

Relation: A two-dimensional array containing single-value entries and no duplicate rows. The meaning of the columns is the same in every row. The order of the rows and columns is immaterial.

Relational database: A database consisting of relations. In practice, relational databases contain relations with duplicate rows. Most DBMS products include a feature that removes duplicate rows when necessary and appropriate. Such a removal is not done as a matter of course because it can be time-consuming and expensive.

Relational data model: A data model in which data is stored in relations and relationships between rows are represented by data values.

Relational schema: A set of relations with interrelation constraints.

Relationship: An association between two entities, objects, or rows of relations.

Relationship cardinality constraint: A constraint on the number of rows that can participate in a relationship. Minimum cardinality constraints determine the number of rows that must participate; maximum cardinality constraints specify the largest number of rows that can participate.

Relationship constraint: Either a referential integrity constraint or a relationship cardinality constraint.

Remote Data Services: A set of ActiveX controls and features that allow data to be cached on a client machine and formatted, sorted, and filtered without assistance from the Web server.

Repeatable read: A level of transaction isolation that disallows both dirty reads and nonrepeatable reads. Phantom reads can occur.

Replicated data: In a distributed database, data that is stored on two or more computers.

Replication: For both Oracle and SQL Server, a term that refers to databases that are distributed on more than one computer.

Replication transparency: In a distributed database system, the condition in which application programs do not know and do not need to know whether data is replicated. If it is replicated, the DDBMS will ensure that all copies are updated consistently, without the involvement of the application program.

Report: An extraction of data from a database. Reports can be printed, displayed on a computer screen, or stored as a file. A report is part of a database application. Compare this with a Form.

Report band: See Band.

Repository: A collection of metadata about database structure, applications, Web pages, users, and other application components. Active repositories are maintained automatically by tools in the application development environment. Passive repositories must be maintained manually.

Resource locking: See Lock.

Resource-sharing architecture: The structure of a local area network in which one microcomputer performs file-processing services for other microcomputers. In a database application, each user computer contains a copy of the DBMS that forwards input/output requests to the file server. Only file I/O is processed by the file server; all database activities are processed by the DBMS on the user's computer.

ROLAP: Relational OLAP using a relational DBMS to support OLAP processing.

Rollback: The process of recovering a database in which before-images are applied to the database to return to an earlier checkpoint or other point at which the database is logically consistent.

Rollback segment: In Oracle, a buffer used to store before images for the purposes of concurrency control and transaction logging. Rollback segments can be archived and used subsequently for recovery.

Rollforward: The process of recovering a database by applying after-images to a saved copy of the database to bring it to a checkpoint or other point at which the database is logically consistent.

Root: The top record, row, or node in a tree. A root has no parent.

Row: A group of columns in a table. All the columns in a row pertain to the same entity. A row is the same as a Tuple and a Record.

Row identifier: In SQL3, a unique, system-supplied identifier, a surrogate key. The row identifier can be made visible by stating WITH IDENTITY in the table definition.

Row object: In Oracle, a table that contains objects as its rows.

Rowset: In OLE DB, an abstraction of data collections such as recordsets, E-mail addresses, and nonrelational and other data.

SAX: Simple API (application program interface) for XML. An event-based parser that notifies a program when the elements of an XML document have been encountered during document parsing.

Schema: A complete logical view of the database.

SCN: See System Change Number.

Schema-valid document: An XML document that conforms to its XML Schema definition.

Scrollable cursor: A cursor type that enables forward and backward movement through a recordset. Three scrollable cursor types discussed in this text are snapshot, keyset, and dynamic.

Second normal form: A relation in first normal form in which all nonkey attributes are dependent on all of the key.

Selection: A relational algebra operation performed on a relation, A, producing a relation, B, with B containing only the rows in A that meet the restrictions specified in the selection.

Semantic object diagram: Same as Object diagram.

Semantic object model: The constructs and conventions used to create a model of the users' data. The things in the users' world are represented by semantic objects (sometimes called objects). Relationships are modeled in the objects, and the results are usually documented in object diagrams.

Semantic-object view: The portion of a semantic object that is visible in a form or report.

Serializable: A level of transaction isolation that disallows dirty reads, nonrepeatable reads, and phantom reads.

Service provider: An OLE DB data provider that transforms data. A service provider is both a data consumer and a data provider.

Servlet: A compiled, machine-independent Java bytecode program that is run by a Java virtual machine located on a Web server.

Shared lock: A lock against a data resource in which only one transaction may update the data, but many transactions can concurrently read that data.

Shrinking phase: In two-phase locking, the stage at which locks are released but no lock is acquired.

Sibling: A record or node that has the same parent as does another record or node.

Simple network: (1) A set of three relations and two relationships in which one of the relations, R, has a many-to-one relationship with the other two relations. The rows in R have two parents, and the parents are of different types. (2) Any set of tables and relationships containing the structure defined in (1).

Simple object: An object that contains no repeating attributes and no object attributes.

Simple object access protocol (SOAP): A protocol for transmitting procedure calls as small XML documents using HTTP.

Single-tier driver: In ODBC, a database driver that accepts SQL statements from the driver manager and processes them without invoking another program or DBMS. A single-tier driver is both an ODBC driver and a DBMS; used for file-processing systems.

Single-value attribute: In a semantic object, an attribute having a maximum cardinality of one.

Slice: In OLAP, a dimension or measure held constant for a display.

Snowflake schema: In an OLAP database, the structure of tables such that dimension tables may be several levels away from the table storing the measure values. Such dimension tables are usually normalized. Contrast with Star schema.

SOAP: See Simple Object Access Protocol.

SQL: Structured Query Language; a language for defining the structure and processing of a relational database. It is used as a stand-alone query language, or it may be embedded in application programs. SQL is accepted as a national standard by the American National Standards Institute. It was developed by IBM.

SQL3: SQL3 is an extension to the SQL92 database standard that includes support for object-oriented database management. Developed by both the ANSI X3H2 and the ISO/IEC JTC1/SC21/WG3 standardization committees.

SQL view: A relation that is constructed from a single SQL SELECT statement. SQL views have at most one multi-valued path. The term *view* in most DBMS products, including Access, Oracle and SQL Server, means SQL view.

Standard generalized markup language (SGML): A standard means for tagging and marking the format, structure, and content of documents. HTML is a subset of SGML.

Star schema: In an OLAP database, the structure of tables such that every dimension table is adjacent to the table storing the measure values. Contrast with snowflake schema. In the star schema, the dimension tables are often not normalized.

Statement level consistency: All rows impacted by a single SQL statement are protected from changes made by other users during the execution of the statement. Contrast with transaction level consistency.

Stored procedure: A collection of SQL statements stored as a file that can be invoked by a single command. Usually, DBMS products provide a language for creating stored procedures that augments SQL with programming language constructs. Oracle provides PL/SQL for this purpose; SQL Server provides TRANSACT/SQL. With some products, stored procedures can be written in a standard language like Java. Often stored procedures are stored within the database itself.

Strong entity: In an entity-relationship model, any entity whose existence in the database does not depend on the existence of any other entity. See also ID-dependent entity and Weak entity.

Subtable: In SQL3, a table that is a subtype of a second table, called a supertable.

Subtype: In generalization hierarchies, an entity or object that is a subspecies or subcategory of a higher-level type. For example, ENGINEER is a subtype of EMPLOYEE.

Supertable: In SQL3, a table that has one or more subtables defined on it.

Supertype: In generalization hierarchies, an entity or object that logically contains subtypes. For example, EMPLOYEE is a supertype of ENGINEER, ACCOUNTANT, and MANAGER.

Surrogate key: A unique, system-supplied identifier used as the primary key of a relation. The values of a surrogate key have no meaning to the users and are usually hidden on forms and reports.

Swizzling: In OOP, the process of converting a permanent object identifier into an in-memory address and the reverse.

System Change Number (SCN): In Oracle, a database-wide value that is used to order changes made to database data. The SCN is incremented by whenever database changes are committed.

System data source: An ODBC data source that is local to a single computer and can be accessed by that computer's operating system and select users of that operating system.

Tabular data provider: An OLE DB data provider that presents data in the form of rowsets.

Target namespace: In an XML Schema document, the namespace that the schema is creating.

TCP/IP: Terminal Control Program/ Internet Protocol.

Third normal form: A relation in second normal form that has no transitive dependencies.

Three-tier architecture: A system of computers having a database server, a Web server, and one or more client computers. The database server hosts a DBMS, the Web server hosts an http server, and the client computer hosts a browser. Each tier can run a different operating system.

Top-down database design: The design of a database that works from the general to the specific. The resulting database can serve an organization's overall needs; the danger is that it may never be completed. See Bottom-up database design.

Transaction: (1) An atomic transaction. (2) The record of an event in the business world.

Transaction boundary: The group of database commands that must be committed or aborted as a unit.

Transaction isolation level: The degree to which a database transaction is protected from actions by other transactions. The 1992 SQL standard specified four isolation levels: Read Uncommitted, Read Committed, Repeatable Reads, and Serializable.

Transaction level consistency: All rows impacted by any of the SQL statements in a transaction are protected from changes during the entire transaction. This level of consistency is expensive to enforce and may (probably will) reduce throughput. It may also mean that a transaction cannot see its own changes. Contrast with Statement level consistency.

Transaction node: In a distributed database system, a computer that processes a distributed transaction manager.

TRANSACT/SQL: A Microsoft-supplied language that is part of SQL Server. It augments SQL with programming language structures such as while loops, if-then-else blocks, and other such constructs. TRANSACT/SQL is used to create stored procedures and triggers.

Transform-oriented language: A data sublanguage such as SQL that provides commands and capabilities to transform a set of relations into a new relation.

Transient object: In OOP, an object that has not been written to permanent storage. The object will be lost when the program terminates.

Transitive dependency: In a relation having at least three attributes, R (A, B, C), the situation in which A determines B, B determines C, but B does not determine A.

Tree: A collection of records, entities, or other data structures in which each element has at most one parent, except for the top element, which has no parent.

Trigger: A special type of stored procedure that is invoked by the DBMS when a specified condition occurs. BEFORE triggers are executed before a specified database action, AFTER triggers are executed after a specified database action, and INSTEAD OF triggers are executed in place of a specified database action. INSTEAD OF triggers are normally used to update data in SQL views.

Tuple: Same as Row.

Two-phase commitment: In a distributed database system, a process of commitment among nodes in which the nodes first vote on whether they can commit a transaction. If all the nodes vote yes, the transaction is committed. If any node votes no, the transaction is aborted. A two-phase commitment is required to prevent inconsistent processing in distributed databases.

Two-phase locking: The procedure by which locks are obtained and released in two phases. During the growing phase, the locks are obtained, and during the shrinking phase, the locks are released. Once a lock is released, no other lock will be granted that transaction. Such a procedure ensures consistency in database updates in a concurrent-processing environment.

Type-valid document: An XML document that conforms to its DTD; contrast with not-type-valid document.

UML: Unified Modeling Language, a set of structures and techniques for modeling and designing object-oriented programs and applications. It is both a methodology and a set of tools for such development. UML incorporates the entity-relationship model for data modeling.

Unified Modeling Language: See UML.

Union: A relational algebra operation performed on two union-compatible relations, say A and B, forming a third relation, say C, with C containing every row in both A and B, minus any duplicate rows.

Union compatible: The condition in which two tables have the same number of attributes and the attributes in corresponding columns arise from the same domain.

Union incompatible: The condition in which either two tables have a different number of attributes or the attributes in corresponding columns arise from different domains.

Updatable view: A SQL view that can be updated. Such views are usually very simple and the rules that allow updating are normally quite restrictive. Non-updatable views can normally be updated by writing application-specific INSTEAD OF triggers.

User data source: An ODBC data source that is available only to the user who created it.

User view: A particular user's view of a database.

VBScript: An easily learned, interpreted language used for both Web server and Web client applications processing; a subset of Microsoft Visual Basic.

Vertical partition: A subset of the columns of a table. For example, in a table with 10 columns, the first five columns.

Vertical security: Limiting access to certain columns of a table or join.

View: A structured list of data items from entities or semantic objects defined in the data model.

WAP: See Wireless Application Protocol.

Weak entity: In an entity-relationship model, an entity whose logical existence in the database depends on the existence of another entity. See also ID-dependent entity and Strong entity.

Web server: In the three-tier architecture, a computer that sits between the client computers and the database server and hosts an HTTP server.

Wireless application protocol (WAP): A communications protocol developed to create a world-wide standard for network access from wireless devices. Also see Wireless Markup Language.

Wireless markup language (WML): A variant of XML developed to enable web pages to be displayed on wireless devices.

WML: See Wireless Markup Language.

WML Script: A scripting language that is part of the wireless markup language. It is a variant of ECMAScript or, as it is better known, Java Script.

XML: Extensible markup language; a standard markup language that provides a clear separation between structure, content, and materialization; can represent arbitrary hierarchies and hence be used to transmit any database view.

XML Namespaces: A standard for assigning names to defined collections. X:Name is interpreted as the element Name as defined in namespace X. Y:Name is interpreted as the element Name as defined in namespace Y. Useful for disambiguating terms.

XML Schema: An XML-compliant language for constraining the structure of an XML document. Extends and replaces DTDs. Under development and very important to database processing.

XPath: A sublanguage within XSLT that is used to identify parts of an XML document to be transformed. Can also be used for calculations and string manipulation. Co-mingled with XSLT.

XPointer: A standard for linking one document to another. XPath has many elements from XPointer.

XQL: A standard for expressing database queries as XML documents. The structure of the query uses XPath facilities and the result of the query is represented in an XML format. Under development and likely to be important in the future.

XSL: (1) first meaning: Extensible Style Language. Originally a facility for transforming XML into potentially very complicated styles. Divided into two parts: XSLT for transforming document structure and producing simple formats and XSL-FO for formatting documents in complicated and sophisticated styles. (2) current meaning: XSLT Stylesheet. The document that provides the {match, action} pairs and other data for XSLT to use when transforming an XML document.

XSL-FO: Extensible Style Language—Formatting Objects. The part of the original XSL left over after XSLT was removed. A very large and complicated standard for sophisticated formatting that is still under development.

XSLT: Extensible Style Language: Transformations. A program (or process) that applies XSLT Stylesheets to an XML document to produce a transformed XML document.

BIBLIOGRAPHY

Database Articles

Check these sites for recent articles about database topics:
CNet—www.news.com
Database Programming and Design—www.dbpd.com
Databased Advisor—www.advisor.com
Intelligent Enterprise—www.intelligententerprise.com
PCMagazine—www.zdnet.com/pcmag
ZDNet—www.zdnet.com

DBMS and Other Vendors

Java—java.sun.com
SQL Server—www.microsoft.com/sql
Oracle—www.oracle.com
MySQL—www.mysql.com
Tabledesigner—www.tabledesigner.com

Standards

JDBC—java.sun.com/products/jdbc
and mmmysql.sourceforge.net
ODBC—www.liv.ac.uk/middleware/html/odbc.html
ODMG—www.odmg.org
SQL3—www.obis.com/x3h7/sql3.htm
Worldwide Web Consortium—www.w3.org
XML—www.xml.org

Books and Publications

ANSI X3. *American National Standard for Information Systems—Database Language SQL*. ANSI, 1992.

Berson, Alex, & Stephen J. Smith. *Data Warehousing, Data Mining, and OLAP*. New York: McGraw-Hill, 1997.

Boumphrey, Frank. *Professional Stylesheets for HTML and XML*. Chicago, IL: Wrox Press, 1998.

Bowen, Rich & Ken Coar. *Apache Server Unleashed*. Indianapolis, IN: SAMS, 2000.

Bruce, T. *Designing Quality Databases with IDEF1X Information Models*. New York: Dorset House, 1992.

Chamberlin, D. D., et al. "SEQUEL 2: A Unified Approach to Data Definition, Manipulation, and Control." *IBM Journal of Research and Development 20* (November 1976).

Chen, P. *Entity-Relationship Approach to Information Modeling*. E-R Institute, 1981.

Chen, P. "The Entity-Relationship Model: Toward a Unified Model of Data." *ACM Transactions on Database Systems 1* (March 1976).

Coar, Ken A. L. *Apache Server for Dummies*. Foster City, CA: IDG Books, 1997.

Codd, E. F. "Extending the Relational Model to Capture More Meaning." *Transactions on Database Systems 4* (December 1979).

Codd, E. F. "A Relational Model of Data for Large Shared Data Banks." *Communications of the ACM 25* (February 1970).

Coffee, Peter. "No-sweat Database Design." *PC Week* (March 11, 1996).

Corning, Michael, Steve Elfanbaum, & David Melnick. *Working with Active Server Pages*. Indianapolis, IN: Que Corporation, 1997.

Deitel, H. M, & P. J. Deitel. *Java: How to Program, 3rd Edition*. Upper Saddle River, NJ: Prentice-Hall, 1999.

Embley, D. W. "NFQL: The Natural Forms Query Language." *ACM Transactions on Database Systems 14* (June 1989).

Eswaran, K. P., J. N. Gray, R. A. Lorie, & I. L. Traiger. "The Notion of Consistency and Predicate Locks in a Database System." *Communications of the ACM 19* (November 1976).

Fagin, R. "Multivalued Dependencies and a New Normal Form for Relational Databases." *Transactions on Database Systems 2* (September 1977).

Fagin, R. "A Normal Form for Relational Databases That is Based on Domains and Keys." *Transactions on Database Systems 6* (September 1981).

Feuerstein, Steven with Bioll Pribyl. *Oracle PL/SQL Programming*. Sebastopol, CA: O'Reilly, 1997.

Fields, Duane K. & Mark A Kolb. *Web Development with Java Server Pages*. Greenwich CT: Manning Press, 2000.

Flanagan, David, Jim Farley, William Crawford, & Kris Magnusson. *Java Enterprise in a Nutshell*. Sebastapol, CA: O'Reilly, 1999.

Fronckowiak, John W. *Microsoft SQL Server 7.0 Administration*. Microsoft Press, 1999.

Goldfarb, Charles F. & Paul Prescod. *The XML Handbook*. Upper Saddle River, NJ: Prentice Hall, 1998.

Goodman, Danny. *Dynamic HTML: The Definitive Resource*. Sebastopol, CA: O'Reilly and Associates, 1998.

Hall, Marty. *Core Servlets and Java Server Pages*. Upper Saddle River, NJ: Sun Microsystems Press, 2000. Highly recommended!

Hammer, M., & D. McLeod. "Database Description with SDM: A Semantic Database Model." *Transactions on Database Systems 6* (September 1981).

Harold, Elliotte Rusty. *XML: Extensible Markup Language*. New York: IDG Books Worldwide, 1998.

Kay, Michael. *XSLT: Programmer's Reference*. Birmingham, United Kingdom: WROX Press, 2000.

Keuffel, Warren. "Battle of the Modeling Techniques." *DBMS Magazine* (August 1996).

Kroenke, David. "Waxing Semantic: An Interview." *DBMS Magazine* (September 1994).

Loney, Kevin & George Koch. *Oracle 8i, The Complete Reference*. Berkeley, CA: Osborene/McGraw-Hill, 2000.

Loomis, M. E. S. *Object Databases, The Essentials*. Reading, MA: Addison-Wesley, 1995.

McLaughlin, Brett. *Java and XML*. Sebastopol, CA: O'Reilly, 2000.

Meyers, Nathan. *Java Programming on Linux*. Indianapolis, IN: Waite Group Press, 2000.

Monson-Haefel, Richard. *Enterprise Java Beans, 2nd Edition*. Sebastopol, CA: O'Reilly, 2000.

Moriarty, T. "Business Rule Analysis." *Database Programming and Design* (April 1993).

Muench, Steve. *Building Oracle XML Applications*. Sebastapol, CA: O'Reilly, 2000.

Muller, Robert J. *Database Design for Smarties: Using UML for Data Modeling*. San Francisco, CA: Morgan Kaufmann Publishers, 1999.

Nijssen, G., & T. Halpin. *Conceptual Schema and Relational Database Design: A Fact-Oriented Approach*. Englewood Cliffs, NJ: Prentice-Hall, 1989.

Nolan, R. *Managing the Data Resource Function*. St. Paul: West Publishing, 1974.

Red Hat, Inc. *Linux 6.2 Getting Started Guide*. Durham, NC: Red Hat, Inc., 2000.

Ricart, Manuel Alberto. *The Complete Idiot's Guide to Linux, 2nd Edition*. Indianapolis, IN: Que Publishing, 2000.

Rogers, Dan. "Manage Data with Modeling Tools." *VB Tech Journal* (December 1996).

Schumate, John. *A Practical Guide to Microsoft OLAP Server*. Boston, MA: Addison-Wesley, 2000.

Sturm, Jake. *Data Warehousing with Microsoft SQL Server 7.0*. Redmond, WA: Microsoft Press, 2000.

Thakkar, Meghraj. *Teach Yourself Oracle 8i on Windows NT*. Indianapolis, IN: SAMS, 1999.

Thomsen, Erik. *OLAP Solutions: Building Multidimensional Information Systems*. New York: John Wiley and Sons, 1997.

Weissinger, A. Keyton. *ASP in a Nutshell, 2nd Edition*. Sebastopol, CA: O'Reilly, 2000.

Zloof, M. M. "Query by Example." *Proceedings of the National Computer Conference*, AFIPS 44 (May 1975).

INDEX

E

N

O

R

S

T